Society in

Transition

PRENTICE-HALL SOCIOLOGY SERIES

Herbert Blumer, Editor

Society in Transition

by

HARRY ELMER BARNES

SECOND EDITION

New York PRENTICE-HALL, INC. *1952*

To

JEAN

Who has borne with gay fortitude the deprivation
of companionship produced by my labors on this
and other books

Preface

The original edition of this book sought to present a comprehensive panorama of the social problems of our age, interpreted against the background of rapid social change. A drastic revision was necessary, however, for a suitable exposition of social problems at the mid-century. New trends, especially those introduced by the Second World War, the cold war, and the current critical state of international affairs, have profoundly affected our national social institutions and problems. The social transition examined in the original book has become more rapid and far-reaching. This new edition not only brings the book down to date in recording social data, but also takes into account the novel and accelerated trends of the postwar social world.

The new edition retains two outstanding features that characterized the original book: (1) the most complete survey of important social problems to be found in any book in the field; and (2) illuminating historical perspectives on each of these problems, without which no contemporary social problem can be approached in an intelligent and adequately informed manner. The size of the book has been reduced somewhat by the elimination of those chapters that were most peripheral to *social* problems, strictly interpreted. The result is, however, that the new edition is distinctly a better *social problems* text than the original. The historical sections, which were, perhaps, the most unique feature of the original edition, have been retained in essentially their original form. New chapters have been added on the family, on housing, and on community organization, because of the belief that their absence in the original edition was its only serious deficiency.

The frame of reference—cultural lag—remains basic in the new edition. But it has been extended beyond the lag between institutions and technology to include: (1) the lag in growth and adjustment among institutions themselves: and (2) the failure, thus far, to provide any adequate substitutes for the fast disintegrating personal and primary societies of the agrarian era, which lasted from the dawn of history until the end of the nineteenth century. The concept of personal and social disorganization, interpreted as the most acute manifestation of cultural lag, has been introduced to explain the immediate basis of most of our serious social problems. This frame of reference is adequate to account for the leading social problems of today and is as far as one can go without distorting the presentation by intruding theoretical considerations, which are usually of a highly subjective or abstract nature.

The presentation of the frame of reference is concentrated mainly in the first chapter of the new edition. The problem material that follows is presented objectively. Hence, teachers who do not accept the frame of reference suggested by the author will find no difficulty in interpreting the problem material according to their own ideas and convictions.

Certain pedagogical aids to teaching from the text have been introduced. Blackface subheadings have been inserted to emphasize and clarify the sequence of treatment. The bibliographies have been made more selective and descriptive and have been placed at the end of each chapter. Pictures and graphs appear for the first time in the new edition.

Those teachers who desire a reasonably complete survey of the facts and trends in our main social problems at mid-century will find this the most useful extant textbook in the field. The original edition had considerable appeal for the general public. These readers will find the new edition equally relevant to their interests.

The author wishes to thank those who aided him in preparing the original edition, who are named in the Note of Acknowledgement to that edition, and also the several able sociologists who offered valuable suggestions in guiding the preparation of the new edition. Professor Oreen Ruedi has been of indispensable assistance in preparing the first drafts of Chapters 11 and 12; the *Social Work Yearbook* has been of much value in gathering and checking information.

Harry Elmer Barnes

Cooperstown, New York

Contents

ix

Part III

SOCIAL PATHOLOGY

CONTENTS

Part I

Socio-Biological Aspects of Contemporary American Life

CHAPTER 1

Cultural Lag and Social Disorganization

The Basis of Our Social Problems

THE FOUR GREAT WORLD REVOLUTIONS

Importance of historical perspective in understanding social problems. Despite the fact that most of the social problems of today are relatively new and are a product of twentieth-century economic and social situations, it is quite impossible to understand their origin and nature without giving attention to the historical background of our age. This introductory chapter will seek to present at least a brief summary and appraisal of the factors that have created American society and social problems as they exist at the beginning of the second half of the twentieth century. We may start by placing our era in the larger panorama of the historic human past, relating it especially to the former great periods of social change and social crisis.

The four great world revolutions. The vital aspect of contemporary social experience is its place in the world trends of our time—its relation to the great movements in contemporary civilization as a whole. When we approach current social history from this fundamental point of view, we perceive that the United States, with the rest of the Western world and much of the Orient as well, is passing through what we shall call the fourth great world revolution in the historic experience of mankind.

The social historian's conception of a world revolution is not limited to the violent changes we usually associate with the word *revolution*, although thus far in human experience war and violence have accompanied the disintegration of old social orders and the inauguration of new ones. By a world revolution we mean a fundamental change in social conditions and patterns of life and in the social and economic basis of power. A new class of leaders arises. New institutions spring up and sweeping changes are made in those that remain from an earlier pattern of culture. A new type of civilization comes into being. The basic patterns of society are reconstructed.

The first world revolution produced the dawn of history in the ancient Near East. In these earliest recorded times the military chieftains of tribal society slowly built up small feudal kingdoms and city-states.

3

Adroit and powerful rulers of such political units conquered others and, in time, created kingdoms and empires. Vast wealth was amassed by rich landlords and a prosperous commercial class. A powerful priesthood, so it was thought, kept the favor of the gods and brought supernatural aid to the conquerors. The same process was repeated when the Roman Republic and the Roman Empire were gradually established millenniums later.

The second great world revolution took place when Roman imperial society disintegrated after 300 A.D. and the Germanic tribal chieftains and kings seized control of Western Europe. They built a new social order centered primarily around powerful landlords, thus creating what we know as medieval feudalism. In time, strong national monarchies arose. The manors and gilds dominated economic life. The medieval Church and Scholastic philosophy reigned supreme in the moral and intellectual realms.

Following 1500, a third world revolution came along, this time brought about chiefly by the rising power of the merchant class—the new bourgeoisie. At first, they supported the kings against their traditional enemies, the feudal lords, thus promoting the growth of royal absolutism. However, the kings themselves became a greater menace to the mercantile classes than the feudal lords had been; so the bourgeoisie took up arms against the kings and either dethroned them or subordinated them to a system of representative government dominated by the middle-class merchants and businessmen. The wars of Cromwell against Charles I, the ousting of James II, the American Revolutionary War, the French Revolution, and the Napoleonic Wars were only incidental military episodes in this great social revolution, in the course of which the merchant class replaced the feudal landlords as the dominant group in Western society. Napoleon, in a profound historical sense, was mainly an agent of social change.

This third world revolution, which produced modern times, probably bears the closest resemblance to our age. In the three centuries following 1500, the typical medieval institutions (such as a decentralized feudal government, a manorial economy, gild control of urban industry, local markets and national fairs to facilitate exchange of goods, the theory of the just price and other moral limitations on greed and sharp business practices, the unified international ecclesiastical state, and Scholasticism) were undermined or completely supplanted.

In their place arose the basic institutions and trends of the early modern age—the centralized national state, at first absolutistic and then representative, farming by free tenants under squires or great landlords, an increasingly commercial and industrial economy, the domestic or putting-out system of industrial control, national and world trade, capitalistic ideals and methods, the quest of private profits by any means not flagrantly illegal, the great split in Christendom produced by Protestantism and the ascendancy of humanistic ideals in education.

Had a scholar suggested in 1400 that the civilization of his age was about to undergo a sweeping transformation, he would have been ignored or ridiculed. But that is just what happened. By 1800 medieval civilization was no more, except in the backward parts of Europe.

Likewise, today, in the middle of the twentieth century, it is hard to believe that we may be in about the same situation in which the Western world found itself around 1400. Yet, plenty of evidence supports the opinion that more far-reaching changes, based chiefly on our new empire of machines, have already been instituted since 1850 than any previous century has ever witnessed—perhaps the most fundamental transition in man's experience. We are already far advanced in the fourth great world revolution, which will either bring man into an unprecedented era of peace, plenty, and security or produce world chaos and return us to barbarism. The outcome will depend mainly upon whether or not we are able to modernize our institutions and thereby enable ourselves to utilize our great scientific and mechanical resources for the benefit of man rather than for his impoverishment and destruction.

CULTURAL LAG

The failure of institutions to keep pace with science and material culture. The chief cause of all four of the world revolutions has been a discrepancy or maladjustment between material and nonmaterial culture. About 1750 began the rise of modern science and engineering and the successive industrial revolutions that have given us modern industry, transportation, and communication, thus completely changing the nature of our material culture.

Today, we have giant turbines, a few of which can generate more energy than the entire working population of the United States. We possess automatic machinery of the most amazing efficiency. One plant, for example, can turn out 650,000 light bulbs each day, or 10,000 times as many per man as was possible by the older methods. This automatic machinery can be controlled by thermostats and the photo-electric cell, or "electric eye," which are absolutely dependable and all but eliminate the human factor in those forms of mechanical production where they can be utilized. We have giant trim autobuses; clean, quiet, Diesel-motored trains; safe, swift airplanes. We have enormous skyscrapers. Our bathrooms would fill a Roman emperor with envy. Our system of communication is incredibly extensive and efficient. Radios and television would appear miraculous to persons who died in so recent a period as that of the First World War. Radar is even more momentous in its possibilities. Our modern printing presses would stagger Gutenberg. We could thus go on indefinitely through all the provinces of our "Empire of Machines." The striking developments associated with aviation—jet and rocket planes that can fly faster than sound and could encircle the globe in a few hours, the atom bomb, and the like—are only the most recent and dramatic aspects of the manner in which our mechanical world has forged ahead of our social institutions.

Never before has there been such a gulf between technology and social institutions as in our own day. We have a thoroughly up-to-date material culture, diverse and potentially efficient beyond that of any earlier age. On the other hand, the institutions and the social thinking through which we seek to control and exploit this material culture are an antiquated mosaic, compounded of accretions from the Stone Age to the close of the eighteenth century.

It is, therefore, quite obvious that the main key to understanding the reasons for the decay of modern institutions, the decline of our civilization, and the onset of the fourth world revolution lies in the phenomenal growth of contemporary science and technology and the failure of our institutional life and social thinking to keep pace with this growth of material culture.

This ever widening gulf between our science and technology, on the one hand, and our institutional development and social thinking, on the other, is the most important and crucial aspect of what we call *cultural lag*, to use the phrase that William F. Ogburn introduced a generation ago in his book, *Social Change*.

Other phases and aspects of cultural lag. An important aspect of cultural lag, aside from the ever widening gap between technology and relatively archaic institutional life, lies in the fact that our new methods and techniques of transportation and communication have produced many *new* social situations and social pressures for which the simple life in the personal societies that have dominated human existence down to recent times has not prepared us. We live today in a world society, but we have been conditioned in our social outlook and responses mainly by restricted local institutions and family and neighborhood life.

Cultural lag is also manifest in the fact that our primary societies, such as the family, local play groups, neighborhoods, and the like, of a rural civilization are breaking down far more rapidly than public activity and community organization are being developed to take over their functions. This has led to a lack of personal and moral discipline and much social chaos. Since personality and character have been produced primarily by these simple personal societies, their breakdown has led to personal as well as social disintegration.

Also important is the cultural lag among institutions themselves. Certain institutions change more rapidly than others. As a rule, economic institutions can be modified more quickly than religious and moral institutions, probably because economic life has been more thoroughly secularized and is less enveloped in strong emotions. This failure of institutions to readjust themselves in relatively uniform fashion is responsible for many of our leading social problems. No sane sociologist would contend that every last social problem is caused *exclusively* by cultural lag, however comprehensively conceived; it seems fair to say, however, that most social problems are produced by cultural lag, and that all of them are intensified by it.

War brings the cultural lag problem to a critical stage. The increasingly devastating character of war has brought the problem of cultural lag into its most critical period. We are able to produce ever-better battleships, tanks, bomb-sights, automatic rifles, long-range artillery, and atom bombs. We pool every intellectual resource of university laboratories, scientific foundations, and industrial research to discover how we may wage war more effectively. There seems to be no limit to the intelligence that we apply to the technical problem of war.

On the other hand, we approach the whole social and cultural problem of war with attitudes dating back to the period of the bow and arrow.

Whatever social services war may have rendered in early days, it has become a fatal anachronism and the chief threat to the preservation of contemporary civilization. The institution of war is today a stupid monstrosity. As Omar N. Bradley has put it bluntly, war is fundamentally immoral as an agency of settling human relations. Yet the very best brains of the world are still being employed to bring war to new heights of horror and destructiveness. As matters now stand, our archaic institutional approach to the problem of war and peace will do little more than permit us to stand by helplessly while atom bombs, atom rockets, disease germs, and lethal chemicals wipe out human civilization.

This discussion of war as an example of cultural lag brings us to the heart of the matter. For a long time, the issue of cultural lag has been of great practical importance. It has produced our economic problems of waste, under-consumption, low standards of living, poverty, unemployment, and the like. It accounts for our inadequate housing and much of our unnecessary disease, sickness, and death. It has produced most of the wars in contemporary times and prevented the emergence of really adequate and constructive plans for peace.

In spite of all these handicaps and evils produced by cultural lag, most of humanity could survive in the past. But the development of atomic energy, the new strides in bacterial warfare, and the like, have introduced an altogether new and more alarming trend into the situation. At this time, and from now on, the lessening and elimination of cultural lag are bound up with the very survival of the human race. Unless we are able to bring up to date the institutions most directly involved in war, it will not be long before humanity will be in part extinguished and in part consigned to barbarism. Nothing short of an institutional readjustment sufficient to hold all wars in check—and that without barbarizing fears and preparations—will suffice to preserve anything deserving the name of civilization. Otherwise, cultural lag will exact its final penalty in the destruction of human civilization, just as physiological maladjustments once doomed the dinosaurs.

It will avail nothing to retreat from this challenge into the fog of mysticism that is proving so popular with those who lack the courage to face the issues. Less than nothing will be gained by seeking refuge in dogmatic cults or in the mystical writings of a Toynbee or a Sorokin. We must face our problems with the resolute courage of men like the late H. G. Wells, who saw that scientific and mechanical marvels can bring untold benefits to man, if he will but learn how to turn them to his advantage.

HOW THE CURRENT ALARMING DEGREE OF CULTURAL LAG CAME ABOUT

Relatively rapid institutional changes from 1500 to 1800. A little reflection on the history of modern times makes it easy to understand how this dangerous disparity between our material culture and our social institutions has come about. It is not, as some suppose, because our institutional development in modern times has been slower than in earlier ages. As a matter of fact, institutional progress has been more rapid since 1500 than in any other comparable period of human history.

Unfortunately, science and machinery have progressed even more rapidly over the same period. There has been greater scientific and mechanical progress since 1450 than in the whole million or more years of human experience before modern times. Institutional development, even though relatively rapid in the last five centuries, has simply not been able to keep pace with scientific and mechanical progress. Another important element in the situation, as we shall see, is that the business classes have, particularly since 1800, thrown the whole weight of their influence behind stimulating science and machinery, at the same time seeking to stabilize institutions and frustrate social change.

In early modern times, there was actually a greater social impulse to institutional changes and to new types of social thought than there was to the progress of science and invention. Between 1450 and 1750, as the Middle Ages came to an end and modern times came into being, it was institutional changes that were sought by the rising middle class. The middle class repudiated most types of medieval institutions and social thought. It helped along the growth of the national state and transformed it from an absolutistic to a representative basis. It developed the ideas of natural law, which placed jurisprudence behind the protection of property. In conjunction with the Protestant leaders, the middle class created and fostered the capitalistic system. It took an active part in colonialism and the creation of modern imperialism, developed an appropriate type of political and economic theory to justify the new bourgeois system, and brought into being the liberal political philosophy that justified revolution against the privileged aristocracy. It defended outstanding civil liberties, such as freedom of speech, press, assembly, and religion. In economics, it extolled the freedom of trade and the immunity of business and trade from extensive government regulation. These institutional changes were far more rapid and extensive than the mechanical advances between 1450 and 1750.

Middle class opposes social change after 1800. Most of these innovations in economics and politics had been achieved by the close of the eighteenth century. The bourgeoisie believed that they had created an ideal social order. The system thus created tended thereafter to crystallize and to resist change. In this way, the very social class that for three hundred years had strongly encouraged the transformation of institutions and social thought, placed itself in the path of comparable social changes in the nineteenth and twentieth centuries.

The business and financial classes then threw all their tremendous power into the maintenance of things as they were in our institutional life. At the same time they were becoming more and more enthusiastic about science and technology, which many of them looked upon as potential guardians of the dearly loved status quo. This set of values has persevered from about 1800 to the present time and is the main reason for the strange and alarming state of affairs we face today—namely, the juxtaposition of a thoroughly up-to-date science and technology with a heritage of social institutions and social thought that date, for the most part, from around 1800 or earlier.

Material culture now secularized. Another reason why material culture advances far more rapidly than social institutions in our day is that our material culture has become far more thoroughly secularized than our institutional equipment. Therefore, there is not the same emotional and quasi-religious opposition to changes in science and machinery as there is to any proposal to alter our social institutions.

In primitive times, material culture was regarded as sacred, a gift of the gods. Although material benefits were, perhaps, not quite as holy and sanctified as social institutions, yet material things—e.g., tools and weapons—were venerated. The would-be innovator placed himself in jeopardy if he proposed the use of a new tool or weapon. Primitive peoples often used an obviously inferior tool for fear that they might offend the gods by switching to a more efficient tool, and material progress was slowed down by this "technological piety," as Veblen called it.

The superstitious element in material culture was reduced in mature primitive society, and the invention of superior tools and weapons carried mankind to the threshold of civilization. By modern times, the notion of the sanctity of any particular pattern of material culture had been pretty well broken down, and science and machinery had become essentially secularized. There were some attenuated hangovers for generations, well-represented by fantastic opposition to new methods of transportation, such as railroads. Nevertheless, by and large, the secularization of science and technology was well advanced by early modern times and the completion of this process is one of the outstanding accomplishments of modern civilization. We are no longer fearful of the gods or evil spirits if we discard an ancient tool, vehicle, or machine and choose a newer and more efficient one.

In contrast with this, we find that social institutions still retain much the same halo of sanctity with which they were endowed in primitive society. While we may not fear so directly the vengeance of the gods if we alter a social institution, as was the case in primitive days, we act as though we did. We appear to assume that, if we change the social pattern of life, some horrible disaster will result, even if the gods do not obliterate the nation. This was well illustrated as late as 1937 by the popular horror at the proposal to reform the Supreme Court. While part of this apparent terror was drummed up to discredit the Roosevelt administration, there were millions who sincerely believed that the Court was invested with some sort of divinity and that to alter its composition and challenge its tyranny would bring social chaos to the country. No sort of propaganda, however clever and lavishly subsidized, could have raised a similar outcry about any change in material culture. Henry Ford's change of his automobile from Model T to Model A was greeted with nationwide eagerness and enthusiasm.

WHY WE FAIL TO CLOSE THE GULF BETWEEN MACHINES AND INSTITUTIONS

Social attitudes toward technology and institutions. Since the gulf between machines and institutions is the chief cause of current difficulties and disasters, from poverty to war, why is so little being done to remedy this situation? Social psychology and cultural history explain our lamentable defects and failures in this respect.

So long as we are proud of our institutions and ideas in direct ratio to the antiquity of their origin, we have less than any incentive to bring them up to date. Until we are as much embarrassed by an archaic idea or social practice as we are by an obsolete gadget, there is little prospect of making any headway in modernizing our institutional equipment. We shall have to be just as insistent in demanding experts in legislative halls and administrative offices as we are in demanding their presence in power plants and hospitals.

Widening the gulf between institutions and machinery. Far from taking steps to bridge the gulf between our institutions and machinery, the intellectual attitudes and social values of our era actually tend to widen it. We provide various lucrative rewards for scientists and engineers who make important discoveries, even though we stand in no great present need of further scientific discoveries, save perhaps in the field of medicine. But, though we require more than anything else today the contributions of the social inventors who can bring our institutions and social thinking up to date by devising new and better forms of government, economic life, legal practices, moral codes, and educational systems, we bestow few or no prizes or rewards on the social inventor. Indeed, he is more likely at best to be ridiculed as a well-meaning crank or nitwit, and in certain countries he is imprisoned or shot. The net result is an extension of the already menacing abyss between our science and machinery on the one hand and our institutional life and social thought on the other.

RECENT REVOLUTIONARY ENLARGEMENT OF SOCIAL GROUPS, STRUCTURES, AND INTERESTS

Cultural lag in the institutional scene. Although we usually think of cultural lag as implying mainly the disparity between technology and relatively archaic primary institutions, this concept must be extended if we are to understand fully the origin and causes of our social problems today. There is also a marked lag among institutions and social groups. This is most critically manifested in the decay of the basic institutions—

the primary groups—of the agrarian society, which dominated human experience from the dawn of history to the opening of the present century, and our failure to plan and develop new institutional forms to replace or supplant those that are falling into the discard as a result of technological advances and the social changes produced thereby.

The expansion of social experience. One of the chief reasons for social disorganization and the related social problems of our day is the revolutionary changes in the nature of new social groups, structures, interests and controls, changes that have followed upon the rise of contemporary technology. This has resulted chiefly from the new agencies of transportation, communication, and opinion building which have transformed many of the most important processes of human life and social activity from a local to a national or international basis and have created social structures and interest groups so vast that neither the social experience nor the social science of the past is today capable of coping with the problems thus produced.

Present-day social processes transcend personal and local societies. The socializing processes of the not too distant past grew out of human experience in small, personal, and simple societies, chiefly primary and small secondary groups—family, neighbors, friends and play groups, the local community, township and the like. Action and thought were controlled chiefly by relatively stable local customs and the cultural heritage of a limited area. Most sociological thinking about the elementary socializing processes has also been concentrated on what goes on in such small and simple groups. Local group life and the sociological analysis thereof are obviously important, but neither prepares the citizen of today to recognize the world he lives in or to deal with its problems effectively or happily.

Many of the most important problems and experiences of the citizen of the mid-twentieth century have been expanded by our technological revolution to a national or world scope. The knowledge and experience gained in primary and small secondary groups provide no adequate preparation to understand even the problems involved, to say nothing of their efficient solution. We are, as it were, trying to participate in the United Nations on the basis of knowledge and experience drawn from a husking bee, an urban service club, or a trade union local.

Examples of broadened social contacts and problems created thereby. Vast movements of peoples involving several great racial stocks native to different continents have produced extensive racial contrasts and mixtures. The contemporary world has brought about a sweeping interdependence of groups and peoples, but has not subjected the members to any socializing and educational experience that would fit them to understand each other and cooperate effectively. We have a multiplicity of groups on a national scale, such as business organizations, labor unions, and other interest-groups made up of millions of persons with a widely diversified racial and cultural background. Even wider in scope and diversity are international organizations, cartels, relief and rehabilitation organizations, international federations, and so on. In a profound social sense, members of these groups are strangers to each other, with all the suspicion and blockage of action that this produces. This situation produces struggles for power, prestige, and adjustment that involve conflicts in social philosophies, economic creeds, political ideologies, and moral patterns, for the solution of which individual experience gained in the socializing processes of local groups provides slight guidance.

Wider social pressures. Along with new and much larger groups and social structures, new and more extensive forms of social control, social pressure, and channels of information have come into being to supplement or replace family teachings, neighborhood gossip, local public opinion, and stereotyped community customs. These have been produced by the new agencies of communication, such as newspapers, radio, movies, television, and the like. We are subjected to a comprehensive, varied, and continuous barrage of deliberately planned and inculcated propaganda which reaches whole nations simultaneously in the effort to shape opinion and control action to preconceived ends. Such pressures are even international in range. "The Voice of America" speaks in many languages by short-wave radio all over the world with the aim of promoting American policies abroad. All of the mammoth interest-groups which we mentioned above have access to the newspapers and to the air and carry on propaganda to promote their several causes. The individual is overwhelmed by pressures thrown at him from every political, social, and economic direction.

Reaction of new experiences and contacts upon the individual. All this has greatly modified the status and operations of the individual citizen. At the turn of the century, the citizen was preponderantly a dweller in a small community. He was largely self-controlled within the confines of local opinion and practice, and exerted a more or less significant influence on the events and activities of his time. Now he is caught up in the great social structures and movements over which he can exert little influence as an individual personality and the nature of which he often understands only imperfectly. Moreover, while individuals are now becoming even more conscious of their basic rights and privileges they are also constantly growing more dependent on organizations, many of them of wide scope and membership, in order to attain their desired goals and to protect their achievements. They are poorly fitted by past experience to function intelligently as individuals within such organizations.

Sociology must reckon with new trends. Both society and sociological analysis must become reoriented in the light of these new and revolutionary trends in social organization, control, and functioning, and adapt thought and action to take account of the sweeping changes in the technological and institutional nature of the era in which we now live. Neither social action nor sociological description will have much relation to basic realities if it stems solely from life in, or study of, the simple, local, and personal societies which dominated life down to a generation or so ago.

In this book we shall endeavor to present social processes and problems in the light of these new trends, always remaining conscious, however, that many individuals still continue to live in small groups, carry on a congenial life therein, seek to make a living in this local social setting, strive there for position and prestige, and are in part controlled by local codes of opinion and moral patterns.

SOCIAL DISORGANIZATION AS A CAUSE OF SOCIAL PROBLEMS

Group basis of the human personality. Human nature and personality are products of group life, social conditioning, and the cultural heritage. Without these forces, any man, even of the mid-twentieth century, would be an undisciplined animal. A number of so-called wild men, or feral men, have been discovered who have spent their lives without any human association whatever, at least from early childhood onward. They were found to be devoid of all the usual attributes of human nature, such as discipline, sympathy, sociability, kindliness, and the like. While able to make sounds, they have no coherent language. They represent nothing more than the highest form of primate animal life.

We are separated from such an animal-like existence today only by those products of socialization that have grown out of our group life, formed our social habits, and added to our knowledge. These products are handed down from generation to generation; they are the total cultural heritage of mankind. Since the very dawn of history this shaping of human nature and creation of the cultural heritage have essentially been the work of what we call primary groups, the small personal and local societies such as the family, neighborhood, play group, local religious association, and the like.

During the last seventy-five years or so, chiefly as a result of the Industrial Revolution, and especially of the revolution in transportation and communication and the growing predominance of city life, these primary groups have been undermined and their influence steadily weakened. This has produced a type of cultural lag of the greatest significance in understanding social problems—social disorganization. Unless we can find some form of group conditioning and community planning that will provide substitutes for the socializing influence formerly supplied by primary groups, the outlook for social stability and progress is ominous indeed.

Nature of social disorganization. The eminent sociologists, W. I. Thomas and Florian Znaniecki, described social disorganization as any serious "decrease of the influence of existing rules of social behavior upon the individual members of the group." Kimball Young, a student of Thomas, clarifies the idea in the following manner: "Social disorganization refers to the breakdown of the societal order to such an extent that the former controls are dissipated, the former correlation of personality and culture is destroyed, and a certain chaos or disorder arises in which old ways of doing have been lost and new ways not yet developed." [1]

[1] Kimball Young, *An Introductory Sociology*. New York: American Book Company, 1934, p. 54.

There is nothing difficult about the notion of social disorganization. If social organization, operating through the ideas and institutions that control group life, is essential for an orderly, secure, and prosperous social existence and individual scheme of life, it is evident that when social organization breaks down, we lose the advantages and guidance of normal group controls and a greater or less degree of social chaos results. For example, if the family controls, neighborhood cooperation, and religious sanctions that formerly sufficed to guide life no longer function effectively, and no improvements or substitutes are provided, living conditions will become disorganized and pathological.

Social disorganization produced by cultural lag. It may appear that there is a discrepancy between the idea that social disorganization causes most social problems and the statement frequently made in this book that social problems are mainly a manifestation of cultural lag. But there is no contradiction whatever. Cultural lag means that social institutions do not keep pace with the material conditions of life, or that some social institutions lag behind others in the process of readjustment to changing conditions. This is precisely what causes social disorganization to arise. Social disorganization is only another way of describing some of the more acute and pathological results of cultural lag.

SUMMARY

At the mid-century, we are passing through a great social transition, comparable to the dawn of history, the decline of pagan society in the later Roman Empire, and the break-up of medieval civilization after 1400.

In all of the great world revolutions or social transitions of history, the main cause of such drastic readjustments has been the discrepancy between technology and the social institutions of each period.

Today, the chief reason for the momentous social problems of our age is the fact that science and machinery have far outdistanced their institutional setting. We have a mid-twentieth century science and machinery which we seek to control with institutional equipment built up in the rural economy and society that preceded 1800.

The result is what sociologists and cultural historians call cultural lag; in this case, the lag of institutions behind science and machinery.

But cultural lag embraces other forms of social maladjustment—the failure of some institutions to change as rapidly as others, and our inability, thus far, to find wider and more substantial substitutes for the personal, primary societies of a rural age that are disintegrating under the impact of a mechanical and urban era.

All these forms of cultural lag help to produce social disorganization, by which we mean the failure of existing forms of institutional structure and social control to provide the guidance and discipline needed in our time. Social disorganization is the most acute manifestation of cultural lag and the main cause of the social problems now besetting us.

SELECTED REFERENCES

Barnes, H. E., *Can Man Be Civilized?* New York: Brentano, 1932. An elementary and readable introduction to the rational interpretation of our contemporary life and its problems.

Bloch, H. A., *Disorganization: Personal and Social.* New York: Knopf, 1951. Most recent treatment of social disorganization and social problems.

*Chapin, F. S., *Cultural Change.* New York: Appleton-Century, 1928. Introductory treatment of the main cultural changes since primitive times, ending with a clear theoretical discussion of the nature of cultural transformation and the lag in institutions.

Elliott, M. A., and Merrill, F. E., *Social Disorganization.* New York: Harper, 1941. Excellent book on the institutional disorganization of our time, caused by cultural lag and the disruption of primary institutions.

*Faris, R. E. L., *Social Disorganization.* New York: Ronald Press, 1948. Most recent sociological analysis of social disorganization and its implication for the social problems of today.

Fosdick, R. B., *The Old Savage in the New Civilization.* New York: Doubleday, Doran, 1928. A very readable and thoughtful discussion of the manner in which our civilization is menaced by projecting our cave-man mentality into the age of machines and world-wide communication.

Laski, H. J., *Reflections on the Revolution of Our Time.* New York: Viking Press, 1943. Stimulating and thoughtful discussion of the public implications of the current fourth world revolution produced by cultural lag in our time.

Lee, A. M., and E. B. (Eds.), *Social Problems in America.* New York: Holt, 1949. Valuable collection of readings, with much attention to cultural lag.

North, C. C., *Social Problems and Social Planning.* New York: McGraw-Hill, 1932. A good discussion of the possibility of bringing our institutions up to date and solving the problem of cultural lag through social planning.

*Ogburn, W. F., *Social Change.* New York: Viking Press, 1950. A pioneer discussion of the nature of culture as a sociological concept, notable for the introduction into popular usage of the notion of cultural lag. Still the best theoretical introduction to the subject.

Pitkin, W. B., *A Short Introduction to the History of Human Stupidity.* New York: Simon & Schuster, 1932. Really a massive, but vastly entertaining, onslaught on the credulity of mankind. Reveals quite a different Pitkin from the author of his more widely-read books.

*Robinson, J. H., *The Human Comedy.* New York: Harper, 1937. Popular introduction to our contemporary problems, viewed from an historical point of view, by the most thoughtful of all American historians.

Soule, George H., *The Strength of Nations.* New York: Macmillan, 1942. An able statement of the thesis that our social problems are due to cultural lag, growing out of our failure to apply scientific knowledge and rational methods to our institutions. Suggests ways of doing so.

Wells, H. G., *The Salvaging of Civilization.* New York: Macmillan, 1921. Notable appraisal of our social crisis, stressing the "race between education and social catastrophe." The latter appears to have won.

White, L. A., *The Science of Culture.* New York: Farrar and Straus, 1949. The most competent discussion of the cultural interpretation of history and society, and a formulation of a new science of culturology.

[*Note:* Books marked with an asterisk in chapter bibliographies are regarded by the author as especially cogent for supplementary reading.]

CHAPTER 2

Population Trends in Modern Society

THE GROWTH OF POPULATION IN MODERN TIMES

Age-old interest in population problems. Population problems have held the attention of writers from a very early period. For instance, in one of the earliest references to the Devil in the Old Testament (I Chronicles 21), we find David being tempted to take a census of the Israelites. As early as the middle of the sixth century B.C., the Greek poet, Theognis, provided us with the first extant reference to the principles of eugenics. He recommended that the practice of selective breeding be extended from domestic animals to the human race. In his *Republic,* Plato presented the first systematic plan for a scheme of eugenics applied to mankind. From the days of Plato to those of Malthus, writers have considered one or another aspect of population problems. In this chapter we shall consider some of the more important population trends in modern times, note explanations that have been offered therefor, and seek to indicate some of the more significant implications of modern population changes.

Slow growth of population before modern times. The growth of the population of the world was relatively slow before modern times, mainly because of the high death rate before the rise of medicine as a science, and the lack of the food necessary to supply a large population. The latter was chiefly the result of crude agricultural methods, the absence of modern machinery, and inadequate means of transporting, storing, and preserving food. During the last 150 years, the net increase in the number of human beings on the planet has been greater than in the previous million or more years in which the race has been in existence.

Julian Huxley, in *Harper's Magazine,* September, 1950, estimated that the population of the world in the so-called food-gathering period of late tribal society was between two and ten million, with five million as a reasonable figure. Around 6000 B.C., when an organized hunting economy had developed, world population stood somewhere between five and twenty million, with ten million as a fair estimate. By 3500 B.C., when early civilization was well established, the figure was about twenty million. World population had increased to 100 million by 500 B.C. and to 200 million by the height of the Roman Empire. By around 1650, it had reached about 550 million; by 1800, nearly one billion; and, by

16

1925, the two billion mark had been passed. Huxley predicts a world population of three billion by the year 2000. He cites the following figures for the rate of increase in world population within historic times:

Period	Rate of Increase
5500 B.C.–3000 B.C.	0.04%
3000 B.C.– 850 B.C.	0.06
850 B.C.–1650 A.D.	0.07
1650–1750	0.29
1750–1800	0.44
1800–1850	0.51
1850–1900	0.63
1900–1950	0.75
1937–1947	0.82

Turning now to figures of population growth in Europe, students of the history of population growth, such as the eminent German scholar, Karl Julius Beloch, believe that between the later Roman Empire and the seventh century after Christ the population of Western Europe steadily declined. Beloch estimated that the population of Western Europe in 200 A.D. was approximately 40 million. By 700, it had shrunk to something like 30 million. From this low point it slowly increased during the early Middle Ages, until in the year 1000 it amounted to approximately 35 million. More settled conditions and the growth of urban communities led to a more marked increase between 1000 and 1300, so that at the later date Beloch estimated that the population of western Europe had reached approximately 53 million. During the later Middle Ages population growth was steady, if slow. Despite the ravages of the Black Death in the fourteenth century, Beloch estimated that the population of western Europe in 1600 stood at about 73,500,000 and he believed that the total population of all Europe at this time was approximately 100 million.

Two students of population who actually lived in the seventeenth century also offered estimates of the population of Europe in their day. An Italian, Francesco Riccioli, believed that the population of Europe in 1661 was 100 million, while in 1696 the English statistician, Gregory King, also gave the estimate of 100 million for his day. Since there were devastating epidemics and wars in the seventeenth century, such as the London plague and the deadly Thirty Years' War, modern students of population history are inclined to credit all these estimates. They believe that the population of Europe in 1696 was not much, if any, greater than it had been in 1600. The total population of the world in 1643 is estimated to have been about 450 million.

Acceleration of population growth in Europe after 1700. By 1700 the expansion of Europe, the commercial revolution, greater material prosperity for at least the middle class, and improved medical care were making themselves felt. Johann Peter Süssmilch and Walter F. Willcox have estimated that, by 1750, the population of all Europe had grown to approximately 140 million. By 1800 it had increased to some 187 million.

We have fairly reliable statistics for the population growth of some representative European states in early modern times. For example, in 1500 the population of England and Wales is estimated to have been about three million. By 1600 it had reached four million; in 1700, six million; and in 1800, nine million. At the close of the Middle Ages it is believed by the chief authorities that France had a population of about 12 million. By 1700 its population had increased to 21 million, in 1770 to 24 million, and in 1800 to 27 million. The population of Italy in 1700 is estimated as 14 million, and in 1800 as 18 million; of Prussia in 1740 as 3,300,000, and in 1800 as 5,800,000; of Austria in 1754 as 6,100,000, and in 1800 as 8,500,000. There are no reliable statistics for the population of Russia. It is estimated that in 1720 it amounted to about 14 million, and in 1800 to around 30 million.

Though there was a marked acceleration of population growth during the eighteenth century, a far more striking increase in the population of Europe set in as a result of the combined impact of improved agricultural methods, the Industrial Revolution, and the advances in medical science and care. In 1800 the population of Europe was 187,693,000; in 1830, 233,962,000; in 1860, 282,893,000; in 1890, 362,902,000; in 1930, 505,100,000; and in 1940, over 540,000,000. In 1801 the population of England and Wales was nine million. In 1950 it had risen to 44 million. Germany was little affected by the Industrial Revolution down to 1871, when it had a population of about 41 million. By 1940 this had increased to 69,640,000. Italy grew from 18,124,000 in 1800 to 43,864,000 in 1940; Russia, from about 30 million in 1800 to 207,000,000 in 1951.

POPULATION OF EUROPE SINCE 1800

Year	Population (in thousands)	Annual Increase per 1000
1800	187,693	. . .
1810	198,388	5.6
1850	266,228	5.9
1900	400,577	9.9
1940	540,000	7.4

Population growth in the United States and Latin America. The United States was relatively an empty country in 1789, with a white population of less than four million. This had grown to 150,697,361 in 1950. This growth of the population of the United States since the establishment of the national government in 1789 has thus been even more striking than population increases in Europe. This has been due to the fact that a large natural growth of population (excess of births over deaths) has been supplemented by immigration on a scale never before witnessed in the history of humanity. From 1790 to 1860 the population of the United States increased at the rate of about 35 per cent a decade; and from 1860 to 1910 at over 20 per cent a decade; but from 1910 to 1920 it dropped to less than 15 per cent, and between 1930 and 1940 to only 7.3 per cent. But there was a great spurt in population growth in the 1940's, when the increase reached 14.3 per cent.

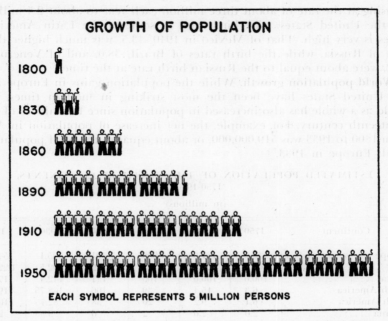

GROWTH OF POPULATION

1800

1830

1860

1890

1910

1950

EACH SYMBOL REPRESENTS 5 MILLION PERSONS

Pictorial graph indicating growth of population in the United States.

POPULATION OF THE UNITED STATES SINCE 1790

Year	Population (in thousands)	Annual Increase per 1000
1790	3,929	....
1800	5,308	35.1
1810	7,239	36.4
1820	9,638	33.1
1830	12,866	33.5
1840	17,069	32.7
1850	23,191	35.9
1860	31,443	35.6
1870	38,558	22.6
1880	50,155	30.1
1890	62,947	25.5
1900	75,994	20.7
1910	91,972	21.0
1920	105,710	14.9
1930	122,775	16.1
1940	131,409	7.3
1950	150,697	14.3

Although the rapid growth of the population of the United States has been the most striking trend in the New World for a century or more, it is now being eclipsed by the record of Latin America, where the population is now growing more rapidly than in any other large sector of the world. Its population is today about the same as that of the United States, approximately 150 million. The Latin American population is now increasing at the rate of about three million each year to about 2.5 million for the United States. The birth rate in some of the Latin American states is very high. That of Mexico in 1940, 43.5, was much higher than that of Russia, while the birth rates of Brazil, 38.0, and of Venezuela, 37.2, were about equal to the Russian birth rate at the time.

World population growth. While the population gains in Europe and the United States have been the most striking in modern times, the world as a whole has also increased in population since the middle of the eighteenth century. For example, the net increase of population in Asia from 1800 to 1933 was 519,000,000, or about equal to the total population of all Europe in 1933.

ESTIMATED POPULATION OF THE EARTH BY CONTINENTS, 1750-1950 [1]

(in millions)

Continent	1750	1800	1850	1900	1930	1950
Europe	140.0	187.0	266	401	505.1	547.7
Asia	406.0	522.0	671	859	992.5	1,223.1
Africa	100.0	100.0	100	141	142.4	175.8
North America	6.3	15.4	39	106	168.75	192.6
South America	6.1	9.2	20	38	82.75	101.3
Oceania	2.0	2.0	2	6	9.88	23.7
TOTAL WORLD POPULATION	660.4	835.6	1098	1551	1901.38	2,264.5

If the population of the world were to increase for 250 years more in the same ratio that it increased from 1900 to 1950, it would then reach a total of over 10 billions. This would be an alarming figure, for it might be difficult to do more than to maintain sheer existence for such a population on the planet, even assuming remarkable progress in technology and distribution techniques during these 250 years.

It is hardly likely, however, that the population of the world will increase to anything like this extent because in the majority of the more thoroughly industrialized states the birth rate has been falling off rapidly, and the populations have been tending to stabilize themselves with respect to the matter of growth. Before many more generations it is probable that the countries which are not now industrialized will have introduced machinery, the factory system, and urban life. Population stability may then take place.

In 1923 Edward Murray East estimated that the total population of the world, by the year 2000, would stand at approximately five billions. Others, such as biologist Raymond Pearl, put the figure much lower— at not more than half the estimate given by East. In 1936, Pearl estimated that the world's population peak would be reached in 2100 with

[1] From *The Encyclopaedia of the Social Sciences*, Vol. XII, pp. 241, 245. By permission of The Macmillan Company, publishers. 1950 figures are latest estimates.

a total population of 2,645,000,000. As we have noted, Julian Huxley predicts a population of three billion for the world in 2000.

All estimates regarding world population during the next hundred years are guesswork, even if we are fortunate enough to escape any more world wars. If India and China are affected to the same extent by industrialization, better agricultural methods, and improved medical care that Europe was between 1700 and 1950, the Chinese population would grow to over 1.5 billion and that of India to much over a billion. After urbanization and other factors reducing the birth rate set in and the death rate stabilizes, we could then expect population stabilization and decline to take place, as it has done in the mature civilizations of the Western world. But there are too many unknown factors to make any precise or dogmatic predictions at all reliable.

SOME CAUSES OF RAPID POPULATION GROWTH IN MODERN TIMES

Fecundity and fertility. Before attempting to discuss the reasons for the important changes in the rate of population growth noted above, we should define two terms which are bound to recur frequently in the pages following, namely, *fertility* and *fecundity*, as these are applied to population analysis.

Fertility means the actual rate of production of offspring in any given population, as measured by the birth rate. It does not measure the innate biological power of reproduction, but rather the extent to which this power is manifested at any given time in a particular population. Fecundity means the potential power to produce offspring, in other words, the real capacity of a people for reproduction. In practice, it has reference primarily to female fecundity. The male powers of reproduction are relatively so great that they are never likely to fall below a level which would make possible a rate of reproduction far beyond the capacity of the most fecund females. This is due to the fact that the number of available male spermatozoa enormously outnumber the female ova—to the ratio of millions to one.

The notable decline in the birth rate during the last century in many countries means that fertility has been declining, but there is little evidence of any reduction in fecundity or the physiological power to reproduce. Indeed, A. M. Carr-Saunders believes that there has actually been an increase in human fecundity in the course of historic times.

Population growth not due to increased birth rate. It is very commonly assumed that the enormous increase in population during the nineteenth century and the opening decades of the twentieth was due chiefly to a striking increase in the birth rate. This is a complete misapprehension of the facts. We have fairly reliable statistics on birth rates for the Western world since about 1825. Almost without exception the birth rate has fallen off markedly in this part of the world during this period. For example, the birth rate of Sweden dropped from 35 per 1,000 in 1800, to 25 in 1900 and to 15.0 in 1940. In England and Wales the birth rate for the years 1860-1865 was 35 per 1,000, but by 1940 it had dropped to 14.6. In France it dropped from 35 in 1800 to 25 in 1880, and to 14.6 in 1939. The German birth rate dropped from 36.1 in 1848-1852 to 20.0 in 1940. The Italian birth rate dropped from 36.9 in 1868-1872 to 23.4 in 1940. Turning to a less industrialized country, Russia, the birth rate dropped from 48.9 in 1868-1872 to 43.8 in 1924-1926, to 38.3 in 1938, and to about 25 in 1951. This shows that in predominantly rural countries the birth rate has fallen off less markedly than in industrial states; but, nevertheless, there has been a definite decrease in the birth rate even in the agricultural nations.

BIRTH RATE IN WESTERN AND NORTHERN EUROPE, 1841-1937 [2]

Year	Birth Rate	Year	Birth Rate
1841-1845	31.9	1891-1895	29.7
1846-1850	30.9	1896-1900	29.4
1851-1855	30.8	1901-1905	28.4
1856-1860	31.7	1906-1910	26.6
1861-1865	32.1	1911-1914	24.2
1866-1870	32.0	1915-1919	17.0
1871-1875	32.7	1920-1921	23.8
1876-1880	32.8	1922-1923	21.0
1881-1885	31.4	1924-1925	19.9
1886-1890	30.2	1937	17.0

We have no complete statistics for the birth rate of the United States during the nineteenth century, but such facts as we have prove that our country has shared in the general European tendency toward a markedly lower rate. This was offset in the last half of the nineteenth century as the result of the influx of a vast number of immigrants of child-bearing age. Since immigration has greatly declined during the last 35 years there was also a striking falling off in the birth rate and population gains in the United States, a matter to which we shall devote considerable attention later on.

It has been estimated that the birth rate in the United States was about 55 in 1800, 43.3 in 1850, 38.3 in 1870, and 30.1 in 1900. It stood at 18.9 in 1930 and at 17.9 in 1940. Due to very special conditions, there was a notable spurt in the American birth rate during the war decade, until it reached 25.8 in 1947. We shall consider the causes and results of this phenomenon later in the chapter.

Reasons for declining birth rate: birth control. Professional students of population problems have offered a number of explanations for this striking decline in the birth rate during the last century. They are agreed that birth control and the use of more effective contraceptive methods are unquestionably the chief deliberate method whereby the marked falling off of the birth rate has been brought about. We now have far more effective and reliable means of preventing conception than were known a century ago. In addition to these mechanical and medical advances

[2] From *The Encyclopaedia of the Social Sciences*, Vol. II, p. 569. By permission of The Macmillan Company, publishers.

in the field of birth control, there are even more important psychological, sociological, and economic factors at work. People seem ever more desirous of utilizing these better contraceptive devices. Some of the reasons for the increasing enthusiasm for contraception will become apparent as we examine other causes that are offered to explain the drop in the birth rate since 1800.

False notion of decline in fecundity. Certain students of population accepting the general doctrine of Herbert Spencer—that the growth of civilization produces a definite decrease in human fecundity—have alleged that growing industrialization and increased education have brought about a real, if involuntary, increase in human sterility. In short, they allege that the race is becoming biologically less capable of maintaining a high birth rate, even if it wished to do so. Some authorities, such as Corrado Gini and R. A. Fisher, hold that there has actually been a physical change in the race and that there is a real physiological basis for this decline in human fertility. They believe that a decrease in fecundity has preceded and produced the observable decline in fertility. Few serious students of population problems today accept the ideas of Spencer, Gini, or Fisher. There would appear to be no physiological basis for a declining birth rate. Even late marriages, which may be associated with an actual reduction in female fecundity, are produced primarily by cultural and psychological factors, and the resulting lowering of fertility cannot be assigned to any physiological changes in the population.

Vital effects of city life. Such population experts as F. H. Hankins, W. S. Thompson and Raymond Pearl admit that there has been a sharp decrease in fertility among highly civilized peoples, but they do not believe that there is any physiological change in the race so far as latent fecundity is concerned. They find the chief explanation for the lower birth rate in the changed social and cultural conditions that have appeared in modern urban life following industrialization. Hankins, Thompson, and Pearl believe that reproductive activity has become diverted and frustrated as the result of the great increase of urban life and the habits that go with it, late marriages in professional and business groups, sedentary existence, overeating of rich foods, heavy drinking, retiring late at night in a fatigued condition, nocturnal recreational distractions, and increasing nervous tension, all of which often reduce sexual interest and vigor. Special stress is laid by Hankins upon the decrease of fertility in families as the result of those innovations in contemporary urban culture and social life that have a direct relation to the frequency of sexual intercourse, general physical and sexual vigor, and the prevalence of diseases that bear directly upon sexual activity. It would seem that these authorities who explain the apparent increase of involuntary sterility as the result of urban living conditions are on firmer ground than such writers as Gini who postulate some mysterious decline in fecundity, especially on the part of the upper classes. City populations, exclusive of migration from country areas, are not holding their own today in population.

In addition to all this, there is, of course, the fact that children no longer have the economic value in urban surroundings that they formerly had in a rural society. Indeed, they are usually an economic liability and a source of increased worry in city environments. So, added to the less obvious effects of city life in reducing sexuality and fertility, there is a strong impulse deliberately to prevent conception. It seems reasonable, therefore, to hold that the total impact of city living conditions on sexual activity and procreative intent is the main reason for the contemporary decline in the birth rate.

Influence of social ambition. Among other influences leading to a decline in the birth rate, it is obvious that the ambition to improve one's economic and social status is important, especially among city populations. The French scholar, Arsène Dumont, stressed this fact many years ago. In order to enjoy a greater degree of security, luxury, and social prestige, people are inclined to limit the size of families, and this has involved an increasing use of contraceptive devices. This ambition to improve economic and social conditions has also been very influential in bringing about the notable movement from country to city areas in the last hundred years. It is in the cities that we find the most marked tendency toward a declining birth rate—the larger the city the more notable the decline. This trend toward a lower city birth rate was partially offset for many years by the tendency for the young and most prolific elements from the country to seek employment in cities. With the present slowing up of migration from country to city, we may expect the birth rate in cities to fall even more markedly in generations to come.

Within cities we find a striking differential birth rate at work. It is among the most ambitious groups that we find the most extreme decrease in the birth rate. The unskilled workers have the largest families; the skilled workers rank next; then follow the clerical and professional workers; and the rich usually have the smallest families of all. In many instances this attempt to improve well-being or maintain good economic conditions has also produced a lower birth rate even in country areas. This has been particularly true in France, where even among peasants small families are the rule, partly because of the effort to prevent breaking up small landed holdings by dividing them among too many heirs.

Feminism. Some students of population have made much of the allegation that feminism and the increased emancipation of women have helped notably to decrease the birth rate. Having carefully reviewed the evidence for this contention, Thompson is inclined to discount it. He admits that this is true of the more thoroughly emancipated women who have gone into the professions, but he does not believe that this factor has as yet materially affected the fertility of the majority of women. He concludes that "We may dismiss such changes as being of but little importance in producing the decline in the birth rate in western lands."

Religion and the birth rate. Religious liberalism is frequently alleged to be a cause of the decrease in the birth rate. In general, Protestants have exhibited a lower birth rate than have Catholics. Complete rejection of institutional religion undoubtedly has had even more influence upon the restriction of the birth rate. Such emancipated persons have no religious incentive for procreation. Since they do not believe that there are any souls to be saved, they do not heed the scriptural injunction to "be fruitful and multiply." Nor do they have any religious or moral qualms about using contraceptive devices.

Thompson believes, however, that social, economic, and psychological factors are at work in changing population trends even in the religious field. For example, he does not think that the general tendency of Catholics to increase more rapidly than Protestants is due wholly to the encouragement to have large families that is given to Catholic communicants by the priesthood. He points out that Catholics are, by and large, economically the poorest element in both rural and urban populations. Hence, they are subject to the general tendency of those at the bottom of the income ladder, relatively immune to any driving social ambitions, to increase most rapidly in numbers. Whenever Catholics attain a better economic and social status, they seem to follow the general tendency of the well-to-do class to restrict the birth rate in order to improve their general social and cultural conditions.

An extensive study of fertility levels and changes among Catholic families between 1919 and 1933 was made by Samuel A. Stouffer. He found that the birth rate among Catholics remained considerably higher than that among Protestants down to 1933, but the decline in the Catholic birth rate from 1919 to 1933 was more rapid than the decline in the birth rate among Protestants. Indeed, some expert students of population problems, such as Lorimer and Osborn, doubt that religion, by itself alone, exerts any decisive influence on fertility and the birth rate.

Greater cost of rearing children. Finally, as Elbert H. Clarke has done well to emphasize, the rising standard of living and the greater cost of bearing and rearing children, especially in cities, has had no little influence in discouraging procreation and leading people to take steps to prevent conception:

Children are costing more. It costs more to clothe a child, for standards are being set by families which have only one or two children to dress, instead of five or six. There must be more schooling. Self-support comes several years later than it did a generation ago. Then there are mounting expenses which we all must meet. Taxes are going up. Social security must be paid for. More and more burdens are waiting to bear down with greater force on the tired shoulders of the fathers of families in the future.[3]

To sum up, then, the remarkable population growth since 1750 or 1800 has not been due to any increase in the birth rate—any gain in fertility. Actually the birth rate has fallen off sharply in this period, especially after the First World War. This decline in the birth rate is due to many causes, but all are closely related to the great increase of city populations and the diversified complexities of urban living conditions and mental attitudes. These unconsciously distract energy, interest and attention from procreative activity and produce many socio-psychological reasons for desiring smaller and smaller families. Increasingly

3 "Birth Control and Prosperity," *The Forum*, February, 1938, p. 108.

effective contraceptive devices and wider knowledge of their existence have facilitated the success of all deliberate efforts to reduce the birth rate.

Reduced death rate the main cause of population growth. We may now look into some of the more obvious causes for the marked increase of population from 1750 to 1914. Students of population are almost universally agreed that the chief cause of modern population gains has been the reduced death rate. This has been a result of the progress in sanitary engineering, medical science, and preventive medicine. Of course the industrial and agricultural revolutions have played their part, for without their contributions those saved from death by disease would have perished from exposure or starvation.

Evidence of a decreased death rate. During recent generations in civilized countries of the Western world, the death rate has fallen much more rapidly than the birth rate. For example, in England and Wales the death rate fell from 22.1 per 1,000 in 1838-1842 to 11.9 in 1930-1931. In the same period the French death rate fell from 23.6 to 16. In Germany it fell from 28 in 1868-1872 to 10.8 in 1932. Between 1868 and 1930, the death rate in Italy fell from 29.8 to 14.5. In Sweden, where we have reliable statistics for 150 years, the death rate dropped from 27.9 in 1790 to 11.7 in 1940. There has been a comparable decrease in the death rate in the United States, which in 1880 was about 19.8, in 1920 was 13.1, in 1948 was 9.9, and in 1949 was 9.7, an all-time low.

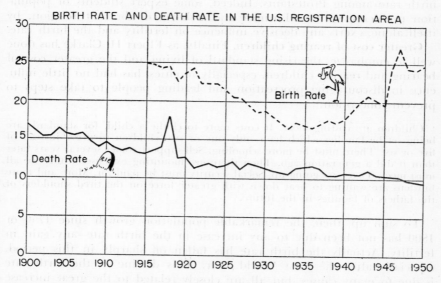

BIRTH RATE AND DEATH RATE IN THE U.S. REGISTRATION AREA

Reasons for declining death rate: sanitary engineering and better medical science. The reasons for this striking decrease in the death rate, during the last 75 years particularly, are readily apparent. First and foremost were the development of sanitary engineering and the improvements in medical science. Sanitary engineering made possible more healthfully constructed cities, better sewage disposal plants, the improvement of water supply, and other factors that notably decreased disease, especially epidemic diseases.

Medical science has notably improved in the last century and, as a result, has saved many lives which were hitherto doomed. Most important has been the decrease in infant mortality. This is especially important in relation to population growth because it is young people who have children. It has been estimated that in 1775 only 532 out of every 1,000 children born in Germany survived to the end of the tenth year. By 1926 this figure had been raised to 863. In England and Wales the figures are 703 for the period 1838-1854 and 868 for the period 1920-1922. These statistics are representative of civilized countries where sanitary engineering and medical science have reached a high stage of development. In the United States the death rate among children between the ages of 1 and 14 was reduced by over 79 per cent in the 35 years between 1911 and 1946. The death rate from the chief communicable diseases of childhood—measles, scarlet fever, whooping cough, and diphtheria—was reduced by more than 90 per cent during these years, and that from diphtheria, formerly the most fatal of the group, by some 97 per cent. In the year 1948 alone, child mortality dropped 17 per cent from 1947. The lowered child mortality has been a result of the better feeding and more sanitary care of infants; the decline in the number of infants born, which makes possible better home care; the more competent medical care of children; and the general gains in mass prosperity and well-being, which make possible better nutrition and more healthy surroundings.

Along with the decrease in infant mortality there has also been a very notable reduction in the death of mothers at childbirth. This has been a product of the progress in aseptic obstetrics since the discovery of the causes of childbed fever by Oliver Wendell Holmes and Ignaz Semmelweiss in the middle of the nineteenth century. Nevertheless, until the discovery of the sulfa drugs and the antibiotics in the years since 1935, the deaths from childbirth infections remained scandalously high.

Improved medical science has achieved wonders in reducing what were once deadly epidemic and contagious diseases. Illustrations of this may be seen in the remarkable success in reducing the prevalence of typhus, yellow fever, typhoid fever, smallpox, diphtheria, scarlet fever, and malaria. Tuberculosis, which ranked first as a cause of death in 1900 in the United States, dropped to seventh in the list in 1947. Pneumonia, which ranked second in 1900, stood in sixth place in 1947. In thoroughly civilized countries notable progress has been achieved in battling the ravages of venereal diseases. The development of aseptic surgery has also played a large part in the reduction of the death rate. The sulfa drugs and the antibiotics have played a leading role in curbing the death rate in the last 15 years, both in treating diseases and promoting aseptic surgery.

Death rate tending to become static. At the same time there has been a relative failure to check or reduce the death rate from chronic diseases that are usually most prevalent in mid-life or old age, such as heart maladies, cancer, kidney disease, and other degenerative disorders. Most of these are alarmingly on the gain. Heart diseases, which stood fourth as a cause of death in 1900, now rate first in order as a "killer" and in 1948 accounted for 44 per cent of all deaths from disease in the United States. Cancer, which ranked tenth as a cause of death in 1900, has now moved up to second place. Even in 1949, when the death rate was at an all-time low, deaths from heart diseases and cancer were still on the gain.

Since we can hardly expect an indefinite continuance of revolutionary medical progress in reducing deaths from diseases more commonly occurring in youth, from epidemics, or from contagious diseases that are now pretty well conquered, population students believe that we are nearing the end of any spectacular decrease in the death rate.

Any marked decrease in the death rate in the future can only be brought about by greater success in treating the chronic diseases, in making good medical care available to the whole population, and in raising the standard of living of the underprivileged masses so that their resistance to disease will be increased. But all such possible advances, desirable as they are, will probably be offset by the greater mortality that will be inevitable among the greatly increasing number of older persons in the population—12 million now over 65, and probably 25 million by 1980. Many medical and population experts believe that our death rate may have touched bottom at 9.7 per 1,000 in 1949, that it may rise somewhat in the next two decades, and that it may stabilize around 14 or 15 in the 1980's.

Effects of mechanization and industrialization. It is probable that the other major influences bringing about the notable gains in population since 1750 are those related to the advances in industry and agriculture and the growing mechanization of life. These also have exerted much influence in decreasing the death rate. For example, sanitary engineering has thus far been more directly related to the Industrial Revolution and engineering than to medical science. In a direct way the Industrial Revolution made it possible to support a larger population through more efficient manufacture and transportation of goods, introduction of mechanical methods in agriculture, more rapid and efficient transportation of food products, more extensive and successful preservation of foods through the canning industry and improved refrigeration, and the opening up of new lands to settlement and cultivation.

It would not be inaccurate to say that sanitary engineering and medical science have brought about most of our population gains through decreasing the death rate, and that the mechanical revolutions in industry, transportation, and agriculture have made it possible to support the larger population that the decreasing death rate has produced.

Minor causes of population growth. In addition to these two major causes of population growth, we should note certain less important social and economic influences. For example, indiscriminate charity has sometimes increased the birth rate. Such was the case with the deplorable poor laws, notably the Gilbert Act of 1782 and the Speenhamland Plan of 1796, enacted in England in the last two decades of the eighteenth century. They provided for poor allowances in proportion to the cost of living and the size of the family, thus encouraging both legitimate and illegitimate births. The high economic value of child labor was also a stimulant to the birth rate and population growth in the past. In the early days of the Industrial Revolution children were often preferred to adult males because of the lower wages for which they would work. There was a direct incentive to bear children who might work in factories and help support the family. In the rapidly developing agricultural economy of the nineteenth century, child labor was also at a premium, particularly upon the American frontier. It is obvious that such social and economic influences, making for a higher birth rate, have become much less potent in recent years.

Life expectancy and the life span. Intimately related to the reduction of the death rate through improved medical science and other influences has been the increase of what population students call life expectancy, or the average length of life at any given time. In those countries of the Western world that have good medical care life expectancy has just about been doubled since 1800. In western Europe in the eighteenth century the average expectation of life at birth was only about 35 years, approximately that in India today. By the time of the outbreak of the Second World War it had increased to nearly 65 and is still on the gain. The likelihood of dying in any given year has essentially been cut in half, and more people live to middle and old age.

Some relevant figures will illustrate this increase in life expectancy. In England and Wales the life expectancy of males was 39.9 years and of females 41.8 years in 1838-1854. By 1936, the life expectancy of males had increased to 61.5 years, and of females to 65.8. In the nineteenth century the life expectancy of a citizen of the United States was probably about the same as a resident of England and Wales. In 1947, the life expectancy of white females in our country was 70.6 years, and of white males 65.2. Among non-white females it was 61.79, and for non-white males 57.9. The average for the whole population in 1947 was 66.8 years, about 18 years more than in 1900 and about two years longer than in the 1930's. By 1951, the life expectancy for the total population, male and female, stood at about 68 years.

The life span of man is quite another matter. This refers to the usual extreme length of human life as compared to the extreme length of life of other mammals. While this varies with individuals, there is no indication that it has changed at all during historic times for the human race as a whole. Although more people live to an extreme old age now than formerly, there is no evidence that any person lives longer today than some did several thousand years ago. Biologists and physiologists have estimated that the natural life span of man is between 115 and 125 years. In future centuries, with the perfection of medicine and hygiene, the life expectancy could almost reach the life span.

Various efforts have been made by chemists, physiologists, and physicians to increase the life span, a problem which seems mainly that of preventing cells from aging. Two generations ago, Jules Bordet developed a serum made from connective tissue of the liver, but it proved ineffective. About the same time, the great Russian biologist and physician, Eli Metchnikoff, tried to stave off old age by recommending the drinking of sour milk, and later vainly tried to perfect the cytoxic serum that Bordet had envisaged. Perhaps more useful will be the serum devised by the Russian physiologist, Alexander A. Bogomolets, who believed that the degeneration of connective tissue is a main cause of senescence and developed a serum to prevent this. Its effectiveness still remains to be fully tested.

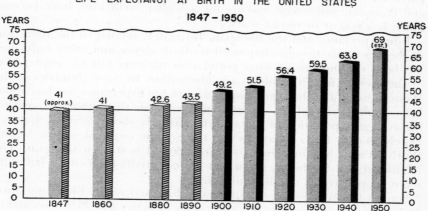

LIFE EXPECTANCY AT BIRTH IN THE UNITED STATES
1847 – 1950

The increase in life expectancy has some important results bearing on population trends and problems. Since a larger number survive to old age, this means an increase in the total population unless offset by a concurrent decrease in the number of births and a lessening of the younger elements in the population. But it also means an increase in the death rate, because of the higher incidence of death among persons over 60 or 65 years of age. The most important effect is, of course, the great increase in the number of older persons in the population and the many special problems that this involves, a matter to which we shall turn our attention later.

THE DECLINE OF THE RATE OF POPULATION GROWTH IN THE TWENTIETH CENTURY: POPULATION STABILIZATION

The "demographic transition." While the nineteenth century was notable for population growth, urban living conditions and some other factors have brought about a notable decrease in the birth rate in many of the northwestern European countries as well as in America—a decrease so marked that some of these populations have been scarcely more than reproducing themselves, even with a constantly lowering death rate. In France the population was almost static until 1946; in England it promises to reach a static point within thirty years or so, and in the United States in perhaps forty years. As has been pointed out by a number of observers, particularly L. I. Dublin and R. R. Kuczynski, it is in the highly industrialized and urbanized countries that the birth rate has fallen off most rapidly. Industrialization is associated first with marked population increases and then with a trend toward a lower birth rate and population stabilization. The reason for this phenomenon is that industrialization at first produces more food and better transportation, as well as improved sanitation. But it also brings about extensive urbanization, and the latter, in turn, creates various social and psychological conditions opposed to rapid population growth.

This trend towards the stabilization of population growth as a result of (1) a falling birth rate, caused by better living standards, social ambition, the conditions of urban life, and the deliberate prevention of conception, and (2) of an approximately static death rate, caused by the difficulty of conquering the growing incidence of chronic diseases and the higher mortality among the increasing number of old persons in the population, is what students of population call "the demographic transition," or the "demographic revolution." It has been the most important factor in the population picture of the Western world in the twentieth century.

Effect of the First World War on population trends. A special and temporary, but extremely potent, cause of this falling off in the rate of population growth after 1914 was the First World War and its ravages. About 12 million soldiers were killed, and an equal number of civilians were killed or died of starvation and disease. Some 20 million were wounded, and an equal number suffered as widows, orphans, and refugees.

Such cataclysmic results could not avoid affecting the population situation in Europe in a profound fashion. It represented perhaps the most striking example of Malthus' "positive" checks to population growth in all human history until 1914. During the war a large portion of the males of procreating age were absent from home in the army or navy. Many of them were killed and never returned to resume their normal procreative activities and responsibilities. Others who did return were wounded and maimed, or were greatly reduced in vitality, so that they could not procreate with their usual efficiency. The influenza epidemic killed off millions, some students of this episode believing that it took a far greater toll of lives than the Black Death. Millions suffered from malnutrition. This resulted in a loss of vitality and fertility. Malnutrition also enormously increased infant mortality and other manifestations of the death rate. The British blockade, which lasted for over six months after the Armistice of November, 1918, killed over 800,000 in Germany through malnutrition and starvation.

No complete and final estimate of the extensive effects of the First World War and the influenza epidemic of 1918-1919 on population trends has yet been made, though Dudley Kirk has offered much information in his valuable book on *Europe's Population in the Interwar Years*.[4] The

_____

[4] New York: Columbia University, League of Nations Publications, 1946.

rate of population growth in all belligerent countries was far less than in the decade of 1901-1910, and in several of them there was a net population loss for the years 1911-1920. The losses were heaviest in eastern Europe, being especially severe in Russia, Jugoslavia, Poland, and the Baltic states. W. F. Ogburn has shown that the war cut the birth rate by half in France and Germany; there were 1,500,000 less babies born in France than would have been born in time of peace. The net reproduction rate dropped in Germany from 1.5 in 1913 to 0.97 in 1921-1925. The British birth rate was cut from 24.1 in 1913 to 17.7 in 1918. The war increased the death rate in the countries involved by about 25 per cent. Kirk estimates the total population loss from the war as about 30 million. The quality of the population was also reduced, because the best physical types were in the army and made up the larger part of the casualty lists.

Population trends and policies between the two World Wars. The birth rate continued to fall in Europe between the two World Wars as follows:

	1908-1912	1921-1925	1937
England	25.2	20.4	15.3
France	19.4	19.3	14.7
Germany	30.0	22.1	18.8
Italy	32.7	29.7	22.7

The death rate, too, fell, but not so rapidly as the birth rate:

	1921-1925	1935
England	12.4	11.7
France	17.2	15.7
Germany	13.3	11.8
Italy	17.3	13.9

While Malthus believed that countries would have to become progressively solicitous and active in restricting the birth rate, exactly the reverse of this policy became fairly prevalent between the two World Wars. Instead of trying to cut down the birth rate still further, several states adopted almost frantic measures to encourage population growth and to increase the birth rate. D. V. Glass wrote a book on *The Struggle for Population*,[5] solely devoted to a description of the measures which were employed by England, Germany, Italy, France, and Belgium to increase the birth rate in these countries. Such measures included family allowances, marriage loans, bachelor taxes, prizes for large families, homestead allotments, and the like. In January, 1940, France adopted a program embodying all of these measures, designed to cost $25,000,000 the first year and to increase thereafter. No revolutionary results in the way of increasing the birth rate were produced in these countries, nor does Glass have much hope that there will be any in the immediate future unless the economic organization of society is thoroughly reconstructed to give the working classes a greater portion of the social income.

In Italy where these new forms of stimulation to population growth

---

[5] New York: Oxford University Press, 1936.

were in force longest there was a steady drop in the birth rate after Mussolini came into power—from 30.8 in 1922 to 23.4 in 1940. The slump in the birth rate was most noticeable after 1928, by which time most of the encouraging measures were in effect. In Germany the birth rate rose in the first six years of Nazi rule from 14.7 to 20.7, but students of the problem believe that this was due mainly to partial recovery from the depression as a result of the revived armament industry and public works. The restriction of abortions also played its part in increasing births. The French experiment after the Second World War will be described shortly.

Population losses in the Second World War. It is quite evident that the mortality in the Second World War was far greater than in the First, but the figures are even more elusive and incomplete. Kirk estimates the loss of life in Europe to be about 19 million. If one includes the losses in the Far East and those from starvation and chaos all over the world after the war, it is not unreasonable to hold that the total direct mortality in all continents from the Second World War was at least 40 million. One competent estimate puts it at 70 million. In Berlin, the birth rate dropped from 15.7 in 1939 to 4.9 in 1946. Even France, only briefly involved in hostilities, entered the war with a 41.5 million population and ended with 40.5 million. Of course, the ultimate population loss from the Second World War will be far greater than the direct mortality during hostilities.

Drastic French program of stimulating the birth rate. Alarmed by the decline in population and by the growth of the Russian military threat, the French government instituted the most ambitious program for stimulating the birth rate that has ever been instituted by any country save, perhaps, Soviet Russia. This is called the *Allocation Familiale*.

A bonus of $100 is given for the first child, and one of $66 for each additional one. A subsidy of $6.60 is given monthly for the support of the first child. A family with four children gets a monthly subsidy of $52. A monthly subsidy of $13 is paid for each child above the number of four. These subsidies continue until the child is 15 years of age, and until 20 years if he goes ahead with his education. There are many other special aids to families with children. An unskilled laborer may make as much, or more, out of his family subsidy, if he has four children, as he will from his wages.

The program costs about a billion dollars yearly at present and the expense is likely to increase. But it is beginning to produce the results sought. The French birth rate has risen from 14.6 in 1939 to 20 in 1950, most of the gain coming since 1946. About 850,000 French babies were born in 1950. But the increased birth rate is already creating serious problems, especially those connected with housing and education. These are likely soon to outweigh any imagined military advantages.

Basis of population stabilization. It will be distinctly worthwhile for us to examine in somewhat greater detail the bearing of these current tendencies in population growth upon the problems which society will be compelled to face in the not distant future. We shall consider first the growing stabilization of population in those areas where population increase was most notably slowing down.

We have already briefly indicated the reasons for the decline in population growth and a trend toward the stabilization of population. The birth rate was steadily falling until about 1940, while the rapid lowering of the death rate, which was characteristic of the last century, is now coming to an end, since sanitation and medical science have already produced their more revolutionary effects. Hence, the marked increase of population due to the fact that the death rate fell far more rapidly than the birth rate no longer continues in the same ratio as in the past. City life is becoming ever more predominant in industrialized states. We have already noted that various aspects of city life, living habits, recreational activities, food tastes, and the like, with their reaction upon sex relations and marriage, seem to be rather unconsciously and involuntarily lessening the fertility of the race. Further, it is in cities that we find the most complete expression of economic ambition, social climbing, and other tendencies that make people less willing to burden themselves with large families.

Population stabilization in the United States. Let us look for a moment at the facts concerning population stabilization in the United States, for it is the situation in our own country which most directly affects our interests. The following statistics, dealing with the period from 1915 to 1949, will illustrate the fact that the death rate is no longer falling as rapidly as in earlier years. This is true even though the death rate did reach an all-time low of 9.7 in 1949. By 1940, it began to appear that the birth rate had begun to reach the end of its downward trend for an unpredictable period. It increased from 16.5 in 1933 to 17.9 in 1940. But the rate of population increase from 1930 to 1940 was only 7.3, as compared with 16.1 for 1920 to 1930. We shall deal later on with the remarkable increase in the birth rate due to the unusual social conditions in the war decade.

BIRTH AND DEATH RATES IN THE UNITED STATES, 1915-1949

(Per 1,000 of Total Population)

Year	Births	Deaths	Excess of Births
1915	25.1	14.1	11.0
1920	23.7	13.1	10.6
1925	21.5	11.8	9.7
1930	18.9	11.3	7.6
1935	16.9	10.9	6.0
1940	17.9	10.7	7.2
1949	24.1	9.7	14.4

Certain representative figures will emphasize this remarkable trend toward population stabilization in the United States until 1940. From 1930 to 1940 the number of women between 14 and 44 years of age in the United States increased from 30,418,336 to 33,184,405. One would have expected a corresponding increase in the number of children. But the number of children under five declined in the same period from 11,444,390 to 10,597,891. There were 1,600,000 fewer children under ten in the country in 1938 than in 1933. There seemed to be a definite disinclination to bear children, especially on the part of city women. We may now turn to a consideration of the increase of urbanization, which, as we have seen, produces a marked decline in the birth rate.

Growing urbanization of the American population. The increase in the relative urban population of the United States is well illustrated by the fact that, in 1880, 28.6 per cent of the population lived in cities; in 1890, 35.4 per cent; in 1900, 40 per cent; in 1910, 45.8 per cent; in 1920, 51.4 per cent; in 1930, 56.2 per cent; in 1940, 56.5; and in 1950, about 59.0 per cent. In 1930 only one family out of four lived on farms. By 1950 the ratio had dropped to less than one out of five. Despite the fact that the rural birth rate is far higher than the urban, no less than four-fifths of the total national population increase from 1940 to 1950 took place within the 168 standard metropolitan areas of the United States. The new method of computation used in the 1950 census puts the actual urban population at 64.0 per cent of the total.

The following figures indicate clearly the fact that the birth rate is lowest in urban areas. In 1920, in rural states, the number of children under four years of age to each 1,000 women between the ages of 16 and 44 was 629; in partially industrialized states it was 534; and in thoroughly industrialized states, with an overwhelming predominance of the population living in cities, it was only 458. In 1940, the crude birth rate of the urban population was 16.8, and of the rural population 18.3. When corrected for differences in age distributions, the figures stood at 15.8 for the urban population and 19.5 for the rural population. These latter figures provide the best measure of the differences in urban and rural reproduction rates on the eve of the war decade.[6] Comparable information for 1950 is not yet available, but estimates for 1941-1946 indicated that the rural birth rate still remained far higher than the urban.

When will population growth cease in the United States? On the basis of these and other facts, Thompson concluded in the 1930's that the population of the United States was likely to stabilize itself around the years 1955-1960 at about 145 or 150 million. Thereafter it would begin to decline, at first slowly for a decade or two, and then more rapidly. Others predicted that it would stabilize at between 130 million and 155 million between 1955 and 1965. It has been necessary to modify these predictions considerably in the light of the unique population growth in the war decade, though the trend predicted was sound.

The sudden and striking increase in the birth rate and population during the 1940's made necessary a marked revision of the estimates regarding the size of the American population at which the stabilization would be likely and the time when this stabilization would probably take place. Instead of the former figure of somewhere between 130 million and 165 million, that which has now been suggested is between 165 million and 190 million, with about 185 million as the most likely

6 T. L. Smith, *Population Analysis*. New York: McGraw-Hill, 1948, p. 195.

figure. The time of stabilization is now estimated to be about 1985 instead of 1955 to 1965.

Population stabilization in Europe. If prewar population trends ultimately prevail, this leveling off and stabilization of population will also take place in many other countries. More and more Europeans are living in cities. Of the total population increase of 93.5 million in Europe between the two world wars, no less than 80 million of this increase was in city population, mainly produced by migration from country to city areas.

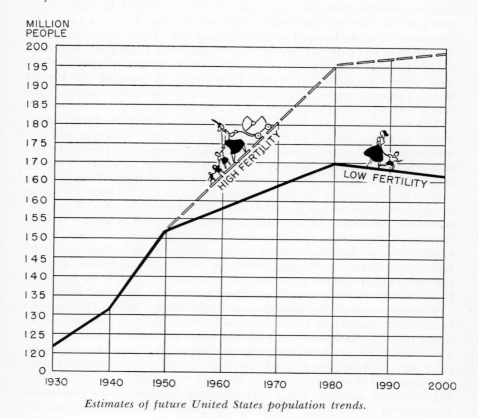

Estimates of future United States population trends.

It has been estimated that England and Wales, with a population of 43,753,000 in 1950, will have a population of about 28,600,000 in 1976, and 22,500,000 in 2000. Germany (within the March, 1938, boundaries), with a population of approximately 66 million in 1934, has been estimated to have a prospect of 70 million in 1970, and of 67 million in 2000. Indeed, some statisticians have predicted a German population as low as 46 million in 2000. As a result of losses during the Second World War, the seizure of German territory by Russia and Poland, the deprivations, starvation, disunity and economic chaos after the war, even the figure of 46 million may be too large. France, with a population of 40,500,000 in 1946, will, it is estimated, have a population of 35,000,000 in 1960, and about 30,000,000 in 2000. Italy, with a population of some 42.5 million in 1934, has been estimated to have a prospective population of 50 million in 1961, and 40 million in 2000.

While as late as the 1940's students of population were pretty generally agreed in predicting population stabilization and decline for the Western world, recent population trends may lead to the necessity of a marked revision of the above predictions. It has been thought that the spurt in population following 1940 would be a highly temporary matter produced by wartime conditions. But there is already considerable evidence that this marked increase in the birth rate may prove fairly permanent and that even in Europe and the United States populations may continue to grow during the remainder of the century. Unusual conditions, especially those demanding greater manpower to meet the alleged Russian threat, may upset previous population trends and predictions. The whole situation is too fluid as of today to warrant any dogmatism on the matter. There is, of course, no prospect of population stabilization in Asia, Oceania, Africa or Latin America for decades to come.

Possible effects of population stabilization. Thompson, Fairchild, and others have suggested that important problems of a social, economic, political, and cultural character will arise from any general tendency toward population stability such as we have described. We may, therefore, consider briefly some of the social and economic consequences of a possibly more restricted population growth in the United States. It should be kept clearly in mind, however, that the full effect of population stabilization on American society will be postponed for a generation or more later than seemed likely before the Second World War because of the striking population gains since 1940. Of course, if the spurt in the birth rate since 1940 should continue indefinitely, the previously predicted population stabilization will not take place at all, unless produced by great losses of life in war.

Some writers have held that a certain advantage may be found in that there will be a lessening of unemployment as the number of workers decreases. This benefit will, however, be limited by the fact that it is the unskilled workers and the poorer classes in the cities and country alike who are increasing most rapidly at the present time. Therefore, the working class is declining less rapidly than other groups. Further, if machines, especially automatic machinery, are introduced ever more rapidly, the growth of technological unemployment may outrun the rate at which the population growth decreases, especially among the working class. Moreover, if it continues to be difficult for older persons to obtain employment, the increasing size of this group in the population will aggravate rather than lessen the unemployment problem.

Any possible gain in diminishing unemployment will also be countered by a comparable decrease of customers or consumers. This will be particularly significant because the largest consumers of food and goods per capita are the relatively well-to-do groups which are increasing least rapidly in the population at the present time. A falling off in the number of producers would not be so important, for future inventions can supply machines that will more than offset any loss of man power. But machines cannot consume goods and services. It should be noted that this decline of customers will come in a period when improved technology is making possible the production of more goods than ever before.

Some have thought that an increased foreign market will compensate for our loss of customers at home. This hope has been encouraged by the great increase in our foreign "trade" since 1945. But most of the goods sent abroad have been given away directly in relief measures or indirectly through the Marshall Plan. This foreign charity cannot be continued indefinitely without ruining American solvency, and Americans ultimately have to pay through taxation for the goods sent abroad. Other industrialized nations will find themselves in the same situation that we are, for their populations will also be stabilizing themselves—some of them more rapidly than the United States. They, likewise, will be looking for foreign customers rather than seeking to buy goods from us. The Marshall Plan and the Economic Co-operation Administration, which is carrying it out, are building up strong competitors for the foreign trade of the world, the potentialities of which have been greatly diminished by the impoverishment of the world through war and by the barriers erected to trade with Soviet Russia, its satellites, and Communist China. The Marshall Plan seemed likely to be wrecked by the inadequacy of markets for the increased volume of goods the nations aided would be able to produce, until it was virtually transformed into an armament project in 1950-1951.

Certainly, important new developments will be likely to take place in our economic life if customers grow relatively fewer. The competition for their trade will grow ever more keen and intense. High pressure advertising may become even more the order of the day, and it may be still more irresponsible than at present, unless checked by stringent legislation. Perhaps business will make a desperate effort to create more monopolies, so that they may offset fewer sales by higher prices for the sales which can be consummated.

As population growth falls off, there will also be a smaller market for farm products. This will be particularly serious, since we can already produce more of many basic farm products than the people can buy with their existing incomes. This may mean increasing unemployment and misery for the rural population, which will be especially disastrous because it is here that the rate of population increase is greatest today.

The total effect of population stabilization may thus require extensive economic readjustments. The only plausible way of adjusting the continuation of the capitalistic system to a marked falling off in the rate of population growth will be to provide increased mass purchasing power. If there are fewer persons to make purchases, each person must have more income with which to buy food and goods. This will render necessary steadier employment and higher wages and salaries.

Yet, with a more efficient and equitable economic system this falling off of population growth could prove a real blessing. As the National Resources Committee pointed out in 1938, in its report on population trends in the United States:

The transition from an increasing to a stationary or decreasing population may on the whole be beneficial to the life of the nation. It insures the continuance of a favorable ratio of population to natural resources in the United States. Each citizen of this country will continue to have, on the average, a larger amount of arable land, minerals, and other natural resources at his disposal than the citizen of any of the countries of the Old World. This supplies the material basis for a high level of living, if these resources are used wisely and if cultural conditions are favorable to initiative and cooperative endeavor.

If capitalism is to handle this population trend successfully, it will, as we indicated above, have to provide for a far more rapid elevation of the standard of living than has ever taken place in the past. If we have bigger and better machines and fewer persons to use their products, from either factory or farm, purchasing power and consumption must increase with unprecedented rapidity. As Elbert H. Clarke remarks:

If the capitalistic scheme of things, so successful on the whole in the past, is to be preserved in the relatively near future, then the standard of living in the next American generation must rise with twice the rapidity with which it has generally risen in the past.[7]

While we may hope that this marked increase in purchasing power and living standards will actually take place, there is little current evidence that such will be the case. This was demonstrated by the vigor required in the battle of the New Deal to keep living conditions on a fair par with those in the past. Even these moderate efforts to promote human well-being were fiercely opposed by those who control contemporary American economic life. The same has been equally true of Mr. Truman's Fair Deal program. Though posing as the protagonist of a "welfare state," he has asked for only 6 per cent of the Federal budget for welfare purposes, and has received from Congress about half of what he has requested. Even this has been assailed as socialism by his critics, and welfare legislation has been virtually abandoned.

One timely and interesting result of the marked decrease in the birth rate from 1925 to 1939 is that which bears on armament and the relative proportion of males of military age today. While the total population of the country increased by about 19 million in the 1940's, the number in the age group of 10 to 19 years decreased by about 230,000, and those in the age group of 19 to 26 increased by only about 300,000. This means that, if the present conscription legislation continues, the armed forces will need virtually all physically fit males reaching 19 for some years to come.

False alarm over trend to population stability. The slowing down of population growth in the twentieth century has produced a large amount of popular nonsense and public hysteria. As Henry Pratt Fairchild has observed:

---

[7] Clarke, *loc. cit.,* p. 111.

There is scarcely any aspect of applied social science so infused with emotion, tradition, prejudice, convention, fear and romantic mysticism as the question of population. In spite of the large and increasing amount of scientific study given to the question in recent years, there still remains a vast amount of misunderstanding, and ill-informed and biased thinking on the subject.[8]

Particularly notable in this connection is the general alarm expressed in many quarters lest we are facing race suicide and the extinction of humanity. Such a notion arose from a number of causes. The rate of population growth in the nineteenth century, which was utterly unprecedented in human history, has accustomed us to look upon rapid population growth as a normal thing. Quite naturally, therefore, any stabilization of the population is viewed as a sign of racial decay and degeneration. The intense manifestations of nationalism and militarism of late have revived and strengthened the "cannon-fodder" psychosis. The first two attitudes are contrary to science and common sense. The last represents a partisan and vicious concept that does not require serious scientific discussion, however much it may demand practical social resistance. As Julian Huxley well states this point:

Why in heaven's name should anyone suppose that mere quantity of human organisms is a good thing, irrespective either of their own inherent quality or the quality of their life and experiences? . . .
It is clear that men's more ultimate aims and more satisfying satisfactions are in their essence qualitative, and are liable to be frustrated if overridden by purely quantitative aims, the mere demand for more. And that holds for the demand for more people just as much as for more material goods.[9]

As the totality of human history amply proves, the law of normal nature is a relatively stationary rather than a rapidly growing population. The nineteenth century was an unusual episode in the biological history of man. The discovery of new land and the Industrial Revolution, together with the rise of medical science, made possible an unprecedented population growth. New land has been relatively exhausted, the Industrial Revolution has passed through its main stages, and medical science has done its major work, for the time being, in reducing the death rate. Hence, we need not expect any permanent continuation of the abnormal population growth of the nineteenth century in the Western world. Indeed, if it should continue, its results would be so disastrous as to push humanity back into savagery. Further, a declining birth rate is proof of higher evolution and of racial maturity. It possesses great advantages for the race. Without it, population would have to be kept down by disease, death, famine, war, and other such agents. Moreover, the decline of population growth could make it possible to raise the standard of living and to make mundane existence really worth while for more of the population. It also enables us to give more attention to the quality rather than the mere quantity of the population.

We need not worry about the disappearance of man from the globe as

8 "Let Malthus Be Dead," *North American Review*, March, 1932, p. 202.
9 *Harper's Magazine*, September, 1950, pp. 43-44.

the result of a falling birth rate. If this trend gets at all dangerous it still might be possible to establish social sanctions and rewards for large families which will stimulate population growth. We are still, however, taking the world as a whole, threatened by population growth rather than physical decimation. We have already mentioned the possible intense national problems and serious international reverberations which may take place as a result of the probable great population gains in Asia when this continent is affected by industrialization and medical science, as the Western world was after 1750. We shall deal with this topic more thoroughly later.

If we are alarmed about the failure of recent generations to bear enough children, then our first step to correct the situation is to make this a better world into which to bring children. We must offer some incentive, in the way of security and plenty, to the bearing and rearing of children.

Increase of the aged in American population. One of the most important results of the sharp drop in immigration (in peak immigration years over 90 per cent of the arrivals were under 45), the declining birth rate, population stabilization and increased life expectancy, is the fact that there will be more old people in the population. In 1820, the average age of the whole American population was only 16.7 years; in 1880, it had risen to 20.9 years; and in 1940, to 29.0 years. By the time the population stabilizes around 1985, there may be nearly as many persons in the population over forty as under forty—over 65 million between the ages of 40 and 65, and over 25 million 65 years of age or over.

In 1860, only 2.7 per cent of the population, or 860,000, were over 65, and in 1900, only 4 per cent. In 1945, 7.2 per cent, or 9,920,000 were past 65, and in 1950, 8.1 per cent, or some 12,322,000. If this trend continues, there will be nearly 20,000,000, or more than 12 per cent, over 65 in 1970, and at least 25,000,000, or around 17 per cent, over 65 when the population of our country stabilizes about 1985. It is predicted that by the year 2000 more than 20 per cent of the population will be over 65 years of age. And, with the increasing life expectancy, an even larger percentage of those past 65 will go on to a riper old age. Theoretically, life expectancy may be extended until it approaches the natural life span of 115 to 125 years.

This increase in the number of old persons in the population is bound to produce several striking results. Consumer habits will be considerably altered. As the number of old people becomes relatively greater in the population, they will tend to spend more of their money on wheel chairs and canes and on the arts and on leisure activities, such as books, concerts, lectures, travel, and the like. They will spend less on dolls, toys, skis, roadhouses, jazz orchestras, college football, and so on. Unemployment and social security payments to the aged are bound to increase. A careful study showed that in 1890 about 70 per cent of all men over 65 were gainfully employed. By 1951, this had dropped to about 35 per cent, and it was estimated that by 1960 only about 30 per cent of those over 65 would be employed. The increasing number of aged means greater public expenditures for their support. A recent report of the Census Bureau stated that 3,500,000 over 65 have no cash income at all, and that the remainder have a median income of $808 as compared with $2,332 for the age group of 45 to 54. Total payments to the aged in 1950 amounted to nearly 3 billion dollars.

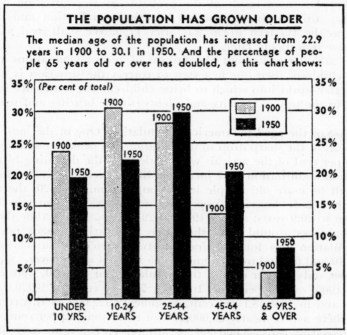

THE POPULATION HAS GROWN OLDER

The median age of the population has increased from 22.9 years in 1900 to 30.1 in 1950. And the percentage of people 65 years old or over has doubled, as this chart shows:

COURTESY NEW YORK TIMES.

Since, on the whole, social conservatism seems to go hand in hand with increasing age, a population in which older persons predominate will likely become far more conservative in both business and politics. If this is true, a serious situation may arise—the period between now and the end of the twentieth century will probably call for the most rapid and extensive institutional readjustments in the whole history of mankind. A conservative population will be poorly adapted to making such swift and sweeping changes in satisfactory fashion. Perhaps this potential conservatism of the future population of the United States will be tempered and restricted by the hardships to which the masses may be subjected in the period of readjustment and also by the greater amount of time which increased leisure will provide for reflection upon the difficulties and miseries of the period.

Another cultural change of importance will be that in the field of education. If, ultimately, there are relatively fewer children attending the schools, the latter will be less crowded and there will be less necessity for mass production methods in the educational realm. Enrollment in schools will become more stable and predictable. There will be more time and, possibly, more inclination to improve the quality of education. The necessity for adequate adult education will also be intensified. There will be relatively more older people in the population to require adult education, and they will have a greater need for adult education because of the necessity for sweeping readjustments in their life habits and modes of earning a livelihood.

All these changes due to the increasing number of old persons in the population, especially changes in the educational realm, will be postponed or modified for a generation or more because of the remarkable spurt in the birth rate in the 1940's, due to wartime conditions, and the resulting increase in the number of children. To this subject we will now turn our attention.

SOME PROBABLE RESULTS OF THE SPURT IN POPULATION GROWTH SINCE 1940

Spurt of birth rate in the 1940's. Although there was a steady falling off in the rate of population growth between the two world wars, a sharp reversal of this trend took place in the 1940's, due mainly to the special conditions produced by the war. Among these were the following: over 15 million young men were taken into the armed services and auxiliary aids. Most of these required a considerable period of training before being sent overseas. This gave many the opportunity to marry before embarking, and a large number did so because of romance, passion, or apprehensiveness concerning their fate. Many of those who married left pregnant brides behind. The higher wages and full employment of the war period encouraged a higher marriage and birth rate among civilians. Then, after V-E and V-J Days, millions of veterans returned home filled with procreative frenzy; this led to a great increase in the birth rate for several years after 1945.

Though this marked spurt in the birth rate in the 1940's may be a temporary matter, it is bound to affect social conditions in this country for a generation or more. First, let us look at some of the basic facts.

The birth rate in the United States increased from 17.9 in 1940 to 25.8 in 1947, 24.2 in 1948, and 24.1 in 1949. The marriage rate increased from about 100 per 10,000 of the population in the 1930's to 163 in 1946. Whereas there were only 2,203,000 children born in 1937, some 3,700,000 were born in 1947. The census of 1950 revealed 29,665,000 children under ten years of age, an increase of 39.3 per cent over the pre-war decade. The total population growth from 1940 to 1950 was 19,028,086, an all-time record for a decade. The previous high had been 17,064,426 for the decade between 1920 and 1930. Most of this record population growth during the 1940's was due to the excessive number of births. Any decline in the civilian death rate was offset by war casualties, and immigration, while higher than in the 1930's, added less than a million to the native population. The following table shows the shift in the number in the various age groups of the population between 1940 and 1950. Those under 10 years of age and those over 65 made the most striking gains.

Age	1940	1950	Per Cent Increase
All ages	131,669,275	150,697,000	14.5
Under 10 years	21,226,146	29,656,000	39.3
10 to 24 years	35,667,293	33,420,000	6.4*
25 to 44 years	39,672,246	44,945,000	13.3
45 to 64 years	26,084,276	30,444,000	16.7
65 years and over	9,019,314	12,322,000	36.6

*Decrease

Those European countries least affected by war losses also experienced an unusual increase in the marriage and birth rate in the 1940's, but none as marked as the United States.

Results of recent gains in the birth rate. What are some of the existing and probable results of this striking variation in normal population trends? In the first place, by 1950, those under 15 were the largest single group in the population. This reduced the disproportionate percentage of the group over 65. It restored a better balance between youth and old age in the population. Second, it postponed by two decades, from 1965 to 1985, the time when the total population growth of the nation may be expected to level off, and made the figure at which the stabilization occurs considerably larger, about 185,000,000, as against the earlier estimate of 130,000,000 to 165,000,000. Third, unless teachers are better provided for and so induced to enter and to remain in the profession, there will be a real crisis in our public schools. Some 26,774,000 were enrolled in our public schools in 1951, but it is predicted that there will be 33,561,000 enrolled in 1957. Yet, due to inadequate pay and other unattractive features of the teaching profession today, the number of teachers is decreasing rather than increasing. Over 400,000 teachers have left the profession since 1940. Many have not been replaced, and many of the replacements are inferior to the teaching force of 1940. Fourth, there is bound to be a boom in industries that furnish food and supplies to babies and youth, and fifth, a further intensification of the already menacing housing shortage. Finally, this group of 8 million additional children born in the 1940's beyond prewar expectations are bound to affect the employment problem later, if we avoid a third world war.

Population trends of the 1940's may continue. During the 1940's most students of population believed that the high marriage and birth rates were chiefly a product of wartime conditions and that there would be a return to the trends of the 1930's following 1950. As yet, there seems little evidence that this will be the case, at least for some years to come. Some 3.7 million babies were born in 1950, this making the fourth year in a row that more than 3.5 million babies had been born each year. The net population of the United States increased by 2,475,000 during 1950. During the last six months of 1950, the annual rate of increase was 2,792,000, the highest in our history. Some students of population predicted that the country would reach a population of 165 million before 1960—a figure earlier predicted as attainable only by 1980 or later.

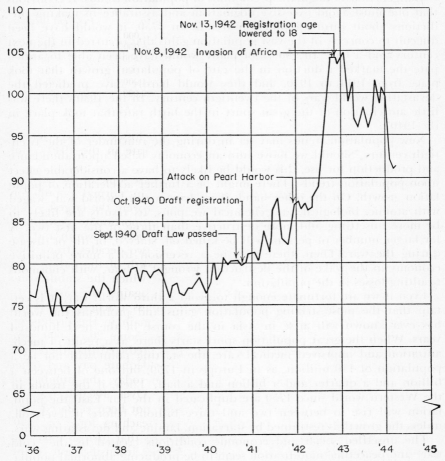

Graph indicating how the Second World War stimulated the birth rate in the United States.

The most probable explanation for the continuance of this trend towards many births and rapid population growth lies in the biological impact of the numerous marriages in the period since 1945 and the revival of social conditions like the wartime days of the 1940's in the intensified cold war, the draft, the Korean war, and the announcement of many years ahead of emergency military mobilization. All these things revived the notable trend towards the high marriage rate and procreative activity of the war years. The marriage rate rose sharply during the last six months of 1950, and the birth rate went up markedly during 1951. There is no great likelihood of any permanent reversion to prewar population trends until political and social conditions return to a more normal state. This may be postponed for a generation.

Dangers in over-dogmatic predictions of population trends. It is obvious that one must avoid excessive dogmatism and assurance in making predictions about future population trends. In 1750, it would have been difficult to conceive of the vast population gains that occurred in the next century and a half. In 1900, not many would have been able to anticipate the marked reduction in the rate of population growth that took place from 1914 to 1940, and they would hardly have predicted the devastating world wars of the twentieth century. In the 1930's there was little anticipation of the great spurt in the birth rate that took place in the 1940's.

New population trends may set in during the remainder of the twentieth century. Should we move into an economy based upon abundance and production for use, this would be likely to have a considerable effect upon population trends. There might be a further acceleration of population growth. On the other hand, if we have a third world war, waged with atomic, biological, and chemical weapons, its results are likely to be more unsettling and more destructive than those of the first two. A far larger number of persons will be killed off, starved, or die of disease during the war. Then, there may be a reversion to a more primitive economy in the wake of the destruction wrought by war, with enormous resulting losses in the population.

Even if we are fortunate enough to avoid a third world war, it is certain that the most striking population gains and problems the world has ever known will arise in Asia in the course of the next hundred years. When the great population spurt starts there, as a result of mechanization and improved medical care, the starting point will not be a population of 140 million, as in Europe in 1750, but one of between a billion and a quarter and a billion and a half. Then, if the trends in the Western world since 1750 are duplicated in the Far East, the population will rise to between two and three billions before it levels off, unless the growth is restrained by starvation, famine and devastating wars.

The unsettled social and economic conditions created by the "cold war" and peacetime mobilization seem to be producing abnormal population trends not unlike those of the 1940's. This is sure to be the case if these conditions persist for many years, as is now predicted.

SOME LEADING SOCIAL IMPLICATIONS OF DIFFERENTIAL
POPULATION GROWTH

Contrasts in rate of population growth. We may now look somewhat more thoroughly into the more important implications of the differential rate of population growth as manifested among the regions of the world, the major countries of Europe, and the various areas, social classes, and age groups in the United States. By differential population growth we mean such facts as that some continents have a higher rate of population growth than others, that on each continent some nations grow in numbers more rapidly than their neighbors, that the rural birth rate is higher than that of the city, and that the poorer and least educated elements in the population have a higher birth rate than the well-to-do and the well educated.

A few statistics on the population situation will prove illuminating. The differential rate of population increase among the various continents of the world is revealed by the following figures giving the annual natural increase per 1,000 from 1900 to 1930:

Europe	7.8
Asia	4.8
Africa	0.3
North America	15.6
South America	26.3
Oceania	16.8

The following statistics show percentage of population increase in European countries between 1920 and 1939:

England and Wales	8.0	Czechoslovakia	14.0
France	7.0	Albania	32.3
Germany	13.9	Bulgaria	30.0
Netherlands	28.7	Greece	43.5
Italy	15.6	Rumania	28.2
Spain	20.2	Jugoslavia	31.0
Poland	29.9	U.S.S.R.	27.0

Relative population density in world regions. The relative pressure of population, which is related to the birth and death rates, past and present, differs greatly among the various countries of the world, and thus creates an unstable equilibrium in world society. The following table presents relative and typical contrasts in population pressure, as measured by the number of inhabitants per square mile in each of the countries mentioned:

Great Britain	504.7
Japan	469.
India	176.3
China	145.6
United States	44.2
Brazil	14.0
Argentina	12.2

The relatively low density of India and China compared to Great Britain and Japan is due to the vast areas of mountains and desert in both of these countries. Those portions that are the real centers of population have an extreme density of population, some of them much greater than Britain or Japan.

Population pressure may cause war. This situation has made for international tension and war in the present economic and political order. Britain could support its population only by the receipts from a great colonial empire; hence, she fought to maintain this empire. Japan thought she must expand in order to relieve population pressure and to get income from colonies. In this way, Britain and Japan clashed. The United States refused to acquiesce to Japan's expansion; hence, we tangled with Japan, and so on.

Differential population growth in Europe. Although in the Western world the twentieth century has been characterized by a marked slowing down of population growth and a tendency toward the stabilization of population, this has by no means been universally true, even of all of Europe. In what are still predominantly agricultural areas, such as Poland, Russia and southeastern Europe, population growth remains relatively rapid. In agricultural economies the various socio-psychological conditions of city life that make for a lower birth rate do not operate as extensively as in industrialized nations. The latest estimates, those for 1937, give the birth rate for northwestern Europe as 17, for southern Europe as 23, and for eastern Europe as 30-34. The crude birth rate for Poland in 1938 was 24.8; for Bulgaria in 1940 it was 22.2; for Rumania in 1940 it was 26.5; and for Jugoslavia in 1939 it was 25.9. It has been estimated that the population of southeastern Europe will increase by some 27,000,000 between 1940 and 1970.

Economic and political aspects of differential population growth in Europe. In Europe in the 1930's one could observe the reaction of Germany and Italy against Russia and the French and British empires. Germany was a highly industrialized state that needed both food products and raw materials from outside as well as a greater market for German goods. Italy needed to find an outlet for what was an exceedingly large population in certain parts of Italy. Italy also required raw materials and markets. There was a feeling that Russia, Britain, and France had more of this world's goods, in the form of territory and resources, than was compatible with reason and justice.

The Second World War grew in part out of this situation of population pressure and the rivalry between have and have-not nations. The so-called peace settlements since V-J Day have only intensified this situation, which played so prominent a rôle in producing the Second World War. And perhaps even more unsettling today as a factor in the world politics of the future is the promise of vast Russian population growth, to which we shall now call attention.

It is obvious that the decidedly differential rate of population growth among the states of Europe will, if it continues for any length of time, bring about a readjustment in the relative power and prestige of the European countries. Those in which the population growth is steadily falling off will be outdistanced by hitherto less powerful and important states that have a far more impressive rate of population growth. This will certainly be true if man power continues to be of primary importance in determining the relative political and military strength of modern states. If air, tank, and submarine warfare supplants, to any considerable degree, the old types of conflict waged by infantry and by capital ships, sheer man power may, however, count for less in the future of warfare. But certainly no predictable changes in the nature of war will entirely eliminate the importance of huge reserves of man power for both military and industrial purposes. The German defeat by Russia in 1941-1945 demonstrated this.

Implications of rapid population growth in Soviet Russia. One of the most remarkable aspects of differential population growth in relation to world politics today is the contrast of the situation in Russia and southern Europe with that in Western Europe. Countries in the latter region seem to be approaching a stable population, but the prospect is for an enormous increase of population in the next twenty years in Russia and southern Europe. Our ablest students of population believe that European Russia, even within its 1938 boundaries, will have an increase in population of some 77,000,000 from 1940 to 1970, and will have a total population at the latter date of some 250,000,000. The increase will be greater than the total population of Germany in 1937.

In 1970, Russia will have more males of working age than those in all the countries of Western Europe. She will have 32,000,000 men of prime military age, between 20 and 34—more than the next seven largest European countries combined. The United States in 1970 will have only about 18,000,000 men in the 20-34 age group. Moreover, there will be a relatively larger number of young men in Russia in 1970, which means that the population will go on increasing rapidly, whereas that of Western Europe will probably have stabilized before 1970. These figures do not take into account the fact that, since 1938, Russia has annexed territory inhabited by about 25,000,000 persons, all of a highly fertile group.

The remarkable increase in the Russian population has been stimulated by an extensive system of punishments and rewards. There are heavy taxes on spinsters, bachelors, and small families. Special care is provided for mothers, and a bonus is paid on every child after the second one. These bonuses increase notably in cases of large families. The bonus at the birth of a fourth child is 400 rubles and that at the birth of the eleventh child is 5,000 rubles. There is an allowance of 80 rubles per month for the fourth child, which rises to 300 per month for the eleventh. Illegitimacy is not discouraged; indeed, it is indirectly encouraged, for unmarried mothers get an allowance after the birth of their first child. There are medals for mothers of many children, and honorary titles and orders for these, such as "Heroine Mothers" and the "Order of Motherhood Glory." Abortions were outlawed in 1936, and birth control is now discouraged.

Interestingly enough, such efforts have failed to increase the Russian birth rate. An official report in November, 1951 stated that although the Russian population, including annexed areas, had increased from 193,000,000 in 1939 to 207,000,000 in 1951, the birth rate had dropped from 38.3 to about 25. The marked population increase seems to have been produced by a reduction in the Russian death rate.

Population growth and density in the Far East. Equally striking is the contrast between population trends in the Western world and those in the Far East. In the Far East, the birth rate increased from 1870 to 1940. For example, in Japan in 1878-1882 the birth rate was 24.7 per 1,000, while in 1921-1925 it was 34.6, and 34.0 in 1948, even after the Second

World War. The annual net increase of population before the Second World War was about 900,000. It has risen since, being estimated by Juitsu Kitaoka, a Japanese population expert, as about 1,750,000 in 1950. At the present rate of increase the population of Japan, now about 83,000,000, would be over 120,000,000 in 1975.

Although we do not have precise figures available for China, students of population agree that the birth rate has also increased there rather markedly during the last half century. It is estimated that China now has a population of about 500 million, with an excess of births over deaths of 15 per 1,000 annually. This would mean an increase of over 7 million a year now, and would lead to a doubling of the present population by the end of the century. Such Chinese provinces as Kiangsu have the highest population density of any political unit of comparable size in the world. The Chinese birth rate is still high, but there is a large infant mortality, to say nothing of the prevalence of infanticide and famines. In Shanghai alone, some 35,000 bodies of dead newborn infants are picked up on the streets each year. The birth rate in India is also very high, and the population growth is rapid, despite the high death rate. In 1920, India had a population of about 340 million. By 1940 it had increased to nearly 390 million. Including Pakistan, it had reached the 420 million mark by 1951.

Although the death rate in these oriental countries is still high—on the increase in most of them—there is every prospect that it will begin to fall as industrialization and improved medical methods are introduced. Indeed, in Japan the death rate has already begun to fall rather strikingly, dropping from 21.8 in 1921-1925 to 20.5 in 1936 and 12.0 in 1948. It is very possible that, as a result of industrialization, improved agricultural methods, and better medical care and sanitation, the Orient will, in the second half of the twentieth century, reproduce the experience of the Western world during the nineteenth century by a striking increase of population—possibly followed later on by the stabilization of population growth. A leading population expert, P. K. Whelpton, estimates that the population of Asia will increase by 135 million in the next 20 years.

Political and international consequences of the Far Eastern population situation. Let us now consider the significance of population differentials among the main regions of the world, the existence of which has produced what Thompson calls "danger spots in world population." Since the population pressure is far greater in the Orient than in the Occident, we may find a future line-up of East versus West. The countries with large populations, limited areas, and relatively slight natural resources may use their impressive future man power to seize a foothold in the territory of the more fortunate states.

Important military and political consequences resulted from the fact that the oriental countries had a rapid population growth in the twentieth century while most of the West grew more slowly. Some of these countries were tempted to enlarge their boundaries to support more people. Japan began to seek more "living room" early in the twentieth century, when it annexed Korea after wars with China and Russia. In

1931 Japan entered and conquered Manchuria and in 1937 invaded China proper. At the height of her successes in the Second World War Japan had occupied much of eastern China, had captured the American bases in the Philippines, had driven the English back from Malaya and Hong Kong, had ousted the French from Indo-China, and had overrun Thailand and much of the East Indies.

Although the defeat of Japan in the Second World War temporarily ended Japanese expansion, the halt to population growth was only temporary and no permanent equilibrium can be expected. Indeed, the Japanese situation is getting worse than it was before the expansion movement of the 1930's. All Japanese have been brought back to Japan. There, the population has increased from 78,000,000 in 1945 to 83,000,000 in 1950. It will reach 90,000,000 by 1955. Even now, the 83,000,000 Japanese are being saved from starvation mainly by American taxpayers, who bear the occupation costs. The great prospective population growth of China and India may well lead them to repeat later the Japanese expansionist trends of the first half of the twentieth century. India has thrown off the British yoke. Whatever form the unrest due to population growth in the Far East may take, it is likely to exert a disturbing influence in world politics. It will be stimulated by growing nationalistic trends and resistance to foreign imperialism.

Emigration, even if freely allowed, would not take care of the excess population in Asia. Japan's annual increase in population today is about 1,750,000. This number cannot leave for other areas without profound economic and political disturbances. Moreover, even if such emigration were possible and peaceful, it would not greatly lessen the rate of population increase at home. If the United States took in only those suffering from famine in China (5-10 million in average years and 20 million in bad famine years), it would swamp the country without greatly reducing the frequency or severity of famine in China.

Differential population growth among social classes. The Old World provides evidence of differential fertility rates and population growth not only among continents and nations, but also among social and economic classes. In all advanced and industrialized countries in Europe the lowest birth rate is found among the professional and business classes, and the highest among the unskilled workers who see little hope of climbing the social ladder. This can be illustrated by a study of English fertility rates in 1931. The number of family births per 1,000 married men in England in this year ran as follows: professional men, 98; business men, 102; clerical workers, 111; skilled workers, 140; semi-skilled workers, 162; and unskilled workers, 174.

As we shall soon see, this class differential in fertility rates holds good for the United States. It is obvious that this situation has serious and unfortunate social implications with respect to social well-being and intellectual attainments.

Differential fertility and population growth in the United States. Since the United States is a politically unified country, the most important facts about differential fertility rates and population growth here at present are: (1) the tendency of the rural birth rate to be higher than that in cities; and (2) the fact that the differences in the birth rate are associated very definitely with gradations in the social hierarchy according to income and education.

We have already pointed out that the corrected rural birth rate of 19.5 in 1940, as compared with the urban rate of 15.8, demonstrated the excess in the rural reproduction rate. Other statistics bear out this fact. If we take the period from 1925 to 1929 and limit ourselves to the white population, we find that the rural farm women were providing a natural population increase (excess of births over deaths) of 60 per cent each generation. The rural non-farm women provided a natural increase of about one-half this amount. Women in rural villages and small cities were just about insuring mere replacement or population stability. In cities with a population between 25,000 and 250,000 the fertility of the women was so low as to produce a loss of 10 per cent in the population, and in the very large cities the loss was 20 per cent.

In 1929-1931 married native white women living in urban areas produced during their child-bearing period only 2.1 children on the average; rural non-farm women bore 3.2 children; and rural farm women produced 3.7 children. This represented a fertility differential of about 80 per cent between urban and rural women. In 1940 the current generation of women of child-bearing age was reproducing itself only to the extent of 96 per cent. The rate for urban women was 74 per cent; for rural non-farm women, 114 per cent; and for rural farm women 144 per cent. Calculations for the period of 1941-1946 place the net reproduction rate for the urban population at 98, for rural non-farm groups at 136, and for the rural farm population at 193. Not only is rural fertility much greater than urban, but the death rate in rural areas is, on the whole, lower than that in cities, even with the inferior medical care. In rural areas, the fertility is greatest among the most submerged rural groups: the farm laborers, farm renters and owners of marginal farms.

Perhaps even more significant than the fertility differential as between urban and rural areas is that among socio-economic and socio-cultural groups.[10] Frank W. Notestein made a careful study of this differential fertility based on the 1910 census and found that the fertility groups ranked in the following order, from highest to lowest: farm laborers, farm renters, farm owners, unskilled urban laborers, skilled workers, business classes, and professional classes. As T. L. Smith has pointed out, subsequent studies of this situation only confirm Notestein's findings: "All recent work in the United States has done little more than substantiate more fully the conclusions reached by Frank W. Notestein in his thorough analysis of the 1910 census data."[11] The general nature of this differential ratio of population increase in the United States has been summarized by Notestein:

---

[10] For the most illuminating survey of the sociological implications of the differential fertility of socio-economic and socio-cultural groups, see P. H. Landis, *Population Problems.* New York: American Book Company, 1948, Chaps. VI-IX.

[11] Smith, *op. cit.,* p. 220.

During 1930 to 1935, 55 per cent of the nation's excess of births over deaths was contributed by that third of the population living in the principal agricultural areas. Within these areas the largest contributions came from the poorest sections. In 1930 the fertility of the population in the agricultural problem areas was 76 per cent above the permanent replacement level. On the other hand, in cities with 25,000 or more inhabitants, fertility averaged only 85 per cent of that necessary for permanent maintenance of the population, and in one-quarter of those cities it was less than 75 per cent of that level. Within each city fertility was highest among the poor and unskilled and lowest in the business and professional classes.[12]

The following table, based on figures from representative American cities, brings out the fact that the largest urban population increase tended to come in families of unskilled workers with a low income and inferior educational equipment. With respect to education, the only group which was replacing itself through the net reproduction rate was that having less than a seventh grade education. Those on the college level were only about half replacing themselves.

DIFFERENTIAL NATALITY IN AMERICAN CITIES
(Births per Thousand Native White Married Women, 1935)

Occupation of Head		Family Income per Year		Educational Attainment of Wife	
Business	93	$3,000 and over....	88		
Professional	101	2,000–2,999	73	College	97
Skilled	101	1,500–1,999	77	High School	98
Semi-skilled	116	1,000–1,499	94	7th-8th grades	114
Unskilled	137	Under $1,000	137	Under 7th grade....	140

Contrary to the general impression, there is not, at the present time, any striking differential in the birth rate as between native and immigrant stocks, except for the recent Mexican immigrants, who are increasing more rapidly than any other group in the United States, while the Negroes and the whites today have both reached what is approximately an equilibrium as to true reproduction rates, though the Negro birth rate remains higher than that of the white in normal times.

General consequences of contrasting rates of population growth. The social consequences of these contrasting rates of population growth for the future of American society are of extreme significance, even if one eschews any single-track biological interpretation of society and culture. The issues involved were the main theme of a scholarly and comprehensive work by Frank Lorimer and Frederick Osborn,[13] in which they divided the effects of the differential rate of population increase into four types: (1) economic; (2) intellectual trends; (3) changes in hereditary vitality; and (4) alterations in the social environment.

The most important economic effects of differential population growth

---

[12] *Birth Control Review*, April, 1938, p. 76.

[13] Frank Lorimer and Frederick Osborn, *The Dynamics of Population*. New York: Macmillan, 1934.

stressed by Lorimer and Osborn were the accumulation of a surplus population in agricultural areas with limited natural resources and low living standards, and a comparable prevalence of a surplus of unskilled rural and city workers.

The excess of agricultural population not only means low standards of rural life but also produces a large crop of migratory farm laborers without any fixed habitat or any satisfactory family life. It is particularly significant that this high birth rate in the farm population takes place, in part, in rural areas where farming opportunities have become progressively less attractive and productive—areas that have been denuded by dust storms and other results of generations of senseless destruction of grasslands, forests, and other natural resources. Moreover, after many years of migration of the abler and more alert types from the country to the cities, it is probable that the rural element is inferior to what it was several generations back.

The striking increase in the number of unskilled workers is also particularly ominous because it comes in an era characterized by the unprecedented introduction of labor-saving machinery, automatic machines, and the resulting technological unemployment. These unskilled workers, at best, have inadequate income, are insecure in their employment, live in misery, have restricted educational opportunities, and often represent a relatively low quality of population with respect to intellectual attainments. Unless there are marked changes in the economic basis of society, their condition is bound to grow worse.

Accepting even a moderate view of the situation, the fact that the greatest population increases take place among those of the lowest economic, social, and intellectual status, in country and city alike, means that we are lowering, slowly but surely, the "average hereditary capacity for intellectual development." Lorimer and Osborn concluded, with respect to the significance of these population differentials:

Present reproduction tendencies seem to be having especially serious effects at both extremes of the scale of intellectual development, tending disproportionately to reduce the number of individuals with unusual ability to be expected from any given number of births, and significantly to increase the proportion of individuals of low-grade intelligence.[14]

This deplorable trend in the intellectual realm is further intensified by the fact that, since the poorer groups provide most of the population increase, their children have the most restricted opportunity for educational training and advantages.

Lorimer and Osborn did not believe that any changes of great importance are taking place with respect to hereditary vitality, that is, inherited capacity for health and longevity. A longer study of the problem may, however, lead to a modification of this interpretation.

The differential rate of population increase among various groups of the American population is having a definitely deleterious effect upon the social environment in which children are reared. Those who can provide

---

[14] *Ibid.*, p. 346. By permission of The Macmillan Company, publishers.

the best educational and cultural advantages are not reproducing rapidly enough:

It is evident that those who enjoy the greatest cultural resources are not having enough children to replace themselves in the next generation, and that the most undeveloped groups in our national life are the chief sources of population increase.... Thus, each new generation of Americans is tending to be disproportionately recruited from areas with low standards of living and inferior educational resources.[15]

In the light of all these facts, Lorimer and Osborn sensibly recommended a comprehensive program of research to reveal all the facts as to the nature and implications of the differential rate of population increase in our country and the adoption of resolute and adequate social policies to solve the problems which are emerging therefrom.

The need for this remains unchanged after the Second World War. It was estimated by competent social economists that, in 1950, some two-thirds of our children were born in families that do not have a sufficient income to provide the sheer physical necessities required for a decent standard of living, to say nothing of adequate educational and cultural opportunities.

Uncertain future fertility trends. Whether the new trends in population growth and fertility which accompanied the spurt in the birth rate during the war decade will seriously modify past trends with respect to differential fertility in the United States will become evident only with the passage of time. The recent developments connected with the "cold war," extensive peacetime draft of civilians, mobilization, and threat of a third world war may revive and perpetuate the abnormal marriage and fertility trends that dominated the 1940's.

Economic complications. The problems of differential population growth and the adaptation of the population to its environment are complicated by economic changes. There are many places in the country where we have a marked overpopulation. The slum areas harboring the mass of the poor in our great urban centers will immediately come to mind. But they do not by any means exhaust the situation. In the Great Lakes area there are many persons living on a low standard who once worked in the forestry industry there. As the latter became extinct they could not find ready employment elsewhere. The Dust Bowl and adjacent regions in the West, which have been temporarily ruined by dust deposits, can no longer support their former populations. Moreover, intensive agriculture without proper fertilization has disastrously affected many areas in the South and has made it difficult, if not impossible, for many of the inhabitants to eke out a bare existence. Improved farm machinery has decreased the need for farm labor in both South and West. To solve such situations, resettlement efforts must be combined with birth control. Ever since 1920, there has been a widespread movement of people from the whole central portion of the United States, from the Gulf of Mexico to the Canadian border, to the Pacific coast or the northeastern

---

[15] *Ibid.*, p. 345. By permission of The Macmillan Company, publishers.

portion of the country, tempered only by the flocking of workers to the automobile manufacturing centers in Michigan and adjacent areas.

SUMMARY

The population of the world increased very slowly prior to the middle of the eighteenth century. The reason for this was the high death rate that preceded the development of modern medical science, and the inadequacy of the food supply before the rise of scientific agriculture, mechanical industry, and contemporary transportation methods.

Population has grown rapidly since about 1750. The world population has increased from about 660 million to more than two and one quarter billion; European population has grown from 140 million to about 550 million; and the population of the United States, from 4 million to about 151 million.

Though some believe that the rapid growth of population in modern times has been the result of an increase in the birth rate, this is not true. The birth rate has been falling in all industrialized countries for more than a century. The chief reasons for this are the total conditions of city life, which discourage large families, and the appearance of new means of preventing conception.

Population trends in industrialized countries seem to follow this pattern: first, rapid increase of population; then, a slackening of the rate of population growth; and finally, stabilization of population, with births about equalling deaths. This pattern is called by students of population "the demographic transition."

War conditions and postwar international situations have produced a remarkable spurt in the birth rate in the Western world which may at least temporarily upset the prewar trends toward population stabilization and decline.

As a result of the declining birth rate and the increase of life expectancy, more and more old persons are to be found in the population. This creates a number of new social problems, some of them extensive and serious.

Taking the world as a whole, there is a marked contrast in the rate of population growth between the more backward agricultural countries and those which have been mechanized and urbanized. This is especially notable in comparing Western Europe with Soviet Russia and the Far East where the rate of population growth is still high. This situation produces grave political and international problems.

There is also a marked contrast in birth rates within each country— at least in all industrialized countries. The highest birth rate is found among those who are the least well-to-do and those who are least educated. This raises serious problems of social welfare.

The main population problem of today in all civilized countries is that of population quality rather than quantity. We have plenty of people. There is no need for larger populations. The great problem is to insure a high quality of children and to provide proper opportunities for the development of those who are born. Hence, the problem of population shades off into the fields of eugenics, economic reform and education.

SELECTED REFERENCES

*Carr-Saunders, A. M., *The Population Problem*. Oxford: Clarendon Press, 1922. A standard work on basic aspects of the population problem. Especially notable for elucidation of the principle of an "optimum population."

————, *World Population: Past Growth and Present Trends*. Oxford: Clarendon Press, 1936. A comprehensive historical treatment of population tendencies in recent times, including a survey of the world situation before the Second World War.

*Cook, R. C., *Human Fertility*. New York: William Sloane Associates, 1951. An able, if slightly alarmist, book dealing with the present trends towards a revival of rapid population growth.

Davis, Kingsley, *The Population of India and Pakistan*. Princeton: Princeton University Press, 1951. Excellent recent monograph discussing one of the main areas of the Far East which is subject to massive overpopulation.

Dublin, L. I., and Lotka, A. J. *Length of Life*. New York: Ronald Press, 1950. Able general statistical study of the increase in life expectancy and related population trends.

Glass, D. V., *Population Policies and Movements in Europe*. Oxford: Clarendon Press, 1940. Survey of the prewar European population situation, with special emphasis on efforts to increase the rate of population growth.

Kirk, Dudley, *Europe's Population in the Interwar Years*. New York: Columbia University, League of Nations Publications, 1946. Best discussion in English of the impact of the First World War on population trends, and of developments between the two world wars. Ample tables and statistical data.

*Landis, P. H., *Population Problems*. New York: American Book Company, 1948. One of the more recent manuals on population problems. Especially valuable for emphasis on social and cultural aspects of population growth.

Lorimer, Frank, *The Population of the Soviet Union: History and Prospects*. New York: Columbia University, League of Nations Publications, 1946. Comprehensive analysis of current population trends in Russia, with predictions of remarkable future growth in next half century.

*Lorimer, Frank, and Osborn, Frederick, *Dynamics of Population*. New York: Macmillan, 1934. Very important for a discussion of the social implications of differential fertility and population growth.

*Lorimer, Frank, Winston, Ellen E. B., and Kiser, L. K., *Foundations of American Population Policy*. New York: Harper, 1940. An excellent book on prewar population trends in the United States and their social implications.

Mather, K. F., *Enough and To Spare*. New York: Harper, 1944. A counterargument to the views of Vogt and Osborn. Contends that the world still has plenty of natural resources if wars and waste are curbed.

Myrdal, Gunnar, *Population: A Problem for Democracy*. Cambridge: Harvard University Press, 1940. Able discussion of public and political problems of population trends.

National Resources Committee, *Problems of a Changing Population*. Washington: Government Printing Office, 1938. The official summary of prewar population tendencies in the United States and predictions of future trends. Stresses the slowing down of population growth and the increasing number of old people.

*Notestein, F. W., *et al.*, *Future Population of Europe and the Soviet Union.* New York: Columbia University, League of Nations Publications, 1944. Best analysis of the extent and implications of the differential rate of population growth in eastern and western Europe.

Smith, T. L., *Population Analysis.* New York: McGraw-Hill, 1948. Extensive descriptive demographical material dealing with the population situation in the United States today.

Thompson, W. S., *Population Problems.* New York: McGraw-Hill, 1935. A standard book on population problems. It deals with many related social problems, such as the growth and redistribution of city populations.

*————, *Plenty of People.* New York: Ronald Press, 1948. Supplements the previous book by bringing it down to date in light of subsequent population trends.

*————, *Population and Peace in the Pacific.* Chicago: University of Chicago Press, 1946. Thoughtful discussion of local and international implications of future population prospects in Asia. Essentially supplants author's previous book on *Danger Spots in World Population.*

Whelpton, P. K., *et al.*, *Forecasts of the Population of the United States: 1945-1975.* Washington: Government Printing Office, 1947. Probably the most expert and authoritative prediction of population trends in the United States.

CHAPTER 3

Population Theories, Birth Control, and Eugenics

LEADING THEORIES OF POPULATION

The Malthusian law of population growth. Changes in population levels have naturally aroused the interest of observers of social conditions. Population problems have been discussed by writers for thousands of years. A scholar in the field of population questions, Charles E. Stangeland, actually wrote a good-sized book on the many theories of population growth that had been set forth before the time of Malthus, with whom many people believe that the discussion of population problems began.

We have no space here for the discussion of historical curiosities in the field of population theory, so we shall begin our review of some leading theories of population growth with a discussion of the notions of Thomas Robert Malthus (1766-1834). It has been deemed most fruitful to treat the theories of population after we have had an opportunity to consider the actual facts about population growth throughout the course of the history of Western society.

In 1798 there appeared the first edition of Thomas Robert Malthus' *Essay on Population,* which was destined to have a remarkable influence on economic and social discussions for more than a century. The substance of Malthus' argument was: (1) population tends to increase at a geometric ratio (1, 2, 4, 8, 16, and so on), but the food supply cannot possibly be made to increase at more than an arithmetic ratio (1, 2, 3, 4, and so on); and (2) as a result, population tends always to press upon the underlying means of subsistence.

Malthus has been subjected to much unfair and irrelevant criticism by those who have not read his doctrines with care. For example, he has been alleged to hold that the food supply actually increases at an arithmetic ratio. Then it is pointed out that the food supply often fails to increase at any such ratio. Or, it is observed that population does not increase at an exact geometric ratio. Malthus' real statements on these points seem well within the bounds of reason. He only alleged a definite tendency to approximate such ratios.

Malthus saw two kinds of checks to the tendency of population to outrun its food supply—(1) positive: war, pestilence, and starvation; and

(2) negative: postponement of marriages to a later age, and what he described as "moral restraint." In the England of his day, Malthus sincerely believed that a considerable part of the population could hardly escape a life of poverty and misery. He feared that, for the immediate future at least, any increase in the means of subsistence would tend to bring about a more than corresponding increase in the size of the population.

Malthus issued later and more complete editions of his famous work on population. Though he did not alter his basic ideas, as contained in the original edition of his book, later versions did modify certain important details. In the later statements of his doctrines, Malthus tended to lay less stress upon the precise ratios between the increase of human numbers and the means of subsistence. He was more inclined to emphasize only the general tendencies implied in these ratios. He also was willing to admit that many factors, in addition to the pressure of population on the means of subsistence, help to determine the growth of numbers in any given population. Finally, he became rather more optimistic, in that he believed that his proposed negative or preventive checks on population growth were actually beginning to work and were rendering unnecessary the more harsh and drastic conditions involved in the positive checks, such as famines and wars.

The validity of the Malthusian theory of population today. So important has been the Malthusian theory of population that it will be worth while to examine its validity quite dispassionately in the light of historic changes. It is obvious that, in Western Europe, the population has increased notably since 1800. Yet, the rate of increase has not been greater, but actually less, than the increase of the food supply available. This does not necessarily invalidate the so-called Malthusian law, but it does point to other factors at work in the actual situation, most notably scientific agriculture, the artificial preservation of food, and better transportation methods. In fact, a careful statement of the law would immediately destroy many of the criticisms. For example, sudden and extensive increases in food supply cannot instantaneously lead to equal increases in the population.

Obviously, Malthus' law was intended to apply to a given population within a definite area. If the boundaries of the area are changed, as has been the case with Russia, the United States, or the British Empire, it must naturally take some time for numbers to reach what might be called the saturation point. The same qualification is obviously true when one considers the new sources of food supply from outside, which modern transportation has made available. Moreover, increasing human material demands and a higher standard of living tend to bring into play the voluntary abstention or "moral restraint" that reduces the birth rate. Finally, increasing knowledge of birth control and deliberate sterilization have led to restriction of the size of an increasing number of families without the "moral restraint" or abstention from sexual intercourse which Malthus recommended. As we noted in the preceding chapter, the improvements in machinery, transportation, agriculture, canning and refrigeration have completely revolutionized our ability to produce, transport, distribute and preserve food. There are surely social considerations that justify population limitation, but in the Western world we could produce and transport enough food today to support any reasonable or probable population.

Another consideration which neo-Malthusians often disregard is that the biological and food-producing issues are today complicated by the inequalities of social income and the inability of the masses to get money enough to buy the food that actually exists in abundance. Men starve or go hungry in the midst of plenty—indeed, even in the face of deliberate destruction of food that cannot be sold at a profit. Witness the deliberate destruction of millions of bushels of potatoes and the rotting of millions of bushels of wheat and corn in an underfed United States and a starving world in postwar years, especially in 1949 and 1950. It is possible that population increases could go on to a point where, even in an equitable and efficient economy, men could not produce enough to eat. But in advanced economic civilizations today, the food problem is mainly one of getting an income with which to buy available supplies, rather than of any actual shortage of food. It is more a problem of securing purchasing power for an adequate diet than one of sufficient food production. In short, we may say that, as a result of technological changes in industry, transportation, and agriculture, which make possible more extensive production, transportation, and preservation of food, and of the marked tendency before 1940 for population growth to fall off rapidly, Malthusianism, for the Western world at least, is distinctly a horse-and-buggy concept that no longer possesses any practical validity.

Present waste of natural resources and human misery no vindication of Malthusianism. The severe postwar famine in central Europe, Japan, China, and India, and the publication of two striking books in 1948, William Vogt's *Road to Survival,* and Fairfield Osborn's *Our Plundered Planet,* have tended to give a new vogue to Malthusianism among superficial thinkers. Vogt and Osborn have cogently stressed the great waste of land and resources due to erosion, floods, dust bowls, soil exhaustion, and war devastation. This is all true, but there is nothing new in such information, striking and appalling though it may be. The same story was told in Paul Sears' *Deserts on the March* (1935), except that the postwar books could add comment on the devastation caused by the Second World War.

Any attempt to link this with Malthusianism is quite beside the point. Malthus held that the products of biological nature must inevitably outrun those of physical nature—that the products of procreation are bound to exceed those of cultivation. History has proved this to be signally untrue in the twentieth century. The rate of population growth has fallen off rapidly in every industrialized and urbanized country at the very time when science and technology have enabled us vastly to increase the food supply and all other material needs of mankind. We now know that population growth will level off in most countries long before limits are reached in increasing the food supply.

Causes of present-day starvation and famines. What causes famine and starvation today is not the fact that population must always get ahead of the food supply, unless checked by war and famine, but the social, economic, and political stupidity of mankind that prevents us from increasing and distributing the food supply as rapidly as science and technology have made possible. Famine and starvation today are caused by cultural rather than natural factors.

Wars, both foreign and civil, and excessive armaments, have absorbed or diverted the scientific knowledge, technical energy, and monetary resources that should have been put into agricultural research and better methods of agricultural production. Wars, and their aftermath of political stupidities, have greatly reduced the potential output of crops and other material necessities. It has been civil strife, foreign wars, economic exploitation, and the diversion of scientific and technological talent from food production and distribution that account for the starvation and famine in central Europe, Japan, China, and India. These have also been mainly responsible for the economic waste and soil exhaustion that Vogt and Osborn so widely deplore.

Bullets instead of bread. The answer to all revivals of Malthusianism in our day is contained in O. W. Willcox's *Reshaping Agriculture* (1934) and *Nations Can Live At Home* (1935), and in K. F. Mather's *Enough and To Spare* (1944). Using a thorough mastery of agricultural science in his analysis and generalizations, Willcox shows that even the least well-endowed of the so-called have-not nations, such as Great Britain (exclusive of her empire), Italy, Germany, and Japan, could, if they adopted and applied the best agricultural science of our day, not only provide subsistence but even be able "to supply their every essential need for food and clothing in overflowing abundance from their own land."

Even China and India, the classic lands of famine, could provide enough food to eliminate all famine if they would curb civil strife and adopt modernized methods of production. The wars of China are much more responsible for recent Chinese famines than Malthusian ratios, though of course the real responsibility goes back to the whole archaic and exploitive character of Chinese agrarian feudalism and the failure to attain political unity and economic efficiency. The vital fact is, that, if the countries which have the most acute food shortages had put even a fraction of what they have spent on armament and war into developing the best agricultural methods, there would have been no such shortages.

The books of Vogt and Osborn are to be commended for their call to reduce the wicked and needless waste of our natural heritage, but they afford no reason for reviving Malthusianism. Moreover, there are some 1,300,000,000 acres of good farm land in the world that remain entirely uncultivated. Much of this is located in the tropics and possesses almost unbelievable fertility and potential productivity. There is no rational basis for seeking to obscure or deny our current political and economic stupidity by "passing the buck" to Malthus.

Biological theories of population. Since Malthus published his famous *Essay,* there have been many theories offered to explain population growth and overpopulation, as well as declining birth rates. We have space here only for the more important of these. The various writers may be broadly divided into three major schools: (1) those who have emphasized biological factors affecting human growth; (2) those who have laid most stress upon economic influences; and (3) those who are most inclined to find socio-psychological forces the most significant in determining the rate of population growth.

The first important statement of the biological position was set forth by Thomas Jarrold. In his *Dissertations on Man* (1806), shortly after Malthus published his essay, Jarrold contended that the true explanation for the decline of the birth rate is not to be found in such economic and social factors as the pressure of population on the means of subsistence. Rather, it is due to the operation of some unknown but very real physiological factor which reduces both fecundity and fertility.

A few years after Jarrold had set forth these ideas, an effort was made to explain why this physiological factor comes into play. Such was the burden of the population theory of Michael Thomas Sadler, which he prefixed to a work on *Current Evils in Ireland* (1828), and of Thomas Doubleday's *The True Law of Population* (1842). It was Sadler's idea that hardship and privation encourage human fecundity, but a state of plenty tends to decrease it. The greater the density of population, all other things being equal, the greater the prosperity and the less the fecundity. Therefore, as soon the population becomes dense, the natural law of decreased fecundity comes into operation and reduces the population. Doubleday held that the availability of food is the chief factor affecting human fecundity and fertility. Whenever there is a scarcity of food, nature steps in and increases fecundity. Abundance of food, on the other hand, tends to decrease fecundity. In short, he held that births will, in general, tend to increase in about the same ratio as the extent of poverty.

More influential was the famous population theory set forth by Herbert Spencer in 1852. He held that there is a fundamental antagonism between what he called "individuation" and "genesis." As civilization becomes more complex, a larger proportion of available physiological energy is used up in problems of personal development and expression; hence, there is less energy available for reproductive purposes. In short, advanced civilizations seem to be antagonistic to high fecundity. Spencer's theory was widely adopted, especially by the influential American economist, Henry C. Carey, who used it as a means of combating the pessimism of Malthus. It was upon the basis of this idea that Carey transformed the perspective of classical economics in the United States from a pessimistic to an optimistic attitude.

Among the most extreme of all these theories which relate population changes to the physiological factor of declining fecundity is that which has recently been set forth by the Italian student of population problems, Corrado Gini. He likens the growth of population in any nation to the cycle of life in the individual. A young nation, like the youthful individual, is most prolific. As the individual grows older he becomes less potent in reproductive activity. Likewise, the more mature nations become less prolific. Social factors influence this tendency. Declining fecundity first affects the upper classes, but in due time it becomes operative among all classes. In every instance it is the weakening of the reproductive instinct and reproductive power that determines the lessening of population growth. Gini does not, however, explain the physiological basis of this lowered fecundity ˙or account for its appearance. He adopts the notion, but offers no substantial biological explanation. His doctrine remains essentially mystical. This same general theory of declining fecundity, or "germinal vitality," on a physiological basis has been accepted by the English student, John Brownlee, in his study of the relation between population density and the death rate (1920), and by the English geneticist, R. A. Fisher, in his examination of hereditary fecundity in the English nobility and of the differential birth rate among social groups in the United States. A comparable study has been made by Willy Wagner-Manslau on the fertility of European nobility (1932).

Few population experts ascribe any validity to such views as those of Gini, Brownlee and Fisher. We have already noted that there seems no scientific basis for the contention that human fecundity has diminished in modern times.

The German sociologist, Georg Hansen, offered an interesting bio-social theory of population in his notion of the three major vitality classes (1889). First, we have the high vitality class, which is found in the rural regions. This has a high birth rate and a low death rate. The medium vitality class is found among the middle-class residents of cities. It has a moderate birth rate and a low death rate. Finally, we have as the low vitality class the urban proletariat. This is characterized by a high birth rate and a high death rate. Hansen explained the dynamics of population growth by contending that the first class tends to migrate to the cities and augments and sustains the third class. His notions about the low vitality class have been somewhat upset by the subsequent improvement of city sanitation.

Economic interpretations of population growth. The most famous effort to relate population tendencies to economic factors was embodied in the work of the founder of modern scientific socialism, Karl Marx. Marx denied that there is any universal law of population. We must seek an explanation of population changes in the light of conditions prevailing in each stage of civilization. Under modern capitalism, over-population is primarily the result of an inadequate distribution of the social income. Enough wealth and goods are produced to make possible permanent well-being on the part of all the population. But capitalism prevents the masses from having access to the wealth they produce. The solution of the population problem, then, is to reconstruct the method of the distribution of income.

Henry George was as much convinced as Marx that economic factors account for overpopulation and poverty. But he was less interested in general industrial conditions and capitalistic exploitation than he was in the land problem. He believed that the main reason for overpopulation and misery resides in the fact that men are denied access to free land and that private interests absorb the increased land values produced by social activities. He contended that this situation could be remedied by applying the single-tax doctrine to land values, thus appropriating the unearned social income for the benefit of society.

The French statistician and social economist, Pierre Émile Levasseur (1828-1911), set forth in his *La population française* (3 vols., 1889-1892) a theory of population that combined economic and technological factors. He rejected the Malthusian theory on the ground of the remarkable recent progress in technology which has brought with it increased ability to produce, transport, and preserve the food and goods essential to human existence. He held that technology is advancing more rapidly than the population is increasing. Moreover, its future possibilities are limitless. Hence, we may expect that there will always exist an adequate margin between the means of subsistence and the population that depends upon it. Levasseur was, perhaps, a little overoptimistic, since he generalized mainly from French data.

The Italian publicist and social economist, Francesco S. Nitti (1868-), offered some interesting theories in his *Population and the Social System* (1894). He agreed with Spencer's theory that fertility declines with individuation and the progress of civilization, but he sought an economic and psychological explanation of this phenomenon. He held that equality of wealth promotes individuality and, hence, brings about a restriction of the birth rate. On the other hand, where gross inequalities of wealth or a caste system prevail, individuality is suppressed and the birth rate rises. Nitti believed that the pressure of population on the means of subsistence in the past has been a leading cause of human and cultural progress.

Socio-psychological approaches to the population problem. The first important socio-psychological theory of population growth was set forth in England by Sir Archibald Alison in his work, *The Principles of Population* (1840). He stressed the fact that population growth must be subjected to rational control. He believed that this would be brought about by the progressive development of "artificial wants." In other words, he emphasized the powerful influence exerted on population trends by rising standards of living.

The most influential explanation of population trends from this point of view was contained in the work of the French scholar, Arsène Dumont, *Depopulation and Civilization* (1890), and in later books developing the same theme. Dumont's population theory has been designated as "the law of social capillarity." In free, democratic societies population growth is controlled in a voluntary fashion by socio-psychological influences. Ambitious individuals, like the oil in the wick of a lamp, tend to rise to higher levels in the social system. Cultural interests become more important than family interests and reproductive activities. The individual wishes to climb up the social ladder and in doing so finds family burdens ever heavier and more obstructive to his social ambitions. As S. J. Holmes puts the matter: "The desire to climb higher on the social ladder is not so easily accomplished with children hanging about the skirts." As the individual rises in the social scale, he deliberately restricts the number of children in his family.

Where there is a very high general prosperity, however, there may be a high birth rate, since under such conditions the individual can make headway even with a large family. Dumont accepts Spencer's idea that the higher the development of individuality the smaller the population of the nation becomes. This principle can operate, however, only in societies on a democratic basis. In countries where the caste system prevails, such as in India, the principle of social capillarity cannot function because there is no chance of improving one's social status. Hence, there will be no tendency for the birth rate to be restricted or for the population to fall.

The biological and the socio-psychological explanations of population growth have been brought together in a suggestive and constructive fashion by Frank H. Hankins in his essay on "Civilization and Fertility" (1931). Hankins recognizes that there has been a decline in the fertility of Western peoples since they have become thoroughly industrialized and life has become predominantly urban. But he does not follow Gini in assuming some mysterious hereditary decline in fecundity. Rather, he seeks an explanation in the decreasing fertility of families as the result of changes in urban social life that affect physical vigor, food habits, frequency of sexual intercourse, relevant diseases, and the like. This interpretation gives a more realistic and sensible explanation than the views of Gini and Dumont. While Hankins can scarcely be said to have formulated a "law" of population growth, this conception of the primary importance of the totality of city life conditions in reducing fertility and the birth rate and producing a trend towards population stabilization may well be regarded as the most important principle expounded in the history of population theories since the days of Malthus. W. S. Thompson and others have set forth similar ideas.

The idea of an optimum population. An effort to work out a comprehensive law of population growth is embodied in the important work of the English student of population problems, Alexander M. Carr-Saunders, *The Population Problem* (1922). Carr-Saunders takes into consideration all the biological, economic, and socio-psychological influences that have determined population trends in the past. He would give each its due and proper weight. He believes, however, that from early times people have, consciously or unconsciously, sought a certain definite level of population growth. This ideal he describes as the "optimum number," the population that, under any given set of conditions, is believed to give the highest per capita return to society. Naturally, this optimum changes with the transformation of cultural conditions, the degree of industrialization, and social ideals. Students of population problems are inclined to accept this theory of Carr-Saunders relative to an optimum population. But so far there has been little actual research and analysis designed to reveal just what this optimum number would be for any given people at any stated time. Therefore, it still remains essentially an idealistic formulation, whatever its theoretical validity and its potential social utility.

Carr-Saunders' theory is, in general, supported by Harold Wright (1883–), another English student of population problems, in his book on *Population* (1923). He believes that, up to a certain point in human history, population increases and the pressure of population on subsistence have stimulated the growth of human culture and have promoted prosperity. But this point had already been passed by 1914, and notable increases in population now tend to reduce the prosperity and comfort of humanity. Wright is notable for stressing the fact that the contemporary pressure of population on subsistence in certain countries is a powerful contributing factor to war. He thus agrees with Thompson that marked differences in population growth and natural resources do constitute real danger spots in the contemporary world.

In addition to these broader sociological interpretations of population trends, attempts have been made by such students as Raymond Pearl, L. J. Reed, L. I. Dublin, A. J. Lotka, and R. R. Kuczynski to reduce the facts of population change to mathematical laws, capable of statistical proof and graphic presentation.

Basic principles and trends in population. The question is often raised as to whether there can be any valid universal law of population growth. Our brief review of population facts and population theories would seem to require that a negative answer be given to this query. Cultural changes, which affect population growth, are too sweeping and unpredictable to make possible any universal law which would not, at the same time, be so general as to be more or less useless for the guidance of immediate population policy. Perhaps such a conception as that of Carr-Saunders with respect to an optimum population may have some general social significance. We can only generalize from the trends of the past and from current tendencies in population growth. Both often prove how risky it is to generalize from either. Population problems represent preëminently a field that must be guided by current research and by the tentative generalizations derived from such research.

Though there is, perhaps, no universally valid law of population growth, there are undoubted principles and trends which explain population developments in modern times. Industrialization, mechanization, improved transportation methods, better ways of preserving foods, improved agricultural techniques, sanitary engineering, and the progress in medical science have combined to produce great increases in population in the more advanced countries of the world. These increases have been brought about primarily as a result of lowering the death rate. The birth rate has fallen, not due to any lessening of human fecundity but rather to socio-psychic factors, primarily the total effects of city life. Industrialization produces urbanization, and the latter leads to a reduction in the rate of population growth and a trend towards population stabilization and ultimate decline. This tendency is also helped along because the factors encouraging the declining birth rate still remain potent, although the decline of the death rate is approaching a static condition and is likely to remain so. Whatever further progress is made in conquering disease will probably be offset by the increasing number of non-preventable deaths among the ever increasing number of persons in the population above the age of 65 years. Probably the nearest approach to a valid law of population is the general conception of the "demographic transition" referred to in the preceding chapter.

THE BIRTH CONTROL MOVEMENT

Development of the birth control program. We have already made it clear that birth control, or deliberate and conscious efforts to prevent conception, whatever the many reasons therefor, is the main direct method whereby the remarkable decline in the birth rate since 1850 has been achieved. We may now briefly review the history and social implications of the birth control movement.

Malthus himself believed in the desirability of limiting conception and reducing the birth rate, but his method was what he called "moral restraint," or the postponement of marriage and sexual intercourse until the persons in question possessed enough resources to support a family. As a pious former minister, he was vigorously opposed to deliberate contraceptive methods that would permit more or less complete freedom of sex relations in the family.

Those who have advocated the reduction of the birth rate and the control of population growth through deliberate prevention of conception have rather generally been known as "neo-Malthusians." The first group of thinkers to support this program were the English Utilitarians and Philosophical Radicals. Their leader in this phase of thought was Francis Place (1771-1854). As the father of fifteen children, Place had good reason to doubt the effectiveness of Malthus' prescription of moral restraint as a means of preventing children from being born. In his *Illustrations and Proofs of the Principle of Population* (1822), Place vigorously advocated the use of contraceptives, and in later pamphlets he suggested a specific method of bringing this about. He also converted to the cause an English journalist, Richard Carlile, whose *Every Woman's Book* (1826) was the first work in the English language to be devoted exclusively to the problem of contraception. In 1830 Robert Dale Owen, son of the famous Robert Owen, published his *Moral Physiology,* which was widely read. It openly discussed contraception and the methods whereby it could be achieved.

From the United States came the first book on contraceptive methods by a physician. This was *Fruits of Philosophy; or The Private Companion of Young Married People,* by a Massachusetts physician, Charles Knowlton, published in 1832. This quickly became a best seller in both the United States and England. Following 1848, the American Utopian, John Humphrey Noyes, introduced *coitus reservatus* as a method of contraception in his famous Oneida Community in central New York. He popularized his views in his periodical, the *Oneida Circular.* The experiment was broken up by religious persecution in the 1870's, and the group turned to remunerative industry in manufacturing steel traps and silverware.

A broad sociological and economic consideration of the whole problem of birth control was embodied in *Elements of Social Science* (1854) by George Drysdale, a socially minded English physician. In 1860, the English reformer and free-thinker, Charles Bradlaugh, launched the most important neo-Malthusian periodical of the century, *The National Reformer*. Much publicity was attracted to the birth control movement in 1877 by the famous trial of Bradlaugh, Annie Besant, and Edward Truelove for selling Knowlton's treatise. The trial had the natural and inevitable effect of enormously increasing the circulation of Knowlton's work, as well as that of Mrs. Besant's own book, *Law of Population*. Another popular treatise of this period was Dr. H. A. Allbutt's *The Wife's Handbook* (1870). The Bradlaugh trial also led to the formation of the Malthusian League in 1877. Bradlaugh was its first president and Mrs. Besant its secretary. In 1878 C. R. Drysdale succeeded Bradlaugh and the League was reorganized. In the twentieth century, the outstanding English exponent of birth control has been Marie Stopes. She opened the first English clinic for birth control in London in 1921, and organized a society which issues the *Birth Control News*.

Progress of the birth control movement in the United States. We have already referred to American beginnings of the birth control movement in the writings of Knowlton and the methods of Noyes. The method proposed by the latter, which was probably physiologically and psychologically harmful, was popularized, though condemned, by Dio Lewis, an American purist and a forerunner of Anthony Comstock. A very influential pamphlet, *Sexual Physiology*, was issued in 1866 by R. H. Thrall, an American physician.

In the twentieth century the first ardent American medical advocate of birth control was the sexologist, William J. Robinson (1860-1936). Perhaps his most important service to the movement was his conversion of the famous American physician, Abraham Jacobi. In 1912 the latter, with great courage, advocated birth control in his presidential address before the American Medical Association. This enormously improved the prestige of the birth control movement in the United States. Even Jacobi's eminence in the medical profession and the dignity of his presentation did not, however, save him from insults and caustic criticisms. One physician, Austin O'Malley, for example, wrote that "Dr. Abraham Jacobi has become careless in his associations and has joined this estimable galaxy whose cult is the lonely cradle. As everyone knows he used to be a very useful physician. He was imprisoned for high treason against the government of Germany in 1851, and he is a revolutionist against the government of God in 1915."

The most active propagandist of birth control in the United States during the twentieth century has been Margaret Sanger, who was trained as a nurse. In 1914 she was arrested for distributing her publication, *The Woman Rebel*. This attracted much publicity to the birth control movement in this country, and in 1915 the American Birth Control

League was established. The change of American sentiment is well reflected by the fact that, 20 years after her arrest, Mrs. Sanger was voted by a highly reputable organization to have been the most notable woman of the year in her services to American society. Mrs. Sanger's own courageous campaign was mainly responsible for this change of attitude. She tells the story in her book, *My Fight for Birth Control* (1931), and, more completely, in her *Autobiography* (1938).

In 1919 the Voluntary Parenthood League was organized, and Mary Ware Dennett, an American lay sexologist, became its first president. In 1923 Mrs. Sanger and her associates established in New York City the first successful birth control clinic in the United States. Its chief medical advisers have been Hannah Stone and James F. Cooper. A police raid on the clinic in 1929 gave the movement additional publicity. The clinic was vigorously defended by the New York *Telegram* under the editorship of Roy W. Howard. Birth control clinics, following the model of the parent clinic in New York, have been established in many other leading American cities. The New York Clinic issues the invaluable *Journal of Contraception*. By January, 1949, there were 537 birth control centers in 34 states and the District of Columbia, serving at least 175,000 patients.

Contraception was also brought prominently before the American public through the advocacy of "companionate marriage" by Benjamin B. Lindsey in the 1920's. The companionate marriage implied complete and successful use of contraceptive methods. Perhaps the greatest victory for the birth control movement came in June, 1937, when the American Medical Association finally reversed itself and came out in favor of birth control under medical supervision, about 25 years after the advocacy of such action by Abraham Jacobi. Better unification and consolidation of the birth control movement was promoted by the formation of the Birth Control Federation of America in 1938. It merged the American Birth Control League and the Birth Control Clinical Research Bureau, thus combining the educational and medical work of the birth control movement in the United States. Partly to reduce popular prejudice, the Birth Control Federation changed its name in 1942 to the Planned Parenthood Federation of America. It now describes its birth control work by the less inciting but equally effective terms of "family planning" and "child spacing."

The birth control movement in the United States was long hampered by obstructive legislation. In 1873 Anthony Comstock induced Congress to deny the use of the mails to birth control information and devices, even when sent by members of the medical profession. Drastic laws were also quickly passed by a number of states. Twenty-four of them made the giving of contraceptive information a crime. On November 30, 1936 the United States Circuit Court of Appeals, in the notable case, *United States of America* vs. *One Package Containing 120, more or less, Rubber Pessaries to Prevent Contraception,* for all practical purposes nullified the Federal Comstock laws, so far as the medical profession was concerned. Birth control is legal today in 19 states, and legal, with restrictions, in 27 others. In Massachusetts and Connecticut it is still illegal even for physicians to give contraceptive advice or to hand out contraceptive devices. As late as 1938 all birth control clinics in Massachusetts were raided and closed down.

Birth control trends in continental Europe. The birth control movement spread to continental Europe in the nineteenth century. Birth control met an especially hearty response in Holland, where developments paralleled those in Britain. The leaders of the birth control movement in Holland, in its early days, were Aletta Jacobs, of Amsterdam, and Johannes Rutgers of The Hague. Indeed, Jacobs opened the first birth control clinic in the world in Amsterdam in 1878, making it a free clinic four years later. When the International Medical Congress met in Amsterdam, in 1879, C. R. Drysdale, of the English Malthusian League, was invited to address it, and a branch of the League was established in Holland. The Dutch government has been very tolerant of birth control work. The movement took on an international character, and International Neo-Malthusian Conferences have been held, beginning with the initial one at Paris in 1900. In 1922, Mrs. Sanger made a world trip in behalf of the movement.

After the First World War, however, there was a reaction against the movement in several European states. The Fascist countries, with their desire to produce more soldiers, were naturally antagonistic to birth control. Even democratic France became alarmed over the decline of the French population, when viewed from a military angle, and placed decided restrictions on the birth control movement. Following the rise of Hitler and his military threat, Soviet Russia reversed its earlier attitude and frowned on birth control, thus adopting the same policy as the Fascist nations. The Roman Catholic Church has been steadfastly opposed to birth control. So far as it has sanctioned the movement at all, it has advocated the "natural" method of observing the so-called "safe period" in women. Students of genetics have cast doubt upon this safe period.[1]

Social benefits from birth control. The sociological arguments in favor of birth control are well known. They have been ably summarized by Frank H. Hankins. By helping to keep the population adjusted to the desirable optimum number, birth control improves the general material well-being of society. Birth control elevates the status and increases the independence of woman. Through the institution of voluntary parenthood, woman is freed from her former slavery to the reproductive function. Birth control relieves the many evil results of unwanted pregnancies, the sufferings of women who are already afflicted with more children than can be supported and reared effectively, the prevalence of abortions, and the practice of infanticide. By keeping the number of children in the family within reasonable bounds, birth control tends to reduce infant mortality, improve the general health of children, and make possible an improved education for them.

---

[1] D. D. Bromley, *Birth Control*. New York: Harper, 1934, Chap. IV.

Birth control tends also to increase family stability and lessen divorce. With smaller families the existing family income will go further, and a very important economic cause of divorce is thus markedly reduced. If one attaches much importance to companionate marriage for the young, as a means of lessening fornication, prostitution, and the like, as well as affording excellent training for future permanent marriages, the birth control movement is highly important. The companionate marriage system is unthinkable without adequate contraceptive measures. Finally, while the birth control movement and the eugenics movement should not be confused, the latter would be impossible without the former. We cannot make births selective unless we can first subject them to control.

Untenable objections to birth control. A number of definite objections have been raised to birth control by its critics. Although these objections are ostensibly based on physiological and psychological grounds, they are, for the most part, only rationalizations grounded in traditional religion and morality. It is alleged that birth control is physically injurious through promoting sterility, producing various pathological conditions in female organs, and upsetting feminine physiology in many and far-reaching ways. It is held to be psychologically unfortunate in its effect upon sex relations and upon the normal feminine attitude toward conception and procreative activities. It has been alleged to create neurotic conditions in both males and females, particularly the latter.

The best medical and psychiatric opinion is that these objections to contraceptive practices have no foundation in fact, provided the devices are used by normal persons and represent the best scientific methods available. That there may be failures and unfortunate aftereffects growing out of amateurish use of contraceptives, especially self-devised types, without medical advice is undoubtedly true. In this respect, however, the opponents of birth control, who do everything in their power to prevent it from becoming legal, respectable, and subject to scientific medical control, are really aiding in the production of the unfortunate results which they deplore.

Effectiveness of present birth control methods and devices. There is much debate as to how effective even the latest and most highly perfected contraceptive devices really are. While no known device is as yet foolproof in the hands of every person, contraceptive methods are becoming ever more effective, safe, and harmless. That they have already proved relatively effective is to be seen in the marked decline of the birth rate in countries and groups where their use is widespread. Extended clinical research and experimentation are constantly going on in the effort to test the efficacy of devices already known and to invent new and more efficient ones. It may be safely predicted that relatively perfect contraceptive devices will be generally available by the time society is ready to accept them without question and to legalize their use without restriction.

One important reason why birth control devices are not more uniformly effective lies in the fact that thoroughly efficient contraception depends upon two elements: namely, (1) the efficiency of the device itself, and (2) the personal or psychological factor of care and persistence in the use of the device. Slight carelessness or neglect at even rare intervals may suffice to defeat the objective sought and to nullify the effects of contraceptive precaution in the ninety-and-nine times when the best devices are used with care and precision. Lapses into carelessness, or willingness to take a chance, even if relatively unusual, may well suffice to build up a large family. Intercourse under the influence of alcohol is, of course, one of the chief causes of lightheartedness or carelessness in using contraceptives.

These facts have important sociological significance. They mean that birth control devices are likely to be used most effectively by the classes who least need them, namely, by the most intelligent elements in the population who are already failing to reproduce themselves.

The underprivileged groups, who most need the aid of contraceptives, are more ignorant of effective contraceptives, cannot afford to procure them, or tend to be relatively less endowed with the alertness and apprehensiveness essential to the successful employment of contraceptive methods. Some authorities have suggested that nothing short of actual sterilization will serve as a really effective mode of contraception for the lower classes who produce more children than they can support and rear effectively. If this is true, it may safely be predicted that it will be a long time before birth control will become generally effective among the submerged classes in the population. It will require a long civilizing and educational process before we shall be able to use extensive sterilization to correct the unfortunate differential in population growth that permits the less capable elements in the population to be responsible for most of the net increase in population. Other students, however, believe that, since the main activity in the birth control movement is now being carried on among the low-income groups, significant results may soon be achieved even among these submerged groups.

The abortion scandal. Inasmuch as abortion is closely related to the birth control problem, something should be said about it as a sociological issue. Abortion is, of course, a method of birth control, but it is to be sharply differentiated from contraception, which means literally the prevention of conception. Abortion, on the other hand, means the interception and prevention of the normal birth of a child already conceived. While a large proportion of up-to-date medical opinion is now definitely ranged on the side of the general use of contraceptive devices, few medical men, at least outside of Soviet Russia, have possessed the courage and realism to advocate the legalization of abortion under proper medical supervision and execution. But in the United States several enlightened physicians, such as William J. Robinson and A. J. Rongy, have openly come out in support of this policy. Since one of the main arguments in favor of contraception is that it will reduce the need for abortions, the necessity and prevalence of the latter are being increased, even if unconsciously, by those who oppose contraceptive devices.

The actual facts as to abortion are truly appalling. Students of the problem have estimated that there are between 700,000 and 2 million abortions performed annually in the United States. It is conservatively estimated that a minimum of 10,000 deaths result annually from these abortions. Margaret Sanger estimates that out of every four mothers who die in the United States in relation to pregnancy, one dies as the result of an abortion. In New York City, in 1932, 21 per cent of all maternal deaths were estimated to be due to abortions. In addition to the actual deaths, there is the indescribable suffering of those who seek and undergo abortions under the depressing atmosphere and unscientific procedure which the illegality of the practice renders inevitable. Perhaps there is no more dolorous and impressive monument to the persistence of human bigotry and savagery than the statistics relative to abortions under conditions as they now prevail in the United States.

The fact that most abortions are illegal and render the performer thereof liable to criminal prosecution makes it difficult for any except the very rich to have abortions performed under medically safe and psychologically satisfactory conditions. The poor have recourse only to quacks and midwives, or they resort to dangerous amateurish efforts at self-induced abortion. Even competently trained physicians who perform illegal abortions have to operate under conditions which necessitate haste, brutality, and inadequate after-care. Only the very few exceptionally prosperous and well-protected abortionists can feel free from the possibility of detection and prosecution and be able to take their time and give proper care.

All the danger and most of the suffering connected with abortion today grow out of the fact of its illegality. This situation was amply demonstrated by the experience of Soviet Russia, which temporarily legalized abortion and made it possible to have abortions executed calmly by trained physicians. It was officially reported that, in a record of over 50,000 abortion cases, not a single death resulted. The Russian experience also proved that the legalization of abortion produced no epidemic of abortions. There were probably fewer abortions per capita in Soviet Russia than in the United States during the same period. Following the rise of the Nazi threat and the need for increased manpower, Russia outlawed abortion in 1936 save in rigorously essential medical cases.

Since it is entirely evident that no amount of social, religious, or moral pressure can do away with the prevalence of abortions, many sociological and medical authorities are coming to take a realistic view of the problem and to recommend the complete legalization of abortion under the supervision of trained medical authorities. They argue that if we are bound to have abortions, we might better make them both legal and safe. Further, our current efforts to punish those who perform abortions fall down miserably. According to Dorothy Dunbar Bromley, there were only two actual convictions of abortionists in New York City in the fourteen years between 1920 and 1934. The fact of illegality suffices merely to produce terrorism, secrecy, haste, and serious physical risks, and to make adequate medical attendance unavailable or so expensive as to be prohibitive for the majority. That matters might, for the time being, get worse rather than better seemed evident from the reign of terror instituted against Brooklyn abortionists as an outgrowth of the Amen investigation. The fact is, however, that outlawing abortion results only in sporadic persecution and terrorizing of abortionists rather than in suppressing abortions, and in continuing the physical mortality and mental morbidity inevitably involved in the illegal practice of abortion. Most drives against abortion are inspired by religious fanatics and engineered by those who seek to gain votes or increased newspaper circulation thereby.

EUGENICS AND PROBLEMS OF POPULATION QUALITY

Rise of the eugenics movement. In the preceding portions of this chapter we have been concerned mainly with problems related to the quantity of the population. We may close the chapter by examining briefly the origins and nature of the eugenics movement, which is primarily devoted to improving the quality of the population. The need for this has been made clear in earlier pages, where it was pointed out that population trends have, of late, been antieugenic, namely, have seemingly been leading to a decrease of mental ability in the population.

Interest in improving the quality of the human population goes back to early days. We have already referred to the eugenic proposals of Theognis and Plato. The Spartans actually put into operation rather extensive eugenic practices. In early modern times, the utopian writer and monk, Tomaso Campanella (1568-1639), revived the doctrines of Plato. One of the first proponents of eugenics in the nineteenth century was John Humphrey Noyes, who designated his program as "stirpaculture" and combined it with his contraceptive ideas. But the rise of the modern eugenics movement was primarily an English contribution to social thought and practice. Its development has grown up mainly around the work of Sir Francis Galton (1822-1911) and his disciple, Karl Pearson.

The work of Sir Francis Galton. For nearly fifty years Galton devoted his high intelligence, unusual industry, and enormous enthusiasm to the promotion of the eugenics concept and program. The respect accorded his work was increased as the result of his earnest concern for deep study, prolonged research, and moderation of statement. His first attraction to the subject resulted from observing the plasticity of animal types under selective breeding. He became convinced that mental qualities in man were equally subject to hereditary influences, and could be markedly improved by deliberate selective breeding of superior types. Galton's *Hereditary Talent and Character* (1865) marks the starting point of eugenics literature. His other more important books were *Hereditary Genius* (1869), in which he defended the thesis that outstanding mental ability is hereditary; *Inquiries into Human Faculty and Its Development* (1883), in which he first coined the term "eugenics"; and *Natural Inheritance* (1889).

Galton's writings had a powerful influence in promoting interest in eugenics both in England and abroad. The Galton Laboratory of National Eugenics was established at the University of London in 1907, and was directed by Karl Pearson, an eminent mathematician who was converted to an interest in eugenics by Galton. The Eugenics Education Society was founded in 1908, with Galton as honorary president and Leonard Darwin, son of Charles, as president. This society publishes the *Eugenics Review,* the most important periodical devoted to this field of thought and science.

When Galton reached old age, it proved very fortunate for the eugenics movement that he had found so capable and energetic a disciple as Karl Pearson. Pearson's most significant statements of his views on the eugenics problem are contained in his brief books on *National Life from the Standpoint of Science* (1900) and *On the Laws of Inheritance in Man* (1903). In these he made it clear that he believed that eugenics offers the most promising mode of procedure in solving our current social problems. More important than his theoretical writings have been the extended researches into human heredity which he has conducted or directed at the Galton Laboratory. The most sensational of these, perhaps, was his demonstration that chronic alcoholism in parents seems to have no hereditary effect upon the mentality or physical vigor of their children. While the progress of eugenics in intellectual circles in England was due mainly to the work of Galton and Pearson, the popularization of the movement was promoted by the more enthusiastic but less critical work of Caleb W. Saleeby, *Parenthood and Race Culture* (1909).

The eugenics movement in the United States and continental Europe. The eugenics program has received sympathetic attention from scholars in the United States. The first enthusiastic convert was the inventor, Alexander Graham Bell. One of the first important works by an American scholar who sought to present a comprehensive view of the eugenics conception was William E. Kellicott's *The Social Direction of Human Evolution* (1911). But the American whose work in eugenics has been most closely analogous to that of Galton and Pearson in England was Charles Benedict Davenport, a professsional biologist and geneticist. The best exposition of his general eugenic philosophy is contained in his *Heredity in Relation to Eugenics* (1911). Davenport was the author of many later technical studies in specialized fields of eugenic research. With the financial aid of Mrs. E. H. Harriman and the medical advice of Lewellys F. Barker, William H. Welch, and E. E. Southard, he organized in 1910 the Eugenics Record Office in connection with the Biological Laboratory at Cold Spring Harbor, Long Island. He also was instrumental in founding the Eugenics Research Association. Davenport, Irving Fisher, and others founded the American Eugenics Society in 1926. This organization publishes the *Eugenical News.* Davenport's most active professional associate was H. H. Laughlin.

Interest in the eugenics movement spread to other countries, though the influence of Galton was dominant in all cases. In France we have the writings of de Candolle, a French-Swiss botanist, and of Ribot, Jacoby, Guyau, and Vacher de Lapouge; and in Germany the works of

Hansen, Ammon, Schallmayer, and Woltmann. The movement became international, and an International Federation of Eugenical Organizations was established. Several international eugenical congresses have been held.

The goal and types of eugenic programs. The fundamental goal of the eugenics movement is to improve the quality of the human population through increasing the desirable elements and qualities and correspondingly reducing the undesirable. It aims to correct the unfortunate differentials in the existing birth rate, whereby the less capable elements in the population are producing the greatest net growth. In short, eugenics aims to introduce the principle of selective fertility as a determining factor in future population growth.

There are two major types of eugenics proposals. These are, quite logically, supplementary: (1) *positive eugenics,* which aims to encourage the breeding of superior human types, with the general aim of bringing about a relative increase of such types in the population; and (2) *negative eugenics,* which seeks to restrict the breeding of inferior human types and ultimately hopes to get rid of these altogether. By superior types, the eugenicists mean primarily those with superior mentality, though they are not neglectful of improving physical vigor. Inferior types, according to the earlier and more extreme statements of eugenic theory, are the feebleminded, the insane, habitual criminals, and certain diseased types arising from hereditary taints. The methods proposed for negative eugenics are segregation and sterilization.

Present obstacles to positive eugenics. Positive eugenics is still almost wholly an idealistic conception. There is no practical program which has yet been elucidated to put positive eugenics into actual operation. Human breeding is still too much under the control of amatory sentimentality and traditional religious and moral dogmas to permit any truly selective breeding of human beings. The conventional democratic dogmas are also opposed to the notions of positive eugenics, since democracy proceeds on the hypothesis of the equality of man. Moreover, since the ablest mental group in the population is, on the whole, to be found among the professional classes who are rarely able to achieve relatively large wealth, it will obviously be necessary to subsidize superior parents if they are to be induced to raise large families.

There is, however, no legitimate doubt of the soundness of the eugenics principle that mental ability is not equally distributed in the population and that superior mentality is distinctly an hereditary trait. We can agree with Samuel J. Holmes that "one may concede to the environment a generous measure of influence in the development of intelligence without affecting the validity of the conclusion that the mental differences among our fellow creatures are largely the product of their allotments of genes." [2]

There are other difficulties which arise in formulating and executing the program of positive eugenics. It is hard to secure agreement on the question of just who are the desirable types to be increased in the popula-

---

[2] S. J. Holmes, *The Eugenics Predicament.* New York: Harcourt, Brace, 1933, pp. 78-79.

tion, save for the fact that there is unanimity of opinion that we want fewer defective and pathological types. Especially dangerous is the injection of race prejudice into eugenic philosophy.

In addition to the social and cultural difficulties in promoting positive eugenics, there is the further obstacle—ironically—that the very progress of genetic research, which eugenics has powerfully encouraged, has served to discredit some of the eugenic dogmas and to undermine many optimistic expectations of the earlier and more naïve exponents of the eugenics program. Particularly important here have been the revelations of geneticists relative to the complexity of hereditary mechanisms and processes, especially the rôle of the genes in heredity and the operation of the Mendelian law. These recent discoveries in genetics eliminate the hope of achieving speedy and direct results in the way of improving human types through selective breeding, even though society were to wholeheartedly accept the idea at once. It has been shown that parents may, and often do, produce children markedly different from the parental types. An extreme manifestation of this is the fact that Mongolian imbecility is most frequently found among children of parents of relatively high mentality. It is now pretty clear that the only way to execute the program of positive eugenics would be to promote breeding on a large scale by generally desirable parental types and to be willing to see results accomplished in slow and gradual fashion. It is unquestionably true that positive eugenics represents the only possible mode of improving the general quality of the population, but we can no longer hope for the rapid and revolutionary results in a few generations which Galton anticipated.

Possible services of negative eugenics. Negative eugenics represents a more immediate and practical field of operation, for most sensible persons are willing to admit the desirability of reducing the number of defective and pathological types. But even here it has been necessary greatly to qualify the theories and expectations of the earlier eugenicists and reformers. For example, it was not so many years ago that it was believed that if we prevented breeding by the insane, the epileptic, the feeble-minded, and the habitual criminals, we would quickly eliminate these classes from the population. We are now in possession of information which definitely disproves any such optimistic hopes.

In the first place, as Abraham Meyerson and others have shown, only a very small percentage of insanity is literally hereditary. Therefore, cessation of all breeding by insane types would not eliminate even the majority of cases of insanity. Likewise, we have also learned in recent years that not more than half of the cases of feeble-mindedness are hereditary. Further, hereditary feeble-mindedness is apparently based upon recessive Mendelian traits which are hard to breed out. As H. S. Jennings has pointed out, if we were to prevent all propagation among the hereditary feeble-minded types in a given generation, we would reduce the number of feeble-minded in the next generation by only about 11 per cent, under normal conditions. Holmes has shown that, to get rid of the larger portion of hereditary defectives, we would have to sterilize at least the lowest 10 per cent of the population, a measure which we could not hope to adopt for many years on account of religious and social prejudice.

The same qualifications relative to earlier eugenic hopes must be applied to the case of criminals. We now know that even our convicts—generally, the lowest class of criminals—are not mentally inferior to the general run of the population of the United States. The criminal class, as a whole, is distinctly more intelligent than the average of the population. Hence, even if we could eliminate all feeble-mindedness through selective breeding it would hardly solve the problem of crime. Further, we now realize that there is no such thing as an hereditary habitual criminal type. It has been amply demonstrated that crime is primarily a social product which cannot be bred out of the community.

Social reforms more essential and practical than eugenics. Even more unsound is the contention of certain extreme eugenicists to the effect that we cannot hope to solve our major social problems until eugenics has produced a superrace through selective breeding. It is obvious that any such program would be far too difficult of realization to be of any great practical utility. It would probably require a century or more to realize important results, even after society had sanctioned such a policy.

Our social problems of today are too acute to wait for a century or more before we begin to attack them realistically. Further, we do not so much need a better race as we do better opportunities for those now alive. There is no reason to believe that the human race is incapable of coping with present-day problems. The obstructions in the way of solving our social problems are primarily institutional rather than biological. A human type which has advanced from the cave age to mid-twentieth century civilization without any marked changes in physical or mental qualities may be presumed to be biologically capable of dealing effectively with current social perplexities. It is social conservatism and cultural lag that are holding us back today rather than physiological defects or any mental deficiency in the race. As Carr-Saunders has observed: "Those who think that germinal changes in mental characters will affect the evolution of society and mould the course of history are on the whole mistaken. The course of history is in the main dependent upon changes in tradition which are, for the most part, independent of germinal change." Moreover, great mental ability is no guarantee of a progressive outlook and of opposition to cultural lag. Many men with a superlative intellect—as, for example, Prince Metternich, Pobedonostsev, and Arthur J. Balfour—have been arch reactionaries and a greater menace to society than a million dull normal persons or morons.

There is also a danger that eugenics could be made a handmaiden of Fascism and dictatorship through undue emphasis upon aristocratic theories. That this is no idle illusion may be discerned by noting the influence exerted upon Italian Fascism by the writings of the Italian sociologist and eugenicist, Vilfredo Pareto, and by observing the sterilization policies of Nazi Germany. The latter have, however, been very unfairly exaggerated and exploited by opponents of eugenics, who have sought to smear eugenics as a Fascist or, particularly, a Nazi program. This is palpable nonsense. Most of the leading eugenicists have been democrats and libertarians. There is no more ground for rejecting eugenics because Hitler abused the movement than there would be for abandoning education because Hitler degraded it.

When all is said and done, there can be no doubt whatever that the eugenics program is a noble social ideal which should be heartily supported by all intelligent and forward-looking citizens. There can be no intelligent quarrel with the larger objectives of eugenics; there is justification for sane reservations only with respect to the thoroughness and rapidity with which these objectives may be realized under existing social conditions.

Flimsy and unconvincing case against moderate eugenics program. The critics of eugenics do not make out a very convincing case for their position. Clarence Darrow's rather ill-fated opposition to eugenics was best summarized in his article on "The Edwardses and the Jukeses." [3] It was based more upon commendable human sympathy, of which Darrow had an unusual supply, than upon extensive sociological or biological knowledge. He did, however, expose some of the excesses of the naïve or old-fashioned eugenicists. Darrow later admitted to the present writer, quite generously and quite frankly, that he had probably been mistaken in his earlier opposition to eugenics.

Some anti-eugenic writers have made much of the following quotation from Walter B. Pitkin:

Would not such a eugenic program simply add to our burden of discontent? Would we not be overwhelmed by grey hordes of neurotics, hypochondriacs, and murderous malcontents? What can cause more trouble than a highly intelligent man who has been trained far beyond his opportunities? Better an army of morons than that! For the morons are at least healthy and contented. And is not contentment in sound body more to be desired than a defeated intelligence? [4]

Those who know Pitkin and his writings well will at once realize that he wrote this with his tongue in his cheek and in a sarcastic vein. Further confirmation is added by a perusal of his most important book, *Short Introduction to the History of Human Stupidity*. No such excuse can be offered for the following pronouncement by Charles Bernstein, a trained physician with a life-long experience in dealing with mental defectives:

When we observe what fine physical specimens the majority of the morons are, we may well wonder if it may not be nature's plan through evolution to develop, through the moron, a physical man upon whom may be later engrafted a more highly organized and stable brain and nervous system than we have so far known and this more perfect physical man will not break in his various organs under the stress of such increased intellectual burden, especially with other morons in line of development to cater to his physical and labor needs. [5]

[3] *The American Mercury,* October, 1925.

[4] Quoted in Paul Popenoe, "Feeblemindedness Today," *Journal of Heredity,* October, 1930, p. 422.

[5] *Ibid.,* p. 429.

That such a statement, so contrary to all known laws of biology and physical anthropology, could have been written by a scientifically trained man indicates that the friends of eugenics must battle against prejudices of others than the ignorant man-on-the-street.

Sterilization: the effective technique of negative eugenics. Since sterilization represents a method of birth control and is absolutely indispensable to the promotion of the eugenics program, we may profitably summarize at this point the nature and achievements in the field of human sterilization. First, we should get a clear conception of just what is meant by sterilization, as practiced today among civilized peoples.

In the popular mind, sterilization is all too often confused with the older method of removing the sex glands in males and females, namely, castration in the male and ovariotomy in the female. Such operations as these usually destroy sex powers and end sexual intercourse for males. When we discuss sterilization in contemporary terms we have no reference whatever to such drastic operations. The sterilization of males is a minor operation, vasectomy, which may be performed under a local anesthetic, and from which complete recovery may be expected in a week at the most. It consists of cutting out a small section of the *vas deferens,* a duct which carries spermatozoa from the testicles to the seminal vesicles. In the case of females, the operation is known as salpingectomy. It is a somewhat more serious operation than vasectomy, but not at all dangerous when executed by competent surgeons. It consists of cutting out a section of the Fallopian tubes and thus preventing the ova from proceeding to a point where fertilization is possible. Intrauterine cautery sterilization has recently simplified the technique.

These operations in no way interfere with the sex function. They neither reduce sexual powers nor decrease the pleasure derived from sexual intercourse. Indeed, a certain school of medical and physiological opinion holds that these operations actually increase physical and sexual vigor. They are, in fact, identical with the so-called Steinach operation for rejuvenation, except that in the Steinach operation only one of the *vas deferens* or one of the Fallopian tubes is excised, thus not interfering with the power of procreation and conception. They certainly do not lessen physical and sexual capacity. Through removing worries relative to unwanted pregnancies and eliminating the inconvenience attendant upon the use of the cruder birth control devices, sterilization actually increases the pleasure derived from sexual intercourse. In elaborate investigations of persons who have been subjected to these operations, there is rarely any report of lessened sexual vigor and pleasure, and a large percentage invariably report an increase. Therefore, the common objections to sterilization on the ground that it prevents the execution of a normal and desirable function are entirely groundless.

Progress and legalization of sterilization. The discovery of the effectiveness and relative simplicity of sterilization operations has led to a widespread recommendation that it be extensively adopted as a method of restricting the birth of undesirable types of the population. The man to whom credit should be given for introducing vasectomy as a eugenic measure is H. C. Sharp, a physician at the Indiana State Reformatory, who introduced the practice (1899) long before it was legalized in 1907. The first eugenic sterilization bill in the United States was introduced in the state of Michigan in 1897, but it failed to pass. The Pennsylvania bill, passed in 1905, was vetoed by the governor. The first actual law to get on the statute books was that passed in Indiana in 1907. Altogether, some thirty-two states have passed such laws, and twenty-seven of them still retain this legislation on their statute books.

These sterilization laws have had to run the gauntlet of the courts, and those passed in New Jersey, Nevada, Iowa, New York, Michigan, Indiana, North Carolina, Alabama, and Washington were declared invalid. In some of these cases modified statutes were later enacted. States which passed laws that are still unconstitutional and inactive are New Jersey, Nevada, New York, Alabama, and Washington. At present it is unlikely that any reasonable sterilization laws will be declared unconstitutional. The issue was carried to the Supreme Court of the United States, in the case of *Buck* vs. *Bell,* in an effort to test the Virginia law. The decision was handed down on May 2, 1927. The court upheld the statute; and, in delivering the opinion, Justice Oliver Wendell Holmes made the laconic observation that "three generations of imbeciles are enough." Justice Pierce Butler disagreed with this opinion. This decision of the Supreme Court in the Virginia case exerted a decidedly restraining influence upon state courts in invalidating sterilization laws. For example, in two famous state cases since, *Davis, Warden,* vs. *Walton* in Utah (1929) and *Board of Eugenics* vs. *Troutman* in Idaho (1931), the supreme courts in these states upheld the state sterilization laws.

In general, sterilization laws apply mainly to certain types of insane, the feeble-minded, epileptics, and criminals. Unfortunately, most of these laws have remained all but dead letters because public opinion has not demanded their enforcement. Down to January 1, 1949, only some 50,193 sterilization operations had been performed under the authority of the various state laws. California stood far in the lead in this activity with 19,042 of the total. The next state in order was Virginia with 5,366. That sterilization is mainly an achievement of the last two decades or so may be seen from the fact that only 8,515 operations had been performed down to January 1, 1928. Over forty thousand operations have, thus, been performed since that date. But we have only touched the surface of the problem, since there are over 115,000 feeble-minded and epileptic persons and over 500,000 insane persons in public institutions. These are only a fraction of the total of these types in the population. The number sterilized to date has been about equally divided between insane and feeble-minded persons. Statistics gathered and published by *Birthright Inc.* present the quantitative picture of sterilization operations in the United States to 1949.

As to how many informal and voluntary sterilization operations, not compulsory according to law, have been performed in public and in private, there is no means of knowing, because in many states such operations are illegal unless justified on drastic medical grounds.

TOTAL STERILIZATIONS OFFICIALLY REPORTED UP TO JANUARY 1, 1949

State	Year First Statute Adopted	Cumulative Total of All Operations		
		Total	Male	Female
Alabama	1919	224	129	95
Arizona	1929	20	10	10
California	1909	19,042	9,845	9,197
Connecticut	1909	505	31	474
Delaware	1923	783	404	379
Georgia	1937	636	106	530
Idaho	1925	14	4	10
Indiana	1907	1,840	919	921
Iowa	1911	891	274	617
Kansas	1913	3,001	1,747	1,254
Maine	1925	235	24	211
Michigan	1913	2,982	795	2,187
Minnesota	1925	2,211	502	1,709
Miss.	1928	596	154	442
Montana	1923	241	67	174
Nebraska	1915	688	323	365
N. H.	1917	557	113	444
N. Y.	1912	42	1	41
N. C.	1919	2,152	466	1,686
N. D.	1913	784	271	513
Oklahoma	1931	553	122	431
Oregon	1917	1,821	713	1,108
S. C.	1935	81	8	73
S. D.	1917	745	275	470
Utah	1925	555	260	295
Vermont	1931	251	83	168
Virginia	1924	5,366	2,135	3,231
Washington	1909	685	184	501
W. Virginia	1929	48	1	47
Wisconsin	1913	1,658	342	1,316
Puerto Rico	1937	986		986
TOTALS		50,193	20,308	29,885

The inadequacy of present sterilization practice as a protection against the birth of feeble-minded children may be seen from the fact that it has been estimated that the average number born per 100,000 of the population is about 45.5 per year, and the average of sterilization is about 2 per 100,000 annually. There were only 1,526 eugenic sterilizations in 1950.

The 1950 sterilization rate in the six leading states, per 100,000 of the population, was North Carolina 7.3, Georgia 6.6, Virginia 6.2, Utah 4.9, Iowa 4.3, and Delaware 4.1. The following table gives the total number of reported sterilizations per 100,000 of the population down to 1949.

STERILIZATIONS REPORTED PER 100,000 POPULATION
Prior to 1949

Delaware	293.9	Nebraska	52.3
California	275.5	Montana	43.1
Virginia	200.4	Washington	39.4
Oregon	167.2	Iowa	35.1
Kansas	166.6	Connecticut	29.5
North Dakota	122.3	Maine	27.7
South Dakota	116.0	Mississippi	27.3
New Hampshire	113.4	Oklahoma	23.6
Utah	100.9	Georgia	20.3
Minnesota	79.1	Alabama	7.9
Vermont	69.9	South Carolina	4.2
North Carolina	60.2	Arizona	4.0
Michigan	56.7	West Virginia	2.5
Indiana	53.6	New York	.3
Wisconsin	52.8	Idaho	.2

The movement for eugenic sterilization in Europe goes back to 1892 when the famous Swiss sexologist and psychiatrist, August Forel, advised the sterilization of hereditary defectives. In Germany, sterilization bills were introduced in the Prussian legislature as early as 1903. But it was many years before any sterilization law was actually passed. The first one in Europe was put through by the Canton de Vaud in Switzerland in 1928. A number of other states soon passed such laws: Denmark in 1929, Germany in 1933, Sweden and Norway in 1934, and Finland and Danzig in 1935. Estonia passed a comprehensive sterilization law in 1937 which provided not only for sterilization but also for voluntary abortion in cases of hereditary insanity, feeble-mindedness, and incurable hereditary physical defects.

The German laws of 1933 and thereafter attracted the most attention. Although it was officially maintained that the Nazi sterilization operations were designed wholly for eugenic purposes, it was widely charged that racial and social prejudice played an important rôle in the selection of those to be sterilized.

Whether justified or not, there is no doubt that its association in spectacular fashion with the Nazi régime has increased the popular prejudice against the eugenics movement and led to much unfair smearing of the program, even when entrusted to competent non-political hands.[6]

---

[6] For a good summary of European sterilization legislation, see Marie E. Kopp, "Eugenic Sterilization Laws in Europe," *American Journal of Obstetrics and Gynecology*,

As the nature of sterilization becomes more clearly understood and its simplicity, especially for males, is fully comprehended, it is likely to be used more widely, in a purely voluntary fashion, as a means of birth control for those who are certain that they no longer desire to procreate. Those who thus voluntarily adopt sterilization for themselves are bound to be the most intelligent types in the population. Therefore, it may turn out that sterilization will, for a considerable time, operate in a manner counter to the general program of the eugenicists. There is little probability that sterilization will become general among the lowest types in the population unless it is made compulsory. It will surely be a long time before any such mandatory policy is adopted, however desirable it may be from a sociological standpoint.

YET each day the feebleminded and the mentally defective are entrusted with the most important and far reaching job of all
The job of **PARENTHOOD!** the creation of new life
and the responsibility of rearing children

SUMMARY

Interest in the population problem has led many to seek to discover and formulate some valid *law* of population growth. This aspiration long

September, 1937. The sanest description of the Nazi sterilization laws and practices is to be found in Clifford Kirkpatrick, *Nazi Germany: Its Women and Family Life.* Indianapolis: Bobbs-Merrill, 1938, pp. 182 ff.

antedated Malthus, speculation on the subject having existed since Greek days. But Malthus' law of population is the most famous of all.

Malthus maintained that population tends to increase more rapidly than the food supply and can be held in check only by war, famines, and other calamities, unless persons voluntarily refrain from marriage or from sexual intercourse in marriage.

Although reasonably sound when Malthus set forth the theory at the beginning of the nineteenth century, it no longer possesses any validity for industrialized nations. We can now produce, transport, and preserve plenty of food for any probable population. The problem, today, is primarily economic, that of providing an adequate personal income to buy the food already at hand.

Since Malthus' time, others have sought to discover laws of population growth from biological, economic, psychological, and sociological methods. All of these have been stimulating, but there is probably no valid law of population beyond that implied in the so-called "demographic transition"—the tendency towards rapid population growth on the heels of industrialization, a slackening of the rate of growth as urbanization sets in, and an ultimate stabilization of populations.

The misery caused as a result of the poverty often found among very large families, and other considerations, gave rise to the birth control movement, which is devoted to encouraging the deliberate prevention of conception in those instances where this is justified in the interest of health and good living standards. Birth control began to be advocated early in the nineteenth century, but it took more than a century to secure its legalization, even in relatively civilized countries.

The leader of the birth control movement in the United States was Margaret Sanger. After a long struggle birth control was legalized by the Federal courts in 1936, but it is still illegal in Massachusetts and Connecticut. Important educational and social gains have resulted from the development of the birth control movement. It has suffered a rebuff in certain European countries as a result of the rise of totalitarianism and the demand for a large and ready supply of fighting manpower.

Interest in the effort to improve the quality of the human population has produced what is known as the eugenics movement. The idea behind this goes back to early Greek days, but an English biologist, Sir Francis Galton, founded the movement in its modern manifestation about the time of our Civil War.

The eugenics program aims to improve the quality of the population by increasing the number of children born of superior parents and decreasing the birth rate among the feeble-minded, degenerate, and other undesirable or inferior types.

SELECTED REFERENCES

Bromley, D. D., *Birth Control: Its Use and Abuse*. New York: Harpers, 1934. A very readable, sane and reliable account of birth control in its biological, medical and sociological aspects.

Brown, F. W. S., *et al., Abortion*. London: Allen and Unwin, 1937. Competent symposium by English medical and sociological authorities.

Burlingame, L. L., *Heredity and Social Problems*. New York: McGraw-Hill, 1940. Population and other socio-biological problems discussed within the framework of the concept of hereditary forces and influences.

Cooper, J. F., *Technique of Contraception*. New York: Day-Nichols, 1928. Reliable pioneer book from medical standpoint.

Darwin, Leonard, *What Is Eugenics?* London: Galton, 1926. A competent, readable and friendly essay in support of the eugenics program.

Dennett, M. W., *Birth Control Laws*. New York: Hitchcock, 1926. Able account of early efforts to legalize birth control in the United States. Published before the victories in the Federal courts.

Dickinson, R. L., and Bryant, L. S., *Control of Conception*. Baltimore: Williams and Wilkins, 1938. One of the most readable medical discussions of the technique of birth control.

Hankins, F. H., *The Racial Basis of Civilization*. New York: Knopf, 1926. Contains valuable passages on theories of heredity and biological quality in relation to social progress.

Himes, N. E., *Medical History of Contraception*. Baltimore: Williams and Wilkins, 1936. Most comprehensive treatment of the subject in English.

Holmes, S. J., *The Eugenics Predicament*. New York: Harcourt, Brace, 1933. A sensible and tolerant discussion of the biological and sociological aspects of the problem.

Kopf, M. E., *Birth Control in Practice*. New York: McBride, 1934. A competent review of birth control practices and results, based on an elaborate study of actual case histories.

Landman, J. H., *Human Sterilization*. New York: Macmillan, 1926. Excellent survey of the whole problem from the biological, medical, and sociological standpoints.

Osborn, Frederick, *Preface to Eugenics*. New York: Harper, 1940. Probably the best book on the subject. Authoritative, but modest in its claims as to immediate benefits from the eugenics program.

Robinson, Victor, *Pioneers of Birth Control*. New York: Voluntary Parenthood League, 1919. Brief survey of the leaders in the birth control movement from Malthus to Margaret Sanger.

Robinson, W. J., *The Law against Abortion*. New York: Eugenics Publishing Co., 1933. Vigorous argument by a physician for the legalization of abortion.

Rongy, A. J., *Abortion: Legal or Illegal?* New York: Vanguard, 1933. Sane discussion of the problem in its sociological aspects by an able physician.

Sanger, Margaret, *Autobiography*. New York: Norton, 1938.

————, *My Fight for Birth Control*. New York: Farrar and Rinehart, 1931. Two books by the American leader of the birth control movement, describing her successful battle for the legalization and establishment of birth control.

Siegel, Morris, *Population, Race and Eugenics*. London: Davis, Lisson, 1939. Good presentation of the biological argument for eugenics.

Stangeland, C. E., *Pre-Malthusian Theories of Population*. New York: Macmillan, 1904. Scholarly review of population theories in the pre-Malthusian era.

Thompson, W. S., *Population: A Study in Malthusianism*. New York: Longmans, Green, 1915. The standard book on the Malthusian theory and its sociological evaluation.

CHAPTER 4

Human Migrations and the American Immigration Problem

HUMAN MIGRATIONS

Leading causes of human migrations. In this chapter on the migrations of peoples we shall describe very briefly the more important migrations in human history, then consider in more detail the nature and consequences of immigration into the United States, and finally deal with the more important migrations within the boundaries of the United States.

Human migrations have played a dominant rôle in the distribution of peoples over the face of the globe and in the development of historic civilizations. Among the chief causes of human migrations, we may note the following: The search for food and pasture lands has started many historic peoples on the move in quest of these objectives. Increasing density of population and resulting food shortages have been a potent cause of human expansion beyond the original habitat of a social group. Wars have frequently compelled peoples to move, and conquests have often been followed by the forcible removal of the conquered and their deliberate colonization in distant areas. Better economic opportunities, especially since the Industrial Revolution, have led to mass migration from rural to industrialized areas. Political oppression has induced men to flee from tyranny to settle in freer lands or to endeavor to set up their own governments in relatively unoccupied areas. Intolerance and religious persecution have driven men from their homes in the effort to discover regions where they might worship according to the dictates of their own consciences.

Social and cultural results of migrations. We may look briefly at some of the more important social and cultural effects of human migration. Migrations have brought peoples into contact and conflict and have set in operation among human beings the struggle for existence in the form of war and group competition. Since the stronger and better organized social types have tended to triumph and survive, it is held that this competitive experience has improved the race and promoted human civilization. Certainly it was primarily responsible for the termination of primitive tribal society and the rise of the large political societies after the "dawn of history."

Migrations have also had a profound effect upon the biological constitution of peoples. They have brought about protracted and extensive race contacts and ethnic mixtures. As a result, it is difficult to find any pure races among the civilized peoples of the globe. In this manner, also, the biological diversity and plasticity of the human race has been notably forwarded.

Cultural progress owes much to human migration. It is generally admitted by historians of civilization, such as W. R. Shepherd and F. J. Teggart, that the contact of cultures is the most dynamic and civilizing process that has ever operated upon mankind. It breaks down stagnation, encourages criticism, arouses curiosity, and promotes the imitation of new customs. Migration has been a leading cause of cultural contacts throughout the historic experience of man. It has been through migration that cultures have been bodily transplanted from one region of the earth to another, the most dramatic and impressive example being the Europeanization of much of the world after 1500.

Through the mingling of different cultures and peoples produced by migration, new and often higher types of civilization have been built. Different racial types are assimilated, and there is an interchange of cultural contributions. The outstanding illustration of this creation of a great civilization through the intermingling of diverse types brought together by successive migrations has been the development of American civilization in the last four centuries.

Leading examples of human migrations. We have space here to mention only some of the chief migrations in the history of mankind. One of the outstanding migrations in primitive or preliterary times was the first invasion of America by mankind. Anthropologists agree that this earliest settlement of the western hemisphere was accomplished by Mongolians who moved in successive waves of migration through the Bering Straits area and down the west Pacific coast as far as South America. There is no agreement as to exactly when this migration began, but archeological discoveries in 1949 indicate that it may have been as long as 40,000 years ago. Africa and Oceania were peopled by migrations in primitive times. Africa was presumably populated by groups which spread from the central area north and south, though recent spectacular discoveries of very primitive types of prehistoric men in South Africa may mean that the migration spread from there. Oceania owes its population to migrations from Africa and Asia. Some believe that the burden of historical evidence, together with archeological investigations in China, would seem to indicate that central Asia may have been the literal "cradle of the human race" but more recent discoveries cast doubt on this contention. At any rate, Asia has been subjected to repeated waves of migration from preliterary times to the invasion of China by Japan within the last few decades.

Although it is possible that the transition from an ape-like ancestor to man was made in Europe, this is not likely. It would seem that since early prehistoric times Europe has been settled by peoples who came from Asia and Africa. The more widely accepted opinion is that the ancestors of the long-headed racial types in Europe were a race that came in from Africa across the land bridges then connecting Europe and Africa. Hence, they are known as the Eurafrican race. Others believe that the Nordic types originally migrated from the Caspian Sea area. In either case, they originally came from outside of Europe. We are reasonably certain that, in late Paleolithic times and during the Neolithic age, the round-headed Alpine peoples came into Europe from Asia and settled along the highland area from the Balkans to France. They were, in part at least, the progenitors of the present Celtic and Slavic types. In the fourth century B.C., the Gauls crossed the channel into Britain, swept down over Italy, and overran most of Germany and the Balkans, even invading Greece, Thrace, Phrygia, and Galatia. Their empire thus extended from Britain to the Levant, and dwarfed the later dominions of Charlemagne or Napoleon. Indeed, it almost rivaled in extent the Roman Empire in the days of Augustus.

Beginning early in the Christian era, the Germanic tribes gradually drifted into the Roman Empire, and by the fourth century they began those migrations which we used to know under the title of the "barbarian invasions." Their movements did not entirely cease until the Norsemen finally settled down at the height of the Middle Ages. It now appears that the Germanic peoples were pressed out of their habitats in central and eastern Europe by the movement of the Mongoloid Huns, who were driven from Asia by the gradual drying up of their pasture lands. The invasion of the Huns brought terror to Europe, but they retired as quickly as they came. From the seventh century onward the Arabs and other Muslims moved across northern Africa and crossed into Spain, for a time threatening to occupy western Europe before they were turned back by Charles Martel at the Battle of Tours in 732. The Mongols and Tartars menaced eastern Europe in the thirteenth century, and in the middle of the fifteenth the Turks captured Constantinople and ended the existence of the Byzantine or Eastern Empire. They moved on and seemed likely to overcome Europe, when in 1683 they were turned back in defeat from the gates of Vienna by a Christian army under the leadership of John Sobieski, king of Poland.

At the close of the fifteenth century Columbus and Vasco da Gama discovered sea routes to the Indies and America and launched the most impressive migrations in the history of mankind. This expansion of Europe was the chief factor in creating modern civilization. It built up the civilizations of the New World and went far toward Europeanizing the Old World. The greater part of human history since 1500 revolves about one or another manifestation of this expansion of Europe overseas and the reaction of the expansion movement upon European civilization itself. Since 1500, some 60 million Europeans have left that continent for new homes overseas. The Industrial Revolution opened up new avenues of employment for the peasant populations of Europe and led them to migrate to urban centers in Europe and America. The later aspects of this movement created the immigration problem in the United States.

Migrations as a key to the history of civilization. According to Andrew Reid Cowan, a stimulating English writer on history and politics and the author of *Master Clues in World History,* the main reason for the fall of civilizations in the past has been the invasion of mature, rich, and settled cultures by warlike and more barbarous nomads. Culture and prosperity apear to reduce warlike capacities and military prowess. Hence, as soon as a civilization was able to produce prosperity and display, it offered itself as an invitation to attack and spoliation by envious nomads. Cowan points to such historic episodes as the Kassite invasion of Mesopotamia, the invasion of Egypt by the Hyksos, the Median and Persian conquest of Babylonia, the Macedonian conquest of Hellas and the Near East, the Germanic and Hunnish invasions of the Roman Empire, and the Mongol invasions of Western Asia and Eastern Europe as examples.

The settled and mature civilizations rarely seemed able to hold off the marauding nomads by hand-to-hand fighting with spears, swords, battle-axes, bows and arrows, and the like, which the nomads could also procure. But the invention of gunpowder changed all this. This provided the settled civilizations with implements of warfare which they could procure in greater profusion and better quality than the poorer nomadic peoples. From this time onward, civilized groups could more than hold their own against nomadic invaders, and established civilizations had a greater prospect of permanent existence. As an explanation of many leading trends in history down to modern times, this view possesses much merit. But Cowan failed to reckon with the fact that improved military technology might also provide mature civilizations with the means for their own destruction.

Another very important idea in regard to the effect of migrations on the course of civilization has been offered by Frederick J. Teggart in his book, *The Processes of History.* According to Teggart, the most dynamic factor in the rise and spread of civilization has been human migrations. If a civilization is cut off from external contacts, it tends to become stagnant; migrations must bring in new ideas and impulses if civilization is to thrive. These influences stimulate the conflict of social ideas, create new cultural patterns and hasten the abandonment of outworn practices. New vistas of thought and behavior are thus opened and the way is cleared for social innovations and the further progress of civilization.

An important qualification in regard to the notion of human migrations has been set forth by the eminent English physical anthropologist, Sir Arthur Keith. He holds that, while migrations have been very important in shaping history in the last ten thousand years or so, they began very late in human experience, which runs back well over a million years. In his *New Theory of Human Evolution,* Keith holds that it was the fixity of the habitat and the isolation of social groups for tens of thousands of years that led to the inbreeding which he regards as the explanation of the origin of the various types of prehistoric men and the main races of mankind today.

Even this brief review of the part played by migrations in human history will suffice to indicate the importance of this phenomenon in the development of human civilization. We may now turn to that significant episode in the history of human migrations which most directly concerns us, namely, immigration into the United States.

ORIGINS OF THE IMMIGRATION PROBLEM IN THE UNITED STATES

Emigration and immigration. Before we begin to discuss the question of immigration to the United States, we should clear up the matter of terminology. The term "migration" covers all forms of population movements, including emigration and immigration. Emigration refers to the movement of peoples out of their own habitat to another. Immigration means the coming of outside peoples into a given area which they have temporarily or permanently chosen as their new dwelling place.

The immigration problem in the United States deals with the coming of various peoples to this country since the time of Columbus. As a social problem it involves not only the actual migration of outsiders to the area now occupied by the United States but also the numerous and complex social processes which have been set up by this unprecedented migration of peoples. No other migration in human history in any way compares with this one. Between the discovery of America and the First World War over 40 million persons came to that part of North America which we now know as the United States. Even the Mongol and Turk invasions of the Middle Ages dwarf into numerical insignificance compared to immigration into the United States. We may first consider migrations to this area in the colonial period, before the United States became an independent nation.

Motives of colonial immigration. The motives of immigration in colonial times were religious, political, and economic. Some desired to convert the natives to Christianity. Others wished to achieve freedom to worship as they pleased. The political motives were also mixed. Some fled from the tyranny of absolute monarchs and others sought to advance the prestige of the mother country through sweeping conquests in the New World. There were all kinds of economic motives involved. Some were on the lookout for the real and reputed treasures of precious metals and gems in the New World. Others were primarily interested in trading possibilities. Many of the poorer classes sought freedom from bondage or poverty in the opportunities which the New World was supposed to open up. Thousands of indentured servants and redemptioners hoped to work out their freedom here. There was also a considerable amount of forced and compulsory migration from the Old World to the New. Criminals and paupers were sent in considerable numbers from Europe to America, and there was widespread kidnapping of members of the lower classes in order to get a labor supply for colonial enterprise. William Robert Shepherd once said that the chief motives for migration overseas after 1500 could be comprehended within the three words, "gospel, glory, and gold." Viewed broadly, we may accept this succinct descrip-

tion of the motives of immigration during the colonial period as substantially correct.

Chief types of colonial immigrants. The majority of the colonial immigrants were of English and Scotch-Irish stock. It is estimated that about
500,000 came in the seventeenth century and approximately 1,500,000 in
the eighteenth. The Scotch-Irish contingent from Ulster is estimated to
have amounted to at least 500,000. They came mainly in the middle of
the eighteenth century. While economic, political, and religious considerations lay behind this great migration, particularly important was the
great famine in Ulster in 1740. These Scotch-Irish carried the great
frontier movements as far as Tennessee and the South. Unfortunates and
criminals, as we have shown, made up a considerable element in the
English migration to America in colonial times. Transported criminals
are estimated to have amounted to around 50,000. They were sent mainly
to the southern colonies. Indentured servants and redemptioners, who
sought their freedom through labor in the colonies, were decidedly more
numerous than the criminals. They were scattered throughout the colonies
but were particularly plentiful in Pennsylvania. More than half of the
population of colonial Pennsylvania at the time of the Revolution were
descended from indentured servants and redemptioners. Many English
debtors were sent to the colony of Georgia, most of the earlier settlers
in this colony being persons of this type.

A considerable number of Germans were encouraged to come to
America by the British, who in part subsidized their migration. Many
of them settled in Pennsylvania and have come to be known as the Pennsylvania Dutch. It is estimated that the British also brought around two
million Negroes to the colonies on the mainland and the British West
Indies. Spanish and French migration to America was relatively slight
and highly selected, compared to the English migration. And only a
small portion of the total came to regions now included within the
boundaries of the United States. Most of those who did so settled in
Louisiana and in the southwestern portions of the United States. There
were a considerable number of Dutch, who settled in New York and
New Jersey, along with a few Swedes and Finns in Delaware.

Quality of colonial immigrants. The question is often raised as to
whether we have received as good a type of immigrant within the last
fifty years as we did when the country was being settled in colonial times.
It is usually assumed that we have not. An extreme version of this point
of view was set forth in Wilbur Cortez Abbott's *The New Barbarians,*
in which he compared our more recent immigrants to the barbarians who
overran the Roman Empire.

A calm examination of the facts would seem to indicate that those who
came to the United States from Europe after 1870 were, qualitatively
considered, quite equal to the original colonial immigrants. It has been
alleged that toward the close of the nineteenth century we began to get
the "dregs" of Europe. This is probably an exaggeration, but even if we
were to accept this view of the situation, it is certain that the "dreg"

element was relatively as great in colonial times. Certainly, the recent immigrants have not included as relatively large a contingent of criminals, paupers, and bond servants as did colonial immigration. So far as social status is concerned, colonial immigrants were not superior in quality to those who have come to us since the Civil War. The notion that there was any large group of the English nobility among the colonial settlers has been laid at rest by T. J. Wertenbaker, who made a study of the famous "first families of Virginia." He has shown that there were not more than three families in colonial Virginia drawn from this class— and these were of the lesser nobility.

The only basis on which one could hold that colonial immigrants were superior would be on the assumption that Anglo-Saxon and Nordic types are racially superior in mentality and physical vigor to the peoples from southern and central Europe who have dominated in the immigration since 1870. We shall have occasion to point out in the following chapter that there is little substantial scientific foundation for any such racial arrogance. If we criticize the type of immigration to the United States after 1870, this attack must be based mainly upon the great number and cultural diversity of recent immigrants.

IMMIGRATION TO THE UNITED STATES SINCE 1789

Napoleonic wars and Industrial Revolution stimulate immigration. Although immigrants came to the United States in somewhat varying numbers when the country became independent and set up a new national government, it was not until after the close of the Napoleonic wars that we encounter another important wave of immigration. This was produced by the economic crisis after the long period of devastating wars and by the reactionary political policies of the time, which clamped down on revolutionaries and republicans. In 1816 about 8,000 came to the United States, but in 1817 the number jumped to 22,400. After this, immigration gradually fell off, until in 1820 only 8,385 came in. Although some of these immigrants went to the new industrial towns, a considerable proportion of them sought farms in the new area opened up west of the Alleghenies. Migration into this region was facilitated after the opening of the Erie Canal in 1825.

Increase of immigration after 1830. A more liberal land policy and improved methods of transportation, together with the continuance of political reaction in Europe, led to a marked revival of immigration following 1830. In the year 1832 some 60,482 immigrants came here. Even more marked was the influx in the 1840's and 1850's. Although the English contingent remained a large one (over 650,000 English came between 1840 and 1860), the most striking innovation in the immigration of these two decades was the migration of large numbers of Irish and Germans to America. The Irish immigration was increased by the disastrous potato famine of 1846-1847. In the year 1849, 219,000 Irish came to the United States. In the two decades from 1840 to 1860 approximately 1,700,000 Irish came to this country. They were the first group that settled mainly in the cities. This explains the large influence exerted by the Irish on the development of political machines in the United States, especially urban political organizations.

IMMIGRATION FROM EUROPE TO THE U.S.

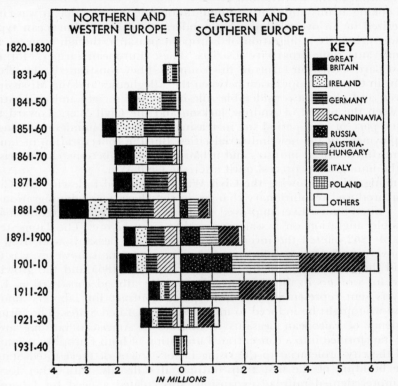

GRAPHIC ASSOCIATES FOR PUBLIC AFFAIRS COMMITTEE, INC.

Though the Germans were attracted here by economic opportunities, such as cheap land and the growing industrialization, the most powerful motive behind their migration to the United States at this time was political. The revolutions of 1830 and 1848 were crushed and a period of dark political reaction set in thereafter. Great numbers of German liberals sought refuge under the free and republican government of the United States. In the period from 1840 to 1860 some 1,380,000 Germans came to this country. In 1854 alone, some 215,000 Germans arrived in our ports. The fact that the majority of these German immigrants were of liberal political inclinations led them to sympathize with the frontier liberalism and idealism of the United States. They were disposed to combat slavery, and many of them enthusiastically joined the Republican party when it was organized in 1856 as a distinctly liberal party.

The total immigration from 1840 to 1860 is impressive, for it amounted to over 4,300,000—more than the total population of the country in 1789. It continued to be heavy during the decade of the Civil War, totaling some 2,315,000. The appearance of successful steam navigation on the oceans helped to make possible this enormous relative increase of emigration to the United States.

Looking at this mid-century immigration one may say that it was characterized by an overwhelming preponderance of North European types. It was primarily a migration of European peasants, though some of the immigrants came from city districts. These European farmers, for the most part, settled on farms in this country. They constituted a large element in the rural population between the Alleghenies and the Mississippi River, and played a considerable rôle in frontier society and civilization between the period of Andrew Jackson and the Civil War. Toward the latter part of this period an increasing number of immigrants sought employment in the new industrial cities. But the concentration of immigrants in American industry and urban life did not become characteristic of the immigration process until after the Civil War.

Immigration following the Civil War. The period following the Civil War produced revolutionary changes in the character of immigration to the United States. Ever improved methods of ocean transportation made possible migration on a scale vaster than ever before. The Homestead Act of 1862 offered the incentive of free land to peasants who lived in the overcrowded areas of Europe. Even more important, however, was the rapid industrialization of the United States after 1865 and the growing need for workers in the new factories and in railroad construction. Employers sent representatives to Europe to contract for laborers among those who might be induced to migrate to the United States. The former tendency of European peasants to migrate to American farming areas was transformed into a concentrated migration of both European peasants and the city proletariat to the rising factory towns of the United States. The building of the first transcontinental railroads, with other forms of unprecedented railroad expansion, also created a need for laborers. So intense and greedy was this demand that even a large number of Chinese coolies were imported after the Civil War for work on the western railroads. After this construction was finished, the coolies were left stranded in the West, where they created serious social problems. Another important mode of employment of immigrant labor was in urban construction work. City growth was very rapid at this time, and immigrants were widely employed as unskilled labor in every type of urban construction, as well as in road building in the country areas.

Not only was there a marked change in the industrial distribution of European immigrants after the Civil War; there was also a sweeping alteration in the racial composition and nationality of European immigrants. Those coming from the North European areas dwindled in numbers, and in their place came an ever greater volume of the peoples from central, eastern, and southern Europe. Between 1890 and 1914, two-thirds of our immigrants came from these areas, with Italy, Austria-Hungary, and Russia leading the list. In the early twentieth century there was an ever larger immigration from Russia and Russian Poland, a considerable number being Jews who fled from the brutal pogroms and also hoped to better their economic condition. The Jewish element settled mainly in urban areas and tended to move rather heavily into the needle trades and into mercantile and professional activity.

TRENDS OF IMMIGRATION

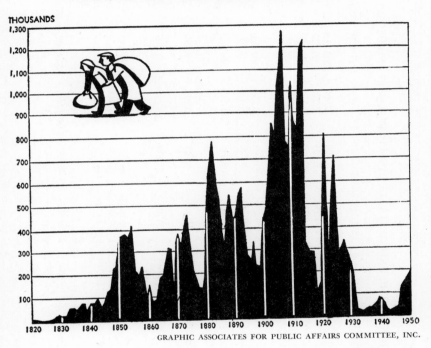

GRAPHIC ASSOCIATES FOR PUBLIC AFFAIRS COMMITTEE, INC.

Graph showing the great influx of immigrants from 1900 to 1914, and the remarkable decline since the restrictive legislation of the 1920's.

Marked increase of immigration after 1890. The increase in the number of the immigrants during the period from the Civil War to the First World War was also highly impressive. A veritable deluge of immigrants came in after 1905, and in a number of single years, such as 1905, 1906, 1907, 1910, 1913, and 1914, the number of immigrants in each year was in excess of one million. In the decade from 1901 to 1910 no less than 8,795,000 came to our shores.

The problems related to the social and cultural assimilation of our immigrant population were enormously intensified not only by the volume but also by the cultural diversity of immigrants in the two generations before the First World War. Indeed, the chief valid objections to immi-

IMMIGRATION TO THE UNITED STATES, BY NATIONALITIES AND DECADES

COUNTRY	1831-1840	1841-1850	1851-1860	1861-1870	1871-1880	1881-1890	1891-1900	1901-1910	1911-1915
Austria-Hungary				7,800	72,969	353,719	597,047	2,145,266	889,427
Belgium	22	5,074	4,738	6,734	7,221	20,177	20,062	41,635	25,447
Denmark	1,063	539	3,749	17,094	31,771	88,132	52,670	65,285	29,798
France	45,575	77,362	76,358	35,984	72,206	50,464	36,006	73,379	40,432
Germany	152,454	434,626	951,667	787,468	718,182	1,452,970	543,922	341,498	137,711
Greece							15,996	167,519	118,916
Italy	2,253	1,870	9,231	11,728	55,759	307,309	655,694	2,045,877	938,984
Netherlands	1,412	8,251	10,789	9,102	16,541	53,701	31,816	48,262	31,344
Norway	1,201	13,903	20,931	109,298	211,245	568,362	95,264	190,505	47,527
Sweden							230,679	249,534	72,055
Russia (Russian Poland)	646	656	1,621	4,536	52,254	265,088	593,703	1,597,306	894,003
Spain	2,954	2,759	10,353	8,493	9,893	6,535	6,723	27,935	27,921
Portugal							23,010	69,149	48,580
Rumania							14,559	53,008	11,187
Switzerland	4,821	4,644	25,011	23,286	28,293	81,988	33,149	34,922	17,020
Turkey (in Europe)							2,562	118,202	73,741
United Kingdom:									
England	73,143	263,332	385,643	568,128	400,479	657,488	271,094	388,017	193,623
Scotland	2,667	3,712	38,331	38,768	87,564	149,869	60,053	120,469	62,944
Ireland	207,381	780,719	914,119	435,778	436,871	655,482	403,496	339,065	121,740
Wales							11,186	17,464	10,250
TOTAL FROM EUROPE	495,688	1,597,502	2,452,657	2,064,407	2,261,904	4,721,602	3,703,061	8,136,016	3,795,797

COUNTRY	1831-1840	1841-1850	1851-1860	1861-1870	1871-1880	1881-1890	1891-1900	1901-1910	1911-1915
TOTAL FROM EUROPE (brought forward)	495,688	1,597,502	2,452,657	2,064,407	2,261,904	4,721,602	3,703,061	8,136,016	3,795,797
AMERICA	33,424	62,469	74,720	166,597	403,726	426,523	42,659	361,808	528,098
China	8	35	41,397	64,301	123,201	61,711	23,166	20,605	10,499
Japan	......	......	......	......	......	......	26,855	129,797	36,400
Turkey (in Asia)	......	......	......	......	......	......	8,398	77,393	72,231
Other Asia	40	47	61	308	622	6,669	28,396	15,772	4,479
TOTAL FROM ASIA	48	82	41,458	64,609	123,823	68,380	86,815	243,567	123,719
OCEANIA	9	29	158	221	10,913	12,574	8,793	12,973	6,126
AFRICA	52	55	210	312	229	437	1,343	7,368	5,847
ALL OTHER COUNTRIES	69,801	52,777	25,921	15,232	1,540	1,299	1,749	33,654	200
GRAND TOTAL	599,125	1,713,251	2,598,214	2,314,824	2,812,191	5,246,613	3,844,420	8,795,386	4,459,800

IMMIGRATION TO THE UNITED STATES, BY YEARS
(Year ending June 30)

1890	455,302	1903	857,046
1891	560,319	1904	812,870
1892	479,663	1905	1,026,499
1893	439,730	1906	1,100,735
1894	285,631	1907	1,285,349
1895	258,536	1908	782,870
1896	343,267	1909	751,786
1897	230,832	1910	1,041,570
1898	229,299	1911	878,587
1899	311,715	1912	838,172
1900	448,572	1913	1,197,892
1901	487,918	1914	1,218,480
1902	648,743	1915	326,700

gration, as it took place in this era, are not so much related to the quality of the immigrants as to the numbers involved and the cultural contrasts that the immigrants presented not only to the culture of the United States but among themselves as well.

IMMIGRATION TO THE UNITED STATES, BY NATIONALITY
1820 TO 1936

Albania	2,846	Turkey in Europe	155,568
Austria and Hungary	4,138,333	Yugoslavia	53,394
Belgium	155,024	Other Europe	21,309
Bulgaria	65,424		
Czechoslovakia	110,928	TOTAL FROM EUROPE	32,434,685
Denmark	333,900		
Estonia	1,839	China	379,982
Finland	18,310	India	9,704
France	588,023	Japan	227,162
Germany	5,938,822	Turkey in Asia	205,317
Great Britain:		Other Asia	38,858
England	2,629,335		
Scotland	732,587	TOTAL FROM ASIA	911,023
Wales	86,233		
Not specified	793,741	Canada and Newfoundland	2,957,422
Greece	427,006	Mexico	768,453
Ireland	4,588,464	West Indies	46,919
Italy	4,692,447	South America	117,649
Latvia	3,918	Other America	40
Lithuania	7,166		
Luxemburg	854	TOTAL FROM AMERICA	4,329,116
Netherlands	249,059		
Norway and Sweden	2,018,640	AFRICA	25,311
Poland	407,366	AUSTRALIA-NEW ZEALAND	53,739
Portugal	254,499	PACIFIC ISLANDS	10,610
Rumania	155,496	NOT SPECIFIED	254,066
Russia	3,343,088		
Spain	168,913	TOTAL FROM ALL	
Switzerland	292,153	COUNTRIES	38,018,550

Recent restriction of immigration. The latest important period of immigration tendencies has been that since 1914. This may be called the period of restriction, proceeding to an extent that borders upon exclusion. Hostility to immigrants is no new thing in American history. It played its part in the Know Nothing Party back in the middle of the nineteenth century. It was strong enough in the 1880's to lead to the passage of laws excluding oriental labor and outlawing the bringing of immigrants into the country under labor contracts. But the opposition was not able to bring about serious restriction of immigration until after the First World War.

The main grounds for the development of opposition to immigration were racial, religious, and economic. The original immigrants had been mainly of Anglo-Saxon or Teutonic stock, and they grew more and more alarmed at the tremendous influx of Italians, Slavs, and Jews. Since these original Nordic immigrants were mainly Protestants, they were also opposed to the new immigration on religious grounds. They were disconcerted by the fact that the Slavs and Italians were chiefly Catholics, as well as by the large Jewish immigration from Russia and elsewhere. Finally, American laborers, especially organized labor, were frightened by the prospect of extensive competition with cheap European labor. The latter were, at first, easily exploited by American employers willing to accept less than prevailing American wages, and accustomed to living standards lower than those that native Americans cherished and enjoyed.

We shall later consider more in detail the restrictive legislation. Here we need only observe its general character. After years of agitation, a literacy test was imposed in 1917. By laws of 1921 and 1924, the so-called quota system was introduced. This method of restriction, as normally enforced, limits the immigration from all non-American countries to an annual figure of 150,000. The operation of this quota plan was also intensified by the economic depression of 1929 and succeeding years, which led to other temporary restrictions. Prospective European immigrants recognized the futility of coming to a country where millions already were unemployed.

In the administration of Herbert Hoover, new energy and alertness developed in the deporting of aliens, so that in the years 1931-1932 more aliens left the country than came in. The net loss was some 68,000. Between 1931 and 1935, the number of emigrants leaving the country exceeded the number of immigrants entering by some 103,654. It has been estimated that the alien population of the United States decreased by 3,838,578 between 1924 and 1938.

When conditions improved under the New Deal, the number of immigrants coming here increased somewhat, and between 1936 and 1940 arrivals exceeded departures by 172,347. Immigration fell off during the war years, but picked up notably after 1945. Some 188,317 immigrants came in during 1949, as compared with 38,119 in 1945. The entry for 1949 was, thus, about 40,000 above the 150,000 limit. Sympathy with the suffering and persecuted in Europe is also thought to have led to winking at a considerable volume of illegal or unrecorded entry. The "Red" and war scares and emergency precautions led to a revival of deportation activity unparalleled in our previous history in 1950. Nearly 600,000 aliens were deported in that year.

IMMIGRATION TO THE UNITED STATES, BY YEARS
(Year ending June 30)

Year		Year	
1917	295,403	1933	23,068
1918	110,618	1934	29,470
1919	141,132	1935	34,956
1920	430,001	1936	36,329
1921	805,228	1937	50,244
1922	309,556	1938	67,895
1923	522,919	1939	82,698
1924	706,896	1940	70,756
1925	294,314	1941	51,776
1926	304,488	1942	28,781
1927	335,175	1943	23,725
1928	307,255	1944	28,551
1929	279,678	1945	38,119
1930	241,700	1946	108,721
1931	97,139	1947	147,292
1932	35,576	1948	170,470

Because these restrictive laws do not apply to immigrants coming from countries in the western hemisphere, they do not restrict immigration from South America, Central America, or Mexico. There has been a large influx of Mexicans into the southern part of the United States, especially the Southwest, since the First World War. A large number—estimated by some to be more than 500,000—cross and recross the Mexican border each year to engage in seasonal work. According to the 1940 census, there were 377,433 Mexicans of Mexican birth resident in this country and 699,220 native born of Mexican parentage. Some expert authorities estimate that there are at least 3,000,000 persons of Mexican descent in the United States today. This has created problems which we shall consider in the following chapter. On the whole, however, we may say that the problem of immigration into the United States has now come to a stage in which the quantitative issue is not at all acute. From now on, it will be mainly a matter of providing for the better assimilation of those who are already here.

LEGISLATION AFFECTING IMMIGRATION TO THE UNITED STATES

Main stages or periods of immigration policy. We may now review some of the more important phases of the history of legislative efforts to regulate immigration. The attitudes dominating this country have been thus summarized by Ridenour and Brown: "Cordial reception, attempted assimilation, brusque restriction, and hysterical deportation—these four phases, risking a possible oversimplification of terms, tell the story of

America's attitude toward the immigrant." [1] The legislation that we shall review represented, in a broad way, the effort to write these attitudes into the law of the land.

There have been four major periods in the development of public attitudes and legislative policies with respect to immigration. These are summarized by Rufus D. Smith as:

1. The Period of Colonization, to 1782.
2. The Period of Uncontrolled Immigration, 1783-1830.
3. The Period of State Control, 1831-1882.
4. The Period of Federal Control, 1882 ff.
   (a) Regulation, 1882-1921.
   (b) Restriction and the Quota Act, 1921 ff.
   (c) Emigration Greater Than Immigration, 1931-1935.
   (d) Increase of Immigration, 1935 ff.
   (e) Some Relaxation of Limitations, 1945 ff.
   (f) Intensified Deportation of Aliens, 1950 ff. [2]

During the colonial period, as we have already noted, immigration was not only welcomed but was even made compulsory in many instances as the result of British policy. Not only did England subsidize the migration of Germans who settled in Pennsylvania and elsewhere; she also sent thousands of criminals and paupers to this country. English companies interested in colonization also kidnapped a considerable number from the English lower classes and sent them over to the American colonies. There was also an extensive propaganda literature written both by Europeans and those already in America seeking to induce more of their countrymen to leave their homeland and migrate to America.

Alien and Sedition Laws. The first important legislation relating to immigration was the Alien and Sedition Laws, passed in June and July, 1798. These represented the earliest instance of alien hatred in our country. The Alien and Sedition Laws were incited by the pro-French agitation of many aliens and their Jeffersonian sympathizers. These laws were not designed to restrict immigration but rather to control the behavior of aliens already here. They provided for the deportation of obnoxious aliens, the control of aliens in the time of war, and the punishment of seditious conduct and writing by both aliens and natives. Fiercely opposed by the Jeffersonians, their passage hastened the decline of the Federalist party, and they were quickly repealed when Jefferson became president.

Rise of opposition to immigration. So far as immigration is concerned, the policy of the new nation was at first extremely cordial and liberal. Laborers were needed in the new factories as well as in the building of roads, canals, and railroads. Settlers were also welcomed so that they might take up land beyond the Alleghenies. The government did not even take the trouble to gather statistics about immigration until 1820. The only immigration laws passed in this period were state laws, which

---

[1] F. J. Brown and J. S. Roucek (Eds.), *Our Racial and National Minorities*. New York: Prentice-Hall, 1937, p. 607.

[2] *Ibid.*, p. 629. Sections (e) and (f) added by author.

were mainly designed to encourage immigration and to promote the welfare of immigrants. States desiring a large immigration tried to outdo each other in their efforts to attract immigrants.

In the 1830's in certain northern states there first appeared definite evidence of a sentiment against immigration, fomented, in part, by laborers who feared the competition of foreigners and, in part, by Protestants who were worried about the increasing number of Catholics who were coming here. Social reformers were also apprehensive about the immigration of foreign paupers and criminals. This alarm led to the passage of a resolution by the House of Representatives in 1838 calling for a committee of inquiry to look into the matter of immigration and to consider the desirability of restrictive legislation. No practical effect, however, resulted at the time.

When Irish immigration developed the proportions of a tidal wave after the potato famine of 1846-1847, the anti-immigration movement developed added momentum. It was increased somewhat by the marked growth of German immigration after 1848. The opposition of labor and Protestants remained the dominant factor in this movement. It constituted the basis of the Know Nothing Party, which reached the height of its power in 1856, when the Whig party endorsed its candidate for the presidency. This was a phase of what Ray A. Billington has called "the Protestant Crusade." But, again, no restrictive legislation grew out of this anti-immigration sentiment of the middle of the century.

Indeed, during the Civil War decade there was a reversal of attitude, and legislation was passed during this period in the hope of encouraging immigration. We needed foreign workers to take the place of the men who had joined the army from both the industrial cities in the North and the farms in the West. The Homestead Act of 1862 offered free land to immigrants who wished to settle down on farms, and a law of 1864 sought further to facilitate immigration to this country. It was repealed in 1868 after war conditions had passed.

Origins and development of restrictive legislation. The period of legislative restriction of immigration under Federal control began with the famous general immigration law of August 18, 1882. This established the precedent of national control of immigration and provided for the exclusion of criminals, paupers, the insane, and other undesirables. Another act of the same year excluded Chinese laborers for ten years. In the 1880's, labor unions, first under the leadership of the Knights of Labor, became more powerful. They united with the antiforeign agitators to bring about the passage of the famous law of 1885 that forbade the immigration of laborers under contract and of strike-breakers. This law worked a considerable hardship upon actors, artists, musicians, and other desirable persons who were accustomed to come here under definite contractual relations. As a result, the law of 1885 was modified in 1891 to make exceptions with respect to these types. In 1888 and 1892 additional restrictive laws were passed barring from immigration alien races that refused to assimilate directly with the native stock. These laws were designed to restrict the immigration of Chinese. A strong anti-Catholic influence appeared in the American Protective Association, organized in 1887. This doubtless helped on the trend toward the criticism and restriction of immigration.

The first decade of the present century produced important developments in immigration policy and legislation. In 1903 a law was passed providing for American inspection of immigrants at European ports of departure. It also gave our government the right to deport within two years after arrival any immigrant who had come here in violation of the terms of this act. In 1906 the Bureau of Immigration was created to keep careful records respecting immigration and to collect important information bearing thereupon. In 1907 a law was passed designed to check the white slave traffic and the importation of actual or potential prostitutes. An Immigration Commission was also created to investigate the immigration problem and make a report to Congress. In this same year President Roosevelt negotiated the famous "Gentleman's Agreement" with Japan whereby the Japanese government agreed to refuse passports to the United States to all Japanese laborers, whether skilled or unskilled. This agreement was meticulously observed by the Japanese government and virtually put an end to Japanese immigration to the United States.

In 1910 the Immigration Commission submitted its famous report, which was of epoch-making significance for the later history of immigration legislation. It became the point of departure for laws that had, by 1924, advanced from a policy of restriction to one of virtual exclusion. The Commission advocated a radical restriction of immigration. It recommended that restriction be secured through imposing a literacy test; excluding unmarried and unskilled laborers; preventing excessive immigration from any particular country or race; increasing the amount of money which immigrants were to possess upon landing; and raising the head tax on immigrants.

A bill embodying most of these recommendations was passed by Congress, but it was vetoed in February, 1913, by President Taft because it incorporated a proposal for a literacy test. Similar bills were vetoed in 1915 and 1916 by President Wilson, who likewise objected to the inclusion of the literacy test. Finally, in 1917 a bill embodying a literacy test was passed over President Wilson's veto. The head tax on immigrants was raised to $8. The first head tax, a small one of fifty cents, had been imposed by the law of 1882. It had subsequently been raised to $2.

The act of 1917 constituted the beginning of legislation that in the course of twenty years produced what is virtually the exclusion of immigrants, when judged by the policies that earlier prevailed. This new legislation not only embodied a sweeping restrictive policy but also reflected a definite prejudice against peoples from central, eastern, and southern Europe, a policy produced, in part, by the then popular Nordic propaganda literature stressing the superiority of the Teutonic and Anglo-Saxon peoples. The famous quota system of immigration restriction was introduced by the act of May, 1921, limiting the annual immigration of foreigners to a number equal to 3 per cent of the persons of each nationality who had been resident in the United States in 1910. It also declared that not more than 20 per cent of this annual quota could be admitted in any one month.

The National Origins system. This did not satisfy the opponents of immigration. H. H. Laughlin of the Eugenics Record Office, and others, went before Congress with data which, they alleged, proved the high preponderance of immigrants in crime, vice, and general degeneracy. Thus, another law was passed in 1924 that notably extended the system of quota restriction. Under the law of 1924 the number of immigrants who could lawfully enter in a year was limited to 2 per cent of the population of each nationality resident in the United States on the basis of the census of 1890. This choice of 1890 in the place of 1910, as the basis for quota calculation, was particularly designed to give preference to Nordic immigrants. The law of 1924 also provided that, beginning in 1927, restriction was to be extended so as to limit the total immigration in any given year to 150,000. The 1924 quota proportions in determining the national distribution of this total were to remain in force. This policy is still in operation. This quota policy, established in 1921, 1924, and 1927, is usually referred to as the "National Origins Plan."

The law of 1924 sweepingly excluded Japanese immigration, thus offending Japan. Many felt that this was an altogether unnecessary affront to Japan because the latter had so faithfully respected the Gentleman's Agreement of 1907. Not only was immigration sharply restricted as the result of the application of the 150,000 limit in 1927 but also, under Secretary of Labor William Doak (1930-1933), a policy of drastic deportation of aliens, unprecedented in our history, was deliberately adopted. The adverse economic conditions created by the depression following 1929 also stimulated voluntary departure. After 1931, the emigrant aliens leaving the United States outnumbered the arriving immigrants. For the period 1931-1935, the excess of departures over arrivals amounted to a little over 100,000.

The law of 1924 has rightly been regarded by students of immigration as of fundamental and revolutionary significance. Rufus D. Smith contends that it divides American population history into two epochs. He goes so far as to state that it constitutes "a second declaration of American independence" and is the most far-reaching legislation ever enacted by the Congress of the United States. He thus summarizes his view of the historic significance of the immigration law of 1924:

The United States, in consequence of the Immigration Quota Act of 1924, stands at the beginning of an epoch, a turning point in its social and economic history. This law constitutes the most revolutionary factor in the evolution of American civilization, much more so than the depression of 1929, the election of the President, or the introduction of the New Deal, although these for the moment loom significant in the mind of the average citizen. As history is written one hundred years from now, it may well be that historians will accept the 1924 Immigration Quota Act as the most profound decision among the social and economic policies of the American people.[3]

---

[3] Brown and Roucek, *op. cit.,* p. 642.

While the National Origins system still governs our immigration policy, our sympathy with those suffering under foreign persecution led to some relaxation of the limits originally imposed. The number formally admitted in 1949 exceeded the 150,000 limit by about 40,000, and it is

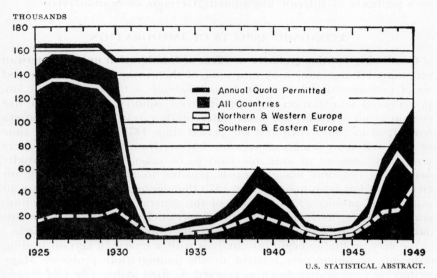

Quota Immigrants Admitted: 1925-1949.

U.S. STATISTICAL ABSTRACT.

thought that there were even more unrecorded entries. The laws of 1948 and 1950 permitting the entry of displaced persons were another instance and reflection of this new trend. There has been strong pressure to relax greatly the limitations laid down in 1924 and 1927, but thus far this has not succeeded. Indeed, the alarm about disloyalty, espionage, and the like, and emergency mobilization precautions, led to unprecedented activities in deporting aliens in 1950. Some 580,000 aliens were deported in 1950, and another 470,000 were arrested while seeking entry. Both figures were double those for 1949, and the number deported was ten times as many as in 1940. Many of these aliens deported in 1950 were Mexicans seeking to cross the border illegally to find employment in the United States.

Unscientific character of present restrictive legislation. Although there were many valid reasons for bringing to an end immigration on·the vast scale which took place between 1900 and the First World War, our present policy has probably gone to the other extreme, and the methods employed for discriminatory selection of immigrants are highly unscientific. It would have been far better to provide for more moderate restrictive measures about 1890 and to maintain these in force, than to permit the great inundation by immigrants until the First World War and then to rush into virtual exclusion. Further, the National Origins Plan is based more upon unsupportable race prejudice than upon sound sociological procedure. Intelligence tests and other comparable devices would be far more effective than race prejudice in selecting the limited number of immigrants allowed to enter the country. An able Italian, Pole, Russian, or Rumanian is superior, as a potential American citizen, to a mediocre or inferior Englishman, German, or Scandinavian.

ECONOMIC ASPECTS OF IMMIGRATION

Conflicting opinions relative to effect of immigration on the American economy. We may now look into some of the outstanding economic and social problems that have been brought about as the result of the un-precedented immigration of aliens into our country. To make the discussion at all relevant, one must differentiate carefully between the era from 1800 to about 1870 and the period since 1870. Down to the time of the Civil War, immigration was relatively limited in numbers, there was a vast amount of available land to be taken up, and the rapidly developing economy made it easily possible to absorb the immigrant element. It has been mainly since 1870 that immigration has become an acute social problem. Our analysis of the general social effects of immigration will be restricted primarily to tendencies and results since this date, and particularly since 1890, when the frontier was finally closed.

We may profitably begin our analysis with a review of certain leading economic considerations relative to the immigration problem. Many writers on immigration, such as Edward A. Ross in his *The Old World in the New,* have presented a very unfavorable verdict on the effects of immigration since 1890. Ross believes that it has disastrously affected the economic life and living standards of our country. It is the contention of such authorities that immigrant laborers have been willing to work for lower wages than native workers, have thrown many of the latter out of employment because of unfair competition, have been willing to exist on a far lower standard of living than American workers have wished to accept, and have thus lowered cultural traits and the standard of life in our country.

A contrary thesis has been upheld by other authors who have looked into the problem. They have contended that immigration has not had any unfortunate effect upon wages and standards of living in this country. Such a point of view is expounded by Isaac A. Hourwich in his *Immigration and Labor.* Those who thus defend immigrant laborers contend that the latter have not permanently been willing to accept lower wages and that they have not, on the whole, debased living standards in this country. Let us look at some of the more obvious facts and conclusions.

Immigration and American labor standards. If it be true that immigrants have accepted lower wages and a less satisfactory standard of life than prevails among the native born, the responsibility for this can, in large part, be laid at the door of American capital and employers. There is no evidence that the immigrants would not have gladly accepted higher wages and better living conditions if they had been given the

ENTRY AND DEPARTURE OF ALIENS IN THE UNITED STATES, 1932-1948

	1932	1933	1934	1935	1936	1937	1948
Total aliens admitted	174,871	150,728	163,904	179,721	190,899	231,884	646,576
Immigrant	35,576	23,068	29,470	34,956	36,329	50,244	170,570
Non-immigrant	139,295	127,660	134,434	144,765	154,570	181,640	476,006
Total aliens departed	287,657	243,802	177,172	189,050	193,284	224,582	448,218
Emigrant	103,295	80,081	39,771	38,834	35,817	26,736	20,875
Non-emigrant	184,362	163,721	137,401	150,216	157,467	197,846	427,343
Increase or decrease of immigration	−112,786	−93,074	−13,286	−9,329	−2,385	7,302	198,358

opportunity to do so. American employers welcomed—even encouraged—the enormous influx of immigrant labor, which they could exploit more effectively than native labor. They were only too glad to offer immigrants employment at low wages. Whenever immigrants realized that they were being exploited, they resented this fact and endeavored to remedy the situation. In so far as immigrant labor has been disastrous to the economic well-being of the United States, this loss must be partly attributed to the short-sighted industrial and social policies that have characterized American employer policy since the Civil War.

All important studies of labor conditions among immigrants in recent times agree that immigrants have at least temporarily been willing to accept wages below the level prevalent among native-born workers. This condition has been due in part to the helplessness of recently arrived immigrants and in part to the fact that what were low wages when judged by native American standards, were relatively high wages when viewed in the light of what these people had earlier been able to earn in Europe.

Although immigrants have been more active in endeavoring to improve their wage scale since the turn of the century, as late as 1910 the Immigration Commission discovered that the income of foreign labor was still below that of native labor. For example, the average weekly earnings of immigrant labor were $11.92, the average weekly earnings of the children of these immigrants over 18 years of age were $13.89, and the average weekly earnings of the native born of native parentage were $14.37. The comparable figures for yearly incomes among these groups were $455, $566, and $666. There seems no doubt, then, that immigrants were long paid less than native labor. Whether thereby they debased the wage scale for native laborers is less certain, but it would seem that a definite tendency in this direction must have been the fact. Not only did wages paid to immigrants tend to be less than those to native laborers, but immigrants were also very commonly driven into the least desirable types of employment.

One of the chief methods whereby native American labor has been able to increase wages and improve living standards has been through labor organization and the development of collective bargaining. Hence, it is important to look into the effect of immigrant labor on labor unionism in the United States. The Immigration Commission, in 1910, declared that immigration had weakened and disrupted American labor organizations. On the other hand, Hourwich and other apologists for immigration have pointed to the large number of immigrants in labor unions, to the prominence of certain foreign-born labor organizers, and to the fact that some of our strongest unions are made up almost entirely of immigrants and their children. Hence, they allege that immigration certainly has not served to undermine the American labor movement.

The facts, as presented in a sympathetic but highly competent analysis by William M. Leiserson, a leading labor expert, in his *Adjusting Immigrant and Industry,* would seem to be about as follows: Every new wave of immigration tended to weaken American labor organization, but in subsequent generations many descendants of immigrants became aggressive labor unionists. As unionism has become better developed, immigrants have been more quickly absorbed into the ranks of union labor when the way was open for them to do so. Each great wave of new immigrants had a disastrous temporary effect upon the American labor movement, but by the present time immigrants and their descendants have entered so widely into labor organizations that their net effect has been to strengthen the labor movement in our country. It must also be remembered that the immigrants are not the only ones who have obstructed labor unionism. Native American workers helped to hold back labor organization in the southern textile factories and steel towns and in the mining areas of Illinois. We may agree with Leiserson's judicious summary of the situation with respect to immigrants and labor organization in our country:

Although the finding of the United States Immigration Commission that immigrants were weakening and disrupting American labor organizations has been questioned, it must be admitted that the rapid influx of new labor did tend to weaken the existing labor organizations. But that this was a temporary result of the necessity of finding a footing in American industry, and not due to the racial character of the more recent immigrants from southern and eastern Europe, is evident from the strong unions of mine workers, garment workers, and shoe workers, that have been built up by these immigrants; and from the fact that every other race of newcomers in industry, including rural native Americans as well as North European immigrants, have also weakened labor organizations. English, Scotch, and Irish immigrants were used to break the strikes of native workers early in our history. When these in turn formed unions and struck, German workmen took their places. Bohemians, Scandinavians, and Jews were the strike breakers of the eighties, and in later years the south and east Europeans merely repeated the experience of the previous comers.[4]

Not only have immigrant laborers been exploited through low wages and living standards, but there has also been a tendency to mass and concentrate them in special industries and particular localities where they make up the overwhelming majority of the population. This has both facilitated economic exploitation and intensified cultural segregation. It has been customary in such industrial and mining communities made up of immigrants for the employers to control the stores and shops of the locality, thus often providing an additional form of exploitation. Employers, likewise, frequently provided and usually controlled the police in such company towns, thus easily quelling any protest and suppressing labor agitation. This topic is discussed in detail in J. P. Shalloo's *Private Police*.

There was long a tendency for immigrant labor to be particularly hard hit by our great industrial crises. Having been in the past poorly organized and mainly outside the American labor movement, the immigrants have been unable to protect themselves from rapid discharge,

---

[4] W. M. Leiserson, *Adjusting Immigrant and Industry*. New York: Harper, 1924, p. 174.

prolonged unemployment, and abject misery. Moreover, it is during the tense periods of depressions, when native labor is more widely unemployed, that the prejudices against immigrant labor flare up most violently. During the depression following 1929 there was an extensive deportation of alien laborers. Further, there has frequently been much discrimination against alien laborers in the actual administration of relief during crises.

Immigration and the unemployment problem. One very important consideration with respect to immigration and labor is frequently lost sight of, namely, the relation of the tremendous mass migration between 1900 and 1914 to the critical problem of unemployment after the First World War, and especially after 1929. Most unemployment in the United States has been laid to technological changes and business slumps, but a considerable part of the responsibility rests with those who permitted the tremendous mass movement of immigrants into this country after 1890.

Over 17 million persons came to the United States between 1890 and 1914. The great majority of these settled in industrial towns and mining areas. Very few took up a rural habitat. At this same time there was still a considerable migration of native American stock from the country to the city. This led to a marked concentration of population among the laboring element of our cities. During the First World War the enormous demands for labor served to absorb most of this new surplus of manpower. The extensive construction work after the war, due to the suspension of building operations in war time and the remarkable expansion of the automobile industry, helped to take care of this great army of urban industrial workers during the 1920's. But not even the unusual industrial activity of the Harding-Coolidge era could absorb all this new industrial army. There were several million unemployed before the depression set in in the autumn of 1929.

During the depression unemployment passed any previous marks, competent estimates running as high as 15 to 18 million unemployed. The unemployment census in 1937-1938 seemed to indicate that the number of unemployed in late New Deal times was pretty close to 10 million. The 17 million who came in from 1890 to 1914 have, naturally, reproduced copiously and greatly added to the potential laboring group in urban communities. As we noted in the preceding chapter, it is the poorest sector of the laboring class that reproduces more abundantly than any other group in the cities. It may turn out that this undoubted contribution to extensive unemployment has been the most disastrous influence exerted by immigration upon economic conditions in the United States. Had this creation of a vast additional army of potential workers come during the time when the United States was an expanding economy the result would not have been so serious. But it was most potent in its results after the First World War, when the economy was becoming stabilized and technological unemployment was first becoming a serious menace to the working class. Wartime industry after 1940, the cold war economy after 1945, and the Korean war and mobilization after 1950 have temporarily relieved the unemployment problem, but it is unlikely to be a permanent solution.

Net effect of immigration on American economic life. We may now consider certain broader aspects of the relations between immigration and American economic life. In the matter of the production of wealth, immigrants have constituted an enormous asset in the way of increased manpower. Much of our industrial expansion and transportation construction has been achieved through their efforts. It has been pointed out by some students, however, that the cheap manpower provided by immigrant labor probably retarded mechanical invention in this country. If so, it has also, to this extent, checked technological unemployment.

With respect to the consumption of wealth in this country, the immigrants have provided a vast army of consumers and have created a market for many goods that could not otherwise have been sold. Yet it can hardly be maintained that, as consumers, they have been as effective per capita as have been the native born. They have lived on lower standards, and their lower income has provided them with less money to spend on goods and services. Here again, however, it has been the avarice of some American employers that was partly responsible. There is no doubt that the immigrants would have been glad to spend more money if they had been able to earn it. Another reason why the immigrants represented a relatively less effective type of American consumer is the fact that certain groups of them, especially the Italians, have not spent in this country all of even the low income which they earned. Many have endeavored to save stringently, accumulate a competence, and then return to Europe to live more cheaply and pleasantly on what they have saved in America. From 1902 to 1924 the Italians who returned to Italy equalled no less than 62.8 per cent of those who came to this country in this period.

On the whole, we may probably conclude that the net effect of immigration upon our economic life in the last sixty years has, to some degree, brought about a depression in wages and living standards. It has also helped along the somewhat overrapid industrial expansion of the country, which neglected many details and resulted in a somewhat unsound economy. Of all the deplorable effects of immigration in economic affairs, however, it would seem that the most serious was the creation and expansion of a great army of surplus laborers, which it may be progressively more difficult to provide with steady and remunerative employment within the general structure of the capitalistic system, in case our taxpayers finally weary of the intolerable burdens of the cold war and unlimited handouts abroad, and force a return to normal American economic conditions.

The problem of the total influence, for good or evil, of immigration since 1870 on American economic life is so complicated and so involved in guesswork that no summary or categorical verdict is possible. But it is safe to say that any allegation that our economic ills of the mid-century can be traced mainly to post-Civil War immigration is untenable.

IMMIGRATION AND SOCIAL PATHOLOGY

Immigrants forced into bad living conditions. One of the most unfortunate aspects of the life of immigrants in the United States has been the depressed living conditions into which they have been forced by exploitation at the hands of both employers and avaricious landlords. This fact has been vividly stated by Langdon W. Post:

Of all the deliberate exploitation of the masses, that of those immigrant hordes who poured into the United States of America from abroad is probably the most shameful.... Millions of dollars and huge fortunes were created out of their thin pocketbooks.... So terrified are they of being put out on the street that the first thing they take out of their pay is the rent.... They have had to accept what was offered, or else sleep on the streets, and so busy have they been trying to earn enough money to pay for even that little, they have had neither the time nor the opportunity to demand something better. It is this apparently philosophical acceptance of indecent conditions which has led the ruling class to excuse and accept these conditions on the ground that the people enduring them were perfectly happy. In other words, because they do not revolt or go on the rampage as a result of these conditions they must be perfectly contented under them. This has been the approach of America to housing for the past 150 years.[5]

The overcrowding and other bad conditions that characterized the housing of immigrants as late as 1880 is well described by Smith Hart, who cites the following not extreme case:

In Ludlow Street, for example, a Jewish tailor with a wife and two children rented a two room tenement. The tailor, his wife and children, and two male boarders occupied the larger room. The bedroom, eight feet square, was sublet to another tailor and his wife. The second tailor and his wife hung a curtain across the middle of their room and rented out the surplus half to a third tailor with a wife and child. The sanitary police arrested the original tailor. His wife appeared before the authorities the next day to lodge complaint that the sanitary police "were robbing her of her tenants." [6]

In late years, however, certain immigrant groups have shown much energy and vision in taking the leadership in improving urban living conditions. A notable example is the excellent apartments erected by the Amalgamated Clothing Workers in New York City.

Immigration and crime. Another important problem connected with the immigration issue is the question of the relation of immigration to the increase of crime and vice in this country. There have been sharp differences of opinion among students of the situation. For example, H. H. Laughlin of the Eugenics Record Office believed that he found a great preponderance of crime and vice among immigrant groups, particularly recent immigrants and their descendants. On the other hand, the Wickersham Commission on Law Observance and Enforcement took exactly the opposite position and contended that the foreign born committed fewer crimes per capita than did the native born.

Laughlin's statistical methods have been sharply attacked as biased

---

[5] Langdon W. Post, *The Challenge of Housing*, copyright, 1938, and reprinted by permission of Farrar & Rinehart, Inc., publishers.

[6] *The New Yorkers*. New York: Sheridan House, 1938, p. 186.

and unreliable. It would also seem that objections may be made to accepting the Wickersham verdict at its face value. In estimating the percentage of crime committed by the foreign born in relation to the criminal record of the native born, the commission compared the crimes committed by the foreign born with those committed by all of the native born American stock. The latter, of course, included the children of the foreign born. Most studies of immigration and criminality have shown that the most markedly criminal elements in the population are these very children of foreign-born parents. At least, this seems to be true in most of our larger cities. Hence, the deductions of the commission must be analyzed with this important qualification in mind. Had it eliminated the children of the foreign born from the native stock in their comparison of relative criminality, the superior showing of the foreign born would have been much less impressive.

Superficially, on the face of the figures, the foreign born do seem to commit less crime per capita than does the native stock. We have to keep in mind, however, the fact that many who commit what are, by American standards, regarded as crimes are often not arrested in communities made up overwhelmingly of foreign-born persons. The police in such localities are also frequently made up of the same nationalities and are usually tolerant in such matters. If there is actually a relatively lower crime rate among the foreign born, it is probably due to the fact that they have learned the lessons of law observance in the better-disciplined countries of their origin. Their cultural segregation in the United States permits their original respect for law to carry over during their residence here.

We have already suggested that the children of the foreign born commit more crime per capita than does any other group in the population. This fact is due primarily to problems of social and cultural maladjustment. The customs and folkways of the parent culture have a less potent influence over the second generation of immigrants—the children of immigrant parents—and are less effective in restraining them from criminal conduct. At the same time, the children of immigrants have not been sufficiently assimilated into American culture to permit American folkways to exert an effective disciplinary influence. This group, then, falls between two forces. Not finding themselves culturally adjusted to the old or the new, they seek an adjustment of their own, too often in gangs that may turn their energy into criminal activities. The facts in this situation have been admirably summarized by Frederic M. Thrasher, a student of juvenile delinquency:

The facts recounted above can lead us to but one explanation of the excessive delinquency of the children of foreign-born parentage. They are the unknowing victims of disorganized social conditions and a superficial Americanization that goes little beyond contacts with the vice, crime and political corruption which are characteristic of the blighted areas in which they live. The solution of the problem, then, is clear. It lies, on the one hand, in curtailing the evil influences which play upon the children of these areas, and on the other, in opening up to them more adequate opportunities to participate in the cultural heritages which we like to think of as being most truly representative of American life.[7]

7 Brown and Roucek. *op. cit.,* p. 710.

If it be true, as many authorities contend, that misery and low living standards promote crime, this factor undoubtedly operates with special force among the children of the foreign born who are brought up under less favorable surroundings than comparable groups among the native stock. The fact that immigrants and their children were long compelled to live in slum areas—what Clifford Shaw calls "delinquency areas"— makes it all the more remarkable that their ratio of criminality has not been greater than it is shown to be.

On the whole, so far as the recent past is concerned, one may fairly conclude with Donald R. Taft that "immigration has increased the crime hazard in this country." We cannot assume, however, that there is any racial basis for this fact. It is a problem of cultural nonassimilation and social maladjustment. We shall point out, however, in a later chapter dealing with crime, that Earnest A. Hooton sharply challenges prevailing opinion on this subject and contends that there is a definite racial and immigrant basis for crime in the United States. His statements have stirred up much controversy over this problem.

What we have said above about criminality has referred primarily to traditional crimes. When it comes to organized crime and racketeering, there is little doubt that the foreign born and children of foreign born, from Capone to Costello, have taken a lead in organizing and conducting such large-scale delinquency.

Immigration, vice and gambling. Investigations of the relation of immigration to organized vice bring us to about the same conclusions that we have reached with regard to immigration and crime. There may be a greater sexual laxity among some of the foreign born, but much of this can hardly be classed as vice or immorality, when judged by the standards of the immigrant. They frequently bring a far more civilized and broadminded sexual morality with them than has prevailed in American communities. They are also familiar with prostitution in their native habitat. It is not surprising that there is a relative preponderance of the children of the foreign born among those who are engaged in organized vice. The more general prevalence of poverty among the immigrants has naturally facilitated the recruiting of many prostitutes from this second generation of foreign stock. Organized vice has been preponderantly under the control of the foreign born or second generation immigrants.

The same observations apply to gambling. Foreigners are often more tolerant and realistic on the matter of gambling and bring gambling habits with them from the fatherland. The trend of the second generation toward delinquency naturally induces them to flirt with gambling enterprises as a means of acquiring an income, and some of them have assumed a prominent rôle in controlling the mammoth organized gambling business in our country today.

In the more recent period of the development of organized crime, vice, and gambling, there seems little doubt that those who are foreign born or are of foreign descent have assumed leadership in the control of this important development in the American crime picture. Expert students of the problem allege a close tie-up between these immigrant American leaders in organized crime, vice and gambling and the Italian *Mafia,* a powerful underworld criminal organization. Here the name of "Lucky" Luciano immediately comes to mind.

IMMIGRATION AND POPULATION PROBLEMS

Immigration has contributed greatly to our rapid population growth. The relation of immigration to population quantity and quality raises interesting sociological issues. It is obvious that today current immigration plays little part in the increase of the population of our country. But in the past it has exerted an influence on population growth unprecedented in the history of mankind. Not only have about 40 million immigrants come to our country, but also they have been very prolific in the reproduction of their kind, though today in comparable income groups there is not much difference in the birth rate of immigrant and native stocks.

Viewing the matter simply from the standpoint of quantity, immigration has been a great asset to population growth in the United States. But it is a grave question whether our population has not increased too rapidly to permit the proper institutional and cultural readjustments. Moreover, as we suggested above, immigration may have produced a potential army of unemployed that will create ever more critical situations in the economic field. Of course, it is probably true that if we were to adopt an economy based on production for use we could easily support the present population of the United States at a decent standard of living. But within the capitalistic structure and in the light of capitalistic practices, there is some ground for the contention of many authorities that we have already reached a state of serious overpopulation so far as the labor supply is concerned. If so, immigration has contributed notably to this deplorable result. The abnormal employment situation that has existed under the war and quasi-war economy since 1941 cannot be expected to be permanent.

There are some who maintain that we should welcome immigration as a means of relieving population pressure in European countries. This presumes a degree of international altruism that exceeds the bounds of reason. Further, extensive emigration from European countries has only temporarily relieved overcrowding in these areas. Increased births and a decrease of deaths have quickly brought the population back to the original level. If overcrowded European states wish relief from overpopulation, the answer is that birth control, like charity, should begin at home.

Immigration and population quality. Perhaps the fiercest controversies over immigration have revolved about the question of whether or not it has reduced the quality of the population of the United States. It is here that racial and national prejudices have their freest play. We have already referred to the "new barbarian" complex of certain critics of immigration such as Wilbur C. Abbott of Harvard. This has been countered by other extremists who maintain that there is no such thing as racial differences or cultural superiority.

We shall point out at some length in the following chapter that there is no scientific basis for the theory of comprehensive racial superiority. We have already indicated that, so far as the relative preponderance of submerged classes is concerned, even the immigrants who have come to us since 1890 can make relatively as good a showing as the original colonial immigrants. Intelligence tests administered to immigrant children have seemed to many to indicate that in certain nationalities and social levels among the later immigrants the innate mental powers are less than those of the native stock. Other equally authoritative students have contended that these mental tests have not been designed to eliminate the cultural disadvantages and handicaps under which these immigrant children operate. Hence, they claim that the tests do not reveal actual mental inferiority. Although we may concede some mental inferiority on the part of certain groups among the immigrants, it is doubtful that this has exerted any extensive deleterious influence upon the quality of the American population. The most important point to note here is that the relatively high rate of fertility among the lower classes, immigrant and native, may constitute a serious challenge with respect to the maintenance of the quality of the American population.

Certainly there is no ground for belief that the immigrant stock represents a lower order of innate physical vigor and mental capacity than the native element. It is true that the great increase in the American population as the result of immigration and reproduction by immigrants has probably restricted the rate of increase among the native white stock, but it can hardly be shown that this has been particularly disastrous to the physical quality of the American people. The notion that intermarriage between the native stock and any of the European types that have come to this country is physically objectionable or mentally deleterious lacks any substantial scientific foundation. Any detrimental effects of immigration upon the United States are of a cultural and institutional rather than of a biological order.

CULTURAL IMPACT OF IMMIGRATION

Theories of immigrant assimilation. In considering the effects of immigration upon the American cultural complex we find two schools of thought about cultural assimilation. One is the so-called "melting pot" theory that has been popular with many American students of the immigration problem. This group contends that the foreign cultures should be rapidly sloughed off and immigrants adjusted to American civilization through prompt assimilation. The other school, which is chiefly upheld by those of foreign descent, contend that the foreign elements should be allowed to perpetuate a large portion of their alien culture. They hold that civilization is promoted by the contrast and conflict of cultures, and that these foreign cultures have important contributions to make to American civilization.

It is the melting pot theory that has been most persistently followed in American policy. But it must be conceded that the melting process has not proved entirely successful thus far. Immigration has been too rapid, and the institutional provisions for assimilation have been slow and inadequate. The theory may work out better in practice in future generations, now that immigration is dwindling.

Whatever the relative value of these alien cultures to the United States, there is no doubt that the actual cultural nonassimilation due to overrapid immigration has produced many serious social problems in our country. The greater criminality of the children of foreign-born parents is a case in point. The educational problem has been intensified. Immigrants who came to us in the period after 1890 tended to be less literate upon arrival than were the earlier aliens. This has increased the extent of illiteracy in our country and made the problems of adjustment more difficult. Language differences have also handicapped the children of immigrants in the educational process.

Problems of assimilation. The problem of adjusting the immigrant to American civilization through cultural assimilation requires tact and discrimination. Blunt attempts at overrapid assimilation are likely to be disastrous, for the culture of immigrants is based upon age-old traditions that are very valuable to them and are reluctantly cast off casually and speedily. If immigrants are forced to throw aside their old culture too rapidly, we waste the possible contributions that it might make to American civilization. We also tend to introduce cultural confusion and maladjustment into the lives of immigrants. This produces an especially difficult situation for the children of immigrants, who take on a sort of half-and-half cultural status resulting in a confusion of outlook and maladjusted behavior. It is this situation which leads to the proclivity of this second generation to crime and vice.

The other extreme policy of isolating foreign communities as alien islands in American culture and leaving the immigrants to shift for themselves also creates unfortunate results. It perpetuates extreme divergencies in American life and culture. We expect the immigrant to become naturalized and to function as a good American citizen. This he can hardly do if he lives in what is essentially an alien community and has little conception of American ideals and institutions. Moreover, immigrants, if left to themselves, are likely to continue to dwell in slum quarters and to perpetuate low living standards that encourage crime, vice, and degenerate communities. The better educated and more ambitious immigrants or children of immigrants tend to leave these unattractive surroundings and make their way into the native stock through intermarriage and professional achievements. The mass of immigrants are thus left culturally stranded and deprived of their ablest and most ambitious elements.

We may hope that with the falling off of immigration, which is making the problem of cultural assimilation easier to control and direct, the laxity, inadequacy and crudities of American policies in the past will be remedied. We may expect, or certainly wish for, a policy that will either preserve or absorb the more beneficial contributions inherent in alien cultures, at the same time producing sufficient assimilation to enable the descendants of immigrants to function successfully as members of the American cultural and political community.

Immigration and the arts. We may summarize briefly the positive contributions that immigrants unquestionably have made to American culture and civilization. In the first place, they have certainly helped to lessen American cultural stagnation, inertia, and smugness. Through the clash of cultures they have tended to break down the "cake of custom" in the United States. They have brought to this country many skilled crafts, which, unfortunately, are not of so great immediate utility in our mechanized civilization as they were in the Old World. If we are able in the future to make more and better use of leisure, these skilled crafts may be a contribution of permanent value to American life. There is no doubt of the fact that immigrants have made an overwhelmingly greater per capita contribution to the arts than have the native stock. Merely to mention architecture, sculpture, painting, music and the dance will emphasize this point. It is perhaps in the field of music that the immigrants have made their most distinctive contribution to American esthetic life.

This stimulation of American culture by immigration has been offset to a considerable degree by the indirect contribution of immigration to the intensification of the censorship of art and literature. Immigration has notably increased the political and psychological strength of religious bodies and organizations opposed to literary and artistic freedom. This may be illustrated by the example of the city of Boston, once rightly regarded as the "Athens of America" and the custodian of the "Cradle of Liberty." Because of the influence and pressure of certain religious organizations that owe their predominant power to immigration, we have witnessed in Boston since the First World War the operation of an absurd censorship of books, art, the drama, and the movies unparalleled in the recent history of any other first-class American city. This religious pressure supporting censorship is not limited to Boston or any other large seaboard town built up by immigration. It permeates the nation and is today perhaps the most stultifying single factor in American literary and artistic life.

Immigration and American religious and moral life. From the broad point of view of the relation of immigration to American religious life, it is probable that immigration, by bringing to our shores many different religious groups, has made for greater religious tolerance. Some reservations, however, must be made to this general statement. Religious contrasts have also provoked some of our more flagrant examples of religious intolerance. The great influx of Catholics in the two decades before the Civil War produced the so-called Protestant Crusade of that era. The American Protective Association, which was organized back in 1887, was violently anti-Catholic. The revived Ku Klux Klan, which flourished after the First World War, was dominated by antagonism against both Catholics and Jews. Of late there has been an increase of Catholic militancy which has alarmed many who have no particular prejudices. Some felt

that the Farley and Flynn influence in the Roosevelt administration unduly increased Catholic power in the field of public affairs. Father
Coughlin alarmed others. Catholic activity against radicals and artistic
freedom in the United States alienated still more. Anti-Semitism has
flared up on occasions, especially since the First World War.

With respect to morality, one may safely conclude that the immigrant
contribution has been, on the whole, a salutary and valuable one. It has
helped to modify one of the least lovely and least defensible elements
in American culture, namely, the harshness, crudity, and narrowness of
the old Puritan moral outlook. The immigrant contributions in this respect will become progressively more valuable as we are compelled to
cope more extensively with the problems of leisure. In any final estimate, however, of the relation of immigration to morality, it is necessary to keep in mind the fact that the religious powers that have been
strengthened by immigration have often taken the lead in seeking to
censor art, literature, and the drama.

Promotion of international interests. Immigration has also tended to
increase the growth of an international outlook, at least in times of
peace. In great crises, however, this has not always proved to be the case.
The various nationalities in this country tend, in time of war or sharp
international controversy, to sympathize with their fellow nationals back
home. This has led to the charge of "hyphenated" Americanism. At the
same time, if the safety of this country is threatened, a burst of super-
patriotism results and an effort is made to make all types in this country
conform to the patriotic ideal and to the dictates of American public
policy. The First World War offered a peculiarly instructive instance of
both these tendencies—hyphenism and mob psychology on a national
scale. During the Second World War, the foreign born and those of foreign descent fell into line with the war effort more thoroughly. Indeed, the
enthusiasm of some of these groups for the war exceeded that of the
native stock. On the whole, it would seem that most of the superpatriotic
worries about cultural diversities and foreign loyalties among immigrants
have not been warranted.

Immigration and American educational life and policy. Among the
institutions that have promoted cultural assimilation and applied the
melting pot philosophy to immigrants, the American public school system stands first. With its exclusive use of the English language for instruction and its curriculum constructed by Americans for Americans,
it has been sweeping and direct in its method of promoting assimilation.
Its very virtues in this respect have been weaknesses in other regards. It
has been lacking in consideration for the persistence and value of alien
cultures and has moved too rapidly and directly. It has thus often resulted in disorganization and defeat instead of true assimilation. This
fact has been well brought out by E. George Payne:

Unfortunately, public school educators did not have the philosophy, the
vision, or the technique of the social workers in their relations to the immigrant
and his problems. Because of this deficiency the public schools received immigrant children, treated them as natives, totally disregarded their cultural back-

grounds, and judged their performance by American cultural standards of conduct. They provided for them a conventional and for the most part an academic subject-matter, built out of American traditions and standards. This program had very definite results. A limited number broke with their traditions, discarded them as quickly as possible, forgot them, and accepted American standards as they conceived them, and, having broken completely with their families and their traditions, were readily absorbed into American life. A larger number sought to forget their traditional backgrounds, regarded them as inferior, and held their elders in disrespect for continuing practices out of harmony with American traditions. This led to family disruption and disintegration, for the traditional family authority was broken. Some of the youths of this group made their ultimate adjustment to American life and were absorbed into the American stream, but a larger number made up the delinquent and criminal group, providing a source of unending problems. Finally, the largest group could not make their adjustment to the school, persisted for a time in failing to make the grade, and finally fell by the way, discouraged and with a feeling of inferiority and failure. As they grew to adulthood, they were fed into the industrial machine as common laborers and thus advanced our material culture.[8]

It may be that our schools in the future will handle the problem of the education of immigrants in a more discriminating fashion. Thus far, the improvements in this respect have not kept pace with advances in other phases of public education. The harsh and direct methods of promoting assimilation in the public schools have been one of the reasons, along with religious prejudices, why the foreign born have so widely supported parochial schools.

Special types of educational procedure have been set up to deal particularly with immigrants. Most notable have been the English language classes, which have been particularly demanded and supported by employers who realize the utility of giving instruction in English to their employees. Probably the most intelligent work in assimilation has been done by the social settlements, such as Hull House in Chicago and the Henry Street Settlement in New York. They have had more regard than the school system for the culture of aliens and have been more successful than any other institution in bringing about a happy mean between forced assimilation and cultural segregation. Unfortunately, the settlements are unable to reach more than a very small percentage of the immigrant population.

Immigration has intensified the problems of education in another way. Certain religious groups, on the one hand, seek to educate as many children as possible outside the field of public education through parochial schools. But, through their political power in certain states and cities they also endeavor to control the public school system in which children outside their religious circle are educated. They thus shun public education for their own children, so far as possible, but, at the same time, wish to dominate it. Recently the movement has gone even beyond this, and we have witnessed a determined drive to get public funds allotted for the support of private religious parochial schools. The power of these religious groups in state and national politics, which is constantly on the gain, makes it seem likely that this drive will succeed in the not-distant

---

[8] Brown and Roucek, *op. cit.*, pp. 601-602.

future. This has alarmed many eminent educators who are not impressed with the logic or justice of the situation.

Intermarriage of natives and aliens. Actual amalgamation of aliens and natives through intermarriage naturally promotes assimilation. Thus far, the intermarriage between the aliens who have come in since 1890 and the native stock has been relatively limited. We have no adequate figures on the subject, but those we have indicate that the intermarriage of the foreign born with native Americans does not account for more than from 3 to 15 per cent of the total marriages of the foreign born. Intermarriage between children of the foreign born and native Americans is somewhat more frequent, running to somewhere between 15 and 30 per cent of the total marriages of the second generation immigrants. The immigrants from northern and western Europe have shown the greatest inclination to intermarry with the native stock.

Cultural segregation. We may now consider the institutions that promote cultural segregation, or at least retard rapid assimilation. Religion and the church have exerted much influence in this respect. The majority of the "old immigrants," those coming from northern and western Europe, were Protestants, the only notable exception being the Irish Catholics. On the other hand, the overwhelming majority of immigration from central and southern Europe since 1890 has been made up of Catholics and Jews. With the exception of English and Irish immigrants, there has been a tendency to conduct church services, in part at least, in the language of the aliens. Religious customs and social activities that were brought from the homeland are also perpetuated. The immigrant churches, particularly the Catholic church, are also a strong force in establishing and maintaining parochial schools, which frequently give some part of their instruction in alien tongues. The Jews, owing in part to persecutions in the past, in part to the nature of their religious views and institutions, and in part to the fear of anti-Semitism in this country, have tended to perpetuate Jewish culture in their religious life. This is particularly true of the orthodox Jews.

For these reasons it is generally agreed by students of the immigration problem that the net effect of the religious life of the aliens has been to preserve and perpetuate the immigrant culture. As Kaupos has put it: "The most powerful bond which unites immigrants of the same nationality in a foreign country is that represented by religion and the church. . . . In the churches they feel at home." It is possible, however, that, as the immigrant churches gain greater insight and maturity through their experiences in America, religion may in time become an effective agency of assimilation. Such is the opinion of G. M. Ridenour and F. J. Brown:

It may well be in the days ahead that the churches of America will have made a genuine contribution to a national program of assimilation; an assimilation based upon a mutual exchange of cultural gifts; an assimilation neither hurried nor coercive, which will evoke a friendly response from the foreign born because it recognizes the value of their racial contributions to the people of the United States. Far better the assimilation of the immigrant through mutual adjustment than a coerced Americanization which tore him by the roots from Old World cultures.[9]

One important way in which the church helps to perpetuate alien culture and to obstruct rapid assimilation among the immigrants lies in the powerful support that it gives to the foreign language press. We may profitably say a word about the nature and extent of the immigrant press in the United States.

The foreign language press arose as a natural response to many definite needs on the part of the foreign born. They wished to keep in touch with problems of interest in the fatherland, and at the same time they desired to read news about American events in a language that they could understand. There are at present over a thousand foreign language publications in the United States, issued in some 38 different languages. There was a considerable decline in the number of foreign language publications after 1917, when the United States went into the First World War and there followed a drive against certain foreign language publications. The loss in numbers is also, to a certain extent, accounted for by the growing tendency toward mergers and chain newspapers in the foreign language field.

The foreign language press is an extremely diversified affair, running all the way from metropolitan dailies, like the *New Yorker Staats-Herold*, the *Jewish Daily Forward*, the *Jewish Morning Journal*, the *Jewish Day*, *Il Progresso*, and *Dziennik Polski*, to small and struggling personal organs of a few pages to each issue. There are a total of 322 foreign language newspapers published in the United States today, with a total circulation of 3,382,000. In addition, there are about 700 more social and religious publications whose total circulation is not precisely known.

The foreign language press gives more than usual attention to news items and national issues drawn from the fatherland. Religious news also plays a prominent part in the majority of the foreign language publications. But the common charge that the foreign language press is "Red" or revolutionary is ill founded. Considering the fact that the foreign language papers are read primarily by the working classes, they have been remarkably conservative in tone. Editors of foreign language papers have a natural vested interest in retarding the full cultural assimilation of immigrants. If their readers mastered the English language and became primarily interested in American news, most of the foreign language papers would have to cease publication.

IMMIGRATION AND AMERICAN POLITICAL LIFE

Naturalization of aliens. The problem of the aliens in American political life revolves mainly about two fundamental issues: namely, (1) the naturalization of aliens and their entry into the duties of American citizenship, and (2) the part played by immigrants in American political life.

---

[9] Brown and Roucek, *op. cit.,* p. 622.

Not all immigrants can become American citizens if they wish to. Orientals were long excluded from the right of naturalization. The exception today is the Chinese who were granted the right of naturalization in 1946. For others than Orientals, the qualifications for American citizenship are essentially the following: The person must

... be a member of either the white or the African race and twenty-one years of age; have resided in the United States continuously for five years; be able to speak English; be devoted to the principles of the Constitution; be of good moral character; have entered the country legally; renounce his former allegiance and take the oath of allegiance to the United States; prove that he is neither an anarchist nor a polygamist; pay the required fees...; and follow the prescribed procedure.[10]

There are quite needless technicalities imposed in the procedure for naturalization. These have doubtless restrained a considerable number of aliens from going through the process of acquiring citizenship. The increased charges for naturalization instituted in 1929—namely, first

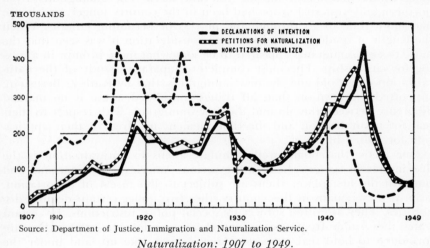

Source: Department of Justice, Immigration and Naturalization Service.

Naturalization: 1907 to 1949.

papers increased from $1 to $5, and second papers from $4 to $10—may have discouraged some from becoming citizens. The fixed and incidental cost of attaining citizenship may run in many cases as high as $50.

By and large, the volume of naturalization has been impressive and hardly supports the contention of some writers that many immigrants wish to stand aside from the responsibilities of American political life, while benefiting by residence in the American political community. The number of aliens in the country declined between 1930 and 1940. In 1930, there were 14,204,149 foreign born in the country, of whom 6,284,613 were aliens. An act of 1940 compelled alien registration, and the number discovered was 4,889,770. The number of aliens revealed by the 1940 registration act was less than half of the total foreign born and

---

10 D. R. Taft, *Human Migration*. New York: Ronald Press, 1936, p. 314.

less than 4 per cent of the total population of the United States. In 1940, there were 11,594,896 foreign born. Of these, 7,280,265 had been naturalized, 924,534 had taken out their first papers, 2,555,128 had not taken out any papers, and the remainder of the aliens were of undetermined citizenship. The number of aliens fell off during the war, and in 1945 there were 3,050,803 aliens in the country.

Students of immigration problems noted that between 1900 and 1910 there seemed to be a relative slowing down of the tendency for immigrants to naturalize themselves. In 1910 it was also pointed out that whereas some 74 per cent of the immigrants from northern and western Europe were naturalized, only about 37.7 per cent of the newer immigrants from central and southern Europe had been naturalized. This led to the conclusion that the more recent immigrants were more reluctant to assume the responsibilities of American citizenship. Later students pointed out, however, that this generalization was based upon an incomplete comprehension of all the relevant facts. The immigrants from northern and western Europe had been in the country longer, and hence had more time to go through the process of becoming citizens. When the length of residence was taken into consideration it was seen that the more recent immigrants appeared to be somewhat more prompt in applying for citizenship. The most complete comparative study of the naturalization of the old and the new immigrants, that by Ruth Z. Bernstein, supported the position that, all things considered, there is no marked difference between the old and the new immigrants with respect to their zeal for naturalization and the time element involved in their application for citizenship.

One factor that might well stimulate aliens to naturalization is the discrimination against aliens in the various American laws, national and state. In the first place, aliens are subject to the threat of deportation. Even if they remain in this country, they live under certain definite disabilities. They are often subject to special police restrictions. In certain states they suffer from discrimination in taxation. In others they are forbidden to hold real property. They cannot take up land under the provisions of the Homestead Act. Aliens are also definitely discriminated against in the various provisions for receiving relief and obtaining work on public works enterprises. In the winter of 1938-1939 such discrimination passed all former bounds through wholesale dismissal of aliens from the rolls of the Works Progress Administration.

Political alignments of immigrants. Immigrants have entered readily into American political and party life. Our political parties were eager to enlist immigrants in their ranks and to gain voting strength thereby. In the earlier and more corrupt days of city politics many immigrants were allowed to vote before they became citizens. Mark Twain's classic description of an Irish immigrant landing in New York in the 1870's, being greeted at the dock by Tammany politicians, and then taken to the polling place to vote on his way from the wharf to a rooming house, is slightly overdrawn, but it reflects the spirit and practices of the time. The immigrants, on their part, welcomed the enthusiastic partisan embraces of American politicians. It was one of the few outstanding evidences of cordiality which they met on coming to this country.

The Irish immigrants long exerted greater influence upon American political life, in proportion to their numbers, than any other immigrant group. The Irish quickly aligned themselves with the Jacksonian Democrat party. Jackson was himself an Irishman, and his party was opposed to the American aristocrats who naturally reminded the Irish of the hated English nobility. The Democrat party was also liberal in the matter of immigration and naturalization. Further, the anti-immigration and anti-Catholic Know Nothing party was affiliated with the Whigs, who partly fathered the Republican party. Finally, the Irish were opposed to abolition and to the emancipation of the slaves because they feared the competition of cheap Negro labor. The Irish have remained faithful to their original Democrat affiliations, though there have been some signs of a shift. The latter was reflected in the nomination of an Irishman, William F. Bleakley, as Republican candidate for the governorship of New York State in 1936, and the simultaneous "walk" of Al Smith out of the Democrat ranks.

In some ways more important than the Irish support of the Democrat party was the relation of Irish immigration to the development of party machines in the cities and the growth of the political boss. In this period following 1850, the Irish were peculiarly qualified to succeed in city politics. They had a marked clannishness, they were strongly united by devotion to Irish nationalism, and they were also solidified by a common devotion to the Catholic Church. Thus, they speedily took over control of city politics in many parts of the United States. In 1894 it was observed that New York, Brooklyn, Jersey City, Hoboken, Buffalo, Albany, Troy, Boston, Pittsburgh, St. Paul, St. Louis, Chicago, Kansas City, Omaha, New Orleans, and San Francisco were all dominated by Irish political machines. This control of the politics of great urban centers also gave the Irish a large influence in state and national politics.

The German contingent among the immigrants at first affiliated with the Jeffersonian Democrat-Republican party. This was particularly true of the Pennsylvania Dutch. But after 1848 there was a very definite shift, mainly to the Republican party, which was launched in 1856. The great majority of the Germans who came in after the failure of the Revolution of 1848 in Germany were liberals and radicals. The new Republican party was, at the outset, idealistic, progressive, and antislavery. All these things appealed to Carl Schurz and the German liberals who had come to this country. When the party became more conservative and corrupt after the Civil War, Schurz and the German liberals were leaders in the movement for civil service and political reform.

The fact that the First World War was waged by a Democrat administration under Woodrow Wilson and that the Wilson administration bitterly discriminated against German-Americans in certain instances temporarily intensified the enthusiasm of German-Americans for the Republican party. Many who had hitherto voted the Democrat ticket helped to elect Harding and Coolidge. Yet, in the 1920's a definite rift developed between many German-Americans and the Republicans because the latter were identified with the enforcement of prohibition. The German element failed to remember that this amendment had been submitted to the people by a Democrat war administration. Although the majority of German-Americans still vote the Republican ticket, they are by no means as unanimous as they were at the turn of the century.

The fact that many German radicals came to the United States after 1848 and during Bismarck's persecution of German Socialists in the 1880's has made such Germans a prominent element in American radicalism and Socialism since 1850.

The great bulk of the Scandinavians who came to this country settled in the north central United States, particularly in Minnesota, Wisconsin, and the Dakotas. Most of them were farmers at the outset. They were inclined to follow the Germans in aligning themselves with the Republican party. In due time, however, the Scandinavians awakened to the fact that the Republicans tended to become the party of the financial interests, which in various ways exploited the western farmers. Hence, the Scandinavians became more of an independent and reformist element in western politics. The La Follette reform movement in Wisconsin was originally built up on the solid foundation of Scandinavian support. The Farmer Labor party was most successful in the heavily Scandinavian state of Minnesota. Floyd Olson was for a time a national figure.

The Slavs, especially the Poles, have recently become an important element in American political life and organization. They settled mainly in the cities, and have often contested Irish supremacy therein. At first they joined the Republican party because this was the organization favored by most of their employers. Prohibition under Republican auspices, however, helped to turn them against the latter, and their sufferings under a Republican president during the depression from 1929 to 1933 hastened their withdrawal from Republican ranks. They have now rather generally become a powerful element in the Democrat party in Illinois, Michigan, New York, and Pennsylvania. They elected Anton Cermak mayor of the second largest American city—Chicago.

The Italian immigrants have followed much the same pattern of political alignment as have the Slavs. They settled in cities and entered the Republican party of their employers. But Prohibition and the depression led them rather definitely into the Democrat party. They have also produced important liberal and independent figures in American politics, the most notable of whom have been Mayors Fiorello H. La-Guardia and Vincent Impellitteri of New York City.

Balance-sheet of immigrant influence on American political life. The balance sheet of immigrant contributions to American political life is not easy to assess. As positive benefits, we may list the German-American contribution to liberalism, radicalism, and the spirit of reform. They helped to make the Republican party less responsive to the business interests than it might otherwise have been, though this influence was rarely or never decisive. Inasmuch as the Democrat party since the Civil

War has been decidedly more liberal than the Republican and more devoted to interests of the common man, the powerful support given to this party by the Irish and others has indirectly served to stimulate democracy and social justice in our party life.

Among the deplorable results of immigration upon American politics, the foremost has been the close relation of immigration to urban political machines, political graft and corruption, organized crime, and the degradation of the democratic process. Further, since immigrants have tended to be relatively less literate and informed upon American political matters, they have been less capable of functioning intelligently in a democratic system of government. To a limited extent, at least, we can assign the relative failure of democratic government in the United States to the impact of immigration. But we must remember that the native Americans share this responsibility through our failure to educate the immigrants to the responsibilities of citizenship and through our all too great eagerness to profit by the political ignorance of immigrant groups. Immigration has increased the Catholic and Jewish influence in American politics, which has provoked such responses as the ultra-Protestantism of the Ku Klux Klan. Certainly the increasing religious activity in politics has notably frustrated the intention of the Fathers of the country to divorce completely church and state. Immigration has also contributed to the growth of special pressure-groups that exert an important, even disproportionate, influence on American political life and strategy, especially in the so-called close states.

The effect of immigration upon our foreign relations and international politics has been mixed. It helped us to get a better notion of foreign cultures and gave us more of an international point of view. On the other hand, refugees from the Old World have often carried their European quarrels and hatreds to the United States. Eager to rescue their native lands from the tyranny that has overtaken them, many immigrants have sought to arouse an unnecessary belligerency in our own countrymen.

FORCED MIGRATION OF PEOPLES DURING SECOND WORLD WAR AND THE PROBLEM OF DISPLACED PERSONS

Forced migrations during and after the Second World War. Because the matter directly touches American public problems, both our appropriations for relief abroad and our policies about temporarily relaxing immigration restrictions, we should say a word about the movement of peoples during and after the Second World War. In the course of the war, both the Nazis and the Russians moved millions of persons about as labor battalions and the like. Other millions fled before the advances of the Nazis and the Russians. It is estimated that about 7,000,000 had returned to their home countries or had been repatriated by the end of 1947. But, it was believed that at least 1,500,000 were still what we call "displaced persons," scattered from Great Britain to China and living on a veritable subsistence level under the most distressing conditions. About 850,000 were living in crude and crowded camps in Europe, mainly in Germany and Austria. This number had been reduced to about 500,000 by 1950.

Main groups of displaced persons. These displaced persons fell into some four main groups in Europe: (1) the survivors of the Nazi labor battalions of the war period, mainly Slavs and Rumanians, and the German slave laborers still held by the Russians; (2) anti-Communist refugees from the Baltic states who fled before the Russian invasion as the Soviet armies closed in on Hitler; (3) slave laborers, mostly Germans, held by Czechoslovakia and France (in addition to the vastly larger number held by the Russians); and (4) Jews, mainly refugees from the postwar anti-Semitism in Poland.

Along with the indescribable horrors and cruelties in forced migrations and the bestial living conditions involved, these displaced persons have provided the basis for serious international crises. The Jews sought entry into Palestine, but the British objected. This resulted in much violence, the British withdrawal from Palestine, the Israeli-Arab War, and general confusion for a time in this region. The retention of many German slave laborers by Russia, Czechoslovakia, and France has increased and perpetuated the ill-feeling and bitterness in central Europe. Efforts have been made to permit around a half-million displaced persons to enter the United States. In 1948, Congress passed a law permitting the entry of 200,000 displaced persons during the next two years, but agitation continued for a more liberal law, which was passed in 1950 and provided for the admission of 344,000. About 250,000 had entered by August, 1951.

Expellees and refugees. Much more numerous than the groups usually classified as displaced persons are the Germans who have been expelled from Czechoslovakia, Hungary, the Balkans, Poland, and those portions of eastern Germany handed over to Poland. The number is estimated as between ten and fifteen millions. They were forced to crowd into a Germany that had lost its main food-producing areas and was able to provide even inadequate rations only through extensive foreign relief.

In addition to the expelled persons in Europe, many millions of Japanese were forcibly brought back from Korea, Manchuria, and China to intensify the struggle for existence in an already overcrowded Japan whose economy and capacity for self-support were shattered by the war. These Germans and Japanese are usually known as "expellees" rather than displaced persons.

Although most displaced persons and expellees are or have been refugees, the latter group is more inclusive and much larger than both of the former combined. J. Donald Kingsley, director-general of the International Refugee Organization, estimated in June, 1950, that there were between 30 and 60 million refugees in the world. And they were increasing all the time as, for example, Germans fleeing from eastern into western Germany. Not only are personal situations tragic, but the refugee problem creates serious economic and political difficulties.

HISTORIC MIGRATIONS WITHIN THE UNITED STATES

Indian migrations. Aside from immigration, there have also been a series of historically significant migrations within the boundaries of the United States.

The first important example of migration within the boundaries of what is now the United States was, of course, the migrations of the American Indians, whereby they spread from the western coast to Maine and Florida. Much later, as a result of white occupation of American territory, the Indians were pressed back, and many of them were finally subjected to forced migrations westward when they were restricted to residence on the reservations selected by the government. We shall have more to say about the white man's contact with the Indians in a later chapter.

The frontier movement. The most important of all the migrations that have taken place within the United States has been what is known as the frontier movement, whereby the United States was populated and American dominion over the whole continent effected. This frontier expansion ranks with the growth of industrialization as one of the two outstanding features in our achievements down to the present time. Its effects upon American life and society were studied in particular by Frederick Jackson Turner and his disciples, who created a whole school of historical interpretation in terms of frontier processes in American cultural development. The Turner thesis has recently been interpreted and illustrated by Ray A. Billington in his book on *Westward Expansion* (1949). The relation of the frontier to American culture and ideals has been graphically portrayed by Marjorie Barstow Greenbie in her *American Saga*.

The Scotch-Irish element was the first important contingent to promote the frontier movement. They settled at first mainly in Pennsylvania, but after the close of the French and Indian War they penetrated into the region beyond the Alleghenies, going as far as Tennessee and some of the southern states. After the United States became an independent nation, many of them settled in what was then the Northwest Territory. But the filling up of the area between New York and Pennsylvania on the east and the Mississippi River on the west was achieved mainly by New Englanders and the English and German immigrants between 1790 and the Civil War. Slavery disputes in the Kansas-Nebraska area led to a considerable migration into these territories by antislavery elements from the New England states in the decade preceding the Civil War. The Homestead Act of 1862 encouraged further expansion into the West, a trend which was remarkably facilitated by the building of railroads into this region. Large numbers of Scandinavians migrated to Minnesota and the Dakotas. By 1890, most of the desirable farming land had been taken up under the Homestead Act. It is generally agreed by historians that the year 1890 marks the end of the historic frontier movement.

Many of the more characteristic traits of American civilization either grew out of the frontier movement or were intensified by it. Frontier society strengthened the sentiment of nationality. The frontiersmen were intensely loyal to the national government and had little sympathy with the states-rights movement. The hard struggles of families to subdue nature and make a livelihood on the frontier naturally stimulated the development of an individualistic philosophy. The frontiersmen were intensely democratic, and were suspicious of the rule of the "rich and the well-born," which had been recommended by Alexander Hamilton, John Adams, and the Federalists. The democratization of the American system of government owed much to the frontier society. Their democratic sentiment made the frontiersmen, for the most part, vigorous opponents of slavery. The frontier settlers were also prone to social idealism and optimism. To this frontier spirit we owe in large part the development of what James Truslow Adams has called "the American dream" psychology. By this we mean the irrepressible optimism that pervaded even the lower strata of American society and led to the belief that every American child might be on his way to the White House, or at least to material prosperity and social prominence. This psychology has notably retarded the development of an American labor party and other reform programs based upon the assumption of a permanent proletarian status.

The frontier gave birth to most of the programs of social and economic reform that have developed in our history. The main movements which have attacked plutocracy, exploitation, graft, and corruption in American life were born on the frontier. Such were the Greenback, Granger, Populist, and similar movements, and the Bryan Democracy. There was a strong spirit of frontier reformism in the Roosevelt Progressive movement of 1912, in the La Follette Farmer-Labor revolt of 1924, and in the development of the Non-Partisan League and the Farmer-Labor movement in the West after the First World War. The strongly individualistic strains in frontier philosophy have, however, circumscribed and limited the value of many of these reform movements which have arisen in the West. The frontier also stimulated religious life and a Puritanical morality. The great religious revivals of the middle of the nineteenth century were most successful in frontier regions. Religious orthodoxy still retains a fairly firm grip upon the West, and the Puritanical morality has given support to such movements as Prohibition.

The Mormon migration. A number of special migrations contributed to this westward movement. An important one was the Mormon migration to Utah. The Mormons are a religious group whose activities and achievements have also reached out into social, economic, and political fields.

The sect took its origins from revelations said to have been made to Joseph Smith early in the last century. Smith stated that in 1823 an angel of the Lord had appeared to him in a little town in central New York, telling him of some strange golden tablets containing the records of the aboriginal inhabitants of North America. According to the Mormon story, these people were Hebrews—some of the lost ten tribes—who had migrated to America under the guidance of God about 600 B.C. They were responsible for the high civilizations early established in America. Owing to warfare among various groups about the fifth century A.D., they became extinct, with the exception of certain degenerate descendants, namely, the American Indians, who had no knowledge of the sacred revelation of Mormon.

The Book of Mormon, the record of these aboriginal Hebrew-Americans and the essence of their religious beliefs and practices, is supposed to have been compiled by Mormon, one of their later prophets, and completed by his son, Moroni, who finished his work about A.D. 420. He is said to have deposited these plates near Palmyra, New York, to have reappeared in the guise of an angel in 1823 to inform Smith of these remarkable facts, and to have returned in 1827 to guide Smith in digging up these plates and to tender him divine aid in translating them into English. Smith said that Mormon and Moroni had originally written on the plates in hieroglyphic script, similar to that used by the ancient Egyptians. Aided by miraculous spectacles, Smith completed the translation of the Book of Mormon in 1830, and founded the Mormon congregation on April 6th of that year, at Fayette, New York. The Book of Mormon, as one would suspect, is remarkably similar to the Hebrew Bible in its conception of God, the creation, the patriarchs and the prophets; but it claims for itself, rather than the New Testament, the textual basis of true religion.

Smith and his converts migrated to Missouri between 1831 and 1838. They were driven out of there by their Christian neighbors and sought refuge in Nauvoo, Illinois, in 1838. Here dissension started within the Mormon group, and the "Gentiles" (Christians) of Illinois soon became hostile. Smith was killed by a mob. To escape further persecution, an advance guard, under the leadership of their new prophet, the indomitable Brigham Young, started on the long and perilous journey across the untraveled West in search of the "land of promise." This they located on the shore of Great Salt Lake, Utah, on July 24, 1847, the year before gold was discovered in California.

This was a most unattractive and unpromising area when first discovered, being a desert inhabited by the warlike Ute Indians. The Mormon prospectors decided, however, to settle here, and Young returned to Iowa to bring the rest of the faithful from their temporary place of refuge at Council Bluffs. The land about Salt Lake City proved very fertile when irrigated. The Mormons introduced irrigation in the West and cleverly placated the Indians. Considerable money was also made through trading with those who passed through Salt Lake City on their way to and from the West after the discovery of gold in California. The Mormons have proved very thrifty, industrious, cooperative, and well disciplined, and have acquired great wealth and power. Especially important in promoting their prosperity in recent years has been the development of the sugar-beet industry.

The Mormon Church now has some 1,184,595 members in Utah and adjoining states and has an extensive missionary organization extending even to Europe and other areas overseas. Many Gentiles are fearful and intolerant of Mormonism, but most of the charges made against the Mormons by fanatics are unfounded. There is no reason why the Mormons should be either specially favored or persecuted; they should be left in peace, in keeping with the American tradition of religious toleration. Popular feeling against the Mormons was intensified by their practice of polygyny, which was officially repudiated by the Mormon Church in 1890. Utah was admitted to the Union as a state in 1895.

The power of Mormonism is based upon other than religious considerations. It is a social, economic, political, and cultural organization, as well as a religious movement. The excellent discipline of the faithful, matched only by the Catholic organization of believers, gives Mormonism a strength out of proportion to the bare number of its adherents.

The Gold Rush. Another dramatic western migration followed in the wake of the discovery of gold in California in 1848. The news spread rapidly and soon a great army of gold-seekers from all parts of the world rushed to California. Americans went by thousands. The greatest number went overland by way of the Oregon Trail, and many others by the Santa Fe Trail to the south. The hardships endured by these travelers can scarcely be imagined. For the greater part of the way there were no roads or bridges. The Indians were hostile and often plundered wagon trains and massacred the migrants; long stretches of desert had to be crossed where food and water were scarce. Others of the gold-seekers took the long voyage by sea around Cape Horn, and still others went by water to Panama, crossed the isthmus on horseback, and waited until they could secure passage on a ship bound for San Francisco. Thousands died of yellow fever at Panama. The "forty-niners," as they were called, were hardy, adventurous men. Although many died on the way, more than eighty thousand had reached the "golden land" by 1850.

Negro and Mexican migrations. There are two important examples of recent racial migrations in the United States. One is the remarkable migration of Negroes from the South to northern industrial cities. This migration took place mainly in the years 1916-1919, 1921-1924, and 1941-1945. In the course of these three migrations nearly three million Negroes migrated to gain the advantages of industrial employment and other opportunities in the North. We shall deal with this matter more thoroughly later. This overrapid migration of Negro labor produced serious race riots and many new problems of adjustment for the Negro arrivals in the North.

Since the First World War there has been a large increase in Mexican immigration into the southwestern states, and Mexican labor is spreading over this area. It is estimated that at the present time there are at least three million persons of Mexican birth or Mexican descent in this country, most of them concentrated in Texas, California, and the southwest generally. The census formally lists only about a million and a quarter persons of Mexican birth or parentage. The ease of crossing the Mexican border makes it difficult to control Mexican immigration. It has been estimated that nearly a million Mexicans attempt to cross and recross the border each year to work on American soil.

Migration to cities. We have already referred to the marked migration from the country areas to the cities, and we shall deal with this problem more thoroughly in a subsequent chapter. Hence, we may pass over the matter here with casual mention. By 1930, 56.2 per cent of the population had come to live in cities, leaving a rural population of only 43.8 per cent. Those actually living on farms constituted only 24.8 per cent of the total population in 1930. After the depression in 1929 made industrial conditions worse in the cities, a considerable number left urban areas and returned to the country. This served to intensify the already serious conditions in the agricultural economy and population of the country. With the growth of armament and war industry after 1940, workers once more flocked to the cities. In 1950, over 59 per cent of the population lived in cities. Indeed, the new method of computing urban population used in the 1950 census put the city population as 64 per cent of the total. The rural farm population made up a little less than 19 per cent of the total.

Migratory seasonal labor force. A special but very important phase of migration within the country is that of our migratory or seasonal labor. Under modern industrial and agricultural conditions migratory labor is a world phenomenon. Tens of thousands of workers have gone each year from Italy and Spain to the harvest fields of the Argentine. More than a quarter of a million Chinese laborers were accustomed to move in and out of Manchuria annually.

Seasonal migratory labor is an important item in the economy of the United States and creates serious social problems. There is no precise information as to the number of such migratory workers; even Federal estimates run from 500,000 to 5,000,000. An estimate of a million and a half would be very conservative. A quarter of a million follow the harvest line from Texas to Canada. California employs about 125,000 in the fruit and vegetable industries. Many find work in the beet fields of Utah and other states. The introduction into harvesting of the tractor-drawn combine cut down the number of migratory farm laborers in the grain states, but this loss was more than offset by the reinforcements received from migratory youth after the depression started in 1929, and by wholesale migrations from the western "Dust Bowl" to the Pacific Coast. Mexican immigrants, legally or illegally entering the country, now constitute a major source of our seasonal labor, especially in the Southwest.

The Social Science Research Council made a thorough study of migratory labor. It found that there are five major seasonal migrations in addition to seasonal work in harvesting grain: (1) the southern migration of winter and spring to pick citrus and truck crops, all the way from Florida to New Jersey; (2) the berry crop migration, in which workers migrate all over the eastern United States, from the Gulf States to the Great Lakes; (3) the western cotton migration, involving about 50,000 workers who pick cotton from Texas to California; (4) the sugar-beet migration, mainly restricted to western plateau states; and (5) the Pacific Coast migration, embracing everything from fruit-picking to lumbering, and involving several races and 125,000 migratory workers in California alone.

Some of the migratory workers were taken into the armed forces in the

Second World War and others obtained work in munition factories. A number of returning veterans and war workers have continued to find work in the cold war economy of postwar days. But the condition of the migratory workers as a class remains deplorable, and they are one of the chief under-privileged groups in the country, along with the sharecroppers of the South. The problem was deemed so serious that President Truman appointed a commission to investigate the matter in June, 1950.

Living conditions and social situations among these migratory laborers have been notoriously abnormal and unsatisfactory. The workers live in all kinds of habitations, from hobo jungles and flop houses to crude automobile camps. Before the First World War many were recruited into the membership of the Industrial Workers of the World (IWW). The attacks upon the IWW during and after the war all but destroyed this organization and removed its contributions to disciplining and protecting migratory labor. The families of migratory workers, if they have any, suffer with them from various kinds of deprivation. The educational situation is especially bad. The National Education Association estimates that there are a million children of migratory workers with virtually no education facilities whatever.

Refugees from the dust bowl. To this virtual standing army of migratory workers, there was added in the 1930's another even larger and equally depressed group—the refugees from the dust bowl on the plateau east of the Rocky Mountains, and from other eroded and worn-out farming areas nearby.

Because of the plowing under of the protective buffalo grass in the great marginal agricultural area along the eastern border of the Rocky Mountain plateau during and following the First World War, the top soil in this region became peculiarly susceptible to the ravages of the wind, which has darkened the sky with dust as far east as the Atlantic seaboard. Serious drouths contributed their quota to the intensification of the disaster. Not only have the dust storms rendered this marginal area unproductive, but millions of tons of dust were deposited by the wind upon areas farther east which were formerly relatively fertile and productive. As a result, thousands of persons who were, only a quarter of a century ago, independent farmers, tenant farmers, and sharecroppers, were forced by sheer necessity to take to the road in the hope of finding employment and subsistence in more fortunate regions. They went especially to California and other Pacific Coast states. It was satirically observed that "Oklahoma has captured California without firing a shot." Carleton Beals thus described this migration:

They travel along in old hooded wagons, with bony nags, or in old rattly cars, sometimes with elaborate homemade trailers, or in light trucks. Each vehicle is stacked high with dirty bedding, cots, bedsprings, tents, an iron stove. On the running board may be seen a battered trunk, a galvanized tub, perhaps a dog or an accordion. Each vehicle is crowded with children, grandfolks, aunts, cousins, neighbors. They all set a great store by kinsfolk.[11]

[11] Carleton Beals, "Migs. America's Shantytown on Wheels," *The Forum*, January, 1938, p. 11.

Even when they reached their destination, the lives of these newer migrants were incredibly miserable. Beals has depicted one of their typical camps:

> Rows of tents, trailers, shacks, lean-to's, side-by-side close, with perhaps a single faucet for several hundred families, with half a dozen privies usually set in the very center of the camp. Imagine the lack of privacy, the misery of rain and sickness. It had been raining for two weeks when I visited the camps around Pima, Oceano, and Nipomo; the tents were literally swimming in mud.[12]

The United States has in this way been building up a new gypsy proletariat, which is a challenge to constructive statesmanship and economic reform:

> Whatever the contretemps of their lives, they represent a dramatic population shift, they are part and parcel of a new economic development in the Far West. The only life they can lead is a gypsy life. They are the new American gypsies on wheels, following the crops from the early harvest in hot Imperial Valley, on up the coast to the pea harvest, over into San Joaquin for the grape harvest, finally the cotton picking. They have no homes; their children attend half a dozen or more schools during the year. Each year they become more definitely a group with cultural frontiers, less adaptable to any other kind of life. Most of them would no longer have any success as settlers. Once they were farmers; now they are nomads. They are agriculturalists without roots in the soil whose wealth they garner.[13]

It is obvious that any such element in the population is entirely incompatible with the ideal of "the more abundant life" promised by the New Deal and the subsequent Fair Deal. Many of these refugees were drafted or found work during the Second World War and the cold war which followed. But their places may soon be taken by refugees from the new dust bowl, which has been in preparation since 1940 around the borders of the dust bowl of the 1930's.

Northward migration of southern mountaineers. Ever since the First World War decade, there has also been a large migration of mountain folk from Kentucky, Tennessee, and other southern regions to Detroit and other northern industrial centers. This has been, in the main, a voluntary search for employment in the automobile and other industries, but it was also encouraged by open-shop employers, who believed that it would prove more difficult to enlist these newcomers in organized labor movements. This migration reached mass proportions during the Second World War.

Persistent inter-regional migration of Americans. Owing to the popularity of John Steinbeck's *Grapes of Wrath* and newspaper publicity, there is a rather general conviction that our continental migration is a seasonal affair, is the product of special natural calamities, or is made up mainly of poverty-stricken farmers fleeing the dust bowl. All this is a misapprehension.

There has been a widespread and gradual movement during the last three decades from the whole central section of the country (from the

---

12 *Ibid.*
13 *Ibid.*, p. 15.

Appalachians to the Rockies and from the Canadian to the Mexican border) to the Pacific Coast states, and, to a lesser extent, to the northeastern states. In the 1940's, some 4 million persons migrated to the Pacific Coast region alone. Proof that those who go to California are not all dust-bowl refugees is amply shown by the fact that less than one-fourth of those who settled in the state in the 1930's were former farmers or farm laborers.

The magnitude of interstate migration in recent times is shown by the careful estimate that there were at least 4 million migrants in each year from 1930 to 1940, and in 1937 there were some 5 million. The causes are complicated:

> Not only climatic reverses and soil depletion but also a large number of other situations—factors such as seasonal jobs, fluctuations in wages, the depletion of mineral and other natural resources, rise and decline of industries, technological displacements, population pressures, fluctuations in market conditions, migratory industries, and special demands for labor (such as New Deal construction projects and war and defense industries).[14]

Wartime migrations. Interstate migration was greatly increased by employment offered by war industries during the Second World War. The new migration drifted mainly toward manufacturing centers, especially in the Middle West and in the Pacific Coast area, which experienced a great industrial expansion due to war orders. It has been estimated that from 15 to 20 million civilians voluntarily left their homes between 1940 and the end of the war, to move into other counties and states, mainly to secure employment. There are no reliable figures as yet on what proportion returned to their homes after the war, but the Census Bureau reported in August, 1948, that some 12,338,000 persons were living in a different state in 1947 from the one in which they were living in 1940. Some 19,500,000 persons were living in a different county in 1946 from the one in which they lived in 1940.

In addition to these voluntary migrations of civilian workers, there was one forced migration during the war. Some 110,000 out of 127,000 Japanese in this country were evacuated from their West Coast homes and placed in barbed-wire concentration camps in inland states, from Arizona to Arkansas. Less than two-thirds had been able to return to their former homes by 1950.

Increased mobility of peoples. We could find no more appropriate conclusion to this section of recent migrations than a few observations on the increased mobility of populations due to the development of new facilities of transportation. Until the Second World War, the steamship and the railroad played the major role in bringing about increased mobility of the peoples of the world. The effect of these media is to be observed in the fact that in a single year more than a million persons came from Europe to the United States by steamboat, and our railroads enabled them to be scattered quickly throughout the country. Even this record was exceeded by the transportation of American troops during the First World War, when a total of 300,000 per month was reached. Slightly over

---

[14] *National Education Association Bulletin,* November, 1941, p. 216.

two million soldiers were sent to France in a little over one year. Some 60,000 Italian and Spanish workers have migrated in a single year to the wheat fields of the Argentine. After 1914 the automobile and the bus added notably to the mobility of the migratory population. There are, as we first noted, around a million and a half of these migratory persons roving over the United States annually—a number equal to more than one-third of the total population of the United States when Washington became president. The transportation feats of the Second World War greatly exceeded those of the First because we sent more than four times as many soldiers and civilians overseas. Tens of thousands of these were transported in airplanes, which are becoming an ever more prominent means of travel in both peace and war.

SUMMARY

The civilization of the world today is the product of human migrations which have taken place over tens of thousands of years. These migrations, although often accompanied by much bloodshed and destruction, have been a dynamic factor in human history. They have broken down cultural stagnation and introduced new ideas and ways of living.

The most extensive migrations in all history have taken place since the discovery of America and the Industrial Revolution, following 1750. Although the migration of Europeans to the United States began in the earliest colonial period, a revolution in our immigration took place following 1870. Many more came to our shores and most of them came from central, southern, and eastern Europe rather than from northern Europe.

Despite much agitation to limit or exclude foreigners, there was no serious movement to restrict immigration until about the time of the First World War. The only restrictive laws passed related to Chinese and contract laborers. Restriction begun in 1917 developed into something approaching exclusion under the National Origins policy of the 1920's. The rigorous restriction policy has not been based on wise criteria of selection. It has been founded on nationality and race rather than ability.

Although there has been some increase in immigration since the mid-1930's, the quantitative problem no longer exists. The immigration problem in the United States today is chiefly one of getting the best quality of new immigrants and completing the assimilation of those who came earlier.

The economic effects of immigration to the United States have been mainly the creation of a vastly larger labor force and greater productive capacity, and the development of a great body of urban workers whose full employment in recent years has been possible only because of war and armament emergencies.

Immigration has produced a disproportionate amount of crime and vice, found chiefly among second-generation immigrants who are inadequately disciplined by either Old or New World culture. Much of the responsibility for this crime and vice may be assigned to the fact that immigrants have been forced into crowded city areas with bad living conditions. There is no evidence of any special racial proclivity to crime and vice.

Biologically, immigration has greatly increased our population. There is no evidence that it has brought about any physical deterioration of the population. The immigration problem has been chiefly one of cultural assimilation, and our melting-pot procedures may have been too rapid and harsh, as well as somewhat ineffective.

Immigrants have made a disproportionate contribution to American art, music, and literature. Religious friction has been increased, but not to an alarming extent. Greater interest has been developed in world affairs, though this may have reached excessive proportions in recent years.

Most immigrants have become naturalized and have entered into American political life. Broadly speaking, those from northern Europe have affiliated with the Republican party, with the exception of the Irish, and the others have joined the Democrat party. But there have been many exceptions and much shifting of party loyalties has taken place in recent years.

During and since the Second World War there have been serious problems of forced migrations in Europe and Asia. Displaced persons have been driven out of central and eastern Europe by persecution. Millions of Germans were expelled from their older homes and sought refuge in Western Germany. Millions of Japanese were driven out of Asia and brought back to their former island homes.

Extensive migrations have taken place within the United States. Our country was peopled by the great westward frontier movement. Special migrations were associated with the Mormons, the Gold Rush, and the more recent flight from the dust bowl of the Rocky Mountain plateau area. There are between 500,000 and 1,500,000 seasonal migratory workers whose economic condition is becoming worse as a result of the increasing competition of machine methods in agriculture. Southern mountaineers are seeking employment in the industrial centers of the mid-West. There is a large and persistent movement of peoples from the mid-West to the Pacific Coast, some 4 million going there in the 1940's.

The most striking recent migration within our country was that during the Second World War. The civilian migration during this period numerically exceeded the military movements. Some 15-20 million civilians migrated, and about 13 million moved from their homes to participate actively in war operations.

SELECTED REFERENCES

Adamic, Louis, *From Many Lands*. New York: Harper, 1940. Interesting propaganda for immigration and immigrants.

*Anderson, Nels, *Men on the Move*. Chicago: University of Chicago, 1940. The best book on hoboes and migratory workers.

*Baldwin, R. N., Holmes, J. H., and Dewey, John, *The Land of the Dead*. New York: Committee against Mass Expulsion, 1947. A vivid, brief survey of the forcible expulsion of Germans, Jews, and others from their homelands after 1945. A narrative of incredible brutality, showing that the postwar action of the victors was in many ways more harsh than Hitler's treatment of conquered peoples.

Bernard. W. S., *et al.*, *American Immigration Policy: A Reappraisal*. New York: Harper, 1950. Critical history of the period since 1921, and a moderate argument for a more liberal policy.

Bloom, Leonard, and Riemer, Ruth, *The Socio-Economic Effects of the War on Japanese-Americans*. Berkeley: University of California Press, 1949. Good account of the impact of wartime evacuation experiences upon the Japanese.

*Boudreau, F. G., and Kiser, C. V. (Eds.), *Postwar Problems of Migration*. New York: Milbank Memorial Fund, 1947. A very valuable symposium on postwar migrations, including several useful chapters on civilian migration in the United States during the period since 1939.

Brown, F. J., and Roucek, J. S. (Eds.), *Our Racial and National Minorities*. New York: Prentice-Hall, 1937. A comprehensive symposium on the ethnic and national groups which have come to the United States, the problems of assimilation, and some leading contributions of immigrant groups to American life.

Brown, L. G., *Immigration*. New York: Longmans, Green, 1933. A competent manual treating the whole field of immigration.

Davie, M. R., *World Immigration*. New York: Macmillan, 1936. General study of migrations, with special reference to the United States.

Dees, J. W., *Flophouse*. Boston: Marshall Jones, 1948. Valuable sociological study of the life and attitudes of the homeless man.

*Fairchild, H. P., *Immigration*. New York: Macmillan, 1928. The standard and classic textbook on the immigration problem. Judicious in its appraisal of the effects of immigration.

————, *The Melting Pot Mistake*. Boston: Little, Brown, 1926. Criticism of the melting-pot procedure in the assimilation of immigrants by the leading American authority on immigration.

Garis, R. L., *Immigration Restriction*. New York: Macmillan, 1927. Authoritative treatment of the subject through the "National Origins" policy.

Gold, Michael, *Jews without Money*. New York: Liveright, 1930. A graphic account of the life of the poorer Jewish immigrants to America.

Hansen, M. L., *The Atlantic Migration, 1607-1870*. Cambridge: Harvard University Press, 1940.

————, *The Immigrant in American History*. Cambridge: Harvard University Press, 1940. Two very valuable historical studies of immigration to America.

*Hartman, E. G., *The Movement to Americanize the Immigrant*. New York: Columbia University Press, 1948. An excellent historical and sociological study of the American melting-pot technique in dealing with the immigrants.

Isaac, Julius, *The Economics of Migration*. Oxford: Oxford University, 1947. Best study of economic forces encouraging human migration.

*Kirkpatrick, Clifford, *Intelligence and Immigration*. Baltimore: Williams and Wilkins, 1926. The most scientific and objective study of the intellectual level of our immigrant population.

Konvitz, M. R., *The Alien and the Asiatic in American Law*. Ithaca: Cornell University Press, 1947. This is probably the best volume on the legal aspects of the rights of aliens and Asiatics in American society and the problems of naturalization.

Kulischer, E. M., *Europe on the Move*. New York: Columbia University Press,

1948. Excellent review of European population movements from 1917 to 1947, including migrations overseas.

Leiserson, W. M., *Adjusting Immigrant to Industry*. New York: Harper, 1924. Pioneer study of the relation of immigration to American industrial life by a leading authority on labor relations.

Ross, E. A., *The Old World in the New*. New York: Century, 1914. A great sociologist's brief, critical analysis of the social effects of unrestricted immigration to America.

Schermerhorn, R. A., *These Our People: Minorities in American Culture*. Boston: Heath, 1949. Recent and thorough study of minority group cultures and their impact on American life.

Seabrook, William B., *These Foreigners*. New York: Harcourt, Brace, 1938. A highly favorable view of the contributions of immigration to American life.

Smith, Bradford, *Americans from Japan*. Philadelphia: Lippincott, 1949. Authoritative study of Japanese immigration.

Stephenson, G. M., *A History of American Immigration*. Boston: Ginn, 1926. The standard treatment of the history of immigration to this country prior to the "National Origins" legislation.

*Taft, D. R., *Human Migration*. New York: Ronald, 1936. A careful work, well fortified with statistics, correcting many common prejudices about the immigration problem.

Thomas, D. S., and Hishimoto, Richard, *The Spoilage*. Berkeley: University of California Press, 1946. The definitive account of forced Japanese evacuation during the Second World War.

*Utley, Freda, *The High Cost of Vengeance*. Chicago: Regnery, 1949. Most reliable survey of postwar Europe. Fully reveals the disasters resulting from the policies of the victorious United Nations since July, 1945.

Willcox, W. F., *et al.*, *International Migrations*, 2 vols. New York: National Bureau of Economic Research, 1929, 1931. Elaborate survey of the migrations of peoples.

*Wittke, Carl F., *We Who Built America*. New York: Prentice-Hall, 1939. An appreciative interpretation of immigration, especially of that before 1890.

Young, Donald, *American Minority Peoples*. New York: Harper, 1932. A standard sociological treatment of minorities.

CHAPTER 5

The Race Problem in Sociological Perspective

THE NATURE AND ORIGINS OF RACES

Recent interest in the race problem. We may now look into the question of race and its relation to contemporary social and cultural problems, especially in the United States. The race problem has assumed an unusually prominent position in public discussion because of the popularity of propagandist literature upholding the notion of the cultural supremacy of the Nordic (Aryan) race, the later thoroughgoing adoption of this theory by Adolf Hitler in Germany, and the strong reaction against these Nazi doctrines and practices after 1933.

Uses and meaning of the term "race." First, we may look at the meaning of the term "race." Few words have been used more loosely. This has been well pointed out by Julian Huxley:

The term "race" is currently used in several quite different senses. In the first place, it is used to denote one of the major divisions of mankind—black, white, yellow, and brown. Secondly, it is used to denote the actual human material of a particular country, group, or nation and its biologically transmissible characteristics: for instance even the most ardent upholders of the Nordic theory cannot mean by the "British race" anything more than the actual inhabitants of Great Britain and their descendants overseas. Thirdly, it is used to denote a hypothetical "pure race" which is taken to have existed in the past and later to have become contaminated by admixture with foreign elements: this, for instance, lies behind the ideal of the "Germanic race." Fourthly, it is sometimes used as equivalent to a recognizable or supposedly recognizable physical type, as Arab, Irish, etc. Fifthly, it is occasionally applied to a local population which by reason of isolation, has become or is supposed to have become fairly uniform and stable in physical type—for example the "Cornish race." Sixthly, it is also sometimes used in a wholly inadmissible sense to denote the peoples who speak a certain type of language, for example in such a phrase as "the Aryan race," the "Latin races." [1]

Only the first of these uses of the term has any true scientific validity. To this we may now turn our attention.

The main races of mankind. The term race, in any scientific sense, is a concept of physical anthropology and refers to a definite set of physical

---

[1] J. S. Huxley and A. C. Haddon, *We Europeans*. New York: Harper, 1936, pp. 215-216 (quoted by permission of Harper & Brothers and the authors). See also J. M. Reinhardt, *Social Psychology*. Philadelphia: Lippincott, 1938, Chap. X (an excellent exposé of race myths).

traits that characterize the largest groups or divisions of mankind. The most distinctive racial groupings are the yellow, white and black races. The distinguishing physical traits of these main races are more than simple contrasts of complexion or pigmentation of the skin. The yellow, or Mongolian, race not only is yellow in color but also has a very round or broad (brachycephalic) head and very straight hair, round in cross section. The black, or Negro, race stands at the opposite extreme with a very long (dolichocephalic) head and curly hair, flat in cross section. Between these two extremes falls the white, or Caucasian, race with an intermediate head form and wavy hair, elliptical in cross section.[2] The American Indians, the so-called red race, are actually a branch of the Mongolian racial type, and so are the Eskimos. The so-called brown, or Malayan, race appears to be a mixture of Negro and Mongolian elements, with some white admixture possible as well. There are many other minor physical characteristics of race, such as the facial angle, but we need not consider them here.

There are several subdivisions of the white race. The relatively long-headed type falls into two groups: the Mediterranean race of southern Europe, relatively short and swarthy; and the tall, blond Nordic, Baltic, or Teutonic race of northern Europe—the Aryan race of the racial mythologists. Between these has settled the relatively roundheaded Alpine race, made up of the so-called Celtic and Slavic types. They reside from Ireland to Russia but have mixed greatly with the Mediterranean and Nordic types in the last twenty thousand years. It is thought that the ancestors of the Mediterranean and Nordic types originally came from Africa and those of the Alpines from central Asia. Some students of racial history of man are inclined to believe that the Nordic race originally came from the Caspian area rather than from Africa.

Subdivisions of the Mongolian and Negro races are equally or more numerous, but since they have played little part in the history of Western civilization, less attention has been paid to them.

Race is, thus, a physical matter. It has nothing directly to do with cultural or mental traits. That certain races have distinctive mental traits may be true, but it is virtually impossible to determine to what extent they are a result of the physical fact of race and how far they are a product of cultural factors independent of race. All attempts to demonstrate the comprehensive superiority of one or another of the races or subraces of man have been unsuccessful. Tests have been unable to exclude those cultural factors that upset the possibility of isolating the purely racial elements.

The origin and dispersal of races. Within the last generation it has been necessary to modify somewhat the accepted theories of the origin and dispersal of races. Until recently, most anthropologists and sociologists accepted the so-called monogenist theory of the transition from a

---

[2] Miss Madeline Kneberg has challenged the notion that cross sections of the hair are indicative of race. See *American Journal of Physical Anthropology*, Vol. XX, No. 1, and Supplement, April-June, 1935, especially p. 61.

high form of anthropoid ape to man. According to this theory, the transition from anthropoid to man was a unique feat of nature—a marvellous sport or mutation which presumably could happen but once in the physical history of the simian world. If this theory was accepted, it appeared likely that the original human race was born in one area through such a mysterious mutation (long believed to have been in the area around Java), later spreading from this region over the Old World and still later into the Americas. All the races, according to this doctrine, had a single and common parentage.

Within the present century, and especially since the First World War, physical anthropologists and archeologists have turned up in the course of excavations a considerable number of very primitive types of man, comparable to the *pithecanthropus erectus,* or Java Man, who was long believed to represent the first demonstrably human type and was the prize exhibit of the monogenist school. These early types of man, who seem to represent transitions from anthropoid to human types and have been discovered since Eugene Dubois happened upon *pithecanthropus erectus* in Java in 1891, have been unearthed in widely separated parts of the Old World—northeastern China, South Africa, and England. It appears very unlikely that men of such limited capacity, virtually without any useful material culture to assist them, could have travelled from Java to Peiping, South Africa, and the extreme northwestern part of Europe. Moreover, although all these scattered early types are distinctly human, there are minor structural differences which seem to disprove the theory of a common and unique parentage. Hence, the polygenist theory that the transition from anthropoid to man was made in a number of widely distributed areas of the Old World now seems to be greatly strengthened, if not conclusively demonstrated. Further, there is no good reason to believe that this transition had to be an heroic mutation that could happen but once and only in one place. It is more likely that it was the product of organic evolution and could have taken place in several regions.

At any rate, whatever the origin of the human race and its present racial divisions, it is rather generally agreed that the races of mankind as we know them today were produced by several cooperating forces. Primitive peoples, hundreds of thousands of years ago, must have lived in relatively permanent habitats for tens of thousands of years. Here, they were subjected to the influence of a common physical environment that helped to shape the physical character of the residents. Likewise, inbreeding for many thousands of years tended to give uniformity to the physical type in any given environment. Subsequent dispersal of the main races presumably took place long after the physical traits of these races had become fixed and permanent.

Except for the Eskimos and the American Indians, the Mongolian race may have expanded chiefly around its place of origin in eastern Asia. Recent finds of very primitive types in South Africa seem to give weight to the view that the Negroes spread north from there. But they may very well have dispersed from Central Africa where equally primordial types of man may still lie undiscovered. Many believe that the white race orig-

inated in western Asia and later spread into Europe. Others believe that
the longheaded white types of today—the Mediterranean and Nordic—
came into Europe from Africa over landbridges across what is now the
Mediterranean Sea. If so, they came in after Europe had been populated
for several hundred thousand years by earlier types of men of whose
racial characteristics we cannot be precisely certain because they have left
no evidence of their pigmentation or hair structure.

In the course of the dispersion of races from a single area or from
multiple regions of origin, there has been a great deal of racial mixture,
so that there are no longer any completely pure races that perfectly represent the racial types of 100,000 years ago or more. Many subdivisions of
each major race have been produced by racial mixtures and environmental pressures in the intervening period. We are well aware of the subdivisions of the white race. But there are even more striking contrasts
among the subdivisions of the Mongolian and Negro races. The extremes of both of these latter races show greater physical contrasts than
those that exist between the Mediterranean, Nordic and Alpine subdivisions of the white race.

Controversy over racial traits. The whole subject of racial traits and
racial differences needs far more scientific study than it has received. As
we shall make plain when dealing with the origin and development of the
Aryan myth, most discussions of race prior to 1900 were based on emotion, mythology, and racial arrogance. Little attention was given to the
scientific facts. Racial traits were confused with the cultural heritage,
and too much stress may have been laid on the historical importance of
race. Then, early in the present century, a vastly influential anthropologist, Franz Boas, in the laudable effort to combat racial mythology and
prejudice, launched an equally extreme attempt to minimize the potency
of racial factors and the significance of racial differences in history. This
trend rendered a valuable service in combating Hitler's revival of the
mischievous racial arrogance of the nineteenth century, but it contributed little to a better scientific understanding of the facts of race or the
significance, if any, of racial differences.

Race and culture. We have said that race is primarily a matter of physical traits. But, among the many peoples of the world, different patterns
of living have been adopted. There are, thus, cultural as well as physical characteristics of the several races. Every individual belongs not only
to a racial but also to a cultural group. All human groups in adjusting
themselves to their environment have developed definite habits and ways
of doing things; they have made tools and weapons, and devised customs
and laws to regulate group life. Each generation receives what the last
has done and thought: weapons, buildings, automobiles, machinery,
shoes, and typewriters; belief in gods or God, ideas of right and wrong,
and all the other customs and folkways of any particular group.

Man must adapt himself to both the material and the non-material
culture. Each racial group has its own cultural environment, which plays
a major rôle in its life. It is common for people to confuse the cultural
heritage of a group with its racial traits and this has led to all sorts of

misunderstandings. Most racial mythology and much racial arrogance have developed as a result of confusing the cultural heritage of racial groups with their physical traits, or identifying rather uniform cultural traits with the false assumption of a definite racial basis for such traits. Anti-Semitism has been an outstanding product of such erroneous identification of cultural traits with racial realities.

THE QUESTION OF RACE SUPERIORITY

Confusion in discussions of race superiority. As we may gather from the preceding section, the question of whether one race is superior to another is a matter of warm controversy. The problem of race superiority has been greatly confused because there has not been a sufficiently sharp differentiation between the terms "race equality" and "racial similarity." It is obvious that races are not similar. As we have noted above, the marked physical differences among races provide us with the foundations of racial divisions and of the classification of races. Races have developed traits suiting them for varied physical environments. Certainly, some seem better adapted to life in the Arctic regions, and others seem to be more capable of adapting themselves to tropical conditions. There are also, in all probability, mental differences among the several races, though these are more difficult to ascertain and evaluate. The mental traits of races are deeply affected by the cultural heritage and institutions of any given people, though these same cultural patterns have little, if any, effect upon the physical characteristics. It may well be that certain races have greater capacity for abstract thinking, others for deep emotional expression.

Complicated nature of problem. A basic question in the problem of racial superiority is whether or not these physical and mental racial differences imply or demonstrate the comprehensive superiority of any one race. In the first place, one has to ask the question, "Superior for what?" Suppose we are able to demonstrate that one race is superior in intellectual capacity to others. Does this mean that such a race would have to be regarded as superior to other races in an all-embracing way? A positive answer to this question would be doubted by most unbiased students of the race problem.

Again, we must take into consideration the natural habitat of the various races. For all practical purposes, a race may be regarded as superior only in its relative capacity to live most successfully in its physical environment. For example, even if we were to accept the judgment of those most antagonistic to the Negro and hold that the Negro is markedly inferior to the white in America today, we would be compelled to recognize that the Negro appears to be far superior to the white when it comes to life in the original African habitat of the Negro.

Further, it seems to be very generally admitted by students that the Negro is far more richly endowed emotionally than the white man. This leads to the interesting question of whether intelligence or emotion is the most valuable human trait. For several generations, this question constituted the chief bone of contention between two great schools of European philosophy. The Rationalists upheld the superiority of the intellect, and the Romanticists the primacy of the emotions. No one has since been able to decide with any finality which group of philosophers had the better of the argument.

It has been held that the Negro seems very backward and lacking in talent when set off against the white, in such matters as technology and business. This has been held to be true even when one allows for social handicaps imposed upon the Negro in the United States. Yet most of those who make this allegation overlook the fact that there were many extremely clever and talented Negro mechanics in slavery days, when the Negroes were encouraged to develop along these lines of endeavor. They also ignore the capable Negro scientists and technicians of our day, such as George Washington Carver. But suppose we concede for the moment that the Negro is at a disadvantage in these matters, which are of such importance in our industrialized capitalistic system of society. Greater success in acquiring wealth is obviously no proof of comprehensive racial superiority. Capacity for the enjoyment of leisure, as well as talent for breadwinning, must be considered in evaluating racial ability. This will be even more true in the future age of leisure than it has been in the past. Moreover, facts set forth in the following chapter throw much doubt on the validity of the common assumption that the Negro is inferior to the whites in the realm of sheer intelligence when afforded comparable opportunities to manifest and develop intellectual qualities.

Scientific testing of racial superiority. The question of racial superiority cannot be settled in any satisfactory fashion unless the issues involved are subjected to rigorous scientific testing. Such testing cannot be valid unless we take large samples from the races involved. The study of a few selected cases is bound to be misleading because variations among members of the same race are often more impressive than the generalized differences which are held to exist between the various races.

With respect to physical superiority, few competent students of the racial problem contend that there is any demonstrable and comprehensive physical superiority or inferiority on the part of any race. An exception might possibly be made in the case of certain primitive pigmy types, but their seeming physical insignificance may be more suitable for the rudimentary culture and the harsh type of physical environment in which they often live. It is in this realm of physical differences among races that the question of relative adaptation to the geographical environment is particularly relevant.

The question of mental differences of races is a subject of far more heated controversy. There are certainly marked mental differences among the various races. Disbelievers in racial superiority contend, however, that these differences do not necessarily demonstrate any comprehensive superiority. They maintain that what is apparently superior capacity for cultural achievements is complicated by factors that cannot be eradicated in the administration of intelligence tests. Frank H. Hankins, who is one of our most competent students of the problems of race and, in general, sympathetic with the efforts to establish racial superiorities, if they do exist, is candid enough to admit, after a complete review of all the evidence, that "in view of these considerations and the difficulties due to language and cultural readjustments, we may admit that interracial comparisons that are entirely fair and absolutely conclusive do not yet exist." [3]

There have been many attempts to administer mental tests to racial groups in the effort to settle the question of relative mental capacity. Those who incline to accept the theory of a hierarchy of racial ability hold that these tests demonstrate that the primitive races now extant are mentally inferior to those which attained civilization. They further assert that the Negro race ranks lower in the matter of intelligence than the white and yellow races. But even they concede that the white and yellow races are essentially equal in mental capacity and that the same generalization applies to the three white subraces constituting the majority of the peoples of Europe. William I. Thomas, one of our most judicious students of anthropology and race problems, after examining all the important efforts to test the intelligence of races, held that the results of these tests were inconclusive:

From this general approach it will be seen that the significance of racial endowment for the interpretation of behavior reactions tends to disappear. It is to be emphasized, however, that there are no proofs that the mind is of precisely the same quality in all races and populations, and no such claim is made by anthropologists. It is not improbable that there is a somewhat different distribution of special abilities, such as mathematics, music, etc. The most scientific approach to the problem is through mental testing, but the results of intelligence tests as applied to races and populations have always been negative. Positive results have, in fact, been reached by this method but it has always been clearly shown that these results have depended on the nature of the tests. That is, the tests employed have always measured mental ability plus a cultural factor, namely, learning. There is thus no clear-cut evidence that differences in abilities exist per se, since it can always be shown that the variables mentality and culture have not been isolated by the tests.[4]

Sooner or later, we may be able to devise mental tests that will eliminate the cultural factor. It may then be possible to ascertain more clearly the actual mental differences between races and to come closer to a settlement of the controversy as to whether there is any real mental superiority involved. Perhaps the most sensible conclusion at present is that the evidence still remains inconclusive. But we may certainly state with complete assurance that the older and cruder dogmas of racial superiority involved in the Aryan myth are utterly without scientific foundation. The allegation that any of the European subraces is markedly superior mentally to the others may be regarded as unproved. Nor is there any apparent probability that improved mental tests will lead to modification of this verdict.

Race superiority and racial prejudice. Most of the justification of racial prejudice, which figures in controversies over European immigration to the United States, has no scientific support whatever. If it be conceded that the yellow race is equal in mental capacity to the white, the same

---

[3] F. H. Hankins, *The Social Basis of Civilization.* New York: Knopf, 1926, p. 326.

[4] W. I. Thomas, *Primitive Behavior.* New York: McGraw-Hill, 1937, p. 799.

statement applies to race prejudice against oriental immigration to our country. We shall consider the question of Negro mentality more thoroughly in the following chapter. It hardly needs to be pointed out that the Aryan mania, which raged in Nazi Germany, is unadulterated nonsense when viewed in the light of the most elementary scientific facts about the mental and physical capacity of races.

Hence, we may fairly say that, although the matter of race superiority is not yet a closed question in regard to some refinements of detail, most of the race prejudice in the world today stands outside the bounds of science and logic alike. The problem of racial capacity and of differences therein has been summarized by Earnest A. Hooton:

> Now it is quite evident that the status of the problem of racial intelligence is about as follows. Anthropologists have not yet reached the point of an agreement upon criteria of race which will enable psychologists to isolate with any degree of facility the racial types which are to be studied. Psychologists have not yet been able to develop mental tests which anthropologists are willing to trust as fair gauges of mental capacity. Neither group has yet perfected its technique of measurement. Until we know exactly how to distinguish a race and exactly what intelligence tests test, we shall have to hold in suspension the problem of racial mental differences.
>
> That such differences exist I have not the slightest doubt; that with our present methods they can be summarized quantitatively so that we are justified in assigning one race a position of superiority as contrasted with another, I deny. I hold no brief for racial equality; I do affirm with conviction that it is unfair to apply the standards of our own environment and our own race (whatever that may be) to groups of people differing from us in hereditary physical and mental characteristics and, as a result of such alleged "tests," hastily to stigmatize certain races or certain national groups as mentally inferior.[5]

THE QUESTION OF RACE MIXTURE

Racial mythology opposes race mixture. The problem of race mixture is closely related to the issue of race superiority. The earlier upholders of the thesis of racial superiority, such as Count de Gobineau, were vigorously opposed to extensive race mixture on the ground that the allegedly pure and superior races were bound to deteriorate. But we have to keep clearly in mind the fact that there is no such thing as a pure race in the world today. We would have to go far back into the anthropological past to find anything that even approximated racial purity. All existing races are hybrids, some of them of an extremely complicated and diversified type. Even what seems to be a relatively high degree of racial homogeneity is no conclusive proof of racial purity. This physical homogeneity may be no more than a product of long continued inbreeding, emphasizing and intensifying traits that originated in hybridity.

Race mixture appears to have promoted social progress. The evidence of history would seem to indicate that race mixture can be a decided asset in promoting cultural achievement. Since there is no evidence of any pure race in historic times, there is no proof that a pure race has ever created

---

[5] From E. A. Hooton, *Up From the Ape.* New York: Macmillan, 1931, pp. 596-597. By permission of The Macmillan Company, publishers.

a high form of human culture. One may go further and say that all
the great historic cultures of mankind have been produced by relatively highly mixed racial types. If we investigate the racial basis of the
great historic cultures of Europe, we shall find that a mixture of Nordics,
Alpines and Mediterraneans seems to have been most favorable to cultural
progress. In a preceding section, we have already made it abundantly
clear that no one of these races, in relatively unmixed form, has ever
created an outstanding European civilization. In his notable study of
British genius, Havelock Ellis found that by far the greatest relative number of distinguished men came from those regions in England where race
mixture in the past had been most marked and extensive. No other important world civilization has been so distinctly a product of extensive
and persistent race mixture as that of the United States. History would
thus seem decisively to have put the stamp of its approval upon the mixture of races.

Fallacy of most biological arguments against race mixture. We may
now consider some of the biological aspects of the case against race mixture. Those biologists and anthropologists who are critical of race mixture allege that this process of crossing races may have the following deleterious effects: (1) superior races will undergo degeneration as they mix
with inferior races; (2) hybrids tend to exhibit decreased physical and
mental efficiency; (3) even if hybrids give evidence of a brief period of
increased vitality immediately after the crossing of races, this temporary
spurt collapses and there soon comes a decline to a level of vitality lower
than that of either of the parent stocks; (4) hybrids manifest a distinct
decline in fecundity; and (5) hybridity tends to produce organic disorganization, the inheritance of mutually incompatible traits, and the prevalence of physical disharmonies. The American eugenicist, C. B. Davenport, particularly stressed this last point.

It is obviously true that all these alleged disastrous effects of hybridization, or racial crossing, can hardly exist in actual fact. As all known races
are highly complex hybrids, they could hardly have survived and pros-
pered under all these handicaps. Since, as we have seen, there are no
examples of pure races and no demonstrable comprehensive superiority
of any one race, the traditional dogma of racial adulteration through
racial mixture hardly holds water. Of course, if the lower types of one
race cross with lower types from another, the children will naturally tend
to be less capable than the superior members of these groups.

There is no evidence of any loss of physical or mental vigor from racial
crossing, even of an extreme type. The German scholar, Eugen Fischer,
made a thorough study of a very extreme type of racial mixture, that
between the white Dutch Boers of South Africa and the Hottentot Negroes who constituted their native neighbors. Their offspring are known
as the "Rehobother bastards." Fischer studied the latter over five generations and found no evidence of any decline in physical or mental vigor.
Indeed, most students of race crossing believe that the process seems to be
biologically advantageous. Race mixture brings about a greater organic
variability; and, hence, gives the process of natural selection a wider

variety of material upon which to work. Following out the Mendelian principle of heredity, race crossing also reduces the appearance in the hybrid type of recessive defects common to the parental stocks.

There seems to be pretty general agreement among biologists that racial crossing does definitely increase the vitality of the hybrids for several generations. Many question the rather generally accepted view that this new store of vitality is lost after some generations. At any rate, there is no evidence that the vitality of hybrids tends to decline to a point below that manifested by the parental stocks. There is, in other words, no ultimate deterioration of vitality below the level of the races mixed. So whatever increase in vitality takes place as a result of race mixture constitutes a clear gain, even if it is temporary.

There is no evidence to support the theory that race mixture brings about a definite decrease in human fecundity, in other words, that it produces sterility in the hybrid type. Fischer found that even in the extreme case of the Rehobother bastards there was no sign of increasing sterility. There was an average of 7.7 children per family in the fifth generation.

Nor do the facts seem to bear out Davenport's theory of physical disharmonies and incongruities in hybrids. The latter usually tend to be well-proportioned individuals. This is true in the instance of mulattoes, who come from the Negro-Caucasian mixture. In a broad way, hybrids tend ultimately to blend into an intermediate type lying between the norms of the stocks that have crossed, although this blending process is not so rapid and simple a matter as it was believed to be before the Mendelian law of heredity was understood. Certain distinctive parental traits, however, do persist among the hybrids. But these rarely represent any serious physical disharmonies. Further, if the extreme variability caused by race crossing should produce defective monstrosities, it would be equally likely to produce types of unusual excellence and high capabilities.

Most instances cited to support the theory of physical degeneracy as a result of hybridization have failed to take account of the relative quality of the stocks that have mixed. If race mixture takes place among the lower types of each race, it is obvious that the hybrid result will fall below the average of the crossing stocks. The same principle, however, would apply to mixture between inferior types of the same race. Much race crossing has been carried on among those from lower levels of the races involved, and this has given rise to the popular view that race mixture produces mutual physical degeneration. These considerations undermine the contentions of the famous study by Jon A. Mjøen of Scandinavian data on the crossing of racial strains. His examples represented a low quality of the population, carrying an abnormally heavy freight of hereditary defects. After a careful review of all the important theories and of accumulated research materials, Hankins concludes that "the widely prevalent notion that mixture is bad in itself and that all crosses are to be avoided on general principles is wholly without foundation." He goes on to say that:

Our general conclusion, therefore, is that race crossing as such is not biologically injurious. It may and doubtless does lead to some alteration in bodily proportions and mental potentialities. But that it leads to disharmony or instability is far from established and in view of the operation of the influence of the internal secretions on embryological development it seems highly improbable that from race crossing alone serious disharmonies could result.[6]

If it be true that intermarriage between extremely divergent races is not biologically harmful, then it is quite obvious that no biological evils could grow out of the intermarriage of white immigrant types in the American population, all drawn from one or another of the subraces of Europe. We may, therefore, agree with Donald R. Taft that there is no biological reason for opposing the intermarriage of white immigrants in the United States or of immigrants with the native American stock.

The majority of the states in the United States still have some form of anti-miscegenation laws—that is, laws preventing the intermarriage of certain racial groups, for example: in South Carolina, a white male may marry a Chinese woman, but a white woman cannot marry a Chinese male; in North Carolina, a white person may not marry a Negro or an Indian. Negroes, however, may marry North Carolina Indians except the Cherokees of Robeson county; in Maryland, whites may not marry Negroes or Malays, nor may Negroes marry Malays; in Wyoming, whites may not marry Negroes, mulattoes, Mongols or Malays. Negroes, however, may marry Malays; in Nebraska, a white may not marry a person who is one-eighth or more Chinese or Japanese; in North Dakota, a white person may marry a full-blooded Chinese or Japanese, but not a person whose great-grandfather was a Negro.

Dangers of race mixture mainly cultural. It would, of course, be inaccurate to deny the fact that there may be disastrous social results from race mixture. But these are of a nonbiological character. If social handicaps or cultural obstructions are imposed upon the hybrids, these may be sufficiently severe to outweigh even the biological benefits of race mixture. Such considerations as these raise questions of a different order, which will be dealt with elsewhere.

RACE CONFLICTS AND RACE PREJUDICE

Racial conflict as a social philosophy. A whole philosophy of history has been built up around the doctrine of race conflict. This philosophy is what we know as "Social Darwinism," the dogma that the conflicts among human races have promoted the progress of civilization in the same way that the struggle for existence has stimulated natural selection and biological improvement. The leader in the development of this type of thought has been the Polish-Austrian jurist and sociologist, Ludwig Gumplowicz. Recently, this view has been given added weight by the writings of Sir Arthur Keith, the most distinguished of present-day physical anthropologists. The ideas of the Social Darwinists have been fiercely

---

[6] F. H. Hankins, *op. cit.,* p. 343.

attacked by critics such as the famous Russian sociologist, Jacques Novicow.

But the notion of the virtue and justice of the conquest of one race by another rose long before Darwin's time. We find it in the boasts of Assyrian conquerors, in the Jewish idea of a chosen people, and in Aristotle's assertion that certain races are superior and are destined by nature to rule the earth. From ancient times to those of the "white man's burden" of modern imperialistic lore, there has been a tendency to assume racial superiority and then use it as a justification for wars and conquest.

Rebellion against racial subjection. Today the supposedly inferior and subject races are asserting their independence. This rebellion is important in both domestic and international affairs. We see it manifested in the Negro problem in the United States. The peoples of India have finally thrown off the yoke of the British Empire. There is a white-yellow conflict of serious proportions being prepared in the Pacific area, which is being speeded up and intensified by the nationalism that has accompanied the emancipation of India and the Communist conquest of China. That the Negroes in Africa will indefinitely submit to white dominion is unlikely. Race prejudice has recently flared to a new intensity in South Africa. The pseudo-racial quarrels between the Jews and the Arabs threaten the peace of the Near East. Even when there is no actual race conflict, a fictitious one is trumped up. This may be even more fierce and brutal than real racial conflicts, witness the anti-Semitism of Hitler's Germany.

Future prospect of racial conflicts. There seems every prospect that racial and pseudo-racial conflicts will grow more serious in the next few generations. Hitler has been disposed of, but anti-Semitism continues in central and eastern Europe. Many of the so-called displaced persons are the product thereof. The final showdown between the Orient and the Occident in the Far East lies ahead of us, if not immediately, at least eventually. Growing white toleration and good-will toward the Chinese as a result of a common cause in battling Japan during the Second World War (which went so far as to lead the United States, in 1946, to permit the naturalization of the Chinese) may now be reversed because of the Communist invasion of Korea. A new "yellow peril" myth of even greater intensity than that at the time of maximum Chinese immigration or the Boxer Rebellion may well arise. The insurrection of the Negroes is just beginning to gather momentum. Some of our most careful students of international affairs and racial contacts predict that interracial wars, more terrible than any human struggles in the past, may characterize the next hundred years of human experience. The prospect is ominous. It will require international statecraft of a high order to avert the calamity.

Race prejudice a mental and cultural problem. The problem of race is primarily a state of mind which may be best described under the caption of race prejudice. Certainly, most of the prevalent ideas about race today are mainly a product of race prejudice. If we could deal with the matter of race in the calm and dispassionate fashion in which it is handled by many anthropologists, our race problems might rapidly evaporate.

Race prejudice is believed to originate mainly as a sort of secondary or incidental manifestation of what Franklin Henry Giddings used to call "the consciousness of kind." Persons and things that are familiar to us are congenial and comfortable, but those that are strange provoke in us sentiments of fear and hostility. Strange peoples, as well as strange objects and customs, alarm and offend us. The cultural by-products of race often arouse more hostility than the physical racial differences. This spontaneous and elemental reaction to race differences has been intellectualized, rationalized, and elaborated into systems of philosophical and historical interpretation. Notable examples are social Darwinism, anti-Semitism, the Aryan myth, and the Anglo-Saxon theory which will be dealt with later on.

Of course, this automatic hostility to differences in the physical traits and customs of peoples is not the only cause of race prejudice. Economic and political influences operate strongly here, especially in advanced societies. Theories of racial superiority and inferiority are often used to justify an economic hierarchy, the domination of the political scene by certain groups, and the exclusion of others from political life. Social snobbishness also plays its rôle in creating and perpetuating race prejudice.

Sir Arthur Keith's argument in behalf of race prejudice. There are some men of real intellectual distinction who contend that race prejudice must be encouraged and conserved as a positive and constructive influence in human culture. Such, as we noted above, is the contention of the British physical anthropologist, Sir Arthur Keith. In his little book, *The Place of Prejudice in Modern Civilization,* he looked with horror upon the prospect of intermarriage to the point of universal deracialization. He holds that we must preserve racial purity, and that race prejudice must be fostered in order that the selective influence of wars may not be lost. The following paragraph summarizes his views:

Thus I come deliberately to the opinion that race prejudice has to be given a recognized place in our modern civilization. I have asked you to count the price we must pay for a deracialized world. In turn you may demand of me whether I have reckoned the cost of maintaining our racialized world. Yes, I have. It means a continuation of Nature's old scheme of intertribal rivalries and eternal competition. Without competition Mankind can never progress; the price of progress is competition. Nay, race prejudice and, what is the same thing, national antagonism, have to be purchased, not with gold, but with life. Nature throughout the past has demanded that a people who seeks independence as well as peace can obtain these privileges only in one way—by being prepared to sacrifice their blood to secure them. Nature keeps her human orchard healthy by pruning; War is her pruning-hook. We cannot dispense with her services. This harsh and repugnant forecast of man's future is wrung from me. The future of my dreams is a warless world. As a gardener, Nature has two sides, a good and a bad. She plants and she also prunes. If we accept her, we have to accept her altogether. Sooner or later she brings the false prophet to book.[7]

In a later and larger book, *A New Theory of Human Evolution,*[8] Keith has from these and similar ideas formulated a philosophy of history.

---

[7] Keith, *op. cit.* New York: John Day, 1931, pp. 49-50.
[8] New York: Philosophical Library, 1949.

Fallacies in race prejudice theory. Although we respect Sir Arthur's eminent contributions to physical anthropology, we must observe that his eulogy of race prejudice and interracial wars implies a rather narrow view of human behavior. This doctrine, a belated expression of Social Darwinism, was mercilessly exposed years ago by Novicow in his work, *A Critique of Social Darwinism* (1910). As Novicow pointed out, wars may have exerted a constructive influence in early days by creating large political states out of primitive tribal groups. But as civilization advances, the struggles that promote cultural improvement should also become of a progressively higher character. The biological conflicts should be subordinated to economic competition, and this in turn to intellectual conflict.

Cultural and educational solutions of race prejudice. Race hostility can gradually be overcome through proper cultural influences. In certain European countries, in which many different physical types have been compelled to live together and mingle daily for centuries, there is often a minimum of race prejudice. This may be observed even in rather extreme instances of racial contrast.

It is probable that the only agency upon which we can fully rely to battle effectively against race prejudice is sane education about the problem of race and racial contacts. The more we learn about the frail scientific foundations of any dogmatic race prejudice, the less potent it may become. Race prejudice is preëminently capable of flaring up in an unpredictable manner. There were many, at the opening of the present century, who believed that civilization was so far advanced that race prejudice was about to become a thing of the past. Yet, after the First World War, race prejudice exploded with an intensity unparalleled in modern times, and even today it seems to be gaining momentum steadily. To combat race prejudice, education must be relevant to racial realities. A generally high level of education is no adequate safeguard against race prejudice. Germany in 1933 was surely one of the two or three best educated nations of the world, but this did not suffice to prevent the development of bitter race prejudice. Further, emotional reactions may temporarily suppress the influence exerted by sound race education, and excesses in the name of anti-racism may provoke new outbreaks of racial prejudice.

Anti-Semitism a product of racial mythology. It was pointed out earlier in this chapter that there is a popular tendency to mistake racial cultural traits for hereditary characteristics. The most notable example of this error in history has, perhaps, been the tendency to regard the Jews as a physical race and to regard pro-Semitism and anti-Semitism as true race prejudice. Whatever the merits or evils in either of these attitudes, they are based on cultural patterns and reactions and not on any actual racial foundation. Therefore, one of the most bitter and enduring historic prejudices has been founded on racial mythology.

Though many Jews regard themselves as a race, physically considered, and the enemies of the Jews so regard them, it has long been made clear by scientific students of race that the Jews in no sense whatever constitute a distinct physical race. In fact, there was never any real Semitic race. The term Semitic can be used correctly only in a linguistic sense. The peoples who used the Semitic languages in antiquity were highly mixed in their racial composition, being mainly made up of various Mediterranean and Alpine types. It is probable that the Jews were the most extremely mixed of all the Semites in the ancient Near East. Peoples came into Palestine from north, south, and east in successive waves of migration. Even the so-called Jewish element in Palestine is believed by scholars to have come in at different times. The exaggerated aquiline nose, commonly regarded as the most distinctive physical trait of the Hebrews, is a characteristic that was acquired through intermarriage with the Hittites. It has been more common among some other peoples than among the Jews.

If the Jewish people were hopelessly mixed before the famous dispersion—the Diaspora—after the destruction of Jerusalem in A.D. 70, there has been even greater race mixture since that time. The Jews have spread all over the Mediterranean area, into northern Africa and every part of Europe, and to the United States. Despite all attempts to make them exclusive, intermarriage with Gentiles has taken place extensively. It is very hard to distinguish Jews, in a physical sense, from the surrounding peoples among whom they have dwelt for generations or centuries.

Therefore, to regard the Jews as a physical race and to persecute them on racial grounds is scientifically preposterous. It may be fairly observed, in passing, that it is equally absurd for extreme Jewish nationalists to put forward claims for Jewish superiority on any racial grounds.

THE ARYAN MYTH: A CASE-STUDY IN RACIAL MYTHOLOGY AND PREJUDICE

Philology and the origins of race myths. Since the chief example of racial mythology and racial arrogance in contemporary times has been manifested in the development of the so-called Aryan Myth, we may well review its genesis and dissemination as an instructive example of how fallacious conceptions of race may arise and exert a powerful and disastrous influence upon the course of history and human thought.

The origins of race myths must be sought in the vestiges of the primitive, tribal "aversion-complex" exhibited toward strangers, symbolized by the old phrases of "Jew" and "Gentile," and "Greek" and "Barbarian."

In its modern form, the race myth gradually arose out of the dogmas of the Romantic philosophers at the close of the eighteenth century. They emphasized the dominating importance of "national character" as the basis of the culture and institutions of every state. This doctrine was given a particularly forceful statement by Johann Gottlieb Fichte in his famous *Addresses to the German Nation* in 1807.[9] Here he stated that perhaps the most precious element in the German cultural heritage consisted of the unique German language, or *Ursprache*. This emphasis of Fichte

---

[9] J. G. Fichte, *Addresses to the German Nation*. LaSalle, Ill.: Open Court, 1923.

and others upon the importance of language in national character encouraged the origins of modern scientific philology, which came to fruition in the notable works of Sir William Jones, Franz Bopp, the Grimm brothers (Jacob and Wilhelm), Friedrich Max Müller, William Dwight Whitney, and others.

The rise of philology promoted the comparative study of the languages and institutions of Europe and Asia. This led to the discovery of certain basic similarities in the root words and word structure of the Eurasiatic languages, particularly the similarity between some European languages and the Sanskrit of ancient India. Friedrich Schlegel, a leading Romanticist, believed that Sanskrit was the original tongue from which the others descended. The establishment of this similarity among the Eurasiatic languages was due primarily to the work of Franz Bopp, who published his *Comparative Grammar* in 1833.

False identification of race and language. During the next generation much important work was done in the way of describing the origins, migrations, and affinities of these so-called "Indo-Germanic," "Indo-European," or "Aryan" languages. It came to be rather commonly maintained that there was not only an original Aryan language but that a primordial Aryan race spoke it and was responsible for these linguistic similarities and identities. By the 1850's this had become a rather common assumption on the part of many essayists, philologists, and anthropologists, including F. F. A. Kuhn and F. A. Pott. In fact, Müller himself, though he later repudiated the view, confirmed this general impression in his very influential lectures on *The Science of Language* (1861), supporting the view of the identity of Aryan language and race.

This false assumption of linguistic and racial identity would not, however, have furnished the basis for a racial psychosis taken by itself alone. Müller, indeed, assumed that even the Bengalese and the British were related racially. What was needed to complete the myth was a vigorous statement of the cultural importance and historic mission of particular races. This indispensable impetus to racial arrogance was supplied in the famous *Essay on the Inequality of the Human Races* by Count Joseph Arthur de Gobineau (1816-1882), published in 1854.[10]

Gobineau's doctrine of white Aryan superiority. Gobineau, seeking to find the key to a philosophy of history, discovered it in a theory of race. He held that there are three primary races, the white, the yellow, and the black. The white he believed to possess energy, courage, and leadership to a preëminent degree; the yellow race, outstandably stable and fertile qualities; and the black race, sensuality and artistic impulses to a unique extent.

Gobineau was a somewhat paradoxical critic and eulogist of race mixture. His philosophy of races ran somewhat as follows: a certain amount of race mixture is essential to produce any high civilization; but civilization, in turn, is always destroyed by too great an amount of race mixture.

---

[10] For a good review of the work of Gobineau and his followers, see Jacques Barzun, *Race: A Study in Modern Superstition*. New York: Harcourt, Brace, 1937.

Gobineau believed that the white race is superior to the other two, and that the highest and purest branch of the white race is the Aryan, derived from the Hindu Kush plateau of Asia. The Germans are the best, although by no means pure, representatives of the Aryan race today. Since no one race possesses all the traits necessary for a high civilization, there must be a mixture of the Aryan leaders with an inferior race that harbors certain desirable qualities, especially those of high fertility. All civilizations have actually arisen through Aryan conquests of inferior races. Yet, while this race mixture creates high civilizations, it contains within itself the seeds of its own destruction. The race mixture proceeds until the Aryan blood has become fatally diluted with inferior strains, whereupon the civilization declines and disappears.

Gobineau's eulogy of Aryan superiority naturally evoked the desire to prove that one's nation is made up primarily of the Aryan race, though Gobineau himself felt that, outside of Germany, the Europeans were almost hopelessly degenerate and decadent through extreme race mixture. Himself a Frenchman, he was one of the first to proclaim the Latins a decadent race. At any rate, intense racialism as a social theory and historical hypothesis dates mainly from Gobineau's work and influence.

Spread of the Aryan myth. At first, however, this Aryan hypothesis gave rise to relatively little nationalistic chauvinism in Europe, because it was assumed that the broad similarities among the European languages, with the exception of Basque and certain of the so-called Turanian dialects, implied and demonstrated that the overwhelming majority of all Europeans, within whatever national boundary, were good Aryans. This benign illusion was demolished by a number of Germanic writers, particularly J. G. Cuno (1871), Theodor Pösche (1878), and Carl Penka (1883), who proved convincingly that the assumption of the identity between race and language was entirely untenable.

Their contention is confirmed by anthropological facts. A fairly well unified race, like the American Indians, has more than a hundred distinct stock languages, to say nothing of the enormously greater number and variety of dialects. On the other hand, in some European states obviously different races speak the same language, as the result of cultural pressure and historic associations. Hence, it became apparent that not all Europeans were Aryans. From the 1880's onward, there was a feverish effort on the part of the writers of every European country to prove themselves the only true Aryans and their neighbors of inferior non-Aryan clay. The Germans argued that the true Aryans were the blond, blue-eyed Teutons— the Nordics.

It has frequently been held that these Teutonic writers were the only ones who succumbed to this fanaticism, but any such notion is a product of propaganda since 1914. In fact, every state had its group of philologists, anthropologists, and historians who interpreted national culture in the light of alleged racial superiority due to the Aryan heritage, England and France quite matching the Teutons in this respect. These views also found expression in the obsessed writings of Houston Stewart Chamberlain, Maurice Barrès, Rudyard Kipling, and other literary figures. They influenced the nationalistic historical literature, which held a supreme place in historical writing until around the close of the nineteenth century. It was represented by such works as those of Droysen, von Sybel, von Treitschke, Michelet, Martin, Kemble, Stubbs, Freeman, Fiske, Burgess, and others only slightly less distinguished and widely read.

The Aryan myth spread to the United States and we find the well-known American publicist, William Allen White, declaring in his *The Old Order Changeth* (1910), a generation before Hitler, that:

> The best blood of the earth is here—a variated blood of strong, indomitable men and women brought here by visions of wider lives. But this blood will remain a clean, Aryan blood, because there are no hordes of inferior races about us to sweep over us and debase our stock. We are separated by two oceans from the inferior races, and by that instinctive race revulsion to cross-breeding which marks the American wherever he is found.

Teutonism and Nordicism. The most influential work to stress the identity between the Aryans and the Teutonic race, thus exalting Teutonism, was that of Houston Stewart Chamberlain (1855-1927), *Foundations of the Nineteenth Century,* which first appeared in Germany in 1899.[11] Chamberlain was a native of Britain, was educated in France and Germany, and married the daughter of the famous German composer, Richard Wagner. He became a member of the German circle that worshipped Gobineau, and he soon outdid the Germans themselves in eulogizing the genius of the blond Teutonic race. When he found conspicuous examples of cultural leadership in men who were apparently non-Germans, he had little hesitation in claiming that such persons were in part, at least, of German descent. He even contended that Jesus was not of Jewish descent and had a large infusion of Aryan blood in his veins. Chamberlain's book was the most eloquent and comprehensive statement of the thesis of Teutonic superiority ever published.

A more discriminating, but an extremely enthusiastic, defense of the Teutonic thesis was brought to the United States by the distinguished political scientist and historian, John William Burgess. Burgess laid great stress upon the Teutonic foundations of American culture and political institutions. His views were most influential in the two decades from 1890 onward, his classic work on political science being published in 1890. His friend, President Nicholas Murray Butler of Columbia University, helped to popularize Burgess' views in American intellectual, educational, and social circles. The famous Historical School, established at John Hopkins University by Herbert Baxter Adams in 1876, also enthusiastically stressed the Germanic and Anglo-Saxon origin of American institutions.

Far more popular excitement was created a quarter of a century after Burgess' book appeared by the publication of the work of a New York lawyer, Madison Grant, *The Passing of the Great Race* (1916).[12] It was given unwarranted scientific prestige through the fact that a laudatory preface was provided from the pen of the eminent zoölogist, Henry Fair-

---

[11] New York: Dodd, 1912.
[12] 4th ed., New York: Scribner, 1921.

field Osborn. As a matter of fact, Grant's book was simply a spirited and eloquent revival of the Aryan and Teutonic racial mysticism that had been accumulating from the days of Gobineau to Chamberlain. All its theories had already been exploded by scholars in Europe and America. Grant substituted the term Nordic for Teutonic, but his general thesis was the same as that of Chamberlain. A conspicuous example of pseudo-science and race prejudice, the book was persuasively written, had a great vogue, and gave new currency to the Nordic myth. Grant wrote later books attacking immigration from central and southern Europe. His views had some influence upon those who advocated drastic immigration restriction after the First World War.

Grant's views were adopted and expounded in the even more popular writings of T. Lothrop Stoddard, *The Rising Tide of Color*,[13] and *Racial Realities in Europe*.[14] When Adolf Hitler came into power in Germany, he put Aryanism into actual operation with a vengeance and launched a sweeping campaign against the German Jews. Alfred Rosenberg was the Nazi leader most interested in promoting Aryanism, anti-Semitism, and other racial vagaries of the Hitler régime. Julius Streicher led in the Nazi campaign against the Jews in the press. In the summer of 1938, Mussolini defied Gobineau's dogma relative to the decadence of the Italians as a result of the breeding out of Aryan blood. He proclaimed the Italians to be true Aryans and adopted, in rhetoric, at least, the same racial policies that Hitler had put into operation in Germany five years before.

The Aryan myth exploded. While this racial obsession was taking on its most vigorous and cocksure form, scientists were patiently assembling the data which were to reveal with pitiless thoroughness the fundamental inaccuracy of all the assumptions underlying the racial interpretation. An American scholar, W. Z. Ripley, using the extended researches of European anthropologists, wrote a comprehensive work on *The Races of Europe* (1899), which thoroughly demolished the theory that there ever was any such thing as an Aryan race.[15] The term "Aryan" was shown to be applicable, if at all, only to certain linguistic items common to some peoples of Europe and Asia. It was also proved highly dubious whether the term Aryan could be accurately used even to describe the cultures of those peoples who spoke the so-called Aryan languages. Above all, Ripley, Giuseppe Sergi, and others contended that the Teutonic peoples were not of Asiatic derivation and could not have been the original bearers of the Aryan languages and culture. If there are any such facts as a definite Aryan language and typical Aryan institutions, it is the consensus of the best anthropological opinion that they were probably brought into Europe by the roundheaded Alpine or Eurasiatic race.

The absurdity of the whole notion of the Aryan race was humorously but cogently emphasized in his later years by Friedrich Max Müller, in

---

[13] Scribner, 1920.
[14] Scribner, 1924.
[15] New York: Appleton, 1899.

the following words: "An ethnologist who speaks of Aryan race, Aryan blood, Aryan eyes and hair, is as great a sinner as a linguist who speaks of a dolichocephalic [longheaded] dictionary or a brachycephalic [round-headed] grammar."

Likewise, the term "Indo-Germanic," [16] if used to describe a unified race or culture, is a scientific and historical monstrosity. Yet, it crops out in so authoritative an historical work as the third volume of the *Cambridge Medieval History*. Indeed, it is still in common use among many conventional historians, particularly the English. Moreover, the term "Indo-European" certainly cannot be accurately employed as descriptive of either the Mediterranean or the Nordic groups. Therefore, it cannot very well include all the races and cultures of both ancient India and modern Europe.

Lack of foundation for theory of Teutonic or Nordic superiority. We shall now review the great historic civilizations and indicate the essentially non-Nordic basis of the majority of them.

All the great civilizations of Oriental antiquity were, for all practical purposes, definitely non-Nordic. This is especially apparent as soon as one accepts the modern scientific view that the Nordics are in no important sense racially related to the peoples of ancient India or to the Eurasiatic Alpines who came from this region to Europe following the close of the Paleolithic age. The great European heritage that came from Egypt was devoid of any Nordic basis. Nor is there good ground for believing that Nordics played any significant part in the creation of the successive cultures of Mesopotamia. The high civilization of the ancient Aegean area was a purely Mediterranean culture without any significant Nordic admixture whatever. At the most, some Nordics may have taken part in the destruction of Aegean civilization.

Further, we must revise the ordinary notion that all highly advanced human civilization has been limited to the area between the Tigris and the Thames. As a matter of fact, in most respects aside from science and material culture, the ancient civilizations of China and India were more complex and mature than those of the Occident. That they are of non-Nordic derivation would scarcely need to be pointed out even to Lothrop Stoddard and Madison Grant.

To pass on to classical times, there was only a small minority of Nordics in the racial composition of ancient Greece and Italy, as Harold Peake, Sergi, V. Guiffrida-Ruggeri, and J. L. Myres have amply demonstrated. Certainly the Nordic element in early classical culture, if present at all, was so slight as to be almost negligible. When the Germanic peoples entered the classical scene in large numbers during the Roman Empire, they only served to help on the decline of classical civilization. The foundations of medieval culture were laid in pre-Roman and Roman Gaul, which developed its civilization prior to any extensive Germanic invasions.

---

[16] First applied about 1825 by the German writer, Heinrich Julius von Klaproth.

The highest culture of the Middle Ages was not to be found in western Europe but in the Eastern, or Byzantine, Empire and among the Muslims of the Near East, northern Africa, and Spain. The contrary view has become popular solely because of the misleading nature of our conventional textbooks on medieval history, which usually concentrate their attention on the Latin-Christian culture of northwestern Europe during the medieval period. The Muslim culture was, of course, entirely non-Nordic, and there was but a small Nordic minority among the peoples that maintained the Byzantine culture unbroken down to the final conquest by the Turks in the middle of the fifteenth century.

Even the civilization and institutions of medieval Europe, as Numa Denis Fustel de Coulanges, Camille Jullian, and others have proved, took their origin not so much from the crude Teutonic institutions of the Franks as from the Teuton assimilation of the Gallo-Roman culture of Italy and Roman Gaul. Even in a political and military sense no convincing case can be made for Nordic supremacy during the medieval period. The strongest national monarchies of the Middle Ages were those of France and England, while the Holy Roman Empire remained throughout the medieval age a loose and weak organization. We now know that medieval France was predominantly non-Nordic, and that the non-Nordic element was certainly as large as the Nordic even in medieval England. One must, however, in fairness note the high political military capacity of the Nordic Normans who settled in northern France and later invaded England.

The most striking political organizations of early modern Europe were the despotisms of Spain and Bourbon France, while the Germanic states in central Europe continued to be politically backward and loosely organized. The German countries remained the "weak sister" in the political family of Europe down to the period of Bismarck's impressive statesmanship following 1860.

If one were to accept for a minute the thesis of racial causation in politics, European history since the fall of the Roman Empire would thus constitute an effective argument for the relative political incapacity of these very Nordics whose unique political force and subtlety were upheld by the whole school of writers from Droysen and the Maurers to Stubbs, Freeman, Fiske, Herbert Baxter Adams and Burgess. The facts of history certainly constitute much more of an apparent indictment of the political ability of the Nordics than they do a demonstration of their unusual capacity in this field. Of course, the sane historian will disregard the whole racial interpretation of political history and will understand that, in all probability, the backwardness of Germany for centuries was caused by peculiar historical handicaps of an ecclesiastical, geographic, and economic character.

No basis for recent theories of Nordic inferiority. In revealing the lack of any scientific or historical validity in the older theories of Nordic superiority, it is also helpful to call attention to the fact that there is no more support for the recent fantastic theories of the racial inferiority and viciousness of the Nordic peoples, such as the views set forth by Lord

Vansittart, Paul Winkler, and Richard Brickner. Any reprehensible conduct on the part of certain groups among the Germanic peoples in contemporary times is a cultural rather than a racial product.

The Anglo-Saxon myth. In England and our own country the most
popular race myth has been that variant of the Nordic obsession known
as the "Anglo-Saxon myth," which was so effectively exploded by Professor Henry Jones Ford in *The American Mercury,* September, 1924.[17] The
Anglo-Saxon myth was based essentially upon the contention that most
of the unique political talent of the Nordics migrated from Germany,
along with the Angles, Saxons, Jutes, and Danes, and took up its abode
among these Nordic immigrants to the British Isles. The latter were supposed to have swept this area clean of the fickle and decadent Celts. The
American version of the Anglo-Saxon myth, developed by writers like
John Fiske, contended that the best in the Anglo-Saxon political genius,
in turn, left the British Isles during the period of the colonization of
America. It attained expression in the democratic township government
and other local institutions of colonial New England and, on a larger
scale, in the Federal Republic established by the Constitution of 1787.

The Anglo-Saxon myth came to full bloom in the United States at the
turn of the century when our writers were filled with exuberance over
winning the Spanish-American War. William Allen White wrote in his
Emporia *Gazette* on March 20, 1899:

> It is the Anglo-Saxon's manifest destiny to go forth in the world as a world
> conqueror. He will take possession of all the islands of the sea. He will extermi-
> nate the peoples he cannot subjugate. That is what fate holds for the chosen
> people. It is so written. Those who would protest will find their objections over-
> ruled. It is to be.

The same sentiments were uttered by Albert J. Beveridge in his first
speech in the United States Senate on January 9, 1900:

> We will not renounce our part in the mission of our race, trustee under God,
> of the civilization of the world. . . . He has marked us as His chosen people to
> lead in the regeneration of the world. . . . The question is elemental. It is racial.
> God has not been preparing the English-speaking and Teutonic people for a
> thousand years for nothing but vain and idle contemplation and self-administra-
> tion. No! He has made us the master organizers of this world to establish system
> where chaos reigns. He has given us the spirit of progress, to overwhelm the
> forces of reaction throughout the earth. He has made us adepts in government
> that we may administer government among savage and senile peoples. . . . And
> of all our race He has marked the American people as the chosen nation to
> finally lead in the regeneration of the world. This is the divine mission of
> America. . . . We are the trustees of the world's progress, guardians of its righteous
> peace.

It may fairly be remarked that Hitler's racialism never attained greater
heights of ecstasy and fantasy than these extracts from White and Beveridge. It is also interesting, as evidence of social and policy changes, that
the United States, a half-century after their time, is now engaged in lead-

---

[17] See also F. G. Detweiler, "The Anglo-Saxon Myth in the United States," *American
Sociological Review,* April, 1938.

ing a world crusade to overwhelm the forces of radicalism rather than of reaction.

The researches of physical anthropologists and cultural historians have demonstrated both the racial and institutional fallacies in the Anglo-Saxon myth. England remained, even after the Germanic conquests, certainly as much non-Nordic as Nordic. The United States has been settled from the early colonial period by a very mixed population. Finally, most of the institutions that are looked upon as primarily Anglo-Saxon were in few instances derived from Germany. They have been the result of the interaction of various historic forces and situations more or less uniquely English or American, and in some instances wholly modern in origin. A conspicuous example is the myth that our modern democratic institutions were derived from the *folk-moot* of the primitive German backwoods. As a matter of fact, democracy was a product of modern industrialism and the rise of the working class. In the United States the western frontier also made its contribution to the democratic movement.

Race mixture in past undermines any racial interpretation of the history of Western civilization. It is scarcely necessary to call attention to the manner in which the demonstrable racial mixture in the history of Europe rules out as utterly impossible any literal racial interpretation of European history. Even if we were to assume, for example, that the culture of France or the culture of Germany is both unique and the product of a definite racial heritage, shall we attribute French culture to the Nordics of the northeast, the Celts of the central portion, or the Mediterraneans of the south? Or, in the case of Germany, is its culture primarily the product of the Nordics in the north or the Alpines in the south?

Even if we could feel sure, which we certainly cannot, that there is any definite relation between race and culture, particularly in the case of the subraces of Europe, the wholesale mixture of all European types which has been going on since the Neolithic period would most assuredly rule out as nonsense any attempt to defend a racial interpretation of the history of the various European states. There is nothing in Europe approaching a pure racial stock. This fact can probably best be driven home by a concrete illustration. There is no better one than the following summary by Karl Pearson of the racial heredity of Charles Darwin, long pointed to as, physically and mentally, a typical Englishman:

He is descended in four different lines from Irish kinglets; he is descended in as many lines from Scottish and Pictish kings. He has Manx blood. He claims descent in at least three lines from Alfred the Great, and so links up with Anglo-Saxon blood, but he links up also in several lines with Charlemagne and the Carlovingians. He sprang also from the Saxon emperors of Germany, as well as from Barbarossa and the Hohenstaufens. He had Norwegian blood and much Norman blood. He had descent from the Dukes of Bavaria, of Saxony, of Flanders, the Princes of Savoy, and the Kings of Italy. He had the blood in his veins of Franks, Alamans, Merovingians, Burgundians, and Longobards. He sprang in direct descent from the Hun rulers of Hungary and the Greek Emperors of Constantinople. If I recollect rightly, Ivan the Terrible provides a Russian link. There is probably not one of the races of Europe concerned in folk-wanderings which has not had a share in the ancestry of Charles Darwin. If it has been possible in the case of one Englishman to show in a considerable number of lines how impure is his race, can we venture to assert that if the like knowledge were possible of attainment, we could expect greater purity of blood in any of his countrymen? [18]

SUMMARY

There has been much lamentable confusion in the use of the term "race." Race has often been mistakenly identified with the cultural traits of peoples. Race is, scientifically speaking, a strictly physical concept and involves only the somatic or bodily traits of the various peoples of the earth. On the basis of such physical traits, they have been divided into three main branches—white, yellow, and black, but there are many subdivisions of each of these major races.

It was once believed that all the races of mankind go back to some single parent stock, the transition from higher forms of ape life to man being accomplished, presumably by a mutation, in one place, once and for all. More recent discoveries of very primitive types of mankind, from Peiping to South Africa, and from England to the East Indies, now make it seem more reasonable that the transition from anthropoid to man took place in several widely-separated areas at a very remote period. If this be true, the races of mankind had a multiple rather than a single origin.

There has been a common tendency to view the folkways and customs of various peoples, their culture, as racial traits. These cultural types and activities have been attributed to racial influences. There may be some slight ground for this explanation, but cultural patterns are mainly a socio-psychological and historical product, rather than an outgrowth of racial traits. Most race prejudice has grown out of this false confusion of race with culture.

There may be definite mental traits and abilities that are associated with specific physical racial types, but there is no definite proof of the comprehensive superiority of any main race or of any subdivision of a main race. At least, no tests thus far devised can demonstrate all-around racial superiority.

All important historic peoples reveal the existence of a greater or less degree of racial mixture. It was once believed that any race mixture is disastrous, both physically and culturally. More careful studies have overthrown this illusion. There are no pure races and there is no proof that racial mixture, even of an extreme type, is physically disastrous to the offspring. Cultural handicaps and race prejudice may make race mixture a temporary liability, but this is another matter. The long existing mixture of races excludes the validity of any racial interpretation of history.

Race prejudice is wholly a cultural product. There is no scientific justification for it, but it has been the cause of much strife and injustice in the course of history. Adequate education in the realities of the race problem is the only real solution of race prejudice.

---

[18] "The Problems of Anthropology," *Scientific Monthly*, 1920, p. 455.

Anti-Semitism is a classic example of both racial mythology and race prejudice. There is no such thing as a Jewish race. All the characteristics of the Jewish people are, as with all other peoples, a cultural manifestation.

The Aryan, Nordic, and Anglo-Saxon "myths" are another important historical example of racial superstitions and prejudices. Language was mistakenly identified with race in creating the Aryan myth. We now know that there never was any Aryan race. The Nordic subrace is an actuality, but there is no scientific or historical justification for believing in the superiority or the inferiority of the Nordic peoples. However one estimates the conduct of the Nordic peoples throughout history, their behavior has been the outcome of cultural influences and habits.

SELECTED REFERENCES

Barzun, Jacques, *Race: A Study in Modern Superstition.* New York: Harcourt, Brace, 1937. Brilliantly written critical and historical exposition of various racial interpretations of history.

Benedict, Ruth, *Race: Science and Politics.* New York: Viking, 1940. A spirited attack on race myths and prejudices, especially their exploitation in the political policies of contemporary Europe.

Boas, Franz, *The Mind of Primitive Man.* New York: Macmillan, 1911. Vastly influential pioneer work minimizing the role of race in history and cultural building.

———, *Race, Language and Culture.* New York: Macmillan, 1940. Brings data and arguments in earlier work down to date.

Coon, C. C., *The Races of Europe.* New York: Macmillan, 1939. Scholarly survey of the physical anthropology of European peoples. Brings down to date, with many additions, the classic work of W. Z. Ripley listed below.

Cox, O. C., *Caste, Class and Race.* New York: Doubleday, 1948. An extended critique of those doctrines and practices that are based on ideas of social aristocracy and racial superiority.

Dixon, R. B., *The Racial History of Man.* New York: Scribner, 1923. Panoramic survey, from the standpoint of physical anthropology, of all the major races of mankind, including theories of their origin and dispersion.

Fairchild, H. P., *Race and Nationality as Factors in American Life.* New York: Ronald, 1947. Sane and thoughtful book on racial ideas and influences in American society. Valuable as a supplement to the book by F. H. Hankins listed below.

Graber, Isacque, and Britt, S. H. (Eds.), *Jews in a Gentile World.* New York: Macmillan, 1942. Symposium on Jewish life and anti-Semitism in the United States.

Grant, Madison, *The Passing of the Great Race.* New York: Scribner, 1916. An influential exposition of the theory of racial superiority, especially of the Nordic race.

Hankins, F. H., *The Racial Basis of Civilization.* New York: Knopf, 1926. Perhaps the best single volume on the race problem in its sociological aspects. Debunks the popular theories of race superiority without surrendering a scientific attitude toward racial problems and eugenics.

Hooton, E. A., *Up From the Ape.* New York: Macmillan, 1931. Probably the ablest American book on the physical derivation and evolution of the historic races prior to recent discoveries.

Huxley, J. S., and Haddon, A. C., *We Europeans*. New York: Harper, 1936. Popular but reliable work by a biologist and an anthropologist on the racial composition and traits of European peoples. Critical of theories of racial superiority.

Keith, Sir Arthur, *The Place of Prejudice in Modern Civilization*. New York: Day, 1931. Defense of race prejudice and conflicts as a dynamic force in history by a British physical anthropologist.

———, *A New Theory of Human Evolution*. New York: Philosophical Library, 1948. Continues theory of earlier book, but main emphasis is on close group life and inbreeding as the basis of the origins of races.

Klineberg, Otto, *Race Differences*. New York: Harper, 1935. Competent analysis of the problem of race superiority and racial abilities.

Park, R. E., *Race and Culture*. Glencoe, Ill.: Free Press, 1949. Important collection of essays by a leading American expert on race problems. Stresses cultural factors.

Radin, Paul, *The Racial Myth*. New York: McGraw-Hill, 1934. Able exposition of the Boas position on race and culture.

Ripley, W. Z., *The Races of Europe*. New York: Appleton, 1899. Classic work on the physical traits of European races, which exploded the idea of an Aryan race.

Simar, Théophile, *The Race Myth*. New York: Boni, 1925. Scholarly review and critique of theories of racial superiority and the racial basis of history.

Snyder, L. L., *Race: A History of Modern Ethnic Theories*. New York: Longmans, Green, 1939. A readable account of the origin and spread of the theories of race superiority.

Stoddard, T. L., *Racial Realities in Europe*. New York: Scribner, 1924. Survey of European races and racial traits following the general attitude of Madison Grant.

Valentin, Hugo, *Anti-Semitism: Historically and Critically Examined*. New York: Viking, 1936. Probably the best general work on anti-Semitism.

CHAPTER 6

Race Contacts and Problems
In Contemporary American Society

THE RELATIONS OF THE WHITE POPULATION WITH THE AMERICAN INDIANS

Importance of race problems in American society. The relations of the white population of the United States with other racial groups have played a very important role in our American society, and many expert students regard race relations as the most critical social problem of the mid-twentieth century. Much of our national history, especially our military exploits and territorial expansion, from the time of the landing of the English in Virginia in 1607 to the defeat of General Custer in 1876, was intimately associated with white relations with the Indians. Indeed, it went back even earlier, to the first landing of Columbus and the Spanish penetration of the American continent in the sixteenth century. Today, the problem of white relations with Negroes is agitating the country as never before. It has pressed the civil rights issue to the forefront of public discussion on political strategy and constitutional problems. It is having a major effect on urban social problems and on our industrial development. Few other social problems today present more baffling obstacles to a rational and amicable solution.

In this chapter we shall consider historically and sociologically the nature, impact, and possible solutions of the contacts between our white population and other races now resident in the United States. We shall start with white relations with the Indians and then consider contacts with the Chinese, Japanese, Mexicans, and Negroes.

The American Indians in colonial times. The American Indians have lived on the North American continent for thousands of years. Some were probably here as early as 20,000 or 15,000 B.C. New discoveries indicate that the first Indians may have arrived 40,000 years ago. Anthropologists estimate that at the time Columbus discovered America, there were between 600,000 and 850,000 pure blood Indians occupying what is now continental United States. When the white man first trespassed on his land, the Indian remained relatively indifferent; but when the whites demanded ever more territory, the Indian tribes were roused to savage opposition. Even while the two races were in conflict, the white man was

169

learning Indian customs which he needed to know before he could fully adjust himself to the New World. If the whites had not adopted Indian methods of getting food, preparing shelter, and making clothes, they would have suffered even more than they did from hunger and cold. Colonists became skilled in paddling canoes, an Indian method of transportation. They found Indian dress comfortable and practical. Pictures of frontiersmen show them in skins and soft-soled Indian moccasins. Our language has been enriched with such commonplace Indian words as skunk, hickory, squash, pecan, toboggan, tomahawk, and squaw.

Not all white settlers treated the Indians alike. The French adopted many Indian customs and lived much like the red men in the backwoods. French trappers often married Indian women. The Spanish and Portuguese attempted to raise the Indian's standard of living to something like the European level. The remains of ancient missions throughout the Southwest are memorials to the Spaniards' attempt to convert the Indians to Christianity. Other colonial nations, the English and Dutch, refused to mingle with the "savages." Following the Revolutionary War and the adoption of the Constitution, the Indian problem fell into the lap of the newly constituted government of the United States.

The treaty system. From 1804 until 1871, the relations of the government with the Indians, during rare times of peace, were governed mainly by specific treaties, many of which early involved the settlement of Indians on reservations. The treatment of those Indians who were put on reservations and were regarded as wards of the nation was careless and demoralizing. The Indians were fed, clothed, and housed at government expense, but were given little incentive to develop a self-sufficing economy or self-respect. Private individuals and corporations were permitted to absorb much of their lands. With the settlement of the Far West after the Civil War, a series of new Indian wars broke out, one of the most dramatic incidents being the annihilation of General George Custer's command at the battle of the Little Big Horn (1876) by the Sioux chief, Sitting Bull. The inefficient and corrupt treatment of the Indians inspired Helen Hunt Jackson to publish her *A Century of Dishonor* in 1881. This book did much to arouse public interest in the plight of the Indians. Eventually legislation was passed that has gradually improved the lot of the Indians.

Administrative machinery for handling Indian affairs. The first official action of the Federal government in dealing with the Indian problem was the passage of a law in 1795 authorizing the president to appoint temporary agents, who were to "reside among the Indians." In 1796, a law was passed creating trading posts in Indian areas, and in 1798 a Superintendent of Indian Trade was appointed.

The trading-post system was ended in 1822, and, in 1824, Secretary of War John C. Calhoun organized the Bureau (now Office) of Indian Affairs. In 1832, a Commissioner of Indian Affairs was appointed, and this office has continued as the apex of the administrative machinery dealing with Indians. In 1834, a law known as the "Indian Intercourse Act" was passed. This law, providing for 12 field agents to handle Indian matters, was long the basis for regulating the administration of Indian affairs. In 1849, the Bureau of Indian Affairs was transferred from the War Department to the newly-created Department of the Interior. This action was sharply resented by the War Department and the army, and the friction and bickerings between military and civilian officials over Indian problems seriously impaired a scientific and fair handling of the Indian situation for many years. In 1869, an unpaid Board of Indian Commissioners was created to advise the Commissioner.

The reservation system. The utterly inadequate nature of the treaty system was so apparent that, in 1871, it was abandoned in favor of congressional legislation on Indian matters, and the reservation system became completely dominant in our public Indian policy.

A typical Indian reservation is a tax-exempt tract of land owned by the tribe and held in trust for the Indian inhabitants by the government. In theory at least, it cannot be levied upon or alienated, and the Indians are free to go and come as they wish.

The first important reform legislation was the Dawes Act of 1887, which provided for the division of tribal lands among individual Indians, under certain limitations, particularly a government trusteeship of 25 years. The land allotment system was liberalized by the Burke Act of 1906, which eliminated the 25-year waiting period before full ownership could be conferred.

Among the chief defects of this legislation were: (1) that the land included in the reservation was usually not sufficient to support the Indian inhabitants and was of inferior quality, and (2) that no adequate provision was made to prepare the Indians to own and cultivate land. But probably the greatest weakness in the administration of Indian affairs was the failure to protect the Indians from the alienation of their land by greedy private interests. Between 1887 and 1933, the land belonging to Indians under government grants shrank from 130,000,000 acres to 49,000,000 acres.

Citizenship was conferred on the Indians in 1924, but in Arizona and New Mexico they were either not permitted to vote at all or only under severe limitations for over 20 years after this date. Many Indians refuse to exercise the right of suffrage even when they are legally qualified.

Belated development of Indian education. One of the main reasons for the unsatisfactory nature of Indian affairs has been the failure of the Federal government to provide adequate educational facilities for Indian children.

Federal interest in the education of Indian children first appeared in the passage of a law in 1819 appropriating $10,000 annually for this purpose, but no government schools were established. Rather, the money was paid over to missionary organizations operating among the Indians, a system which prevailed until 1873, when the law of 1819 was repealed.

The next step was the provision of a small number of inferior non-reservation boarding schools. The first and most noted of these was opened in 1879 in an abandoned military post at Carlisle, Pennsylvania, by Captain R. H. Pratt. The most famous graduate of Carlisle was Jim Thorpe, voted the outstanding American athlete of the first half of the twentieth century. The school was closed in 1918. Until the reforms following the Meriam Report of 1928, the great majority of Indian children who received any education at all did so in boarding schools. Between 1879 and 1928 a number of reservation boarding schools were established. In 1926, out of 24,591 Indian pupils enrolled in government schools, 20,092 were in boarding schools and only 4,499 in reservation day schools. The program of supplanting boarding schools by day schools did not really get under way until 1934; even ten years later, in 1944, more than a third of all Indian children in government schools were still attending boarding schools.

A major defect of the boarding-school system was the prevalence of harsh military discipline, copied from that established by Pratt in 1879. The education was inferior. The teaching force was numerically inadequate and often ill-prepared, and insufficient attention was paid to vocational education.

The Meriam Report of 1928 revealed that, at the end of the first quarter of the present century, only about 65,000 out of 77,577 Indian children of school age were getting any education. About 34,500 were in public schools, with the Federal government paying tuition for most of them, and the rest were in government boarding and day schools and in mission schools. The appropriation for an Indian child in a boarding school was usually only about $225 a year, as against $700 a year for a child in a low-cost white boarding school, and the service and teaching were inferior.

When Charles J. Rhoads was appointed Commissioner of Indian Affairs in 1929, he began to improve the education of Indian children. Many new school buildings were built, military discipline was abolished, better vocational instruction was provided for, more reservation day schools were created, and the per capita allowance for children was increased to $375 a year. When Rhoads was succeeded by John Collier in 1933, these reforms were continued, and special stress was put on the creation of more government community day schools on the reservations. Perhaps the most important law affecting Indian education was the Johnson-O'Malley Act, passed in 1934. This authorized the Bureau of Indian Affairs to make contracts with the states to educate Indian children with the aid of Federal funds. Indian education is, however, still inferior to that provided for whites. Many children are not in school at all, the educational staff remains inferior to that provided for white children, not enough good vocational courses have been introduced, and there are still not enough community day schools. Indian children are frequently discriminated against in public schools, and are entirely excluded in some instances.

But the fault is not all with the government. Many Indians do not wish to send their children to school, at least for a whole year. Compulsory education laws have been on the books since 1892; they were made more rigid in the 1920's, but this has not assured anything like full attendance by Indian children, even when good schools are available. Indians often like to keep their children home to help until the year's work is over. Moreover, the memory of the harsh military discipline of earlier times has not been blotted out.

The present status of Indian education may be summarized on the basis of 1945 figures, the latest available. The Federal government operates 238 schools for Indian children in the United States, from rural schools with one room and a dozen pupils to consolidated or centralized schools with 400 to 500 pupils. Some 155 of these schools are reservation day schools; 66 are reservation boarding schools; and 17 are non-reservation boarding schools. The Federal government encourages Indian children to attend public schools whenever they are available, and more Indian children now attend public schools than Federal schools. For the most part, the Federal day schools are maintained only in areas in which public schools do not exist or are inaccessible to Indian children. In 1945, of 92,296 Indian children between 6 and 18, some 31,927 were attending public schools, 27,252 were enrolled in Federal boarding or day schools; 7,813 were attending mission boarding or day schools; 19,375 were not in any school (some 15,000 of these being children on the Navajo Reservation); and 5,929 were unaccounted for. In 1948, some 7,204 children were attending reservation boarding schools, and 6,269 non-reservation boarding schools. In Alaska, the Federal government operates 78 elementary day schools, with 3,750 pupils, and 2,852 attend the territorial public schools. About 1,500 Indian children in Alaska are without any educational facilities. Federal education for Indian children ends with high school since there are no Indian colleges, but several Indian high schools offer two years of post-graduate vocational training.

Serious medical and health problems among the Indians. Medical care for Indians, like educational opportunities, has lagged behind that provided for whites. The medical and health problems among Indians have been complicated and intensified by a number of special factors, such as the necessity of readjustment to a sedentary life on reservations, bad economic conditions making for inadequate food, clothing, and shelter, the special susceptibility of Indians to such diseases as tuberculosis and trachoma, and the lethal effect of alcoholic excesses on Indians. But the sickness and mortality could have been greatly reduced had adequate and competent medical care been provided.

The first casual effort to provide medical care for Indians was embodied in the Indian Appropriation Act of 1856, which allotted pay for doctors in Indian agencies. But not much was accomplished, since, even as late as 1873, only half of the agencies had any doctor at all. In 1873, a medical division was set up in the Bureau of Indian Affairs. Though the medical division was abolished in 1877, some improvements continued to be made in the medical service. In 1878, the Commissioner of Indian Affairs ordered that all doctors on Indian reservations must be graduates of an approved medical college. The first hospital for Indians was opened in 1882. The paucity of medical care at the turn of the century, however, is shown by the fact that in 1900, there were only 86 doctors in the entire Indian service and only 5 Indian hospitals, though the number of Indians in 1900 was 237,196.

A number of improvements took place in the next quarter century. The medical division was revived in the Bureau of Indian Affairs in 1909, a medical supervisor was appointed, and $12,000 was appropriated to study and treat trachoma. In 1912, President Taft earnestly recommended better medical care for the Indians. Indian medical appropriations increased from $60,000 in 1912 to $700,000 in 1926. In the latter year, the medical service in the Bureau of Indian Affairs was reorganized in cooperation with the Public Health Service. Four medical districts were created for the country, and a medical director was provided for each. The Meriam Report of 1928 stressed the fact that medical care for Indians still remained far below the standards maintained by the Public Health Service and the Veteran's Bureau. Commissioners Rhoads and Collier strove to improve the Service, adding more medical districts, doctors, and hospitals. Medical appropriations rose from $700,000 in 1926 to a little over 4 million dollars in 1936, at which time there were in the Indian Service some 160 full-time and 78 part-time doctors and 500 nurses. At the present time, the Indian Service operates some 64 hospitals and sanatoriums in the United States, with approximately 4,000 beds, and 7 hospitals in Alaska with over 700 beds. In addition, the Indian Service makes contracts with a number of public and private hospitals to render hospital care to Indians in places where the Service does not maintain its own facilities. Over 50,000 receive hospital care each year. In 1950, there were 150 full-time and 119 part-time doctors in the Indian Service, and 833 nurses, and the total appropriations for the Indian Health Service were $11,883,917.

But medical care for Indians still lags far behind that for whites. A number of doctors left the Indian Service during the war, and not all of them have returned or been replaced. Doctors are poorly paid, hospitals have to operate on a much lower appropriation than Public Health hospitals, and the number of doctors and hospitals per capita is far less than among whites. There is a high prevalence of tuberculosis and trachoma, particularly among some of the more economically unfortunate Indians of the Southwest, especially the Navajos. Nevertheless, the improvement of medical care in the last half century is reflected in the fact that the Indians are now increasing in numbers more rapidly than any other racial minority in the country, except for Mexican immigrants. The use of sulfa drugs and the antibiotics has cut down the prevalence of trachoma in some areas, more scientific methods of treating tuberculosis are being introduced in Indian hospitals, and deaths from typhoid, smallpox, and diphtheria have been notably reduced. Despite all this, however, the situation is still far from satisfactory, as the following statistics supplied by Howard A. Rusk will make amply clear:

1. Compared with an over-all tuberculosis death rate of 33.5 in 100,000 among the general population in 1947, the rate was 336 for Indians in North Dakota, or ten and nine-tenths times higher than among whites, and 302 among the Navajos, or nine times higher.
2. In 1948, the infant mortality rate for the nation was 32 in 1,000 children born; among Montana Indians it was 116; among the Navajos, 227.

3. Typhoid occurs four times more frequently among Indians than among the general population.
4. Trachoma, which has largely disappeared among the general population, is increasing in several Indian tribes.
5. Pneumonia death rates were 8 to 1 higher in Nebraska and 17 to 1 higher in Wyoming among Indians than among non-Indians in the same states.
6. Corrective dental service for Indians is so limited that only emergency work for school-age children is provided.
7. Despite the general lack of needed beds, 1,055 of the Indian Service's hospital beds are closed by lack of funds.

The famous Meriam Report of 1928 and subsequent improvements in the Indian Service. We have already mentioned several times the Meriam Report, which was published in 1928. This gave the greatest impetus to the study and improvement of Indian conditions since *A Century of Dishonor,* published half a century before.

Various organizations interested in Indian affairs seriously criticized the Indian Service during the years following the First World War. They asserted that there was little to show for the increased expenditures on the Indian Service, that the Indians were being cheated out of their lands, that poverty was widespread among the Indians, and that health and educational conditions were scandalous. Herbert Work, Secretary of the Interior, was impressed by these charges and determined to learn the truth about Indian affairs. He requested the Institute for Government Research to make a survey of the Indian situation and of the government service to the Indians. The survey was conducted under the direction of Lewis Meriam, and the Report was published by the Brookings Institution in 1928 under the title, *The Problem of Indian Administration.*

Among the recommendations made were the following: that a Division of Planning and Development be set up in the Bureau of Indian Affairs to carry on studies of the Indian situation and reorganize the Indian Service; that 5 million dollars be appropriated at once to rehabilitate the Indian Service; that the Civil Service Commission should set about to provide the number of qualified employees needed in the Service; that $75,000 be appropriated to strengthen the medical research staff; and that the educational system should be reorganized, strengthened, and liberalized.

Most of these recommendations were carried out in whole or in part. Charles J. Rhoads, a public-spirited Pennsylvania banker, was made Commissioner of Indian Affairs in 1929. He took his responsibility seriously and tried to put into operation the steps and measures suggested in the Meriam Report, especially those pertaining to education and medical service.

In 1933, President Roosevelt appointed as Commissioner of Indian Affairs the first true expert on the Indian problem ever to hold this office. This was John Collier, who had been secretary of the Indian Defense Association, one of the organizations responsible for the Meriam survey, and editor of the *American Indian Life Magazine.* He set up a relief system, established an Indian unit of the Civilian Conservation Corps, cancelled some of the Indian debts to the government, checked the alienation of Indian lands, and bought more land for the Indians. He improved the educational system by introducing more government community day schools on the reservations, and enlarged and improved the medical service. He sought to educate the public on Indian matters by publishing a Bureau magazine known as *Indians at Work*.

Especially important was the passage of the Wheeler-Howard Indian Reorganization Act of 1934. This repealed the earlier land allotment acts, put an end to the alienation of Indian lands and other physical resources, established an indefinite government trust period for Indian lands, returned to tribal ownership the surplus reservation lands, enabled the Commissioner to buy more land for the Indians up to an expenditure of 2 million dollars a year, and created a revolving credit fund of 12 million dollars for the Indians. Perhaps the most important political feature of the Act was the effort to revive Indian self-government. The Indian tribes were authorized to draw up constitutions and by-laws and to elect officers to handle tribal matters and negotiate with the Federal, state, and local governments. The Indian Service has been much expanded and strengthened since 1934. In 1948, it had 7,496 full-time civil service employees, and 3,563 part-time workers.

Collier's work with the Indians was restricted during the Second World War, but he remained in office until 1945, when he resigned. He was succeeded by William A. Brophy, another expert on Indian affairs, whose main achievements have been to enlarge and reorganize the field service and to devise a more flexible system of administering the Indian Service.

The intelligent administration of the Bureau of Indian Affairs by Rhoads, Collier, and Brophy, together with our absorption in war matters during the 1940's, lulled many into a false sense of satisfaction concerning the Indian problem.

Economic difficulties of the Indians. Except for some valuable Indian reservation holdings in forest and mineral lands, the Indian economy has revolved chiefly around argiculture and stock-raising. Here the Indians have been handicapped by poor land, lack of irrigation, and primitive farming technique. At the present time, some 60,000 Indian families own about 56,000,000 acres of land, with some 40,000,000 acres owned tribally. About 15,000,000 acres are semi-desert and unfitted for any kind of economical operation. Only about 12,000,000 acres have enough rainfall to make possible dry farming, and only 3,000,000 acres are classified as good farm crop land.

As a result of the progress in the Indian Service since 1928, and especially since 1934, the situation has been somewhat improved. Better farming methods have been introduced. Government grants and loans to Indians have increased, and some progress has been made in irrigating Indian lands. The income from Indian agricultural operations, exclusive of stock-raising, grew from around a million dollars in 1932 to $25,000,000 in 1948. The improvement in the livestock industry has been comparable. The income from livestock grew from $1,224,000 to $31,000,000. Income from wage-work increased from 12 million dollars in 1933 to about 25 million dollars in 1945, partly because of the extensive entry of Indians

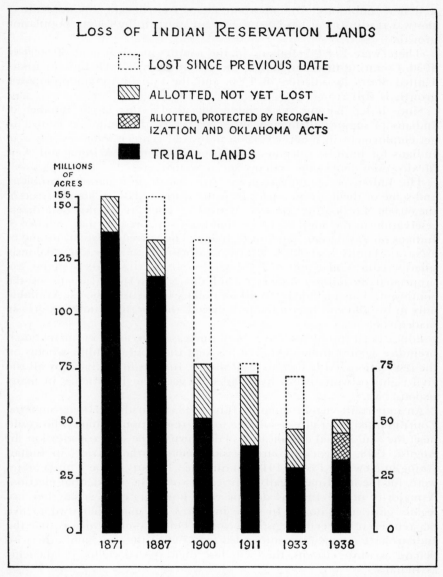

LOSS OF INDIAN RESERVATION LANDS

▢ LOST SINCE PREVIOUS DATE

▨ ALLOTTED, NOT YET LOST

▦ ALLOTTED, PROTECTED BY REORGAN-
IZATION AND OKLAHOMA ACTS

■ TRIBAL LANDS

MILLIONS
OF
ACRES

155 150 125 100 75 50 25 0

75 50 25 0

1871 1887 1900 1911 1933 1938

into war munitions factories. Despite this improvement in the Indian economic situation, there has been an increasingly critical period since the end of World War II.

Indian problems after the Second World War. The administrative and humanitarian work of the Bureau of Indian Affairs was seriously restricted by the diversion of Federal interest, personnel, and resources to the war effort after Pearl Harbor. Some 65,000 Indians who served in the armed forces, or worked in war industries, acquired new perspectives and new ambitions. An important factor contributing to problems of postwar readjustment has been the recent spurt in the Indian population growth.

There were 244,437 Indians in the country in 1920, and 392,000 in 1950. Counting those in Alaska, there were over 450,000 Indians under United States jurisdiction in 1950, and the rate of Indian population growth is still rising.

Since it has become increasingly difficult for this larger number of Indians to support themselves on reservations, they must be helped to get employment in non-reservation industrial centers. Veterans' loans to Indians for business purposes have been inadequate. Arizona and New Mexico even denied the Indians Social Security aid.

The Indians as a minority group still constitute a national problem, and some of them are in especially acute distress. This is notably true of the 60,000 Navajos, the largest Indian tribe. They are isolated on a desert reservation in the Southwest that could not support half that number of Indians on any decent standard of living. The current median income of a Navajo family is about $500 a year. Moreover, they have scandalously inferior educational and medical service. In April, 1950, Congress appropriated 88 million dollars to aid the Navajo-Hopi Indians of the Southwest. This included 25 million dollars for better schools. Available only in installments over a ten-year period, the appropriation was grossly inadequate.

Educational problems have been increased because in many areas prejudice against Indian children has kept them out of public schools off the reservations. Although, in legal theory, Indians formally enjoy all the civil rights of whites, they have failed to get them in practice in many regions.

An important victory came in July, 1948, when the Arizona Supreme Court granted the right of suffrage to the reservation Indians who could meet the educational qualifications laid down in the state constitution. In August, 1948, a Federal court decision removed the barriers to Indian voting in New Mexico. In 1948, all qualified Indians in the United States were, for the first time, legally entitled to vote in a presidential election. A majority of the Indians do not vote, however, even when they are legally entitled to do so. In some instances not more than two to five per cent even bother to register as voters. One reason for this is that the Indians have a somewhat unfounded fear that, if they vote and otherwise behave as white citizens, they will lose their special rights and benefits as Indians.

A number of voluntary organizations are assisting the Indians to secure their rights and to improve their economic and educational status. Such are the Indian Defense Association, the Indian Rights Association, the Association on American Indian Affairs, the National Congress of American Indians, and the American Civil Liberties Union. They have plenty of work ahead, and it is obvious that the American Indians are far from a "disappearing race," as some believe. Of course, most of the approximately 450,000 Indians now under American jurisdiction are no longer "pure-blooded" Indians; Indians have mixed extensively for many years with whites and Mexicans. It is estimated that less than 25 per cent of the Indians today are pure-blooded Indians who speak their tribal language. There is less white prejudice against race mixture with Indians than with Negroes, Chinese, and Japanese.

Deceptive emancipation program of Indian relief. The main subterfuge employed by those who still wish to exploit the Indians is to urge the ending of the reservation system and thus bring about the complete "emancipation" of the Indians. Until the Indians are fully prepared by education and economic aid to fare for themselves on an equal basis with white citizens, nothing could be more fatal to their cause than to remove the protection they derive from the reservation system and Federal wardship. As Oliver La Farge has said, this proposed emancipation, which has a noble ring to it, would actually "emancipate the Indians out of everything they have."

Probably the best conclusion to our review of Indian problems is the suggestion of Howard A. Rusk to the effect that, while it may be a noble aspiration to raise the standard of living of natives in Asia and Africa, "we could well practice some of our Point IV philosophy in our own backyards."

CHINESE, JAPANESE, AND MEXICANS

The arrival of the Chinese. Another important contact of white Americans with peoples of another race came as a result of Chinese immigration. The first wave of Chinese immigrants came to this country rather suddenly. In the 1840's and 1850's there were many political disturbances in China, including the Opium War and the famous Taiping rebellion. These caused much misery and destruction, and many Chinese looked longingly for better conditions outside of their own country. Just about this time gold was discovered in California, and some 25,000 Chinese came into California within three years after gold was found in 1848. They were heartily welcomed at first and put to work in the mining camps. Further need was found for Chinese coolie labor in the next generation when the Pacific coast and transcontinental railroads were being constructed. The railroad promoters welcomed the Chinese labor because of its relative cheapness and docility.

Growing opposition to Chinese immigration and labor. In the 1870's the completion of the first period of railroad construction left thousands of Chinese unemployed and stranded in the West. Their idleness created a special and serious problem. During the two preceding decades much anti-Chinese sentiment had developed in the West, and the crisis in Chinese labor after 1880 enabled this opposition to crystallize effectively.

White labor complained of the disastrous competition of the Chinese, who could live on a much lower standard than Americans were willing to accept. There were also charges that the Chinese were especially addicted to sexual vices and traffic in opium. The fact that these Chinese immigrants were overwhelmingly males and that they did use opium

extensively provided some basis for such protests. Doubtless the charges
of immorality and degeneracy were exaggerated, but the most was made
of them in order to secure legislation ousting the Chinese. We have
already called attention to the immigration legislation excluding the
Chinese and Japanese, which began in 1882 and was completed in 1924.

Present relations with the Chinese. Despite the rigorous exclusion provided for in the law of 1882 and its subsequent extensions, a considerable
number of Chinese trickled into the United States after that time. In
1940 there were 77,500 Chinese in the country, about 50 per cent of
whom were resident in California. The Chinese live almost exclusively
in segregated colonies in the American cities which they inhabit. These
are the so-called Chinatowns which are visited by curious whites. There
is not much competition in the industrial and business fields between
the Chinese and the whites. The Chinese have withdrawn from most of
the enterprises in which they would come into direct competition with
the whites. They devote themselves mainly to serving the needs of their
own countrymen. The main competitive businesses that they still maintain are the laundries and the restaurants. The social and cultural contacts between the whites and Chinese are very limited. Moreover, there
is only a slight degree of intermarriage between Chinese and whites. This
restriction of cultural contacts between the whites and the Chinese has
prevented us from exploiting the cultural advantages which might have
come from learning more about Chinese philosophy and ways of life.

Although Chinese immigration has ceased, the Chinese element in the
country is increasing because of an excess of births over deaths. But
foreign-born Chinese are declining rapidly. In 1940 they constituted less
than three-fifths of the total Chinese population. Owing to their industrial and social segregation and the slight number of Chinese in the
country, they do not produce a race problem of any great seriousness,
even in California and other Pacific coast states. Furthermore, our sentimental attachment for Chinese culture has restrained the development of
any such race prejudice against them as exists against the Japanese. The
fact that the Chinese have been less ambitious and aggressive upon arriving in this country has also contributed to this same general situation
of relative tolerance for the Chinese who are here. The fact that China
was our ally against Japan in the Second World War temporarily increased our cordiality towards American Chinese, and legislation was
passed which permitted native-born Chinese to become citizens of the
United States, beginning with July 4, 1946. Now that China has fallen
to the Communists, there is considerable likelihood that this more cordial
attitude may be reversed.

Japanese immigration. The main wave of Japanese immigration to
the United States came after the passage of the Chinese Exclusion Act of
1882. There are more Japanese in the country than Chinese. In 1940
there were 126,947 Japanese in continental United States, about 85 per
cent of whom lived in the three Pacific coast states and 70 per cent in
California alone. They did not drift eastward, as did the Chinese. Unlike
the situation with the Chinese, the Japanese population of the United

States is decreasing. The hostile American attitude and legislation led many to return to Japan before Pearl Harbor. There were 138,800 Japanese here in 1930.

Friction between whites and Japanese on the Pacific coast. The Japanese did not prove nearly as docile as the Chinese, nor were they as willing to be segregated. They were ambitious to get ahead in the world. They came here in a poverty-stricken condition, were hard workers, and were willing to accept a lower standard of life than would the whites. They went predominantly into agriculture, both as owners and tenants. A whole family would work in the fields. This fact, together with the lower living standards, made it possible for them often to win out over the whites in agriculture and other competitive pursuits. On the eve of the passage of the laws excluding the Japanese from the right to hold land in California, Japanese farmers produced 90 per cent of the asparagus, about half the green vegetables and sugar beets, and much fruit and berries. Another reason for opposition to the Japanese was the fact that they were far more patriotic and politically minded than the Chinese and many remained loyal to the Japanese fatherland.

Intense antagonism to Japanese immigration soon developed in the western states. It was alleged that the Japanese presented insurmountable economic competition with whites, that they rapidly increased in population, that they threatened the purity of the white race through a tendency to intermarry with whites, and that they refused assimilation with American culture.

Japanese competition in Californian agriculture was somewhat serious in some districts, but in industry and other pursuits the Japanese showed no general willingness to work for much less than the whites. The charge of overrapid reproduction is not borne out by the facts. Nor is there statistical evidence of any marked tendency toward intermarriage with the native population. So far as nonassimilation is concerned, the western whites did their best to prevent assimilation from taking place, even had the Japanese desired it. There was a minimum of vice and dependency in the Japanese population.

Nevertheless, race prejudice dominated the whites' attitudes toward the Japanese, and they were subjected to severe forms of discrimination. They suffered under important legal disabilities, such as the Federal legislation refusing them the right of naturalization and California laws designed to prevent them from owning land. The latter type of legislation was often evaded by the Japanese and some of it was set aside by the courts. Generally speaking, much of it became a dead letter and until Pearl Harbor the Japanese were active in Pacific coast farming and gardening. But these laws made a permanent impression on the Japanese mind and increased resentment over discrimination. E. G. Mears passes the following verdict upon them: "These acts are economically unsound, morally questionable, and internationally unfortunate; and their lax enforcement sets a bad example both to Americans and Orientals, especially serious in the case of the younger generation." Social discrimination also existed. Japanese were accorded less than normal courtesy in many establishments and were often excluded entirely from such places as dance halls, swimming pools, and the like.

Exclusion of the Japanese. It was the antagonism of the Pacific states which led to the negotiation of the Gentleman's Agreement in 1907, providing for the cessation of the immigration of Japanese labor to this country. These states were also mainly responsible for the unnecessary affront to the Japanese in the immigration legislation of 1924. The Gentleman's Agreement had been carried out with fidelity by the Japanese government. Though Japanese immigration has now ceased, there is considerable tension between the whites and Japanese in the coast states. Moreover, it may safely be said that the controversies over Japanese immigration, particularly the attitude of the coast states toward the Japanese, had much to do with the cooling off of the formerly friendly relations between Japan and the United States.

Forcible movement of Japanese in wartime. The most extreme action taken in discrimination against the Japanese was the forcible evacuation of the Japanese from the western states. At the time of Pearl Harbor, there were about 127,000 Japanese in the country, some 113,000 of whom lived in California, Washington, Oregon, and Arizona. About 94,000 resided in California.

On the ground that these Japanese would be a military risk if allowed to remain on the coast, some 110,000 persons of Japanese ancestry were evacuated from their homes in these western states by order of the War Department and moved to relatively isolated assembly centers and relocation projects, enclosed within barbed wire. These were situated in California, Arizona, Idaho, Wyoming, Colorado, Utah, and Arkansas. If any work was provided, wages were low, and living conditions were usually bad. In retrospect, this action now appears to have been a needlessly harsh product of wartime hysteria. Less than two-thirds of the evacuated Japanese have been able to return to their homes.

Although Chinese-American friendship may deteriorate as a result of the Communist conquest of China, it is possible that our relations with the Japanese may grow more cordial now that Japan has become more indispensable as an ally to checkmate the advances of Russia and Chinese Communism in the Far East.

Mexican immigration. The latest problem of race contacts in the United States involves Mexican immigration, especially to the Southwest. Mexican immigration has not been impeded because the drastic restrictive legislation of 1921 and 1924 does not apply to immigration from other American countries. The Mexicans are a mixed race of Spanish and Indian descent, the relative proportion of these bloods varying in the particular areas of Mexico. Although Mexicans have been drifting into the country for generations, the greatest volume of entry has come during and since the First World War. The census of 1940 listed as resident in the United States 377,433 Mexicans, 699,220 native-born of Mexican parentage, and 67,568 of Central or South American derivation. The exact number of persons of mixed Spanish-Indian-Mexican derivation is unknown, but the leading American authorities, such as Carey McWilliams, estimate their number as between 2,500,000 and 3,000,000. Nine-tenths of them live in six states—Texas, California, Arizona, New Mexico, Colorado, and Utah. Nearly half of the total live in Texas, and about half of the remainder in California. As the result of the unemployment growing out of the depression, a large number of them returned to Mexico after 1930, but another Mexican immigration movement set in with the beginning of the business upturn of 1934, and an even larger one followed our entry into the Second World War.

In addition to more or less permanent and lawful emigration from Mexico into the United States, there is a large amount of illegal and seasonal entry which has of late attracted a great deal of attention and led to extensive deportations. It has been estimated that over 500,000 Mexicans cross the border and enter the United States each year to participate in seasonal labor, many of them returning to Mexico when the work is finished for the time being. In 1951, the Federal government began taking more drastic steps to check this mass migration of seasonal Mexican labor. A temporary quota of 100,000 to 200,000 was established.

Problems of Mexican immigration. Many Mexican immigrants have brought with them a low standard of living and are relatively illiterate and superstitious. They are occupied mainly in agricultural labor. They have tended to live in segregated quarters, which are almost invariably overcrowded and often dirty and unsanitary. Judged by American standards, there is a disproportionate amount of crime and vice among the Mexican immigrants. The proximity of some of the main Mexican settlements to large army barracks has doubtless intensified the prevalence of prostitution among the Mexican women.

There is considerable social discrimination against the Mexicans. Indeed, in the southern and southwestern states much the same practices of segregation are applied to the Mexicans as to Negroes. But the Mexicans differ from other racial groups in refusing to try to force themselves into places where they are not wanted. They are relatively proud and remain aloof. This has facilitated the effort of the American states in the Southwest to segregate the Mexicans. In one way the Mexicans surpass their American neighbors. They are far more artistic, especially musically, and they have a much better conception of the value and uses of leisure. The wise procedure in dealing with Mexican immigration would be to educate the Mexicans, particularly about sanitation and health, and then let the Americans profit by imitating the esthetic talents of their Mexican neighbors. Since the Mexicans are a cross between Europeans and the American Indians, there is no real ground for race prejudice against them, even when judged by conventional American notions of racial qualities.

Mexicans in American industry. The Mexicans have become important in agriculture in the Southwest and in California. They produce much cotton and citrus fruits in Texas and New Mexico and provide much of the agricultural labor in the beet-growing areas of the Southwest, California, Colorado, and Utah. They are very popular as seasonal agricultural laborers, since they work for relatively low wages and do not aspire to land ownership to any marked degree. Thus, they have checked the spread of Negro labor to the Southwest. The Mexicans are also extensively employed as railroad laborers in the latter region and on the Pacific coast. They are beginning to enter the heavy industries, some of them having already penetrated as far east as the steel mills of Pennsylvania. The intense demand for manpower during the Second World War still further encouraged Mexican immigration and many Mexicans entered war industries, especially in the Southwest and on the Pacific Coast, and some permeated even to the Middle West. The concentration of Mexicans in cities such as Los Angeles during the war led to tension and riots, notably the so-called zoot-suit escapades.

The relations of native whites with Mexicans is bound to be an increasingly important item in our minority problems. The Mexicans are already numerous and the increased demands for manpower associated with the peacetime draft of native civilians and the tremendous program of armament expansion are bound to bring more of them into this country. The Mexican birth rate—the highest in Latin America—will produce greater pressure for emigration to the United States. In some single counties in the Southwest where the Mexican population is most dense there are over 10,000 Mexicans. Moreover, the birth rate of Mexican immigrants is the highest of any group in our country.

THE NEGRO PROBLEM IN THE UNITED STATES

Origins of the American Negro problem. Of all the problems of race contacts in the United States, the Negro problem has possessed the outstanding historic significance. It is also oldest in point of time, excepting only white contacts with the American Indians. The first Negro slaves were brought to the Spanish colonies in the sixteenth century. The first importation of Negroes to the English colonies on the mainland came when some twenty were deposited in Jamestown in 1619.

At first there was no great demand for slaves, and it was not until the end of the seventeenth century that they became numerous in the English colonies. It is estimated that the British brought over altogether about two million Negroes to the English settlements in the West Indies, the Bermudas, the Bahamas, and the mainland during the colonial period. In 1770, more than half the population of South Carolina was Negro, and half the population of Virginia was Negro. Even in New York state, a seventh of the population was composed of Negro slaves. It is estimated that Negroes constituted a fifth of the entire population of the country on the eve of the American Revolution.

The question of the importation of slaves came before the Constitutional Convention of 1787. It was provided that the slave trade should not be interfered with until 1808, when it should terminate entirely. There was, however, much smuggling of Negroes into the country between 1808, when the Constitution prohibited their importation, and the Civil War. The invention of the cotton gin in 1793, and the enormous stimulation of cotton culture which it produced, created an unprecedented demand for Negro slave labor. This demand stimulated the smuggling of slaves after 1808. Even more important in the growth of slavery was the development of systematic breeding of slaves in the southern states. Most of the slave breeding was carried on in Virginia, Kentucky, Tennessee, and Maryland, which supplied not only their own needs but, in part, those of the deeper South.

Treatment of Negro slaves. There has been much controversy as to the economic and social condition of the Negro slaves in the South. Their treatment differed with region and occupation. They were best treated in domestic service and in the older and eastern portions of the South, and most harshly in the newly opened cotton areas of the deep South and Southwest. On the whole, it is probably safe to say that they were materially as well off as the unskilled workers in the new northern factories. Their livelihood was assured by their owners as the result of sheer self-interest on the part of the latter. Against this may be set off their legal servitude and the breaking up of Negro families.

Arguments in behalf of slavery. Since most Southerners were convinced that large-scale cotton production was impossible without Negro slave labor, slavery came to be regarded as absolutely indispensable to southern prosperity. It was argued that slavery was good from every point of view: (1) the Negroes benefited because they had been rescued from savagery and, unlike free laborers, they were sure of care in sickness and old age; (2) the masters benefited because they could direct Negro labor to an extent impossible with free workmen, and because, relieved of all manual toil, the slave owners could devote themselves to intellectual and cultural pursuits and to the duties of government; and (3) American society as a whole benefited because there was no unrest or real poverty among the slaves, and the extensive production of cotton not only brought prosperity to the southern United States but also supplied the world with an essential article of industry.

Arguments such as these, explicitly stated on many occasions, were probably believed by a majority of Southerners. Many who could not accept every one of them still defended the continuance of slavery because they felt that abolition would be disastrous to all concerned.

Disadvantages of a slave economy. There were some very serious drawbacks to the system of slavery, however, which received relatively little attention in either the North or the South. In the first place, slave labor was necessarily inefficient, ignorant, and wasteful. Consequently, while the North and West were progressing rapidly through the use of labor-saving machinery and improved methods of production, labor and industry in the South remained much as they always had been. Because slaves could be employed most effectively in cotton culture, plantation owners tended more and more to raise little except cotton. Since fertilizers were rarely used then, lands which were devoted to cotton year after year soon became exhausted. With an inefficient labor supply, if one were to prosper, it was imperative to have extremely fertile soil. Therefore, the more enterprising planters were constantly abandoning their lands and moving westward with their slaves, to take up, and in time to exhaust, fresh land. One result was that the land of the South, taken as a whole, produced much less than its full capacity. This situation also helps to explain the "land-hunger" of the South.

Again, at the best, only a small proportion of the white population of the South benefited by slavery; probably fewer than one man in twenty owned slaves. The nonslaveowning whites were looked down upon, and it was very difficult for them to rise in the social or economic scale. They had to eke out a miserable living as small farmers on poor land not good enough for plantations. The injury done to the great mass of Southerners, especially the white workers, by the institution of slavery was effectively explained in a book published in 1856 and entitled *The Impending Crisis,* by Hinton R. Helper, a "poor white" of North Carolina. Although it was composed chiefly of statistics, its appearance created an explosion of wrath in the South; postmasters refused to deliver it, and all copies that could be found were burned. There are many who believe that it alarmed the slaveowners even more than did *Uncle Tom's Cabin.*

Notwithstanding an occasional bitter critic like Helper, the great bulk of the "poor whites" defended slavery. For one thing, they believed that cotton culture, and therefore southern prosperity, depended upon it. For another thing, nearly all southern politicians, and most of the editors, teachers, and ministers—the groups that have the most influence in forming public opinion—were of the slaveowning class or dependent upon it, and they had convinced the population as a whole that slavery was a necessary and beneficent institution.

Sane attitude towards slavery and the Civil War. We have now reached a period in American history when both Northerners and Southerners should be able to discuss slavery and the Civil War in detached and judicious fashion. Most educated Southerners readily admit today that slavery was an undesirable social and economic system, which was seriously undermining the prosperity and well-being of the South long before the Civil War. Sane Northerners are equally willing to concede that abolitionism was an ill-chosen method of proceeding against slavery. Enlightened Northerners and Southerners alike admit that the Civil War was a tragic mistake, for which both the North and South must share the responsibility.

The freeing of the slaves, as the result of the Emancipation Proclamation (1863) and the Thirteenth Amendment (1865), threw upon the country the burden of taking care of slightly over 4 million Negroes. The slave system was at an end, and some new social order had to be devised to adjust the Negroes to a life of freedom.

Race crossing and the future of the Negro race. In considering the problems raised by the Negro population in the United States, we may first consider certain physical issues, particularly those related to race crossing, amalgamation of the two races, and the prospect of breeding out the Negro race through mixture with whites.

Although the interbreeding of whites and Negroes has never been approved in an institutional sense by the white population, such race crossing has been going on in an informal way ever since the first Negroes came to the country. The extent can only be guessed at, though the figures as to the number of Mulattoes in the total Negro population throws some light on the general situation. In 1910 it was estimated that, in the country as a whole, Mulattoes (2,050,000 in number) constituted 20.9 per cent of the total Negro population. The fact that this percentage had dropped to 15.9 in 1920, with 1,660,000 Mulattoes, would seem to indicate that this race crossing is on the decline. Students have attributed this trend to the improved education and increased race pride of the Negroes. It may also have been affected somewhat by the increased freedom of sex relations among whites in this same period, thus making it less necessary for white males to have recourse to Negro females. The whole problem of Mulattoes is very uncertain, due to the inability of census enumerators to make a scientific discrimination between Negroes and Mulattoes. Mulattoes were not enumerated in the census in 1930, 1940, or 1950.

There was long a great amount of prejudice on the part of some groups against Mulattoes. It was alleged that they were physically feeble, low in fertility, and likely to be morally degenerate. Our review of the scientific evidence on race mixture in the preceding chapter has shown that such notions have no scientific foundation whatever. The Mulattoes have exhibited as satisfactory physical and mental qualities as could be expected from their parentage. If a low-grade white crosses with a low-grade Negro, one could expect only low-grade offspring as a rule. On the other hand, the mating of high-grade whites and Negroes will normally produce high-grade Mulattoes. Mulattoes who are offspring of normal parents tend to be physically harmonious and well formed. Any disadvantages which have surrounded American Mulattoes have been social and cultural rather than biological. It is a sufficient answer to the charge of Mulatto inferiority to point to the fact that a disproportionate number of the Negroes distinguished in intellectual and cultural pursuits in this country have been Mulattoes. This may be accounted for in part by the fact that the white parentage involved was of an unusually high character, and it may be due as well to the fact that better educational opportunities and a cordial acceptance by whites are more accessible to Mulattoes. Whatever the cause, it is obvious that Mulattoes cannot be regarded from any standpoint as an inferior group.

The fact that racial crossing between whites and Negroes may be definitely on the wane and may decline more sharply in future generations thoroughly explodes the popular illusion that the Negroes will ultimately disappear because of absorption into the white population. Indeed, Warren S. Thompson believes that the Negro population in the United States is likely to grow darker in the future. There will be fewer Mulattoes, and, as they intermingle and cross more and more with whites, they will tend to move out of the Negro population altogether. Moreover, it is in the southern areas where there are the fewest Mulattoes, namely in the rural areas of the black belt, that the pure black Negroes are increasing most rapidly today. This leads Thompson to conclude that:

Since there is some reason to think that there is less racial mixture going on now than at any time since the Negro was first introduced to this country and since the southern Negro is increasing faster than his whiter northern cousin, it would not be at all surprising if our Negroes were to show an increasing darkness of color. The passing into the white population of the near-whites would also aid in producing this change and we may witness the seeming paradox of a race growing steadily darker on the average at the same time that the number of its members having some white blood is increasing.[1]

A study of health conditions among the Negroes, as well as the statistics of population growth among the Negro population, also disposes of a frequently held conviction that the Negro problem will disappear in time, as the result of the fact that the Negro element will gradually die off. This illusion has grown out of the observed fact that since 1860 the Negro population has increased far less rapidly than has the white. Those who have drawn from this fact the deduction that the Negroes are dying out have failed to take account of recent population trends among both whites and Negroes. The rapid growth of the white population was partly due to immigration, which is now of slight importance, and the rate of population growth among native whites is falling off in normal times. Even during the population spurt of the 1940's the Negro population is believed to have grown more rapidly than the white.

Growth of Negro population. The Negro population of the United States has more than trebled since emancipation. In 1860, there were 4,441,830 Negroes in the country; in 1940, the number had increased to 12,865,518; and by 1950 there were over 15,000,000. But the proportion of Negroes to the total population has fallen off considerably during the same period. In 1860, Negroes constituted 14.1 per cent of the population, in 1940, only 9.8 per cent, and in 1950, about 10.0 per cent. The Negro birth rate has been consistently higher than the white since 1860; in 1943 it was 24.1 as against 21.2 for whites. But the rate of population growth among Negroes until very recently has been lower than that of whites, because of the higher Negro death rate. The death rate for Negroes of all ages in 1943 was 12.18 compared with 10.7 for whites: the death rate of Negro infants is 63 per cent higher than that of white infants. Such serious forms of illness as tuberculosis, venereal diseases, kidney diseases, and pneumonia are especially frequent among Negroes. The life expectancy of Negroes in 1947 was 57 years, compared to 67.9 for whites.

Negro health problems. The high death rate and incidence of sickness among Negroes is due in part to the increased concentration of the Negro population in congested, substandard areas of northern cities, with bad living conditions, and in part to the notorious inferiority of medical care for Negroes. In 1948, there were only 3,800 Negro physicians (about 2 per cent of the total) in the United States, or one for every 3,777 Negroes, as contrasted with one doctor for every 750 persons in the whole population. In Mississippi, there is only one Negro physician to about 18,000 Negroes. There are only about 1,650 Negro dentists out of a total of some 75,000 American dentists. The hospital situation is even more

---

[1] W. S. Thompson, *Population Problems,* 2nd ed. New York: McGraw-Hill, 1935, p. 184.

deplorable. There are only 124 Negro hospitals, many of them substandard, with a total of only 20,800 beds, out of the total of 1,500,000 beds in the hospitals of the country. The outlook for any rapid improvement in Negro medical care is not good because of barriers to Negro medical education and interne training, and the increasing difficulty and expense of medical education.

Negro population shifts. The location of the Negro population has undergone considerable change since emancipation; most notably there has been a movement from the rural South to the industrial and urban North. In 1860, 92.2 per cent of all Negroes lived in the South, 7.7 per cent in the North, and 0.1 in the West. In 1940, only 77 per cent lived in the South; 21.7 per cent in the North, and 1.3 per cent in the West. The percentage of Negroes in the North and West has, of course, greatly increased since 1940. The main reasons for this shift of the Negro population have been the increasing difficulty of the growing Negro population in making a living on the farms of the South, the better economic opportunities in the industrial cities of the North, and the lesser social and legal disabilities of the Negro in the North.

Although there was a gradual drifting of Negroes northward from 1865 to 1916, the extensive Negro movement to the North has come since 1916, and in three major waves of migration: (1) in the years from 1916 to 1919, between 200,000 and 400,000 Negroes came North; (2) between 1921 and 1924, over 500,000 moved North; and (3) during the Second World War, perhaps as many as 1,500,000 migrated to the North and West. Stanley High has thus described the sources and destination of these Negro migrations:

There were three main streams in this movement. One came through the tobacco fields, rice swamps and sugar farms of the Eastern seaboard and headed straight for New York. Another arose in Mississippi, Alabama and Georgia, and ended, eventually, in Chicago. A third stream came out of Texas, passed through Arizona and Oklahoma, and led into St. Louis and Chicago.

The most notable fact about the third migration lay in the large number of Negroes who migrated to the Pacific coast.

In the first wave of migration, the Negroes were attracted mainly by war industry; in the second they were impelled by the bad farming conditions in the South and the postwar revival of industry in the North; and in the third by the manpower demands and higher wages in the northern armament industries. But there were other than economic attractions. The Negroes believed that by coming North they could enjoy more civil liberties, lessen social discrimination, and secure better educational opportunities for their children.

The significance of the extensive and continuing migration of Negroes from the South to the North and West has been variously appraised by students of the Negro problem. Jessie P. Guzman, editor of the *Negro Year Book,* summarizes the situation as follows: There has been a gain for the Negroes who have migrated. Despite difficulties in the way of obtaining decent housing and avoiding overcrowding, Negroes who have gone North and West have gained the civil liberties they seek, have earned more money, and have increased their independence and self-respect. The Negroes in the South have not been greatly affected by the migrations, though the latter may have slightly reduced the competitive struggle of southern Negroes for a living. The southern whites may have lost by the migrations through lessening the labor force and their purchasing power. The withdrawal of masses of Negroes from the South may lower the artistic and cultural level of that region. But the reduction of the Negro population may lessen apprehensiveness on the part of southern whites and lead to a more liberal attitude toward the Negroes who remain there. At any rate, if the South wishes to check Negro migrations, it will have to provide better economic opportunities, higher living standards, and a greater extension of civil liberties.

Increasing urban concentration of Negroes. Since the great majority of Negroes who have come to the North and West have settled in cities, this northward migration has also produced a marked dislocation of the Negro population in respect to rural and urban distribution. In 1860, not over 10 per cent of Negroes lived in cities; by 1949, well over 50 per cent were city dwellers. In 1940, 44.7 per cent of Negroes who lived in the South still dwelt on farms, but over 90 per cent of those in the North and West lived in cities.

Almost invariably, Negroes have fared worse than whites in housing conditions and sanitation in both southern and northern cities, with the resulting greater amount of Negro sickness and the higher Negro death rate previously mentioned. Further, the marked growth in the number of Negroes in cities inevitably increased the moral, cultural, economic, and political problems connected with city living in general, intensified for Negroes by the adverse living conditions forced upon them. Stanley High thus describes the economic, social, and hygienic aftermath of Negro migration and urbanization in northern centers of population:

In the matter of food, fuel and shelter, life was generally worse, by a good deal, than it had been in the South. This was particularly true of shelter. Even before the migration, the Black Belt of the average Northern city was a down-at-heels area which had probably been occupied by low-income foreign groups before the Negroes took it over. Many buildings had already been condemned and there was no new construction. The new population found that the only areas into which it could move were already overcrowded and that the number of available living quarters was steadily declining. The congestion that resulted was—and, especially in New York and Chicago, still is—worse than the worst of tenement districts.

To make matters worse, white tenement owners—known to the Negroes as "rent hogs"—took immediate advantage of the situation. They still take advantage of it. There is, so far as I know, no Northern city in which the Negroes are not obliged to pay considerably more for decidedly poorer quarters than any other section of the population. Negro tenants in Chicago, for example, pay from eight to twenty dollars per month for the same room for which the previous white tenants had paid from four to five dollars. In New York, apartments which were rented to whites for $55.00 a month were rented to Negroes for $110. In most cities, when the Negroes take a street, rents are raised from 10 to 40 per cent. In consequence, a large number of Negro families are obliged to lay out half or more of their entire monthly incomes to pay for what passes as a place to live.

This largely accounts for the fact that, day and night, Sunday and holidays, the streets of the Black Belt are always filled with people. Detroit's Paradise Valley, for example, is as much awake at two in the morning as at high noon—perhaps even more so. Harlem hardly ever starts dancing before eleven o'clock at night, and no one with any sense of timing and the proprieties would think of showing up at a party before midnight. In other words, in the average Negro neighborhood, no one wants to go home. And that, in turn, is, in part at least, because of the kind of homes so many Negroes have to go to. The streets, the pool and dance halls, the lodge rooms and all manner of less legitimate hangouts are far more cheerful.

But this overcrowding has had other more disastrous consequences. Tuberculosis among Negro children under five years of age is double that of white children; for those between five and nine, it is four times as great; and from ten to nineteen, it is five times as great as that of whites. In Chicago, recently, one third of the female occupants of the jails were Negroes. In New York, the number of arrests of Negroes in proportion to population has run as much as five times ahead of that for whites.[2]

The Negroes in agriculture. The most notable development in the economic life of Negroes since emancipation has been the relative decline in the number engaged in agriculture and the increase in the number employed in various industrial pursuits. In 1860, the overwhelming majority of Negroes in the South were farm laborers under the slavery system. In 1940, only 33.2 per cent of all employed Negroes were engaged in agriculture. But the preponderance of agricultural laborers among the Negroes who are still engaged in farming pursuits has continued to our own day. In 1890, there were 1,105,728 Negro farm laborers, or some 64 per cent of all Negroes employed in agriculture. In 1940, the number of Negro farm laborers in the South had dropped to 468,126, but they still greatly outnumbered any other Negro agricultural group: owners and managers, 173,628; cash tenants, 64,684; other tenants (except sharecroppers), 142,836; and sharecroppers, 299,118. The pay of Negro agricultural laborers has remained relatively low; in 1945, the average weekly income of an employed Negro farm laborer was $8.60, and his average annual income, $224.

Between 1890 and 1910, the level of Negro prosperity in southern agriculture—95 per cent of all Negro agriculture is carried on in 16 southern states—improved somewhat, and by 1910 there were 218,972 Negro farm owners who owned some 12,847,348 acres of land valued at $620,587,241. After 1910, this development of Negro farm ownership was checked, chiefly by the ravages of the boll weevil, the depression of southern agriculture, and the general depression of the country after 1929. The depression of Negro agriculture, reflected in the decrease in Negro farm owners who owned some 12,847,348 acres of land valued at a larger proportion of Negro farmers in the tenant group, especially the sharecropper group. In 1910, Negro cash tenants constituted about one-half of the total tenant group; by 1940, they made up only a little over one-sixth of the tenants. In 1940, 74.5 per cent of all Negro farmers, exclusive of farm laborers, were tenant farmers. The lowest of these

---

[2] Stanley High, "Black Omens," *Saturday Evening Post*, May 21, 1938, pp. 7, 64.

Negro farm tenants in income and economic well-being, as well as by far the largest element in the tenant group, are the some 300,000 share-croppers (in 1940), who barely live on a subsistence level.

Although the New Deal farm legislation provided some benefits to Negro farmers and although the increased demand and prices for farm products since Pearl Harbor also helped them out, neither or both sufficed to check the decline in Negro agriculture; it is estimated that over a million Negroes left southern farms between 1940 and 1948. The median money income of the rural non-white family in the United States in 1945 was $559, and the figure for the southern Negro farm family was even lower. On the other hand, the median income of the urban non-white family was $2,052 for the country as a whole. This helps to explain the vast migration from southern Negro farms to urban areas during the 1940's.

Even the comparatively prosperous Negro farm owners operate under distinct disadvantages. The Negro farm units are usually of inferior fertility and too small acreage to permit the use of the most efficient agricultural methods. There is too much concentration on a limited number of crops, sometimes on one crop. And few Negroes are able to purchase the best and latest farm equipment. The obstacles to efficient farming by the poorer farm owners and farm tenants are, naturally, greater, and the efficiency of these groups is lower. With the increased mechanization of southern farming, the outlook for the Negro farmers is even less promising than their past experience.

The main group of Negro farmers who have improved their condition recently are the handful—some 37,763 families in 1944—who have been aided by the Rural Rehabilitation Program of the Federal Farm Administration. A sampling of these Negro farmers showed that they had an average annual farm income of $1,006; small indeed, but a great gain over their previous near-destitute condition.

Negroes enter American manufacturing industry. As Negroes, slowly at first, turned from farms to other forms of industrial employment, they began, chiefly after 1890, to find employment in southern labor camps, cotton factories, tobacco factories, and steel mills. They were mainly employed at heavy labor and unskilled tasks, receiving very low wages, usually not over 75¢ to $1.50 a day even in steel mills, around 1900. In the tobacco factories, their wages ran from 50¢ to $1 per day. It was difficult for Negroes to compete for employment and wages with the numerous southern poor whites in the rising cotton factories of the new South. After 1914, with the increased demand for labor in the North, Negroes were able to make their way more generally into many forms of factory employment and other types of industrial occupations.

The fact that millions of Negroes have shifted from farming to industry and from the rural South to the industrial and urban South and North has greatly modified the economic picture of Negro life. But most Negroes still live in the South and are concentrated in agriculture and domestic service. A disproportionate number of employed Negroes still remain domestic servants. In 1940, Negro men made up only 10.3 per cent of the total male working population but they constituted 60.2 per cent of all males in domestic service, 21 per cent of all urban laborers, and also 21 per cent of all farm laborers and foremen. Farmers, farm laborers, and other laborers accounted for some 62.2 per cent of all employed Negro men, but for only 28.5 per cent of all employed white men. Negro women, who made up 18.9 per cent of the total female working population, provided 46.6 per cent of all female domestic servants. The following table from the *Negro Year Book* gives the distribution of Negro workers, according to industrial groups in 1940:

MAJOR INDUSTRY GROUP OF EMPLOYED NEGROES 14 YEARS OLD AND OVER (EXCEPT ON PUBLIC EMERGENCY WORK) BY SEX, FOR THE UNITED STATES, 1940

Employment Status and Major Industry	Total	Male	Female	PER CENT DISTRIBUTION Total	Male	Female
Employed (except on emergency work)	4,479,068	2,936,795	1,542,273	100.0	100.0	100.0
Agriculture, forestry and fishery	1,484,914	1,238,301	246,613	33.2	42.2	16.0
Mining	52,981	52,754	227	1.2	1.8	...
Construction	142,419	141,261	1,158	3.2	4.8	0.1
Manufacturing	515,514	467,286	48,228	11.5	15.9	3.1
Transportation, communication and other public utilities	200,191	196,762	3,429	4.5	6.7	0.2
Wholesale and retail trade	348,760	286,930	61,830	7.8	9.8	4.0
Finance, insurance, and real estate	68,117	56,309	11,808	1.5	1.9	0.8
Business and repair services	48,863	47,783	1,080	1.1	1.6	0.1
Personal services	1,292,524	243,700	1,048,824	28.9	8.3	68.0
Amusement, recreation, and related services	32,187	27,516	4,671	0.7	0.9	0.3
Professional and related services	176,685	84,014	92,671	3.9	2.9	6.0
Government	56,921	48,632	8,289	1.3	1.7	0.5
Industry not reported	58,992	45,547	13,445	1.3	1.6	0.9

Despite the increasing diversification of Negro industrial employment, the great majority of Negro workers have remained unskilled laborers. In 1940, 15.6 per cent of all employed white men were skilled laborers, but only 4.4 per cent of employed Negroes were so rated. Some 30 per cent of employed white men were engaged in professional, proprietary, managerial, clerical, and sales occupations that embraced only 5 per cent of employed Negroes.

The wages and salaries of Negro workers have usually, with only the few exceptions that prove the rule, been lower than those received by employed whites. This has been true even when Negroes and whites performed the same tasks requiring the same skills. In a Chicago foundry, in 1927, the average weekly wage of white laborers was $37 per week, that of Negroes $29. In the clothing industry in Chicago at the same period, white workers were paid $37.40 per week, and Negroes $18 to $25 for the same type work. A study of the median wages of Negro women in 1929 in fifteen states showed that in only two of the states were the median weekly earnings as high as $9, while in four states they were below $6. These examples could be multiplied, but they sufficiently reveal the general situation before the Federal wage legislation of 1938 and thereafter.

Since Negroes have had to work to survive, discriminatory wage policies were easy to enforce; one reason why Negroes could not obtain higher wages was that they found it difficult to get into labor unions to secure the prevailing union wages. The American Federation of Labor, the only strong labor organization until the Congress of Industrial Organizations was formed in 1935, was long opposed to admitting Negroes to membership.

Moreover, the AFL is a craft organization made up mainly of skilled workers, and there were few Negro skilled laborers, even if the AFL had been willing to admit them. The new CIO, by admitting unskilled laborers, including Negroes, compelled the AFL to liberalize its policies.

This new development in union policy, along with growth in the number of Negro industrial laborers, has led to a great increase in the unionization of Negro workers. By the year 1946, the number of gainfully employed Negroes reached 5,500,000 and the Negroes in labor unions numbered about 750,000, as compared with only about 100,000 in 1930. Perhaps the most successful Negro union has been the Brotherhood of Sleeping Car Porters, organized by A. Philip Randolph. After this union was recognized by the Pullman Company in 1937, hours of labor were reduced and pay increases totaling $1,250,000 per year were granted.

Other factors that have helped to raise the wage level of Negro workers have been the Wage-Hour Law of 1938, which reduced discrimination against Negro workers in industries engaged in interstate commerce, and the Fair Employment Practices Laws, outlawing wage discrimination because of race. Adequate laws, along with some enforcement machinery, have been passed by Connecticut, Massachusetts, Rhode Island, New York, New Jersey, New Mexico, Oregon and Washington. Discrimination is prohibited on public works in California, Minnesota, Nebraska, Kansas, Illinois, Indiana, and Pennsylvania. A weak FEPC bill was passed by the House of Representatives in February, 1950, but it did not get through the Senate.

Despite all these improvements since the turn of the century, Negroes have a long way to go to gain economic equality with whites; they will require more complete unionization, and they will have to be protected by a greater number of state laws—or a Federal law—prohibiting wage discrimination solely on the basis of race. Establishing anything like economic equality with whites will also involve increasing the number of Negroes in skilled trades and in professional and clerical work. The chief gain here in recent years has been the growth of the relative number of Negro employees in the Federal government. A careful check made in 1944 revealed the fact that the 300,000 Negroes made up about 12 per cent of all Federal employees in that year, as compared with 9.8 per cent in 1938.

Negroes in American business. Some Negro leaders, especially those in the National Urban League and the National Negro Business League, have suggested that one solution of the Negro problem is to build up a strong Negro middle class of bourgeois businessmen. Some progress has been made along this line. It is estimated that there are over 800,000 Negroes now engaged in some form of business activity. There are today something over 80,000 Negro business establishments, most of them relatively small. The majority are grocery stores, cleaning shops, restaurants, night clubs, beauty parlors, barber shops, and funeral parlors, enterprises in which there is the greatest amount of racial discrimination against Negroes in establishments conducted by whites. These Negro economic activities are conducted mainly for Negroes, though the restaurants have considerable patronage from the whites, as do also the increasing number of Negro night clubs.

The most important Negro ventures in larger business and financial operations are in insurance, banking, department stores, and real estate investment, with insurance heading the list. These Negro business and financial enterprises are relatively shaky because they are frequently loosely organized and financed and they cannot rely upon effective support from the whites who control the capital of the country. The failures of Negro banks have been even more striking and frequent than the scandalous failures since 1920 among the white banks, though Negroes have demonstrated ability to operate sound and solvent banks.

The depression after 1929 was especially disastrous to Negro business and financial activity, wiping out almost overnight even the wealthy Chicago Negro banker, Anthony Overton, the most conspicuous finance capitalist thus far produced by the Negro race. The pump-priming and relief policies of the New Deal helped to restore the lost business of the Negro establishments, and the increased prosperity of the Second World War period was even more effective, though even at the close of the war Negro business had not regained the 1929 levels.

In 1945, it was reported that there were 205 Negro insurance companies doing business, 46 of them members of the National Negro Insurance Association. These 46 had $57,000,000 in assets, 3,695,000 policy holders, $630,000,000 worth of insurance in force, and $33,000,000 in annual income from premiums. There were 111 Negro banks in 1943, with combined resources of $15,176,000, most of it in government war securities. Deposits amounted to about $14,000,000. There were 91 Negro credit unions in 1945, doing as well as comparable white organizations. In 1939, there were 29,827 Negro retail stores, with combined sales of $71,466,000. This was a marked gain over the figure for 1935. But the blow dealt to Negro business by the depression is evident from the fact that the sales of Negro stores in 1929 amounted to $98,603,000, some 27.5 per cent more than the 1939 sales.

Some students of the Negro problem are rather pessimistic about the future development of Negro business and banking enterprises because of the special handicaps under which they have to operate. Sterling D. Spero and Abram L. Harris conclude that "because of these serious obstacles, Negro business affords no real foundation for the growth of a black middle class." Nevertheless, Negro business has provided goods and services for many thousands of Negroes who would have found it more difficult to secure these from white enterprises.

Negro living conditions. The living conditions and habitations of the great majority of American Negroes are substandard. Only the better class of Negro farm owners in the South and the more prosperous Negro business and professional men live under desirable physical conditions. Often, not even the relatively highly paid skilled Negro laborers can secure decent habitations, though they may have the money to pay the

COURTESY FEDERAL PUBLIC HOUSING AUTHORITY.

Beecher Terrace, Louisville, Ky., before.

high rentals required. The Negroes who live under the worst conditions are the sharecroppers in the shacks of the South and the unskilled Negro workers who are herded in tenements in the slum areas of the industrial cities of both the North and the South.

Since a Federal report before the Second World War showed that about 60 per cent of all urban dwellings are substandard, and since Negroes usually get the worst of these substandard habitations, the bad conditions under which they live in the cities today can easily be pictured. Listed as overcrowded in 1940 were only 8 per cent of urban dwellings for whites as against 25 per cent of those occupied by Negroes. This was a very modest estimate. Negro tenements are notoriously in a state of disrepair and lacking in conveniences, especially modern plumbing. But, except when restrained by rent ceilings, the so-called rent-hogs among the landlords unmercifully gouge the Negroes by charging them high rents for these miserable living quarters. Such substandard living quarters naturally breed disease and are one of the causes of the high sickness and death rate among Negroes; they also increase immorality and delinquency, because the unattractive living conditions drive Negroes out of their homes into the street, dives, and gambling joints. There are relatively few home owners among urban Negroes, about one-third as many per capita as among whites.

COURTESY FEDERAL PUBLIC HOUSING AUTHORITY.

Beecher Terrace, Louisville, Ky., after. These two photographs show improvements in Negro Housing conditions. Unfortunately, there are too few instances of such progress.

These conditions existed before Pearl Harbor, and the bad situation was greatly intensified by the crowding of many more Negroes into urban centers to take part in war industries. The acute housing shortage for all urban dwellers during and since the war has hit Negroes especially severely. Overcrowding has increased, the dilapidation of unrepaired buildings has grown apace, and new building comes last in Negro districts. The gist of the whole matter of Negro housing has been well summarized in the *Negro Year Book* (1947):

Informed observation and available facts indicate that the vast majority of Negroes and other non-whites live in substandard housing and in slum or blighted areas, and they are bound to such housing neighborhoods by reason of their income limitations, resulting from racially restricted job opportunities, and imposed residential segregation reinforced by racial restrictive covenants, traditions, or law.

There is little prospect for any great immediate improvement in Negro living conditions. Negro agriculture in the South is depressed and likely to become more so. The new urban housing program for both whites and Negroes is pathetically inadequate, and improvement will come most slowly in Negro quarters. Only 19 per cent of the low-rent units of the Federal Public Housing Authority, or some 145,584 units, were occupied by or planned for Negroes in 1945. This is a mere drop in the bucket. The struggle to break down restrictive covenants, if successful, may minister to Negro pride, but it will do little for a long time to provide better habitations for Negroes. The main improvement in the Negro housing situation during the war decade was the increase in the number of urban Negro home owners, which rose from 24 per cent to 34 per cent. This was made possible by greater earning power during the war, the savings and government grants of service men, and increased government loans.

The Negro in American politics. One of the most bitterly disputed issues in the status and activities of Negroes in American political life is the right of the Negro to vote in primaries and elections. The Fifteenth Amendment (1870) forbids suffrage discrimination on the basis of race, and the Fourteenth Amendment (1868) orders that any such limitation of the right to vote shall be penalized by reducing the representation of the offending state in Congress to a corresponding extent.

It is now rather generally admitted by students of the problem that it was a mistake to give the Negroes the right to vote immediately after emancipation, without any preparation for the duties of citizenship. At any rate, Negroes not only exercised the right to vote after 1865, but for a time participated prominently in the government of the South under the direction of northern carpetbaggers and the protection of northern armies. White Southerners determined to prevent the recurrence of this situation. By various devices they have since made every effort to keep Negroes from the polls.

When the whites recovered control in the South, they imposed very high and numerous qualifications for all voters, both white and black. This device, however, excluded many southern whites. The dilemma was solved by the so-called "grandfather clause," invented by Louisiana in 1898, which provided that those who were excluded by existing qualifications could, nevertheless, vote if their male ancestors had been able to vote before 1867. This ruse continued the exclusion of Negroes but removed the barriers to most white voting.

When the Supreme Court declared the grandfather clause unconstitutional in 1913, other devices were found to keep the Negroes from voting. One such device is to set up tests and qualifications for registering voters that will operate to the disadvantage of Negroes. Another much debated method of preventing or discouraging Negroes from voting is the poll tax or head tax, which Negroes are often unable to pay or neglect to pay. Many efforts have been made to pass Federal legislation outlawing the poll tax, but they have all been blocked by filibustering southern Congressmen. Interestingly enough, it has been estimated that the poll tax legally disqualifies more than twice as many whites as Negroes—about

7 million whites to 3 million Negroes. But the fact that whites have not paid their poll tax is often overlooked at the polls.

Another way of nullifying the political power of southern Negroes has been to keep them away from the primaries, since primaries are far more important than elections in most southern states, which are usually safely Democrat. Though Negroes make up about 47 per cent of all persons of voting age in Mississippi, it is estimated that only between 1,000 and 3,000 Negroes voted in the primary elections in that state in July, 1942. Some states, including Texas, made the primaries a sort of "association" or "club" and denied membership to Negroes. The United States Supreme Court, in the Louisiana primary case in 1941 and the Texas primary case in 1944, ruled that primaries are an integral part of the election procedure and declared the club stratagem unconstitutional. Following these decisions, some other southern states dropped their restrictions on Negroes at primaries. An important legal victory was won in South Carolina in 1947, when Federal Judge J. Waties Waring revealed great personal courage in ruling that Negroes must be given the full right to vote in South Carolina primaries. His decision was upheld by the Circuit Court of Appeals in 1949. South Carolina has, however, been able to continue in part Negro exclusion or intimidation by refusing to adopt the secret ballot.

These court decisions and other liberal trends in the South led to a marked increase in the number of qualified Negro voters in the South. The following table gives the gains from 1940 to 1947 in twelve southern states, and there has been a considerable increase in some of these states since 1947, notably in Alabama and South Carolina:

States	1940	1947
Alabama	2,000	6,000
Arkansas	4,000	47,000
Florida	18,000	49,000
Georgia	20,000	125,000
Louisiana	2,000	10,000
Mississippi	2,000	5,000
North Carolina	35,000	75,000
Oklahoma	60,000	50,000
South Carolina	3,000	50,000
Tennessee	20,000	80,000
Texas	30,000	100,000
Virginia	15,000	48,000

Despite these legal gains in clearing the way for Negro suffrage, Negro leaders contend that the great majority of southern Negroes are still denied the right to vote. It is worth remembering, however, that the non-southern portions of the country as well as the South have violated the Constitution. The South has defied the Fifteenth Amendment, outlawing discrimination, but the non-southern majority in Congress has ignored the mandate of the Fourteenth Amendment to penalize such discrimination by reducing the congressional representation of offending states.

Since the Republican party was the party that carried through Negro emancipation, southern Negroes long remained loyal to the Republicans, even if they could not cast many votes for Republican candidates. Incidentally, this led to some abuses in selecting Republican delegates from the South to the national nominating conventions. In the last 25 years, following the migration of so many Negroes to northern industrial cities, there has been a slackening of the bonds attaching the Negroes to the Republican party. Especially during the New Deal era did Negroes turn to the Democrats, who passed much legislation favorable to their race. Many southern Negroes, perhaps less socially and economically alert than those in the North, may still cling to Republican leadership, but Negroes in the northern cities incline to be bi-partisan, giving their support to whichever party promises the most favorable legislation to Negroes.

At present, Negroes thus tend to pursue a program of political expediency in party support, backing in any election the party most likely to promote Negro interests. Negroes of voting age number approximately 7,500,000, with about 3,000,000 eligible to vote. About half of the eligibles are in northern states. The Negro vote is powerful out of all proportion to its numerical proportion because the active and effective Negro voters are concentrated in close northern states with a large electoral vote. It has been estimated that the eligible Negro vote in New York in 1950 was 950,000; in Pennsylvania, 470,000; in Illinois, 350,000; in Ohio, 330,000; in California, 310,000; in Michigan, 230,000; and in Missouri, 205,000. Negroes hold a potential balance of power in 17 states with some 281 electoral votes. Indeed, some expert political observers have contended that President Truman may have owed his election in 1948 to the Negro vote. They point out that he won by carrying Ohio, Illinois, and California. In these states most of the Negro vote went for Truman and in each instance was considerably larger than the Truman majority. The Negro question, at least temporarily, split the Democratic party in 1948, the Truman following in the party sponsoring a civil rights plank which was directly opposed to the traditional southern policies of states rights and the subordination of the Negro.

Civil rights for Negroes. The question of conferring full civil rights on Negroes and all other racial minorities is now prominently before the country and has precipitated a national crisis. Civil rights problems are intimately related to the issue of the Negro in politics, for the right to vote is a major civil right. The civil rights controversy has come to a head primarily for three reasons: (1) the favorable attitude of the Roosevelt New Deal administration to increased civil rights for Negroes and the personal encouragement given by Mrs. Roosevelt to the Negroes to battle for their civil liberties; (2) the important part taken by Negroes in the Second World War: some 700,000 Negroes were in the army on V-J Day, and 167,000 in the navy, and about 3 million Negroes took some part in wartime industry; and (3) the appeal of the Truman administration to the political support of racial minorities, and its proposal that Federal legislation confer full civil rights on Negroes and other racial minorities.

We have already referred to the abuses that arose under the Negro-carpetbagger rule in the South following the Civil War. This provoked a white defense reaction in the form of the Ku Klux Klan and the passage by southern states of the so-called Black Codes, which rigorously restricted Negroes in their civil liberties and social privileges. Congress responded, in 1875, with the Civil Rights Act, designed to guarantee Negroes equal privileges in hotels, theatres, and conveyances. This law was set aside by the Supreme Court in 1883.

Today, restrictive laws and ordinances in the South, commonly known as "Jim Crow" regulations, usually compel Negroes to use a separate portion of railroad stations, to occupy special coaches on railroad trains and separate sections of street cars and buses, to live in segregated areas of cities, and to have separate schools for Negro children.

The National Association for the Advancement of Colored People was founded in 1909 by Morefield Storey, an eminent Boston lawyer, and other white and Negro leaders who were interested in eliminating the civil disabilities of Negroes. Its leading figure down to 1931 was W. E. B. Du Bois. Since 1931 it has been led by Walter F. White. The Association has devoted itself particularly to the struggle to obtain civil equality for Negroes, but not much progress was made until late New Deal days. In recent years there have been a number of legal victories in the courts, which have at least extended the legal basis of Negro civil liberties, whatever the failure to realize them as yet.

In the Mitchell case, in 1941, the Supreme Court ruled that railroads must provide accommodations for Negro passengers equal to those supplied for whites. In several cases in state and lower Federal courts, it has been ruled that Negroes must be served in dining cars in regular order and not restricted to service on the "last call." In 1950, in the Henderson case, the Supreme Court ruled that Negroes cannot be legally compelled to eat in dining cars at tables restricted to Negroes. In 1946, a Supreme Court ruling that it is illegal to segregate Negro passengers in buses crossing state lines affected state laws in some ten states requiring such segregation.

Equal rights for Negroes in state-supported universities have been upheld by the Supreme Court. In the Gaines case in Missouri, in 1938, the Supreme Court held that students could not legally be barred from admission because of race and color and ordered that equal educational facilities must be provided for Negroes. In 1950, in the McLaurin case in Oklahoma, the Supreme Court decided that it is illegal to compel Negro students to sit apart from white students in classes, the library, or the university cafeteria. In the Sipuel case in Oklahoma, in 1947, the Supreme Court ordered the state of Oklahoma to provide legal education for a Negro girl equal to that given white law students.

During the summer and autumn of 1950, a number of court decisions laid the legal basis for the elimination of segregation in southern institutions of higher education. In June, 1950, in the Sweatt case in Texas, the Supreme Court ruled that students cannot be limited to Negro law schools, on the ground that the latter are not equal in educational facilities to law schools for white students. In Missouri, in July, 1950, the Federal court, following the same line of reasoning, ordered the University of Missouri to open its graduate schools to Negro students. In September, 1950, in the Swanson case, the Federal court in Virginia directed the University of Virginia to cease excluding students from its Law School because of race or color. In October, 1950, the Attorney-General of Tennessee rendered the opinion that the University of Tennessee could not bar students because of race or color. On the other hand, Federal Judge J. J. Hayes ruled that the Law School of the North Carolina College for Negroes provided as good facilities as the University of North Carolina Law School and that the latter could continue to bar Negroes if it wished to do so. A law was passed in New York State, in 1948, outlawing discrimination in university admissions on the basis of race, color, or creed.

In the Alston case, the Supreme Court upheld an earlier (1940) decision by a lower Federal Court ordering that Negro teachers must be paid as well as white teachers for comparable work. A number of instances in which Negro pupils were denied admission to northern public schools have been taken to the courts, and, in some instances, the Negroes have won.

Outside the field of education, pressure has been put on the upholders of Negro segregation by such groups as the Actors' Equity Association, which voted to refuse to put on plays in cities that segregated or excluded Negroes.

Some gains were made by Negroes in the armed services. On July 8, 1944, the army was ordered to abolish segregation of Negroes in army recreational and transportation facilities. Limited experimentation was carried on in 1945 in mixing Negroes and whites in replacement units in combat. When the peacetime draft was being debated in 1948, Negro leaders demanded the abolition of all racial segregation in the armed forces. Considerable progress has been made along this line recently. There is no formal segregation in the armed forces. President Truman ordered it abolished in July, 1948. Army and navy schools are now open to Negroes, Negroes may be promoted to the higher grades in the military forces, and they may be assigned to any army unit. There is no segregation in military service and housing facilities.

Efforts to give Negroes equal rights in urban residence have of late centered mainly on the attempt to outlaw restrictive covenants, namely, agreements by property owners to refuse to sell, lease, or rent their property to Negroes or to permit any Negro occupancy. Several state and lesser Federal courts have ruled that such covenants are illegal. But the final settlement of the matter depends on the working out of a 1948 ruling by the Supreme Court, that, although restrictive covenants are not unconstitutional, neither Federal nor state courts have any right to enforce them. A study of segregation in housing made by Alexander L. Crosby and Marion Palfi during 1950 revealed the fact that the segregation of Negroes in urban housing is more rigorous and complete in some northern cities like Chicago, New York and Detroit than in most southern cities. The trend away from segregation is most notable in Los Angeles and Denver. Efforts have been made to secure Negro admission to good northern hotels, and in the Bowman case in New York City, in 1944, the state court upheld the Negro complainant.

As we have already stated, the whole civil rights issue for Negroes and all other racial minorities has been brought actively to the fore by the proposal of the Truman administration to extend full civil rights to racial minorities by Federal legislation. This has provoked heated resistance from southern leaders, because it not only threatens white supremacy in the South but also challenges states rights in handling racial controls and restrictions. At the Democrat National Convention in Philadelphia in 1948, the civil rights clause in the platform, inserted by pressure of the Truman following, provoked an active revolt by the southern Democrats and a threat to desert the Democrat party in the coming election. The threat was made good in South Carolina, Alabama, Mississippi, and Louisiana, in which states the states-rights Democrats nominated Gov. J. Strom Thurmond of South Carolina for President. Thurmond received a popular vote of 1,006,363 and 38 electoral votes.

In the 81st Congress, the Truman forces sought to amend the Senate debate rules so that the civil rights program could be pushed through Congress. This met with a determined filibuster by southern Democrats in the Senate in February and March, 1949, and President Truman had to beat an ignominious retreat. The civil rights program seemed to be indefinitely postponed, so far as Federal legislation is concerned.

When legislation to remove disabilities from minorities, especially Negroes, seemed blocked for the time being, President Truman and his supporters turned to the courts, and in the spring of 1950, Attorney-General McGrath appealed to the Supreme Court to set aside the whole foundation of the policy of segregation, which is based on the idea that civil rights and social status can be "equal" though "separate." It was argued that there can be no equal rights in a situation in which segregation exists, even when the facilities and conveniences are literally equal. The Supreme Court decisions in June, 1950, in the Henderson, Sweatt, and McLaurin cases, and the Federal Circuit Court decision in the Swanson case in Virginia, seemed to indicate that the Federal courts would uphold this doctrine when specific public cases were brought before the courts. The *United States News & World Report* thus summarizes the main gains in civil rights for Negroes in recent years:

A Negro in the south is now entitled to the same chance to get a university education as a white youth. Negroes can't be segregated in the classroom. A Negro riding on a railway train is entitled to the same service as a white passenger. Real estate titles cannot contain enforceable covenants barring sale to Negroes or persons of other creeds and races. A Negro charged with crime cannot be convicted if members of his race are barred from juries. States cannot stop Negroes from voting in elections, general or primary, for national officials.... The armed forces have abolished segregation.[3]

There remains, however, a wide range of possibilities for private enforcement of segregation in private schools, housing leases, restaurants, hotels, theaters, clubs, and fraternities. Thus far, the Supreme Court has

---

[3] June 16, 1950, pp. 18-19.

refused to hear cases involving purely private arrangements for segregation. What the final outcome will be remains to be seen; it can only be said that the issue of civil rights for racial minorities is now, more than ever before, facing the country.

Reduction of lynchings. An important gain in a matter closely related to Negro political and civil rights has been the reduction in the number of Negro lynchings in recent years. Lynching was widely used in the past as a part of vigilante justice in our frontier society. Before the Civil War it was far more usual in other parts of the country than in the South and was more frequently used on whites than on Negroes. As late as the year 1884, 160 whites were lynched and only 51 Negroes. After this time an ever greater proportion of lynchings were of Negroes and in the South, primarily for the alleged purpose of discouraging sex crimes by Negroes. Actually, only about a third of southern lynchings of Negroes have been for sex crimes, real or alleged; nearly half the lynchings have been for homicide. Between 1882 and 1946, some 4,716 persons were lynched, of which 3,425 were Negroes. In the decade of 1920-1929, no less than 95.5 per cent of lynchings took place in the South.

Owing to the leadership of both enlightened southern whites and Negro crusaders for civil rights, lynching has now been almost eliminated. The movement against lynching was directed primarily by the Commission on Inter-racial Cooperation, organized in Atlanta, Georgia, in 1918, and made up of 100 white and Negro leaders drawn from the whole South. The number of recorded lynchings has been reduced from 83 in 1919 to 6 in 1946, 1 in 1947, and 2 in 1948, one of these being of a white person.

Negro education. The outstanding facts about Negro education today are (1) a vast improvement since 1900, and (2) still a marked inferiority to the education of whites. It is estimated that about 97 per cent of Negroes were illiterate in 1860. In 1940, only about 10 per cent were so rated, as compared with 1.3 per cent for native whites, and 12.2 per cent for foreign-born Americans.

The number and proportion of Negro children in schools have greatly increased since 1900. In that year, 1,083,516 Negro children, or 31 per cent of all those between 5 and 20 years, were attending school. In 1940, 2,698,901, out of a total of 4,188,500, or 64.4 per cent, were in school. For the age-group of 5-17 years, the figures were even more impressive. In 1940, about 86 per cent of all Negro children between 5 and 17 were enrolled in public schools. Not only is Negro school attendance getting better in the South, but the larger number of Negroes in northern public schools has boosted the record of Negro school attendance in the last quarter of a century.

The number of years of Negro school attendance has also increased. In 1940, the median number of years during which Negroes attended school was 5.7; this was still much below the figure for whites, which was 8.8 years. A better record is also being made for the average number of days attended by Negro pupils; in 1945-1946, the average attendance in a school year was 139 days for Negro children and 149 for white.

Moreover, Negro public school education is no longer so markedly concentrated in the lower elementary grades. Many more than formerly get into the higher grades and considerably more go on to high school though the ratio is still far below that for white children. The length of the school term for Negroes is beginning to catch up with that for white children. In 1945-1946, the Negro school year had increased in 17 southern states and the District of Columbia to 170 days, as compared with 175 for whites. The teacher-pupil ratio has also improved; in 1945-1946, it was 35 for Negroes and 28 for whites.

All this is encouraging, but other figures bring out additional facts about the lag between educational facilities for Negroes and those for white children. The median percentage of Negro teachers who had four years or more of college education in 1940 was 28.9 as against 52.7 for white teachers, and, as a rule, the Negro colleges offered poorer instruction than the white. The school buildings for Negro children are usually inferior to those for whites in the South, though there are some notable exceptions and the situation is improving. The amount of capital invested in school buildings and equipment for white children in southern states is over four times that invested in buildings and equipment for Negro children. In 1940, the median expenditure for a standard classroom-unit in southern states was $376 for Negroes, and $1,160 for whites. The spread of such equipment cost for Negroes was great, running from $154 in Mississippi to $1,250 in West Virginia. The expenditure per pupil is much less for Negroes, $57.57 for Negro children in 1945-1946, to $104.66 for white. In 1944-1945, some ten southern states spent 189 per cent more per white pupil than per Negro pupil enrolled in the public schools. The court decisions ordering equal educational opportunities are bringing improvements here.

Transportation facilities for Negro children in rural areas lag far behind those for white pupils. In ten southern states, the transportation appropriation for white children was $6.11 per child, when for Negroes it was 59 cents. Many Negro children still have to walk long distances to one-room rural schools.

The pay of teachers in Negro schools remains lower than that of white teachers. In 14 southern states, in 1941-1942, the average annual salary of Negro teachers ran from $226 in Mississippi to $1,593 in Maryland; the pay of white teachers varied from $712 in Mississippi to $1,796 in Delaware. The United States Supreme Court has upheld a Federal court decision of 1940 ordering Negro teachers to be paid the same salary as white teachers for comparable work, but the salary situation has not yet been equalized. In 1945-1946, the average salary of Negro public school teachers was $1,134 as against $1,640 for white teachers.

The general picture of Negro public school education is, thus, one of steady and gratifying improvement, but much additional progress must be made in southern states to bring Negro education up to anything like a parity with white education. Negro education in urban northern areas is better than in the South, but even in the North the level is often below that for white children, both for the educational plant and the quality of instruction.

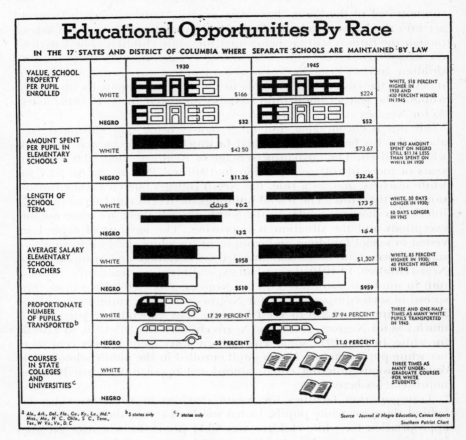

Despite many handicaps, more and more Negroes are getting a college education. In 1940, 1.1 per cent of Negroes had one or more years of college education; this figure was far below that for whites, which stood at 5.4 per cent. In 1950-1951, there were 108 Negro institutions of higher learning, with 74,526 enrolled, a marked gain over the 43,000 enrollment of 1941-1942, the previous peak year. Some fourteen of these institutions offer instruction on the graduate level, and, in 1944-1945, some 576 graduate students were enrolled. Among the best of these Negro colleges and universities are Atlanta University, Fisk University, Florida A&M College, Hampton Institute, Howard University, Knoxville College, Langston University, Lincoln University, North Carolina A&T College, Talladega College, Tuskegee Institute, Virginia State College for Negroes, West Virginia State College for Negroes, and Wilberforce University. Negro collegiate enrollment has grown from 2,624 in 1900 to 74,526 in 1950. The proportion of Negroes in Negro college faculties has about doubled. There are now over 100,000 Negroes who have college degrees. A very large number of students in Negro colleges and universities, which are concentrated mainly in southern states, come from the North.

It is obvious that the opportunities for higher education for Negroes are far below those for whites. The legal struggle for Negro admission to state-supported colleges and universities has taken on a new impetus since the court victories in the Gaines, Sipuel, McLaurin, Sweatt, Swanson, and other cases mentioned above. If states admit Negroes to the regular state universities, the situation will be markedly improved. Northern states may follow the example of New York, which, as we noted, has passed a law barring discrimination against Negroes in college and university admissions.

The decision of the Federal courts in the McLaurin, Sweatt, and Swanson cases in 1950, brought the matter of Negro education in the South to a critical impasse. It appeared that the South might either have to abolish segregation in the schools and colleges or take steps to equalize the educational facilities and opportunities for white and Negro youth. The latter would involve stupendous expenditures, estimated by experts to run to at least a billion dollars. The Southern Regional Council estimated that the cost of equalizing school buildings alone in the 17 states that practiced segregation in 1949 would run to more than $725,000,000.

The drive against segregation in education has thoroughly aroused some southern leaders. Governor James F. Byrnes of South Carolina frankly stated that if the courts upheld the complete abolition of segregation in southern schools, the only practicable procedure would be to close the schools.

The anti-segregation movement in southern schools met a rebuff in June, 1951, when a three-judge Federal court, in the Clarendon County (South Carolina) case, held that "segregation of races in the public schools ... is a matter of legislative policy for the several states, with which the Federal courts are powerless to interfere." The court did, however, order that Negro schools should be made equal to those for white children. The "segregation" and "equality" question for public schools will not be finally settled, legally, until this case is carried to the Supreme Court.

Special aid for Negroes. A number of foundations have given special assistance to the improvement of Negro education, especially in the South. Such are the Julius Rosenwald Fund, the Rockefeller General Education Board, the Carnegie Corporation, the Peabody Fund, the Russell Sage Foundation, and the Phelps-Stokes Fund. There is much agitation for Federal aid to Negro education, but the South has not been very cordial to this movement because it challenges states rights and because it is feared that Federal aid may be contingent on the abolition of racial segregation in the school system.

Negroes in scholarship, journalism, the arts, and sports. The number of Negroes who have distinguished themselves in various fields of scholarship, journalism, the arts, music, and sports is so extensive that they cannot be listed completely. For a complete list, with a description of their work, one must consult the *Negro Year Book*. Some of the best known scholars are the great Negro chemist, George Washington Carver; the historians, William E. B. DuBois and Carter G. Woodson; the economist, Abram L. Harris; the sociologist, E. Franklin Frazier; and the philosopher, Alain Locke.

Negro education outside the schools has been promoted by the increasing number and improved nature of Negro newspapers. In 1943, there were 164 active Negro newspapers, of which about 120 were weeklies. Some 144 of these had a combined average net circulation of 1,613,255 per issue. The circulation of 106 of these increased by 27 per cent between 1943 and 1945. There are 15 Negro newsgathering agencies which serve these papers.

Some of the Negro newspapers, such as the *Pittsburgh Courier,* are of high quality. George Schuyler, columnist for the *Courier,* is regarded by other commentators as one of the best in American journalism, and he does not stand alone. The Negro newspapers are abandoning their former more or less exclusive concern with Negro problems and interests and are giving more coverage to public affairs and world events. Important newspaper awards and prizes have recently been won by Negroes. In addition to newspapers, there are over 100 Negro magazines. In 1943, the combined average net circulation per issue of 79 of these was 1,850,378, and their content and coverage are improving in the same ways as the Negro newspapers.

Even those who are skeptical about the Negro intellect have to admit the success of that race in literature, music, and art. There are the novelists, Frank Yerby, Walter F. White, Jessie Fauset, and Claude McKay; and the poets, Paul Laurence Dunbar, James Weldon Johnson, Langston Hughes, and Countee Cullen. Samuel Coleridge-Taylor (a British Negro), W. C. Handy, William Grant Still, and H. Lawrence Greeman are outstanding Negro composers. Able Negro singers can be counted by the dozen, the outstanding being Paul Robeson, Roland Hayes, and Marian Anderson. Other important Negro artists are the conductors, Dean Dixon and Duke Ellington; the pianists, Hazel Scott and Roy Tibbs; the violinist, Louis Vaughan Jones; the composer and pianist prodigy, Philippa Schuyler; the painter, Henry Farmer; the sculptor, Richmond Barthe; and the architect, Paul R. Williams.

The Negro has competed successfully with whites in sports. Among pugilists, Peter Jackson, Joe Gans, Jack Johnson, Henry Armstrong, Ray Robinson, and Joe Louis are notable. Jesse Owens is one of the greatest modern athletes. A great gain, recently, for Negroes in the world of sports has been their admission to membership in major league teams. "Jackie" Robinson of the Brooklyn Dodgers was voted the most valuable player in the National League in 1949.

Although some mental testers claim to have shown the Negro to be inferior to the white man in intellectual capacity, there is no scientific evidence whatever to support the view that the Negro belongs to an inferior race. The brief survey of distinguished Negroes should remove any doubt that the Negro is capable of achieving greatness in any chosen field if given the opportunity.

Negro religion. The church has been one of the main cultural factors in the Negro's life, for there he feels no color or racial inferiority. Negro

DO YOU NEED HELP?   If you have questions about use of the card catalog, ask the Reference Librarian.

HELP US SERVE YOU BY – Prompt response to Library communications.
Renewing books on or before due date.

FINE D.	RET.
IST NOT.	2ND
CALL-IN	BILL
REMIND.	

SHELF LIST				
NEW BK	TO BE SH	RES SH	MEND	DB-BK-TR
FILE-D	FILE-LC	STAX-D	STAX-LC	NL

church membership increased by over 450,000 between 1926 and 1936, an increase of 8.6 per cent in the decade, although the percentage of increase in total church membership during this period was only 2.4 per cent. The increase in Negro church membership accounted for 37 per cent of the gains in total church membership in this country from 1926 to 1936. There were 5,661,000 Negro church members in 1936. The majority of Negro church members are highly orthodox and fundamentalist in their religious beliefs. Contrary to the general opinion, however, Negroes are not overwhelmingly and universally religious. The above figures indicate that over one-half of American Negroes do not attend any church.

The most recent dramatic demonstration of Negro religious enthusiasm has been the work of Father Divine in New York City and Philadelphia. The Father has attracted thousands of Negroes into his religious establishments, or "heavens." More realistic has been the religious leadership of Adam Clayton Powell, Jr., minister of the great Abyssinian Baptist Church in Harlem, New York City. Powell carried his leadership from religion into politics when he was elected to Congress in 1945.

Main Negro plans for solution of Negro problem. We may conclude this treatment of the Negro problem with a discussion of the major policies that have dominated various Negro leaders in their effort to improve the status and well-being of their race. Abram L. Harris and Sterling D. Spero have summarized these under the four following headings: (1) interracial conciliation; (2) civil libertarianism; (3) militant race consciousness; and (4) Negro class consciousness as an exploited industrial proletariat.

Interracial conciliation. Of these four attitudes and policies, the first has been the most popular and has received the greatest approval from both Negroes and whites, but it is today subject to severe criticism by the more progressive Negro leaders and by many realistic white students of the Negro problem. This program of interracial conciliation is founded on what has been called the "Uncle Tom" psychology, in that it places its reliance chiefly upon the benevolence of "good white men." Its more prominent sponsors have generally opposed the unionization of Negro labor, and they have been bitterly antagonistic to any attempt to arouse Negroes as a class-conscious proletariat. Of all the Negro programs, it has been most closely related to the idea of creating a Negro middle class, based upon the expansion of Negro business enterprise. This theory was the guiding influence in the organization of the National Negro Business League. It is natural that this policy is also the one most vigorously promoted by the northern foundations that have interested themselves in Negro welfare.

The outstanding leader of interracial conciliation was Booker T. Washington (1856-1915). Washington was the founder of the famous Tuskegee Institute, established in 1881 in Alabama. He became easily the most renowned Negro leader at the opening of the present century. Theodore Roosevelt risked the wrath of the South by making Washington the first Negro leader ever to be invited to dine at the White House. Washington appealed to white self-interest by contending that it would be impossible for the South to rise so long as it imposed disabilities on the Negro. His basic text was that: "You cannot keep a man down in a ditch unless you remain down there with him." The two chief organizations devoted to promoting interracial conciliation are the Commission on Interracial Cooperation in the South, and the National Urban League in the North. Washington's successor as president of Tuskegee Institute and his ablest supporter was Major Robert R. Moton.

One's attitude toward the policy of conciliation must depend upon the solution one seeks for the Negro problem. If one wishes to promote peace and good will, along with a regime of Negro docility, this policy is undoubtedly superior to any other that has been suggested. Since it accepts as inevitable the persistence of social inequalities at the expense of the Negro, it can hardly be expected to free the Negro race from all its handicaps. Those who look forward to the removal of these obstacles have been logical in criticizing interracial conciliation. They are not opposed to conciliation as such, but they are critical of any conciliation which presupposes extended continuation of Negro inferiority.

Civil libertarianism. If Washington was the foremost exponent of interracial conciliation, preeminence in the policy of civil libertarianism must be accorded to W. E. B. DuBois, and Walter F. White, who have demanded political, legal, and social equality for Negroes. DuBois helped to found the National Association for the Advancement of Colored People in 1909. This has been the most effective Negro organization working for the civil liberties of American Negroes. It seeks to do away with all forms of discrimination against Negroes and to accord them full equality with their white neighbors. Much stress is also laid upon Negro education, but the educational policy advocated is far less docile and complaisant than that promoted by Washington. Yet, the NAACP agrees with Washington in wishing to promote harmony between the two races, provided that this harmony is not purchased by the overhigh price of perpetual Negro bondage. In connection with the American Civil Liberties Union, the National Association for the Advancement of Colored People has done more than any other organization to battle for the civil and social rights of Negroes. It also issues *The Crisis,* perhaps the most important Negro publication. In 1931, Walter F. White became secretary of the NAACP and has since directed its activities.

Pan-Negroism. Another movement designed to aid the Negro was the pan-Negro program launched by Marcus Garvey about the time of the First World War. Often wrongly described as a "back-to-Africa" policy, it was really economic in its basis. The central thought of the Garvey movement was "Africa for the Africans." This envisaged the creation of a great independent Negro state in Africa with which the Negroes in the United States would have extensive and prosperous trading relations, thus placing the economic and commercial status of all Negroes on a firm basis. The whole idea was chimerical. Garvey was especially hostile to white laborers, whom he regarded as the chief enemy of the Negro.

Garvey was discredited by certain extravagances and unwise financial ventures, and he was deported to Jamaica in 1927. His movement gained its chief support from the Negro migrants in the northern cities. Their first invasion of the North came at about the same time that Garvey launched his movement in 1914. The two chief organizations organized to promote the Garvey policy were the Universal Negro Improvement Association and The African Communities League. If Garvey's policies and methods were more glamorous and dramatic than those of Washington and Du Bois, they were also less worthy of serious consideration. This need not be taken to imply, however, that there is nothing to be said for the wisdom of a pan-Negro movement. It will probably be stimulated by the rebellion of Old World Negroes against continued white dominion.

Negro Communism. The effort to promote proletarian class consciousness on Marxian principles among Negroes has been mainly the work of American Communists, particularly the Communist party. It is their contention that the capitalistic system of society is the chief obstacle to race equality. They maintain that the Negro can never reach a position of social and economic equality until capitalism is destroyed. Consequently, the Communists do their best to carry on their propaganda among Negroes of both the North and the South. Whatever one thinks of the wisdom of the Communist program, there can be no doubt that this policy has stirred great bitterness and alarm among the southern whites. This proposed marriage of Moscow and Africa naturally greatly excites the southerners of the lower as well as the upper classes. Though James W. Ford, a Negro, has repeatedly been the vice-presidential candidate of the Communist party, there are relatively few Negro members of the party.

The communist propaganda in the South was widely publicized by two cases in the 1930's, the Scottsboro case in Alabama and the Angelo Herndon case in Georgia. In the first case the Communists, through the International Labor Defense, came to the rescue of Negro boys accused of rape on very flimsy and dubious evidence. The Herndon case involved a life sentence imposed upon a Georgia Negro for possessing radical pamphlets. He was finally released by the Supreme Court of the United States.

The Scottsboro case admirably illustrates the methods and results of this fourth policy of Negro leadership. It made admirable publicity for the Communists, but it performed a dubious service for the Negro boys. If the case had been left in the hands of the National Association for the Advancement of Colored People, there is the best evidence that the boys would have been freed within a few months. When the Communists insisted upon interjecting the Red issue into the case, it dragged on for years and several of the boys were held for a considerable time in prison and narrowly escaped hanging. Contrary to a general impression, the Scottsboro Negro youths were martyred to the cause of communist propaganda. This may have been worth while for the Communists, but the latter can hardly claim to have made a courageous and straight-forward battle for civil liberties. But the case did, incidentally, direct world-wide attention to the gross discrimination against Negroes in the southern courtroom. One important legal gain for Negroes did grow out of the

Scottsboro case, namely, a Supreme Court ruling that jury trials are not valid if Negroes are excluded from jury service.

Of all the programs for the solution of the Negro problem, this fourth one is charged with the greatest amount of social dynamite, whatever one thinks of its wisdom or fundamental validity.

Local organization to improve race relations. Many who are directly concerned with race problems believe that these national programs for improving the condition of the Negroes and promoting better race relations should be supplemented by plans and activities to improve interracial relations in local urban areas. In such efforts as have already been initiated along these lines, Negroes and other racial minorities are brought together with native whites and share in educational, cultural, and recreational activities, all designed to promote better interracial understanding and tolerance. The basic idea is that these, like charity, should begin at home. A good example of such local organizations to better racial relations is the Fellowship House established in Philadelphia, which has been imitated in several other cities.

The outlook for Negro-white relations. The problem of racial adjustments and conflicts in the United States is in too fluid a condition to justify any dogmatic predictions. Not since the slavery controversies before the Civil War and during Reconstruction has the issue of civil rights for racial minorities been so vigorously before the American public or the matter of racial equality and race relations been so warmly debated. The fact that the forces supporting race equality are more powerful and better organized than at any earlier time has provoked correspondingly stronger reactions on the part of those who wish to continue white supremacy. The developments in the future will depend not only on public education and debate but also on the general economic and social situation in the country. Continued prosperity will be likely to restrain interracial violence, but prolonged depression may encourage various elements to find a scapegoat in racial minorities. Moreover, economic and social chaos is a natural breeding ground for intolerance and violence.

It was natural that the increased prominence and movements of Negroes during the Second World War and the readjustments immediately thereafter would tend to promote clashes between whites and Negroes. The most important of these race riots were the Mobile, Alabama, riot of May, 1943; the Beaumont, Texas, riot of June, 1943; the Detroit riot of June, 1943 (the most bloody of all); the Harlem riot of July, 1943; the Columbia, Tennessee, riot of February, 1946; and the Athens, Alabama, riot of August, 1946. Although these incidents were unfortunate, they were not as numerous as might have been anticipated, nor as bloody as several earlier race riots following the First World War.

The main interest in interracial relations has recently tended to shift from the prevention of sporadic race riots to the promotion of a comprehensive movement for civil rights for all racial minorities. In this movement, the leaders have been drawn from all racial minorities as well as from native whites who believe in racial equality and interracial toleration.

Although the material in the preceding pages on the Negro problem demonstrates marked progress in the education, alertness, and public power of Negroes, this does not mean that the problem of racial prejudice and conflict has been solved or even reduced. Indeed, the opposite may be more nearly true. The greater the advances made by Negroes, the more impatient they become over their remaining handicaps and the more determined to remove them. This, in turn, encourages the champions of white supremacy to take stronger steps to keep Negroes under control. Further, the idea that all prejudice against Negroes is a monopoly of the South is a gross misconception. The South has been in greater contact with more Negroes for a longer period of time. When Negroes have seemed to threaten vested white interests in the North, there has been no dearth of anti-Negro sentiment and action. Some of the worst race riots have taken place in northern cities. Southerners are mainly interested in perpetuating white supremacy.

Undoubtedly, the most important single factor in promoting greater Negro strength in public affairs and more success in securing Negro civil rights has been the migration of large numbers of Negroes to northern cities located in states in which the vote is fairly evenly divided between the two major parties. Here, Negroes can hold something like a balance of power, especially if they join forces with other racial minorities. This new situation has led northern politicians of both parties to pay more attention to Negro demands. Politically speaking, Negroes can no longer be ignored as a voteless minority, segregated in a group of southern states. This, again, does not promote either political or racial harmony. It has stimulated southern political leaders to resist proposed Federal legislation to better the lot of the Negroes. Another factor in winning more civil rights for Negroes is the fact that the present United States Supreme Court reflects New Deal policy, which was very friendly to the idea of racial equality.

These concluding considerations are offered mainly to make it clear that, although the race problem in the United States is far from solved, sporadic recent gains may point to the eventual triumph of racial tolerance and ideas of racial equality.

SUMMARY

Race problems have played a prominent role in American history from the very days of discovery. The whites conquered and occupied the continent at the expense of the original Indian inhabitants, who were members of the Mongolian race. The slavery issue and the Civil War turned on the question of Negro labor and rights. Relations with Mexicans have existed since the Mexican War of the 1840's. Oriental immigration became an important problem following the Civil War.

Our handling of the Indian problem was loose, inefficient, and exploitative for a hundred years after the Revolutionary War. During this period Indian policy was administered under the treaty and reservation systems. The Indians were ignored or exploited, and their lands were taken over by white settlers. Under the reservation system, dominant after 1871, conditions among the Indians remained unsatisfactory. Absorption of their lands by whites continued, Indian education was grossly inadequate, medical care was virtually non-existent, and economic standards and efficiency were low.

The famous Meriam Report of 1928, revealing the shocking conditions of Indian life and our inefficient Indian policy, led to reforms instituted by the Roosevelt Administration and carried out by John Collier as Commissioner of Indian Affairs. Educational facilities for Indians were improved, better medical care was provided, and economic aid was forthcoming. But Indian economic conditions remained depressed·in many areas, especially after the shock of the Second World War. Indian lands and agricultural methods are often inferior, and Indians have had difficulty in securing non-agricultural forms of employment. Conditions are especially critical in some areas, notably among the Navajos and other Indians of the Southwest, where the majority of Indians outside Alaska are concentrated.

Chinese were first encouraged to come to America in large numbers after the discovery of gold in California and during the great era of railroad building after the Civil War. When the railroads had been constructed in the West, Chinese laborers were left stranded and hostility to the Chinese increased. As a result, Chinese immigration was suppressed. Most of the Chinese are now segregated in a few cities, mainly on the West coast. Due to our alliance with China in the Second World War, Chinese were admitted to American citizenship in 1946, but this more sympathetic attitude may be reversed now that the Communists have conquered China.

Japanese began coming to the United States in large numbers, especially to the Pacific coast, a generation or so after the maximum Chinese immigration. They entered agricultural pursuits on the West coast and developed sharp competition with white farmers and gardeners. Friction and hostility developed, followed by the Gentleman's Agreement of 1907, which ended the immigration of Japanese, and by the needless Exclusion Act of 1924, which was an affront to the Japanese. During the Second World War, most of the Japanese inhabitants of Pacific coast areas were forcibly evacuated to inland camps, and many have not been able to return to their homes or possessions. Relations with the Japanese may improve as Japan becomes more important as a possible ally against Soviet Russia and Communist China.

The abolition of Negro slavery after the Civil War created the urgent problem of adjusting Negroes to a life of freedom. The process was carried out too hastily during Reconstruction days, and Southern hostility was aroused. The Northern Reconstruction program surely set back the sane handling of white-Negro relations by many years.

The Negroes are increasing in population—from about 4,400,000 in 1865 to well over 15,000,000 in 1950. But the increase has been restrained by the high Negro death rate, a result of bad living conditions, excessive exposure to disease, and inadequate medical care.

Another notable Negro population trend has been the migration of Negroes to the North since 1914 and their concentration in northern industrial cities. Nearly three million Negroes have left the South in three major waves of migration since 1914. Reaching the North, they have settled mainly in cities. Even in the South there has been a migration from country to city. In 1860, only 10 per cent of Negroes lived in cities; in 1950, over 50 per cent were urban dwellers. Negro city living conditions have been unsatisfactory. Negroes have been forced into slums, they have been exploited by "rent-hogs," and they have been denied healthy living conditions.

Negro economic conditions have been depressed ever since emancipation. Negro farmers have been compelled to operate on small farms, often of low fertility, and they have not been able to get good mechanical equipment. Hence, they cannot compete successfully with large, mechanized southern farms. Negro farm labor is in an even more critical condition today as a result of the invention of new machinery, such as the cotton picker, improved corn harvesters, tractors, and combines. This unfortunate situation is likely to grow worse in the years to come.

Negroes have increasingly entered the ranks of industrial labor, but even here they have operated under such handicaps as rough forms of employment, low wages, and inadequate protection by labor unions. Even Federal labor legislation has not put Negro industrial labor on terms of practical equality with white labor. Negroes have begun to enter business pursuits—some 800,000 are now thus engaged. But Negro business establishments are usually small retail or service units. There has been some progress, however, in developing Negro banking, insurance, and real estate enterprises. Negro business has not yet recovered from the blow it suffered in the depression following 1929.

Negroes were long excluded from political life in the South by various forms of legal strategy. These have been attacked in the Federal courts and most of them outlawed. But in the Deep South, many Negroes are still excluded from the polls. The most notable recent development in Negro politics has been the increasing number of northern Negroes, and their adoption of political expediency rather than adamant and sentimental affiliation with the Republican party. As a result, the Negro power in national politics has been greatly increased, especially in close states. The Negro vote now holds the balance of power in 17 states with a total of 281 electoral votes.

Negroes have long been subjected to segregation in living quarters, agencies of transportation, and service facilities. This segregation has also been successfully attacked in the courts, but has not been completely abolished. President Truman's Civil Rights program led to a revolt of many southern Democrats in the presidential campaign of 1948, and has been blocked in Congress by filibustering tactics.

Negro education, although distinctly gaining in both school enrollment and facilities, is still markedly inferior to that of whites. Segregation of the races in education, especially in higher education, has recently been undermined by Federal court decisions. But it will take much time and great expense to bring Negro education in the South up to the standards which prevail in the education of whites.

Negroes are coming to play an ever larger and more impressive role in American art, music, literature, science, scholarship, and sports, a fact which serves to discredit the idea of Negro intellectual and artistic inferiority. Those Negroes who embrace religion have remained strongly emotional and orthodox. But the common idea that all Negroes are strongly religious is exploded by the fact that at least half of the Negro population have no religious affiliations.

There have been several notable Negro programs to solve the Negro problem. Booker T. Washington founded the plan of interracial conciliation, devoted to the idea that both whites and Negroes suffer from imposed Negro inferiority. W. E. B. DuBois and Walter White have led in the battle for Negro civil liberties, which has won so many recent court victories. Marcus Garvey set up a pan-Negro program to enlist the interest of Negroes in Africa as well as in the United States. More recently, Communism has appealed to some Negroes as the solution of the Negro problem. Others believe that cordial white-Negro relations can best be promoted by local programs of white-Negro association in education, the arts, and sports.

Despite recent court gains, the problem of white-Negro relations still remains critical. The greater the victories won in the courts, the greater has been the alarm and hostility of many southern leaders. The solution of the problem will require many years and much patience and tolerance by both white and Negro leaders.

SELECTED REFERENCES

Allen, J. S., *The Negro Question in the United States.* New York: International Publishers, 1936. Lays special emphasis on the relation of the Negro situation to industrialization and the labor problem. One of the most searching studies of the economics of the Negro question.

Bond, H. M., *The Education of the Negro in the American Social Order.* New York: Prentice-Hall, 1934. A standard account of the education of the Negro.

*Collier, John, *The Indians of the Americas.* New York: Norton, 1947. Comprehensive historical and sociological treatment of the Indian problem by the former Commissioner of Indian Affairs.

Dale, E. E., *The Indians of the Southwest: A Century of Development under the United States.* Norman: University of Oklahoma Press, 1949. An unusually intelligent, interesting, and expert account of the sector of Indian life most important in our time.

*Davie, M. R., *Negroes in American Society.* New York: McGraw-Hill, 1949. A sociological study of Negro life and Negro-white relations from the African background to the current struggle for FEPC laws. An outstanding recent book on the Negro problem.

*Davis, Allison, and Dollard, John, *Children of Bondage.* Washington: American Council on Education, 1940. Competent and interesting analysis of the efforts of Negroes, especially Negro youth, to adjust their life to city conditions and mechanical industry in the South.

Du Bois, W. E. B., *The World and Africa*. New York: Viking, 1947. An able book on the historical African background of Negro culture and social experience. Fills an important gap in the literature on the Negro problem.

*Franklin, J. H., *From Slavery to Freedom*. New York: Knopf, 1947. Comprehensive historical survey of American Negroes, from their African background to the gains in race equality since the Second World War.

*Frazier, E. F., *The Negro in the United States*. New York: Macmillan, 1949. Regarded by many as the most competent and important single volume on the Negro problem. A professional sociological analysis.

Herskovits, M. J., *The American Negro*. New York: Knopf, 1928. A useful little book, presenting the main facts about the origins and physical traits of the Negro in the United States.

———, *The Myth of the Negro Past*. New York: Harper, 1941. Deals realistically with the African element in the cultural heritage of the American Negro.

Kardiner, Abram, and Ovesey, Lionel, *The Mark of Oppression: a Psychosocial Study of the American Negro*. New York: Norton, 1951. An attempt to provide a sociopsychological analysis of Negro problems and discrimination. Valuable for case studies.

*La Farge, Oliver, *As Long as the Grass Shall Grow*. New York: Longmans, Green, 1940. Sympathetic treatment of the Indian peoples and cultures, and of the relations of the Indians with the government.

——— (Ed.), *The Changing Indian*. Norman: University of Oklahoma Press, 1942. General symposium on Indian life, social conditions, and public treatment.

Lee, G. W., *River George*. New York: Macaulay, 1937. A social novel portraying the difficulties of educated Negroes in the South after the First World War. Gives information which does not get into textbooks and throws light on Negro folkways.

MacLeod, W. C., *The American Indian Frontier*. New York: Knopf, 1928. Best single book on Indian life and culture prior to white domination.

McWilliams, Carey, *Prejudice; Japanese-Americans: Symbol of Racial Intolerance*. Boston: Little, Brown, 1944. Critical analysis of racial contacts between Americans and Japanese in this country.

———, *North From Mexico*. Philadelphia: Lippincott, 1949. Best book on American racial contacts with Mexicans and Spanish-speaking Americans.

Myrdal, Gunnar, *An American Dilemma*, 2 vols. New York: Harper, 1944. The most elaborate study ever made of the American Negro problem.

Ottley, Roi, *Black Odyssey*. New York: Scribner, 1948. Intensely interesting journalistic history of the Negroes in the United States.

*Powdermaker, Hortense, *After Freedom*. New York: Viking, 1939. Probably the best case-study ever made of contemporary Negro life in the Deep South. It is an account of life in a Negro community in a cotton-growing section of Mississippi. An indispensable book on the Negro problem.

*Rose, A. M., *The Negro's Morale*. Minneapolis: University of Minnesota Press, 1950. Important treatment of Negro reaction to race discrimination and the effect of this on Negro relations with whites.

Sandmeyer, E. C., *The Anti-Chinese Movement in California*. Urbana: University of Illinois Press, 1939. A study of Chinese-American racial conflicts in California.

Schermerhorn, R. A., *These Our People*. Boston: Heath, 1949. Able descriptive panorama of American minority groups and their problems.

Spero, S. D., and Harris, A. L., *The Black Worker*. New York: Columbia University Press, 1931. An authoritative account of the relation of the Negro to problems of employment and unionization. Written before the CIO, it needs to be supplemented by H. R. Cayton and G. S. Mitchell's *Black Workers and the New Unions,* University of North Carolina Press, 1939.

*Tannenbaum, Frank, *Slave and Citizen.* New York: Knopf, 1947. Authoritative brief study of various historic policies relative to treatment of Negroes by whites.

The Negro Year Book, edited by J. P. Guzman, V. C. Foster, and W. H. Hughes, Tuskegee, 1947. Most comprehensive compendium of facts on Negroes. Especially valuable for description of Negro achievements in scholarship, science, literature, arts, and sports.

Weaver, R. C., *The Negro Ghetto.* New York: Harcourt, Brace, 1948. Comprehensive study of racial segregation of Negroes in northern cities and the Negro struggle to get decent housing.

White, W. F., *Man Called White.* New York: Viking, 1948. Autobiography of Walter F. White of NAACP, the most active proponent of Negro emancipation from civil disabilities. Contains much interesting and cogent information on Negro-white relations.

CHAPTER 7

Health, Disease, and Medical Care

THE HEALTH PICTURE IN THE UNITED STATES AT THE MID-CENTURY

Impressive progress in medical science. In few fields of human endeavor has greater progress been made in the past hundred years than in medical science. The brilliant work of physicians, surgeons and of research scientists in the medical realm has revealed the causes and cures of many diseases once thought incurable. Impressive advances have been made in surgery and medical treatment. Ultra-modern hospitals, with the newest and finest equipment, stand on the sites of dingy "nursing homes" of a century ago. Indeed, if we speak of an industrial revolution as having occurred within the past century, we must also acknowledge a "medical revolution."

Inexcusable extent of bad health. Yet, medical examinations of selectees for the United States army during the Second World War revealed a startling condition of poor health among the very group who should be physically most fit. About 5,000,000 out of 15,000,000 men called up by the draft boards were rejected because of physical and mental defects which made them unfit for military service. The same general situation prevailed with respect to the extensive number of inductees called up in the latter part of 1950. Some 32 per cent of all those called up in the draft in December, 1950, were rejected because of physical and mental defects. The results of these examinations have led medical authorities to declare that the health of the American population is definitely below par. This opinion is confirmed by examination of our annual statistics of sickness and death. Competent medical authorities have stated that only about one person in a hundred in the United States today can be regarded as in truly perfect health. In 1949, some 1,449,000 persons died from all causes. It is estimated than some 325,000 or 23 per cent, of these deaths could have been prevented by timely and sufficient medical care.

Summary of the health and disease situation in the United States. Perhaps as good a summary of the whole illness and disability picture in the United States as has ever been assembled is that presented by Howard A. Rusk in *The New York Times:*

(1) One person out of every twenty is disabled by sickness or accident in any twenty-four hour period.

(2) Twenty-five million persons suffer from chronic ailments, many of which are disabling, with 50 per cent of the sufferers under 45 years of age.

219

(3) One million deaths occur yearly from chronic disease.

(4) Ten million days of disability each year result from chronic disease.

(5) Those suffering disabilities from accidents number over 10,000,000, mental diseases, 8,000,000, diseases of the heart and arteries, 6,850,000.

(6) Seventeen million Americans now living will die of cancer unless a cure is found. Some 167,464 unfortunates died in 1945 of this dread disease.

(7) Fifty-eight million Americans now living will die of the number one killer, heart disease, unless we learn more about its cause and cure. Some 588,009 of our citizens died in 1945 from this cause.

(8) About 97,000,000 persons in the United States need financial help to meet the cost of serious illness. This averages two persons out of three.

Major Causes of Disability

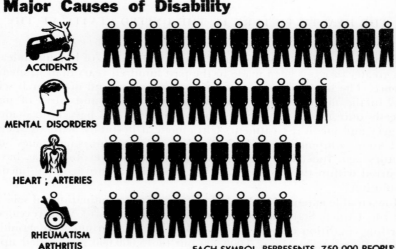

EACH SYMBOL REPRESENTS 750,000 PEOPLE

COURTESY PICTOGRAPH CORPORATION.

Social and economic aspects of the health problem. This paradox of great advances in medical science along with a high sickness and death rate demands serious consideration. Since our birth rate has been falling in normal times, population growth depends upon our ability to lower the death rate. Furthermore, the quality as well as the quantity of population is affected by health. Loss of work due to illness loses 500 million man-days a year, 4.2 billion dollars in wages and salaries, and a corresponding reduction in production and profits. It has been reliably estimated that the total direct and indirect monetary cost of illness, preventable deaths, and accidents amounted to 38 billion dollars in 1947. Bodily illness also produces a vast amount of misery and worry, which increases mental disease.

HISTORICAL ASPECTS OF THE DISEASE PROBLEM

Diseases in primitive times. In this section we shall consider certain of the outstanding historical facts relative to the nature, theory, and causes of disease and shall summarize briefly the diseases that today constitute the chief menace to mankind in civilized communities.

It was formerly widely believed that primitive peoples were relatively free from disease. There was a myth about "the healthy savage," akin to Rousseau's fanciful ideas about "the happy savage." A study of the skeletal remains of primitive man, along with more careful investigation of existing primitive types, proves very decisively that many diseases well known today were prevalent among early peoples. For example, lesions discovered in the skeletons of early man suggest the existence of tuberculosis. The prevalence of diseases of the brain—perhaps also of insanity— is demonstrated by the common primitive practice of cutting open, or trepanning, the skull. There were also magical reasons for this operation.

Ancient and medieval diseases. When we come to historic times, there is evidence of most of the diseases known in our day. This is not surprising, in the light of the fact that more than 99 per cent of the period of man's physical existence as a biological type had already passed by the time of the dawn of history. Moreover, man has existed in precisely his present physical make-up for at least 30,000 to 70,000 years. We have evidence showing the existence in the ancient Orient of cholera, the bubonic plague, typhus fever, smallpox, and leprosy. The Old Testament tells of a pestilence which wiped out tens of thousands of persons in the reign of King David. It also contains a number of references to insanity and nervous diseases, as well as to most common physical diseases, including venereal disease. Our knowledge of diseases in oriental antiquity has been greatly extended by the medical examination of Egyptian mummies and the discovery of ancient Egyptian medical records.

Medical science was notably extended by the Greeks, and their medical literature attests to the existence of the more important diseases known today. The Middle Ages are historically notorious as an era of epidemics, at least in the urban areas. Contrary to general impression, however, pestilence was even more prevalent in early modern times. The expansion of Europe overseas increased the contact with the older epidemic diseases of Asiatic lands. Syphilis first became a scourge in western Europe in the early sixteenth century. Medical historians have usually held that syphilis was first brought into Europe by the early European explorers of America. More recently, evidence has indicated that it may have been in existence in the Old World throughout historic times. Since the Indians are of Mongolian derivation, they may have brought it from the Old World to the New, from whence it may have been reintroduced with a new virulence by Columbus and subsequent explorers.

The disease picture in contemporary times. The most important revolutions in the nature and incidence of diseases in recent times are not, therefore, the appearance of new diseases. Rather, they relate more to the increased prevalence of certain types of diseases as the result of new living conditions produced by industrialization and urban life. The increased strains and stresses of modern life have brought a notable increase in serious heart disorders and in mental diseases. Digestive diseases have also been increased as the result of richer foods and increased nervous tension. Diseases of the teeth have been increased by cheap processed foods, especially candy. The apparent striking increase in the ravages of cancer in recent times has suggested to some that this may be a disease which is aggravated by modern conditions. But it may be mainly due to greater alertness and precision in detecting cancer since the rise of modern medicine and surgery. At any rate, disease is a problem that has afflicted man throughout historic times. Disease problems in our day represent only a difference in degree and not one of kind, when compared with diseases in earlier days.

Theories as to the causes of disease. Theories as to the cause of disease have passed through a notable evolution within historic times. Until the Greek period the prevalent explanation of disease was what has been called the demonic or diabolic theory. Disease was looked upon as the product of evil spirits. As a result of this theory of disease, medicine in the ancient Orient was chiefly a phase of magic. There is some evidence, however, that Egyptian physicians had, in a number of instances, suggested naturalistic causes for certain diseases.

Among the Greeks, we first find the emergence of definitely physical interpretations of disease, however absurd their theories may appear in our day. Hippocrates, the so-called father of medicine, offered two major theories of disease. He held that the body was composed of four humors; blood, phlegm, yellow bile, and black bile. Health consisted in the proper mixture of these humors in a given individual, and disease in a disturbance of this ideal mixture. He held that the heavenly bodies exerted an influence over this mixture, thus linking up medicine with astrology. His other main theory of disease was what is known as the miasmatic doctrine. He contended that certain diseases, particularly malaria, were acquired as the result of breathing bad gases from marshy areas, or lagoons. These theories prevailed until modern times, when the conception of contagious and degenerative diseases finally triumphed.

The doctrine of contagion as the cause of many diseases appeared originally as a by-product of magic rather than of true medical observation. It was held that diseases might be spread as the result of malign magical powers. The Hebrew theory of contagious diseases, which appears in the Old Testament, seems to have originated in this manner. The Christian Church took over these Hebrew doctrines from the Scriptures. More thoroughly divorced from religion and magic was the conviction of Thucydides, the Greek historian, that the plague was spread as the result of physical contact and direct contagion. The Muslim physicians of the Middle Ages also reinforced this theory of contagious diseases, especially notable being the study of the Black Death by the Spanish Muslim physician, Ibn Khatima, whose work was perhaps the first important treatise on contagious diseases. The first specific statement of our modern medical theory of contagion, as a product of pathogenic microörganisms (disease germs), was made by Jacob Henle, who published his *Pathological Researches* in 1840. But the thorough demonstration of this basis of contagion came in the last half of the nineteenth century, as the result of the work of the famous bacteriologists, Louis Pasteur and Robert Koch, the latter a pupil of Henle. The history of medical understanding of communicable diseases constitutes an interesting chapter in medical science and social welfare.

MAIN TYPES OF DISEASE

Contagious diseases. There are several types or groups of contagious diseases. An important group of communicable diseases are transmitted by germs contained in body discharges from the intestinal and genito-urinary tracts. Representative examples of such diseases are typhoid fever, cholera, dysentery and other intestinal diseases, and hookworm. The media of transmission of these diseases are numerous. Hookworm is transmitted chiefly through contacts with infected soil. Recognition of this fact, mainly as the result of the researches of Charles Wardell Stiles at the turn of the century, led to preventive medical measures which, in Richmond County, Virginia, for example, reduced the proportion of school children infected with hookworm from 83 per cent in 1910 to 2 per cent in 1921. This remarkable achievement was the result of soil sanitation and of compelling people to wear shoes. Typhoid fever is carried chiefly by polluted water, though a polluted milk supply may also play a deadly role. Cholera is transmitted both by water supply and by flies. The same applies to dysentery and other epidemic intestinal disorders.

Another important group of contagious diseases owe their spread chiefly to insects. One of the most important triumphs of medical science has been the demonstration that malaria and yellow fever are carried mainly by certain types of female mosquitoes. African sleeping sickness was also shown to be transmitted mainly by the bite of the tsetse fly. The deadly typhus fever is carried mainly by body lice. Bubonic plague, of which the foremost historic example was the frightful Black Death at the close of the Middle Ages, is normally a disease confined to rodents, such as rats and squirrels. It is brought to man primarily as the result of flea bites.

A third class of contagious diseases is transmitted mainly by direct contact with infected human beings. Such are measles, diphtheria, smallpox, pneumonia, influenza, tuberculosis, venereal diseases, leprosy, mumps, meningitis, scarlet fever, and whooping cough. Of course, a polluted water or milk supply, as well as direct human contacts, may transmit some of these diseases.

Bacteriologists have been able to isolate and study the bacteria—that is, bacilli, cocci, and spirilli—or viruses responsible for most of these contagious diseases. Some diseases, such as common colds, influenza, measles, smallpox, and infantile paralysis (polio), are not caused by ordinary germs but by extremely small organisms known as viruses. These disorders are known as virus diseases.

The recognition of a second large field of diseases, which we know of as constitutional and degenerative diseases, grew primarily out of our improved knowledge of human physiology during the last hundred years.

This helps to explain such pathological conditions as heart disorders, cancer, and other diseases connected with senility.

Chronic and degenerative diseases. So successful have medical science and bacteriology been in their efforts to cope with contagious diseases that today, in civilized countries, the most deadly disorders are the non-communicable diseases, chiefly constitutional and degenerative. Among these are heart and circulatory disorders; cancer; kidney diseases, such as nephritis (Bright's disease); diabetes; serious brain diseases; liver disorders; acute rheumatic fever; pernicious anemia; appendicitis; and thyroid disorders, such as goiter. Heart and circulatory diseases, which cause death in several ways, are our most deadly maladies today. They cause over 650,000 deaths annually—nearly half of the total. Even in the field of non-contagious diseases, medical science has made great headway, as we shall indicate.

Mental and nervous diseases. Another category, also comprised for the most part of noncommunicable diseases, is made up of mental and nervous disorders, which are becoming increasingly prevalent amidst the strains and stresses of modern urban life. Today, more than half of the public hospital beds in the United States are occupied by patients suffering from mental and nervous diseases.

EXTENT OF DISEASE AND ACCIDENTS IN THE UNITED STATES

Amount of illness in the United States. In the autumn and winter of 1935-1936, the United States Public Health Service, aided by grants from the Works Progress Administration, made a house-to-house canvass of illness in 740,000 urban families in 19 states and 36,000 rural families in 3 states.

On the basis of this survey it was estimated that, in the United States, 6 million persons were not able to work on any average day during the winter months because of illness resulting from disease, or injury caused by accident. This figure is higher than it would be for the summer months, since in winter there are more cases of influenza, pneumonia, and colds. An official estimate in 1948 held that at least 7 million persons are incapacitated every day by illness.

"The great killers." The most serious diseases are the "great killers," those which are most likely to produce death and do actually bring about the greatest number of deaths. Heart disease and circulatory disorders head the list. Technically, they are known as cardiovascular diseases, and they embrace some 21 distinct types of heart and circulatory disorders. They cause the death of over 650,000 persons annually—some 44 per cent of all deaths from disease. There are over 10,000,000 persons in the United States who are disabled by heart and circulatory diseases, and they lose about 152,000,000 work-days annually. An estimated 60,000,000 persons now alive in the United States will die of heart disease and circulatory troubles unless treatment is radically improved and applied in the immediate future. It is amazing that, in the light of these appalling figures, only about 200 out of some 150,000 practicing physicians in the

United States limit themselves solely to the specialized treatment of heart disorders, and less than 450 others are even part-time specialists in this field. The amount of money that has been spent for research in the study of heart disease is also distressingly low. In 1948 the per-death expenditure for research purposes was $525 for infantile paralysis, $2.13 for cancer, but only 17 cents for heart disease. Despite all the money spent on infantile paralysis research, the epidemic of 1949—about 40,000 cases—was the worst in our history.

Cancer ranks next to heart and circulatory diseases as a killer today. Some 500,000 persons died from cancer from 1942 through 1944, or nearly twice as many as were killed in battle among the American armed forces

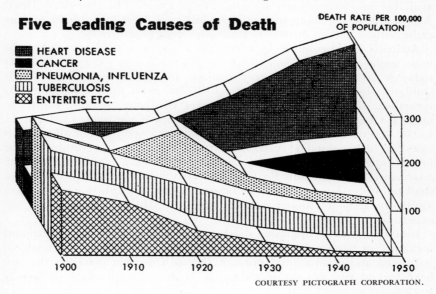

Five Leading Causes of Death

DEATH RATE PER 100,000 OF POPULATION

- HEART DISEASE
- CANCER
- PNEUMONIA, INFLUENZA
- TUBERCULOSIS
- ENTERITIS ETC.

300

200

100

1900   1910   1920   1930   1940   1950

COURTESY PICTOGRAPH CORPORATION.

in the Second World War. About 200,000 persons died of cancer in 1950. Around 22 million persons now alive will die of cancer unless the present death rate is lowered by better treatment. About 300,000 develop cancer each year. In 1951, the National Cancer Institute reported that cancer has increased notably in recent years. The number of new cases increased by some 37 per cent between 1937 and 1947. Some of this may have been due to the increase in the population, but no great amount, since the main population increase was in the number of young persons who are not so much affected by this disease. Lung cancer is increasing most rapidly, perhaps due in part to increased cigarette smoking and the dust-laden air breathed by the ever growing city populations.

Medical statistics indicate that third in order as menaces to health and life come the various brain lesions and pathological brain conditions, and fourth, the chronic, degenerative kidney diseases, sometimes lumped together under the term nephritis.

As we have hinted above, the money we spend to fight the more deadly diseases has been illogically apportioned. The National Foundation for Infantile Paralysis collected 22 million dollars in 1948, and had a reserve of over 10 million. The National Tuberculosis Association collected about 20 million, and the American Cancer Society over 13 million. But the American Heart Association, which has to combat the greatest killer of all, collected only $1,600,000 in 1948, and only $2,656,000 in 1949. The most important achievement in the campaign against heart diseases came in 1948. The Federal government passed the National Heart Act, which provided for the establishment of the National Heart Institute as a unit in the United States Public Health Service. Some three million dollars was appropriated for this work in 1949, and over 10 million was available in 1950 to carry forward the program. The American Heart Association raised about four million dollars in 1950, and sought to raise eight million dollars in 1951 to study and treat heart diseases.

Arthritis and rheumatic disorders. Not a leading cause of death but the most serious chronic ailment and the second largest cause of disability today is arthritis, with other rheumatic ills. Arthritis is a peculiarly stubborn disorder, the causes of which are little understood even by specialists. But the ravages from this type of disease are due mainly to neglect. One of the leading medical specialists in the field, LeMoyne C. Kelley, has recently estimated that "more than 75 per cent of all arthritis cases can be benefited or cured if adequate treatment is begun during the first year. Even more advanced cases can be helped." And many of the established remedies thus far found effective are relatively cheap. As we shall point out later, we seem to be on the eve of revolutionary curative agents for arthritis, though most of them are still expensive and in the experimental stage.

Industrial and occupational diseases. Any discussion of the nature and incidence of disease would be incomplete if mention were not made of industrial and occupational diseases. One of the great penalties that we have had to pay for our machine age is the harmful effect of factory work upon human health.

These industrial and occupational diseases may take many forms, from the general undermining of the health of miners and office workers, who fail to get enough fresh air and sunshine, to such specific ailments as lead poisoning, from which painters often suffer, and silicosis, contracted by stone cutters. It would be difficult to estimate the amount of ill health for which modern working conditions are responsible.

There is also little doubt that the fatigue associated with many jobs, especially in some mass-production factories, has a serious effect upon health. The sheer boredom of factory work produces nervous reactions that keep many people from work. An English medical journal, *The Lancet,* stated in 1931 that boredom caused industrial workers in England to lose more time from their jobs than all the recognized industrial diseases combined.

The accident menace. Disease is not the only leading cause of death. There are around 30,000 accidents every day, and about 10 million a year serious enough to keep a person from work for a day or longer. Each year about one out of every 16 persons is killed or disabled by accidents. Fatal accidents have decreased from a high of 110,000 in 1936 but the figure is still far too high, around 100,000 annually. The year 1950 was the "safest" in recent years, but even in that year 90,000 persons were killed and 8,900,000 injured. Some 275,338 Americans lost their lives in the armed forces during the Second World War, but during this same period the deaths from accidents numbered over 355,000. About 670,584 Americans were wounded during the war, but during the same years those injured in accidents numbered 36,000,000.

Automobile traffic is the leading cause of fatal accidents. Some 31,500 persons were killed in automobile accidents in 1949. They increased by 11 per cent—to over 35,000—in 1950. Nearly as many persons have been killed by automobiles as in all the wars in American history. Through the year 1949, 970,000 persons had been killed in battle in the course of all American wars, and 910,000 had been killed by automobiles. There were some 1,125,000 non-fatal automobile accidents in 1950.

Accidents are especially frequent and mortal among children. More children are killed in accidents in the United States each year than die from all children's diseases combined. Over 14,000 children are killed each year in accidents; 1,500,000 are injured in accidents, and over 50,000 of those injured are permanently disabled. Even in the epidemic years of 1945 to 1949, the death toll from polio for children under 15 years of age was only 4,343, but some 71,000 were killed in accidents. There has been little progress in reducing the death rate from accidents among children. In the last 15 years the death rate from non-accidental causes has been reduced by 44 per cent, while that from accidents has dropped only 2 per cent.

In 1940, accidents produced a loss of man-days in industry some twenty times greater than the loss of work time due to strikes. It has been pointed out that the loss of 340 million man-days through accidents in the first nine months of 1941 might have built 20 battleships, 200 destroyers, and 1,000 heavy bombers.

The economic cost of accidents is appalling. Even in 1950, with the lowest accident toll in recent history, it was estimated by the National Safety Council that the economic loss from accidents in that year totalled some $7,700,000,000. This included wage losses, medical expenses, overhead costs of insurance, production delays, damage to equipment, and property damage from fires and traffic accidents.

The total cost of caring for all the physically handicapped—deaf, dumb, blind, and crippled, many of the latter maimed by accidents—is over 500 million dollars annually. Only a few of these afflicted men and women are employed.

Causes of accidents. The causes of accidents are an overpowering desire for profits, which keeps employers from installing safety devices on dangerous machines; the mania of motorists for speed on the highways and on city streets; and carelessness in construction work, factories and mines, on the streets, and, above all, in the home. Accidents in the home rank next to traffic accidents as the chief cause of accidental death. Some

27,500 died in this way in 1950, while only 15,500 were killed in occupational accidents. In a normal peacetime year, about one-third of all accidents causing death take place in the home. Nearly 20 per cent of the 100,000 deaths from accidents in 1947 occurred on farms.

Progress in reducing accidents. In late years there has been a per capita decline in industrial accidents, because workmen's compensation laws have forced employers to provide better safety devices such as goggles to shield the eyes of the metal or stone worker, steel covering for dangerous machinery, and emergency levers to stop a machine before it crushes a man's hands. Pressure by John L. Lewis and his United Mine Workers and enlightened self-interest by some mine operators have markedly reduced the mining accidents in recent years. Since 1912, the vast steel industry of the United States has given special attention to accident prevention. In 1949, its accident record was about half that of the average for all industries. Safety measures have also reduced railroad accidents, except in the environs of New York City. The year 1937 was the safest in railroad history, with a passenger fatality rate of 0.073 per hundred million passenger miles. Lack of repair and replacement on road beds and equipment, as well as greater speeds and traffic, led to a considerable increase of accidents after Pearl Harbor, but they were still far fewer than thirty years ago, and new equipment has once again brought the accident rate down to prewar levels—0.074 per hundred million passenger miles in 1949. Cities have sought to reduce the hazards to pedestrians. In 1950, it was announced that per capita accidents to pedestrians in New York City had been reduced to half the 1930 level.

Rise of the safety movement. The accident menace has been countered by the rise of the safety movement. Safety campaigns in large cities are waging war on the careless motorist who does not "Stop! Look! and Listen!" Special educational movies have been prepared showing the dangers of drunken driving and carelessness at home. The striking and shocking educational pamphlet, *And Sudden Death,* on automobile accidents, by J. C. Furnas, made many persons more careful on the roads. We shall deal with some of the more successful community safety campaigns in a later chapter.

Handicapped persons. An important item in the health and medical problem is the matter of handicapped persons. There are at least 28 million handicapped children and adults in the country, distributed, according to an estimate in August, 1948, as follows: deaf and hard of hearing, 9 million; orthopedically handicapped, 8 million; dumb and lesser speech defects, 6 million; cardiac troubles, 4 million; blind and defective vision, 4 million; epileptic, 6 million; and rheumatic fever, 500,000. That this estimate is moderate can be seen from the fact that a special survey of those suffering from hearing ailments alone in 1949 put the number at 15 million. It was estimated that, of this number, 3 million were children, the great majority of whom could be cured if they received adequate treatment in time. The more usual estimate of the number disabled by heart (cardiac) diseases is 10 million rather than four.

ACCIDENTAL DEATHS BY PRINCIPAL TYPES

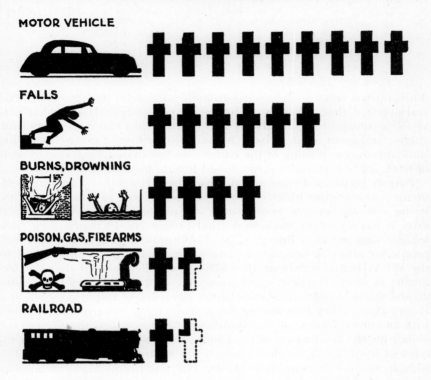

MOTOR VEHICLE

FALLS

BURNS, DROWNING

POISON, GAS, FIREARMS

RAILROAD

BUILDING AMERICA

COURTESY *Building America* AND THE METROPOLITAN LIFE INSURANCE COMPANY.

As we have noted, the cost of caring for the handicapped surely runs to at least half a billion dollars a year. When one also considers the loss of labor and of professional and industrial skill involved, the economic cost of having so many handicapped persons is astronomical, presumably running into more than a billion dollars a year. Since many of these handicaps result from preventable diseases and accidents, the problem is directly linked with that of medical care and safety precautions to prevent accidents. The incidence of blindness has been greatly reduced by using nitrate of silver and, more recently, penicillin on the eyes of new-born infants.

ECONOMIC AND SOCIAL ASPECTS OF ILLNESS, ACCIDENTS AND PREVENTABLE DEATHS

Tremendous economic cost of disease, accidents and preventable deaths. The economic cost of illness, accidents, and preventable or premature deaths is tremendous—some 38 billion dollars or about 15 per cent of our total national income. The Federal Security Agency has broken down this total cost for 1947 as follows:

Short-term sickness	$ 5,000,000,000
Incapacitation	$11,000,000,000
Partial disability	$11,000,000,000
Premature, preventable deaths	$11,000,000,000
Total	$38,000,000,000

This cost was equal to even our astronomical Federal budget before 1951 and over ten times what we spend for all public education annually. If saved (as much of it could be by adequate medical care and safety campaigns) and spent constructively, it would go far toward raising the living standards and well-being of the nation. No less than 4,300,000 man-years of work are lost annually through bad health, much of it preventable.

Poverty increases disease and deaths. There is another important economic consideration which needs to be pointed out in this place. That is the relation between poverty and disease, and poverty and medical care. It has long been understood that people are, in many cases, poor because they are sick. But, as C. E. A. Winslow does well to point out, people are also sick because they are poor. This fact was emphasized in the WPA Health Survey of 1935-1936. It was here shown that the frequency of illness is much higher among the poor than among the well-to-do and the rich. Illness that disabled for one week or longer occurred at a 57 per cent higher rate among families on relief than among families with an annual income of $3,000 or more. Chronic illness ran 87 per cent higher for the families on relief. Families not on relief, but with an income of less than $1,000, had twice as much illness disability as families with an income of more than $1,000. The number of heads of families who could not seek employment because of illness was much higher among families on relief. Among the latter, one head of a family out of every 20 was unable to seek work because of disability. For families not on relief with incomes of $1,000 and under, the ratio was 1 in 33, and in families not on relief with incomes of over $3,000 the ratio was 1 in 250.

Other interesting conclusions were drawn from this survey by Josephine Roche, Assistant Secretary of the Treasury in charge of Public Health, who directed the survey. She pointed out that the death rate from the ten major diseases (those which cause three out of every four deaths in the United States) for the more than 40 million Americans with incomes of less than $1,000 a year was twice that of the rest of the population. The death rate from all causes was more than twice as high for the unskilled workers as it was for the professional classes. The death rate from respiratory tuberculosis was seven times as great among unskilled workers as among the professional classes. Pneumonia killed three and a half times as many unskilled workers as it did professional workers. Infant mortality was five times as high in families that had an income of less than $500 as in families with an income of over $3,000. Yet, half the babies born in the United States at the time were born to families on relief and families not on relief but with an income of less than $1,000. Poverty was also responsible for most of the preventable deaths of mothers in childbirth. As Bernhard J. Stern puts it: "It is clear that ill health and high mortality are products of poverty and low income and do not arise from any postulated organic inferiority of those belonging to the lower income groups." The following table, taken from the Report of the 1935-1936 Federal Health Survey, will give a clear picture of the close relationship between low income and the frequency of illness and disability:

RELATION OF ANNUAL PER CAPITA VOLUME OF DISABILITY[a] IN THE
UNITED STATES FOR LOW INCOME GROUPS TO THAT IN THE
HIGHEST INCOME GROUP, 1935-1936 [b]

| | | Income Status of Family | | |
Diagnosis	Relief	Under $1,000 per year	$1,000 to $1,500 per year	$5,000 and over
All Diagnoses	266	166	121	100
Tuberculosis	875	388	250	100
Orthopedic Impairments	420	283	175	100
Rheumatism	369	213	138	100
Digestive Diseases	340	180	114	100
Nervous Diseases	287	204	135	100
Degenerative Diseases	268	156	109	100
Accidents	221	173	129	100
Respiratory Diseases	189	121	91	100
Infectious Diseases	124	93	93	100
Diagnoses not elsewhere grouped	261	160	127	100

[a] Defined as the product of the frequency of illness and the duration of illness.
[b] Adjusted to the age composition of the Health Survey total white population, 1935-36.

Source: National Health Survey 1935-36, Preliminary Reports, Sickness and Medical Care Series Bulletin 9: *Disability from Specific Causes in Relation to Economic Status* (Washington, 1938), p. 9.

It is often taken for granted that health conditions among the poor in city slums are bad, but we assume that even the poor in country districts are robust and healthy. This illusion was shattered by a health survey of low-income farm families conducted by the Farm Security Administration in 1941. The findings have been summarized as follows:

Farm security officials were shocked to find that only four per cent were in good health while the number of physical defects averaged three and a half per person. An appalling rate of defective teeth, vision, and hearing is disclosed in the report, and clinical diagnosis revealed that one child out of every 12 under 15 years of age suffered from malnutrition and one out of 17 from rickets.

The greater mortality among the poor is due to three main causes. First, their crowded and unsanitary living conditions expose them to greater danger of infection, so that they are more likely to contract disease. Second, their low income usually makes it difficult or impossible for them to get adequate medical care when they become sick. Third, there is the fact that malnutrition among the poor lowers their resistance, renders them more susceptible to disease, and makes them more likely to die even when given proper medical attention.

Poverty limits medical care. The same discrepancy is seen when we consider the relation of poverty to inadequate medical care. The proportion of families who receive no care from a physician in the instance of disease is far higher among the poor. Among families on relief in 1936, 30 per cent of the cases of illness received no care from a physician. Among families with an income above $3,000, only 17 per cent of the cases of illness were without the care of a physician. A comparable situation existed in lack of nursing and hospital care received by poor families. This was particularly true of poor families in small cities and rural areas. Forty per cent of the counties in the United States, comprising a population of 17 million, did not have available a registered general hospital. Some 40 million persons, those with an annual income of less than $1,000 could not pay for adequate medical services and in many instances did not receive medical care. It was then estimated that a family needed an income of $100 weekly to assure adequate medical care under private practice, unless covered by voluntary insurance. The figure would need to be $200 weekly today.

Very important in the light of these facts was the large number of persons who were receiving free, if often inadequate, treatment from competent physicians. It was estimated in 1936 that there were about 1,230,000 persons daily receiving medical treatment in the United States. Approximately 500,000 of these were treated in free clinics. Of the 730,000 who were treated by private doctors, some 225,000 did not pay their bills. In short, about two-thirds of the nation's sick, who get any medical treatment at all, were on the free list. It was estimated that American doctors donate over a million dollars daily in free medical attention, when we take into account both free clinics and non-payment of bills.

MEDICAL SCIENCE AND THE CONQUEST OF DISEASE

Medical science reduces the death rate and infant mortality. In this section we shall concentrate upon certain outstanding achievements of medicine in combating disease. We have already referred to the effect of medical progress in reducing the death rate and especially in lowering infant mortality. Just to refresh our memory on this matter, we may recall attention to the fact that the death rate in Sweden dropped from 27.9 in 1790 to 11.7 in 1940. The death rate among children in the United States was reduced remarkably in the first half of the present century—from 116 per 1,000 of the population in 1901-1910 to 45 in 1950. The death rate from the main communicable disease of childhood—measles, scarlet fever, whooping cough, and diphtheria—was reduced by 90 per cent during this period. Between 1898 and 1948 the infant death rate in New York City was cut from 140.9 per 1,000 to 30.4.

Medical science depends on natural sciences. The progress of modern medical science rested upon prior discoveries in the field of natural science, especially in biology, physiology, chemistry, and physics. Indeed, medical science has tended to lag behind scientific discoveries in general. For example, blood transfusions were first performed in the seventeenth century, but were not generally introduced into medical practice until the time of the First World War. Sir Christopher Wren first employed the intravenous injection of drugs in 1656, but this did not come into general use until syphilis was thus treated early in the twentieth century. Sir Humphry Davy discovered the anesthetic, nitrous oxide, in 1799; but anesthesia was not successfully introduced into surgery until it was employed by the Georgia physician, Crawford W. Long, in 1842, and the Boston dentist, William T. G. Morton, in 1846. It took the British Navy over forty years to introduce James Lind's cure for scurvy. Surgeons long combated Lord Lister's notions of aseptic surgery, and Louis Pasteur had to battle for many years against the opposition of physicians and surgeons alike to his bacteriological discoveries, which have since revolutionized the conceptions of infection.

Quarantine. One of the earliest achievements of medical science in controlling disease was the origin of quarantine. A semireligious basis for this appeared among the Hebrews and the early Christians. But the adoption of quarantine as a truly medical practice did not come until the time of the Black Death in 1348-1349. The very word quarantine is derived from the words *quaranta giorni,* or forty days, the period of time set by town authorities for the segregation of those suffering from the Black Death.

Inoculation, vaccination, and immunity. Another important phase of medical progress in combating disease was the rise of the theory of promoting immunity through inoculation and vaccination. Inoculation was first associated with the attempt to control smallpox and seems thus to have been introduced into Turkey about 1675. In this form of treatment, persons were inoculated with smallpox virus taken from those who were suffering from a mild case. Knowledge of this procedure was brought to England in practical fashion by Lady Mary Wortley Montagu, wife of the British Ambassador at Constantinople, in 1718. The practice was first introduced into Western medicine by a Boston physician, Zabdiel Boylston (1679-1766), in 1721. He was threatened with death for his innovation, but he was successfully protected by none other than Cotton Mather.

It was the English physician, Edward Jenner (1748-1823), who improved upon this method by substituting vaccination for inoculation. He found that immunity to smallpox could be produced by vaccinating persons with virus taken from cows suffering from cowpox (*vaccina*), from which we get the term vaccination. He proved the value of this method in 1798. It has subsequently been applied to other diseases. Pasteur discovered a method of inoculation against rabies in 1885. Vaccination against typhoid fever was introduced by Pfeiffer and Kolle in Germany and by Wright in England in 1896. The use of vaccination or mild inoculation has been greatly extended since that time.

Discovery of curative drugs. The discovery of the use of potent drugs to check deadly diseases has been an important aspect of medical progress. The first revolutionary achievement was the introduction of what was originally known as Jesuit's bark, brought to Europe from Peru in 1638. It was called "cinchona" because it was first successfully used in the treatment of the Countess of Cinchon. The remedy derived from it came to be known as quinine. Its use was first established in England by Thomas Sydenham in 1658. It worked a veritable revolution in the treatment of malaria, which had hitherto been one of the major maladies afflicting the human race. From this time until the introduction of salvarsan, sulfanilamide, and antibiotics in the twentieth century, drugs have played an increasingly important role in the human control of disease.

Bacteriology and the germ theory of disease. Perhaps the most important achievement of medical science in the way of understanding and controlling disease is that connected with the rise of bacteriology. Forecast by Henle in 1840, it took its practical origins from the investigations of fermentation by Louis Pasteur. From this field it passed into human pathology. Pasteur had already established the relation of bacteria to a deadly disease of the French silkworm. Pasteur's work was paralleled by that of the German pathologist, Robert Koch (1843-1910). In the late 1870's, Koch investigated the causes of infection in wounds, and in 1882 he made the revolutionary discovery of the bacillus that causes tuberculosis. After this, as Harvey Cushing graphically expressed it, new bacteriological discoveries came along "like corn popping in a pan." Among the more important of these, which followed between the 1870's and 1905, were Koch's discovery of the germ of Asiatic cholera; Neisser's discovery of the gonococcus; Hansen's discovery of the germ of leprosy; Laveran's discovery of the germ of malaria; Nicolaier's discovery of the tetanus bacillus; Kitasato and Yersin's discovery of the plague germ; Loffler's discovery of the diphtheria germ; the discovery of the pneumonia coccus by Friedlander, Frankel, and Sternberg; Eberth's discovery of the germ which causes typhoid fever; Weichselbaum's discovery of the meningococcus; Bruce's discovery of the germ of Malta fever; Schaudinn's discovery of the spirillum which produces syphilis; and Stiles' isolation of the hookworm parasite.

Other physicians and laboratory specialists have shown that some diseases are not caused by germs but by viruses, living organisms but closer to the inorganic realm than germs. They are so small that they could not be seen until the recent development of the electron microscope. Some are so small that they are no more than a millionth of an inch in diameter. We have already mentioned some of the leading diseases caused by virus infections.

A more recent development in bacteriology has been what is known as "preventive" bacteriology. This is based upon the discovery that otherwise healthy persons may carry germs of deadly disease in their systems without contracting the disease themselves. This suggested the necessity of treating or isolating such dangerous disease carriers. Bacteriology also revolutionized surgery by suggesting the use of antiseptics to kill germs in operations, and later promoting aseptic surgery, which gave the surgeon a germ-free field of operation to start with. It has also greatly reduced deaths from childbirth.

Epidemiology. A fundamental branch of medicine that has waged war against disease is what is known as epidemiology, or the science of epidemic diseases. It rests upon a growing apprehension of the facts about contagion. We have already noted that a Spanish Muslim physician studied contagious diseases in relation to the Black Death of his own time. But the first decisive book on the theory of contagion was that written in 1546 by the Italian physician, Girolamo Fracastoro, on *Contagions and Contagious Diseases*. Likewise, Richard Mead in England studied the spread of the plague in 1720. The introduction into medical science of a clear understanding of the nature and method of contagion—the germ theory of disease—was contained in the *Pathological Researches* by Jacob Henle (1809-1885), published in 1840. The advances in bacteriology outlined above have, of course, been of very great value in promoting epidemiology.

The first important specific contribution to the science of epidemiology was the study of the Devonshire colic by Huxham in 1739 and by Sir George Baker in 1767. This was continued in John Haygarth's study of the epidemiology of smallpox and typhus in 1767-1793. As the result of the further development of epidemiology, the major pestilences of previous centuries have been pretty thoroughly eradicated among civilized peoples. This achievement has been due to a growing understanding of the germs which produce these epidemic diseases, and of the living conditions which favor their growth and spread. Medicine has suggested ways of preventing infection, promoting immunity, and killing the germs. An important contribution to epidemiology was the demonstration by the English statistician, James Brownlee, in the twentieth century, that there are cycles of epidemics and that their return may be predicted, thus preparing physicians and the public to cope with the situation without being taken by surprise. Brownlee's investigations were instigated by the influenza epidemic at the close of the First World War. Our knowledge of epidemic diseases has been advanced by such students as Simon Flexner in America and William Topley in England, who artificially induced and experimentally controlled epidemics in laboratory animals.

Tropical medicine. Many important contributions to our knowledge and technique of disease control have come from what is known as "tropical medicine." In 1877, Patrick Manson discovered that certain female mosquitoes play an important part in transmitting diseases. He suggested in 1884 that they are responsible for malarial infection, a theory which was demonstrated to be true by his colleague, Ronald Ross, in 1898. In 1900 the American physician, Walter Reed, showed that the deadly yellow fever is also carried by a female mosquito. In 1904 Dutton and Todd discovered that the African tick fever—"relapsing fever"—is produced by the bite of the tick. About the same time, Sir David Bruce found that the African sleeping sickness is transmitted to man by the tsetse fly.

Serums and serology. Important in the war on disease has been the development of what is known as serology, or the science of the uses of serums and antitoxins to cure diseases. This began by experiments with diphtheria antitoxin, carried on mainly by Roux and Yersin in 1888 after Loffler's discovery of the diphtheria bacillus in 1884. This antitoxin was first applied to a human patient in von Bergmann's clinic in Germany in 1891. It has been improved by von Behring, Kitasato, and others and has become very effective.

The use of serums has been enormously extended since the original experiments with diphtheria antitoxin. Some are prophylactic, or protective, and are injected to render the person immune to the disease. Such serums have been found very effective in preventing tetanus, rabies, scarlet fever, typhoid fever, and certain other diseases. Other serums are curative, and are used to insure and hasten the successful treatment of those suffering from a particular disorder. Such are the serums used in treating certain types of meningitis, infantile paralysis, tick fever, pneumonia, and the like. The most remarkable recent development in serums has been the discovery by a noted Russian bio-chemist, Alexander Bogomolets, of a serum that is alleged to check the chemical changes in the body cells which cause senescence (old age). This may increase the normal life span to 100 years or more.

Aseptic surgery. Aseptic surgery, based on bacteriology and chemistry, has greatly reduced the death rate. The founder of aseptic surgery, Joseph Jackson (Lord) Lister (1827-1912), found that the death rate on amputations performed by him between 1864 and 1866 was 45 per cent. Pasteur's early experiments fell into his hands, and Lister became convinced that their lessons could be fruitfully applied to surgery. Therefore, he advocated the cleansing of the surgeon's hands and the patient's wounds by antiseptics, particularly carbolic acid. The results he achieved were revolutionary, but for years he was ridiculed and combated by conventional surgeons. The earliest antiseptics were such crude and simple chemicals as carbolic acid and iodine. During the First World War, such improved antiseptics as Dakin's solution (commercially known as Zonite) were introduced. In recent years much safer and more effective antiseptic drugs have been found. Sulfa preparations and such antibiotics as penicillin, streptomycin, tyrothricin, and gramicidin have been introduced to supplement the older germicides.

Aseptic obstetrics. The all-important introduction of the conception of antisepsis into obstetrics was due to the work of Oliver Wendell Holmes in the United States and of Ignatz Semmelweiss in Vienna. Simultaneously, they arrived at the conviction that childbed fever or puerperal infection is due to the presence of contagious factors, that is, pathological bacteria. This discovery came in the 1840's. Semmelweiss was ridiculed and battled by the Viennese doctors, and in disgust he resigned from his position in Vienna and went to Budapest to teach obstetrics. He was so pained and disappointed over the rejection of his doctrines that he ultimately died in an insane asylum. But his views revolutionized obstetrics and saved the lives of hundreds of thousands of mothers, who had earlier been sacrificed to the ignorance, carelessness, and stubbornness of physicians.

In spite of the work of Holmes, Semmelweiss, and their successors, the deaths from childbirth infections remained scandalously high until the coming of the sulfa drugs and the antibiotics after 1935. Today, such infections are proof of virtually criminal carelessness and neglect on the part of the physician or midwife.

Development of anesthesia. Pain, illness, and death have been reduced by the development of anesthetic surgery, another important contribution of chemistry to medicine. In 1800 the English chemist, Sir Humphry Davy, pointed out that nitrous oxide gas could be inhaled, sleep produced, and pain eliminated. He suggested that this fact might be made use of in surgery. But it was half a century before this discovery was utilized in medicine, first in dentistry. On December 11, 1844, nitrous oxide gas was used by Henry Wells in Hartford, Connecticut, to extract a tooth without pain. In the meantime, in March, 1842, Crawford W. Long, of Georgia, used ether to remove a tumor from the neck of a patient. But the decisive introduction of anesthetic surgery was the work of William T. G. Morton, originally an assistant of Wells as a dentist and later a physician. On October 16, 1846, Morton administered ether to a patient of John C. Warren at the Massachusetts General Hospital in Boston, and Warren removed a tumor painlessly. The medical world was then convinced that a new era had dawned in surgery. Sir James Simpson introduced chloroform for surgery in England in 1847. Anesthesia has been greatly improved during the last century through the discovery of new anesthetics and novel combinations of traditional ones, and through the provision and increasing use of local anesthetics, such as cocaine and novocaine.

The sulfa drugs. The greatest contribution ever made by chemistry to the struggle against disease has been the discovery and introduction, since about 1935, of the sulfa drugs and, subsequently, of the various so-called antibiotics.

The first of the sulfa drugs was sulfanilamide, derived from a dye product and first introduced in Germany in 1935. A large number of improved sulfa drugs have since been discovered and made available, such as sulfapyridine, sulfathiazole, sulfadiazine, sulfasuxidine, sulfamerizine, and sulfaguanidine. These later improvements are, generally speaking, more effective against germs and less toxic (less harmful to the system) than the original sulfanilamide.

The sulfa drugs do not kill germs; they paralyze them until the white corpuscles in the blood can destroy them. The sulfa drugs have not only been very valuable in reducing infections arising from surgery and childbirth, but have been unprecedentedly effective in treating meningitis, serious streptococcic infections, kidney infections, gonorrhea, certain types of pneumonia, erysipelas, and several other maladies. In 1948, a new sulfa derivative, known as thalamyd, was reported to be effective against ulcerative colitis, bacillary dysentery and even cholera. Derivatives of sulfanilamide, the so-called sulfone drugs, have proved the only effective remedy in treating leprosy.

Unfortunately, certain persons cannot use sulfa drugs safely. In some instances the application of sulfa drugs appears to reduce the number of red corpuscles in the blood and, more rarely, to kill off the white corpuscles which usually produces death.

The new antibiotics. It is very fortunate that, about the time the sulfa drugs were beginning to work their wonders on those who could use them safely, a whole new range of so-called antibiotic substances were discovered, most of which can be used without any disastrous results to patients. Antibiotics are microbes that are able to cluster or clump together disease germs in the body so that the white corpuscles can quickly and easily dispose of them. Most of these antibiotics are derived from molds or from soil bacteria.

The most famous and useful of these antibiotics is penicillin, derived from a blue-green mold like that which forms on bread and cheese. It was first discovered by Alexander Fleming in London, in 1929, and was made available for general medical use during the Second World War. Penicillin is far less toxic than the sulfa drugs and can, therefore, be given in very powerful doses. It is probably the greatest single discovery in the whole history of medical science and has checked and cured more infections and diseases than any other single drug ever known. Further research has provided ever more powerful types of penicillin, such as the one known as penicillin X. Penicillin is invaluable in destroying infections in ordinary wounds and in surgical incisions. It is potent against most of the diseases which have yielded to the sulfa drugs and is more effective since it can be used in unlimited doses under proper medical supervision. Penicillin has completely revolutionized the treatment of venereal diseases: one large injection of a special preparation called duracillin will cure gonorrhea nine times out of ten, and it has become the most widely used drug in preventing and treating syphilis.

There are, however, a number of disease germs, called gram-negative microbes, which do not yield to penicillin. To overcome these, Selman Waksman of Rutgers University discovered in 1943 another remarkable antibiotic known as streptomycin. It appears to be the first antibiotic that is fairly effective against certain types of tuberculosis and the hitherto almost fatal tubercular meningitis. Other powerful antibiotics, derived from the soil bacteria, such as tyrothricin and gramicidin, are highly toxic and cannot be injected into the system, but they are very effective in curing refractory surface infections.

Among the latest important additions to the antibiotic arsenal are chloromycetin, discovered by P. R. Burkholder in 1947, and aureomycin, discovered by B. M. Duggar in 1945. Chloromycetin has been found to be extremely effective against typhoid fever and scrub typhus. Aureomycin works rapidly in the treatment of virus pneumonia, Rocky Mountain spotted fever, and undulant fever, the latter of which has previously proved an extremely stubborn disorder. No important toxic after-effects have yet been discovered in the use of either of these drugs.

Waksman, the discoverer of streptomycin, announced the discovery of a new antibiotic, neomycin, in 1949. It promises to be effective against paratyphoid fever, tuberculosis, and boils and abscesses. In 1949, the Charles Pfizer Laboratories discovered a new antibiotic called viomycin, which promises effectively to supplement streptomycin in the treatment of tuberculosis. Enzymes, such as streptodornase and streptokinase, have recently been found very useful in cleansing infections in body locations inaccessible to practicable surgical treatment.

A great revolution in the future provision of antibiotics came in 1949, when Mildred Rebstock learned how to produce chloromycetin synthetically by chemical methods. If this technique can be applied to other antibiotics it will greatly increase production and lessen costs.

Resistance of germs to new drugs. It might be thought that, with the discovery of the sulfa drugs and the antibiotics, many dread diseases and serious infections are now fully conquered. But this is not so; there seems to be a struggle for existence in the realm of disease germs, and new strains of these germs appear that are highly resistant to both the sulfa drugs and the antibiotics. However, chemical and medical researchers are making these remedies more powerful all the time and are discovering new antibiotics to conquer the newer and more resistant disease germs. It now seems that the chemists and doctors can always keep one step ahead of new and more resistant strains of germs.

An interesting juncture of the old and new in medical history came with a recurrence of a few cases of bubonic plague on the 600th anniversary of the famous and devastating epidemic of the Middle Ages (the Black Death of 1349). These cases were promptly treated and quickly and easily cured by use of the sulfa drugs and the new antibiotics. Some cases were cured by a combination of sulfadiazine and streptomycin, and others by combining penicillin and aureomycin. This dramatic therapeutic achievement demonstrated impressively how modern medical science can readily conquer one of the most fatal and dreaded diseases of all recorded medical history.

Other contributions of chemistry to the war on disease. Chemists have discovered a number of other useful new drugs. One is thiouricil, which is effective against the worst form of goiter. Then, there is the new group of anti-histamine drugs, which are useful in treating the great range of allergic diseases from asthma and hay fever to skin diseases and serum sicknesses. Chemistry has also been very important in developing our ideas about increasing human vitality and resistance to disease. Especially important here has been the discovery of vitamins.

Those chemists and physiologists who study nutrition have found that certain foods have elements vital to health, but others lack such nourishing qualities. Joseph Goldberger of the United States Health Service discovered that the poor whites in the South who were afflicted with pellagra lived mainly on an unbalanced diet of cornbread and molasses. Goldberger pointed out that the pellagra sufferers lacked proper diet for body needs. When these people were fed green vegetables, rich in vitamins, pellagra all but disappeared. Knowledge of vitamins is causing many people to eat more sanely. For example, fat people who yearn for slender figures are warned to keep plenty of vitamins in their diet.

This discussion leads us logically to the next topic, resistance to disease, because vitamins and other essential items found in milk, eggs, butter, green vegetables, and citrus fruits help to build up bodily resistance to illness.

Building up resistance and immunity to disease. Doctors learned from their study of tuberculosis that certain diseases apparently could not be cured by drugs alone. The only way to check them was to adopt healthier diets and habits, thus enabling the body to become strong enough to throw off disease. This was demonstrated by E. L. Trudeau, who established a famous sanatorium for tuberculosis patients at Saranac Lake, New York, in 1884. His pioneer work in treating tuberculosis was the inspiration for the Public Health Service in much of its experimentation with preventive medicine. It now seems possible that in streptomycin, neomycin, viomycin, and para-aminosalicylic acid we have at last found remedies that will check tuberculosis, which claimed 48,000 lives in 1947.

Though the death rate from tuberculosis dropped from 200 per 100,000 of the population in 1904 to 30 in 1948 and has been cut by 50 per cent since 1930, the announcement of over 133,000 new cases in 1948 indicated the persistent seriousness of this disease. It is estimated that there are over 500,000 persons suffering from active tuberculosis in the population, not over half of whom recognize that they are so afflicted. They thus endanger their own health and spread the disease to others.

Glandular therapy. Another very important type of bio-chemical therapy is that which has grown out of our increasing knowledge of the glands of internal secretion. In many instances we have learned how to produce artificially a substitute for their mysterious hormones and to employ these products in the treatment of glandular disorders. The earliest achievement was the demonstration that some forms of goiter could be cured by administering doses of thyroid extract. This extract was first derived from the thyroid glands of sheep and later manufactured synthetically. Another outstanding discovery in the field of the glandular treatment was the production and administration of insulin after its discovery by F. G. Banting in 1922. This has proved the first effective remedy for coping with diabetes. Further progress was made in diabetic treatment with the development of protamine zinc insulin, which requires only one injection daily, instead of three needed, in serious cases, of the older type of insulin. It has been necessary, thus far, to inject insulin with a needle. In 1949, it was discovered that ACTH, a master hormone derived from the pituitary gland, is effective in treating serious and hitherto incurable diseases of the eye and arthritis. Cortisone is another glandular product which has proved helpful in treating arthritis. It is now believed that cortisone can soon be produced synthetically, thus cutting the present almost prohibitive cost and increasing the supply available. Certain glandular products have also been important as an aid to surgery, particularly in the way of stimulating recovery from surgical shock. Adrenalin has been extensively used for this purpose. Pituitrin is valuable as an aid in restoring intestinal action after an operation, and in inducing child-bed labors.

The latest discovery in this field is that relating to the so-called steroid compounds which many biochemists and physicians believe may come to have great utility in treating cancer, rheumatic fever, arthritis, leukemia, serious skin diseases, and sterility.

Physics aids the battle against disease. The science of physics has also been of great value to the improvement of medical science. X-rays, discovered by Wilhelm von Roentgen in Germany, in 1895, and radium, discovered by the Curies in France, about 1900, are the two main contributions of physics to medicine. X-rays are a great aid to surgeons in ascertaining the need for operations and in locating tumors, fractures, and the like. Both X-rays and radium are valuble in treating numerous disorders, especially cancer. Diathermy has proved useful in relieving many forms of pain. The most recent discoveries in physics that may be of great utility in medicine have been a by-product of the research in intra-atomic energy. Here, radioactive isotopes have been discovered that may open a whole new and promising type of treatment for cancer. Recently, the University of Illinois Medical College has made what may be revolutionary progress in the treatment of cancer by applying massive doses of high-voltage X-rays through the use of a 26-million volt betatron. The many important recent applications of electro-physics in psychiatry, such as electric shock and electroencephalography, will be described in a later chapter.

Psychology and psychosomatic medicine. Biology, physiology, chemistry, and physics are not the only sciences enlisted to battle disease. Recently, psychology has been called in, especially in the new field of psychosomatic medicine. This lays great stress upon the effect of bad mental states and hypochondria in causing illness. It has been estimated that as many as 4 out of ten persons who consult physicians are suffering more from mental symptoms than from physical disorders. This is aside from all who are victims of obvious nervous and mental diseases. Psychosomatic medicine stresses the importance of using sound psychology and psychiatry to deal successfully with such persons. It also emphasizes the fact that the mental attitude of physicians may be quite as important in bringing about cures as their use of drugs. Some regard psychosomatic medicine as the greatest medical advance of the twentieth century next to the discovery of the sulfa drugs and the antibiotics.

Recent advances in dealing with chronic diseases. Although we are as yet only in initial stages in this field, important advances have been made in checking or curing the more important chronic diseases. Antibiotics, especially penicillin, are coming into use to prevent rheumatic fever, one of the serious ailments associated with heart disease, and sulfa drugs have been found effective in preventing its recurrence. Drugs are effective in reducing high blood pressure and coronary occlusion. Recently, a non-toxic remedy popularly known as "the salt sponge," has been discovered which eliminates much of the salt intake which is dangerous to persons suffering from high blood pressure. Remarkable advances in heart surgery, touching such matters as congenital abnormalities and defects of the heart and acute heart infections, have been made since the Second World War. Especially notable is the operation on "blue babies." But most cases still have to be treated by reducing the strain on damaged hearts and lessening fear and anxiety.

Although there is as yet no specific cure for cancer, mortality can be greatly reduced through prompt diagnosis and immediate treatment by surgery and by the use of radium, X-rays, and isotopes. The greatest hope, so far, resides in speedy diagnosis and diversified treatment. Emerson Day, one of our leading cancer specialists, estimated in 1951 that 70,000 out of the 300,000 new cancer cases that develop each year could be "absolutely cured" if diagnosed promptly and treated efficiently. But decisive victory over cancer will probably have to await more knowledge concerning its causes.

Dramatic new medical discoveries in the late 1940's give much promise of soon producing revolutionary gains in the treatment of arthritis and allied disorders. Thus far, four new drugs—cortisone, ACTH (adrebicortico-tropic hormone), pregnenolone, and percoten—are the outstanding recent discoveries that promise to check or cure many arthritic troubles. Cortisone may soon be produced synthetically.

Other examples of recent medical progress. With the growing prevalence of industry and factory employment, industrial medicine has an ever more important role. This branch of medicine began in Great Britain in the middle of the nineteenth century, when Thackrah and Greenhow began to investigate the effect of industrial occupations on human health. It has included the study of poisons contracted in certain occupations (to which Alice Hamilton has given special study), of the effect of dust and other particles inhaled during work, and of the influence of certain occupations upon human fatigue. The application of the principles of scientific management has helped to reduce the effects of fatigue and boredom, and even more effective has been the introduction of industrial and clinical psychology by some enlightened employers. But thus far only the surface of this important economic and medical problem has been scratched. Increased attention has been given to safety appliances in factories, mines, and stores, and to the reduction of accidents.

The increase of mental and nervous diseases has promoted the development of neurology and psychiatry, through which the various organic and functional mental and nervous disorders are studied and treated. The fever and penicillin treatment for paresis, the shock treatment for dementia praecox and depressive psychoses, psychosurgery, and Freud's psychiatric theories represent the most notable progress. The mental hygiene movement was founded to check the growth of nervous and mental diseases.

Success in surgery has been greatly improved by recent developments. The sulfa drugs and the antibiotics have greatly reduced deaths from infection. Improved and more complex methods of anesthesia have aided surgeons. Very important have been blood testing and the provision of blood banks that enable surgeons to attempt far more prolonged and complicated operations than they would have thought of risking a generation ago.

Dentistry has advanced from a crude mechanical technique to a complex medical science. This progress has had significance for curative and preventive medicine generally. Not only have teeth been better cared for, but it has been shown that our teeth may play an important role in producing focal infections that cause arthritis, rheumatism, and other chronic disorders of a serious character. Less weight can be assigned to a theory once popular in certain medical quarters that these focal dental infections are a prominent cause of insanity and criminality. New methods of preventing tooth decay have been provided by the use of fluorine and ammoniated tooth powders and pastes.

It was natural that physicians would give more and more attention to public health measures and to preventive medicine. This is a field which we shall discuss later.

Lack of attention to special medical problems of the aged. Despite all the notable progress in medical science, there is one field of medicine to which little attention has been given as yet. That is the unique medical needs of the aged. A few special students of the problem have developed what they call geriatrics or the science of dealing with the needs and disorders of the aged, and considerable information has been accumulated in this field. But anything like adequate specialized medical care has not yet been extended to the aged group. Howard Rusk recently observed that we have not even scratched the surface in meeting the special medical requirements of the 12,300,000 persons now in the population over 65 years of age. Specialized medical attention for this group would greatly reduce the incidence of disease among them, would enable them to be more productive, and would save much money now lost through unnecessary disease and idleness. The problem is bound to become more serious and extensive as the numbers in this age group increase in the wake of present population trends.

Improved training of physicians and surgeons. We have more trained doctors in proportion to the population than any other country: one to every 750 persons, as compared with 870 in Great Britain, 950 in Denmark, 970 in Canada, 1,300 in France, 2,400 in Union of South Africa, and 25,000 in China. The better medical schools now have at their disposal the medical lore and knowledge of the whole world. They have fine laboratories and excellent clinics. They usually require a college degree for admission, and demand special pre-medical training during college. Four years of work are required in medical college, with several years of internship thereafter. Young physicians who wish to specialize must follow their internship with several years of an all but unpaid medical or surgical residency in a hospital. This means that the young doctor who has the best medical training today will have spent from ten to sixteen years after graduation from high school in getting his medical training before he starts remunerative practice. This is a strenuous and expensive process, and the average reward is pitifully low—an average of about

$5,000 a year in 1940 and $10,000 in 1949. But, whatever the exactions imposed on the incipient physicians, the public gains from the vastly increased competence of the medical profession.

Development of hospital facilities. An important aspect of better medical and surgical treatment has been the establishment and improvement of systematic hospital service. The first important hospitals were built by the Romans. During the Middle Ages the majority of the hospitals were provided by the Catholic church. After the Reformation public authorities were compelled to give more attention to the provision of hospital service. In continental European countries the majority of the hospitals are public institutions maintained by taxation. In Great Britain and the United States, hospitals for general diseases have thus far been provided in considerable part by philanthropic activity and are governed by private trustees.

The present trend is, however, even in the United States, toward public construction and control of hospitals. This is notably true of hospitals for nervous and mental cases. The trend toward public hospitals was promoted particularly as the result of the extensive hospital construction by the United States government to care for disabled veterans. The extent of publicly owned hospitals in the United States is amazing to those who have not investigated the subject. Publicly owned hospitals contain over 70 per cent of the 1,425,000 hospital beds in the country; they provided the care for about 80 per cent of the 445,478,000 patient-days spent in all hospitals in 1948.

Despite the fact that we now have some 6,355 hospitals, with the 1,425,-000 hospital beds mentioned above, and some 87,500 bassinets, there are not available for private patients more than 900,000 hospital beds which measure up to decent medical and surgical standards. At least another 900,000 would be needed to provide the hospital facilities required for good medical and surgical care of the total population. Some 15,000,000 persons receive hospital treatment each year. In addition to the inadequacy of hospital facilities, another serious problem in connection with hospital care is its almost prohibitive cost to all except the rich and the very poor, the latter of whom can get some care in charity wards of hospitals.

Persistence of quacks and nostrums. We have now dealt with some of the major outstanding advances in medical science which most directly relate to the war on disease. But one should not imagine that the results have become universally accessible or effective. Among certain groups of the American population, particularly in rural areas, the status of medical belief is not much above that of the Mesopotamian peasant of four thousand years ago who relied upon magic and incantation. There is recourse to all sorts of quacks and bogus remedies. And in both rural and metropolitan centers, drugs that have no more curative powers than many traditional herbs of the backwoods areas are advertised over the radio. Not even the first flush of New Deal enthusiasm and reform was able to make headway against the intrenched interests of medical and drug quackery and to put on the statute books a really effective pure food and drugs act. Never has the public been more at the mercy of bogus or harmful drugs. If the laws are a little better today than in 1900, so also are there more questionable drugs on the market and far better sales propaganda to promote them. We spend over $600,000,000 annually on quacks and nostrums.

THE RISE AND GROWTH OF SANITARY ENGINEERING

Sanitary conditions in ancient and medieval times. The progress of sanitation and sanitary measures was long regarded as chiefly an aspect of preventive medicine, but their development has been in reality more a phase of engineering than of medicine. Most public health measures until the middle of the nineteenth century were primarily related to the development of sanitary engineering. This field of work is concerned with the manner in which human wastage—bodily and other—and rubbish have been disposed of.

In the ancient cities, rubbish, garbage, and human excretions were thrown into alleys or the main streets. This was true even in Athens. Aristophanes gives us a colorful picture of the filth that blocked the Athenian streets. This was cleaned up occasionally when the time for a public or religious festival drew near. Rome possessed wider and better paved streets and had some arrangements for flushing them off with surface water. Roman streets were thus less congested with filth than were those of Athens and other Greek cities. Juvenal's picture, however, of the throwing of garbage and slops into the streets of the Roman tenement areas reminds one of Aristophanes' gibes at the Athenian thoroughfares. The medieval cities were notoriously filthy, though Lynn Thorndike has warned us against exaggerating this fact and has shown that some medieval cities were fairly well paved, had a good water system, and took reasonable care of rubbish. Urban filth particularly characterized the mushroom and ramshackle industrial cities that sprang up in the wake of the introduction of machines and factories in the eighteenth century. This condition was particularly true of the horrible and hastily erected tenement buildings in the early factory towns. All sorts of waste and garbage were thrown out of the door or through a hole in the floor.

Filth and disease in early American national history. The almost total absence of the most elementary sanitary provisions in the United States some years after the Revolutionary War is revealed by Smith Hart's description of the situation in disposal and water supply in New York City when this city was the capital of the United States:

The problem of sewage disposal rested lightly on the city fathers. Processions of slaves from the abodes of the town's first families wended their way to the river banks at dusk each with a tub of dung perched on his shoulder. The generality, however, still disposed of excrement by flipping it through the handiest window. In accordance with a city ordinance, on Tuesdays and Fridays from April to December, all good householders scraped it bi-weekly from sidewalk and gutter and pushed it into the center of the streets. In winter, they let it lay where it landed. There was a pleasant fiction current that these mounds of offal (known to the jocular citizenry as "Corporation Pudding") were to be removed by cartmen in the employ of the city and occasionally a captious critic would address a newspaper broadside to the Commissioner of Streets labeled "Awake Thou Sleeper," but it was generally felt that it was a small matter to make such a fuss about. Unless there was an epidemic, the "pudding" was left in the center of the streets where in due course of time it was kicked about by the feet of unwary passersby until it got lost.

The wells from which drinking water was drawn were situated for the most part in the middle of the extremely filthy streets. Much of the supply came from the famed Tea Water pump in Chatham Street (Park Row). The Tea Water was fed by seepage from the Collect Pond, once a beautiful limpid pool surrounded by hills, which had long since become a receptacle for dead dogs and cats and the contents of slop buckets. The white and black residents of the shanties on its banks laundered their odds and ends of linen and "things too nauseous to mention" in it.[1]

Sewers, garbage collection, and street cleaning. The growth of sanitary engineering is, therefore, mainly a product of recent history. Until modern times, sewers were used chiefly to take care of excess surface water. This was true of even the famed Roman sewers. For example, the *cloaca maxima* drained the excess surface water from the Roman Forum. In 1596, Sir John Harrington, one of the major benefactors of the human race, whose praises have not been sufficiently sung by humanity, invented the indoor toilet. The use of this humanitarian device created, for the first time, a real and extensive need for sanitary sewers. The earliest of these sewers came in the late seventeenth and early eighteenth centuries. They were at first mainly natural water courses, or dug ditches. In time they were covered over. By 1808 Paris had fourteen miles of such sewers. Until 1850, however, cesspools were the chief repository of human waste in cities, and privies or the dry vault in country areas. As late as 1877 there were still 82,000 cesspools in the city of Philadelphia.

The menace of water pollution from cesspools was the main reason for the systematic construction of sewers. London began extensive sewer construction in 1847, and had provided itself with a fairly good system of sewers by 1865. Comparable developments took place in continental and American cities. Sewage was first chiefly disposed of by letting it pour into lakes, rivers, or the sea. But in some areas this was not safe or feasible, and disposal by the method of chemical precipitation and disintegration was widely introduced. The first important city disposal plant of this kind in the United States was set up in Worcester, Massachusetts, in 1890. This mode of disposing of sewage is now very common where neighboring water courses are not available or water pollution is dangerous. An extensive improvement of American sewer systems came about after 1933 as the result of liberal allocation of Federal public works funds for such purposes.

In cities garbage is usually collected in rack or tank wagons, or trucks. In seaboard towns it has very frequently been dumped in the ocean, but this practice is now being curbed. Garbage has also been used for filling up low and marshy lands and for feeding hogs. Methods of commercial reduction have been tried out in the effort to produce grease and fertilizer.

---

[1] Smith Hart, *The New Yorkers.* New York: Sheridan House, 1938, pp. 15-16.

But systematic incineration is the most popular present-day method of disposing of garbage and rubbish.

Street cleaning has been revolutionized through the introduction of mechanical sweepers and water flushers. The better contemporary cities are today models of external cleanliness, at least outside of slum and tenement areas. Pericles would stand aghast on Park Avenue in New York City—as much for its cleanliness as for its vast apartment houses and its parade of automobiles.

Providing an urban water supply. An important aspect of sanitary engineering has been the provision of a healthful and adequate water supply. The first people to provide systematically for a clean and abundant supply of water were the Romans. This, rather than their sewers, was the main Roman contribution to sanitary engineering. The Romans not only constructed aqueducts to bring an adequate supply of water to Rome, but built them throughout the empire. One of these Roman aqueducts is still in active use in the city of Metz. During the Middle Ages there was a reversion to dependence upon springs and local wells. These were often infected by drainage from cesspools and privies. The invention of adequate pumps worked a revolution in providing a water supply for the flat countries of Europe. The pumping of water in this manner became fairly common in the sixteenth century.

But the creation of an adequate and safe water supply for both European and American cities was often incredibly delayed. London, for example, had no decent public water supply until after 1900. The main factor which made the construction of modernized water systems obligatory was the discovery that typhoid fever is due primarily to polluted water supply. As the result of this, the construction of municipal water systems has been a leading phase of sanitary engineering in the last half century.

The chief sources of the water supply for cities are ground or surface water, streams, lakes, and springs. With ground water, spring water, and water from streams, the supply has to be accumulated in great reservoirs to make it dependable at all seasons of the year. The acute water shortage in New York City in 1949-1950 sharply called attention to the fact that the increased per capita use of water in our great cities has created a serious water problem. Experts revealed that the increased use of water is also accompanied by a general depletion of the natural supply of water throughout the country.

Frequently, water can be used directly by city dwellers only after systematic treatment. It may be discolored, laden with bacteria, or both. If discolored by mud and other substances, it is treated by what is known as the process of sedimentation. It may also have to be subjected to filtration. This latter process not only clears the water but removes most of the bacteria. The water is forced over sand and gravel for a considerable distance. Aeration is also commonly used to purify water. When systematic disinfection is necessary, chloride of lime, or, more recently, liquid chlorine is used. Some cities have tried the experiment of adding iodine to the water supply as a protection against the prevalence of goiter. This, of course, is resorted to only when the water is notoriously defective in iodine content. The administration of city water systems involves such significant and extensive responsibility that it has become a major department of municipal engineering and municipal government.

The Public Works Administration and the Works Progress Administration under the New Deal worked a revolution in American sanitary engineering after 1933. There was unprecedented activity in building sewage disposal plants and public water works and in clearing up stream pollution.

THE DEVELOPMENT OF THE PUBLIC HEALTH MOVEMENT

Slight development of public health measures before modern times. The remote origins of public health measures are to be detected in the magical ceremonies of primitive and oriental peoples who thereby sought to drive off the evil spirits believed to bring disease. There was, of course, no conception of the scientific idea of contagion. The Greeks widely used the method of fumigation, designed to counteract what they believed to be unhealthy—miasmatic—odors. This technique was suggested by the then common miasmatic theory of disease, to which we have made reference earlier. The Romans made some real contributions to public sanitation in the way of providing a good water supply and attempting to keep the streets clean.

During the Dark Ages there was a pretty general abandonment of sanitary measures. The early church tended to glorify uncleanliness and disease as a disciplinary preparation for the heavenly abode. In the later Middle Ages this attitude was abandoned to some extent; cities adopted a few elementary sanitary precautions and had some regard for public health. At the close of the Middle Ages, segregation and quarantine were frequently introduced, particularly to cope with plagues like the Black Death.

Origins of the public health movement. The modern public health movement arose chiefly in the late eighteenth and the early nineteenth centuries, as the result of the conviction of social reformers that disease produced an unwarrantable amount of human misery and economic loss. The psychological and social background of the movement is to be found in the spirit of reform and social betterment expressed by writers from Francis Bacon to Thomas Paine. The first notable pioneer in public health measures was the prison reformer, John Howard. Following 1774, he vigorously promoted the movement for better sanitation of prison ships and prisons. Howard proved a martyr to the cause, dying of a fever which he contracted while studying Russian prison conditions.

Jeremy Bentham, Edwin Chadwick and the development of the English public health movement. Thomas Percival, Sir Robert Peel, and Anthony Ashley Cooper, the seventh Earl of Shaftesbury, well represented the influence of the early Industrial Revolution on the public health movement. Ashley took the lead in advocating more sanitary conditions and better safety devices in the factories and the mines. But the great influence in the origin of the public health movement was that of Jeremy Bentham (1748-1832). Public health was one of his many reform proposals. It was one of his disciples, Edwin Chadwick, who was the dominant figure in the practical instigation of public health activities in England. He was ably aided by Southwood Smith, another disciple of Bentham. As Secretary of the Poor Law Commission in 1838, Chadwick was deeply impressed by the widespread effects of sickness in producing poverty. Together with English doctors, he studied the various factors contributing to ill-health, especially stressing those elements in the physical surroundings of city dwellers having a direct relation to illness. In 1842 he submitted his famous report on sanitary conditions among the working classes of Great Britain.

This report, confirmed by a royal commission in 1844-1845, is the most important document in the history of the public health movement. It not only produced a revolution in English sanitary science and preventive medicine but also provided the model upon which other countries in Europe and America later proceeded. It was as a result of Chadwick's report that the British government, in 1848, took steps to establish what Richard H. Shryock has called "the most effective local and national sanitary institutions which modern society had yet devised." These sanitary improvements were carried out by Chadwick's disciple, John Simon, who was the health officer of London from 1848 to 1855 and chief medical officer of the kingdom from 1855 to 1876. The Royal Sanitary Commission made its famous report on sanitation and public health in 1869. This English public health development, culminating in the great Public Health Act of 1875, was the fountainhead of the modern public health movement. It had a social and economic, rather than a medical, foundation. This fact has been well stated by C.-E. A. Winslow:

> The foundation of the modern public health movement was thus laid during the latter third of the nineteenth century, primarily as a result of the assumption that disease as an economic burden upon the community was largely preventable. The movement was given strength and impetus by the demonstration that certain kinds of disease were caused by microbes and that such diseases could often in fact be easily and completely controlled by simple scientific procedures.[2]

These English innovations set the pace for public health developments in the last half of the nineteenth century. Sanitary engineering and the prevention of contagion through control of the physical environment and personal movement were the measures most stressed. Such measures served to reduce very greatly the prevalence of smallpox, cholera, the plague, and typhoid fever. Toward the end of the nineteenth century the progress in bacteriology served to give the public health movement more of a medical cast. Medical science came to vie with sanitary engineering as a major force in public health achievements.

In the twentieth century preventive medicine and public health work branched out in even broader fashion, taking into account social and

---

2 From *The Encyclopaedia of the Social Sciences,* Vol. XII, p. 648. By permission of The Macmillan Company, publishers.

educational factors affecting health. This more comprehensive approach has been well summarized by Sir George Newman in describing English public health measures since 1900:

With the twentieth century came a series of laws dealing with mothers and children; with midwives and nursing; with notification of birth, employment of children, school meals; with the medical inspection and treatment of school children, physically and mentally defective children and the Children Act itself; with the protection of food; with pensions for the aged, for widows and orphans, and the insurance of the adolescent and adult against sickness, accident and unemployment; with dentistry; with infectious diseases and fever hospitals; with tuberculosis, mental deficiency, lunacy, blindness and venereal disease; with factories and workshops and the industrial welfare of the workers.[3]

Origins of the public health movement in the United States. The development of public health activities in the United States directly followed the English movement and was influenced by the latter. Interest was first aroused by John Griscom, a New York City humanitarian who had traveled extensively abroad. The first sanitary convention was held at Philadelphia in 1857. It discussed quarantine regulations, adequate sanitary codes, and pure food and drug regulations. This movement was directly stimulated by the work of Chadwick, Smith, and Simon in England. A very important impetus to public health in the United States was the creation of the American Public Health Association in 1872. This organization effectively promoted research and propaganda in the field of public health. The investigations by William T. Sedgwick and others, following 1877, touching upon water supply and sewage disposal, were the outstanding American contributions to sanitary engineering in the last half of the nineteenth century. We have seen that bacteriology emphasized the importance of medical science in the public health movement in Europe after 1875. It was equally true in the United States. George Miller Sternberg discovered the pneumonia bacillus in 1880, independent of the work of Fränkel in Europe, and Theobald Smith first scientifically investigated Texas fever a decade later. The great landmark in American bacteriology at this time was, however, the establishment of a public health laboratory by Hermann M. Biggs in New York City in 1892.

Health education. The systematic public health movement in the last half of the nineteenth century had taken the form of improved sanitary engineering and the introduction of bacteriological science to combat disease and prevent contagion. The problems created by tuberculosis about 1900 brought a revolution in the motivation and emphasis of the public health movement at the turn of the century. Tuberculosis did not seem to yield to improved sanitation or to immunization through chemical and bacteriological methods. The only effective treatment seemed to be increasing human resistance by more hygienic living. Though this attack was first applied in the war on tuberculosis, which was the

---

[3] J. A. Hammerton (Ed.), *Universal History of the World,* Vol. VIII. London: Amalgamated Press, 1928, p. 5055.

most important single cause of death in 1900, it was soon extended to other fields and has colored the whole public health movement in the twentieth century. The reason for this was that a better regimen of human hygiene could be assured only through systematic health education. Thus, in the twentieth century, although sanitary engineering and bacteriology are still vigorously cultivated, they have had to give way to health education as the dominant trend in the public health movement.

Health education was chiefly local before 1900. The most important achievement was the publicity given to the antituberculosis movement by Hermann Biggs in New York City in 1897. But health education soon took on a national character. We may illustrate this by calling attention to the National Tuberculosis Association, organized in 1904, which launched national propaganda against the "white plague." Then the movement became international. An international conference on tuberculosis was held in Washington in 1908. Other public health organizations were established in various fields and threw themselves into the work of health education. Among these were the American Conference for the Prevention of Infant Mortality (1909), the National Mental Hygiene Committee (1909), the American Society for the Control of Cancer (1913), the American Social Hygiene Association (1914), the National Society for the Prevention of Blindness (1915), the Association for the Prevention and Relief of Heart Diseases (1915), the National Child Health Council (1920), and the American Child Health Association (1922). At this same time the teaching of hygiene was introduced in limited fashion into the schools.

Conferences on "well babies" were held. Clinics were opened for the instruction of the poor and the treatment of diseases among them. District or visiting nursing associations became more common and promoted health work among the submerged classes. Social settlements often undertook health education. Health lectures were held systematically. Health demonstration centers were set up, the most notable of which has been the Bellevue-Yorkville Health Demonstration maintained in midtown New York between 1926 and 1936 under the auspices of the Milbank Memorial Fund. Perhaps the outstanding educational propaganda in the last decade has been the publicity directed against infantile paralysis, cancer, heart disease, and venereal diseases. This has usurped the primacy held by antituberculosis propaganda at the beginning of the century.

Health education was notably seconded by impulses to the public health movement which came from the field of economics. As we have noted, observers supplemented Chadwick's contention that people are poor because they are sick by the assertion that, likewise, they are sick because they are poor. The public health movement became interested in wiping out slums, in increasing wages, and in stabilizing employment. Its sponsors also advocated health insurance. The costs of medical care attracted attention and helped to produce the famous Federal study of this subject which began in 1927 and was completed in 1932. The movement for pure food and drugs was launched with real vigor by Theodore Roosevelt and Harvey W. Wiley in 1904.

Development of public health administration in the United States. The development of public health administration in the United States followed a similar movement in England. Some local health boards were established between 1800 and 1840. A Federal public health service, based on a law of 1798, was gradually built up in the latter part of the nineteenth century and was administered by the Treasury Department until 1939. A National Board of Health was created in 1879. The United States Public Health Service was formally established in 1912. It was transferred from the Treasury Department to the Federal Security Agency in 1939.

Active support has been given to public health administration by the states, especially since the Civil War. The first state health board was that set up in Massachusetts in 1869. The first state law providing for the medical inspection of school children was that passed in Connecticut in 1899. There are now health departments in nearly every state, county, and city. Publicly owned and operated hospitals provide about three-fourths of the hospital beds and hospital service in the United States.

Slight expenditures for preventive medicine. The main defect in American public health today is the relatively small amount of money spent on preventive medicine. The Committee on the Costs of Medical Care discovered that, in 1929, only 1.4 per cent of the total expenditures for medical care went to support preventive medicine. The situation has been improved somewhat by the Federal Social Security Act of 1935, which permitted the government to appropriate 8 million dollars annually to aid the states in public health activities. The United States Public Health Service has recently extended these activities, but they are still very inadequate.

The public health program today. The public health movement has spread throughout the modern world. It is especially well established in Europe. The Health Organization of the League of Nations after 1921 helped to give the public health movement a distinctly international character. The perspective and program of the public health movement in our day have been admirably summarized by Sir George Newman:

What does this change in the center of gravity really mean? It means that there is a larger understanding of the purpose of preventive medicine, both in the object and the methods of securing the health of the people. It is no longer a question of stamping out pestilence or of providing a sanitary environment. The purpose of preventive medicine is how to develop and fortify the physique of the individual and thus increase the capacity and powers of resistance of the individual and community; to prevent or remove the causes and conditions of disease or its propagation; to postpone the event of death and thus prolong the span of man's life.

The basis of public health must always be a sanitary environment; but the new hygiene seeks to develop the innate capacities of man, physical, mental and moral; it aims at the avoidance of disharmony and disease in its early stages, in order to escape its later results in the body. Let us see what its modern programme is.

First, wise human nurture, an effective maternity service, infant welfare and child hygiene are designed to build a healthy race. Secondly, good housing, a pure and abundant water supply, drainage and sewerage, the reduction of nuisances and the abatement of smoke, a wholesome and sufficient food supply and industrial hygiene are to create a sanitary environment. Thirdly, the provision of sound nutrition, life in the open air, exercise and rest, vaccines and antitoxic sera are to establish immunity and a resistant body. Fourthly, the control of epidemics, the destruction of infective agents, the isolation and treatment of infectious persons, disinfection, quarantine, avoidance of cough-spray or expectoration are methods of reducing mass infection. Lastly, adequate and sufficient medical practice for the sick and disabled of all ages, classes, clinics, dispensaries, hospitals, sanatoria, and a health insurance system are medical services for the early diagnosis and treatment of disease.[4]

PRESENT DEFICIENCIES IN MEDICAL CARE AND FACILITIES IN THE UNITED STATES TODAY

Inadequacy of medical care today. The inadequacy of medical care in the United States was demonstrated by the number of men rejected for service in the United States Army under the Selective Service Act of 1940. Despite the progress in medical science since 1917, a greater proportion of recruits were turned down because of physical and mental defects in 1941 than in 1917—less than 33 per cent in 1917 and more than 43 per cent in 1941. Although the examinations and standards were more rigorous in 1941 than in 1917, it is clear from these figures, after making all due allowances, that the nation has not been able to benefit sufficiently from the progress of medical science. That it has not been able is due mainly to the expense of medical care under the prevailing system of private practice and to the failure to educate communities to appreciate the great advantages and economies of cooperative medicine and health insurance. As General Hershey summed up the situation: "The fact remains that while we may not be worse now than 24 years ago we seem certainly to be no better. . . . We are physically in a condition of which nationally we should be thoroughly ashamed." The extensive rejection of draftees in 1951 indicated that conditions had not changed for the better in the decade after Pearl Harbor.

Need for more trained physicians. Though the inadequacy of medical treatment today is due more to the defective system of medical practice than to the shortage of doctors, it has been estimated that we could well use today 20 per cent more well-trained physicians than we have, and we shall soon need even more, for the population is currently growing more rapidly than the supply of newly admitted practitioners. There are only 79 good medical schools in the country, with an enrollment of 25,103 students in 1950. Their output of gradautes each year is only about 6,000—6,389 in 1947. Since about 4,000 doctors die each year the net gain is only a little over 2,000 yearly. There should be twice that many medical graduates if we are to have the 250,000 doctors we shall need by 1960. The problem was intensified by the Korean War in 1950 and by the draft which envisaged from 3 to 5 million under arms and requiring medical care. Howard A. Rusk predicted early in 1951 that there would be a shortage of at least 22,000 doctors by 1954. An expert committee after two years of study reported in February, 1951, that an additional 40 million dollars

---

4 Hammerton, *op. cit.*, p. 5055.

would be needed annually to enable the medical schools to turn out enough doctors.

There were only about 201,000 licensed physicians and surgeons in 1950 and only about 150,000 were in active practice. About 50,000 of these were specialists or were absorbed in research, government service, and similar work, leaving only about 100,000 general practitioners, or about one to every 1,500 persons. There are fewer doctors today per capita than there were forty years ago—one to 750 today as compared with one to 636 in 1900. Some 25,000 qualified young men applied for entrance to medical schools in the autumn of 1950, but only a little over 7,000 could be admitted. In New York State, in 1950, the number of applications for admission to medical colleges outnumbered the facilities for admission by a ratio of twenty to one.

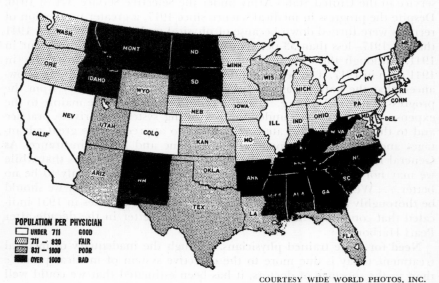

POPULATION PER PHYSICIAN

☐ UNDER 711	GOOD
▨ 711 − 830	FAIR
▩ 831 − 1000	POOR
■ OVER 1000	BAD

COURTESY WIDE WORLD PHOTOS, INC.

This graphic map reveals the very uneven distribution of physicians and medical care in the United States.

In some branches of medicine, such as psychiatry, there is a desperate shortage of trained doctors. There are only about 4,500 psychiatrists in the country, and we need at least 20,000. One of the reasons for the shortage of psychiatrists is the attempt of physicians to monopolize this field and to exclude clinical psychologists, though the latter often have a much better professional training in psychotherapy than the average M.D., especially for treating the functional mental and nervous diseases.

Recently, the eminent scientist of Yale University, Paul V. Sears, made a practical suggestion of much merit pending the time when we are willing to spend enough public funds to train an adequate corps of doctors. He proposed that most of those applicants for admission to medical schools now turned down because of the miserably inadequate facilities for training doctors could be given less rigorous training and turned out as "bachelors of medicine." Such "limited practice" doctors could care for ordinary injuries and minor ills, thus giving the insufficient supply of completely trained physicans and surgeons more time to care for serious ills and injuries.

The shortage of dentists, good nurses, medical technicians, and trained hospital personnel is even greater than that of doctors. Federal and state aid will be needed to enable more capable young men to undertake the arduous and costly task of preparing for the practice of medicine. Today, only a young man of independent means can afford the time and expense required to prepare for the practice of surgery or for most other medical specialization.

Attitude of many established physicians and surgeons restricts medical and surgical care. One of the reasons for the shortage of good medical and surgical service in many cities and towns is the attempt of older, established physicans and surgeons to monopolize the practice in these areas, on the wholly fictitious ground of their superior training and ability.

The average physician and surgeon now past 50 years of age usually entered medical college directly from high school or after only two years of college training. After completing his four years of work in medical college, he usually took a year of internship in medicine or surgery and immediately started to practice, often with no residency training at all, or such training of one or two years at the most. Today, in order to specialize, a young man takes four years of pre-medical work in college, four years of medical college instruction, two years of internship, and from two or three to as many as eight years of residency training, before beginning to practice.

During his residency the young physician or surgeon does most of the routine work in hospital medical treatment and surgery, the older doctors limiting themselves chiefly to the more lucrative cases, except for an occasional charity operation. Hence, much of our medical and surgical care is provided by men who are well trained but get virtually no pay. Even when a doctor has finished his long residency, he finds his progress blocked by the staffs of the urban and community hospitals, who refuse to admit him on terms of equality and limit his practice.

This deplorable situation was aired by J. D. Ratcliff in an article in the *Woman's Home Companion* of October, 1948, which was prefaced by a statement from no less an authority than Allen O. Whipple, former president of the American Surgical Association, to the effect that: "There is no question that (younger) well-trained physicians and surgeons ... are far better qualified and more competent than many of the older practitioners in the smaller cities of this country. There is no doubt that these younger qualified doctors are prevented from demonstrating their ability in a good number of communities by the failure of the local physicians to give these younger men an opportunity to practice in the hospital or hospitals of the community."

A helpful suggestion on how to make better use of the services of young doctors was recently made by Dean William Lee Hart of the University of

Texas Medical School. He recommended that all internes should put in at least one year of their interne training as assistants to general practitioners. This would also relieve the financial problem of internes. They could be paid $300 a month, as compared with the average of about $50 a month which they receive in hospitals.

Urgent need for more and better hospital facilities. Though we need more well-trained physicians, technicians, and nurses, the shortage of hospital facilities is even greater. We do not have half the number of acceptable hospital beds we need. Including the Federally owned and operated hospitals, we have a total of 6,355 registered hospitals and about 1,425,000 hospital beds in the country. Of the 1,020,000 hospital beds outside the Federal system, some 150,000 are obsolete and sub-standard. This means that we have less than 900,000 hospital beds acceptable for use. Of these there are only about 470,000 beds in general hospitals, which care for most of the ordinary medical and surgical cases. The others are for mental, tubercular, and chronic cases. In some 40 per cent of the counties of our country, with a total population of 15,000,000, there is no hospital whatever. It is conservatively estimated that we need an additional 900,000 hospital beds immediately.

Inadequacy of current sanitary engineering. Although we take justifiable pride in our achievements in sanitary engineering, they are today about as inadequate as health provisions. To bring them up to our requirements would involve an immediate outlay of 7.7 billion dollars— 3.7 billion for sewage disposal systems, 2.2 billion for water works, 1.6 billion for rural sanitation facilities, and 166 million for garbage disposal facilities. Some 9,000 towns and cities, with a total population of over 6 million, need entirely new sewage systems. About 10,000 cities and towns, with a population of 80 million, need improved systems; and only 6.5 million persons live in towns and cities with wholly adequate and satisfactory systems. In rural areas, some 33 million persons live without adequate sewage disposal facilities.

THE CRISIS IN MEDICAL PRACTICE

Lag between medical science and medical care. In the opening chapters of this book, we called attention to the fact that the most striking characteristic of our civilization is the enormous gulf between scientific achievements and the institutions whereby we attempt to control the results of science and technology. This situation applies to a marked degree to the practice of medicine today. From a purely scientific view, the progress in medicine and allied sciences has been remarkable indeed. Many diseases that were in former years a scourge of mankind have been curbed or conquered. Impressive progress has been made in preventive medicine and organized public health movements. The chief problem today is to bring the best resources of medical science to the aid of the whole population—in other words, the problem of medical care and getting adequate treatment for the masses. In most instances the better doctors know what to do for patients, but many patients do not have access to good medical care. The science of medicine has attained a relatively high level of achievement, but the social organization of medical practice presents a strikng example of cultural lag. It has been estimated that, if all persons in the United States had access to the best medical care, the current number of deaths could be reduced by at least 325,000 each year.

Although medical training given even in 1925 is already sadly out of date, the practice of medicine in the United States is still dominated by ethical ideals, economic practices, and social procedures very similar to those which prevailed in the days of blood-letting. Medical practice is veritably threatened by anarchy and disorganization. The ideals which dominated the struggling rural doctor of 1850 still prevail in the medical practice of our urban industrial age.

The very rich and the very poor fare best under our present archaic system of medical practice, for the former can afford to pay high fees and the latter are able to obtain much free service in clinics and in charity wards in hospitals. But the poor who obtain this free treatment are usually subjected to much inconvenience and humiliation and are menaced by carelessness and neglect. Moreover, the doctors waste much time because of inefficient organization of their practice, and, on the whole, they are inadequately paid when the high cost of prolonged medical education and the relatively high prices of equipment and drugs are taken into consideration. The medical crisis of today is, thus, a crisis in methods of practice rather than in the scientific aspects of the craft.

Expert summary of deficiencies in present system of medical care. The deficiencies in the present system of medical practice were brought forcefully to the attention of the Committee on the Costs of Medical Care, and in their famous report of 1932 the defects of contemporary medical practice were summarized as follows:

1. The people need a substantially larger volume of scientific medical service than they now utilize. This is particularly true of persons with small incomes. In spite of the large volume of free work done by hospitals, health departments, and individual practitioners, and in spite of the sliding scale of charges, it appears that each year nearly one-half of the individuals in the lowest income group receive no professional medical or dental attention of any kind, curative or preventive.

2. Modern public health services need to be extended to a far greater percentage of the people, particularly in rural areas, towns and small cities.

3. There is need for a geographical distribution of practitioners and agencies which more closely approximates the medical requirements of the people.

4. Current expenditures for medical care in rural and semirural areas are insufficient to insure even approximately adequate service, to support necessary facilities, or to provide satisfactory remuneration to the practitioners.

5. Many practitioners, particularly well-trained recent graduates, should have opportunities to earn larger net incomes than they now receive. Incomes of general practitioners and of specialists should be more nearly equal than at present. The opportunity and incentive for "fee-splitting" should be removed.

6. Better control over the quality of medical service is needed, and opportunities should be provided for improving quality as rapidly in the future as it has been improved in the past. Improvement of the quality of service would include: elimination of practice of unqualified "cult" practitioners; control over practice of secondary practitioners (like midwives, chiropodists, and optometrists); restriction of practice of specialties to those with special training and ability;

more opportunity for post-graduate study for physicians, particularly rural practitioners; more opportunity for physicians to exchange experiences and to assist each other; better control, through supervision and further education, over the work of certain physicians and dentists who even though regularly licensed are not competent for many functions.

7. There should be more effective control over the number and type of practitioners trained, and their training should be adjusted to prepare them to serve the "true" needs of the people.

8. There is a need for reduction of waste in many directions, such as the money spent on unnecessary medication, on services of poorly qualified or utterly unqualified "cultists," and wastes due to idle time of practitioners, high "overhead" of private medical and dental practice, unused hospital accommodations, and the sending of patients from place to place for medical service.

9. There is need for some plan whereby the unequal and sometimes crushing burden of medical expenses can be distributed. The prevailing methods of purchasing medical care lead to unwise and undirected expenditures, to unequal and unpredictable financial burdens for the individual and the family, to neglect of health and of illness, to inadequate expenditures for medical care, and often to inequable remuneration of practitioners.

As a solution of the medical dilemna, the committee made the following specific recommendations:

1. That medical care be furnished largely by organized groups of physicians, dentists, nurses, pharmacists, and other associated personnel, centered around a hospital, and rendering home, office, and hospital care.

2. That all basic public health services be extended until they are available to the entire population, according to its needs.

3. That the costs of medical care be placed on a group payment basis through the use of insurance, taxation, or both methods, without precluding the continuation of the individual fee basis for those who prefer it.

4. That a specific organization be formed in every community or state for the "study, evaluation, and coördination of medical service."

5. That the professional education of physicians, dentists, pharmacists, and nurses be reoriented to accord more closely with present needs, and that educational facilities be provided to train three new types of workers in the field of health; namely, nursing attendants, nurse-midwives, and trained hospital and clinical administrators.

Nothing which has happened in the last twenty years has seriously challenged the wisdom of the observations of this distinguished Committee about the inadequacy of conventional private medical practice. Most developments have served to emphasize the cogency of their recommendations.

Total cost of medical care in the United States today. At the present time the total cost of all medical care and health services, both public and private, is about $8,500,000,000. Of this sum, private individuals and organizations spend about $6,500,000,000. The rest is spent by Federal, state, and local governments for medical care and the prevention of illness, including public health services and preventive medicine. Of the total spent for medical care, some $3,500,000,000 goes into our hospital bill, on which the government spends over a billion dollars. Of the civilian hospital bill of about $2,000,000,000, the Blue Cross pays over $275,000,000.

The amount spent per family on medical care varies greatly according to the income of the family. In 1944, the last year for which the facts are available, families with an income from $500 to $1,000 a year spent, on the average, only $88 for all medical care, and those earning more than $5,000, spent an average of $265. In 1948, it was estimated that the average expenditure for all medical care was $160 per family. This was nearly twice as much as would have been required to protect each family by the Blue Cross and Blue Shield insurance plans, which provide partial coverage for most medical and surgical cases.

Financial obstacles to adequate care under the present system. Under our present system of medical practice in which the doctor furnishes his services on a personal business or fee basis, the very rich and the very poor fare the best, though medical care for the latter is usually miserably inadequate. Theoretically, the poor can receive free clinical care, but it is rarely actually available, least of all in rural areas. On the great mass of people, in between the extremes of wealth and poverty, the cost of medical care often falls as a heavy burden.

The average man can plan to lay out a definite sum for rent, food, and clothing, but he does not know how to budget for illness. Who can estimate how many will be sick in the family during the coming year? Most family incomes are not high enough to afford sudden large sums for hospital care and physicians' fees. Sickness causes families to do without many necessities in order to pay their medical bills; often, it is necessary to borrow money. It has been estimated that five-sevenths of the population would have to borrow money to pay promptly for medical care if any serious or protracted illness occurred. The upshot of the matter is that many families do not call the doctor until too late; they hope to get by without medical care. Also, treatment may be cut short before the patient is cured. Necessary physical examinations are neglected. Poor eyesight and abdominal pains are borne in silence. In every way efforts are made to cut down doctor's bills.

A few statistics will clarify the situation. The Federal health survey of 1935-1936 showed that 30 per cent of the families on relief had no medical help at all. Another expert estimate states that four out of ten Americans who are ill normally receive no attention from a doctor. Oscar R. Ewing has pointed out that about half of our American families, those with incomes of $3,000 or less, "find it hard, if not impossible, to pay for even routine medical care." It is said that death takes 325,000 persons every year in the United States who would live if given proper medical care.

Doctors are poorly paid. Yet, the doctors, on the whole, are very poorly paid for their services. In 1936, the median net income of doctors in the United States was only $3,235; in 1938, $3,027; and in 1940, $3,245. The average net income in 1940 was $5,047. The most authoritative recent estimate of the income of physicians and surgeons was published in *Medical Economics,* September, 1948. This placed the average net income of physicians and surgeons in independent or private practice at $11,300. Department of Commerce figures for 1949 gave the average income of all doctors as $11,308 net. Even if these estimates of income are correct, the doctors would be little better off than in 1940, since their living costs and other expenses have also doubled. There is a common illusion that at least specialists, whose training is particularly long, arduous, and expensive, are rewarded by a lavish income. This is not true. In 1949, it was estimated that the average income of general practitioners was $8,850 a year, and of specialists, $15,000.

Only in a few instances do doctors receive large incomes. Nearly two-thirds of the patients receiving treatment are on the free or partly-free list. Most of these go to free clinics, but a large number of private patients do not pay their doctor bills. Despite all this, it is claimed that the total cost of medical care is too high and could be reduced by an improved system of medical practice that would average medical costs to the individual patient, give everybody adequate care, and pay the doctors far better than they are paid today.

The problem of health insurance. Here, indeed, is a paradoxical situation. Large numbers of people cannot afford any medical attention, medical care is far too expensive for the majority of patients, and yet many good doctors are poorly paid. What is the answer to the riddle? Leading experts have suggested the introduction of a new system of administering medical care, designed to reduce costs as far as possible and to place financial arrangements on an insurance basis. Toward this end many plans have been devised.

The more extreme would have the government take over the provision of medical care, the hiring of doctors, and the running of hospitals. But this would require costly governmental machinery and considerable appropriations of money. Other plans, however, are not so drastic.

The nearest we have come to state or government medicine in the United States is in the army and navy hospitals, the Federal hospitals for war veterans, state hospitals for the insane, the state and county clinics, and the public health services. Out of a total of about $8,500,000,000 spent in 1947 for all medical care and health service in the United States, the Federal, state, and local governments contributed $1,962,000,000, or nearly one-fourth of the total. About three-fourths of the hospital beds in the country are in publicly owned and operated hospitals, though many of the physicians and surgeons who make up the staffs supply treatment on the basis of private practice.

The time is not yet ripe, according to the late Kingsley Roberts, formerly director of the Bureau of Co-operative Medicine, for the domination of all health activities by the government. We would have to pass drastic legislation to meet the needs of the sick in this country by such extreme methods. The best way to avert complete state medicine is to make available adequate medical care by a more moderate form of health insurance.

We may think of health insurance as based on averages, just like any other insurance plan. If people could budget payments for medical insurance, as they do payments for life insurance, the costs would not seem so great, especially if payments were arranged on the basis of the worker's income.

Practical nature of a health insurance system. We spend only about one-fifth as much to check and treat disease and accidents as they cost us each year. It is believed that, if the money were expended efficiently through a system of health insurance, the amount we pay for all forms of medical care and health service would provide first-class medical care for all and pay all doctors handsomely. The American people could readily pay this amount and more, despite the disproportionate number of persons in the low-income brackets, if payments were handled through an efficient type of health insurance.

Look, for example, at our annual bill for alcoholic beverages, which amounts to about 10 billion dollars and to which even the very poor contribute their quota. The reason the poor and the moderately well-to-do can buy liquor is that they usually make small purchases at frequent intervals. They are not suddenly or unexpectedly called upon to pay a liquor bill that may be ten times what they normally spend for liquor in a whole year—but this is just what they are faced with in the event of a prolonged illness or a serious operation. If a poor family spent only $1 to $1.50 per week for liquor, this sum diverted to medical care through a sound health insurance system would be ample to take care of all the expenses involved in providing decent medical care for the whole family. Combined Blue Cross and Blue Shield insurance against most medical and surgical cases costs only about $6 per family each month, or $75 each year. Henry Kaiser, in the scheme of industrial group medicine that he set up for his workers during the Second World War, made good medical care available to each employee for about seven cents a day. It is probable that the sum spent each week by the average poor family on tobacco alone would, if put into a good plan of health insurance or cooperative medicine, amply provide for all needed medical care.

Outline of existing methods of dealing with the problem of better medical care. There are at present in the United States a number of organizations and methods that seek, in one way or another, to eliminate some of the defects in our present system of private medical practice. The late Kingsley Roberts, while director of the Bureau of Co-operative Medicine, summarized most of these schemes. Revised to take account of more recent innovations, his outline follows:

1. Urban medical centers.
2. Private group clinics worked on a fee-for-service basis (Mayo, Crile, Ross-Loos).
3. Post payment plans to meet medical bills (Wayne County Society).
4. Voluntary associations that enter into agreement with doctors for reduced rates (Peoples Medical League, New York).
5. Lodges and Trade Union Beneficial Societies giving medical services (Elks).
6. Unions that have similar plans (United Office and Professional Workers, New York).
7. Employer-sponsored medical service, operating for the benefit of employees and their families (Endicott-Johnson).
8. Medical practice under workmen's compensation laws.
9. Industrial medical practice, combining workmen's compensation, public liability, and industrial hygiene protection (National Broadcasting Company).
10. The practice of medicine in institutions built, equipped, and maintained by local, state, and/or national funds, tax derived, and staffed by doctors who

are paid either partially or completely for their service by the state (Federal hospitals, state hospitals, Bellevue, New York City).

11. Public health departments—national, state, and local.

12. Health insurance by policy and cash profit systems (Commercial health insurance).

13. Non-profit medical and surgical insurance (Blue Cross-Blue Shield plan).

14. Associations of individuals, either on a profit or nonprofit basis, which collect monthly dues and pay for medical services on a fee-for-service, free choice of physician basis (Coöperatives set up under R.A. and FSA).

15. Group hospitalization associations.

16. Coöperative health associations giving complete medical coverage (Elk City, Group Health Association, Washington, D.C.).

17. Voluntary health associations with state subsidy.

18. Compulsory health insurance systems.

19. State medical practice in countries that are not capitalistic in character, such as the U.S.S.R.

We shall consider a few of the more important methods outlined by Roberts. The last two that we shall consider, compulsory state health insurance and state medicine, are not, strictly speaking, utilized in the United States as yet, except for mental patients' and veterans' hospitals. Of course, all government expenditures for health purposes are, in a sense, state medicine, and workmen's compensation laws come close to being a sort of compulsory health insurance.

Medical centers. In cities of any size, there is a tendency for doctors to congregate in office buildings mainly or wholly restricted to physicians and surgeons as tenants. The doctors are thereby able to make the most economical use of office space, secretarial help, and nurses, and to have enough aid to make it unnecessary for physicians to waste their time at clerical work.

This development has sometimes gone so far as to create urban medical centers, the most notable of which is the great Columbia-Presbyterian Medical Center, opened some years ago in New York City. This procedure also brings together general practitioners and specialists and facilitates the reference of patients to specialists. The practice of medicine remains an individual matter, however, and the personal fee system persists. These medical centers probably represent the furthest we can expect individual medical practice to go in the way of meeting the challenge of efficient and economical medical care.

Group clinics and hospitals. There are doctors who divide expenses by employing the same office help and renting a suite of offices together. This reduces costs. Each doctor collects his own fees. There are famous medical and surgical clinics, like the Mayo establishment at Rochester, Minnesota, where the poor man pays what he can and the rich pays what he is charged. Such devices are, of course, only highly efficient private medical practice. They do not even approximate socialized medicine or health insurance. But group clinics can, if they choose, provide a fairly satisfactory form of cooperative, socialized medicine. One of the best examples is the Ross-Loos Medical Group in Los Angeles, in which a large staff of physicians and surgeons serve over 100,000 members for a specified yearly sum, determined by contract in advance.

Fraternal health insurance. Another way of budgeting medical care is by voluntary insurance. One of the oldest forms of this procedure is fraternal insurance, under which a fixed sum is collected monthly from members, and doctors are employed to treat them. But this scheme is too limited and inefficient to be of any general use. Employers' mutual benefit associations and trade union medical benefit plans have proved more satisfactory, but even these are no answer to the problem of providing for adequate medical care on a larger scale.

Industrial prepayment health insurance plans. Employers like the Endicott-Johnson Shoe Company near Binghamton, New York, have successfully used an industrial group-insurance plan. The employer deducts a small amount from the employee's wages for medical and hospital care, and the costs are averaged as in any insurance plan. One of the most successful of these industrial group insurance plans is that maintained by the Standard Oil Company in Baton Rouge, Louisiana, in which excellent medical attention has been provided for about $42 a year. This includes hospital service. About 2,500,000 persons are now covered by industrial insurance plans.

Universities and colleges use similar group-insurance plans, in which the students pay a small yearly sum for the infirmary services of doctors and nurses.

Commercial health insurance service. Life and other commercial insurance companies are entering the field of health insurance. They both issue policies to individuals and offer group insurance to the employees of industrial concerns. In the latter instance, the employer deducts the premium to be paid from the wage of the workers. Cash payments of specified sums are made in somewhat restricted types of medical care and hospitalization. The adequacy of this form of health insurance depends mainly upon the terms of the contract, the reliability of the company, and the size of the group covered.

The Blue Cross and Blue Shield Plans. More persons have some form of protection against hospital, medical, and surgical costs through the Blue Cross and Blue Shield services than by any other type of coverage or organization. The Blue Cross Plan originated in 1937 as "a non-profit corporation organized under community and professional sponsorship and approved by the American Hospital Association for the purpose of enabling the public to defray the cost of hospital care on a prepayment, group basis." All of the 90 Blue Cross plans are sponsored by local hospitals, doctors, and surgeons, and those of the public who wish coverage. Usually the initiative in setting up such a plan in any community is taken by the state or county hospital association.

Blue Cross plans provide only for hospital care, but most of the 90 plans now in operation cover room and board, nursing care, operating room, laboratory service, routine medication, and use of the delivery service. A majority of the plans also provide for special services, such as special diets, emergency room, anesthesia, basal metabolism tests, oxygen therapy, X-ray, and electro-cardiograms. These benefits are available to subscribers for 21 to 30 days, and most of the plans pay about half the costs for an additional 90 days. The plans and rates are determined locally to meet the particular community need. Although rates vary from locality to locality, the national average monthly rates are $1.25 for one person, $2.00 for husband and wife, and $2.75 for an entire family. More than 36,000,000 persons are now protected under some Blue Cross plan, and subscribers have access to some 4,000 hospitals containing 85 per cent of all general hospital beds. The total income from the 90 Blue Cross hospital plans in 1948 was $317,473,030, of which $270,928,123 was paid to hospitals for the care of subscribers.

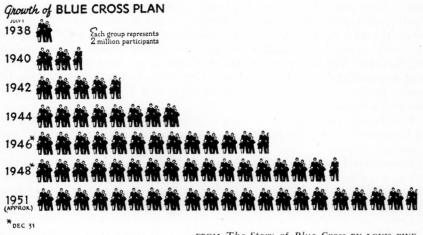

Growth of **BLUE CROSS PLAN**

FROM *The Story of Blue Cross* BY LOUIS PINK.
COURTESY PUBLIC AFFAIRS COMMITTEE, INC.

The Blue Cross plans have been satisfactory for hospital care, but they do not provide for medical and surgical treatment. To meet this need, the Associated Medical Care Plans, Incorporated (now known as the Blue Shield), was founded in 1946, under the auspices of the American Medical Association. This is a non-profit, prepayment plan, with three main types of contracts: (1) the service-benefit contract, in which all fees due physicians and surgeons are paid by the Blue Shield organization; (2) an indemnity contract, by which the subscriber receives credit towards the fees; and (3) a combination of the two. The latter is the best and most common contract. Of the 90 Blue Cross plans, some 79 are combined with a non-profit plan to provide medical and surgical care; of these 79, some 64 are Blue Shield and have a combined membership of about 14,000,000. Blue Shield coverage costs on a national average $1.17 per month for one person, $2.26 for a husband and wife, and $2.75 for an entire family. These charges for Blue Cross and Blue Shield coverage were raised slightly in 1951, due to increased costs produced by rising prices generally.

There is little doubt that the Blue Cross and Blue Shield combination provides the most extensive facilities for budgeting medical, surgical, and hospital care in the United States. But, large and rapidly growing as is the list of subscribers, not enough of the population is as yet covered, many take the cheaper and less adequate contracts for coverage, and there is a large turnover of subscribers. Moreover, in Blue Cross and Blue Shield coverage, the first few office or home calls by physicians have to be paid for by the patient. This may be necessary to protect the scheme from hypochondriacs and malingerers, but it also means that in this type of insurance the patient is protected only against serious and protracted illness and surgical cases. Pending the adoption of some general public health insurance plan, the Blue Cross and Blue Shield plans are, however, the most popular and adequate protection that the American public has against the disasters from sudden, protracted, and serious illness.

Medical Society Coverage. Prior to the Second World War, several city medical societies, such as the Cleveland Academy of Medicine, worked out economical plans for hospitalization insurance. Since the rise of the Blue Cross and Blue Shield Plans, the tendency has been to abandon city plans and to provide coverage through the Blue Cross and Blue Shield. Some state medical societies have provided plans for health insurance. The State Medical Society of California has such a plan under which a person can receive fairly complete medical and surgical care for a payment of about $8 monthly.

Rural community medicine. Some towns in the Canadian Northwest hire the local doctor at a fixed salary, to which each family contributes its share. Before the Second World War, the cost averaged around $20 per family. This is one example of the plan known as rural group medicine. The Federal Farm Security Administration has aided such plans in the United States through cooperation with local associations of farmers.

Community cooperative medicine. One of the most discussed and successful plans of voluntary socialized medicine is community cooperative medicine, such as the Farmers' Union Co-operative Association of Elk City, Oklahoma. Under this program, the community, through a selected committee, hires physicians and surgeons and builds or leases a hospital. The members who subscribe pay a fixed annual health insurance fee and receive complete medical and hospital care. The community then pays the doctors. If there is any money left, it is returned to members or spent for additional medical equipment. No one person can predict his illness, but the cost of medical care for an entire community can be accurately estimated.

This cooperative plan has advantages for both patients and doctors. The doctors do not have to wait for patients; they can spend their spare time working to reduce illness. The less illness, the less doctors have to do. The people of the community are guaranteed prompt and competent medical care at low cost. Perhaps the most famous of these community cooperative medical plans is the Group Health Association of Washington, D.C., for government employees. When it was attacked by the American Medical Association, Thurmond Arnold sued the latter under the anti-trust laws and won his case.

Full yearly medical and hospital care under the system of cooperative community medicine can be provided for a maximum of $50 per person, or $100 per family, and physicians can be far better paid than the average doctor is today. This system has proved adequate where it exists, and it avoids the bureaucracy and red tape of compulsory health insurance and state medicine. The main argument against the community system, and for compulsory health insurance, is that not enough communities will voluntarily install cooperative programs to meet the needs of more than a handful of the total population.

Extent of insurance coverage. Limited though the coverage still is, there has been a marked increase in the subscription to some sort of insurance protection against medical, surgical, and hospital costs. In 1950 about 40 per cent of the population had some type of coverage, mainly through the Blue Cross and Blue Shield systems and commercial insurance plans. Some 61 million had some form of hospital insurance, over 55 per cent of this through the Blue Cross system and over 40 per cent through commercial insurance companies. About 34 million also had some degree of insurance against at least a part of surgical costs. Some 13 million had partial insurance against physicians' charges. Only about $3\frac{1}{2}$ million, however, had fairly full insurance coverage for nearly all medical, surgical, and hospital expenses. About 33 million had some form of insurance against loss of income from sickness and accidents.

Relative inadequacy of voluntary insurance against non-surgical and non-hospital cases. Despite the gratifying spread of voluntary insurance providing some payment for medical and surgical expenses, the protection is still grossly inadequate for the mass of the American people. This is especially true of non-surgical and non-hospital cases. Insurance systems providing payment for physicians' calls for illness not requiring surgery are very incomplete and unsatisfactory in most cases. This is due in part to the far greater possibility of malingering on the part of patients in non-surgical cases and to the possibility of graft by a small minority of doctors. Insurance covering general medical care usually requires the patient to pay the entire cost of the first several calls by a physician and rarely provides complete payment for later calls. The only good protection for doctors' calls is usually for post-operative cases, when the patient has returned home. In short, the Blue Cross and Blue Shield systems and some commercial health insurance policies assure reasonably adequate provision for payment of hospital bills but any adequate plan for insurance against non-hospital cases remains to be provided, so far as the mass of Americans are concerned.

The English system of state medicine. Prior to 1948, England had a rather comprehensive system of compulsory health insurance for low-paid workers. But the Labour Party government broadened this into what is virtually a complete system of health insurance. Under this scheme, each physician is paid a basic salary of $1,200 annually and is allotted an additional $3 for each patient under his care. The cost of the new plan is paid for almost entirely by taxation. There is complete free medical and hospital service, and dental and optical care for every man, woman, and child in England who wishes to register under the plan and make the required contribution. Physicians are allowed to engage in private practice in their spare time, and anybody who wishes can get private medical care if he can pay for it.

The majority of English doctors vigorously opposed this plan; some 89 per cent of them voted against it in February, 1948, but the Labour Government, led by Aneurin Bevan, Minister of Health, persisted and the doctors gave way. The new system was put into operation in July, 1948. Critical judgment of the merits of the plan will need to be applied cautiously in the light of the obvious fact that many of the doctors may seek to prove it a failure. Nevertheless, after three years' experience with the new system, it had proved so popular that even the British "Tories" did not dare to attack it directly. During the first year of the operation of the system England had the lowest death rate in its history. In its issue of August 7, 1950, even *Newsweek,* traditionally hostile to "statism," was led by considerations of integrity and honest reporting to present a long and favorable appraisal of the operation of the British system to date.

Soviet state medicine. There is no private practice of medicine in the U.S.S.R. All medicine is state medicine. Doctors are paid a fixed salary by the state. The Russian system is more extreme than the British, in that no Russian doctor is allowed to engage in private practice under any circumstances. Russia's experience with state medicine affords a good basis for comparing the merits of state medicine with the relatively individualistic medical practice that still persists in the United States.

The following figures give a precise picture of the improvement of Russian medical care under the Soviet Union: hospital beds had been increased from 175,000 in 1913 to 875,000 in 1941; urban medical centers from 1,200 to 13,500; nurseries from 500 to 850,000; physicians and surgeons from 20,000 to 130,000; and the annual health budget from 300 million rubles to 12 billion. To give some comparisons with the United States, there are about 1,425,000 hospital beds in the United States and about 150,000 physicians in active practice. What many people here do not realize is the extent of the public control over medical treatment in the United States. Publicly-owned and -operated hospitals contain about 75 per cent of the hospital beds in the country, and provide about 80 per cent of patient-days of hospital service rendered. The government pays about 25 per cent of the total bill for medical care and health services.

The movement for public health insurance in the United States. In 1945, the Wagner-Murray-Dingell Bill was introduced in Congress. It provided for compulsory health insurance, supported by Federal and state aid, to the annual amount of some 4 billion dollars, about the cost of carrying on the Second World War for a week in 1945.

This bill, which had the hearty support of President Truman, embodied a number of proposals. First, the Federal government would provide aid, along with the states, to construct new hospitals and enlarge existing ones. The Federal government did not propose to construct or operate such hospitals, but would help to pay for them and their operation. Second, provisions were made to extend maternal and child care facilities, to improve the public health services, and to aid in the campaign of preventive medicine. Special attention would be given to improving the health of children in schools. Third, considerable Federal aid to medical students and medical research was planned. Fourth, and most important, a system of compulsory health insurance was to be set up to cover the majority of the population. Finally, there would be disability insurance against wage losses from sickness and accident disability.

The system of health insurance provided for medical, hospital, and nursing care and laboratory service. It was to be made an integral part of the Social Security System under the Federal Security Administration. The funds were to be raised by payroll tax on employers and employees —first a tax of 3 per cent and later of 4 per cent. As in the Social Security System in general, Federal standards and requirements of medical, surgical, and hospital service were mandatory to secure Federal funds. The details of administering the plan and the methods and rates of paying the participating physicians and surgeons were to be worked out by local authorities. The latter were to be advisory committees made up of physicians and laymen.

The plan was extremely flexible, in that physicians were free to decide whether or not they would participate at all, and, if they did, how much of their time they would give to patients treated under the insurance system. All citizens were to remain perfectly free to get their medical care through private practice if they wished to do so. But those who were covered by the system were to be compelled to contribute whether they used it or not, just as persons who send their children to private or parochial schools are required to pay school taxes. The administration of private hospitals would remain as previously, except that they would have to maintain the required standards to receive Federal aid. This plan of health insurance was far less extreme than the British system and fell far short of state medicine, under which doctors work as employees of the government. Whether this plan was needed or wise, it was certainly as moderate as any scheme of compulsory health insurance could be expected to be.

On November 19, 1945, President Truman sent a strong message to Congress in favor of this bill, but certain conservative members of Congress, like Senator Robert A. Taft, thought the measure too socialistic and demanded a more moderate bill. Senator Taft introduced such a bill, which was an improvement over the slight Federal aid to health that now exists, but its proposals were inadequate and difficult to enforce. Even the timid Taft bill was not brought to a vote before the adjournment of Congress in June 1948, nor was it seriously discussed in the next two sessions.

In his address on the state of the nation at the opening of the 81st Congress, President Truman reiterated his support of national health insurance and state-supported medical care. The American Medical Association, girding for the battle, assessed members $25 each to raise a giant fund of three million dollars to fight the President's program. High priced public relations firms were employed. Faced by such opposition on the part of the AMA and many other conservative forces, all stressing the alleged failure of the British state medical plan, the Truman medical program has not even been brought up for serious debate and has been unceremoniously shelved. Indeed, the creation of a Federal Department of Welfare, recommended by former President Hoover's committee on governmental reorganization, was rejected mainly because it was feared that Oscar R. Ewing, head of the Federal Security Agency, and the chief government proponent of the Truman medical plan, might be appointed Secretary of Welfare.

Better medical care is indispensable. We have now outlined the leading plans of socialized medicine and state medicine. Whether or not we approve of any of them, we must think in terms of community well-being and the future of medicine. John P. Peters, in the *Virginia Quarterly Review*, remarks, "Today, the scientific practice of medicine demands knowledge, expert technical training, diagnostic and therapeutic facilities undreamed of ten years ago; the armamentarium which it will require in another ten years is beyond prediction. If the world is to reap the benefits of these scientific discoveries, they must be made available to the public."

Will we continue to advance in our fight against disease, while we lag behind in our administration of medical care? Why should we learn how to cure ailments if people generally do not benefit from the knowledge? Is cooperative medicine the answer, or should we allow the government to assume complete control of the medical world? Most doctors in our country disapprove of state medicine. Regardless of the plan chosen, we should hasten the day when people will receive adequate medical service. The greater the current opposition of the vested medical interests to such moderate plans as those of President Truman, the greater the probability that we will later adopt some such drastic program as that of Britain or Russia.

HYGIENE, EUGENICS, AND EUTHANASIA

Earnest A. Hooton's views on race hygiene. Although the medical profession must, necessarily, devote most of its attention to the care of the sick and the attempt to save the ailing, there are important social considerations which challenge this concentration on the preservation of individual patients. This generally overlooked point has been clearly brought out by the distinguished anthropologist of Harvard University, Earnest A. Hooton.

Hooton finds that there are two major defects in contemporary medical philosophy. In the first place, we take too seriously the sanctity of human life and concentrate too much upon saving the individual, often at the expense of the community. In the second place, doctors devote so much time to studying the sick that they have never learned just what a well man is really like. By seeking primarily to save the life of the individual ill person, without considering the welfare of the social group, medical practice has helped along the physical and mental degeneration of the race and the needless suffering of innumerable patients and their relatives. Hooton continues:

There can be no doubt that the effect of medicine today is to increase enormously the proportion of the physically and mentally unfit in society. While medical science, as yet, is unable to prevent and to cure many diseases, it has succeeded in lowering infant mortality, in raising the expectation of life, and in preserving for long periods many persons of inferior constitution whose bodily processes have been impaired by the ravages of disease. It has, in short, rescued the perishing as well as cared for the dying. I venture to question the desirability of this remarkable achievement from an evolutionary and social point of view. It is as if farmers should concentrate their veterinary skill upon the preservation and natural increase of the runts which turn up in their litters of pigs. The result would be more and more of worse and worse pigs. A sympathy and fellow-feeling for swine would not excuse such a policy. Christ was a good deal wiser when, having allowed the devils to go into the Gadarene swine, he unperturbably watched the latter rush down from a high place into the sea.[5]

The solution of this problem lies in preventing those who are mentally and physically defective from breeding and in disposing of the incurable sufferers in humane fashion: "Euthanasia, under proper restrictions, ought not to be either illegal or unethical as the final resort of medical practice."

Hooton suggests that it is difficult to make a man well unless we understand a well man. He calls attention to the amazing fact that, although we have millions of case studies of sick persons, there is not in the world one single full case study of a well and normal being. He recommends the establishment of a scientific institute for the intensive and prolonged study of healthy human beings. This might accomplish even more than the study of pathology in the promotion of sound medical practice. And, as Hooton does well to point out, "for half the cost of the building of one destroyer, it would be possible to establish and maintain, perhaps in perpetuo, an institute for the study of well human beings."

Rise of the euthanasia movement. Unnecessary suffering from incurable diseases, pain and anguish in fatal lingering illnesses, physical monstrosities, low-grade imbecility, idiocy, and the like, have raised from time to time the question of mercy deaths, or euthanasia, as this process is called. This means the termination, in painless fashion, of the life of incurable sufferers and of such hopeless burdens on society as idiots and low-grade imbeciles. The program does not envisage mercy deaths in any case in which reasonable doubt exists as to possible recovery or the restoration of a socially useful life. They would be applied only in obviously hopeless cases. Many believe that there is everything to be said for such a movement, from the standpoint of economics, humanity, logic, and medical science. They hold that there is not a single argument that can be brought against it, save those drawn from an antiquated theological arsenal. The following statement presents the arguments against euthanasia and the answers to them:

1. No one can say that disease is incurable.
Ans. The law would not read "incurable disease" but "incurable stage of any disease," and certainly three competent physicians in consultation could determine the question of curability.
2. Physicians are not trustworthy and might be influenced to agree to do away with a wealthy sufferer for the benefit of his relatives.

---
5 *The Forum,* December, 1937.

Ans. This charge is ridiculous on the face of it; but, as stated before, the word of three physicians would be required by law and it is difficult to believe that three physicians would conspire in the fashion suggested.

3. Euthanasia is murder.

Ans. The definition of murder in all dictionaries is "killing with malice afore-thought." Since euthanasia is done in kindness, it cannot be classified as murder.

4. Dying persons are emotional and not responsible for what they say.

Ans. This argument is baseless because the proposed law would require agreement on the matter by three physicians and the decision would not depend on the emotion of the dying person.

5. Euthanasia would destroy the sacredness of human life.

Ans. On the contrary, life is too sacred to be degraded by useless suffering.

6. Only God has the right to give and take life.

Ans. This is a statement for which no proof can be given. It is based on an interpretation of the commandment, "Thou shalt not kill," more correctly translated, "Thou shalt do no murder."

7. The knowledge that euthanasia was possible would create fear in the mind of a patient that it might be used on him.

Ans. The law provides that euthanasia shall not be used except with the consent of the person if the person is sane.

8. Euthanasia would destroy much of the incentive for medical research.

Ans. The argument is based on the idea that the thought of the terrible suffering in the world is the incentive which leads scientists to seek cures for such diseases as cancer. But even were euthanasia legalized, there would still be plenty of suffering, sufficient at least to spur scientists to discover cures.

9. God ordains pain as penance for sin and to perfect us for heaven.

Ans. This argument was one employed against anaesthetics, which are now universal. If some people choose to endure pain, very well, but they have no right to prevent the merciful use of euthanasia by others. Judging from actual cases, extreme suffering is more often degrading than elevating.[6]

In 1938 the eminent New York clergyman and sociologist, Charles Francis Potter, organized a National Society for the Legalization of Euthanasia—now the Euthanasia Society of America, Incorporated. It was designed to conduct a national campaign of education as to the social need for legalizing euthanasia; to maintain a central headquarters for information, consultation, and distribution of literature; and to prepare, introduce, and urge the passage of euthanasia bills in Congress and state legislatures. Potter gathered a large and distinguished group of supporters for his movement, drawn from physicians, biologists, sociologists, publicists and clergymen. Foreign notables, such as Havelock Ellis, Julian Huxley, H. G. Wells, H. H. Greenwood, Sir James Purves-Stewart, Canon F. R. C. Payne, and others, lent their aid to the program.

Interest in euthanasia has grown in the last ten years, and the problem has been widely debated. There have been a considerable number of "mercy killings." In four important cases, those disposed of by euthanasia were hopeless and low-grade idiots. Three others involved the disposition of persons hopelessly ill in the terminal stages of cancer. One of the latter took place in Manchester, New Hampshire, on December 4, 1949, when Herman Sanders gave a patient dying of cancer intravenous injections of air. The case gained nation-wide attention and did more than anything else in the history of euthanasia to arouse public interest in the matter.

---

[6] Prepared by Charles Francis Potter.

Although the case was not fought out on its merits in the courts, it served a valuable educational purpose. The public interest which the case attracted was amazing. The Euthanasia Society polled a fair sample of Australians at the time and found that no less than 85 per cent had read about the case. In all mercy-killing cases in late years, there have been only two convictions, and in one of these the sentence was commuted—the John Noxon case in Massachusetts. But, by a 2-1 decision in 1947, the United States Circuit Court of Appeals condemned mercy killings.

Public opinion in support of euthanasia has grown amazingly in recent years. A poll of the whole country, taken late in 1950, showed 46 per cent opposed, 43 per cent in favor, and 11 per cent undecided. In the light of the almost universal horror expressed at the very idea not so long ago, this represents a veritable revolution in the public attitude.

Whatever the ethical and theological aspects of the matter, there is surely little ground for the extreme sensitivity or horror expressed by some critics of euthanasia about the loss of life that would result from any reasonable application of euthanasia. Compared to the loss of 325,000 or more lives annually as a result of inadequate medical care, the number who would be put out of misery through the adoption of euthanasia is trivial indeed. Many more die each year through the failure of doctors to make calls. Moreover, many of those who die from inadequate medical care are persons of normally good physique and health, not hopeless and incurable invalids.

SUMMARY

The health situation in the United States today provides a striking example of how cultural lag produces serious social problems. The development of medical and surgical science has been most impressive, and work in these fields is thoroughly up-to-date and abreast of the latest scientific knowledge. On the other hand, medical care lags along in the same general pattern that prevailed in the days before the Civil War.

The result of this lag is that only a small proportion of the American people can enjoy the advantages of the remarkable achievements in medical and surgical science. Less than half the American people obtain adequate medical care, and at least a fourth of them receive virtually no medical care at all. Nearly 350,000 persons die each year who could be saved if they received timely and sufficient medical care. The cost of unnecessary illness and death, due to inadequate medical care, runs to nearly 40 billions of dollars each year. The amount of ill health found among the draftees in 1917-1918 was described as a national scandal by physicians and military officials, but the situation had not improved in 1941-1945 or in 1951.

There have been enormous advances in medicine and surgery in the last hundred years, and especially in the last two decades, due to the introduction of sulfa drugs and the antibiotics. Sanitary engineering and public health measures have also undergone remarkable development in this same period.

As a result of such advances, the older epidemic and contagious diseases, and the main diseases of children, have been pretty thoroughly conquered and brought under control. Infantile paralysis, or polio, is about the only exception. The chief menace to health today—the "great killers"—are the chronic or degenerative diseases most common among persons of middle and old age. Heart diseases of various kinds, brain lesions, cancer, chronic kidney diseases, and arthritis are leading examples of these chronic disorders. These diseases are on the increase, partly the result of the growing tension, worries, and excitements of modern urban life and partly the result of the increase in the number of people in the age-groups most susceptible to these diseases.

There is today a serious shortage of physicians, surgeons, nurses, and hospitals, but the main reason why so many persons do not get adequate medical care is the archaic organization and inefficient administration of medical care.

Doctors, nurses, and hospitals are not used efficiently. Few except the rich can afford to pay for competent medical care, because they do not budget medical costs on some insurance plan. Health insurance, either private or public, is the only solution for the problem of bringing medical care to the level of efficiency that has already been attained in the realm of medical science.

Private health insurance plans have been the most popular in the United States, and the Blue Cross and Blue Shield Plans are the most efficient and highly developed of these. Such coverage and protection is still extremely inadequate to meet the health needs of the American people, but it is the best solution we have thus far been able to provide.

President Truman has repeatedly recommended a plan for modest and limited Federal aid to health insurance, hospital construction, and medical training, but his program has been fiercely opposed by the majority of the leaders of the medical profession and bluntly shelved by Congress.

Pending some effective solution of the problem, the issues of private practice versus socialized medicine will be warmly debated, and millions of Americans will suffer from unnecessary and prolonged illness, and hundreds of thousands who might be saved by good medical care will continue to die.

There is a growing sentiment in favor of sane and adequately safeguarded euthanasia, or the practice of allowing a council of physicians to decide when it is wise to put a suffering and hopelessly incurable patient out of misery through the use of some painless drug.

SELECTED REFERENCES

*Alexander, Frans, *Psychosomatic Medicine: Its Principles and Applications.* New York: Norton, 1950. The most authoritative introduction to the psychiatric approach to medical treatment, by a leading American psychiatrist.

Armstrong, B. N., *The Health Insurance Doctor.* Princeton: Princeton University Press, 1939. Excellent account of public health insurance in England (prior to the 1948 system), Denmark, and France. Shows how this method of averaging medical costs works in practice.

Blake, R. P., *Industrial Safety*. New York: Prentice-Hall, 1943. Standard work on safety campaigns and methods, especially in industrial operations.

Cabot, Hugh, *The Doctor's Bill*. New York: Columbia University Press, 1935. A sensible and liberal analysis of the crisis in medical care and the budgeting of its cost.

Clark, Evans, *How to Budget Health*. New York: Harper, 1933. One of the pioneer books on plans to average the costs of medical care.

*Davis, M. M., *America Organizes Medicine*. New York: Harper, 1941. Important work by an expert on medical care, dealing with development of trends towards community and socialized medicine and public health insurance.

De Kruif, P. H., *Microbe Hunters*. New York: Harcourt, Brace, 1926.
———, *Men Against Death*. New York: Harcourt, Brace, 1932.
———, *The Fight for Life*. New York: Harcourt, Brace, 1938.
———, and De Kruif, Rhea, *Why Keep Them Alive?* New York: Harcourt, Brace, 1936. Four lively books by the chief popularizer of the war on disease by medical science. Entrancing and generally reliable. The last book is a powerful statement of the relation of poverty to disease and problems of medical care.

*Dietz, David, *Medical Magic*. New York: Dodd, Mead, 1938. One of the better popular treatments of the present status of the more deadly diseases and the triumphs of medical science in the last generation.

Dunbar, Flanders, *Mind and Body: Psychosomatic Medicine*. New York: Random House, 1947. Pioneer work on new field of medicine which stresses mental influence on bodily disorders and their treatment.

*Ewing, O. R., *The Nation's Health*. Washington: Federal Security Agency, 1948. Official argument and cogent data supporting the Wagner-Murray-Dingell bill and President Truman's program of national health insurance.

———, *Environment and Health*. Washington: Federal Security Agency, 1951. Very valuable summary survey of sanitary engineering and preventive medicine developments in the United States.

Garrison, F. H., *An Introduction to the History of Medicine*. Philadelphia: Saunders, 1929. The standard one-volume history of medicine.

Gray, G. W., *The Advancing Front of Medicine*. New York: Whittlesey House, 1941. Good review of progress in American medical science and treatment.

Heiser, V. G., *Toughen Up, America!* New York: Whittlesey House, 1941. Vigorous argument for better medical care for the mass of Americans.

*Kingsbury, J. A., *Health Security for the Nation*. New York: League for Industrial Democracy, 1938. The best introductory treatment of the principles of socialized medicine and the averaging of the costs of medical care.

Long, P. H., *A-B-C's of Sulfonamide and Antibiotic Therapy*. Philadelphia: Saunders, 1948. Competent treatment of the medical use of the sulfa drugs and antibiotics.

Moore, H. H., *Medical Care for the American People*. Chicago: University of Chicago Press, 1932. Good analysis of the problem of medical care, based on the findings of the Committee on the Costs of Medical Care.

Reed, L. S., *Health Insurance*. New York: Harper, 1937. Authoritative and objective description of the principles and techniques of health insurance.

*Rorty, James, *American Medicine Mobilizes*. New York: Norton, 1939. A slashing attack on professional greed and reaction in the medical profession and a graphic account of the steps taken by progressive physicians to socialize medical practice.

*Shadid, Michael, *A Doctor of the People*. New York: Vanguard, 1939. Good account of an experiment in community cooperative medicine.

Shyrock, R. H., *Development of Modern Medicine*. New York: Knopf, 1947. Admirable book for the lay reader on the origins and development of contemporary medical science.

Sigerist, H. E., *Socialized Medicine in the Soviet Union*. New York: Norton, 1937. Account of state medicine in Russia by the greatest living medical historian.

————, *A History of Medicine: Primitive and Archaic Medicine*. New York: Oxford University Press, 1951. The first volume of a monumental history of medicine. Covers diseases and medical treatment among primitive peoples and the Egyptians and Babylonians.

Sokloff, Boris, *The Miracle Drugs*. Chicago: Ziff-Davis, 1949. Popular but reliable treatment of the nature and therapeutic role of the sulfa drugs and antibiotics.

*Stern, B. J., *Society and Medical Progress*. Princeton: Princeton University Press, 1941. An able and progressive study of the social factors which have affected, and often retarded, medical progress and medical treatment.

Tannenbaum, S. A., and Branden, P. M., *The Patient's Dilemma*. New York: Coward-McCann, 1935. A criticism of medical treatment under the system of private practice.

Chapter 8

Marriage and the Family

HISTORICAL DEVELOPMENT OF THE HUMAN FAMILY

Biological basis of human mating. Our simian heritage provides some of the leading traits that account for the relative permanence of human mating. Man has the unique physiological trait of having no distinct mating season. Among most animals the females are not usually susceptible to sex stimulation except during the mating season, and the males are sexually aggressive only when the females are receptive to their attentions during the mating period. The primates and other simians, on the contrary, are constantly accessible to sex stimulation. This trait naturally has facilitated and encouraged permanent sex pairing.

Other simian traits are the tendency to bear fewer young than most animals and the longer period of helplessness of the offspring. These characteristics are particularly developed in the human race. Much stress has been laid by sociologists on the long period of dependence of the human child upon its mother. John Fiske, for example, attributed the very origins of organized human society to this fact.

Certain sociologists have tried to find unique qualities in the human pairing relation. They hold, for example, that man has an innate antipathy to incest and inbreeding, that there is an inborn feeling of modesty or shame about sex, that the affection between human males and females is not encountered in lower animals, that chastity is universally insisted upon for unmarried women and fidelity for married women, and that human beings crave social approval for their sexual behavior.

That many of these traits have usually dominated the historical family is evident, but this fact must be attributed to cultural factors rather than to psychological or physiological qualities unique in the human race. Modesty, chastity, aversion to incest, social control of sex activities, and the like, are purely cultural in their origin. None of these things can be called instinctive with man. They have been brought about by social experience and the growth of folkways.

Although human love is obviously different in degree from the affection shown in the pairing arrangements of even the higher apes, it can scarcely be demonstrated to be different in kind. Moreover, much of the difference in degree in human love is a matter of culture rather than of biology. The human family, very obviously, rests upon physiological facts

276

and tendencies that antedate the origins of the human race. The highly varied forms of sex relations, marriage, and the family group among human beings are, however, a distinctly human contribution and an outgrowth of the cultural and institutional experience of the human race.

Controversy over earlier forms of the family. Before the rise of anthropology and historical sociology, it was thought that the monogamous family, the permanent pairing of one male and one female, had been universal among all peoples at all times. This was a fundamental Christian dogma. Every known form of family other than the monogamous arrangement was held to be exceptional and the work of the devil. Indeed, before the Christians, the Jews had denounced the polygyny (often confused with polygamy) of the Gentile peoples, even though the man who was traditionally the wisest of all the Jews, Solomon, is reputed to have been exceptionally successful in maintaining one of the largest harems of recorded history.

When the science of anthropology, or the study of primitive peoples, came into being in the wake of Darwin's enunciation of the doctrine of evolution, the earlier theories of the predominance of monogamy were roughly handled. According to many anthropologists of the early evolutionary school, something rather close to promiscuity prevailed in the first stages of primitive society, and there was little permanent mating. The first system of pairing was group marriage, out of which polygyny arose. In the earliest period of polygyny, relationships in the family were traced through the mothers only. In due time, as a result of wife capture, wife purchase, and the economic conditions of pastoral life, this maternal system was transformed into the paternal family, in which relationships were traced through the males. Out of this paternal but polygynous family, monogamy gradually evolved as the final stage of family life.

Some of the early writers on family origins, such as the German-Swiss philologist, J. J. Bachofen, alleged that there had not only been a maternal family but also a definite period during which women exerted the dominant authority in political and military life, the age of the so-called matriarchate. Even in the twentieth century, reputable writers have revived something like this earlier notion of the evolution of monogamy from primitive promiscuity and subsequent maternal rule. Especially notable was the voluminous work of Robert Briffault on the *Mothers,* published in 1927.[1] His views were less extreme than those of the older anthropologists but in a general way he upheld the notion of female sociopsychological ascendency in the primitive family. While doubting the existence of any such thing as political domination of males by females in primitive society, Briffault believed that the original family was a biological group consisting of the mother and her offspring. They were supported by members of the clan of which the father or sexual partner was not a member.

Monogamy the usual form of family. The dogmas of the older evolutionary anthropologists about the gradual evolution of human monogamy

---

[1] Three Vols. New York: Macmillan.

out of a primordial promiscuity were first attacked in sweeping fashion by a Finnish anthropologist, Edward Westermarck, who published the first edition of his famous *History of Human Marriage*,[2] in 1891. After an extensive survey of marriage relations among many primitive peoples, Westermarck contended that monogamy, founded originally on masculine jealousy and possessiveness, has been the prevalent type of human family relationship from the earliest days. Other forms of family arrangements Westermarck believed to be exceptional, even though frequent at certain times and places. He tried to support his theory by an appeal to biology. He pointed to fairly permanent pairing relationships among the higher apes and laid special stress upon the prolongation of human infancy as a force making for human monogamy. Westermarck's conclusions have been generally accepted, with a few qualifications, as the accurate interpretation of the nature and development of the human family. They were the more convincing because Westermarck, a tolerant liberal on sexual matters, had no personal axe to grind in defending monogamy.

The theory that women once ruled over society—the notion of a so-called matriarchate—has been rather ruthlessly disposed of by contemporary anthropologists. They have shown that most of the evidence upon which Bachofen and others relied to support any such contention was either unreliable, misinterpreted, or both. It is well known that, in primitive society, we have both maternal and paternal families, that is, families in which relationships are traced exclusively through the mother or solely through the father. But Franz Boas and his disciples have raised serious doubt whether the maternal family was an older type than the paternal family, and they are even more inclined to doubt that the paternal family arose out of the maternal. It seems that historic conditions, in time, favored the paternal family. Briffault's work gave evidence of immense industry and great learning, but his efforts to rehabilitate the older notions about human promiscuity and the predominance of maternal society have been undermined by Bronislaw Malinowski, Robert H. Lowie, and other present-day anthropologists. Malinowski's books on the *Father in Primitive Psychology* [3] and *The Sexual Life of Savages* [4] are a convincing answer to Briffault's notions. The attempt of Mathilde and Mathis Vaerting to revive the theory of the matriarchate on sentimental and feminist grounds in their book, *The Dominant Sex*,[5] is less impressive than Briffault's erudite labors.

Anthropologists warn against reading into primitive times our own notions about the monogamous family. In historic times the monogamous family has been the basic social unit, dominating sex habits and controlling many other forms of social usage. But in primitive society it frequently did not exert any such clear dominion over social life. The

---

[2] Fifth ed., 3 Vols. New York: Macmillan, 1921.
[3] New York: Norton, 1927.
[4] New York: Liveright, 1929.
[5] New York: Doran, 1923.

monogamous family was often affected by many other social usages—for example, by the marriage class system among the natives of Australia and by other complicated relationship systems in primitive society. Further, the clan and gens system definitely modified the status of the monogamous family among primitives. This system proclaimed a fictitious relationship among all members of a clan or gens, even though any direct blood relationship was non-existent in many instances. Therefore, although monogamy has dominated marriage customs, we must not think of primitive monogamy as being identical in social status and functions with the monogamy of the rural Christian family prior to the Industrial Revolution and the rise of our urban civilization.

Polyandry and polygyny. There have been other types of family relationships, such as polyandry and polygyny. Polyandry means the marriage of one woman to several men, who may or may not be brothers. In Tibet, where it was usual for several brothers to marry one woman, the elder brother usually enjoyed certain special privileges and powers. In other polyandrous situations the husbands might have equal rights to their common wife. Polyandry has been a relatively rare form of human family. The main explanation offered for its existence is that it best serves the sex needs of man in regions in which nature is extremely unproductive and the resources of the community do not permit universal monogamy—areas in which one man finds it difficult to support a family. Polyandry has also been explained as a result of an excess of males in any given locality, but this is probably more unusual as a cause than limited natural resources.

In contrast to polyandry, polygyny, or the marriage of one man to several women, has usually been produced by exceptional riches and prosperity. In no instance has polygyny prevailed among all the inhabitants of any given region. It has almost always been restricted to the more wealthy in the population. It has persisted into our own times in a sub-rosa and non-institutionalized manner, namely, in the frequent tendency of rich males to support, besides an institutionalized wife and family, one or more mistresses.

A number of clearly evident factors have tended to encourage polygyny. Sexual ardor, adventurousness, the desire for display and prestige, and the zeal for novelty have almost invariably provided strong psychological motivations for polygyny. Among primitive peoples, and in early historic societies, the capture of women in war made it natural for victorious males to appropriate a number of captive women. Slavery also facilitated polygyny; attractive slave women often became concubines of their masters, who were already provided with an institutionalized family.

Political and military considerations have also been operative. Polygyny made it possible for the males of the ruling class to beget many more children than would have been possible under a monogamous system. Polygyny was also frequently conferred as a reward for military valor and strategic prowess. Religion often rationalized and approved the prevailing practice of polygyny among the ruling class, which the priests desired to placate and favor in return for political support of the prevailing cult.

Of all the moral influences that have helped to undermine polygyny as a fairly open and general practice among wealthy males, the Hebrew and Christian religions have probably been the most powerful. But they have usually driven it underground into non-institutionalized manifestations rather than completely extinguished it. Male sexual ardor and zest for novelty have proved too powerful for any type of religion thoroughly to uproot or completely to discipline.

Factors strengthening monogamy. Although the Jewish and Christian religions have supplied the chief moral sanction for monogamy, and have exerted the strongest psychological pressure in its behalf, many other factors have tended to make it the predominant type of family. The extremes of poverty and prosperity that favor polyandry or polygyny, respectively, have not been characteristic of human society as a whole. Also, the relative equality of the two sexes in numbers has inevitably encouraged monogamous forms of pairing. Moreover, monogamy facilitates devotion to children, since both parents can give their undivided attention to the offspring of a single woman. Monogamy also tends to promote sentimental affection. The monogamous family provides a more cohesive social unit and simplifies blood relationships. Monogamy also creates better protection and greater solicitude for the wife than can prevail under polygyny. When, to these many natural and social advantages of monogamy, was added the strict formal sanction of an authoritative religious system, it is not difficult to understand why monogamy has predominated in western Christian civilization.

Family life in the ancient Near East. In the ancient Near East, the monogamous family was prevalent among the masses, with polygyny relatively common among the richer males. The position of women in Egypt was a favored one, not matched in subsequent history until very recent times. Many queens ruled the country, and, more than that, the property and inheritance rights of women were fully recognized. Perhaps most important of all was the fact that property was inherited through the mother:

Egypt had kept very ancient traditions of the eminent right of women to inheritance . . . the wife, though subordinate in fact, was independent by right. . . . The wife of a prince gave her sons the right to rule. The wife of royal race was the keeper of the royal heritage and transmitted the right of kingship to her children alone.[6]

It is thought by many Egyptologists that these facts indicate the prevalence of the maternal family and matrilineal relationships in prehistoric Egypt.

Among the Semites of early western Asia, the paternal system dominated and rigorous patriarchal authority frequently evolved. Polygyny was very common among Semites in the Near East other than the Hebrews, and the latter were unable to stamp it out entirely within their own domains. One of the chief contributions of the Hebrews to the history

---

[6] Alexandre Moret, *The Nile and Egyptian Civilization.* New York: Knopf, 1928, p. 306.

of the family was their sanctification of monogamy and the introduction of the strong patriarchal tendencies revealed in the Old Testament. The authoritarian family, which emphasized both monogamy and male dominion and was adopted by the Christian Church in the later Roman Empire, is primarily a heritage from the Hebrews. But polygyny continued to prevail in the Near East from ancient times to our own. It was common among the Persians and also among the Arab sheiks. From these sources it was taken up by Islam and was practiced by the richer Muslims from the days of Mohammed himself to our own time. Only in 1926 was it abolished in Turkey, with the introduction of the new social system of Mustapha Kemal.

The family in Greece and Rome. Among the Greeks, particularly the Attic Greeks, the family occupied a special position. It was rather thoroughly divorced from romance and sentiment, thus proving that the monogamous family can prevail without any romantic foundation. The Greek family was a practical affair, which existed primarily for the purpose of breeding and rearing children. The Greek wife was kept in the home and denied any legitimate sexual freedom outside. Greek men often found their romantic attachments outside the family with mistresses of a high intellectual order, or satisfied their promiscuous sex cravings by relations with prostitutes. In Sparta, male adultery was given a quasi-institutional sanction among the ruling classes as a method of producing more male children, who were highly prized as future members of the Spartan army and military caste.

The Roman family passed through a notable historical evolution. It started out as a rather extreme manifestation of patriarchal monogamy, in which the father or eldest living male had almost absolute authority over his wife and children, even to the extent of inflicting death for what were considered legitimate reasons. Adultery on the part of the wife was severely punished and divorce was rare. Religious, social, and military pressures all made the early Roman family extremely cohesive.

During the later Republic and the early Empire, this type of Roman family all but disappeared. The free Roman peasantry, which provided the social and economic foundation for the patriarchal Roman family were decimated as a result of wars, the growth of great estates, and the working of the land by slave gangs. With the growth of wealth, as a result of conquest and commerce, the richer Romans desired to free themselves from the older restrictions upon promiscuity. The presence of many beautiful captives and slave women encouraged their zeal. The dispossessed peasants and others who flocked to the cities, especially Rome, became an urban rabble, herded together in miserable slums and apartments.

These conditions undermined the old religious and patriarchal family of early rural Rome among the urban masses. Marriage was no longer a sanctified social institution, but became a civil contract. There was a limited feminist movement at this time, by which women gained the right to hold some property and other new privileges, all of which made for a greater degree of female independence. It was natural that divorce became far more common under these conditions. Indeed, it became extremely prevalent, particularly among the upper classes, and not even Augustus was able to check the trend. There was a great deal of vice among the city rabble.

The downfall of the old Roman family was most marked at the end of the Republic and during the first century of the Empire. During the latter part of the Roman period, marriage was once more restored, at least among the masses, to something of its former sanctity and cohesiveness. The predominance of Christian ideals during the later Roman Empire has suggested to scholars that we must qualify the view that the Roman Empire disintegrated because of the downfall of the Roman family and the increase of sexual promiscuity. The Empire actually fell apart during those centuries when the Christian influence was becoming effective in checking the earlier immorality of the Romans. But, no doubt, the conditions that had prevailed before the Christian triumph exerted a powerful influence for many generations thereafter.

Medieval Catholic influence on the family. Due to the influence of Paul, Augustine, and other sex purists, marriage was made a sacrament and brought under ecclesiastical dominion. Divorce was outlawed, though separation and the annulment of marriage were sanctioned. Patriarchal parental authority was encouraged by church doctrine. The chastity of women was extolled, and virginity became a veritable cult. The fact that medieval life was primarily rural made it possible for the church to carry through the revolution in morals and family relationships with relative success. Country life is far more favorable to authoritarian monogamy than the more complicated conditions of city life. The chivalrous ideals held about noblewomen eased the conscience of feudal lords, who ravished unprotected non-noblewomen almost at will. By ultimately forbidding marriage of the clergy, the Catholics deprived religious leaders of the benefits of family life, at the same time ridding them of its responsibilities. Although the formal celibacy of the clergy was taken for granted during the medieval period, it was not uncommon for priests, monks, and friars to maintain concubines, and to have children by them. The church frowned on this but was not able to eliminate the practice until after the reforms of the Counter-Reformation.

Protestantism and the family. Protestantism brought with it a number of important changes in sex practice and ideals. Protestants were as strongly against sexual sin and promiscuity as were Catholics, but they believed that the celibacy of the clergy increased rather than reduced clerical immorality. Inasmuch as the Protestant leaders drew many of their moral ideals from the Old Testament rather than the New, they tended to stress patriarchal authority in the family. With the Calvinistic emphasis on thrift it was natural that the economic value of the housewife would not be overlooked. The Calvinistic emphasis upon the moral virtues of hard work was held particularly relevant for the wife. The Protestant ideal of the good wife was one who was both obedient unto her husband and passionately devoted to industry and thrift. The Protestants laid considerable stress upon the value of education as a necessity for reading the Bible. Since there were few public schools for the masses, the family long had to assume most of the responsibility for such education as the average child received.

The Protestant ideas about the family were brought to America and received their most complete development on the rural frontier. The sparsity of population and the isolation of the rural family in America made the family the center of economic, social, educational, and recreational life. Dangers from natural and human enemies encouraged parental authority, discipline, and respect. The economic value of the family was very great, because there was intense need for the labor of women and children. Social contacts being relatively few, the family divided with the rural church the leadership in social, intellectual, and recreational life. And the time spent in the home was far in excess of that devoted to the worship of God, even in those days when families frequently spent all day Sunday in devotions. The predominance of the family during some two centuries of American rural life gained for it a preëminent place in our institutional equipment and our respect.

Foundations of rural family cohesion. The rural American family illustrated the cohesive power of a primary institution. It rested on four foundations: First, there was the economic and social importance of the home. Before the Industrial Revolution women were subordinated to males in the domestic economy to the extent that few women had economic, occupational, or legal freedom. Second, one notes the patriarchal authority of the husband and father, given to him by custom and law. Since public opinion and the conditions of life were added to the force of law to buttress male authority, it is small wonder that divorces were relatively infrequent. Third, the dependence of all individual members on the united family was a prime factor in family stability, and few individuals had status except as a member of a family group. Girls were expected to marry young and raise large families, and a spinster's usual lot in life was to take care of the children of some more fortunate sister. Women, except in their family function, were relatively helpless. This point must be stressed because of its importance in the discussion of the current weakening of family bonds. A fourth foundation of the traditional rural American family was the strong religious sanctions that supported it. The family was regarded as a religious institution resting upon supernatural approval. Adultery was regarded as a serious sin, and divorce was viewed almost as seriously. William F. Ogburn thus summarizes the social role of the rural American family:

The American family was many things to its individual members. There was not only its economic importance, but other institutional functions of the family were at the same time strongly developed. It furnished protection to its members, with less aid from the community than is expected today: it might even, as in the case of feuds, carry on private wars. The authority of the father and husband was sufficient to settle within the family many of the problems of conduct. Religious instruction and ritual were a part of family life. For a successful marriage it was considered important that couples should have the same faith. In general, the home was the gathering place for play activities though there were some community festivities. Educationally the farm and home duties constituted a larger part of learning than did formal instruction in schools. Farm life furnished what we now call manual training, physical education, domestic science instruction and vocational guidance. The individual spent much of the daily cycle in the family setting, occupied in ways set by the family pattern.[7]

HOW MODERN SOCIAL TRENDS HAVE UNDERMINED THE HISTORIC MONOGAMOUS FAMILY

Evidence of disintegration of the traditional patriarchal family. The traditional patriarchal monogamy is now undergoing thorough reconstruction in our urban era. The divorce rate has increased steadily in the years since 1900; today there is one divorce for about every four marriages in our country. Family desertions are extremely common, although such evidence as we possess about their number does not indicate that they are increasing as rapidly as divorce. As divorce becomes easier, desertion is less necessary or attractive, for the legal responsibilities of family life are not removed by desertion. There is a greater prevalence of sexual freedom outside the family than was common a half century ago. Many of the functions of the family are now taken over by other agencies. In certain circles, especially in cities, children are no longer an economic asset but are a notable financial liability. Some of the most sacred ideals of the older family and sexual morality are today often regarded very lightheartedly, especially by the younger generation.

New economic influences. Among the chief forces undermining the traditional family are the economic developments associated with modern industrialism, especially the growing economic independence of women, and the growth of a secular outlook on life, which challenges the authoritarian religious foundations of the conventional family. Although secularism has been very influential in changing our attitudes toward the family, there is little doubt that economic influences have been more immediately and comprehensively potent. The rural family group is no longer the center of economic life. Many more people buy their food than produce it for themselves. Most goods are now made in factories and purchased from distributors. The work of women and children becomes progressively less important to the family in an urban era. Legislation limiting the work of women and children, especially the latter, has made it less possible for these younger persons to contribute to the income of the family group. Indeed, in urban life, children are generally a serious economic liability. Industrialism made possible the remunerative employment of women and has given them an economic independence which they have never previously known as a class. Hence, millions of women no longer have to depend upon a husband for their maintenance.

Effect of city life. Of all the indirect effects of modern industrialism upon the family, it is probable that the rise of city life has been the most demoralizing. We have pointed out that the French sociologist, Dumont, stressed the fact that social ambition in city life has tended to reduce the

---

[7] W. F. Ogburn, *et al., Recent Social Trends*, 2 Vols. New York: McGraw-Hill, 1930, Vol. I, p. 667.

birth rate and the size of families. It even discourages marriage in some instances. Further, the total conditions of city life have been the most potent factor in reducing the birth rate. Almost everything used by the city family is produced outside the family circle. The delicatessen shop is slowly but surely replacing the kitchen in the urban family. Indeed, many city families eat almost exclusively in restaurants, so that not only the kitchen but the dining-room, as well, has been taken out of the home. Likewise, amusement and recreation are sought mainly outside the family circle. The radio and television have modified this somewhat, but it is likely that novel forms of outside entertainment will appear to offset this new trend.

City life has made children a liability, and the growing popularity, effectiveness, and accessibility of birth control devices have made it ever easier to avoid the responsibility of child bearing. They also encourage the seeking of sexual satisfactions without contracting the responsibilities of matrimony. The social radicalism promoted by modern industrialism and urbanism has developed a philosophy antagonistic to the conventional family. Early in the seventeenth century a radical friar, Tomaso Campanella, called attention to the fact that the family is the chief bulwark of the institution of private property. Many radicals have, therefore, sought to break down the sanctity of the family.

Corrosive influence of secularism. Secularism has directly attacked supernatural religion, which provided the intellectual and moral foundations of the traditional family. Thoroughgoing secularism denies the existence of any form of supernatural sanction for any type of social institution. Probably the most important influence of secularism upon the modern family is the divorce of sin from sex. For the first time since the days of Augustine, the notion of the sinfulness of sex has been candidly and sharply assailed. The family and other accompaniments of sex are to be judged solely by their contributions to human welfare, here and now.

Secularism is not necessarily hostile to the family as a means of satisfactorily handling the problems of sex and reproduction. Indeed, it recommends monogamy as the normal and most satisfying method. But it is certainly comprehensively hostile to the tyranny of a monogamy that is regarded as indissoluble for any cause whatever. The growth of secularism has lessened repugnance to the use of birth control devices by wiping away any such notion as the traditional religious view that birth control is also "soul control" and prevents immortal souls from coming into existence. It is quite probable that the growth of secularism may ultimately lead to a family system more in accord with scientific facts and social realities than the old-time monogamy. If so, it will increase the success and stability of family life. But, certainly, the secular outlook has thus far exerted a corrosive and disintegrating influence upon the traditional American family and its moral bulwarks.

Undermining the traditional functions of the family. An able student of contemporary family problems, W. F. Ogburn, has suggested that the best way of discovering the degree to which the old rural type of family has declined is to investigate what has happened, of late, to the traditional functions of the authoritarian family. He lists seven of these functions: (1) affectional; (2) economic; (3) educational; (4) protective; (5) recreational; (6) family status; and (7) religious.

The affectional function has been less hard hit than the other family functions and is probably the most powerful function today. But its weakness is shown by the fact that about one family in four ends by divorce, that there are many family desertions, and that innumerable unhappy families persist without resort to divorce.

That the economic function of the family is being undermined by modern technology and urban life may be seen from relevant statistics. The output of bakeries increased four times as much between 1914 and 1925 as did the general population. During the same period, the products

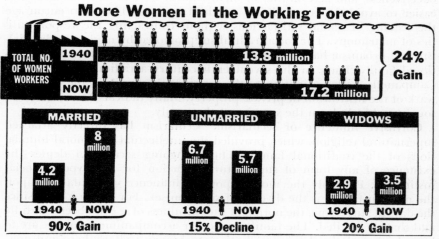

More Women in the Working Force

TOTAL NO. OF WOMEN WORKERS	1940	13.8 million
	NOW	17.2 million

24% Gain

MARRIED	UNMARRIED	WIDOWS
1940: 4.2 million NOW: 8 million	1940: 6.7 million NOW: 5.7 million	1940: 2.9 million NOW: 3.5 million
90% Gain	15% Decline	20% Gain

of canning factories and other food factories increased over six times as much as the population. From 1900 to 1920, the number of restaurant-keepers and waiters increased about four times as much as the population. The number of delicatessen stores increased about three times as rapidly as the population. The amount of work done in laundries increased nearly four times as rapidly as the population from 1914 to 1925. The sales of sewing-machines per capita for home use have markedly declined since 1914. So have the number of domestic servants employed in the home, despite the great increase in wealth between 1914 and 1929. These trends before 1925 continued during the next quarter of a century. The number of married women per capita in the population that are gainfully employed has more than quadrupled since 1900. In 1951, out of a total labor force of 63,700,000, no less than 19,467,000 were women. Of these, 50.9 per cent were married women, with another 16 per cent widowed or divorced, many of them with young children.

Education has become almost entirely a function of the schools. The number of teachers has increased more than twice as rapidly as has the number of parents since 1870. Children are being taken into the schools at an earlier age and for longer periods—the school year increased from 132 days in 1870 to 176 days in 1946. The protective function of the family is also being appropriated by the state. The number of policemen and other official protective functionaries has increased by over 85 per cent since 1910—about four times as rapidly as the population. Juvenile courts, probation services, and social legislation affecting children are other extensions of the protective function outside the family. The recreational function has passed beyond the family. Card playing, listening to the radio, and television are about the only forms of recreation that remain primarily centered in the home.

Family status also changing. Fewer persons live in separate houses; more live in city apartments, which cramp the living habits of the former rural family. Children are no longer the aid and protection they once were. They tend to disperse, and the parents rely more and more on insurance and annuities to protect them in old age. The state has also aided with old age insurance.

As secularism undermined the religious functions of the family, religious exercises in the home became less frequent. Automobiles, movies, radio, television and other secular diversions help on this secularizing trend. All in all, we may agree with Ogburn's general conclusion:

> There is no doubt that the family, as a social institution, is declining. This is the conclusion from a series of quantitative studies. Many of us do not realize that the family is declining or even changing. For we are accustomed to think of the family as we do of the Rock of Ages, something that in the nature of things must always remain essentially unchanged as the foundation of society, otherwise civilization itself would not exist. And then when the day-by-day changes are slight we do not notice them. It is when we return after a long absence that we can see the cumulative changes that have occurred.[8]

As we shall see later in this chapter, the unsettled wartime conditions in the 1940's made the family even more unstable than it was when Ogburn wrote.

The problem of marriage and the home in a changing civilization is receiving more than usually serious attention from others than alarmed traditionalists and purists. Enlightened persons recognize the transition through which home and family life are passing and agree that this is directly related to the increase of divorce, desertion, juvenile crime, juvenile drunkenness, and other evidences of social demoralization. The home is invaded and challenged by new distractions and amusements. Marriage itself has become strikingly unstable. According to United States government statistics, the average family holds together for less than six years, even in normal times.

Lack of serious and thoughtful approach to marriage. Social historians recognize the broad economic and institutional changes that have helped

---

[8] W. F. Ogburn, "Decline of the American Family," *The New York Times Magazine*, February 17, 1929.

bring about the instability of marriage and the revolution of the home. The growth of modern industrialism, the rise of the factory system, the entry of women into industry, the progress of universal education, the appearance of the single standard for the sexes, the impact of the automobile upon the social life and habits have, as we noted above, all played their part. But along with these factors we must consider the personal attitudes of those who approach the altar seeking holy wedlock. Some light is certainly thrown on the complex problems of modern marriage by a study of the state of mind and expectations of those upon the eve of marriage. The Marital Relations Institute of New York submitted over 40,000 questionnaires to couples applying for marriage licenses in the larger cities of the United States, from New York to San Francisco. The most important questions asked were:

(1) Why are you marrying?
(2) What do you expect out of marriage?
(3) How long do you think your marriage will last?
(4) Do you expect to raise a family?
(5) Do you expect to help support your home? (Asked of women only.)

Some 5,000 men and 13,000 women answered the questionnaire. The lack of serious consideration of the purpose and justification of marriage was brought out by the answers to the first question. Only 1,620, or 9 per cent of those who replied to the questionnaire, even attempted to answer this question. Apparently over nine-tenths of the couples could offer no logical explanation. About half of the small fraction that did answer claimed that they were doing so for love. About a fourth of those who answered said that they were marrying for security. About a third of those who claimed that they were marrying for financial security were men. Less than one per cent of those who answered declared they were marrying for the purpose of bearing children.

As to what the couples expected out of marriage, "financial security" and "a good home" ran neck-and-neck for first place among answers to question 2. These far out-distanced romance and the like. Four women declared that they expected "nothing."

As to how long the expectant couples believed that their marriages would last, the estimates ranged from two years to "forever." The average of all answers submitted to this question produced a composite figure of a little over 16 years, indicating almost a 300 per cent optimism when compared with government figures as to the duration of the average marriage in this country today.

Though only a small fraction gave the bearing of children as their primary purpose, a larger per cent answered that they expected to raise a family. The men seemed far more interested in propagation than the women; some 82 per cent of the men and only 21 per cent of the women intended to raise a family. The inroads on the theory that woman's place is in the home were revealed by the fact that 43 per cent of the women who answered question 5 expected to help support their home.

From answers to these questions it would seem that important reasons for the instability of marriage are the absence of any intelligent or rational consideration of the object of matrimony, and the incidental role of children in the desire for marriage. The chief stabilizing influence would appear to be the zeal for economic security, but this is mitigated by the fact that so many women expressed their intention to contribute toward the support of the home. Such women are highly unlikely to submit for long to an unpleasant or oppressive home environment.

Inasmuch as the chief evidence of the growing instability of family relationships is the increase of the divorce rate in contemporary times, we may now turn to a brief survey of the history of divorce and the extent, nature, and causes of divorce in our day.

A BRIEF HISTORY OF DIVORCE PRACTICES, ATTITUDES AND LEGISLATION

Divorce among primitive people. Divorce seems to have an antiquity as great as that of the family itself. The pairing arrangements of higher apes and of the earliest primitive peoples were often broken up. In well-developed primitive society divorce was common; but it was not usual to sanction it, except for some reasonable cause. Wives were divorced for barrenness, adultery, general laziness and shiftlessness, poor cooking, neglect of children, disagreeable personality, invalidism, and old age. Women were permitted to divorce their husbands for laziness, neglect, and cruelty. The economic value of wife and husband to each other in primitive society helped to limit the frequency of divorce. The woman needed a hunter and protector, and the man required somebody to do housework, agricultural labor, and other forms of manual occupation. These economic factors were probably stronger than either religion or romance in preserving family life in primitive times.

Divorce in the ancient Near East. The high position of women in Egypt limited the freedom of the husband in divorcing his wife, a practice that was fairly general in those oriental countries where the patriarchal system prevailed. Among the Babylonians and the Assyrians, patriarchal society gave the husband relative freedom to divorce his wife, but even here divorce for trivial causes was frowned upon. Adultery was universally recognized as an almost compulsory cause for divorce because of its menace to the efficacy of ancestor worship. A male heir whose bastardy was not known would nullify the whole scheme of ancestor worship in any given family.

The Jewish law, mainly drawn up in the patriarchal period, also gave the husband great leeway in repudiating his wife and terminating the family arrangement. The Mosaic law declared that for good purpose a man could write his wife "a bill of divorcement, and give it in her hand and send her out of his house." Divorce was also permitted by the mutual consent of both parties, and the wife could divorce her husband for persistent cruelty, notorious immorality, and neglect.

Mohammedan law and tradition generally favored the easy repudiation of a wife by her husband, though in certain Muslim areas divorce has been relatively rare. The wife could divorce her husband, but under greater restrictions and only for extreme cruelty or neglect. The Koran did, however, permit a wife to obtain a divorce with relative ease if she could obtain the consent of her husband. When the divorce was a judicial proceeding, it was not granted until three months after the application.

Divorce in classical times. In Attic Greece, divorce was relatively easy. Either the husband or the wife might have a bill of divorce drawn up and presented to an archon, who submitted the question to a jury. The sexual freedom allowed to the Greek husband, the economic value of his wife, and the domestic servility and dependence of the Greek wife all combined to minimize the actual frequency of divorce. In Sparta, divorce was restricted, because children were looked upon as the property of the state, and adultery was tacitly encouraged in order to increase the number of children.

In early Rome, the patriarchal father could eject his wife from his home at will, as a manifestation of his extensive authority. Formal divorce was permitted for infanticide, adultery, and sterility. The religious and economic conditions of the early Roman family, however, made divorce relatively infrequent. The law of the Twelve Tables increased the freedom of Roman divorce. In the later Republic and the Empire, marriage came to be looked upon as primarily a civil contract. It could be terminated by mutual consent, as essentially a private agreement. Both men and women could dissolve marriage by the legal formality of notification of intention to do so. Augustus tried to check the frequency of Roman divorce by imposing certain economic and social penalties, but divorce remained common throughout the Empire, and the legislation of Theodosius and Valentinian in the middle of the fifth century contained few drastic restrictions. Men were given fifteen grounds for divorce and women twelve.

One may say that relative ease of divorce was provided for throughout classical civilization, though in practice the Romans availed themselves of the opportunity far more frequently than the Greeks. Greek notions of the family and resort to mistresses and prostitutes without any notable social stigma seem to have worked in the interest of family stability.

Divorce in the Catholic Middle Ages. Christianity, by making marriage a sacrament, exerted a powerful influence in restricting the freedom of divorce. But it was not able to influence Roman law in this regard for some centuries, the legislation of the middle of the fifth century A.D. being favorable to easy divorce. But, under Justinian in the sixth century, Christian theories triumphed in Roman law. The old practice of divorce by mutual consent was done away with, and divorce was permitted only for certain specified and actually serious offenses, delinquencies, or deficiencies. For example, a husband was allowed to divorce his wife only for her failure to reveal plots against the state, plots against her husband's life, adultery, chronic social dissipation in the company of other men, running away from home, defying her husband by attendance at the circus or theater, and procuring abortion against her husband's will. In the canon law of the Roman Catholic Church, no formal divorce was allowed. Only separation was permitted. This could be secured only through recourse to an ecclesiastical court and was permitted only for adultery, perversion, impotence, cruelty, entrance into a religious order, or marriage within a tabooed degree of relationship.

The Roman Catholic substitute for divorce was what is known as annulment. This could be permitted on the ground that there had been some form of deception or ignorance of premarital sin, impotence, or other impediments to complete family life, which had not been known to one or both of the parties prior to marriage. Therefore, in Catholic theory, the marriage had never actually been consummated and was null and void from the beginning.

Effects of Protestantism. Though under Protestantism the attitude towards divorce was relaxed, freedom of divorce made only very gradual headway in Protestant countries. For example, although the Church of England was actually born from the divorce case of Henry VIII, it has maintained a very stern attitude toward divorce through the reign of Edward VIII. The Protestant clergy were, however, highly favorable to increased political authority at the expense of the Catholic Church. Divorce tended to become a matter of civil rather than ecclesiastical law, though religious dogmas retained a predominant influence over the content of civil legislation on family and divorce problems.

In Germanic countries divorce was permitted for adultery, perversion, bigamy, murderous assault, desertion, and extreme cruelty, as well as for insanity and certain other more unusual causes. Under the Nazis there was, paradoxically, both a tightening and a relaxation of divorce legislation, in conformity with the racial and eugenic program of the new regime. Marriage between robust "Aryans" was made rigid, and divorce was possible only for serious cause. On the other hand, mixed marriages (of an "Aryan" and a Jew) and marriages of persons with an inheritable disease were readily annulled. France long opposed any relaxing of divorce laws, but in 1884 legislation was passed that permitted divorce for adultery, cruelty, disgrace, assault, and conviction for an infamous crime. Italy, strongly Catholic, has had relatively strict divorce laws; Fascism strengthened them in the interest of a higher birth rate.

Until 1857, absolute divorce could be secured in Great Britain only through an act of Parliament. In that year, legislation was passed to enable a husband to divorce his wife for adultery and the wife to divorce her husband for adultery, or adultery combined with bigamy, rape, perversion or extreme cruelty. A Royal Commission recommended liberalization of divorce legislation in 1912. This was achieved by legislation in 1914, 1920, 1923, 1926, and 1930. The legislation of 1923 placed the sexes on terms of equality, and legislation of 1926 severely restricted newspaper publicity of divorce cases. But the causes for divorce were not notably extended, with the result that there has been frequent perjury and collusion in trumping up adultery evidence to secure divorce. After the Second World War there was a marked increase of divorce in England—from

14,614 divorces in 1945 to 56,033 in 1947—but even then the rate was only about one-fourth that of the United States.

In America, divorce was discouraged by religious influences in colonial times, but the more rigorous attitude has been gradually relaxed since the Revolution, and especially in the present century. Divorce legislation differs among the states. Until 1949, there was no legal ground for divorce in South Carolina, but there are 14 recognized grounds for divorce in New Hampshire. In many states, including New York, the only usual legal ground for divorce is adultery. This has produced a vast amount of hypocrisy, subterfuge, perjury, and collusion, in some instances amounting to a veritable divorce racket, which is morally more reprehensible than the free-and-open divorce system that prevails in Nevada, where divorce can be procured on the vague and flexible ground of extreme cruelty.

Recent divorce legislation. The best-known liberal and civilized divorce legislation is to be found in the laws and practices of the Scandinavian countries, of American states like Nevada, Idaho, and Florida, of Mexico, and of Soviet Russia prior to 1940. In 1915, Sweden enacted a law based upon extended study of the whole divorce problem. It provided for divorce by mutual consent in all instances where persistent family discord exists. The parties must make an application to be followed by a year's separation during which efforts at reconciliation are made under court authority. If the application is renewed after a year, the divorce is granted. For more serious causes divorces can be granted without the lapse of the year specified in discord cases. The example of Sweden was followed in 1918 by Norway, and in 1920 by Denmark. The radical government in Mexico eased divorce legislation, and Soviet Russia provided for divorce by mutual consent or by the request of either party, without the necessity of specifying the grounds.

This relaxing of Russian legislation was not followed by any overwhelming epidemic of divorces, though the rate rose somewhat. The divorce rate in the Scandinavian countries, in Mexico, and in Soviet Russia is far lower than that which has prevailed in the United States since the First World War. The divorce legislation of the Scandinavian countries, Mexico, and Soviet Russia is epoch-making in that it is the first legislation of the sort in human history that has been separated from religious considerations and has been based upon scientific facts and social investigation. As a result of patriotic, military, and defense considerations, the freedom of divorce in Russia was restricted just prior to the Second World War.

Need for improved divorce legislation in the United States. There is no doubt that changes should be made in contemporary divorce legislation. The United States has 48 state divorce laws, which vary from extreme laxity to absolute rigor. Because of the difficulty of securing a divorce in some states, thousands of persons go to states where divorce is easy, secure a divorce, and return to their home state. This has resulted in serious legal problems: for example, a person may have established temporary residence outside his state, secured a divorce, and returned to his home and remarried. He may then find that, under his state law, he is not legally married and the children of his second marriage may be considered illegitimate. In recent years, with the rising divorce rate, there have been increasing problems because of the lack of uniformity in state laws. Numerous cases involving disputed divorces have been brought before the courts.

On June 7, 1948, the Supreme Court handed down four important decisions that seemed likely to aid the pressure for uniform divorce laws. In two similar cases, the Court held by 7-2 decisions that Nevada divorces, although legal to dissolve a marriage, do not cancel the obligations of former husbands to make monthly payments ordered by New York courts in separation proceedings. Since New York has only one ground for divorce, many couples legally separate and, in some cases, the courts order husbands to continue to support their wives. Justice Jackson, disagreeing with the decision, said that the rulings merely added to the existing confusion, for people today do not know, and even a lawyer cannot tell them with assurance, how their out-of-state divorce and later remarriage might be regarded legally by the state in which they make their home. He urged the Court to issue a ruling by which people can live. In the other two cases, also similar, the Supreme Court ruled that the Massachusetts courts could not challenge divorces obtained in Nevada and Florida if both the husband and wife had full opportunity before the divorce to argue in the courts the question of legal residence.

Another ruling regarding Nevada divorces was handed down by the Supreme Court on April 18, 1949. By a decision of 5-4 the Court ruled that divorces obtained in Nevada can be overruled by other states under certain circumstances. Justice Jackson, one of the dissenters, protested that this makes the nation's divorce laws more confused than ever. The majority held, however, that Connecticut had acted properly in setting aside a Reno divorce and granting the ex-wife a widow's share in the property of her former husband, who died without leaving a will.

There has been increasing agitation for a uniform Federal divorce law. Much opposition has developed from two sources: from commercial interests in states in which easy divorce laws bring in large sums of money, and from those persons who believe in the right of states to manage their own problems and who fear infringement by the Federal government. But a Federal law modeled on the legislation of the Scandinavian countries would help to remove some of the divorce evils prevalent today.

INCREASING PREVALENCE OF DIVORCE

Divorce rates in leading countries. The outstanding fact about divorce is its steady increase in most civilized countries during the last generation. Japan is an exception: it once had easy divorce laws but later made divorce more difficult. The following table shows the trend toward greater frequency of divorce since 1890:

DIVORCES PER 100,000 POPULATION [9]

	1890	1900	1910	1920	1935
United States	53	73	92	139	171
Japan	269	143	113	94	70
France	17	25	37	71	50
Germany	13	15	24	63	74
Sweden	8	10	16	29	63
England and Wales	1	2	3	17	41

[9] J. P. Lichtenberger, *Divorce: A Social Interpretation*. New York: McGraw-Hill, 1931, p. 110. The figures for 1935 were kindly computed for me by Frank H. Hankins, from W. F. Willcox, *Studies in American Demography*. Ithaca: Cornell University Press, 1940, p. 342; *League of Nations Yearbook*, 1940; and S. A. Stouffer and L. M. Spencer, "Recent Increases in Marriage and Divorce," *American Journal of Sociology*, January, 1939, pp. 551-554.

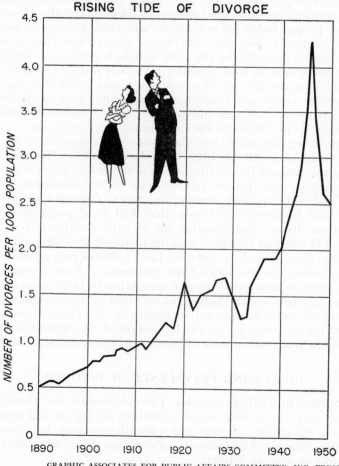

RISING TIDE OF DIVORCE

NUMBER OF DIVORCES PER 1,000 POPULATION

GRAPHIC ASSOCIATES FOR PUBLIC AFFAIRS COMMITTEE, INC. FROM
How Can We Teach About Sex? BY SIDONE GRUENBERG.

More recent statistics give the number of divorces to each hundred marriages as follows: United States (1945), 30.8; Switzerland (1944), 9.0; Japan (1938), 8.2; Germany (1938), 7.6; France (1940), 6.5; Scotland (1944), 4.6; England and Wales (1945), 3.9. Although the divorce rate in the United States leads all others, it has increased more rapidly in Great Britain, Sweden, Netherlands, Denmark, and France since 1900 than in the United States.

Increasing divorce rate in the United States. In the United States, the divorce rate has increased more than five-fold since 1890. Divorces in the United States are more frequent among freethinkers and Protestants than among Catholics; more frequent among the native born than the foreign born, and among Negroes than whites; more frequent in the city than in the country; more frequent among the rich and the poor than among the middle class; and far most frequent among childless couples. Some idea of the increasing instability of the monogamous family in America today can be gleaned from the following table, in which marriage rates, divorce rates, and divorces per marriage are assembled:

Year	Marriages per 1,000 Population	Divorces per 1,000 Population	Ratio of Marriage to Divorce
1887	8.7	.5	17.4
1890	9.0	.5	18.0
1895	8.9	.6	14.8
1900	9.3	.7	13.2
1905	10.0	.8	12.5
1910	10.3	.9	11.3
1915	10.0	1.0	10.0
1920	12.0	1.6	7.5
1925	10.3	1.5	6.8
1930	9.2	1.6	5.1
1935	10.4	1.7	6.1
1937	11.3	1.9	5.9
1940	12.1	2.0	6.0
1941	12.7	2.2	5.7
1942	13.2	2.4	5.5
1943	11.8	2.6	4.5
1944	11.0	2.9	3.8
1945	12.2	3.5	3.5
1946	16.4	4.3	3.8
1947	13.9	3.4	4.0
1948	12.4	2.8	4.4
1949	10.7	2.6	4.1

Should divorce continue to increase at the present rate, there would soon be one divorce for every marriage. It may be hoped that, before this happens, marriage and the family will be brought under scientific and sociological controls that will eliminate a number of the factors that work most powerfully today to increase the divorce rate.

The divorce rate by states varies greatly, mainly as a result of their widely different divorce laws. The following table shows the frequency of divorce in the ten highest and the ten lowest states in 1947:

Highest		*Lowest*	
Nevada	99.3	South Carolina	0.0
Florida	9.0	North Dakota	1.5
Idaho	6.5	Pennsylvania	1.5
Texas	6.1	Connecticut	1.7
New Mexico	5.8	North Carolina	1.9
Wyoming	5.5	Wisconsin	1.9
Montana	5.0	Minnesota	2.0
Arkansas	5.0	New Jersey	2.0
Washington	4.7	Vermont	2.0
Missouri	4.4	Nebraska	2.6

It is obvious that the extremely high rate for Nevada is due to the short residence requirement of six weeks for outsiders who wish to avail themselves of the Nevada legislation. The overwhelming majority of the divorces are granted to non-residents. The divorce rate for permanent residents of Nevada is relatively low, only about 5 per cent of the total divorces granted in the state being given to permanent Nevada residents—another proof that ease of divorce does not lead to divorce excesses.

Increasing resort to annulment of marriages. We referred earlier to the practice of the Catholic Church of granting annulments of marriage instead of divorces, which the Catholic Church has never sanctioned. Of late there has been an increasing tendency for non-Catholics, especially in the states with rigorous divorce laws, to resort to annulments. In New York State, which permits divorce only for adultery, the trend has become so notable that Supreme Court Justice Daniel F. Imrie recently called attention to it and described annulments as "backdoor divorces." At present, it is estimated that there are two annulments granted in New York State for every three divorces. It is doubtful if the rate is as high in any other state. Annulments offer the same opportunity for perjury and collusion as prevails in divorce cases. There are about a dozen legal grounds for annulment in various state laws. The most common ground advanced is "fraud," which is about as broadly interpreted as "mental cruelty" has been in the divorce courts of states with easy divorce laws.

Sex and residence of divorce applicants. A study of divorce statistics reveals that over two-thirds of all divorces are granted to the wife. More women than ever before are economically independent of their husbands and thus able to refuse to continue marriage under unfavorable conditions. Another factor encouraging women to initiate divorce proceedings is the greater number of legal grounds on which a wife can secure a divorce. The fact that the wife sues for divorce and carries through the divorce action may not mean that she was the one who originally proposed the move; she may file the suit so that her husband can keep on with his work and thus be better able to finance the cost of the divorce.

The rural divorce rate is still about 50 per cent less than in the urban areas, possibly because rural public opinion, to some extent, still serves as a deterrent to divorce. Further, there are usually more children, there are not as many opportunities for remarriage or for economic independence, and unhappily married persons often leave the rural community, establish residence elsewhere, and then secure a divorce.

Some reasons for the increase in the divorce rate. A number of explanations have been offered for the marked increase of divorce in the United States. Bertrand Russell, for example, thinks that "family feeling is extremely weak here, and the frequency of divorce is a consequence of this fact. Where family feeling is strong, for example in France, divorce will be comparatively rare, even if it is equally easy." Divorce is a symptom of deeper social trends, which have undermined the moral and economic basis of monogamous family life. Adultery, cruelty, and desertion may not be more prevalent today than sixty years ago. We have no way of telling. It is possible that the lessening of the social taboos and the general easing of conventions have given many couples the courage to end their incompatibility by legal divorce. Moreover, divorce has also been made cheaper in many areas.

The growth of industry and the increase of wealth in the United States in the twentieth century undoubtedly provide one explanation of the phenomenon of increasing divorce. General social cohesion and, consequently, family cohesion, has declined, and all classes have been infected with an eagerness to live on an ever-rising scale. The unhappiness produced by readjustments and disappointed ambitions has had its repercussions in the family, particularly for young married couples. A psychological explanation for increased divorce is the strong feeling of individualism among contemporary men and women. This has reacted against the tolerant give-and-take attitude required in the monogamous family relationship. Concurrently, female emancipation has bolstered woman's ego and independence, and helped to destroy the paternal type of family. The feminist movement, although not handing woman a passport to license, has made her more self-assertive and so endangered the old type of family stability. Equally demoralizing to stable marriage is woman's increasing participation in industry. For the urban working class, the home has tended to become little more than a night lodging place. When the effects of the prevailing

WHO gets divorces?

2/3 of all divorces are granted to women

The divorce rate in the cities is twice that in our country areas

About 2/3 of the people who obtain divorces have no children

The Atlantic coastal region has the Lowest divorce rate; there is a rapid increase as we go west

COURTESY PUBLIC AFFAIRS COMMITTEE, INC.

Chart showing effect of some personal and social situations on the divorce picture.

zeal for pleasure are added to the abnormal life in tenement or apartment house dwellings, it can be seen that conventional family life, particularly in urban centers, is fading away. Since industrialism has been undermining the home for many years, we now have a generation of undomesticated children who, in turn, when they marry, are prone to form unstable unions.

Bertrand Russell insists that the modern father is losing his former position in society. Among the proletariat, he is so busy earning a living that he rarely sees his children, and when he does see them, usually on Sundays, he scarcely knows how to behave towards them. Further, Russell observes that the state is increasingly taking over parental responsibilities, most emphatically among the submerged classes, where the father frequently cannot afford to feed or clothe his offspring decently. It may be noted that the depression after 1929 produced a notable increase in desertion. Children bred in the shadow of home relief lost that pride in the father which was formerly a natural heritage. The paternal status in the family has certainly deteriorated as contemporary civilization has advanced. This is true both among the upper classes, among which family instability seems most marked, and among the lower classes, among whom poverty does not permit the father to be much of a parent. Among the middle classes, at present, the father is of most importance; so long as he earns a good income he can provide adequately for his offspring, and he has a certain amount of leisure to devote to their care and direction.

Another vital factor in the increase of divorce, frequently overlooked, is that we have strict formal standards of sexual morality. Hence infidelity is commonly regarded as an unpardonable transgression, and the wronged partner usually feels that both pride and decency require a divorce action. In a country like France, fidelity is not considered the most important factor for the success of a marriage, and adultery is not so likely to provoke the husband or wife to petition for divorce. In France the family is not so frequently split and shattered through divorce and separation. The stress laid by our mores on sexual fidelity as the indispensable factor in the marital relationship develops a spirit of hypocrisy in marriage which, combined with the amazing ignorance of sex facts, is a potent force for divorce.

LEADING CAUSES OF DIVORCE AND OF DIVORCE INCREASE IN THE UNITED STATES

Formal and actual causes of divorce. The formal grounds for the granting of divorces in the United States are listed in the table on page 299.

These formal grounds of divorce, which are listed as the legal grounds in actual divorce cases, are frequently accepted by writers as the literal and true causes of family instability. To do so is, however, extremely naive, and such authors give a misleading view of the chief causes of divorce.

The ground that is offered in court is, all too frequently, entirely or partly fictitious and is dictated mainly by legal and other considerations

GROUNDS FOR GRANTING DIVORCES, 1887-1932

Cause	1887-1906	1922	1932
Cruelty	21.8%	34.5%	42.7%
Desertion	38.9	32.8	27.9
Adultery	16.3	10.9	7.3
Combination of Causes	9.4	8.7	8.0
Failure to Provide	3.7	4.2	4.1
Drunkenness	3.9	1.0	1.4
Others	6.1	7.8	8.6

that make it convenient to submit that particular reason for divorce. In New York State, for example, where adultery is the only usual ground on which divorce is granted, the applicant must allege adultery by the other party. Consequently, it is extremely common to "frame" a case of fictitious adultery, to be brought into court as evidence. If friends will not perform this service, there are professional adultery "fixers" of both sexes who will stage the frame-up. They are known to every good divorce lawyer. Hence, adultery may be the ground advanced to cover a score of different reasons for wishing the divorce. In Nevada, the most common grounds for divorce are "extreme cruelty," or "mental cruelty." These suffice as adequate legal grounds and are, at the same time, less likely than most others to afford the basis for sensational newspaper publicity. The fact that Nevada and several other states with relatively easy divorce laws accept "cruelty" as a legal basis for divorce accounts for the great increase in cruelty as the ostensible ground for demanding divorce and as the leading reason for granting it.

Even when the reason for divorce alleged in court is an actual cause, it is all too frequently a superficial one. Suppose, for example, that the cause alleged is desertion and that a husband has actually deserted his wife in the case. The real cause for the divorce lies in the reason for desertion. Was it from sheer boredom, the result of frequent quarrels, the product of sexual incompatibility, or the effect of chronic economic impoverishment? Moreover, if it was boredom, why was the man bored? For the real causes of divorce we thus have to turn to studies of sex life and family instability, such as have been made by Alfred C. Kinsey, G. B. Hamilton, Katharine Bement Davis, Dorothy Bromfield Bromley, Ernest R. Groves, W. F. Ogburn, W. F. Robie, and Lewis M. Terman, and to statistics of family income and studies of family budgets.

Marriage too easy to contract. Certainly one of the leading reasons for the downfall of the monogamous marriage and the emergence of a desire for divorce is found in the current ease of marriage. In most states, marriage can be contracted almost instantaneously. Marriages that are entered into as a result of a week-end flair for adventure or during a period of intoxication are not likely to prove successful or enduring. Modern advertising constantly encourages a frivolous attitude towards marriage. Countless advertisements imply that all that is needed to get and hold a husband or wife is the right kind of perfume, toilet soap, jewels, brassiere, coiffure,

shaving soap, hair oil, tweeds, automobile, or yacht. There is a fundamental hypocrisy and inconsistency in our whole attitude towards marriage, the family, and divorce. We maintain an air of the utmost lightheartedness and casualness to marriage, and at the same time regard the
family which results from it with an attitude of awesome sanctity. If the
family is a serious matter, then it is obvious that marriage is equally
serious. One of the best ways of promoting family stability would be to
make marriage a far more thoughtful and deliberate affair. The most
practicable first step would be to require a considerable delay between the
announcement of marriage intentions and the granting of a marriage
license.

Marriage without enthusiasm. Another often neglected but important
incitement to divorce is brought about when marriages are entered into
without any particular enthusiasm on the part of one of the parties involved. These marriages may proceed out of kindheartedness and an un-
willingness to rebuff pathetic affection and intense devotion. In such
instances, it is frequent that the man has not even realized he has proposed marriage. Some casual remark has been misinterpreted; the man
finds himself trapped in an embarrassing situation and does not have the
courage to be candid. Sinclair Lewis's portrayal of how Babbitt entered
into his engagement and marriage is a more frequent occurrence than one
appreciates. Women also frequently give an impression of consent to a
proposal when they have no such intention, a soft answer being used to
turn aside disappointment. Later, they find themselves so implicitly committed to marriage that they consent. The well-known quest of marriage
and security by women often induces them to accept an offer of marriage
when they feel no romantic impulses in the situation. Marriage and the
family impose enough difficulties and responsibilities upon those with
great initial enthusiasm. When this is lacking, there is likely to be resentment and restlessness from the beginning.

Childless families. The failure to have children seems to promote divorce and family instability, especially when there are few other cohesive
forces. About two-thirds of all divorces are granted to persons who have
no children. About 20 per cent of the divorces are given in instances
where there is only one child. One authority has estimated that 70 per
cent of childless marriages in the United States ultimately wind up in
the divorce court. The impact of increasing divorce upon children is,
thus, less serious than many suppose, since there are few children in most
of the families broken by divorce.

Economic factors. Studies of family discord and instability reveal the
frequency of economic causes of divorce. The pride of the wife and her
natural desire for display suffer severely when her husband cannot provide enough income for even the necessities. A man may become dis-
gruntled with his wife because she does not maintain a neat and tidy
home and an attractive table, although the responsibility for this failure
may rest primarily upon his own inadequacy as a provider. The mechan-
ism of projection frequently comes into play here. The guilty party does

not recognize his or her faults and blames the partner for the inadequacies. Economic insecurity and worries put the nerves of both husband and wife on edge and lead to quarrels, a sense of discouragement and futility, and an unwholesome atmosphere in the home. At times, the economic inadequacy becomes so great that it is literally impossible to keep the home together. The fact that divorce is also common among the rich is, however, sufficient reason to warn against any single-track economic explanation of divorce.

Sexual ignorance and incompatibility. Certainly one of the most important causes of family instability is basic sexual ignorance. Husbands are all too frequently over-aggressive and brutal at the outset. Wives suffer from emotional frigidity, morbid fears, and psychological unpreparedness. Sinclair Lewis's portrayal of the wedding night of Elmer Gantry provides an excellent illustration of a deplorably frequent situation. As Kinsey points out, a very large proportion of even married women never realize complete sexual satisfaction. Closely related to sex ignorance is the matter of sexual incompatibility, a fact that is likely to become known only after the marriage relationship has been consummated. Another associated cause of unsatisfactory marriage relations is venereal disease, whether known or unknown to one or the other of the partners before marriage. A husband who imagines that he has been cured of gonorrhea may have a chronic case and infect his wife after marriage. Or a woman may be suffering from syphilis, knowingly or unknowingly, and the husband may not discover it until the wife has a series of stillbirths.

Although it is rarely mentioned in any divorce statistics or publicity, it is generally agreed by expert students that sexual ignorance, incompatibility, and inadequacy are the foremost causes of marital discord. Judge George A. Bartlett, one of the most experienced of Reno divorce court judges, who presided over more than 20,000 divorce cases, was of the opinion that more marriages fail because of sexual incapacity or ignorance on the part of one or both of the partners than from any other cause: "Of all the factors that contribute to happy marriage, the sex factor is by far the most important. Successful lovers weather storms that would crush frail semi-platonic unions." As Lewis M. Terman has pointed out, other psychological factors, such as the happiness of the parents of the husband and wife, and the childhood happiness and sexual experience of the couple, are also closely related to marital happiness.

Monogamy and monotony. But even marriages that are originally founded upon romantic enthusiasm and in which the sexual adjustment is satisfactory may fail because of an unsatisfactory technique in keeping the monogamous relationship attractive. This problem has become more important with increasing leisure brought about by the machine. Formerly, when almost the entire energy and time of husband and wife were devoted to supplying the family needs, it was less necessary to find in each other a stimulating companion. With more and more leisure time, the deadly intimacy of the average monogamous relationship may be a menace to the family. Inadequate housing and overcrowding in city life have intensified this problem. With living conditions what they are today, it would be difficult to avoid excessive intimacy even though the persons involved were fully aware of the desirability. If one were to try to design a situation perfectly adapted to the destruction of the sentiment and novelty so essential to long-continued amorousness, he would arrive at something bearing a very close resemblance to the monogamous family, as it exists today. It is difficult to refute the facts pointed out by H. L. Mencken in the following quotation:

> Monogamous marriage, by its very conditions, tends to break down strangeness (between the sexes). It forces the two contracting parties into an intimacy that is too persistent and unmitigated; they are in contact at too many points, and too steadily. By and by, all the mystery of the relation is gone, and they stand in the unsexed position of brother and sister. Thus that "maximum of temptation" of which Shaw speaks has within itself the seeds of its own decay. A husband begins by kissing a pretty girl, his wife; it is pleasant to have her so handy and so willing. He ends by making Machiavellian efforts to avoid kissing the every-day sharer of his meals, books, bath towels, pocketbook, relatives, ambitions, secrets, malaises and business; a proceeding about as romantic as having his boots blacked. The thing is too horribly dismal for words. Not all the native sentimentalism of man can overcome the distaste and boredom that get into it. Not all the histrionic capacity of woman can attach any appearance of gusto and spontaneity to it.[10]

Growing independence of women. The increasing independence of women has been a significant cause of the increase of divorce. Women are no longer economic slaves bound to their husbands. Many a woman, if she does not like her husband or if he is a poor provider, need not continue to suffer from domestic unhappiness or impoverishment. She can earn her own living, divorce her unsatisfactory spouse, remain independent of him, and finally make a more satisfactory marriage.

Secularism and reduced reluctance to seek divorce. The lessening of public opprobrium against divorce and the tendency to accept it more as a matter of course, both the result of the growing secularism and the decline of orthodox religious controls, undoubtedly have made divorce more frequent. But it can hardly be alleged that this is an underlying cause of divorce. It simply makes dissatisfied parties to a marriage less reluctant to take public steps to terminate the unsatisfactory union.

There are other real causes of divorce, but those that we have listed—ease of marriage, indifference to marriage at the outset, childlessness, economic insecurity, sexual maladjustment, monogamous boredom, the growing economic independence of women, a more tolerant public opinion on divorce, and the decline of supernatural religion—account for the overwhelming majority of divorces and desertions, and the unhappy families in which divorce never actually takes place. The latter instances are frequently overlooked by students of marital problems, but, as Ludwig Lewisohn suggested in his book, *Don Juan,* they may account for a greater volume of human misery and suffering than complete marital ruptures involving divorce.

---

[10] *In Defense of Women.* New York: Knopf, 1922, pp. 109-110.

THE EFFECTS OF THE SECOND WORLD WAR ON THE FAMILY

Family instability intensified by war. War speeds up social change. All of the reasons for divorce noted above were given new impetus by the Second World War. Divorce rates, already high, rose alarmingly in the United States after Pearl Harbor. Statistics show, however, that long before the Second World War, the traditional patriarchal family pattern of the frontier and rural areas was disintegrating. The war increased the instability of the family considerably. War, especially if large-scale and long-continued, always disrupts family relationships and promotes conjugal instability.

Nearly 15 million persons were taken from their home surroundings by enlistments and the draft between 1940 and 1945. In addition, another 15 million men and women left their homes to work in defense and war plants. Large numbers of families left their homes and migrated hundreds, or thousands, of miles to find employment in war industries. The movement of war workers to already crowded urban areas made it difficult to find a place to live. Sometimes only temporary shelters were to be found, often in trailer camps or hastily erected shacks. Over-crowding and poor sanitation were common. Under these conditions, it was inevitable that family tensions would grow and family cohesion would suffer. Even when women and children did not migrate, many men left their homes to work. As a result husbands and wives drifted apart and found it difficult to resume life together again.

In some instances, changed income brought a weakening of family ties. Income was sometimes lowered when the husband was drafted, but for war workers, in spite of increased living costs and higher taxes, income increased. Women, as well as men, earned high wages in war plants. For many women, it was their first industrial employment. Wives became self-reliant and economically independent of their husbands and found it exciting to be free from home responsibilities.

Increased marriages during wartime. War conditions greatly stimulated marriages, many of them hasty, ill-considered, and regretted later. The marriage rate in the 1940's increased much more rapidly than population growth—23.9 to 14.5. Married couples increased from 28,516,937 to 35,320,000, the number of marriages being 3,670,000 above normal. In 1940, about 59 per cent of the female population, 14 years of age and over, were married; by 1946, over 63 per cent were married. The greatest increase in the rate of marriage was among young women between the ages of 20 and 24. In 1940, slightly over 50 per cent were married; in 1946, over 58 per cent. The marriage rate for the group of women 25-34 years of age increased by 4 per cent during this same period. The marriage rate for the country as a whole rose from 10.7 in 1939 to 16.4 per 1,000 of the population in 1946—an all-time high. About 1,500,000 soldiers married during wartime at home or abroad. About 100,000 soldiers married women of different race or nationality from their own. Although a large percentage of the marriages in the United States during wartime were marriages of servicemen, the tendency to marry hastily was also common among those at home, who were encouraged by high wages and more opportunities to marry.

Some of those who married during the war had previously planned marriage, but for thousands of couples marriage was the result of wartime conditions. In the frenzied haste of war, there was even less consideration of suitability among partners. The glamour of a uniform, the desire to

Marriages Boom Again With War . . . Births Stay High

FROM *U. S. News and World Report,* AN INDEPENDENT WEEKLY NEWS MAGAZINE PUBLISHED AT WASHINGTON. COPYRIGHT 1950, UNITES STATES NEWS PUBLISHING CORPORATION.

share in the excitement of the moment drew many girls into marriage after a whirlwind courtship of a few weeks or even days. Sometimes, either one or both of the parties had been drinking too much and had no clear recollection of the event or the person they married. Some girls married not because of the excitement, but for fear they would have no further opportunity; others married for the service allotment or the possible insurance if the soldier husband were killed. Some men married with the mistaken idea that it would keep them from being drafted; others hoped to have a child to leave behind in case they were killed in battle; some married because they hoped marriage would bring some sense of security in a time of uncertainty.

In considering the large number who married in haste, those who delayed marriage are often overlooked. Some marriages were prevented entirely by the death of the serviceman or the subsequent engagement of the girl or the man to another person.

Families undermined by wartime separation. After the parting, in the case of service men, thousands of couples who had married in haste, decided it had been a mistake, that there was little basis for a happy marriage—no similarity of background, no interests in common, no desire to resume the marriage relationship. It was no wonder that many of these couples decided to be divorced during or after the war.

Postwar family chaos. After VJ Day, demobilization took place rapidly. Veterans returned to take up civilian life. Some of them were changed, maimed, disfigured, or mentally ill, and could not successfully resume normal family life. Many returned to find their wives so accustomed to financial independence and a feeling of freedom that they were not willing to go back to home-making. Some veterans, although guilty of extensive infidelity themselves, were outraged to find their wives had occasionally been unfaithful; and there were wives who, finding that their husbands had taken advantage of the more liberal sex mores abroad, began suit for divorce. Probably not as many wives sued for divorce on grounds of unfaithfulness as did husbands after discovering the infidelity of their wives in their absence.

In some instances, even with prewar marriages of several years' duration, long separation brought about a feeling of strangeness. Both husbands and wives were older. The war had given them varied experiences. The husband had very often seen a life far different from the one he had previously known; he had matured and had developed a new philosophy. Such men often returned to find their wives had not changed their points of view and had been little matured by the war. Many men were bitterly disillusioned to find that the war years had so little effect on their wives. In some instances it was the wife who had matured, had established new values, had found new independence and was disillusioned with her returning husband. Many couples had idealized each other during the long absence, had built up an attractive but illusory mental picture of the absent one, and were disappointed when they saw each other again. Sometimes, it was the emotional let-down following protracted worry that produced great difficulty in readjustment. Children often caused rifts between parents. There were children who had never seen their fathers and resented the intrusion of a stranger. In like manner, many fathers also resented the fact that their children and their wives had been able to get along without them.

Housing shortages intensify family crises. There is no doubt that the housing crisis was a factor in the rising divorce rate and the unstable family situation after the war. Thousands of couples had never had a settled home; war brides had followed their husbands and lived in hotels, trailers, or tourist camps near the fort, air base, or naval station. After the war, they hoped to find a permanent home. But the housing shortage and the exorbitant cost of available homes forced large numbers of veterans and their families to double up with relatives or other couples. Crowding made readjustment even more difficult.

The problem of crowded housing was especially acute for veterans who went to college to finish, or to begin, their education under the educational opportunities offered by the Federal government. Over five million veterans, many of them married, jammed into colleges and universities. They lived in trailer camps and quonset huts, or moved in with other married couples and tried to manage on the limited stipend allowed.

Postwar economic problems. Economic problems after the war encouraged GI divorces and broke up marriages of long standing. Although most of the returning veterans could get a job, their wages were, in part, eaten up by higher taxes and increased living costs. There was no money left to enjoy the night-club life that had intrigued many of them in wartime and the demobilization period. The housing shortage made home living conditions very unattractive, even to couples whose income was sufficient to have enabled them to rent pleasant homes under prewar conditions. Many women who found employment while their husbands were in service announced their intention of continuing to work. A survey in 1945 showed that 40 per cent of the working wives intended to continue if they could secure a job after the war. The economic problems faced by returning veterans intensified this desire. Many husbands, objecting to the desire for independence, bitterly resented this decision of their wives to continue work. The friction over money matters and the intention of the wife to continue work frequently led to the divorce court.

Cultural tensions. The large number of marriages of American soldiers with foreign women also put a strain on the American family. About 100,000 soldiers married foreign girls during the war. The cultural, and sometimes the racial, differences posed many problems for the new family. Friends and relatives of the man often did not like the foreign wife and, even while trying to welcome her in her new country, they resented her presence. The wives, in a new and strange environment far from home, often found American ways unpleasant. This was especially true if the foreign bride discovered on her arrival in this country that her husband had exaggerated his wealth and position or had, as was sometimes true, outrageously lied about them. Bitter disillusionment was inevitable and divorce practically certain.

Increase of divorces in postwar period. Although the divorce rate increased tremendously after the war for the reasons we have noted, it had risen even during the war. This was not true of the First World War, but the Second World War was so much more disruptive of normal life, took so many more men into the services, put so many more women into war work, and encouraged so many hasty marriages, that it was almost inevitable that the divorce rate would continue to rise over 1940 levels. Although the divorce rate rose during the war, many marriages that were then almost at the breaking point were temporarily saved until a later time. Some husbands solved their problems by enlisting "for the duration," and many women, who otherwise would have sued for divorce, waited until the end of the war so that they might receive the wartime allowances to dependents. There was thus a back-log of already broken marriages which came into the divorce courts at the end of the war. Another important factor restrained divorce during the war. Wives who seek a divorce when their husbands are serving their country are not regarded so kindly by their communities. Many wives, to retain respect of public opinion, waited until after the war to dissolve a marriage which, as a matter of fact, had long before been broken. In 1945, the divorce rate had risen from the 1940 ratio of one divorce to six marriages to an all-time high of one divorce to 3.5 marriages. By 1950, over half of the marriages contracted during the war had ended in divorce, and many marriages of longer duration had broken under the strain of war.

High divorce rate may have reached its peak. There is much evidence that the high divorce rate of the mid-1940's has reached its peak and is declining. By 1949, this downward trend was noticeable for the nation as a whole. The divorce rate dropped from 4.3 in 1946 to 2.6 in 1949. Undoubtedly, those couples waiting for the end of the war to file for divorce have already been through the courts, and the majority of the hasty war marriages have been legally dissolved. As yet, however, there is little reason to believe that the divorce rate will decline to the prewar level.

The high rate of marriage between 1940 and 1946 also began to decline after 1946. It dropped from 16.4 in 1946 to 10.7 in 1949. However, in July, 1948, an act was passed to draft young men between the ages of 17 and 25 for a year's training in military service. By August, 1948, the marriage rate had again begun to rise in many communities. The increase was due, in part, to the belief that married men would be deferred by the draft boards for a longer period of time.

An even greater increase in the marriage rate was produced by the Korean War, the extensive peacetime draft to create an army of some 3,500,000 men, and the threat of the outbreak of a third world war. During the second half of 1950, the marriage rate rose to about 15 per cent above the rate for the last six months of 1949. Experts forecast some 1,825,000 marriages in 1951, a number exceeded only by the 2,291,045 marriages in 1946 and 1,991,878 in 1947. If the state of emergency and a vast peacetime army are continued for 20 years or more, as some civilian and military officials now predict, it is obvious that there will be no return during that period to anything like normality in the marriage, divorce and desertion situation. A third world war would probably upset the marriage and family picture even more completely than did the Second World War.

SOME REMEDIES FOR DIVORCE AND FAMILY INSTABILITY

Prevent thoughtless and precipitate marriage. The rational solutions of the deplorable prevalence of divorce are naturally suggested by the foregoing realistic approach to the causes of divorce. In the first place, marriage should be made more difficult. Only companionate marriage of youth, if this is ever widely adopted, should be permitted without prolonged reflection. Even a companionate marriage should not be contracted lightheartedly. So slight a restriction as the New York State law, which requires a delay of 72 hours between the acquisition of the marriage license and the wedding ceremony, reduced the number of marriages in the state by 6,610 during the first year of its operation. At least, there was this decrease in the number of marriages in 1937. It would seem reasonable to suggest that at least a six-month period be required between the declaration of intent to marry and the consummation of this intention. If Sweden can demand that married couples wait a year to decide whether or not they wish a divorce, certainly it is not excessive to demand that half this time be required for reflection on the part of those who are going to undertake an experiment with far more serious social consequences than divorce.

Nothing much can be done about marriages that are unwisely contracted as a result of pity or kindheartedness, without either passion or enthusiasm on the part of one of the persons. This is purely a personal matter, which can hardly be reached either by public education or legislation. It may well be emphasized, however, that a temporary "broken heart" over a broken engagement is less pathetic than a prolonged broken heart during a long and unsuccessful marriage or after divorce.

Employment and adequate income for all. We can never expect any satisfactory solution of the problem of divorce and desertion unless we make it possible for all able-bodied and energetic persons to earn a decent and respectable livelihood. Few families, however satisfactorily adjusted in other respects, can successfully weather prolonged misery and impoverishment. Even if there is no actual desertion or divorce, there is found to be much suffering and discontent. Moreover, children cannot be adequately cared for in the midst of economic inadequacy and insecurity. Just how we shall be able to bring about this adequate income for all is quite another question, but it is plain that we have the natural resources and technological equipment in the United States to provide plenty for everybody with the greatest of ease. However, the frequency of divorce among the rich shows that economic well-being alone is no complete solution of the divorce problem.

Sex education. Perhaps the most important remedy for divorce is realistic sex education about the facts and responsibilities of the marriage relationship. And it is highly desirable that this education be acquired before marriage. A few weeks of bungling at the outset may undermine what might otherwise be a thoroughly satisfactory marriage. If we wish to keep the monogamous family intact, marriage manuals like those of W. F. Robie and his successors will probably accomplish far more than savage legislation against divorce. The sex purists, who are most violent against freedom of divorce and are most scandalized by its prevalence, are themselves mainly responsible for the existence of the mental attitudes and ignorance that bring about most family discord. Most social scientists believe that, as a phase of sex education, there should be thorough instruction in birth control methods. Many a family is undermined by being burdened with children who come before the family is ready to take care of them, or arrive in too great numbers. Compulsory medical examination of both persons before a marriage license is granted would aid in removing the factor of venereal disease as a cause of marital difficulties.

Making monogamy more attractive. Much more should be accomplished in improving the attractiveness and novelty of monogamous situations. Marion Cox once suggested that periodic vacations from marriage relations should be provided for. Students of sex relations and pairing arrangements among apes have found that this works well in stabilizing primate affections and keeping the pairing arrangement intact. It might achieve as much for human beings. But it will prove difficult to improve the attractiveness of monogamy unless decent living standards can be secured and maintained. There is little possibility of novelty and surprise when a large family is packed into a slum apartment or a run-down farm dwelling. The desperate housing shortage during and since the Second World War has aggravated the overcrowding and has probably had some bearing on the increased divorce rate, especially with GI marriages.

Family counselling. Many have sensibly suggested that we emphasize the work of domestic relations courts rather than rely upon divorce courts in the handling of marital problems. There is much to be said in support of this proposal. A reconciliation may often be substituted for what would otherwise be separation, desertion, or divorce. Domestic relations courts have hitherto been as much concerned with discovering the family basis of juvenile delinquency as with lessening family discord.

Much interest has developed of late in marriage counsellors, family advice bureaus, and family clinics. In these, an effort is made to discover the causes of marital discord and to reduce or remove them by the application of psychology, psychiatry, and social work principles. One of the more successful of these clinics is the Bureau of Marriage Counsel and Education, which has been maintained for some years in New York City by Valeria H. Parker. It has been stated that Parker has prevented thousands of divorces. The American Institute of Family Relations, directed by Paul Popenoe in Los Angeles, has done much good by bringing about better family understanding and greater family cohesion. Other important developments along this line have been the Marriage Counsel of Philadelphia, founded in 1932, and the Family Consultation Service of Cincinnati, a joint enterprise sponsored by the Council of Churches and the Family Welfare Society. Certainly, much can be done in family clinics when the chief cause of discord is not rooted in such factors as economic stress or sterility, which lie beyond the reach or control of the counsellor.

On the other hand, there is always the danger that, despite good intentions, the basic principles of social science may be violated in these clinics. This danger has been well stated by Kingsley Davis, who concludes that to regard family clinics "as applying scientific efficacy to the tragic problems of personal relations strikes me as a violation of fact."

It is obvious that no good will be achieved in any campaign against divorce by attempting to reduce the economic independence of women or to arouse public opinion against divorce, even if such things were possible in our day.

Rational divorce legislation. When it comes to the matter of suggesting rational divorce legislation, it would probably be difficult to propose anything more satisfactory than the Scandinavian laws, described earlier in the chapter. These provide for divorce in all cases of marital discord after a year of reflection. Temporary anger, sulking, or despondency are not likely to endure for a year. When the application is renewed after the passage of twelve months it is assumed that the family should be dissolved, with due provision for proper support of dependent children. The Scandinavian legislation also makes possible immediate divorce for causes sufficiently serious to warrant expeditious action. Some more radically-inclined persons recommend following the lead of Soviet Russia, which made divorce immediately available upon the desire of either party. It seems to the writer that the Swedish procedure is preferable, though the early Russian practices are certainly far saner than such absurdities at the other extreme as the legislation of South Carolina, which until 1949 permitted no divorce.

It is often asserted that easy divorce laws inevitably lead to a veritable wave of divorces. The evidence does not bear out any such assertion. The divorces in Sweden increased only from 847 in 1915 to 1,040 in 1917, and 1,310 in 1920, the latter being an insignificant figure in proportion to the total population of Sweden. The rise of the divorce ratio in Sweden to 3.2 in 1950, about equal to the rate in the United States, can be attributed to the same wartime and postwar influences that seem to have increased the number of divorces in most of the countries of the Western world. In Soviet Russia as a whole, under the freest possible divorce procedure, the divorces per capita were fewer than those in the United States. Sex education, sexual freedom, and elementary economic security for the whole body of the people evidently proved more effective in Russia in preventing a high divorce rate than has severe restrictive legislation in many other countries. The experience of the State of Nevada is also illuminating. It is literally true that, so far as the legal aspects are concerned, a permanent resident of Nevada may decide at the breakfast table that he wishes a divorce and may get one before luncheon. Yet the percentage of divorces per capita among the permanent residents of Nevada is lower than the per capita divorce rate in New York State, with adultery as the only ground for those who seek divorce.

Curb the alimony racket. Any intelligent solution of the divorce problem must carry with it the termination of the abuses of the alimony racket. This is one of the two leading rackets connected with divorce, the other being collusion and fixing of evidence, particularly evidence of adultery. At the present time, the alimony racket is a fertile field for thrifty and ruthless gold-diggers. They snare wealthy husbands, live with them long enough to provide a semblance of honest intent, sue for divorce, and get awarded a large alimony—sometimes as much as one third of the husband's income. Often these large alimonies are awarded when the wife who secures the divorce is perfectly able to take care of herself.

Aside from the purely racketeering aspects of alimony procedure, there are other abuses in the contemporary practice. Alimony for the divorced wife has more logic behind it when the husband divorces the wife. But alimony is very frequently given today when the wife asks for the divorce of her own volition. Although no sane person can doubt the moral right of temporarily granting reasonable alimony to a dependent divorced woman, providing the marriage relationship has been long enduring, there is little justification for alimony payments to a young and recently married woman who is perfectly capable of caring for herself. The courts, all too often, fail to consider the question of need and merit when awarding alimony. One of the most illogical abuses is the frequent practice of imprisoning husbands for nonpayment of alimony. This is akin to imprisonment for debt, which has long since been abandoned as ethically reprehensible and financially illogical.

Alimony goes back to the earliest historical times. The principle was clearly embodied in the Code of Hammurabi, some 1700 years before Christ. Such practices were developed more thoroughly by the Greeks and Romans, though in divorce by mutual consent the parties involved had to make their own private arrangements in such matters. The medieval church strongly influenced the development of alimony practices. Since it regarded the family as indissoluble, alimony payments were made perpetual after separation. The Protestant cults introduced definitely punitive concepts, alimony being a punishment for the guilt of a husband. This concept has survived; the courts tend to base the amount of alimony more upon the degree of the husband's guilt than upon the needs of the divorced wife.

The more enlightened divorce codes of our day have eliminated the earlier concepts and abuses of alimony payment. Sweden allows alimony only in cases of actual want. In Soviet Russia, where divorce by mutual consent prevailed for some time, any question of payment to one of the parties was a matter for private arrangement without any legal compulsion. Certain American states, such as Massachusetts, North Dakota, and Ohio, have granted the husband the right to alimony under certain specific conditions when the husband is the injured party in the divorce case. Few expert students of alimony, however, approve the granting of alimony to both sexes as a solution of the problem. This device is simply a manifestation of the old error that two wrongs can make a right.

Any sane solution of the problem of alimony would require that the punitive aspects of alimony be completely wiped away and that imprisonment for nonpayment of alimony be terminated. The matter of alimony awards should be determined wholly by the needs of the dependent wife and children. Legitimate rights of both of these should be fully protected in divorce cases, though there should never be alimony payments that would encourage the divorced woman to avoid seeking remunerative work or satisfactory remarriage. Least of all should a divorced woman be allowed to collect alimony from a former husband after she has remarried. At present, alimony does not automatically cease upon the remarriage of the divorced woman. There have been instances in which married women have collected alimony from two or more former husbands at the same time.

DESERTION AS A SOCIAL PROBLEM

Extent and causes of desertion. We have already noted that desertion has been called the poor man's divorce. Estimates enable us to know that there is a considerable volume of desertion. About one third of the divorce cases brought to court list desertion as a cause of action. Whether desertion is the fundamental cause of family discord, it is likely to be a contributing cause if so stated in the divorce proceeding. Over 20 per cent of all ex-

penditures for family relief go for aid to deserted women and their dependents. The most competent estimate that we have places the annual
number of desertions in the United States at 150,000 to 200,000.

The causes of family desertion are numerous and complicated, but they
boil down to two basic situations, namely, that family life is unattractive,
or that, for one reason or another, it cannot be successfully continued.
The reasons for the latter are primarily economic insufficiency, personal
inadequacy to meet the responsibilities of family life, and lack of proper
techniques for making marriage relations successful. Poverty and low
income probably play a larger rôle in desertion than in divorce. The great
majority of desertions are by men. Men depend less upon their wives for
support and are more easily drawn away from family situations in search
of sexual novelty and new contacts.

Aspects of desertion problem. A number of conditions most frequently
associated with family desertion result from the fact that it is mainly a
lower-class phenomenon. Deserters have an inadequate education in many
cases. They rate high in lawlessness; some 20 per cent of them have court
records. Many of the desertions are the result of hasty youthful marriages.
Personal instability seems to play its part, since over 50 per cent of male
deserters are repeaters at the process. Excessive alcoholic indulgence is
frequently associated with desertion. There is a relatively high proportion
of feeble-minded and psychopathic persons among family deserters. Desertion is much more common in city families than in rural families, probably because the family renders less indispensable services in the city than
in the country and there are many more temptations in the city. Desertions
are more likely to take place in mixed marriages, in which conflicts of
race, religion, or language increase the problems of family adjustment. In
an important study of 1,500 representative cases of desertion, Joanna C.
Colcord found that about 76 per cent arose from various sex difficulties
and from the use of alcohol and narcotic drugs, 39 per cent from the
former and 37 per cent from the latter cause. Temperamental causes and
economic insufficiency accounted for the majority of the remaining cases.

The social problems arising out of desertion are not markedly different
from those which grow out of divorce, bereavement and widowhood, except that the element of personal sorrow in desertion may be less. Desertion imposes a heavy burden upon public and private relief agencies that
take care of the destitution produced by desertion. The problems of both
mother and children are much the same as in divorce and widowhood. In
some instances, when there are no children, desertion may be a blessing
rather than a calamity, since it may terminate a family relationship that
involved more discord than satisfaction.

Solution of desertion problem. In attempting to solve the problem of
desertion we must recognize that it is chiefly a problem which calls for
economic reform, mental hygiene work, and sex education. As much as
possible should be done to provide more adequate sex instruction, to bring
neurotic persons into guidance clinics, and to increase the scope of the
work of domestic relations courts and family clinics. Legislation to prevent
hasty marriages and to discourage altogether the marriages of the psycho-

pathic and the feeble-minded is desirable. Special social agencies to deal with desertion cases would be extremely helpful. It is particularly essential that any assistance for those already married should be given in the early years of marriage. There is little prospect of effective aid after discord and quarreling have become chronic. More adequate income would prevent a number of desertions, but this is a matter beyond control by the social worker or the mental hygiene adviser.

THE FUTURE OF THE FAMILY

Increasing marriage rate. Few social problems are more frequently or solemnly discussed than that of the future of the human family. There are many who predict that it will ultimately disappear, but even if this should prove true it will not take place for many generations.

One should be clear as to what is meant by any rational discussion of the future of the family and the possibility of its disappearance. What is

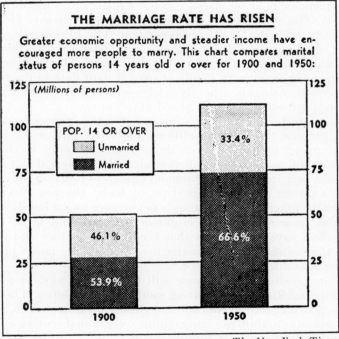

THE MARRIAGE RATE HAS RISEN

Greater economic opportunity and steadier income have encouraged more people to marry. This chart compares marital status of persons 14 years old or over for 1900 and 1950:

(Millions of persons)

POP. 14 OR OVER
Unmarried
Married

33.4%

46.1%   66.6%

53.9%

1900   1950

COURTESY *The New York Times.*

seriously threatened by contemporary developments is the old rural patriarchal family and the notion of indissoluble monogamy. Definite pairing arrangements between males and females do not appear to be in the slightest jeopardy. In fact, there are more marriages, and at least temporary families, than ever before in history. This is notably true of the United States, where the marriage rate has been increasing—from 8.3

in 1870, to 16.4 in 1946. If companionate marriage is introduced, the marriage rate will be even more markedly increased. Even the radical developments in Soviet Russia before 1940, which represented as drastic a social change as we may expect in the civilized world for many years to come, did not seem to lessen the popularity of marriage. Therefore, although the older type of family, which developed in a pastoral and agricultural economy, does seem to be disintegrating and may disappear entirely, there appears no reason whatever to predict •the end of marriage or even any decline in its popularity. Indeed, if divorce becomes easier, it is likely that many persons who now recoil from the idea of assuming a life-long responsibility will be encouraged to contract matrimony and may be induced to continue the arrangement indefinitely. Indeed, the higher divorce rate has brought with it an increased marriage rate. The more frequently persons are divorced the more frequently they can remarry. Some 75 per cent of those divorced between 1943 and 1948 were remarried by 1948. Of those divorced between 1934 and 1943, 86 per cent had remarried by 1948.

The percentage of those married in the United States has increased in the last fifty years. In 1900, 53.9 per cent of the population over 14 was married. In 1950, the figure stood at 66.6 per cent. The 1946 marriage rate of 16.4 per 1,000 of the population in the United States was an all-time high.

New social conditions and effects on the family. The question of the disappearance of the human family at some distant date in the future is, therefore, quite obviously a purely academic one. But future tendencies in the family are a matter of real practical concern.

Anderson and Lindeman have suggested that the increased prevalence of urban life and the living conditions associated with it are likely to bestow far greater importance upon the mother. Obviously, no changes in our cultural and social set-up will ever alter the biological fact that the women must bear the children. Woman's biological function thus remains constant, whatever the degree or type of social changes affecting the family. On the other hand, the father's importance in the family has been considerably lessened by recent economic, cultural, and social changes. Social workers have pointed out that keeping the mother and child together is a far more important matter than keeping the father present in the family, desirable as this may be.

It is quite possible that the state will take over a good many of the father's responsibilities of supporting mothers and children. The government now provides for the education of children. Public health agencies, nursing associations, child guidance clinics, recreational centers, and many other child welfare agencies supply aid to families that were formerly purely domestic responsibilities. The increasing prevalence of mothers' pensions, especially the provision under the Social Security legislation for grants to dependent mothers and children, is another indication that the government may assume an ever greater responsibility for supporting mothers and dependent children. The rural family under male parental dominion owed its cohesiveness and enduring qualities primarily to the fact that there were indispensable responsibilities which only the family could assume. Now that this set of conditions has been greatly modified we cannot doubt that there will be a marked effect upon the future family.

If civilization survives the present world crisis, we may safely predict that the family will be greatly modified, but that marriage will continue to be as popular as ever, though undoubtedly readjusted in terms of social rationality. Affection must play a larger role in keeping the family together than sheer economic pressure. Those influences that increase affection, such as children, mutual interest, avoidance of excessive intimacy, and the like, will need to be encouraged. Supernaturalism, intolerance, ignorance, and dogma must have an ever lessening influence over family life. The latter will be reconstructed in harmony with scientific facts and a reconsideration of social welfare. Such a readjustment must certainly involve thoroughgoing sex education; possibly, the sanction and encouragement of companionate marriages; the imposition of greater restrictions and responsibilities upon permanent unions; rational divorce legislation and easier divorce; and the provision of economic conditions that will bestow upon the family the material foundations for an enduring and successful matrimonial arrangement. The family of the future will have to be kept together because the partners wish to have their marriage endure and because the family situation is worth preserving. If we desire to increase the number of marriages that can be both personally congenial and socially worth while, this will impose upon society the responsibility for bringing about economic security and other general living conditions reasonably compatible with successful monogamy.

Family of the future held together by internal cohesive forces. Perhaps the best conclusion to the consideration of the future of the family would be to call attention once more to W. F. Ogburn's thesis that the family of the future must be held together by increasing the internal cohesive factors stabilizing family life, such as sentiment, romance, affection, better sexual relations and adjustment, and the improvement of congenial companionship. The older external factors of economic pressure, fear of the supernatural world and hellfire, timidity in the face of local gossip, and the economic helplessness of women have broken down or been greatly reduced in potency. Our main attention to the problem of preserving the human family must be concentrated on strengthening the internal cohesive influences which Ogburn has enumerated. In the past husbands and wives had to stick together whether they wished to or not. In the future, the family can be preserved only by providing conditions that will make them wish to go on living together.

UNMARRIED ADULTS

Number of unmarried adults. Discussions of sex and marriage problems frequently revolve solely about the consideration of the family and divorce. But a very considerable social problem is the situation of unmarried adults. There are, today, many more single persons than divorced or separated. In 1947, out of a total male civilian population of 52,350,000 over 14 years of age, some 34,638,000 were married, 14,760,000 were single, 2,134,000 were widowed, and 818,000 divorced. In the female population of 54,806,000, on that date, 35,212,000 were married, 12,078,000 were single, 6,376,000 were widowed, and 1,140,000 were divorced. The exact number of deserted is unknown. There were, thus, in 1947, nearly 27,000,000 single persons above the age of puberty in the population, along with over 10 million widowed, divorced, and separated persons.

Reasons for number of single persons. A number of reasons have been offered to account for the fact that so large a proportion of the population refrain from what Malthus called "the delights of domestic society." Economic inadequacy and insufficiency undoubtedly account for a considerable amount of non-marriage. There may not be sufficient income available to support children. This is particularly important today, when children, under conditions of city life, are an almost unmitigated financial liability.

The growth of economic and sexual freedom encourages and enables many to obtain sexual satisfaction outside of matrimony. The extensive entry of women into industry and the professions makes it unnecessary for an ever larger group of women to marry solely for pecuniary reasons. The proportion of gainfully occupied women, 15 years and older, who have entered industry and professions has increased very markedly in the last 50 years in the United States. About two-thirds of these are single, widowed, or divorced. In 1940, there were 12,850,000 women in all occupations, of whom one-half were single, one-sixth widows and divorcees, and one-sixteenth separated from their husbands. During the war the number of gainfully employed women rose to 19,700,000 in 1944. Even in 1949, there were 17,325,000 so occupied.

Many psychological factors help to explain the existence of the unmarried contingent of the population. Feelings of inferiority and other neurotic states may hold one back from seeking matrimonial opportunities. Fixations on the parents and faulty sex education may effectively obstruct normal sexual aspirations and the consummation of conjugality. Serious disappointments in love may exert their influence, as well as having too high ideals in the quest of a partner. Homosexuality and other sexual abnormalities very obviously stand in the way of normal marriage relationships.

Social and personal effects of non-marriage. We may now consider some of the chief results of non-marriage. The most conspicuous one is the fact that a large group of persons of child-bearing age are not contributing to population growth. Although there is a considerable amount of illegitimacy, procreation outside of wedlock is not institutionally accepted and non-marriage certainly contributes markedly to a lower birth rate. Whether this is a disaster or a benefit to society depends upon the philosophy with which one approaches the population problem. But the existence of any large number of unmarried persons of high ability does have its effect in lessening the potential level of population quality. If marriage confers upon the married an enviable state of mind and superior social surroundings, these advantages are obviously lost by the non-married. Yet, since many of those who remain unmarried are psychologically unfitted for normal marriage relations, their entry into wedlock might well produce more discord and unhappiness than satisfaction and well-being.

Certain authorities contend that various evils, particularly neurotic symptoms, arise from the absence of normal sexual relations by the unmarried, but, as Ira S. Wile and others have pointed out, we must not assume that all the unmarried are celibate and innocent of sexual experience. Ellen Klatt studied a group of unmarried women and found that 18 per cent of those under 18 years of age, and over 60 per cent of those between 18 and 22 years of age had engaged in some active form of sex experience. G. V. Hamilton investigated a group of professional men and women and found that 59 per cent of the men and 47 per cent of the women had engaged in sexual relations before marriage. This seems to have been a result sometimes of the fact that marriage was anticipated. Other studies have confirmed the impression that a large portion of the unmarried have normal but noninstitutionalized sexual relations, and many more practice autoerotic and homosexual relations. It is mainly among those who are both unmarried and celibate that we need fear any marked development of neurotic tendencies because of repression of the sex instinct. It must also be remembered that there are many who enter into marriage relations and develop neuroses because of their inability to initiate or sustain normal sex relations.

When we turn to the social pathology of the unmarried we find that the unmarried show a per capita preponderance among cases of dependency, mental instability, vagrancy, crime, and among the patrons of prostitution. Except for the latter, we cannot assign the responsibility directly to the unmarried state. We would expect to find a larger number of dependents among the unmarried because the economic inadequacy is a major cause of the failure to marry. Likewise, many fail to marry because they have been neurotic types from childhood. We cannot assume that all unmarried neurotics are neurotic because of their failure to marry. Marriage responsibilities would be likely to make many of them even more neurotic. In the same way, vagrancy is likely to be an outgrowth of mental instability and economic insufficiency, which are more a reason for failure to marry than a direct result of such failure. It is only natural to suppose that the absence of family restraints and responsibilities would remove some of the factors that deter people from committing crime. It is frequently true, however, that criminality arises from the very conditions of mental instability and poverty that prevent marriage. Of vice and prostitution it may be safely assumed that the patronage of prostitutes is notably increased by the presence of a large number of unmarried males in the population. But studies have revealed the fact that prostitutes have many married customers. Moreover, with the growing freedom of sex relations, unmarried males are satisfying their sex desires to an even greater extent through relations with females who are not prostitutes.

Remedies for the problems of the unmarried adult. A number of remedies suggest themselves for failure to marry and its frequent unsound social and personal results. Higher wages and salaries and steadier employment are necessary if we are to make it possible for many of those now unmarried to support a family. So long as they are unable to do so, it is better that they should not marry and beget a number of dependent or inadequately reared children. Sex education and mental hygiene services would help to eliminate many of the neurotic conditions which sometimes prevent marriage. Companionate marriage would offer a solution for those who are biologically and psychologically fitted to marry but cannot or do not wish for the moment to assume the responsibilities of a permanent union. But there will be no permanent solution of the problem until we have sufficient economic readjustment to provide the material basis for successful conjugality on the part of all able-bodied and mentally healthy citizens.

WIDOWS AND WIDOWHOOD

Extent of widowhood. The number of widows in American society has increased with the general growth of population, but there is probably little more widowhood per capita than at earlier periods in our history. In 1947, there were in the civilian population over 6,375,000 widowed females and over 2,130,000 widowed males. It is estimated that some 500,000 newly widowed females are added each year. The preponderance of widowed females is easily explained. Males are more numerous in industry and are otherwise more exposed to the dangers of contemporary life. More males are killed in accidents, travel, and in ordinary occupational activities. Moreover, males who have lost their wives usually find it easier to contract a second marriage.

The deaths which produce widowhood result from a few outstanding causes. About seven deaths out of every ten that cost the life of the male wage-earner before old age are produced by heart disease and high blood pressure, cancer, tuberculosis, pneumonia, kidney disorders, syphilis, and accidents. Most of the recent progress in reducing the mortality that leads to widowhood has taken place in the successful medical attack upon pneumonia, tuberculosis, and syphilis. The other leading causes of mortality remain relatively constant or are on the increase.

Effects of widowhood. The problem of dependency is aggravated by the loss of the earnings of the bread-winner. But the problems of a bereaved home are more than economic. If the mother has to leave the home to secure employment or children have to go to work, it is difficult to provide a normal and desirable home life and education. The emotional difficulties of widowhood are serious and numerous. The sorrow frequently brings a serious psychological shock, and the transferring of all affection from the husband to the children may create important psychological difficulties for both the mother and the children. This is particularly true if there is only one child. Mental breakdowns and sheer dependency are the extreme ravages created by widowhood.

Remedies for problems of widowhood. The remedies for widowhood naturally fall under the heading of immediate relief and preventive measures. Until recently, younger widows and their children have ordinarily been taken care of either by public or private agencies. Most elderly widows have been provided for in private homes for the aged and in our almshouses. Children who are dependent as a result of widowhood have been cared for both by outdoor relief and by being placed in public or private institutions for orphaned children.

A more adequate and civilized method of supporting widows and dependent children has been provided by the system of widows' pensions. The first comprehensive mothers' pension law was passed in Illinois in 1911. By 1930, all states except Alabama, Georgia, South Carolina, and New Mexico had passed some sort of mothers' pension legislation carrying with it an annual expenditure of about 30 million dollars in relief aid. The Social Security Act of 1935 and its more recent amendments have provided extensive Federal and state aid to widows and dependent children. More liberal and uniform workmen's compensation laws are essential to provide immediate income for widows of men killed in accidents. Both personal and social insurance need to be extended to lessen the economic impact of the death of wage-earners. Savings and thrift should be encouraged, but this should be accompanied by more fully assuring the solvency and reliability of banks. Many an American widow has lost the family savings because of our scandalous and numerous bank failures or the carelessness and delinquencies of trust companies. Mental hygiene clinics have provided some psychological relief for both widows and children, but such facilities need to be greatly extended before they will be sufficient.

If we are to reduce widowhood, we must provide better medical care for ·the masses. Improvements in preventive medicine and in methods of dealing with certain fatal and hitherto unconquered diseases, less carelessness in home life, and more stringent control of occupational and transportation hazards are mandatory.

ILLEGITIMACY

Extent and cause of illegitimacy. Illegitimacy, or children born out of wedlock, is a surprisingly common phenomenon in modern countries. For example, in 1914, the illegitimate births in Austria amounted to 11.9 per cent of the total live births; in Denmark, 11.5 per cent; in Bavaria, 12.6 per cent; in Saxony, 16 per cent; in Portugal, 11 per cent; and in Sweden, 15.8 per cent. In certain European cities the rate was much higher. Over a five-year period from 1905 to 1909, the illegitimacy rate in Budapest was 26.3; in Copenhagen, 25.5; in Lyons, 22.2; in Moscow, 24; in Munich, 27.8; in Paris, 25.5; in Stockholm, 33.5; in Vienna, 30.1. These urban figures are somewhat inflated, however, because a number of illegitimate births in urban hospitals represented deliveries of rural mothers who had come to the city for delivery. Recent statistics on the illegitimacy rate in northern European countries put the 1949 rate in Sweden at 9.16; in Denmark, 7.4 per cent; in Finland, 5.6 per cent; and in Norway, 4.9 per cent.

In the United States, although the illegitimacy rate is growing steadily it is still far below representative European rates, especially for the white population. Among Negroes the illegitimacy rate tends to equal that of the European countries. In 1934, the illegitimacy rate for American Negroes was 15.5 per cent.

Samuel J. Holmes made an authoritative survey of illegitimacy in the United States based upon 1934 figures. Taking into account both the white and Negro population, the illegitimacy rate was 3.9 per cent. Out of every thousand live births, 39 babies were born out of wedlock. There were 35,000 white illegitimates and 43,000 Negro ones. But the ratio of illegitimacy was more than seven times higher among Negroes than it was among whites. The rate for whites was 2.04 per cent and for Negroes the 15.5 per cent mentioned above. Holmes showed that illegitimacy was increasing in this country and accounted for the increase in the following ways: (1) overconfidence in the effectiveness of simple and inadequate birth control methods; (2) the economic effects of the depression, which checked the marriage rate and produced a certain amount of sexual and family demoralization; and (3) a lessening of the stigma attached to illegitimacy. There are no adequate postwar figures on illegitimacy in the United States.

Causes and problems of illegitimacy. Among the direct causes of illegitimacy are sexual ignorance and inexperience, inadequate birth control devices or incomplete knowledge of how to use effective devices, pathological carelessness and indifference, intercourse during intoxication, and mental defect. There are other more general, indirect causes of illegitimacy. Such are increased sexual freedom, low economic status, which is often associated with ignorance, bad living conditions which make for sexual promiscuity, mental instability or defect, and so on.

The burdens of illegitimacy fall most heavily upon the poor. Many of the evils of illegitimacy are due as much to social intolerance and wrongheadedness as to the responsibility of the persons involved. The antipathy toward the illegitimate mother and child and the tendency to make them both outcasts is an outrageous social anachronism. The fact that illegitimate children rank relatively high among juvenile delinquents is also due mainly to the stigma and handicaps that society places upon illegitimate children.

If one eliminates the traditional aspect of sin, it is apparent that most of the evils associated with illegitimacy are socially created and that all of them are aggravated by our archaic social attitudes. If these were changed, the most important problem of illegitimacy would be providing economic support for the mother and child.

Rational approach to the problem of illegitimacy. Remedial steps against illegitimacy are clearly indicated by the situation. There should be better sex education, particularly better instruction in the use of birth control methods. Improved economic conditions might enable many to marry who now risk illegitimacy through sex relations outside of wedlock. Wholesale sterilization of the feeble-minded would prevent the large volume of illegitimacy among feeble-minded persons. Until the time when illegitimacy can be reduced, the whole idea of bastardy, and the mental complexes and social attitudes associated with it, should be completely swept away. After an illegitimate child is born it is too late to accomplish anything by terrorizing the mother or humiliating the child. The child's future transcends any other social consideration. Its opportunity for development into a useful citizen must not be lessened as a result of antiquated ethical prejudices and mob psychology.

SUMMARY

The biological and social bases of the human family are results of traits we share with the anthropoid apes: our main sex drives and a trend towards permanent mating.

Evolutionary theory once seemed to support the idea of original promiscuity among primitive peoples and the gradual evolution of monogamy, the rather permanent pairing of one man with one woman. More careful later studies, by Edward Westermarck and others, have, however, established the fact that monogamy has been the usual form of family life throughout human experience from the earliest times. Other types of the family have been special deviations produced by unusual economic and other factors.

The Jewish and Christian religions provided strong support for the monogamous family, and the conditions of rural life added many strong external pressures to encourage an enduring monogamy. Economic and religious considerations were especially influential.

Modern intellectual forces and social customs have weakened the traditional historic patriarchal family, founded on rural life and supernatural religion. The increasing economic independence of women has given them greater opportunities for existence outside the traditional family. City life has reduced the economic functions of the family, lowered the birth rate and reduced the size of the family, lessened the economic value of children, and increased the burdens of rearing children. Educational facilities and social work have taken from the family many former functions. Secular trends have undermined the religious pressures that supported rigorous monogamy. The traditional functions of the family have been reduced by contemporary social life and technology. There is little serious preparation for marriage and family responsibilities.

The breakdown of the traditional monogamous family is most clearly revealed by the recent marked increase in divorce. Divorce has existed from the earliest recorded period. It became especially common in later classical society. This trend was powerfully checked by the rise of the Catholic Church which made marriage a sacrament and has never countenanced divorce. Protestantism also exerted a restraining influence on divorce. Secular, economic, and social conditions of modern life have undermined the opposition to divorce, and it is increasing in all civilized countries.

Divorce has increased rapidly in the United States, and, due to disintegrating influences during the Second World War, the number of divorces increased until, in 1945, there was one divorce to every 3.5 marriages. The formal and legal grounds offered in applications for divorce rarely reveal the real underlying causes for the disintegration of the family. The basic cause is that many of the external pressures which, in earlier days, assured a cohesive monogamy have been reduced or extinguished.

The remedy for divorce lies in making marriage more attractive and in preparing couples more adequately for the responsibilities of family life. In other words, internal cohesive influences must supplant the external pressures that are now fast disappearing.

Economic security is indispensable for successful family life. Sex education is essential to satisfactory marriage. Marriage counselling may be of great utility in helping to solve family difficulties. Rational divorce legislation will be of value. We need Federal divorce legislation, based on the realities of modern living conditions and on the tenets of sound social science. Marriage is increasing, partly as a result of the growing number of divorces. There is no need to fear the elimination of the family, but its stabilization is a major requirement of orderly social life.

Preoccupation with marriage and family problems has often led to the neglect of the problems of unmarried adults. There are half as many unmarried as married in the population of the United States. The problems of their sex life and social adjustments cannot be ignored by social scientists and social workers. Without proper aid and guidance, the sex life and psychological adjustments of the unmarried often take on pathological aspects.

Illegitimacy is an important by-product of the sex life of unmarried persons. Conventional religious prejudices against illegitimacy should be softened, and sane sociological principles applied to the problem.

SELECTED REFERENCES

*Apstein, T. E., *The Parting of the Ways*. New York: Dodge, 1935. A clear introduction to the divorce and separation problem by a writer professionally concerned with marriage and divorce situations.

Baber, R. E., *Marriage and the Family*. New York: McGraw-Hill, 1939. A standard and competent text on family problems.

Becker, Howard, Hill, Reuben, *et al.*, *Family, Marriage, and Parenthood*. Boston: Heath, 1949. Comprehensive and informing symposium.

Bergler, Edmund, *Divorce Won't Help*. New York: Harper, 1948. Excellent psychiatric analysis of the causes of marital discord and possible remedies.

Bowman, H. A., *Marriage for Moderns*. New York: McGraw-Hill, 1942. A clear and lucid introduction to marriage preparation and problems.

Christensen, H. T., *Marriage Analysis*. New York: Ronald Press, 1950. Able analysis of the main problems of family life, with special stress on personality situations.

Cuber, J. F., *Marriage Counseling Practice*. New York: Appleton-Century-Crofts, 1948. A brief but competent account of the development of marriage clinics and marriage counseling service.

*Das, S. R., *The American Woman in Modern Marriage*. New York: Philosophical Library, 1949. A highly enlightened and stimulating account of the reaction on family life of the emancipation of woman, increased economic opportunities for women, greater tolerance of sex freedom, and divorce.

Duvall, S. M., and Hill, G. W., *When You Marry*. Boston: Heath, 1949. Stresses preparation for marriage and family responsibilities.

Elmer, M. C., *The Sociology of the Family*. Boston: Ginn, 1945. A mature and well-informed analysis of family problems discussed in the light of sociological principles.

*Folsom, J. K., *The Family and Democratic Society*. New York: Wiley, 1948. A rather reassuring answer to recent alarmist books on current trends in family life.

Frazier, E. F., *The Negro Family in the United States*. Chicago: University of Chicago Press, 1939. The ablest study of the special problems of the Negro family.

Goodsell, Willystine, *A History of the Family as a Social and Educational Institution*. New York: Macmillan, 1915. Useful history of the family and matrimonial institutions.

Groves, E. R. and G. H., *Sex in Marriage*. New York: Emerson Books, 1940. A conservative and restrained but important book on the relation of satisfactory sex adjustment to success in marriage. One of the best introductions to the subject for the general reader.

*———, *The Contemporary American Family*. Philadelphia: Lippincott, 1947. Perhaps the most up-to-date and authoritative presentation of family problems.

———, *Dynamic Mental Hygiene*. Harrisburg: Stackpole, 1949. Comprehensive study of possible applications of mental hygiene to family problems, especially family counselling.

Harper, R. A., *Marriage*. New York: American Book Company. 1949. Readable summary of the more practical problems of marriage and family life.

Hill, Reuben, *et al.*, *Families under Stress*. New York: Harper, 1950. Important case studies of the impact of the Second World War on family stability.

Jung, Moses (Ed.), *Modern Marriage*. New York: Crofts, 1940. Symposium on all aspects of marriage and family problems. Sane and well-balanced.

Kinsey, A. C., Pomeroy, W. B., and Martin, C. E., *Sexual Behavior in the Human Male*. Philadelphia: Saunders, 1948. A much discussed book which was the first frank effort to discover and print the realities about human sexual behavior and habits. Incidentally revealed much about female sex behavior, but is to be followed by another volume explicitly on this subject.

Knox, S. T., *The Family and the Law*. Chapel Hill: University of North Carolina Press, 1941. A useful book on the laws relating to marriage, family usages, and divorce.

Landis, J. T., and M. G., *Building a Successful Marriage*. New York: Prentice-Hall, 1948. Able and up-to-date treatment of marriage and the family in sociological perspective.

Lichtenberger, J. P., *Divorce*. New York: McGraw-Hill, 1931. A standard sociological manual, discussing the extent, causes, and possible remedies for divorce in the United States.

*Lindsey, B. B., *Companionate Marriage*. New York: Boni and Liveright, 1927. A much discussed book, advocating early trial unions as the best preventive of mental disease, prostitution, and venereal disease, and as the best preparation for successful permanent unions.

*Locke, H. J., *Predicting Adjustment in Marriage*. New York: Holt, 1951. Valuable recent survey of factors affecting success and failure in marriage, based on numerous case studies.

Mangold, G. B., *Children Born out of Wedlock*. Columbia, Missouri: University of Missouri Press, 1921. A standard sociological study of illegitimacy and its problems.

Merrill, F. E., *Courtship and Marriage*. New York: Sloane, 1949. Readable book laying emphasis on preparation for family life and problems.

Mowrer, E. R., *Family Disorganization*. Chicago: University of Chicago Press, 1927. Important study of family instability, divorce and desertion.

———, *The Family: Its Organization and Disorganization*. Chicago: University of Chicago Press, 1932. Brief but penetrating discussion of family problems, with emphasis on family disorganization.

Neumann, Henry, *Modern Youth and Marriage*. New York: Appleton, 1928. A sane discussion of the marriage problem, based on sound ethical principles divorced from superstition.

*Nimkoff, M. F., *Marriage and the Family*. Boston: Houghton Mifflin, 1947. One of the best recent manuals on the family in contemporary society.

Reuter, E. B., and Runner, J. R. (Eds.), *The Family*. New York: McGraw-Hill, 1931. Valuable collection of readings and source-materials on most aspects of family life.

Rougemont, Denis de, *Love in the Western World*. New York: Harcourt, Brace, 1940. Stimulating historical and psychological account of the social and cultural import of romantic love.

*Stern, B. J. (Ed.), *The Family, Past and Present*. New York: Appleton-Century, 1938. A symposium providing a good historical and sociological study of the family.

Terman, L. M., *et al.*, *Psychological Factors in Marital Happiness*. New York: McGraw-Hill, 1938. While not neglecting sexual aspects of marital unhappiness, it presents many other factors involved.

*Truxal, A. G., and Merrill, F. E., *The Family in American Culture*. New York: Prentice-Hall, 1947. Comprehensive exposition and analysis of the role of the family in American civilization.

Vaerting, Mathilde and Mathias, *The Dominant Sex*. New York: Doran, 1923. One of the later efforts to defend the thesis of female ascendency in the sexual and social history of humanity.

*Waller, Willard, *The Family*. New York: Dryden Press, 1951. One of the most complete textbooks on the family, and the best analysis of personal relationships within the family. Strong on the psychological side.

Wile, I. S. (Ed.), *The Sex Life of the Unmarried Adult*. New York: Vanguard, 1934. Candid and expert symposium on all aspects of the problem.

Winter, Ella, *Red Virtue*. New York: Harcourt, Brace, 1933. An interesting and competent discussion of the sex and marriage situation in Soviet Russia. Many restrictions have been imposed since 1933.

Zimmerman, C. C., *Family and Civilization*. New York: Harper, 1947. Valuable for its emphasis on the interrelation between cultural change and family trends.

Part II

Institutional Impact of Urban
Industrial Life

CHAPTER 9

Rural Life

THE ROLE OF THE FARM IN HUMAN HISTORY

Past human experience mainly rural. The farm and rural life have played a long and important role in the history of humanity.[1] The farm dates back to the Neolithic or New Stone Age. Thousands of years before the dawn of history groups of men had settled down to systematic cultivation of the soil and were familiar with the more important grains and fruits which have since been produced in farming operations. The great majority of human cultures since the origins of civilization have been worked out within the patterns of a farming culture. If we include within the general category of farming the nomadic or pastoral peoples, it would be accurate to say that down to the Industrial Revolution an overwhelming proportion of mankind have lived within a rural economy. It is true that, since the dawn of history, cities have been the center of the highest cultural achievements and the source of most social progress. But the farmers and the herders were the bulwark of the existing economy, the political order, and the military forces of historic states. Moreover, it is from the country districts that the great majority of city dwellers have been drawn, from the days of the ancient Near Orient to the era of great industrial cities following the rise of machinery and the factory system.

Rural basis of ancient and medieval civilization. In ancient Egypt the administrative bureaucracy and the whole fiscal policy of the state were, for several thousand years, devoted mainly to establishing control over the grain supply and the herds of the Nile valley. Impressive though the Egyptian arts and crafts may have been, agriculture was the foundation of the Egyptian economy and gave color and character to Egyptian civilization and politics. The unparalleled military triumphs of the Assyrian armies were based primarily upon the virile peasantry who supplied a vigorous and dauntless body of soldiers. The culture of the ancient Greek city states rested on an agrarian foundation, and even many of the inhabitants of Periclean Athens lived part of each year on farms in the neighboring rural districts of Attica. Much of the Greek commercial life was devoted to securing an adequate grain supply.

Though the Roman empire is often described as a municipal civiliza-

---

[1] See N. S. B. Gras, *A History of Agriculture in Europe and America*. New York: Crofts, 1940.

tion, it is a well-known fact that the military conquests which created this empire were the work of the free Roman peasantry of the Roman republican period. The suppression of the small Roman landholders and the rise of great estates, or *latifundia,* cultivated mainly by slaves, was perhaps the outstanding social and economic change in the whole history of Rome. It was also the most fatal transformation. The decline of the free peasantry contributed notably to the later military weakness of Rome, her economic disintegration, and the growth of political corruption. The defiance of law and taxation by the great landlords in the later Roman empire put the finishing touches on Roman decline and laid the basis for medieval feudalism.

Medieval civilization rested on a preponderantly agricultural foundation. The great mass of medieval people lived on the rural manor or on farms conducted by other methods. The governmental system of the Middle Ages, chiefly feudalism, was the natural offspring of an agricultural civilization and was specifically adapted to the circumstances created by the manor and other phases of the provincial and localized medieval rural economy. The decline of the manor and the rise of capitalistic farming at the close of the Middle Ages was one of the more important harbingers of the appearance of modern times.

Rural forces in modern and contemporary history. Agriculture and the farm were still dominant for centuries after the modern age was established. Even in western Europe the majority of the people still lived on farms until well along in the nineteenth century. The agricultural revolution which came, particularly to England, in the seventeenth and eighteenth centuries increased the productivity of farms and made it possible to feed the ever larger number of workers who flocked to the new industrial towns. The increased efficiency of the new farming methods freed more agricultural laborers for the new demands of the city. Further, the enclosing and engrossing of land in England between 1750 and 1825 drove many thousands of English peasants from their rural holdings and made them willing to accept miserable living conditions in the new factory cities as the only alternative to sheer starvation. Agriculture also colored the dominant political processes of early modern times, which, in their more fundamental aspects, were a struggle of the new business classes against the vested agrarian interests.

The even more impressive agricultural revolutions of the nineteenth and twentieth centuries freed still more rural residents for migration to industrial centers, and the increased farm production supplied the food for the ever mounting urban populations. It was land hunger that brought the Russian revolution of 1917 to a head and took Russia out of the First World War. The opposition of the Russian peasantry to Soviet economics was a major reason for the launching of Five Year Plans by Stalin and the ruthless but efficient nationalization of Russian agriculture. From the Swiss Lake Dwellings to the mechanized Soviet farms, rural life and agrarian interests have thus exerted a powerful influence over the evolution of human culture.

Agrarian pattern of modern institutions. The dominant social institutions of modern times have been deeply influenced by rural life. When we talk of the family in sociological terms, we still mean essentially the rural family. Contemporary discussions of the weakening or downfall of the family refer, in reality, to changes in what has been the traditional rural kinship group. The rural population has provided the major support of the Christian church, especially of the Protestant church. The latter has been the center of social life in the American rural community. Country dwellers long remained relatively immune to the discoveries in scholarship which undermined traditional views of the Bible and religion. Hence they have been a bulwark of Christian orthodoxy.

Nor can we overlook the reaction of rural life upon modern politics. The farming population has made important contributions to the rise of democracy and representative government. Colonial local government in the township and the country laid the basis for American democratic institutions. The western frontier first put democratic theories into practice on a large scale and made democracy a truly national achievement in the United States. It was from the rural West that we derived many of the more important reform movements which swept over the United States between the days of Andrew Jackson and Franklin Roosevelt.

Human mental patterns shaped by rural experience. Until almost our own generation the farm mentality provided the dominating psychological patterns of the human race. Conditioned sharply by the repetition of seasons and agricultural processes, farm life tended to encourage stability and conservatism. Relatively isolated from the rest of the world, the rural mentality was provincial and exclusive. There was a natural suspicion of strangers and of novel ideas and methods. Having to depend mainly upon his own efforts, the farmer acquired traits of independence and personal resourcefulness. Being at the mercy of the weather and other manifestations of natural phenomena, the farmer inevitably developed a tendency to give a large place in his thinking to the elements of chance, fate, and magic. It was also logical that he should create a multitude of superstitions with respect to the heavenly bodies and weather conditions which had so marked and fateful an influence over his very livelihood.

Subordination of rural life: a social revolution. Now, in our day, the "empire of machines" has drawn more and more of the population into great urban centers. New developments in transportation and communication have tended to urbanize the ever smaller proportion of the population which remains in farming districts. The relative decline in the importance of rural life and the partial urbanization of that which lingers on certainly constitutes one of the major turning points in the cultural and institutional history of mankind. The reduction of rural life and institutions to a subordinate position in Western civilization has veritably introduced a new epoch in human history in which urban industrialism has supplanted the agrarian pattern of life that dominated human culture from Neolithic times to the twentieth century.

THE EVOLUTION OF AMERICAN FARMING

Colonial farming. The agricultural economy of North America dates from a period even before the European invasion of America which began in the seventeenth century. Several of the Indian tribes, notably the Iroquois in central New York, had developed a settled agricultural economy and were efficient in the production of a number of crops, particularly Indian corn, or maize.

The period of European settlement, from 1600 to the American Revolution, roughly coincided with the first agricultural revolution in Europe. The improved methods of European agriculture and stock breeding, as well as the new crops which had been introduced, especially clover and turnips, were brought to America by the colonists. From the Indians the colonists learned how to cultivate maize and other typically American crops.[2] In other words, colonial agricultural technique combined the best in the agricultural methods of the Old and the New Worlds.

In New England and the Middle Atlantic colonies small farms were the rule, except for the great estates of the quasi-feudal Dutch patroons located along the Hudson River. In New England it was the custom to assign a certain number of acres to each colonist for his personal cultivation. In the South great plantations, sometimes as large as 5,000 acres, were extremely common. Because of the plentifulness of land, colonial agricultural methods were often wasteful, and there was little development of fertilization or intensive agriculture.

From independence to the Civil War. From the period of the Revolution to the Civil War the chief development in American agriculture consisted in carrying the colonial farming methods to the West. The westward movement took place in three "waves," each with its typical culture. First came the hunter and trapper, who explored the country and made known its possibilities. He was followed by the pioneer farmer, who cleared the land and began subsistence cultivation. These two types of frontiersmen were usually driven on further by the appearance of the settled farmer, who brought in more of the comforts of civilization and was able to produce a surplus of agricultural products, for which he sought the markets of the East and South.

This period also brought improved techniques into agriculture. Better iron and steel plows, mechanical mowers and reapers, and a crude threshing machine were devised. These inventions remarkably accelerated farm production and made it possible to supply the food demands of the rising commercial cities in the East.

---

[2] Few realize our debt to the American Indians for food products. There were over two hundred of these of practical importance. Representative examples are such cereals as maize and wild rice; fruits like avocado pears, blackberries, raspberries, blueberries, huckleberries, cherries, plums, pineapples, strawberries and persimmons; many vegetables like potatoes, sweet potatoes, yams, pumpkins, squashes, peppers, cassavas, and tomatoes; nuts, such as peanuts, chestnuts, black walnuts, butternuts, hickory nuts, pecans, and Brazil nuts; and beverages, such as cocoa and chocolate. See A. H. Verrill and O. W. Barrett, *Foods America Gave the World*. New York: Page, 1937.

By the middle of the last century there were three rather distinct sections of the country, so far as agricultural interests and methods were concerned. In New England, commerce and manufacturing came to occupy an ever larger proportion of the population, and the number engaged in farming fell off. Such farming as existed was devoted mainly to producing dairy products, beef, wool, fruit, or tobacco. A similar trend also took place in the Middle Atlantic states, though much grain was produced here as well.

The second main section was the new Northwest, between the Alleghenies, the Mississippi, and Lake Michigan, which was opened up to settlement by the canals and railroads. Here crop farming dominated the scene and was mainly devoted to the production of grain and livestock.

Finally, in the third region, the South, cotton was the chief product after the invention of the cotton gin. It was grown, for the most part, on large plantations worked by Negro slaves. There were also a number of depressed poor whites who worked small farms, growing cotton, corn, and other products, whereby they eked out a relatively miserable existence. The raising of beef cattle began in the Southwest at this time.

Effects of the Civil War period. The era of the Civil War brought about a real revolution in American farming life. The demand for grain during the war encouraged the settlement of a further Northwest: Iowa, Minnesota, and the Dakotas. This was facilitated by the famous Homestead Act of 1862, which gave farms of 160 acres to those who wished to take advantage of the offer. By 1900, some 4½ million farms had been taken up under the Homestead Act. The 160-acre farm became the most characteristic unit in western farming. Further agricultural inventions, such as steam threshing machinery and the mechanical binder and header, notably increased the efficiency of agricultural activity in the West, which specialized in the production of grain.

The Civil War broke up most of the great southern plantations and led to an era of small-scale farms in the South, worked by both Negro and white farm laborers. There was also a considerable development of tenant farming and sharecropping in the southern region.

In New England and the Middle Atlantic area the more diversified types of farming persisted. This period witnessed the sweeping industrialization of the eastern United States. This trend not only provided a market for the vastly increased volume of farm products but also reduced the relative proportion of Americans engaged in agricultural pursuits.

Twentieth-century farming. The cultural and institutional developments of the twentieth century have been more momentous than any earlier trends with respect to the character and future of American farming. Agriculture, particularly in the West, has been far more thoroughly mechanized since the invention of the gasoline tractor, gang plows, gang harrows, and the giant harvesting combine. Western farms have tended to become ever larger. Irrigation has been provided for on a large scale in order to render this area more independent of drought. The efficiency of western farming has been vastly increased, but this has served to throw many farm laborers out of employment and to create other serious maladjustments to which we shall refer later. In the South two extremes have been notable in recent farming trends. Farm tenancy and sharecropping have become more prevalent and more depressed. In contrast to this we find the rise of great estates, in many cases far larger than the earlier plantations. They are often owned and managed by farming corporations. Instead of depending on Negro slaves they are worked mainly by new iron slaves: the gasoline tractor, the Rust mechanical cotton picker, and chemical weed eradicators are the most recent and portentous innovations in this field. In the Northeast, specialized farming remains the rule, but with a very general tendency to diminish the production of grain in favor of dairy farming, market gardening, and fruit raising.

Not only has farming been mechanized to an unprecedented degree in the twentieth century, thus greatly increasing its efficiency and per capita production, but our general economy has grown ever more complicated. Agriculture has to face many more diversified problems. As the farmer has made himself more efficient by machinery and more independent of nature through irrigation, he has at the same time piled up agricultural surpluses which are frequently difficult to dispose of in the home market at profitable rates. Our protective tariff system has restricted the world market for grain which is open to the American farmer. The urbanization of life has opened new contacts for the farmer and has revolutionized his outlook upon life. The cities have absorbed an ever greater proportion of the population, leaving today less than one-fifth of the total inhabitants of our country directly engaged in agricultural pursuits. American farming in the middle of the twentieth century is in an even greater state of flux and transition than the American urban community.

THE FARM IN AMERICAN LIFE BEFORE
THE FIRST WORLD WAR

Farmer's dependence on physical nature. In this section we may consider some of the outstanding patterns of the traditional American rural life. But it must be made clear that in this discussion we are referring to conditions antecedent to the First World War. The situation since that time has been so dynamic and unsettling that it has produced an era far different from that which prevailed at the turn of the century. Indeed, it requires a separate treatment that will be presented in a later section of this chapter.[3]

Many social historians have emphasized the fact that cities depend very directly upon geographical factors and physical nature. But rural life is even more closely and directly dependent upon geography than is municipal growth. Climate, weather, and the state of the soil condition the character, variety, and production of the main farm crops. Agricultural productivity holds the balance between prosperity and misery for

---

[3] For a good treatment of traditional American rural life and society, see M. N. Rawson, *Forever the Farm.* New York: Dutton, 1948; and for a briefer survey, T. L Smith, *The Sociology of Rural Life.* New York: Harper, 1946, Chap. II.

the farm population. The production and distribution of farm products create the chief economic problems of farmers and give color to the prevailing rural culture.

The farmer is very directly and immediately tied down to his rural habitat and is more sharply affected by nature than any city dweller can possibly be. The various natural phenomena, from storms to soil composition, condition his very means of existence. The highway terrain determines the access of the farmer to cities and towns, and facilitates or restricts his marketing activities. To a certain extent, the farmer has, in the twentieth century, been able to triumph over topographical handicaps through the development of railroads, better highways, automobiles, auto trucking, and the like. Finally, geographical factors have colored the social life of American farming areas. Before the automobile era geographical proximity determined the extent of social intercourse. The local neighborhood has been, in all rural areas, the basis of acquaintanceship, friendship, and social intimacy.

American culture shaped by rural life. Down to the outbreak of the First World War the farm was the most fundamental institution in American civilization. The great mass of the population had lived in rural areas during the nineteenth century, and a clear majority was still dwelling in such regions in 1910. Even the remarkable growth of the American cities after 1850 was due chiefly to rural influences and contributions. The superior physical vitality and fertility of the rural population provided the marked population increases that helped to fill up the growing cities. The great majority of the native-born inhabitants of our municipalities came from country areas. Resourcefulness and leadership in American industry were derived primarily from young men who had been born in the country and later moved to urban regions. The foreign-born immigrants helped to expand our cities, particularly after 1890, but much of the financial, industrial and commercial leadership still came from native-born and country-bred young manhood. The rural mentality avoided both the flashy brilliance and superficiality of the urban intelligentsia and the docile servility of the urban proletariat, who worked in deadly monotony in the factories and lived in drab misery in the city slums.

The American farm gave character to American life. This was true in all parts of the country. The typical farm virtues, such as chastity, thrift, industry, and independence, were looked upon as the great moral virtues of the nation. The rural mentality provided psychological traits that dominated our culture. The general rural stability was tempered by a tendency toward revolution, or at least militant discontent, when oppression became unendurable. The farming frontier exerted a deep and lasting influence on American life. It stimulated idealism, nationalism, and social and economic reform. It strengthened democracy and gave prestige to individualism. This frontier spirit not only dominated the frontier itself but reacted profoundly upon the intelligentsia and the leaders of the East. Theodore Roosevelt was only one of the more conspicuous examples.

The rural family. The influence of the farm in creating American social institutions can hardly be overestimated. As we have already indicated, the American family, in conventional phraseology, really means the rural family which came to be regarded as basic to, and characteristic of, all that is good in family life. There was an economic basis for the importance and integrity of the rural family. The wife and children were economically valuable as a result of the services they contributed in farming occupations. The assistance rendered by child labor tended to encourage large rural families. The patriarchal ideals which dominated rural family life colored and facilitated family discipline. Both the wife and the children were, as a rule, subordinated to the will of the husband and father. The family and the fireside provided the setting and tempo of moral and social life in the rural community. The idle moments of life were generally spent under the paternal roof. The folkways and moral ideals of the community were effectively inculcated through family instruction.

The rural family was extremely cohesive, and divorce was infrequent. The wife was very dependent upon the husband in an economic way and was therefore loath to place her very sustenance in jeopardy for the sake of a flirtation. The rural mores were decidedly antagonistic to infidelity and divorce, particularly in the case of women. Further, it was harder to hide promiscuity in rural areas, and less opportunity or incentive for conjugal infidelity was provided. Esteem for kinship beyond the immediate family has also been very important in rural areas. All the kin, extending to various grades of cousins, were expected to be proud of their relationship and ostentatiously cordial to their relatives. Our notions of the older rural family and its virtues may be somewhat sentimentalized and exaggerated today, but the rural family was extremely well suited to the culture out of which it grew. It may be that community organization will bring about some satisfactory revision of the rural family or find substitutes for it. So far, however, it has not been notably successful in doing this.

Extensive influence of the rural church. Rural life exerted a tremendous influence in sustaining the orthodox church, especially of the Protestant variety. Protestants controlled rural areas, as Catholics dominated many urban regions during the last seventy-five years. There are two main reasons why the farmer manifested a loyal enthusiasm for the church.

In the first place, as we have noted, the farmer was brought much more into direct contact with the vicissitudes of physical nature and adopted a somewhat mystical view of life processes. God was assumed to be responsible for unpredictable natural occurrences. A favorable attitude on God's part seemed desirable to the farmer in order to make the weather, climate, and the like, more beneficent. Church attendance and pious observances operated as a sort of permissible rural magic, designed to keep God on good terms with the farming population.

In the second place, the church occupied a central position in rural social life. Outstanding events of life like births, marriages, and deaths were usually celebrated under religious auspices. In many rural areas it was literally true that the church was the only building which was large enough to house a major wedding, funeral or party ("sociable"). The church provided and enforced, to a considerable degree, the moral ideals of the community, and exerted a strong influence upon various aspects of social control. It gave continuity to community traditions, and occupied a position of stability and prestige in the neighborhood. Moreover, the church exerted a large amount of control over rural recreation and the lighter phases of social life. Church attendance provided an opportunity for the invidious display of feminine styles and attire. The several neighborhoods in the community met within the church and renewed acquaintances. Church services, especially in the evening, were particularly fertile in promoting sociability between the sexes. Until recently, permanent matings in rural areas were frequently initiated through chance meetings at church services or church parties. Revival meetings, which were common in rural church circles, provided occasions which were both sanctified and exciting.

Because of its isolation, the rural church was protected against the more corrosive and disintegrating influences of urban life and culture. The farmer had less to distract him from church-going in the way of substitute and alternative diversions. Moreover, the higher criticism and other forms of scholarly questioning of Biblical infallibility were slower in making headway into rural regions. Rural religion remained more orthodox and more a matter of personal experience.

The influence of the rural community on the church, however, brought with it certain weaknesses, too. A rigorous orthodoxy tended to keep religion apart from secular activities of daily life and made it more difficult to link up religion with the social problems of the community. There was a persistent demand that the preachers stick to the gospel of salvation and refrain from discussing sociology. Sectarianism and denominationalism tended to produce a narrow-minded view of religion and religious communicants, to create an excessive sectarian arrogance, and to produce more churches than a rural community could effectively support. As a result of this "overchurching," there was often an inferior rural ministry, with financial returns to the latter as low as the quality of the services rendered.

Orthodox Christianity, still laying much stress on the Old Testament, gave rise to an autocratic attitude toward both salvation and human conduct. God was presented in the guise of an arrogant and impatient deity, and the rural minister was frequently prone to imitate the ways and attitudes of his divine superior. This made it difficult to introduce a persuasive attitude and an air of sweet reasonableness into rural religion. The emphasis placed upon individual salvation rendered it hard to adapt the rural church to the task of promoting community projects. Finally, the overwhelmingly puritanical, solemn, and ascetic tendencies of the rural church became progressively more distasteful to modern youth and more out of accord with the general trend of modern life. This led to extensive desertion of the rural church by the youth of a later generation. The traits of the rural community, long a major source of strength to the rural church, have helped on the marked crisis in religious life which is today characteristic of most of the rural regions of the United States.

Education in rural society. The rural community has been placed in a somewhat contradictory position with respect to education.[4] Like all persons of democratic inclination, the farmers had a sentimental devotion to education. But the high economic value of child labor on the farm tended to restrict the amount of time which could be given over to "schooling." The leading American democrats, such as Horace Mann, Henry Barnard, James G. Carter, and the followers of Jackson, laid great stress upon the social and personal importance of education. The farmers fell in heartily with this general philosophy. They were the chief bearers of the "American dream" legend, with its notion that every American boy is potentially on his way to the White House. Education would increase his prospects of gaining distinction. The frontier region was particularly characterized by enthusiasm for education.

At the same time, the head of the farm household found himself faced with practical considerations which tempered this enthusiasm for education when translated into practical terms. Except in the dead of winter, the labor of children was highly valuable. Even in winter, they were needed for shoveling out roads and cutting wood and doing sundry chores. Hence, the average farmer was loath to part with his children for any great period of the year, even to head them in the direction of the White House. This attitude led to the restriction of the school year to a period far shorter than that in city areas. Further, it favored removing children from school entirely at a relatively early age. By and large, it may be said that the practical hostility of the farmer to education in fact has long outweighed his sentimental loyalty to the theoretical benefits of instruction.

The "little red schoolhouse" of the rural community has been sentimentally extolled in American prose and poetry alike. It unquestionably rendered an important service to American intellectual life, for it was a matter of either the little red schoolhouse or nothing. But only the most extreme bucolic nostalgia can prevent one from recognizing the gross defects of the conventional rural school. H. B. Hawthorn sharply but correctly speaks of "its boxcar buildings, its thirty-five minute classes, its five-months school year, its migratory girl teachers, its traditional three r's, and its educational inefficiency." Secondary education was even more at a disadvantage in rural areas.

Rural influence on American political life. The importance of the farmer in the world of politics is readily apparent to all students of American history. The frontier farmer played a dominant role in the creation of American democracy. Indeed, Thomas Jefferson was convinced that American democracy would survive only so long as the country remained predominantly rural. The importance of the farming element in American party history, from the Jeffersonian Democrat-Republican party

---

[4] Lowry Nelson, *Rural Sociology*. New York: American Book Company, 1948, Chaps. 19-21.

to the Farmer-Labor party that supported La Follette in 1924, is a matter of common knowledge. Not only have the less prosperous farmers generally aligned themselves with the more democratic of the major parties, but they have created important special parties of protest, such as the Populist party and others to which we shall devote attention later. Moreover, they have frequently consolidated the farming elements in both parties, in order to promote bipartisan—farm bloc—support of agrarian programs. Northeastern farming communities, especially those of the Middle States and New England, have shown rather persistent conservative tendencies. As a general rule, most of the farmers in the Middle States and New England supported the Republican party after the Civil War. The main strength of the progressive and radical rural political movements came from the western and some southern states.

The rural element has also contributed in important ways to local government in the United States. The rural neighborhood has been one of the strongest bulwarks of democratic feeling in American culture. It has been narrow-minded and provincial, but it has also been democratic. It was the rural township of New England which provided Americans with their first real training in democratic politics. The township precedents were carried over into state and Federal practice. In the South the county was the characteristic unit of local government, and it lent itself better to aristocratic control. In the Atlantic states and the West a mixed form of local government, combining the township and the county, has been dominant. County government has usually had a sheriff as its chief executive officer; a board of supervisors, each elected by a township, as its legislative body; and a county judge as the chief judicial officer. A county clerk looked after such records as deeds to property. A superintendent of highways cared for the increasingly important function of building and repairing highways. The tremendous sweep toward urbanization in the last half century might have engulfed what remains of American democracy but for the counterbalancing influence of rural local government.[5]

By and large, rural politics were free of the gross venality and corruption of machine rule in the cities. Although there has been trivial commercialism and manipulation in rural politics, these abuses have been far less serious than municipal graft. A rural citizen might be induced to sell his vote for a drink of hard cider or cheap whiskey, poured down his throat back of the local church, but the scattered population and limited resources of rural areas were not well suited for the operation of machine politics. In other words, it was not superior political morality in rural areas but lack of economic opportunity for remunerative graft which kept down political venality and corruption in agricultural regions.

Role of fraternal organizations in rural life. The lodge or fraternal organization has exerted a strong influence on rural life, especially among the well-to-do class of farmers. There were a number of reasons for this popularity of the lodge in rural areas. Most of the fraternal societies

---

[5] P. H. Landis, *Rural Life in Process*. New York: McGraw-Hill, 1940, Chap. 21.

adopted in their ritual certain phases of Biblical pageantry and Christian philosophy. Therefore, the popularity of the church in the rural community provided a natural link with a quasi-religious fraternal group. The rural mentality has been particularly susceptible to mystery and superstition, and the ritual of the lodge ministered to these urges. The striking and bright-colored vestments and the awesome ritual of the lodge tended to lift the rural dweller above the drab and commonplace level of his daily life. The ranks and grades of lodges gratified the latent ambition for the social superiority which was generally absent from routine life in the democratic rural community. The ritual, ceremonial, and dress of the lodge constituted one of the few artistic expressions in the rural neighborhood and appealed to whatever urge may have existed for pageantry and esthetic life. Since the rural church was usually a Protestant church, there was no pageantry in religion like that to be found in the Catholic churches in the cities. The ideals of the lodge also fitted in well with the cooperative, fraternal, and neighborly feelings of the rural community, and the lodge often served as an instrument of neighborhood philanthropy.

Some of the more important farmers' organizations grew directly out of the lodge pattern. Such was the Grange or the Patrons of Husbandry, the most popular and enduring of all fraternal rural organizations. This has been, from its beginnings, a quasi-fraternal and secret order. Numerous local farmers' organizations, such as Farm Institutes, developed with much success. They were designed to promote interest and instruction in farm problems and to create avenues of sociability through farm picnics and the like.

Dominance of local democracy and gossip and neglect of art. The social organizations of the rural areas tended to have a neighborhood and community basis. They were democratic, and social equality prevailed. There was little of the "social distance" which is to be observed between the dwellers in penthouses and the inhabitants of city slums. Democracy in the farming communities was sustained in social relations as well as in political machinery.

The rural press exerted a large influence on the social and intellectual life of country communities before the rise of the large city dailies and their facile circulation in rural regions as a result of rural free delivery of mail and private distribution by automobiles. Unfortunately, these local rural papers tended to be more diverting than informing. They were devoted chiefly to the systematic collection and dissemination of local gossip, well characterized by Ernest R. Groves:

> One might define gossip as a depraved product of curiosity. Country people are fond of gossip; indeed gossip may become one of the popular recreations of the country group. It is difficult to bring together any gathering without at least one who personifies gossip ... any group of people with little interest and much hard work and few contacts finds relief in gossip.[6]

---

[6] *The Rural Mind and Social Welfare.* Chicago: University of Chicago Press, 1922, p. 152.

An outstanding reason why gossip had such potency and interest in rural regions was the highly personal nature of rural life and the intimate acquaintance which existed among the inhabitants of a farming neighborhood. Family rivalry and personal envy also contributed to the popularity of the neighborhood gossip spread before the community in the rural paper. The high-grade, impersonal and professional farm journals have been primarily a product of the twentieth century. There are, however, several notable exceptions which originated well back in the previous century.

The artistic phases of life in rural communities were notoriously neglected or scarcely existed at all, except in connection with the pageantry of fraternal societies. Indeed, the country dweller tended to be actually suspicious of art, looking upon it as mischievous or wicked and a reflection of the degeneracy of the "city slicker." The observation of a farmer father, upon hearing that his son has been convicted of a serious felony while in college, "Thank God he does not play the piano," fairly reflects the older rural attitude toward art and artistic expression.

Though farmers were generally suspicious of art, there were some meritorious contributions to art in certain farming regions. Conspicuous examples were the rural New England architecture and interior decoration, and the excellent decorative craftsmanship of the Pennsylvania Dutch farmers.

Mental patterns produced by rural life. Students of rural problems are convinced that the traditions and processes of farm life have produced a definite type of rural mind or bucolic psychology. This has been well stated by Kenyon L. Butterfield:

> For the fact is that farmers are different. They are not peculiar, not unique nor inferior. They are just different. They live under different conditions from city people; they think in different terms; they breathe a different atmosphere; they handle their affairs differently—perhaps because they have different affairs to handle. This difference is not a difference in essential human qualities, but merely the effect of environment upon the inherent traits. Farmers are quite like other people in their fundamental instincts; but these instincts discharge through different channels from those that exist in the crowded city, and hence bring different results, so different as to produce the "rural mind." [7]

The typical rural mentality which prevailed before the rise of the technology of our day and the urbanization of rural life was a direct and natural expression of the conditions of rural existence. Repetition, as expressed in the recurring seasons of the year, the duplication of crops, and the daily regimen of life, helped to breed conservatism in the rural mind. There was a natural inclination to believe that life in the future would and should go on as it had in the past. The farmer tended to be suspicious of innovations and new proposals, and he was inclined to resist them even when they were obviously advantageous to him and his family. This rural mental attitude stands out in sharp contrast to the marked curiosity, the urge for the novel, and the constant shifts and changes characteristic of the urban mental outlook.

---

[7] Preface to Groves, *ibid.*, p. xiii.

The farmer and religious magic. The farmer was to a unique extent at the mercy of the phenomena of nature. His prosperity depended upon favorable climatic and weather conditions. Prolonged droughts, floods, and other natural disasters threatened or brought temporary ruin to him. Since nothing could be done about controlling these aspects of physical nature which so deeply affected the farmer, he tended to assume an attitude of resignation in the face of nature and an inclination to trust to fate. He believed that all he could do was to work hard and trust to a lucky outcome with respect to the weather. Yet the farmer was not without all hope that he could exert some indirect influence upon these natural phenomena. He believed in a special Providence which might watch over him if he did his part. A characteristic rural phrase was that "God helps those who help themselves."

Still, something more than personal effort was necessary to invoke the assistance of this beneficent Providence. The latter needed to be propitiated by due and proper ceremonial observances. It was this feeling which supplied the main utilitarian motive underlying the strong tendency toward church attendance in rural communities. A churchgoing community was believed to be more likely to be blessed with favorable weather than a godless group. This conviction gained headway when the farm of a scoffer suffered especially severely from some natural calamity. If, however, a church leader met some especially grievous reverse at the hands of nature, this was interpreted as the will of God, executed as a fond effort of the celestial parent to discipline the character and to strengthen the faith of the sufferer. This rural attitude of resignation in the face of Providence was a strong factor contributing to the development of rural stolidity and self-restraint. It was believed to be eminently fit and proper for the rural dweller to control his feelings—whether of sorrow or of joy.

The belief that God was on the side of those who made the greatest effort to help themselves abetted the common rural tendency to eulogize hard work and to look askance upon idleness as the most effective instrument of diabolical ingenuity and temptation. But the traditional industriousness of rural areas all too often lacked any intelligent plan. It was, in part, a product of the feeling of uncertainty in the face of nature and partly an outgrowth of the fatalistic notion of inevitability and repetition. Related to this attitude was a marked tendency to rely upon personal intuition and private opinion. The farmer was suspicious of the expert; and, above all, he delighted in an opinionated argument. This made it difficult to introduce scientific knowledge and a planned economy in rural communities.

Rural superstitions. The rural dweller inevitably developed a large range and variety of superstitions, which were, for the most part, directly based upon natural phenomena.[8] He sought for signs in nature which would give him some hints and guidance in the face of the general and gnawing uncertainty of what nature might have in store for him. These

------

[8] See especially J. M. Williams, *Our Rural Heritage.* New York: Knopf, 1925, Chap. V.

signs and portents, in which the farmers tended to believe, are classic. Such were sundogs, halos and coronas around the sun and the moon; the nature and formation of clouds; atmospheric conditions affecting the transmission of train whistles and other sounds; the behavior of common animals and plants; the falling of the leaves in autumn; squirrels' accumulation of nuts; and the flight of birds.

It is probable that more superstitions gathered about the moon than around any other manifestation of nature. The position of the new moon —whether upright or flat—was believed to determine whether the ensuing month would be wet or dry. A first sight of the new moon over the right shoulder was believed to bring good luck. Procedure with respect to crops and domestic animals was closely related to moon superstitions. Certain crops should be planted only in the "light" or "dark" of the moon. Pigs should be bred, castrated, and killed according to the appropriate phase of the moon. The same applied to the tapping of trees and other rural operations.

The farmer was usually hard put to it when asked for an explanation of these beliefs, though at times he had what seemed to be a quasi-logical answer. In general, however, it may be said that these superstitions arose in primitive communities in very early days, when they were closely associated with magic. They were handed down and followed primarily as a matter of rural tradition.

Mental isolation and personal independence of the farmer. The conditions of rural life encouraged both personal and cultural isolation. This produced provincialism, smugness, and hostility to what was new and different. But at the same time it promoted a strong feeling of individualism and personal responsibility and stimulated the resourcefulness of the farmer. Because the farmer had to face a wide variety of tasks, both of an agricultural and a mechanical type, he often achieved a personal versatility and confidence unknown to the city dweller, whose usual helplessness in the face of even the slightest mechanical emergency has been a standing joke in rural areas. Moreover, the diversities and informalities of rural existence helped to safeguard the farmer against the depressing standardization which characterizes urban communities.

The fact that the farmer had to work hard to obtain a sheer living inevitably produced a marked tendency toward acquisitiveness. A little additional gain was an important item in his life. Since his property existed in concrete things, such as land, buildings, and animals, rather than in paper claims to ownership, as in the case of urban security holders, the farmer had a robust sense of private property rights. He valiantly resisted any proposal to limit the status of private property. Nowhere was socialism more fiercely resisted than in prosperous rural regions. The property sense and a strong spirit of individuality constituted powerful obstacles even to the development of cooperation among farmers. Only the direst distress was able to create rural cordiality toward radicalism and collectivism. The radical reform parties which have had a large farm following have always gained their main rural support in areas where the farmers have been suffering from severe economic depression. Prosperous farming areas were a bulwark of political conservatism. Not until the serious farming depression of the period from 1921 to 1934 was rural individualism shattered in what had been prosperous farming areas and the average farmer slowly converted to relying more and more on government support and cooperative societies.

Rural puritanism. In his moral perspective the farmer usually tended to be a rigorous puritan. In one way this was a natural outgrowth of the religiosity of the farmer. The rural religion emphasized conventional virtues and fiercely denounced the wickedness of the city. Another foundation of rural puritanism was economic pressure and the necessity for thrift. Not only might indulgence condemn the soul to damnation, but it cost money and used up personal energy which should be devoted to productive labor. To a considerable extent rural puritanism was a rationalization of the actual necessity of working hard and long. Other writers, especially H. L. Mencken, have laid great stress upon the potency of envy and the sentiment of the invidious in stimulating the rural puritanism. The rural folk read of the glamorous and colorful sins of the city and inwardly resented the fact that such sins were monopolized by the urbanites. Hence, they denounced with special fierceness those acts which they secretly envied but actually could not share.[9]

Nature of rural crime. In the same way that the lack of economic opportunity kept down political graft in the country areas, so also it tended to restrict crime, especially those forms of crime which are of an acquisitive character and represent the theft of various forms of property and goods. Most rural crime, until recent years, has been some form of crime against persons. Only since the Second World War has there been a great wave of rural crimes against property. As Earnest A. Hooton observes:

> Rural residence puts a premium upon physical hardihood and restricts the choice of crime. Countrymen are prone to violence against persons, partly because of their physical equipment and partly because rustic life affords few opportunities for acquisitive offense. In general, one must rape, murder, or behave.

Embattled farmers a revolutionary force. While the farmer was conservative and stolid, he presented a good example of the fact that a worm will turn. The farmer can endure much misfortune and oppression, but he also tends to store up resentment. When this resentment has accumulated to the point where it can no longer be contained, the farmer possesses the personal courage to rise up and make a determined protest, by force of arms if necessary. There is much talk in radical literature about revolution by the urban proletariat, but so far in American history the farmers have made a far better showing in actual revolt. From Bacon's Rebellion in colonial Virginia to recent milk strikes and "necktie parties" for foreclosing judges, the farmers have engineered most of the revolts in American history. Lamar Middleton has shown

---

[9] H. L. Mencken, *Notes on Democracy*. New York: Knopf, 1926, pp. 35 ff.

that out of the nine major revolutions and rebellions in the United States, six have been engineered almost exclusively by the embattled farmers.[10]

FARM ORGANIZATIONS AND FARM MOVEMENTS

Main farmers' organizations. The American farmers have created a number of national organizations designed to promote the well-being and prosperity of the farming class.[11] The earliest and most enduring of these was the so-called Grange, or Patrons of Husbandry, founded by Oliver H. Kelly in 1867. A quasi-secret society and fraternal order, it devoted its earliest efforts to securing a fair deal from the railroads, increasing the political unity and power of farmers, and promoting co-operative marketing in rural areas. After 1880 it declined markedly, but it was revived after the First World War and now enjoys consider-able vitality and prestige as an organization for advancing the general interests of farmers and for promoting community sociability among the farming groups in local neighborhoods. It supports certain types of agricultural cooperation, holds social meetings, and aids in dis-seminating educational information pertaining to rural problems. In 1950, it had a membership of 850,000.

Next came the Farmers' Alliance, which was organized in Texas in 1878 and enjoyed a rapid growth, partially as a result of the declin-ing prestige and popularity of the Grange. It stepped into the breach created by the temporary eclipse of the latter. By 1890, it had more than 2,000,000 members. The Alliance adopted a comprehensive plan of social reform embodying free silver, banking reform, an income tax, an eight-hour day, more direct democratic methods in government, and an alliance of farmers with union labor. In 1892 the Farmers' Alliance merged with the Populist party and terminated its independent existence.

The year 1902 witnessed the birth of two new farm organizations. The American Society of Equity was born in Indiana in December, 1902. It aimed to promote the national economic interests of the farming class and to stimulate fraternal, benevolent, and social activities among farmers in local communities. Its strength has been shown mainly in the north central portion of the country. Also limited mainly to this region has been the Farmers' Equity Union, organized in 1910 and now having about 25,000 members. The National Farmers' Union was launched in the state of Texas in the summer of 1902. Its leader at the outset was Newt Gresham. It is a secret organization and somewhat radical and militant in its aims, being primarily a champion of de-pressed and marginal farmers. It maintains that there must be a fundamental change in our economic system if our farm problem is to be solved. It lays much stress upon agricultural cooperation and a

---

10 *Revolt: U.S.A.* Harrisburg: Stackpole, 1938.
11 On farmers' organizations see C. P. Loomis and J. A. Beegle, *Rural Social Systems.* New York: Prentice-Hall, 1949, Chap. 19.

readjustment of the farm mortgage and debt situation. Like the Farmers' Alliance, the Farmers' Union favors a united front with organized labor. In 1907, it had nearly a million members, but this has declined to about 150,000 today. It is strongest in the Southwest and the Plain states of the West.

One of the more recently organized and most powerful farm organizations is the American Farm Bureau Federation. It was founded in New York State in 1913, but did not become influential until the 1920's. Its membership is made up mostly of the more well-to-do farmers and has a family basis. About 500,000 families are now members. The Federation devotes much of its activity to Congressional lobbying in behalf of farmers, to promoting large-scale cooperative agricultural markets, and to education and propaganda in farming localities. It is especially interested in stimulating scientific farming. It is more conservative than the Farmers' Union, and its main strength is found in the Middle West. None of these national farm organizations makes any direct effort to protect or aid the nearly 3 million farm laborers in the country. The National Farm Labor Union is young, weak, and inadequate.

There have also been many important sectional organizations of farmers, perhaps the most notable being the Non-Partisan League of Minnesota and the Dakotas which arose during and immediately after the First World War. The militant spirit of the League was revived in the early 1930's by the Farmers' Holiday Association which was organized to frustrate the foreclosure of farm mortgages.

It is obvious that the farmers are not nearly as well organized as urban labor. The American Federation of Labor claims 7,500,000 members, and the Congress of Industrial Organizations 6,000,000.

Farm institutes. Probably the most important type of local farm organization has been the farm institute. The holding of such local institutes dates back to the period immediately following the Civil War. They have accomplished much in acquainting farmers with new scientific trends in agriculture and in offering suggestions with respect to the improvement of home and living conditions in rural areas. Farm institutes have become less popular and influential since 1920.

The decline of rural interest in traditional fraternal societies (lodges) in recent years accounts not only for the increased popularity of the Grange but also for the growth of farmers' clubs. These extend even to rural children, the popular 4-H Club being limited to children between four and sixteen years of age.

The farmers and cooperatives. The cooperative movement has made increasing headway among American farmers, though it cannot as yet be compared in scope and membership to the movement in some European countries, particularly in the Scandinavian countries and England.

The most extensive and powerful cooperatives in the United States are marketing organizations. There are more than 8,300 marketing cooperatives, with about 2,500,000 members, doing an annual business of approximately three billion dollars. The largest agricultural marketing cooperative is the California Fruit Growers' Association. Next in order would rank certain large dairy cooperatives, such as the National Cheese Producers' Federation and the Land O'Lakes Creameries, both of which have their main strength in Minnesota, Iowa, and Wisconsin. Cooperative marketing of grain has assumed greater importance. The outstanding organization in this field is the Farmers' National Grain Corporation, founded in 1929.

There have been a number of rural experiments with consumers' cooperatives. For a long time, they were mainly local in character and relatively small in size. The movement is, however, gaining headway. There are today about 3,000 rural consumer and farm-supply cooperatives. They have a membership of about 2,500,000, and they do an annual volume of business of $1,500,000,000. Included here are the bulk of the petroleum cooperative associations. There has been a notable development of cooperative insurance companies. There are thirteen large companies of this nature, and much of their business lies in rural areas. They insure about 4,500,000 families, have $850,000,000 of life insurance in force, have a premium income of $75,000,000 annually, and have more than $100,000,000 in assets. If all the farmers' mutual fire insurance companies were to be included, the number of families insured would mount to about 12,000,000. There are approximately 1,000 rural electric cooperatives, with a membership of 3,000,000. In 1948, they collected $173,000,000 in payments by their members for electric energy.

The National Council of Farmer Cooperatives, which was organized after the First World War, remains the central organization that promotes cooperative enterprises in rural areas. It is estimated that there are about 35,500 rural cooperative units in the United States today.

THE FARMERS AND THIRD-PARTY POLITICAL REFORM MOVEMENTS

Political democracy supported by farmers. The farmers have exerted an important influence in the political history of the United States, as we have seen. They provided the main support for Thomas Jefferson and his Democrat-Republican party. They formed the largest element which put Andrew Jackson into the presidency in 1828. The Jacksonian democracy was the only instance in American history in which a farmer-labor movement has been successfully consummated on a national scale. The farmers also enthusiastically supported the new and then liberal Republican party after it was formed in 1856. Since the Civil War, the farmers—particularly the western farmers—have been most conspicuous in politics as the backers of special reform movements.

Greenback, Granger, and Populist movements. The first of these movements was the Greenback movement which arose as a protest against the proposal to resume specie payment after the Civil War and to restore the greenbacks to par. This meant that the debtor farmers would have to pay their debts in money of much greater value than it had when they borrowed it. During the Civil War the greenbacks had fallen as low as

39 cents on a dollar in gold. Debtors who might have borrowed money which was worth only 39 cents in gold might be compelled to pay it back in money worth 100 cents in gold, thus having to return a far greater sum when computed in purchasing power. The Greenback party reached its greatest strength in 1878, when it cast a million votes in a Congressional election. But specie payment was resumed in 1879 and the Greenback party collapsed, many of its followers later falling in line behind the free silver movement.

The next important farmer movement was what is known as the Granger movement of the 1870's and 1880's, so called because the Grange was one of the strongest elements in this new development. It came into being to fight what were regarded as oppressive rates and arbitrary methods on the part of the western railroads in the shipment of grain, cattle, and farmers' supplies. The movement was temporarily successful in passing state legislation subjecting the railroads to rate control. But the Supreme Court soon all but nullified this achievement and the movement came to an end. It did, however, help to create the Interstate Commerce Commission.

Perhaps the strongest of all the rural political movements was that inspired by the so-called Populist party which began in the 1880's and which demonstrated its greatest strength in the election of 1892. It then polled over a million votes and secured 22 votes in the Electoral College. It had an ambitious and comprehensive platform, advocating not only measures directly designed to advance farming interests but also the free coinage of silver; an income tax; a postal savings bank; government ownership of railroads, telegraphs, and telephones; tariff reduction; and the readjustment of the taxation system. The radical program of William Jennings Bryan attracted the Populists in 1896, and they dropped their independent organization and went over to Bryan under the Democrat banner.

Recent political opportunism of farmers. The more radically inclined farmers supported Bryan in 1896 and 1900, but many of them swung over to Theodore Roosevelt in 1904 and supported Taft in 1908. But they were repelled by the reactionary Taft administration and bolted to Roosevelt and the Bull Moose movement in 1912. In 1916, the farmers were inclined to support Woodrow Wilson's neutrality platform, but in 1920 they did not line up decisively with either party.

The depression in American farm life after 1921 tended to revive agrarian discontent in active fashion. The farmers fell in behind Senator Robert M. LaFollette in 1924, and their candidate polled a remarkable popular vote of 4½ million, more than the vote for either Taft or Roosevelt in 1912. Franklin D. Roosevelt's New Deal after 1933 involved, as we have seen, legislation of unparalleled extent and scope in behalf of the farmers. The latter showed their gratitude by turning in a tremendous Democrat vote in the campaigns of 1936 and 1940. The future of the farm vote is as uncertain as the ultimate outcome of the farm problem itself, but just now the Democrat party has a pretty firm grip on the majority of farmers, especially those in the West and South who have been most directly aided by New Deal and Fair Deal legislation and by the prosperity produced by wartime demands, postwar relief needs, the cold war, the Korean war, and the like. It is only in the Northeast that most farmers still remain true to their old allegiance to the Republican party and conservatism.

If we consider the rural population as a whole, the most important political trend in the present generation has been the tendency to abandon the traditional rural individualism and opposition to "statism," and to demand and accept government aid from whatever party happens to be in power.

THE TECHNOLOGICAL REVOLUTION ON THE AMERICAN FARM

Farming technology before the Civil War. In preceding pages we have frequently referred to the progress of mechanical invention in relation to the farm. Now it might be well to bring together a discussion of all the leading phases of those technological changes which have directly affected agricultural methods and rural life. This is desirable, particularly because the more recent technological changes have already revolutionized American farming and promise to exert an even more momentous influence on the future of American rural life.

We have pointed out how the colonists brought from England and other parts of Europe the plow, the cultivator, and other rudimentary agricultural machinery. There were few other improvements in the mechanical basis of agriculture until the nineteenth century. In the first half of this century a number of striking inventions appeared in the realm of agricultural machinery. Thomas Jefferson, John Deere, and others devised better types of iron and steel plows. A rudimentary seed drill was invented and better harrows were provided. A mechanical mowing machine was brought out. Perhaps the most momentous of the inventions of this period was that of Obed Hussey and Cyrus H. McCormick, who produced the mechanical reaper between 1833 and 1845. Crude threshing machines put in an appearance about the middle of the century.

Inventions following Civil War period. From the Civil War onward agricultural inventions became more numerous and impressive. The grain binder (self-binder) was invented in the 1870's, the wire binder in 1874, and the twine binder in 1879. William Deering invented the latter. At the end of the century the mechanical header was introduced and greatly hastened the harvesting process in areas where it was not thought worth while to preserve straw from the wheat stalk. The steam threshing machine worked a revolution in the separation of grain from the husk. At the turn of the century the corn harvester and the corn husker made their appearance and completely transformed the handling of the corn crop. It is estimated that the mechanical inventions of the nineteenth century effected a saving of about 80 per cent in farm labor and cut down farming costs by nearly 50 per cent.

Tremendous mechanization of farming since 1900. But the most sweeping and unsettling advances in agricultural machinery were still to come. They revolved chiefly about the improvement of the internal combustion engine, which made possible a successful gasoline tractor, first introduced by Benjamin Holt in 1903. This, and the automobile truck, tended to displace the horse and mule in agricultural processes. Along with the tractor came ever more effective gang plows and the disc harrow combine. These innovations revolutionized the preparation of the soil for the sowing of crops. Larger grain drills, tractor-drawn in veritable fleets, greatly hastened the sowing of crops. Airplanes used for the sowing of both rice and wheat have also greatly increased efficiency.

The harvesting of grain was equally facilitated by the invention of the harvesting combine which cuts, threshes, cleans, and bags grain all in one process. Corn harvesters of far greater capacity than those of a generation

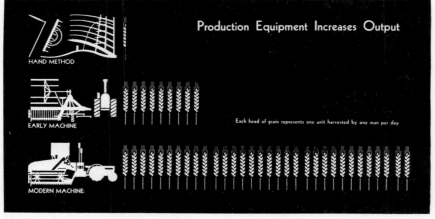

Production Equipment Increases Output

HAND METHOD

EARLY MACHINE

Each head of grain represents one unit harvested by one man per day

MODERN MACHINE

FROM *Building America*, VOL. 1, NO. 1.

ago have been invented. The product per worker in grain agriculture has been incredibly increased in comparison with the old days of the horse-drawn plow and binder. The cotton-picker, invented by the Rust brothers, and the chemical weed eradicator are producing a comparable revolution in southern agriculture.

How chemistry affects farming and food production. The contributions of chemistry to greater agricultural efficiency have also been notable. Scientific soil analysis and efficient fertilization have been made possible on a scale hardly dreamed of in previous generations. The mechanical inventions and better fertilization have created a potential agricultural production in the United States which seems almost incredible, even to scientific students of the problem. One expert, O. W. Willcox, has made it clear in his *Reshaping Agriculture,* and *Nations Can Live at Home,* that we could produce all the food needed for a high standard of living with one-fifth of the number of persons now employed in agriculture, working only one-fifth of the land now under cultivation, if we were to utilize the most efficient mechanical methods and the best modes of fertilization. The import of all this for the future of the American farm and rural community is too momentous for even the most astute economist or sociologist to discern today or to forecast with accuracy.

But this is not all. Not only has the production of food from the soil been put on a far more efficient basis than ever before, but we are on the eve of remarkable achievements in the field of synthetic chemistry. These will both insure a better utilization of farm-produced products and create foods artificially by purely chemical methods. Cornell University recently experimented with sheep fed in the conventional way with natural grains and grasses, and with others which were raised exclusively on synthetic laboratory products. The latter were definitely superior in weight, wool and other important points.

Agricultural surpluses now the main problem of the American farmer. We have already had occasion to call attention to the fact that these agricultural advances have completely upset the theories of Malthus, to the effect that population growth was bound to crowd hard on the heels of food production. In the twentieth century, population growth slowed down notably until 1940, while potential food production increased at a most impressive rate.

The inventions mentioned above have also altered some of the main problems of the farmer. In the old days, his chief ambition was to get a good crop. Today the chief task is more often one of how to dispose of it profitably, once it is harvested. The new machinery, fertilization, irrigation, and insecticides have reduced the tyranny and vicissitudes of nature. But new worries, in the form of agricultural surpluses, arise to plague the farmer.

These agricultural surpluses are not due to better technological methods of production alone. They also grow out of more efficient modes of preserving and transporting food. The canning industry has been greatly improved in recent years. But even more revolutionary has been the ever increasing use of refrigerators and deep-freeze lockers in private homes. This means that less and less food is wasted through spoiling and decay. Particularly notable has been the introduction of so-called dry ice as a type of superrefrigeration and the associated invention of the method of refrigeration employed with frozen food products. Not only does this make possible almost indefinite preservation of food, but it also does this with little loss of the original taste and savor.

The revolution in transportation and communication. The technological changes which have affected rural life have by no means been limited to new methods of producing and preserving food. The revolution in transportation methods has been equally striking. Here again, it has been the internal combustion engine which has played a leading role. The automobile, the auto truck, and the motor bus have completely transformed transportation between the country and the city.

Without improved roads, however, the automobile would have been extremely restricted in its utility, especially during bad weather. At the outset of the twentieth century there was hardly a surfaced road in the United States, with the exception of the paved city streets. Consequently, there has been enormous activity in building new roads and improving the surface of those in existence. There are about 3,250,000 miles of roads in the United States today, of which 1,500,000 are surfaced; 200,000 miles have first-class surface. Mechanical snowplows have been made available to help keep roads open and passable during even the most adverse weather conditions. In horse and buggy days a speed of five miles an hour was normal. Today the person who averages 40 miles an hour on interurban trips is regarded as a somewhat conservative driver. The significance of all this in increasing rural mobility and rural-urban contacts is as apparent as it is revolutionary. The isolation of the rural neighborhood is a thing of the past, and with its extinction have gone many of the more characteristic phases of earlier rural life.

The communication of information has undergone changes which are in many ways more dramatic and impressive than the evolution of agricultural machinery or transportation methods. Here electricity has been most influential. The daily newspaper gathers news almost instantaneously from all parts of the earth and the rural free delivery and private automobile deliveries put the great metropolitan dailies speedily in the hands of rural readers. The telegraph and telephone place rural areas in rapid contact with distant regions, while the telephone also facilitates communication within the rural community. The movie newsreels provide a visual portrayal of happenings throughout the world, while the feature movies enable the farmer to share in the marvels of Hollywood, along with his urban neighbor. Most impressive of all have been the inventions in the field of radio. A farmer in the American Far West can now listen to a report from Tokyo or an address from Paris. Instead of upbraiding his wife and children at the close of the evening meal, he can regale himself with the edifying discourses of a radio commentator or comedian. Like the city dweller, the rural inhabitant has been made world-conscious. Television is also now coming to rural regions and is likely to work an even greater mental and social revolution than moving pictures and the radio have accomplished in shaping the rural mind.

Electricity has not only brought a new world to the farmer in the realm of communication, it has also produced on many farms innumerable new conveniences in the way of light and power. The so-called "power age" is now dawning even in rural communities. There has been a great increase in the rural use of electricity since early New Deal days. By 1950, 85 per cent of the nation's farms had electrical service, as compared with only 11 per cent in 1935. The rural use of electrical current in 1950 was over 80 times as great as it had been at the close of the First World War. Farmers now have motor-driven grinders, saws, lathes, milking machines, and cream separators, and farmers' wives have their electric mixers, flatirons, and stoves. The industrial revolution, in most of its phases, is now the common property of the farm as well as of the city.

SOME EFFECTS OF THE NEW TECHNOLOGY UPON FARM LIFE

Mechanization: its menace to the small farmer, marginal farmer, and farm labor. It was inevitable that such stupendous technological changes as we have only briefly summarized in the preceding section would bring about sweeping readjustments in every phase of rural existence. Indeed, they threaten the very future of the farm, a matter which we shall discuss more at length later on in the chapter.

The far greater efficiency of the new machinery renders any successful competition of the archaic farmer with mechanized farming entirely out of the question. The farmer who cannot provide the best of machinery is in much the same condition today that the hand weaver found himself in during the era of Silas Marner. In the smaller and diversified farms of the East this situation is less acute, but even here the farmer who can provide himself with good fertilizers, more scientifically planned crops, milking machines, and motor trucks possesses a distinct advantage over his less fortunate neighbors. On the western ranch farms the situation of the ill-equipped farmer is truly desperate. Indeed, the farmer who possesses fairly up-to-date equipment on a small scale is at a marked disadvantage when compared to the sweeping and high-powered mechanization of the extensive farms of the West and South. Wheat produced on the extensive farms of the West can be sold at around a dollar a bushel and return a profit, whereas the average western farmer must sell it for two dollars to break even. The gasoline tractor and other improved farm machinery in the South have put the small farmer and sharecropper at an equal disadvantage in that area.

The plight of farm labor is even more desperate than that of the small farmers. The new agricultural machinery threatens them with an era of unemployment as widespread and serious as that which confronts the urban worker in an era of automatic machinery and photoelectric and thermostatic controls. It is estimated that the harvesting combine alone took seasonal work away from more than a quarter of a million farm hands.

In the light of these advances in agriculture, the folly of cultivating marginal lands becomes ever more transparent and shocking. Many millions of acres of land now cultivated must be returned to forests and pastures, of which we are in real need. Intensive cultivation of good land is the only sensible procedure for American agriculture. In short, one may observe that any discussion of rural problems which ignores the tremendous technological changes of recent years, and those which doubtless lie ahead, is comparable to a solemn discussion of transportation which leaves the automobile and airplane out of the picture or an analysis of communication which does not reckon with the telegraph, telephone, radio, or television.

Older rural culture and interests undermined by mechanization. The technological revolution, accompanied by the relative reduction of the rural population, has markedly lessened the uniqueness and significance of rural culture in American life. The rural neighborhood has tended to lose its identity and distinctive characteristics. The farming neighborhood has been almost literally jerked out of isolation and thrown into contact with world culture. With increasing urbanization, the relative prestige of rural institutions and attitudes has markedly declined. This trend has been emphasized by Paul H. Landis:

> The nation's past is one of rural experience; its present is a blending of ruralism with urbanism, the latter holding the dominant place in the mechanization of experience and at the same time encroaching on the more psychological aspects of behavior, making deep inroads into the mores, customs and traditions of the people.[12]

While urbanization has exerted a great influence upon rural life, the cities have not, however, entirely wiped out the hold of the larger rural villages and small cities upon farm economics and culture. Farmers still market some of their milk and food products in villages, buy much of their groceries and feed in villages, take their automobiles to villages for repairs, consult village physicians, attend village churches and movies, and send their children to village high schools. Rural social and community life also still tends to center in villages.

Although the nature of rural life has been revolutionized, and its position in the national economy and culture greatly deflated, these changes have not all been disastrous to country dwellers. The latter have been freed from the oppressive isolation and limited contacts of the old farming neighborhood. Better transportation facilities enable them to have access either to the best rural talent or to the cultural advantages of urban centers. Many of the less appealing aspects of the farm mentality have been altered for the better.

The isolation, provincialism, and smugness which dominated the old rural mentality have been notably modified. The radio has provided a substitute for petty neighborhood gossip and scandalmongering. The doings of the neighbor's hired girl have been subordinated in interest to the musings of the hired girl in the radio soap opera. The banterings of radio comedians prove more diverting than local scandals and drab rural adultery. The movies have also tended to lessen interest in neighborhood gossip. Ingrid Bergman and Rita Hayworth are far more colorful targets for the rural scold than is any erring housewife. The general puritanical outlook has been restricted, as a result of contact with the manners and customs of urban centers, indeed of the whole world.

The importance of the providential element and of fatalism is now less apparent in rural thinking. By means of irrigation, fertilization, chemical protection against insect pests, and other innovations, the farmer has rendered himself more independent of the eccentricities of nature. It is economics rather than meteorology which provides him with his greater obstacles today. Therefore he tends to look less to God and more to the government as a means of helping him out of his difficulties.

Rural individualism and mental patterns collapsing: This growing tendency to rely upon governmental aid and direction has reduced the

---

[12] Landis, *op. cit.,* p. 3.

intensely individualistic traits of the oldtime farmer and his adamant resistance to governmental controls. Few groups now look more eagerly for government aid and support than the farmers. Many believe that President Truman owed his election in 1948 to the heavy farm vote for him. At any rate, the farmers today tend to support the party and candidate which offer them the greatest prospect of high prices and wide sales for farm products. As a result of all these changes the rural mentality which we described in an earlier section now persists in any complete form only in backward or marginal farming areas and among the older generation of farmers.

Neither the typical urban mentality, with its shallowness, superficiality, and ever shifting interests, nor the smug and provincial rural mental attitudes can be regarded as ideal. It is possible that the impact of urban life and interests upon the country will produce a new rural mentality which will be a happy mean between the urban traits and the older rural pattern. This would be a fortunate development. It would seem, however, that there is some danger that the city mentality, operating both by direct contact and through the new instruments of communication, will overwhelm the country and submerge it under an essentially urban type of mental outlook. Of course, if cities are broken up and there is a general movement toward suburban and rural areas, the impression of metropolitan mentality on the country may be less complete.

Rural life now more pleasant but less distinctive. The new technology, communication, and electricity have obviously made the country a far more pleasant region in which to dwell. From a physical standpoint there are many more conveniences in homes which have felt the impact of the new technology. The rural dweller can now participate in the advantages of both city and country life. In past generations, country life was often indicted because of its drab and monotonous character and its oppressive isolation. Such a charge is rarely leveled against the better developed rural areas today. The main problem now is for the farmer to make enough from his farm to be able to go on living in what has become, admittedly, one of the most attractive dwelling places on the continent, the mechanized rural community. The greater attractiveness of rural life under modern advantages has led to a notable migration from the city to outlying areas, within easy range by automobile. More and more, people work in the city and live in the country.

Rural culture has been profoundly modified by improved transportation and increased contacts with urban life. City styles in clothing and household furnishings now predominate in rural areas. The distinctive "rube" is a thing of the past in most rural areas. Recreational interests of the country have similarly been shifted to the city. Country dwellers use their automobiles to attend baseball and football games in urban centers. Instead of playing checkers or dominoes in the evening, they turn on their radios and listen to ringside reports of a championship prize fight or view the contest on the television screen. Jazz and swing music have superseded folksongs and hymn singing. The characteristic city trait of "keeping up with the Joneses" is now swiftly permeating rural localities.

RURAL SOCIAL INSTITUTIONS SINCE THE RISE OF THE
NEW TECHNOLOGY

Changes in the rural family. In an earlier section we discussed rural social institutions and mental attitudes prior to the rise of mechanized farming, the automobile, and new modes of communicating information. We may now briefly review the outstanding changes in rural life and society which have been produced by the comprehensive revolution in technology.[13] The outstanding fact about recent developments in rural regions is the impact of the new technology and urban influences upon farm life.

The farm family—the idealized American family—has been undergoing notable changes in the twentieth century. It was long the product and reflection of a specific form of farm technique and social surroundings. These have undergone a marked alteration in the last half-century, and the family has naturally experienced comparable changes as a result. Machinery has supplanted to a considerable degree the prevalence and value of child labor. Fewer children are born in farm families today. Birth control methods derived from city centers have helped in this process. Women and girls in rural areas are less at the mercy of men than they were in the old days. Women can now leave the country, get work in the city, and support themselves. The emancipation of women has thus affected rural regions. The farm home is no longer the center of social and recreational life. Automobiles take all members of the family out of the home to rural villages and cities in quest of various types of amusement. Even when they stay at home, the farmers are usually diverted by material originating outside the home circle, such as the daily paper, farm journals, popular magazines, and radio and television programs of every variety.

Indispensable services once performed by the family are now being taken over more and more by community or school nurses, clinics, and playground directors. The rigorous morality of the rural area is also breaking down. The temptations of the city are now more accessible, and infidelity consummated by rural pleasure seekers in urban centers is easier to conceal. City influences are also undermining the puritanical philosophy of the rural neighborhood. The movies have been especially influential in this respect. As a result of all these tendencies, the divorce rate is increasing in country districts, and the old stigma of divorce is being rapidly erased. With the undermining of the rural family, even in country areas, it is inevitable that its influence upon the city family is becoming progressively reduced.

Reduced influence and vitality of rural neighborhood and church. The rural neighborhood is disintegrating and losing its former distinctive characteristics even more rapidly than is the rural family. Better transportation facilities and increased urban contacts have destroyed the unity and lessened the cohesiveness of the country neighborhood. The

---

[13] See E. des. Brunner and J. H. Kolb, *Rural Social Trends*. McGraw-Hill, 1933.

farming population no longer depends upon the neighborhood for either sociability or cooperative assistance. The progress of mechanized farming tends to cut down the number of persons carrying on farming activity in any given rural region. Better machinery lessens the need for cooperative endeavor. As we have seen, the rural neighborhood tends ever more to seek its amusement and recreation in villages and cities. This has destroyed the old rural congeniality group. Most neighborhood groups are gradually disappearing, and in their place we find a tendency to substitute a rural community life, with the larger villages as its center. The social perspective of the rural neighborhood is being extended to villages, cities, and the world in general.

A vigorous effort has been made to prevent the complete destruction of rural social life through the institution of community center projects. This undoubtedly represents a real improvement over the less enlightened and more provincial rural neighborhood associations. But it is often hard to make the community center idea take root in rural villages on account of the overwhelming attraction of neighboring cities. The rural community center movement has been most successful where there are few large adjacent cities and the rural village retains its social ascendency.

The old rural church, as a center of the intellectual and social life of the farming community, has also been hard hit by new developments. Where the rural church has proved non-adaptable and has insisted upon remaining doggedly loyal to the drab and dour orthodoxy of old days, it is losing out in its fight against falling numbers. The younger generation finds little attraction in the type of religious doctrine and social life which dominated rural regions a half century ago. There is, moreover, a general trend away from all forms of religious interest. Although it is not as marked as in the city, this trend is readily observable today in country districts. The secular influences of the city have made their impression. Better education of rural youth tends to undermine many of the old orthodox doctrines. Moreover, the great increase of material distractions has been particularly disastrous to orthodox religion. The automobile, the movies, and the radio have unquestionably done more to wreck rural religion than all the critical scholarship and atheistic propaganda combined. With new methods of amusement and recreation, the country no longer depends on the church for its social life. Secular diversions abound on every side.

The most notable effort to rehabilitate and preserve religious life in the country is the introduction of the federated church and the community church. Even in the older days, the rural community was "over-churched." This was due to narrow denominational divisions and sectarian bitterness. Financial pressure has tended to overcome this more thoroughly of late. Rural churches simply have to combine and pool their resources or go out of existence altogether. This amalgamation has been facilitated by better methods of transportation. The community church represents a distinct advance not only in its suppression of denominational narrowness, but also because it frequently produces a type of preaching and social activity better adapted to the social needs of today. But the secular diversions of contemporary life are proving a real obstacle even to the community church.

Enormous recent improvement in rural educational facilities. In the realm of education we find outstandingly favorable and constructive changes in rural institutions. A greater amount of state aid is now available to support rural education. Teachers can be better paid and schools more adequately equipped. State legislation has also become more rigorous in prescribing a longer school year and raising the minimum age for compulsory school attendance. Better transportation renders it easier to combine school districts and thus make a more economical use of available educational facilities. The progress towards combination and better school systems is revealed by the fact that the number of one-room schools has declined from about 200,000 in 1920 to 75,000 in 1950. Nevertheless, these 75,000 one-room rural schools still account for nearly half of the school buildings in the United States, employ one-twelfth of the teachers, and have an enrollment of one-sixteenth (1,500,000) of the school children in the country.

The greatest recent advance has been achieved in the consolidated and centralized school districts. Here a thoroughly modernized plant, equal in quality to most city schools, can be provided and a first-rate faculty brought together. The centralized rural school represents, perhaps, the most impressive aspect of recent progress in public education in the United States. Indeed, it is not going too far to state that centralized rural school systems constitute the greatest single achievement in American education since the days of Horace Mann over a century back. The consolidated school also renders an important service in building up a common community sense and community spirit. Moreover, rural education is not only becoming more efficient from the standpoint of plant and personnel, but it tends to be more practical. Greater attention is being paid to natural and social science, domestic economy, and the manual arts. But there is still room for improvement in this respect in even the very best of the consolidated schools.

Lag in rural political institutions. In the field of politics there have been few marked changes in rural regions as a result of technological advances. Local politics in rural districts operate according to the older structures and mental patterns. The political units of the pioneer age such as the township and county persist in an urban and industrial era. The maintenance of political units that were laid out for a horseback or horse-and-buggy era in an automobile and electric age has proved an unnecessary expense and handicap in the administrative and social services of local areas. This has been especially true of rural county jails and crime detection. Few rural counties can afford to build and operate adequate jails or provide a good rural police system.

The farmer is, however, becoming more aware of national and international issues as they bear upon farm problems. But the increased information of the farmer frequently leads only to confusion, because of the difficulties and complications involved in the national economy and world situation. Conflicting currents of propaganda and the distractions of partisanship also often confuse the political perspective of the rural population.

Government rather than divine aid now sought by farmers. The most characteristic fact which emerges from the political life of the farmer today is the revival of radicalism and reform enthusiasm and the demand for government aid to farmers. This was brought about as a result of the great depression in agriculture after 1921 and the strong economic pressure exerted on the farmer. Such panaceas as the Townsend old-age revolving pension plan aroused great interest in farming areas. The growing tendency, noted before, to look to the government rather than to God for aid has made the farmer more tolerant of collectivism and has enormously weakened the adamant individualism which formerly prevailed in prosperous farming communities.

Rural communication agencies. The competition of the city daily, distributed by rural free delivery, has been well-nigh fatal to the local rural newspaper. The latter, if in existence at all, is now made up almost entirely of local gossip and imported "boiler plate." Its chief appeal is local news and gossip. But, as we have seen, the comic sections in the dailies, Mickey Mouse and other movie features, soap operas and other radio trivialities, and television programs have crowded in upon the gossip mongering of the rural area. The main advance in rural journalism has been the recent growth of greatly improved farm journals. These are often edited by scholarly and well-trained experts in the field of agriculture, having a good grip upon underlying agricultural issues, and present a truly constructive vision with regard to farm problems. The city daily, of course, gives the farmer an unprecedented array of national and world news.

The increasing popularity of the rural telephone in the present century has tended to break down rural isolation, to intrude on rural privacy, and greatly to extend the facilities for gathering and disseminating gossip. Moreover, its practical services in rural life have been almost limitless. Over half of the rural population now have telephone service.

The most striking recent revolution in rural communication has, of course, been the radio and television. Along with an incredible amount of drivel, there is a residual element of valuable information. News broadcasts give the farmer frequent reviews of "hot" world news. Farm problems and other public issues are often discussed over the air. The more prosperous farmers are already buying television sets. Television may prove more revolutionary in rural communication and entertainment than radio. It may make the rural home something like the entertainment unit that it was in older farming days.

THE ECONOMIC CRISIS OF 1923 TO 1941 AND THE AMERICAN FARM

Higher living standards demanded by farmers. We shall now consider the economic problem of American farming in the light of the recent technological revolution. Too much stress cannot be laid on this point.

The economic problem is the crux of farm life today. In most other respects life on the farm has improved—in education, cultural opportunities, home conveniences, transportation, and the like. Yet, with all these gains, the ability of the average farmer to make a mere living, to say nothing of accumulating a sizable surplus, has correspondingly declined in normal times. If a man on a farm can barely live, he is unable to avail himself of all the advantages which modern technology has laid at his feet. Of course, there is the other side of this picture. Farmers desire more today than formerly. What constitutes a "living" today on the farm embraces many more gadgets than it did in 1900.

Relative prosperity of American farming from 1850 to 1920. American farming prosperity, which was maintained, with some serious lapses, on a fair level from 1850 to 1920, with a relative depression from 1880 to 1900, rested upon certain definite historical conditions. In the first place, English capitalism was unable to feed itself. After the repeal of the Corn Laws in 1846, England very frankly depended upon cheap foodstuffs from abroad, and the American farmers were the major source of this supply. At the same time, our capitalistic system was then in a state of rapid evolution. We were a debtor economy and sent our farm products abroad to help pay the interest on our foreign borrowings and the bills for the raw materials and semifinished goods that we needed for the building up of American industrial prosperity.

The remarkable growth of American capitalistic industry after the Civil War created such a tremendous demand for foreign products and services that every effort was made to stimulate the expansion and productivity of American agriculture as a leading means of meeting our foreign obligations. The marked growth of the American urban population, following the development of our manufacturing industries and the rise of mass production, also served to postpone for two or three decades the final reckoning with Canada, Australia, the Argentine, and Russia. American farmers were already on the verge of evil days when the First World War broke out and sent the prices of farm products to the dizziest heights known in the history of American farming.

Serious depression in American agriculture after the First World War. With almost cruel suddenness, after 1921, American farming was plunged from the clouds into the abyss. British and Continental capitalism was hard hit by the war, could no longer spend so heavily for food products, and bought much of its agricultural imports elsewhere. American capitalism, in the meantime, had reached a state of monopolistic maturity. We became a creditor nation. We no longer needed to pay heavy interest charges on foreign investments or import such large quantities of foreign aid and goods. Therefore, we could not export agricultural products to pay debts. The further development of mechanization and efficiency in American farming greatly increased the agricultural productivity per unit of labor and capital expended, thus encouraging the tendency to produce more farm products at a time when the foreign demand for them was decreasing. The high protective tariff system, which American farmers have been beguiled into supporting by politicians, worked against the farmers. Europeans curtailed wheat purchases here because they could not send manufactured goods in payment. At the same time, this shutting off of effective foreign competition enabled American manufacturers to charge farmers high prices for their goods.

As we have seen, the striking growth of the American population, which created an ever larger market for our farm products, slowed down decisively in the second and third decades of the present century. Our home market growth was thus reduced at the very time when the foreign demand was also slackening. Further, new dietary conceptions, based upon our recently acquired knowledge of vitamins and the like, brought about shifts in food uses, greatly to the detriment of the older and heavier standard farm products, such as cereals and potatoes. There has been a greater consumption of fruits and vegetables. The hay market was undermined by the rise of the automobile and the decreased use of horses and mules. The new foreign farm areas, such as Australia, the Argentine, and Canada, entered into the food producing race with full force after 1920. We find it as difficult to compete with them today as western European farmers found it to compete with us between 1850 and 1900. Further, many of our former customers in foodstuffs abroad were so seriously affected by the economic results of the First World War that they had no surplus left to buy foreign foodstuffs from us on anything like the scale that prevailed before 1914. Moreover, they made desperate efforts to create self-sufficiency in foodstuffs through intensive cultivation, land reclamation, and the like. Further, the American farmer suffered somewhat from the fact that the world price for grain was fixed at Liverpool, although but a small proportion of American wheat was sold abroad.

In the region east of the Alleghenies, in particular, many farmers were forced out of wheat farming or diversified farming and compelled to concentrate on dairy farming. But the rise of holding companies in the milk industry dealt the dairy farmers a severe blow. These holding companies greatly increased the "spread" of the price between producer and consumer without rendering any comparable service to the public. They reduced the price of milk paid to the farmer and increased the cost of milk in cities. To the author's personal knowledge, farmers in central New York in depressed times were paid less than two cents a quart for milk which was sold in New York for twelve cents. Although the "spread" is not usually as atrocious as this, it is sufficient to impoverish the dairy farmers and curtail milk consumption in cities. After price rises following 1946, the spread has run from 5 to 7 cents a quart for producers to from 20 to 24 cents a quart for consumers.

The refrigerator car and modern methods of refrigeration have also depressed certain types of American farming, especially market gardening in the North. While refrigeration has stimulated production notably in California, Texas, and certain other areas, it has undermined market gardening in many portions of the northern United States. Garden products from warmer areas arrive in northern cities before production can begin in the colder sections of the country and take the "edge" off the market. Moreover, they glut the northern markets and often make it difficult for the market gardener to sell his products at any price.

In the years from 1921 to 1933, it veritably seemed as though the heavens had fallen in on the American farmer. As late as 1920 he was still enjoying an almost fabulous and unprecedented prosperity. A decade later he was in a condition that made his state back in the days of Populism seem almost opulent by comparison. Such a tremendous and sudden shift in destiny not only quickly absorbed the farmer's reserves from the past but shook his morale to its very foundations.

Statistical picture of the depression. The mortality list on the "morning after" 1920 is a long and sad one. In 1919 the gross farm income in the United States was nearly 17 billion dollars. By 1932 it had shrunk to $5,377,000,000. The share of farm income in the total national income dropped from 18.5 per cent to less than 10 per cent in the decade from 1919 to 1929. In June, 1932, the prices of farm products were only 52 per cent of their 1914 level, whereas the prices of the commodities the farmer had to buy were 10 per cent higher than they were in 1914. The farmer, therefore, could purchase with his farm products only about 47 per cent of what he could have bought in 1914. The per capita income of the American farming population, even in the general boom year of 1929, was only $273, as compared with $908 for the nonfarming groups.

On top of all this came a tremendous break in the value of farm property. Until 1920 farm real estate had held up at a high price in spite of temporary setbacks to farming prosperity. Therefore, a farmer who could no longer make what he believed to be an adequate living could at least sell out to some more optimistic person and live for a time on the proceeds. Even this escape was partially closed after 1921. The value of farm property in the United States dropped from 78 billion dollars in 1919 to 44 billion dollars in 1932. At the same time, the farm-mortgage indebtedness increased from $3,300,000,000 in 1910 to $7,900,-000,000 in 1920 and to $9,500,000,000 in 1931. In 1931 the interest on mortgage debts absorbed no less than 8 per cent of the gross farm income of the United States, compared to 3 per cent in the days before 1914. Paralleling this rise of mortgage indebtedness and interest charges went a comparable increase in taxes. In this same year, 1931, farm taxes equaled 11 per cent of the gross farm receipts, compared to 4 per cent in the period before 1914. So staggering were these charges on the farmer that in the five years prior to March 1, 1932, 9.5 per cent of the farms of the country passed out of the hands of their original owners through mortgage foreclosures and the like, and 3.5 per cent of American farms were sold because of failure to pay taxes.

These hard times naturally brought an increase in farm tenancy. In 1880 only 25.6 per cent of farm occupants were tenants. Over half of these were located in the South. From 1880 onward there was a steady increase in farm tenancy, with the most marked growth in the present century. Moreover, it spread from the South all over the country. In 1890 the tenants made up 28.4 per cent of the total farm occupants; in 1900, 35.3

per cent; in 1920, 38.1 per cent; and in 1930, 42.4 per cent. By 1930 tenancy was on the gain in some 41 states.

The most depressed group of tenant farmers are the southern share-croppers, a group of poor whites and Negroes who are virtually agricultural laborers paid in their produce rather than in cash. They are most numerous in Alabama, Arkansas, Louisiana, Mississippi, and parts of Texas. They were particularly hard hit by the depression of cotton prices and by mechanical inventions, such as the farm tractor. Along with the farming population forced out of the Dust Bowl area to become migratory workers, these sharecroppers constitute, perhaps, the most miserable and depressed group in American economic society. Their life and ways were immortalized in Erskine Caldwell's *Tobacco Road*.

American deserts on the march. Another serious blow to American agriculture was the almost annual recurrence of ever more serious droughts. General climatic conditions—perhaps climatic cycles—have something to do with this. Another important cause of agricultural tragedy has been the ruthless denudation of the American continent and the resulting soil erosion. Out of some 500 million acres of land which was once fit for cultivation, wind and water erosion have seriously damaged 300 million acres, with 100 million acres of this damaged land utterly ruined for cultivation. At the present rate of erosion there will be less than 150 million acres of fertile land in the year 2000. Not only have our forests been destroyed; millions of acres of grasslands have been transformed into marginal farming lands, with the result that both the newly cultivated grasslands and the adjoining older farming areas have been changed into near-deserts by great dust storms. The greed for grain during the First World War led to the plowing up of millions of acres of land on the eastern border of the Rocky Mountain highland. This had been covered with buffalo grass which held down the top soil. It was fine grazing land. Once the grass was removed and a drought came, the top soil was at the mercy of the winds. A great Dust Bowl was created in Oklahoma and adjacent regions from which the top soil was blown away, leaving this area a veritable desert and burying hundreds of thousands of acres to the eastward under the drifting dust. This is only the most conspicuous instance in our general movement toward creating a great American desert. Hundreds of thousands of unhappy and ruined farmers from the Dust Bowl area had to leave and seek a pittance elsewhere. Their tragic trek was graphically portrayed in John Steinbeck's *Grapes of Wrath*.

From a geographical and climatic point of view we have tended in the United States to live optimistically and complacently in a fool's paradise. We have taken it for granted that we inhabit a new and rich country which will forever remain fertile, outside of a few unimportant desert areas. We look with smug pity upon the great parched districts of the Old World. But if we understood history in any complete fashion, we would know that these dry and burning regions are the most cogent possible warning to us. There is not a great desert area of our day which has not been a fertile district within historic times. The Sahara, the desert areas of upper Mesopotamia (Sumeria), the Gobi desert in China were all of them moist and fertile at one time and supported large and hopeful populations. Now they are the most striking grave-yards of departed civilizations.

COURTESY FARM SECURITY ADMINISTRATION. PHOTO BY ROTHSTEIN

*A grim picture of poverty and desolation on a submarginal farm
ruined by erosion, drought, and dust.*

Although most of us do not realize it, the United States is not only moving on in the same course, but at a relatively dizzy pace. It took some of the great deserts of the Old World a thousand years or more to lose their fertility and dry up. If trends continue unchecked in this country for another hundred years, much of our country will be desert or semi-desert. Today the denudation is accomplished by much more effective instruments, such as our tractors, gang plows, sawmills, dynamite, and nitroglycerine. And we are dominated by a much more dynamic philoso-phy of wholehearted greed and exploitation than were the earlier historic peoples. Although this same modern technology might be turned about to work the opposite results in vast irrigation projects, exploitation rather than conservation has motivated our empire of machines. In his important book, *Deserts on the March*, Paul B. Sears has well sounded a note of warning:

Wherever we turn, to Asia, Europe, or Africa, we shall find the same story repeated with almost mechanical regularity. The net productiveness of the soil has been decreased. Fertility has been consumed and soil destroyed at a rate far in excess of the capacity of either man or nature to replace. The glorious achieve ments of civilization have been builded on borrowed capital to a scale un-dreamed of by the most extravagant of monarchs. And unlike the bonds which statesmen so blithely issue to—and against—their own people, an obligation has piled up which cannot be repudiated by the stroke of any man's pen...

The story on the older continents has been a matter of millennia. In North America it has not been a matter of more than three centuries at most—generally a matter of decades. Mechanical invention plus exuberant vitality have accomplished the conquest of a continent with unparalleled speed, but in doing so have broken the gentle grip wherein nature holds and controls the forces which serve when restrained, destroy when unleashed.[14]

Though we might still save from a great American desert enough good land to give us one-fifth of that now cultivated, which Willcox assures us will be all that we need, it would be a national calamity and disgrace to witness the rest of the country in a state of aridity and desolation.

RELIEF EFFORTS IN BEHALF OF FARMERS, AND THE NEW DEAL AGRICULTURAL MEASURES

Movements to secure Federal aid for farmers. The various farm organizations mentioned earlier worked hard to benefit their members, but the plight of the farmer became so desperate in the 1920's that the private organizations were unable to cope with the situation. Government aid was sought. Under the leadership of Senator Arthur Capper of Kansas, a farm bloc was organized in the Senate in 1921. Like the previous farmers' organizations, it urged the government to undertake a program of farm relief.

Many plans were set forth, most of them seeking to increase and stabilize the price of wheat, of which there was a large surplus production. The most widely discussed plan was that embodied in the McNary-Haugen bills, which were passed by Congress in 1927 and 1928, but were twice vetoed by President Coolidge. They advocated the export of surplus wheat at the world price. The losses sustained on wheat exported at the world price, because of the difference between the world and domestic prices, would be made up to the farmers through an equalization payment. The farmers would gain by this plan, since the great bulk of the wheat could be sold at the domestic price, protected by our tariff wall. The losses on the surplus exported at the world price would be relatively slight by comparison.

Another much discussed scheme was the Moline Plan, set forth by George Peek and Hugh S. Johnson. It proposed to create a financial corporation, supported by American farmers, which would buy up all surplus wheat and sell it at the world price plus 40 per cent, the latter being about equal to the tariff on wheat in the Fordney-McCumber Tariff Act of 1923. The farmers would be assessed through a sales tax to make up this 40 per cent addition to the world price. The advantage to American farmers would be that the domestic price of wheat could not be forced down to the level of the world price. Although these plans were not adopted, they demonstrated the widespread and well-organized interest in solving the farm problem.

---

[14] *Deserts on the March.* Norman: University of Oklahoma Press, 1935, pp. 9-11.

In 1929, a Federal Farm Board was established, with Alexander Legge as chairman. This board undertook the task of controlling the farm surplus and of stabilizing wheat and cotton prices; but it could not make much headway against the adverse trends of the depression years, and the farm situation went from bad to worse. About 350 million dollars were spent in a fruitless effort to stabilize prices, while farm surpluses piled up.

New Deal farm measures. The farm problem, one of the most pressing issues confronting President Roosevelt after his inauguration in 1933, was promptly faced by the new administration. On May 12, 1933, the Agricultural Adjustment Act (AAA) was passed. The government, by the Act, endeavored to control and reduce excess production of crops. It agreed to pay bounties to farmers who retired land from the cultivation of wheat and cotton. The revenue for these bounties was to be obtained chiefly from the manufacturers and the millers in the form of processing taxes. The AAA was declared unconstitutional by the Supreme Court in January, 1936, but government aid had at least temporarily increased farm income. Gross farm income grew from 5.3 billion dollars in 1932 to 8.5 billion in 1935. It is estimated that, under the AAA, cotton growers benefited by 780 million dollars, wheat farmers by 356 million, and hog producers by 320 million.

The basic policy of the short-lived AAA was revived, without the processing tax, in the Soil Conservation and Domestic Allotment Act of 1936, superseded by the second Agricultural Adjustment Act, passed in 1938. The latter Act also intended to keep up farm prices by restricting production. The 1938 law was upheld by the Supreme Court, and many farmers signed contracts with the government whereby they agreed to take certain land out of production and place other sections in soil-building crops. The government payments for crop control helped to provide the farmers with money for taxes and interest on mortgages. Government subsidies to farmers under the new act were actually higher than under the original AAA. In 1939, government payments to farmers were 807 million dollars, as compared with 573 million in 1935. In 1946, the government payments were still nearly as large as in 1939.

Although the New Deal farm legislation helped to solve the immediate farm crisis, it was fundamentally wrong, for it subsidized scarcity at a time when only about 10 per cent of the American families were getting what government experts regarded as a liberal or desirable diet, and when over half the population was ill-clothed and ill-shod. What the New Deal should have done was to stimulate urban production and employment and raise wages and salaries sufficiently to produce the mass purchasing power needed to enable the city workers and white-collar groups to buy the farm products needed to insure a high standard of living. This was not done, partly through lack of vision and initiative in the early days of the New Deal, and partly because of the resistance of conservative economic groups as they recovered more power after 1936.

The financial crisis in American agriculture brought forth a number of other acts designed to tide farmers over the emergency. The AAA had provided 2 billion dollars of government bonds for farm loans at

FACTS ABOUT THE FARM PROBLEM

	CASH FARM INCOME FROM CROPS AND LIVESTOCK	GOVERNMENT PAYMENTS
1930	●●●●●●●●● $ 8,883,000,000	NONE
1932	FARM POPULATION 1930 – 30,169,000 1948 – 27,440,000 ●●●●● $ 4,682,000,000	NONE
1933	◑●●●●● $ 5,278,000,000	◖ $131,000,000
1935	●●●●●●● $ 6,969,000,000	◖ $573,000,000
1937	◑●●●●●●●● $ 8,744,000,000	◖ $367,000,000
1939	◑●●●●●● $ 7,733,000,000	◗ $807,000,000
1948	◑●●●● ●●●●●●●●● ●●●●●●●●● ●●●●●●●●● $31,018,000,000	◖ $256,000,000

Each disc equals one billion dollars

COURTESY *The New York Times.*

This graph reveals amazing increase of gross farm cash income as a result of the Second World War and the cold war.

4 per cent interest. The Farm Credit Act (1933) centralized the credit agencies extending loans to farmers and set up banking facilities to handle the loans. The Farm Mortgage Refinancing Act (1934) created the Federal Farm Mortgage Corporation to supervise refinancing of farm mortgages and loans and to forestall foreclosures. The Crop Loan Act (1934) helped farmers to carry on their farming operations during the difficult season of 1934. The Farm Mortgage Foreclosure Act (1934)

enabled the Federal Farm Land Bank to extend loans to farmers to redeem the farms they had lost by foreclosure. The number of mortgaged farms was reduced from 40.1 per cent in 1930 to 38.8 per cent in 1940.

Superficial and contradictory character of much New Deal farm legislation. It is difficult to see how the farm problem can be solved by any of the methods which were proposed and tried under the New Deal. They were superficial both in fundamental conception and in detail. The American people have never been able to buy all the cereal products required for a liberal and decent diet. Even in the prosperous year of 1929 only 10 per cent of American families had income enough to purchase a liberal diet. While we have never since had any such complete study of American consumption as the Brookings Institution study on which the 1929 figures are based, it is probably true that the same general situation still prevails. The increased income of the American population has been largely offset by rising prices. Moreover, we have never produced food enough for the American people. R. R. Doane has shown that even in 1929, out of twelve major food items in the American diet, we had a production deficiency in eight. Despite this, the government attempted to restrict wheat and other forms of agricultural production.

Yet, if we had a sufficient redistribution of income to enable the masses to obtain a liberal diet, this would not solve the farm problem. Much of our wheat is now produced by the extremely inefficient methods followed by marginal farmers. If we applied the most efficient technique to all the land now under cultivation we would produce a wheat crop which would completely swamp the nation, even with a high level of mass purchasing power. If, to avoid this, we combined the greater efficiency with a restriction of the area cultivated, it would mean the ousting of far more than half of the present farmers and farm laborers.

What has been said about the crisis in cereal production applies also to cotton farming. The American people have never had all the cotton clothing really needed. Yet we could produce far more than the masses could readily use, whatever the increase in their purchasing power in a sound and prosperous rural economy.

Moreover, there were contradictions and paradoxes of detail in the farm relief measures. While the Federal Farm Board was urging crop restriction after 1929, the Department of Agriculture and its subordinate organizations were teaching the people how to grow bigger and better crops. The AAA aimed at crop restriction and the retirement of land, while the CCC and other reclamation projects sought to bring more land into a condition where it could be effectively cultivated.

Farmers still depressed at end of New Deal. Although there is little doubt that the New Deal farm measures at least temporarily benefited the farming class, irrespective of whether the program was sound or not, it is also certain that the New Deal failed conspicuously to solve the farm problem in the United States. This may plainly be seen from a few representative facts about the state of farm life and the farm economy in 1940, at the end of the New Deal and before armament and war had worked a temporary revolution in farm production and income for the better class of farms and farmers.

In 1940, there were about 6,100,000 farms, of which at least a million were submarginal and barely able to provide subsistence for their operators. There were about two million small, family farms, not well equipped or very productive, which provided no more than a "living" for the operators. The remaining half of the farms produced 90 per cent of all the farm products to reach a market. Clearly the poorest half of the farms produced only a microscopic income per farm in the form of revenue from products marketed. About 39 per cent of the farms of 1940 were operated by tenants.

The figures for farm income in 1940 are equally instructive and dolorous. The total farm income from one-fourth of the nation's farms was less than $400 each. The income from nearly an additional fourth of the farms was less than $750 each. Farm families received only 7.8 per cent of the total national income, although some 22.9 per cent of the people lived on farms. The farmer's share of the consumer's dollar spent for staple foods in 1940 was only 42 cents, whereas it had been 53 cents in 1913. At least one-third of all the farms in 1940 were so small, poorly equipped, or lacking in fertility that the operators could not be fully employed throughout the year in their farm work.

TEMPORARY EFFECT OF THE SECOND WORLD WAR ON AMERICAN FARMING

Temporary farm gains produced by Second World War and relief programs. The New Deal measures did not bring full employment or prosperity to either American manufacturing industry or American agriculture. It remained for the Second World War and postwar conditions to provide such results, at least temporarily. The demand for food for our armies and workers, and for those of our allies, during the war, quickly wiped out the farm surpluses of the previous two decades and provided a market for everything the farmer could raise. Various circumstances, especially demand for farm products for foreign relief and the parity system which guaranteed high farm prices, actually increased farm prosperity for several years after the close of the war.

Statistical picture of revived farming prosperity. Somewhat more crop land was brought under cultivation during the war years and immediately thereafter. For some 52 main farm crops the acreage harvested increased from 321 million in 1940 to 351 million in 1948. The total crop yield increased even more notably. For all crops the gain was from an index of 110 for 1940 to 138 in 1948. The total cash receipts for all farm products, exclusive of government payments, rose from 9.1 billion dollars in 1940 to 31 billion dollars in 1948. The average value, per farm, of all farm products, both those sold and used at home, rose from $1,309 in 1940 to $3,148 in 1945, and $4,350 in 1950. Farm income continued to gain steadily from the close of the war through the year 1948. Net farm income increased from 13 billion dollars in 1945 to 18.3 billion dollars in 1948.

Gross farm income rose from 25.4 billion dollars in 1945 to 35.2 billion dollars in 1948. It was approximately 30 billion in 1950.

The marked rise in farm prices was more responsible for this astonishing increase of farm income than the gains in acreage and production. The price index of food grains rose from 84 in 1940 to 250 in 1948; of

FARM PRICES THROUGH TWO WARS

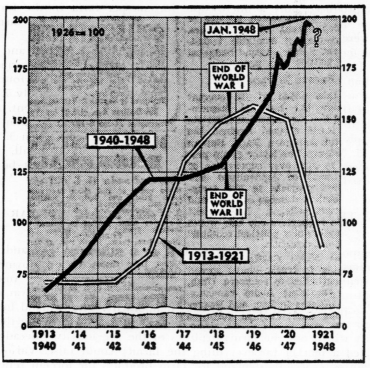

COURTESY *The New York Times.*

feed grains and hay from 82 in 1940 to 249 in 1948; of meat from 111 in 1940 to 361 in 1948; of dairy products from 119 in 1940 to 297 in 1948; and of cotton from 77 in 1940 to 270 in 1948. For all farm products, including livestock, the price index rose from 100 in 1940 to 301 at the beginning of 1948.

Other statistics further reveal the temporary improvement of the economic state of American farmers during the 1940's. The value of all farm property increased from 41.2 billion dollars in 1940 to 87.7 billion dollars in 1948 and 91 billion in 1950. The average net property of the American farmer in 1950 was estimated to be $17,000. The total farm indebtedness fell from 8.3 billion dollars in 1940 to 7 billion dollars in 1947. The total farm mortgage debt fell from 6.6 billion dollars in

1940 to 4.9 billion dollars in 1948. The number of mortgaged farms was reduced from 38.8 per cent in 1940 to 29.2 per cent in 1945.

The spectacular gains in farm income were, of course, offset in part by increased farm costs. Although the prices of farm products rose in spectacular fashion, so did the prices of everything the farmer had to buy. The food, clothing, machinery, fertilizer, and cattle food that the farmer had to purchase rose in cost approximately in proportion to the prices of what the farmer had to sell. The wages which the farmer had to pay to farm labor also jumped to unprecedented heights. In 1940, the average daily wage of farm hands, exclusive of board, was $1.59; in 1946 it had risen to $4.74, and in 1948 to $5.30. Monthly farm wages, exclusive of board, rose from $36 in 1940 to $117 in 1948. The total cash expenditures of farmers increased from 6.4 billion dollars in 1940 to 18.2 billion dollars in 1948.

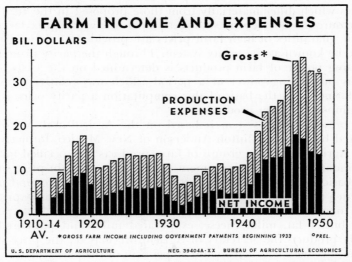

FROM *U. S. Statistical Abstract, 1950.*

Gross farm income and net income and production expenses of farm operators: 1910-1950.

In this way, much of the impressive apparent improvement of the farmer's economic situation, as a result of increased production and sales and much higher prices, was absorbed in higher costs of operation and living. Nevertheless, on the whole, the farmer's condition was more prosperous and secure, for the moment, than that of the urban wage-earner who also received much higher wages than in 1940. This was due to the fact that most farmers were relatively free from rent costs and many other expenses imposed on the urban dweller. In short, the farmer's living expenses were normally less than those of city workers.

In addition to large purchases of farm products by the more completely employed and higher paid industrial workers and white-collar employees and for relief abroad, the high income of the farmers after 1945 was also maintained by an elaborate and rather lavish farm price support program, the nature of which we shall explain.

Although the mass of farmers enjoyed relative prosperity in the postwar years, nothing of the sort existed for the millions of sharecroppers and farm laborers, especially the migratory workers. Many of these groups faced stark destitution like that of the 1930's. In March, 1950, about 100 children were found starving in a farm labor camp in Arizona and this was not an isolated instance. These destitute farm laborers and share-croppers were overlooked in the concern with relief measures for the distressed abroad. The efforts of the National Farm Labor Union (not to be confused with the Farmers' Union) were not adequate to the task of giving the necessary aid to these poverty-stricken rural dwellers.

The parity system and farm price support. Since the Second World War the farmers have been able to keep up farm prices through government measures which differ materially from those proposed in the 1920's. The new measures do not depend so directly upon the world price levels. Full domestic guaranties of high farm prices are provided. This program has come to be known as the parity system. Through the parity principle the purchasing power of farm products is determined on the basis of their previous purchasing power at a period which was relatively favorable to the farmers. On the basis of this computation a parity price is found for all important farm products.

The present parity system is based on the Agricultural Act of 1949, sponsored by Senator Clinton Anderson of New Mexico, formerly Secretary of Agriculture. Two groups of farm products are specified for which it is mandatory that the government specify and maintain price support: (1) six basic commodities—corn, cotton, wheat, rice, tobacco, and peanuts —on which the support level is fixed at 90 per cent of the parity price; and (2) ten non-basic commodities—wool, tung nuts, honey, Irish potatoes, butter, butter fat, milk, cheese, evaporated milk, and powdered milk. On milk products the Secretary of Agriculture may set the price support levels at anywhere between 75 and 90 per cent of the parity price; and, on the other of these ten products, anywhere between 60 and 90 per cent. Further, the Secretary of Agriculture may, at his discretion, establish support prices for virtually any type of agricultural product, up to 90 per cent of parity prices. In the summer of 1950, support prices were being paid on all mandatory farm products and on five discretionary products.

The government system of price support under this plan operates in two ways: (1) crop loans to farmers in which case the government holds the crop as collateral until such time, if ever, that it can be sold on a favorable market; and (2) outright government purchases of farm products to maintain the general price level of any farm product. The Commodity Credit Corporation is the government agency which handles these operations. To keep the system under control, the government maintains acreage allotments and marketing quotas. The former limits the number of acres which a farmer can plant to a given crop. If the farmer exceeds this limit, he becomes ineligible for price supports. The marketing

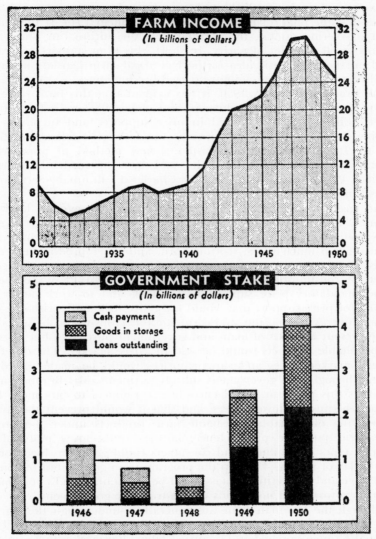

COURTESY *The New York Times.* FACTORS IN THE FARM PRICE DEBATE.

The upper panel shows the trend of farmers' cash income. The lower panel shows how much the Federal Government has invested in the farm program in the form of (1) payments to farmers under the Conservation Program and the Sugar Act, (2) crops in storage, and (3) loans outstanding. The first category represents an outright expenditure. The second and third figures are cumulative and represent the Government's stake in the price support program at the end of the fiscal year (or on March 31 in the case of 1950). They do not mean that the Government has lost that much money. If farm prices fall, the net loss to the Government could be heavy, but if prices rise the Government can avoid loss on stored commodities.

quotas may only be applied to the six basic farm products—the main reason that the potato situation got out of hand in 1949. If the farmers reject marketing quotas, the Secretary of Agriculture can lower price support to 50 per cent of parity. In short, this farm support program is based on the same basic idea as the New Deal farm legislation, that is, to help farmers by encouraging restricted production.

The Brannan Plan. By 1950, it was evident that this farm price support program was breaking down. The Commodity Credit Corporation had 4.7 billion dollars invested in price supports, and surpluses were growing. In spite of this, farm income was falling (it fell about 27 per cent in 1949). This crisis suggested a new method of approach to maintaining agricultural prosperity and brought forth the so-called Brannan Plan, proposed in 1949 by Charles F. Brannan, Secretary of Agriculture.

The basic conception of the Brannan Plan is to expand food consumption and, presumably, agricultural production, and to diversify farm production more rationally. It is assumed that farmers have been producing too much wheat, cotton, corn, and other products especially needed in wartime, and not enough of the crops better adapted to peacetime consumption requirements. The Brannan Plan proposes to extend mandatory price support to livestock and to work out a new formula for price support that would favor livestock and perishable farm products over wheat, cotton, and corn. Storable crops would be supported by the present methods of loans and government purchases, but livestock and perishable products would be sold in a free market. The difference between market prices and support prices would be made up to the farmers through cash government subsidy payments. Mr. Brannan maintains that this program would encourage consumers to buy more farm products because of lower prices, and that it would prevent the rotting and wasting of valuable perishable farm products under the present government purchase plan. Hence, farmers could grow more of the desirable types of products, and consumers could get more food for the same outlay of money. To keep the program from getting out of control, the acreage and marketing quotas would be maintained and noncooperating farmers would get no subsidy checks from the government.

Although the Brannan Plan was generally sounder than the Agricultural Act of 1949, the American Farm Bureau Federation and the National Grange opposed it. Organized labor, however, rather generally supported the Plan on the ground that it would mean lower food prices for city populations. Of the main farmers' organizations, only the National Farmers' Union supported the Brannan Plan. The Democrat losses in the Congressional election of 1950 made it likely that the Brannan Plan would at least be temporarily shelved.

Why there was no depression in American farming after the Second World War. We noted earlier that after the First World War, there was a rapid and serious decline of farming prosperity which lasted for virtually twenty years, though mitigated somewhat from 1933 to 1940. After the Second World War a decline did not come at once, mainly because of the great demand for goods to meet current needs, delayed wartime orders, rearmament, and foreign rehabilitation, which kept city workers employed and able to buy food in large quantities, and because of the shipment of large quantities of food abroad for relief. What are the prospects of continuing this set of favorable conditions for the farmers in the future?

The Marshall Plan, or the European Recovery Program, as it is now known, is in operation under the Economic Co-operation Administration, and is expected to continue in one form or another for years. This is believed to mean that large quantities of American farm products may continue to be sent abroad. Since the demand for manufactured products is still ahead of the supply, city workers can be expected to go on buying farm products in large quantities for some time to come. We now have in operation a plan of government support for farm products— the parity—which, as we have seen, guarantees minimum prices each year and will make up the difference to farmers in the event that actual prices fall below this minimum. This encourages farmers to keep up a large production, for they do not have to fear any immediate probability that the bottom will fall out of farm prices.

Temporary and precarious nature of present farm prosperity. These conditions and circumstances would appear to assure farm prosperity for some years, but there are limits and dangers. The more completely the foreign nations recover, the less will be their demands for American food and the greater their ability to produce their own, as was the case after 1920. The economic recovery program has now been transformed from relief to armament, which will call for less food products, though this may be in part offset by increased food shipments to famished foreign countries like India. What a generation of great peacetime armies or a third world war would produce is unpredictable.

The parity and price support program seemed to be falling apart at the seams as we entered the second half of the century. By the summer of 1950, the government had 4.7 billion dollars tied up in its price support program. But cash farm income fell off from $31,332,000,000 in 1948 to $28,100,000,000 in 1949, and net farm income from 18 billion to 15 billion. A drop of another 2 billion was predicted for 1950. The old problem of agricultural surpluses, which had plagued the Coolidge, Hoover, and New Deal administrations, returned once more. For example, early in 1950 the government had on its hands 25 million bushels of potatoes, purchased at $1.10 a bushel, which it was selling back to the farmers at three-fifths of a cent a bushel for cattle feed or fertilizer— though there were still millions of Americans who could not get enough potatoes to eat.

In the summer of 1950, the Commodity Credit Corporation had 516,250,000 bushels of wheat and corn stored up—enough to fill a freight train reaching halfway around the world; some 3,600,000 bales of cotton, or enough to make 90 million bedsheets; 88 million pounds of dried eggs— all that the bakers of the country would need for eight years; 99 million pounds of butter; 316 million pounds of dried milk; and a large supply of cheese, soybeans, tobacco, dried fruit and peas, cottonseed meal, and similar items. The situation was reminiscent of New Deal days when wheat and cotton were being plowed under while the country was ill-fed and ill-clothed. The trends and figures for 1949 and the first half of 1950 seemed to indicate that the first big break in postwar "prosperity" might come in agriculture.

In the event of an impending recession, it is proposed by farm leaders that the farm economy be protected by government subsidy of greater food consumption by American citizens; and by the establishment of a new sort of AAA which will pay the farmer for reduced production of crops. It is rather obvious that, even if such measures can be provided, they will be mainly temporizing rather than any permanent solution of our farm problem.

Farm income sharply increased by Korean war and armament program. By May, 1950, it seemed that there might be a break in farm income with the crisis in the parity system, and that the farmers might at last be

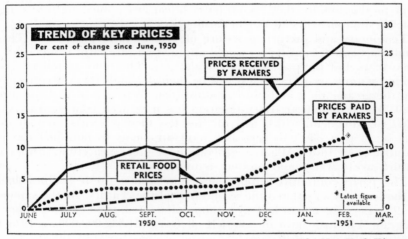

COURTESY *The New York Times.*

headed towards a postwar depression. But when the United States intervened in Korea to lead the United Nations movement, there was a sharp change for the better in the outlook for the economic status of the farmers. Employment of city workers increased to take care of the vast armament program and thus revived the demand for more farm products. More food was needed for American soldiers in Korea and the training camps, and for relief in Korea and India. Farm prices felt the impact of rising prices generally as inflation proceeded, and they rose no less than 27 per cent between June, 1950, and April, 1951. The average gross income of American farmers in 1950 was $4,350, and the net income was $2,225, as compared with a net income of $350 in 1900 and $960 in 1925.

Basic reforms essential to permanent rural prosperity. The great problem of the farmer in the postwar period is to keep his present larger market and high prices. So long as full industrial employment in cities, large shipments of food abroad for relief, and a great rearmament program continue, it appears likely that the farmer may hold his own. In short, the farmer's prosperity is tied up to the same general abnormal and necessarily temporary conditions that give prosperity to the urban workers and provide a powerful but passing "shot in the arm" to an otherwise wobbly capitalism.

A farm program to maintain rural prosperity. Anticipating the time when the abnormal conditions of the Second World War and its aftermath, which have proved a momentary blessing to American farmers, will come to an end, the leading farm organizations have formulated the following policies and objectives, designed to assure some measure of prosperity and security for farmers in the years to come:

1. Maintaining abundant or adequate production of food and fiber products.
2. Securing an equitable share of the national income for farmers.
3. Conserving and building up our soil resources.
4. Improving the coordination of the Federal agencies that work with farm people.
5. Improving and modernizing the parity formula.
6. Using price supports and production control.
7. Improving facilities for rural development, including health, education, nutrition, and recreation.
8. Improving marketing, processing, and distribution of farm products.

Farmers embrace the welfare state. Amid all this uncertainty as to the future of farm conditions, one certainty exists: that the former vigorous individualism of the American farmer and his opposition to government interference in business and to government aid to individuals are now dead, apparently forever. No group in American society today is more insistent upon government aid than the farmers. This was well demonstrated not only by the ardent farmer support of the New Deal, but also by the fact that it was the farmer vote that helped to defeat Mr. Dewey and to elect President Truman in November, 1948.

LARGE FARMS AS A SOLUTION OF THE RURAL PROBLEM

Large collective farms under government supervision. Many students of rural economics believe that the only solution of our farm problem, in many areas, is the large collective farm; that is, government ownership or control of lands, buildings, and equipment, and the cultivation of the land by families under a cooperative organization with a government contract. This has worked successfully in some government projects in New Mexico. The advocates of the collective farm contend that, if we hold to the old American tradition of exclusive private farm ownership, the improvements in technology will make the agricultural class ever more dependent on the government for sheer relief and farm subsidies, without gaining the advantages that the large collective farm promises in the way of greater mechanical efficiency, larger production, a higher standard of living, and greater security for the cultivators of the soil. This collective farm program is a drastic plan, and if tried, should be sharply scrutinized.

Trend toward larger farms. While as yet there has been only a very slight development of large collective farms under government control, there has been a very marked tendency towards much larger farms. Between 1910 and 1945, the farms of 1,000 acres or more increased in number from 50,135 to 112,899, and the acreage in these larger farms increased from 167 million acres to 460 million; by 1945, these farms contained over 40 per cent of all farming land.[15] At the other end of the scale, the number of farms between 20 and 260 acres decreased by 694,781 between 1910 and 1940. The largest one-third of our farms produce about four-fifths of all our farm products for the market. In 1945, the largest 8.7 per cent of the farms produced 45.5 per cent of the gross value of all farm production. These farms have only 12.2 per cent of the total farm population. The concentration of farming units is even more impressive than such statistics suggest, for great farming corporations have leased and united many small farms in actual operation, though they are still listed in the census as separate, small farms.

Social and cultural disadvantages of large-scale farming. This tendency toward the growth of very large farms has usually been hailed as a great advance and an important step toward the solution of our farm problem. Such an attitude has been based on the consideration that large farms permit the most complete utilization of advanced types of farm machinery and, hence, are more efficient. But this appraisal leaves aside the matter of the effect of such large-scale, mechanized farming on the personal and social side of the picture. Studies have been made of large-scale and small-scale farming areas, under comparable conditions, and these indicate that personal independence and dignity, public utilities, and social services are far superior in the small-farm districts. The large farms are more efficient in sheer production, in terms of manpower units, but they tend to reduce the social aspects of the process to the status of servility and neglect. There is a danger that these large corporate farms may develop into great mechanized *latifundia*.

The Bureau of Agricultural Economics recently made a study of a large-scale farming area and a small-farm district in the San Joaquin Valley in California, the former known as Arvin and the latter as Dinuba. General agricultural conditions and population make-up were virtually the same in the two areas. But personal relations, local business, and social services were far superior in Dinuba. The latter had two banks, Arvin none. It had two newspapers to one in Arvin. Its streets were paved, those in Arvin were not. Its housing facilities were far superior to those in Arvin. It had a high school and four grammar schools to one grammar school in Arvin. Its service and social clubs were far more numerous and active. There were more recreational facilities and there was far less juvenile delinquency. There were more retail business establishments,

---

[15] A considerable portion of the 460 million acres in these large farms was ranch and pasture land.

		ARVIN (LARGE FARMS)	DINUBA (SMALL FARMS)
	POPULATION	6,300	7,800
	TRIBUTARY TRADE AREA (APPROX.)	70,000 ACRES	77,000 ACRES
	BANKS	NONE	TWO
	NEWSPAPERS	ONE	TWO (one vigorous, a real force in the community)
	ALL BUSINESS ESTABLISHMENTS	60	156
	SCHOOLS	ONE GRAMMAR SCHOOL (no high school)	Four grammar schools (one high school)
	LOCAL GOVERNMENT	COUNTY ONLY	Incorporated, elects own local officials
	SERVICE AND COMMERCIAL CLUBS	TWO	FIVE
	FRATERNAL AND WOMEN'S CLUBS	NONE	SEVEN
	VETERANS' ASSOCIATIONS	NONE	TWO
	CHURCHES	SIX (only three are adequately housed)	Fourteen (mostly substantial and in good condition)
	HOUSING	Very poor; houses badly crowded on small lots; very few brick or other permanent buildings	Modest but generally adequate; most houses on lots of 50x120 ft.; lawns, trees, etc
	YOUTH AND JUVENILE DELINQUENCY	Fairly serious, few recreational opportunities	Almost nonexistent; numerous recreational facilities

PICTOGRAPH CORPORATION FOR PUBLIC AFFAIRS COMMITTEE, INC.

A comparison of the communities of Arvin and Dinuba.

doing an amount of business about double that in Arvin. Only five out of ten of the inhabitants of Dinuba worked for wages, while eight of ten of those who lived in Arvin did so. In short, as Carey McWilliams puts it, "Dinuba was a real farming community while Arvin was more of a camp than a community." Few who lived in Arvin contemplated identifying their lives with any permanent habitation or career in the region.

Such comparisons need not be taken as any blanket condemnation of large-scale farming, which certainly could be so conducted as to combine technical efficiency with a well socialized community life, but they do show that the situation involves something more than merely the matter of expensive mechanical equipment and high crop output. In the light of these facts, it is both instructive and ominous that in January, 1949, the United States Department of Agriculture issued a report indicating that the future economic outlook for the million small farms in the nation that produce only from $500 to $1,000 worth of products annually, at the high prices of 1949, is highly dubious, even in the current period of temporary rural prosperity.

Probably the best solution of the farm problem is to obtain the increased efficiency which the latest mechanization on large farms makes possible, and then to insure a parallel development of community spirit and facilities by systematic community organization service supplied, if necessary, by the Federal government. Such a solution would be more in harmony with American traditions and temper than collectivized farms under government ownership or control.[16]

The farm laborers displaced by increased mechanization could very properly be employed on public works and in the service industries which we shall require if a condition of security, abundance and leisure, which would constitute true civilization, is ever attained in this country.

CURRENT RURAL SOCIAL PROBLEMS

Rural population trends today. We touched on the population situation in rural areas in the chapter devoted to population trends. There we made it clear that the total rural birth rate is higher than the urban, and the rural farm birth rate continues to be higher than that in any other segment of the population. Yet, due to adverse economic conditions and other causes, the rural farm population is dwindling not only relatively but absolutely. The relative proportion of the population of the United States living on farms has declined strikingly in the last forty years. In 1910, out of a total population of about 92,000,000, there were some 32,000,000 in the rural farm population. In 1950, out of a total population of 150,700,000, the rural farm population stood at only 26,200,000. Though the total population of the country grew by 18.7 per cent in the decade of the 1940's and the rural population as a whole grew by 7.4 per cent, there was an actual loss in the rural farm population. It declined from 30,200,000 in 1940 to 26,200,000 in 1950.

---

[16] On rural community planning, see Earl Hatch, *Rebuilding Rural America*. New York: Harper, 1950.

This produces a curious and paradoxical situation in present rural population trends: the total rural farm population is declining, and yet the rural farm birth rate is the highest in the country and many farm families are far too large to be supported on a decent standard of living. This is to be explained by several factors: the vast improvements in rural technology have reduced the demand for farm labor, the surplus has sought employment in cities, and the highest rural birth rate is among the marginal farm families that have insufficient income to provide a good living for large families. The problem can be solved only by introducing birth control methods among marginal farmers. There is little prospect of improving their economic well-being.

This means that the rural population problem today involves population quality as well as quantity. Many of the marginal farm parents are below the average in physical quality and intelligence. This consideration has been especially stressed by Fritts and Gwinn in their book, *Fifth Avenue to Farm*.[17] They have called attention to the fact that the best types from the country have been drained off to the cities. Hence, they allege that the current population increase in country areas is being brought about by the least capable and promising of the rural groups. At the same time, the superior persons of rural origin who have gone to the cities have failed to reproduce as rapidly as the rural groups. Although this menace to population quality may be exaggerated, there is no doubt that the situation described is essentially true.

Rural health. The health situation in rural areas has been definitely improved in the last quarter of a century. This has been due to the improved training of doctors and to advances in communication and transportation which make it easier to summon and receive medical aid. This is offset by the reluctance of well-trained young doctors to settle in rural communities and by the scarcity of good hospitals in country areas. A detrimental trend in the realm of rural medicine today is the increasing temptation to dangerous self-medication as an outgrowth of radio buncombe.

As matters stand, there is slightly more disease in the country today than in the city, when per capita comparisons are made. But, as we have noted, this is partly due to the fact that the age groups which are most free from disease, namely those between 16 and 35, are those which leave the country to migrate to the city. As we have already pointed out in the chapter on health, the country is really healthier than the city and the chances of survival to a relatively old age are decidedly greater in rural regions. By comparison with the city, the country makes an especially good showing with respect to mental and nervous diseases.

Increase and transformation of rural criminality. There is a greater degree of criminality per capita in cities than in country districts. But rural crime is distinctly on the increase. There are a number of fairly obvious reasons for this. The social controls and disciplinary agencies of the older rural life are rapidly disintegrating. No adequate substitutes

---

17 New York: Harper, 1938.

for these have as yet appeared. City contacts are increasing, and the psychological factors that stimulate crime in urban centers are beginning to operate in country regions. Crime news in the press, crime movies and crime radio programs, which may stimulate delinquency, are as available to the farming population as to city dwellers. The rural criminal, because of his greater personal courage and resourcefulness, is likely to be a more dangerous criminal than the city offender—at least in forms of criminal activity outside the realm of organized crime and racketeering. Courtney Ryley Cooper has pointed out that many of the leading gunmen have come from rural districts.

The public enemies of the last five years, for instance, with very few exceptions, came from the village, the small town, or the "typically American city." With the exception of Alvin Karpis and a half-dozen others, they were of supposedly clear American stock. Many of them had been reared in an atmosphere supposedly the best of all—that of the little community, and even of the farm.[18]

Because of the unsettling effects of the Second World War, increased prosperity among farmers, and the impact of urban influences on rural regions, there has been a marked increase in rural criminality. This increase has been most evident in crimes against property, whereas in previous years rural crimes had been mainly crimes of violence against persons. The rural crime rate is still lower than the urban, but since 1945 it has increased more rapidly than the urban.

Declining rural puritanism. The old puritanical morality of the country areas has been undermined of late. So far as commercialized vice in rural areas is concerned, it is probable that there are fewer prostitutes in rural villages than was the case a generation back. But it is much easier to make contact with urban prostitution by automobile transportation. The automobile has probably done more to stimulate increased freedom of sex relations in rural regions than has any other institution or device since the termination of colonial bundling. The close scrutiny formerly exerted over rural youth is no longer possible in the days of motor touring. The movies and the increase of drinking among the youth of both sexes have contributed to this increased laxity of sex relations in rural regions.

It may also be pointed out that, while this is a special case, it is undoubtedly true that the worst vice and immorality known anywhere in the United States is to be found in the more backward and semi-abandoned farm areas. Here we frequently run upon the most appalling degeneracy, including complicated forms of incest and widespread illegitimacy. In due time a more sane and healthy type of moral code than the older narrow-minded puritanism may be worked out in country regions, but at the present we find a definite trend toward moral laxity and vulgarity. The combination of greater accessibility to urban vice, clinging vestiges of rural puritanism, and inferior rural medical care are in part responsible for the fact that the highest venereal disease rate

---

[18] C. R. Cooper, *Here's to Crime*. Boston: Little, Brown, 1937, p. 382. See also S. H. Holbrook, *Murder out Yonder*. New York: Macmillan, 1941.

today is frequently found in rural regions. Venereal disease is also prevalent because country folk are ashamed to consult the local doctor, and fear local gossip if they do. Ignorance is an important factor, too, in many instances.

THE FUTURE OF COUNTRY LIFE

General outlook for American farming. In the following chapter we shall see that the city has come to a turning-point in its development.[19] Either the city will continue to grow until it collapses as a result of congestion or atom bombing, or there will be a marked trend toward breaking up large cities into suburban areas and small "Greenbelt" communities.

COURTESY J. C. ALLEN & SON.

This typical, prosperous Indiana farm in the era of good times following Pearl Harbor reveals the charming setting of rural life for well-to-do farmers.

The rural community is in fully as critical a stage today as are the urban centers. Farm life, as it existed fifty years ago, is seemingly doomed. The day of the small farm is coming to an end in many areas. There is every reason to believe that more and more cereal and cotton farming will be carried on in the future by large-scale operations, using the newest and most efficient machinery. Outside of cereal and cotton farming, the trend is likely to be toward specialized agriculture, such as fruit raising, vegetable growing, and dairy farming. These cannot be mechanized as completely as cereal farming. We have already dealt with the economic situation of American farming and indicated the measures and policies essential to insuring farm prosperity in the future.

---

[19] D. E. Lindstrom, *American Rural Life.* New York: Ronald Press, 1948, Chaps. 19-20.

Rural life takes on a new pattern. Although the long-range outlook for many farmers is dark, there is little possibility that the rural areas will be abandoned in wholesale fashion. On the contrary, there seems to be a marked trend of population movement from the city to the country. Henry Ford once started a system of small industries—model small plants located in country areas—which he hoped would make possible an ideal combination of manufacturing and rural life. Their success proved the wisdom and practicality of such a program. Improvements in transportation will probably cause an ever greater migration of urban workers to rural regions bordering on urban centers. Even today, many thousands of workers live in the country and daily commute to the city.

Movement from city to country. The movement from the city to the country has already begun. The rural farm population declined by about 1.9 million between 1910 and 1930. But, during that same period, the rural population not engaged in farming increased by 5.9 million. Some of this latter gain came from births within that segment of the former farm population that had abandoned farming but still remained in the country; most of it, however, came from the migration of former urban dwellers to the country. After the depression began in 1929, the movement to the country was even more rapid. In 1932, the rural population gained over a million and, in this year, exceeded the city population growth by over 500,000. This was the first time in recent American history that cities had suffered a relative loss in population.

After economic conditions improved in 1933, some of those who had migrated to the country returned to the city. But it is evident that the rural non-farming population is already making steady gains and that this trend is likely to increase as time goes on. The rural farm population has ceased to grow and has begun to decline. It was 30,157,513 in 1930, 30,216,188 in 1940, and 26,200,000 in 1950. On the other hand, the rural non-farm population increased from 23,662,710 in 1930 to 27,029,385 in 1940, and 31,092,000 in 1950. Moreover, the counties containing or adjacent to cities increased more rapidly than any other section of the country. As a result of the abnormal conditions during the Second World War, the American farm population shrank by over 4 million between 1940 and 1950, but current tendencies indicate that the non-farming rural population will continue to increase. It more than held its own in the period from 1940 to 1950 in contrast to the shrinkage in the rural farm population. By 1950 the rural non-farm population had become larger than the rural farm population; in that year the rural non-farm population constituted 20.6 per cent of the total population, and the rural farm population only 17.3 per cent.

This movement to the country and suburbs by thousands who remain employed in cities, and commute back and forth, may have important social and cultural results for the nation. The urban centralization and the contact of cities with rural conditions may produce a mixed urban-rural type of life and culture, combining the good (or the bad) features of both. The stabilizing trends in rural life may be united with the greater tolerance and breadth of interests characteristic of city life. The possible benefits from this trend have been clearly stated by Landis:

The nation's future is unpredictable, but if present trends continue urban patterns may be expected to continue to dominate. It is possible, however, that the future trend may be towards a balance between metropolitan urbanism and progressive ruralism; it is possible that the rural life of tomorrow, by combining the better elements of the folk culture of rural society with the selected phases of urban culture, may achieve a level of human adjustment that has been unparalleled in either rural or urban cultures of the past.[20]

Of course, there may be unfortunate results from urbanization in bringing certain pathological aspects of city life out into the country, but even these are likely to be less flagrant in a rural environment. One ominous symptom indicating that the urbanization of country mores may produce bad results has been the great increase in rural crimes, especially crimes against property, since the Second World War.

THE OUTLOOK FOR COUNTRY YOUTH

Farm youth and the "American Dream." For no rural group has the farm crisis been more serious than for youth.[21] The great "American Dream" has usually revolved around the country boy who has made good. The Horatio Alger and Rover Boys stories, which have become part of the folklore of America, often depicted the country boy, born of poor but honest parents, who went to the city and fought his way to the top, ultimately becoming President of the United States, a captain of industry, an urban banker, or something of the sort. Many of the more notable achievements in our national history were actually those of rural youth who went to the cities, bringing with them the energy, ambition, and natural ingenuity taught by rural life, the initiative and independence characteristic of the country, and the strong physique gained by living in healthful surroundings. The youths remaining in the country bought farms, and although, with few exceptions, they did not become wealthy, they acquired economic stability and personal independence. These persons built up and carried on the sturdy farm character that had made our farming population the backbone of the nation.

In former days, and even down through the First World War, young people born on a farm had a fairly promising future in prospect. The more venturesome and alert often went to the city, found positions, and established themselves in business or the professions. Those who did not go to the city could set themselves up in some form of village industry or retail trade, or become owners of farms and able to support themselves and their families on a decent standard of living.

---

[20] Landis, *op. cit.,* p. 4. See also D. E. Lindstrom, *American Rural Life.* New York: Ronald Press, 1948, pp. 163 ff.

[21] Landis, *op. cit.,* Chap. 23.

Bleak outlook for many rural youth. What are the prospects of farm youth today? The outlook is not too bright. With rural life losing its distinctive characteristics, the long-range outlook for rural youth is one of economic instability and relative cultural decay in many rural areas. We have already noted that the highest birth rate takes place among families on the marginal and small farms that are not able even now to maintain a decent standard of living. During the decade from 1930 to 1940, farm families received less than 10 per cent of the national income, but had to shoulder the task of educating 30 per cent of the nation's children.

Farms are getting larger and, therefore, are becoming fewer in number. In 1930, the average size of farms was 157 acres; by 1940, it was 174 acres, and concentration has gone on even more rapidly since 1940. All this means that there will be a smaller number of farms available for young men to take over as owners and operators. In the coming generation there will be about three boys born and reared on farms for each farm left open for occupation as a result of the death or retirement of the owner.

The cities, in normal times, have a large number of unemployed persons who must go on relief or work on government projects. It has, therefore become increasingly difficult for country youth to find work in the city. Small-scale village industry is often unable to compete with efficient large-scale production. The automobile has taken much of the trade from the country store. Rural dwellers now do much of their shopping in city stores, where there is a greater volume and variety of goods and usually lower prices. Mail-order firms like Montgomery Ward and Sears, Roebuck have also helped to undermine the small town and village establishments. These companies also have large local retail stores in many American cities.

Attempts to aid rural youth. The country areas have improved their educational facilities, but they are still backward by comparison with those of the city. Even the marked improvement in rural education is of little practical use if farm youths cannot secure jobs after they have been trained for them. Although rural facilities for recreation and leisure time have been increased, the provisions are still far less adequate than in urban areas.

The government set up a number of programs designed to help rural youth. The United States Department of Agriculture, working through the state colleges of agriculture, has promoted 4-H Clubs designed to teach young people better farming methods, home economics, new ideas of community life, and better types of recreation. Many high schools have received Federal grants for courses in agriculture and home economics, and the Office of Education has contributed radio programs and public forums. The now abandoned National Youth Administration, organized chiefly for youth on relief, aided those who could not attend school without financial assistance, provided special courses in agricultural schools for farm boys and girls, supplied work projects for unemployed youth, and offered some guidance in choosing a job and finding employment. The Farm Credit Administration has provided financial aid to young farmers who want to get a start in agriculture. Whatever farm aid came as a result of the various agricultural acts of the New Deal has, directly or indirectly, helped rural youth. The United States Employment Service helps young people in the country as well as in the city to secure jobs.

Despite these many and varied government programs and agencies to help rural youth, no proposal has yet been launched which in any way copes with the seriousness of the situation. The most thorough study ever made of the problem, *Rural Youth; Their Situation and Prospects,* conducted by the Works Progress Administration at the close of the New Deal period, declared that: "A concerted frontal attack has yet to be made on the long-time factors responsible for the widespread destitution and restricted social opportunities of rural youth." Concentration on war and on rearmament after the war have prevented, and apparently indefinitely postponed, any such "frontal attack."

War temporarily alters the picture. The coming of war in 1941 improved the picture to a certain degree. Many farm youths joined the armed services; others found profitable employment in the booming war industries. The great increase in the demand for farm products, coupled with the drafting of farm boys and the migration of many rural youth to war-industry centers, temporarily created an actual shortage of farm labor. This temporary improvement in the prospects of rural youth does not, however, alter the bleak general prospect for the future.

To be sure, the large demand for farm products could be sustained in part if we were to adopt, before foreign relief and armament aid falls off, such means of assuring steady employment and high wages for urban workers as a large Federal housing program, extensive highway construction and other public-works projects, adequate Federal support for recreational and other service facilities, Federal aid to public education, national health, and the like, but there seems no probability that such steps will be taken, at least to the extent needed to produce substantial results. In President Truman's "welfare" national budget of 1950 only six per cent of Federal expenditures was allotted to such purposes.

Even the generally improved conditions during the war decade did not increase the well-being of children born on the marginal and small farms, except insofar as rural youths from such areas secured employment in cities. The same will be true if rearmament and conscription continue indefinitely after 1951. Unless the fundamental reforms in American agriculture summarized in earlier pages are executed, there is no prospect of any permanent improvement in the opportunities and living standards of American rural youth, least of all for those on marginal and small farms where the rural birth rate remains highest.

SUMMARY

During the thousands of years from a period antedating the so-called dawn of history to the middle of the nineteenth century, human life and culture were predominantly rural. Human nature was conditioned chiefly by rural living and institutions. The gradual submergence of rural culture during the last hundred years has been, perhaps, the chief cultural revolution in human experience.

American society was overwhelmingly rural in its traits until 1900. It was based on the traditional personal and primary groups—a cohesive patriarchal family; a cooperative and closely knit neighborhood life; a powerful rural church, which was as important in social as in religious life; inadequate educational facilities; popularity of fraternal organizations to meet the craving for ritual, mystery and pageantry; and a local government structure adjusted to the limited transport and communication facilities of a primitive rural economy.

From a socio-psychological point of view, rural life was characterized by mental isolation and conservatism, belief in magic, superstitions of nature, fatalism, strong individualism, and personal self-reliance. There was little interest in art. The rural delinquency rate was low, but most rural crimes were serious. They were chiefly crimes of violence.

To promote better rural living conditions and income, the farmers have brought into being some notable farm organizations—the Patrons of Husbandry, or Grange; The Farmers' Alliance; the Farmers' Union; The American Farm Bureau Federation; and the National Council of Farm Co-operatives. Farm cooperatives represent the most promising type of contemporary rural organization and economic experimentation. There is no strong organization to aid farm laborers, and the farmers are far less thoroughly organized than in industrial labor.

Rural depressions and the exploitation of farmers have induced the more depressed farmers to form radical third-party organizations, such as the Greenback, Granger, and Populist parties. Later, these farmers supported Bryan Democracy, the Progressive party, and the Farmer-Labor party. Today, most farmers are politically opportunist and support the party which promises the most in the way of farm aid. The strong individualism and anti-statism of earlier rural life is fast fading away.

The technological revolution since 1900, including mechanization, better transportation facilities, improved rural communication agencies, and electrification, has profoundly changed the material basis of rural life. The marginal farmer who cannot provide himself with the most efficient mechanical equipment is apparently doomed to failure.

Technological changes have produced an equal transformation of rural institutions and mentality. The rural primary groups are disintegrating, rural mental isolation is being wiped out, and farming areas are being urbanized in their tastes and demands. Rural life has been made more pleasant for the prosperous farmers, but it is becoming ever less distinctive.

American farming suffered a severe depression in the 1920's. New Deal farm relief measures were helpful but inadequate. Only war, foreign relief, and government price supports for farm products sufficed to restore at least temporary prosperity for the bulk of American farmers. But the marginal farmers, sharecroppers, and much of farm labor has continued to be depressed. The price-support program is now in a critical condition, and farm income dropped off rather sharply until late in 1950. Farm prosperity may be seriously threatened unless stimulated by the continuance of war preparations or actual war.

Basic economic reforms are essential to assure permanent rural prosperity. The most promising trend now is the increasing development of large mechanized farms. But, along with these, we shall need a comparable development of rural community organization to assure decent living standards and supply consumer needs.

The rural farm population is declining rather rapidly, but the rural non-farm population is growing. The outlook for more and better country life is promising, whatever the future destiny of the farm population itself.

For the time being, the prospects of rural youth are bleak, indeed, as American agriculture faces a future of increasing mechanization, reduced opportunities for new farmers, and a decreasing need for farm labor.

SELECTED REFERENCES

*Baker, O. E., Borsodi, Ralph, and Wilson, M. L., *Agriculture and Modern Life*. New York: Harper, 1939. An appreciative discussion of the place of the farm and rural life in contemporary American civilization.

Blumenthal, Earl, *Small Town Stuff*. Chicago: University of Chicago Press, 1932. Good sociological study of the small rural town.

Breckling, G. J., *The Brief Year*. New York: Westminster Press, 1951. A novel providing a colorful reconstruction of life in a rural town prior to the First World War.

Chang, Pei-kang, *Agriculture and Industrialization*. Cambridge: Harvard University Press, 1949. Summary and analysis of sociological theories as to the effects of industrialization of agricultural countries.

Cole, W. E., and Crow, H. P., *Recent Trends in Rural Planning*. New York: Prentice-Hall, 1937. Valuable for impact of New Deal philosophy on rural life.

Gee, Wilson, *Social Economics of Agriculture*. New York: Macmillan, 1942. Important analysis of economic aspects of American rural life.

Gras, N. S. B., *A History of Agriculture in Europe and America*. New York: Crofts, 1925. The best brief survey of the history of agriculture and the agrarian economy.

Hawthorn, H. B., *The Sociology of Rural Life*. New York: Century, 1926. A substantial and sane manual on rural social life before the New Deal era.

Haynes, F. E., *Third Party Movement*. Iowa City: Iowa Historical Society, 1916. The standard book on the radical political movements of the last century which were backed chiefly by farmers.

*Hibbard, Benjamin, *Agricultural Economics*. New York: McGraw-Hill, 1948. An unusually readable and penetrating analysis of rural economic life and resulting social patterns.

Hicks, Granville, *The Small Town*. New York: Macmillan, 1946. A brilliant and very readable analysis of the cultural character and social problems of the rural town.

Holmes, R. H., *Rural Sociology*. New York: McGraw-Hill, 1932. Good textbook stressing the primary institutions and personal society of rural life.

Kolb, J. H., and Brunner, E. deS., *A Study of Rural Society: Its Organization and Changes.* Boston: Houghton Mifflin, 1940. Excellent analysis of rural social patterns and the changes wrought by technological advances.

*Landis, P. H., *Rural Life in Process.* New York: McGraw-Hill, 1948. Authoritative and very readable treatise, with emphasis on social forces in rural life.

*Lindstrom, D. E., *American Rural Life.* New York: Ronald Press, 1948. Remarkably clear and interesting survey of rural life and society at the mid-century.

Loomis, C. P., and Beagle, J. A., *Rural Social Systems.* New York: Prentice-Hall, 1949. Voluminous statistical description and comprehensive analysis of the structure and functions of rural society.

McDonald, Angus, *Old McDonald Had a Farm.* Boston: Houghton Mifflin, 1942. Inspiring and absorbing account of how toil, intelligence, and persistence turned a run-down Oklahoma farm into a model and profitable homestead.

*McWilliams, Carey, *Ill Fares the Land.* Boston: Little, Brown, 1942. Able and thoughtful description of the farm problems created by drought, the mechanical revolution. and marginal farming.

Nelson, Lowry, *Rural Sociology.* New York: American Book Company, 1948. Brings the resources of sociological theory to bear on the analysis of rural society and social problems.

*Rawson, M. N., *Forever the Farm.* New York: Dutton, 1948. Based on New England materials, this book gives perhaps the best impression of what farm life was like before the rise of modern machinery and transportation.

*Sanderson, Dwight, *The Rural Community.* Boston: Ginn, 1932. A study of contemporary rural life by a leading rural sociologist, who stresses the continuing importance of the rural village as a social community.

*————, *Rural Sociology and Rural Social Organization.* New York: Wiley, 1942. Comprehensive treatment of rural social life by the dean of American rural sociologists.

Schafer, Joseph, *Social History of American Agriculture.* New York: Macmillan, 1936. Best general historical account of evolution of American rural society.

Sims, N. L., *Elements of Rural Sociology.* New York: Crowell, 1940. One of the best introductory studies of rural life and institutions.

Smart, C. A., *R.F.D.* New York: Norton, 1938. An interesting analysis of rural life, laying special stress on the way farm life promotes originality and ingenuity in meeting practical problems.

*Smith, T. L., *The Sociology of Rural Life.* New York: Harper, 1946. One of the ablest presentations of the leading social processes involved in rural life.

Sorokin, P. A., and Galpin, C. J., *A Systematic Sourcebook in Rural Sociology* (3 vols.). Minneapolis: University of Minnesota Press, 1930-1932. Elaborate collection of materials on rural life and rural social processes.

Taylor, C. C., Raper, A. F., *et al., Rural Life in the United States.* New York: Knopf, 1949. Excellent recent description of rural life in the main farming areas of the United States.

Williams, J. M., *Our Rural Heritage.* New York: Knopf, 1925.

————, *The Expansion of Rural Life.* New York: Knopf, 1926. Two thoughtful books on rural sociology, notable for their socio-psychological approach to rural life and problems.

Woofter, T. J., and Winston, Ellen, *Seven Lean Years.* Chapel Hill: University of North Carolina Press, 1939. An able analysis of the distressed farmers under the New Deal and convincing evidence of the inadequacy of New Deal measures in solving the problems of the marginal farmers.

CHAPTER 10

Leading Problems of Urban Life

THE NATURE AND GROWTH OF MODERN CITIES

Modern cities set a new pattern of civilization. Having now surveyed the leading traits and social patterns of rural life, we may now turn to living conditions and social processes in urban life. The latter really represent a new stage and a different pattern of human civilization. At several places in this book, we make it clear that contemporary, industrialized urban life, by undermining or displacing the rural primary groups that had created and shaped human personality and character for many thousands of years, constitutes one of the most sweeping social revolutions in the history of civilized mankind. This fact has been well described and emphasized by Louis J. Wirth:

City and country are not merely distinct types of physical entities; they are also contrasting modes of life. Life on the farm or in rural areas is relatively stable and simple compared with life in the city. Rural life is close to nature, relatively isolated, uncomplicated by an advanced technology, and self-sufficient. The rural community involves few people and these few are much alike in their origins, their occupations, and their ways of living. Rural life rests upon intimate associations. It is held together by rumor, gossip, personal controls, and a common culture.

City life on the other hand is carried on remote from nature in a highly complex man-made technological environment. The city is interdependent and in close contact with the outside world. It gives rise to a great division of labor. The urban community consists of great numbers of heterogeneous persons both as to origins, occupations, and ways of living. Although densely crowded together, people in the city do not rely upon intimate associations with all of those who live near them to carry on an orderly life. The inhabitants of a city are held together by news and publicity, by formal laws, and by impersonal controls. In contrast with life in the country, urban life is characterized by complexity, instability, and indirect interrelations.[1]

The contemporary city as a social and cultural entity. Among the numerous institutional and cultural developments of modern times, it is probable that the larger industrial and commercial cities of our day are the most novel and complex product of social evolution. They are a highly complicated social, economic, political, legal, cultural, and psychological

---

[1] L. J. Wirth and Ray Lussenhop, *Urban and Rural Living*. Washington: National Education Association, 1944, p. 7.

phenomenon which has never appeared before in the experience of mankind. This fact has been well pointed out by the late Frederic C. Howe, an expert on urban problems and urban evolution, in a passage which is far more impressively true today than in 1915 when it was written:

> The twentieth-century city bears but slight resemblance to the city of the past. It is no longer a place of refuge, of protection from attack. It has lost the cohesion of the family and the clan. No single religion unites the citizens; no legalized caste divides the free from the slave, the master from the apprentice. It is no longer sovereign as it was in Italy and Germany. It has become an integral part of the state. Its life, too, is no longer local, it has become international. Every corner of the world contributes to its population, as does every race and creed. The steamship and the railroad have made the city a clearing-house; they have brought New York and Pekin into closer commercial relations than were the neighboring communities of England two centuries ago. The power of the hand operative has been multiplied into many horse-power by steam and electricity, while the division of labor has increased the productive capacity of the individual a thousandfold. The industrial city is a new force in the world.[2]

The modern city is a social and cultural innovation not only because of its relation to new industrial and commercial achievements in recent times. It is also a novelty because of its complex character as a social unit. This has been emphasized by William Bennett Munro:

> The modern city is an endlessly complicated phenomenon. It is sometimes defined as "a large body of people living in a relatively small area"; but this definition is altogether inadequate. It conveys no intimation of the fact that the city has a peculiar social structure, a specialized governmental organization, a unique legal status and a highly intricate economic life. A comprehensive definition of the modern city must indicate that it is a social, political, legal and economic unit all rolled into one. It is a concentrated body of population possessing some significant social characteristics, chartered as a municipal corporation, having its own system of local government, carrying on multifarious economic enterprises and pursuing an elaborate program of social adjustment and amelioration. . . .
> The city has more wealth than the country, more skill, more erudition within its bounds, more initiative, more philanthropy, more science, more divorces, more aliens, more births and deaths, more accidents, more rich, more poor, more wise men and more fools.[3]

Number and nature of ancient and medieval cities. Cities are not, of course, exclusively a phenomenon of contemporary times. There were important cities in the ancient and medieval periods. But modern cities differ from previous urban centers in size, number, and character. City life figured more prominently in the civilizations of the ancient Near Orient and classical times than it did in the medieval period, at least outside of Muslim areas. The commercial cities of the ancient Orient— Babylon, Sidon, Tyre, Gaza, Damascus, Aleppo, and Susa, for example— were relatively numerous and important, though far and away the greater

---

[2] *The Modern City and Its Problems.* New York: Scribner's, 1915, pp. 47-48.
[3] From *The Encyclopaedia of the Social Sciences*, Vol. III, pp. 478-479. By permission of The Macmillan Company, publishers.

part of the population of all ancient kingdoms lived in the country and engaged in agricultural and pastoral activities. Greek and Roman civilization had an important urban basis. Indeed, it was Rome which gave a predominantly urban cast to the society and culture of the ancient world. Gaining control over the urban communities of the ancient East, Rome built her empire on the basis of municipal life and administration.

ROTHENBURG-ON-THE-TAUBER

Rothenburg, Germany: A fortified town of the Middle Ages. This picture of one of the best preserved cities of the Middle Ages shows the small and restricted character of most cities prior to the era of industrialization.

One of the main reasons for the decline of the Roman Empire was the undermining and impoverishment of municipal life. But, when compared with the situation in the industrialized countries of today, the cities of antiquity and the Middle Ages were relatively few and small. It is probable that only Alexandria, Baghdad, Constantinople, and Cordova reached the million mark in population. There are many authorities who doubt that even these cities had a million dwellers within their confines.

Ancient and medieval cities could not be very large, by modern standards, because of defects in transportation. Before steam transport was introduced, it was difficult to bring together enough food and other supplies to support a great population concentrated in one area. Moreover, most of the relatively large cities of antiquity and the medieval period were scattered over a considerable area. They were like a series of small cities joined together mainly as a political unit. They were, to use a modern technical term, "polynucleated" cities. They were not concentrated, as in the modern industrial metropolis. In the medieval period there were very few cities with a population of 100,000 during the Middle Ages. The largest were located in the Eastern, or Byzantine, Empire, and in Muslim areas.

The larger ancient and medieval cities usually owed their origin and growth mainly to geographical and political advantages. They were located in positions that were easy to defend. Or they attained their dominant position through political ascendancy. The latter not infrequently grew out of the fact that their superior strategic position enabled them to extend their conquests and thus increase their political power. Commercial contacts and advantages were also present in many cases. The cities of Babylonia, Syria, and Greece frequently owed their large population and their prosperity to commercial activity. Cultural factors also served to attract inhabitants, as in the case of Athens, Alexandria, Paris in the Middle Ages, and the Italian cities of the Renaissance.

In early modern times, some of the important historic cities, such as London, Paris, Berlin, Vienna, Madrid, St. Petersburg, and Washington, also gained in numbers and prestige as the result of their political predominance. But the cities of recent times depend far less upon an easily defended location or political primacy. As Munro points out, not one of the ten largest cities in the world today owes its position to the possession of a defensible location and only three of them are political capitals. The great cities of today, as well as most of the lesser cities, owe their primacy chiefly to modern industry and trade.

Origins of the urban, industrial era in civilization. We may now consider some of the outstanding facts with regard to the actual increase of urbanization in modern and contemporary times. It will be illuminating to start off with a few representative figures with respect to the population of important European cities on the eve of modern times.

In the fifteenth century Paris was far and away the largest city in western Europe. It had a population of about 300,000. London had a population of only 40,000, and no other English city had as many as 15,000 inhabitants. Such famous German cities as Nüremberg and Cologne had only slightly more than 20,000 inhabitants, and a great commercial and banking center like Frankfurt did not have even 10,000 permanent inhabitants. The most highly urbanized area in Europe at this time was Flanders, but even its main cities, Bruges, Ghent, and Ypres, had only between 50,000 and 75,000 inhabitants. Berlin at this time was an unimportant town, with only a few thousand dwellers. In 1709 when the city was merged with three other neighboring towns, the total population of the newly amalgamated Berlin was only 57,000. Outside of Flanders, the overwhelming majority of the population of Europe was found in rural areas or in villages with less than 500 inhabitants.

The first notable stimulus to urban growth came as the result of the expansion of Europe and the Commercial Revolution after the discovery of sea routes to America and India about 1500. By 1800 London was the largest city in the Western world, with 864,000 inhabitants. Paris had a population of 547,000, and Berlin 172,000. Vienna at the time of the famous Congress of 1815 had a population of about 240,000. The population of New York City in 1800 was 79,000. Despite this striking growth of some of the larger cities between 1500 and 1800, urbanization was by no means general outside of Flanders. In 1801 there were only 15 cities in England with a population of over 20,000. Their total population amounted to only 1.5 million.

The metropolitan era. The main era of urbanization followed on the heels of the agricultural and industrial revolutions which began in the eighteenth century. The great metropolises of the world became far larger. According to the latest estimates, the population of Greater London is 8,350,000; that of Paris (Greater Paris) 6,658,000; Berlin, 4,332,000; and Vienna 1,930,000. On the eve of the First World War the population of

COURTESY FAIRCHILD AERIAL SURVEYS.

An Aerial View of Modern New York City.

Vienna was 2,150,000, but it fell off considerably as the result of the disastrous effects of the war upon both Austria and Vienna. The latest estimate for the population of Greater New York is 7,835,000. If New York City were as inclusive of adjoining cities as is Greater London, thereby taking in the large cities of New Jersey across the Hudson River and Westchester centers, the population would be four million greater than that of metropolitan London.

Not only have the metropolises of the world grown in size, but urbanization has also increased enormously within each country. For example, as early as 1891 there were 185 English cities with a population of over 20,000, their aggregate population amounting to more than 15.5 million.

The following table will indicate the rapid and impressive urbanization of the Western world since the Industrial Revolution was well established.

PERCENTAGE OF THE TOTAL POPULATION LIVING IN
URBAN AREAS, WESTERN WORLD [4]

Year	United States	England and Wales	France	Germany
1800	6.0	20.0	....	....
1850	15.4	50.2	25.5	....
1860	19.7	54.6	28.9	....
1870	25.7	61.8	31.1	36.1
1880	28.6	67.9	34.8	41.4
1890	35.4	72.0	37.4	47.0
1900	40.0	77.0	40.9	·54.3
1910	45.8	78.1	44.2	60.0
1920	51.4	79.3	46.3	64.4
1930	56.2	80.0 (1931)	49.1	67.1 (1933)

[4] Adapted from W. S. Thompson, *Population Problems*. New York: McGraw-Hill, 1935, p. 274.

The latest available statistics give the urban population of the United States in 1950 as 59.0 per cent; that of England and Wales in 1930 as 80 per cent; that of France in 1936 as 52.4 per cent; and that of Germany in 1939 as 69.9 per cent. It is an impressive fact that, of the 93.5 million increase in population in Europe and the Soviet Union between 1919 and 1939, 80 million went into urban population.

Growth of the urban population in the United States. In 1790, the United States did not have one city with 50,000 inhabitants; today, we have 231 such cities, five of them with over a million inhabitants, though it was not until 1880 that we had even one city with a population of a million. In 1800, about 6 per cent of our inhabitants lived in cities; in 1950 about 85 per cent lived in cities or so close to cities that their life pattern was primarily urban. We had not one metropolitan district in 1800; by 1950, we had 168 of them, and in them lived some 84 million persons out of a total of 150 million. Perhaps the most striking fact about our urbanization is that we have today 260 times as many urban dwellers as in 1800 and less than 15 times as many rural inhabitants.

The unusual economic conditions produced by the Second World War reversed the trend in the 1930's and greatly accelerated urban growth. This was due mainly to the erection or expansion of great war plants within urban boundaries and the flocking of war workers to such centers of employment. When computed on the basis of census methods of 1940 and before, the urban population of the United States grew by some 13,946,298, or 18.7 per cent, as compared to 14.3 per cent for the whole population and 7.4 per cent for the rural population. If computed according to the 1950 census practice of including the densely settled areas around urban fringes, the urban population grew by 21,469,298 in the 1940's. By the 1940 method of computation, the urban population con-

Year	Total Population	Urban Population		Increase in Per Cent Urban during Preceding Period	
		Number	Per Cent of Total	Absolute Increase	Percentage Increase
1790	3,929,214	201,655	5.1	...	...
1800	5,308,483	322,371	6.1	1.0	19.6
1810	7,239,881	525,459	7.3	1.2	19.7
1820	9,638,453	693,255	7.2	−0.1	−1.4
1830	12,866,020	1,127,247	8.8	1.6	22.2
1840	17,069,453	1,845,055	10.8	2.0	22.7
1850	23,191,876	3,543,716	15.3	4.5	41.7
1860	31,443,321	6,216,518	19.8	4.5	29.4
1870	38,558,371	9,902,361	25.7	5.9	29.8
1880	50,155,783	14,129,735	28.2	2.5	9.7
1890	62,947,714	22,106,265	35.1	6.9	24.5
1900	75,994,575	30,159,921	39.7	4.6	13.1
1910	91,972,266	41,998,932	45.7	6.0	15.1
1920	105,710,620	54,157,973	51.2	5.5	12.0
1930	122,775,046	68,954,823	56.2	5.0	9.8
1940	131,669,275	74,423,702	56.5	0.3	0.5
1950	150,697,361	88,370,000	59.0	2.5	18.7

stituted 59 per cent of the total in 1950, while by 1950 reckoning it made up no less than 64 per cent. Some four-fifths of the total national population increase during the 1940's took place in the 168 standard metro-

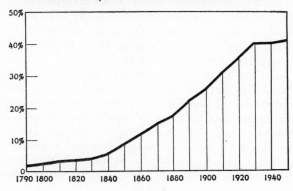

PERCENT OF TOTAL POPULATION IN CITIES 25,000 AND OVER SINCE 1790

politan districts of the country. The number of cities with a population of over 25,000 grew from 397 in 1940 to 477 in 1950; those over 100,000 from 92 to 106.

Urban growth would now seem to be on the increase, but this is taking place mainly in suburban areas. In the 1940's the central cities in the 168 metropolitan districts grew by only 5,652,000—13.0 per cent, while the outlying urban districts grew by 9,000,000—34.7 per cent. The table and graph on page 395 present the essential facts on the urbanization of the United States since 1790.[5]

Agricultural improvements promote an urban age. The causes of the impressive urbanization of society in modern and contemporary times are numerous and complex, but they all gravitate about the outstanding economic changes since the seventeenth century. Specifically, new developments in agriculture, industry, transportation, and the resulting growth of trade have produced the large, modern cities.

It has been very generally understood that rapid urbanization has been closely related to the Industrial Revolution and the rise of machines and the factory. But the very significant contributions of the agricultural revolution to urban growth have frequently been overlooked. It was the increasing efficiency of farming which made it possible for cities to become larger and more numerous after industrial changes had supplied the vital stimulus to urban growth. It would not be inaccurate to say that machines and factories made the industrial city necessary, while improved agriculture, transportation, and trade have made it possible for large cities to exist in unprecedented numbers.

Agricultural improvements made it possible to produce a far greater amount of food than ever before. Enough food could be grown by a limited portion of the population to support a large nonagricultural group concentrated in urban areas. Further, as farming became more efficient, the number of farmers needed to produce food became less, and more farmers' sons and daughters were free to seek employment in the cities. It has been predicted that, with the relative decrease in the size of the rural population, cities will not be recruited so markedly from country areas in the future. But it seems likely that this process of migration from country to city is bound to go on for a considerable time. Agricultural efficiency is likely to increase more rapidly than the rural population will fall off in numbers. As we promote mechanized efficiency in farming, we shall continue to free a large rural group which can go to the cities, if there is any employment to be found for new recruits in urban areas. In other words, the country is likely to be able to go on replenishing the cities, if there is any economic need for such replenishment. The probability is, however, that technological unemployment in the cities will increase as rapidly as the mechanization of farms and will augment the large army of excess laborers who are already in cities. We shall probably need a great expansion of service industries and public-works enterprises to absorb the surplus labor of both country and city areas unless we continue to keep a large sector of our manpower under arms.

The rôle of the Industrial Revolution and steam power in creating urban civilization and population concentration. The rise of the empire of machines and the factory system, as basic products of the Industrial Revolution, has constituted the main stimulus to urban growth since the middle of the eighteenth century. The gilds were usually located in towns

---

[5] *Postwar Problems of Migration.* New York: Milbank Memorial Fund, 1947, p. 162.

during the Middle Ages, but there were not enough gildsmen to create large urban populations. The putting-out system, which followed upon the heels of the gilds in many countries, was located, in large part, in the country areas. Machines made the factory system necessary because they could not be set up conveniently in the homes of workers. Factories required the concentration of a working population in the nearby neighborhood, especially in days when working hours were long and transportation facilities crude and meager.

Another very important reason for the congregation of the population near factories was that the main power relied upon in those days was steam, which had to be applied to machinery right on the spot where it was generated. Workers could not then be scattered about in small units, as they may be today since the rise of the electric age. Steam power was, thus, the primary factor in promoting massed urban growth in modern times. It not only made necessary the concentration of workers near factory sites, but it also made it possible to transport food and raw materials from distant parts of the country or from foreign lands. Of all the many influences which brought about the tremendous concentration of working populations in urban regions, steam power should probably be assigned first rank.

Machines and steam power created the first factories, but then cumulative factors contributed to ever greater urban congestion. Factories that were successful tended to grow ever larger. Since steam power continued to be the main form of energy employed, additions to plant facilities were made right adjacent to the earlier buildings. The larger the plant, the greater the number of people who had to live near it in order to work in it. Satellite industries also tended to collect around the larger factories, thus adding their plants, workmen, and workmen's homes. So the congestion of factory towns rolled up like a snowball.

The problems of business administration also helped to promote urban congestion. At first the offices of factory owners and managers were located in the factories themselves. This brought still more persons to live in the factory neighborhood. For various logical reasons, these newly located administrative offices tended to group themselves together in the same building or in buildings situated in the same section of the town. Before the days of the telephone, it was relatively necessary to keep administrative subordinates and clerks personally accessible and under immediate supervision. This produced an ever greater congestion of the white-collar element in city populations. Wholesale and retail merchants also congregated in the same general sections of the city, thus bringing about a congested population among those who dominated the process of distribution. The professional classes serving both industrialists and laborers, such as lawyers, doctors, engineers, and teachers, also naturally flocked to the new urban centers.

In the earlier urban period, when these tendencies were first manifested, construction methods in office buildings produced a certain limitation upon the possibilities of extreme congestion. Office buildings could not be very high, and hence the area which they occupied was fairly extensive. But improvements in steel and reinforced concrete construction, especially in the twentieth century, have made possible a degree of urban congestion hitherto undreamed of. They created the epoch of the sky-scraper. Improved methods of city and suburban transportation all but removed any limitations from urban population growth and its characteristic congestion. More numerous railroads, faster train service, and bigger and better ships made it possible to bring an ever larger supply of food and raw materials from all parts of the earth to metropolitan centers.

In this way there grew up the monstrous urban leviathans of our era. They were not only far larger than the cities of antiquity, but they were highly concentrated within a given area. They became what are called mononucleated cities, in contrast to the scattered and diffuse, or polynucleated, urban settlements of antiquity and of the Far East today.

We shall consider later the future of the great industrial and commercial centers of our era. Suffice it to say at this point that the earlier economic and social reasons for very large cities and extreme urban concentration no longer exist since the rise of electricity and improved methods of communication by means of the telephone, the telegraph, and teletype systems. The main forces perpetuating and encouraging our absurd current urban congestion are the vested interests of real estate owners and investors and the profit motive, encouraged and administered by real estate promoters. Most of these have an interest in stimulating urban congestion. Under normal conditions the more congested the area, the higher the price of real estate holdings. Of course, there is a counter-influence in the ambitions of those real estate speculators who are engaged in promoting suburban developments. Certainly, the trend of enlightened opinion today emphasizes the logic and convenience of urban decentralization.

Lewis Mumford's panorama of urban evolution. We are indebted to Lewis Mumford for a very suggestive prospectus of the evolution of cities.[6] He correlates definite urban types or stages with the social and cultural conditions which produced them and which were fostered by them. His theory of urban evolution represents a valuable sociological contribution to our conception of the stages of urban growth. This may well serve as a very appropriate summary of our discussion of urban origins and development.

The first type or stage of urban society recognized by Mumford is what he designates *eopolis*. This is the village community which arose in Neolithic times. It was based upon a pastoral and agricultural economy of a simple sort, but with a surplus production which provided security and continuity. Permanent dwellings were constructed and a rudimentary type of village planning was worked out. The village social organization was based upon blood relationships and community association. This agricultural village community was the germ or prototype of the true city which appeared later.

---

[6] *The Culture of Cities.* New York: Harcourt, Brace, 1938, pp. 285 ff.

The second stage or type of urban development was the *polis,* represented by the first oriental city-states and early Greek and medieval village communities. The *polis* had a citadel suitable for defense, a common shrine or temple for the worship of the local deities, and a market place for the exchange of products and ideas. While the *polis* was usually associated with a rural economy, we find here the beginnings of mechanization in water mills, metal working, wheeled vehicles, and paved roads. The social division of labor was further developed, giving the urban elite free time and energy for the cultivation of philosophy and art. Special buildings, such as temples, stadiums, theaters, gild halls, cathedrals, and schools, were constructed to house these new cultural activities. But the traditions and social customs of a rural age still dominated the mentality of town dwellers.

Third in order came the *metropolis.* This type of large urban community arose when some one city, as a result of strategic location, better natural resources, and superior trading facilities, attracted an unusually large number of inhabitants. This enabled it to assume a predominant position in the region or in the country as a whole. Mechanization of life was carried still further. The division of labor multiplied. Manufacture and trade finally supplanted agriculture as the dominant factor in economic life. In order to assure an adequate food supply, foreign trade was elaborately developed. These trading contacts, together with the immigration of foreigners, produced a cross-fertilization of cultures. New habits and ideas were introduced. Greater wealth and leisure stimulated the development of philosophy and art.

It was in these vigorous urban centers, such as the Athens of Plato, the Florence of Dante, the London of Shakespeare, and the Boston of Emerson, that human culture attained its very finest expressions. Yet, even as early as the metropolitan stage we find symptoms of urban decay. The various cultural elements are not adequately integrated, a selfish individualism springs up, war is professionalized, and a fatal gulf develops between the wealthy class and the workers. The metropolis soon comes to be dominated by the rich and by the ideals entertained by this class.

The fourth stage of urban development is what Mumford describes as *megalopolis.* Here we come even more definitely upon evidences of social pathology and urban decline. The city is dominated by the financial and business elements. Mere bigness and power become the ends most sought in urban development and city life. The lust for power and wealth crowds out the finer human sentiments. Mechanization is carried on to new extremes. Bureaucratic government is established. Standardization dominates life, even in culture and the arts. Scholarship descends to sterile compilation and statistical research. Education is devoted primarily to encyclopedic instruction, and knowledge is divorced from the realities of life. The workers are exploited by the wealthy classes, and the class struggle between the *bourgeoisie* and the proletariat becomes sharper and more comprehensive. Representative examples of this megalopolitan stage of urban development have been Alexandria in the third century B.C.; Rome in the second century after Christ; Constantinople in the tenth century; Paris in the eighteenth century; and London, New York, and some other large American cities today.

The megalopolis degenerates into the *tyrannopolis*. This is represented by Rome in the later Empire, and it is a type into which most large contemporary cities are already entering. Here the whole urban economy becomes essentially parasitical. Both economics and politics are carried on primarily for the purpose of exploitation. The politicians build up a coalition with organized criminals. Hence, the tyrannopolis is dominated by "respectable people who behave like criminals and by criminals whose activities do not bar them from respectability." This is the age of organized racketeering and commercialized crime. Political idealism is replaced by cynicism and loss of nerve. The predatory mentality spreads even beyond the boundaries of the state and leads to imperialistic wars and the excessive drain of great armament programs. Dictators, with all the characteristics of local gangsters, take over the control of entire states. Intellectual and artistic independence is repressed and censorship grows more usual and vigorous. All original work in the arts and sciences ceases.

Finally we come to the sixth and last stage, that of urban collapse, or the period of the *nekropolis*. In this terminal stage of urban evolution the cities are laid waste by war, famine, and disease. The cities themselves become little more than empty shells, the graveyards of ancient glories and the centers of contemporary degradation. The buildings fall into ruins, stores are looted, and the economy collapses. Foreign invaders may come in to wipe out what remains, or the process may be brought to an end by dry rot from within. In the nekropolitan era we find "the city of the dead: flesh turned to ashes; life turned into a meaningless pillar of salt."

Although Mr. Mumford does not contend that cities must inevitably pass through all of these stages, he shows that we have had examples of every one of them in the past, even including Nekropolis, which has been exemplified by the later stages of Babylon, Nineveh, and Rome. Most of the larger cities in Europe and America have reached the stage of megalopolis, and many of them have entered that of tyrannopolis. Many great American cities present that collusion between predatory politicians and organized criminals which is characteristic of the tyrannopolitan era. The only sure defense against these terminal calamities of urban evolution is adequate city planning, undertaken in time.

FACTORS IN URBAN ORIGINS AND GROWTH

Geographical elements in urban growth. Geographical factors have played a leading part in determining the location and the growth of cities. Indeed, as Niles Carpenter has pointed out, city life began in the ancient Near Orient where an arid climate and the necessity of irrigation made community life and a dense population both natural and desirable. The location of many ancient cities was also closely related to geographical advantages favorable to defense. Hilltops and places surrounded by water were prized. Natural defensive considerations do not loom as important today as in ancient times, but geographical forces have continued to exert a deep influence upon the location of cities.

Geographical situations affecting trade and transportation have been of great potency in determining where cities will be built. Wherever we find a break in transportation sufficient to cause delay, storage, or transfer, we are likely to find that a city has grown up. Breaks between land and water transportation are especially notable in this regard. New York City affords a good example. The necessity of transshipment always favors the rise of a city. Where trade routes cross or converge, cities will usually spring up. Many cities are located on some form of navigable water which makes it possible for them to exploit the advantages of cheap water transportation. Mouths of rivers, river and lake ports, canal terminals, and similar waterways, are favorable to city growth.

Water power, as well as water routes, is often a determining factor. No other type of power is as cheap as water power where it can be found in sufficient quantities. With the coming of the electrical age, factories do not have to be located directly on the water power sites, for water-driven turbines can generate electricity which can be distributed cheaply to all plants in the region. Adjacency to rich agricultural regions will stimulate the growth of certain types of cities which may specialize in the manufacture of farm machinery and act as a distributing agency for farm products. The proximity of minerals and oil has helped many an important city to come into existence and to prosper. In some cases cities are located where they are relatively midway between readily accessible sources of minerals. For example, Gary, Indiana, has become a great iron and steel city because it can draw upon the coal mines to the south and the iron ore of the Lake Superior district.

Any large and growing city must have a considerable hinterland to draw upon and to serve. When the city of Vienna was deprived of its natural hinterland by the Treaty of St. Germain, it was struck a fatal blow. The improvement of transportation facilities, of course, invariably enlarges the hinterland; this affects city growth and prosperity. Sometimes, a city with its special type of industry may be located and grow up purely by accident. But even in such cases this very priority of location and industrial development comes in time to constitute a geographical item of real importance.

Geographical factors making for health and salubrity—for example, high altitudes, dry climate, and medicinal springs—may encourage city growth. Colorado Springs; Saratoga Springs; Hot Springs, Arkansas; and Warm Springs, Georgia, will come to mind as examples, as well as such Old World cities as Carlsbad and Vichy.

In short, one may say that no city is likely to thrive and attain importance without one or more of these various types of geographical advantage. As Carpenter puts it, the geographical causes of city growth today are "polyvalent"—that is, there are usually numerous and varied physical factors promoting city development. Other things being equal, maximum city growth is likely to take place where there are special advantages with respect to the availability of raw materials, a good labor supply, and transportation facilities. Any drastic transformation of the geographical importance of certain locations may profoundly modify urban trends which have depended thereupon. A classic instance was the reaction of the discovery of America and an ocean route to the Far East upon the Italian cities of the later Middle Ages.

We have, of course, only scratched the surface of the geographical basis of city life. A whole school of sociology and urban reconstruction, led by Frédéric Le Play, Patrick Geddes, Victor Branford, and Lewis Mumford, has grown up about the study of the relation between city growth and the natural geographic background of the more important urban communities.

Economic causes of urban development. We have already mentioned many of the important economic factors in recent urban development and we need do no more than summarize and characterize these at this point. We have noted that machines and the factory system made the city indispensable, while agriculture made the growth of great cities a possibility. Industrial cities grew because they provided extended and diversified employment for those who came from the rural areas and the more backward countries. The increased demand for goods which followed urban development, together with improved transportation facilities, provided a more extensive commercial foundation for urban prosperity than had ever before existed. We have already noted how steam power and its industrial and administrative by-products served to promote urban concentration.

Such factors as these furnished what is known as "the economic base" of contemporary urban growth. Perhaps trade has been a more enduring foundation of urban economies than any other single factor, though it is often relatively far less important than productive industry. The accessibility of iron ore and coal has given us our great steel cities and metallurgical centers. Many of the cities of the Rocky Mountains area owe their origin and prosperity to precious metals and other mineral resources. The increasing importance of petroleum in the twentieth century has led to the appearance of wealthy mushroom cities founded on the oil industry, especially in Texas and Oklahoma.

The most stable and permanent economic base for urban expansion is found where there are natural incentives or advantages which make possible the growth of several flourishing industries. Technological changes, or the exhaustion of a particular type of natural resource, are less likely to upset economic stability in such cities. Especially impregnable are cities which combine diversified industrial facilities with elaborate trading opportunities. Such cities naturally tend to develop into metropolitan centers. The latter possess important basic industries and extensive trading activities and dominate the field of credit and finance. What G. R. Taylor has called satellite cities, with subsidiary industries, tend to cluster about metropolitan regions, clearing their products and activities through the metropolis. This interrelation of satellite cities and their metropolis has created what R. D. McKenzie described as "metropolitan communities." The development of the railroad and, even more, the motor vehicle, played a dominant rôle in building these metropolitan societies.

Socio-psychological factors promoting urban expansion. Another important economic consideration, highly influential in creating large urban

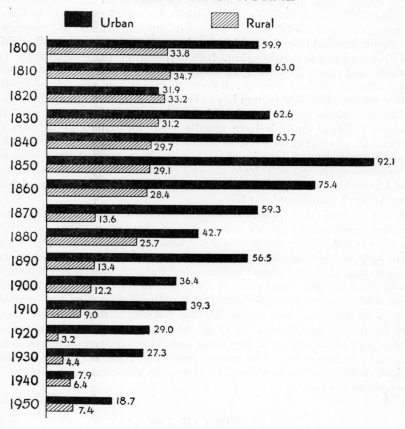

PERCENTAGE OF POPULATION INCREASE
OVER EACH PRECEDING CENSUS
URBAN AND RURAL

■ Urban   ▨ Rural

Year	Urban	Rural
1800	59.9	33.8
1810	63.0	34.7
1820	31.9	33.2
1830	62.6	31.2
1840	63.7	29.7
1850	92.1	29.1
1860	75.4	28.4
1870	59.3	13.6
1880	42.7	25.7
1890	56.5	13.4
1900	36.4	12.2
1910	39.3	9.0
1920	29.0	3.2
1930	27.3	4.4
1940	7.9	6.4
1950	18.7	7.4

centers, is intertwined with psychological factors. It represents the urban manifestation of the old adage that "nothing succeeds like success." This has been described by some writers as the "bigness psychosis." For generations, cities have prided themselves upon their size and rapid growth, wishing to become even larger. Urban growth has been stimulated by deliberate boosting through exploiting the prestige of size and its supposed advantages. Urban pride and prestige have depended, to a certain extent,

upon increasing size and rapid growth. There is also a firm conviction
that bigness in business, finance, and merchandising enterprises inevitably
brings with it greater efficiency in these lines of economic activity. Large
cities often draw to themselves superior organizing talent in industry. Professional men flock to the larger cities because of the increased prestige of
having an office there. Residence in a large city provides more of an opportunity to make a big showing in almost any line of endeavor. There is
a tendency to prefer being a small toad in the big pond to being a big
toad in a little pond; and, of course, all the little toads in the big pond
entertain ardent hopes of becoming big toads. The fact that a few succeed
in so doing keeps alive the aspirations of those who are less successful.
Further, large cities offer greater facilities for social snobbery, lavish entertainment, and social levity. They are, on the whole, less restrained
by the puritanical impulses which dominate rural areas and smaller cities.

Other causes of urbanization. Influences other than geography, economics, and psychology have, of course, played a role in locating cities.
Especially in ancient times, religious shrines often grew into leading
urban centers. Political factors have also been important. In ancient times
political capitals might be selected for their defensive advantages, but
modern political capitals have usually been located so as to gain the
advantages of central location, as regards both territory and the distribution of population. Educational advantages have exerted their influence
in promoting city growth, from the rise of the medieval cities of Oxford
and Cambridge to the origin of American cities like Princeton, Ithaca,
Ann Arbor, Urbana, and the like.

It might be well to point out in this place that our larger cities have
become important economic enterprises in themselves. They have built
up a great administrative bureaucracy which provides extensive employment and pays out vast sums of money in salaries and wages. The sanitary
engineering, transportation facilities, and lighting enterprises which are
maintained by cities have created a colossal industrial venture involving
tremendous outlays for construction and maintenance. The cost of public
education, policing, and fire protection constitute impressive economic
and financial expenditures. In 1949, the 397 cities of the United States
with a population of over 25,000 spent 4.05 billion dollars on public activities and administration. The annual budget of New York City is over a
billion dollars, an amount equal to fifty times the total public income of
the Roman Empire.

THE ECOLOGY OF THE CITY

**The Park-Burgess conception of the ecology of urban life and popula-
tion distribution.** Having surveyed the evolution of urban communities
and the outstanding factors connected therewith, we shall examine in this
section some of the leading characteristics of the city as a social community. We shall also consider the main social groupings which are found
in city life and the urban types which have emerged as the result of
some generations of urban experience.

Realistic sociological and ecological analysis of the urban community was mainly inspired by the pioneer work of Robert E. Park of the University of Chicago, and such disciples of Park as Ernest W. Burgess, R. D. McKenzie, Louis Wirth, and others. Urban *ecology*, as the term is used here, refers to the spatial distribution of the leading urban population types and the interests and activities they represent.[7]

We may now describe ecological areas or zones as they develop in the usual city, and the population types that dwell in them. It will be well to note, at the outset, that very little of this spatial distribution of city functions, activities and population groups has been planned in any intelligent fashion. It has grown up, in part, as the result of the functional differentiation of urban activities and, in part, as the result of accident and habit. The congestion and the helter-skelter character of urban development have been produced by this very planlessness. Only recently has there been any real effort to plan the functional distribution of city activities and structures. The most important outcome of this movement to date has been the rational but arbitrary "zoning" of city areas, with the aim in mind of keeping given types of businesses and related structures in specified urban regions, by such regulations as separating residential from manufacturing and shipping districts, and by restricting the size, design, and type of buildings in each district.

Burgess's concentric zone pattern of urban ecology. One of the most widely followed patterns for analyzing urban ecology is the concentric zone theory propounded by Ernest W. Burgess. The heart of any of our typical larger cities is what is known as the "downtown" area—the central business district. This is the zone of finance and commerce and of the services which are most directly related to them. It is the area of great skyscraper business structures. Along with these giant office buildings, which bring about a tremendous concentration of urban population during working hours, we find the restaurants, hotels, and stores, which serve the business area. Wholesale and public markets are also frequently located in this district. While some may live permanently in the hotels located here, human habitation is usually incidental and transient in this urban zone. It is the financial and commercial core of the city.

Adjacent to or surrounding this downtown zone is a residential, industrial, and more highly specialized commercial zone. It is sometimes known as "the inner industrial zone." Here we find a massed working population devoted primarily to the manufacturing of clothing, furs, leather goods, cigars, and the like. For the most part, these businesses are run by small-scale firms. The workers who dwell here live in relatively inferior residential areas, sometimes the abandoned homes formerly occupied by the richer elements of the city. The workers form their own special social communities, usually organized on the basis of trades and industries.

Surrounding this second zone we find the tenement and slum districts

---

[7] For an excellent presentation of the whole problem of human ecology as applied to the city and community, see A. H. Hawley, *Human Ecology*. New York: Ronald Press, 1950.

and the back street areas, inhabited by the lower class workers. Here the
sweated industries tend to congregate, with much of the work carried
on in the miserable dwellings of the poor. In this district we find the
massed misery of city life, though "bohemian" communities and night
clubs may locate here, and vice and gambling tend to center in this
area. Healthy recreational facilities are limited or wanting altogether.
Good sanitary facilities are deplorably lacking. Here are located most of
what Walter Rollo Brown calls the "short wheelbase churches."

Between the tenement district and the apartment house region is
usually a rooming house area for white-collar employees. Here we find
the homes of "the great middle class of clerks, salesmen, skilled mechanics,
and other industrial workers—many unmarried and coming from outside the city." These dwellings are usually in districts undergoing a
transformation from residential to commercial uses, and run all the
way from former residences of the rich to more commonplace middle-class
homes.

Bordering on the rooming house area are found the middle-class apartments and the stores, the "middle wheelbase" churches, and the schools
which serve this large element in the urban population. Except in the
larger cities, we also find in this area single dwelling houses. Interspersed
in these areas are a number of palatial skyscraper apartment houses inhabited by the well-to-do or the very rich. In the larger cities, like New
York, the lavish apartment houses of the rich may constitute a special zone
or district, such as Central Park West and Park Avenue in New York.
The "long wheelbase churches" are found in such districts.

Finally, most remote from the downtown section are the suburban
apartments and single homes, populated chiefly by commuters who
carry on their daily labors in the more congested areas of the urban community. With the increasing congestion of the city proper and the
growing facilities of rapid transit, these suburban areas have become
more populous and more widely scattered on the periphery of the city, and
today they are growing much more rapidly than any other urban area.

In addition to this quasi-functional ecological distribution of city
districts, we find the segregation of racial and national groups, particularly in American cities that have been built up largely as the result
of foreign immigration. These racial and national colonies tend to be
situated chiefly in the inner industrial zone and in tenement areas.
In industrial cities, they often cluster about the great factories.

The concentric ecological pattern only general and relative. It should
not be supposed that this concentric distribution of urban districts is
clean cut and uniform among all cities.[8] This concentric ecological survey simply describes the general trend of the distribution of urban structures, activities, and inhabitants. Important redistributions of zones and
population are going on all the time in the larger cities. The rich
abandon one section and the less well-to-do move in. Slum sections may be

---

[8] For a critical appraisal of this concentric pattern, see E. E. Muntz, *Urban Sociology*.
New York: Macmillan, 1938, pp. 33-34.

cleared and palatial apartments erected in their place. This is well illustrated by the erection of expensive apartments along the eastern waterfront of Manhattan in New York City, and the vast apartment developments, such as Stuyvesant Town and Peter Cooper Village, erected by the Metropolitan Life Insurance Company in what were slum areas of downtown New York. Above all, it cannot accurately be held that any particular region of the city houses all the retail establishments. The more important ones tend to be located on the borders of the downtown area, but they are distributed throughout the entire urban community, taking on their special character from the type of clientele which predominates in the neighborhood.

Homer Hoyt's sector-growth scheme of urban ecological analysis. Another scheme for urban ecological analysis has been suggested by Homer Hoyt. This he calls the sector-growth pattern. Instead of concentric rings of spatial and type distribution outlined by Burgess, Wirth, and others, Hoyt contends that urban distribution may more resemble the layout of an octopus, with the tentacles following the main transportation lines. The body of the city is concentrated around the downtown business, industrial, and residential districts, and the high rent areas may be located on the outer edge of several outlying sectors of the city.

The metropolitan community. In addition to the city proper, or the concentrated urban district, we should also consider the larger metropolitan community, a phase of urban development to which R. D. McKenzie has given special attention. In his suggestive book, *The Metropolitan Community,* he points out how our earlier towns in the colonial period were located by chance or accident or where there were special advantages as to fishing, raw materials, or trading opportunities. After 1850 railroad construction played the most important role in determining the nature and location of our cities. Urban life followed in the wake of the railroads. Cities were located at railroad junctions or at places where manufacture and trade could be carried on most advantageously in connection with the new railway traffic. They were primarily gateway centers or distributing points.

A new era in city life was introduced in the twentieth century—and especially since the First World War—by the appearance of the motor vehicle propelled by the internal combustion engine. This new mode of transportation brought cities into close and speedy contact with outlying rural towns and farming districts. Bus and truck transportation systems were installed, joining city and country. What had formerly been sharp urban boundaries were erased or shaded out. The Bureau of the Census took cognizance of this fact in its computation of the urban population in 1950. The great city, its suburbs, and the adjacent rural areas were all brought within what is essentially a great metropolitan community dominated by the densely populated city at its center. There are 168 of these metropolitan districts in the United States today. They have a population of 84,000,000 out of a total population of 150,700,000, and four-fifths of all population growth during the 1940's took place in these metropolitan districts. The metropolitan community of today thus reaches out from the congested financial districts of the metropolis to the adjacent farming regions which seek the city for their markets, their ideas, and their entertainment. The great city of today extends far beyond the boundaries of the urban corporation in its economic and cultural influences.[9]

Greater New York City, as an urban, if not a legal, community, is the most extreme development of a metropolitan community. It covers a circle fifty miles in diameter around Manhattan Island and spreads over twelve counties in New York and New Jersey. It contains a population of nearly 14 million, six million of whom live outside the city corporation in 500 suburban cities, towns, and communities.

THE CITY AS A SOCIAL COMMUNITY

Main social effects of the rise of city life. The rise of the modern industrial city has produced many important social changes. Indeed, a new era in human culture and social life has come about. In his important book on *Problems of City Life,* M. R. Davie lists what he believes to have been the outstanding social consequences of the arrival of an urban social age: (1) the disintegration of the institutions and conditions which have come down from the older rural era; (2) a sweeping revolution in the nature of family and home life; (3) an increasing complexity of social relationships; (4) a zeal for innovation and radical departures from old standards of life and social values; (5) a sharper separation of socioeconomic classes; and (6) an increasing volume and speed of intercommunity mobility.

Social distance and social clashes in the metropolitan community. One of the most striking things about the great city of today as a social community is the unprecedented combination of physical proximity with social distance. All social types are thrown together by the tens of thousands within the same urban boundaries. Yet we find in one large urban community social differentiations and barriers as great as those that formerly separated the medieval feudal lord from the most lowly serf or cotter. As Munro has pointed out, between the occupants of palatial apartments and penthouses and the slum dwellers, who may live within a stone's throw of one another, there is "the greatest social distance" to be observed anywhere on this planet.

Disappearance of neighborhood life. Until the emergence of the great urban areas, the local neighborhood was the center of social life. Geographical proximity was directly related to personal acquaintance and sociability. This has all passed away in the typical large city. Urban dwellers not only are unacquainted with those who live in the neighboring apartment houses; it is rare that they even know personally all of those who live on the same floor of their own apartment house. Social relations are chiefly selective, functional, and professional in character.

---

[9] R. D. McKenzie, *The Metropolitan Community.* New York: McGraw-Hill, 1933, especially Chap. I.

Urban inhabitants choose their friends on the basis of trades and professions, fraternal associations, recreational interests, and other considerations which have little or no relation to the proximity of their residences.

Class differentiation in city life. Every type of class differentiation known to modern society emerges in city life. We have the plutocrats, the well-to-do middle class, the lesser *bourgeoisie*, the white-collar proletariat, the industrial proletariat, the down-and-out bums, and the underworld. Though we pride ourselves upon being a democratic country, where all men are free and equal, these class distinctions are real and potent, even though their boundaries may be somewhat vague and fluid. Cultural and racial distinctions also prevail. We have foreign colonies, Negro districts, Chinatowns, and the like.

Complex and heterogeneous nature of metropolitan life. On the main city thoroughfares, carrying on their various economic activities by day and seeking amusement by night, are the most inchoate and heterogeneous crowds that the world has ever witnessed. Only ancient Rome and Alexandria could present any remote comparison with the situation typical of our greater cities. But it may be doubted whether, even in these ancient cosmopolitan centers, the streets were ever mobbed by such diversified throngs as infest the "great white ways" of our metropolitan communities. Yet even in these maulings and jostlings, the trade marks of class differentiation are clearly visible and usually respected.

It is obvious that, with such diversity of social status, economic interest, and cultural background, it is extremely difficult to bring about any considerable community of interest or unity of attitude in urban public affairs. In rural communities, those who associated in schools, business, and the like, were drawn from a common cultural heritage, which their activities perpetuated. In our cities, the population is drawn from different parts of the same country, and from many different countries. They have highly diversified mores, traditions, and social habits. There is no continuity of tradition to perpetuate, no common community standards to confirm and apply.

But the very exigencies and emergencies of urban life force the city to maintain a certain minimum of social coherence and community of policy. Rich and poor alike, foreigner and native born, seek to educate their children, protect their health, and defend their homes and property against robbery and fire. Hence, the city has to unite upon an educational policy and the provision of a vast educational plant. All classes find it necessary to drink water and dispose of waste. Hence, we have the development of vast sanitary engineering enterprises to promote the health and well-being of all types of urban dwellers. Public health activities and hospitals are provided. Police departments are created to preserve law and order. The fire-fighting force is brought into existence to protect both penthouses and intolerable slums. In order to alleviate suffering and to ward off mass indignation and mob violence on the part of the desperately poor, the rich unite to develop and maintain charitable enterprises.

Secondary groups and functional organizations predominate in urban society. The altruistic impulses and social consciousness which formerly functioned within the primary family and neighborhood groups of agrarian society now find their outlet in various secondary groups designed to promote some form of social uplift. As the home and neighborhood become less important in city civilization, various functional groups and civic centers have gained in relative influence. In New York City alone there are over twelve hundred of these organizations which aim to serve others without remuneration.

This trend well illustrates the process whereby the small and simple personal or primary groups of rural society are being supplanted by larger secondary groups which dominate urban society. We find such functional organizations as chambers of commerce, labor union centrals, and the like. Service clubs of numerous types abound, and fraternal organizations tend to thrive as a mode of providing social contacts for urban dwellers. Nels Anderson and E. C. Lindeman thus summarize the various types of groups which emerge in urban life and provide varied if inadequate substitutes for the neighborhood activities and associations of an earlier day:

1. Functional groups: organized primarily on behalf of a specific and objective interest; trade unions, manufacturers' associations, chambers of commerce, etc. (Conflict groups.)

2. Occupational groups: organized on behalf of a professional interest, but less concerned with directly objective issues; medical societies, engineering societies, etc.

3. Philanthropic and reform groups: organized to protect the unfortunate members of society, or to propagate such constitutional changes as will improve society.

4. Religious groups: held together by virtue of a common subjective goal or interest.

5. Nationality groups: clusters of immigrants who fall into natural groups because of language, culture, etc.

6. Memory groups: organized for the purpose of projecting a past experience (pleasant or unpleasant at the time but somehow since risen to importance) into the present and future: war veteran societies, alumni associations, etc.

7. Symbolic groups: formed about a set of symbolisms or rituals which often are valued in direct proportion to their inappropriateness to the present environment: lodges, fraternal societies, secret societies.

8. Service-recreational groups: informally organized about the wish for playful adult activity coupled with a sense of doing good: Rotary, Kiwanis, Lions, etc.

9. Political groups: clubs or societies which are often, at least in part, memory groups, but which exist for the purpose of perpetuating a set of political principles; Tammany Hall, Jefferson Clubs, Lincoln Clubs, etc.

10. Feminist groups: women organized in the interest of cultural, educational, civic purposes; women's clubs, leagues for women voters, etc.

11. Atypical groups: groups which exist in all cities, and lend color to the urban scene, but which must be regarded as departures from the norm: on the positive side, bohemians, intellectuals, esthetic groups, etc.; and on the negative side, "gangs," or groups organized for effective law violation.[10]

---

[10] Urban Sociology. New York: Crofts, 1928, pp. 298-299. For another interesting classification of urban social types see N. P. Gist and L. A. Halpert, *Urban Society.* New York: Crowell, 1948, pp. 328 ff.

With groups so numerous and diverse as these in city life, it is a tremendous task, as we have noted, to produce the community of interest and unity of public opinion that are needed to cope with the complex and difficult problems of urban political and social policy. Unity and consistency are all but impossible. At best, all that can be hoped for is a workable compromise and a loose adjustment among these multifarious urban groups. The existence and consequences of this situation have been graphically emphasized by Munro:

This social disintegration, this complete absence of psychological homogeneity, is what burdens the city with many of its most difficult problems. It makes virtually impossible the securing of a consensus on any project or program of civic betterment. What the business interests propose is usually viewed with suspicion by the industrial workers. Intelligentsia and middle class, politicians and reformers, stand-patters and go-getters pull apart in the city, not together. Unified social leadership becomes next to impossible and group leadership takes its place. The city dwellers think in groups; they become strongly group conscious; hence many of the community's social problems have to be handled by makeshift and compromise rather than by vigorous, unified, constructive effort.[11]

Reactions of city life on the traditional home and family. One of the most important changes which the city has brought in the fundamentals of social life has been its impact upon the home and the family. The prevailing conceptions of the home, both in popular phraseology and in sociological discussion, revolve about the rural home and family of the pre-urban epoch. These rested upon a definite social and economic foundation associated with the conditions of rural life and a farming economy.

In the city these original bases of the family have been wiped out as ruthlessly and as thoroughly as has been the old rural neighborhood life. Moreover, the majority of city dwellers have no fixed and permanent abode such as was characteristic of rural life. Moving day on May first and, especially, on October first has been a characteristic institution of urban existence. People have shifted from one apartment to another or from one tenement to another as rabbits change their holes. This is true even of the relatively well-to-do. This excessive mobility of the urban population has continued despite the recent housing shortage. A government report in 1951 indicated that in the twelve months before April, 1950, one-sixth of the American population, or some 25,500,000 persons, moved from one house to another.

Life patterns of the urban proletariat. This novel and excessive mobility of the urban workers, their lack of the permanent homes, and the absence of that direct contact with nature which was characteristic of earlier rural society, are well presented in the following striking passage from the writings of the eminent economic historian, Werner Sombart:

---

[11] From *The Encyclopaedia of the Social Sciences,* Vol. III, p. 479. By permission of The Macmillan Company, publishers. For the best treatment of the success achieved by cities in attaining common social values and community integration in thought and action, see R. C. Cooley, *The Moral Integration of American Cities.* Chicago: University of Chicago Press, 1951.

First, there appears the important fact that the proletarian is a typical representative of that type of man who is no longer in relation (either internal or external) to Nature. The proletarian does not realize the meaning of the movement of the clouds in the sky; he no longer understands the voice of the storm.

He has no fatherland, rather he has no home in which he takes root. Can he feel at home in the dreary main streets, four stories high? He changes his dwelling often either because he dislikes his landlord or because he changes his place of work. As he moves from room to room, so he goes from city to city, from land to land, wherever opportunity (i.e., capitalism) calls. Homeless, restless, he moves over the earth: he loses the sense of local color; his home is the world. He has lost the call of Nature, and he has assimilated materialism.

It is a phenomenon of today, that the great mass of the population has nothing to call its own. In earlier times the poorest had a piece of land, a cottage, a few animals to call his own; a trifle, on which however he could set his whole heart. Today a handcart carries all his possessions when a proletarian moves. A few old scraps are all by which his individual existence is known.

All community feeling is destroyed by the iron foot of capitalism. The village is gone; the proletarian has no social home; the separate family disappears.[12]

Decline of urban home as a social unit. Just as urban social life no longer revolves about the neighborhood, so the basic unit has almost ceased to be the family home. During the temporary family occupancy of urban apartments, these are little more than cages and cubicles from which one goes out in quest of most pleasures and interests. There is little opportunity for diversified recreation in an apartment. Children become an economic liability in the urban home, at least during the period prior to the termination of their education. They can render no economic assistance of any importance, as they formerly did on the farm or in the factories during the days of child-labor. They are expensive to rear, and they complicate the problems of urban apartment life. Renting restrictions in the better apartment houses operate against a high birth rate. Renting to families with babies is frowned upon, and in some apartments such families are excluded altogether. In addition to the increasing financial expense of children in large cities, they also cause an unusual expenditure of nervous energy, due to parental worries over the acute traffic and play hazards in urban life and the new and varied temptations to juvenile delinquency.

It is not surprising, then, that urbanization has been accompanied by a striking increase in the divorce rate, until about one urban family in three winds up in the divorce courts. The father is becoming less important as a disciplinary force in the home. Woman's child-bearing traits compel her to continue to be the center of such family life as does exist. Anderson and Lindeman believe that urban life has brought us to a critical turning point in the history of the family. They think that it is possible that a new type of family life may emerge, with woman occupying a position of ascendency:

Doubtless the family of today, in adapting itself to the strange and disturbing environment of the modern city, will have to seek some new definition of status for its members and a new orientation in the total cultural situation. Woman

---

12 Werner Sombart, *Das Proletariat*, cited in Milton Briggs, *Economic History of England*. London: 1914, pp. 213-214.

will probably rise out of the role of a menial leashed to the routine of household work and child-bearing. She will probably not return to the old-time male domination, certainly not to the [Theodore] Rooseveltian ideal of family life. She is learning that the city is hard upon the children of the dying patriarchal family and that it undomesticates the male. Some observers of the situation look hopefully to the role the modern woman is going to play in bringing order out of chaos in building a new family life which may be more suited to the city. This period of chaos is only the chaos of transition from the paternal to a maternal family pattern. The man of the urban family is becoming less of a factor in the home. Perhaps there never was a time when he was more removed. He eats one and often two meals a day away from home.[13]

In the chapter on population we emphasized the fact that social ambition on the part of the great urban middle class and the distractions and energy-consuming activities of urban life as a whole constitute the most potent factors in reducing the birth rate in our day. We need not repeat the evidence or data on this matter here.

Park benches and night clubs replace the rural neighborhood. While there may have been an unnecessary amount of sentimentalizing over the antique rural family and the agrarian neighborhood, it is nevertheless true that they supplied the answer to certain social needs for which there has as yet been no comparable urban substitute.

The rural family and neighborhood have shaped human personality and character since the dawn of history. Community facilities may at some later day provide adequate substitutes, but they have not done so thus far. This lag, lapse, or interlude between rural family and neighborhood control of personal life and social discipline and the delayed development of community agencies is the chief cause of social disorganization in our day. We have already pointed out that social disorganization is the most acute form of cultural lag and a chief cause of our many and varied social problems.

The poor spend their leisure hours in a crowded existence within a drab tenement, looking at passing crowds or city lights through dingy windows, or they aimlessly pound the sidewalks with thousands of others like themselves. In summer months they may flop down on park benches. Many drift into dives and saloons which neither elevate nor amuse them in any satisfactory fashion. The younger element may seek a substitute for the lost rural social institutions in gangs which often verge on the criminal. The wealthier element find a frothy distraction in what is known as "café society." This was, in its origins, a product of the "night club era," a contribution of prohibition days to urban recreation and amusement.[14]

Clarence Day once suggested that if man had been descended from cats rather than from monkeys he would have had far greater proclivity and talent for a strenuous and diversified night life. There is no denying that café society, the popularity of night clubs, and increasing night life have introduced such characteristically feline social habits among the

---

[13] *Op. cit.*, p. 351.
[14] See Stanley Walker, *The Night Club Era*. New York: Stokes, 1933.

upper-class circles of our urban communities. The alarming increase of mental and nervous disease in urban areas may be, in one sense, a demonstration that a simian organism is unsuited to the adoption of feline behavior. The stimulating intellectual discussions which once characterized the old urban coffee houses are notorious for their absence from these contemporary nocturnal gambols of café society. The floor show has supplanted, as a dominant point of interest, all intellectual discussion and conversational élan. In short, for better or worse, the social life and intellectual interests of urban communities are essentially novel and a decadent departure from traditional thought and behavior.

SOME PROBLEMS OF CITY GOVERNMENT

Early developments in municipal government. City government has played an important rôle in the history of political institutions. In the ancient city-states we find the first examples of representative government, with the possible exception of certain tribal assemblies in primitive times. It is in the medieval cities, especially those of Spain, that we discover the origins of representative government in the form in which this has come down into modern times. Municipal government in the medieval towns was the most intelligent and efficient type of government known to the Middle Ages. Our modern conception of constitutions, charters, and liberties comes in considerable part from the communal revolutions of the medieval period and the struggles of towns against kings and feudal lords. Most of the terminology and much of the structure and methods of modern municipal government are a direct heritage from the institutions of the medieval town. It is apparent, thus, that medieval town government had important influences upon both the local and national political institutions of our day.

Urban government has also affected political theory. The most famous book ever written on political theory, Aristotle's *Politics,* was based on a study of ancient urban political life. The English statesman of the late nineteenth century, W. E. Gladstone, described it as still the most important book ever written on politics. Machiavelli's *Prince* and the theocratic doctrines of John Calvin are other illustrations of the effect of urban experience on political theory.

We have no space for any detailed discussion of European municipal government. Except for the recent developments in totalitarian countries, city government in Europe represents a modified heritage from the Middle Ages. The administrative officers and the representative bodies are, for the most part, still known by their medieval names.

The English borough government comes down directly from the medieval period, having been modernized by the famous reform bills of 1832 and 1835. The cities are governed by a mayor, a common council, and a board of aldermen. Together, they make up what is known as the City Council. English cities enjoy a considerable amount of local autonomy in matters pertaining to their own affairs. Municipal self-government gained much headway in Germany in the nineteenth century.

It got its start in the famous reforms of Baron von Stein in Prussia in 1808. The old medieval officers, such as burgomasters and councilors, were continued, in name at least. German city government was further liberalized in the Weimar Republic after the First World War. But under Hitler and the Nazis, after 1933, urban autonomy was severely curtailed, along with other manifestations of political centralization. The communal government of France represents a heritage from the French Revolution. The municipal council is the dominant group. The mayor is elected by the council, but is important chiefly as a representative of the central government, which may remove him at its pleasure. The capitals of the more important countries of Western Europe, London, Berlin, and Paris, have a special and more complicated form of government than that which exists in other cities. In this respect they resemble the government of Washington in our own country. Municipal government is undergoing considerable reorganization in post-war Europe since 1945.

Political graft and corruption in American city government. City government has played an important part in American political development. As we have already noted, the political machine first developed on a large scale in American cities, especially those cities which had a large foreign-born population. These machines dominated not only city politics but state politics as well, often even exerting a powerful and deplorable influence over national politics. Graft, corruption, and exploitation were rampant in city government for generations. This situation received its first classic description in the work of Lincoln Steffens, *The Shame of the Cities,* first published in 1904. The books by Jack Lait and Lee Mortimer, *Chicago Confidential* and *Washington Confidential,* while more sensational and less substantial than Steffens' classic, surely sufficed to show that metropolitan governments remain as corrupt, vice-ridden, and graft-ridden at the mid-century as they were fifty years before. Political reforms, to which we shall make reference shortly, have improved city government in many of the lesser cities, but it has been difficult to introduce honest and efficient types of government into our great metropolitan centers. Their populations have been too large, unwieldy, and disorganized to make it easy to secure a united front for reform. Moreover, the greater opportunities for graft in metropolitan areas have made the politicians more determined to retain these sources of spoils.

The city of Chicago has, perhaps, been most notable for the creation and perpetuation of graft, corruption, and the spoils system in municipal government. Both parties have shared in this plunder. As Charles E. Merriam of the University of Chicago once put it, "The Republican and Democratic parties are but the two wings of the same bird of prey." The city political machine in Chicago has acted as an intermediary between the great banking, real estate, traction, and public utility interests above, and the gangster element below. The big financial and business interests desire to secure freedom from public regulation and to bring about a reduction of taxation. They contribute heavily to the campaign funds of friendly machines and candidates and offer other rewards to complaisant politicians. At the other end of the scale the gangsters, racketeers, and gamblers wish to be let alone in their remunerative activities in organized crime, gambling, and vice. They pay protection money, stuff ballot boxes, intimidate independent voters, discourage political reformers by threats, and otherwise aid the political machine in emergencies.

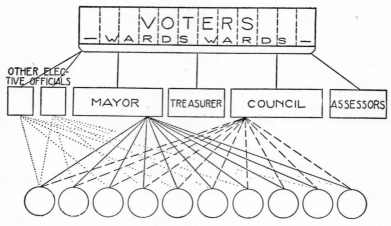

Mayor-council Form of City Government.

It has been estimated that in the days of the Thompson rule in Chicago the plain and outright graft ran to somewhere between 75 million and 125 million dollars annually. This was made possible in a number of ways. Inflated contracts were awarded. In one 2.5 million dollar paving job there was 1 million dollars of pure graft. A political printer was paid $120,000 to print the annual message of the president of the board of trustees of the Sanitary District. Payrolls were padded. On the average, 16 out of every 100 names on the public payrolls in Cook County were bogus and fraudulent. In campaign years approximately 2 million dollars was paid out in bogus salaries. Tax rebating was used as a form of political blackmail.

Coal companies were organized by friends of assessors and the Board of Tax Review. In case of protests about assessments and taxation, agents of these coal companies would call and promise relief if orders for coal were placed with them. One coal company openly printed cards with the encouraging slogan, "Buy your coal of us and cut your taxes." Ninety per cent of the coal in the Loop District was bought from such companies, and in one year alone there was an assessment reduction of 500 million dollars. High prices were paid for real estate bought by the city. City property was often sold or leased at scandalously low rates. Public funds were placed with favored bankers. Offices and promotions were sold to the highest bidders.

Large sums of money poured in from the racketeers, bootleggers, gamblers, and operators of organized vice. In campaign years the scandals were particularly notorious. In one case $2,250,000 was supposedly paid to experts for their opinions on a city bond issue. But the experts received only a nominal salary and the bulk of this sum went into the Thompson campaign fund. The difficulty of organizing intelligent public opinion behind municipal reform is revealed by the fact that Mayor Thompson was able successfully to distract public indignation from municipal scandals by waging a colorful rhetorical campaign against King George V of England. The régime of Anton J. Cermak, who succeeded Thompson, was regarded by many as more corrupt than that of Thompson. It was cut short by Cermak's assassination in March, 1933. The Kelly-Nash machine, which followed that of Cermak and endured for more than 15 years, was smoother in its operations but scarcely less venal and exploitive. Indeed, an able Chicago publicist, Milton S. Mayer, writing on the eve of the Second World War, contended that under the Kelly-Nash machine, conditions had not improved since the Thompson days:

> The sum and substance of the current situation is that there isn't going to be any reform in Chicago. National reformism has passed its crest, leaving its mark on most American cities, even Kansas City and Los Angeles. But the worst city in America went right on getting worse and is going to get worse faster from now on.[15]

Some hope was expressed by reform elements after the election of 1948, but they were as much disappointed as were those who expected relief under the Cermak and Kelly-Nash regimes. The sensational book of Jack Lait and Lee Mortimer, *Chicago Confidential,* published early in 1950, fully demonstrated that civic corruption in Chicago at the mid-century was, if anything, worse than in the Thompson era. Indeed, it revealed such an appalling tie-up between officialdom and the underworld that the book is generally regarded as the main inspiration for the creation of the Kefauver Committee to investigate organized crime. And the revelations of this Committee regarding Chicago political conditions is believed to have been a chief reason for the defeat of Senator Scott Lucas in 1950.

New York City could not quite match the achievements of Chicago in municipal graft, but it made an excellent showing nevertheless. During the terms of Mayor "Jimmy" Walker, who reigned contemporaneously with "Big Bill" Thompson in Chicago, the Tammany Tiger enjoyed an unusually rich diet in Manhattan. Even before the Seabury investigation, notorious scandals, such as those in the sewer contracts in Queens County, had been exposed. Judge Seabury and his associates revealed many juicy scandals in the Tammany government. There was much graft in connection with city docks and piers. Fee-splitting was common. One employee of the Bureau of Standards made $25,000 monthly out of this form of graft. The firm of a fee-splitting lawyer who was in the zoning department deposited $5,283,000 between 1925 and 1931. The sheriff of New York County banked $360,000 in seven years, though his salary and other official income were not more than $90,000 for the same period. The sheriff of Kings County banked $520,000 in six years, although his

---

[15] *Nation,* February 25, 1939.

salary ran to less than $50,000 for the period. A deputy city clerk deposited $384,000 in six years. His chief official duty was to marry couples. There was much graft in the city bus system. Organized vice and gambling flourished under police protection. In the spring of 1932 Mayor Walker resigned under pressure and fear of removal.

The corruption under the Walker régime led to a revolt of the voters and Fiorello La Guardia was elected on a reform fusion ticket in 1933 and reëlected in 1937 and 1941. He gave New York an efficient and honest administration. His successor, William O'Dwyer, though a Democrat organization candidate, had earned a reputation as a "gang-buster" while serving as District Attorney in Brooklyn. He was long believed to have been a relatively honest and competent mayor, but the Kefauver Committee uncovered evidence in 1951 that he was not uncontaminated by contacts with the top figures in organized crime and gambling. The election of Vincent Impellitteri on an independent ticket in November, 1951, may have marked a return to something like the reputed honesty and efficiency of the La Guardia era, but it is too early as yet to be certain about this matter.

In Jersey City a machine far more "reform proof" than that in New York was built up by Mayor Frank Hague and it resisted all reform forces for two decades. It was always able to deliver the Democrat votes needed to carry New Jersey. Equally venal and powerful was the machine created in Kansas City by Thomas J. Pendergast, the political mentor of President Truman. He ruled with an iron hand until he was dethroned and imprisoned as an incident of Democrat political strategy under President Roosevelt, who had previously warmly welcomed Pendergast support. James M. Curley operated a powerful political machine in Boston very successfully in spite of repeated charges of gross corruption and his conviction of fraudulent use of the mails.

Origins of the reform movement. For a time, most reforms in municipal government took the form of periodic rebellions against the machine "rascals." But this proved futile. It was hard to keep the rascals out, and sometimes the reformers later turned rascals. Therefore, the really significant achievements in the reform of municipal government have been brought about through striking changes in the whole structure and method of urban rule.

The important turning point in the institution of vital reforms in city government was the holding of a national conference on city government in 1894. Out of it grew the National Municipal League, which has since been a driving force in the improvement of urban administration. This conference laid down certain basic principles which should apply in honest and efficient city government: (1) urban communities should be granted full rights of self-government by the states; (2) democratic principles and practices should prevail in city rule; (3) city property and franchises should be protected against political and private utility grafters; (4) municipal government should be placed directly in the hands of experts; (5) these experts should be made subject to popular control; and (6) to make this feasible and practical, adequate popular checks upon city administration must be set up. The outstanding products of this movement for expert, but democratic, city government have been the commission form of city government, the city manager system, and civil service standards for city officials.

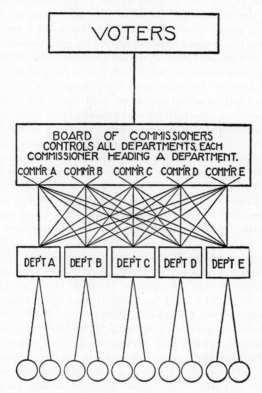

Commission Form of City Government.

The traditional mayor-council form of city government. The earliest and most common form of city government in the United States reproduced in a small way the pattern of the state governments which had imitated the Federal system in setting up three distinct departments of government. The city executive in such cases is the mayor. The common council is the counterpart of the state senate, and the board of aldermen of the state assembly. A city judiciary controls the judicial situation.

This form of government is complex and often irresponsible and inefficient. It has easily lent itself to domination by corrupt political machines with results that we have just described. In spite of its notorious defects, however, it still remains the most frequent and popular form of urban government. In 1949, some 1,163 cities with a population over 5,000 were using the mayor-council system—some 57.2 per cent of the total of such cities.

The commission form of city government. The commission form of government began during an emergency—the destruction of the city of Galveston by a great tidal wave in September, 1900. It spread rapidly from Galveston, and by 1914 had been adopted by some 400 cities. Since the First World War it has lost ground to the city manager plan, as well as to a revival of the traditional form of city government. In 1949, some 302 cities with a population of over 5,000 each, 14.9 per cent of such cities, were using the commission form of city government.

Under the commission form of urban government, all the powers are lodged in an elective council, usually of five members or commissioners. One of the five acts as chairman and frequently has the title of mayor, though he has no independent executive authority. Each of the five commissioners assumes responsibility for certain specific administrative functions. This commission form of government greatly simplifies municipal government, centralizes authority, and increases expertness. But it often degenerates into partisan and personal squabbles, though party designations are formally excluded from the primary and election ballots. Three members of the commission frequently line up against the other two, and there are many cases of bickering and delay. These defects, together with the organized hostility of the party machines, have been mainly responsible for the decline in the popularity of the commission form of city government.

The city manager plan. The city manager plan of city government began in Staunton, Virginia, in 1908, but it became important and popular chiefly after it was adopted by Dayton, Ohio, in 1914. It gained much headway after 1918, and by 1950 it was operating in about 500 cities. A few large cities—Cleveland, Cincinnati, Rochester (N.Y.), and Kansas City (Mo.)—adopted this system. It has been conspicuously successful in Cincinnati, which had previously been a notorious sore spot of boss rule. Unlike the commission form of government, the city manager plan is still on the gain, and the increase has been especially rapid during the last five years, some 42 cities being added to the list between March, 1949 and April, 1950. In 1949, among cities of over 5,000 population, 495, or 24.3 per cent, were operating according to the city manager plan, and the number had increased to nearly 550 by the end of 1950.

Under the city manager scheme, the commission structure is utilized but is enlarged and known as the city council. An administrative expert, called the city manager, is hired to direct all the chief city departments except education, which has usually continued to be controlled by a separate board of education. Legislative and political responsibility are lodged with the mayor and the council, thus separating administrative activities from politics. With the consent of the council, the city manager appoints the lesser city officers, usually attempting to be guided by considerations of merit rather than of political favors.

On the whole, the city manager plan has worked satisfactorily. In fact, it has worked in splendid fashion when the politicians have kept their hands off and given the scheme a fair trial. The disastrous experience of

Kansas City under the Pendergast-MacElroy combination illustrates the evils which may result when political machines exploit the city manager plan. Even in some cities which have not adopted the city manager plan, the latter has served, through imitation, to strengthen the administrative powers of the mayor.

Outlook for city government. Looking upon city government in the light of its evolutionary record in the United States, one may say that for some generations it exerted an unusually disastrous influence upon American government. In the twentieth century, however, urban government, by using the commission and city-manager plans, has made greater strides than has any other phase of American politics in freeing itself from partisanship, corruption, and inefficiency.

The exceptions here remain the larger urban communities. But in New York City, reform, under Fusion auspices, temporarily broke the power of Tammany Hall in 1933, by electing Fiorello La Guardia as mayor. For the first time in New York political history, a Fusion candidate was re-elected in 1937. Indeed, Mayor La Guardia's majority in 1937 was more impressive than the plurality which he received in 1933. Many believed that the La Guardia triumphs might mark the turning point in the long and deplorable record of partisan graft and corruption in the great metropolitan centers of the country, especially as La Guardia was reëlected for a third term in 1941. The first Fusion campaign was managed by Ben Howe, probably the greatest genius of his time in the reform movement in American municipal politics. The election of Vincent R. Impellitteri, the Independent candidate, as mayor of New York City in 1950, indicated an almost unique revolt of the voters against traditional party rule. It was even more impressive than previous Fusion victories.

As we have noted, the reform element in Illinois has not been able to make comparable headway against the political machine in Chicago. The Pendergast and Hague machines have been at least temporarily crippled, but the Curley machine in Boston remained triumphant, despite the fact that Curley served a term in a Federal prison for illegal use of the mails.

Limited success of urban civil service systems. Cities have made wide use of the civil service system in seeking to improve the honesty and efficiency of city officials. But the enormous metropolitan budgets, with their potentialities for political graft and manipulation, have made it difficult in many cities to maintain an efficient urban civil service procedure.

Municipal finances. A word or two should be said about municipal finance. It is too complicated a subject to be discussed in detail in this book, but it is an economic item of great moment in the nation's life. The more than a billion dollar budget of New York City is as large as that of the State of New York. The degree of efficiency and honesty in determining, raising, and expending city budgets differs markedly. It depends upon the extent to which urban reform has been achieved in any particular city. As we have indicated above in discussing urban graft, municipal finance was long a rich source of political spoils. But the better governed cities of today have systematized their budgetary procedure and pay their bills with relative expedition and honesty. Nevertheless, corruption and chaos have been allowed to persist in an unbelievable manner in many municipalities. Anarchy and division of responsi-

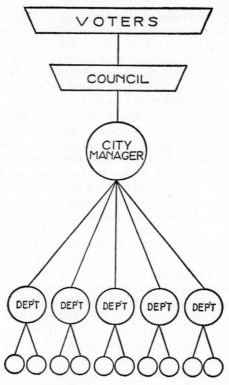

City Manager Form of Government.

bility inevitably facilitate graft and waste, and make honesty and economy almost impossible to achieve.

"Keeping up with the Joneses." City finance has been adversely affected not only by the spoils system but also by an irresponsible—or, at least, irrepressible—type of "booster" psychology. This became particularly apparent in the period between the First World War and the great depression of 1929 and following years. Although most of this city expansion was motivated by good intentions, it had little regard for financial realities. Its nature has been well summarized by Lothrop Stoddard:

Despite a much higher standard of honesty, despite marked improvement in technical economy and efficiency, the average American city government, great or small, has been living beyond its means. The current depression has merely brought to a head unsound spending and borrowing evils that have long been going on.

Of course, students of municipal affairs warned us of what was happening. But the general public did not listen, because the average American citizen had come to believe in permanent prosperity and blithely discounted the future. Municipal governments thus merely reflected popular optimism in their civic policies. They boosted tax rates and floated bond issues, not wrongfully or recklessly, but for causes which, though individually right and proper, collectively made up too ambitious a program to be undertaken in so short a time.

One of the chief causes for this general trend toward municipal extravagance is our national mania for "keeping up with the Joneses." Almost every American city has some municipal rival which it dearly loves to outdo. Suppose Jamestown installs a new system of cluster lights on its Main Street. Instantly the patriotic citizens of Johnstown, over in the next county, yearn for an equally good miniature imitation of the Great White Way. Again, suppose Johnstown erects a fine brick high school. The old wooden structure at Williamstown becomes an eyesore to its loyal boosters, who clamor for a bond issue to erect a new seat of learning that will go Johnstown one better. And so it goes with parks, playgrounds, boulevards, World War memorials, and a hundred other matters. Each one good in itself, of course. But, taken together, not so good—from a solvency and credit point of view.[16]

The bankers encouraged this type of civic extravagance in the predepression boom days because investment and trading in municipal bonds offered a large source of revenue to banks. Then came the crash of 1929 and the booster balloon was rudely punctured. The bankers thereupon withdrew their support or in some cases virtually took over the cities in a financial sense. The depression after 1929 brought extensive new burdens in the way of relief expenditures, while taxpayers were confronted with serious financial losses, reduced incomes, and extended unemployment. When this situation was combined with the heavy overhead that had come down from the boom period, a veritable crisis in city finance resulted. The Federal government had to step in and pass the Municipal Bankruptcy Act of May 24, 1934, to ease up the debt situation in American cities.

Well-governed cities, with an efficient budget system, were, however, able to weather the financial crisis. Milwaukee, under the moderate socialist government of Mayor Daniel Hoan, ended the year 1931 with all bills paid and a bank balance of 4 million dollars. Cincinnati was unusually efficiently governed under City Manager Clarence A. Dykstra. It also ended the difficult year of 1931 with all bills paid, and with a good balance in the bank. At the same time it had paid off over a million dollars of its bonded debt and cut its tax rate. In marked contrast to this was the virtual bankruptcy of the city of Chicago, which for many months was even unable to pay its teachers.

Critical state of urban finance. Some of the distressed municipalities improved their condition since 1933 as the result of Federal aid, but the high fixed charges in their financial setup, along with continuing burdens of relief, left American municipal finance as a whole in a rather critical condition on the eve of Pearl Harbor. The following table will give one an idea of the relative financial standing and credit of leading American cities on the eve of the Second World War.

---

[16] "Why Cities Go Broke," *The Forum,* June, 1932, p. 378.

RELATIVE CREDIT STANDING OF THE MAJOR MUNICIPALITIES
ON JAN. 1, 1941.

(Ranged in order of yields on their bonds—those with lowest yield
enjoy the highest credit—data from *The Bond Buyer*)

Cincinnati	1.45%	San Francisco	2.10%
Baltimore	1.60	Philadelphia	2.25
St. Louis	1.60	Los Angeles	2.40
Pittsburgh	1.65	Newark	2.50
Kansas City	1.70	Metropolitan Water District of	
Minneapolis	1.85	Southern California	2.55
Boston	1.90	Detroit	2.70
Chicago	1.95	New York	2.85
Cleveland	2.00	Port of New York Authority	2.87
Buffalo	2.10	Jersey City	3.25

The Bond Buyer's index of municipal bond yields stood at 2.14% on Jan. 1, an all-time low. A year earlier it was 2.59%, while the high was 5.69% on May 1, 1933.

City expenditures have been increasing since the Second World War. In 1949, the 397 American cities with a population of over 25,000 spent $4,052,000,000. Since there were 15,823 cities with a population under 25,000, a total urban expenditure of five billion dollars would be a very restrained estimate. This exceeds the total Federal Budget in 1932 and 1933. As a group, American cities have piled up a tremendous debt burden. In 1949, the gross debt of American municipalities totaled over 10 billion dollars, or more than eight times our total national debt in 1916. Urban debt is now on the increase.

It is important to point out that this increased urban indebtedness has not all been due to extravagance. It has also been a result of rising essential expenditures, of the increasing movement of urban populations to the suburbs, and of failure to solve the slum problem. Migration to the suburbs has affected urban finance adversely in two ways. In the first place, when metropolitan districts are abandoned by relatively well-to-do dwellers, the property value drops and taxes fall correspondingly. Further, when the abandoned homes are occupied by less prosperous groups, tax delinquency increases. Second, inhabitants of the many suburbs that are entirely outside urban corporation limits cannot be taxed at all by the city in which they formerly dwelt. But the suburban dwellers come to the city during the day to work and shop, and they enjoy all of the urban services and facilities tax-free, except for incidental or indirect taxation—city sales taxes, hotel and restaurant taxes, bridge and tunnel tolls, and increased fares on city transportation facilities. New York City has suffered notably from migration to the suburbs. It has been reduced to desperation in the effort to raise enough money to provide for essential urban services. It can do so only by state aid and by imposing an excessively high city sales tax. Another cause of urban financial difficulties has been the fact that the lack of housing construction and repair has hastened the deterioration of urban housing and the increase of the slum areas. These are a great financial liability to any city, for slum districts usually contribute less than 10 per cent of urban real estate tax income, while they absorb nearly half of all urban expenditures.

Impressive value of urban property. Another interesting item in the urban financial picture is the great value of urban property. For example, the taxable real estate and special franchises in Manhattan alone in 1947-1948 amounted to $7,743,603,790, or a sum about equal to the municipal debt of the larger cities in the United States—those with a population of over 25,000. The total assessed valuation of all taxable property in Greater New York in 1948 was $17,584,492,413. The total assessed valuation of all taxable property in Chicago in 1948 was $7,527,708,198; in Detroit $3,745,817,710; in Philadelphia, $3,417,497,435; in Los Angeles, $2,306,818,400; and in Baltimore, $2,052,954,229. It has been estimated that the total assessed valuation of all urban property in the United States in 1948 was between 125 and 150 billion dollars. The assessed valuation per capita in 300 cities of over 25,000 population was $1,788; and the average tax per $1,000 of assessed value was $42.66.

The average urban taxpayer's ignorance of urban financial operations. One reason why political machines can continue with so much graft is that the average taxpayer lives in essential ignorance of the facts of city finance. Clarence E. Ridley, executive director of the International City Managers' Association, listed some "major sins" in the reporting of municipal finance. In the first place, most cities make no adequate financial report. In 1937 some eighty annual reports were issued by cities in the United States. But these eighty represented only 5 per cent of the total number of cities of over 10,000 population. Such reports as are issued are filled with irrelevant, uninterpreted, or misinterpreted statistics. The valid statistics that are included and interpreted are usually intelligible only to a certified public accountant. They are a closed door to the average citizen. Further, these annual reports are all too often a chaotic collection of departmental reports which lack any essential unity.

Urban police systems. One of the most important city departments, and one often undermined by graft, is the Department of Public Safety, which usually includes the police and fire departments. The police force in our great metropolitan centers constitutes a miniature army. In 1949, New York City had 19,521 men on its police force, Chicago 7,265, Los Angeles 5,173, Philadelphia 4,870, and Detroit 4,721. The per capita cost of the police force in all cities over 10,000 inhabitants stood at $6.17 in 1947. The total expenditures for the police in these cities in 1949 was $367,161,000.

Inefficiency in apprehending criminals. The police systems in our municipalities probably compare well with most other city departments as to honesty and efficiency. But our urban policing still leaves much to be desired as a means of coping with the scandalous American crime situation. A large proportion of criminals are never even arrested. The report of the National Crime Commission on "The Relation of the Police and the Courts to the Crime Problem" gave us a precise summary of the situation in the 1930's. The number of arrests for burglaries reported ran from 35 per cent in Cleveland to 5 per cent in Kansas City: for robberies reported, from 49 per cent in Cleveland to 3 per cent in Buffalo; for murders reported, from 84.5 per cent in Cleveland to 32 per cent in St. Louis. In an elaborate study of 610,000 reported crimes, published in 1942, C. C. Van Vechten found that there were arrests for 25 per cent, convictions for 5.5 per cent, and prison sentences meted out for 3.5 per cent. The Federal Bureau of Investigation claimed some improvement during postwar years. In 1948, arrests were made for 28.9 per cent of reported crimes. Of all those formally charged by the police, 77.1 per cent were found guilty, but the high percentage of convictions was for petty crimes. Convictions for the more serious crimes ran from about a third to a little over half of the cases in which persons were formally charged with a crime. Why is there so low a rate of arrests?

Reasons for police inefficiency and corruption. In the first place, the criminals are more intelligent as a group than are the police. Few will contend that the police rank above the average of the population as to intelligence. But Carl Murchison and others have proved that even the convicts are as intelligent as the men studied in the army mental tests—certainly a fair measure of the general American population. But the convicts are, as a group, the stupid minority among the criminal class as a whole. Therefore, if the convicts are as intelligent as the army men—or as the police—then it is likely that the criminal class as a whole ranks above the average police force in native intelligence.

In the second place, many of the police are lacking in honesty and integrity. Many are dishonest before entering the service. They are friends of corrupt politicians and are often actually appointed to the force in order to insure protection for the guilty. If honest when they take up their duties, they often fall victim to the temptation of protection money and other graft. They blandly ignore the crimes of their friends and those who have paid for protection.

The police scandal in New York City, especially in Brooklyn, in 1950-51, exposed the venality which can exist in what are supposed to be among the best police systems of the country. It probably also revealed the unwisdom of outlawing gambling and driving it into the underworld which craves protection.

But there are honest policemen. Perhaps most of them are honest. They actually desire to arrest criminals. But they are given orders by those higher up in the city government or city politics to "lay off." Doubtless there was many a Chicago policeman who felt outraged when "Scarface" Al Capone and "Bugs" Moran brazenly announced that they had merged their criminal gangs, but no group of Chicago policemen could break up either gang and hold their jobs. In the 1938 trial of James J. Hines, the ruling figure in the "numbers game" and the chief power behind the throne in Tammany politics, it was admitted that New York City policemen were transferred or disciplined whenever the underworld leaders complained that they made even a pretense of enforcing the law in any particular precinct. As an expert police reporter, James P. Kirby, has well observed:

If policemen are corrupt, their corruption is hardly greater than that of the atmosphere in which they work.... It is the politician on the bench, in the prosecutor's office, and in the council chambers of our great cities—to their shame—who has set the pace which the policeman follows.

In the third place, there is not enough differentiation and specialization in the police service. Policemen are compelled to combine routine inspection, control of traffic, and other perfunctory duties with the detection of skilled professional criminals. There are special detectives but, for the most part, only the larger cities have made any effort to provide a group professionally trained in the repression of crime and the apprehension of law-breakers. Finally, honest and efficient policemen have to give too much of their time to trivial malefactions which should be left to the control of public opinion. This is a result of our tendency to try to make everybody good by law.

Suggested improvements in police systems. What is the remedy? The answer is easy enough, but to get practical action may be slow and difficult. We should divide the police force into two groups: (1) those who carry on routine inspection and patrolling; and (2) those specializing in crime detection. We would do well to increase the quality, payment, and integrity of the first group, but special attention should be paid to the second. Municipal engineers should do more to assist the police with traffic problems. As one police expert puts it: "It is obvious that traffic engineering is not a proper function of the police. Police should not be burdened with traffic engineering any more than they should be required to design streets or specify pavements."

The crime detection force should be recruited from a superior and well-educated class in the community—preferably college-trained men. They should be given prolonged and intensive training in criminology and all sciences auxiliary to it. They should be absolutely divorced from politics. Their position, status, tenure, and promotion should be based solely upon ability, training, and personal record. Their appointment should be made from a civil service list. They should have all the physical equipment necessary to run down the most adroit crooks. In other words, they should be competent, honest, fearless, and well-equipped.

If we turned such a group loose on the criminals we might catch most of the crooks who now run our crime bill up into the billions. This is no idle dream. Chief August Vollmer built up such a force in Berkeley, California, and could build up another in any place where a city government would give him proper support. Arthur Woods was on his way to giving New York City a real police force. He was compelled to leave the office of Police Commissioner before his efforts could bear permanent fruit. In California in recent years there has been the greatest progress in developing a technically trained, efficient, and independent police force to be observed anywhere outside the Federal Bureau of Investigation.

Too much emphasis cannot be laid upon the necessity for a police force equal to the present emergency. We can make little headway with either punishment or treatment of criminals unless we catch them. We shall be forever exposed to their onslaughts as long as they escape arrest. Further, greater certainty of arrest has a powerful effect in restraining criminals. This is proved by the example of England and other European countries. Their punishments are far milder than ours, but they apprehend more of their criminals. The improvement of the Federal detective system in the Bureau of Investigation of the Department of Justice under J. Edgar Hoover has led some to believe that we may be able, sooner or later, to build up a system of crime prevention and detection comparable to that provided by Scotland Yard in England. During the last two decades the largest cities have made an effort to build a professional crime detection force modeled on the FBI, and it is in these larger cities that we usually find today the best record of arresting and convicting criminals, at least those criminals guilty of the traditional crimes. The master minds of organized crime and gambling and the more clever traditional criminals are rarely arrested in any city. Even if arrested, they are often freed through legal chicanery and political influence.

Fire fighting and fire protection in cities. The improvement of fire protection constitutes one of the more notable phases of progress in urban administration, though the losses from fire are still scandalously high. Cities have far better fire protection than have rural areas, though the risks of fire are infinitely greater in urban regions. In the United States as a whole, fire losses amounted to 715 million dollars in 1948—nearly five dollars per capita. Impressive as the sum may be, it is insignificant compared to the crime bill of cities. It has been estimated that rackets and organized crime in New York City alone cost annually a sum in excess of the total fire losses of the whole country. Indeed, many of the fires in our larger cities are due to the work of the arson racket, now a well-developed phase of organized crime. The detective branch of the Fire Underwriters Association has done much in recent years to curb the arson racket.

Experts have estimated that one-half of the fire loss in the country today is preventable. This has led to increasing stress being laid upon fire prevention and upon public education in this field. Fire zoning and careful control of current and future urban construction are notably reducing the fire hazard of cities. But this still remains high in tenement areas and other sections where buildings are extremely congested and not of fireproof construction. Some of the larger cities have introduced regulations making it necessary to reconstruct the older tenements in such a fashion as to retard the rapidity with which fires have previously spread.

The fire departments of our larger cities rival the police departments in size and payrolls. In 1949, New York City had 10,565 employees in its fire department; Chicago 3,288; Philadelphia 3,202; Los Angeles 2,505; and Detroit 1,821. The expenditure for fire departments in all cities with a population of over 10,000 in 1949 was $312,071,000. Usually fire departments are far more free from graft and corruption than police departments, though in 1950-1951 in New York considerable graft was uncovered in the fire department. But it is very rare indeed that any such thing occurs as collusion between fire departments and arson rings or that fire departments protect those in the arson racket.

There have been impressive advances in the technique of fighting fires during the last century. A larger force of firemen has been provided and in the better cities firemen are given technical education in fire-fighting. Firemen are better paid and are now being put on twelve- and eight-hour shifts. Fire-fighting equipment has been revolutionized. We have moved on from the leather bucket and handsquirt to motor-propelled engines that can deliver 2,000 gallons of water a minute under a pressure of 300 pounds per square inch. Special high-pressure water mains have been constructed to aid in fire-fighting. Fireboats have been constructed to fight fires along the waterfront. Electric fire alarm systems have been installed. Chemicals have been widely introduced into fire-fighting. Factories, mercantile establishments, and hotels are extensively introducing chemical protection and automatic sprinkler systems. These automatic sprinklers are usually so arranged that when they start action they simultaneously send in a fire alarm to the nearest fire department station.

Improved methods of saving lives in fires have also been provided, a trend which is highly desirable since the deaths from fires run to between 6,000 and 8,000 lives per year, with a far larger number who are seriously injured. Spectacular losses of life have occurred in fairly recent night club and hotel fires. Some 491 persons lost their lives in the burning of the Coconut Grove night club in Boston on November 28, 1942; 61 persons lost their lives in the LaSalle Hotel fire in Chicago on June 5, 1946; and 121 in the fire in the relatively new Winecoff Hotel in Atlanta, Georgia, on December 7, 1946. The latter was the most disastrous hotel fire in American history.

Fire-fighting has made enormous strides since Mrs. O'Leary's cow kicked over the lantern that started the great Chicago fire in 1871. But it is probable that fireproof construction is a better safeguard than any available method of fighting fires.

MUNICIPAL OWNERSHIP AND URBAN SOCIALISM

Meaning of urban socialism. As we suggested above, modern cities have gone into various forms of business enterprise in extensive fashion. This so-called municipal socialism has been particularly well developed in Europe. Cities have operated transit systems, electric utilities, gas plants, and other enterprises. Occasionally they have entered extensively into building and housing projects.

In the United States the amount of urban socialism has varied greatly, but on the whole it has been far less extensive than in European cities. It has been taken for granted in every American city that certain types of business should be handled by the municipality. Such is the case with public education, sanitary engineering, fire protection, and the like. But there have been wide differences in the reaction to the proposal that cities should control and manage transportation and other utilities. Looking at the matter broadly, one may say that American cities have

been relatively resistant to the blandishments of urban socialism. Nevertheless, there have been certain interesting experiments. By 1938 four-
fifths of all American cities of more than 5,000 population owned some
form of public utility. There are still, however, some 240 cities in this
group that owned no public utilities in 1949.

Examples of municipal ownership. The most striking and uniform
triumph of urban socialism in American cities has been accomplished in
the public ownership of water works. The health of the city is so closely
interrelated to the water supply that cities have been reluctant to entrust
this to the whims and uncertainties of private business. In 1800 only 6
per cent of municipal water plants were publicly owned. This had grown
to 69 per cent in 1949. The alarming water shortage in New York City
in 1949 and 1950 emphasized the importance of adequate municipal
planning and control of the water supply. Many cities make a large
profit out of the water business. In 1923 the city of Milwaukee had a net
profit of $1,396,429 on the operation of its water plant. Some 48.5 per cent
of the sewage disposal plants were owned by cities in 1949.

City transportation has usually remained in the hands of private
enterprise, but several cities of importance have undertaken to own and
operate their street railways. The man mainly responsible for the movement for municipal ownership of street railways was Tom L. Johnson,
himself originally a rich traction mogul in the Middle West. He started
his campaign in Cleveland in 1901. Although he did not succeed with
his program in that city, he attracted much attention to the crusade and
deeply influenced movements of the sort elsewhere. San Francisco was
the first large city to make this experiment, beginning in 1912. Seattle
took over the entire street railway system of the city in 1918. In 1922
Detroit also bought its street railway system, and has operated it profitably.
A year previously, the Canadian city of Toronto had done the same thing.
New York City is gaining an ever greater degree of ownership of its transit
systems. On the whole, however, cities have made little headway in owning and operating transportation systems. In 1949 only 11 cities in the
group having a population of over 5,000 (0.5 per cent) owned their
street railway systems. They have done a little better in taking over bus
lines. In 1949, 41 cities in this class (2.0 per cent) owned bus lines.

Slight progress has been made in the way of municipal ownership of
gas plants, amounting to only 2.2 per cent in 1949. The largest and most
impressive of these municipal gas enterprises is that launched by Omaha,
Nebraska, in 1920. It has been estimated that municipal gas plants sell
gas on the average from 15 to 20 cents cheaper per 1000 cubic feet than
do the private plants. Moreover, most of the some 45 municipal gas
plants now in existence make a sizeable profit, which is turned over to
the city treasury.

In spite of vigorous opposition from the private utilities, there has been
a notable trend toward municipal ownership in the field of electric utilities. In 1949, some 261 cities, or 12.8 per cent, owned and operated electric
light and power plants. On the basis of a careful estimate, it is stated that
the private utility plants charge about one third more, on the average,

than do the municipal plants for comparable services. It has also been held that the country would save half a billion dollars a year on its electric bill, if all the light and power were generated in municipal plants.

There are various and sundry other forms of economic ventures into which municipalities have entered. A few cities have municipal coal and fuel yards. The public can profit by lower prices, since the city can buy fuel on a large scale. Our larger seacoast towns have invested heavily in municipal ports, piers, and wharf terminals. This has been particularly the case with New York, Baltimore, New Orleans, Los Angeles, and Seattle. Approximately 3.8 per cent of ports are today city property. Municipal markets have been popular for many years. Considerably more than half of the cities with a population of over 30,000 have municipal markets, and over three-fourths of the cities with a population above 100,000 have one or more municipal markets. Particularly notable have been the municipal markets in New York, New Orleans, and Cleveland. Some 32 per cent of all urban cemeteries and about 21 per cent of the airports are owned by cities.

Present extent of municipal ownership. The following table from the *Municipal Year Book* summarizes the status of municipal ownership in the United States at the mid-century. It is based upon data reported by some 2,033 cities of over 5,000 population in 1949:

EXTENT OF MUNICIPAL OWNERSHIP

Items	Number of Cities	Percentage of Cities
Airports	425	20.9
Abattoirs	41	2.0
Auditoriums	382	18.8
Bus systems	41	2.0
Electric utilities	261	12.8
Gas systems	44	2.2
Incinerators	288	26.7
Port facilities	78	3.8
Sewage disposal plants ...	986	48.5
Street railways	11	0.5
Water supply	1405	69.0

Balance sheet of municipal ownership. We shall deal with municipal housing projects in a later chapter. One may observe that, on the whole, municipal ownership has worked reasonably well in every field where it has been given an honest trial. This has been true despite political partisanship and corruption in city government. One important advantage in municipal ownership is that the public can directly control and oust political grafters in municipal enterprises. But the public is relatively helpless in the face of the graft and exploitation by private finance and business. The greatest need right now is for increased municipal control of the milk supply of our urban centers. In the New York state constitutional convention of 1938 it was proposed that milk be made a public utility, but no steps were taken to bring this about.

MUNICIPAL TRANSIT AND TRAFFIC PROBLEMS

Street cars and buses. The problems of municipal transportation have been among the most formidable ones in the experience of modern cities. In the early days municipal transport was chiefly a problem of getting enough conveyances to take care of the needs of citizens. There was relatively slight congestion of traffic. Today we not only require more and better conveyances of certain types, but we have the new and tremendous problem of controlling the body of traffic that floods the contemporary city streets.

The early street railways were served by horse-drawn cars, the first of which began operation in 1832. But horse-drawn cars did not become common until after the Civil War. A revolution was worked in surface-car transportation when electrically-propelled cars were introduced in the 1890's. These were handed over mainly to private enterprise, and considerable political graft and corruption entered into the awarding of street railway franchises. In our day the coming of automobiles and motorbuses has struck a blow at electric surface cars comparable to that which the latter delivered against the horse-drawn cars fifty years ago.

In certain important ways the bus era has even more thoroughly disrupted the former methods of street transportation. The electric street railway system is today one of our major sick industries. There is little private building in this field at present. But economically managed electric street railways can still render good service and make money. It is definitely assured, however, that motor buses will become the well-nigh universal method of public surface conveyance. These motor-buses are constantly being improved in speed, safety, and comfort. Urban and suburban bus transportation has now become a tremendous enterprise. In 1949 some 8,918,143,000 revenue passengers were carried in urban buses by 1,740 bus companies and 57,800 buses.

Elevated railroads and subways. Elevated railroads, first propelled by steam and then by electricity, have played an important part in city transportation since the first elevated line was opened in New York City in 1870. They are still very important in some large cities. For example, Chicago still depends upon them almost entirely for nonsurface transportation.

The financial and political vested interests in the great elevated systems radiating out of the Chicago Loop district have thus far been able to hold at bay any extensive development of subways in Chicago save for a few suburban lines as they pass through the heart of the city. But plans are now being developed for a subway system for Chicago. Only in New York City, which has over three-fourths of the total subway mileage of the country, have the elevated railroads been eclipsed and mostly dismantled. Of course, the outlying extensions of nearly all the subways become elevated systems.

The first subway in the United States was opened in Boston in 1897, but the major subway development has taken place in New York City. The earlier New York subways were built through the collaboration of private enterprise and city contributions. New York City labored under definite handicaps in collecting revenue from these earlier subway lines because private enterprise had a prior lien on the earnings. As a result, recent subway construction in New York City has been a municipal enterprise. Subway construction is extremely expensive, the average cost for construcing a mile of the Eighth Avenue subway in New York being $11,500,000 at the time of construction, and it would be more than double this figure today.

Travel on the subways, however essential and convenient as a mode of transportation, is actually a phase of urban pathology. This is particularly true in rush hours. Lewis Mumford thus comments on what he calls hell on the subway:

> Rushing beneath geological strata, rivers, tall buildings, avenues, the fortunate travellers who have seats struggle to assimilate the day's dispersed events recorded in the newspapers. For those who stand, the subway becomes a cloister; a place of enforced inactivity and contemplation; if you will, a travelling prison.[17]

Taxicab traffic. Another important and novel type of urban transportation is provided by taxicabs. These have supplied extremely important service in transportation for the well-to-do in both business and social engagements. Taxicab service came in with such a rush that it has been inadequately regulated by most municipalities. There are usually too many cabs, which results in low income per driver. Since the drivers seek customers by cruising about, they greatly increase traffic congestion. Some steps have been taken toward regulating taxicab transport. The number of cabs is controlled and restricted in certain cities; in others, a taxicab franchise is granted to one or a few operators who accept definite city regulations.

Urban traffic problems. The simultaneous use of the streets by private automobiles, taxicabs, commercial trucks, motorbuses, and surface cars, to say nothing of pushcarts in certain urban sections, has brought about a tremendous congestion of traffic. Moreover, the honking of automobile horns makes our streets a bedlam, compared to which the Tower of Babel might be regarded as a convention of deaf mutes.

Our cities have struggled heroically to provide scientific traffic regulations and to supply signals and police supervision to control traffic. But the congestion is still scandalous and the lives of pedestrians are rendered extremely precarious. On some of the main New York City thoroughfares, one can walk more rapidly than he can be transported in a motor bus during the more congested hours of travel. During business hours on rainy days one can often literally crawl on his hands and knees more rapidly than a bus progresses along the busier streets. In the more congested sections one can often out-walk even a taxi. There seems little doubt that the larger cities will soon have to provide elevated streets for vehicular transport, especially for the main arteries of traffic. Indeed, certain of the metropolitan communities have already undertaken such construction.

---

[17] Mumford, *op. cit.*, p. 261.

Better entrances and exits are being provided for vehicular traffic by means of elevated streets, bridges, and tunnels. To a certain degree, however, this is self-defeating, for the easier it is made for cars to get into town, the greater the urban congestion in the morning and evening and during

COURTESY *The New York Times.*

Fifth Avenue and 47th St. New York City: Problems of traffic congestion in large American cities.

theatre hours. If more progress is made in the way of breaking up population congestion in the chief urban districts, this will help notably to reduce the problems of city traffic. Thus far, rapid transit and suburban life have mainly served to increase congestion in cities during working hours. If, however, business and commercial life come to be scattered about as a result of better city planning, this will no longer be the case.

Parking difficulties. Important among city transportation problems is that of parking automobiles and motor trucks. It is becoming an ever more serious problem to find parking space for motor cars. In some areas of cities, such as the crosstown streets in New York between 14th Street and 42nd Street, traffic is all but paralyzed as a result of parked motor trucks depositing and receiving merchandise. Cities have tried to cope with this problem in numerous ways. New York City is placing severe restrictions on the parking of merchandise trucks on crosstown streets. Many cities have installed parking meters, requiring payment in proportion to the time parked. These have helped to some extent. Other cities have extended their zoning laws to cover parking regulations. Some have mandatory off-street parking and have required apartment house owners to build garages for families occupying such structures. Many cities have provided municipally owned parking space near the central business districts. Parking fees run from 25 cents to $1 per day. A traffic expert writing in 1951 estimated that it would cost between 60 and 100 million dollars to provide adequate off-street public parking facilities in New York City alone. The following figures giving the percentage of cities, according to population, which have installed parking meters and established municipal parking lots will help to indicate the extent to which municipalities have sought to deal with the serious parking problem.

Population	Percentage with parking meters	Percentage having city-operated parking lots
Over 500,000	47	60
200-400,000	90	25
100-200,000	80	42
50-100,000	79	47
25-50,000	69	52
10-25,000	58	45

Urban airports. Air navigation, too, has entered the urban scene. Out of the total of 6,414 airports in the United States in 1948, no less than 2,050 were municipally owned. Buses bringing in the ever increasing number of air passengers cause further congestion in city streets.

SANITATION AND PUBLIC HEALTH

Health situation in cities. In the chapter devoted to health and medical care we described the incredible lack of sanitation in early American cities, and described some of the progress that has since been made. We also detailed the need for extensive additions and improvements in urban sanitary facilities. We have pointed out that urban sanitary facilities and operations are usually controlled by the municipal corporation and constitute an impressive demonstration of the success of municipal ownership. Nothing more need be said on these subjects in this place, except to recall the aid provided by Federal funds after 1933.

We may, however, profitably examine the question as to whether cities are healthier than country areas. They certainly were not before the rise of urban sanitation and public health measures. Water supplies were easily polluted and epidemics were frequent. It is often stated, however, that today our larger cities are far healthier than rural areas. This assertion is buttressed by citing the crude death rates, in which the cities make a somewhat better showing than country districts. There is no doubt that the cities have more and better doctors per capita than country areas, though these better doctors are more expensive to procure and their services are not so readily available to the lower middle class and the poor. A very important fact, of course, is that the larger cities have far better hospitals and a more thoroughly organized public health service. This helps to offset the fact that, because of population density, the congestion of buildings, lack of fresh air and ventilation, restricted exercise, and all-too-frequent gloom and darkness, city life is less hygienic than country life. Other things which contribute to make city life less healthful are the increased amount of noise, smoke, dust, and gases and a marked increase of exposure to possible infection. The slums are notoriously unhealthy dwelling areas.

Inaccuracy of crude death rate tests. Careful students of morbidity and mortality statistics are inclined to doubt the frequent assertions of city boosters that cities are more healthful than country areas. As W. S. Thompson has done well to point out, the crude death rates in contemporary cities are misleading as a reflection of urban versus rural mortality. In our cities there have been and still are a disproportionate number of young persons, especially young women. Many of these have been drawn in from the country areas. Both sickness and death are less frequent among youth. Young women have the lowest death rate of all. In this way, the healthier age-groups have been drawn away from the country and brought into the cities. For these reasons one must properly correct the crude death-rate test of the relative morbidity and mortality of the city, as compared with rural areas. Thompson believes that the country has much the better of the argument as to salubrity and longevity.

It hardly needs to be pointed out that, especially since the rise of automobile traffic, the prospect of serious accidents or accidental death is enormously greater in urban areas. About one other matter there can be no legitimate doubt, namely that nervous and mental diseases occur far more frequently in cities because of the greater extent of slum life, overcrowding, social and personal disorganization, and the additional strains, stresses, and noises.

PROBLEMS OF SOCIAL PATHOLOGY AND DEPENDENCY IN CITIES

How city life favors crime and vice. We shall treat the questions of crime, vice, and dependency more thoroughly in later chapters. But something should be said here about the relation of city life to various types of pathological social behavior. In the rapidly growing industrial cities it was inevitable that the crude living conditions would bring about extensive social maladjustment. Men and women accustomed to a simple farming life and controlled by country folkways and rural public opinion poured by the thousands into the new mushroom cities. There were no well-established city folkways and mores to guide and control the new city populations. The serious problems of readjustment to an altogether different mode of life, together with low income and depressed living conditions, naturally increased the prevalence of crime, vice, and degeneracy. This fact has been emphasized by Niles Carpenter.

In the author's opinion, many of the disorganizing effects of the city upon the individual (crime, mental breakdown, etc.) are to be interpreted not so much as effects of city life as such, but rather as the effects of the *sudden impact of the characteristically urban set of conditioning influences upon a personality that has been accommodated to a characteristically non-urban set of influences.*[18]

Also fundamental to any understanding of the greater prevalence of crime and vice in cities is a recognition of the fact that it is in cities that we find the greatest amount of social disorganization, which brings with it the personal disorganization of which crime, vice, alcoholism, drug addiction, and the like are leading pathological manifestations. In the slum areas we find an overwhelming prevalence of the overcrowding, broken families, unwholesome environment, inadequate recreational facilities, impoverishment, and other unfavorable situations which encourage all forms of delinquency, viciousness, and degeneracy.

The fact that young people predominate among those who come from the country to the city is another reason for the disproportionate amount of urban crime and vice. Crime and vice have been disproportionately prevalent among those under thirty years of age, and this situation has become worse in recent years. In the cities of the United States the situation has been further aggravated and complicated by racial and cultural maladjustments because the populations of the American cities have been made up, to a large extent, of immigrants. Many of these came from rural areas in Europe, and they have had a double problem of adjustment to both a new way of life and a new civilization. Moreover, as we have seen, it is the children of the foreign-born who have had the greatest proclivity to crime and vice of any group in the population.

So much for the general historical factors which have contributed to make crime and vice more prevalent in cities. Let us now look at some of the more specific reasons for the greater prevalence of social pathology in urban life. In the first place, there is far more opportunity for crime per square mile in the city than in the country. There is more wealth and, hence, better prospect for bigger "hauls" in criminal depredations. The same is true of vice and commercialized gambling. Cities provide a larger and more opulent clientele for these types of excitement. Despite the better policing of cities, it is a fact that the criminal and the vicious elements can hide themselves away more safely in urban districts than in most rural regions. The living conditions most favorable to the development of criminals are found mainly in the cities. Here are located most of the typical "delinquency areas" studied by Clifford Shaw and others.

Since there is less opportunity for wholesome outdoor recreation in cities than in the country, substitute forms of expression must be found, and these often border upon or actually enter the realm of the vicious and the criminal. We have already noted that urban life tends to break up the old rural family and to destroy its disciplinary power. Since nothing adequate has been substituted for it as a type of social control, city youth tends to run wild. Juvenile gangs take the place of the old

---

[18] *The Sociology of City Life.* New York: Longmans, Green, 1931, pp. 217-218. (Italics are Carpenter's.)

rural hearth circle. City youths, instead of sitting around the home fires, as in olden days, are now given to "turning on the heat" in dance halls and cheap night clubs. Criminal and vicious juvenile gangs have actually threatened to get out of hand in some of our large cities in recent years.

Nature of urban crime. As a result of the many factors favoring greater criminality in urban regions we can readily understand the conclusion reached by the eminent criminologist, Edwin H. Sutherland, that: "The number of serious crimes in proportion to the population seems to increase with the size of the community." At least this holds true in cities up to those above 250,000 in population where the better crime detection service and more thoroughly developed crime prevention programs appear to restrain the commission of serious crimes somewhat more successfully. Since the Second World War, however, the crime rate per capita has risen more rapidly in country than in urban areas, though the urban crime rate still remains considerably higher than that in country regions.

Until fairly recently urban crimes were predominantly crimes against property as compared with the crime picture in rural districts. The following table, comparing rural and urban crime rates in the state of Minnesota for the period 1936-1938, illustrates the far greater prevalence of crimes against property in urban areas down to the eve of the Second World War:

COMPARATIVE RURAL AND URBAN CRIME RATES [19]

	Rural	Urban
Murder and voluntary manslaughter	1.3	1.3
Negligent manslaughter	1.1	0.6
Rape, including carnal knowledge	3.6	3.7
Robbery	9.5	42.1
Aggravated assault	5.2	10.2
Burglary	61.6	257.8
Larceny (except auto theft)	97.6	567.9
Automobile theft	25.2	220.9

[19] Thorsten Sellin, *Crime*. Washington: National Education Association, 1942, p. 20.

Following the Second World War, there has been an increase in urban crimes against persons which has reached almost epidemic proportions in some cities. These crimes do not usually have an economic motive but seem to be caused by psychopathic compulsions, degeneracy, sadism, and craving for morbid excitement. These crimes take the form of "mugging," vicious physical assaults, knifings, rapes, degenerate sexual assaults, molesting of children, and the like. While some of this form of crime gets reported in the newspapers, much of it is so morbid, degenerate, and personally humiliating that it is not even reported to the police or, if reported, is not discussed in the newspapers. This alarming new development has received its first complete description in the recent book by perhaps our ablest journalistic writer on crime, Howard Whitman, in his *Terror on the Streets*.[20] As we point out elsewhere, there has been a comparable reversal of the character of rural crimes during the same period, namely, a growing preponderance of crimes against property.

Vice, gambling, alcoholism, and drug addiction. Organized vice and gambling are far more prevalent in urban regions than in rural areas. The reasons are clear enough. There is a larger clientele interested in such matters, among other reasons because they do not have more normal and healthful outlets. There is also a greater proportion of unmarried persons in cities. The tense nervous life of cities favors indulgence in more artificial and extreme forms of diversion and excitement. There is less of normal family life in the city than in the country. Those who manage vice and gambling have a far greater prospect of remunerative returns in city communities. Non-commercial sexual promiscuity is also far greater in urban centers than in rural districts. Liquor consumption and drinking habits are relatively far more common in the cities. This has become particularly true since the repeal of prohibition, partly as the result of the fact that the urban resorts in which drinks may be obtained are far more attractive and drinking more respectable than in rural saloons and barrooms. Drug addiction is more usual in the cities. Many resort to drugs in order to deaden or reduce the strains and distractions of city life. This drug habit takes the form of everything from relatively mild remedies for inducing sleep to indulgence in the more potent forms of narcotics. Since the drug addict is notoriously given to proselyting and spreading the habit, cities offer far more favorable opportunities for this type of degenerate activity. Drug addiction among city youths, even those of high-school age, has become an increasingly serious problem of late.

Higher urban suicide rate. The suicide rate is far higher in cities than in rural communities. In 1929, for example, the urban suicide rate was 58 per cent higher than the rural rate. It went beyond this figure in depression years. This excess of urban suicide probably arises from the breakup of the rural family and neighborhood life and of the accompanying social attachments and life patterns in the urban environment. The eminent French sociologist, Émile Durkheim, attributed suicide in considerable part to this breakdown of personal groups and the traditional mental attachments and emotional supports which accompanied them. The social and personal disorganization which city life and depressed urban living conditions have created or intensified bear their pathological fruit in a higher suicide rate as well as in a greater amount of crime, vice, and degeneracy. The problem of suicide will be discussed more fully later.

The problem of poverty and old age in cities. Poverty, measured merely in terms of monetary income, may not be any more prevalent in the city than in the country. In fact, the per capita income of city dwellers is from two to three times that of the farming population in normal

---

20 New York: Dial Press, 1951.

times. In 1929 the ratio was $908 to $273. In 1948 the ratio was about $1,400 to $800. But the expenses of life in cities are correspondingly greater. Moreover, poverty in the city renders the poverty-stricken person far more helpless than it does the country dweller. The latter can supplement his income and provide sustenance through various forms of agricultural activity, or he can gather fuel and other necessities in more informal fashion. But the city dweller who has lost his income or has a grossly inadequate income immediately becomes a subject for relief and charity if he is to survive at all. As we indicate in other places in this book, the raising of funds for private charity is handled mainly by community chests, and the administration of private charity is conducted by charity organization societies, sometimes known as federated charities or associated charities. Since the depression of 1929, public charity, supplied by the city, state, and Federal governments, and social security payments have greatly exceeded the contributions of private charity.

The problems of old age are particularly acute in urban regions. Because there is relatively less chance of surviving to old age in cities, the latter have a slightly lower ratio of old persons. But our social and economic system deals in much more ruthless fashion with the old person who dwells in the city. A farmer may be productively engaged until he is 70 years old, or even older. But in industry and clerical occupations, and in retail trades in our cities, it is becoming ever more difficult to secure employment after one is 45 years of age. Indeed, it is difficult in many lines to obtain employment after 35. Those who have steady employment are more frequently turned out of their jobs after they have reached the period of middle life. To the reality of physical old age has thus been added the even more serious fact of fictitious economic old age. Therefore, our cities pile up a large proportion of unemployed old people who become a personal or a public charge. It is harder to take care of this surplus of unemployed old persons in the city than it is in the country. There is less room in city apartments, especially in tenement districts, for the idle aged who must sit around at home. Moreover, it costs more to support an unemployed person in idleness in urban districts. The ever more serious economic and social problems of old age are thus primarily an urban problem.

Urban provisions for dealing with personal dependency and social pathology. While recognizing the undoubted fact that delinquency, degeneracy, and dependency are much more prevalent per capita in the large cities than in any other sections of the country, save for some of the more backward small-town and marginal farming areas, it is necessary to keep in mind that the cities also make the best provision for combating and relieving these conditions. Social work is best developed here. Community chests, which now raise nearly 200 million dollars a year, devote nearly all of their efforts and resources to assisting the urban needy and unfortunate. Social settlements exist only in cities. There is better policing and more adequate provision for crime prevention. Venereal prophylaxis is generally better known in cities and more easily accessible. Various agencies for suppressing the drug habit are most numerous and effective in urban areas. This situation tends to keep down what would probably otherwise be far more impressive and dangerous manifestations of social pathology in urban communities.

CULTURAL LIFE IN CITIES

The urban mental patterns. Cities have played the dominant role in the evolution of human culture. As Maurice R. Davie correctly remarks, "all great cultures have been city born." From ancient Memphis and Thebes to contemporary Paris and Moscow, most of the cultural achievements of mankind which are studied by historians have been produced by city populations. Hence, we may profitably analyze the character of urban culture in our day.

Before we begin to describe specifically the cultural life and institutions of our cities, it will be well to say a word about what experts on city life regard as the somewhat typical urban mentality. This is important because the psychology of city life directly and powerfully influences the cultural interests and activities of urban communities. Attention has been called to the fact that city life presents so many diversified stimuli and such an ever-shifting range of impressions and personal contacts that the urban mind is characterized by a sort of dynamic superficiality. As Munro expresses it:

The city dweller leads a life so crowded with impressions that little time is left to him for reflection. These impressions are quickly and easily made, but just as quickly and easily erased, for the city mind craves novelty and is impatient of repetition. Its yearning is always for something new, something strange, something bizarre. Thus the urban mentality is restive, impulsive, intolerant of delay, although it is docile enough in its continued submission to public abuses.[21]

Anderson and Lindeman develop this same line of reasoning, laying stress upon the transient, tense, superficial, and flashy character of urban mental reactions. They further point out that even mental calm and self-possession on the part of city dwellers is artificial and self-induced. When the strains of city life become too great, pathological developments, both personal and social, become unusually rapid and devastating:

The city flows on relentlessly with ever-increasing speed, touching its inhabitants here and there with stimulation that demands quick, varied, and exact response. New situations are always arising and must be met quickly and precisely. As there is little time to "stop and think," a stamp of alert precision is made upon the city dweller's personality. He develops a quick and sharp decisiveness which makes him appear nervous, but his is the kind of nervousness necessary for survival. He also appears to be a person whose life is given over to externals, and to the rural-minded he may seem superficial. Although his life is filled with color it is difficult for the rural person to understand his inducements and motivations. His values seem determined by outward appearances. Whatever his personality, he essays to flash it on the surface where it can be taken in at a glance. His contacts, as brief as they are numerous, make it necessary for him to concentrate on "the first impression." The psychology of sales-

---

21 From *The Encyclopaedia of the Social Sciences,* Vol. III, p. 481. By permission of The Macmillan Company, publishers.

manship, for instance, lays great emphasis on the first contact. Thus the city man takes in impressions and gives them in the most pithy, dynamic form. Accordingly, he dresses for each occasion and gives a great deal of attention to dress.

Possessing a wide knowledge of many things, he seems to be profound about nothing. In conversation he glides over many things with the same haste that he rushes after a street car or as he reads the newspaper, by devouring the headlines. Making studied attempts to impress or "get away with it," much of his so-called "class" or style or culture is designed for flash and display.... In the rush of life and the hasty contacts that characterize urban existence, these sketchy impressions are about all the cosmopolitan modern man has time for. If there is not actual sophistication, there must at least be a pretense. This invitation to parade one's wares, and sometimes it becomes a compelling imperative, is essentially urban. . . .

If selection and accommodation go toward producing the urban personality—the urban habit of mind—the negative phase of the same process makes the city a center of multitudinous unadjustments and maladjustments. The businessman who seems so self-possessed under strain may have gained his calm by smoking innumerable cigarettes. The society woman who greets her guests with so much *savoir-faire* may be upon the verge of hysteria. In order to conceal the fear of unadjustment and the nervous strain, urban personalities develop a lively feeling of self-regard. Indeed, one of these characteristics as distinguished from rural personalities is egoism, and so long as their nervous systems support them, this carries them far toward achievement. But once the race becomes too swift, and the strain too great, the nervous system breaks and this same egoism turns into abnormal self-degradation. Or whenever the egoism becomes absorbed in a crowd movement, the result may be a frightened exhibition of uncontrolled enthusiasm, following crazes, manias, and fads, or in extreme cases, giving way to mob action with all its manifestations of hatred and violence.[22]

N. P. Gist and L. A. Halbert agree in general with this appraisal of urban mental traits, but they also single out for special emphasis the qualities of self-assertiveness, aggressiveness, and egotism as the most characteristic traits of the urban mentality. These may be merely an overcompensation for an underlying sense of uncertainty and insecurity. At least, R. D. McKenzie observes that: "From the point of view of individual welfare, most of the graver problems of metropolitan living may be grouped under the general category of insecurity or instability."[23]

Influence of urban mental traits on national life and culture. These facts about the mentality of city dwellers are not only important in their relation to the cultural activities of the city but are also extremely significant on account of the dominant urban influence over the mental and institutional life of the nation. City life now pervades and colors national life in all industrialized countries. The superficial and mercurial urban psychology is a particularly serious handicap in an age which requires profundity and intellectual reflection as never before in history. This fact is clearly brought out by Munro:

The city, in any event, is bound to be a controlling factor in the national life. As the city is, so will the nation be. Its population supplies most of the national leadership. Through its daily press the city dominates public opinion far outside its own bounds. It is stronger in its influence upon political thought than its ratio of population warrants. It sets the fashion—in morals and in

---

[22] Anderson and Lindeman, *op. cit.,* pp. 232-234.
[23] McKenzie, *op. cit.,* p. 316.

manners as in attire. The demeanor of the city is not, therefore, a matter of concern to itself alone. It is of vital concern to all who desire high national aspirations to be established and maintained, for the ideals of a nation are determined by the most influential among the various elements of its population.[24]

Characteristic personality types in cities. Anderson and Lindeman believe that city life has produced certain definite urban personality types, which can be fairly easily distinguished. Among them are the following: First, we have the rich man, or the great "captain" of finance and industry. He gains his distinction because of conspicuous success in the acquisition of wealth. His mythical austerity and aloofness have gained for him a sort of reverential awe.[25] More amiable and congenial is the philanthropist, whose repute rests upon conspicuous giving rather than conspicuous acquisition. The philanthropist, often aided by his public relations counsel, has done much to create a more cordial attitude toward the rich on the part of the "have-nots" in society.

The booster type has been immortalized by Sinclair Lewis in *Babbitt*. This type is loyal, above all else, to city prestige. He constitutes the dynamic element in contemporary urban growth and enthusiasm. The city club-man is the typical cosmopolitan sophisticate and is the most cultivated product of upper-class urban society. More of an exhibitionist esthete is the bohemian, who seeks to combine the pleasures of the flesh with intellectual curiosity and an urbane outlook. In this class we find types that run from emancipated critics to self-indulgent degenerates. An interesting city type which has grown out of immigration is that which Anderson and Lindeman call the "allrightnick." This type is usually a son of the foreign born. He is an amiable pusher in business and an exhibitionist social climber in city society. By conspicuous expenditures on dress and the like, he seeks to over-compensate for his rejection by polite society. Then we have the rebel type, whose rebellion may be against city life as a whole, but more usually takes the form of an intense hostility to the differences in wealth and social opportunity that city life presents. This type is the recruiting ground for the more intelligent radicals. The great moguls of organized crime, racketeering, and gambling syndicates have in the last three decades supplied a new and glamorous, if pathological, city type. They are the "captains of industry" of the underworld. Rarely arrested or convicted, they have enjoyed undue publicity and prestige, and they probably have done much to encourage persons of impressionable or unstable minds to enter a life of crime. Finally, we find the various types of social outcasts, such as chronic mendicants, hoboes, and the like.

The city also brings out certain definite female types. Socially most conspicuous, and the most complete representative of caste society in the United States, is the society woman, usually the wife of one of

---

24 From *The Encyclopaedia of the Social Sciences,* Vol. III, p. 481. By permission of The Macmillan Company, publishers.

25 For a very different appraisal see William Feather, "The King of Loafers," *The American Mercury,* October, 1924, pp. 143 ff.

the great moguls of finance, industry, or trade. She is mainly concerned with the stereotyped functions of polite society, which has been extremely exclusive. The society woman is the most perfect example of Veblen's theory of the leisure class, with its zest for honorific display and conspicuous extravagance. Immediately related is the emergent society dame or debutante. It has been estimated that the annual cost of presenting debutantes to society averages over $19,000 per "deb." But the old days of a caste society seem to be drawing to an end as a result of the social and economic changes going on in our cities. The main purpose of the debut in the past was to get the society girl presented to society so that she could procure an eligible bachelor from the same lofty social stratum. But there are few of these left.

Very prominent in the twentieth century has been the feminist, who has promoted the emancipation of women. The older agrarian and aristocratic foundations of feminine prestige and security having been undermined by industrialization and urbanization, the feminist seeks to discover new methods of restoring respect and stability to the female sex. Her efforts take both economic and political forms of expression. The most extreme and influential type of feminist is the clubwoman, who has sufficient economic independence to devote herself almost exclusively to the task of emancipating her sex and increasing female social self-consciousness in urban communities. The clubwoman is a powerful force in urban social work and civic agencies.

Aspects of urban cultural life. The cultural life of cities is inevitably conditioned very sharply by the mentality of its inhabitants. Our contemporary urban communities present ample resources for those who wish to carry on a full, studious, and reflective cultivation of literature, the arts, and music. But the urban zest for the flashy, the sensational, and the superficial reduces or frustrates anything like a full appreciation or exploitation of the cultural advantages which the cities extend to their inhabitants. One will find the musical comedies, burlesque shows, and night clubs much more enthusiastically patronized than museums or the public libraries. Café society attracts the socially elite to a far greater extent than does a lecture by Einstein or any other great intellectual celebrity.

When it comes to spreading before their numerous inhabitants the accumulated culture of the past, the cities certainly provide extensive and varied facilities. The public schools are relatively excellent. Diversified provisions are made for adult education. The New School for Social Research and the People's Institute in New York City are excellent examples. Our better public libraries in the cities have abundant literary resources and are efficiently administered. Elaborate museums of science and technology and richly endowed art museums abound. Musical tastes are ministered to by operas and public concerts. It is in the cities that we find the public forums at which city populations may listen to the more distinguished intellects of the country. In many cities the department of education maintains such forums and offers free admission. Never before in human history has the average man had placed before him such rich and varied cultural facilities as the greater cities of today put at his disposal.

City life and creative work. When it comes to originality and creativeness in the realm of culture—making additions to extant cultural achievement—the cities possess far less outstanding advantages. Of course, much depends upon the type of culture and personality involved. Some forms of cultural activity are best carried on in cities, and certain types of persons can do their best creative work in an urban environment. But, on the whole, city life is too distracting to make for the better and more permanent types of creative effort, and many authors and artists tend to retire to rural areas to execute their best work.

For the most part, the cultural activities of cities have tended to be a leisure class matter, or at least a culture of the leisure and professional classes. But more recently there have been important examples of cultural activity by the lower middle class and the proletariat. Notable instances were the achievements in the theater under the auspices of the Works Progress Administration, and the extremely popular musical comedy, "Pins and Needles," put on by the International Ladies' Garment Workers in 1937. The WPA did much to promote art and music among the masses and met a hearty response.

Urban sports and recreation: "spectatoritis." In the realm of sports and recreation we find much activity and enthusiasm on the part of city dwellers. This is due primarily to the fact that the older and more spontaneous outlets of rural life are denied to them. Mumford points this out in observing that city life involves the

... acceptance of a day that includes no glimpse of the sun, no taste of the wind, no smell of earth or growing things, no free play of the muscles, no spontaneous pleasure not planned for a week in advance and recorded on a memorandum pad: in short, that day without an hour given to sauntering, which so amazed and horrified Henry Thoreau. Hence the need for synthetic stimuli.[26]

Commercialized sport depends for its revenue primarily upon urban patronage. This is particularly true of baseball, boxing, wrestling, and hockey. It is also becoming ever more true of football, with the increased popularity of professional teams which play exclusively in large urban centers. Basketball, still played chiefly by amateur college teams, began to attract great crowds in the 1940's. All this has developed a mental pattern, if not a disease, known as "spectatoritis."

Millions attend baseball, football, hockey, and basketball games; boxing, wrestling, and professional tennis matches; and horse, auto, and dog races. Many more millions enjoy reading about them in the daily papers, listening to play-by-play accounts over the radio, or following the games on television. At a conservative estimate, Americans spend between four and five billion dollars a year on various forms of commercialized recreation, and most of it is spent by city dwellers.

Almost 21 million persons attended major league baseball games in 1948, and a record 389,763 persons paid more than two million dollars

---

[26] Mumford, *op. cit.*, p. 261.

to see the 1947 World Series. The largest attendance at a single baseball game was on October 10, 1948, when 86,288 fans saw the World Series game between Cleveland and Boston at Municipal Stadium, Cleveland. The gate receipts for the game were $378,778.

Boxing matches, particularly in the heavyweight class, have produced greater attendance and larger receipts than any other commercialized sporting spectacle. On occasion, boxing fans have spent over a million dollars to see a single fight; the Dempsey-Tunney fight at Chicago in September, 1927, set a record of $2,650,000 that remains the all-time high for boxing receipts.

In spite of our efforts to curb race-track gambling, horse racing has become an important commercial sport. Large sums of money running into billions of dollars are won and lost each year in gambling on horse races. It is estimated that nearly six billion dollars were bet on horse races in 1949.

Football, both intercollegiate and professional, has become a big business since the First World War. In 1948, there was a total attendance of more than 13 million at games played by 99 leading college and university teams. Since there are 1,800 institutions of higher learning, it would be reasonable to assume that the total attendance at intercollegiate football games in 1948 was in excess of 25 million, and that total gate receipts approached 100 million dollars. An expert estimate put the gate receipts from college football in 1950 in excess of 100 million dollars, compared to 20 million for major league baseball. Professional football, too, has grown by leaps and bounds in the last decade.

We have already called attention to the fact that basketball, still dominated mainly by amateur college teams, has gained greatly in popularity in recent years and attracts great metropolitan crowds in attendance. The games are frequently played in large indoor amphitheaters such as Madison Square Garden in New York City.

We shall discuss urban recreational development in a later chapter on Community Organization, but a few figures here will indicate the growth of this movement in the first half of the present century. Between 1906 and 1914, approximately 350 cities established public recreation systems. By 1929, the number had increased to 950, and by 1950 to 2,195. The number of urban playgrounds increased from 1,300 in 1910 to 14,747 in 1950. In 1950, there were 58,029 paid recreation leaders and 104,590 volunteer leaders. Some 6,784 paid leaders were employed on a full-time year-round basis. Total expenditures for recreational and park activities were $269,000,000 in 1950. Total attendance at urban recreational facilities in 1950 was estimated at about 500 million persons.

Attempts to rate or grade cities in cultural attainments. Robert L. Duffus attempted to rank the larger cities of the United States in the order of their relative interest in culture and recreation as determined by their per capita expenditures for health and sanitation, schools, libraries, and recreation. He arrived at the following result:[27]

---

[27] Duffus, *loc. cit.*, p. 355.

Boston	$30.90	Washington, D. C.	$22.48
New York	26.37	Philadelphia	19.51
Chicago	23.83	San Francisco	17.95
Los Angeles	23.39	St. Louis	17.30
Detroit	23.12	Baltimore	16.25
Cleveland	22.94	New Orleans	13.54

Duffus recognized that this was only a rough and incomplete attempt to rank these cities as cultural centers. Boston, though at the top of the list, compelled chorus girls to wear stockings, refused to permit a performance of *Desire under the Elms,* and has indulged in a ridiculous censorship of books. Boston also has one of the lowest ratings with respect to civil liberties. An important criterion of urban culture and civilization is the tolerance which is represented by the reaction to civil liberties. On the basis of their respect for such civil liberties as freedom of speech, press, assemblage, and tolerance of radical opinion, Roger Baldwin of the American Civil Liberties Union ranked the leading American cities in the following order: Cleveland, New York, St. Louis, San Francisco, Milwaukee, Pittsburgh, Buffalo, Philadelphia, Baltimore, Chicago, Boston, Detroit, Los Angeles.

DISADVANTAGES OF LARGE, CONGESTED CITIES

Serious social problems created by urban growth and concentration. Though urban growth has been sensational during the last half-century and many cities have taken pride in their rapid increases in size and population, expert students of urban problems fear that city growth and congestion have carried with them serious social, economic and cultural disadvantages. In his *Problems of City Life,* M. R. Davie lists four of the outstanding handicaps or disadvantages of life in great, congested metropolitan centers: (1) the increasingly serious problem of providing decent and adequate housing facilities; (2) the difficulty of obtaining and continuing a sufficient water supply and a good sewage disposal system; (3) the growing problems of urban transportation and the increasing congestion of traffic; and (4) the inadequacy of transit facilities between the suburbs and the city-centers.

Disadvantages of life in great metropolitan centers. Stuart Chase believes that urban concentration in our larger cities has come to the point where it places in jeopardy the safety of city dwellers and the very integrity of the urban community:

Megalopolis is not a pleasant home for many of its citizens, awake or asleep. Even for those—and they may be the majority—whose pleasure quotient exceeds the pain, the gross volume of the latter, however unconscious, does much to retard a gracious and civilized life. Look at the faces in the street. The machine has gathered us up and dumped us by the millions into these roaring canyons. Year by year more millions are harvested, the canyon shadows deepen, the roar grows louder. No man, no group of men, knows where this conglomeration of steel and glass and stone, with the most highly complicated nervous system ever heard of —a giant with a weak digestion—is headed....

In brief, Megalopolis, for all its gaudy show, its towering architecture, its many refinements and cloistered comforts, is not physically fit for ordinary people to live in. And as the noise, dust, accident, explosion, and traffic congestion figures show, it grows continually worse. The technological limits of the machine have been repeatedly outraged until now the tangle of vital nerves is so complicated and involved that it is safe to say no one understands them or realizes in the faintest measure the probability and extent of some major lesion.[28]

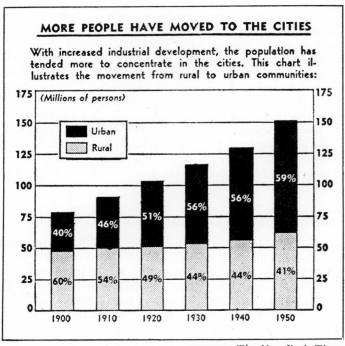

MORE PEOPLE HAVE MOVED TO THE CITIES

With increased industrial development, the population has tended more to concentrate in the cities. This chart illustrates the movement from rural to urban communities:

COURTESY *The New York Times.*

Redistribution of congested urban populations made possible by electric power and communications. Expert students of urban problems, notably Warren S. Thompson, have laid great emphasis upon the fact that the large city is no longer a necessity from an economic, social, or cultural standpoint. This is so because of the development of electricity as a major factor in contemporary power and communication. We have already noted that it was the rise of steam power which not only made possible, but also inevitable, the earlier urban congestion. Today, electricity not only makes it possible to move industry and business administration out of congested urban centers, but also actually makes it desirable to do so from the standpoint of both economic and social efficiency. Electric power can be transmitted from the source of generation with very little cost, unless the distances are greater than is at all necessary for the decentraliza-

[28] "The Future of the Great City," *Harper's Magazine,* December, 1929, pp. 83-84, 89. For one of the best case studies of a megalopolitan society and culture, tending toward tyrannopolis, see Robert Sinclair, *The Big City: A Human Study of London.* New York: Reynal and Hitchcock, 1938.

tion of urban populations. The telephone and teletype systems have conquered distance with respect to communication, thus facilitating the decentralization of office administration. This statement does not imply any sentimental "back to the country" philosophy, but rather calls attention to the hard-boiled and realistic arguments for a greater development of suburban industrial life and the creation of smaller urban communities.

Alleged advantages of vast metropolitan communities are largely mythical. It is difficult for many to understand the desirability of urban decentralization because we have for so long had drilled into us the fiction of the greater advantages and increased efficiency of very large cities—the so-called megalopolis psychosis. It is fairly easy to convince most reasonable persons that our great cities are not really habitable from the truly human standpoint. But it is usually taken for granted that we must make such sacrifices of human convenience and mental calm in the interest of the overwhelming advantages of the metropolis from the point of view of every type of efficiency. Thompson endeavors, with much success, to overthrow this popular conception. We may now review his arguments, which are shared on most points by many other students of the problem.

Contrary to the general impression, manufacturing costs are demonstrably greater in plants located in the great cities. Labor is also relatively less efficient. Similarly, the clerical force employed in business administration is less efficient and more quickly exhausted in the great metropolitan areas. The wear and tear of getting to and from work is especially hard upon this group. Many either live in the suburbs or ride long distances on the subways and elevated trains. There is an enormous waste of time and energy growing directly out of overcongestion. Thompson thus summarizes the disadvantages of the congested metropolitan city:

I dare say that in most large cities a major part of the electricity generated is used to keep people out of one another's way and to overcome other handicaps of congestion rather than for the actual accomplishment of productive work or for night lighting. Think of the stupendous amount of electricity used in vertical transportation in the large city, of the amount of daylight lighting required where buildings are crowded together, of the amount of power consumed by the street railways, and of the energy expended in supplying water and heat to the upper floors of the great office buildings, hotels, and apartment houses.

There is the same inefficient use of all other types of power. More gasoline is consumed by standing automobiles than by moving ones, more man power is spent in reconstructing than constructing, and more nervous energy is expended in keeping out of other people's way than in doing one's work. In every direction one finds this enormous waste of physical and mental energy when population is heavily congested. The stage of diminishing returns both economically and humanly has apparently set in some time back in most of our cities of over 250,000.[29]

The great cities are also less healthful than are smaller towns. In many of the greater cities of Europe and the United States the true birth rate is lower than the true death rate. The values of family life can be better conserved in smaller cities. The real cultural values provided by cities

---

29 W. S. Thompson, *Population Problems.* New York: McGraw-Hill, 1935, p. 293.

with a population of less than 250,000 can be made as satisfactory, for all practical purposes, as those possible in metropolitan communities. This is particularly true since the advent of the movies, the radio, and television. Moreover, smaller cities provide a better atmosphere for creative cultural activity, as well as much greater opportunities for recreation.

Alternatives in dealing with overgrown cities. Stuart Chase suggests that we face two alternatives with respect to our overgrown cities. We may allow the concentration to go on until the whole vast mass breaks down as the result of over-complexity and top-heaviness or we may begin rationally to redistribute the mass populations of metropolitan areas. He favors the second possibility. The arguments for the advantages of the smaller city have been brought together effectively by Thompson:

> One need not let his imagination have much rein to see in the small city or the polynucleated large city of the future the nearest approach to the ideal place in which to live and work for those who carry on our manufacturing and commercial activities. In such cities no one need spend more than a few minutes going to and coming from work and yet may have adequate space around his dwelling in which his children can play and in which he himself can relax. With the more general use of electricity all cities can be kept fairly clean—free from smoke and dust, and they can also be kept free from many of the devastating noises of our present large cities. When congestion is lessened, real-estate values will become more reasonable and parks and playgrounds for all can be had at a cost which is not prohibitive. Such cities will also offer ample opportunity for the development of the more desirable civic virtues and for the maintenance of a human friendliness that it is impossible to retain when one must force one's way continually among the great crowds of large cities.[30]

Obstacles to the decentralization of cities. The two major obstacles to the realization of this ideal of urban decentralization are the convictions which support the myth of the advantages and greater efficiency of large cities, and the metropolitan real estate interests. We have already shown the falsity of the efficiency fiction. It will take much education along this line, however, to bring the general public to a realization of the fact that big cities are relatively inefficient. The real estate interests will be an even more difficult nut to crack. Most urban real estate operators favor increased congestion in order to boost the value of a given area of urban property. Yet we shall have to face the issue realistically, for, as Stuart Chase puts it: "If we want a city to use and enjoy, we must give up great sections of the real estate racket." This may be less difficult than it seems. There may be a chance of fighting fire with fire. The breakup of the great cities offers an unusual opportunity for suburban real estate development. The suburban realty interests may become powerful enough to compete effectively with the vested interests and propaganda of the metropolitan realtors.

Evidence of decline of big city psychosis. There are a number of symptoms that the big city psychosis is losing some of its former prestige. For example, during the boom era between 1920 and 1930, many of our larger cities made tremendous annexations. For example, Los Angeles

---

30 *Ibid.,* p. 332.

added 90 square miles; Detroit, 60 square miles; and New Orleans, 18. Extensive annexations were also made by Milwaukee, Cleveland, Pittsburgh, Seattle, Chicago, and Minneapolis. Walter H. Blucher, Executive Director of the American Society of Planning Officials, has pointed out that this same group of cities made virtually no annexations between 1930 and Pearl Harbor. The former enthusiasm for great size, and the rivalry upon this point, have definitely subsided. It was found that the advantages of annexation were heavily outweighed by the disadvantages in assuming the burdens, financial and otherwise, of the annexed towns and rural regions.

The suburbs are on the gain. Since 1930 suburban areas have grown much more rapidly than the congested parts of our large cities. The census of 1930 presented impressive facts on this tendency between 1920 and 1930. The central area of New York City increased its population by 27 per cent; its suburbs, by 80 per cent. The proportionate growth of the central city to the suburbs in other cities was Chicago, 25 to 73 per cent; Philadelphia, 7 to 42.6; St. Louis, 6.3 to 106.5; Cleveland, 11.8 to 125.8; Buffalo, 13.1 to 50.4; Baltimore, 9.7 to 72.2; Indianapolis, 15.9 to 80.4; Knoxville, 36 to 66; Pittsburgh, 7.2 to 19.8; and so on through the list.

The reports of the 1950 census indicate that suburban areas continued to grow much more rapidly than the central city districts during the war decade. The population of the central cities increased by 5,652,053, or 13.0 per cent, while the population of the outlying urban areas increased by 9,001,329, or 34.7 per cent. Today, about one person out of every four in the United States is a suburban dweller, and there is one suburbanite to every two persons who dwell in crowded city centers. In addition to this large suburban trend there was, of course, a considerable movement from cities to country homes.

THE CITY PLANNING MOVEMENT

Development of the city planning movement. The future of city development is not likely to be left to spontaneous tendencies or to unguided change and accident. Already there is a notable movement on foot thoroughly to survey modern cities and their regional hinterland, with the aim of planning rationally for the devolution of cities and a sane redistribution of their populations. This trend is usually known as the *city planning movement* which has developed rapidly since 1900 and follows a number of different patterns.

City planning dates back to ancient oriental times. Even in medieval towns there was some conception of planning. Sir Christopher Wren worked out a plan for the rebuilding of London in 1666 after the great fire. This would have made London one of the most beautiful of the world's cities, but the plan was disregarded. Paris was partially rebuilt according to definite plans by Louis XIV, Napoleon I, and Napoleon III. Especially important was the work carried out by the latter under the direction of Baron Georges Haussmann. Germany has given more attention to city planning than any other large country. The city planning movement was given an initial impetus in the United States when Major Pierre L'Enfant laid out the design of the new capital at Washington.

But scientific city planning on a social, as well as architectural, basis really began with the work of Frédéric Le Play in France in the last half of the nineteenth century. By his day the Industrial Revolution was sufficiently advanced to indicate the necessity of considering the underlying geographical, biological, and economic factors involved, as well as planning for architectural and scenic beauty. Le Play recognized that in any social planning of cities one must have a full knowledge of the city and its outlying environs, including population, resources, and topography. Hence, he proposed the scientific social survey of urban areas and their environs.

Le Play's ideas were taken up and related more directly to city planning by the eminent Scottish biologist and sociologist, Patrick Geddes. Geddes organized and conducted the Edinburgh Survey and gave it publicity through the Town Planning Exhibition of 1910. His ideas have gained support among pioneers in the city planning movement elsewhere. They were brought to the United States by Lewis Mumford. This planning movement led by Geddes under the Le Play influence has been notable for the stress laid upon the social elements involved. It is a truly ecological and sociological program, linking city planning, industrial conditions, and topography. The garden-city planning movement led by Ebenezer Howard, and the greenbelt program of Lewis Mumford are outgrowths of the Geddes influence.

Chief city planning programs. There are three major types of proposals which dominate the city planning movement of today: (1) the New York City tendency toward the massing of skyscrapers in the mid-urban areas, along with extensive development of suburbs; (2) the opposite extreme, known as the "garden-city" conception of Ebenezer Howard, of England, which spreads the population widely over suburban areas and avoids urban congestion; and (3) the proposals of a Frenchman, M. Le Corbusier (C. E. Jeanneret), which aim at a compromise between these two extremes.

The New York trend is, as we have seen, toward massing the great business skyscrapers and tall apartments in the center of the city and encouraging the suburban spread of the shopping and working population. The garden-city program denies any necessity for urban congestion and distributes the population so that there shall never be more than fifty persons per housing acre. The plan of M. Le Corbusier is, perhaps, more immediately practicable than either extreme. His plan is thus described by Patrick Abercrombie:

His City of Tomorrow (planned for 3,000,000 people) is as opposed to the New York tendency of jostling skyscrapers at the center, as it is to the Garden City low-over-all density. He proposes to maintain or slightly to increase the over-all Continental density but to reduce the ground covered by buildings to 15 per cent of the total area and to confine all business to a few isolated skyscrapers ¼ mile apart and 700 feet high; the intervening ground is open gardens and woodlands of extremely naturalistic type, through which run great unimpeded traffic arteries. All housing is in two types of tenement, which being at least 110 feet high also leave a great deal of open space....This is the extreme use of height in order to free ground space, rather than greatly to increase density. The four basic principles are given as follows:

1. We must de-congest the centers of our cities.
2. We must augment their density.
3. We must increase the means for getting about.
4. We must increase parks and open spaces.

M. Le Corbusier is, however, sufficiently human to allow...garden villages, both for those who wish to work in the factory zones (kept outside the city) and those who work in the skyscrapers but prefer to bring up their families in "garden" houses. There is an essential protective zone of woods and fields—a fresh-air reserve—between the city proper and these suburbs.[31]

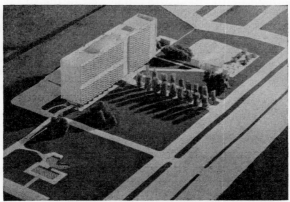

COURTESY INSTITUTE OF CONTEMPORARY ART, BOSTON.

A Le Corbusier apartment in Marseille, France. Shows the broad open spaces provided for in this method of city planning to relieve congestion.

The chief obstacle to the adoption of so rational a plan is that it would require the abandonment or destruction of billions of dollars' worth of buildings already constructed in our planless era of city building. This would be opposed by the vested real estate interests. Nevertheless, Le Corbusier has recently been able to carry out his plan to a considerable degree in rebuilding a section of the French city of Marseilles. In the construction of urban buildings, Le Corbusier lays great stress on extensive use of glass and extreme solar lighting. Hence, the ideal Le Corbusier city is often described as "the radiant city."

City planning had an auspicious start in the United States when L'Enfant was brought over to plan the city of Washington at the beginning of the nineteenth century. Alexander Hamilton also arranged with him to plan Paterson, N. J. But for nearly a century there was a lapse in organized city planning in the United States as the result of the pressure of industrialization and the dominion of a short-range profit motive. In the twentieth century the city planning movement was revived

---

31 *Town and Country Planning.* New York: Holt, 1933, pp. 116-118.

on a more extensive and scientific scale. Early in the present century the Chicago plan was worked out under the direction of Daniel Burnham. This was the first important American development in contemporary times.

Perhaps the most ambitious of all regional urban surveys in this country was that carried out after the First World War by a committee appointed to conduct the regional survey of New York City and its environs. A voluminous and comprehensive report was published embodying an impressive set of recommendations for the reconstruction of the metropolis of the New World. This has been summarized and interpreted by Robert L. Duffus in his book, *Mastering a Metropolis.* In a report submitted by Dr. Rexford G. Tugwell in the spring of 1939, the New York planning commission vigorously recommended urban decentralization. The Chicago and New York plans have been widely imitated by other municipalities. As yet, however, the main development in New York City planning has been the building of skyscraper apartments, but with better provisions for at least small parks. Good recent examples are Stuyvesant Town and Peter Cooper Village in downtown New York. The leading figure in inspiring such planning is Robert Moses, who has carried out gigantic projects in improving transport facilities and park areas. This program has been condemned by Lewis Mumford as one of "planned congestion."

The most fertile mind devoted to problems of urban reconstruction in the United States is that of Lewis Mumford, who has set forth his ideas in comprehensive fashion in *The Culture of Cities.* Inspired by Geddes and Branford, he rejects the program of Le Corbusier and the New York City program as inadequate evasions of the crisis facing modern cities. He sees much good in the garden-city proposal, but he is more inclined to favor such more drastic reconstructions of city life as are provided by the Tennessee Valley Authority projects, the Columbia River development, and the "greenbelt" towns planned by the Resettlement Administration. While it will be necessary to demobilize and redistribute our present metropolitan centers, he believes that future city planning should avoid entirely the undesirable traits of the metropolitan and megalopolitan communities.

Even more drastic is the movement led by Ralph Borsodi. He proposes to abandon the great cities altogether, to build up small cooperative rural groups, and to establish self-sustaining homesteads that carry on home production by means of mechanical devices adapted to installation in the home or small community shops. Subsistence agriculture will also be developed.

Zoning plans and systems. Pending the reconstruction of our cities, some progress in improving urban architecture and ecology is being made through what is known as the "zoning movement," first systematically adopted by New York City in 1916. This is an attempt to plan city building and redistricting so that similar kinds of buildings—residences, apartment houses, skyscrapers, stores, or factories—will predominate in a given section of the city. Building permits are granted for only certain kinds of structures in a given zone. Supplementary zoning ordinances restrict the height, area, weight, and bulk of buildings by specific districts. This zoning program is designed to end the ugliness and confusion which arise when all kinds of structures and activities are found in a single city district. In 1949, there were 1,072 cities with a population of over 10,000; of these, 667 had an official city-planning agency, 51 had an unofficial planning agency, and 144 had none. The others, some 210 in all, did not report. About 550 of these cities had comprehensive zoning ordinances in operation. Of the cities with a population over 25,000, no less than 88 per cent had such ordinances; for cities between 10,000 and 25,000 the figure was 74 per cent.

Certain regulations of the zoning system, especially that of New York City, have brought about a marked change in skyscraper architecture. The stipulation is that a tower of any height may be erected on one-fourth of the building space and that the height of the rest of the building fronting on the street must be in proportion to the width of the street. High towers are erected, flanked by massive terraces. The New York Telephone Building, designed by Ralph Walker, and the Hotel Shelton, by Arthur Harmon, were good early examples of this type of architecture in which beauty is combined with an effort to secure the maximum efficiency in strength, floor space, light, and ventilation. These buildings are mostly free from any trace of classic or Gothic influences. Indeed, this style is reminiscent of the hanging garden architecture of ancient Babylonia.

The atom bomb and the future of cities. Fear of the atom bomb may do more to break up great metropolitan centers than has ever been achieved through common-sense considerations, especially if the cold war continues between Russia and the United States. In less than a decade atom bombs may be fifty times as devastating as those used on Japan in 1945. Several of them might destroy the whole metropolitan district of Greater New York. One hydrogen bomb might accomplish this. If this ominous threat remains, we may expect a shifting of cities from the seaboard areas to central and mid-western portions of the country, and a scattering of urban populations in order to make them less vulnerable to the atom bomb. Some preliminary moves along this line have already taken place.[32]

City growth and life reaching a turning-point. Whether we make progress in the reconstruction of cities mainly by piecemeal activities or by wholesale reorganization and redistribution, it is obvious that urban development has reached a new epoch or era. The new world of power and communication introduced by electricity and atomic energy is likely to have as far-reaching an effect upon the urban development of the next hundred years as steam power did upon city growth in an earlier era. The

---

[32] On the relation of fear of atomic bombing to the possible decentralization of cities, see W. F. Ogburn, *The Social Effects of Aviation*. Boston: Houghton Mifflin, 1946, pp. 354 ff.

changes will probably be as potent in their effects upon city society and culture as upon urban architecture and transportation.

As a conclusion to our survey of contemporary urban life we could probably do no better than to point out that city life, like country life and the farming economy, has reached a critical turning point. Unless urban concentration is checked and cities are redistributed through sane regional planning, the outlook is dark indeed. Our urban communities, many of them already in the stage of megalopolis, and some of them in that of tyrannopolis, will probably pass into the nekropolitan phase of utter collapse and extinction. If, on the other hand, regional planning can be instituted in time and on a sufficient scope, urban life may supply a high type of life and culture, hitherto unrealized on our planet. Only a rash person would presume to state dogmatically today which road future urban development will follow.

SUMMARY

Cities have existed since the rise of civilization, but the modern industrial and commercial city presents a new epoch in human experience— especially in its dominant position in contemporary culture. In the industrialized countries, between 50 and 85 per cent of the total population dwells in cities.

The invention of machines and the introduction of factories made the modern cities necessary; better agricultural and transportation methods made them possible. The use of steam power, which had to be applied where generated, lack of transportation facilities for urban workers, and haste in unplanned city construction led to urban congestion, slum areas, and serious overcrowding.

Our large cities fall into a common general pattern with respect to the spatial distribution of economic activities and residential types. This pattern is known among sociologists as the ecology of urban life. The most notable recent change has been the remarkable development of suburban areas. This has been made possible by new methods of rapid transit.

Cities have brought about new ways of living markedly different from the older rural patterns of life. City life is characterized by many stimuli and distractions, diversity of tastes and types, increased mental tension, greater speed, and growing superficiality. City life destroys the older rural primary groups, and there has been no comparable development of urban community programs to provide substitutes. This accounts for the acute social disorganization in the urban life of today.

City government has become increasingly important in our state and national political life, since the leading political machines are located and maintained in urban centers. There was deplorable corruption in urban politics in the generation following the Civil War. This stimulated the formation of the National Municipal League in 1894, which marks the beginning of consistent efforts to improve city government.

The older mayor-council form of urban government still predominates, but there has been a notable development of better government types in the commission and city manager plans. The latter is growing rapidly now, and is in control of about 25 per cent of our cities with a population of over 5,000. The police, fire, sanitation, and public health departments of our city governments constitute impressive public enterprises.

City finances create vast and serious problems. During the 1920's, irresponsible spending, due mainly to the "booster" psychology, caused bankruptcy or serious financial crises in many cities following 1929. Other factors promoting urban financial crises have been the growth of suburbs, which use metropolitan facilities while escaping direct taxation for their support, and the growth of slum areas. The latter absorb a disproportionate amount of the urban budget without comparable financial returns.

Traffic congestion, coming on the heels of automotive transportation, has created one of the most serious of our urban problems. It has been intensified by the congestion and planlessness of most city construction. There seems to be no ultimate solution except for drastic decentralization of cities, which the electrical age now makes possible.

Crime and vice are disproportionately prevalent in cities. This is due in some degree to the concentration of immigrants in urban centers, but chiefly to the social disorganization of urban life, the prevalence of delinquency areas in urban slums, and the greater urban opportunities and incitements in regard to crime and vice.

Cities are the center of most of the literature and arts of our day. But the conditions of city life are an obstacle to creativeness in literature and the arts and there is an increasing tendency for authors, artists, and musicians to retreat to the country to produce their creative work. The most striking development in urban culture today has been the extensive development of commercialized sports, and the provision of public, supervised recreational centers.

Our cities are now reaching a critical period. They are overgrown and top-heavy. They must be broken up and their populations redistributed. The remarkable growth of suburbs will not provide an adequate solution to the problem. The use of electric power now makes it feasible to scatter urban populations, but the heavy investment in city real estate and the social habits of our day still constitute effective obstacles to such a trend. Decentralization may be hastened by the threat of the atom bomb to congested urban areas.

There are three main plans for the reconstruction of cities. The New York City plan proposes to concentrate skyscraper buildings in the center of the city and to distribute an ever greater proportion of the population in suburban districts. The garden-city plan, developed by an Englishman, Ebenezer Howard, calls for a wide spatial distribution of the city populations in buildings of low or medium height. The plan of the Frenchman, Le Corbusier, envisages cities with high, well-lighted buildings, surrounded by ample parks and open spaces. The most advanced thinkers in this field are not satisfied with any of these plans, but insist that the great cities of our day must disappear entirely and be replaced by a multitude of small towns, often described as "garden cities" or "greenbelt towns."

SELECTED REFERENCES

Abercrombie, Patrick, *Town and Country Planning*. New York: Holt, 1933. A brief and authoritative description of the leading types of city planning by a leading English writer on this subject.

*Anderson, Nels, and Lindeman, E. C., *Urban Sociology*. New York: Crofts, 1928. Perhaps the best introduction to urban social life, its culture and problems.

Anderson, William, *American City Government*. New York: Holt, 1925. A standard manual, clear and comprehensive.

Angell, R. C., *The Moral Integration of American Cities*. Chicago: University of Chicago Press, 1951. Important recent monograph dealing with achievements of cities in attaining common values and community integration.

Bogue, D. J., *The Structure of the Metropolitan Community*. Ann Arbor: University of Michigan Press, 1949. Sociological and statistical analysis of 67 metropolitan communities, illustrating the social position and influence of metropolitan areas.

Borsodi, Ralph, *This Ugly Civilization*. New York: Harper, 1932.

———, *Flight from the City*. New York: Harper, 1933. Two books by the leading American critic of city life, mass production, and the ugliness of the factory town. The first book attacks the ugliness of the industrial city and its ideals, and the second suggests an escape by going to the country and carrying on a subsistence economy. If somewhat idealistic, they are a valuable corrective for current beliefs and practices.

Carpenter, Niles. *The Sociology of City Life*. New York: Longmans, Green, 1931. A standard sociological treatment of urban social trends and problems.

Davie, M. R., *Problems of City Life*. New York: Wiley, 1932. Able sociological description and analysis of urban social problems.

Dickinson, R. E., *City, Region and Regionalism*. New York: Oxford University Press, 1947. The application of regional concepts to urban ecology and city planning programs.

Dobyns, Fletcher, *The Underworld of American Politics*. Chicago: Dobyns, 1932. A fearless analysis of the incredible Cermak machine in Chicago.

Duffus, R. L., *Mastering a Metropolis*. New York: Harper, 1932. Clear account of the trends toward urban planning in New York City.

*Gist, N. P., and Halpert, L. A., *Urban Society*. New York: Crowell, 1948. A standard and competent manual on urban sociology.

Griffith, E. S., *History of American City Government*. New York: Oxford University Press, 1938. The development of leading types and problems of American municipal government by one of the chief experts in the field.

*Hart, Smith, *The New Yorkers*. New York: Sheridan House, 1938. An extremely entertaining history of New York City, revealing its seamy side, which is usually glossed over in such accounts. A vivid little book.

Hawley, A. T., *Human Ecology: A Theory of Community Structure*. New York: Ronald Press, 1950. A comprehensive exposition of the ecological doctrine first formulated by Geddes, Park, McKenzie, and others, on the basis of which theories of urban ecology have been founded.

Lait, Jack, and Mortimer, Lee, *New York Confidential*. New York: Crown Publishers, 1949.

———, *Chicago Confidential*. New York: Crown Publishers, 1950.

———, *Washington Confidential*. New York: Crown Publishers, 1951. Three somewhat lurid and sensational journalistic books on political and personal corruption and graft in large American cities. The residual element of truth amply demonstrates that, while some patterns of corruption have changed in the half-century since Lincoln Steffens wrote his classic book,

The Shame of the Cities, conditions are in many ways worse and more alarming than in 1904. The books underline the connection between municipal, state, and Federal corruption.

*Lewis, H. M., *City Planning*. New York: Longmans, Green, 1939. Perhaps the best introduction to the whole social and architectural problem of city planning and the redistribution of urban populations.

McKean, D. D., *Boss: the Hague Machine in Action*. Boston: Houghton Mifflin, 1940. Good picture of the Hague political machine in Jersey City.

McKenzie, R. D., *The Metropolitan Community*. New York: McGraw-Hill, 1933. Important discussion of the sociology of city life, by a leader of the ecological school.

Milligan, M. M., *The Inside Story of the Pendergast Machine*. New York: Scribner, 1938. Spirited exposure of the Pendergast era in Kansas City.

*Mumford, Lewis, *The Culture of Cities*. New York: Harcourt, Brace, 1938. The most original and stimulating book in the English language on the modern city and human living. Critical of the great city and favorable to the substitution of small communities, like the greenbelt towns fostered by the New Deal.

*Muntz, E. E., *Urban Sociology*. New York: Macmillan, 1938. One of the best sociological texts on the life and social problems of the modern city.

Peterson, E. T. (Ed.), *Cities Are Abnormal*. Norman: University of Oklahoma Press, 1946. Important symposium by experts, urging the decentralization of our overgrown urban centers of population.

Queen, S. A., and Thomas, L. F., *The City: a Study of Urbanism in the United States*. New York: McGraw-Hill, 1939. Important contribution to urban sociology which skilfully integrates geographical and social factors in urban life.

Saarinen, Eliel, *The City, Its Growth, Its Decay, Its Future*. New York: Reinhold, 1943. A criticism of congested metropolitan areas and a rational planning program, by one of the leading architects of the twentieth century. Makes homes, rather than boulevards and plazas, the core of his plan.

*Sinclair, Robert, *The Big City*. New York: Reynal and Hitchcock, 1938. An extremely interesting study of the effect of the city of London viewed as a typical great metropolis, on human life and culture. A devastating indictment of the contemporary metropolis.

Steffens, Lincoln, *The Shame of the Cities*. New York: McClure, Philips, 1904. Classic study of urban corruption at the turn of the century.

Thompson, C. D., *Public Ownership*. New York: Crowell, 1925. Pioneer study, which includes chapters on early trends towards municipal socialism.

Woolston, H. B., *Metropolis*. New York: Appleton-Century, 1939. Able treatment by leading sociologist of outstanding traits and problems of life in large American cities.

CHAPTER 11

The Housing Problem and Proposed Solutions

SOCIAL IMPORTANCE OF THE HOUSING PROBLEM

Inadequate and inferior housing is now regarded as an important and acute social problem. The acute housing shortage of the present time has focused attention on a problem which has long existed. At no time since the Industrial Revolution have enough houses been built in our cities to make it possible to discard worn-out structures and to meet the demands of a rapidly increasing population for additional housing units. Technical progress in other fields has usually made possible the replacement of the old by the new. The housing industry, however, has been unable to develop techniques which would enable it to build homes for all families who need and want housing at a price they are able to pay. As a consequence, even before the depression, following 1929, it is estimated that 10 million American families—more than 40 million persons—lived in dwellings which did not meet the very minimum standards consistent with our material civilization. This situation is even worse today, due to stoppage of building during the Second World War and the spurt in population growth.

No dwelling can be called adequate today if it does not meet both physiological and psychological needs. A dwelling with sound walls, roof, and foundation; a private toilet; water in the house; windows for sunlight and air; and sufficient privacy provides no more than minimum requirements. If family life is to be strengthened and preserved, every family must be adequately housed. The kind of home in which a child is reared determines to a large extent his attitude toward the community and the government. The house alone does not make a home, but a child whose home is dilapidated, unsanitary, and overcrowded is not always likely to have much incentive to become a responsible citizen. The future welfare of America depends, in a large measure, on a housing program which will clear the slums and make decent housing available to everybody.

Housing gives the average American the least satisfaction for money expended. The housing situation in the United States is perhaps the weakest single link in the socio-economic aspects of the capitalistic system. As *Fortune* has pointed out, the average American workman can get far less for his money in the way of shelter than in any other form of essential expenditure. Aside from his housing, the average American making $30

460

a week in prewar days could live fairly well and could get his money's worth for what he spent:

> With an income of $30 a week a man can get meat six days a week and fish on the seventh. He can provide his family with clothing adapted to the climate in which it lives and to the mores around which its social life revolves. He can offer his children education more than equal to their capacities to absorb and use knowledge. He can surround his wife with electrical and mechanical gadgets to make her work easier and her temper more amiable; and he can drive an automobile that no amount of money could have purchased fifteen years ago.
>
> In his leisure time, of which he has a fair amount, he can and does spend a good deal for entertainment and gets a good deal in return. When he is ill he can as a rule obtain some sort of medical care and hospitalization. And when he dies his insurance will provide a "four-coach funeral with metal casket," and a backlog of cash to tide his widow over the aftermath.[1]

When it comes to housing, it is another story entirely. The $30-a-week city dweller is usually able to get nothing more than an archaic old barn of a dwelling or a bleak apartment often fashioned out of an abandoned mansion:

> What he receives, far too often, are the hand-me-down leavings of the income groups immediately above him—houses designed originally for other needs and other incomes, and now out of date, expensive to heat and maintain, wasteful of space. It is as though the automotive manufacturers built no cars below the $4,000 class.
>
> Many of these cars would eventually filter down to the lower income levels, but they would arrive in the hands of their final owners as candidates for the scrap heap, expensive to operate and utterly unsuited to the transportation needs of the average man. Apply this principle to housing in the lowest income groups—down through the fifth- and tenth-hand house, into the slums and blighted urban areas—and housing becomes something characterized chiefly by its crimes, its infections, and its smells.[2]

In the light of price and wage increases since 1938, when the *Fortune* article was written, the figures cited would be approximately doubled in each case today, but the facts remain as true in principle as they were a decade and a half ago.

Housing and health. Although the problem of housing and the provision of adequate dwellings is often overlooked entirely in treating social problems—or is handled incidentally in connection with city life and urban planning—it is surely important enough to warrant independent consideration as one of the major problems of contemporary society.[3]

The housing problem is immediately and directly related to the matter of physical health. There is no doubt that overcrowded slums and miserable apartments, without adequate sanitation, air, or sunshine, notably increase the incidence of disease and the probability of serious illness. Such conditions also facilitate the spread of contagious diseases. Studies of disease conditions in cities show a tremendous preponderance of illness in crowded slum areas. The relatively slight amount of serious

---

[1] *Fortune,* May, 1938, p. 63.

[2] *Ibid.,* p. 64.

[3] For a good study of the effect of adequate housing on health, family life, crime, vice, etc., see Jay Rumney and Sara Schuman, *The Social Effects of Public Housing in Newark, N. J.* Newark: Housing Authority of the City of Newark, 1944.

illness and the low death rate in Sweden in recent decades can undoubt-edly be attributed to some extent to the erection of many model apart-ments in Sweden. These apartments, of course, are available to the working population.

We ordinarily think of bad living conditions and the illness resulting in part from those conditions as limited chiefly to urban slums. To a lesser extent, however, a similar situation exists in rural areas. As we shall point out, half of the dwellings of the American farm population are substandard. Living conditions in such habitations invite disease and reduce the resistance of those who suffer from illness. This situation is intensified by the difficulty experienced by poorer people in the country of obtaining good medical care.

The health conditions which are undermined by life in city slums are not limited merely to physical disorders. The increased tensions, worries, dissatisfactions, and confusion which are inevitably associated with slum life also produce by far the greatest volume of mental disease per capita. As we shall point out in the chapter concerning mental disease, the researches of R. E. L. Faris and others have shown that the rate of mental disease in the city slum areas is vastly out of proportion to that in the better residential sections of a city.

Housing affects family life. There can be no doubt that bad housing conditions have also contributed to the disorganization of family life. There is little opportunity for a happy family life in a rundown slum apartment which makes no provision for comfort or decency, either within or without the place of dwelling. This is especially important in our day, when, as we have seen in an earlier chapter, families must be held together primarily by internal cohesive forces and the pleasures of domestic association rather than by external pressures based upon fear and necessity.

Housing, vice, and crime. The housing problem is also immediately associated with the problems of crime and vice. We shall point out in the chapter on crime that delinquency tends to be concentrated in the crowded slum areas of our cities which Clifford Shaw and others have correctly designated as "delinquency areas." Moreover, to the degree that unsatisfactory housing conditions promote demoralized and broken fami-lies and unsatisfactory family life, they contribute directly and potently to juvenile delinquency. What we have just said about the contributions of slum areas to the increase of crime also applies to their promotion of vice and degeneracy in general.

Housing and life satisfactions. In addition to the relation of the housing problem to such acute problems as those of health, family condi-tions, crime, and vice, perhaps the most important aspect of housing is its bearing upon the general contentment and comforts of life There is little value in having a multiplicity of other satisfactions if one cannot live decently and comfortably in his own home. Such is not the condition with more than half of the American population today. This is true of both country and city life. The only answer to the problem is an adequate number of pleasant and sanitary dwellings, whether in city or country.

To some of the efforts to make such provisions we shall now turn our attention.

EUROPEAN EFFORTS TO PROVIDE SATISFACTORY HOUSING

Development of housing in Great Britain. Perhaps the first important effort to provide decent housing for the new working population brought about by the Industrial Revolution and the rise of factories was the erection of model dwellings by the Scotch reformer, Robert Owen. Early in the nineteenth century, he built a well-planned village for his workers at his plant in New Lanark, Scotland. About the same time, the French

FROM REED AND OGG, *New Homes For Old,* HEADLINE BOOKS, FOREIGN POLICY ASSOCIATION.

New Housing Project at Kensal Rise, London, England.

social philosopher and reformer, Charles Fourier, emphasized the importance of providing good housing for workers in his ideal communities for the working classes.

The first serious attention to the problem of housing for the masses in England came about as the result of the prevalence of cholera and other epidemics in the working-class slums. This led to the first English Public Health Act, which was passed in 1848 and greatly strengthened in 1875. In 1851, England passed the first housing law of modern times. This law permitted local governments to build dwellings for laborers, but it did not make such action mandatory. During the remainder of the century a number of laws were passed in Britain that increased these powers of local governments and specified minimum standards for housing construction.

After the First World War, England began to take active steps to relieve the great shortage of dwellings. It launched a program of low-rent housing construction in 1919, when it passed the Housing and Town Planning Act. This required the town governments to provide low-rent houses and to prepare a town planning program which could be examined and approved by the national government. This act was supplemented by new laws in 1923 and 1924 which compelled the towns to contribute toward the cost of low-rent housing.

Later, about 1930, England began an extended movement to move large numbers out of the worst slums and to rebuild slum areas. Since that time more than 300,000 slum dwellings have been torn down and an equal number of new houses constructed. Approximately a million slum dwellings were reconstructed by public mandate, mainly at the expense of the owners. But this was only a beginning, and even today there are about four million English urban houses that are at least 100 years old.

In 1935 the English government moved on to a more ambitious program of relieving overcrowding. The government provided subsidies for the construction of low-rent housing. By 1939, 15 per cent of the British population were living in homes subsidized by the government and owned and managed by the municipalities. This program was seriously restricted by wartime conditions after 1939. With the victory of the Labour Party in 1945, there was a trend toward the nationalization of the housing program, and the Labour Government has undertaken an extensive program of government housing construction.

In addition to public housing projects in England, model company workers' towns were erected, such as that built at Bourneville by the Cadbury cocoa firm, and at Port Sunlight by the Lever soap manufacturers.

German housing trends. Although Friedrich Krupp had built some model homes for his workers in 1865, it was not until 1880 that Germany began to pass housing laws that established minimum standards of construction for workers' housing.

Following the First World War, the Weimar Republic launched an extensive program of subsidizing low-rent housing construction. This was aided by extensive foreign loans. Between 1925 and 1931 about three million new dwellings were constructed. Most of these were expertly planned and admirably constructed. The Nazi government under Hitler continued to support housing construction for workers. The Nazis sought to decentralize housing by granting special support and aid to workers who built homes in the areas surrounding the industrial cities. The Nazis encouraged the construction of low-cost housing which workers could buy rather than rent.

Housing in France. France was very slow in taking any action to provide better housing for the masses. Some private housing societies were formed in 1853, but not until 1912 did France pass a law which even permitted local governments to provide low-rent housing for the working classes. This law proved ineffective.

The devastation wrought by the First World War, which destroyed about a million buildings in France, compelled action on the housing problem. But for a decade the laws passed were ineffective. For although the laws permitted housing construction, they did not require it. Nor was any public money appropriated to support such action.

The first effective French law was the Loucheur Act of 1928, which provided low-interest government loans up to 90 per cent of the cost of construction of low-cost dwellings. By 1932, about 200,000 such dwellings had been constructed. The financial support of the French government has, however, been very inadequate. In 1934, some help was given to limited dividend housing agencies, but little construction resulted from this. Also ineffective was the French effort to exempt low-rent housing from taxation. There is still an excess of slums in the French cities.

Much of the building progress has resulted from certain special planning projects like those worked out by Le Corbusier in Marseilles. The Second World War checked even the little French building that was taking place. Since the war there has been some renewed French housing construction, funds for which have been provided in part by aid received under the Marshall Plan. This is now being held up by concentration on armament construction.

Housing innovations in Holland. Holland was the first country in Europe to pass a law which made it mandatory for the town governments to provide satisfactory housing for their citizens. This law, passed in 1901, ordered all towns of over 10,000 to draw up plans for future housing. These plans had to be approved by the national government, which helped to finance the new houses. Under this act, Holland has constructed more than 250,000 new dwelling units that have been financed by public funds. These make up about 10 per cent of the total dwellings in the country as a whole. About one-fourth were built by municipalities, the rest by public housing societies. Holland was thus the first country to start public housing in real earnest before the First World War. The program continued until the Nazi occupation and was resumed after the war.

Cooperative housing in Sweden. Sweden has been remarkable for its housing construction, which, since 1923, has been carried on chiefly by the cooperatives. These have been able to obtain needed money at low interest from the Swedish government.

At first much of the cooperative housing construction in Sweden was designed for middle-class families. After 1936, cooperative building was extended to working-class families. For such construction by the cooperatives the town provides free land, and the government gives to the cooperative society a subsidy determined by the size of the family.

Since 1929, most of the funds for Swedish housing have been provided by the Swedish Housing Loan Fund, an organization to which the government made a large grant of money. But the cooperatives have taken the lead in financing the new housing construction under this plan. The government has come to their aid liberally in providing aid for the construction of houses for the poorer group of workers. In 1939, about 15 per cent of the urban population of Sweden was living in homes that had been financed at least in part by the government.

Swedish housing is probably the best in Europe today. It is rivalled only by some of the better apartment developments erected by the Weimar Republic, and some of Mussolini's model apartments in Rome and a few other Italian cities. The cooperative apartments are models of up-to-date housing construction. Slums have been virtually wiped out in Sweden. This has paid off well not only in increased comforts of life, but also in the reduction of disease. Between 1916 and 1936, deaths from tuberculosis, for example, fell by about 40 per cent in Sweden.

Other housing trends in Scandinavian areas. While perhaps not as impressive as the Swedish achievements, there have been notable gains in housing in neighboring areas, such as Norway, Denmark and Finland. Denmark has been more successful than any other country in the world in providing good housing for the rural population. This has been accomplished mainly through the efforts of the cooperative societies which have attained a greater strength in rural life than the cooperatives of Sweden. Some partisans of Finnish cooperatives rate the housing advances in Finland equal to those in Sweden.

Housing progress in Vienna after the First World War. The Socialist government in Vienna carried on an extensive experiment in apartment construction after the First World War. Vienna had to work under serious handicaps. The peace treaty left the city an unnatural metropolis, containing one-third of the population of Austria, with the supporting hinterland shorn away. The great city was left high and dry, compelled to import most of its food and raw materials. Austria had to compete with the new states which had been especially favored by the treaties. It was crushed by taxation and by financial burdens imposed by the treaty. Standards of living were abominably low. If Vienna could overcome such conditions, any American city should have easy sailing in any plan of municipal housing.

Until 1919, housing conditions in Vienna were a menace to health, decency, and efficiency. Three-quarters of all domiciles consisted of small flats of two rooms or less. Overcrowding in limited quarters was almost incredible. The typical flat was built and equipped as follows:

> It provided a kitchen and one other room, constructed in large units by speculative builders. Many rooms had no direct light and air, or opened on a shaft of such limited area as to be entirely inadequate. The lavatories and running water were usually situated in the common hall and were used by several families on the same floor. Very few dwellings had gas or electricity. The houses, as a rule, covered practically the entire site, providing inadequate courts and no play space except the streets.[4]

The postwar government of Vienna faced this situation with energy and resolution. It reorganized the taxation system in such a manner as to make profiteering in rentals no longer possible and to reduce land values. The city bought up about one-third of its entire land area. The new tax

---

[4] R. E. Chaddock, "Housing in Vienna: A Socialistic Experiment," *American Journal of Sociology*, January, 1932, pp. 562-563. Copyright, University of Chicago Press.

system gave it funds and land on which to build. Between 1919 and the Fascist triumph in 1934, Vienna spent over 100 million dollars on these municipal apartments. About 65,000 new dwellings were constructed— enough to rehouse one-tenth of the citizens. Compare with the prewar flats a typical flat in a new Vienna apartment:

It consists of a very small entrance hall, a kitchen, one larger and one smaller room, and a lavatory—covering in all 430 square feet. All have lavatories and running water within the flat. Each flat has electric light, a gas stove for cooking, and a small metal stove burning coke for heating, both furnished by the municipal gas company....

The flats are arranged in units built around large courts, with gardens, play-grounds, and sometimes wading pools for children in the center.... The building must not cover more than one-half the area of the site, and often occupies less. All rooms have direct light and air.... In buildings housing three hundred families or more a central steam laundry has been constructed, equipped with the most modern devices.... Here housewives may do their own laundry work. ... Central baths for tenants are provided in the large housing units.... Kinder-gartens to the number of 100 have already been established in these municipal buildings.[5]

These flats rented for seven shillings (about $1.05) per month, a charge designed to take care of their upkeep. There was a slight additional charge for the use of the central laundry and baths. The good results were quickly apparent. A large number of Vienna's working population could live in good quarters at low cost. The number of householders greatly increased in spite of the shrinkage in the population of the city as a whole. Infant mortality and tuberculosis rates were lowered notably.

After the depression that set in about 1930, garden colonies of very simple dwellings were constructed, in part to house the unemployed. When the Fascists took over under Dollfuss in 1934, some of the apart-ments were destroyed by bombardment. The Dollfuss régime did little for workers' housing except to build some barrack-like apartments, or "family poorhouses." Unfortunately, the Viennese slums were left largely untouched by both the Socialists and the Fascists.

State housing in Soviet Russia. The state economy of Soviet Russia facilitated the extensive development of public housing projects in that country. Housing conditions and slums had been bad in Tsarist Russia. The industrialization of Russia carried on by the Soviet rulers made it necessary to provide much new urban housing. The favorable situation for public housing planning in Soviet Russia has been clearly stated by Jacob Crane, an American engineer and architect:

For the first time in the modern world, cities may be built according to plans which utilize all of the land to the best advantage of city living because the land is publicly owned. In America big city building, and to a large degree city planning, has necessarily failed to produce good results because it has to be done within the very severe limitation of recognizing private property interests and the increase in and inflation of land values. This alone gives Russian city planning a tremendous advantage over that of America.[6]

---

[5] *Ibid.*, pp. 564-566.

[6] "A New Conception of City Planning," *Economic Review of the Soviet Union*, January 15, 1932, p. 36.

Striking advances in housing have been executed in Russia in the course of its vast town planning program. Slums have been eliminated to some extent in the older cities, new workers' apartments have been constructed, and whole new industrial cities have been constructed, not only in European Russia but in many districts beyond the Urals and in Siberia. In 1925 the capital investment in housing projects was 63 million rubles. In 1930 it was 775 million; in 1931, slightly more than a billion; and in 1935, almost two billion. In the coal regions alone investments for housing amounted to 201 million rubles in 1931 as against 95 million in 1930. Better than these figures are those in terms of square meters of floor space constructed. In 1925, almost two million square meters (approximately 30,000 houses) were constructed. For 1930 it was six million square meters (105,000 houses), and for 1933, more than seven million square meters (approximately 150,000 houses).

The Third Five Year Plan (1938-1942) embraced a program of providing 377 million square feet of new housing. How much of this was built is not fully known. War conditions unquestionably slowed down construction, and much Soviet housing in European Russia was destroyed by the German invasion and by the Soviet "scorched earth" policy, carried out by retreating Russian forces.

A systematic reconstruction of Moscow was launched in 1935. About 54 million square feet of new housing had been constructed there between 1923 and 1938. In Leningrad, new workers' apartments, housing over 400,000 persons, had been built by 1938. Many of these were destroyed by the long German bombardment of the city. At the time of the German invasion in June, 1941, half of the nonfarm housing space in Soviet Russia had been built by the Soviet régime. But the fact that the urban population of Russia had trebled between 1917 and 1941 still left Russia with an acute housing shortage at the time of the outbreak of hostilities. This shortage has increased as a result of the stoppage of building during the war and the destruction wrought by the war.

Virtually all Russian housing has been built by state authorities since the institution of the Five Year Plans in 1928. Before that time, the cooperative societies had carried on much of Soviet housing construction. A law of August, 1918, abolished private ownership of real estate in Russia, but former owners were given some special rights to their homes. Such private homes as still exist are leased to occupants under state supervision. New housing is financed by the Soviet public budget. Actual construction is carried on chiefly by city soviets and state industrial enterprises. Rents are low, since they are intended to cover only maintenance costs. They absorb only about 5 per cent of the family income. Most of the urban housing constructed by the Soviet authorities prior to 1941 were large apartment houses, many of them without elevator service.

The difficulty of penetrating the "Iron Curtain" since 1945 has made it difficult to obtain detailed information concerning the Russian housing situation today, but there can be little doubt that the housing shortage is at least as great as it was in 1941.

In 1945, almost two billion rubles were appropriated for the construction of housing in European Russia alone. The postwar trend is reported to be away from large workers' apartments and toward prefabricated single-family houses and two-story apartments. Individually constructed houses are encouraged by means of grants of land, loans for building, technical assistance, and aid in securing building materials. Veterans of the Second World War are given special preference both in the building and in the occupancy of new housing. Soviet housing is interesting and instructive mainly as the most complete example of the nationalization of housing construction and administration.[7]

NINETEENTH-CENTURY AMERICAN SLUMS

Slum life in New York City a century ago. Slums are nothing new in human experience. There were plenty of them in the cities of antiquity. The masses that the Roman emperors controlled through "bread and circuses" lived in miserable, crowded frame buildings which the great historian, Ward Fowler, has well described as resembling "rabbit warrens." Even the small medieval cities had their slum quarters. But the urban slum problem did not become universal until the time of the Industrial Revolution.

Social historians have long since made it plain that in the early days after the introduction of machinery and factories, many of the workers lived like hogs. Indeed, the early tenements were often inferior to the better cow stables. Since industrialization and urbanization began in America later than it did in some European countries, our tenements and slums were not quite so vile and bleak as those which existed in certain European cities. But they were bad enough, as may readily be discerned from Smith Hart's description of "Sweeney's Shambles" in Gotham Court, New York City, an apartment inhabited under the following conditions at the time of the Civil War:

Gotham Court had been erected as a model housing project by a Quaker in the 1850's. It was a barracks of the worst type. Within twelve years of its erection it had been condemned as unfit for human habitation by the Council of Hygiene. Under the "Shambles" ran an underground vault some twelve feet wide and two hundred feet long. It was reached by a flight of stairs in the entrance of one of the Court buildings—"every step oozing with moisture and covered with filth." The paved floor of the vault "yielded to the slightest pressure of the feet a suffocating odor compounded of bilgewater and sulphuretted hydrogen." A hundred open toilets reeking with filth ranged on one side of the cave.

The "Shambles" contained two hundred tenements. The occupants were very poor widows supporting their children on microscopic earnings as charwomen, unskilled laborers and chronically sick and disabled craftsmen who were unable to obtain employment at their trades. A typical Gotham Court tenement, one room 12 feet square and a windowless bedroom 6 feet by 6, contained nine

---

[7] For more information on Soviet housing, see Hans Blumenfeld, "The Soviet Housing Problem," *The American Review on the Soviet Union,* November, 1945; and J. N. Hazard, *Soviet Housing Law.* New Haven: Yale University Press, 1939.

people—a crippled veteran of the Civil War and his wife, their three children, a woman lodger with two children, and a male lodger who paid 15¢ per night for his shelter. The rent was $5 a month.[8]

The great increase of immigration after the Civil War added to urban crowding in the United States and made housing conditions even more deplorable. The way in which the submerged classes lived prior to the passage of the Tenement House Act of 1867 may be discerned from a not unusual case which has been thus described by Edward Crapsey in his famous book, *Nether Side of New York:*

In a dark cellar filled with smoke, there sleep, all in one room, with no kind of partition dividing them, two men with their wives, a girl of thirteen or fourteen, two men and a large boy of about seventeen years of age, a mother with two more boys, one about ten years old, and one large boy of fifteen; another woman with two boys, nine and eleven years of age—in all fourteen persons.[9]

Persistence of slums. Many of the slums of today have descended from what was regarded as the "model apartment" of the 1880's, the so-called "dumbbell tenement." This has been described as follows by Lewis Mumford:

Its ground plan provided for two narrow side courts at the middle of the site. The windows on these courts looked bleakly on the windows, only a few feet away, of the next-door dumbbell tenements. The apartments in these buildings were called "railroad flats," because one room formed the corridor to the next. These flats had little light and air and no privacy.[10]

Once occupied by fairly prosperous middle-income families, they have deteriorated into slum tenements.

Even today, when much is made of the remarkable advances in city lighting in the era of electricity, there is still an altogether too great amount of darkness and gloom in tenement areas:

New York is the best lighted city in the world. Yet in the midst of this abundance of light, there are 3000 miles of dark and gloomy tenement halls through which millions of men, women and children pass daily.

It is in these dark public hallways that inadequate lighting permits accidents to occur, allows unsanitary conditions to pass unnoticed, endangers the morals of the young and the health of young and old and permits hold-ups and crimes to take place. These dark halls permit pyromaniacs to work unseen, to menace the lives of sleeping families. . . .

In a city where millions of lights blaze against the skies, it is tragic that so many must be subjected to the dangers of darkness. This situation arises out of inadequate lighting in old law tenements.[11]

Though it may seem incredible to some, Charles Abrams, one of our leading students of housing problems, pointed out early in 1950 that cellar apartments, not unlike those described by Crapsey in 1867, are still occupied by human beings in Harlem today.

---

[8] Smith Hart, *The New Yorkers.* Sheridan House, 1938, pp. 156-157.

[9] Cited in Smith Hart, *ibid.*

[10] *New Yorker,* May 20, 1950, pp. 73-74.

[11] *Let There Be Light,* Charity Organization Society, 1935, p. 3.

HOUSING CONDITIONS IN THE UNITED STATES

WPA survey of national housing conditions. It has long been recognized that a large proportion of the population of the United States has
always been poorly housed. In the past two decades, thorough surveys
made in both urban and rural areas have gathered impressive evidence as
to the extent of our housing needs. The Real Property Inventories
(1934-36) assembled data from 203 urban communities in various parts
of the country, including a complete survey of New York City.[12] Eight

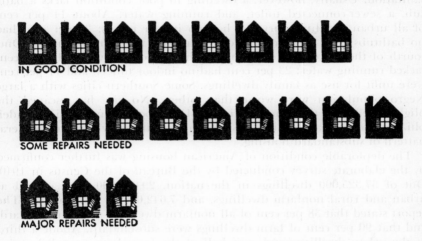

AMERICAN HOUSING CONDITIONS
(203 URBAN COMMUNITIES)

IN GOOD CONDITION

SOME REPAIRS NEEDED

MAJOR REPAIRS NEEDED

UNFIT FOR USE

Each house represents 5 per cent of all dwelling units surveyed

FROM *Can America Build Houses?* BY MILES L. COLEAN, PUBLISHED BY THE PUBLIC
AFFAIRS COMMITTEE, INC. CHART BY PICTOGRAPH CORP.

*Pictorial graph showing housing conditions and needs in the mid-New Deal
period (1936).*

million dwellings, representing about 40 per cent of all urban households, were judged according to minimum standards, such as the structural condition of the dwelling, the sanitary facilities provided, and the
number of families in a dwelling unit. Only about 39 per cent of the
housing units were in good condition. About 17 per cent were overcrowded. More than half of them had been built before 1915, and one-

---

[12] *Report on Urban Housing.* Washington: Works Progress Administration, 1939.

fourth of the dwellings were over 40 years old. Almost 45 per cent urgently needed repairs, and about 13 per cent of the houses surveyed needed major repairs. Leaky roofs, cracked foundations, and rickety stairways were common characteristics. About 3 per cent of the houses were found to be structurally unsafe and beyond repair.

Regional variations in housing deficiencies. The housing survey showed regional variations and also marked differences in housing conditions within the regions. In general, the cities of the Southeast had the largest number of substandard dwellings and those of the Northeast, the lowest. The data collected on sanitary facilities and room space provide a vivid picture of the wretched conditions of living for many American families. A deteriorated physical structure does not always mean absence of sanitation. Usually, however, a dwelling in poor condition lacks a bathtub, a sewer-connected toilet, and running water. About 14 per cent of all urban dwellings surveyed had no indoor toilets; 20 per cent had no bathtubs; and 5 per cent had no running water in the house. One-fourth of the urban homes of the South were overcrowded; 16 per cent lacked running water; 23 per cent had no indoor toilets; and 17 per cent were unfit for use as family dwellings. Some Southern cities with a large Negro population were worse than others. No city has escaped the blighting effect of the slum. Studies of Minneapolis, Cincinnati, Philadelphia, St. Louis, Kansas City, Missouri, and Butte show the same general pattern of substandard housing.

The deplorable condition of American housing was further confirmed by the elaborate survey conducted by the Bureau of the Census in 1940. Out of 37,325,000 dwellings in the nation, 29,683,000 were classed as urban and rural nonfarm dwellings, and 7,642,000 as farm homes. The report stated that 38 per cent of all nonfarm dwellings were substandard, and that 90 per cent of farm dwellings were substandard. About a third of the urban dwellings and over half of the farm homes needed major repairs. A third of the substandard dwellings were so dilapidated that to delay repairs would make them hazards to both health and safety.

Negro housing especially inadequate. The 1940 housing survey showed that substandard housing is, in general, the only kind available to the Negro in all urban areas; to the Mexican in the Southwest; and to the Chinese on the West Coast. In Charleston, South Carolina, in 1936, 48 per cent of the houses occupied by Negroes had no indoor toilets and 56 per cent had no tub or bathing facilities. In Louisville, Kentucky, over 95 per cent of the Negro families lived in substandard homes. In 1940, only one out of 10 homes of Southern urban Negroes met minimum standards. More than one-third of the Negro dwellings, with no sanitary facilities of any kind, were unfit for use. In Chicago, the majority of the Negroes lived in the worst slum areas of the city. Negroes were living at a ratio of 90,000 to the square mile, whereas whites in neighboring apartment houses lived only 20,000 to the square mile.[13]

---

[13] R. N. Anshen (Ed.), *The Family: Its Functions and Destiny*. New York: Harper, 1949, p. 302.

Postwar survey of housing conditions. In 1947, a sample study of housing needs was made by the Bureau of the Census. This housing inventory, though incomplete in detail, does provide data on the changes since the 1940 Housing Report. Urban and rural nonfarm dwellings had increased to 41,625,000 but rural homes had declined slightly—to 7,492,000. The quality of some dwellings had improved slightly, due in part to Federal aid and in part to higher private income during the war years. Some 27 per cent of the urban and rural nonfarm dwellings were classed as substandard and 80 per cent of the farm homes were so classed. The prevalence of overcrowding was revealed by the 1947 census and by a special study conducted in 1948. In the latter year it was found that 2,333,000 married couples, or 7.1 per cent of all married couples, were living "doubled up" with other families. In addition, there were 112,000 families living in institutions, motels, rooming houses or hotels for transients.

Most of the improvements during the war years were made by white nonfarm families. It was estimated by the Census Bureau that the proportion of substandard dwelling units occupied by non-whites was six times as high as that for whites. Over one-third of these dwellings lacked essential plumbing facilities. Overcrowding was four times greater among non-white families.

In view of the current discussion of veterans' housing needs, it is significant that the sample survey of 1947 reported that 35 per cent of married veterans were living "doubled up" or in rented rooms, and that 10 per cent of all veterans were living in substandard housing. The Negro veteran was even worse off in regard to housing than the white veteran. More than one-third of the Negro veterans in the South and 30 per cent in the North were living in dwellings needing major repairs and lacking standard plumbing facilities. Over one-half of all Negro veterans were living "doubled up" or in rented rooms. Writing in Miss Anshen's symposium on the family, the housing experts, Charles Abrams and J. P. Dean, declared that the "housing disorder was worse in 1947 than at any time in American history."

Although some progress in making repairs has been made by some families since 1940, great numbers of substandard units have continued to deteriorate, and the greatly increased number of new families has continued to exceed the number of new dwelling units made available. Thus the housing problem remains about as acute as ever.

THE SOCIAL COSTS OF BAD AMERICAN HOUSING

Bad housing and disease. The staggering social cost of the slums in terms of misery and blighted lives cannot be overemphasized. In almost every community, the areas of disease, death, and crime conform to the areas of poor housing. Bad housing is not the only cause of the social maladjustments of the slum-dweller. Criteria for determining to what precise degree the substandard home is responsible for the pathologies of slum life have not been established. Nevertheless, overcrowding, scattered common toilets, dark living quarters, dampness, and poor ventilation are surely breeders of disease and misery. It is difficult for a family to turn out good citizens under such conditions. The rates for tuberculosis, typhoid, contagious disease, rickets, and venereal disease appear to confirm the general conclusion that where housing is poorest, disease rates are highest. In Tampa, Florida, the records show a death rate of 17.2 per 1,000 in a slum area, as compared to 4.5 per 1,000 in the rest of the city. In Indianapolis, a slum area was responsible for 30 per cent of the city hospital costs. The City Housing Commission of Detroit reported that the pneumonia death rate in a slum area was triple that of a normal residential area, and the tuberculosis death rate 10 times as great.

Slums promote crime and vice. Crime and juvenile delinquency are highest in slum areas. Crowded conditions and lack of recreational facilities force children into streets and alleys to play. The National Conference for the Prevention and Control of Juvenile Delinquency stated that the relationship between unsatisfactory and inadequate housing and juvenile delinquency is clearly established: "A family lost in the slums and blighted area of a metropolitan center, or the inadequate housing and community facilities of a depressed rural section, finds itself victimized by anti-social forces beyond its control." [14] Numerous studies have verified this general conclusion. In Cleveland, a slum area containing less than 3 per cent of the population contributed over 4 per cent of the larcenies, 6 per cent of the robberies, 8 per cent of the juvenile delinquencies, 11 per cent of the illegitimate births, and almost 22 per cent of the murders. In a Detroit slum, the crime rate was seven times as great as that for the city as a whole. In one Chicago slum area, one-fourth of the boys between the ages of 10 and 17 appeared in the juvenile court in a single year.[15]

Slum areas a financial drain on cities. Good housing costs money but to maintain bad housing is even more costly. The cost of slums to the taxpayer can be measured in dollars and cents, since various cities have made studies on the costs of depressed areas. The taxes which the slum-dweller cannot pay to support the services he receives must be borne by those who live outside the slum. The City Planning Board of Boston, after a study of city finances in 1935, reported the per capita deficit to the city from a slum area to be $48.24; from all other residential areas, the per capita deficit was $10.81. A survey made by the Chamber of Commerce in a mid-west city showed that a slum area, housing only 10 per cent of the population, absorbed 25 per cent of all public funds; 30 per cent of the municipal hospital costs; 26 per cent of the family welfare budget; and 16 per cent of the total cost of fire protection. A report on Baltimore slums estimated that the slums contributed only about 6 per cent of urban tax income and absorbed nearly half of urban expenditures.

---

[14] *Report on Housing, Community Development and Juvenile Delinquency*. Washington: National Conference for Prevention of Juvenile Delinquency, 1946.
[15] *Ibid.*

Whatever the other factors may be in the total causes of social and personal maladjustment, it seems clear that the social costs of poor housing are too high to justify the continuance of slum areas. They constitute a disproportionate drain on community resources.

ESTIMATES OF OUR HOUSING NEEDS

Prewar estimates. During the depression after 1929, private industry practically ceased house-building. The optimistic theory of previous decades that private enterprise would supply all needed houses was no longer plausible. It was evident that housing had become a major social problem. Surveys were made to determine the amount of housing needed to replace old, worn-out structures; to build new dwellings; to accommodate those living doubled up; and to give a margin of choice which would enable the renter to select a dwelling to meet his needs.

According to Edith Elmer Wood, an outstanding authority on housing, a sum of 13-17 billion dollars would have been needed even in 1939 to carry out slum clearance, provide new housing, and allow a ratio of 3-5 vacancies to every 100 houses.[16] Harold L. Ickes, Secretary of the Interior, was much more conservative, stating that two billion dollars should be spent on housing. Both of these estimates were based on the 1930 census, which showed 4.5 million homes out of 17,373,000 needing major repairs. They were gross understatements as to the need for new housing, both urban and rural, at the time. On the eve of Pearl Harbor, realistic students of our housing problem estimated that it would cost about 50 billion dollars to rehouse the American urban population in such a manner that good living standards would be available for all. The figure today would be more than double that amount.

Postwar housing requirements. Since 1940, estimates made of the amount of housing needed have ranged from a million to a million and a half new dwellings needed annually for 10 to 40 years. The National Housing Agency stated in 1944 that 16,100,000 units were needed to replace substandard housing and to meet the demand for new housing. The Congress of Industrial Organizations, the American Federation of Labor, and the National Association of Housing Officials estimate housing needs at an average of 1.5 million dwellings to be built annually for 10–20 years.

The above estimates were for needed urban dwellings only. If we include the 5,150,000 farm dwellings needing repairs, the total number of substandard housing units that should be replaced is close to 20 million. A recent report on housing needs is that of the Administrator of the National Housing Agency, who stated in 1949 that the minimum housing needs had now reached 17-18 million dwelling units.

It is essential to build houses, but the planning and building must be closely related to the monthly rents which can be paid. A statement

---

16 *Introduction to Housing: Facts and Figures.* Washington: Government Printing Office, 1940, p. 82.

of the National Housing Administrator in the hearings on the Taft-Ellender-Wagner Bill before the Committee of Banking and Currency said that, based upon 1940 price levels, nonfarm housing needs should be met as follows:

1. About 3,600,000 units, or 28 per cent of the total, to rent for less than $20 a month.
2. Over 4,800,000 units, or 38 per cent of the total, to rent between $20-30 a month.
3. Over 4,200,000 units, about 34 per cent of the total, to rent above $40.

The housing problem of veterans has received the attention of many housing groups and Federal agencies since 1945. It was estimated in March, 1946, that before the end of 1947 almost 3 million married veterans would need homes. Only 14 per cent felt they could afford to pay more than $50 a month; 54 per cent could pay $30-50, but one-third could pay only $30 a month.[17]

It seems clear from the above estimates that a comprehensive housing program, providing both for replacement construction of new buildings and a margin for vacancies, would require the building of about a million and a half houses each year for a period of 10-20 years. The longer the program is delayed, the greater the problem will be.

WHY THERE IS A HOUSING PROBLEM IN THE UNITED STATES

Housing problems follow on the heels of the Industrial Revolution. The housing problem in America began with the introduction of the factory system. Workers from rural communities and foreign countries crowded into urban areas to be near their jobs in the factories. As industry expanded, the number of workers increased and the need for housing grew. Thousands of box-like structures were built close together to save ground space. They proved to be profitable business ventures for builders who, as yet unhampered by law, gave no thought to planning for ventilation and sanitation. The factory workers, unable to afford better housing, moved into these tenements, and the era of city slums began.

As demand for goods increased, industry further expanded. The well-to-do families, wishing to escape the ever-increasing congestion, built homes farther away from the business areas. Their cast-off homes, no longer kept in repair, were rented to the middle-income families who could not afford to pay a high rent or build homes of their own. In time, the middle classes passed these dwellings on to the working classes. This pattern, established in the earlier days of the growing city, has been continued until the present. Much of the housing occupied by the middle-income group and the working classes was originally built by those in a higher income bracket.

---

[17] *War Department Survey of Separation Centers,* December, 1945.

Low income creates the most serious housing problems. The reasons for poor housing today are not difficult to discover. Homes are built for those who can afford them. Inadequate income forces families to take what they can find at the price they can pay. In 1929, one of our most prosperous years, a survey made by the Brookings Institute showed that more than one-fifth of American families had incomes under $1,000, and that about one-fifth received incomes between $1,000-$1,500. More than 71 per cent of all family incomes were under $2,500.[18]

The amount paid for rent gives a fair idea of the conditions under which low-income families lived in 1929. Approximately 34 per cent of the urban dwellings rented under $20 a month; one-third were rented at $15 or less; and 15 per cent were rented at under $10 a month. Even at that date, although a home renting for $20 a month was generally substandard, more than one-third of the families in the United States paid less than $20 a month for rent.

In 1934, the average annual income of one-third of the families in urban areas was less than $800. It is generally agreed that to maintain a reasonable budget, no family should pay more than 20-25 per cent of its income for rent. On an $800 income, even a rent of $15 a month, providing the poorest kind of housing, was beyond the reach of many families.[19] It is easy to see why only one-tenth of one per cent of urban dwellings built in 1938 were within the reach of the families with incomes below $1,500. It is equally obvious that private industry cannot afford to build houses for the low-income group. Nor is building for the middle-income group always a profitable venture. It was estimated in 1938 that no private builder in New York City could afford to erect a dwelling unless he could rent it for $10 a room per month.

Disastrous results of speculative rather than investment real estate ventures. Another serious cause of the housing chaos and inadequacy is speculation rather than sound investment in urban real estate. This factor has been well described by the eminent architect and housing-planner, Clarence S. Stein, who planned Radburn, New Jersey, the first community designed for the automobile age, and, later, Chatham Village, in Pittsburgh, and Sunnyside Gardens, in Queens, New York City:

> The failure of speculative housing is not only in the physical havoc it produces in blighted areas, present and future. Its practices are leading to municipal bankruptcy.
>
> In contrast with the failure of speculative housing, it is heartening to review the long record of financial success of investment companies, going back in one case 68 years. Through the worst real estate depression this country has known these enterprises have continued to pay interest and amortize their mortgages. Their capital structure has come through the storm unimpaired....
>
> As a result of speculative practices in Los Angeles in 1931 there were 175 square miles of subdivided land vacant and useless, spotted throughout the county—enough land withdrawn from agricultural use to house an additional population of 83 per cent (1,820,000). The wasted annual cost of maintaining the 2222 miles of street on which the empty lots face is $1,450,000. The yearly

---

[18] *America's Capacity to Consume.* Washington: Brookings Institution, 1934.
[19] Wood, *op. cit.,* p. 6.

cost to the owners of carrying the vacant lots in which $750,000,000 is invested—including interest on investment, taxes and assessment—is some $66,500,000. Much of this is passed on to the community due to uncollected taxes and assessment. Speculation in land and housing is at the root of municipal bankruptcy.

The blight of the central core of our cities, like the ruthless waste of outlying improved but unused land, is the result of speculation in housing. Detroit has allowed seventeen square miles to decay because of disorganized speculation in land and living places. In Cleveland, twenty-one of the seventy-seven square miles are unfit for human habitation and unremunerative as to property. Chicago has forty-four square miles of blighted areas. The inhuman living conditions in these areas are causing the population to evacuate. The empty and blighted properties bring in little or no income to their owners. As a result, they are far in arrears in the payment of taxes. They are a dead loss to the municipality. Meanwhile, the speculators are spreading the seeds of future blight on the outskirts of our cities. The antiquated, individualistic, small scale method of planning, building, land ownership and community disorganization continues to make these new sections obsolete even before they have reached their first state of physical decay.[20]

EARLY EFFORTS TO PROVIDE BETTER HOUSING FOR THE POOR IN THE UNITED STATES

Origins of American housing reforms and planning. Slums did not develop as early in the United States as in England, because rapid industrialization did not occur here until the nineteenth century. In the first half of the century, the plight of the slum-dweller received little attention. Slums were increasing in number. Speculators erected tenements on high-priced land and vied with one another in building the largest number of rooms in the smallest amount of space. The traditional attitude that good housing is only the housing which brings in a high margin of profit was all too evident in the construction of dwellings. During this period, there were few protests against the many tenement apartments without toilets, bathtubs, or outside exposures.

In 1842, John Griscom, reporting on New York City, expressed the fear that disease would spread as a result of the bad housing in the slums. The first tangible result of the series of investigations which followed the Griscom report was the Tenement House Law of 1867. This law, although wholly inadequate, required cellar apartments to have the ceiling at least one foot above the ground and set a limit of 20 persons to one water closet. In 1879, the building of apartments without windows was prohibited.

Tenement House Act of 1901. The first important housing law was the New York City Tenement House Act of 1901. This Act made it illegal to erect dwellings which did not provide fire escapes, adequate ventilation, and sanitary facilities. Many of the tenements built before 1901 are, however, still used today. In 1940, it was estimated that 2 million persons lived in the buildings condemned at the turn of the century. Nevertheless, the Act of 1901 was important, even though the housing of slum-dwellers showed little improvement, for it set a minimum standard

---

[20] *Survey Graphic,* January 29, 1940.

for future building. Tenement house laws based on the New York statute were passed in Pennsylvania, New Hampshire, Michigan, and Iowa.

RISE OF LIMITED-DIVIDEND HOUSING PROJECTS

Early limited-dividend housing projects. Outright gifts from philanthropists to rehouse slum-dwellers have been negligible. The limited-dividend idea, the investment of philanthropic capital with voluntarily limited returns, was due to the influence of Octavia Hill, an English reformer. Her ventures in the field of housing for the slum-dwellers of London demonstrated the soundness of her belief that limiting returns on investment would still bring a profit to the builder. Her ideas spread to the United States.

In 1885, the New York Society for Improving the Condition of the Poor built a model tenement for Negroes on the limited-dividend plan, restricting its returns on the investment to 6 per cent. In 1890, Alfred T. White built Riverside Dwellings in Brooklyn on the limited-dividend plan. The City and Suburban Homes Company, organized in 1896, carried on numerous building projects; it invested over 11 million dollars and provided for 3,500 families.

By the First World War, a score of limited-dividend projects had been built in New York City, but they housed only about one per cent of the slum population—approximately 5,000 families.[21] During this period, the influence of Ebenezer Howard's English "Garden Suburbs" had resulted in the formation of city planning groups in some of the larger cities.[22] The Russell Sage Foundation financed the building of Forest Hills Gardens on farm land on Long Island outside the public transportation lines. The project had originally been planned for the modest-salaried worker, but it was actually used chiefly by a more prosperous class. The Queensboro Corporation at Jackson Heights, Long Island, began building garden apartments for a lower-income class than the occupants of the Forest Hills project.

The New York Housing Act of 1926. In 1926, New York passed the State Housing Act, establishing a State Board of Housing, and granted partial tax exemption to real estate, insurance companies, banks and investment houses in order to stimulate the building of dwellings for sale and rent. Eleven housing companies took advantage of this law, and 5,896 apartments had been constructed by 1937, representing an investment of about 30 million dollars. But few were constructed for the low-income group of renters.

The New York innovations in limited-dividend housing were imitated elsewhere. The Ginn estate erected the Charlesbank Homes in Boston. The Buhl Foundation financed the construction of Chatham Village in Pittsburgh. The Marshall Field estate and the Julius Rosenwald Fund

---

21 G. H. Gray, *Housing and Citizenship.* New York: Reinhold, 1946, p. 14.
22 See below, p. 549.

provided model apartments in Chicago, the latter giving attention to apartments for Negroes.

Cooperative housing. During this period, some cooperative housing ventures were attempted on a small scale. The first successful example was a Finnish apartment begun in Brooklyn in 1917. In general, however, cooperative apartments were not built for the low-income groups. The Amalgamated Clothing Workers built two projects: Amalgamated Housing in the Bronx (1926) and Amalgamated Dwellings on East Grand Street (1930). In order to live in these projects, the tenement-owners made a payment of $500 a room, part of it in a lump sum and the rest in rent of $11 per room. In 1948, the down-payment was still $500; rent had increased to $12.50 per room.

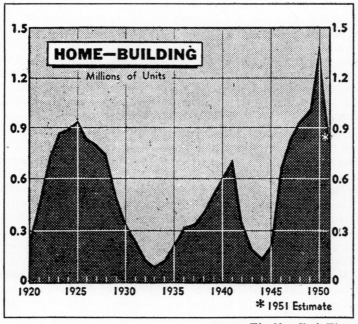

COURTESY *The New York Times.*

Graph illustrating volume of housing construction since the First World War.

Little public housing before the New Deal. It is evident that during the first three decades of the twentieth century, with the exception of the limited-dividend projects, little attention was paid to the over-all housing of Americans. Meanwhile, industrial horizons were widening, and power was being transmitted over long distances. The extension of communication made it possible to develop new residential areas, but the same patterns of high land values, real estate speculation, substandard dwellings, and too few houses remained. There were some zoning laws and some legislation to regulate building and to curb irresponsible activities of landlords, but, for the most part, the housing of families was unaided and unregulated, and was left to private enterprise.

INSURANCE COMPANIES EXPAND IN HOUSING CONSTRUCTION

Insurance companies revive private housing construction on the eve of the Second World War. During the depression, private enterprise could not build houses. By the time the program of the United States Housing Authority was begun in 1938, however, there were indications that private building industry could begin operations on a larger scale. Accordingly, President Roosevelt launched a "House America" program. There was little general response, however, to the appeals of the President to build houses in order to reduce the housing shortage and to provide employment. Between 1939 and our entrance into the Second World War, private enterprise provided new housing for only 1.2 per cent of the families with incomes under $1,200 and only 4.9 per cent for families with incomes between $1,200 and $1,500. The rest was supplied to families in the higher-income brackets. In this period, however, the entrance of large insurance companies into the field of housing is of special interest.

Five insurance companies—Metropolitan Life, Equitable, New York Life, John Hancock, and Prudential—entered the housing field. Several of them had taken part in limited-dividend housing construction following the New York Act of 1926. The Metropolitan Life has had, by far, the most extensive program. As early as 1922, Metropolitan Life funds had built Sunnyside Gardens in Long Island City.

Metropolitan Life Insurance projects. In 1938, the Parkchester development in the Bronx was begun by the Metropolitan Life. This vast project houses 42,000 persons. The average income of the families living in the Parkchester Development was $3,000 in 1941, and the average monthly rent ranged from $35-70 a month. Obviously, the project was not planned to re-house the slum-dweller. The community of Parkchester is grouped into four superblocks, separated by main thoroughfares. Each superblock has its own stores, recreation center, and movies. For sheer size, Parkchester is impressive. A city within a city, it provides efficient living. There is, however, little emphasis on community life, since no provision for this has been made by the Company. The complete ownership of the community by the Metropolitan Life makes it impossible for tenants to have any voice in their own affairs. During the political campaign of 1948, distribution of pamphlets within the city of Parkchester was prohibited.[23]

In 1943, the New York legislature passed the Urban Redevelopment Corporations Law, which gave cities the power to make land in blighted areas available to housing corporations for building purposes. In order to encourage building, the bill provided tax exemption for 25 years. The limitation on rents, written into earlier acts, was dropped from the 1943

---

[23] Kathryn Close, "New Homes with Insurance Dollars," *Survey Graphic*, November, 1948.

bill. The Metropolitan Life promptly took advantage of this law and began to plan large projects. Stuyvesant Town, Peter Cooper Village, and the Riverton (Harlem) projects were the results. These projects were planned to accommodate about 9,000 families.

In 1941, two Metropolitan Life projects were begun in California: Parklabrea, in Los Angeles, and Parkmerced, in San Francisco. War priorities delayed construction, but one-half of Parklabrea and two-thirds of Parkmerced were opened in 1943. They were finished with buildings 13 stories in height, instead of the original two-story apartments planned. The rents, though not exorbitant, are hardly fitted to the pocketbooks of the poor. One-bedroom apartments rent for $60 and three-bedroom apartments rent for $90.

COURTESY FAIRCHILD AERIAL SURVEYS, INC.

Stuyvesant Town and Peter Cooper Village, two gigantic housing projects in lower New York City recently completed by the Metropolitan Life Insurance Company. They well illustrate the New York City type of city planning.

All the Metropolitan Life projects are similar in plan, but the California projects cover less ground, and more space is thus provided for land and park areas. For instance, Parkchester covers 50 per cent of ground space. Parklabrea and Parkmerced, when completed in 1950, covered only 18 per cent. The total financial investment of the Metropolitan Life is estimated as approximately 300 million dollars in the seven developments—the New York and California projects and one outside Washington. The total number of families rehoused is over 35,000—or about 125,000 persons.

Critical estimates of the Metropolitan construction. There has been both praise and criticism of the insurance projects, particularly of the New York projects of the Metropolitan Life. Lewis Mumford has condemned them as only a lavish recent example of "planned congestion." There is no doubt that the City of New York has lost considerable revenue under the Redevelopment Law. It is estimated that the loss will run about 50 million dollars for Stuyvesant Town alone. Since the Metropolitan Life sought a sound investment for its money, no attempt has been made to house low-income families. About 3,800 families were displaced by the Stuyvesant Town project and were forced to find homes in even worse slum areas. In 1944, the New York legislature passed a bill to make funds available for building housing projects for families displaced by the projects of private industry. This, however, was over a year after construction had begun on Stuyvesant Town.

Stuyvesant Town has been criticized for its tall apartment houses; for the little area remaining for lawn and parks; for the relatively small apartments; for the fact that there are over 400 persons to the acre in these projects; and for the lack of community life. One problem will be of great importance to the residents of Stuyvesant Town and Peter Cooper Village in the near future. There is no centrally located school within the project. Legal restrictions made it impossible for the Metropolitan Life to construct a school. When the children of residents become of school age, they will have considerable distance to go to school, and all will have to cross main streets of city traffic. Lewis Mumford, writing to the editors of the *New Yorker* (November 27, 1948) to defend his criticism of Stuyvesant Town, said: "These new housing projects are not cut to fit the requirements of family life; family life must be cut to their required large scale of living ... Many generations of New Yorkers will have to pay for the mistakes that have already been made."

Inadequate community life and facilities. One main weakness of the law under which the New York Housing Authority operates is that it forbids the erection within housing developments of schools, markets, and amusement centers. As Lewis Mumford says:

> Under the terms of the law, this housing has been separated from every other manifestation of neighborhood life, so although these estates are physically neighborhoods, or even small cities, they lack most of the organs and attributes of a full-fledged domestic community. The fourteen thousand people who live on the thirty-four acres occupied by the adjoining Jacob Riis and Lillian Wald Houses in lower East Side Manhattan, haven't a single church or synagogue or motion-picture house, or public market within their whole area.[24]

This defect was remedied in the Fresh Meadows Development erected by the New York Life Insurance Company in Queens.

Prudential and New York Life projects. In 1939, The Prudential Insurance Company began two projects in Newark, N. J. The City of Newark was empowered by law to condemn needed land and to sell to a company for building purposes. As a result, some of the most dilapidated houses in the slum areas were demolished. The Prudential Company built two groups of homes: the Douglas-Harrison for Negroes and the Chellis Austin for whites. Recently the Prudential has cooperated with the Fed-

---

24 *New Yorker*, May 20, 1950, p. 76.

eral government in making extensive loans for giant low-cost mass-produced housing projects, notably the Lakewood Park development for veterans in Los Angeles. The New York Life Insurance Company built Fresh Meadows in Queens on Long Island after the war. Many regard it as the best of the insurance company housing projects.

Commendations of insurance housing ventures. Although the insurance ventures have their critics, they also have their supporters. Those who support the insurance projects point to the fact that a blighted area is now replaced by a wholesome area; that employment has been created; that veterans in the income group not eligible for subsidized housing, but unable to buy or build, will now have a chance to find a place to live. Other supporters point to the fact that, although tax exemption is a loss in revenue, the neighborhoods in which the projects were built never paid adequate revenue to the city—indeed, were a financial liability.

Problem of racial discrimination. The policy of racial discrimination adopted by the insurance companies in their housing projects resulted in the filing of suits against both the Metropolitan Life and the New York Life Insurance Companies. The suit against the Metropolitan Life was instituted by three young Negro veterans who protested the barring of Negro tenants from Stuyvesant Town and Peter Cooper Village. The court decision was in favor of the insurance company's policy. The Supreme Court of New York and the Appellate Division upheld the decision of the lower court. The United States Supreme Court refused to review the New York case.

There was much criticism of the court decisions by civic groups. Plans for renting apartments in the insurance housing projects for United Nations employees were cancelled by UN personnel because of the alleged display of racial bias. The publicly-announced policy of nonracial discrimination by the New York Housing Authority and the provision in the Wicks-Austin Bill (March, 1950), which forbade racial and religious discrimination in housing projects assisted by tax exemption, influenced the Metropolitan to alter its attitude toward Negro tenants. In August, 1950, the Metropolitan Life Insurance Company announced that, in the future, carefully selected Negro tenants would be admitted to Stuyvesant Town and Peter Cooper Village.

At the present time, the rôle of insurance companies in the solution of our housing problem is not fully apparent. But one thing is certain: their investment in housing projects, although sound, profitable, and socially constructive, hardly solves the problem of providing housing for the low-income groups who most urgently need good housing today.

The same fact holds true for private housing construction of all kinds. There has been a great boom in the private housing field since 1948. In 1949, a million new housing units were started, and in 1950 no less than 1,400,000 were launched. This can be compared with the 894,000 units built in 1925, the previous peak of private construction. Exponents of private construction have hailed this boom as proof that private building operations can solve the American housing problem. But it fails even to touch effectively the most serious of our housing shortages

—namely, that for the low-income groups in both city and country. More-over, the Korean War, the defense program, and priorities in materials have halted much of the private construction which has been started.

STATE AND CITY HOUSING PROGRAMS

New York State takes the lead. Neither private construction nor Federal housing operations began to meet the need for new housing. Some states attempted to step into the breach. In 1938 New York State, under the prodding of Governor Herbert Lehman, amended its constitution so that the state could make loans to assist "low-rent housing and the clearance, replanning, reconstruction, and rehabilitation of substandard and unsani-tary areas." By 1949, New York had authorized loans of about $735,000,000 and annual subsidies of $25,000,000. About 20 important projects had been completed and many more had been planned. Other states that followed the example of New York were California, Connecticut, Illi-nois, Massachusetts, New Hampshire, New Jersey, Ohio, Pennsylvania, and Wisconsin.

City housing aid. New York City also began to aid housing develop-ments for both low-income and middle-income groups. These have been financed by the sale of New York Housing Authority bonds, and the dwellings are operated on a nonprofit basis with rentals from $15.45 to $17.49 per room. About 200 other cities have adopted roughly similar plans to build new housing or to assist in financing construction. But the majority of new urban housing has been constructed either by private enterprise or through Federal aid, made possible by the United States Housing Act of 1937 and the Lanham Act of 1940. About 350,000 permanent dwellings had been built by 1950 under the provisions of these acts.

THE FEDERAL GOVERNMENT ENTERS HOUSING

Public housing begins during the First World War. Until the First World War, the Federal government had remained out of the housing field. But the demand for war essentials, even before the United States entered the war, resulted in a migration of workers to the munition centers. Overcrowding in already congested areas required action. Private industry had built some new dwelling units but not enough to meet the needs. Two emergency Federal agencies were created—the Emergency Fleet Corporation and the National Defense Council. The Fleet Cor-poration, under the auspices of local housing corporations, used Federal loans and built 9,000 houses in 27 towns on land provided by shipbuild-ing companies. The National Defense Council, operating through the United States Housing Corporation, built new "garden villages" on a large scale. At the end of the war, projects to care for 15,000 families had been built by the two Federal agencies. The total result of the Federal program was negligible when compared with the needs, but certain of the procedures adopted by the government at the time of the First World War were used later in the peacetime housing program.

Housing shortage after the war. It was estimated that at the end of the First World War, there was a shortage of over a million dwelling units. Private industry was slow to begin construction, since building costs had increased tremendously during the war. By 1921, the number of houses built had slowly increased, and it was confidently believed that private enterprise could handle the housing needs. The mood of the 1920's was one of optimism. At first, it would seem that the optimism was justified, for between 1920-29 almost seven million dwelling units were built. In the year 1925, the peak year of building by private industry, 925,000 were built. Most of the construction during this period was for the high-income group. Over three-fourths of the dwellings built were within the rental price range of only one-fifth of the population.[25]

After 1929, building activity practically ceased. Only 59,000 homes were built in 1934. Slums grew worse, and, as unemployment increased, there was even greater overcrowding. Few buildings were torn down, and no repairs were made on buildings already in a bad state of deterioration. The middle-income group, wanting new homes, either went without them, or paid too much for a house and lost it later during the depression.[26]

In 1929, President Hoover, concerned about the desperate situation confronting many slum-dwellers, called a Conference on Home Building and Home Ownership to discuss low-cost housing from various angles. The Conference made numerous recommendations. The first feeble Federal step to aid housing was incidental to the Home Loan Act of 1932, which created the Federal Home Loan Bank Board. It was designed more to save homes from foreclosure than to provide new dwellings. In 1932, also, the Reconstruction Finance Corporation was established under the Emergency Relief and Reconstruction Act. It was authorized to make loans to corporations organized solely for the purpose of building homes for the low-income groups. The only project that met specifications and received aid from the RFC was Knickerbocker Village in lower Manhattan (1933). Financed by a 10-year loan and exempt from city taxes under the New York law of 1926, it cleared three of the worst slum blocks in New York City.

THE NEW DEAL HOUSING PROGRAM

New Deal interest in housing. Unemployment increased rapidly after 1930, and the emergency became acute. Much attention was paid to housing by President Franklin D. Roosevelt and the New Deal. The Federal aid, made possible through emergency legislation, was designed, in part, to encourage home owners to begin construction and make repairs by granting loans to them. In this way, jobs for the unemployed would be provided, money would be put in circulation, and recovery would be

---

[25] Nathan Strauss, *The Seven Myths of Housing*. New York: Knopf, 1944, Chap. IX.
[26] E. E. Wood, *Introduction to Housing*. Washington: Government Printing Office, 1940, pp. 73-85.

aided. The New Deal program was, however, more than a pump-priming program. It was part of a broad social philosophy—that of providing a "more abundant life" for Americans.

COURTESY *The New York Times* AND BARNEY WEINBERG.

A Manhattanville vista that the community seeks to erase.

The housing program during the Roosevelt Administration falls into two categories: One was aid to increase the opportunities for home ownership through easier loans and more protection to both borrowers and lenders. The other type was Federal aid for housing through the building of slum clearance projects. The Federal Housing Administration, authorized by the National Housing Act (1934), and the Home Owners Loan Corporation (1933) were agencies set up to administer the first aspect of the New Deal program. Between 1933 and 1950, the HOLC lent over 3.5 billion dollars to cover more than a million homes, and the investment was 93.5 per cent self-liquidated. The FHA makes no loans but insures them. It has insured over 12 million mortgages involving about 18 billion dollars.

Operations of the Public Works Administration. The National Industrial Recovery Act (1933) authorized the creation of the Public Works Administration (PWA), which undertook the construction of slum-clearance projects. The housing powers of the Reconstruction Finance Corporation were transferred to the PWA, and a Housing Division was set up. The PWA controlled Federal housing projects until 1937. During those years, 51 projects in 36 cities were completed, and more than 21,800 families were rehoused at a cost of 134 million dollars.

PUBLIC HOUSING ADMINISTRATION.

Laurel Homes, Cincinnati, Ohio. Picture shows how dilapidated and congested slum area looked when rebuilt as a modern apartment development.

This work of the Federal government in new housing construction was altogether admirable as a demonstration of what can be done in clearing away slums and erecting suitable habitations for human beings. The Williamsburg Houses in Brooklyn, Old Harbor Village in Boston, the Lake Terrace Apartments in Cleveland, Laurel Homes in Cincinnati, the Jane Addams Houses in Chicago, the Lockefield Garden Apartments in Indianapolis, Summerfield Homes in Minneapolis, the Techwood Project in Atlanta, Smithfield Court in Birmingham, and Lauderdale Courts in Memphis are characteristic examples of such Federal slum-clearance and housing construction. But the entire program, including all construction finished by 1941, housed only a pitifully small fraction of our slum population.

The PWA was a pioneer, and its stormy career was filled with criticism of its costliness. In spite of obstacles and criticisms, however, the program was successful, if inadequate. Rents charged on projects averaged about $5.10 per room per month, which was comparable to many slum rents. The program also served to dramatize to the public the need for providing shelter for the slum-dwellers. One of its concrete accomplishments was to encourage 29 states to pass legislation which led to the establishment of 46 local housing authorities. The PWA encouraged mass planning and undoubtedly was responsible for the passage of the Wagner-Steagall Housing Act (known as the United States Housing Act) in 1937, which created a permanent Federal housing agency—the United States Housing Authority (USHA). Pursuant to the Housing Act of 1937, the projects of the PWA were taken over by the USHA in 1939.

The United States Housing Authority. The United States Housing Authority established subsidized public housing as a national policy. Responsibility was placed on local communities for planning, building, and managing the projects. Local-Federal partnership was made possible in this way. The USHA was authorized to make loans up to 90 per cent of total cost of low-rent projects for 60 years at a low rate of interest. The community supplied the materials and the remaining 10 per cent of the money. Subsidies equal to at least 20 per cent of the Federal contribution were authorized to bring the rents down to a level which families drawn from sub-standard housing could afford. Only families from groups whose incomes were less than five times the amount of rent set were eligible for rehousing.

The Housing Act of 1937 made available 800 million dollars in loans and annual subsidies not to exceed 28 million dollars for these low-cost and low-rent public housing developments. Under this Act and the authority of the USHA, 387 developments with 120,000 dwelling units were constructed. In addition, 201 developments with 51,698 dwellings were built for defense and war workers after 1940 and turned over for low-rental civilian housing at the close of the war. This work was accomplished by 568 local housing authorities which were brought into being in accordance with the 1937 housing law.

Negroes were given full consideration in this New Deal housing program. Nearly 20 per cent of all low-rent housing constructed or planned was designed for Negro occupation. Since the Negroes constituted about 10 per cent of the population this was a generous, if much needed, allotment.

THE WAR HOUSING PROGRAM AFTER PEARL HARBOR

Public housing during the Second World War. The defense emergency of 1940 interrupted the program of the USHA and the insurance companies, and focused the attention of all housing agencies on the task of providing housing for defense workers. In June, 1940, all the funds of USHA were diverted to defense housing, and in the next 18 months acts were passed to make about 800 million dollars available for emergency housing. An Executive Order of February, 1942, created the National Housing Agency, with the Federal Housing Administration, the Federal Home Loan Bank Board, and the Federal Public Housing Au thority as the three constituent agencies.

As the United States moved into the war program, the government housing program assumed tremendous proportions. Some 8 million persons were rehoused in one way or another. More than 850,000 publicly-financed housing units—at a cost of 2 billion dollars—had been built or were under construction by June 30, 1945. The construction proceeded at the rate of 30,000-40,000 units a month in 700 war production areas. Sometimes 1,000 units a day were built. This included dwellings, dormitories, and temporary units. Some programs were in metropolitan areas, involving the fitting of housing into already crowded communities. Other projects were in small communities, whose facilities were undeveloped and ill-equipped to meet the needs of the large number of war workers. Entire towns of 50,000 or more inhabitants were built. The City of Vanport (Oregon), built for the shipyard workers in the Portland-Vancouver region, grew to a population of 40,000 and became the second largest city in Oregon. More than 8,000 dwellings were built in Orange, Texas. Part of the construction was on swampland, 12 feet below sea level.

All sorts of obstacles confronted the task of construction. Materials and equipment for building were scarce even from the beginning. Delays in delivery further held up construction. All kinds of substitutes had to be used. Temporary buildings, some of them substandard from the beginning, were built by the thousands. The War Production Board gave blanket priorities to divert all possible materials not needed for war plants into housing for war workers. As young men were called into service and into war work, there was a scarcity of labor for construction. By 1944, the need for housing grew even more urgent.

Crudity and temporary nature of wartime housing. The sharp criticisms of the housing built for war workers were for the most part valid. Less than half of the war housing was of material or quality which could be permanently useful to the communities in which it was built. The rest, built for temporary use—especially after 1942—was to be dismantled after the war. The average cost of the permanent dwellings was held to about $4,500, and the cost of temporary shelter to about one-half of that amount. Temporary shelter included the use of trailers, portable shelters, and the conversion of warehouses, factory buildings, and railroad cars into shelters. The total housing units built or converted into temporary dwellings numbered nearly 2 million. The total cost of the war housing program was about 8 billion dollars.

At first, war housing was limited to civilian war workers. By 1944, returning service men found it increasingly difficult to find a place to live.

In June, 1945, in response to the demands of veterans, Congress authorized the opening of some war housing units to veterans and their families.

THE POSTWAR HOUSING CRISIS AND CONGRESS

Acute housing shortage after the war. After VJ day, the housing shortage, which had been bad enough 20 years before, grew steadily worse. The depression in home building which had slowed down construction after 1929, the complete cessation of residential construction for non-war workers during the war, and the ever-present shortage of houses all combined to produce a housing crisis which experts declared was the worst in American history. There was an immediate need for at least 4,500,000 non-farm dwelling units, to say nothing of the more than two million farm dwellings which were beyond repair. Many veterans could find no place to live. About one and one-half million service men had married during the war and were eager to find homes for themselves and their wives. War workers who had left their communities for work in war plants found that there was no place for them to go. Many of the 6.25 million urban homes reported as substandard in 1940 had further deteriorated during the war, since no repairs could be made. Even those whose income was large enough to buy or build found that materials for building were often unobtainable.

By the end of 1946, it was conservatively estimated that 6.5 million families were "doubled up." An additional 500,000 were living in trailers or other temporary accommodations. Almost one-fifth of the urban population were living with relatives or friends. Many veterans demanded that temporary war housing be turned over to them for homes. Only about 100,000 units were available. Surveys of the housing of married veterans were made by the Bureau of the Census in 1946 in 111 cities. These surveys showed that the extent of doubling up ranged from 15 per cent in Boise, Idaho, to 47 per cent in Atlanta, Georgia. More than 70 per cent of Negro veterans in Washington were doubled up with other families.[27]

Provisions of the Taft-Ellender-Wagner Bill. In August, 1945, the Taft-Ellender-Wagner Bill, designed to provide public low-cost housing, was introduced into Congress for the first time. The bill, according to its preamble, "seeks to realize as soon as feasible, the goal of a decent home and a suitable environment for every American family."

The Housing Bill proceeded on the plan that had been developed by the USHA. In order to encourage private enterprise to build for middle- and low-income families, the bill would insure up to 95 per cent of the loan (90 per cent was the limit insured by the Federal Housing Administration). Veterans were to be given the opportunity to secure housing through a government loan. Repayment of the loan was to be within 32 years instead of the 25 years provided for under the USHA procedure.

---

[27] Anshen, *op. cit.*, pp. 300, 318 ff.

The interest rate would be reduced from the 4½ per cent of the FHA to 3 per cent.

To encourage builders to engage in larger operations, and thus to permit more building, construction loans were to be made to builders so that marketing risks might be reduced. In order to give the middle class an opportunity, loans were to be limited to houses costing no more than $5,300. In order that the homeowner might be further protected, the bill proposed to permit him to defer his monthly payment if he became unemployed through circumstances beyond his control. Long-term loans of 40 years, at a low rate of interest, would be made to local housing authorities as inducements to invest in rental or cooperative housing. It was hoped that the bill would also stimulate and direct investment by insurance companies that build, own, and manage middle-income projects.

Embodied in the proposals were provisions for an expenditure of almost 13 million dollars for a 5-year Federal program of research into the best methods of management, and ways to encourage long-term investments by private enterprise. The bill, under the familiar formula of the USHA, would provide financial aid to communities. This Federal aid would build 500,000 additional units of low-cost housing at a rate of 125,000 a year for four years.[28]

The rural community would not be neglected if the Taft-Ellender-Wagner proposals became law. Programs amounting to about one-third of those planned for the urban areas would be put into operation in the rural community. The Secretary of Agriculture would be authorized to make long-term low-cost loans to farm owners to build houses for themselves and their workers. There was also provision in the bill for the subsidizing of housing for farm workers, sharecroppers, migratory labor, and others.

The high cost of land is one of the chief factors in the high cost of housing. Urban redevelopment has been made difficult because land has been too costly to make re-use profitable. The Taft-Ellender-Wagner Bill would use loans and subsidies to help cover the difference between the cost of land and its value in re-use. Two-thirds of the cost would be borne by the Federal government. The local community would bear the remainder of the cost—such as donation of land, remission of taxes, cash, materials, or labor. The framers of the bill estimated that about 1.5 billion dollars' worth of rural slums would be eliminated. It is evident that the bill was very restrained in the light of the needs.

Congress rejects the Taft-Ellender-Wagner Bill. The Taft-Ellender-Wagner Bill was planned as a long-range program—not to meet the current emergency. The veteran without housing would have preferred immediate help. However, no Congressional action was taken. Part of the reluctance of Congress to pass the bill was due to the pressure from the real estate companies, insurance companies, and those who feared

---

[28] Summary of TEW, from Leon Keyserling, "Homes for All and How," *Survey Graphic,* February, 1946.

increasing government control. Opponents' arguments fell into several types: public housing involves an expenditure of public funds and adds to the total tax burden; public housing means competition with private enterprise; public construction is more expensive; housing is a local problem; and if the government will stay out, private industry will build houses. Another argument used by the opponents of a Federal housing bill was that a building boom was on the way, and that as soon as materials became available in quantity, private enterprise itself would build many houses.

THE FEDERAL EMERGENCY HOUSING PROGRAM

Need of an emergency housing program. It was apparent by the end of 1945 that Congress was not prepared to pass a housing bill at that time. By December of that year, the housing crisis had reached a state of emergency. President Truman appointed a Housing Expeditor, Wilson W. Wyatt, former mayor of Louisville, Kentucky. Wyatt was asked to plan a full-scale housing program, to handle the emergency, and to set up a long-range program to replace unsafe, inadequate dwellings with permanent structures.

In 1947 the housing administration of the Federal government was reorganized. The temporary National Housing Agency of 1942 was replaced by the permanent Housing and Home Finance Agency, made up of the Federal Housing Administration, the Public Housing Administration, the Home Loan Bank Board, and the National Housing Council. The Public Housing Administration now replaced the United States Housing Authority of the 1937 Act.

The emergency housing program was launched at the beginning of 1946. The goal was set at 2,700,000 houses to be built in two years— 1,200,000 the first year and the rest the second year. To reach the goal, Wyatt advocated: (1) further restrictions on private building to channel scarce material into veterans' houses to sell for $6,000 or less and to rent for $50 or less a month; (2) a system of subsidies to certain producers to increase production of needed materials; (3) market guarantees to encourage manufacturing of prefabricated or factory-built houses; (4) restoration of Federal wartime authority to provide liberal financing as a means of encouraging private construction; and (5) a continuation of price ceilings.

In May, 1946, Congress passed the Veterans Emergency Housing Act to implement the Wyatt program. There was doubt from the start that the goals set could be achieved. The boom year in housing, 1925, had produced only 935,000 units, and at that time there had been no problems of reconversion or scarce materials. The pessimism seemed justified. Less than 750,000 homes were built during the first year of the Wyatt program. Discouraged by the lack of cooperation, Wyatt resigned at the end of the year. His successor, Frank R. Creedon, tried to carry on the program as originally outlined. During 1947, however, only 850,000 units were completed. In that same year, there were 900,000 marriages.

Obstacles to the emergency program. Several major obstacles prevented the emergency program from reaching its goals. Of these, the increase in construction costs was the most important. By August, 1946, costs of residential construction had risen 37 per cent since 1945; cost of living had risen 27 per cent; but earnings had risen only 14 per cent. Those veterans who could have paid $50 a month rent in 1945 were no longer able to pay the higher rentals. By the fall of 1945, the $6,000 house promised by Wyatt could not be built for less than $7,500. In 1947, the same house cost $11,500. The postwar house was thus beyond the reach of the majority of veterans, as well as of most others in direct need of housing.

The rise in building costs was also due to increased costs of materials. The price ceiling on building materials was lifted in November, 1946, and many basic materials reached exorbitant levels before the ceilings were replaced three months later. For example, 1,000 common bricks, costing $13 in 1939, sold for $25.50 in 1947. Hardwood flooring, which cost $118 per 1,000 board feet in 1939, now cost $250. Lumber and mill-work had risen by more than 100 per cent by 1947. Wall plaster, which cost $12 a ton in 1939, cost $19 a ton in 1947.

Part of the high price of materials was due to the trade-restraint practices of both manufacturers and labor unions. These practices have been of long duration in the housebuilding industry. Manufacturers attempt by combination to maintain high prices and to restrict competition. For instance, the manufacturers who provide 80 per cent of the plumbing supplies sell only to jobbers. The jobbers, in turn, agree to resell only to plumbing contractors; they refuse to deal with builder or buyer. The net result of this combination is to keep prices high, restrict the possibility of introducing new techniques, and retard the distribution of materials. Sometimes, manufacturers and contractors agree not to compete with each other. They set identical prices so that the buyer has no chance of getting a lower bid.

Unions have been forced to engage in various restrictive practices in order to contend with the general insecurity of the housebuilding industry. To lengthen the time spent on the job, the width of a paintbrush is limited and the use of a spray gun is prohibited. The use of power tools on certain jobs is also regulated. Skilled workers are used for tasks which might be performed by unskilled labor. Certain work is required to be done on the building site, as, for example, the making of wooden molds into which concrete is poured. Jurisdictional disputes have developed between different craft unions and have slowed down the work. Such disputes as whether carpenters or metal workers should install metal doorknobs on wooden doors, or who should place the brick work on a tile-faced fireplace in a frame dwelling, have been knotty problems.

Wages rose to new levels. This rise was due, in large measure, to the restrictive practices and the shortage of workers in the housebuilding trades. The prevailing rate for construction workers in 1940 was $1.00 an hour. In 1947, the wage rate was $2.50 an hour, or $100 for a 40-hour week. In 1947, bricklayers received $2.75 an hour and restricted their members to the laying of 400 bricks a day instead of the 800 of a decade before.

Uncertainty in delivery was a factor in the failure of the housing program. A builder might be forced to suspend operations for a period of time until he could secure a needed item. The average time required to build a small home in 1947 was nine or ten months. Before the war, three or four months was sufficient.

Another factor hampered the progress of building. Materials were still scarce. Despite the subsidy payments authorized by the Emergency Housing Act, shortages continued. Nails, millwork, plaster base, brick, concrete block, pipe for sewer connection, and bathroom fixtures were often unobtainable. This shortage was due, in the main, to the competition of other industries needing steel and lumber to reconvert to peacetime industry.

Still another reason for the failure of the housing program may be traced to the hesitation of buyers and builders to invest in expensive houses for fear of a sudden deflation. Builders feared to erect houses for rental. Buyers—even those who could afford to buy—objected to investing $12,000 in a former $6,000 house when they had no assurance that prices would not collapse rapidly.

Prefabricated houses, suggested by Wyatt as a way out of the housing shortage, did not materialize in large numbers. Building codes were partly responsible for this failure. For example, some codes require a certain thickness of walls for dwellings; specify the kind of materials which can be used; and prevent the use of new materials. Some codes require a corner post of a certain width or certain widths of studs to be used in ceilings. Some states like California and Florida have been prevented from using the prefabricated house because of peculiar local conditions. The California and Florida building codes provide for special bracing in the event of earthquakes and hurricanes. Certain northern cities have building codes governing the kind of roofing necessary to resist heavy snows in winter.

POSTWAR HOUSING ACTS

President Truman's vain efforts to secure an adequate housing law. In his message to Congress on February 25, 1948, President Truman urged Congress to pass a housing program which would set a goal of one million houses a year for the next ten years. He said that overcrowding had increased by 50 per cent since 1940, and that 2½ million married couples still lived with other families. He reminded Congress that less than one million homes had been completed in 1947, and that less than 15 per cent of them were for rent. The sale price of homes built was too high for those who needed housing most acutely. He referred to the overcrowded conditions of long standing and to the failure of private industry to meet the needs, and he recommended a number of measures to end the shortage. Most of the President's proposals were included in the Taft-Ellender-Wagner Bill, passed by the Senate but stalled in the House.

Specifically, President Truman urged improvement in the distribution of materials and revision of local building codes to permit a wider use of prefabricated houses. He urged that steps be taken to ease the immediate situation of doubling up and overcrowding that had shown no improvement in over two years since the end of the war. He exhorted Congress to pass a law which would provide government aid for low-rent public housing project, and encourage private investment to erect rental housing. Congress took no action on the President's message and adjourned without passing any housing bill.

Inadequacy of the 1948 housing law. In the Special Session of Congress called by the President in July, 1948, a modified Housing Act was passed, a substitute and much weaker bill than the Taft-Ellender-Wagner Bill. This action was taken by Congress despite the fact that at the Nominating Conventions in June both party platforms had pledged the speedy passage of legislation designed to relieve the housing shortage.

The 1948 Housing Act failed to make any provision for urban public housing, urban redevelopment, or rural housing aid. For the most part it only extended and liberalized existing Federal mortgage insurance policies. It made it easier to finance homes by guaranteeing loans made through the FHA to builders of apartment units and to contractors erecting 25 or more homes costing $6,000 or less. Government loans were permitted on veteran and non-veteran cooperative housing projects. The President reluctantly signed the bill, realizing that it was better than no legislation. In a prepared statement, he declared that the Housing Act fell far short of the goal and that "Congress in enacting this bill has deliberately neglected those large groups of our people most in need of adequate houses—the people who are forced to live in disgraceful rural and urban slums."

The attitude of many Congressmen and real estate promoters toward any long-range housing bill which might be proposed is illustrated by a statement made by Senator Willis Robertson, of Virginia, explaining his negative vote on the proposed housing bill. Senator Robertson said that he was unwilling to be committed to a housing program which, "if carried to its ultimate conclusion would result in driving private enterprise out of the field of housing." The Senator maintained that in 1948, "we had the largest privately financed home-construction program in our history, totalling about 1 million units and all financed within the framework of a system of private enterprise." Robertson also referred to the constant drain on the Federal treasury for a period of 40 years if the subsidy grant provisions were included, "even if during that period, the Government is not forced to finance more than one-seventeenth of the estimated need for so called low cost houses." [29]

Gains in the 1949 housing law. The 81st Congress passed a Housing Act in July, 1949, which contained some of the ideas embodied in the Taft-Ellender-Wagner Bill introduced four years previously. It was far

---

[29] Statement in Richmond *Times-Dispatch*, February 24, 1949.

from adequate, and in operation would do little more than meet the yearly demands for additional housing required for newly-formed families.

The 1949 Act authorized financial assistance—loans and a capital subsidy—for the construction and operation of 810,000 low-rent dwellings to be built over a six-year period. These would just about keep pace with the growth of slums; in other words, over 800,000 now suitable housing units would deteriorate into slum districts in six years. Slum clearance was encouraged through providing that up to one billion dollars in Federal funds would be provided to pay two-thirds of the difference between the actual cost of acquiring slum and blighted land and its eventual re-use value.

The basic loan formula established by the 1937 Housing Act remained the same. Local housing authorities plan and build low-rent housing projects which they finance with the assistance of loans from the Federal government. Since the rental revenue from the projects will not be enough to cover the cost of building and operating the housing, the cash deficit is to be made up by a subsidy. This Federal payment, known as the *annual contribution,* is limited to a maximum of 4.5 per cent of the development cost. The local government contributes to the low rent of the projects by exempting the projects from all taxes. The Act raised available loan funds to 1.5 billion dollars, and as much as 308 million dollars annually for 40 years was authorized to subsidize the program.

Included in the Act was a program of Federal assistance for new housing on productive farms to be administered by the Farmers' Home Administration. Special concessions were made to large families. Preference as tenants was given to veterans of the two world wars. It was hoped that this provision in the Act would stem the criticism of veterans' organizations for the failure to provide adequate housing for veterans.

The 1950 amendments. Amendments were made to the housing legislation by an Act passed in April, 1950. The original bill, as backed by the Administration, had sought to provide more aid for low-cost housing, especially through creating housing cooperatives backed by government guaranties. This vital item in the bill was defeated in Congress. As passed, the 1950 Act mainly benefited middle-income groups. The powers of the FHA were broadened and loan policies somewhat liberalized. Veterans' cooperatives and nonprofit housing organizations were permitted to receive FHA insurance up to 95 per cent of the replacement cost of their projects. Discrimination against families with children was discouraged.

The 1950 Housing Act also provided for the disposition of all temporary and permanent war and veteran housing projects. Some 544,000 units had been disposed of prior to the passage of the 1950 Act, but over 360,000 units remained. Increased benefits were provided for veterans' housing. The maximum government guarantee was raised from $4,000 to $7,500 per veteran and provisions were made for direct loans to good credit-risk veterans. This made possible the gigantic Lakewood Park development for veterans in Los Angeles. Another addition to housing policy was the provision for loans to educational institutions to finance the building of dormitories and family housing for students needing such accommodation.

LEVITTOWN AND LAKEWOOD PARK: RECENT MASS-PRODUCTION METHODS IN PRIVATE HOUSING ENTERPRISE

The Levittown development. Although a venture by private industry, housing projects such as Levittown, Long Island, have been encouraged and aided by the Federal government. The Federal Housing Administration, now insuring loans up to 95 per cent of the value of a house, made it relatively easy for a builder to borrow money to build low-cost houses.

COURTESY *American Legion Monthly.*

Homes at Lakewood Park, Los Angeles, California.

Purchase terms on low-cost houses with a government-guaranteed mortgage made it easier for prospective home owners in the low- and middle-income groups to buy.

Levittown, near Hicksville, Long Island, is a community of 17,546 houses built by Levitt and Sons, Inc. About 50,000 persons live in Levittown. Mass produced, the houses are all alike and sell for $9,000. Each house has four rooms and bath, and includes an attic which can be converted into two more bedrooms and bath. The houses have radiant heating, the kitchens come equipped with refrigerator, stove, and Bendix washer, and in the living rooms is a built-in television set. Few of the residents of Levittown are over 35 years of age. There are numerous children.

Levittown is unincorporated. It has no mayor or officials, no movies, and no nightclubs. Levitt and Sons, the builders, have made numerous rules. The grass must be cut every week; washing cannot be hung on ordinary clotheslines but only on removable drying-racks that must be taken in on weekends and holidays. In spite of these arbitrary regulations, there are many advantages. There are parks and playgrounds for the children, baseball diamonds, handball courts, swimming pools, and convenient shopping centers. All families in Levittown have about the same income—around $3,800 a year.

Lakewood Park project in Los Angeles. Even more impressive than Levittown is the project at Lakewood Park in Los Angeles constructed by the Aetna Construction Company and Biltmore Houses Inc., under the authority of the Veterans Administration and financed by loans by the Federal government and the Prudential Insurance Company. The project covers 3,500 acres or ten square miles. It was started in February, 1950, and was planned to be completed in two years. Nearly 7,000 dwellings were finished in the first year. The program calls for 17,150 houses to provide homes for about 70,000 persons. The houses are two- and three-bedroom stucco structures. The former will sell for $9,100 to $9,250 and the latter for $10,150 to $10,300. The prices are set by the Veterans Administration. Veterans can buy without any down payment by virtue of joint guaranties and loans by the government and the Prudential. Monthly payments are about $44. The development will have its own schools, playgrounds, churches, hospital, theatres, shopping center, and offstreet parking centers to accommodate 10,000 automobiles. It is the most impressive example to date of mass-production low-cost urban housing. Another California project is the plan of Paul Trousdale and Joe Louis to build 4,000 homes for Negroes in Richmond.

Defects of Levittown and Lakewood projects. There has been much praise and many criticisms of Levittown and similar projects. The most frequent critical comment concerns the monotony of style, the lack of space between dwellings, and the fear that the slum pattern of the future is now being formed by mass-production methods. In some of these projects the walls and floors have a tendency to sag a bit after a time, and the plumbing is far from good. There are numerous unsolved problems in projects of this type. Transportation is inadequate and, even now, Levittown needs more schools, hospitals, and sewage facilities.

The one obvious advantage of the mass-produced housing projects is that they demonstrate that, if private industry is interested in supplying low-cost housing, it is able to do so. If armament and war do not bring about a complete alteration of our way of living, there will be more projects like Levittown. Indeed, defense needs have led to plans for one in Bucks County, Pa. They will not solve the housing problem, but may serve as examples to other builders in the housing industry.[30]

---

[30] See "Up from the Potato Fields," *Time* 56:67-72 (July 3, 1950) for a fuller discussion of Levittown. For the Lakewood project, see Hannibal Coons, "The Way They Put Them Up," *American Legion Monthly*, January, 1951, pp. 20 ff.

THE PROSPECTS FOR THE FUTURE IN HOUSING URBAN AMERICA

Korean War slows down public housing projects. By the summer of 1950, the tense international situation caused President Truman to announce that the number of public housing units which could be put under construction during the second half of 1950 would be cut to 30,000. This limitation to 30,000 units represents an estimated cut of 25 per cent from the anticipated number. As of August, 1950, only 81 projects with a total of 27,644 units had been given final contracts, and over 200 projects (representing almost 100,000 units) were awaiting final approval. President Truman also announced that the disposition of all war and emergency housing units was to be halted, pending international developments and the possible needs of new housing for defense workers.

In addition to the curtailment of the public housing program, tightened credit restrictions made it virtually impossible for those in the middle-income bracket to buy homes. Only homes costing over $25,000 remained free from the drastic restrictions.

Revival of defense housing, 1951. The launching of emergency mobilization and a vast armament program at the end of 1950 and early in 1951 made it necessary to give attention to a new defense housing program. By the summer of 1951 there were serious housing shortages around the plants that were expanding their production of war materials. President Truman asked Congress to appropriate money to promote a defense housing program. A bill was introduced and passed the Senate. This provided for extensive Federal aid to private building interests in such a program, but sharply restricted any government construction of defense housing and limited it to such areas and projects as would not normally appeal to private construction companies. Late in 1951, Levitt and Sons contracted to build a 16,000-home defense project in Bucks County, Pennsylvania.

Our urban housing problem remains unsolved. The housing problem is still unsolved. Though during the four years from 1946 through 1949 an average of about 870,000 dwellings were started each year, this only scratched the surface and did not meet the new annual needs. Some 83 per cent of these new dwellings were single-family homes that sold for the highest prices in American experience. The overcrowded slum continues to breed disease and juvenile delinquency. The curtailing of the grossly inadequate public low-cost housing program and the price restrictions on the middle-income group in buying privately-constructed homes leaves the majority of families in America facing the same situation that has been prevalent during the first half of the twentieth century. There is no adequate housing available at a price they can afford to pay.

We mentioned above that conversion to a war economy not only curtails the Federal housing program, but drastically restricts the activities of private builders. If the international situation had not necessitated the building curbs, builders like Levitt and Sons, Inc., probably would have continued to build more housing projects with private funds. Due to defense restrictions, Levitt and Sons had to abandon their plan for an ideal housing community at Landia on Long Island, which was to have houses selling for $13,000.

NATURE AND EXTENT OF THE RURAL HOUSING PROBLEM

Acute deficiency of rural housing in the United States. Bad housing is usually thought of as restricted to urban areas. The average American likes to think of neat, well-painted farmhouses set in picturesque surroundings as characteristic of rural life. In reality, rural housing is far below the level of urban housing. In the rural areas, housing deficiencies take the form of single structures widely scattered and therefore not as noticeable as the crowded tenement districts of the city.

The Farm Housing Survey of 1934, covering about 8 per cent of farm homes in all states except Pennsylvania and New York, indicated the condition of rural housing at the outset of the New Deal. Almost 70 per cent of the homes were without running water; 88 per cent lacked bathtubs; and more than 90 per cent had no indoor toilets. Writing in 1947, Abrams and Dean maintained that "the poorest housing conditions in the United States are found among farmers."

The Farm Housing Survey of 1938 showed that one-fourth of all rural homes were in bad structural condition—that is, they had leaky roofs, unsafe floors, or bad foundations. The buildings were frequently of the poorest construction, unpainted and unsightly. Crowded conditions are not limited to cities. In his book on *Rural Sociology,* Lowry Nelson calls attention to the fact that the largest farm families have the poorest dwellings. Three times as large a proportion of farm homes have over 1.5 persons per room as urban homes. Large families of tenants or farm laborers live in one- and two-room shacks. A survey of rural housing conditions in Virginia in 1940 revealed that one family out of six had more than 1.5 persons per room (the minimum standard for housing). In one community, 12 persons were found living in a one-room shanty. The furnishings consisted of a table, a rusty stove, and pallets on which the family slept. In another community, 17 persons were found in two rooms. Six persons slept in two beds; 11 others had only straw mattresses. In still another community, a family of six lived in a one-room sheepshed with a dirt floor. In this same area, a family of three lived in one corner of a barn.[31]

It was estimated that, in 1940, the homes of over two million of the 7,642,000 farm-operator families in the United States were in such bad condition that they were nonrepairable.[32] Only one-fourth had running water; less than one-sixth had inside toilets. In 1945, former Secretary of Agriculture, Claude Wickard, testifying at a hearing of a Senate Sub-Committee on Housing, said that two-thirds of the farm families in the United States were inadequately housed and one-half of the farm homes unfit for use.

[31] *Farm Housing in Virginia.* Charlottesville: University of Virginia, Extension Division, 1942.

[32] D. B. Lasseter, "Rural Housing Is Business of Farmers' Home Administration," *Journal of Housing,* December, 1948.

Rural housing in the South. Although every rural section of the United States had bad housing, the South, with 60 per cent of its population living on farms, had the worst conditions. At least half of the farm homes needed major repairs to make them even habitable. Overcrowding on Southern farms was twice as great as on farms in the rest of the nation. One in every six families lived under overcrowded conditions. In Mississippi, Arkansas, Alabama, and Georgia, extreme overcrowding was found in one out of four farm homes. In 1940, nine out of 10 Southern farmers depended on springs or open wells for their water supply. We have no way of knowing how many of these sources of water were contaminated, but studies made in Georgia, Virginia, and Kentucky by the Department of Agriculture revealed that 94 per cent of the wells investigated were either improperly covered or entirely uncovered. The North Carolina Department of Health discovered a high degree of pollution of the rural water supply. In one area, 96 per cent of the water tested contained harmful bacteria. About 80 per cent of the Southern farms had outside privies, and approximately 15 per cent had none at all.[33] Among the few areas of the South in which there are a number of acceptable farm homes are the Kentucky Bluegrass region and the Shenandoah Valley of Virginia.

It hardly needs to be pointed out that rural housing conditions for Negroes in the South are even more lamentably backward and inadequate than those which prevail among white farmers and sharecroppers.

RELATION OF RURAL INCOME TO HOUSING

Low incomes restrict rural housing. The rural housing problem is in one important respect similar to that of urban housing. Inadequate income to afford a better place to live is the cause of poor housing in both the urban and the rural community. In 1935-36, the National Resources Committee made a study of consumer income and reported that 50 per cent of the farmers received less than $1,000 a year; more than one-third had incomes under $750. These figures, low as they are, are probably higher than the actuality. The valuation placed on food grown in the garden, fuel furnished, and value of the house were included in the farm income figures. Even during the war years, when prices for farm produce were at a high level, income was inadequate. The 1945 Census of Agriculture revealed that one-half of the farmers of the nation had a gross income of less than $1,500 a year.[34]

Special difficulties in financing rural housing. Although rural and urban housing are both poor because of inadequate income, the rural housing problem offers special difficulties. This applies particularly to any form of home financing for the owner, cash renter, sharecropper, or farm laborer. The kind of housing available depends on the productivity of the land, the form of tenancy, and the conditions affecting prices. Lowry Nelson gives us relevant information on this point. In 1940, the value of the homes of farm owners averaged $1,421; of farm tenants $704;

---

[33] "Housing in the South," *New South*, Vol. 3, April, 1948.
[34] D. B. Lasseter, *Journal of Housing*, December, 1947.

and of sharecroppers $283. A report issued by the Interbureau Committee on Post-war Planning in 1945 stated that, in general, the quality of farm housing corresponds to the capacity of the farm to support the housing.[35] The rural dwelling cannot be considered apart from the potential productivity of the farm. In 1940, some 1,600,000 farm dwellings were occupied by families whose income would not permit them to own or operate a decent habitation.

The rural nonfarm dweller presents an even more difficult problem. He is neither urban nor rural. He may supplement his income from a garden or a small plot of ground, but since he is not a farmer, he is not eligible for the public aid available to the farmer. The rural nonfarm dweller is too far away from the city to be included under a slum-clearance program. So far, no practical solution to his difficulties has been found, although an overall housing program must include aid to the rural nonfarm dweller.

ATTEMPTS TO SOLVE THE RURAL HOUSING PROBLEM

Early efforts to aid rural housing. The first approach to the problem of aid to the farmer was through the extension of credit. Beginning in 1917, a system of Federal Land Banks was set up to provide farmers with long-term mortgages at a low interest rate. The plight of the farmer grew more desperate as the rural depression after 1920 reduced the value of farm products, and, accordingly, the operation of the Land Banks was extended. The Banks were placed under the supervision of the Farm Credit Administration in 1933, and from that time until the beginning of the Second World War, mortgages and long-term loans were made to farmers to make improvements on their property.

New Deal aid to rural housing. But credit did not help the low-income families or those who lived in small towns and mining communities and who faced destitution as their jobs vanished during the depression. One of the earliest programs during the New Deal was that carried on by the Subsistence Homesteads Division of the Department of Interior.

Three types of families were to be served by this emergency program: (1) workers living in small towns who were unemployed as the result of the closing down of the industries; (2) farm laborers and tenants stranded on land too poor to furnish a living; and (3) the industrial workers whose income was reduced by frequent layoffs. These stranded families were moved, wherever possible, to new locations, preferably in communities rather than in individual homesteads. When it was feasible, the industrial worker was located near possible employment. Each home built conformed to minimum housing standards on a plot of ground from one-half to five acres in size. Each family was expected to grow part of its food and to sell the surplus, if possible. Homesteads for stranded miners were established at Readsville, W. Va., Westmoreland, Pa., and Cumberland, Tenn. About 3,200 families were resettled on 33 homesteads in 17 states.[36]

[35] *Report,* Interbureau Committee on Post-war Planning. Washington: Department of Agriculture, January 17, 1945.

[36] Gray, *op. cit.,* p. 236.

In 1935, the Rural Resettlement Administration took over the Subsistence Homesteads. It continued the program begun by the Subsistence Homesteads Division but placed emphasis on the development of entire communities. Rural-agricultural and rural-industrial communities were to be developed. However, only three rural-industrial communities were actually developed. These communities were called the "greenbelt" towns because they were surrounded by a protective strip of meadow to prevent encroachment by other communities. Multiple dwellings, duplexes, and single houses were built on large tracts of land within the area. Automobile traffic was diverted to the outer rim, and a system of underpass walks made it possible for children to go to parks and playgrounds safely. The "greenbelt" communities were so expensive that no scale of rents could be operated that would meet the costs. White-collar workers, not slum-dwellers, became residents. During the Second World War a 1,000-family unit was built for a lower-income group.[37]

In 1937, the Bankhead-Jones Farm Tenant Act was passed to help tenants buy farms, and the Farm Security Administration, authorized by the Act, was created by executive order. The FSA took over the work of the Rural Resettlement Administration. The program of the Farm Security Administration is not a subsidy program; loans are to be repaid by the families who are helped to buy homes or to improve their surroundings. Between 1937 and 1946, over 16,000 families obtained loans to purchase farms, and about 800,000 farmers borrowed funds to buy equipment and make improvements.[38]

The Farmers Home Administration Act of 1946. In 1946, the Farmers Home Administration Act was passed. This Act broadened the scope of the Bankhead-Jones Act. Farmers would now be permitted to borrow money directly from the government to build, improve, or enlarge their homes. Interest of $3\frac{1}{2}$ per cent was to be charged, and the loan was repayable within 33 years. If unable to finance any part of the building costs, the farmer would be permitted to borrow the entire sum needed. Each loan was to be passed upon by a local committee made up of at least two farmers. Borrowers were required to meet certain minimum qualifications. As planned, the program would not be in effective operation before the end of 1949. There were 55,000 applications for loans within 10 months after the law was passed. It was estimated that the actual appropriation of 15 million dollars would permit aid to only 3,500 farmers, although the Act provides that 50 million dollars can be made available. Even this would not scratch the surface in providing the needed rural housing.[39]

By the end of 1951, most of the 50 million dollars provided for in the Act had been loaned or allocated. As of June 30, 1951, a total of 8,954 loans had been made, amounting to $41,325,320. In addition, 474 loans, involving $218,154 had been approved. The improvements carried out or

---

[37] Gray, *ibid.*, p. 237.
[38] *Ibid.*, p. 238.
[39] *Journal of Housing*, December, 1947.

planned as a result of these loans were: new dwellings, 4,663; repairs to dwellings, 3,647; water systems, 3,415; new farm service buildings, 4,932; repairs to farm service buildings, 2,318; land development, 311; and land purchase, 78. It will be noted that farm service buildings received about as much attention as new or repaired homes.

THE PUBLIC HOUSING PROGRAM IN RURAL AREAS

The USHA enters rural housing. According to the United States Housing Act of 1937, the Federal government was to help the states and local subdivisions improve unsafe and unsanitary housing in urban and rural communities. However, the USHA was, for the most part, planned to serve the urban community. It was designed for large-scale projects rather than for single dwellings. The USHA could take no steps toward initiating a rural program until local housing authorities were set up in the rural areas. In 1939, the USHA, in cooperation with the Farm Security Administration, began to plan for work in rural housing. No program could be launched without local housing authorities to own, build, and operate the projects. By 1940, 65 county authorities had been established in states which had passed laws creating county and regional housing authorities.

In 1940, an experimental program was begun in five areas—Indiana, Mississippi, Arkansas, Georgia, and South Carolina.[40] The program proceeded cautiously. Any farmer, who was unable to provide decent housing for himself, his tenant, or wage hand, applied to the local authority. If, in the opinion of the local housing authority and of a representative of the FSA, he was living on a farm potentially capable of supporting him and his family, and if he met certain general qualifications, his application was approved. The farmer then deeded an acre of ground to the local authority, which built a home with Federal aid, based on the USHA formula of a 90 per cent loan. The home was then leased to the farmer on a year-to-year basis. Within 60 years, the loan from the government was to be repaid, after which the title to the house would remain with the local authority. The occupant of the house had a right to purchase the house at any time, if he were able to pay a price sufficient to enable the local authority to pay off its obligation to the government.

Slight achievements of the USHA-FSA program. The houses built under this rural program of the USHA-FSA were designed to meet minimum requirements of decent housing, but they were in accordance with local needs. Sturdy durable homes with storerooms, sanitary outside privies, and covered wells tested for purity of water supply were built at an approximate cost of $1,300-1,800. The result was a home, planned as a part of the farm, rather than as a unit separated from the potential source of income. By April, 1942, only 286 units had been finished. More-

---

[40] R. Vance and G. Blackwell, *New Farm Homes for Old*. Chapel Hill: University of North Carolina Press, 1946, pp. 32 ff.

over, war shortages of labor and materials curtailed the program, and by the end of the war only 515 units were ready for occupancy. At the present time, the states of Alabama, Arkansas, Florida, Georgia, Louisiana, Mississippi, North Carolina, and South Carolina have counties in which some dwellings are completed. Most of the families now occupying these homes hope to buy them. It is expected that this desire for home ownership, which is part of the rural tradition, will continue, and that most of the homes built under this program will eventually be owned by the families aided by the public housing program.

Rural housing problem remains unsolved. In general, the deplorable rural housing situation remains virtually unchanged. All the rural housing built since 1933 has not even begun to scratch the surface of the problem. And what has been constructed has not been provided for those who need it most—the marginal farmers who live in run-down houses, shacks, and hovels. About all that has been accomplished is to make some sectors of the American public more conscious of the desperate need of the farming population for better housing. Continued delay in establishing a full-scale rural housing program will bring greater deterioration and an even more distressing situation. Until Congress passes a satisfactory housing bill to provide a long-range housing program for both urban and rural communities, there appears to be little hope of improving the housing conditions of our rural areas.

SUMMARY

The task of providing decent housing for the populations of all civilized industrial countries constitutes one of the most acute and important problems of our era. In the United States, housing is the only field in which our vastly efficient and productive technology has never been permitted to meet our social needs. Half of our population, both urban and rural, live in substandard homes, but our technology would be able to rehouse our people in a few years if its potentialities were not restrained by political, economic, and social forces. Housing is the area of expenditure from which the average American gets the least for his money. The American public can never be happy, healthy, or law-abiding until its minimum housing needs have been provided for.

European countries endeavored to meet the problem of public aid to housing far earlier than the United States, and some of them have made much more progress in housing than has this country. Inadequate housing in many European countries is due more to historical, financial, and technological limitations than to the political and social policies that retard housing development in the United States. Soviet Russia and Britain (particularly under the recent Labor Government) have advanced the farthest in public housing. American slums still constitute a national scandal in the light of our vast technological and financial resources. Even today, our slums are growing more rapidly than we can provide public housing units for the lower-income groups.

Various surveys have been made of housing needs in the United States since the beginning of the New Deal. Even at the close of the Second World War, about half of the urban population were living in substandard housing, and nearly a third in dwellings not really fit for habitation without major repairs. The rural housing situation was just as bad, if not worse. Two-thirds of all farm dwellings were substandard, and at least half of them were unfit for human habitation.

To rehouse our population adequately would require at least 17 million new housing units. A major reason for this alarming shortage is that private enterprise will not construct units for low-income groups, and Congress will not support legislation which might provide adequate Federal funds to house the low-income groups in the population.

Much of the private urban housing construction has been carried on under the limited-dividend program by insurance companies, estates, and foundations. The Metropolitan Life Insurance Company has been a leader in this trend and has constructed such impressive housing developments as Parkchester in the Bronx and Stuyvesant Town and Peter Cooper Village in Manhattan. These are impressive projects physically, but they have failed to provide for adequate community life and facilities. The New York Life Insurance project at Fresh Meadows, in Queens, has remedied this defect. But this type of construction—and private building in general—has failed to provide housing for the low-income groups. This requires public subsidizing of housing construction.

Public housing activity in the United States began with the limited activity of the U. S. Housing Corporation of the First World War. But it died out after the war. The acute housing shortage after the depression of 1929 led to New Deal housing activities, conducted by the Public Works Administration and the U. S. Housing Authority. Notable construction resulted, but most of it was for middle- and upper-income families, and the total was no more than a drop in the bucket compared with the housing needs of the country. But the experiment did prove that publicly-subsidized housing operations could be successful with adequate financial support.

During the Second World War there was a great deal of housing construction, but the product was generally crude and temporary. Such construction was no contribution to the solution of our housing shortage, which became unprecedentedly acute after the war.

The Taft-Ellender-Wagner (TEW) Bill, first introduced in 1945, was created to deal with this acute situation, but Congress persistently refused to pass it, chiefly because of the pressure of private building and real estate interests. The housing act finally passed in 1949 was extremely inadequate. It provided for the construction of only 816,000 units over a period of six years. At that rate, construction would hardly keep pace with new slum growth. The Federal Emergency Housing Program, begun in 1946, proved a failure because of many political, financial, and technological obstacles.

Private housing construction enjoyed a boom from 1948 to 1951, but the units built were mainly for high- and medium-income groups. Even this is being drastically curtailed as the country devotes more and more of its energies and resources to armament and war preparations.

Little has been done to relieve the dismal picture of rural housing. Since most of the farmers who acutely need new homes are of the low-income group, only publicly-subsidized housing can provide for their needs. But this has not been forthcoming. Federal agencies to assist rural housing through loans have not met the need, and publicly-supported rural housing construction has thus far been no more than an experimental sampling of the situation. The rural housing situation seems to be getting worse annually, and the deterioration will probably be more rapid with the diversion of Federal activities and interest to armament and war.

In conclusion, one may say that the housing situation in the United States is not much better, considering the shortage and needs, than it was in the 1920's. Unless peace and disarmament can be assured, there is every likelihood that our housing situation will become worse rather than better as we move into the second half of the century. In that event, those social problems immediately associated with housing are much more likely to be aggravated than remedied.

SELECTED REFERENCES

*Abrams, Charles, *The Future of Housing.* New York: Harper, 1947. Probably the most satisfactory book dealing with the housing problem in the United States.

Arnovici, Carol, *Housing the Masses.* New York: Wiley, 1939. Good sociological study of the housing situation, with special emphasis on the needs of the low-income groups.

Bauer, Catherine. *Modern Housing.* Boston: Houghton Mifflin, 1934. Authoritative study of the trends, methods and problems of housing in pre-New Deal days.

*Danenberg, E. F., *Get Your Own Home the Cooperative Way.* New York: Greenberg, 1949. Able discussion of the possibilities and advantages of cooperative housing.

Davies, J. E., *Fundamentals of Housing Study.* New York: Columbia University Press, 1939. Scholarly book on educational aspects of the housing problem.

*Denby, Elizabeth, *Europe Rehoused.* New York: Norton, 1938. Interesting and reliable book on European housing ideals and practices down to the eve of the Second World War.

Fisher, E. M., and Ratcliff, R. U., *European Housing Policy and Practice.* Washington: Federal Housing Administration, 1936. Official study and report on European housing developments.

Fitch, J. M., *American Building: the Forces that Shape It.* Boston: Houghton Mifflin, 1948. Analysis of the social, economic, and architectural factors affecting American housing.

Ford, James, *et al., Slums and Housing,* 2 Vols. Cambridge: Harvard University Press, 1936. Monumental work, giving special attention to the problems of slums and slum clearance in New York City.

Goldfeld, Abraham, *et al., Public Housing Management.* New York: New York University Press, 1938. Important symposium on various aspects of the housing problem and housing developments in Europe and America.

*Gray, G. H., *Housing and Citizenship*. New York: Reinhold, 1946. Stimulating book on the public and social aspects of housing.

Hardy, C. O., and Kuczynski, R. R., *The Housing Program of the City of Vienna*. Washington: Brookings Institution, 1934. Authoritative account of the remarkable achievements of postwar Vienna in constructing low-rent apartments for workers.

Hazard, J. N., *Soviet Housing Law*. New Haven: Yale University Press, 1939. Scholarly and detailed study of the legal basis for the most complete system of public housing development.

*Lewis, H. M., *City Planning*. New York: Longmans, Green, 1939. Excellent book on the relation of the general principles of city planning to housing programs.

Merton, R. K., *et al.* (Eds.), *Social Policy and Social Research in Housing*. New York: Association Press, 1951. Valuable symposium which compiles most of the available data on the theory and achievements of housing.

Perry, C. A., *Housing for the Machine Age*. New York: Russell Sage Foundation, 1939. Competent survey and analysis of American housing needs and programs.

*Post, L. W., *The Challenge of Housing*. New York: Farrar and Rinehart, 1938. The best book on the American housing problem in New Deal days.

*Reed, W. V., and Ogg, Elizabeth, *New Homes for Old*. New York: Headline Books, Foreign Policy Association, 1940. Admirable brief introduction to housing needs and developments in Europe and the United States on the eve of the Second World War. Splendid illustrations.

Rosahn, B. G., and Goldfeld, Abraham, *Housing Management*. New York: Covici, Friede, 1937. Authoritative exposition of the principles and practices of contemporary housing management.

*Schnapper, M. B. (Ed.), *Public Housing in America*. New York: Wilson, 1939. A valuable collection of readings on city housing problems, with special stress on New Deal achievements. Contains extensive bibliography.

Simon, E. D., *The Anti-Slum Campaign*. New York: Longmans, Green, 1933. Good summary of English slum clearance and housing developments.

Stapp, Peyton, *Urban Housing*. Washington: Works Progress Administration, 1938. Official survey of urban housing conditions in New Deal times.

Straus, M., and Wegg, Talbot, *Housing Comes of Age*. New York: Oxford University Press, 1938. Good general study of the housing problem and developments.

*Strauss, Nathan, *Seven Myths of Housing*. New York: Knopf, 1944. Able defense of public housing projects.

*Twentieth Century Fund, *American Housing: Problems and Prospects*. New York: Twentieth Century Fund, 1944. One of the most complete books on the American housing problem, but primarily urban housing.

Walker, N. L., *et al.*, *Urban Blight and Slums*. Cambridge: Harvard University Press, 1938. Authoritative cooperative book on the slum problem.

Wood, E. E., *The Housing of the Unskilled Wage Earner*. New York: Macmillan, 1919.

———, *Housing Progress in Western Europe*. New York: Dutton, 1923.

———, *Recent Trends in American Housing*. New York: Macmillan, 1931.

———, *Introduction to Housing*. Washington: Government Printing Office, 1940. Able and informing books by the foremost American writer on housing problems, here and abroad.

Wright, Henry, *Rehousing Urban America*. New York: Columbia University Press, 1935. Clear and authoritative introduction to American housing problems under the New Deal regime.

CHAPTER 12

Community Organization as a Substitute for the Declining Influence of Rural Primary Groups

THE NEED FOR COMMUNITY ORGANIZATION

How primary groups shaped human personality in the past. In the first chapter of this book we mentioned the influence of primary groups on the human personality. In the chapter on rural life we described in some detail how these primary and personal groups dominated rural society and left their potent impression on the personality and character of country dwellers. It has been the breakdown of these primary groups as the result of industrialization and urbanization that has, more than anything else, given rise to the need for community organization. Hence, at this point we should once more emphasize the significance of primary groups both in the building of human character and in the provision of social discipline.

The human infant is helpless for the first few years. It is the family which cares for him, and in this close circle he learns his first words and is taught the things he should and should not do. In other words, the mores and customs of the group are transmitted to him through the family. As the child grows older, he becomes part of a play group or a small neighborhood group. And association and cooperation here adjust him to the institutional pattern of local group life.

Charles Horton Cooley, in his *Social Organization,* called these intimate associations, or face-to-face relationships of man, "the primary groups." In these primary or personal groups, such as the family, play group, neighborhood, and congeniality group, we acquire all the attributes which we regard as human: love, forbearance, sympathy, tolerance, cooperation, and respect for others. The primary groups are characterized by "oneness" of purpose and sentiments of loyalty:

It is in a primary group that the child attains its first awareness of other persons and subsequently acquires self-consciousness. Here the sense of belonging and having a place and a role, which is the essence of personality, is first derived; and here, also, the child learns to talk and acquires its habits of obedience and self-assertion, or their opposites, as well as its moral judgments. It is in the family, the play group, the neighborhood, and other close relations, that

510

the standards and traditions of the larger society, as well as those typical of primary groups are impressed most effectively.[1]

In civilized society primary groups have almost invariably constituted the basis of social life. The family has been the basic biological and social group. The neighborhood consisted of a number of adjoining families which enjoyed their mutual society and aided each other, when necessary, in rural farming activities. The play group was made up of the children of a group of neighbors, though adults occasionally participated in it. The congeniality group was formed by adults drawn from families in the neighborhood who gathered together because of a common interest in games, local problems, and various activities. The rural church was not only the center of the religious activities of the community but also provided most of the social contacts which extended beyond the scope of the neighborhood.

Since the primary groups have played an outstanding role in the development of the social process, they have been vitally important in the socialization of the individual and in the integrity and preservation of all our established institutions. The economic and the social changes of the past 100 years have, however, produced sweeping alterations in our ways of living, and the machine age, along with the resulting transformations of life, has led to an alarming breakdown of these fundamental primary groups.

City life disrupts the rural primary groups. In a preceding chapter on life in cities today we indicated how the conditions of urban life have seriously weakened the strength of the older rural primary groups and, in some cases, have virtually disrupted them entirely. The family still remains the institution which legalizes and controls the reproductive process, but it is no longer the vigorous and coherent social unit that it was in rural society. Industry is no longer centered in the family. The labor of children can rarely be used in the urban home, and, more often than not, children are an economic liability in the city family. Nor is the urban home of today the center of social life and recreation. It is all too often little more than a place in which to sleep. Probably no other rural primary group has been as completely disrupted by city life as the neighborhood. Even in cities where single homes persist, neighbors have little in common and rarely develop close personal relationships. Families that dwell in apartment houses often do not know more than the names of those who live across the hall. Physical propinquity is no longer the basis of association and friendliness.

Because of the nature of urban life, the rural play group has almost completely disappeared. Children linger around the apartments, loiter on street corners, loaf in parks, and join juvenile gangs. If they are fortunate, they can go to playgrounds at some distance from their homes, where their activities are directed and supervised by paid recreational leaders. Similarly, the adult congeniality group no longer has any neighborhood foundation. The city congeniality group is highly selective.

---

[1] Cooley, *op. cit.* New York: Scribner, 1909, pp. 23 ff.

Persons associate with those who have a common interest in business or professional life or in some special form of entertainment, athletics, clubs, and lodges. They may be drawn together from all over the entire city, taking advantage of modern methods of communication and transportation to assemble. The city church, while still the unit of religious life, rarely has any neighborhood or community basis. Like the adult congeniality groups, its membership may be drawn from scattered portions of the entire urban area. Although many urban churches supply social activities to attract and retain membership, especially of urban youth, no city church is today the dominant social center of the community.

Perhaps the greatest social revolution involved in the gradual but wholesale shift of contemporary life from a rural to an urban basis has been the change from a society based primarily on personal relationships to one which is mainly impersonal in most aspects of life and contacts. The entire economic and social setup of urban life has inevitably undermined the intimate personal contacts of the old rural society and has substituted for it impersonal types of association—secondary groups—based upon new patterns of industrial and professional relations.

New industrial and urban influences have undermined primary groups in rural areas. Not only have the conditions of city life tended to weaken or disrupt within cities the primary groups which once dominated the rural era, but the net impact of modern technology and urbanization upon farming areas has decisively undermined the strength and influence of primary groups in rural society itself. Rural families still have more coherence and exercise more social functions than city families, but they no longer encompass, as formerly, all the major interests of the members. Machines have replaced human beings to an ever greater extent, and have thus lessened the economic value of children. The farm home is no longer the center of recreation. Adults and children alike climb into their automobiles and go to towns or cities for entertainment. These new trends have weakened both the unity and the discipline of the traditional family group.

The rural neighborhood has also been undermined by these same influences. Efficient and complicated machinery has lessened the need for mutual aid and cooperation among neighbors. Similarly, neighbors usually prefer to go to towns and cities for their social life and entertainment rather than to gather together in local congeniality groups. Most of the play carried on by rural children today is limited to the playgrounds of the consolidated schools, where the equipment may be superior to that known in the earlier rural play group. But the opportunities available are more restricted in time, and the associations on the playground are no longer of an intimate neighborhood character. The rural church still exists, and perhaps has a more loyal support per capita than urban churches—at least outside of Catholic circles—but it no longer enjoys its former monopoly of most social life beyond the scope of the family and neighborhood. The radio, movies, television and other new types of entertainment have virtually wiped out the social gatherings which were characteristic of the rural church 50 years ago.

The breakdown of primary groups as an example of cultural lag and a social revolution. Though numerous journalists have described and decried the more superficial and dramatic aspects of the decline of the family and the older personal societies, few social historians and sociologists have realized the more fundamental significance of the breakdown of primary institutions in our age. Virtually everything which separates us from untrained animals has been a product of rural primary groups. All that we call the human personality has been developed by them. The mental attitudes and social discipline of mankind have been provided through their operations. We owe to them our basic conceptions of right and wrong and of social values.

It is obvious that their disappearance or transformation constitutes perhaps the major social revolution in the experience of civilized mankind. The decay of the social discipline and social values hitherto developed and maintained by rural primary groups is a leading cause of social disorganization and the numerous social problems which have developed out of this. The failure to provide, through various forms of community organization, substitutes for the services of rural primary groups as rapidly as the latter have deteriorated is one of the most alarming aspects of cultural lag in our day. Unless community organization is speedily enabled to step into the gap created by the disruption of rural primary groups, human society may disintegrate even without the demoralizing impact of future world wars.

Community organization as a remedy for the decline of primary groups. Community organization is moving in slowly to act as a substitute for the social gap left by the breakdown of the primary institutions. C. E. Rainwater, in discussing the rise of the play movement in the United States, wrote that the nineteenth century saw the complete deterioration of the neighborhood but that the twentieth will witness its reconstruction in a larger framework. It is through the medium of the organization of community forces in all phases that this reconstruction is to be accomplished. Most of the processes of urbanization have created obstacles to such a reconstruction of community life. High population density, low rate of permanent residence, and racial and cultural mixture have all greatly stimulated the growth of secondary groups and relationships which break down the primary associations and are inimical to their rebuilding.

Group responsibility in the present social order. The development of community organization as a solution of the problem of disintegrating primary relationships has come about as a result of the gradual growth of group consciousness. When the Industrial Revolution made changes in industry that concentrated a large number of workers in one place and produced division of labor and mass production, the role of the individual was minimized. This is the reason for the rise of corporations, syndicates, and mergers in the business world. In other words, the Industrial Revolution drove the first wedge into the social fortress of the primary institutions but at the same time suggested new techniques to provide substitute agencies.

The growing trend toward group solidarity is to be seen in the entrance of public organizations into what have hitherto been private affairs. Social legislation has expanded in a remarkable fashion to cover fields of activity that heretofore would have been considered a violation of the inalienable rights of the individual by government. Laws relating to housing, tenant regulation and supervision, child labor, child welfare, municipal parks, playgrounds, and other public welfare measures are examples of the recognition of the new approach to the field of group responsibility.

The significance of the group approach in community life may be discerned from the attitude now assumed by education. Education is no longer a purely individual matter. It is now recognized that there is a community responsibility to uphold acceptable standards, so that education for the masses can be made effective. The modern emphasis is on fitting the child into the community rather than the mere training of an individual. Vocational guidance, manual training, domestic science, and the social studies are examples of this group approach. The force of the group in the community is nowhere better demonstrated than in the field of public welfare. Unless the entire community functions fairly well as a group in the matter of alleviating poverty or solving maladjustments, the entire program is doomed and the community as a whole suffers.

The group approach to all aspects of social work represents a new emphasis and orientation. Gone is the old idea that the individual himself is wholly responsible if he fails to make a living or if he drifts into anti-social conduct. The present theory is that society, when operating defectively, is partly responsible for the pathological conduct of the individual. Social agencies have employed this philosophy in their approach to giving aid. A complete picture of the personal background, environment, employment, friends, clubs, lodges, and the use of leisure time, is obtained in each case before any help is given. In other words, the individual is considered in the light of his group or community; he is not viewed as an independent entity. The application of group responsibility may be seen in the field of crime and juvenile delinquency. The entire procedure of the juvenile court revolves around efforts to place the child in the right sort of group relationships.

These community activities need not imply that social scientists accept the idea that the individual has no responsibility for his action. They simply mean that there is a growing realization that the social environment exercises a definite effect on the individual. Illness, unemployment, and delinquent conduct are no longer considered to be unrelated factors of the individual's life, but are regarded as group or community problems, too.

So long as men lived under a system of domestic economy where each family or gild was a separate unity and not greatly dependent on other units, or so long as the welfare of the whole was not at stake, group action on social matters was less common and less necessary. But as soon as modern industry produced a lack of balance between social units, it was to the interest of the whole that the welfare of individuals be made the concern of the group. People living in cities have found it to their advantage to combine their mutual strength and assets and to work together on satisfying common needs. Community of interest is found in the provisions made to protect the group from fire and theft through the fire and police departments. Public utilities are also a recognition of this group approach. In other words, concentration of population, changes of economy, and the rise of cities have made the group approach to social problems indispensable.

Social work in the new community picture. The existence of the social worker offers the best illustration of the substitution of community emphasis for primary relationships. So long as men lived in small groups and moved in more or less isolated units, the spirit of mutual aid and neighborliness operated effectively. There was less need for formal organization to aid distress. But with the growing detachment of individuals from their primary groups, the family and the neighborhood, there arose the need for group social work.

The creed of the social worker, working in the new community perspective, is to be found in the philosophy of Karl de Schweinitz, in his *Art of Helping People Out of Trouble*: that all persons have one main problem in life—adjustment to environment. This also means that the social worker must understand the community and its possibilities in order to be of service to those who are dependent upon him for adjustment to the new life patterns.

THE MEANING OF COMMUNITY ORGANIZATION AND ACTIVITIES

The nature of a community. The trend toward community organization in the twentieth century is one of the more significant movements in modern society. It has developed out of the leading social changes in the last 100 years—the revolution in rural life, the growth of the city, and the disintegration of the traditional rural family pattern.

The term *community* is used in various ways and its meaning is often confused. In the broadest sense, *community* is the mutual awareness among members of a social group of their reciprocal or interdependent relationships. It is limited only by the strength of this "consciousness of kind" or "we-feeling." It may be vaguely extended to "One World" or limited to the boundaries of a small neighborhood.

In this chapter, however, we will use the term *community* in a more precise way—as a group of people who share a more or less common culture and purpose. Thus, the community may be a rural neighborhood, a small town, an entire city, or a section of a city. The economic and social opportunities of the individual, as well as his views on politics, religion, and economic and social issues, are determined in large part by his social environment. The community is thus a vital factor in the life of the individual, and the community organization movement may assume great importance. By *community organization* we mean the promotion of helpful relationships and experiences among all groups in the community, the unification and coordination of these groups to increase their efficiency and social service, and the adjustment of local communities to the larger social unit of which they are an integral part.

Examples of community activities. Many phases of life have come to be regarded as matters of community concern. Nowhere is this fact more clearly illustrated than in the provisions made by communities for the prevention and cure of disease and the protection of health. The public health movement arose out of the community's fear of epidemics and the realization that the community must assume responsibility for the maintenance of health in order to protect all within its boundaries from individuals suffering from contagious diseases. In addition to such routine duties as the inspection of food and milk and the provision of pure drinking water, the public health departments perform a wide variety of functions. Free clinics give examinations and treatment to those unable to pay for medical care; the large cities maintain hospitals for the sick poor; and the visiting-nurse system is now an integral part of the public health program of many communities. The educational program of the public health movement has helped to reduce the incidence of such diseases as tuberculosis, cancer, infantile paralysis, cerebral palsy, gonorrhea, and syphilis.

Another example of the group approach in community life is to be seen in the modern attitude toward child care and education. Once largely centered in the family, the education of the child has become the responsibility of the community, too. Much more attention is given to the prevention and treatment of the diseases of childhood—with striking success. The majority of the mental hygiene clinics serve the needs of children. Children have been protected against the exploitation of child labor and the mistreatment of orphan and dependent children. Special attention has been given to juvenile delinquency, with regard both to prevention and treatment. The rural play group has been superseded by supervised urban recreation. Educational functions have been extended beyond formal education in the classroom. Today the emphasis is on fitting the child to participate effectively as a member of the group in which he lives. Vocational education and guidance and occupational training are examples of the preparation of youth for adult life. The modern public library supplements the work of the school. Adult education also has received much attention in the last decade. Established to meet the needs of adults who wish more specific training, who desire to continue their formal education, or who seek to spend leisure time profitably, adult education courses are made available through high schools, colleges, and state universities.

The group approach to public assistance of the needy, the aged, the blind, the physically and mentally handicapped, the dependent child, and the juvenile delinquent also provides examples of the acceptance of new responsibility on the part of the community. Today no scientifically-trained social worker would attempt to give financial aid or guidance without obtaining complete knowledge of the background of the person involved.

If we look briefly at the history of community organization, we shall see how group action was made necessary by the sweeping economic and social changes of the last 100 years.

BRIEF HISTORY OF COMMUNITY ORGANIZATION

Community organization began in the care of the poor and distressed. Although community organization is a recent development that has not even begun to supply the great social need created by the decay of primary groups, some form of community interest and activity goes back as far as the dawn of history. The sick, poor, and distressed have always aroused some degree of community interest. It may therefore be said that community organization had its origins in the various types of group efforts to aid the helpless. The care of the sick and poor by the church community and the manorial village community during the Middle Ages are notable historical examples of such informal community activity to aid the helpless. But anything like systematic community activity in behalf of the sick, the poor, and the helpless dates from the time of the Industrial Revolution and the origins of modern urban life.

Origins of the charity organization movement. The growth of distress following the Industrial Revolution led to the development of numerous private and quasi-private charitable activities and organizations in urban centers. But, at first, there was much anarchy, inadequacy, and duplication in this relief work. Many reticent needy persons did not get the relief which they actually required, while many astute grafters got assistance from several different agencies. Moreover, there was considerable waste in the duplication of efforts by charitable agencies in the same city.

Early in the second half of the nineteenth century these abuses were observed by such English students of the problem of relief as Henry Solly, Thomas Hawksley, Octavia Hill, and Charles S. Loch. They proposed the creation of a centralized organization of all the charitable agencies operating in any given city and a careful investigation of individual applications for aid. To effect this, they founded in London, in 1869, the Society for Organizing Charitable Relief and Repressing Mendicity. The next year the name was changed to the Charity Organization Society. The movement spread to the United States, where the first city to adopt it was Buffalo. There a Charity Organization Society was created in 1877. By 1893 there were 55 such organizations in the United States. They have grown in number until now there are more than 400 of them. They are now known also as Associated Charities, Federated Charities, or Community Councils.

Functions of a charity organization society. The Charity Organization Society movement sought to eliminate the defects of earlier urban relief: neglect or inadequate grants to the really needy, graft by clever impostors, duplication of efforts by a multiplicity of overlapping relief associations, and the absence of any proper coordination of charitable and relief agencies.

In cities where a Charity Organization Society was established, the claims of those seeking aid were carefully examined, so that the cases of actual need would be adequately handled and fraudulent claims eliminated from consideration. Duplication of effort and administrative waste were lessened by a proper coordination of all relief agencies. Systematic planning was made for the collection of funds, and wholesale financial drives, such as community-chest campaigns, were carried out. Educational activities were conducted in an effort to improve the living standards of those who were inclined to ask for charity, and to acquaint potential givers with the ideals and methods of scientific social work. Finally, everything possible was done to lessen dependency—at least such steps as could be taken without any serious attack upon the existing economic order. Vigorous support was given to social legislation in behalf of better housing and relief. The establishment of social work councils still further consolidated urban relief administration.

The charity organization movement not only brought great improvement in the general administrative features of charitable relief, but it also revolutionized the procedure in investigating particular cases. As we shall see later, it played a leading role in giving rise to what is known as *social case work*—scientific procedure in investigating relief cases. One of the main abuses which led to the charity organization movement was the lack of investigation of the merit in each application for relief. The case-work method was supposed to provide just this sort of personal investigation. It was also devised to ferret out worthy cases of need which had not previously come to the attention of charitable agencies.

The social settlement movement. If the charity organization movement and social case work revolutionized charity in dealing with needy individuals in a scientific manner, the social settlement movement wrought a comparable change in the efforts to elevate the living conditions and morale of depressed urban neighborhoods and groups, especially the slum areas. While the charity organization movement and social case work have sought to relieve immediate and specific need, the settlement movement has sought to improve general social conditions among the poor and to awaken new aspirations among the submerged classes. Social settlements have often been even more closely related to community organization than the charity organization movement. They have been more directly concerned with the personal and cultural problems of the poor and have sought to alleviate their misery through friendly and understanding contact with them. The social settlement movement began in England about 1875 under the leadership of Samuel A. Barnett. He and his associates opened Toynbee Hall in London in 1884. This was the first important English settlement house.

The social settlement movement spread rapidly to the United States. In 1886, Stanton Coit and Charles B. Stover founded the Neighborhood Guild in New York City. Later renamed the University Settlement, this was the first American settlement house. In 1889, the famous Hull House was established in Chicago by Jane Addams and Ellen Gates Starr. In the same year, Jane Robbins and Jane Fine opened the College Settlement in New York City. The South End House was founded in Boston in 1891 by William J. Tucker and Robert A. Woods. Other famous settlements have been the Henry Street Settlement in New York City, under the direction of Lillian B. Wald; Greenwich House in New York City, directed by Mary K. Simkhovitch; Kingsley House in Pittsburgh, long directed by William H. Matthews and Charles C. Cooper; and Hiram House in Cleveland, under the direction of George A. Bellamy. In 1911 a National Federation of Settlements was founded. By 1950, there were over 500 social settlements, neighborhood houses, and community centers. They were located in 175 communities in 42 states, and they served several million persons. The social settlements are supported mainly by volunteer contributions raised by settlement leaders. Some of the more recently established settlement houses are today financed in part by urban community chests.

Main activities of the social settlement. The purposes of the settlement movement are the provision of a social center for improving civic life and social opportunities for unfortunate persons in depressed neighborhoods, and the investigation and elevation of living conditions in such areas. The settlements work with groups and communities—especially with the so-called neighborhood groups—rather than with individual cases of need. They have made important contributions to civic reform and to the training of citizens. Jane Addams, for example, took an active and important part in public recreation work and in the Chicago investigation of vice in 1911-1912. The settlements have also done much to promote better health work among the poor. Their efforts have helped to create clinics, dispensaries, and visiting nurses' associations. In the 1890's, the Henry Street Settlement was organized by Lillian Wald to improve the health conditions of persons living in an area of the lower East Side of New York. The Henry Street Settlement has had great influence on the work in community health. It has been responsible for instituting programs which led to the medical examination of school children, the provision of school lunches, the use of visiting teachers, and many other services.

Settlements have also been vitally interested in improving educational opportunities, recreational facilities, and playgrounds in slum areas. They have also given special attention to providing classes for foreigners and to teaching them the English language and other subjects. The settlements also aided the movement to make the public schools social centers. This development began in the city of Rochester in 1907. Cultural activities have been promoted through the settlement classes devoted to arts and crafts. Training has been provided in metal work, wood carving, basketry, weaving, and other departments of the crafts. Specific instruction has been given in the various fields of art, including dancing and dramatics.

Social settlements have also been very active in promoting social surveys. For example, William H. Matthews, of Kingsley House in Pittsburgh, took a leading part in the Pittsburgh Survey carried out in 1907-1908 under the leadership of Paul U. Kellogg. The information gathered by such investigations is of great value to the settlements in enabling them to plan their work more intelligently.

Social work promotes the community organization movement. Social work has also made a direct contribution to the community organization movement. The community chest trend combined the ideals of the charity organization movement and the community center experiment. Social work agencies in a given city have sometimes combined their efforts on a community basis. The most conspicuous example was the effort of the Cincinnati Social Unit to create a community organization for the administration of the health and social work activities of the entire city.

Development of the social survey technique. Community studies— analysis of a community to throw light on its social problems—are part of the history of community movements because they indicate the growing awareness of the community as a responsible social unit. The social survey technique was first outlined by the French sociologist Frédéric Le Play about a decade before the American Civil War. Many years later, it was brought over to England by Charles Booth, Patrick Geddes, and Victor Branford. As early as 1880, public interest in England had been sufficiently aroused over the squalor and hardships of slum life to warrant a scientific study of the slum areas. The most complete study was the great work of Charles Booth, *The Life and Labour of the People of London,* which appeared in 17 volumes between 1886 and 1902. It was the first monumental example of the social survey method of studying social problems.

In America, the miseries of slum life were dramatically exposed in 1890 in *How the Other Half Lives,* by Jacob A. Riis. Two years later Riis published *Children of the Poor.* These two books did not pretend to be statistically complete, but they stimulated interest in the problem of the slum-dweller as no purely statistical evidence could have done. Other books followed; some were general studies of public conditions in cities, such as Lincoln Steffens' great exposure of city corruption, *The Shame of the Cities* (1904). Jane Addams and other well-known social workers gave firsthand impressions of conditions they encountered, and they urged a constructive program for the treatment of social ills. But, on the whole, the growth of a scientific attitude toward investigating the community was slow.

In 1902, the National Conference of Charities and Correction presented, for the first time, a full discussion of "Neighborhood and Civic Improvements," and, about this time, a new interest in housing reform was taken by New York City and certain state legislatures. Social conditions were scientifically studied in various American cities. The first city to be investigated was Washington, D.C. The evils found in the shadow of the Capitol were so startling that other cities began to investigate their own slum neighborhoods. Pittsburgh, Pennsylvania, was studied in 1906-1907 under the direction of Paul U. Kellogg. The resulting six-volume report was sponsored by *Charities and Commons,* the official magazine of social workers which later became the *Survey,* and published by the Russell Sage Foundation. This report constituted the first comprehensive application of the survey technique in the United States.

The social survey is an important device in the community organization movement. It is impossible to plan for the adequate organization of relief unless a clear-cut picture is obtained of the social setup and needs of the community, and the interrelationship of all the organizations within it. The survey of a town or city thus furnishes a working basis on which to begin the organization of the community. By 1912, the social survey idea had become so popular that numerous American cities began to study conditions within their limits. Some of the resulting surveys, such as that of Springfield, Illinois, by Shelby M. Harrison in 1914, still stand as models.

Not only were surveys made of entire cities, but various organizations also began to make special surveys. The churches began to study rural and urban church communities. The Federal Children's Bureau examined the needs of mothers and children, and the National Child Labor Committee investigated the labor of children in urban textile mills and factories. Both states and cities carried on surveys of crime and its causes, with particular attention to delinquency areas. In 1914, The Cleveland Foundation was established; it began to make surveys in the field of education, recreation, relief, and the administration of justice. The survey method was gradually improved until it was combined with sociological acumen in the classic study of Muncie, Indiana, by Robert and Helen Lynd in *Middletown* (1929), and their later *Middletown in Transition* (1937). It was found that these surveys, by giving publicity to the existing evils, stirred the whole community into action to alleviate them.

Today the social survey is an accepted procedure for beginning any kind of community program. Experts in survey methods are, however, highly paid, and many communities do not have the funds both to employ experts and then to carry out the program. Community Surveys, Inc., a foundation established to aid in drawing up plans for health, welfare, and recreation programs, now seeks to meet this problem and to provide aid and guidance.

ACTIVITIES AND AGENCIES INCLUDED IN COMMUNITY ORGANIZATION

Nature and functions of community organization. From the preceding history of community organization it is evident that varied activities have been included under the general name of "community organization." Any program with a civic or social aim and sponsored by a compact and organized social group has been called a "community" project. A comprehensive survey of any maladjustment within the community has become a community survey. There have been many different conceptions of the real meaning of community organization, because the community offers an excellent laboratory to study all types of human relations. The student of economics finds it an ideal place to study the economic regime and the interplay of the factors of production, distribution, and consumption. The student of sociology tries to illustrate from a community survey his theories concerning the behavior of the individual, human reactions to environment, and the social functions of both primary and secondary social institutions. The student of religion finds the community a fertile field to study religious organizations and their membership, activities, and functions.

An underlying reason for the confusion that has sometimes led to an inadequate conception of the term "community organization" is the failure to distinguish between those vital public activities which are necessary to enable the group to live, such as protection from fire and theft and the establishment of courts of justice, and the well-rounded operations of the community as a whole. The indispensable public activities do not represent community organization as generally understood. The modern community movement is a deliberate attempt to devise means by which the social, economic, political, health, educational, recreational, and artistic forces in the community may be integrated in such a way that all members of the group will be able to adjust and express themselves satisfactorily.

Examples of community spirit and activities. In order to gain a more adequate idea of the types of activities sponsored by the contemporary community movement, we may indicate here the kinds of methods that have been found successful in promoting and sustaining community solidarity.

Sometimes the activity of one agency like the local housing authority will stimulate community interest. Occasionally, a strong leader or small group can be the means of organizing the whole community. For example, the entire community of Holland, Michigan, is engaged in a year-round preparation for the tulip festival it gives each May. Started by a local civic club in 1929, the project has grown to include all groups and social classes.

A crisis such as war, a depression, flood, or fire can provide a stimulus for coordinating and directing the efforts of citizens in community organization. During the height of the polio epidemic in 1947, one of the North Carolina communities, aroused to action because of its inadequate hospital, built and equipped a modern hospital in a short time. Materials, labor, and equipment were either donated or made available at cost. Committees organized to meet such crises, however, often produce group inefficiency and social waste in trying to solve problems in a rapid and improvised fashion without an overall view of the needs and potentialities of the community.

The Council of Social Agencies. The Council of Social Agencies, a federation of all or most social agencies within the community to coordinate their work, is an illustration of desirable organization for overall planning. This should not be confused with the charity organization society or federated charities which organize and direct relief work. Representatives from the public and private agencies that promote health, welfare, recreation, and education make up the council. Meetings are usually held every month. Standing committees on health, housing, delinquency, and family and child welfare survey and evaluate the work done by the responsible agency in each field and report to the council. Often the accomplishments of one committee stimulate action on the part of other committees. The council of social agencies thus acts as a coordinator and clearing house for all separate agencies, and, as a result, the work of each agency is more carefully planned and executed and is more likely to meet the needs of the group it serves.

Community councils. In the last two decades, Community Councils and Coordinating Councils, made up of interested citizens and local government officials, have been formed. These councils are distinct from the Council of Social Agencies. In 1929, a group of citizens in Alexandria, Ohio, formed a community council to discuss common problems. Today there are more than 300 community councils—more than half of them in California.

A great asset to the community council is the inclusion, wherever possible, of local government officials. Part of the task of community organization is to interest local government officials in community problems; to get organizations such as the Chamber of Commerce, Rotary, Kiwanis, Lions, and Elks clubs interested in community progress; to educate the public concerning the rôle played by both public and private agencies in group welfare; and to make it patent that, although Federal and state funds are made available for certain programs, the local community must provide for programs not covered by such funds. It is also necessary for people to learn that private agencies are not supported by public appropriations but are dependent on the generosity of the community. The community council has lessened the conflict between agencies, has reduced misunderstanding, and has been valuable as an interpreter of the welfare program to the community.

Any plan to organize a community must take into consideration the fact that the community is always changing in nature and problems. Because a particular approach to a community problem has once been successful, there is no reason to assume that it will always be equally successful in the future. The community consists of individuals who have personal aims, interests, and ambitions that reflect living conditions at any given time. Therefore, any well-planned program of community organization in order to fulfill its purpose must take into account the changing and complex economic and social situations within the community.

COMMUNITY AND PUBLIC PROVISIONS FOR CHILD CARE OUTSIDE THE FAMILY

Family no longer provides complete care for children. Until modern times the child contributed all of his labor to the family, and the family provided the child with food, clothing, shelter, education, and medical care. The family had nearly complete control of the child and received all his services in return. Now that the old authoritarian family is breaking up and the rural economy is being superseded by an urban industrial age, the family no longer provides complete care for children, does not exert full authority over children, and does not receive all of the service of children. Let us consider briefly some of the ways in which the community and public agencies have assumed many of the responsibilities for the child that once fell to the family.

Child health provisions. During the last century, great progress has been made in protecting the health of the child. Formerly, many women were delivered of babies by midwives, and they doctored their children with various herbs and syrups. Aseptic delivery, antibiotics like penicillin, and proper medical care during pregnancy have greatly reduced maternal mortality in childbirth. The control of communicable diseases and the great reduction of the epidemic diseases of childhood have saved the lives of many thousands of children who formerly died from diphtheria, whooping cough, scarlet fever, measles, and other children's diseases. The death rate from such diseases was reduced by 90 per cent between 1900 and 1950. Improved knowledge of nutritional science has greatly reduced deaths among young children. The community and the state have given special attention to providing public medical care for children. Gymnasium work and supervised play have also contributed to the improvement of the physical health of children.

Equally solicitous has been the action of the more alert communities in looking after the mental health of children. This has been due largely to the fact that psychiatrists recognize the critical importance of childhood in relation to both mental health and disease. Psychological clinics for children appeared in this country as early as 1896. But the movement for mental health clinics for children, usually called child guidance clinics, did not really begin to get underway until the National Committee for Mental Hygiene was created in 1909. Then the movement grew rapidly. By 1914 there were a hundred such clinics; by 1950 there were more than 700 mental hygiene clinics—about 300 exclusively for children. A great stimulus to the movement was given in 1921, when the Commonwealth Fund provided money for setting up a large number of demonstration clinics in important cities throughout the country. These guidance clinics have been of great value in curbing mental diseases and delinquency and in aiding educators to understand "problem children."

Child labor curbed. A hundred years ago very few persons thought of limiting the labor of children. Parents were generally conceded the right to get as much work out of children as possible. If children were employed outside of the family, much the same notions held true. In 1842, however, public authority was asserted to protect children from industrial exploitation. In that year Massachusetts passed a law limiting the work of children under twelve to ten hours daily. But the movement for such protection developed very slowly, and as late as 1938 only ten states adequately protected children from excessive hours of labor. Federal child labor laws were set aside by the Supreme Court in 1918 and 1922. An amendment to the Constitution prohibiting child labor has been before the country since 1924, but has not been adopted. Recent decisions of the Supreme Court indicate that the present bench would uphold legislation outlawing child labor.

That much needed to be done in protecting children from economic exploitation is to be seen from the fact that in 1930 there were nearly 600,000 gainfully employed children under fifteen years of age. The Wage-Hour Act of 1938 sharply restricted the labor of children in industries engaged in interstate commerce, but there were still a considerable number of children employed in intrastate industries. According to the census of 1940, there were about a million employed children between 14 and 17—250,000 of them under 16. During the Second World War, about 3 million children between 14 and 17 were employed, but the number has dropped off sharply since that time.

In addition to negative or restraining activities on the part of the government in relation to the labor of young children the government has, in the last two decades, taken positive steps to provide employment or support for unemployed youth old enough to be permitted to work. The Civilian Conservation Corps provided employment for over 2 million, and further assistance was rendered by the National Youth Administration.

Care of dependent children. A century ago orphaned and dependent children were taken care of mainly in almshouses, and through what is known as indentures—that is, placing the children in families who agreed to support them in return for their labor. Both of these types of care were cruel and unsatisfactory. The almshouses made for demoralization; indenture invited exploitation.

In the middle of the last century, the Children's Aid Society of New York began to take children out of almshouses and to put them in foster homes without the abuse of indenture. In 1868, the Massachusetts State Board of Charities introduced the practice of boarding out children at public expense. It is generally agreed that carefully selected foster homes are a better place for the dependent child than are even very good orphanages. However, the latter are an enormous improvement over the old almshouses, and their administration is constantly improving. The census of dependent children in 1923 showed that out of the total of about 400,000 such children, 204,000 were in institutions, 121,000 in their own homes, 51,000 in free foster homes, and 22,000 in boarding homes. Since the Social Security system was set up in 1935, more and more children have been supported by government grants in their homes; fewer have been sent to institutions. In 1949, there were 1,370,360 children being supported by grants-in-aid; only 150,000 dependent children were in institutions.

Public care has been extended not only to dependent children but also to neglected children. In 1875, the Society for the Prevention of Cruelty to Children was founded to protect neglected children in New York. Similar societies were established in many other important cities. They brought cases of cruelty and exploitation of children to the courts, helped to punish the guilty, and made provisions for the welfare of the child. The progress which has been made in protecting children from abuses can be seen from the fact that, in early days, half the cases related directly to physical cruelty. Today these cases usually do not amount to more than 10 per cent of the total cases. In addition to protecting children from cruelty, the care of neglected children extends to the support of such children and to efforts to prevent them from falling into situations of crime and vice.

Restraining juvenile delinquency. In earlier days the family supplied most of the moral training and discipline for children. But with the decline of the rural family and the greater temptations of urban life, community agencies had to be set up to keep children out of crime. Here the most important agencies have been the child guidance clinics mentioned above, the clinics for juvenile delinquents, and juvenile courts. The leading figures in promoting this movement were Ben B. Lindsey, in Denver, and William Healy, in Chicago and Boston. Judge Lindsey began his important work about 1900. Healy established a juvenile psychopathic institute in connection with the juvenile court of Chicago in 1909. In 1918, he went to Boston and continued his good work with the Judge Baker Foundation. This juvenile court movement under psychiatric guidance has made considerable headway during the last two decades. Frederic M. Thrasher and Clifford Shaw have aroused interest in juvenile delinquency through investigation of the "gang" problem of youth and the special dangers involved in rearing children in delinquency areas.

Better educational facilities. Formerly, the father and mother provided much of the education for the child, guided by the motto that to spare the rod spoils the child. Most children who were given formal education received their schooling in the miserably equipped rural schools. In the 1880's, G. Stanley Hall, a student of progressive European pedagogy, applied scientific psychological principles to the education of children. An effort was made by John Dewey and others to free education from the barbarous discipline and regimentation of the traditional schools. Some kind of education was made accessible for all through the gradual extension of free public instruction for children after Horace Mann set up the first state system of free public instruction in Massachusetts in 1837. The introduction of mental and vocational tests has enabled us to classify and guide children more effectively. Vocational instruction is being provided more adequately for retarded children.

Supervised recreation. Play, which was formerly limited to the family, the neighborhood, and the rural school has now been developed as a major community and national enterprise. Public recreational activities have developed on a vast scale, and supervised play has grown tremendously. In 1950 there were about 2,000 communities carrying on public recreation; about 90 million dollars was being spent for such recreation. Over a third of these communities were aided by Federal funds. Nevertheless, our recreational facilities for children are still woefully inadequate. There are about 8 million urban children who have inadequate facilities for play, and there are 10 million rural children who lack opportunity for organized and supervised recreation. The consolidated rural schools have done something to remedy this situation, but so far only the surface has been scratched. There are certain organizations of youth devoted to recreation and character building, such as the Boy Scouts, the Girl Scouts, the Camp Fire Girls, Pioneer Youth, and 4-H Clubs.

Child welfare agencies. Child welfare activities and organizations are numerous and extensive. Various health agencies look after the physical and mental health of children. Educators and social workers are concerned with education. Criminologists and psychiatrists endeavor to break up gangs and save children from crime. Recreation organizers seek to provide a substitute for idleness, loafing, and the various other unhealthy forms of activity which might lead to delinquency and degeneracy.

Among the various associations which give special attention to child welfare are the National Child Labor Committee, the Child Welfare League of America, the National Child Welfare Association, the American Child Health Association, the National Committee for Mental Hygiene, the Child Study Association of America, and the Association for Childhood Education. There are also various institutes of child welfare conducted by leading universities. The Federal Security Agency's Children's Bureau is devoted to research and education in the field of child welfare. Important national White House conferences on child welfare met in 1909, 1919, 1930, 1940, and 1950.

COMMUNITY ORGANIZATION IN THE RECREATION FIELD

Need for community recreation programs. The old rural neighborhood play group, one of the most important primary groups, has broken down as a result of the growth of the modern city. Community organization has provided a substitute for the earlier informal play group in the form of a planned recreation movement, which arose in the twentieth century in response to a definite community need. Without play, some of the benefits of group life are lost. Play aids in building a wholesome, well-balanced personality. And, since a healthy body can do better work, play helps to develop a more efficient type of social life.

There was a time when the social value of play was not recognized. Although children have always played, their play was formerly regarded mainly as a means of amusement and as a body builder. Little emphasis was placed on play as socialized training for group living. Although the modern city has destroyed the older play group, industrialization and urban life have brought about an extension of leisure, and the growing realization that the wise use of leisure time is important has led to further recognition of the socializing value of play.

The eight-hour day and the five-and-a-half day week, with vacations and time off for holidays, have given workers more spare time than ever before. In the past few decades technological unemployment has increased enforced leisure time. Child labor laws in many states prohibit children from working; and, although compulsory education compels school attendance, many hours are still left for recreation. The demands and policies of modern industry have forced the retirement of men from work earlier in life.

Increased leisure time challenges community action. As a result of increased leisure time, many of our social problems have become more complicated or acute; juvenile delinquency, for example, often occurs because young people have ben led into mischief during their spare time. The increase in adult crime may also be partly due to the increase of leisure time. Some persons believe that many divorces are the result of increased leisure, which gives more time for family boredom and for domestic dissatisfaction of all sorts. The modern electrical home conveniences have made housekeeping relatively simple and have freed women not only for industry but for leisure-time activities. Many women occupy their afternoons by playing bridge or by going to the movies. For some persons increased leisure has meant more opportunities for cultural improvement, but for others it has made for boredom, dissatisfaction, or dissipation.

The recognition that unwise use of leisure is partly responsible for many serious social problems of the modern age has led to emphasis on supervised recreation. Children must have group direction in recreation, in the same way that they must have guidance in education or in building up their health. In a society where the traditional patterns of living have been altered by the transfer to a larger group of many fundamental activities and services which were formerly individual or family matters, we cannot assume that the problems of leisure time and recreation can be handled without community aid.

Rise of supervised community recreation. The organized play movement began in Boston in 1885. By 1887, 10 playgrounds had been opened, and in 1893 a trained supervisor was hired. But it was not until 1899 that the city of Boston contributed even a small sum ($3,000) toward the costs. This is often called the "sand garden" period of the recreation movement, because most of the playgrounds had little equipment except sand boxes. Boston opened the first public gymnasium in America in 1889. New York City bought a tract for recreation purposes in 1897 and opened it at Seward Park in 1899. No city in the United States had a formal recreation department in 1900.

The social settlements were quick to grasp the possibilities of playgrounds as a means of establishing friendly relationships, teaching good citizenship and sportsmanship, and guarding against the development of antisocial tendencies. Through the interest of the settlements—particularly of Hull House in Chicago—the supervised playground movement entered a new period of expansion and supervision after 1890. The first model playground was opened at Hull House in 1892. It was largely due to the success of the settlements in stimulating interest in play that Massachusetts decided to include supervised play as a part of the school curriculum in 1901. Joseph Lee (1862-1937), a wealthy Boston philanthropist, became the leader in creating and promoting the playground movement in the United States.

By 1900, there was considerable organized recreational activity in many cities. Large cities converted open spaces or vacant lots in congested areas into playgrounds where children might play under the watchful eyes of supervisors. Through the influence of Jane Addams, Chicago established excellent municipal playgrounds, appropriating 5 million dollars for 10 playground parks in 1903. President Theodore Roosevelt declared this to be "the most notable civic achievement of any American city." Philadelphia, St. Louis, Washington, Pittsburgh, and Cleveland followed suit. Usually, the beginnings of the playground movement in each city were fostered by small private organizations that were able to secure municipal support. There were a few instances in which a city government itself took the lead in establishing a playground.

The Playground Association of America was established in Washington, D. C., in 1906 and became the leading force in the playground movement. It was rechristened the Playground and Recreation Association of America in 1911, and in 1930 its name was finally changed to the National Recreation Association. At the time of its organization in 1906, only about 40 cities had made even a half-hearted attempt to establish playgrounds. It was difficult to arouse public enthusiasm and to persuade public authorities to turn over elaborately planned parks to "rowdy children" for play; school authorities were loath to allow the use of school property for playgrounds. It was, therefore, left to the National Recreation Association to build up enthusiasm for supervised recreation. The Association launched an active educational program. Today, its national magazine, *Recreation,* still carries on this program of education.

Recently formed organizations promoting community recreation. In recent years a number of other important organizations have come into being that promote recreational activity and supervised play. The American Recreation Society was established in 1938 and is devoted to providing information, improving standards of leadership, expanding recreation programs, and holding conferences. It publishes a valuable quarterly bulletin and frequent news releases. The Education-Recreation Council of the National Social Welfare Assembly focuses attention on recreation on a national scale. It has a Youth division which gives special attention to promoting recreational facilities for juveniles. Other organizations that seek to aid community recreation are the American Association for Health, Physical Education, and Recreation; the Federal Inter-Agency Committee on Recreation; the National Recreation Policies Committee; and the National Industrial Recreation Association.

Growth of supervised community recreational projects. The provision of urban playgrounds and supervised recreation developed steadily and on an increasingly large scale after the turn of the century. States began to pass laws permitting cities to set up public recreation systems and to appropriate funds to construct and operate them. This is now possible in about 35 states. Between 1906 and the outbreak of the First World War in 1914, over 350 cities had established public recreation systems. By 1929, some 950 cities had public, supervised recreational facilities, with 22,920 full- and part-time recreation leaders. The annual expense of operation was 33 million dollars. New Deal aid to recreation through such agencies as the WPA, the CCC, and the like, notably stimulated the growth of urban recreational facilities, and the Second World War still further assisted the movement. By 1950, some 2,175 urban communities provided for supervised recreation of some type, and some 702 cities had formal recreation departments. There were 14,747 public playgrounds for urban children, whereas in 1910 there had been only 1,300.

Statistics given in the Mid-century Edition of the *Recreation and Park Yearbook* (1951) reveal the progress made in community recreation in the postwar period. The number of cities with supervised recreational facilities increased from 1,743 in 1946 to 2,175 in 1950. The number of full-time, year-round paid recreation leaders increased from 4,870 in about 500 cities in 1944 to 6,784 in 794 cities in 1950. The number of paid part-time leaders increased from 35,500 in 1944 to 51,245 in 1950, and the number of volunteer recreation workers increased in the same period from about 85,000 to 104,590. Representative recreational facilities in urban communities in 1950 were 1,933 athletic fields, 5,502 baseball diamonds, 12,266 softball diamonds, 13,085 tennis courts, 504 stadiums, 2,987 recreation buildings, and 6,633 indoor recreation centers. The attendance at all public recreational facilities in 1950 is estimated to have been in excess of 500 million persons. The total expenditures for supervised recreation in 1950 were 178 million dollars. Not only playgrounds but municipal and county parks have shared in the recent development of recreational facilities. Municipal, county, and regional parks reported in 1950 numbered 17,142, comprising 644,000 acres, of which about 430,600 acres are in municipal parks. The total expenditures for recreational activities, parks and related activities in 1950 were about 269 million dollars. Recreational facilities have come to be mainly under public control and direction—a marked contrast to the situation in 1900 and for many years thereafter. In 1950, the public recreational authorities outnumbered the private agencies by about seven to one.

This was far below the needs, and it is obvious that Federal and state aid are necessary to provide anything like adequate recreational facilities both for urban and for rural children. Although the municipal playground movement has spread rapidly, there are still about 350 cities without adequate provision for municipal recreation. Some cities have grown so rapidly that they actually have little space for playgrounds.

Lag in rural recreational facilities. The interest of rural communities in public recreational programs has lagged behind that of the urban areas. Ten million rural children lack good recreational facilities. Probably one reason for this is that the rural community still affords much natural opportunity for outdoor activity. A number of organizations have tried to overcome this backwardness of rural recreation. The Extension Service of the United States Department of Agriculture has promoted recreation for rural youth through the 4-H Clubs, which now have nearly two million members. In addition to recreational leadership for children, the Extension Service has entered adult recreational planning in such fields as folk-games and dancing, drama, handicrafts, camping, and the study of wild life. It trained some 100,000 volunteer rural recreation leaders in the year 1945 alone.

The National Recreational Association holds rural institutes and has trained about 60,000 rural recreational leaders, drawn from the schools, the churches, the Grange, and 4-H Clubs. Some of the WPA projects were devoted to the improvement of rural recreational facilities. The consolidated school has, of course, done much to centralize and to improve recreational activities for rural children. The school playground, however, usually benefits chiefly those children living within the immediate village community, since children who come to school by bus have an opportunity to use the playground only during the noon hour and recess periods.

Community recreational trends since the Second World War. Since the end of the Second World War, a large number of communities, especially towns and small cities, have developed recreation programs on a year-round basis. Recreation agencies report that participation by all age groups in established recreation programs far exceeds prewar totals. One interesting development has been the increasing emphasis on social and hobby groups for older people. Special activities and facilities for older people were reported by over 300 cities in 1950.

Another postwar development has been the growth of Federal and state advisory services for recreation. The Extension Service of the Department of Agriculture is the most important Federal agency assisting local recreational projects. Advisory service is now furnished by 43 states through such agencies as state recreation commissions, youth authorities, conservation and forest departments, colleges of agriculture, state universities, and departments of commerce. In 14 states, full-time consultant service in recreation was available from some state agency in 1948. This was in addition to those states provided with full- or part-time personnel employed in the Extension Service of the Department of Agriculture to help with local recreation programs.

Local recreation budgets have increased since the war. In some cases, the increased costs of living have been the cause; in other cases, recreation services have been greatly expanded. Many cities are now planning long-range recreation projects which include plans for the acquisition of new areas and the improvement of existing facilities.

Provisions for juvenile recreation are still inadequate. Despite the remarkable development of the playground movement, however, there is much work yet to be done in the field of recreation for children. In 1930, it was estimated that only five million of the approximately 32 million children between the ages of six and 18 were served by public playgrounds. In 1938, it was estimated that over eight million urban and 12 million rural children still had no access to playgrounds. The 1950 figures showed that some gains were made during the postwar period, but there are today at least eight million urban and 10 million rural children without adequate recreational facilities. Recreational experts estimated in 1950 that nearly half of our American children are without anything approaching ample recreational facilities.

THE COMMUNITY CENTER

Origin of community centers. As we have pointed out, recognition of the importance of recreation as a socializing force in the neighborhood has been due in part to the influence of the social settlements and especially the initiative of Jane Addams at Hull House. Since the settlement houses were located in the most congested areas, and since they emphasized work with the community, there was no better place to organize a recreation, education, and art center than in connection with the social settlement.

The community center movement grew slowly because it was difficult at first to get persons to volunteer for service in some neighborhood program. Settlements could not afford to hire enough trained workers who understood the local situation. The program of a community social center usually included such activities as sports, games, dancing, music, dramatics, art, parties, and educational classes. The YMCA, the YWCA, the YMHA, the Girl Scouts, and the Campfire Girls have established social centers that conduct programs in health, vocational and general education, recreation, art, and citizenship.

Use of school buildings as community centers. The development of recreation on a neighborhood basis, and its sponsorship by the social settlement, paved the way for the extension of the community movement to the schools. School authorities, for a time, retarded the growth of this program because they did not want the school grounds or building to be used after school hours; many traditional educators believed that the school building should be locked after the day's formal work was over. But, by 1901, because of successful experiments in using school grounds for community purposes in other cities, a few school buildings in New York City were opened for evening meetings. This was a simple beginning, enabling people to get away from home to read, talk, play games, or listen to music. The following year, Boston opened two schools for evening classes for adults.

It was not until 1907, however, that the school community center movement formally began. Eleven organizations in Rochester, New York, formed a school extension committee and persuaded the local board of education to grant $5,000 to develop educational, social, and recreational centers in the public schools. The committee stressed the importance of the school as a meeting-place to discuss questions of public interest and to build up community spirit. The first Rochester centers were chiefly devoted to setting up public forums, and the social and recreational side was not heavily stressed; but, as additional funds permitted, more emphasis was placed on recreation.

The philosophy of the Rochester group was that the school is a logical meetingplace for the entire community and that in it various recreational, social, educational, and cultural needs might be satisfied. The school gymnasiums were opened to adults, and game rooms were equipped and placed under capable supervision. Proceedings were put on a democratic basis and the participants planned their own programs. Within three years the movement had become so popular that an appropriation of $20,000 was made to open 18 public schools as social centers.

The Rochester experiment spread to other parts of the country. Wisconsin passed a law in 1910 giving school boards the right to open school buildings for recreational and educational purposes outside of school hours, and also to allow their use for public forums. In 1941, the National Education Association approved the use of school buildings for community purposes. The movement has grown steadily and has proved to be a satisfactory method of organizing the cultural and recreational activities of the community. In 1946, 44 per cent of all community playgrounds, 51 per cent of athletic fields, and 79 per cent of indoor community centers were located on school property.

Public forums as a community agency. One of the most important developments in the community center movement, whether located in school buildings or elsewhere, has been the provision of public forums where local and visiting speakers can present important public and local issues and then submit them to discussion and questioning after the formal lecture. In this way, the community can be enlightened concerning local, state, national, and international issues. Of course, people can now get information on such issues from newspapers and radio reports, but they have no way of discussing such information directly with editors, columnists, and commentators. The public forum provides not only for the dissemination of information but also for group discussion of the issues presented. In New Deal days, Federal Commissioner of Education John W. Studebaker provided a corps of able forum leaders who traveled throughout the country addressing local forums. The discontinuance of this service was as regrettable as the ending of the Federal theater, music, art, and writing projects.

Effect of the First World War on community organization. Organized community planning rose to a new high level of activity during the First World War. The National Education Association appointed a Coordinating Committee on the Development of Community Centers to unify community activities during the war. Where training camps were located, the National Recreation Association undertook to organize all the resources of the community so that the leisure hours of the soldiers and sailors might be pleasantly and profitably spent.

The request for community organization came at a time when most public energies were devoted to war activities. Community Service, Inc., composed of those who had been most active in the supervised playground movement, was organized to promote recreational activities on a large scale, with full community support. The scattering of training camps among many communities served to focus public attention on the need for a recreational program in peacetime as well as in wartime. Interest developed on a national scale, large sums of money were raised, special recreational buildings were erected, and all social agencies cooperated to provide adequate recreation for the enlisted men encamped in the community. The united spirit shown in this emergency demonstrated the possibilities of community efforts in a common cause. The wartime interest in recreation had a permanent effect. The emergency activities and successes demonstrated that sufficient funds could be found and that trained leadership and a community spirit could be stimulated if the community banded together.

Although the wartime efforts stimulated organized community recreation, they did not effectively promote the school community center movement. An organization known as the Community Center Association, which had been founded in 1915, took over leadership in this field. The original stimulus came from the work of the National Education Association. Since 1924, the *Journal of Social Forces* (now *Social Forces*) has served as the official organ of the Community Center Association.

Community activities extended during Second World War. The Second World War had even greater influence than the first, again because larger numbers of persons were involved. There were more war workers and more members of the armed services stationed in army and navy camps and bases. Some of the recreation programs were provided at the camps by the Red Cross and the USO (United Services Organizations). By 1943, through the efforts of the Recreation Section of the Office of Community War Services, more than 1,500 cities and towns had organized Defense Recreation Committees to develop and correlate their community programs and to direct them toward serving the needs of wartime recreation. Some communities were able to meet the entire cost of the expanded recreation program, but in other communities professional and financial aid was given by the Federal government.

Buildings were hastily erected to serve as clubhouses for servicemen and women. Athletic programs were organized and trained leaders were in demand. Tennis courts and swimming pools were built. Hobby classes were formed. Volunteer helpers served at the USO headquarters, which held almost continual "open house," providing food and entertainment. Private households were urged to invite servicemen as guests for dinner and the weekend. Some communities—especially those in the vicinity of the larger camps and bases—had well-organized programs in which a wide variety of recreational facilities were made available.

Recreation for war workers, too, received considerable attention from many communities. Some firms employing war workers expanded their recreational programs. In 1942, the National Industrial Recreation Association was formed to aid industries to enlarge their recreational facilities. After the war, some firms and some communities continued their programs, partly owing to the demands of the war workers and veterans who returned to their communities. It may be that the impetus given to community and industrial recreation during the war helped to bring about the notable increase in public recreational facilities after 1945.

Community recreation stimulates other community activities. The recreation movement offers an excellent example of community organization. Its early leaders had to utilize all the available forces in the community to put their program across. This meant placing primary emphasis on recreation and neglecting other phases of public welfare, but such overemphasis on one program was to be expected when there was no coordination of activities. When the entire community was ready to support a program of recreation, a step had been taken toward more complete community organization. The school center movement represented a more comprehensive approach to community organization because it recognized that recreation is only one possible community use of a school building. It demonstrated that recreation is only one of several social problems in a congested area of the city, and it thus paved the way for other phases of community action.

COMMUNITY MUSIC, DRAMA, PAGEANTRY, AND ART AS SOCIALIZING FORCES

Community interest in the arts develops after the First World War. Some of the recent community activities in music, pageantry, festivals, and drama show a definite trend toward community organization of a permanent character. The remarkable development of community interest in the arts after the First World War may be seen from the 1924 report of the Carnegie Corporation on "The Place of the Arts in American Life." Out of 660 community houses, 236 had community singing, 219 theatrical performances, 192 pageants, 168 instruction in crafts, 256 bands and orchestras, and 58 community theaters.

BOARD OF EDUCATION, PORT BYRON, N. Y.

A prize-winning centralized school band, Port Byron, New York.

Growth of community music. Since the First World War, music has come to be recognized as a valuable recreational, educational, moral, and cultural force in the community. The emphasis on music springs in part from the fundamental fact that it helps to develop the latent tastes, hopes, and aspirations of the individual. The growing popularity of concerts, the organization of community choruses, pageants, and masques with musical accompaniment indicate the desire for self-expression through cooperation and association with others. Large cities like New York, Boston, and Rochester have long had excellent community choruses, but within recent years the movement has spread to smaller towns and rural communities.

A first attempt to create community music in an isolated rural community in Delaware offers an example. The first meeting took place in a small schoolhouse. At the end of a hard day's work on the farm, 18 or 20 persons came in farm wagons and old buggies to see what the "singin' teacher" wanted. None of them had any musical training, and there was no musical instrument of any sort available. The teacher had to instruct them in simple songs and to encourage them to join in the singing. The first meeting was not altogether successful, but gradually the farmers grew interested because they found they enjoyed singing together.

As time went on, the original group increased to 40. A man with a strong tenor voice gradually became courageous enough to take the lead in some of the songs. The exhilaration of singing together created a friendly feeling that lasted after the meeting. The group lingered around the stove to talk over some of their mutual problems. The interest fostered in the singing class carried over into the daily life of the participants. The radio programs they listened to took on more meaning; the simple folk songs of other countries taught them by their leader gave them a certain amount of sympathy for people of other lands. But most important of all were the expressions of neighborliness, loyalty, and cooperation.

Community music enriches community life. From such modest beginnings, many communities have carried their musical activities much further. Participation in local group singing has led to a desire to combine with other communities. Some communities have worked up county festivals. In larger groups, community music took on wider social significance. It gave new meaning to cooperation, not only along the lines of music but on larger community issues.

Industrial centers have found that, in many instances, music has served a real community need. To workers and their families, the community chorus has meant relaxation and an appreciation of their own efforts. Music has helped to engender community pride and a spirit of fellowship, and it has encouraged participation in a common interest.

The formation of music groups has also led to a growth in initiative and leadership for both the individual and the community. One of the leaders in a community music group was so encouraged by the praises of his association that he began seriously to study vocal music, and he finally secured a scholarship at a conservatory of music. One community music group, meeting in a dilapidated schoolhouse, raised funds to supply a stove, more light, and a piano for the schoolhouse, and to repaint the walls. This same group decided to form a dramatics group, which also was to meet in the schoolhouse, and later formed a handicraft class to make draperies for the room and a woodworking unit to remodel the furniture. Community interest was thus focused around the schoolhouse, and community organization and group unity of a permanent and valuable nature were achieved through an initial concern with music.

Schools and colleges have long been aware of community interest in school bands and orchestras. In many communities, the school band and orchestra have become an important unit in every community celebration. In Richmond, Indiana, interest in the school band led to the appointment of the public school music teacher as the paid leader of community singing. Not all communities can achieve as much prominence as has Bethlehem, Pennsylvania, for its Bach festival, or Lindsborg, Kansas, for its yearly presentation of Handel's *Messiah,* but music as a socializing force can become a significant phase of community organization. The famous Berkshire Music Festival, held each summer in western Massachusetts, though performed by outside artists, has developed not only a community but even a regional interest in good music.

The community theater. The local theater has also encouraged the trend toward community organization. In recent years, graduates of universities and schools of dramatic art have gone to communities where there was no theater and have established drama groups backed either by some local civic organization or by subscriptions sold in the community. The community theater has come to be an important part of community life in many towns. In some instances, the theater is subsidized by the city; in others, it pays its own way; and in still others, it is even built and operated by the city for the benefit of the people.

The growth of the community theater movement was further stimulated by the Federal Theater, a project of the Works Progress Administration. The Federal Theater made it clear that people are interested in attending plays, if they can afford to do so, and that motion pictures have not destroyed all interest in the legitimate stage. The Federal Theater also proved that the theater movement, to be successful, must be "sold" to the people of the community, and that, if the people have a chance to help in creating it and carrying it on, they will heartily support it.

One of the most interesting examples of theater-minded communities is found in North Dakota. Alfred G. Arwold of the North Dakota Agricultural College believed that the theater might play an important part in promoting community life in ordinarily drab areas. Although the movement started in the city of Fargo, it has spread throughout the state. Under the earnest leadership of Arwold, hundreds of men and women have dabbed grease paint on their faces and have appeared before lantern footlights in old barns. In many communities the plays, with themes familiar to the people of the plains, are written by local persons and are performed by local farmers. Plays during the Christmas season, on the Fourth of July, or at harvest time have been most successful, for the festivals give the whole community an opportunity to participate. The community theater experiment in North Dakota indicates that the whole community should be interested to make a project successful.

The St. Louis Little Theater is a combination of professional and community talents. Many of the actors are residents of the community, but the theater also maintains a permanent staff of actors. The St. Louis Little Theater has been operating successfully for more than 25 years. It is supported by the community without any private endowment, because it has made the community not only a spectator but a part of the cast. Summer theaters maintained in healthful and scenic communities by professional urban actors have helped to develop community interest in the drama.

Community pageantry. Most sections of the country have become pageant-conscious. The pageant is an excellent vehicle for community organization because it requires a large cast and because it usually depicts an event of local community interest. The pageant movement has become nationwide. Between 1925 and 1931, history came alive on the battlefields of the North and the South when many communities cele- brated famous battles by portraying them in the form of pageants. In 1938 covered wagon trains left Independence, Missouri, to retrace the trails to the West. In August, 1940, at the sesquicentennial of the found- ing of Cooperstown, New York, a pageant was given with a cast of 400.

One of the most interesting community pageants was that of the "Lost Colony" staged on Roanoke Island, off the coast of North Carolina. Here, in the sixteenth century, legend has it, the first English colony in America was organized and later disappeared. With the help of the Federal Theater, artists, and technicians, the "Lost Colony" became not only a community project but a money-making proposition. It is estimated that, in the summers of 1938 and 1939, over 250,000 persons visited Roanoke Island. Colonial Virginia, as "the seedbed of democracy," is the theme of the community pageant, "The Common Glory," given each summer since 1947 at Williamsburg, Virginia. So far, the pageant has not been a financial success, but it has attracted large crowds.

Community pageants and folk festivals have become popular through- out the Southwest. Each year fiestas are held in various sections to commemorate religious or historical events. For example, in New Mexico, the victory of Diego de Vargos, who in 1692 recaptured from the Pueblo Indians what is now the city of Albuquerque, is celebrated with an elaborate community festival. School teachers instruct the children in native dances so that they can participate in the festival. Such folk dramas as "Our Lady of Guadalupe," "The Lost Child," and "The Comanche" are presented, together with religious celebrations, songs, and folk dances.

Community art and community life. The teaching of art and the appreciation of art is usually a slow process in community life. Often the natural urge of women to beautify the home is a starting point. Most women desire attractive homes, but many do not know how to go about making the necessary improvements. Farm women, living most of their lives in drab dwellings, and women living in rented homes in small towns derive benefit from a community art project.

The methods used by teachers of art groups have been varied. Teaching women how to make hooked rugs, lamp shades, or similar objects, and how to rearrange furniture, set attractive tables, and make the proper use of color in the home are only a few of the effective types of instruction. Working in groups, the women have added to their knowledge and appre- ciation of art, have gained confidence in their own judgment, and have lost some of their prejudices. Moreover, they have gained in friendliness and in appreciation of the ideas of others.

Classes in community art have often led to a desire to beautify the community. In one instance, an adult art class that decided to decorate the schoolhouse worked in cooperation with the parent-teacher organization to decorate the teachers' rest room and the classrooms in an artistic but inexpensive fashion. In one Delaware town, a "clean up" and "paint up" campaign was sponsored by members of the art class, who had become aware of the dingy physical environment in which they lived. A garden club was begun, prizes were given for the neatest lawns and the most beautiful gardens, and a vacant lot was converted into a park. Daily life thus took on a new meaning through community art, which contributed to an enrichment of community life.

Through lecturers brought in by the instructor, the members of an art class learned that a house can be constructed along good lines as cheaply as along poor ones. Several young couples built homes according to the sound architectural ideas learned in the class. One adult art class in a community in which a new town hall was being built was able to bring about a change in the plans, so that the building would be more pleasing to the eye. In one instance, the interest stimulated by an adult art class in civic architecture led to city planning.

Education in art has produced increased appreciation of general community problems. Some communities have found that interest in adult art classes has led to a serious concern with problems of prejudice, health, sanitation, and education. Appreciation of beauty has created a desire to improve the community.

In many communities, adult art and music classes have thus meant that individuals and groups have found a path to a fuller and richer life. Many individuals have often found that they can overcome shyness and timidity by participating in community activities. The improvement in daily living and the extension of the individual's efforts into those of the group have developed better social values. Learning to appreciate beautiful things is of permanent value. In working together, people also learn tolerance, appreciation of others, and cooperation. With an art or music group as an opening wedge, community organization of all activities has frequently been made easier.

One of the reasons why music and art are so valuable as a means of community organization is that they appeal to every age group. There is no limit to the possibilities of the growth of this influence in the community. Today, in particular, when primary groups are dissolving, when the problems of living are becoming increasingly more complicated, and when individual and group needs are greater than ever before, the group must use every means at its command to make community life richer. So far, no better means than community music, drama, and art have been discovered.

COMMUNITY ORGANIZATION AND PUBLIC HEALTH

Rise of the public health movement. The public health movement is also a vital part of community organization. Laws may be passed and regulations enforced; but, unless the whole community cooperates in carrying out unified health education, the program cannot be fully successful.

The public health movement deals with the community rather than with the individual. Persons who are ill have always been the concern of humane persons, but organized efforts of the community to promote better health are relatively new. Any well-organized public health program will be concerned with a safe water supply, the disposal of waste, and the control and isolation of infectious and contagious disease. But there must also be emphasis on health education to acquaint the general public with early symptoms of disease and to enable each citizen to help himself, his children, and his neighbors to keep healthy. In other words, the logical approach to the public health problem is through the community on the theory that the welfare of individuals means the welfare of the community. The public health program is, therefore, an excellent field for stimulating community interest. In many cases, interest in the health of the group leads to well-directed organization in other fields of community activity.

Development of the city health council. The health activities of urban communities are under the direction of the state and local boards of health. Many public health activities, such as the provision of a safe water supply and the sanitary disposal of sewage and garbage, are maintained by law. Other activities, such as the construction of hospitals and the establishment of clinics, are usually carried on voluntarily. It is to the private or semiprivate organizations, such as the American Red Cross, the American Public Health Association, the American Child Health Association, the National Tuberculosis Association, and countless others, that we are indebted for most of the constructive movements in community health.

As might be expected, the intervention of these numerous agencies in community affairs at first caused much confusion and wasteful duplication of efforts. As with public welfare, attempts have been made to coordinate the work of the numerous health agencies. The City Health Council, a federation of all urban health agencies, operates as a clearing house in health matters, and serves to unify the efforts. The health council idea has been adopted by many cities, among them Cincinnati, Boston, and Cleveland.

The community health center. Although the city health council federates the city health agencies, the Health Center is a better example of the possibilities of community organization for public health. The health center is to the urban neighborhood what the city health council is to the entire city. In most cities, the health center represents a step forward in community organization, because it unifies the activities of all the welfare and health agencies operating in one urban neighborhood. So many aspects of the health problem are connected with social work that it is impossible to think of one without the other. The social worker depends to a great extent on the services of the health agency, and the health agency cannot conduct an effective therapeutic program without the welfare agency. The health center operates on the principle that its services will be utilized by the people who need them most.

The first health center in the United States was established in Milwaukee, in 1911, but the movement did not grow rapidly until the First World War, when the American Red Cross adopted it as a project. By

1920, about 900 Red Cross chapters were engaged in some form of health-center activities. More recently, the public schools helped to build up interest in health-center activities and services.

To illustrate its community emphasis, a notable health center may be cited as an example. The East Harlem Health Center in New York City, which serves about 120,000 persons, was organized in 1930. The enterprise was sponsored by the Red Cross and approved by the city department of health. Twenty-three organizations, composed of nursing agencies, family welfare societies, health officers, and settlements, joined the unified program. Representatives from each agency comprise an advisory council that tries to prevent duplication of effort.

The Harlem Health Center is a neighborhood institution, and it is impressed on the people, through the educational program, that the Center belongs to them and that it is for their use. The program is both therapeutic and preventive. Hospitals and clinics are accessible, nursing facilities are available, and the family welfare societies have cooperated by promoting a boys' club and community work in the Center's school. The local physicians and druggists, once they understood the program, gave the closest cooperation. The Harlem Health Center has gained the trust and confidence of the entire community.

In general, health centers have proved very successful. One of their most important contributions to community organization is to serve as a demonstration area or laboratory. The idea of using the community as a laboratory, to show what can be done through social organization, gained favor after the First World War. The usual practice is to choose a particular community with a definite problem and then to develop and carry out a carefully planned program as a model for other communities. The health demonstration idea has been used to show how diseases may be cured and prevented, and how better community health can be promoted. The Federal Hospital Survey and Construction Act of 1946 has helped the health-center movement. About 450 health centers had been set up by 1950.

The health demonstration project carried on in the Bellevue-Yorkville area in New York City is an illustration of the value of health services in a community. With financial assistance from the Milbank Memorial Fund, the project covered the period from 1927 through 1933. The demonstration was carried on under the direct supervision of the Department of Health, and with the cooperation of all agencies. The 175,000 persons living in this crowded area received intensive health services during this 7-year period. During the time when the project was in operation, the infant mortality rate decreased notably; the death rate from tuberculosis, diphtheria, and typhoid also declined. The project cost about $900,000 for the entire period—a per capita annual cost of 61 cents —in addition to the regular expenditures of the health department and the private agencies.

The survey method has also been used as a phase of community efforts to promote public health. As with all social surveys, health surveys may be limited to one phase of the health problem, or they may cover the entire health situation of a community. By means of the survey, an accurate picture of health conditions may be gained, and, with sufficient publicity, the community is often awakened to its needs and encouraged to solve some of its more pressing public health problems.

Community safety campaigns. Closely related to the public health activities of communities are community safety programs. Though sometimes launched by independent community action, they are usually stimulated or guided by the National Safety Council, a nonprofit organization founded in 1912, with headquarters in Chicago.

Most community safety programs are devoted primarily to reducing traffic accidents. For this, the National Safety Council has a tripartite program built around the so-called Three E's—Engineering, Enforcement, and Education. Engineering covers the problem of safer highways, streets, and motor cars, and better traffic facilities and regulations. Enforcement is concerned with the laws covering traffic and its violations, and the arrest and conviction of as many violators as possible. Education involves complete and accurate instruction concerning the safest and most skillful methods of driving on highways and city streets. In 1943, Lansing, Michigan, launched a community safety program built around the Three E's. After it had been in operation for a year, the number of fatal accidents was cut in half.

An interesting case of independent community activity in behalf of safety was conducted by Topeka, Kansas, which in 1945 ranked 57th in traffic safety among 64 American cities with a population of 50,000 to 100,000. In April, 1946, the Chamber of Commerce and various civic groups decided to set up a Safety Council. The Topeka safety campaign utilized the Three E's, but especially stressed safety education. Much use was made of safety forums, radio talks, safety movies, safety pamphlets, warning cards, posters. The Boy Scouts, Girl Scouts, and other groups were drafted into service to carry on safety propaganda and pageantry. As a result of the community safety activities, Topeka reduced traffic deaths by 55 per cent in one year, and instead of being near the bottom of the cities of its class with respect to safety, it rose to fourth place.

The most conspicuous example of success in community safety programs, however, is that of Stillwater, Oklahoma, a city of 30,000 inhabitants which had no deaths from traffic accidents during the 10 years following January, 1939. Engineers worked with the city authorities in mapping out a good safety plan. Streets were marked off properly, and plenty of stop-signs were installed. Traffic officers were strategically placed. The schools, starting with the kindergarten, stressed safety education. The newspapers and radio stations cooperated heartily in the safety campaign. The campaign worked almost perfectly, in spite of the fact that the community had to cope with about 80,000 visitors annually. The city was awarded top honors in the country by the National Safety Council.

The examples of Lansing, Topeka, and Stillwater are only representative of what can be done to promote community safety with a program intelligently conceived and earnestly executed.

COMMUNITY ORGANIZATION AND PUBLIC WELFARE

Coordination of private and public agencies in community work. Brief mention was made earlier of the attempts to coordinate the efforts of private charitable agencies during the nineteenth century. Actually, however, the more constructive efforts in the social welfare field have come only in relatively recent years. In the decades following 1900, there was an awakening of public consciousness and a realization that the community had to assume some of the burden of caring for the needy.

Private and public welfare agencies have long existed side by side. Formerly, a great gulf separated them. Private agencies attempted to deal scientifically with poverty and allied problems, to set up high standards for professional social workers, and to develop the case-work technique. Public agencies, on the other hand, all too often gave funds to those in need without understanding the causes of poverty or how the community was responsible for their plight. More recently, however, the public and the private social agencies have coordinated and unified their activities more successfully. One indication of this is the entrance of an ever greater number of professional social workers into public agencies. Since 1935, the Social Security Act has caused rapid strides to be made in the professionalization of public relief work.

Gradually, the feeling of community responsibility is growing, and, with it, the demand for trained workers to administer relief. Today the majority of persons believe that welfare work has as vital a claim on the community's taxes as education, recreation, or health. Instead of leaving the care of orphans, neglected children, and the handicapped to private charity, the public is beginning to understand that it is the duty of the community to care for its dependents with public funds. Recently there has been much emphasis on coordination and cooperation in the administration of relief, in order that efficient care may be given at a minimum cost. In the future, it is likely that every enlightened community will appraise its needs and coordinate its program both of private and of public social work from the standpoint of the entire community.

Rise of the community chest movement. The financial federation is an important step in the direction of coordinated social work as well as an excellent example of the substitution of group effort for individual action. The financial federation is now ordinarily known as the Community Chest. The first financial federation was launched in Denver in 1887. Elmira, New York, set up a financial federation in 1910. Because of its endorsement by the Chamber of Commerce, the financial federation movement was developed in Cleveland between 1900 and 1913, and in the latter year the Cleveland Federation for Charity and Philanthropy was founded. This was the first true community chest organization, and Cincinnati immediately followed suit. The First World War gave an impetus to the community chest movement. A lump sum of money was contributed to the war chest and was then distributed to member agencies. After the war, the community chest came to be widely used as a means of securing money for civilian welfare activities in peacetime.

The community chest movement rests on sound social and financial principles. The various private agencies determine their monetary needs, based in part on those of the preceding year, and then submit an estimate to the budget committee of the community chest. The combined estimates of all the private agencies sharing in the chest is the gross amount set as the goal to be met in the annual drive. Volunteers canvass the community, and the money raised is then divided among the agencies. Today about 1,320 cities and large towns have community chests that operate on a year-round basis. Community Chests and Councils of America, organized in 1918, is the national organization to which the majority of local chest organizations—some 1,100—belong.

The community chest movement grew remarkably in the 1940's. The number of chests more than doubled (from 560 to 1,320), and the funds raised rose from 83 million dollars in 1938 to 192 million in 1950. The all-time high was 221 million which was raised in 1945, because of wartime conditions. The sources of contributions to community chests over the years have been found to be about as follows: 40 per cent of the funds come from corporations; 25 per cent from employee groups; 25 per cent as gifts of $100 or over from foundations and private individuals; and about 10 per cent from all other contributors. Corporation contributions have notably increased in the last decade, in part as a mode of reducing taxation. The average per capita contribution is about $2.50, ranging from a low of about $2 in the Southeast to a high of about $3.25 in New England. About 23 per cent of the population contribute.

A paid director and staff have the responsibility of acquainting the public with the work of the agencies participating in the chest. The success of this educational program carried on throughout the year determines, to a large extent, the outcome of the drive for funds.

With few exceptions, businessmen favor the idea of the community chest because they prefer to give a lump sum at one time rather than to be called upon for several smaller donations during the year. They also realize that, in the long run, their single annual donation may cost them less. There is also another reason why the community chest is a practical method of raising funds: to social workers and those interested in the community, it provides a unified and coordinated program expressing the will of the community. Another less important result of the establishment of the community chest, but one worth noting, is that the record of each agency's work and expenses is carefully considered by the budget committee of the chest. An agency failing to perform its task will not continue indefinitely to receive funds from the community. The community chest thus represents the efficient organization of a community working toward a common goal—the well-being of all of its members.

COMMUNITY ORGANIZATION IN THE SMALL COMMUNITY

Relative neglect of the small community. The community problems of the city have become so engrossing and evident that the needs of the rural areas and the small towns have often been overlooked. Arthur E.

Morgan, former president of Antioch College and first Chairman of the Tennessee Valley Authority, in his book, *The Small Community: the Foundation of Democratic Life,* contends that it is "high time that the significance of the small community be recognized." Small communities are the sources of the city populations. The birth rate of cities is so low that the population must be renewed from outside sources in order that the city may survive many more generations. The small community is the chief source of local social leadership. Within the small community, the sharing of problems and the development of mutual respect and tolerance are the principles most needed to be taught by one who is to be a leader. Morgan believes that the enduring basis of our civilization is to be found in those traits fostered by the intimate associations of the small community.

Examples of community organization in small communities. There are many difficulties inherent in a small area which hinder community organization. Many towns and rural areas are stagnant and devoid of leadership. There is often jealousy and clannishness between families. Religious and political factions hamper development, and vested interests prevent cooperation. Often, the lack of qualified persons limits welfare activities because most small towns and rural communities insist on having home or county persons handle the welfare work.

During the last 15 years, however, there have been encouraging developments. To secure Federal funds for Social Security programs, minimum standards of social case work must be maintained. The insistence that a social worker must be something more than just a person "who likes people" has helped to bring in better trained welfare workers from outside the narrow limits of the town or county. There are signs of increasing awareness of community problems on the part of both individuals and groups. Some forward-looking ministers of small-town churches have taken the lead in helping their communities to develop a neighborly spirit. The rôle of the church in leading the small community to organize its resources has been limited, but if the church does take an active part in community organization, its influence is likely to be considerable. Consolidated churches in rural communities have at times exerted a notable influence on the promotion of community projects.

As evidence that a town or rural community can successfully develop community organization, a few examples might be mentioned. Schools— as, for example, Squaw Point in the rural area of Minnesota—have become the focal point of many a community. In the Squaw Point area, the school is a practical workshop drawing the whole community into its projects. The children plant gardens in the spring as part of their schoolwork. Not only do the children learn how seeds grow, but the garden supplies vegetables for the school lunches that are prepared by mothers and girls at the school. There is a community store located at the school that sells surplus vegetables at cost to the parents of the school children. One year, sufficient profit was made to purchase 300 "baby chicks," which the children raised and sold. The whole community has become interested in the school project, and cooperation in other enterprises has thus been made easier.

In Montpelier, Vermont, a town of about 8,000, the unused basement in the city hall was converted into a recreation center for the young people. Funds were collected to install a juke-box, and equipment for table pool, table tennis, and basketball was secured. As a result of growing interest, the facilities of the community were studied by a citizens' committee, the municipal park was enlarged, and a recreational supervisor was employed.

Small community finances. The problem of community finance in the small community often creates difficulties because of the fact that county and state officials largely control the distribution of funds. There are a limited number of persons who can afford to give generously to private agencies or community projects. The small businessman, for example, usually cannot afford to contribute large sums. Although finance is a serious problem, many phases of small community organization only require a knowledge of means by which to make the most of the existing community resources and the enlistment of local aid. In part, the organization, Community Services, Inc., sponsored by Morgan, meets this pressing problem of the small community. Community Services offers professional assistance and counsel to small towns and rural neighborhoods that wish to discover their group potentialities and the meaning of "community."

Forums in small communities. The development of the small community is still in its initial stages. There are numerous facilities for encouraging citizen participation. The forum is a device by which community education can be furthered; it also serves as a means of discovering community tensions and discussing them in a democratic fashion. At the forum programs, citizens may hear a lecture on current problems by an outside speaker or one of their own group, and in the discussion period following the lecture they have an opportunity to ask questions. Two or more speakers may present different points of view on subjects of national and international scope. If the forum is developed in the small community, it can serve much the same purpose as the New England town meeting of colonial times. The town meeting depended on intimate face-to-face contacts and the opportunity of every citizen to be heard. The forum movement can be an integral part of the community organization movement, and it can be developed even in the small community where intimate contacts with others can still be maintained.

Community organization a solution to the social problems of corporate farming. In an earlier chapter on rural life in the machine age, we discussed the disadvantages in regard to community spirit and public utilities and services which are to be found in the great mechanized corporate farming communities, which tend to develop into a sort of present-day mechanized *latifundia*. They are far inferior to the small farming areas in comparable surroundings with respect to community spirit, public facilities, health programs, recreational projects, and the like. Yet, economic forces are producing a very definite trend towards large-scale mechanized farming. The solution of this perplexing situation probably lies in the development of systematic community organization in mechanized farming areas. If necessary, Federal and state funds would be provided to support this type of community work, which promises to be the most needed and useful form of organized effort in rural communities, especially in the West and South.

THE REGION AS A COMMUNITY

Rise of regionalism. The idea that a natural geographic region should provide the physical framework for unified community efforts was first suggested by Frédéric Le Play, the founder of the social survey movement. The regional approach was further developed by Le Play's English disciples, Patrick Geddes and Victor Branford, and brought over to the United States by Geddes' disciple, Lewis Mumford. It has been utilized by Howard W. Odum of the University of North Carolina and a number of American ecologists. The regional concept had long before been made use of by a University of Wisconsin historian, Frederick Jackson Turner, in his interpretation of American history.

Nature of regions. Although the idea of regionalism in social reform is relatively new, regional problems have long existed. City, county, or state lines do not act as fences to enclose social problems within their boundaries. Rivers like the Tennessee, the Colorado, the Missouri, the Columbia, and the Ohio serve several states. Whole areas, regardless of political boundaries, have common problems arising from similar natural resources, geographic influences, or cultural patterns. To treat social and economic problems from a regional point of view is to recognize the broad community of interest and to utilize the total resources of entire regions in order to raise the level of living for all.

Socially regarded, the regional concept is sound; politically, there may be difficulty in organizing communities without primary regard for political boundaries. Because state, county, and local municipalities are "sovereign" powers in many matters, they can prohibit the use of funds outside their boundaries or resist the extension of Federal activities into their area of control.

There is some confusion whether regionalism should be applied to a unified geographical and economic area or only to areas in which there are already similar interests. Some regions in the United States, according to Odum, have common interests and problems because they have similar geographic and social conditions. One of the ablest exponents of regionalism, he develops the thesis that, if the Southeast region can transcend state lines and consider its problems on a regional basis, it will improve its economic, social, and political conditions and better develop its potentially great natural and human resources.

Achievements of community organization in the regional framework. One of the best examples of the development of the total resources of a region is the Tennessee Valley Authority, which serves the region drained by the Tennessee River and four of its tributaries. As a result of the development of the river for effective navigation, the generation of electric power, and provision for flood control, an area of over 40,000 square miles, occupied by more than 2½ million persons, has been transformed. Resources have been conserved as well as developed. Erosion has been halted. Demonstrations of new fertilizers and farming techniques have raised the standard of living of the entire area. Health programs have improved the level of efficiency by reducing illness; model schools have improved education; recreation centers and social case work have helped to solve many of the former personal and social problems. Some persons regard the TVA as having produced a new high level in social democracy; others of a conservative cast of mind fear that the planned community, such as the TVA and the "Greenbelt" communities, under the supervision of the Farm Security Administration, represents a dangerous trend toward expanded government control.

Recently, regionalism has received much emphasis in the long-range plans of the Bureau of Reclamation. The projects are planned around the development of western land and water resources through the building of dams and reservoirs, and they have extended irrigation facilities to create new farms, factories, jobs, and homes. If the Bureau's plans are carried out, the 17 western states will have large regions served by power provided by Federal funds. The concept of the social community developed in the TVA may thus be extended to the areas restored by the reclamation projects, and the basins of the Missouri, Colorado, Columbia, and many other rivers may be loci for the development of human and natural resources far beyond the present range of achievement.

THE PLANNED COMMUNITY AS A WAY OF PROMOTING COMMUNITY ORGANIZATION

Origin of community planning. The development of natural and human resources of large areas, such as the Tennessee Valley, the river basins of the West, or a special section of the country, is regional planning on a large scale. However, the rebuilding of a city or a section of a city is also regional planning in miniature.

A community so planned that its physical layout and equipment provide the maximum of comfort and well-being for those groups living within its limits has long engaged the attention of social reformers. Charles Fourier, the French Utopian Socialist, based his scheme for social reorganization on a community limited in size and organized into small groups to promote efficiency and greater enjoyment of life. Robert Owen, the English industrialist and social reformer of the first half of the nineteenth century, put his ideas into practice in New Lanark, Scotland, the site of his cotton factories. Owen regarded the unsanitary, poverty-stricken condition of his workers as a hindrance to their industrial efficiency and personal contentment. Not only did he organize a large-scale welfare program in his textile mills, but he built better homes and set up stores for his workers.

The garden city. At the close of the nineteenth century, Ebenezer Howard, an office worker in London who was appalled by the living conditions of the English slums, planned a model community which he called a "garden city." Howard's idea, inspired by Patrick Geddes, was to decentralize the industrial city by distributing small units over the whole urban area. These small units combined the best features of both urban and rural life—small, one-family dwellings, open spaces for recreation, and an industrial area separate from the residential area. In 1903, the garden city of Letchworth, with a population of 15,000, was founded on the Howard plan; it was the model for several others later.

Radburn, New Jersey. A few model communities were developed in the United States after the First World War. For example, Radburn, New Jersey, within a short distance of New York City, was developed as a "garden city." Designed by Clarence S. Stein and built following 1929, it was a limited-dividend project of the New York City Housing Corporation. Under the limited-dividend plan, philanthropic capital is invested to return only a small dividend. In Radburn, special areas were designed for business, residence, shopping, and recreation, but, unlike the English "garden city," no agricultural area surrounded Radburn. The automobile hazard received special attention. Underpasses were constructed so that persons might go from one part of the city to the other without crossing the highway; children could go to school, to parks, and to playgrounds without danger. Radburn is still a middle-class community with a large number of children, and it has developed a strong feeling of community responsibility. It is a good example of community organization made possible, in part, by good physical planning.

The Federal "greenbelt" projects. During the 1930's, several experiments were tried with planned communities. The most notable of these were the greenbelt projects. Begun in 1935 by the Resettlement Administration, the projects were taken over in 1937 by the Farm Security Administration of the Department of Agriculture. The greenbelt communities were intended to be rural-industrial communities financed by Federal funds and located near cities of rapid growth. Five communities were planned, but only three were developed to any extent—Greenbelt, Maryland, near Washington, D. C.; Greenhills, Ohio, near Cincinnati; and Greendale, Wisconsin, near Milwaukee. Of these, Greenbelt, Maryland, was the most important, because of the size and maturity of development attained. The greenbelt town differed from the garden city program in that it was not expected to be self-sufficient; it was planned to provide homes and community life for the low-salaried workers of the nearby city.

Greenbelt, Maryland, was laid out to give full scope for community life. It was built in the shape of a crescent, with pastures for the community dairy, space for athletic fields and playgrounds, and a wooded area surrounding the crescent for privacy and a rural atmosphere. The residential district was laid out in oversize blocks. Each block formed a natural neighborhood with a small park and playground in its center.

A town common and a business center were within easy distance of the residential and recreational areas. The combination community center and school served as the focal point for all types of activities of the members of the community—religious, civic, and recreational. The citizens organized a Greenbelt Citizens' Association, a health association, a credit union, a community dramatic society, and a public forum. Before the Second World War, a considerable degree of social solidarity had been reached, although the occupants had lived in the project only for a short item. In 1942, however, the Greenbelt community was made a part of the defense housing program. The original plan to admit only families with small incomes who could adjust to community life was abandoned as the need for housing increased.

The Greenbelt communities are illustrations of a planned development, with the government as landlord, in which community organization took shape in a democratic fashion in a relatively short time. It represents a planned community program of great promise if the problem of decentralizing our great cities is ever seriously undertaken.

Low-cost housing projects in community planning. Low-cost public-housing projects are an example of the way in which solidarity may be reached through the cooperation of local, state, and national agencies. These projects have been made possible mainly by the United States Housing Act of 1937. In states that have passed enabling acts, a community decides whether it desires a housing project. Funds may be advanced to the local housing authority on easy terms by the Federal Public Housing Authority, or direct grants, to be matched by community funds, are made to the community to finance the project.

A local housing authority, made up of a paid administrative staff and of citizens of the community who serve without pay, operates the project on a nonprofit basis. The representation of industry, welfare, and the professions on local housing authorities is indicative of the community nature of the project and of the cooperation of groups in a problem of mutual interest. By 1950, 43 states had low-rent housing laws and 450 cities and towns had housing programs. Today more than 200,000 units are completed and in operation. The public low-rent project serves not only to clear the slums and to improve the general level of community living, but also to promote community cooperation.

The unique Baltimore slum clearance program. Although Federal aid has provided or stimulated much desirable slum clearance and housing construction, the city of Baltimore has been the only American urban community to develop a comprehensive and effective plan to enforce slum clearance. In 1941, the city adopted a municipal housing code that embodied minimum housing requirements in specific terms and that gave health officials the power to enforce a program of sanitary housing. Owners of slum housing had the choice of losing their property and income through condemnation proceedings or of bringing their property up to designated standards. A housing court, presided over by a magistrate who was an expert on housing and the housing code, was created to hear such cases. The rebuilding program did not dissipate its efforts over a number of sore spots throughout the whole city but wisely concentrated on the complete reconstruction of one slum block at a time.

The taxpayers have become convinced that the project pays them off handsomely. They learned that 40 per cent of their city budget had gone to operate and support the downtown slum areas that made up only 10 per cent of the city's residential districts. They were paying 14 million dollars more each year on the slums than they got back in taxes from the slum areas. Hence, they have been willing to support city bond issues to carry out the slum clearance program. It is to be hoped that other cities will profit by the Baltimore experiment.

Planning in the community may be broad and include all levels of the population; it may involve the creation of a new community; or it may be the rehabilitation of a section of the city. Physical rehabilitation does not necessarily lead to the mobilization of the entire resources of the community and the awakening of social consciousness, but it is a means to this end. It offers unlimited possibilities for community organization in the future.

COURTESY CITY HOUSING CORPORATION.

An aerial view of the Radburn, New Jersey housing project.

The "Yardville" project in Philadelphia. Improved living conditions through community planning may include projects other than new housing. The so-called "Yardville" program, developed in Philadelphia in 1948, was devoted to transforming the dingy back yards of typical working-class city blocks into a combination of flower-garden, playground, and park. The idea was started by *McCall's Magazine,* under the publicity guidance of E. L. Bernays, and was soon sponsored and supported by the Philadelphia City Planning Commission and related organizations. But the program was not forced on the residents. It was explained to them, and, after considerable discussion, was accepted with enthusiasm.

The residents helped with the reconstruction, which has been summarized as follows:

> The high board fences were replaced by trim wire ones. Each back door received a terrace for sitting outside. The cracked, uneven alley was widened and repaired. Garbage cans were recessed out of sight in attractive little alcoves built alongside the gate of each yard. The alley is now a garden path; instead of garbage, you smell fresh-cut grass and flowers.
>
> The greatest effect has been on the children. They are no longer forced to risk their lives playing at dangerous street intersections, or to suffer loneliness indoors. Yardville has become the play center of all the children in the fifteen houses along the alley.... Teen-agers and adults now have a place for picnics, sings and dances. Some of the residents prefer to spend their vacations at home. Yardville residents are so enthusiastic about their renovated backyards that they describe the old days as "living in a chest of drawers." Yardville has also paid off in dollars and cents. It has boosted its own property values a good 25 per cent.[2]

COURTESY FEDERAL PUBLIC HOUSING AUTHORITY.

St. Thomas Street, New Orleans.

Since *McCall's* has a circulation of about 3.5 million, the Yardville experiment attracted much attention at once. As a result, the Yardville plan became a national movement almost overnight. Within a month after it had been described in *McCall's*, no less than 300 cities from 46 states—among them 21 of the most important cities in the country—requested full information about the project. Over a hundred cities have since instituted their own "Yardville" projects.

---

[2] *McCall's Magazine*, February, 1949.

Community organization as a means of social control. We have seen how economic changes since 1750 have caused breakdown of the primary groups—the family, the neighborhood, and the play group—and how it has been necessary for community organizations to take over the functions of social control formerly performed by the primary groups. Among such organizations have been various agencies for child welfare, the charity organization society movement, the settlement movement, the playground movement, and the agencies working to coordinate public

COURTESY FEDERAL PUBLIC HOUSING AUTHORITY.

The picture on the opposite page shows the drab city slum that was the site of the St. Thomas Street project in New Orleans. This picture shows the project after completion. This is an example of what has been accomplished in planned community housing after bad slum conditions have been revealed by social surveys.

health activities. We might add to these the groups that have promoted the organization of school centers and of community forum programs.

In addition to these modes of socialization and control, there are more specialized forms of community organization. Businessmen form a chamber of commerce; farmers unite in marketing associations or consumer cooperatives; farm women form canning and cooking clubs; farm boys and girls join 4-H clubs; and industrial companies, such as the Endicott-Johnson Company, sometimes organize the communities in which their employees live. All such activities represent the modern trend of community organization for welfare purposes. If unity and coordination are achieved through organization, then the field of community organization is unlimited. For instance, poverty, crime, and juvenile delinquency might be greatly restricted if the community set about to eliminate them.

SUMMARY

Community organization is an attempt to fill the gap created by the breakdown of primary groups, the disintegration of traditional patterns of living, and the changes in economic and social life since the Industrial Revolution.

There are many evidences of group action to protect the community as a whole. Fields of activity that were formerly the responsibility of the family or of small groups of individuals have now become matters of state, county, or municipal concern. Relief, housing, public health, education, and child welfare, for example, are now dealt with by public agencies or by government legislation.

In earlier civilizations there was little need for organized community effort because there were fewer needy persons, communities were small, and families and neighborhoods helped one another.

In the days of the later Roman Republic and the Empire, the state provided "bread and circuses" for the city poor. Slavery took care of many of the destitute. The ideals of the Christian church altered these practices. The church taught that responsibility for one's fellows is a cardinal virtue.

During the first thousand years of Christian history, most of the aid to the unfortunate in Christian countries was under the direction of the church. With the breakup of the manorial system and the coming of the Protestant Reformation, the state had to assume increasing responsibility for the care of the distressed and needy.

Several important developments helped to create and guide present-day community organization: (1) the charity organization society movement; (2) the settlement house movement; and (3) the social survey technique.

The modern community movement is an attempt to devise a means by which the educational, recreational, social, economic, and political forces in the community may be so coordinated that all members can adjust themselves satisfactorily to new ways of life and can make the best use of community resources.

The supervised recreation movement is an excellent example of community organization because it offers a substitute for the old neighborhood play group and fills a definite need—that of taking up the increased leisure time of the twentieth century. Although the play movement was first launched to provide recreation for small children, it has grown until it includes recreation for adults, too. It is carried on in parks, community centers, and school buildings. The social settlements have also stimulated the growth of the play movement because they have offered an excellent opportunity for the establishment of cordial relations between the settlement workers and the people of the neighborhood. Planned and supervised recreation in rural areas, however, is still only in its infancy.

The public health movement has aided community organization because it has focused interest on the welfare of individuals in order to promote the welfare of all. The public health program, to succeed, must include an educational program, and it is only through the efforts of the community that such health education can be carried on. Community interest has been stimulated through health centers, health demonstrations, and surveys.

The public welfare program is closely related to the community organization, because the community must take responsibility for its members and must coordinate its efforts, to meet their needs. The financial federation or community chest is an excellent example of the substitution of group effort for individual action and represents a unified and coordinated attempt to provide for some of the chief social welfare needs of the community.

Small towns and rural areas have received little concern in the community organization movement. Potentially, the small town offers great possibilities for the development of community spirit, and gradually the attention of those interested in community organization is turning toward the small community.

The idea of the region as a community transcending political boundaries and solving its common problems is relatively new. Such projects as the Tennessee Valley Authority, the Columbia River developments, and the regional plans of the Bureau of Reclamation indicate possible trends in the future.

SELECTED REFERENCES

*Bernard, Jessie, *American Community Behavior.* New York: Dryden Press, 1949. Recent comprehensive description of community life and organization. Probably the best sociological study of the community as a social force and agency.

Brownell, Baker, *The Human Community.* New York: Harper, 1951. Vigorous historical criticism of the manner in which urban life has disrupted the earlier rural community, its life, and standards of value.

Burchfield, Laverne, *Our Rural Communities.* Chicago: Public Administration Service, 1947. A useful guide book to published materials dealing with rural problems and community activities.

*Butler, G. D., *Introduction to Community Recreation.* New York: McGraw-Hill, 1949. The standard work on the development of community planning and supervision of recreational activities.

*Colcord, Joanna, *Your Community.* New York: Russell Sage Foundation, 1947. Good study of community organization from standpoint of social work.

Elliott, M. A., and Merrill, F. E., *Social Disorganization.* New York: Harper, 1941. Excellent book on the institutional disorganization of our time caused by cultural lag and the disruption of primary institutions.

Faris, R. E. L., *Social Disorganization.* New York: Ronald Press, 1948. The latest book in the field. An excellent sociopsychological study of the subject.

Fink, A. E., *The Field of Social Work.* New York: Holt, 1942. A comprehensive work which touches on many areas in which social work contributes to community planning and programs.

Fredericksen, Hazel, *The Child and His Welfare.* San Francisco: Freeman, 1948.

Good discussion of child caring activities of the community beyond the family scope.

*Hatch, Earl, *Rebuilding Rural America*. New York: Harper, 1950. Brief, but able and up-to-date survey of rural community planning.

*Hillman, Arthur, *Community Organization and Planning*. New York: Macmillan, 1949. An up-to-date textbook covering most phases of community organization projects.

Holden, A. C., *The Settlement Idea*. New York: Macmillan, 1922. A competent account of the social settlement and its role in community organization.

*Hopkirk, H. W., *Institutions Serving Children*. New York: Russell Sage Foundation, 1944. Authoritative description of the community agencies that care for the needs of children.

Hudson, R. B., and Walker, J. O., *Radburn: a Plan of Living*. New York: American Association for Adult Education, 1934. Illuminating survey of life and activities in one of the best-known planned communities of the United States.

Kennedy, A. J., and others, *Social Settlements in New York City*. New York: Columbia University Press, 1935. A thorough and well-illustrated description of the great social settlements in New York City and their varied community activities.

*King, Clarence, *Organizing for Community Action*. New York: Harper, 1948. Good introduction to the general problem of community planning and organization.

Lee, Joseph, *Play in Education*. New York: Macmillan, 1915. A thorough discussion of play in health and character building by the founder of the playground movement in the United States.

*McMillen, Wayne, *Community Organization for Social Welfare*. Chicago: University of Chicago Press, 1945. A comprehensive and authoritative book covering most of the important aspects of the community movement.

Meyer, H. D., and Brightbill, C. K., *Community Recreation: A Guide to Its Organization and Administration*. Boston: Heath, 1948. Elaborate work on the organization and operation of community recreation projects. Contains valuable source-material.

*Morgan, A. E., *The Small Community: Foundation of Democratic Life*. New York: Harper, 1942. Pioneer book on the role and problems of the small community.

Mowrer, E. R., *Disorganization, Personal and Social*. Philadelphia: Lippincott, 1942. Able analysis of the breakdown of primary groups.

Mumford, Lewis, *City Development*. New York: Harcourt, Brace, 1945. Strong argument for the advantages of urban decentralization and small urban communities.

*North, C. C., *The Community and Social Welfare*. New York: McGraw-Hill, 1931. One of the standard treatments of community work by a veteran sociologist.

Norton, W. J., *The Cooperative Movement in Social Work*. New York: Macmillan, 1927. Contains valuable material on community chests.

Odgen, Jean, *Small Community in Action*. New York: Harper, 1946. Important recent work on the activities of the small community.

Odum, Howard, and Moore, H. E., *American Regionalism*. Chapel Hill: University of North Carolina Press, 1938. Pioneer work on regionalism in the United States, stressing its importance in sociology and social geography and as a technique of social planning.

*Osborn, L. D., *Community and Society*. New York: American Book Company, 1933. A standard work on the relation of the community to contemporary social life.

Parten, Mildred, *Surveys, Polls, and Samples.* New York: Harper, 1950. Gives valuable material on history of social surveys, but main stress is on surveys of public opinion.

Pettit, W. W., *Case Studies in Community Organization.* New York: Century, 1928. Valuable material on early programs of community work.

Quinn, J. A., *Human Ecology.* New York: Prentice-Hall, 1950. A standard sociological treatise on the subject. Valuable in relation to regional planning.

Rainwater, C. E., New York: *The Play Movement in the United States.* Chicago: University of Chicago Press, 1922. An expert account of the early history of the playground movement as a phase of community organization.

Sanderson, Dwight, *The Rural Community.* Boston: Ginn, 1932. An authoritative study of contemporary rural community life.

*————, and Polson, R. A., *Rural Community Organization.* New York: Wiley, 1939. The standard book in this field of community work.

Steiner, J. F., *The American Community in Action.* New York: Holt, 1928.

————, *Community Organization.* New York: Century, 1930. Two pioneer works by one of the leading authorities on community organization.

*Warner, W. L., and Lunt, P. S., *The Social Life of a Modern Community.* New Haven: Yale University Press, 1941. Good case study and analysis of modern community life in industrial society.

Watson, F. D., *The Charity Organization Movement in the United States.* New York: Macmillan, 1922. The authoritative history and description of the movement for scientific organized charity.

Winslow, C. E. A., and Zimand, Savel, *Health under the El.* New York: Harper, 1937. Description of a classic community health project.

*Young, P. V., *Scientific Social Surveys and Research.* Prentice-Hall, 1949. Competent history, description, and analysis of the social survey movement and its bearing on social research techniques.

Zimmerman, C. C., *The Changing Community.* New York: Harper, 1938. Competent survey of the transformations of community living resulting from cultural and institutional shifts in our era.

Part III

Social Pathology

CHAPTER 13

Poverty, Dependency, and Relief

THE NATURE AND EXTENT OF POVERTY

Poverty persists in the mid-century. One of the most venerable and persistent social problems is that of poverty. Even Jesus regarded poverty as a chronic social problem and no cause for special excitement. Despite the progress in mechanical invention and the enormous increase in riches for the few, there are more persons in poverty today than at any other time in the history of mankind. In some countries, the percentage of those in poverty, in relation to the total population, may be less than at some earlier periods, but the gross number of those who are poverty-stricken in the mid-twentieth century far exceeds the figure for any previous age. This is partly the result of the financial costs and physical destruction wrought by two world wars, especially the second. Moreover, those who suffer from poverty in urban surroundings are far more helpless than were the poverty-stricken in the earlier pastoral and agricultural economies. Unless they are supported by private or public charity, they will actually perish.

Definitions of poverty and pauperism. There have been numerous definitions of poverty. *Poverty* means a state of chronic economic insufficiency; or, as Robert W. Kelso puts it, it is "the habitual state of being poor." But this economic inadequacy brings with it many social and cultural handicaps associated with low living standards. Hence, the definition of poverty given by John L. Gillin is especially comprehensive and illuminating. He defines poverty as

...that condition of living in which a person, either because of inadequate income or unwise expenditure, does not maintain a standard of living high enough to provide for the physical and mental efficiency of himself and to enable him and his natural dependents to function usefully according to the standards of the society of which he is a member.[1]

As a description of life in a state of extreme poverty, one may cite Tom Tippett's description of a West Virginia mining family in 1931:

There is the home of a 30-year-old striker, whom I will call Walter Robinson. We went inside. Some coals were burning in a grate, and around it huddled Mrs. Robinson and three small children. All of them were without shoes, all only half clothed. On the bed in the same room was a tiny baby, three months

[1] *Poverty and Dependency.* New York: Century, 1921 (rev. ed., 1926).

561

old. Still another child died this year. From where I stood I could easily see through the house whose walls were single planks separated by wide cracks. It was just as easy to see the sky through the roof. Nothing that is called furniture was in the place nor anything commonly associated in our minds with the word home. All the Robinsons were hungry and had been underfed for months.[2]

Living conditions in a state of poverty in metropolitan slums would present a somewhat different spectacle, but an equally impressive and repellent one.

Most of those who live below the poverty line usually have enough income to enable them to exist without constant aid from private or public sources, though their life is shrouded in misery and may lead to such unhealthful conditions as to hasten death. Those who live in the lowest poverty groups are called *paupers*. Their dependency is sheer and acute. They are in chronic need of public aid or private relief to maintain their very existence.

Popular bias concerning responsibility for poverty and pauperism. Both poverty and pauperism have usually been mentioned in a somewhat derogatory fashion in most conventional literature. These unfortunate conditions have been portrayed as a manifestation of personal pathology, and the unfortunates who live therein have been treated as though they were in some form of disgrace for which they are solely responsible. It has been implied that the poverty-stricken are a socially inferior lot, bordering on degeneracy, crime, and vice. It has been all to frequently asserted that most of them are a low order of human beings, very generally so lacking in capacity and energy as to be literally unemployable.

This plutocratic bias has been quite thoroughly upset by realistic studies of poverty. Poverty is indeed a disgrace, particularly in this twentieth century. But it is a disgrace to the nation and to the economic system rather than to the miserable beings who live in a state of chronic deprivation. Most of them are not directly responsible for their misery. Many studies of poverty have revealed the fact that at least 75 per cent of those who live in this condition are the victims of general economic misfortune, disease, or mental defect over which they have no direct control. Personal responsibility for their distress can be assigned in only about a quarter of the cases. Even here it is rare that the responsibility is purely personal. So-called shiftlessness and laziness are usually the product of malnutrition, illness, psychopathic conditions, mental defect, and the like, for which the individual cannot very well be held personally responsible.

Equally untenable is the idea that most of those in poverty are so physically inferior and degenerate as to be unemployable. This is one of the most transparent and shoddy of capitalistic alibis. The famous *Fortune* survey of workers who were receiving relief under the Works Progress Administration found that the overwhelming majority were thoroughly employable and that the recipients of relief desired to get work. There is certainly a small residual element of shiftless and lazy

---

[2] Brookwood College *Report*, 1931.

individuals who prefer overt relief to any form of remunerative labor. But even the majority of these could probably be rehabilitated through scientific treatment by social workers, physicians, and other appropriate agencies. The responsibility for poverty is overwhelmingly a social rather than an individual one.

Main classes of dependent persons. Dependent persons fall into several classes. First, there are those on direct relief, that is, receiving cash allowances for food, shelter, and clothing from the government. In June, 1938, over 20 million persons were still on the relief rolls. As the Social Security program was extended, the number receiving direct assistance sharply declined; in 1949, there were only 461,000 recipients of cash allowances.

The second class of dependents includes those aided by the Social Security Act of 1935. In 1949, about 2,500,000 persons received monthly benefits under the Old Age and Survivors program, and about 2,600,000 aged were helped by Old Age Assistance payments. In addition, 1,370,360 children and 71,200 blind persons received government pensions in 1949. The number in the Old Age and Survivors group was increased notably by the sweeping amendment to the Federal Social Security Act that was passed in 1950.

Persons in public institutions comprise the third class of dependents. In 1947, the Bureau of the Census reported 540,000 insane and 134,000 feeble-minded and epileptic patients in public institutions. There are about 90,000 dependent aged persons in state, city, and county poorhouses, and about 150,000 dependent children cared for in state and local institutions. There are about 150,000 prisoners in Federal and state institutions. In March, 1949, the Bureau of the Census stated that there was a total of 1,300,000 persons living in institutions, most of them public institutions.

Not all persons in need of aid are eligible for pensions or institutional care. In 1949, there were 6,582,000 widows reported by the census. Some receive pensions under one of the Social Security programs. Many are not eligible, however, and are dependent on the community. We have pointed out earlier that there are about 7 million who are ill on any average day during the year. Some 10 million persons are injured each year by accidents, nearly a half-million permanently. Workmen's compensation laws are not yet adequate, and many victims of industrial accidents become dependent upon private and public agencies.

Early studies of extent of poverty. The earliest scientific effort to ascertain the extent of poverty took the form of social surveys and was devoted chiefly to a study of poverty in certain urban areas. The most famous of these was Charles Booth's monumental *Life and Labour of the People of London,* begun in 1886 and finished in 1902. Booth revealed the fact that 30.7 per cent of the population of London were living in a state of poverty. B. Seebohm Rowntree made a similar study of York, England, which was published in 1901 as *Poverty; a Study of Town Life.* Rowntree discovered that 27.84 per cent of the population of York were poverty-stricken. More than a decade later, A. L. Bowley and A. R. Burnett-

Hurst published, in 1915, their work on *Livelihood and Poverty*,[3] devoted to a study of four other English communities. They revealed the fact that here 32 per cent were living on earnings of less than 24 shillings a week.

This survey method was also applied to a number of American cities, such as the investigations in New York City by Louise B. More in 1906 and by Robert Chapin in 1907; the famous Pittsburgh Survey made by Paul U. Kellogg and associates in 1906-1907; J. C. Kennedy's survey of the Chicago stockyards district in 1910; and nation-wide surveys made by the U. S. Department of Labor in 1901-1902 and in 1918-1919. These revealed conditions not markedly different from those found by the English investigators. Robert Hunter's estimate, made in 1904, that 10 million were living in primary poverty in the United States, was regarded at the time as sensational and exaggerated, but subsequent studies have proved that his estimate was extremely conservative. Maurice Parmelee was closer to the facts when he estimated in 1916 that at least half of the families in the United States were living in poverty.

Extent of poverty in the United States to Pearl Harbor. We have been able to secure a much more realistic and accurate conception of the facts about poverty in the United States as a result of thorough studies of income statistics. In 1919 the National Bureau of Economic Research estimated that about 86 per cent of all American families were living on incomes below $2,000, the latter sum being regarded by the government at this time as the minimum on which a family of five could be supported with any approximation to healthful and decent living conditions. In other words, at least three-fourths of American families were near or below the poverty line at the close of the First World War.

It was very generally believed that during the Harding-Coolidge regime, from 1921 to 1929, the country as a whole was prosperous and that poverty had all but disappeared. This illusion was thoroughly shattered by the Brookings Institution study, made by Leven, Moulton, and Warburton, and published as *America's Capacity to Consume*. This revealed a most disconcerting condition for the year 1929, which was, on the whole, one of the most prosperous years in American history. The stock market crash late in the year did not materially affect the income of the masses. These Brookings authorities showed that in 1929 some 6 million families, about 21 per cent of the total, had incomes of less than $1,000 per family. Some 12 million families, or 42 per cent of the total, had incomes of less than $1,500; 20 million families, or about 71 per cent of the total, had incomes of less than $2,500. *The 0.1 per cent of the families at the top, with incomes in excess of $75,000, received almost as much of the total national income as the entire 42 per cent of the families at the bottom of the income scale.*

Hence, the maldistribution of income was more responsible for mass poverty than inadequate national income as a whole. In 1928, for example, the per capita income was $749. If income had been equally divided, each family of five would have had an average income of $3,745.

---

[3] New ed., New York: Longmans, 1922.

Such an income would have enabled them to live on a "health and decency" budget and to save a considerable margin. It was contended that such a family might maintain health and decency on an annual income of $2,000. But in 1928, 60 per cent of all American families had incomes of less than $2,000 a year, receiving only about a quarter of the national income, while the richest 1.2 per cent of the families received approximately the same proportion of the national income. One may safely conclude that even in our most prosperous years 60 per cent of the families of the United States did not enjoy an income sufficient to make possible a desirable *minimum* standard of living.

During the depression years the situation was, of course, far worse. At the opening of the year 1933, between 12 and 17 million persons were unemployed. An estimate of 60 million persons living in poverty in 1933 would be a conservative figure. The persistence of poverty and relief on a vast scale, even under the New Deal, is graphically set forth in the following table:

INCOME CLASSES IN 1935 [4]

Number in Each Class		How Much They Receive per Capita
Upper class, very rich, about ..	500,000	$10,000 each, or $ 5,000,000,000
Middle class	12,000,000	1,000 each, or 12,000,000,000
Self-supporting workers, farmers, small business men	34,500,000	500 each, or 17,250,000,000
Marginals, earning most of living but receiving some aid ..	15,000,000	300 each, or 4,500,000,000
Submerged idle, mostly on relief	65,000,000	75 each, or 4,875,000,000
Total	127,000,000	$43,625,000,000

Another study of American income during the mid-New Deal period brings the same old sad story of maldistribution of income and the prevalence of poverty on an almost incredible scale. This study was made by the National Resources Committee and covered the year from July, 1935, to July, 1936. It was found that the lowest third of the 39 million American families, from an income standpoint, received $780 or less in that year. The average family income was $471. The middle third of the families received from $780 to $1,450 per year, with an average of $1,076. The highest third of the families received incomes of from $1,450 to much in excess of $1,000,000 annually. The average family income for this group was $3,000. To emphasize the impoverished condition of the lowest third of the families we may point out that 9,200,000 families, or 70 per cent of all in this group, received no help of any kind from a relief agency, though the total family income was $780 or less. It would not be inaccurate to say that even in the mid-period of the New Deal, two-thirds of the American families were living below the poverty line and that more than 10 per cent of our families existed in a state of pauperism.

---

[4] Walter B. Pitkin. *Capitalism Carries On.* New York: McGraw-Hill, 1935, pp. 180-181.

The New Deal under President Roosevelt removed millions from any fear of immediate starvation, but all available evidence supports the contention that the income of the masses remained lower than it was in 1928 and 1929. The farming population was the only segment of the American masses which had its income raised above the level of the 1928-1929 period. The census of unemployment conducted by the government in 1937 revealed that at least 10 million persons were unemployed.

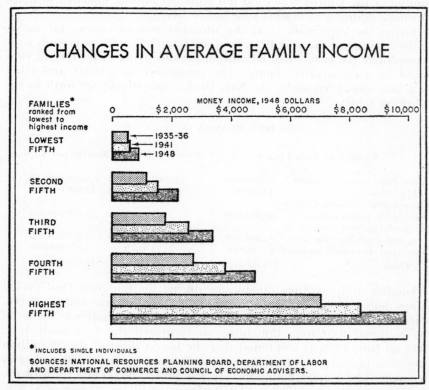

CHANGES IN AVERAGE FAMILY INCOME

FAMILIES*
ranked from
lowest to
highest income

LOWEST FIFTH
← 1935-36
← 1941
← 1948

SECOND FIFTH

THIRD FIFTH

FOURTH FIFTH

HIGHEST FIFTH

MONEY INCOME, 1948 DOLLARS
0    $2,000 $4,000 $6,000 $8,000 $10,000

*INCLUDES SINGLE INDIVIDUALS
SOURCES: NATIONAL RESOURCES PLANNING BOARD, DEPARTMENT OF LABOR
AND DEPARTMENT OF COMMERCE AND COUNCIL OF ECONOMIC ADVISERS.

This graph shows increase in monetary income of five income classes in the United States between 1935 and 1948. This increase was largely offset by increased cost of living and taxes, and reveals little substantial improvement in the lot of the lower income groups as a result of the Second World War and the cold war.

Poverty survives the Second World War. As late as 1942, when the depression was supposed to be conquered, millions of Americans were still living far below a decent standard. Labor Department studies of 33 cities, based on the WPA family budget of 1935 brought up to date for December, 1941, living costs, showed that $29 a week was the minimum income requirement for a worker's family of four. Yet, at that time, the Treasury Department revealed that 3,324,000 workers were earning from

$20 to $30. In other words, millions of families had insufficient income for bare subsistence.

Despite superficial evidence of greater mass prosperity in the postwar period, there was no great change in the inequitable distribution of income that is responsible for inadequate mass purchasing-power—a main cause of poverty and depressions. Taking into consideration the decreased purchasing power of the dollar and the increase in taxation, the situation today is not markedly different from what it was in prewar days. Today it merely costs more to be poor and needy.

One of the best analyses of American poverty today is that found in an article, "Who Are the American Poor?", by Robert L. Heilbroner in *Harper's,* June, 1950. The following table presents the distribution of American personal income in 1948:

Total income received during the year	Total number of families	Total single individuals, not living with families	Total number of people (family members plus individuals)
Under $1,000	4,020,000	4,090,000	16,220,000
$1,000-$2,000	5,580,000	1,830,000	20,060,000
$2,000-$3,000	7,950,000	1,240,000	28,470,000
$3,000-$5,000	12,970,000	810,000 ⎫	
$5,000-$10,000	6,900,000	140,000 ⎬	76,260,000
Over $10,000	1,110,000	30,000 ⎭	

Although the total personal income in the United States rose from 78 billion dollars in 1940 to 212 billion in 1948, 55 per cent of all Americans lived on annual incomes of $3,000 or less. In terms of 1940 purchasing power that income was approximately equal to $1,500. One out of every two single-dwelling individuals had an income of less than $2,000— slightly more than $1,000 in terms of prewar purchasing power. One family out of ten had a weekly income of $20 or less, which is about $10 in terms of 1940 purchasing power. Ten million families and 6 million individuals received incomes of less than $40 a week, or about $20 in 1940 purchasing power. More than 1,700,000 farm families had an annual income of $1,000 or less—about $500 in terms of 1940 purchasing power. Approximately 6 million of the farm population were living in poverty in 1948.

Other statistics were equally depressing. About one-fourth of our wage-earners received less than a living wage. Approximately 4.5 million persons were disabled and were compelled to live on charity or inadequate Social Security payments. Out of almost 6.5 million urban families with an income of less than $2,000, 1.5 million were headed by women, and one-half million of these families depended in whole or in part on relief. Half of all families on relief had an income of less than $1,000, or about $500 in terms of 1940 purchasing power. Therefore, in 1948—generally regarded as a prosperous year—at least 30 million Americans were living in what may technically and accurately be described as poverty or pauperism. Finally, high taxes were absorbing an ever greater portion of the inadequate income of the masses, most of whom paid slight or no income taxes before 1940.

CAUSES OF POVERTY

Physical or natural causes of poverty. In analyzing the causes of poverty, it is customary to list a large number of contributing influences. We shall follow this traditional procedure, but we should make it clear at the outset that political and economic conditions are overwhelmingly responsible for poverty today in the United States.

To a considerable extent, temporary or permanent poverty arises from causes of a physical character. Soil may be inadequate in fertility, thus making it impossible for cultivators to eke out a satisfactory existence. Such unproductive areas are unirrigated marginal lands in the West, particularly those afflicted with drought, dust storms, and the like; exhausted farms in the South; and semi-abandoned farming areas in New England. Inadequate natural resources may restrict the development of industrialization and the employment that might result therefrom. Natural cataclysms like droughts, floods, dust storms, and earthquakes may wipe out wealth and employment and produce serious temporary distress. In many parts of the West drought has been a chronic disaster. There are a number of students like Ellsworth Huntington, of Yale University, who believe that we have definite climatic cycles, accompanied by changes in temperature and rainfall, which directly affect agricultural prosperity and thereby the prosperity of the nation as a whole. Henry L. Moore, of Columbia University, attempted to prove a relation between these climatic cycles and the business cycles of prosperity and depression which have characterized American economic life for more than a century. Insect pests and other parasites may devastate an area and bring misery in their wake. Examples are the grasshopper and locust plagues in the West and the boll weevil in the South. Animal diseases, such as hog cholera, anthrax, and hoof and mouth disease, may markedly reduce the income of the farmers and herdsmen.

Biological factors in poverty. Biological factors make their contribution to the general social pattern of poverty. People may inherit physical or mental defects that reduce their capacity to work or even totally disable them for productive enterprise. The low grade feeble-minded—at least 1,500,000 of them—probably represent the largest single group to be thought of here. The congenitally blind are another, but the feeble-minded and the blind do not exhaust these types. Persons may acquire after birth pathological conditions that incapacitate them. For generations hookworm disease made many thousands of Southerners lazy and shiftless. Industrial fatigue and occupational diseases reduce personal energy and productive capacity. In addition to the mentally ill who are confined to institutions, there are several million more outside of institutions who are incapacitated for consistent productive activity.

In the chapter on public health we called attention to the prevalence of illness and the unnecessarily high death rate. We pointed out there that about 7 million are too sick to work on any average day in the year. In 1948 there were 1,449,000 deaths in the United States, at least half of which occurred among persons of wage-earning age. This meant that many families were deprived of their chief economic support. Each year about 100,000 persons meet death through accidents in the United States, and approximately 500,000 are permanently injured in like manner. All of this increases the volume of dependency. In the past, poverty has been aggravated by a too rapid increase of the population either through natural net gains or through immigration. This has created a working population too large to be absorbed by industry, unless the latter is stimulated by armament production. These population gains have tended to come at a time when labor-saving machines are being introduced extensively, thus reducing the need for human laborers and curtailing opportunities for employment.

Economic causes of poverty. Economic causes of poverty are many and varied. In the most famous work ever written on the subject, *Progress and Poverty,* Henry George attributed poverty to the socially unjust and inequitable system of landholding, according to which we allow private individuals to absorb the increasing land values which are created by society. An underdeveloped economy may be responsible for much poverty. Or we may find that a hangover of primitive industrial methods is associated with poverty. This was notoriously the case with the sweatshop system in American metropolitan centers. Industry may be accompanied by highly wasteful methods. There has been a prevailing impression that the American industrial system is highly efficient. Yet the report of capitalistic engineers on *Waste in Industry* made it clear that in the industrially very active year of 1921 we were wasting about one-half of our potential productive powers within the existing plant capacity. And much more of the responsibility was assigned to industry than to labor. The same general situation persisted until the spasm of industrial organization and effort during the Second World War. Indeed, during the depth of the depression, our industrial plant ran at less than half capacity. The cost of distributing food and goods has been nearly twice that of their production since the First World War.

The whole psychological orientation of our economic system is fundamentally uneconomical. Concentration upon immediate profits—"the ledger psychosis"—tends to reduce the possibility of taking a sound long-time view of the consequences of economic policies. High pressure salesmanship, skillful advertising, and installment buying have helped to bring about incomplete consumption of goods produced—the abandonment of commodities before their possible uses have been exhausted. They are discarded as a result of changes in styles, fashions, and the like. Many of these latter changes are deliberately designed to bring about an uneconomic consumption of goods. A vast amount of money is wasted upon non-essentials like liquor, tobacco, cosmetics, and trivial amusements. In 1947 we spent approximately 10 billion dollars for alcoholic beverages, 4 billion dollars for tobacco, and 2.5 billion dollars for cosmetics, perfumes, and beauty treatments.

Business cycles are primarily a product of a short-sighted greed for immediate speculative profits at the expense of sound industrial policy. They are neither inherent nor inevitable in the capitalistic economy, but they are responsible for a vast amount of unemployment and misery. We have already noted how low wages and an unfair distribution of the economic income make for extended poverty. Indeed, they are the most important direct economic cause of poverty. Protracted unemployment contributes to this common result.

There has been, in the United States, a woeful lack of adequate insurance against the crises and emergencies of life. Only about half of the American population carry private insurance, and the majority of the insured are very inadequately protected. The greatest scandals of all in the insurance field occur in the industrial insurance carried by the poorer classes. Rates are inordinately high, and most policies are allowed to lapse before maturity. Until the passage of the Federal Social Security Act in 1935, about all the public "insurance" that was provided for was to be found in the workmen's compensation laws passed in some of the more progressive states.

Social and psychological causes of poverty. Not a few cases of poverty arise from social and psychological causes. The steady disintegration of the old family system, producing an unprecedented volume of desertion, divorce, and illegitimacy, increases poverty. We have already seen how our lax immigration policy of 1890 to 1914 created a great army of potential workers who cannot be steadily employed in our era of automatic machinery unless we have a vast and wasteful armament program. Domestic methods in the United States are notoriously inefficient and wasteful. Habits of thrift are inadequately developed, and there has been a notorious absence of technical education in domestic science. The average French family could almost exist on what is wasted by the average American housewife. The psychological attitudes which prevail on the part of both employers and workmen are unfavorable to the best productive efforts. From the standpoint of employers, the ideal is to produce the poorest possible quality of marketable goods and to sell the largest possible volume of these for the highest available prices. Taught such lessons by their employers, highly organized American workers translate this into the utmost possible amount of loafing during the shortest possible day for the highest wages they can squeeze out of the employer. Unskilled and unorganized laborers have a general attitude of apathy and indifference toward their unattractive industrial tasks. Their interest is inevitably centered almost exclusively on the pay envelope.

Political basis of poverty. There is a vast amount of waste, inefficiency, and graft in government—particularly in democratic government operated through the party system. Political graft is one of the most lucrative and notorious of the rackets that afflict contemporary America. We have described one phase of it in the chapter on city life. Graft has succeeded the waste and corruption that characterized the dynasties and court society of the former era of absolute monarchs. Governmental waste and inefficiency reduce the possibility of wise political action which might prevent or mitigate other causes of poverty. They also lead to unnecessarily high taxes, which fall to a disproportionate extent upon the middle and lower classes. The sales tax hits the masses with special severity. In addition, there are all sorts of indirect taxes brought about by the tariff system and other forms of public favoritism which penalize the very poor as well as the middle class and the rich. There is a large amount of unwise and indiscriminate public philanthropy, of which one of the most notorious examples has been our lax and corrupt pension system.

One of the outstanding political defects that have been responsible for producing unnecessary poverty has been the failure to make adequate provision for extensive industrial education, manual training, and the like, which would enable the graduates of our schools to obtain remunerative employment. Countless millions of dollars have been wasted upon a type of education that is irrelevant to the needs of a majority of American children. The failures here have resulted in a large volume of unemployment and crime.

But by far the most important type of political defect, which bears upon the poverty problem, has been the failure to work out rational foreign policies that would curb wars and eliminate the necessity for the vast contemporary armament race, with its staggering economic cost. The ravages of the First World War probably contributed more to contemporary poverty than any other single cause, with the sole exception of the weaknesses of the capitalistic system as a whole. One oft-quoted summary, worked out by the Carnegie Endowment for International Peace, pointed out that the cost of the First World War would have been sufficient to furnish: (1) every family in England, France, Belgium, Germany, Russia, the United States, Canada, and Australia with a $2,500 house on a $500 one-acre lot, with $1,000 worth of furniture; (2) a 5 million dollar library for every community of 200,000 inhabitants in these countries; (3) a 10 million dollar university for every such community; (4) a fund that at 5 per cent interest would yield enough to pay indefinitely $1,000 a year to an army of 125,000 teachers and 125,000 nurses; and (5) still leave enough to buy every piece of property and all the wealth in France and Belgium at a fair market price.

If the wealth wasted on the Second World War were available at this moment it would be possible to do all the following things: to provide each family in the United States, Great Britain, Canada, Australia, Ireland, Germany, Russia and Belgium with these benefits—(1) a $15,000 home; (2) $5,000 worth of furniture; (3) $20,000 in cash; and also $150 million worth of schools, hospitals, and libraries, etc. for every city of more than 200,000 population in *each* of the countries listed.

Such vast sums, assuming they were wisely and constructively expended, would have sufficed to eliminate all poverty and create a material utopia.

We may here appropriately summarize the vast cost of wars to the United States. The total cost of the Civil War was about 15.3 billion dollars. The ultimate cost of the First World War to this country will exceed 100 billion. The Second World War cost us about 400 billions to 1946, and its ultimate cost to us, even if it does not bring on a third world war, is estimated by experts to run to 1.5 trillion dollars—enough to transform the United States into a material paradise.

HISTORICAL DEVELOPMENT OF POOR RELIEF POLICIES

Early types of poor relief. In early historical times, the majority of the very poor were slaves, and the institution of slavery acted as a sort of substitute for a system of relief. There were, of course, plenty of free persons who were poverty-stricken, but because they lived in an agricultural or pastoral civilization, they were usually able to provide enough to keep body and soul together without public relief. Poverty on the farm may mean great privation, but it rarely means starvation or death from exposure.

The first notable historical situation in which there was any large number of urban dependents existed in Rome from the days of the late Republic onward. They were provided for by the state through the classic method of "bread and circuses." In this way, the government kept the rabble quiet and loyal to the existing order.

Poor relief during the Middle Ages. With the rise of Christianity, the relief of the poor was gradually taken over by the ecclesiastical authorities. The Roman Catholic Church of the Middle Ages was generally in charge of the activities that we now classify as social work—the custody or relief of dependent classes. Yet, though the Church was the great charitable institution of the medieval period, it regarded the relief of misery as subordinate to its primary task of salvation. A main reason for the special Christian interest in the poor was the development of what was at least a spiritual democracy—a religious solicitude for the common man. The pagans, viewing man chiefly in his secular status, had exhibited less concern for the poor and miserable, who were found for the most part in the class of slaves and menials. While the church fully sanctioned the undemocratic hierarchical organization of medieval society and exhibited in its own organization one of the most powerful hierarchies in the history of human government, it did uphold democracy in a spiritual sense. All men were equal before the throne of God, if not before the throne of the king. The poor man's soul was as worthy as that of an archduke or an archbishop. Hence, the Christians were inclined to give much more attention than did pagans to poverty-stricken fellow believers. Further, Jesus had specifically recommended and praised the giving of alms and the practice of charity. Many of the Christian views on charity and kindness to the poor were, of course, derived from the Jewish social prophets like Amos.

The attitude of medieval Christians toward the poor was clear and decisive. They were not primarily interested in preventive social measures that would eliminate poverty. They were concerned mainly with the immediate relief of suffering humanity and took it for granted that the poor would always remain an integral part of the social order. Indeed, Jesus had implied as much in one of His best-remembered statements: "For ye have the poor always with you." Further, it was thought scarcely desirable to eliminate poverty altogether, for the spectacle of the poor was regarded as a very salutary influence on the rich. By observing their superior and fortunate position in comparison to the lot of the miserable masses, the rich were more likely to be impressed with their good fortune and to express appropriate gratitude to God through extensive gifts to the church.

Aspects of ecclesiastical relief. On these mental and moral foundations the church built up the medieval system of charities and relief. While the church was solicitous about the relief of all dependent classes, it was particularly concerned over the care of orphans. It was necessary to provide these otherwise helpless offspring with living conditions that would make it possible to inculcate in their minds the one true religion. Not only did the church make gifts outright to the poor. It also established, toward the end of the medieval period, a rudimentary loan bank, which loaned money to the poor without interest and thereby saved them from exploitation by usurers.

The medieval church provided institutions to care for the sick and others in special distress. It had charge of and responsibility for the medieval hospitals. It was entrusted with safeguarding public health by supervising travel, isolating suspected disease-bearers, and protecting the population from infected types, such as lepers. Such orphanages and poorhouses as existed in the Middle Ages were supported mainly by the church. Most medieval charity, however, was "outdoor relief"—relief to people living in their own homes. The poorhouse was the exception in the Middle Ages.

So much was the church interested in social work that special religious orders were developed to assume this responsibility. The Brotherhood of the Holy Ghost and the Knights of St. John, or the Knights Hospitalers, gave their attention to the provision and administration of hospitals. The Order of St. Lazarus looked after lepers. The church also took part in medical service of the Middle Ages. Monastic orders supplied many of the more influential professors of medicine in the medieval universities. The Alexian Brothers helped in the burials of the poor. The Trinitarians were particularly interested in the ransoming of captives. The Franciscan friars were extremely active in urging the rich to give liberally to the relief of the poor. They became the chief charitable order in the cities during the later Middle Ages. Although medieval ecclesiastical charity lacked guidance by modern medical and social science, it was otherwise about as adequate to the needs of the times as the average system of relief in an American state was before the rise of social insurance.

In addition to the work of the church, the very institutional set-up of medieval society, we must remember, naturally provided for the relief of some of the misery of that age. The medieval manor—the village community—held within its confines the poor people of the country—and this meant the great majority of all the poor, including serfs and a few slaves. They shared a common poverty and met their crises together in a communal spirit. The gilds of the towns provided charitable relief for many of the indigent artisans. But there were still many poor and miserable people who could rely upon neither the communal manor nor the charity of the gildsmen. To these the church ministered.

Rise of public poor relief in early modern times. Modern times brought in their train new circumstances that made sweeping changes in medieval poor relief methods obligatory. The manor broke up and disappeared in many countries, especially in England. The rise of wheat farming for profit and the inclosure of land for sheep-raising led to the ejection of many of the poor peasants from their paltry holdings and wiped out their sole means of support. This produced a condition of mass misery immortalized in the opening pages of Sir Thomas More's *Utopia*. Monasteries, which had long aided many beggars, were suppressed, and the relief system of the Catholic Church was upset or terminated entirely. In this new era in which the secularization and nationalization of politics was a conspicuous trend, it was logical that the state would seek to supplant the church in relieving the poor, and this is exactly what happened in England, which took the lead in establishing public relief of the poor.

The first important English poor law was that of 1536, in the reign of Henry VIII. It well reflected the transition from religious to public relief. It forbade open begging, directed the local authorities to collect funds to relieve the poor, and ordered that collections be taken up in churches on Sundays, and at festivals and other gatherings. Direct gifts to vagrants were forbidden, and it was directed that professional beggars were to be whipped and driven back to their own parishes. But though the state was now in charge of relief, the churches were still relied upon for a time as agencies for collecting the funds to be disbursed by the public authorities. Laws of 1547, 1555, and 1563 provided that places should be found to lodge the worthy and homeless poor, and that citizens who failed to contribute to poor relief were to be admonished and then publicly taxed to obtain funds. In 1572 a law created special officers, overseers of the poor, and collectors to take charge of poor relief, and in 1576 the first workhouse test was introduced. The justices of the peace were empowered to construct or procure workhouses and to provide raw materials to be used by those who asked for relief. Only those willing to accept such work were to be aided, unless they were obviously incapacitated.

The Elizabethan Poor Law of 1601. This earlier legislation was overhauled and systematically brought together in the famous Elizabethan Poor Law of 1601. The poor were divided into three classes: (1) the able-bodied; (2) the incapacitated; and (3) children. The first were to be relieved solely in the workhouses, as provided in the act of 1576. The second class was to be cared for in almshouses, while the children were ordered to be apprenticed or indentured—that is, bound out to those willing to support them in return for services rendered. A specific tax was to be levied for poor relief, and certain fines and gifts were also to be applied to this purpose. The officials in charge of poor relief—overseers— were taken from each parish, and were appointed by the justices of the peace. This law of 1601 remained the backbone of the English poor relief system until the great act of 1834 was passed, mainly as an outgrowth of long agitation by Jeremy Bentham, noted English social philosopher.

From Elizabeth to Bentham. There were a number of supplementary laws passed between 1601 and 1834. An act of 1662 was designed to prevent the expoitation of rich or generous parishes. It made each parish responsible solely for the relief of those poor who could claim legal residence in the parish. A law of 1691 required more accurate records of poor relief, while another of 1696 extended the workhouse principle that had been embodied in the law of 1576. Then an act of 1723 enabled parishes too small to maintain a separate workhouse to combine in constructing a joint institution to serve as many parishes as united for this purpose. The workhouse test was made obligatory at this time for the relief of all able-bodied poor.

The coming of the Industrial Revolution and the vast increase in the inclosure of lands in England during the second half of the eighteenth century put special strains on the poor relief system. The Gilbert Act of 1782 abolished the farming out of the poor, permitted in many cases relief in private homes instead of in workhouses and almshouses, and introduced the notorious and fatal "allowance system." Only the old, the infirm, mothers of illegitimate children, and young children were to be sent to almshouses; for the able-bodied, relief was to be given in their homes and work was to be found nearby. Paid officials, known as *guardians,* were empowered to collect the wages of the able-bodied poor and then to contribute enough more from poor relief funds to enable the individual and his family to live. This was an open invitation to unscrupulous employers to cut down wages, since the state would make them up in any event.

This disastrous innovation was further extended by the introduction of the famous Speenhamland system. The justices of the peace in the village of Speenhamland in Berkshire met at the Pelican Inn in 1795 and decided to relieve the poor by grants based on the cost of living and the size of the family. The workhouse test for granting relief was to be abolished. This system was adopted by Parliament in 1796 and remained in force until 1834.

The results were what might have been expected: (1) an increase in poor relief expenditures from 10 million dollars in 1783 to 39 million dollars in 1818 and 34 million in 1831; (2) sweeping wage cuts; and (3) the demoralization of the poor and of many of the laboring class.

Despite all its defects, however, the Speenhamland system did tide England over in a period of sweeping social change—that accompanying the early Industrial Revolution, the establishment of the factory system, and the inclosure of peasant lands in great estates. The British statesman, George Canning, held that it probably saved the country from social revolution.

The famous Poor Law of 1834. The poor relief system of England before 1834 thus started out with rudimentary inadequacy at the beginning of the period and terminated in chaos at its end. It was from this condition that the Poor Law of 1834 was designed to rescue England. This great Poor Law of 1834 was an embodiment of the principles of Jeremy Bentham. It was based on the idea of the prevention of pauperism as well as the relief of the worthy poor. It forbade giving relief in homes except to the aged and the sick. It required others to enter a workhouse to get aid. It provided for a logical and efficient unification of local areas in administering relief.

Transition from poor relief to social insurance. The Poor Law of 1834 endured with only a few minor amendments until the close of the nineteenth century. In 1905, a commission was appointed by the Crown to investigate poor law administration in England. The report was submitted in 1909. The majority recommended certain commendable administrative changes in the poor law system, particularly the abolition of the boards of guardians and the poor law unions. It also repudiated the crude deterrent ideas of the law of 1834 and laid more stress upon prevention and curative methods. It urged the creation of special institutions for the housing of the poverty-stricken and for a much more adequate system of outdoor relief.

The minority report made social history. Led by Beatrice Webb, the minority recommended that the poor law be abolished, and that a comprehensive system of social insurance be substituted for it. It held that only in this way could the preventive ideal be honestly and completely realized. It also recommended that the various types of dependents be differentiated and that each be handled by the proper authorities. For example, sick dependents should be under the control of the Health Committee of the County Council, and the mentally defective dependents under the custody of the Asylum Committee. This minority report seems to have had much influence on the passage of the epochal National Insurance Act of 1911.

In 1919, a Ministry of Health was created and given authority over poor-law administration. The Local Government Act of 1929 abolished the boards of guardians and placed the local responsibility for poor-law administration in the hands of the County Councils and the County Borough Councils. The acts of 1919 and 1929 attempted to bring about the desirable combination of centralized authority with local responsibility for the administration of relief. The British system of poor relief after the First World War became ever more closely involved in the social insurance program which will be discussed later.

Colonial poor relief in the United States. The early American system of poor relief was based directly upon the English law of 1601. In some areas, the principles of this famous law were evident in American practice until the twentieth century. In the colonial period, most of the relief to the poverty-stricken was outdoor relief. But there were a few workhouses; many children were bound out or indentured; and in some instances the care of the poor was auctioned off to the lowest bidder. Curtis P. Nettels thus summarizes the outstanding features of colonial poor relief:

The felicity portrayed by promoters of settlement and by writers of the upper middle class is only a part of the picture of colonial life. Many families lived so close to poverty that misfortune reduced them to destitution. . . .

The principles of poor relief introduced into America were those with which the colonists had been familiar in England. After the dissolution of the English monasteries the burden of caring for the poor was assumed by the state, the work being assigned to the localities and the funds obtained through taxes levied on the property owners. All these features characterized the poor relief systems devised in the colonies. . . .

In New England the simplest mode of poor relief was for each family to care for a destitute person during part of the year. Thus Hadley, Massachusetts, voted in 1687 that a widow should be sent "round the town" to live two weeks with each family "able to receive her." Some of the poor, not wholly incapacitated, were given money from the town treasury and allowed to live alone. The most common practice followed by the smaller towns before the Revolution was the "putting out" system. The selectmen paid a householder who agreed to provide food and shelter for a destitute person; the town generally supplied clothing and medical care. Doctors who served the poor received payment from the town. In the larger settlements almshouses soon appeared; Boston had one in 1660. Prior to 1712 it housed criminals as well as the "honest poor," so great was the stigma attached to poverty. After 1712 efforts were made to realize the "primitive and pious design" of the almshouse, i.e., "the relief of the necessitous, that they might lead a quiet, peaceable and godly life there."

Convinced that all able-bodied poor could find work, the New Englanders wasted little sympathy upon vagabonds and sturdy beggars. Such idlers were either bound out as indentured servants, whipped out of town, or clapped into jail. As the number of the able-bodied poor increased, the costs of confining them in prison (or the house of correction) led to the construction of workhouses. . . .

A specialization of function was evident in the system of poor relief at the end of the colonial period. The almshouse cared for the "honest poor," the workhouse employed idlers and minor offenders, the prison housed criminals, and the hospital domiciled the sick. . . .

The prudential New Englanders used prevention as well as relief in dealing with the poor. A master of a vessel who imported immigrants into Massachusetts had to give bond that they would not become a public charge; thus it was hoped "to prevent the importation of poor, vicious and infirm persons." Should an inhabitant bring servants into a town, he must agree to maintain them if they become "diseased, lame or impotent." Again a householder who received outsiders must give notice of their presence; if they seemed likely to become a public burden, they were "warned out" of the town and deported if they would not go willingly. Since each town had to care for its own poor, destitute strangers were speedily returned to their home localities.

Poor relief in the southern colonies may be illustrated by the practices of Virginia, where drifters, runaway servants, and delinquent family heads raised problems akin to those of the northern colonies. The vestries in Virginia disposed of the able-bodied poor, destitute orphans, and the illegitimate children of indentured servants by binding them to masters as apprentices or servants. Almshouses, hospitals, and workhouses do not appear in the parish records; the impotent poor were placed in private homes, the parish supplying clothing and paying the householder the costs of maintenance. Outlays for poor relief, as in New England, varied from 9 per cent to 33 per cent of all expenditures for local purposes. These early forms of relief are the antecedents of modern orphan asylums, poorhouses, public hospitals, widows' pensions, free medical service, and insurance against accidents, unemployment, sickness, and old age.[5]

Almshouses and outdoor relief. After the Revolutionary War and the establishment of independence, there was a general trend toward the building of almshouses. Both the poverty-stricken aged and poor children were cared for in these institutions. In New England the almshouse was usually in the charge of township authorities, while elsewhere

---

[5] *The Roots of American Civilization.* New York: Crofts, 1938, pp. 461-463.

it has generally been a county institution. In the first half of the nineteenth century, almshouses thus became all but universal, and poor relief was chiefly of an institutional character. After the Civil War there was a trend in the opposite direction. Children were, to an even larger extent, taken out of the almshouses and put in special child-caring institutions, either private or public.

The experience of the State of New York not only illustrates the tendency throughout the country but also exerted no little influence upon the general trend of American poor relief. In 1824 the construction of almshouses by all counties was ordered by state legislation. Provision was made for more adequate state aid to private charities in the raising of necessary funds.

This system endured with minor modifications until 1896, when there was a general codification of state legislation dealing with poor relief. The almshouses were continued primarily to meet the needs of the indigent aged. Children were systematically removed from the almshouses and placed in special public and private institutions for dependent children. The provisions for outdoor relief were systematized and made more scientific. Public aid to private charities was definitely curtailed. The supervision over urban poor relief was placed in the hands of the State Charities Aid Association, a private society created in 1872 but having quasi-official standing. In rural areas, the county boards of supervisors still retained control of relief measures.

Indiana reforms system of outdoor relief. Outdoor relief for the rural poor became ever more prevalent in the latter part of the nineteenth century, and Indiana was the pioneer state in introducing efficient supervision of such relief. Before the famous reforms that were begun there in 1895, poor relief in Indiana was administered according to the old law of 1853, which gave the poor relief trustees complete discretion over the amount and methods of relief and did not even require any systematic reports as to the relief given or the need therefor. Grave abuses, waste, and inefficiency sprang up as the result. In 1895, the state spent $630,000 for poor relief under the system of unsupervised relief by township trustees.

Between 1895 and 1899 a series of laws was passed entirely reorganizing the system. They were framed on the advice of experts like Amos W. Butler who were familiar with the famous Hamburg-Elberfeld system of outdoor relief, which we shall describe later. The township trustees were compelled to investigate each case, get what help they could from friends and relatives of needy applicants, compel able-bodied members of the family to work, cooperate with private relief societies, and hand in duplicate reports of the amount given for relief and the reasons therefor. The consent of the county commissioners was required for the granting of more than a specified minimum of relief aid.

Impressive savings were accomplished. The amount disbursed for outdoor relief dropped from $630,000 to $355,000, and the number of those who received aid was cut approximately in half. This Indiana innovation had a marked influence upon the improvement of outdoor relief procedure in other states. It represented something like a modified extension of the charity organization principles to rural outdoor relief.

The charity organization societies and community chests take over urban relief. In urban areas, the control and administration of private relief came to be ever more frequently entrusted to the local charity organization society, the origins and nature of which we discussed in a previous chapter. In the same place we pointed out that the raising of funds for private relief is now carried on mainly by community chests of which there are over 1,300 in the country. They raised 192 million dollars in 1950.

THE RICH AND PRIVATE CHARITY

Do the rich adequately support private charity? Since the charity organization movement, community chests, and the social settlement movement depend primarily upon voluntary contributions, it may be well at this point to consider the question of whether the rich really contribute lavishly to charitable enterprises. The extreme concentration of wealth and income in the United States is frequently justified on the grounds that the rich give liberally to support the poor through private charity, thus putting their money back into circulation and increasing mass purchasing power. In a striking article,[6] Abraham Epstein brands this conception a myth. He says, "Among the masses of well-to-do not many give anything to charity, even in the most generous city, New York. A negligible number of rich individuals support all charities. The vast bulk of the wealthy contribute to none." [7] Epstein concludes that private charity is utterly inadequate to the task of caring for the dependent classes either in normal times or in emergencies.

Indeed, when we talk of caring for unemployment and drought by private philanthropy we talk nonsense. . . . Under this system the burden of social ills falls almost entirely upon the few generous rich and the bulk of poor wage-earners, who cannot refuse to give to charitable appeals when the boss asks them to contribute. It is altogether contrary to the modern principle of a fair proportional distribution of the burden. The bulk of the well-to-do escape entirely from paying their share.[8]

Lindeman's study of wealth and culture. Epstein's conclusions are confirmed by a later and more thorough investigation of the problem by E. S. Lindeman.[9] This is an elaborate study of the relation between great fortunes and humanitarian efforts. It was the product of several years of careful research and is an impressive statistical analysis of the prob-

---

6 "Do the Rich Give to Charity?" *American Mercury*, May, 1931, pp. 23 ff. See also Abraham Epstein, *Insecurity: A Challenge to America*. New York: Random House, 1936, Chap. XI.

7 *Ibid.*, p. 23.

8 *Ibid.*, p. 30.

9 *Wealth and Culture*. New York: Harcourt, Brace, 1936. For even more complete confirmation and documentation with respect to the great foundations, see Horace Coon, *Money to Burn: What the Great American Philanthropic Foundations Do with Their Money*. New York: Longmans, Green, 1938, especially Chaps. II-IV, X, XII, and XIV.

lem. Lindeman presented ample evidence as to the enormous concentration of wealth and income in the United States, such as the fact that one per cent of the people owned 59 per cent of the total wealth of the country, and that 13 per cent of the people owned 90 per cent of the total wealth. On the other hand, 75 per cent of the people owned virtually nothing.

Do those who are fortunate with respect to wealth and income hand back most of it for the benefit of humanity? Lindeman finds that there is no general tendency, such as is usually assumed, for the wealthy to return any considerable part of their incomes to be put at the service of mankind:

> It seems entirely clear that persons who possess large estates do not, at death, redistribute any sizable portion of their wealth to society. They pass their wealth on, so far as is possible, to a small circle of relatives and friends. Only six per cent of the wealthy distribute their estates among agencies and institutions. Moreover, the sum which they thus distribute amounts to only six per cent of the total wealth bequeathed.
>
> And, what is even of greater significance, perhaps, is the fact that the bulk of wealth thus distributed flows into the treasuries of churches, hospitals, and conventional charities. In short, the cultural importance of redistributed personal wealth is slight. This analysis of probated wills and appraised estates reveals that Americans on the whole regard their wealth as personal possessions to be disposed of according to individual interest or fancy.[10]

F. Emerson Andrews' recent survey of philanthropic giving. The data and opinions of Epstein and Lindeman were based on conditions in the 1930's. These have been changed somewhat by new developments in the 1940's, chiefly the marked increase in income, if not in purchasing power, and the higher taxation, especially of large incomes. We are now fortunate to have a comprehensive study of recent conditions and trends made by F. Emerson Andrews of the Russell Sage Foundation and published in his book, *Philanthropic Giving* (1950). This bears out the contention of Epstein and Lindeman that private philanthropy provides only a small portion of the sum needed to take care of the poverty-stricken and other needy persons. Although there has been a considerable increase in the total income from private sources for all charitable and philanthropic purposes, the portion of this devoted to health and welfare agencies today is only about 560 million dollars, as compared to the more than three billion dollars a year paid out in government social security assistance annually under the 1950 Act and an equal sum contributed by employees and employers for private pension and welfare programs.

The most marked increase in contributions to philanthropy of all types has been from living donors, an increase which has been prompted primarily by increases in income and estate taxes. Many have taken advantage of the deduction of 15 per cent for charitable purposes allowed in income taxes. Gifts from living donors stood at 1,052 million dollars in 1929 and dropped to a low of 619 million in 1933. These gifts rose to 1,068 million dollars in 1940, to 2,271 million in 1945, and to 3,609

---

10 Lindeman, *op. cit.,* p. 50.

million in 1949. The total income from all private sources, including corporate gifts and estate bequests, stood at 4,032 million dollars in 1949. Corporate gifts to philanthropy, also stimulated by the higher income taxes, rose from 30 million dollars in 1936 to 241 million in 1947, the last recorded year available. They reached their high point at 266 million in 1945. The most marked increase in the proportion of gifts in relation to income is found in the income class with an annual income of over a million dollars; the rate here increased from 3.1 per cent in 1922 to 8.1 per cent in 1946.

Examining the total contributions to all forms of philanthropy, Andrews found that 60.4 per cent of such contributions comes from those with incomes of less than 3,000 dollars. Some 88.6 per cent comes from those with incomes under 10,000 dollars. Most of this, however, is given to churches and other religious organizations. The low income groups contribute relatively little to agencies relieving poverty and other forms of misery. These latter agencies are primarily supported by gifts from the higher income groups. Churches and religious organizations receive just about half of all the gifts to philanthropy. Health and welfare agencies receive 15 per cent, higher education 8 per cent, and foundations 4 per cent.

Inheritance taxes on large estates have become almost confiscatory in recent years. The inheritance taxes on the estate of Mrs. Horace White, assessed at $9,748,000, were $7,036,000. Those on the 35-million-dollar estate of William K. Vanderbilt were about $30,000,000. Thomas W. Lamont once observed that, in the light of the heavy inheritance taxes, a gift of 500 million dollars by him while living would cost his heirs only about 23 million dollars. Despite this, the rich, as a rule, still prefer to retain their money and other property until death and then have it taken over mainly by a government whose policies and officials they may have bitterly denounced for years. Charitable bequests from estates have actually fallen off since 1930, when they stood at 233 million dollars. They amounted to 186 million in 1947. The high point after 1930 was 202 million in 1944.

This definitive study by Andrews amply confirms the thesis of Epstein, Lindeman, and others that private philanthropy is utterly inadequate to care for the relief of poverty and misery, and that the rich give only a slight proportion of their wealth to philanthropy. Moreover, the total annual contributions to philanthropy by all income classes just about equal the national tobacco bill each year, and are far less than half the amount spent on alcoholic beverages. The statistics on charitable bequests from estates show that the rich have never turned back much of their wealth to society after death. Furthermore, it is evident that their tendency to do this has actually decreased in the last quarter of a century.

The charity of the poor to the rich. In our discussions of the charity of the rich to the poor—inadequate though this charity may be—we usually lose sight of the extensive, if involuntary, charity of the poor toward the rich. This relevant point is well brought out by Gilbert Seldes.

I agree with revolutionaries that the charity system is outworn. But the charity of the rich to the poor is not the only one. There is the appalling charity of the poor to the rich. On the great lists of charitable contributions from the rich to the poor only a few items are anonymous; on the infinitely longer list of charity which the poor have given to the rich no names occur. The unmonied ones have had the exquisite tact to keep heir benevolence a secret. The rich have given to the poor a little food, a little drink, a little shelter and a few clothes.

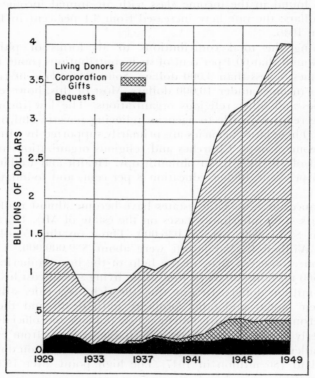

FROM F. EMERSON ANDREWS, *Philanthropic Giving*, RUSSELL SAGE FOUNDATION, 1950.

Graph showing influence of higher income taxes in promoting greater philanthropic gifts since 1940.

The poor have given to the rich palaces and yachts, and an almost infinite freedom to indulge their doubtful taste for display, and bonuses and excess profits, under which cold and forbidding terms have been hidden the excess labor and extravagant misery of the poor. The poor have given ... what is perhaps most precious to them, their security and their peace of mind, and have lived their lives precariously, always on the edge of danger, uncertain of the next day's food or the next month's rent, terrified of living lest they lose their jobs and terrified of dying lest their wives and children starve.[11]

The main generalization that may be drawn from this review of the impossibility of relying upon gifts from the rich to care for the needy is that it was essential to provide for various types of social insurance,

11 *Against Revolution.* New York: John Day, 1932, p. 13.

many of which have been supplied, even though as yet in inadequate fashion, by the Social Security system, which we shall describe later. Community chests, which provide much of the money for direct relief derived from private sources, raise only about 190 million dollars each year, whereas public assistance to the needy amounted to over 2 billion dollars in 1949.

THE DEVELOPMENT OF PROFESSIONAL SOCIAL WORK

Private agencies and charity still required. Public relief under governmental support and supervision has become increasingly important since the 1930's. Private agencies are still necessary, however, to give temporary or permanent care to those persons not eligible for pensions or grants from the government.

The enormous cost of all private and public social benefits today was revealed in a report of the Community Research Associates in 1949, which showed that some 13 billion dollars are being spent annually from public and private sources for such social services as relief, social security, health, correction, education, welfare, and recreation—a sum about equal to all the public expenditures for relief during the entire New Deal period. The relative increase of these social benefits may be seen from the fact that welfare costs were equal to 2.1 per cent of the national income in 1900, but had risen to 17.5 per cent in 1950.

Trained social workers needed for both private and public relief. In view of the fact that social workers have long directed nearly all private relief and are taking an ever greater part in the administration of public relief, it is desirable briefly to describe the development of concepts and practices in social work and the improved training of social workers.

Traditional social work has been limited primarily to alleviating immediate distress, seeking in the course of so doing to introduce preventive measures as far as possible. It has taken the system of society that produces such poverty and misery for granted. It does not anticipate or plan any such reconstruction of society as might eliminate many of the causes of poverty. Hence, social work has been critically described by many intelligent radicals as "the wrecking crew of capitalism." This is the phrase coined by Roger N. Baldwin, himself at one time one of the most distinguished of American social workers. It is charged that social work simply clears away the wreckage produced by the capitalistic system but lacks the courage to advocate a system that would reduce the volume of wreckage. Yet, it must be fairly conceded that, so long as the wreckage exists, somebody must clear it away. Hence, it is far better that this be done by trained social workers, with a professional sense, rather than by well-intentioned amateurs or political grafters. Within the limitations imposed by its temporizing perspective, social work has been reasonably scientific and pragmatic.

Development of scientific social work: social case work. In early days, social workers were motivated mainly by benevolent sentiment. They had little technical training, other than occasionally some slight administrative experience with poor relief. The concepts of informal charity and philanthropy dominated their outlook. Scientific sociology entered very little into the equipment of the early social worker. The first important impulse to scientific training for social work came from the charity organization movement, which stressed careful investigation of individual need. To do this required training in order to familiarize the social worker with the essentials of a thorough investigation of applicants for relief.

The most approved technique of scientific social work is what is known as *social case work*. This has a long history, but one common thread runs through it all—the effort to provide a more thorough personal investigation of relief cases. Its origins may be sought in the scheme of relief work adopted in the city of Hamburg between 1765 and 1788. With improvement, it was copied in the German city of Elberfeld in 1852. Hence, it has come to be known as the Hamburg-Elberfeld system of administering outdoor urban relief.

According to this scheme, a city was divided into small units in which there would normally be no more than three or four dependents. Over each of these districts was placed a poor officer, or *Armenpfleger*. This officer's duties were to become thoroughly acquainted with his district, to ascertain and investigate all needy cases, and to administer such relief as he deemed necessary. These officers served without pay, but the office often was a stepping-stone to some more important post. Fourteen of these units, or sections, were organized into a district, which was supervised by an overseer, or *Vorsteher*. Under his direction, meetings of the poor officers were held every two weeks and their problems thoroughly threshed out. At the head of the entire poor relief system of the city was a central executive committee of nine.

This method of handling poor relief was believed to combine centralization of administration, proper inspection, and personal familiarity with relief problems. The investigation of individual cases by the poor officer marked the origins of social case work, though it was not in any sense disciplined or directed through scientific training in the field. The Hamburg-Elberfeld system of relief administration had considerable influence upon the Indiana system of administering outdoor relief, which we described earlier.

The next important contribution to the development of social case work came from a Scottish clergyman, Thomas Chalmers (1780-1847), a severe critic of the English poor law of 1834. Chalmers attacked the English system of poor relief, which had been extended to Scotland, on the ground that it was not sufficiently discriminating and did not thoroughly investigate individual cases of need. He laid great stress upon investigation, holding that we should weed out those who do not really require help and that we should supply more intelligent and adequate relief to those who are in real need. He also placed much emphasis upon efficiency in raising funds for private charity. His ideals were carried over into the charity organization movement by some of his disciples—Edward Denison, Octavia Hill, and Charles S. Loch.

The need for investigation and for community aid was particularly emphasized by American participants in this charity organization movement, especially by Edward T. Devine, who was for many years secretary of the New York Charity Organization Society and director of the New York School of Philanthropy. To promote more intelligent interest in the charity organization movement, a special department devoted to its study was set up in the Russell Sage Foundation and was put in charge of Mary E. Richmond. Out of her experience came her famous book, *Social Diagnosis*,[12] which appeared in 1917. This became the standard textbook on social case work, and was supplemented by a briefer volume, *What is Social Case Work?* [13] In the latter book she forecast the increasing interest in the psychological point of view and in the study of personality problems. The advances in social case work concepts and techniques in the subsequent twenty years were set forth by Hamilton Gordon in his *Theory and Practice of Social Case Work*.[14]

Mental hygiene and psychiatric social work. Social case work was further enriched by the development of the psychiatric technique and the mental hygiene point of view, which has become increasingly popular in the last three decades. It received its first important expression in the Smith College School for Psychiatric Social Work, created in 1917 and much influenced by Frankwood E. Williams. But the book that first crystallized the psychiatric approach to social case work was *The Kingdom of Evils* [15] by Elmer E. Southard and Mary C. Jarrett, published in 1922.

This trend in social case work provides a better technique for the careful analysis of personality problems in relation to the origins and treatment of poverty. While social case work gained its first great impetus in connection with the charity organization movement, the relief of poverty, and problems of child welfare, the mental hygiene movement supplied other and wider fields for its application. It has been extended with particular success to the problems of juvenile delinquency, probation, parole, and child guidance. Trained social workers have also, of course, supplied much of the professional personnel for the management of institutions for dependents and other segregated classes. The development of a more scientific attitude in social work has promoted much more attention to research in regard to social problems, causes of dependency, and better techniques of relief and administration.

Rise of schools of social work. Since the charity organization movement created the need for a large group of trained social workers, it was natural that such training would be forthcoming. The Boston Training School for Social Workers was opened in 1904, under the auspices of Harvard University and Simmons College. The New York School of Philanthropy, later changed to the New York School of Social Work, was opened in 1905. The Pennsylvania School of Social and Health Work was

---

12 New York: Russell Sage Foundation, 1917.
13 New York: Russell Sage Foundation, 1922.
14 New York: Columbia University Press, 1941.
15 New York: The Macmillan Company, 1922.

launched in 1908. By 1919 there were 15 professional schools of social work, and they then founded the Association of Training Schools for Professional Social Work, later changed to the American Association of Schools of Social Work. There are today 53 schools of social work in the United States, all associated with some institution of higher learning. In 1949, there were over 10,000 students enrolled—4,453 of them full-time graduate students.

In 1950 there were over 100,000 professional social workers in the country, among whom there were about five women to one man. In 1921 social workers founded their professional organization, the American Association of Social Workers, with headquarters in New York City. On October 1, 1950, it had 12,313 members in 115 local chapters. With such training as the above schools offer, social work has attained about as high a degree of professional efficiency as can be achieved in this mode of approach to the relief of dependency. The annual meetings of the National Conference of Social Work provide a sort of national clearinghouse for social work discussion and criticism.

Social changes bring new orientation in social work. Realistic social workers recognize that we are at a turning point in the history of social work. The depression reduced the private resources from which social work had derived most of its financial support. Those whose fortunes had not been depleted were more reluctant to part with their assets, in spite of higher income and estate taxes. The enormous increase of unemployment and other evidences of the weakening of the capitalistic system created relief problems far too expensive for private charity to cope with. The increasing popularity of social insurance and the pension system took many problems of relief away from private agencies.

The prospect of a change of social and economic systems had led many social workers to take a very critical attitude toward the conventional methods and goals of their profession. This attitude has been notably expressed by Roger Baldwin and by Miss Mary Van Kleeck, of the Russell Sage Foundation. Related to this is the current tendency to emphasize the fundamental responsibility of our economic system for dependency. This tends to minimize the importance of relieving individual cases of need. The latter are regarded as simply personal manifestations of the general pathology of our economic order. Hence, there has been a notable shift from emphasis on relief to emphasis on prevention, viewed in a far-reaching fashion. This is in the spirit of the minority report concerning the British poor law in 1909.

There is evidence on every hand that private charity is being supplanted by social insurance in the handling of relief problems. This does not mean that there will be no place for social workers in the future. Much private relief work will continue. But public agencies of relief will have real need for trained agents. Social work is likely to find its main future areas of activity primarily in connection with public relief of one sort or another, especially in connection with the various Social Security programs, and in the fields of public health, mental hygiene, and delinquency control.

THE EXTENSION OF PUBLIC RELIEF UNDER THE NEW DEAL

Early emergency measures of the New Deal. The depression of 1929 will probably come to be recognized as the turning point in relief policies in the United States. The enormous increase of unemployment created a volume of dependency which completely swamped the resources of private charity, though President Hoover insisted upon relying mainly on private charity to the very end. He was only reluctantly persuaded to request a minimum appropriation for the public relief of the dependency caused by unemployment. When Franklin D. Roosevelt came to the presidency, a new philosophy was adopted, and the most extensive program of public relief in American history was immediately set up and put into operation.

A Federal Emergency Relief Administration was created on May 12, 1933, with Harry L. Hopkins, a veteran social worker, as administrator. An initial appropriation of 500 million dollars was made under the terms of the Wagner-Lewis Act of May 12, 1933. This was increased by 950 million dollars in February, 1934, and spent mainly by the Civil Works Administration. The Works Relief Bill of 1935 carried an additional 880 million dollars for direct relief.

In November, 1933, it was decided to take 4 million men and women from direct relief and put them to work. Accordingly, the Civil Works Administration (CWA) was created in that month and put under the general supervision of R. J. Baker, a subordinate of Hopkins. During the winter of 1933-1934, the CWA expended a little over a billion dollars; it was disbanded the following summer. Little work of permanent importance was achieved, but the procedure followed was better than demoralizing direct relief, with its complete idleness. A Federal Surplus Relief Corporation was set up in October, 1933, under the direction of Keith Southard, to purchase foodstuffs as cheaply as possible for distribution to the unemployed, and also to buy up surpluses of clothing, fuel, and the like for the benefit of the unemployed.

The PWA and WPA. More extensive and permanent in character was the effort to provide purchasing power through employment on public works projects. An initial appropriation of almost 3.5 billion dollars was spent under the supervision of Harold L. Ickes, Secretary of the Interior, who was in charge of the Public Works Administration (PWA). In April, 1935, an additional 4 billion dollars was appropriated for public works. Following the passage of the Works Relief Act of April, 1935, a supplementary administrative agency, the Works Progress Administration (WPA) was created. It was administered by Hopkins. It transferred about 3.5 million unemployed persons from direct relief to useful work.

Closely associated with public works was the Civilian Conservation Corps Reforestation Relief Act of March 31, 1933, which set up camps for the unemployed, chiefly young men, to carry on work in reforestation and other conservation activities. In addition to board and lodging, a small cash allowance also was provided. The Civilian Conservation Corps

provided work for about 2 million young men altogether and the value
of its work has been appraised at over a billion dollars.

It is generally admitted by competent students that such "recovery"
as took place under President Roosevelt was mainly the result of this
government spending for relief and public works.

Basic social philosophy of the New Deal. More important than any
specific relief aid—indeed, more important even than the Social Security
Act—has been the social philosophy which·the New Deal introduced:
that the government will not stand idly by and allow the poor to starve
and rot. Public responsibility for a minimum of public weal was probably
the most important single contribution made to American life by the
Roosevelt administration. No longer would it be more difficult to secure
public aid for a man than for a mule.

It hardly needs to be pointed out that the great increase in the scope
and expense of public relief after 1929, and especially since 1933, was not
limited to the Federal government. The various states and local units of
the union have been compelled to shoulder a relief burden unprecedented
in their history. It is officially estimated that the total Federal, state, and
local expenditures for relief from January, 1933, to January, 1939, were
about 13 billion dollars. In both Federal and state jurisdictions, then,
public relief has tended increasingly to supersede private charity.

SOCIAL LEGISLATION AND SOCIAL INSURANCE IN ENGLAND

Origin of British social legislation. Although direct relief, either institutional or outdoor, has been the prevalent method of dealing with
poverty, this procedure has been supplemented and gradually supplanted
by legislation protecting labor and by social insurance schemes designed
to eliminate the need for the direct relief of poverty.

The first considerable success in protective labor legislation was
achieved in Great Britain in the first half of the nineteenth century,
largely as the result of the work of Lord Shaftesbury (1801-1885) and his
associates. These laws were passed chiefly through the initiative of the
Conservatives (Tories). They were motivated in part by humanitarian
considerations and in part by an attempt to get revenge on the Liberal
factory owners who were attacking the British Corn Laws that furnished
protection to the English agricultural group, from which the Conservatives were mainly drawn.

It is impossible in the space available to describe in detail the contents of this legislation, but its general character can be indicated. The
factory acts of 1802, 1819, 1831, 1833, 1844, 1847, 1850, and several minor
laws of the 1860's, established the ten-hour day for the laboring classes in
practically all factories. They also provided effective factory inspection,
safety appliances, better sanitary conditions, and a general discouragement
of child labor. Women and children were excluded from mines, and better
hours and safety devices were provided for in mines by acts of 1842, 1855,
and 1872. The distressing evils in the employment of juvenile chimney-
sweeps were eliminated by laws of 1834 and 1840. Particularly the result

of the efforts of Lord Shaftesbury were the important Factory Act of 1833 and the famous Ten-Hour Bill of 1847. Other important acts were passed in 1850, 1878, and 1901, and a vast fabric of protective legislation and regulations has grown up.

The Liberal program. Although England was the early home of Economic Liberalism, even the party of Cobden and Bright was later converted to social reform through a process of change that Leonard T. Hobhouse clearly explained in his little book, *Liberalism*.[16] The more discerning British liberals at the turn of the century became convinced that if capitalism did not do more to deal with the problems of poverty, unemployment, and the like, socialism might grow and ultimately take over the government.

The vigorous leader of the new Liberal party, David Lloyd George, secured, in the period between 1905 and 1914, the adoption of a legislative reform program sufficient to make Cobden turn in his grave. It was rivaled in content and decisiveness only by the earlier German achievements. Workmen's compensation was provided by an act of 1906. Old age pensions were introduced in 1908-1909. Sickness, invalidity, and unemployment insurance were initiated in 1911. Thoroughgoing reform of the inequitable landholding system was forecast in the Small Holdings Act of 1907, but was cut short by the outbreak of the First World War. The British social insurance system proved of untold value in the relief of the unemployed and sick after the war.

The program of social insurance was considerably expanded in England after 1918. The rules governing eligibility to old age pensions were liberalized by an act of 1919 and the maximum pension rate slightly raised. This legislation was still further extended by the Widows, Orphans and Old Age Pensions Contributory Act of 1925 and the Contributory Pensions Act of 1929. A comprehensive National Health Insurance Act was passed in 1924, and those insured under it also had to be insured for widows', orphans', and old age benefits. On March 1, 1935, the administration of the entire system of English unemployment insurance was placed in the hands of a new National Unemployment Insurance Board.

The Beveridge Report. In June, 1941, Sir William Beveridge was named chairman of a committee, appointed by the Crown, to survey and recommend changes in the British insurance system. The Beveridge Report, made public in November, 1942, recommended the unification and expansion of all existing social insurance in a plan involving complete coverage of all needy citizens, regardless of income. Virtually every person would be expected to contribute.

Under this plan, workers would receive increased unemployment, sickness, and disability payments, based on need rather than on previous earnings, and to be continued as long as necessary. Maternity benefits' were included for women workers and for housewives whose husbands were employed. Funeral benefits were to be provided. Family allowances

---

16 New York: Holt, 1911.

were suggested for those with two or more children under 16 years of age. Free medical care for all persons was recommended. For those cases not covered by contributions, payments would be judged on the basis of need. In addition to the social insurance proposals, minimum-wage legislation was urged. To facilitate the unification and expansion of social insurance, the establishment of a Ministry of Social Security was recommended.

The Labour Government program of cradle-to-grave social insurance. In 1945, a Labour Government replaced the wartime Conservative-Labour Coalition Government. The new Labour Government, soon after its formation, took up the task of extending and applying the security and insurance measures of the Beveridge Report. The National Insurance Act of 1947, which went into effect in July, 1948, extended contributory insurance so as to provide for an improved and more uniform scale of insurance benefits for unemployment, sickness, old age, and death, and for orphans, mothers, and widows.

The insurance plan is financed by contributions from the employer, the employee, and the government. About a dollar a week is deducted from the pay check of an employed man; a working woman contributes about 76 cents weekly. The employer's share amounts to about 83 cents a week for each employee, male or female. To this total weekly contribution of the employer and employee, an additional 50 cents a week is contributed by the government (actually, by the taxpayers). When the worker has made the required number of payments—they vary with different benefits—he and his family are eligible for sickness, unemployment, and other benefits. In the event of illness, for example, the benefits received amount to about $5.25 weekly for the man, plus $3.20 for his wife, and $1.50 for the oldest child. If there are other children in the family, they do not receive benefits because they are covered by the system of family allowances financed by the government entirely out of taxation.

Self-employed persons and those living on private income are required to register and make weekly payments. These payments amount to about $1.23 for the self-employed and about 93 cents for the person who lives on private income. The self-employed and the persons living on income will be eligible for some benefits of the insurance plan. It is expected, however, that few persons from the self-employed or private income groups will wish to apply for the small weekly benefits, but will consider their contributions as additions to their taxes paid to the government. The National Insurance Act covers over 30 million persons; the annual cost of the plan runs to over 2 billion dollars.

The Health Service Act went into effect at the same time as the National Insurance Act. By this Act, free and complete medical, dental, and optical care is provided to every man, woman, or child who desires it. The costs of medical care are financed out of taxation. The plan for free medical care is not to be confused with the sickness benefit provided by the National Insurance Act. The sickness benefit is a small weekly payment made to a worker during periods in which illness keeps him away from work. In order that the sickness benefit be conferred, contributions from the employer, the employee, and the government must have been made for a certain number of weeks.

The new English social insurance system, offering "cradle to grave" security, is one of the most comprehensive plans in existence. It has not been put in operation without opposition. This has been particularly true of the Health Service Act. Many physicians and dentists objected to "becoming civil servants"—that is, receiving their fees from the government—and some of the insurance companies also opposed the socialization of medical services. In spite of these objections, however, the program is operating for 30 million persons who have signed for free medical service. More than 90 per cent of the doctors and dentists have now joined the service, and the health budget for 1950 was somewhat in excess of a billion dollars.

The new medical service plan has met so great a need for medical and dental care that not even the most powerful and reactionary Conservatives have dared to assail it in forthright fashion. When the Labour Government itself sought to tamper with the program in the interest of greater armament expenditures, Aneurin Bevan and other ministers resigned their posts. The English death rate of 10.8 during the first full year of the operation of the new medical plan was Britain's lowest on record—in spite of her austerity regimen.

SOCIAL INSURANCE ON THE CONTINENT

Early German social legislation. The late arrival of the factory system in Germany and the lack of interest of government authorities retarded regulatory labor legislation until 1839. In that year a law was passed in Prussia limiting the working day of children under 16 to 10 hours and prohibiting the employment of children under 9. It also forbade night work for those under 16. The law was miserably enforced but, though recognized as a failure, was not replaced until 1853. Legislation in that year prohibited children under 12 from working, set the working day of children under 14 at 6 hours, and stipulated that child workers were to receive 3 hours of school instruction every day. Here again, the administration of the statute was a farce. Neither employers nor government officials took it seriously. No other German state achieved any greater success with its industrial laws at that time.

Increasing evils called imperatively for more extensive labor legislation, and the formation of the North German Confederation in 1867 set the scene for the adoption of a uniform labor code. After much debate, an industrial code, surprisingly complete for that time, was placed upon the statute books in 1869. This code amplified and reinforced the Prussian laws of 1839 and 1853, extending their provisions to mines and quarries. It also made obligatory the installation of safety devices by manufacturers. Again, lax enforcement, largely as a result of the failure to provide for adequate factory inspection, took most of the teeth out of the measure. When the need for a complete and systematic code of industrial regulation became clearer as a result of the tremendous growth of industry after 1871, the movement for protective labor legislation developed rapidly. In spite of a bombardment of demands from all types of reformers, the imperial government under Bismarck could not be moved toward social radicalism. It remained intent on protecting labor in other ways.

The Bismarckian achievements. In 1891, the movement for protective labor legislation was crowned with success. The industrial code of that year applied to factories, workshops, and home labor, other places of labor being regulated by other means. By its provisions, children under 13 were prohibited from working, and males under 16 and females were not permitted to work at night or to labor more than 10 hours daily. Safety devices were made compulsory, and special regulations covered the more dangerous industries. The industrial code applied uniformly to the whole empire, but inspection and enforcement were left to the several states.

Far more important as social legislation were the remarkable social insurance laws: the Sickness Insurance Law of 1883, the Accident Insurance Law of the following year, and the Old Age and Invalidity Law of 1889. Through such legislation, the empire assumed a policy of paternalistic assistance to the working classes. Though not the originator of the social insurance scheme, Bismarck was the one who supplied the necessary pressure to have the bills put through. Social insurance schemes existed in Germany before 1870, but the achievement of creating a national system and introducing the element of compulsion into its operation was that of the great Iron Chancellor. In 1911 the social insurance laws were unified into a single code, which long stood as a landmark in the history of social legislation.

By the Sickness Insurance Law of 1884, all workers whose income fell below a stipulated amount were compelled to contribute to an insurance fund. Workers' contributions made up two-thirds of the fund, those of the employers the remainder. Free medical attention and one-half of his wages for a period of 26 weeks were guaranteed to the insured person in the event of sickness. The Accident Insurance Law provided compulsory workmen's compensation for nearly all industrial workers. Employers alone contributed to the funds, and they administered them in accordance with the scale set by law. In case of death, a yearly pension amounting to 20 per cent of the deceased's wages was paid to the dependents of the insured person. Employees, employers, and the government all contributed to the fund from which the benefits were paid under the Old Age and Invalidity Law. The pensions varied in accordance with the amount contributed by the worker. Insured persons of 65 (the age limit was first set at 70) could draw their pensions.

There were three reasons that led Bismarck and his associates to the frank acceptance of social insurance by Germany: (1) It was hoped to entice the worker from the doctrines of Marxian socialism, which were spreading rapidly, by assuring him of security and maintenance throughout his life and by showing him that the state had his welfare at heart.

(2) A paternalistic tradition was part and parcel of the Prussian heritage. The government was thought to be the proper authority to care for the workingman. In so doing it would create a healthier, more efficient nation. "In Prussia," Bismarck could say, "it is the kings, not the people, who make revolutions." (3) It was thus held to be the function of the state to protect its citizens. The workingman must be brought to regard the state as his benefactor and friend, not as his enemy. A contented, healthy working class is an asset to the state; a dissatisfied, unhealthy working class is a liability and a problem.

Recent German social legislation. As a result of the First World War, the whole body of German social insurance legislation underwent radical revision. Not only were the old laws liberalized and broadened in their application and the money benefits readjusted to meet the new economic conditions, but in 1927 a measure was passed that provided for unemployment insurance. This type of insurance was also compulsory and applied to all workers whose incomes fell below a set standard. From funds made up of equal contributions by employers and employees, and administered by the state at its own expense, insured persons received a certain percentage of their wages for periods generally not exceeding 26 weeks in the year.

The Nazis considerably modified the German system after 1933. Social insurance benefits—for illness, disability, accidents, old age, and unemployment—were reduced. Moreover, the mutual assistance and insurance associations of the German trade unions were dissolved and their funds turned over to private insurance companies, which paid small benefits. The general Nazi trend was to turn from systematic social insurance to direct relief.

French social legislation and insurance plans. Accompanying the growth of the factory system in France, there appeared the same evils and problems that had faced England. These brought a similar need for regulatory legislation. It is interesting to note that the first steps to regulate the hours and conditions of labor by the state go back to the Revolutionary period and Napoleon I. France was the first continental country to offer legal protection to labor. Legislation subsequent to the Industrial Revolution dates from the child labor law of Louis Philippe's reign. This measure, which was passed in 1841, provided that no children under 8 should be employed in industrial establishments. It limited the working day of children between 8 and 12 to 8 hours and that of children between 12 and 16 to 12 hours. Punishment was prescribed for violation of the law, and special commissions were entrusted with enforcement. The act was sharply criticized and very poorly enforced. The only partially successful and permanent labor legislation that resulted from the Revolution of 1848 was a 12-hour law. There was little additional labor legislation until after the founding of the Third Republic.

Following the report of a commission, a law of 1874 applying to mines and industries provided for: (1) a general minimum age of 12 for children in industry; (2) a 12-hour day for children between 12 and 16; (3) rest periods; (4) the prohibition of night work for females under 21 and for males under 16; (5) sundry sanitary regulations; and (6) schooling for children under 13 in industry. Between 1874 and 1914, labor was further protected by a series of regulatory measures that covered hours, working conditions, the labor of miners, Sunday rest, and provisions for thorough inspection. On the eve of the First World War the government had already published the first volumes of an excellent labor code that systematized the legal material on the question. The Popular Front government under Léon Blum, in 1936-1937, enacted various protective laws, including a 40-hour week and legislation strengthening the status of labor generally.

In social legislation such as old age pensions and unemployment insurance, France lagged behind Germany. The first workmen's compensation law was passed in 1898, and not until 1905 was a system of old age pensions instituted. The old age pension law of that year was replaced by the more satisfactory pensions law of 1910, which was compulsory for all workers not otherwise provided for. By the Social Insurance Law of April, 1930, France finally established a throroughgoing system of social insurance. The workers, the employers, and the government all contributed, and the law provides benefits for unemployment, death, old age, invalidity, maternity, and sickness. This act compels all workers, both male and female, whose incomes do not come up to a certain standard, to insure themselves.

In the chapter on population trends we referred to the vast program and expenditures for family benefits which France has recently established in the effort to increase the birth rate, amounting in payments to about two billion dollars yearly at present.

Social legislation in other countries of the Old World. The example of Germany spread to other European countries. Austria followed closely on its heels in social legislation. The Austrian accident insurance law was passed in 1887 and was subsequently strengthened. Sickness insurance was provided in 1888. After the First World War, under a Socialist regime for a time, Austria extended its state socialism, including one of the most ambitious and commendable experiments thus far in the way of public subsidy of housing facilities. Austria would probably have gone further in social legislation after 1919 had it not been for the fact that the more conservative Christian (Catholic) Socialist party soon captured the country as a whole. True socialism dominated only in Vienna and some other industrial cities. Thus, the Viennese achievements in housing reform and the like were more precisely municipal socialism than state socialism.

In Italy the government first aided the mutual insurance societies. A national accident insurance fund was created in 1885. The year 1898 marked the real introduction of Italian social insurance. In that year laws were passed providing for compulsory accident, sickness and invalidity, and old age insurance. The law of 1898 was extended by the socialist government in 1919 and modified somewhat by the Fascists in 1923. From 1921 to 1930 Italy paid out about 160 million lire for disability, old age, and sickness relief, but the level of benefit payments was reduced under the Fascist regime.

The lesser European countries have also experimented extensively and successfully with social insurance. Especially has this been true of Belgium and the Scandinavian countries. The Australasian colonies of Great Britain have also gone far with social insurance projects. The most extensive assumption of responsibility for the economic welfare of a people by the state in all of human history has, of course, occurred in Soviet Russia. But this has involved a complete destruction of the competitive capitalistic order and the establishemnt of a collectivist society. The Russians have installed a comprehensive system of social insurance which provides protection against old age, incapacity, illness, unemployment, and time lost in labor disputes. There is also a complete system of state medicine which furnishes medical care for all citizens.

SOCIAL LEGISLATION AND SOCIAL INSURANCE IN THE UNITED STATES

American social legislation before the New Deal. Because of administrative difficulties, the division of responsibility and the confusion inherent in our Federal system of government, our laissez-faire philosophy, and the hostile attitude of the Supreme Court toward remedial legislation, the United States for many years made much less progress than most of the European countries in the matter of protective labor legislation and social insurance. Until New Deal days, the greater part of labor legislation passed in the United States was state legislation. This began in 1842, when Massachusetts passed the first law restricting child labor. This prohibited children under 12 from working more than 10 hours a day. In the same year Connecticut passed a similar law but raised the age at which children were protected to 14. Within a decade, a number of other eastern states passed comparable legislation: New Hampshire in 1846, Maine in 1848, Pennsylvania in 1848, New Jersey in 1851, Ohio in 1852, and Rhode Island in 1853. Unfortunately this legislation was not very effectively enforced. Since 1900, nearly every state has passed some sort of legislation to limit child labor as to types of work permitted, hours of work, schooling required, and age restrictions.

Federal legislation to restrict child labor was at first unsuccessful. The two attempts of Congress to legislate against child labor were declared unconstitutional by the Supreme Court, in 1918 and 1922 respectively. In 1924 a constitutional amendment prohibiting child labor was submitted to the states for ratification. Thus far, only 28 states of the required 36 have ratified the amendment, though opinion polls have indicated that an overwhelming proportion of the population is in favor of ratification. The Fair Labor Standards Act of 1938, and especially its amendment in 1949, provided rigorous restrictions on child labor in industries engaged in interstate commerce.

The protection of women in industry began in 1847, when New

Hampshire passed the first law, one limiting the work of women to 10 hours a day. Maine, Pennsylvania, New Jersey, and Rhode Island passed similar laws during the next four years. Today every state in the country has legislation protecting women in industry. Half of them prohibit the work of even adult women in occupations deemed hazardous or injurious to health and safety. There was some state legislation limiting the hours men may work, but much obstruction was met in the attitude of the Supreme Court. In the famous Lochner case in New York State, in 1905, the Supreme Court set aside a law that sought to limit the hours of work

GREAT BRITAIN   62%

GERMANY   56%

UNITED STATES   0.6%
(WISCONSIN)

EACH FIGURE REPRESENTS 2% OF TOTAL

COURTESY U. S. COMMITTEE ON ECONOMIC SECURITY.

Workers of other countries and the U. S. protected by unemployment insurance before passage of the United States Social Security Act of 1935.

in bakeries. On the other hand, the court usually upheld Federal and state laws regulating the hours of public employees. It was also more tolerant of state laws limiting working hours in the interest of public health. On the whole, however, adequate protection of adult male labor was not provided until the Federal Fair Labor Standards Act was passed in 1938.

There was considerable state minimum wage legislation, beginning with the example of Massachusetts in 1912. At first the Supreme Court upheld these laws, the greatest victory being that won in the Oregon minimum wage case which had been prepared by Louis D. Brandeis just before he entered the Court. In this case, in 1917, the court upheld the constitutionality of the Oregon minimum wage legislation. But in 1923 it reversed itself in the case of the law passed by the District of Columbia in 1918. The Court maintained its hostile attitude toward minimum wage legislation until 1936, when it set aside the New York Minimum Wage Act of 1933. In 1937, another reversal took place when the Court upheld the minimum wage law of the State of Washington. A number of states, following the lead of New York, passed new minimum wage legislation after the favorable decision on the Washington act. Today 26 states have such minimum wage laws.

Workmen's compensation laws began in 1902, when Maryland passed such a law, which was declared unconstitutional. A similar fate befell the New York law of 1910. The first law to be upheld by the Supreme Court was that of Wisconsin, passed in 1911. At the present time all the states have workmen's compensation laws, but at least a fourth of the workers are not yet covered by such legislation, notably farm workers, domestic workers, and casual and migratory workers. Compensation payments usually vary from 50 to 80 per cent of previous earnings. The maximum weekly benefits generally are from $25 to $35. The maximum period during which compensation will be paid runs from two years in some states to an indefinite period in others. All but 7 states permit employers to insure with private companies. These 7 require insurance with the state insurance fund. Some 11 others have optional state compensation insurance.

Since the depression and the rise of New Deal policies, the most important social legislation in the United States has been the Federal labor legislation and the Social Security program, both of which we shall now proceed to describe.

The Fair Labor Standards Act of 1938. The first comprehensive Federal effort to regulate hours of work and the wages paid came in the Fair Labor Standards Act of 1938, commonly referred to as the "Wage-Hour Law." It applied to workers engaged in commerce and to those who produced goods shipped in interstate commerce. Most directly affected were the communications, transmission and transportation, iron and steel, saw mill, flour milling, textile, automotive, cottonseed oil, and fertilizer industries.

The law was intended not only to set a minimum wage but also to eliminate labor conditions deemed detrimental to the efficiency, health, and well-being of workers. The minimum wage was set at 25 cents an hour, with a standard maximum of 44 hours work each week. The employer was required to pay his employees time and a half for all hours worked beyond the 44-hour maximum. Only about one-fourth, or 11 million, of the workers of the country were covered by the law when it went into operation. The minimum wage was gradually raised until it reached 30 cents in 1940, and 40 cents in 1945, where it remained until January, 1950. The standard maximum work week was reduced to 40 hours in 1940, where it still remains.

The increased cost of living made the minimum wage of 40 cents extremely inadequate for postwar times, and President Truman urged Congress to raise the minimum to 75 cents an hour. In October, 1949, the 75-cent minimum was approved by Congress and went into effect in January, 1950, but supplementary legislation nullified some of the gain for labor. A little over one million workers, mainly in retail and service trades, logging, and irrigation, were removed from coverage under the

Wage-Hour Law. But the workers now covered—22 million—are about double the number protected in 1938.

There were many problems associated with the enforcement of the law. An extensive body of inspectors and enforcement officers was established to inspect factories and other places of employment, and see to it that the law was complied with. At the outset the work was done comprehensively and efficiently. But, later, decreases in the budget appropriations cut down the number of inspectors and thus hampered enforcement.

The law originally gave the Children's Bureau authority to enforce the child-labor provisions. Later, this authority was transferred to the Secretary of Labor. The minimum age for general employment was set at 16 years; that for occupations declared hazardous was 18 years. The chief opposition to the child-labor sections of the law came from seasonal industries and those textile mills which employed child labor.

The Social Security and Railroad Retirement Acts of 1935. The severity of the depression following 1929 revealed the inadequacy of state and local bodies to cope with the hardships caused by mass unemployment, sickness, and old age. Although by 1930 about 20 states had laws providing aid for the blind, 45 had laws to aid mothers, and 12 had old-age pension laws, many of these laws were inoperative because of lack of funds. Others were so restrictive as to be virtually worthless. No state had a system of unemployment insurance, though bills to provide for it had been introduced in 6 different states.

In President Roosevelt's message to Congress in June 1934, he asked that a Federal law be passed to provide safeguards against "misfortunes that cannot be avoided in this man-made world of ours." He mentioned certain definite objectives; old-age pensions for the needy; a long-term old-age insurance plan; unemployment insurance; health insurance for industrial workers; and pensions for the blind, for mothers, and for dependent children.

The Social Security Act, finally passed in 1935, established three separate programs. Two were insurance plans involving payroll taxes: (1) an old-age pension system, and (2) unemployment insurance. The third program provided Federal grants-in-aid to the aged, the blind, dependent children, and crippled children; to vocational rehabilitation; to maternal and child health services; and to an extension of public health measures. A Social Security Board was established to supervise the plan.

The old-age pension system is based on the contributory insurance method. Not all workers were included. The self-employed, agricultural workers, maritime service, employees of non-profit institutions, and Federal employees were excluded. A tax of one per cent of wages up to $3,000 a year levied on each worker and his employer covered by the plan financed the scheme. Pension payments, based not on need but on previous earnings, were to be made to the insured worker after he reached 65, provided his wages thereafter were less than $15 per month.

The unemployment insurance plan is financed by a payroll tax of 3 per cent of wages up to $3,000 a year on employers of 8 or more workers.

Against this tax, employers could get a credit offset up to 90 per cent for contributions they paid under a state unemployment compensation law. In other words, if a state passed such a law, employers would pay a Federal tax of .3 per cent and a state tax of 2.7 per cent. Benefit payments began in 1938. All states have passed unemployment insurance laws. The weekly payments have varied from $15 to $27, and the payment period ranges from 12 to 26 weeks. In 1949, 60 per cent of all benefits paid by the states were at the maximum permitted by law.

In order to secure Federal grants-in-aid, states were compelled to meet certain minimum general standards set forth in the Federal law. Federal assistance to the needy over 65 was 75 per cent of the first $20 per month paid by the state to the aged recipient, and 50 per cent of the balance up to $50, the Federal ceiling. Old age assistance payments have varied greatly among the states. In June, 1951, they ranged from $76 in Colorado to $18 in Mississippi. Eight other states paid less than $25 monthly. Federal funds for aid to dependent children, the blind, the disabled, and maternal and child health services ranged from one-third to one-half the amount granted by the state certifying agency.

In 1935, Congress also passed the Railroad Retirement Act to be administered by a Railroad Retirement Board. It provided benefits to aged and disabled employees of railroads and express and sleeping car companies. It was amended in 1948 to provide for a 20 per cent increase in benefits, which amounted to 227 million dollars in 1948. Another amendment in 1951 raised benefits by an additional 15 per cent.

Amendments to the Social Security Act, 1939-1950. In 1939, the Social Security Act was amended. The unemployment insurance plan remained the same, but the old-age pension system was put on a sounder basis and became Old Age and Survivors' Insurance (OASI). The payroll tax was raised to 1.5 per cent. The 1939 amendment recognized the family group rather than the individual alone. The amount granted to the worker after age 65 was based on averages, rather than on the total wages earned.

Further amendments to the Social Security Act were made in 1946 and 1947. Old age assistance grants, aid to dependent children allowances, and payments to the needy blind were increased. But, despite this liberalization of Federal grants-in-aid, the payments were still insufficient to care for all those in need.

In his message to Congress in January, 1948, President Truman asked for a broad expansion of the Social Security program, but the law which Congress passed in June, 1948, was vetoed by the President because he believed that it restricted rather than extended the coverage. Congress passed the law over his veto.

In his message of January, 1949, Mr. Truman again took up the problem of Social Security payments and urged that payroll taxes for old age insurance be raised to 2 per cent and that benefits be paid on the first $4,800 of income. In October, 1949, the House of Representatives passed a bill which added about 11 million persons to the coverage, increased benefits about 70 per cent, and raised payroll taxes on both employers and employees, but the Senate did not act. The President

INDIVIDUALS RECEIVING PAYMENTS

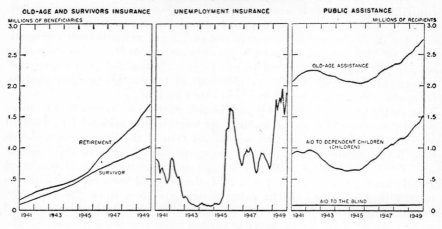

SOCIAL SECURITY PAYMENTS

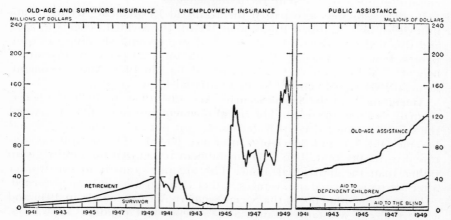

SOURCE: FEDERAL SECURITY AGENCY, SOCIAL SECURITY ADMINISTRATION.

Social Security Operations: 1941-1949. Old age and survivors insurance: *beneficiaries actually receiving monthly benefits (current payment status) and amount of their benefits during month.* Unemployment insurance: *average weekly number of beneficiaries for the month and gross benefits paid during the month under all state laws.* Public assistance: *recipients and payments under all state programs.*

repeated his recommendations for more extended coverage and increased benefits in his message of January, 1950.

Status of social insurance, 1950. Liberalizing action was needed, despite the fact that 35 million persons were already covered by some phase of Social Security legislation in June, 1950. Some 6,400,000 persons were then receiving benefits, and annual disbursements were $2,400,000,000. About 14.5 billion dollars had been collected in Social Security taxes since

1935. The total amount expended by the Federal and state governments for Social Security from 1935 to 1950 was about 24 billion dollars. Of this, about 8 billion dollars had been paid out for unemployment compensation: 3.4 billion for old age insurance; 10 billion in grants to the needy aged; 287 million to aid to the needy blind; and the remainder as aid to dependent children.

In June, 1950, there were 2,800,000 persons on the old age assistance rolls. The average monthly assistance payment was about $44, and the total expenditures in the fiscal year 1950 were $1,437,981,000. In June, 1950, there were 1,700,000 children under 18 on the aid to dependent children rolls. The average monthly assistance payment was $70 per family and $20 per recipient. The total expenditures in the fiscal year 1950 were $520,330,000. At the same time, 77,000 blind persons were being aided under Federal-state plans and 18,000 under state plans. Average monthly assistance was $48, and the total payments were $42,240,000. This was inadequate coverage for the blind, the minimum estimated number of whom is 255,000.

Yet, additional coverage was needed. More than 20 million workers were not covered by Social Security in mid-1950, and the increased payments made possible by the amending acts of 1946, 1947, and 1948 did not match the increase in living costs. Despite the high rate of employment, nearly 1,500,000 persons were drawing weekly unemployment benefits on July 1, 1950.

The Amendment of 1950. Congress heeded Presidential demands, and in August, 1950, President Truman signed the new Social Security Bill, which was even more sweeping than the amendment of 1939. It applied mainly to Old Age and Survivors Insurance. This new Act added about 10 million persons to the 35 million already covered by some phase of Social Security legislation. Those added comprised 4,750,000 self-employed small businessmen; 1,450,000 employees of state and local governments; 1,000,000 domestic servants; 850,000 agricultural workers; 600,000 employees of nonprofit organizations; 200,000 Federal employees; and approximately 1,200,000 in various other categories.

The old age pension benefits under the new law were raised by an average of about 77 per cent. The tables on page 602 reveal the increases in the pensions which will be received by those already retired, and by those who retire in the future at the age of 65.[17]

Other new benefits conferred by the 1950 amendment were the establishment of a new group or category entitled to public assistance up to $50 monthly—the permanently and totally disabled over 14 years of age; and also payments to doctors, hospitals, and clinics for medical services to needy individuals. More liberal assistance was provided for the needy in public institutions. The Federal matching maximums to mothers or relatives of needy children became $27 for the first child and $18 for each additional child.

The tax schedule was revised to meet the mounting costs involved in

[17] Tables from *U. S. News and World Report,* July 28, 1950, p. 25.

the new Act. The tax will remain at 1½ per cent until 1952. Then it will rise to 2 per cent; in 1960 to 2½ per cent; in 1965 to 3 per cent; and in 1970 to 3¼ per cent.

If You Are Already Retired

Here is the new schedule of payments for those whose Social Security pensions have already started. The table shows the amount to be paid monthly to retired couples at various pension levels.

Amount of Present Pension	Pension Under the New Law
$12	$24
15	30
20	37
25	47
30	54
35	59
40	64
45	69

If You Retire After 1950

Pensions that will be available from Social Security to persons retiring after next autumn are shown in the following table. Future pensions are compared with monthly payments now received by workers when they retire. In all cases pensions are payable at 65.

	Average Monthly Wage	MARRIED WORKER		SINGLE WORKER	
		Now	Under Law the new	Now	Under the new Law
	$100	$39	$75	$26	$50
After	150	47	86	32	58
5 Years'	200	55	98	37	65
Employment	250	63	109	42	73
	300	63	120	42	80
	100	41	75	28	50
After	150	50	86	33	58
10 Years'	200	58	98	38	65
Employment	250	66	109	44	73
	300	66	120	44	80
	100	45	75	30	50
After	150	54	86	36	58
20 Years'	200	63	98	42	65
Employment	250	72	109	48	73
	300	72	120	48	80
	100	49	75	33	50
After	150	59	86	39	58
30 Years'	200	68	98	46	65
Employment	250	78	109	52	73
	300	78	120	52	80

Summary appraisal of the Social Security Act. The Social Security Act and later amendments, although still limited in coverage and inadequate as to size of benefits and grants to the needy, the blind, and dependent children, is a beginning in the right direction. It rests on a civilized desire to give a minimum of economic protection to those unable to help themselves; it recognizes the responsibility of the community; and it serves, to some degree, as a means of maintaining the purchasing power of the masses. The extension of old age and survivors insurance to the family unit protects society as well as the individual against dependency resulting from old age and death. So far, the Social Security Act offers one of the few rays of hope to millions of persons who are unemployed, aged, sick or disabled, or fear the time when they will no longer be able to work.

One limitation is certain; the unemployment insurance provisions can only serve to cushion the shock of a mild business recession; they would not carry the country through a serious depression. As Albert L. Warner has stated: "Everyone is agreed on one thing: Unemployment insurance would not rescue us in a real depression. It would be like a couple of leaky lifeboats for a sinking *Queen Mary*. In a business slump or a mild recession, however, unemployment insurance can cushion the shock." Even in 1949, a good business year, no less than 38 per cent of the workers involved exhausted their unemployment insurance benefits before they found another job.

Union social welfare projects. The labor unions have set up additional coverage for nearly 5 million workers in health, welfare, and retirement plans. The best known of these is the one developed for the United Mine Workers by the aggressive policy of John L. Lewis. The UMW collects about 135 million dollars annually in mining royalties and devotes this sum to welfare activities for the miners. The International Ladies Garment Workers and the Amalgamated Clothing Workers have collected about 110 million dollars in their welfare funds. Enlightened employers often contribute to these union welfare funds. In the Philadelphia garment industry they contribute about 8 per cent; a more usual figure is 2 to 5 per cent. The retirement funds are the most important of these union welfare activities. They run from a dollar-for-dollar matching of the Federal payment of $26 per month to the $100 per month paid to retired members of the UMW.

In May, 1949, Mr. Lewis announced that his miners had received 106 million dollars in benefit payments until then. At that time the UMW welfare program provided the following benefits and services: death benefit of $1,000; disability payments up to a maximum of $60 a month to each disabled miner, $20 for his wife, and $10 for each child; widow's assistance grants up to a maximum of $60 a month, and $10 for each child; medical, health, and hospital care; and pensions of $100 monthly for miners over 60 years of age who retired after May 29, 1946.

Noncontributory industrial pensions. John L. Lewis' program of collecting royalties from the coal industry and using the proceeds to provide social benefits for his miners was an opening wedge to what is likely to prove one of the most epoch-making developments in the history of security for the working classes—namely, pensions to workers provided by industrial employers without any contribution from the workers.

A steel strike was called in 1949 mainly to secure non-contributory pensions for members of the CIO steel workers' union. After a bitter struggle, the employers' front was broken when the Bethlehem Steel Company agreed on October 31, 1949, to pay a monthly pension of $100 and some other benefits from company assets. Other steel companies followed suit, as also did the Ford Motor Company, the Chrysler Company, and General Motors. The arrangement with General Motors was especially interesting and significant in that it did not involve even the threat of a strike. It is too early to predict the extent of success of such plans, but they seem likely to dominate the industrial and labor scene and to constitute a great gain in behalf of workers' security. Probably there will have to be some adjustment in connection with government Social Security payments.

Development of a dual system of social security. It was once assumed that the entry of the Federal and state governments into social security programs on an extensive scale would reduce or even eliminate the private agencies and activities working along these lines. The growth of the union welfare and pension projects just described prove that such has not been the case. This important matter is ably discussed by C. Hartley Grattan in an article on "The Social Security Poor," in *Harper's*, December, 1949. As Grattan concludes: "The big point here is that the coming of the government social security system has resulted, not in the fading away of private schemes, but in their rapid expansion. Today it is correct to say that the nation is supporting a dual social security system, private ("union label" increasingly) and governmental, both parts of which are growing rapidly."

The figures here are startling to the uninformed. Employer contributions to private pension and welfare programs rose from 128 million in 1929 to 1,102 million in 1948. Employee contributions to the same private programs increased from 142 million in 1929 to 2,145 million in 1948. Combined, these contributions are approximately equal to all payments to the Federal Social Security system. If present trends continue, the private welfare system may soon cost more than the government welfare system.

THE PREVENTION OF DEPENDENCY

Reducing geographical and biological causes of poverty. Although the relief of existing dependency constitutes an emergency that always requires attention, contemporary social science emphasizes the primary importance of preventive measures and agencies. This philosophy repudiates the traditional theory that the poor and dependent are a necessary and permanent sector of the population. Preventive methods imply a clear understanding of the causes of dependency and a resolute attack upon them, no matter how many toes of vested interests may be stepped upon.

Geographical and other physical causes of dependency may be dealt with. Irrigation projects may temper the calamity of drought. Conservation can conquer dust storms and floods. Chemistry and bacteriology enable us better to war against animal diseases and insect pests. More headway right now is being made against diseases and pests than in controlling droughts, floods, and dust storms.

Biological causes of dependency are not beyond the range of resolute social effort. Birth control has pointed the way to keeping the population down to the number which may be supported within the facilities provided by any given economy. Immigration has already been sufficiently restricted so that there will be fewer future causes of dependency arising from it. Some progress is being made along the line of a better health program. The facilities of free clinics and dispensaries are being increased and extended to ever larger groups of poor people. It is probable, however, that illness will remain a leading cause of dependency until we set up a system of compulsory health insurance. As we shall see, the mental hygiene movement is now developing rapidly and is doing everything possible to cut down the number of the psychopathic and mentally defective. Some help from the eugenics movement may ultimately be expected in reducing the number of feeble-minded. But it is a moot question whether mental hygiene and eugenics will soon be able to cope with those conditions in contemporary life which are tending to increase the number of mentally diseased and defective in the population.

Essential economic and social reforms. In the economic field we might, to some degree at least, adopt the land reform program advocated by Henry George and turn over to society the gains which accompany the development of both rural and urban areas. The competitive system may bring about a greater degree of efficiency in industrial production and may eliminate the large element of waste which still persists. Unfortunately, this will probably be accomplished by more extensive introduction of labor-saving machinery, which will intensify the problem of dependency by throwing more and more men out of work. Labor is becoming more thoroughly organized and it must repudiate the uneconomical and antisocial principle of limitation of output. The initiative of industry, the pressure of public opinion, and governmental action may lead to the provision of more adequate safety devices and the reduction of the still alarming toll of industrial accidents. More thorough government regulation of finance capitalism and speculation would do much to flatten out or eliminate altogether the disastrous cycles of business prosperity and depression. The most alarming economic trend today is the attempt to maintain prosperity and avert depressions by vast armament production, which diverts the products of technology from consumers to materials designed for prospective warfare.

Attacks upon the problem of dependency from the social angle might do much to eliminate or reduce this public burden. Social morale needs to be strengthened through greater activity of social settlements, community agencies, and similar institutions. A socialized religion, laying stress upon the improvement of humanity here and now, would supply a strong social and emotional drive against those evils which contribute to poverty and dependency.

Educational approaches to poverty. An improved educational system could accomplish much in the way of preventing poverty. Educational facilities should be sanely differentiated according to the classes of children which they serve. A far greater degree of attention must be given to industrial education for all students save the minority showing higher intelligence quotients. Vocational training should probably absorb at least half of our educational effort in the public schools. Much greater stress should be laid upon instruction in domestic science, so that wives could make the best possible use of the all-too-limited income which they have to spend. Adequate civic education should train future citizens to understand the types of government policy most desirable in combating the causes of poverty.

Social insurance. The more progressive states of the world have already recognized the necessity for the provision of comprehensive systems of compulsory public social insurance covering sickness, old age, accident, disability, unemployment, and death. The United States finally took a decisive step in this direction through the Social Security Act of 1935. Many nations have also introduced an adequate system of mothers' pensions.

Desirable political measures. Finally, we might accomplish much in eliminating the political causes of dependency. Government efficiency and honesty could be promoted by a more thorough introduction of civil service tests and by the merit system. The notion that the government should act merely as a collective policeman and that it should not attempt to regulate industry and finance must be abandoned. In our day and age the government must assume a wise and positive rôle in the control and direction of economic life. To curb unemployment in private industry, the government must anticipate larger and more complete programs of public works which will absorb the unemployed and redound to the benefit of the nation. Government aid to improve educational facilities, health insurance, and mental hygiene will be indispensable in the reduction of dependency.

Better forms of international organization, a greater use of arbitration, freer trade, and better access to markets and raw materials for all nations will be indispensable if we are to avert the calamity of another world war, with its possibility of complete destruction of civilization. As one commentator has dramatically expressed it, we have now come to a point where we must choose between the atomic race and the human race.

Social education and social reform needed to eliminate poverty. All these preventive measures assume the increase of moral fortitude, scientific knowledge, and social intelligence. Hence, they will have to depend to an ever greater degree upon improved social education. Therefore, we may well recall the assertion that the struggle against dependency is simply one phase of that "race between education and catastrophe" which, in the words of the late H. G. Wells, characterizes modern civilization as a whole.

With respect to both the poverty situation and our general cultural set-up, we stand much as Europe did in the sixteenth century—at the end of a great historic era and on the brink of a new age. In such a setting, it would be futile to predict the course of events for anything more than the immediate future. But it is likely that the poverty and relief situation of the year 2000 will no more resemble that of today than the Poor Law of 1834 resembled the system of monastic charity of the Middle Ages.

If we bring our institutions up to date and put our machines to work in the direct service of mankind, we are bound to move quickly into a material utopia which will permanently abolish all poverty and need for relief. If we fail to do this, we may drift into atomic warfare, chaos, and disorganization which will destroy even the existing relief agencies and will make suffering and misery more bitter, widespread, and unrelieved.

Will we move into a "Nineteen Eighty-four" society? Concerning the future of poverty, the gravest menace is that we may enter a type of society in which poverty is deliberately imposed on the people by the government. In the most important prophetic book of the twentieth century, *Nineteen Eighty-four*,[18] George Orwell pictures a régime based upon perpetual, though limited, war, which is maintained so that the masses can be deprived of the fruits of an efficient technology. They submit to this situation because of the terror and intimidation devised and enforced by the government. World trends of the last fifteen years provide all too much evidence that the main nations of the world are, consciously or unconsciously, slipping into this pattern of life. If this trend cannot be checked, it is obvious that there is no hope of eliminating, or even reducing, poverty.

SUMMARY

Poverty is a state of chronic economic insufficiency. Pauperism is a state of extreme poverty in which a person cannot long maintain life without outside aid of some kind.

Many studies have been made of the extent of poverty and pauperism. In England, until 1918, at least 30 per cent of the population lived in dire poverty. This condition has been bettered somewhat by the growth of British social insurance. In the United States, the amount of poverty has varied with general economic conditions. At the depth of the depression, in 1932, at least half of the American population was living in poverty. Even in 1950, after much social security and other social legislation, there were at least 30 million Americans who lived at or below the poverty line. At least 10 million of those persons existed in a state of pauperism.

There are numerous causes of poverty. Nature contributes to poverty through inadequate national resources and natural catastrophes. There are also biological causes: inherited or acquired physical defects, the ravages of disease, and incapacitating accidents. Economic factors contribute to dependency through inefficient use of our technology, inadequate methods of distributing goods, and inequitable distribution of the national income. Socio-psychological causes exist in the form of extravagance, insufficient social and economic education, and industrial policies which lead to restriction of industrial output. Political corruption and inefficiency also contribute to poverty, but the greatest political cause of poverty is warfare, with its vast devastation and expense.

Methods for the relief of the poor have varied from extermination of the poor and disabled in primitive society to the comprehensive contemporary systems of social insurance. In the Middle Ages, the church, the manorial system, and the guilds provided for most of the relief. With the rise of Protestantism and the national state in modern times, public relief became increasingly important. The first great landmark in this stage was the Elizabethan Poor Law of 1601. Its goal was mainly relief of poverty. The ideal of prevention grew more important during succeeding

---

[18] New York: Harcourt, Brace, 1948.

centuries, and the famous English Poor Law of 1834 stressed prevention as much as relief. In the twentieth century, social insurance has tended to supplant the earlier methods of handling poverty, and its aim is primarily prevention, though sheer relief still looms large in social insurance benefits.

Private relief is still needed and still exists. The funds needed to provide it come mainly from the relatively wealthy groups. Private relief is administered chiefly by trained social workers. There are now many efficient schools of social work to train those needed for private relief work, and trained social workers also play a large rôle in the administration of public relief under social insurance systems.

Social insurance plans embrace protection against accidents, sickness, disability, unemployment, old age, and death of wage-earners. The earliest social insurance system was that devised by Bismarck in Germany in the 1880's. English social insurance began after 1906, during the régime of the Liberal-Labour Coalition Government. It has grown steadily until it now embraces the "cradle-to-the-grave" coverage worked out by the British Labour Government since 1945. Other civilized European countries have also provided social insurance schemes. In Soviet Russia, all relief is government aid to the poor.

There was not much social legislation in the United States prior to the Social Security Act of 1935. Most of it took the form of state laws protecting child laborers and women workers, minimum wage laws, and some provision of public relief under social insurance systems. The depression following 1929 compelled the New Deal administration to provide public relief on an unprecedented scale. New Deal policy moved ahead from outright relief to well-organized plans to provide constructive public works. The most important permanent achievements of the New Deal in handling the relief of the needy were the Fair Labor Standards Act of 1938, which provided for minimum wages, and the Social Security Act of 1935, which set up a comprehensive system of social insurance. This has been amended and extended, and covers unemployment insurance, aid to the needy and helpless of various types, and old age insurance pensions. But private pension systems are also growing and provide benefits approximately equal to those of the Social Security system.

Poverty can only be eliminated, however, by removing the causes of poverty. Conservation, replacement, and better agricultural methods can reduce the impact of natural causes of poverty. Eugenics, better medical care, and safety programs will lessen the biological causes of poverty. More efficient use of our technology, better methods of distributing the goods produced, and some plan for a more equitable distribution of national income would solve many of the economic causes of poverty. Economy and efficiency in political life would aid in reducing poverty, but there is little prospect that poverty can be prevented until universal peace is assured.

If the present international tension continues, there is grave danger that the whole world will move into a system like that pictured by George Orwell in his book *Nineteen Eighty-four,* where the masses remain in perpetual poverty while natural resources and technology are devoted mainly to supporting perpetual phony war.

SELECTED REFERENCES

Abbott, Edith, *Public Assistance*, 2 vols. Chicago: University of Chicago Press, 1940-1941. The most complete account of the entry of the government into the relief of the needy, with special reference to New Deal measures.

*Andrews, F. E., *Philanthropic Giving*. New York: Russell Sage Foundation, 1950. Most complete exposition of the nature, sources, and application of private donations to charity and welfare. Reveals remarkable increase in contributions by living donors since 1941, partly due to the income tax situation. But the book demonstrates the utter inadequacy of private philanthropic gifts to relieve poverty and misery.

*Beveridge, Sir William, *Social Insurance and Allied Services*. New York: Macmillan, 1943. The famous Beveridge Report on the "cradle-to-the-grave" program of social protection of the needy.

————, *Voluntary Action*. New York: Macmillan, 1948. Later supplement to the author's famous report on social insurance.

Brady, R. A., *The Crisis in Britain*. Berkeley: University of California Press, 1950. A reliable, up-to-date and detailed account of the achievements of the British Labour Party since 1945.

Bruno, F. J., *The Theory of Social Work*. Boston: Heath, 1936. Authoritative exposition of the field and methods of social work from the sociological standpoint.

*Burns, E. M., *The American Social Security System*. Boston: Houghton Mifflin, 1949. The most adequate survey of our existing plans and systems of social insurance and relief in the United States.

*Calcott, M. S., and Waterman, W. C., *Principles of Social Legislation*. New York: Macmillan, 1932. A good introductory survey of the nature of modern legislation for the relief and protection of workers and the needy classes prior to the Social Security system in the United States.

Clarke, H. E., *Principles and Practice of Social Work*. New York: Appleton-Century, 1947. Valuable survey of the problems and techniques involved in social welfare work, interpreted from the sociological and psychiatric viewpoint.

Coon, Horace, *Money to Burn*. New York: Longmans, Green, 1938. A realistic study of the resources and activities of the great foundations.

Dawson, W. H., *Social Insurance in Germany, 1883-1911*. New York: Scribner's, 1912. The authoritative account of the rise and development of social insurance in the German Empire.

Douglas, P. H., *Social Security in the United States*. New York: McGraw-Hill, 1939. History and appraisal of security legislation in the United States, including the Social Security Act of 1935.

*Fink, A. E., *The Field of Social Work*. New York: Holt, 1948. The most complete manual on the methods and all major fields of social work. An invaluable survey and summary.

Ford, James, and K. M., *The Abolition of Poverty*. New York: Macmillan, 1937. The most competent survey of the measures and programs needed to abolish poverty and prevent dependency.

*Hamilton, Gordon, *Theory and Practice of Social Case Work*. New York: Columbia University Press, 1941. Supplements Miss Richmond's classic book by assembling and appraising the knowledge and experience gained in the quarter of a century since Miss Richmond's volume was published.

Hayes, C. J. H. (Ed.), *British Social Politics*. Boston: Ginn, 1913. Valuable collection of readings and documents on the rise of social insurance in Britain.

*Kelso, R. W., *Poverty*. New York: Longmans, Green, 1929. Probably the best single volume on the causes and extent of poverty and the pre-New Deal methods of relief.

Lane, M. S., and Steegmuller, Francis. *America on Relief*. New York: Harcourt, Brace, 1938. A brief but reliable introduction to the revolution in relief methods after 1933.

Lindeman, E. C., *Wealth and Culture*. New York: Harcourt, Brace, 1935. Gives a negative reply to the allegation that the benefactions of the rich justify the present concentration of wealth.

Lowry, Fern (Ed.), *Readings in Social Case Work*. New York: Columbia University Press, 1939. Valuable collection of case material.

*McMahon, Arthur, Millett, J. D., and Ogden, Gladys, *The Administration of Federal Work Relief*. Chicago: Chicago Public Administration Service, 1941. The standard history of the Works Progress Administration of the New Deal and its accomplishments.

Meriam, Lewis; Schlotterbeck, Karl; and Maroney, Mildred, *The Cost and Financing of Social Security*. Washington: Brookings Institution, 1950. The best account of the financial aspect of our Social Security system and its future economic implications.

Miles, A. P., *An Introduction to Public Welfare*. New York: Macmillan, 1949. A good up-to-date textbook, providing a historical survey as well as a full treatment of contemporary public welfare techniques and programs.

Muntz, E. E., *Growth and Trends in Social Security*. New York: National Industrial Conference Board, 1949. Informative book on the rise and expansion of social security coverage.

Pipkin, W. W., *Social Politics and Modern Democracies*, 2 Vols. New York: Macmillan, 1931. Comprehensive historical account of social insurance in Britain and France.

Pray, K. L. M., *Social Work in a Revolutionary Age*. Philadelphia: University of Pennsylvania Press, 1949. Keen observations by a veteran social worker on the broader goals and responsibilities of social work.

Richmond, M. E., *Social Diagnosis*. New York: Russell Sage, 1917. The classic formulation of the principles of social case work. On psychiatric social work, see the book by L. M. French in the bibliography for the next chapter.

*Riis, J. A., *How the Other Half Lives*. New York: Scribner's, 1892. The pioneer work in arousing Americans to the sorry plight of the poverty-stricken in great cities.

*Scheu, F. J., *British Labor and the Beveridge Plan*. New York: Island Press, 1943. Good presentation of the background and provisions of the famous Beveridge plan of social security from the cradle to the grave, which has been applied and extended by the British Labour Government.

————, *Social Work as Human Relations*. New York: Columbia University Press, 1949. Valuable symposium on role of social work in human welfare.

*Southard, E. E., and Jarrett, M. D., *The Kingdom of Evils*. New York: Macmillan, 1922. The epoch-making pioneer book on the psychiatric and mental hygiene approach to social problems.

Stroup, H. H., *Social Work*. New York: American Book Company, 1948. Able discussion of the field and the techniques employed.

White, R. C., *The Administration of Public Welfare*. New York: American Book Company, 1950. New edition of one of the best treatments of social work and the operations of public welfare agencies.

CHAPTER 14

Mental Disease, Mental Defect, and the Rise of Mental Hygiene

THE EXTENT OF MENTAL DISEASE AND MENTAL DEFECT

Modern social life, mental disease, and mental defect. Among the social problems which have been greatly intensified as a result of contemporary living conditions, especially those growing out of industrialism and urban life, has been that of mental disease. Mental and nervous diseases have notably increased partly as a result of the strains and stresses produced by modern industrialism and urban living conditions. In 1880, the number of persons confined in hospitals for mental diseases was only 63.7 per 100,000 of the population. By 1946, it had increased to 374.8. Speaking before the American Association for the Advancement of Science, John W. Thompson, of Harvard University, attributed the marked growth of mental and nervous diseases to the increased tensions and overrapid pace of modern life in urban industrial societies.

Although there appears to be no very good reason for believing that the incidence of feeble-mindedness, in proportion to the size of the population, has increased as a result of these conditions, certainly the feeble-minded population has kept pace with the growth of the population in general. Indeed, the number of feeble-minded has probably grown more rapidly than the rest of the population because such persons are less likely to observe rational control over population growth and are less able to use birth control methods effectively. At any rate, their presence in a dynamic urban and industrial age is a more serious problem than it was in pastoral and agricultural society.

Number of mentally afflicted in our population. It has been estimated that over 10 million persons in the United States are temporarily or permanently disabled by mental diseases and serious mental defect at any given time. Those actually disabled have millions of dependents who are thus deprived of their support. In August, 1948, Esther Lloyd-Jones, of Columbia University, using United States Public Health statistics, stated that about 5 million persons were suffering from psychoneuroses and allied mental diseases; 2.5 million had serious character and behavior disorders; 1.5 million were mental defectives of such a low order as to need institutional treatment or segregation; and 600,000 were epileptics. It has been estimated by leading psychiatric experts that, even on the basis of prewar conditions, one person out of every 20 now at the age of 15 will at some time during his life enter a hospital for the treatment of mental illness, and that one person out of 10 will need medical treatment of some kind for a disabling mental disorder. About one million persons now in our grade schools will enter a mental hospital before they die. Lloyd-Jones estimated that 20 to 30 million Americans require, or would definitely benefit by, psychiatric treatment.

An official government census stated that, at the end of 1947, there were 543,727 patients in mental hospitals. There were, on the hospital books at that time, 620,020 patients. These included both persons confined in hospitals and persons either receiving treatment at home or on parole from an institution. Some 248,667 patients were admitted to hospitals in 1947, and the net hospital population increases annually by about 15,000. It would increase even more strikingly if there were room for more patients. There is a long waiting list of patients seeking admission to mental hospitals. State hospitals are now overcrowded to an extent of about 20 per cent of their normal capacity. It is estimated that these institutions cannot now receive much more than half of the really serious cases which should have hospital segregation and treatment. During 1947, more than one million persons received care and treatment in mental hospitals. Over 856,000 men were rejected by the selective service boards during the Second World War as bad psychiatric risks. In addition, there were 700,000 who were later discharged from the army for psychiatric reasons—more than half the number of medical discharges from the army.

In January, 1951, George S. Stevenson, Medical Director of the National Association for Mental Health, made the startling statement that of the 1,250,000 patients then in hospital beds in the country no less than 700,000 were serious mental patients. He went on to say that 200,000 more were suffering from milder mental diseases or disorders of emotional origin, thus indicating that about three out of every four hospital beds were occupied by mental and nervous patients. About 65 per cent of all patients in hospitals conducted by the Veterans Administration are mental cases.

The cost of maintaining public hospitals for the mentally diseased is enormous—over 275 million dollars annually at the mid-century. But this figure is trivial compared to the loss of wages and productive power on the part of the afflicted. Albert Deutsch, a leading writer on the problem, estimates that the minimum annual direct cost of mental disease in the United States is a billion dollars. This is a very restrained estimate, and does not include the cost of caring for the mentally deficient.

The magnitude of the problem of the public care of mental patients can be pointed up precisely by a brief description of the situation in New York State at the mid-century. The cost of the maintenance and construction involved in handling mental cases in the state absorbed no less than a third of the total operating budget of the state. Appropriations for the State Mental Hygiene Department, which is the most expensive department in the state (and growing more so every year), increased by over 300 per cent between 1943 and 1951—from 46 million dollars to 143 million. In New York, the number of patients in state hospitals is increasing by about 4 per cent annually. There were 107,164 in March, 1951.

Modern living conditions, especially in cities, increase mental disease. The marked gains in mental and nervous diseases have been attributed by sociologists and psychiatrists mainly to the enormous increase of mental strain, social stress, and personal worry in the thoroughly industrialized urban existence which encompasses the majority of Americans today. Some of the causes are the direct result of a new type of life that has increased nervousness and mental instability. Noises, crowding, added tension and dangers when on the streets, occupational diseases associated with different forms of industrialism, the monotony of factory life, and inadequate recreation are all contributing factors. Then, of course, there are various forms of indirect influences which tend to promote mental and nervous difficulties. Economic insecurity, for example, produces an untold amount of worry and distress. The older social standards and institutions of rural primary societies have disintegrated, and the former mental moorings have been swept away. No adequate substitutes have been provided as yet. The disintegration of the family and of the neighborhood in urban life, and disturbances of sexual adjustment have contributed their part to increasing nervousness and mental upsets.

That modern city life seems to produce a disproportionate volume of mental and nervous diseases is seen by the fact that the rate of first admissions to hospitals for the insane is about twice as great from urban regions as it is from rural communities. Although it is undoubtedly true that the authorities are more lax and careless about discovering and isolating the mentally diseased in rural areas, this laxness can by no means account for the striking difference in these figures. Further, the rate of first admissions is far higher for those who live in large cities than it is for inhabitants of smaller cities. It is worthy of note, however, that the incidence of mental and nervous diseases is increasing in rural areas as the result of the breakdown of rural institutions and the growth of urban influences upon the country.

Within cities, the incidence of mental disease is far higher in those districts where living conditions are crowded, depressing, tense, and insecure than elsewhere. Robert E. L. Faris and H. W. Dunham found that the insanity rate in the crowded central district of Chicago and in the hobo, rooming-house, and bohemian districts was about 10 times as high as in the outlying residential and suburban areas inhabited by the relatively well-to-do elements of the Chicago population. In other words, the "delinquency areas" revealed by Clifford Shaw and his associates also seem to be "insanity areas" as well, which is not surprising.

The most important consideration in the study of Faris and Dunham, as well as in much of the preceding discussion of the causes of the increasing incidence of mental diseases, is that most of the trends of modern living which have been described have intensified social disorganization. The latter is mainly and most directly responsible not only for the increase of mental and nervous disease but also for the growth of family instability, delinquency, vice, and suicide. In short, the conditions of life which have followed in the wake of industrialization and urbanization, especially the growth of slum areas and depressed living conditions, are mainly responsible for the increase of social disorganization, and the latter produces an ever greater volume of mental disorders.

Greater alertness increases hospital populations. In interpreting these trends, it is necessary to keep in mind the fact that we are today far more alert than formerly in detecting these mentally diseased types and in segregating them in institutions. Better state hospitals and improved popular understanding of the nature of mental afflictions have made relatives more willing to commit patients. Better hospital accommodations have led to keeping patients in institutions for a longer period, thus increasing the total hospital population. The impressive lengthening of the life span by about 20 years since 1880 has also increased the number of old people in the population, and thereby the number suffering from senile psychoses. The number of persons over 65 committed to mental hospitals is increasing yearly. An expert recently pointed out that, whereas about 13,600 persons over 65 were admitted to state hospitals for the insane in 1937, there will be at least 42,000 of this group admitted annually by 1980. Another reason for the large population and congestion of mental hospitals is the fact that dementia praecox (schizophrenic) patients, who constitute by far the largest single group in state hospitals at the present time, live approximately as long as normal persons. Since this disease has been generally incurable, these patients usually become permanent inmates of hospitals and constitute half or more of the total hospital population.

Reasons for the increase in mental disorders are not the cause of individual cases of mental disease. It should be understood that the factors mentioned in the previous pages which have led to an increase in the total number of mental and nervous patients are not the specific causes of any particular mental disease in a given individual. The immediate causes of a mental breakdown, as we shall explain later on, are mainly personal—organic diseases or mental conflicts in the individual mind— and can only be understood after a careful study of each patient by a neurologist or a psychiatrist. What modern life does is to augment susceptibility to mental and nervous disease and to increase the tensions, conflicts, worries, and frustrations that help to cause individual breakdowns.

Number of feeble-minded. Careful estimates of the number of the low-grade feeble-minded in the population give us a figure of about two million. This represents only the very inferior morons and the imbeciles and idiots. There are at least three million serious borderline cases. If we were to regard all persons with a mental age of 12 years or less as feeble-minded, we would find that they embrace approximately 45 per cent of the entire population, or over 65 million persons. Indeed, some 7 per cent of the population, about 10 million persons, have a mental age of 9.5 years, or less, and would certainly have to be classed as feeble-minded even though in most instances they do not require institutional care. Nearly 600,000 were rejected by the draft boards and the Army during the Second World War because of mental deficiency. In February, 1951, it was reported that 38.7 per cent of the draftees from one large section of the country had been rejected because of mental deficiency. There are in our public schools today more than 600,000 seriously retarded children who need special types of educational facilities to prepare them for a self-supporting existence. Of the total of two million relatively low-grade feeble-minded in the population only about 113,000 are segregated in public institutions where they may be adequately cared for, made self-supporting, and prevented from becoming public nuisances. In 1950, Lloyd N. Yepsen, an expert on mental deficiency, estimated that the feeble-minded cost the taxpayers of the country about 1.5 billion dollars annually.

Another serious form of mental disorder, about which neurologists and psychiatrists are not well agreed as yet, is epilepsy. There were some 21,000 epileptics in institutions in 1946, but experts estimate that there are probably 600,000 in the population who actively suffer from the disease. Some students of the problem estimate the latent cases as in excess of 10 million.

NORMAL AND ABNORMAL MENTALITY

Mental life viewed as response to stimulation. Modern psychology no longer holds to the older theological and metaphysical idea of the mind as a separate and mystical entity, existing apart from bodily processes and human behavior, but in some mysterious manner directing these. Mental life is a physio-chemical response to stimulation. The manifestations of such responses are what we know as human behavior.

These responses take place on various levels: physical, physio-chemical, sensory-motor, psychological, and social. The most rudimentary level is physical response, which manifests itself in the movement of the limbs of the body and the like, following the mechanical principles of the lever and the pulley. Next above this we have the physio-chemical responses, operating through the influence of hormones or chemicals secreted by the glands of internal secretion. They are particularly active in relation to the manifestation of leading human emotions, such as sex, fear, anger, and anxiety. Response to stimulation on the next higher or sensory-motor level takes place through what we know as reflexes. We may, for example, remove our hands suddenly from a hot surface. The mastery of the art of walking involves a complex control of reflexes enabling us to stand erect and direct our steps. Responses on the psychological level operate in the shape of ideas, which are slowly built up into a complex, integrated body of information and attitudes from childhood to adult life. Responses to stimulation on the social level make themselves evident in various habits, customs, and folkways prevailing in the group in which a particular individual lives. The total conduct or behavior of the individual represents the integrated result of responses on all these levels of stimulation. Notable defects or inadequacies on any level may create definite departures from what is regarded as normal behavior.

Nature of the normal mind. The normal mind is a mind which is characterized by adequate responses on every level of stimulation. When we come, however, to the conception of "normal" responses on the psychological and social levels, normality has to be judged with reference to the group in which the individual lives. Responses are regarded as normal if they coincide with the ideas and behavior patterns prevailing in the group. These may not necessarily be the most desirable types of responses. Sadly erroneous ideas may prevail in any given group, and the customs and mores of the group may not be in harmony with what is best for the well-being of society or the progress of humanity as a whole. On these psychological and social levels of response, mental normality is viewed primarily as a matter of relatively complete psychic integration and thorough adjustment to the social environment. The ideas entertained by the individual must be relatively consistent and the individual must feel in reasonable rapport with the social habits of the community. The tasks and responsibilities of life should be agreeable to the individual. In short, the individual must respond with enthusiasm and efficiency to the realities of life.

The views of what constitute normal and commendable mental attitudes have differed greatly in the course of human history. The Greeks stressed the desirability of serenity, urbanity, poise, and a sense of personal sufficiency. On the other hand, the attitudes most cherished and heartily recommended by the early Christians were fear, apprehensiveness, worry, a sense of inferiority, and a consciousness of sin. The majority of students of mental hygiene today are inclined to believe that the Greek ideals were the more satisfactory and healthful.

Hazy borderline between normal and abnormal minds. It was long believed that a sharp distinction in kind exists between the normal and the abnormal mind, that a person is clearly and definitely either sane or insane. Such a belief is no longer held by students of mental disease. It is quite apparent that most normal individuals exhibit certain abnormal traits, and that many persons suffering from serious mental and nervous disorders exhibit some degree of mental integration and intellectual lucidity. This is an important consideration for mental hygiene, since it makes clear the vital fact that few persons "go crazy" all of a sudden. They usually exhibit mild forms of abnormal responses long before they are detached from conventional realities and become thoroughly unbalanced. Hence, if we are alert to the nature and existence of early manifestations of abnormal behavior, steps may be taken to treat individuals during the first stages of a mental malady. Then the prospect for the cure or arrest of the disorder is much more promising than it is after there has been a complete breakdown.

Physical basis of mental abnormality. Causes of mental abnormality are both physical and psychological. This is to be expected, because the lower and more fundamental levels of mental stimulation and response are primarily physical in their nature. Abnormal types of behavior may be brought about by disease, toxic or poisonous products in the system, the changes due to age, and the like. A nervous disease known as locomotor ataxia and caused by syphilis paralyzes the limbs and makes it impossible for a man to control basic lever responses. Defects in the endocrine glands prevent normal responses on the physio-chemical level and we then have diseases which manifest themselves in pathological excitability, abnormal apathy, physical monstrosities, and so forth. Paresis, a serious mental disorder caused by syphilis, affects sensory-motor responses and makes it impossible for the individual to control his reflexes in normal fashion. Senility may bring about physical changes which affect the normal responses on all these lower levels.

The flight from reality. Psychologically, mental abnormality is looked upon as a marked inability to face reality, with resulting mental conflicts. The life experiences of the individual, from earliest childhood onward, may have created mental reactions (complexes) which make it very difficult for him to meet adult responsibilities. Harsh living conditions, disappointments in love, professional failures, economic insecurity, and a large number of other unfortunate experiences may make it extremely difficult for many individuals to face enthusiastically or effectively the basic realities of life. Hence, the individual, tortured by mental conflicts and frustrations, tends to escape from this intolerable reality by creating a world of mental fantasy which is more in harmony with his wishes and desires.

This flight from reality may vary all the way from the ordinary daydreaming and mental castle-building, in which we all tend to indulge, to the systematic and enduring hallucinations of the overtly insane. Insanity, viewed from the mental standpoint, is essentially a psychological flight from a repellent and unsatisfactory real world into what is usually a much more attractive world of fancy and myth. Of course, as we shall see later, not all types of hallucinations of the insane are pleasant. In some cases they are quite the contrary. But, in the majority of cases, the flight is made from a harsh practical reality to a relatively satisfactory region of mental fictions. The importance of mental conflict in producing serious mental and nervous diseases may be discerned from the expert estimate that, aside from senile cases, from 50 to 70 per cent of those in state hospitals for the insane are there as a result of emotional and mental maladjustments rather than because of mental diseases due to physical causes.

Inasmuch as few, if any, persons have a completely satisfactory set of experiences from birth onward, or find life entirely to their liking in adulthood, the great majority of normal human beings create for themselves a realm of fancy in which they realize aspirations denied to them in actual life. But, in all such cases, reality occupies the leading rôle in their life interests and activities. With the insane, reality is almost wholly abandoned and the realm of fantasy becomes all-absorbing.

No sharp line between sanity and insanity. These considerations will once more emphasize the fact that there is no sharp line of demarcation between the normal and abnormal mind, between the so-called sane and insane. It is wholly a matter of degree. Nor are all flights into fancy pathological or socially undesirable. Much of art, music, and literature grows out of such flights. In these realms, the line dividing fantasy from constructive imagination is faint indeed. It is a task of mental hygiene to be on the alert to prevent too great a conflict between the individual mental equipment and the reality with which it must deal. Through various remedial measures the mind must be toughened, reality softened, or both results achieved.

One reason for the increasing frequency of mental disorders in our day and age is the fact that many of the realities which we face conflict with the folkways and mores which conditioned mental development in an earlier period of social and economic life and moral convictions. Mental conflicts are thereby greatly stimulated and augmented.

These elementary observations concerning mental normality and abnormality, and the more common causes for the latter, will suffice to indicate that there is nothing mysterious about what we know as insanity. A mentally diseased person usually passes from normal to abnormal mental states rather gradually and by definite stages. The recognition of this fact enables psychiatrists to discern the danger signals and to take steps to arrest those developments which threaten to produce a more or less complete mental breakdown.

THE MORE IMPORTANT MENTAL AND NERVOUS DISEASES

Neuroses and psychoses. We have used the term *insanity* frequently in the preceding pages, but this word is rarely employed today by physicians in describing mental and nervous diseases. It is more truly a legal than a medical term. When we actually look into the field of mental and nervous diseases, we find a great variety of such disorders, some very mild and others of such an extreme form that it is necessary to segregate the sufferer and to prevent him from doing damage to himself and to others. The milder forms of mental and nervous diseases are usually described as *neuroses*. The more serious and extreme maladies are designated as *psychoses*. Although it is not always true, in the great majority of cases a psychosis is preceded by a neurosis. If the symptoms are recognized and given prompt treatment, it is frequently possible to prevent the subsequent development of a psychosis. The usual development of serious mental disorders is, then, from apparent normality to a neurosis, and from the latter to a psychosis.

Though modified somewhat in the light of later knowledge and experience, the classification of mental and nervous diseases is still based on that provided by an eminent European psychiatrist, Emil Kraeplin, in 1896. Both the neuroses and the psychoses are divided into two major types. First, we have the functional disorders which, so far as we know, have no definite physical cause. Neither brain lesions, endocrine defects, physical disease, nor bodily injuries seem to play any important part in the creation of such maladies. They are produced predominantly by mental conditions, and they are preeminently of the type which manifest themselves as a flight from an intolerable reality. The organic neuroses and psychoses are caused by some pathological physical condition, such as brain lesions, endocrine anomalies, disease, bodily injuries, toxic effects, and senility.

The functional neuroses. We may first consider briefly some of the more common functional neuroses, often called psychoneuroses. The symptoms are, naturally, highly diverse, though there is usually one common feature: egocentricity, or the exaggeration of the importance of the patient and his personal difficulties. Alfred Adler, one of the pioneers in psychiatry, believed that the neuroses are chiefly the product of over-compensation for various types of organic inferiority, but most psychiatrists seek a broader explanation. They find that neuroses may grow out of the flight from many phases of reality which have become relatively intolerable for the individual. A sense of organic inferiority is only one of these. There is a wide range of neurotic symptoms. The patients may be irritable and excitable or they may be pathologically depressed and apathetic. Usually, they are abnormally apprehensive and sensitive, and they frequently lack self-confidence. Their mental disturbances may prevent them from enjoying life themselves and make them a serious burden and annoyance to their families and associates.

A common form of functional neurosis is what is called the *anxiety neurosis.* This is believed by many psychiatrists to be chiefly the product of incomplete or frustrated sexual intercourse. Its major symptoms are exaggerated worry, apprehensiveness, and nervous excitability, all of which may superficially appear to have little relation to any realities in the life of the patient. But these worries, obviously based upon some deep-seated form of mental conflict, are real enough to the sufferer. The intense mental symptoms are frequently accompanied by definite physical manifestations, such as palpitation of the heart, perspiration, nausea, and sometimes an actual fear of impending death.

The *obsessive neuroses* are numerous and varied. All sorts of phobias and fears frequently abound, including mild delusions of persecution. Indeed, G. Stanley Hall once collected a list of over six hundred of these phobias—morbid fears and anxieties. Some patients have a pathological fear of open places, known as *agoraphobia,* or an equally morbid fear of closed places, known as *claustrophobia.* In the first instance patients are terrified at the thought of leaving the house and of moving freely out of doors; in the latter case they are morbidly afraid of entering a closed room or space.

This obsessive type of neurotic patient is frequently likely to be subject to all kinds of compulsive ideas and actions, so that sometimes this type of neurosis is called a *compulsive neurosis.* The patient, when out walking, may feel that he must strike every pavement stone with his cane, and he may perhaps return for some distance to strike one that he has missed. Constant washing of the hands is another form of compulsive act. There may be an unconscious sense of guilt, and the repeated washings are a sort of mechanized purification ritual—"an expiatory act, symbolic of repentance." Sometimes such compulsive action takes on a criminal or antisocial character, such as kleptomania, pyromania, and assault. Obsessive convictions and illusion may afflict the individual, and he may cling to fixed ideas which have no factual foundation. Such patients are also often victims of pathological uncertainty and worry. They may be led to inspect a door several times to see that they have actually locked it, or they may worry lest they have failed to turn off the gas, though they have checked up on the situation several times.

Other common forms of neuroses are the *conversion hysterias*. These take the form of hysterical paralysis in which the limbs may be paralyzed without any actual physical foundation for such a difficulty. In one case, an overtimid acrobat developed complete paralysis and thereby escaped from his unpleasant profession—thus standing at the opposite pole in his responses from the "daring young man on the flying trapeze" of traditional glamor. In another case an ambitious young woman entered a hospital for training as a nurse. The sight of blood and hospital smells were very revolting to her. But she was ambitious to succeed. The conflict produced a paralysis of the arms, which disappeared as soon as she left the hospital. There may be hysterical anesthesia, in which portions of the body are rendered immune to normal sensibility. Almost every type of physical disease may be imitated. During both world wars such phenomena were quite common among servicemen. It is with this group of cases that various faith cures may be effective. But there are many types of hysteria which do not simulate physical disorders. There may be uncontrolled hysterical weeping or laughing. Mental fugues are common. The patient may wander away from his home and yet be unconscious of his action. Amnesia, or pathological loss of memory, may be manifested. In the hysterias we usually find what is known as a split-personality, a portion of the mental life being dissociated from reality and from normal personality traits.

At the opposite extreme, in certain ways, from the conversion hysterias, in which the patient falsely appears to have a definite physical disorder, is *hypochondria*. In this form of neurosis the patient imagines that he has or is about to contract every disease about which he has any knowledge, even though he may be in the very best of health. When the hypochondriac reads or hears of any new disease, he feels certain that he is bound to suffer from it immediately. If he has some mild disorder, he exaggerates its nature and implications. A slight cough is sure sign of the onset of tuberculosis; a pimple is proof of infection with syphilis; a slight nausea is evidence of a cancer of the stomach. Foolish though these fears may seem to the outsider, they cause immense misery to the person who is victimized by them.

These are only some of the more important of the common types of functional neuroses, or, as they are now generally known, the *psychoneuroses*. But what we have said about them will suffice to indicate the general nature of such disorders. Usually persons suffering from these neuroses are not confined in institutions. Millions of persons who are victims of neurotic conditions in mild manifestations freely circulate in society and execute their daily tasks. Indeed, many learned psychologists contend that most persons of distinguished ability are, in differing degrees, neurotic. They are most likely to rebel against the conventional and often stupid dictates of the herd, and in this way they develop an unusual amount of mental conflict. There is probably much to be said for this contention. Certainly many of the distinguished historic characters of the past have been neurotic types. Their neuroses have given them an unusual amount of energy and persistence. But, obviously, the majority of neurotics are not persons of surpassing ability, and their symptoms usually deplete their energy and are a serious handicap to their activities.

Organic neuroses. Little need be said in this place about the various organic neuroses, of which there are a large number. Some are caused by physical disease. Others may be produced by focal infections, such as bad teeth, intestinal auto-intoxication, and the like. Others grow out of toxic effects and poisons, such as alcoholic poisoning, lead poisoning, and many other similar cases. There are many organic neuroses which are produced by defects in the endocrine glands, leading to excessive or defective secretions of certain hormones. Such are rickets, trembling palsy, and other disorders. Here, also, we should list tics, neuralgia, neuritis, and the like. Then there are what are called the *traumatic neuroses,* which are due to some type of bodily injury affecting the brain or nervous system.

A serious form of organic neurosis is cerebral palsy, which mainly afflicts children and young persons. It is estimated that about 350,000 suffer from it in the United States today. Until recently, it was rather generally ignored. Due to the stimulus from psychiatrists and psychiatric social workers, a concerted effort is now being made to discover cases and provide effective treatment. This work is directed by the United Cerebral Palsy Associations.

Functional psychoses. We are now ready to describe the more serious forms of mental and nervous disease, the psychoses. Like the neuroses, the psychoses fall into two major types—the functional and the organic.

As will be clear from what we have already said, a considerable number of the functional psychoses are simply more extreme developments of the functional neuroses which we have described. The anxiety neuroses, compulsion neuroses, hysterias, and the like may be unchecked and may develop so far that the person suffering from them definitely breaks off from contact with reality and has to be confined in an institution. Such psychoses simply represent exaggerated symptoms and manifestations of the neuroses which we described above. Functional psychoses account for about 55 per cent of all admissions to state hospitals.

Schizophrenia or dementia praecox. The most serious type of functional psychosis is *dementia praecox,* or *schizophrenia,* as it is usually known in medical usage. Its nature and symptoms were first clearly delineated in psychiatric terms by Kraepelin and Eugen Bleuler. It was called dementia praecox (precocious dementing) because the onset of the disease takes place most frequently between the ages of 16 and 40. So far as is now known, there is no specific physical cause for the disorder, though some have attempted to ascribe it to defective circulation, metabolic disturbances, endocrine defects, and the like.

Schizophrenia is particularly serious from the institutional standpoint, because nearly 60 per cent of all the inmates of our state hospitals for the insane suffer from this disorder. Only about 20 per cent of first admissions to these hospitals are schizophrenic patients, but the latter accumulate more notably than any other type among the psychotic. This is due to the fact that many of the insane, particularly those who are suffering from advanced paresis and senile dementia, die off rather quickly after admission. Others may be released fairly rapidly. Schizophrenic patients, on the other hand, are usually committed at a relatively early age and live about as long as normal persons. Moreover, only a small percentage can be improved enough to be discharged. Even the most advanced methods of treatment by insulin and metrazol, by electric shock and ether shock, and by lobotomy, have as yet produced no mass cures. The improved psychoanalytical techniques for treating this disorder in private practice are impossible to administer in general hospital routine, especially with the limited staff of psychiatrists. Therefore, most schizophrenic patients tend to remain in hospitals. There are over 300,000 of them now in institutions in the United Sttaes.

There is no generally accepted explanation of the specific cause of schizophrenia. Psychiatrists are still at sea on this matter. They generally agree, following Adolf Meyer, that this type is inferior to the normal person in mental and nervous equipment and simply fails to make the grade when faced with the responsibilities of adulthood and social obligations, especially adult sexuality. Such patients are sometimes possessed of brilliant mentalities and make striking records in school. But their emotional makeup seems to be considerably below par. Perhaps later we shall know more about the causes and genesis of schizophrenia, but so far we can merely say that such patients represent a group which is unable to keep up with the social procession. There may be a sex component in the causation of the disorder, as is suggested by the fact that breakdowns usually occur fairly early in life. One eminent psychiatrist, Carl Jung, has suggested that this type "founders on the rock of puberty." At any rate, schizophrenics regress to a lower and inferior order of thought processes—the libido retreats to infantile fixations.

There is more general agreement as to the symptoms of schizophrenia than in respect to its causes. Jung has described the disease as a sort of perpetual walking dream state. The patient, retreating from reality, apparently attains the desired mental adjustment in his obsessive daydreaming and hangs on to it with great tenacity. The schizophrenic type lives decidedly within himself and shows a general indifference to those about him. In psychiatric terms, he represents an extreme form of narcissism, or subconscious self-love. In the earlier stages of normal sex development, the libido fixes upon the ego. Schizophrenic patients regress to this infantile level, turn inward upon themselves, abandon external reality, are inaccessible to ordinary stimuli from the outside world, and live on in a world of narcissistic fantasy.

Complete "cures" of this malady have been very rare until recently, but experimentation with various shock procedures and psychosurgical operations offers at least some hope for schizophrenes. Some psychoanalysts, such as the late Harry Stack Sullivan and his successors, have reported cures as the result of prolonged psychoanalytical therapy.

Other functional psychoses. Another relatively common type of functional psychosis is what is known as the *manic-depressive psychosis*. This disorder was also first clearly isolated and described by Kraepelin. The causes for this form of psychosis are also very incompletely understood. A certain school of psychiatrists believe that it is due primarily to the holdover of infantile antipathies toward parents, but others do not accept this explanation. Classic cases of manic-depressive psychosis pass through a cycle of mental symptoms. In the manic phase they are excessively excitable, full of fantastic plans, generally optimistic; and they manifest a marked flight of ideas—that is, jumping from one topic to another. Later on they pass gradually into a depressed period. In the depths of their depression they frequently sink into stupor and sometimes have to be forcibly fed. They are most dangerous to themselves and others just before going into or just after passing out of this period of stupor and extreme depression. Between the extreme manic and depressed phases they manifest more or less complete lucidity and are often released from institutions.

Some manic-depressive cases exhibit only the manic or the depressed phase and rarely or never go through the complete cycle. Others show at all times mixed symptoms, exhibiting frequent alternations of elation and depression. The manic-depressive patient frequently improves sufficiently to be released, often to be returned later for another period of segregation and treatment. Among the functionally psychotic types, the manic-depressives rank next in number to those suffering from dementia praecox.

The most dangerous of the functional psychoses is *paranoia*. Persons suffering from this disorder may be dangerous because their main symptom is a delusion of persecution, which naturally encourages retaliation against fancied wrongs and plots. Another reason why this disease is dangerous is that the hallucinations are rarely accompanied by any general loss of mental powers. Hence, paranoiacs are often allowed to circulate freely in the general population, where they are regarded as harmless cranks. In mild cases, that is precisely what they are. The delusions of persecution which characterize this psychosis are usually accompanied by the presence of delusions of grandeur and a sense of exaggerated personal importance. In one case known to the writer, a woman had lost her position as librarian through her mental disease. But she ascribed her dismissal to a national political plot and held that the president of the United States had tried vainly to intercede in her behalf. There is no definite knowledge as to the cause of paranoia, though many psychiatrists regard it as a result of repressed homosexuality. Severe cases of paranoia are generally regarded as incurable, though some have been successfully treated by psychoanalysis.

A peculiarly pitiful form of functional psychosis is what is known as *involutional melancholia*. This is a disease which occurs most frequently in middle life, and it often appears in women during the menopause. It is believed that the psychic and social strains induced by this change are at least a contributing cause. While most psychoses have compensatory delusions, which make life more tolerable, there is little of this in involutional melancholia. The patients suffer from extreme worries, psychic agitation, prolonged fits of melancholia, and an exaggerated sense of sin and guilt. They often manifest suicidal tendencies in the effort to escape from their mental suffering. Fortunately, the disease frequently clears up after several years of segregation and treatment. Shock treatment has frequently helped such patients.

The organic psychoses. The above disorders represent the main types of so-called functional psychoses. There is even a greater number of organic psychoses which are caused by brain lesions, physical disease, bodily injury, or toxic products in the body. The most common of these in state hospitals are *paresis,* or general paralysis of the brain due to earlier infection with syphilis, and *senile dementia,* the latter being the psychosis accompanying bodily changes associated with old age.

Until recently, paresis was absolutely incurable and the patients suffering from it usually died a few years after admission. The ordinary specifics against syphilis, such as salvarsan, could not be made to penetrate the brain area where the spirochete is carrying on its ravages in the case of paretics. The choroid plexus prevents poisons from entering the brain, and all known specifics for syphilis, such as mercury and salvarsan, the latter of which is made from arsenic, were poisonous. By the time a nonpoisonous specific, bismuth, was discovered, the much more effective fever treatment for paresis was being applied. Today, by using a combination of bismuth, penicillin, and fever therapy, most cases of paresis can be cured if treatment is begun in time, and even advanced cases can be arrested if it seems desirable to do so. Such treatment has greatly reduced the number of paretic patients in mental hospitals in recent years.

Those suffering from senile dementia, the so-called *geriopsychoses,* are obviously hopeless cases. Their disorder is caused by bodily changes accompanying old age which result in a progressive degeneration of the brain. The most common cause of these psychoses of senility is cerebroarteriosclerosis, or the hardening of the arteries of the brain. Such senile cases make up the largest number of first admissions to hospitals among the patients suffering from organic psychoses.

There are a large number of other forms of organic psychoses. Some are the result of difficulties with the endocrine glands—the *endocrinopsychoses.* If the thyroid secretion is defective in early life it causes cretinism, a sort of pseudo-idiocy, characterized by premature aging of youth, accompanied by extensive dementing almost to the level of the idiot. In maturity and old age thyroid deficiency produces what is known as Gull's disease, so named after the first important physician to study thyroid disorders, William Gull. This disease causes a person to develop into what has been called the "human toad." Parts of the body, especially the hands and face, develop puffy swellings. The features become broad and coarse. There is general mental apathy and loss of memory. Excessive thyroid secretion brings about what is known as Grave's disease, or exophthalmic goiter. This disorder is accompanied by greatly heightened emotions, increased blood pressure, intense excitability, protrusion of the eyeballs, and so forth. The patient literally burns himself up through excessive oxygen utilization.

Disorders of the thymus produce serious mental conditions. A defective thymus may produce feeble-mindedness, and the total absence of this gland usually results in idiocy. It should atrophy after puberty. If it does not do so, it brings about the prolongation of infantile physical and mental traits. Injuries to the parathyroids, resulting in deficiency, produce tetany convulsions, trembling palsy, rickets, and the like. Deficient secretion of the adrenal glands produces a disorder known as Addison's disease, characterized by progressive muscular weakness, decreasing heart action, digestive troubles, and a turning of the skin to a bronze color, either in spots or entirely. Mental states resembling epileptic convulsions, mental confusion, and occasional delirium accompany the disease. Excessive secretion from the adrenals occasionally produces imbecility. An abnormal secretion from the pituitary body brings about gigantism and acromegaly. The latter disorder frequently produces hospital cases. Its physical symptoms are hideous changes of facial features, which become greatly overgrown, as do the hands and feet. Mental changes, including dizziness and hallucinations, usually accompany this disorder. In the terminal stages prolonged drowsiness results, often known as "pituitary hibernation." Disturbances in the sex glands produce a great variety of sex abnormalities, such as homosexuality, satyriasis, nymphomania, impotence, and the aberrant or pathological psychic traits which accompany such situations. There are, of course, many other organic psychoses, but they need not be mentioned here.

Frequency and distribution of the psychoses. These constitute the great majority of the more common organic psychoses. We may add a few interesting details with respect to the problems and distribution of the psychoses. In 1945, the more important mental disorders which accounted for first admissions to all hospitals for mental disease in the United States were, in order of frequency: schizophrenia, 21.1 per cent; cerebral-arteriosclerosis, 10.8; senile dementia, 9.0; manic-depressive psychoses, 8.7; psychoneuroses, 5.1; paresis, 4.6; involutional melancholia, 4.1; alcoholic psychoses, 3.4; and paranoia, 1.6.

Both schizophrenia and manic-depressive psychoses constitute a hospital burden out of proportion to their percentage in first admissions. Patients of the former type are rarely released, while those of the second type are frequently readmitted for treatment. Both live out a normal life span. On the other hand, those suffering from senile dementia and paresis are not so much of a hospital burden as would be indicated by their ratio in first admissions. Both have tended to die off relatively quickly. Since effective treatment has been introduced for paresis, there is either a relatively speedy recovery or quick death for those who are not treated or do not respond to treatment.

As to sex distribution of patients, schizophrenic types are about equally divided between males and females. There is a decided preponderance of males among paretics, since one woman may infect a number of men with syphilis. On the other hand, manic-depressive insanity and involutional melancholia are much more common among women than among men. At the beginning of 1945, of all patients on the books in all hospitals for mental patients, there were 308,285 males and 272,794 females.

Prospect of cure of psychoses. As a summary view of the prospect of permanent cure or improvement in the case of state hospital patients, it may be said that, for the United States as a whole, only between 10 and 15 per cent of the patients are discharged annually as "cured" or improved. In 1945, out of 529,000 patients, 51,000 were discharged, with males and females equally divided (25,575 males and 25,579 females). About 40 per cent of those discharged are later admitted for further treatment, many within a few months.

Epilepsy. Epilepsy is a form of mental disorder concerning which there is as yet no general agreement among even expert specialists as to its nature and causes. Psychiatrists most frequently regard it as a constitutional disorder which produces a definite type of psychopathic personality. The leading psychiatric authorities on epilepsy have been L. Pierce Clark, John T. MacCurdy, and their associates. While conceding that autopsies on epileptics may occasionally reveal brain lesions and other pathologies, they do not believe that it has been proved that these exert any decisive influence on the basic personality traits of epileptics.

On the other hand, the organic neurologists hold that epilepsy is an organic malady which is usually hereditary. They contend that brain lesions and other organic pathologies account for the behavior patterns of epileptics. William G. Lennox, Hans Berger, F. A. Griffs, and others of this school represent leading authorities who thus diagnose and interpret epilepsy. We may now examine the theories of epilepsy as presented by these two schools of thought and experience.

The main symptom of epilepsy, which was formerly concentrated upon by physicians, is the epileptic convulsion or fit, but Clark showed that this is only a superficial aspect of the epileptic makeup and behavior. The epileptic is characterized by extreme egocentricity. For the epileptic, the world revolves around himself to a very intense and morbid degree. Highly generalized and impersonal events are often interpreted by the patient as having a very direct bearing upon his own life situations. The epileptic is hypersensitive, and this makes it very difficult for him to make ordinary adjustments to normal social surroundings. He makes a stubborn and unyielding demand that the social environment shall conform to his wishes and desires. There is a marked lack of rationality and balance in judging events. Immediate personal frustrations stir up irrational excitement. One of Clark's patients received with extreme calmness the news of the death of one of his parents, but he threw himself into an epileptic convulsion when denied a second piece of pie. If an epileptic patient is compelled to wait unduly for a car or bus, he is likely to develop pathological annoyance and regard it as a plot on the part of the transportation company to bring about personal inconvenience to him. The emotional poverty and intense selfishness in the personality makeup of the epileptic greatly increase the problem of acquiring and maintaining friends and otherwise living a normal social existence.

The epileptic convulsion or fit was interpreted by Clark as a temporary lapse of consciousness and the means whereby the patient secures a temporary but intense escape from an intolerable reality. While other psychoneurotics develop fantasies and hallucinations as a mode of escaping from reality, the epileptic gets his release through the convulsion. Some psychiatrists regard the fit as a regressive psychophysical effort to return to the mother and the protective associations connected therewith. Frequently, though by no means always, the epileptic goes into a convulsion in the face of some special annoyance or acute frustration which makes reality more repulsive for the moment.

This severe convulsion is usually preceded by the so-called aura, or warning, which may take the form of physical symptoms or of mental states, such as flashes of light, imaginary voices and other noises, as well as a variety of hallucinations. Then there comes a complete loss of consciousness and the patient falls to the floor with rigid muscular contraction. The contraction of the muscles of the chest and larynx produces a sound which is known as the epileptic cry. Certain psychiatrists regard this as the audible expression of an infantile urge. Following this, the patient goes through a series of convulsions, usually foaming at the mouth. After a few moments he falls into a stupor which may last for an hour or two unless he is aroused. At times these fits may follow in rapid succession. Cases have been recorded where as many as a hundred convulsions have followed each other in rapid succession. The number of these seizures, in the case of epileptic patients, varies greatly. Some do not have more than half a dozen during their lifetime and others may have several daily convulsions. Patients who suffer from what is known as *petit mal* seizures do not have any convulsions at all, but merely experience a temporary lapse of intellectual integration. Such a patient may stare blankly for a moment and drop whatever he is holding in his hand, but he quickly returns to normal alertness. In the case of some epileptics there is no seizure at all. The escape from reality is accomplished through epileptic deliriums and hallucinations. Intense psychic excitement may act as a substitute for the typical convulsion.

The epileptic patient was long regarded as incurable. Drug "cures" and other physical treatment had usually proved essentially futile beyond reducing the frequency of convulsions. Unless competent treatment is given to the epileptic, there may be a progressive degeneration of the personality. The patient becomes ever more shut-in and egocentric. Convulsions usually increase in frequency. A growing mental apathy is usually followed by serious dementing and a general failure of intellectual powers. According to Clark's theory of idiopathic epilepsy, there is, even today, no form of institutional treatment for epilepsy which is likely to effect a cure. Successful treatment can be assured only through prolonged psychoanalysis at the hands of a psychiatrist who is thoroughly informed as to the psychiatric conception of the nature of the disease. Even so, it is difficult to bring about a cure unless the disorder is attacked relatively early in life. But the outlook for a young person who can secure competent psychiatric aid is relatively promising.

Within the last two decades there has been a trend back toward the earlier interpretation of epilepsy as an organic or physical type of mental disorder and the view that it can be transmitted by heredity. This reversal of attitude has been in part the result of the development of the new diagnostic technique, known as electroencephalography, which is used to detect and evaluate brain waves. It is thought that this provides a reliable method of diagnosing epilepsy. A leading exponent of this point of view is William G. Lennox, who believes that there are about 16 million latent cases of epilepsy in the country who, though they may never have seizures, can act as carriers and transmit the disease to off-spring. Some progress has been made, however, in discovering drugs, such as sodium dilantin, paradione, phenurone, and tridione, that reduce the frequency and violence of the epileptic seizures.

Whatever the validity of these two sharply conflicting views of the nature, causes, and treatment of epilepsy, no recent studies have upset Clark's brilliant and epoch-making studies of the epileptic personality or his suggestions as to how to understand and treat the symptoms.

There are about 21,000 known patients suffering from epilepsy now segregated in various institutions. There is no means of knowing how many cases exist outside of such places. It has been estimated that there may be 600,000 epileptics in the country as a whole who suffer from seizures.

Because of the special character of this disorder, it is desirable to have special institutions for the segregation of those afflicted by it. The tendency now is to establish institutions for epileptics on the colony plan. The parent epileptic colony was the Bethel Colony set up near Bielefeld, Germany, in 1867. The first colony institutions in the United States were the Gallipolis colony in Ohio, opened in 1891, and the Craig Colony for Epileptics, established at Sonyea, N. Y., in 1894. The latter attracted world-wide attention. More than 10,000 epileptics are today handled in state epileptic colonies, of which there are eleven in the United States.

Because epilepsy and feeble-mindedness are very different types of mental disorder, the tendency in many states to confine and treat both in the same institution and of the Census Bureau to lump together the statistics for both types, is a grievous medical, administrative, and statistical mistake. It leads to therapeutic handicaps and blunders, to much misinformation, and to the confusion of such information as is available.

INSTITUTIONS FOR THE MENTALLY DISEASED

The humane reforms of Pinel and Esquirol. One of the most notable and gratifying forms of progress with respect to the mentally and nervously diseased has been the improvement in the treatment of these unfortunates and the provision of institutional care for them. Inasmuch as the insane were long regarded as possessed of the devil, they were usually treated with great brutality until the beginning of the nineteenth century. They were frequently thrown into jails and dungeons and also often incarcerated in poorhouses. When they were put into hospitals they were usually chained fast and treated worse than domestic animals.

The man whose name is usually associated with the beginnings of some insight into the nature of insanity and with a modicum of humanity in its treatment was the French physician, Philippe Pinel (1745-1826). In the last decade of the eighteenth century he was appointed physician to a notorious insane asylum in Paris, the Bicêtre. To appreciate fully the improvement which has been attained in the treatment of the insane, we may well quote Albert Deutsch's description of the persons with whom Pinel had to deal:

> The asylum looked like a circle of the Inferno when Pinel entered upon his duties. The lunatics lay all about, raving, riveted with chains and irons. They were regarded as desperate, dangerous animals on a lower plane than criminals, for the latter were not stripped of all their human attributes as the insane were supposed to be. And in truth, the inmates of the Bicêtre had the appearance of wild animals—beards and hair were matted with straw and infested with lice; their clothes were tattered, their nails grown long like claws, their bodies encrusted with dirt and filth. They presented pictures of complete neglect. Their cries of anger, agony and frustration induced by intolerable confinement, mingled with the endless clanging of chains and the crack of keepers' whips.[1]

Against the advice of both physicians and public authorities, Pinel struck the chains off most of the inmates and introduced humane methods of treatment. The predicted disasters did not follow, and Pinel's methods were extended to other Paris asylums. The humane treatment of the insane, "based on a minimum of mechanical restraint and a maximum of intelligent understanding," was thus established. Unfortunately, it was long before any such method became general. The enlightened work of Pinel was carried forward by his successor, another French physician, Jean Esquirol (1772-1840). Esquirol made a comprehensive tour of all French asylums in 1808, became Pinel's assistant in 1811, and planned the famous asylum at Charenton, which was opened in 1826 under his direction. His revelations in 1817 led to the reconstruction of all French procedure with respect to the insane. Esquirol also had a great influence on the improvement of asylum architecture.

William Tuke (1732-1822), an English Quaker, opened the famous "York Retreat" in 1792 and introduced humane methods of treating the insane in England. The work was carried on by Samuel Tuke, and the York Retreat exerted much influence on the rational care of the mentally diseased in both England and the United States. In Germany, Johann Reil took up the cause of humane treatment of the insane. In his work at the Pennsylvania Hospital in Philadelphia following 1780, Benjamin Rush took the first steps in introducing a humane attitude toward insane patients, and he may well be regarded as the American

---

[1] Albert Deutsch, *The Mentally Ill in America*. New York: Columbia University Press, 1949, pp. 88-90.

counterpart of Pinel, Tuke, and Reil in this field of medical and humanitarian efforts.

Early mental hospitals in the United States. In the United States the insane were first treated with the customary brutality that had dominated European practice. Although Boston had long considered plans for building an insane asylum, the first public hospital for the insane in the United States was that opened at Williamsburg, Virginia, in 1773. The next state hospital was opened at Lexington, Kentucky, in 1824. In the meantime there had been various private institutions for the insane, such as the Pennsylvania Hospital in Philadelphia, opened in 1752, the McLean asylum opened at Waverly, Massachusetts, in 1818, and the Bloomingdale asylum, opened in New York City in 1821. The Hartford Retreat was opened in Hartford, Connecticut, in 1824, and a private asylum for "lunatics" was opened for the reception of patients in Cincinnati in 1827. A state lunatic asylum was opened in South Carolina in 1828 and another at Staunton, Virginia, in the same year. Virginia was thus the first state to have two public institutions for the insane. Ohio opened its first state hospital in 1830 at Columbus. New York state passed a law to create a state hospital at Utica in 1836. But as late as 1843, there were only fourteen hospitals in the United States, both public and private, which were devoted wholly to patients suffering from mental disease.

The crusade of Dorothea Dix. By and large, as late as the second third of the nineteenth century, the majority of the insane in this country were still confined in prisons, jails, and almshouses. In 1798 the state of Massachusetts had directed that those "lunatics who are furiously mad" should be sent to the house of correction. The majority of these unfortunates throughout the country were treated brutally in institutions designed for criminals and paupers. They were chained fast or locked in miserable cells, ill fed and half clothed.

The person who was chiefly responsible for rescuing them from their miserable condition was the foremost woman philanthropist in the history of the United States, Dorothea Lynde Dix (1802-1887). At a very early age she took an unusual interest in charity and in cases of unfortunate children. At the age of 25 she fell under the influence of William Ellery Channing, the famous clergyman and reformer. For a time she conducted a model school and, almost by accident, in March, 1841, visited the East Cambridge jail, where she was particularly amazed and shocked to observe the deplorable condition of insane inmates. She then visited other Massachusetts jails and almshouses and found that the same shocking conditions existed throughout the state.

Beginning late in 1841, Miss Dix carried on a vigorous campaign throughout the country, urging legislatures to establish institutions for the insane and to remove these unfortunates from the brutalities visited upon them in prisons, jails, and almshouses. Twenty states responded to her appeals by either establishing or enlarging institutions for the insane, and in some states more than one institution of this sort was erected as a result of her propaganda. The first state hospital directly attributable to Miss Dix's efforts was that opened in Trenton, New Jersey, in 1848.

Dorothea Dix shares with Pinel, Esquirol, Tuke, Reil, Rush, and Beers the main honors in bringing about a more humane, effective, and understanding treatment of those suffering from mental and nervous disorders. We shall have more to say about the work of Beers later.

Today there are 194 state hospitals for mentally diseased patients, 33 Federal neuro-psychiatric hospitals—most of them constructed since the First World War—111 county and city hospitals, and 267 private psychiatric hospitals. The overwhelming majority of mentally-diseased patients are cared for in state hospitals. Out of about 540,000 mental patients in hospitals at the end of 1947, 452,000 were in state hospitals.

Development of mental hospitals since the time of Dorothea Dix. Since Miss Dix's day there has been a great improvement in the institutions designed for those suffering from mental and nervous diseases. In the first place, institutions have been scientifically differentiated. The institutions whose construction was due mainly to the efforts of Miss Dix usually harbored the psychotic, the feeble-minded, and the epileptic in indiscriminate fashion. Today we have separate institutions for all these types, with appropriate specialization of care and treatment. In the institutions devoted primarily to the psychotic, the treatment has been rendered ever more humane and scientific. The earlier "lunatic asylums" were little more than prisons for the insane. Today, in the better institutions, overt physical restraint is reduced to a minimum. Improved treatment has been introduced in the way of drug administration, hydrotherapy, electrotherapy, neurosyphilology, fever therapy, occupational therapy, and the like.

The major defect in mental hospitals at present, aside from inadequate capacity for patients needing treatment, is the absence of a medical staff sufficiently large to apply intensive individual treatment, such as psychoanalysis, to the majority of patients. In some of the state hospitals there are a thousand patients to one psychiatrist. Hence, until the development of fever treatment for paresis, and shock and surgical treatment for schizophrenia and some other disorders, the state hospitals were chiefly useful as institutions for the relatively humane segregation of the psychotic. The majority of patients admitted were either incurable or could be cured only by individual treatment, which, of course, could not be administered. But even so, state hospitals represented a vast advance over the hell holes which Pinel and Miss Dix observed at the beginning of their careers. The hospitals could at least segregate and protect patients, improve their general health, and calm them down.

Ever more numerous psychopathic wards have been established in private hospitals. Important psychopathic hospitals, such as the famous Boston Psychopathic Hospital, opened in 1912, have been provided. There are 267 of them today. The Boston institution is now under state control. It has exerted an unusual influence because of the eminence of its first superintendents, Elmer E. Southard and C. Macfie Campbell. The large Menninger Clinic in Topeka, Kansas, conducted by Carl and William Menninger, has of late gained a wide and deserved reputation for the study and treatment of mental disorders, as also has the Colorado Psychopathic Hospital in Denver, under Franklin G. Ebaugh. We have already mentioned the provision of separate institutions for the epileptic and will describe later the institutions for the feeble-minded. We shall also deal with the development of psychotherapy, or the various theories and practices with respect to treating the insane.

The recent crisis in mental hospital care and treatment. Psychiatric knowledge, despite its impressive development, has been applied only to a limited extent in actual practice in state mental hospitals. It would require a medical staff ten times as large as that in the average state hospital to make extensive use of such individualized treatment as a patient can get from a competent private psychiatrist. Hence, there has remained a great and lamentable lag between our knowledge of psychotherapy and its application to the treatment of patients in public institutions.

Even the segregation and human physical care of patients, which was about all many hospitals could provide, suffered a serious deterioration after 1939. The war period was accompanied by a marked increase in the number of those who suffered from mental and nervous diseases and who needed hospital segregation, but, because of shortages of materials and labor, there was virtually no expansion of hospital plants. The conditions in some state hospitals became almost incredibly bad. A number of intelligent and well-educated conscientious objectors were assigned to duty as orderlies in these state institutions. They were shocked by the conditions they found and gave the facts to newspapers. Their published stories produced sensational publicity and further investigation, and mental hygiene experts joined in the movement of protest against the abominable conditions. Mary Jane Ward's book, *The Snake Pit,* brilliantly portrayed on the screen by Olivia De Haviland, probably did more than anything else to give the public some idea of the nature of the average present-day state hospital.

Conditions in mental hospitals during the 1940's. It was found that in some hospitals the daily expenditure for total maintenance per patient was as low as 45 cents. Even in the best it was only $1.46—although the American Psychiatric Association had estimated that a minimum daily expenditure of $2.50 was necessary to assure even decent physical care. The food provided was inadequate, poorly cooked, and badly served. Patients often lived in indescribable filth. Many were compelled to sleep on the floor. The quality of the hospital orderlies deteriorated seriously, for the institutions could not match the high wages paid in the war industries. The situation constituted a veritable national scandal. It almost seemed as though we had reverted to the period and conditions at the turn of the century that had prompted Clifford Beers to write his immortal book on the cruelties and stupidities of hospital treatment of insane patients.

The publicity given to such conditions led to some improvements, but no action at all commensurate with the needs has yet been undertaken by the majority of states. In an excellent article in *The New York Times* of July 27, 1947, George S. Stevenson, Medical Director of the National Association for Mental Health, thus describes the general physical conditions and operation of a better-than-average state hospital for the mentally diseased in one of the superior state systems:

Some miles outside almost any major American city, on a two-lane macadam road off the main highway, there is a group of large buildings, quite a few of them, probably of red brick. They sit on broad sweeps of beautiful greensward; a little network of small roads, all studded with signs that read "Speed Limit 15 M.P.H." threads among them. This is the State mental hospital. Externally the setting is attractive, the buildings of good architecture. Inside, the impression a visitor gets is something else again.

There is the pervading, indescribable, institutional odor. There is the barrenness of the interior—little furniture, no pictures on the walls, nothing loose anywhere. Everything is colorless. Patients wear loose hospital clothing that has faded with years of laundering. They have no belts, no shoe laces, nothing with which they might harm themselves.

In one of the wards patients sit on benches or on the floor. They seem absorbed in their own private worlds. Some are weeping or groaning miserably; others are staring abstractedly through the barred windows at the grounds, which apparently are kept better than the patients are. In the small rooms where "disturbed" patients are confined individually there are no furnishings, no bed, just a soiled mattress. Perhaps in the next room at the end of the hall a violent case reclines in a tub, his chin held above the water by a canvas harness; the swirling water soothes him. On a near-by table another patient lies swathed in a wet sheet; this is also a sedative device, one that tends to make him drowsy.

What goes on inside the hospital provides a vivid contrast with the orderly external appearance of the institution. And that contrast, to a great extent, symbolizes the status of public psychiatric treatment today. Throughout the United States we are confronted with a seriously ailing system of public psychiatry. The disturbing newspaper and magazine articles of the past few years which have described mental hospitals as "modern Bedlams" have been unpleasant because they couldn't be anything else and still tell the truth.

Stevenson is here describing one of the better state hospitals. Albert Deutsch has this to say in his book *The Shame of the States* about another, the large Byberry State Hospital, near Philadelphia, which was at the time housing 80 per cent more patients than its planned capacity:

I was reminded of the pictures of the Nazi concentration camps at Belsen and Buchenwald. . . . I entered buildings swarming with naked humans herded like cattle and treated with less concern. . . . I saw hundreds of patients living under leaking roofs, surrounded by mouldy, decaying walls, and sprawling on rotting floors for want of seats or benches.[2]

Need and prospect for better hospital facilities. One good effect of this exposure of scandalous deficiencies in our mental hospitals is that it may shock us out of our complacency and lead to adequate remedial steps. Although there were few valid grounds for such a misapprehension, it was taken for granted in the 1930's that our public mental hospitals were good and that they were doing substantial work in curing patients. The recent publicity demonstrating that the opposite is true today may serve to set in motion another era of reform comparable to that which followed the publication of Beers' book and the formation of the Na-

---

[2] New York: Harcourt, Brace, 1948, pp. 40-44.

tional Committee for Mental Hygiene in 1908. Financial grants made possible by the National Mental Health Act of 1946 may ultimately assure an adequate staff of trained psychiatrists for our hospitals, provided that the states appropriate sufficient funds to hire them.

Much could be done to lessen the acute shortage of psychiatrists in these institutions if the medical profession would abandon its short-sighted attempt to monopolize the field of psychotherapy. Clinical psychologists are far more competent to understand the operations of the human mind than is the average physician, and fully as well equipped as the average psychiatrist. For the fact is that our general medical training programs, both in schools and in hospitals, make scant provision for competent training in psychiatry—and it is equally true that the average physician has only grudgingly accepted his psychiatric colleague's views and practices. The clinical psychologist, on the other hand, has usually had fine training in his specialty.

The exposures and investigations during war time, Albert Deutsch's courageous book on *The Shame of the States,* and increased activity by psychiatrists and mental hygiene agencies have actually resulted in some improvements in hospital plants and services at the mid-century. Remedial state legislation has been passed in a number of states, notably California, Florida, Maryland, Minnesota, and Texas. The American Psychiatric Association has created a Central Inspection Board to inspect and rate mental hospitals upon request of the responsible authorities. It has launched a monthly *Mental Hospital Service Bulletin* to provide relevant and timely information on conditions in mental hospitals. At the mid-century, state hospitals remained about 20 per cent overcrowded, the average for the country as a whole.

SOME PHASES OF THE DEVELOPMENT OF PSYCHOTHERAPY

Differentiation of mental diseases from mental defect and the classification of mental diseases. Before much headway could be made in treatmental and nervous diseases, it was necessary to have a clear understanding of what these diseases really are. In other words, it was essential to recognize and classify the main mental disorders. Hippocrates had divided them into two main types: mania and melancholia. There was little real improvement in this classification until the days of the famous German psychiatrist, Emil Kraepelin (1856-1926), though many weird schemes of classification had been suggested. Indeed, feeble-mindedness had been regarded as a form of mental disease by Pinel, though this notion was disregarded in Pinel's own period by Esquirol, who clearly recognized that feeble-mindedness is a matter of mental defect and not of mental disease. A French psychiatrist, Edward Seguin, in the 1840's, completed the distinction between mental disease and mental defect and first outlined a rational plan of treatment for the latter.

Kraepelin was the first to devote special attention to the functional psychoses. In this field he first clearly identified manic-depressive psychosis and dementia praecox. He worked out the first satisfactory classification of mental and nervous disorders. His classification was brought into the United States by Adolf Meyer in the 1890's. Since then the classification of mental diseases has been extended and refined, until today there are about 22 separate groups of mental and nervous disorders which are definitely recognized, some of them having a number of subdivisions. Many pages would be required merely to list the major nervous and mental maladies.

Trend from naive optimism to realism relative to mental disease. Toward the middle of the nineteenth century, after the mentally diseased were beginning to be placed in hospitals for treatment, an optimistic tone colored the opinion of physicians. They believed that insanity would yield easily to scientific treatment. It was held that the psychoses were readily curable. Further observation brought disillusionment about this, and the pendulum then swung to the opposite extreme after 1860. It came to be commonly held that insanity was essentially incurable. Neither of these extreme views prevails today. Opinion is more discriminating, and judgment is expressed only with regard to particular disorders and individual patients. We are ever making new discoveries. In 1920 it was almost universally believed that paresis was utterly incurable. Today, this notion has been abandoned in the face of the success achieved by penicillin and fever treatments. Schizophrenia is still regarded by many as mainly incurable, but treatment by psychoanalysis, electric shock, drugs, and psychosurgery offers much encouragement for the future in treating this mental disorder and several others.

Organic neurology. We have seen that mental disorders are naturally divided into two main groups, functional and organic. It is equally natural to divide the methods of psychotherapy into two types—those which rely upon physical agents and those which depend primarily upon psychological treatment. The first field is commonly described as organic neurology and the latter as psychiatry.

A large number of physical agents and drugs have been relied upon to arrest and cure mental disorders. Drugs have been widely used since the time of Hippocrates. Aside from those employed to combat syphilis, most of the drugs used to treat mental disorders were usually sedatives which help to calm patients but usually do little to cure them. More recently insulin, metrazol, and ether have been used in the shock treatment of mental patients. Important experiments have been carried on in the way of giving narcotics like pentothol to patients to produce prolonged sleep and to recover lost memories—what is known as narcosynthesis. Gratifying results have been obtained in treating some of the functional psychoses by this method. The methods of administering hydrotherapy have been extended and improved. This type of treatment is mainly useful in producing psychic calm rather than in effecting a cure. Electrotherapy is used in treating certain types of mental disorder, especially early cases of brain tumor, certain glandular difficulties, and the like. Electric shock treatment has supplemented or superseded shock induced by drugs, and

the new science of electroencephalography has been of much use in studying brain waves, diagnosing epilepsy, and differentiating organic from
functional mental diseases.

The improvement of brain surgery has helped the treatment of those
suffering from brain tumors. The two men who were mainly responsible
for putting scientific brain surgery on its feet in the United States were
Harvey Cushing in Boston and Charles H. Frazier in Philadelphia. Thyroid surgery has also been useful in treating certain types of mental
patients. The first great thyroid surgeon was Theodor Kocher of Switzerland. His improved technique was brought into this country by George
Crile, of Cleveland, and other able surgeons.

In the last two decades psychiatrists have been impressed by the successful results in the use of insulin, originally employed to check diabetes,
as a mode of treating schizophrenia. This technique was first introduced
clinically in 1927 by Manfred Sakel, of Vienna. He reported that, by
the insulin shock method, he had been able to improve or cure 80 per
cent of his schizophrenia cases. American psychiatrists introduced the
insulin treatment, and as early as 1937 reported the cure or improvement
of 48 cases out of a total of 71 treated. This early report is now regarded
as premature and overoptimistic, though with all the lines of attack now
open on schizophrenia such a percentage of cures or improvement may be
regarded as a reasonable expectation.

The technique employed in insulin shock treatment is to give such a
large dose of insulin as to shock the patient into a coma, in which he is
left for an hour or two. From this he is restored by the administration of
glucose and adrenalin. It would seem that it is the shock rather than
the particular chemical nature of insulin which produces the improvement. Sakel has, however, recently sharply challenged this theory. He
contends that the therapeutic benefits do not come from the shock
but from the chemical and physiological effect of insulin in restoring
hormonal balance in the patient's system.

Other doctors have been successful with shock treatment when using
other drugs, such as metrazol, first used by L. von Meduna about 1929.
As a general rule today, electric shock, introduced by L. Bini and U.
Cerletti in 1934, has tended to supersede the use of insulin or metrazol,
though it is sometimes combined with them. Two important advances
were made in shock treatment in 1949, both by psychiatrists in New
York. It was found that shock treatment was more effective when combined with the use of a drug known as histamine. More important was
the discovery that injections of ether were as effective as any form of shock
treatment, while at the same time avoiding the convulsive seizures and
unpleasant after-effects of earlier forms of shock treatment. Shock treatment has also been found useful in dealing with involutional melancholia
and manic-depressive cases.

Many psychiatrists believe that the value of shock therapy lies in its
ability to temporarily upset the patient's pathological adjustment, making
him more accessible to planned or accidental psychotherapy. They theor-
ize that perhaps the shock constitutes a physiochemical attack on the

neural pathways that have been strengthened by years of habit. The method of intensive-regressive shock therapy is based on such an assumption and has been highly successful. These psychiatrists stress the importance of following the shock treatment with persistent psychotherapy.

Probably the most complete success in using physical agents and drugs to cure serious mental disorders has been the triumph over paresis, long regarded as completely incurable. Now, with combined penicillin, bismuth, and fever treatment, all but the most advanced cases of this disorder—those in which the brain tissues have been too extensively destroyed by the ravages of the spirochete—yield readily to treatment.

The main obstacle to complete success in the field of organic neurology has been the fact that some of the important organic psychoses, such as paresis, were long incurable, and senile dementia will always remain so. Moreover, until recently, organic neurology achieved few cures among the functional psychoses. But the popular interest showered upon psychiatry in the twentieth century should not cause us to overlook the fact that very important contributions to psychotherapy, especially nerve and brain surgery, have come from organic neurology. Moreover, some of the most remarkable revolutions in diagnosis and curative methods which have taken place recently have been contributed by organic neurology, electrotherapy, and psychosurgery rather than by psychiatry.

Revolutionary new developments in psychosurgery. While shock treatment has given us some hope for the hitherto almost hopeless schizophrenia cases, psychosurgery has of late proved very effective, not only for schizophrenia, but also for such other functional mental disorders as involutional melancholia, manic-depressive cases, and severe psychoneuroses. The most common of these psychosurgical operations is what is called prefrontal lobotomy. The neuropsychic basis for this operation was worked out by a Portuguese neurologist, Egas Moniz, in 1935, and the first lobotomies were performed in the same year by a Portuguese neurosurgeon, Almeida Lima. The new technique was introduced into the United States by Walter Freeman and James W. Watts, of George Washington University, in 1936. Over 5,000 such operations have been performed in the United States. Other variations are topectomy and temporal lobotomy. The latest technique is to drill through the skull, and then, with an electric needle, to scar the thalamus tissues. This is known as thalamatomy.

The aim and result of all these operations are essentially the same—to destroy or reduce the activity of the thalamus, which is a sort of emotional center or relay station that transmits impulses to and from the frontal lobes, or thought centers, of the brain. The operations seem to reduce nervous tension and inhibitions, obsession with personal troubles and phobias, morbid introspection, pathological anxiety states, and the like. The record of cures and improvements has been fairly good—in one large series of cases recovery was claimed in 35 per cent and marked improvement in an equal number. The mortality, surprisingly enough, is very low—about one per cent. It is too early to give any dogmatic verdict about the ultimate significance of this newer psychosurgical technique, but there is some ground for believing that it may work as great and beneficial a revolution as Freudian psychoanalysis; it may help types of patients for whom psychoanalysis has not been very effective.

One drawback is that, if the operation has to be severe or repeated, the lowering of inhibitions may extend so far as to cause the loss of a sense of responsibility about personal habits. In extreme cases there may be rather complete loss of intellectual powers. Further, mistakes cannot be corrected, for the portions of the brain removed or tampered with cannot be restored. For these reasons many psychiatrists regard these operations as too dangerous and uncertain to be used widely in general therapy. It may be pointed out, however, that severe lobotomies and the like are usually resorted to only in cases that otherwise seem rather hopeless, so that there is not much to lose by failure. Mild lobotomies and topectomies do not produce any notable loss of self-control over personal habits. On the whole, the results would seem to emphasize caution rather than alarmist abstention.

Growing recognition of the importance of the unconscious mind. The progress of psychiatry has been directly related to the advances in our knowledge of the unconscious phases of mental life, for the functional psychoses have been shown to be primarily disorders of the unconscious. It was once confidently supposed that man is fully conscious of the impulses which move him to action. If any person honestly avowed that he acted from certain motives, there could be little doubt that he did so. If these premises were accepted, the task of the psychiatrist in establishing the facts in any case was the relatively simple one of determining the degree of honesty in the patient's statement. It has now come to be very generally agreed, however, that the great majority of human psychic reactions are produced by impulses or motives that are below the level of consciousness—that emerge from the unconscious sources of psychic life and power. A much-worn but illuminating figure likens the psychic life and activity of man to the iceberg—a great submerged mass of unconscious impulses and a relatively slight visible portion of conscious activity.

This interesting and veritably revolutionary conception in psychiatry has passed through a number of phases or states. It must be regarded as still far from its ultimate development. Although vaguely hinted at from time to time since the Greek period, the first clear conception of the nature and significance of the unconscious in mental life was embodied in the famous work on *The Psychology of the Unconscious* by Eduard von Hartmann, published in 1869. This book was, however, primarily philosophical in its approach. Our actual knowledge of the potency and specific nature of the unconscious mind was subsequently secured through the work of psychiatrists and clinical psychologists.

Actually, the unconscious is almost as important in the mental life of the so-called "normal" individual as it is in that of the sufferer from a psychosis. But the academic psychologists, who had formal custody of the psychology of the normal mind, were rarely interested in the study of human behavior. They were mainly occupied in the effort to measure conscious perception. Hence, they could not very well get on the track of unconscious motives and impulses. The beginnings of scientific study of the unconscious mind were made by physicians.

The major periods in the development of psychotherapy, as related to the study of the unconscious and mental diseases, have been listed as follows by an eminent psychiatrist, Edward W. Taylor:

1. Preceding the eighteenth century—miracles, mysticism, domination of the church.
2. Eighteenth century—charlatanism: Mesmer (1766) and animal magnetism: theory of the domination of the mind by external agents.
3. Beginnings of the scientific method—hypnotism: Braid (1842), Liébault (1866), Richet (1875); hypnotism and suggestion a phenomenon of inner mental processes.
4. Clinical period—study of hysteria and dissociation of personality; Briquet (1859), Charcot (1878), Bernheim (1884), Janet (1892), and Prince (1906).
5. Analytical school—explanation of dissociation: Breuer (1880), Freud (1895), Jung (1897), et al.[3]

Mesmerism. The beginnings of the modern study of the unconscious in relation to mental disorders may be dated from the publication of *The Influence of the Planets on the Human Body* (1766) by Friedrich Anton Mesmer (1733-1815), half scientist and half charlatan. Mesmer was trained as a physician in Vienna but took refuge in Paris in 1777 and developed a considerable following there. He produced remarkable hysterical conduct in patients by the use of various physical agents like tubs, bottles, mirrors, bars, and lights. He relied on the old theory of animal magnetism and held that the mental symptoms he was able to induce were the product of external physical influences operating upon the mind.

Origins of hypnotism. The next stage in the progress of psychotherapy was that in which it came to be understood that the symptoms produced by Mesmer were of purely mental origin and had no relation to the mechanical instruments used. This important fact was first suggested by Alexandre Bertrand, a French psychologist, in his work on somnambulism in 1823. The next significant step was taken by James Braid (1795-1860), who published his *Neurypnology* in 1843. Braid was a famous surgeon of Manchester, England, and a man of scientific standing. He first used the term "hypnotism" and showed that this phenomenon was produced by suggestion operating through purely mental channels. This laid the basis for the future development of psychotherapy. As Bernard Hart puts it: "The formulation of this conception is the historical foundation stone of psychopathology. From it the whole structure can be traced, including all the schools which at present hold the field." [4] This interpretation of hypnotism and suggestion was further developed by Ambroise Liébault and Charles Richet in France.

Early clinical studies of hysteria. The clinical period of psychotherapy opened with the study of hysteria. The first important treatment of hysteria was that by Pierre Briquet in France, who published his *Treatise*

---

[3] *Psychotherapy.* Harvard University Press, 1926, p. 17. I have amplified his prospectus somewhat.

[4] Bernard Hart, *Psychopathology.* New York: Macmillan, 1927, p. 16.

on Hysteria in 1859. This book occupied an intermediate position between Mesmer and Bernheim, since it still regarded hysteria as a product of external stimuli operating upon the mind. A similar point of view was also held by Jean Martin Charcot (1825-1893), head of the clinic at Salpêtrière, and the first great modern clinician in the investigation of mental disorders. He made important additions to our knowledge of hysteria, hypnotism, and suggestion, but his basic interpretations were erroneous. He still contended that hypnotism was brought about by physical agents rather than by the words of the hypnotist and the expectations of the patient.

This misconception was finally repudiated by Charcot's rival, Hippolite Bernheim (1840-1919), head of a rival clinic in Nancy. Bernheim's classic work, *Suggestion in the Hypnotic State,* was published in 1884, and it put the study of mental diseases on a relatively scientific basis by carrying further the notions of Braid and his successors, especially Liébault. Bernheim showed that hypnotism is purely a mental process, that it is not pathological in nature since it can be produced in perfectly normal persons, and that suggestion can be applied outside the hypnotic state. Our conceptions of hypnotism and suggestion, as related to psychotherapy, have made little progress in general principles since Bernheim's day. Subsequent advances have been chiefly in the way of applying Bernheim's conceptions to the further study and treatment of mental diseases.

The first important figure to extend Bernheim's ideas to psychotherapy was Pierre Janet, the ablest of French psychiatrists. His earliest notable work, *The Mental State of Hystericals,* appeared in 1892. He accepted Charcot's undeveloped suggestion that hysterical symptoms are of psychic origin, and he applied to this Bernheim's conceptions of hypnosis and suggestion. To explain hysterical symptoms, he proposed the important notion of the "dissociation of consciousness"—the idea that consciousness in hysterical patients is not unified and under full control but split into two or more streams. The consciousness that recognizes and controls one stream is not able to recognize or control other streams. After applying this interpretation to hysteria, Janet extended it to the study of the other psychoneuroses. In the United States an important contribution of an allied nature was made by Morton Prince, who published *The Dissociation of a Personality* in 1906, and *The Unconscious* in 1914. He examined the problems of the double, or split, personality, making use of the concepts of dissociation, the coconscious, the subconscious, and the unconscious. Both Janet and Prince made important contributions to our understanding of the unconscious.

Janet and Prince fell one step short, however, of explaining the nature of the functional mental and nervous diseases. They were able to demonstrate that dissociation of consciousness goes far toward enabling us to understand the nature of hysterical conduct, but they were unable to explain why the dissociation of consciousness arises in the first place. Further progress awaited the work of Breuer, Freud, and others, to which we may now turn. But we should not ignore the fundamental contributions made by Charcot, Bernheim, Janet, and Prince. They were important pioneers. Their emphasis on a careful study of the symptoms of patients paved the way for the more penetrating investigation by the psychoanalysts.

The work of Sigmund Freud. It was the further investigation of the nature of hysteria which brought about the most important revolution in the history of psychiatry—the development of psychoanalysis by Sigmund Freud (1856-1939). Freud was a native of Vienna but he had studied under Charcot. Upon his return to Vienna, he became interested in the researches into hysteria which were being conducted by another Viennese

Professor Sigmund Freud in London in 1938. With him are his eldest daughter, Mrs. Anna Hollitschek, and Dr. Ernest Jones.

psychiatrist, Joseph Breuer. In treating a patient suffering from hysteria, Breuer had found that under hypnosis the patient could recall psychic experiences which were entirely unrecognized in normal consciousness. By prolonged treatment, Breuer was able to uncover and piece together the hidden psychic past of the patient and to reveal its nature to the latter. As a result, the symptoms cleared up and a cure was effected.

In 1895, Freud and Breuer published their epoch-making *Studies of Hysteria,* in which they contended that this disorder is produced by psychological factors and that it must be cured by psychological methods. From this point, Freud proceeded independently to develop what is known as psychoanalysis, a novel hypothesis as to the nature and treatment of functional mental diseases. Freud laid great stress upon the unconscious basis of mental disorders, the existence of mental conflicts, the significance of infantile and early childhood experiences in producing these conflicts, the repression and forgetting of painful psychic experiences, and the importance of sexual and erotic elements in the unconscious and in the creation of mental disorders. Freud made clear how the earlier unexplained fact of dissociation of personality arises when the libido gets out of the control of the ego, regresses to a fixation on infantile levels of experience, and prevents the normal and harmonious development of the personality. Freud also abandoned hypnotism and worked out what he regarded as a more potent and effective method of exploring the unconscious through free association (of words) and dream analysis.

Wide acceptance of Freudian psychotherapy. Freud's emphasis upon the sexual component of mental diseases, and his extremely comprehensive interpretation of sex, led to bitter attacks upon him by conventional moralists and by the older psychiatrists who held traditional views. Not even Darwin was subjected to so much abuse and vituperation. But Freud gained many supporters in Europe and became especially popular in the United States. In 1909, G. Stanley Hall, president of Clark University, braved the wrath of American puritans within and without the psychological and medical fields by inviting Freud and his disciple, Carl Jung, to expound their doctrines before a distinguished audience at the University.

A number of eminent American psychiatrists soon adopted the Freudian theories. A. A. Brill became the official translator of Freud's works. Such distinguished psychiatrists as Smith E. Jelliffe, William A. White, and James J. Putnam accepted the Freudian doctrines and thus made it quite impossible for antagonistic American psychiatrists to laugh Freud out of court. L. Pierce Clark adopted Freudianism and applied it not only to the functional neuroses and psychoses, but also to a better understanding of epilepsy and mental defect. By the 1920's, psychoanalysis was almost completely accepted in the United States. It was introduced into England by Ernest Jones, W. H. R. Rivers, Bernard Hart, and others.

Essentials of the psychoanalytic technique. The psychoanalytic technique is so important in modern thought and medical practice that we should pause for a moment to describe it very briefly, informally, and untechnically. Freud maintained that the symptoms of functional mental diseases, such as specific phobias, fears, compulsions, and the like, are only disguises of the fundamental disorder which lies in mental conflicts on the unconscious level. Such conflicts are due to psychologically painful infantile experiences, which always involve a considerable sex element. The patient may be able to tell the physician of his specific morbid fears and worries, but he has no real insight into his fundamental troubles. It is the function of the psychoanalysis to uncover the real difficulties, as they exist in the unconscious, and to make the patient understand their nature. If this task is successfully achieved, a cure is presumably effected.

Since progress in psychoanalytic treatment requires a feeling of complete candor and sympathy between physician and patient, it is necessary that the patient learn to trust and respect the analyst. Unless this condition of firm psychic rapport can be secured, there is no possibility of a successful analysis. The attainment of this complete confidence in the analyst is technically known as "transference."

The physician then proceeds to explore the unconscious of the patient by means of free association and dream analysis. In the former process, the physician suggests that the patient talk freely about anything that comes into his head and that he tell what any particular word which comes to him suggests in the way of past emotional experiences. The patient is encouraged to speak freely of all his past experiences, his present difficulties, and his future aspirations. The analyst adroitly guides this psychic reverie, occasionally offering suggestions and observing the patient's reactions. This process is supplemented by dream analysis. It is the contention of the Freudians that dreams symbolize and reveal the hidden conflicts and complexes of patients. So the latter are encouraged to record their dreams and recount them to the doctor. The free association method is also frequently applied to dream analysis by trying out the associations suggested by the dream situations and fantasies.

If the analysis proceeds satisfactorily—it requires a hundred or more hours in most cases—the patient will gradually reveal his deep-seated conflicts, of which he originally had no conception whatever. The analyst, of course, recognizes the underlying situation far more quickly than does the patient. But the psychoanalytic technique forbids the physician to reveal his knowledge directly to the patient. It must be suggested to the latter slowly and indirectly until he himself recognizes it and accepts it of his own initiative. When he does so, he comes to understand the reasons for his troubles and the latter slowly but surely vanish.

The phobias and fears may remain for a time, but they lose their capacity to terrorize the sufferer. The situation has been described by the following analogy: the patient on coming to the psychiatrist for analysis is like a person terrified in the dark by the strange objects which he sees vaguely but does not specifically recognize. They may seem to him to resemble menacing wild beasts and specters. After analysis, these same objects no longer terrify, for they are revealed as in the clear light of day, and are seen to be nothing more, as it were, than tree trunks, stumps, and other harmless inanimate objects.

The cure consists not only in removing the terrifying and all-absorbing fears and phobias, but also in releasing a new fund of psychic energy, which has previously been used up in the repressed mental conflicts. A patient, after a successful analysis, usually has much more mental energy and a greater gusto for life. He is also more self-assured and confident. In instances where the patient had been living under unusually difficult conditions, the physician attempts to redirect the patient's life, though he usually accomplishes this more by suggestion than by direct advice.

Although exaggerated claims for psychoanalysis have been made by some of its less responsible exponents, there is no doubt that skillful analysts have achieved remarkable successes in treating many of the functional mental and nervous diseases which hitherto have been regarded as essentially incurable. Though it cannot be regarded as the sole technique to be followed by psychiatry, it is far from the outright fakery charged by many critics.

Whatever its defects as the initial stage of a great discovery, Freudian psychoanalysis thus constitutes one of the major advances in modern medicine and one of the outstanding contributions to modern psychology. At the celebration of Freud's seventy-fifth birthday, the eminent American psychiatrist, William A. White, made the following estimate of Freud's contribution to psychology and medicine:

To have contributed something to the understanding of man's mind, that most elusive of all phenomena, is to have performed a work of outstanding significance. To have launched such concepts as thinking by the phantasy method, the hypothesis of the unconscious, the theory of determinism in the psychic sphere; to have come to a realization of the factual significance of the emotional cross currents of a personality and the inability of the individual to face his instinctive tendencies; to have done away with such misconceptions as are based upon the body-mind dilemma and to have come to the realization that psychology is a biological science and to an understanding that pathological processes are different from so-called normal processes only in degree and emphasis and that disorder and disease in the mental sphere are experiments of Nature from which the observer can learn about the normal, healthy functions of the mind—to have launched a series of concepts such as these and many others into the field of mental medicine is as significant for man's future as were the contributions of Copernicus, of Newton, or of Pasteur.

If man is the measure of all things, then the measuring rod he uses is his mind, and it is his mind that encompasses all and that is, therefore, greater than all the rest. Professor Freud has brought to the knowledge of the structure and the functions of the mind an entirely new point of view and original contributions of the utmost significance. In doing so, however, he has invaded our secret places, and his invasion has been universally resented. He has dislodged our egotism, wounded our narcissism, as did Copernicus and Darwin, and has been hated as heartily for doing so. He has not been burned at the stake because burning at the stake has gone out of fashion, but he has been attacked by a weapon perhaps more deadly and difficult to defend one's self against than fire. Fire and death in the Middle Ages were weapons that served to weld people together in a common cause, but today, lacking such weapons, man turns to ridicule, which, rapierlike, finds its way truly to the unprotected place in the victim's armor. Professor Freud has, however, been superior even to this weapon, and if I were to express our admiration in a single sentence summing up most of his outstanding characteristics, I think I could do no better than to say, with Havelock Ellis: "When any great person has stood alone against the world, it has always been the world that lost." That, to my mind, expresses the keynote of this evening's assemblage.

Freudianism and sex. Perhaps the most important contribution to Freudianism has been its demonstration of the influence of sexual factors on many forms of behavior, particularly those manifested in mental disorders. Naturally, this has led to wide opposition and misinterpretation. Because the psychoanalyst has pointed out the evil effects of unnecessary taboos and inhibitions, it is too often supposed that he puts the stamp of his professional approval on wholesale adultery, divorce, and license. These fanciful views about psychoanalysis have been justly denounced by C. P. Obendorf and William A. White.

At a meeting of the American Neurological Society in Atlantic City,

Obendorf made it clear that, in handling personal difficulties, the psychoanalyst attempts solely to discover the roots of the trouble and to render such aid as this discovery of causes will offer. He may indirectly strengthen the personality and thus enable the patient to make more effective use of the new knowledge of his problems, but psychoanalysts do not pretend to work miracles. As Obendorf put it:

The only position which the psychoanalyst can assume in these matrimonial tangles is to bring to consciousness those unconscious factors which produce social discord. It is not the function of the psychoanalyst to assume the role of guide either in keeping the couple together or in advising separation.

The allegation that psychoanalysis offers any blanket encouragement to license was laid at rest by William A. White. Answering this charge, directly, he said;

The statement that psychoanalysis gives free rein to all the tendencies and passions on the theory that their repression is bad for the individual is nonsense. Psychoanalysis never taught this and never believed it. The only people who do believe it are those who want to, and they are among the critics of psychoanalysis. Psychoanalysis, as a matter of fact, has, in recent years particularly, laid a great deal of stress upon what other people call moral controls, shown how they have grown up, what are their mechanisms, etc. It has explained how they work, and, like all truly scientific disciplines, it sets forth the facts as it finds them for you or me to do with as we please.

Modifications, if not improvements, of Freudian concepts and techniques. Freud deservedly remained the high priest of the psychoanalytic movement. He was very loath to accept criticism or to modify his doctrines, except on the basis of his own investigations and inclinations. It was thus natural that there would be divergencies from Freudian psychoanalysis, part of them based upon independent judgment and part of them founded upon envy and jealousy. We have space to mention only a few of these.

Alfred Adler began as a disciple of Freud but soon departed from the master's views and was read out of the circle. Adler called his system "individual psychology" rather than psychoanalysis. He laid far less stress than did Freud upon the unconscious, repression, and infantile sex experiences. He was inclined to hold that conflicts and neurotic tendencies grow more out of unsatisfied longings than from repressed disappointments. He put very special emphasis upon overcompensation for a sense of organic inferiority. From Adler's point of view, neuroses are commonly the product of the frustrated ego rather than a conflict between the ego and the sexual libido. Adler exaggerated the psychic differences between men and women, holding that the latter are dominated by instinct and trickery, without any deep consciousness of purpose, whereas a man is motivated by intelligence and a conscious wish for self-realization.

The famous Zürich psychoanalyst, Carl G. Jung, remained faithful to the master longer than Adler, but in time he, too, was cut off and founded a separate school. Much more puritanical in his background than Freud, he was prone to lay less emphasis upon the sexual component in mental and nervous diseases. Jung continued Freud's emphasis upon the importance of the unconscious, and even developed a somewhat fantastic notion of a universal or racial unconsciousness. For example, he derived the night terrors of children from the primitive racial fears of our prehistoric ancestors in caves and forest jungles. In his interpretation of dreams, Jung held that they present the symbolism not only of individual experience but also of the racial unconscious. To Jung we are primarily indebted for the development of the word-association method of psychoanalysis. Jung is also famous for his division of human types into the introvert and the extrovert. The former is a more subjective and reflective type, often given to morbid musings; the latter, more dynamic and aggressive, is a person of action rather than of thought. He represents the objective type of personality. The introvert is naturally more subject to neurotic tendencies. Because of his more aggressive personality, Jung was inclined to rely to some degree upon conscious advice in analysis, a procedure which Freud consistently avoided and vehemently denounced. Jung's most original work was in providing an illuminating psychoanalytical explanation of dementia praecox, to which we have already referred briefly.

Otto Rank developed a very considerable following for his type of analytical procedure. He outdid Freud in stressing the importance of the earliest childhood experiences, being especially concerned with the alleged influence of the birth trauma upon the subsequent development of neuroses. Rank also contended that psychoanalysis should lay much more stress on constructive stimulation of will power as a useful aid to therapeutic efforts, especially in the later stages of analysis.

The most important recent progress in psychoanalysis has been the achievements of Franz Alexander and T. M. French in the Chicago Psychoanalytic Institute. They have been able to speed up treatment without sacrificing curative success, thus making treatment more economical and accessible to more patients.

Trend towards synthesis. An American psychopathologist, E. J. Kempf, endeavored to bring together a synthesis of the ideas of Freud and Adler, Watson's notion of the conditioned-reflex, and the recent contributions of endocrinology to psychiatry. His system, outlined in his *Psychopathology,* is more comprehensive than that of most other psychiatrists, but it has gained few followers because of the popularity of one or another of the more single-track schools. Many American psychiatrists have been eclectics, picking and choosing, and selecting from the various doctrines those which seem to them to have the greatest amount of relevance and substance. Partially in self-defense, many Freudians tended to become even more devout in the worship of the master.

The most healthy recent development has been the tendency to integrate psychoanalytical principles with other basic psychiatric concepts and practices. In this, Eugen Bleuler, J. M. Masserman, and A. P. Noyes have done outstanding work.

Psychiatry as a medical science: the work of Kraepelin and Meyer. In any discussion of the history of psychotherapy some mention should be made of the development of psychiatry as a medical science. In this field of work, the outstanding figures have been Emil Kraepelin (1856-1926) and Adolf Meyer (1866-1950). Kraepelin taught at Heidelberg and Munich Universities. He brought order out of chaos in psychiatry and made the latter a descriptive medical science. We have already called attention to the fact that he was the first to provide a comprehensive and orderly classification of mental and nervous diseases, especially the functional psychoses. He held that these diseases, like all others, run a natural course and must be studied and treated by clinical methods. In this way he introduced laboratory techniques into psychiatry and founded the bio-psychological approach which was later developed much further by Adolf Meyer in the United States. Through his analytical and descriptive studies Kraepelin was able for the first time to isolate and describe leading mental disorders, especially manic-depressive psychoses and dementia praecox (schizophrenia).

The outstanding non-Freudian psychiatrist in America was Adolf Meyer, of Johns Hopkins University. He was well-trained in both medicine and psychology, having been originally a student of Forel and one of the first to master Kraepelin's doctrines. He was later associated with G. Stanley Hall at Clark University. But he early entered into clinical work in state hospitals for the insane, first at the Kankakee State Hospital in Illinois, and then at the Worcester State Hospital in Massachusetts, where he introduced Kraepelin's ideas and methods. Later he became director of the Psychiatric Institute at Ward's Island in New York, where he began work in 1902. One of his responsibilities here was to train the staff physicians for the state hospitals for the insane throughout the state. He was thus able to exert a large influence upon the improvement of psychological understanding and of psychiatric methods in actual state hospital practice. His work was carried on by August Hoch.

Before Meyer's day, notwithstanding the work of Charcot, Bernheim, Janet, Prince, and Freud, main stress had been laid upon the physical aspects of mental diseases and much time had been devoted to performing autopsies on those who had died from some form of psychosis. Meyer contended that emphasis should be shifted from the morgue to the clinic and the laboratory. While the physical pathology of mental diseases can not be ignored, he saw that the symptoms and behavior of patients were more important. Although not antagonistic to Freudianism, Meyer did not accept it wholeheartedly. He referred to his own approach as one of "psycho-biology." He viewed the brain not merely as an anatomical exhibit but more as an agency for the adjustment of man to his social environment—something receiving and giving off stimulation. He regarded mental disorders as a maladjustment of the entire personality rather than narrowly-conceived physiological brain diseases. Meyer carried these broadminded notions to the Phipps Psychiatric Clinic at Johns Hopkins University, of which he was appointed director in 1913. He made this clinic one of the chief psychiatric centers of the Western world. American psychiatry owes Meyer an enormous debt for his insight and industry, and for his sense of balance and realism. Many of the leading American psychiatrists between the two world wars were men who had been trained by Meyer at Johns Hopkins.

Psychosomatic medicine. A very important contribution of psychiatry to medical practice has been the founding of what is known as psychosomatic medicine by Flanders Dunbar, Franz Alexander, and others, to which reference is made elsewhere. This stresses the powerful influence of mental states on many forms of common diseases and the importance of hypochondria in the attitudes of many ordinary patients. It also places emphasis on the importance of a psychiatric approach to general medical practice.

Evils of the medical monopoly of psychotherapy. The development of psychiatry as a medical science was a great contribution to psychotherapy, but a heavy price was exacted thereby. The result was to give doctors of medicine a monopoly of practice in psychiatry and to exclude most clinical psychologists from freedom and legal work in this field. The M.D. degree is required for the normal practice of psychotherapy, though little or no attention is given to instruction in psychiatry in medical colleges. Doctors who enter psychiatry must master the field after gaining their medical degree. A man who has taken his Ph.D. degree with a major in psychology is far better fitted to understand the human mind than the graduate of a medical school—especially if he has taken a number of courses in abnormal psychology and psychiatry and a few basic courses in anthropology. Most medically-trained psychiatrists are rank amateurs in their knowledge of psychology and anthropology, though they depend heavily on both in their concepts and practice. Although there should be constant collaboration between physicians and clinical psychologists in psychotherapeutic practice, there is no doubt that the shortage of experts in this field today is due in large part to the indefensible medical monopoly of psychotherapy.

The Rorschach Personality Test. A sensational contribution to psychiatry and clinical psychology has been the belated application of the Rorschach Personality Test to patients suffering from mental and nervous disorders. This test, developed in 1921 by a Swiss clinical psychologist, Hermann Rorschach (1884-1922), was long ignored not only by educational psychologists but also by psychiatrists. Introduced into psychiatry in recent years, the Rorschach test appears to have had revolutionary results in speeding up the insight of psychiatrists into the personality patterns and emotional difficulties of patients. It utilizes mainly verbal responses to ink blots, which are shown to patients in various ingenious arrangements on different colored cards and evoke numerous symbolic responses, depending upon the subconscious state and patterns of the patients.

Although the methods and results may seem fantastic to the uninitiated at first sight, extensive use of the test and comparison with the results of prolonged psychiatric examination and psychoanalysis of the same patients have both increased confidence in the Rorschach test and demonstrated the vastly greater rapidity with which psychiatrists and clinical psychologists can gain insight into the personality makeup and mental problems of the patient. In a few hours of careful testing by experts, much the same insight can be gained by the psychiatrist as could be obtained in weeks or months of psychoanalysis. Of course, the therapeutic results of Rorschach exploration are not at all comparable to the benefits of psychoanalysis. But the Rorschach test affords much greater possibility of examining individually the personality problems of the mass of patients in mental hospitals, with their perennial shortage of psychiatrists and clinical psychologists, than could ever have been feasible with the older methods.

Lack of adequate number of psychiatrists. Despite all the progress described above in organic neurology, psychosurgery, psychiatry, and clinical psychology, there is a lamentable lag between knowledge in these fields and its actual application to curative therapy. This is mainly due to the lack of enough trained neurologists, psychiatrists, clinical psychologists, psychiatric nurses, and social workers to meet the needs of public hospitals and private practice. The medical understaffing of state hospitals for the mentally diseased is truly fantastic. Even in some of the otherwise fairly progressive states, there may be only one psychiatrist for a thousand patients. George S. Stevenson pointed out in January, 1951, that few of our state hospitals for mental cases provide more than one psychiatrist to 200 patients, whereas one to 85 patients is not unusual in a good English mental hospital. Out of more than 200,000 licensed physicians, there are only about 4,500 accredited medical psychiatrists. At least 15,000 to 20,000—and perhaps twice that number—would be required to care for the mentally diseased and mentally defective. Together with these we would need as many psychiatric nurses and thousands of clinical psychologists and psychiatric social workers.

Psychiatry is one of the most exacting and expensive of the medical specialties in which to prepare for practice, partly because of the paucity of psychiatric instruction before the student leaves medical college and for some time thereafter. After obtaining his medical degree, the would-be psychiatrist must spend two years in a general rotating internship (which excludes training or experience in psychiatry) and then at least three years in psychiatric residency before he will be allowed to practice as a psychiatrist. If he wishes to be a psychoanalyst, he must take two or three more years of specialized training in this field. He must also be psychoanalyzed himself—and must pay for it. Nothing short of public aid in medical training can provide the needed incentive and assistance to lure many young doctors into psychiatry. The National Mental Hygiene Act of 1946 has made a beginning along this line, but it is only a beginning. The medical monopoly of practice in psychotherapy has discouraged able men and women from going into clinical psychology, because the possible types of employment in this field have been highly limited for persons without medical training. Finally, little has been done to encourage or to aid in training the vast additional number of psychiatric nurses and social workers who will be required for any adequate application of our neurological and psychiatric knowledge to the cure and prevention of mental disease.

Unfortunate location of state hospitals a handicap to good service. Another obstacle to good medical treatment of mental patients is the unfortunate location of many state hospitals which makes even the available psychiatrists, nurses, orderlies and volunteer workers less willing to serve in them. Some are located in crowded slum areas of cities, but more often they are situated in remote rural areas which, though scenically beautiful, are isolated from social and intellectual contacts. As George S. Stevenson puts is: "The location of these hospitals results in obstacles for families who wish to visit patients, in barriers against finding good personnel and in using the services of volunteer workers, and in a loss of the impact of the community to a point where the perspective of the hospital becomes limited to the walls of the institution." Out of 900 psychiatrists who served with the armed forces in the Second World War, only 60 expressed willingness to take posts in state mental hospitals. Another consideration here, of course, is the modest salaries paid in state hospitals compared to the frequently impressive incomes of psychiatrists in private practice.

FEEBLE-MINDEDNESS: ITS NATURE, CAUSES, AND TREATMENT

Rise of a scientific approach to feeble-mindedness. As we suggested earlier in the chapter, there was, a century ago, no clear notion of the very real distinction between the psychotic and the feeble-minded. This is not surprising, since some of the more common types of insanity are characterized by dementia and apathy, which closely resemble the attitudes and behavior of the lower-grade feeble-minded types. Hence, "lunatics" and "idiots" were commonly regarded as one and the same thing. The progress in medical science and psychology has, however, enabled us to differentiate clearly between those suffering from mental diseases and those handicapped by mental defect, and to understand that they present quite different problems. Mental defect is a relatively clear and simple matter when compared to the great complexity and variety of mental diseases. Feeble-mindedness could be handled with relative ease were it not for prejudices existing in the social mind against the proper remedial measures and for the reluctance to spend enough money to put them into operation.

From common-sense observation to mental tests. The fact that persons differ in mental capacity is so obvious and is demonstrated in so many different ways that observers have been aware of the fact for centuries. Aristotle discoursed at length on the subject and stressed the fact that some seem born to rule and others to serve. Indeed, the general conviction that there are marked individual differences in mental ability has been the prevailing opinion among mankind except for a brief period in the nineteenth century when extreme democratic notions gained dominion in certain countries. Then only was it believed that all persons are actually equal in innate mental ability. But many leading American democrats never shared this extreme notion. Jefferson, for example, followed Aristotle's belief that some are born to rule and others to serve. Jefferson even went so far as to think that those who are born to serve have sufficient intelligence to recognize those who are born to rule and to put the latter into public office.

Nevertheless, until the twentieth century, both the conviction that people differ in mental ability and the belief that they are equal in capacity were purely a matter of guesswork. It has been only in our century that we have provided a scientific technique for testing the mental capacity of human beings. The beginning of the mental testing movement may be attributed to Sir Francis Galton, the founder of the eugenics movement. Although his interests were primarily biological, he suggested various mental tests to vindicate his thesis of wide differences in human capacity, a matter so very important in his eugenic philosophy. His elementary tests were first set forth in the 1880's. In the latter part of the century the main interest in mental testing was manifested in the United States. During the decade following 1890, J. M. Cattell, Livingston Farrand, and E. L. Thorndike worked on mental tests at Columbia University; Hugo Münsterberg, at Harvard; and Joseph Jastrow, at the University of Wisconsin.

Main types of mental tests for intelligence. The provision of the first adequate mental tests was the achievement of two French psychologists, Albert Binet and Thomas Simon. They devised these tests between 1904 and 1908. Their procedure was to attempt to discover, through an extremely extensive investigation of child knowledge, the questions which the average child could be expected to answer at any given age. A child who could answer correctly the majority of the questions which the average child of his age had been found to be able to answer was regarded as normal. For example, a normal child of six years should be able to answer a majority of the questions which it has been found that children of six can answer. If a child falls behind the average for his chronological age, he is regarded as subnormal or retarded, whereas if he can answer the majority of questions usually handled successfully only by children older than himself, he is viewed as a superior or precocious child. Binet and Simon worked on the improvement of their tests until 1911.

The Binet-Simon tests were first brought to the United States in 1908 by Henry H. Goddard, of the famous laboratory for the study of the feeble-minded at Vineland, New Jersey, in 1908. Goddard improved upon the French tests, especially substituting questions more suitable for children born in an American environment. He was also the first to use these tests to divide the feeble-minded into the three grades of intelligence which are now most generally accepted—morons, imbeciles, and idiots. This more scientific classification took the place of such earlier ones as "simpletons" and "fools."

An improvement on the Goddard tests was devised by Robert M. Yerkes, of Yale University, who introduced the famous "point-scale" system. This made allowance for the difficulties met by foreign children in answering questions. It introduced a decimal gradation, rated according to such environmental handicaps as exist in the case of these children. The next important advance was the so-called Stanford revision worked out by Lewis M. Terman, of Stanford University. This provided more refined methods of testing and a greater uniformity in questions. An effort was made to supply questions which could be answered by any child, whatever his cultural environment. It also devised better tests for superior children.

.Terman was also responsible for popularizing the concept of the Intelligence Quotient, a concept that had been proposed by William Stern. The intelligence quotient reveals the ratio of the chronological age to the mental age. Known as the *I.Q.*, it is obtained by dividing the mental age by the actual or chronological age. At least, this is the procedure if the child is under 16 years of age. For those over 16, the age of 16 is used as the chronological age, whatever the actual age of the individual. For example, a child with an actual age of 8 years, who can answer the questions suitable to a child of 9, has a mental age of 9 years. His I.Q. would be obtained by dividing 9 by 8, and would be 112.5. A child of 12 who could only pass the test for normal children of 9 years would have an I.Q. of 75 (9 ÷ 12). Terman showed that the I.Q. remains relatively constant for any given individual at all periods of his life, tending to become relatively fixed about the age of 5. If there are any changes in I.Q. as the child grows older, the chances are that the superior child will give evidence of an increasing I.Q. and the inferior child will show indications of a falling one.

Mental testing during the First World War. The first extensive mental testing ever carried out was executed by our army psychologists, mainly American academic psychologists, during the First World War. It was necessary to improve on the earlier tests in order to get a method which would be adaptable to mass application. These improvements were chiefly the work of Goddard and Arthur S. Otis, of Stanford University. Moreover, it was found necessary to devise two types of tests. The Alpha test was administered to those who could read and write English. The Beta, or performance, test was provided for those who could not read English. But both tests were supposed to produce identical results in revealing the mental age of those tested.

These army tests revealed a very amazing fact—that 70 per cent of those in the army had a mental age of 14 years and under, while 45 per cent possessed a mental age of 12 years or under. As a matter of fact, the army recruits were probably slightly superior to the population as a whole, since the lower-grade feeble-minded had usually been weeded out by the draft boards. The general results of the army mental tests are revealed in the following table:

Grade	Mental Age	Percentage of the Total
A	18-19	4½
B	16-17	9
C+	15	16½
C	13-14	25
C—	12	20
D	11	15
D—	10	10

These tests struck a body blow at the democratic dogma of the equal mental capacity of all members of the population. They were bitterly attacked by a number of publicists, notably by Walter Lippmann, then an aggressive liberal and democrat. But the critics were effectively answered, if not silenced, by the eminent psychologist, Edwin G. Boring, in a definitive article, "Intelligence as the Tests Test It," in *The New Republic* of June 6, 1923. There is little doubt among fair-minded scientists that the army intelligence tests accurately revealed the above differences in innate mental capacity for individuals, if not for races. And this is all that has ever been claimed for them by the testers.

Since the army tests were administered, there have been many improvements in the testing technique. Such improvements are found in the performance tests devised by Pintner, Paterson, Kohs, Peterson, and others. They eliminate language difficulties almost entirely, and they are particularly adaptable to the illiterate and the deaf. The mental tests have been of very great value to education in enabling us to determine suitable types of instruction for children and to provide specialized classes for retarded types.

We have already called attention to the large number of feeble-minded in the population. At least 65 million are dull normals or lower in intelligence; some 10-20 million are morons or less, and at least two million are of such low intelligence as to need institutional segregation— at least for a time. Actually, only about 113,000 are being thus treated at present.

Main types of feeble-minded. We have also referred to the differentiation of the feeble-minded according to the extent of their mental deficiency. We may make this classification a little more specific. The term *idiot* is usually applied to those feeble-minded persons who have a mental age of less than two years. The *imbecile* is a feeble-minded person whose mental age is between two and seven years. The *moron* has a mental age of between seven and 11 years. The *super-moron* or *dull-normal* type falls within the mental age of 11 and 12 years. The *normal* type of adult is regarded as one whose mental age is 13 years or above.

The details of these distinctions vary somewhat among different classifiers and students, but the range of types and mental ages just described is substantially that followed by the majority. An attempt has also been made to differentiate these defective types on the basis of their intelligence quotient. Idiots are assigned an intelligence quotient of zero to 24; imbeciles, 25 to 49; and morons 50 to 74.

There are also special pathological types among the feeble-minded. The hydrocephalic defectives have abnormally large heads because of the pressure of watery fluid on the skull. The microcephalic have unusually small heads, often of a somewhat pineapple shape. The cretins exhibit a dwarfed physical and mental development, characterized by premature aging and by obstructed body and head growth. One peculiar type of feeble-mindedness is known as *Mongolian imbecility*—often erroneously called Mongolian idiocy. In this type, definitely Mongoloid traits appear, such as slanting eyes and the absence of the usual occipital protrusion on the back of the head. Mongolian imbeciles often have a deeply furrowed tongue. Their mental age is usually four to five years. Curiously enough, Mongoloid imbeciles are most frequently children of parents of superior mental capacity.

Importance of recognizing pseudo feeble-mindedness. While carefully administered mental tests will reveal the mental age of the child and the degree of mental defect in the case of true feeble-mindedness, a very salutary word of caution was uttered by an eminent educator and a leader in the study of school hygiene, William H. Burnham. He called our attention to a very important mental condition which he designated as *pseudo feeble-mindedness.*

As we have seen, true feeble-mindedness is a definite and fixed mental retardation of a physical character which cannot be altered to any notable degree. A true feeble-minded person may be taught how to adjust himself fairly well to simple social situations on a relatively low mental level, but no amount of training of any sort can raise his I.Q. to any marked degree. He has a defective brain.

In the case of the pseudo feeble-minded, the brain possesses normal powers, but various types of inhibiting emotional complications prevent the mind from functioning normally. Therefore, the mental reactions of the child resemble those of the true feeble-minded. This pseudo feeble-mindedness, or mental retardation due to causes other than defective brain power, may result from physical disease, physical shocks, malnutrition, and the like. But the more common causes are serious emotional disturbances, such as fear and the development of abnormal inhibitions of the will as the result of social experiences, emotional conflicts, lack of normal mental stimulation, and the like.

Burnham's conception of pseudo feeble-mindedness is of great practical importance. It means that mental tests alone are not always sufficient to prove actual feeble-mindedness and should not constitute the sole basis on which we may so regard and treat a child. The mental tests must be supplemented by a psychiatric examination of all children involved, in order to discover whether or not there are unusual emotional difficulties which make the child react as though he were feeble-minded when he is not actually such. A physician should also examine children to see if there are present any pathological physical conditions that are retarding mental development and normal mental actions. Unless such precautions are taken, many children who might be restored to normal mental powers and behavior may be railroaded into institutions for the feeble-minded. Under such conditions, their mental retardation may continue indefinitely. On the other hand, if a physician or psychiatrist finds definite and remediable causes for mental retardation, and these are eliminated, the child may be restored to normality, thus becoming an asset to society rather than a social burden. Burnham cites a number of striking cases of pseudo feeble-mindedness. We need select only a couple of representative ones. One is the case of a boy by the name of Don, who was studied by Lightner Witmer. When Don was first brought to Witmer he gave every indication of being a low-grade feeble-minded type:

His father carried him into my office and deposited him, a soulless lump, upon the couch. He sat there with the stolidity of a Buddhist image, absorbed in the inspection of a card which he held in his pudgy hands, as regardless of his father and mother as of the new objects about him. While his gaze moved over the card, he scratched the back of it gently and incessantly with his finger nails. At times he gritted his teeth; and then again he made a crooning, humming sound with which it is his habit to lull himself to sleep.[5]

Witmer found that Don, seemingly a hopeless case of true feeble-mindedness, was actually suffering from emotional inhibitions due to fear. These were removed through skillful treatment and Don became a mentally normal child. At the age of nine, about six years after he was first brought to Witmer, he was in the same school grade as normal children of his age and was rated as among the best 20 per cent of the children of his age in the school.

Another well-known case is that of Father Shields, which Burnham thus describes:

Retarded in his development, and remaining an ignoramus till the age of seventeen or eighteen, recognized as a fool in the community, branded as a moron by his own parents, he was then aroused, took his education into his own hands, passed through college and Johns Hopkins University, and is now a well-known professor in the Catholic University at Washington.[6]

Burnham has thus shown emotional disturbances and neurotic conditions may produce mental reactions resembling feeblemindedness. Related to this is the question of whether or not the true feeble-minded may also suffer from mental and nervous diseases, such as neuroses and psychoses. Formerly, it was believed that those who were feeble-minded could not at the same time suffer from such mental disorders. But more careful study has demonstrated that, occasionally, the feeble-minded may develop neuroses and psychoses. They do so relatively rarely, however, because it is less likely that, with their feeble intellects, they will experience sufficiently serious repression and mental conflict to produce a neurosis or psychosis. Of course, if the feeble-minded person contracts syphilis, he may develop paresis. Other diseases of the brain will also produce mental aberrations in the feeble-minded person as well as in those of normal mental powers. But, on the whole, the problems of mental defect are distinct in kind from those of mental disease.

Only about half of feeble-minded cases are hereditary. We have already discussed briefly the question of heredity and feeble-mindedness in connection with our treatment of the eugenics movement. Half a century ago it was generally believed that the great majority of feeble-mindedness was hereditary, that the feeble-minded are inherently a vicious lot, and that they are prone to crime, vice, and all types of degenerate behavior. Evidence for this was assembled in a number of classic studies of feeble-minded and degenerate families, such as *The Jukes*, by Richard L. Dugdale; *The Kallikak Family*, By Henry H. Goddard; *The Nam Family*, and, *The Hill Folk*, by Charles B. Davenport and his associates; *The Pineys*,

---

[5] *Don*, Psychological Clinic, 1920, pp. 97-111.

[6] W. H. Burnham, *The Normal Mind*. New York: Appleton-Century, 1924, p. 589.

by Elizabeth S. Kite; and *The Family of Sam Sixty*, by Mary S. Kostir. These authors all reached the conclusion that feeble-mindedness was overwhelmingly hereditary and that it was responsible for most of our social evils.

More discriminating investigation since that time has thoroughly upset these older dogmas. It has been shown that no more than one-half of true feeble-mindedness is hereditary, though it is possible that hereditary mental defect is transmitted according to the Mendelian formula. The remainder of all feeble-mindedness is caused by physical disease, bodily injuries, malnutrition, and other unfortunate circumstances to which the individual is subject. This indicates that, even if every living feeble-minded person were prevented from breeding through segregation or sterilization, we could not eliminate all feeble-mindedness.

Feeble-minded not inherently vicious or criminal. It has also been made clear—particularly as the result of more scientific treatment of the feeble-minded—that the feeble-minded are not inherently criminal or vicious. But because the feeble-minded are unusually susceptible to suggestion, they are more easily influenced than normal types in either good or bad surroundings. If they are properly protected and directed, it is easier to keep them law-abiding and moral than it is to procure and maintain such behavior on the part of normal types. On the other hand, if they are exposed to conditions making for crime and vice, they are more likely to fall into evil ways than are normal types of persons. This consideration emphasizes the desirability of proper care and protection of the feeble-minded in the interests of society. These newer and more sensible views of the nature and implications of feeble-mindedness were first set forth systematically by one of our foremost authorities on the subject, Walter E. Fernald, in 1924. Subsequent investigation and treatment of the feeble-minded have served to confirm and extend his somewhat revolutionary conclusions.

Improved institutional treatment of the feeble-minded. The differentiation of the mentally defective from the mentally diseased, and a clearer knowledge of the nature of mental defect, have naturally led to emphasis upon the desirability of providing institutional treatment for these types. The first prominent protagonist of institutional care and treatment for the feeble-minded was Edward Seguin, of Paris, who carried on his educational work in the middle of the nineteenth century. His rôle in the history of the feeble-minded is comparable to that of his fellow-countryman, Pinel, in the handling of the insane.

The first state school for the feeble-minded in the United States was the Massachusetts State School for Idiotic and Feeble-Minded Youth, opened in Boston in October, 1848. It was later moved to Waverly, Massachusetts, and exerted a large influence upon American experience in this field, primarily because of the eminence of its superintendent, Walter Fernald, who served there from 1887 to 1924. In 1855, New York State opened a special institution for the feeble-minded at Syracuse. There are now about 90 public (virtually all of them state) institutions for the feeble-minded and epileptic in the United States. Most of them are overcrowded, though not to so extreme an extent as the institutions for the mentally diseased.

At first these institutions were large, forbidding structures of a semi-penal character. But in the twentieth century there has been a trend

Dr. Walter Elmore Fernald, Superintendent of the Massachusetts State School for the Feeble-minded at Waverly for many years (retired in 1924). To him we owe much of our present knowledge about traits and desirable treatment of the feeble-minded.

toward the cottage and colony system. The man who led in this movement was Charles Bernstein, of the Rome, New York, Institution for the Feeble-minded, who introduced the practice in 1906. He particularly stressed the need for farm colonies for the feeble-minded, as a sort of halfway station between the larger institutions and later release in the general community. But colonies for the permanent segregation of the feeble-minded have been created, the first notable one being Letchworth Village, at Thiells, New York, opened in 1911. This is a true village community and attempts to adapt the feeble-minded to normal social life. Laboratories for the study of the feeble-minded have been created in connection with state institutions. The first was that at Faribault, Minnesota, set up in 1898. That at Vineland, New Jersey, opened in 1906 and conducted by Goddard, has been particularly famous. Others of importance are those at Waverly, Massachusetts; Lincoln, Illinois; and Eldridge, California. The number of the feeble-minded segregated and treated in institutions has increased notably in the twentieth century.

In 1904 there were 14,347 thus segregated; in 1910, 20,731; in 1923, 42,954; and in 1948, approximately 113,000. The facilities are still grossly insufficient, as will be seen from the fact that the best authorities estimate that there are about two million feeble-minded in the country who need institutional care.

Mentally retarded children in the schools. In addition to special institutions for the feeble-minded, ever better provision is being made for handling the 600,000 or more mentally retarded pupils in the public school system. This procedure was first started in Providence, Rhode Island, in 1896. The provisions are still notoriously inadequate, however, since it is estimated that there are over a million mentally retarded children who need a special type of school instruction. It has been found that the best form of education for the mentally defective is manual training. The feeble-minded above the idiot and low-grade imbecile level give evidence of capacity for achievement in the more elementary types of manual trades.

Sound social policies relative to the feeble-minded. In the treatment of the feeble-minded it is generally agreed that the lowest types, such as idiots and low-grade imbeciles, must be permanently segregated in institutions. The more progressive students of the problem recommend that the idiot group should be painlessly exterminated. They are a burden to themselves, to their relatives, and to society. But it will probably be a long time before any such action will be taken. The colony scheme is far better than segregation in large institutions as a means of handling the upper-grade imbeciles and the morons. After the latter have been properly trained, they may readily be boarded out and released on parole.

Those who view the feeble-minded with sympathy but without sentimentality urge that all the feeble-minded should be sterilized—at least those who are released from custody. It is not hoped that we shall thereby be able to get rid of all feeble-mindedness. But the feeble-minded, even of the non-hereditary type, are certainly not fitted to assume family responsibilities. Hence, we would take steps to see that they never are permitted to do so. Some states have laws that permit the sterilization of the mentally defective, and the laws of 27 are in force today. But these laws have been applied with great restraint except in a few states like North Carolina, California, Georgia, and Virginia—and even here their enforcement has been lax. California and Virginia have the best record. The ineffectiveness of such laws to date may be seen by the fact that, while the birth rate of the hereditary feeble-minded per 100,000 of the population is about 45, the average number of operations, even in states that take the law with some seriousness, is about 2 per 100,000 population.

If, as now seems probable, at least half of all mental defect is caused by post-natal factors, such as birth injuries, physical diseases, glandular difficulties, malnutrition, and the like, it is obvious that better medical care and personal hygiene will prevent more mental defect than sterilization, especially as there is no moral opposition to decent medical care. There is great need for more research into the non-hereditary causes of mental defect and for a planned medical campaign based on the information produced by such research. At present the campaign to prevent mental defect lags between growing disillusionment relative to the panacea of sterilization, and apathy and lethargy with respect to post-natal factors and the proper program to cope with the latter.

If the feeble-minded were trained for elementary trades and farming, there is no reason why they could not be made self-supporting.

There is no foundation whatever for a somewhat perverse and sentimental argument that we need to preserve a large number of feeble-minded in the population to "do the dirty work" for society. This dirty work is being performed ever more effectively by machinery today—and mechanical ditch-diggers and road machines do not vote unintelligently, get into prison, engage in vice, go on relief, and otherwise clog the social machinery and pile up social burdens. The problems of modern society are so complex that even the normal person finds it difficult to conduct himself with intelligence and adequacy. The prevalence of a large number of feeble-minded in the population only tends to complicate the situation and to retard social progress. As is the case with mental disease, so with mental defect; the basic goal should be the prevention of as much mental defect as medical science can bring about.

THE DEVELOPMENT OF THE MENTAL HYGIENE MOVEMENT

Nature of mental hygiene. *Mental hygiene,* a term invented by William Sweetzer in 1843, combines all the efforts to deal with mental disease and mental defect through reducing, as far as possible, the prevalence of mental and nervous disorders and mental defects, and by providing humane and scientific treatment for those who are already mentally afflicted. The mental hygiene movement is doing much to suggest more sane and healthful ways of living to those who are still relatively normal. Although mental hygiene has had a large and beneficial influence on methods of curing mental and nervous diseases, its main purpose and program are directed toward preventing mental breakdowns or toward checking them in the early stages. To bring this about, it labors to provide the necessary education, legislation, institutions, and other relevant facilities.

Place of Clifford W. Beers in the mental hygiene movement. The mental hygiene movement had a dramatic beginning in the efforts of Clifford W. Beers to arouse public concern over the inhuman treatment of the mentally ill in state hospitals early in the present century. Beers suffered a mental breakdown a short time after graduating from Yale University, and for three years he was confined in various hospitals for the insane. In 1903, he regained his mental health. He came through his experience with an accurate memory of almost everything that had happened to him in institutions.

Beers was one of the few mentally diseased persons of that time who completely recovered. To enter an "insane asylum" for treatment 50 years ago meant almost a living death. The few persons who ever came out of an "asylum" tried to forget their sufferings and the abuse they

Clifford W. Beers, founder of the mental hygiene movement.

had to endure in the way of discipline and "treatment." Fortunately for the progress of mental hygiene, Beers was an exception. Upon recovery, he determined to devote himself to the elimination of the mistaken medical and social ideas that were responsible for the unintelligent and inhuman handling of mentally diseased persons. In a remarkable book, *A Mind That Found Itself,* published in 1908, Beers related his experiences calmly and clearly. His book attracted wide attention.

Foundation of The National Committee for Mental Hygiene. Beers conceived the idea of organizing state and national committees to promote the study and practice of mental hygiene. In May, 1908, he organized the first state society for mental hygiene, in Connecticut. A National Committee for Mental Hygiene was established a year later. Prominent leaders in many walks of life became interested in the movement. Among the more notable were William James, the famous psychologist, and Adolf Meyer and William Russell, leading psychiatrists. Meyer's advice was decisive in inducing Beers to found the National

Committee. The philanthropist, Henry Phipps, gave indispensable financial assistance at the outset. The Committee was put on a permanent basis in 1909. Its program consisted of: (1) securing money to carry on effective work; (2) taking up "after care" of the insane to prevent relapses; (3) carrying on a program of education to acquaint the public with the salient facts concerning insanity, mental balance, mental hygiene, and healthy mental habits; and (4) attempting to revise the laws and procedure relating to insanity, so that they would be in accordance with scientific conceptions of mental instability.

At first it was difficult to make much headway, because financial aid was neither prompt nor adequate. But, by 1912, sufficient funds had been secured to enable the Committee to commence active work. Progress was still slow, however, because of the prejudice and misinformation concerning mental disorders. Although the treatment of physical illness had been revolutionized in the previous generation, even many educated people in the years immediately preceding the First World War regarded mental disease as beyond the reach of medical science.

Achievements of the National Committee. In 1912, a mental hygiene exhibit was prepared for the International Congress on Hygiene and Demography held in Washington, D. C. This exhibit graphically revealed the extent, cost, and social significance of mental disease and feeble-mindedness and the value of preventive work in the field. At this meeting a section on mental hygiene appeared on the program for the first time, mental hygiene thus receiving formal recognition as a vital element in the field of public health.

The National Committee for Mental Hygiene was especially fortunate in inducing the eminent psychiatrist, Thomas W. Salmon, to become its first medical director, in 1915. Under his guidance, the Committee extended its program beyond hospitals, seeking to prevent mental and nervous diseases. After 1916, new developments in mental hygiene came rapidly. In 1917, a splendid quarterly magazine, *Mental Hygiene,* was launched.

During the First World War, mental hygiene, under the leadership of eminent psychiatrists like Salmon and Pierce Bailey, proved its real worth, not only in the treatment of the mental and nervous disorders usually called "shell-shock" but in bolstering the spirits and morâle of the men in service. In the period following the war, mental hygiene leaders assisted discharged soldiers, sailors, and marines suffering from mental and nervous disorders. In the 1920's, special attention was given to child guidance clinics.

Prominent figures in mental hygiene like William Menninger were able to accomplish even more during the Second World War, for public and military authorities were more willing to listen to psychiatric experts by 1942 than they were in 1917. Research programs were set up to discover new ways of building morâle and controlling the emotionally insecure. Physicians in military service, chaplains, and key officers were given education in mental hygiene. New and more rapid methods were found for curing shell-shock, combat fatigue, and other wartime mental disturbances. Psychologists and social workers were brought in to aid psychiatrists.

The National Committee for Mental Hygiene worked vigorously to improve the lamentable condition of state hospitals for the insane during and after the Second World War and to secure the passage of the Mental Hygiene Act of 1946. It was aided by the Peoples' Committee for Mental Hygiene, founded in 1945, and the National Foundation for Mental Health, established in 1946. Since the Second World War, the National Committee has given much attention to the problem of rehabilitating psychotic patients, and has established a Division of Rehabilitation. In 1950 the National Committee for Mental Hygiene, the National Mental Health Foundation, and the Psychiatric Foundation were merged in a new organization known as the National Association for Mental Health. This is now the official national organization promoting mental hygiene.

Following the Second World War, special attention also has been given to educational work in mental hygiene. In this program the radio and films have helped considerably. Mental health radio programs have been prepared in profusion since 1946. In 1949, a dramatic sketch dealing with the mental problems of teen-age school children was distributed for exhibition in high schools. The Mental Hygiene Film Board was established in September, 1949, with a fund of $250,000 to be spent on films stressing mental health problems. In 1950, seven such films were made and distributed. In recent years, the mental hygiene movement has been aided by foundations, notably by the Commonwealth Fund.

The National Mental Hygiene Act of 1946. The greatest single victory in the history of the mental hygiene movement was the passage on June 3, 1946, of the National Mental Hygiene Act. This provided for the building and equipment of a great National Mental Health Institute at Bethesda, Maryland, in association with the vast Naval Hospital there. This institute is to be an impressive research center on all problems related to psychiatry and mental hygiene. The Act provides for grants to finance the operation of the mental health centers of the United States Public Health Service and for state and local research and therapeutic work. It also makes possible liberal grants to approved training centers for young psychiatrists. This will help to provide many more competent psychiatrists and thus partly to remedy the scandalous present situation where one doctor has to deal with as many as a thousand patients in the poorer state hospitals. But the states will have to increase their budgets for psychiatric staffs if they are to take advantage of the new opportunity to secure adequate medical assistance. The Mental Health Institute is integrated with the work of the United Public Health Service, and its administration is in the hands of the Surgeon General of the United States Public Health Service.

Some figures for 1949 will indicate that the Mental Hygiene Act is likely to work a salutary revolution in psychiatric research, training, and services. In that year, some $3,500,000 was given as grants-in-aid to states for community mental hygiene services. About $2,500,000 was given to promote psychiatric instruction in training centers. The sum of $400,000 was given to 42 medical schools for psychiatric instruction of undergraduate medical students. Grants amounting to about $900,000 were made to support psychiatric research projects. While these appropriations were far below the needs, they constituted a symptom and forecast of prospective substantial public support of psychiatry and mental hygiene.

What mental hygiene has accomplished. The mental hygiene movement has accomplished work of great significance in promoting better mental health. Forty years ago, there was a discouraging lack of public interest in nervous and mental diseases. Even students who graduated from good medical colleges knew little about psychiatry. The significant early manifestations of nervous diseases were all but ignored. In order to be admitted to a hospital for the insane, a person had to be regarded as dangerous and homicidal. The relationship between mental disease and dependency, delinquency, and general inefficiency was not understood even by social workers and other persons concerned with those problems.

Today the situation is different. "Asylums" have become hospitals, and people are beginning to understand that it is no disgrace to be sent to them for treatment. Several states have added mental hygiene divisions to their health departments. Changes in laws are being made, so that persons may be admitted to a hospital for the insane at their own request and receive temporary care. The care and treatment of patients in hospitals have improved, and the proportion of persons who recover is increasing, though the overcrowding of mental hospitals since 1940 has greatly handicapped the work of such institutions. Since good hospital service requires an adequate psychiatric staff, supporters of mental hygiene have labored to increase the amount of attention given to psychiatry in medical schools and to induce more medical students to specialize in psychiatry.

More attention is being paid to the early symptoms of mental disorders. Group therapy, in which a trained psychiatrist may work with 10 to 20 persons at a time, has been developed—especially since the Second World War. Trigant Burrow was the pioneer here. This technique is more economical and can handle more cases than individual practice. It has already proved very effective with children and it has great possibilities of future development in the treatment of adults.

Social workers have come to realize that family, poverty, and delinquency problems may often be approached most effectively through mental hygiene. Marriage clinics and family counselling have become popular. Psychiatric clinics have been established in both juvenile and adult courts, and in prisons and reformatories. Special institutions have been set up for the various types of feeble-minded. Universities and colleges now give courses in mental hygiene, and schools of education train prospective teachers to promote healthy mental attitudes in their pupils. Books, pamphlets, radio programs, and films on mental hygiene have been provided in large numbers, and statistics on mental disease have been systematically collected and distributed.

With the increasing recognition of the place of mental hygiene and psychiatry in general medical practice, a new field of medicine, known as *psychosomatic medicine,* has recently developed. Psychosomatic medicine stresses the interrelation between mental and bodily states, and emphasizes the importance of psychiatric techniques and attitudes in treating physical disorders. It has been estimated that from 40 to 60 per cent of all patients who consult physicians for ordinary diseases are suffering primarily from psychoneurotic difficulties.

The prevention of mental disease. Beers and his associates wanted to do more than cure those already afflicted with mental or nervous disorders. They envisioned a pattern of living that would keep people mentally fit and that would prevent or check mental disease. For this reason, they began with the problems of childhood. Problem children who are antisocial and who refuse to act like normal children furnish the recruits from whom adult neurotics and psychotics, as well as many delinquents, are drawn. By linking the mental hygiene clinic to the public school system, we may be able to discover and treat problem children before their warped personalities have caused them to establish dangerous and incurable habits of thought and conduct. These children can often be saved from mental disorders that might later take them to institutions for the insane or lead them to commit serious criminal acts.

Mental hygiene clinics are growing rapidly. By 1947, there were 485 mental hygiene clinics operating in 1,142 locations. Of the 1,142 service locations, 221 were full-time clinics; 182 were stationary part-time clinics; and the remaining 739 clinics were served by 82 traveling clinic staffs. More than 300 of these clinics were designed to serve children.

Mental hygiene as a new technique of social work. The mental hygiene movement recognizes the importance of mental and nervous factors in every phase of life, and it has extended its work to crime, industry, sex, the family, and education. Scientific criminology is virtually a department of mental hygiene. The use of mental hygiene in industry has been of importance in aiding the worker to adjust himself to new, complex patterns of working and living. Family life may be given a sounder foundation as a result of mental hygiene's effort to create better family understanding and adjustment. In short, all up-to-date social work reckons with psychiatry and mental hygiene, and psychiatric procedure is basic in contemporary social case-work. Even ministers are now given some training in mental hygiene. It is estimated that about 2,500 clergymen now in ministerial service have received mental hygiene instruction and orientation. Elmer E. Southard and Lawson G. Lowrey have been pioneers and leaders in providing a psychiatric basis for social work perspectives and techniques.

Mental hygiene education and publicity. We have mentioned above in passing certain educational activities in behalf of a better understanding of psychiatric and mental hygiene principles and techniques, such as the distribution of books, pamphlets, and films. More systematic efforts have developed recently. One of the most important is the establishment of mental hygiene institutes which are held in various states to instruct physicians, nurses, social workers, teachers, and clergymen. Mildred Scoville has been a leader in this movement, and the Commonwealth Fund has aided states and communities in this work. One of the first institutes was held in Berkeley, California, in 1948. In 1949, some 94 institutes were held in 25 states and the movement is growing rapidly. Mental hygiene instruction is now being introduced in the schools, including even pupil participation in the discussion of important emotional problems. Materials for such school instruction are being prepared and distributed.

Mental hygiene as the basis of a sound code of social ethics. More important, however, than any type of specialized endeavor in mental hygiene is its contribution to the synthesis of biology, medicine, sociology, and psychology, in the effort to create a new body of sound social ethics.

From the outset, Beers and his associates understood that the treatment of the afflicted is not the root of the problem. They saw that in psychiatry, as in other phases of medicine, prevention is the real goal. Hence, they began their nation-wide educational campaign to inculcate healthful and scientific principles of living, which would restrict the ever greater number of mental breakdowns. Consequently, it was inevitable that mental hygiene would slowly become nothing less than a new body of humane and secularized morality. It gives promise of evolving into that dependable guide to life which man has been seeking in vain since the days of the Hellenic secularists of ancient Athens who repudiated the supernaturalism of their age. It represents the only organized program able to give us the new scientific and esthetic morality that is so persistently demanded to guide our lives competently amid the confusion and complexity of modern existence.

Not a few scientists and educators have already proclaimed that mental hygiene will supplant theology. Religious liberals have approved and adopted it, not only as a cornerstone of the new ethics but as a technique for better understanding religion itself. Applied to education, it is revolutionizing our attitude toward the learning processes of children. Precisely to the degree that supernaturalism yields before the onslaughts of mental hygiene will man become capable of meeting the increased strains and stresses which modern life has imposed upon him. Mental hygiene is not only the single body of knowledge scientifically equipped to handle contemporary issues of right living; it is also the only technique likely to appeal to the skeptical younger generation which has lost its faith in the custodians of the supernatural.

At the present time, the problems presented by our social institutions are unusually difficult and baffling because of the rapid changes in many aspects of our life since the scientific and industrial revolutions began in the eighteenth century. Particularly notable are such things as the swiftly altering nature of our technology, the disintegration of primary groups and personal societies, the broad and diversified scope of our contemporary social relations, the extensive and varied stimulation of our present urban life, and the standardization and monotony of conduct in the mechanical age. Along with these new problems presented by the novel socio-economic conditions of the contemporary period, we have the complex issues presented by modern sex life. This we are only just beginning to investigate and control in the light of scientific knowledge, rather than through the dictates of the Pauline, Augustinian, and Kantian theologies. The perspective supplied by the work of Alfred C. Kinsey and his associates is beginning to supplant that of Anthony Comstock.

Essentials of a mental hygiene program. Among the principles of mental hygiene which might be fruitfully applied in the effort to provide a sound code of social ethics and a better basis for the mental health of the individual in mid-twentieth century civilization are the following:

1. Everything possible should be done to promote and increase healthy individual organisms. If mental health means the adjustment of a healthy organism to a compatible social order, we must begin by doing all we can to secure at the start a healthy human organism.

2. We must thoroughly understand child psychology and do everything we can to promote its application, not merely in the school but also in the home. Childhood is veritably the "golden age" for mental hygiene. But it is hard to make headway with such methods in demoralized or broken homes. Hence, family life must be strengthened by better sex and marriage education, psychiatric and sociological counselling, and economic self-sufficiency.

3. Our schools should be made much more attractive and interesting, and we must repudiate entirely the old punitive and penitential conception of pedagogy. Dynamic interest rather than repressive discipline must be the keynote of the new pedagogy. Mental pain and boredom must be abolished. This would virtually eliminate the problem of truancy—the vestibule of much juvenile delinquency.

4. Provision must be made for a highly diversified system of instruction and promotion in the school system, in order to care for the wide variation in human abilities and capacities. Mental hygiene clinics and juvenile courts should be linked with the public school system to detect and treat all problem children as early as possible in their warped lives.

5. We must do everything possible to eliminate the influence of fear on children, which so often results in paralyzing inhibitions and retarded intellectual and emotional development.

6. Much better provision must be made for organized play and recreation, in order to aid the processes of sublimation and facilitate the socialization of the individual.

7. We must provide for a thoroughly scientific body of sex instruction, based fearlessly on the facts of biology, physiology, psychology, psychiatry, and esthetics.

8. Much more should be done to promote the vitality and cohesion of social groups, in order that the individual may participate in many intimate forms of group life. There is no doubt of the truth of Durkheim's contention that mental health cannot be maintained by isolated and detached individuals. This means that community planning must be developed comprehensively and speedily to provide substitutes for the older primary groups that have been shattered by urban life and mechanization.

9. In economic life it is essential to see that every honest and ambitious person has an opportunity for interesting and remunerative employment.

There is nothing which promotes mental ill-health on the part of the working classes more surely and generally than the worries incident to unemployment or the fear thereof.

10. Similarly, we should make much heavier drafts upon industrial medicine and psychology, in order to reduce as far as possible the fatigue and boredom incident to modern mechanical processes and office life. The industrial system should be subordinated to the production of a happier and more prosperous society, instead of exaggerating the profit motive as the core of all economic effort.

11. In our general personal attitudes and social relations we should recognize that it is necessary to depart from the inferiority-complex and psychic apprehensiveness inherent in conventional Christianity and to seek that intellectual serenity and that feeling of personal adequacy which characterized the best Greek philosophy. We must provide means for extroverting our personalities and throwing ourselves more readily into the general stream of social contacts.

Growth of empirical optimism in psychiatry and mental hygiene. As the result of the remarkable advances in psychotherapy and mental hygiene, psychiatrists are recovering some of the optimism which prematurely characterized their work a century ago. But this time the optimism is more discriminating and better founded upon scientific realities. The new and hopeful note in psychiatry, even before the Second World War, was very well expressed by C. Charles Burlingame in the following paragraph:

The dreaded paresis has been partially conquered by von Jauregg's malarial treatment and by pyretotherapy (artificially inducing fever); new educational methods in the modern hospital have supplanted the archaic occupational therapy of basketmaking and rug weaving; the resources of the psychiatrist have been augmented by glandular products and other chemical aids; and, in short, we have left behind the era of "do-nothingism," just as we are leaving behind the metaphysical phases of psychiatry. In this new period the practice of psychiatry will be based on sound medicine, and the psychiatrist will have not one but many arrows in his quiver.[7]

Optimistic as Burlingame may have been in 1938, with some justice, the progress in neurology and psychiatry since that time has been veritably revolutionary. This will be apparent from the merest catalogue of advances in the field since 1938: (1) the successful use of penicillin in treating syphilis, paresis and locomotor-ataxia; (2) the striking development and results of psychosurgery; (3) the introduction of electroencephalography and the Rorschach personality test in helping to diagnose mental diseases more rapidly and accurately; (4) the improvements in shock treatment, especially the introduction of electric shock and ether shock; (5) more extensive and successful use of sedative drugs like pentothal in treatment—the so-called narcosynthesis; (6) the acceleration of psychoanalytic treatment; (7) the development of group therapy; and (8) the remarkable and diversified advances in the last five years in curing or

---

[7] *The Forum,* February, 1938, p. 102.

helping an ever larger percentage of patients suffering from schizophrenia, manic-depressive psychoses, and other functional psychoses.

The chief problem which confronts us in mental hygiene at the mid-century mark, aside from providing adequate psychiatric personnel and hospital facilities, is the question of whether the advances in psychiatry and the increasing facilities of mental hygiene can keep pace with the development of those factors making for the growth of mental and nervous disorders. This is an age of social and cultural disintegration and readjustment. Accordingly, it is an era of unusual strains and stresses. These directly affect our mental life and make for instability and disease. If we successfully make the transition to an era of sexual emancipation, production for use, and world peace relatively rapidly, thus insuring tolerance, enlightenment, prosperity, and security, we may look forward to a steady decrease in mental and nervous disorders. If, however, we proceed toward regimentation, religious and sexual obscurantism, economic collapse, poverty and misery, and more world wars, the ravages of mental and nervous diseases are likely to become ever more extensive and devastating.

SUMMARY

Mental disease is not ordinarily included as part of the health and disease picture of the United States. Nevertheless, along with heart and circulatory disorders, mental disease constitutes the most serious affliction which affects the American population. About one out of every 20 persons now at the age of 15 will require hospital treatment for some form of mental disorder. More than half of the beds in all public hospitals in the country are filled with mental patients, and not more than half of those who need hospital treatment for mental disease can now be admitted to these hospitals.

There has been an alarming increase in mental disease during the first half of the twentieth century, though part of the vast increase in the number of hospital cases of this type can be assigned to our recent progress in detecting and hospitalizing mental cases. This increase in mental disorders can be attributed mainly to the greater complexity, problems, and tensions of modern living. Social disorganization, brought about by institutional disintegration, plays a large rôle. Economic worries have been increased by depressions, inflation, unemployment, and war. Housing and other domestic problems increase family worries.

There is nothing mysterious about what is commonly called *insanity* or serious mental disease, however mysterious some of the causes. There is only a hazy border line between normal and abnormal mental reactions. The latter represent only the intensification and erratic dominion of mental traits present in all individuals. Most grave mental disorders first pass through less serious stages. Hence, if we can detect early symptoms of mental abnormality we can usually check more serious developments and bring about speedier and easier cures.

Mental diseases fall into two major groups—neuroses and psychoses. Neuroses are mild forms of mental disorder which handicap an individual but which usually do not lead him to lose self-control. Psychoses are serious mental maladies which render a person irresponsible and require special medical treatment and at least temporary segregation.

Both neuroses and psychoses are of two types—organic and functional. Organic neuroses and psychoses are caused by physical conditions. Functional neuroses and psychoses are emotional disorders, due chiefly to mental conflicts.

Although institutional treatment of the mentally diseased has undergone vast improvement in the last 150 years, and although the mentally diseased are no longer treated like wild animals and chained down in prisons, jails, and almshouses, conditions remain highly unsatisfactory. Hospital facilities are not sufficient to permit the treatment of more than half of those who need such care. Few hospitals have an adequate medical staff, and most of them are poorly administered. Both of these defects are usually due to inadequate public appropriations.

Similarly, although there have been great advances in psychotherapy in the last 100 years, professional and financial obstacles prevent anything like complete utilization of present-day psychotherapy in treating the majority of those who need this type of care. Psychiatry has been so neglected in medical training that there are only about 4,500 medically trained psychiatrists in the country, whereas at least 15,000 to 20,000 would be the minimum required to handle the mental disease burden.

Private psychiatric care is so costly as to be virtually prohibitive for all except the rich. Few public institutions have an adequate psychiatric staff. Not infrequently, state hospitals have only one psychiatrist to a thousand patients. The medical monopoly of reputable psychotherapy has discouraged the training and use of clinical psychologists, who are often better prepared to understand and treat mental disorders than are many psychiatrists. The National Mental Hygiene Act of 1946 is only a belated and insufficient step in the direction of providing more psychiatrists to cope with the challenge of mental disease.

Mental defect, or feeble-mindedness, implies defective intelligence rather than the diseased mentality of the insane. There are at least two million feeble-minded in the country who have such a low grade of intelligence that they need institutional segregation and care. But less than 10 per cent of these are now so segregated and cared for. There are at least three million serious borderline cases of mental defect that receive virtually no care.

Institutions for the segregation and treatment of the mentally deficient have increased in number and efficiency in the last half century, but they are lamentably inadequate in number and capacity. In the better institutions, the low-grade feeble-minded can be segregated and the more hopeful types trained to be self-supporting. But prevention of mental defect must be the chief goal. Sterilization could accomplish much in this regard, though little is being done here at present. But sterilization is no complete panacea, for at least one-half of all mental defect is not caused by hereditary factors. Better medical care would reduce the causes of post-natal mental defect.

The prevention and treatment of mental disease and mental defect have been undertaken by a comprehensive medical and social program known as *mental hygiene*. This movement seeks to improve and extend psychiatric training; to prevent mental disease and defect—especially by more healthful modes of mental life; and to improve the institutions for the mentally diseased and the mentally defective. It has also promoted psychiatric education. One of the main achievements has been the provision of many psychiatric clinics to aid problem children and to prevent them from becoming serious mental cases or hardened criminals. Many believe that mental hygiene can supply the new body of social ethics—the new moral code—that we require to guide us in an industrial, urban, and secular age.

SELECTED REFERENCES

Barker, Elsa, *Fielding Sargent*. New York: Dutton, 1922. An excellent introduction to the methods of psychoanalysis presented in the form of a novel.

*Beers, C. W., *A Mind That Found Itself*. New York: Doubleday, Doran, 1923. The absorbing autobiography of the founder of the mental hygiene movement. Gives much insight into methods of dealing with the insane early in the present century.

Benedek, Therese, *Insight and Personality Adjustment*. New York: Ronald Press, 1945. Valuable for its concentration on problems of mental health in the period of postwar readjustment, international tension, and social upheaval.

Bisch, L. E., *Be Glad You're Neurotic*. New York: McGraw-Hill, 1936. A popular medical presentation of the frequency of neurotic traits in normal persons and of the constructive functions of mild neuroses. A somewhat reassuring book.

*Bond, E. D., *Thomas W. Salmon, Psychiatrist*. New York: Norton, 1950. A biography of one of the world's greatest practical psychiatrists and one most active in the mental hygiene movement in the United States. An invaluable source of information on the growth of a more scientific and humane treatment of mental disorders in this country.

*Bromberg, Walter, *The Mind of Man*. New York: Harper, 1937. Readable and authoritative history of psychiatry and mental hygiene. Contains a very helpful bibliography.

———, *Mind Explorers*. New York: Reynal and Hitchcock, 1939. Interesting historical survey of the development of psychotherapy and its leaders.

Brown, H. C., *A Mind Mislaid*. New York: Dutton, 1937. Another autobiography revealing the symptoms and experiences of mental disease.

*Burnham, W. H., *The Normal Mind*. New York: Appleton-Century, 1924. A mature discussion of mental hygiene, containing an indispensable chapter on pseudo-feeblemindedness.

Clark, L. P., *The Nature and Treatment of Amentia*. London: Bailliere, Tindall and Cox, 1933. The only comprehensive application of Freudian psychology to the study of feeble-mindedness and its treatment.

*Davies, S. P., *The Social Control of the Mentally Deficient*. New York: Crowell, 1930. The standard work on the feeble-minded in the United States and the methods of dealing with them.

*Deutsch, Albert, *The Mentally Ill in America*. New York: Columbia University Press, 1949. New edition of an admirable book dealing with the treatment of those afflicted with mental and nervous disease. It gives a good history of the stages in the evolution of concepts of mental disease, the improvements in medical treatment, and the evolution of institutions for treating the mentally ill.

*Deutsch, Albert, *The Shame of the States*. New York: Harcourt, Brace, 1948. Shocking but authoritative revelation of conditions in state hospitals for the mentally diseased during and after the Second World War.

Dollard, John, and Miller, N. E., *Personality and Psychotherapy*. New York: McGraw-Hill, 1950. Valuable synthesis of psychiatry, dynamic psychology, anthropology, and sociology in relation to the understanding and treatment of mental disorders.

Faris, R. E. L., and Dunham, H. W., *Mental Disorders in Urban Areas*. Chicago: University of Chicago Press, 1939. Detailed study of mental disease in the city of Chicago, showing variation of disease rates in different residential areas. A pioneer book in indicating the relation between social disorganization and the incidence of mental disease.

French, L. M., *Psychiatric Social Work*. New York: Commonwealth Fund, 1940. Important work on the entry of mental hygiene concepts and practices into social work.

Freud, Sigmund, *A New Series of Introductory Lectures on Psychoanalysis*. New York: Norton, 1933. Probably the best authoritative statement on Freudian philosophy and psychiatry for the general reader.

————, *The Question of Lay Analysis*. New York: Norton, 1950. Authoritative criticism of the monopolistic pretensions of the medical profession in the psychoanalytical field. Calls for broad and well-rounded training, in which routine medical education plays a very small rôle.

Hall, J. K. (Ed.), *One Hundred Years of American Psychiatry*. New York: Columbia University Press, 1945. Symposium by experts on history of American psychiatric concepts and practice.

*Hart, Bernard, *The Psychology of Insanity*. New York: Cambridge University Press, 1922. A leading psychiatrist presents a clear primer of the mental traits which characterize those suffering from mental disorders.

Hoskins, R. G., *Endocrinology: The Glands and Their Functions*. New York: Norton, 1941. Authoritative work on the psychiatric significance of the glands of internal secretion.

Kanner, Leo, *Child Psychology*. Springfield, Illinois: Thomas, 1948. The most extensive application of psychiatry to the mental problems of childhood.

Kempf, E. J., *Psychopathology*. Philadelphia: Saunders, 1922. A landmark in the effort to arrive at a synthesis of psychiatric attitudes and techniques. Needs to be supplemented by Masserman's more recent volume.

*Knight, John, *The Story of My Psychoanalysis*. New York: McGraw-Hill, 1950. Probably the most authentic account of an actual case of psychoanalysis by a well-known scientist who writes under a pseudonym.

Lemkau, P. V., *Mental Hygiene in Public Health*. New York: McGraw-Hill, 1949. Valuable and thoughtful book, stressing the preventive function and responsibilities of psychiatry and indicating the important role that mental hygiene should play in public health.

Lewis, N. D. C., *A Short History of Psychiatric Achievement*. New York: Norton, 1941. A clear and untechnical review of the history of psychotherapy.

Lichtenstein, P. M., and Small, S. M., *A Handbook of Psychiatry*. New York: Norton, 1943. A professional but non-technical description of the main mental disorders.

*Lowrey, L. G., *Psychiatry for Social Workers*. New York: Columbia University Press, 1947. Valuable treatment of psychiatric attitudes and methods for the use of social workers, by an eminent psychiatrist.

Marshall, H. E., *Dorothea Dix*. Chapel Hill: University of North Carolina Press,

1937. A good biography of the first great crusader for the humane treatment of the insane in the United States.

*Masserman, J. H., *Principles of Dynamic Psychiatry*. Philadelphia: Saunders, 1946. Best recent summary and synthesis of psychiatric knowledge. Written from a broad and well-balanced point of view.

*Menninger, Karl, *The Human Mind*. New York: Knopf, 1930. Perhaps the best single book to serve as an introduction to mental disease and mental hygiene. Sound and interesting.

Menninger, W. C., *You and Psychiatry*. New York: Scribner's, 1948. A good introduction to psychiatry for the layman.

Nicole, J. E., *Normal and Abnormal Psychology*. New York: Macmillan, 1948. Excellent introduction to clinical psychology and psychiatry for nurses and social workers.

Noyes, A. P., *Modern Clinical Psychiatry*. Philadelphia: Saunders, 1948. An up-to-date manual covering the field of mental and nervous diseases.

*Rennie, T. A. C., and Woodward, L. E., *Mental Health in Modern Society*. New York: Commonwealth Fund, 1948. The best up-to-date survey of the field of mental hygiene.

*Roberts, Harry, *The Troubled Mind*. New York: Dutton, 1939. An admirable elementary introduction to the nature, symptoms, and treatment of mental disorders.

Spiegel, E. A. (Ed.), *Progress in Neurology and Psychiatry*. New York: Grune and Stratton, 1949. Survey of recent developments, including the best review of the development of group therapy.

*Terhune, W. B. (Ed.), *Living Wisely and Well*. New York: Dutton, 1949. Excellent, popular symposium on mental hygiene by leading American psychiatrists.

*Thompson, Clara, *Psychoanalysis: Its Evolution and Development*. New York: Hermitage House, 1950. A clear and up-to-date account of the development of psychoanalytical concepts and techniques from Freud to the present time.

White, W. A., *Outlines of Psychiatry*. Washington: Nervous and Mental Disease Publishing Company, 1935. A classic synthesis of psychiatric knowledge by an eminent American psychiatrist.

CHAPTER 15

Crime in Mid-century Perspective

THE NATURE OF CRIME

Criminology and penology defined. Since we shall be dealing with criminology and penology in this and the following chapter, it will be well to define them. *Criminology* is the science of crime, including criminal codes, the factors favorable to criminality, the nature and types of criminals, the varieties of crime, the apprehension, conviction and sentencing of convicted criminals, and programs of crime prevention. *Penology* is the science that deals with the treatment of convicted criminals. The term was invented by Francis Lieber a century ago, and he defined it as the science of punishing convicts. Today, most enlightened students of the subject would define it as the science of so treating criminals as to segregate permanently the nonreformable types and to rehabilitate the reformable group.

Crime as illegal antisocial behavior. We may at the outset present a few elementary definitions for the purpose of clarifying our later discussion. The term *crime* technically means any form of antisocial behavior which at present, or at some time in the past, has so far violated public sentiment as to be forbidden by existing law. Crime, then, represents only a rather specialized portion of the totality of antisocial behavior—that which is outlawed. There is a large field of behavior known as immorality which is conventionally regarded as antisocial but which is not punishable by law. It is left to the control of public opinion. The arbitrary border line between crime and immorality is to be seen from the fact that acts which in some countries are regarded as serious crimes are often not even viewed as immoral in other areas. Such are brutalities and intolerance in the family circle, family neglect, economic exploitation, and warfare. Moreover, we have a broad class of cases which are technically known as *torts*. We can go to law about them and recover civil damages, but guilt in this field is not subject to the penalties ordinarily meted out for crime.

Irrational character of criminal codes. It is usually believed that the seriousness of a crime, judged on the basis of its damage to society, is the test that distinguishes criminality from other forms of antisocial conduct. This should be the case, but, to the extent that we allow the criminal code to determine what we regard as crimes, it is not. Many crimes listed in the criminal code are on the statute books solely because they were acts socially disapproved of a century or more ago. Today they may no longer be serious offenses against the well-being of society. Other acts are made crimes by statute because of the distorted fanaticism of ignorant or biased groups. On the other hand, many of the more disastrous recent forms of antisocial behavior are not even regarded as immoral, to say nothing of being branded as criminal. This is so because the dominant groups in society still approve such behavior. This fact is reflected in Bernard Shaw's cynical but all too true quip that if a man steals a loaf of bread he goes to prison, whereas if he steals a railroad he is likely to go to parliament.

The statute books are cluttered up with a vast number of outgrown or useless laws. Writing in *Harper's Magazine,* L. M. Hussey estimated that the average law-abiding citizen of a large modern city unwittingly commits enough crimes in a single day to warrant a sentence of about five years in prison and fines of about $3,000. The citizen's quite unintentional and unconscious criminal acts in a single year would thus call for 1,825 years in prison and over a million dollars in fines. Many criminals are made when poor unfortunate persons are detected in such unintentional crimes, arrested, and convicted because of lack of influence and legal aid. Many laws still on the books reflect ideas and conditions of long ago. In one southern state a third successive failure to attend church on Sunday is still a capital crime. Laws against blasphemy and witchcraft still survive.

In addition to the mass of obsolete laws, more than a quarter of a million new laws have been passed by our states since 1900. To these may be added the many Federal laws and municipal ordinances. We are unduly hasty today in creating new crimes by statute. In 1931, no less than 75 per cent of all the inmates of Federal prisons and correctional institutions had been incarcerated for committing acts that were not crimes 15 years earlier. Such conditions are demoralizing to our legal system and court procedure.

With so many laws on the statute books, we recognize that, in differing degrees, we are all law-breakers. A large number of laws have no direct support in public sentiment and hence cannot be enforced. Unenforced laws are a nuisance. As Dean Young B. Smith, of the Columbia Law School, observed: "A law incapable of reasonable enforcement because of social conditions is absurd. The attempt to control by law conduct which may be more effectively controlled in other ways is a misuse of law and a social waste." Very much to the point is the following comment by an eminent New York publicist, as quoted in *The New York Times:*

Unless both the unenforceable and the obsolete laws are stricken from the federal, state and municipal statute books, the very fundamentals of law enforcement are threatened. If respect for the law is to be tempered by ridicule and limited by personal application, the laws that are essential to the integrity and welfare of the community must suffer proportionately with the laws that are unenforceable or obsolete.

Economic basis of most crime today. Realistic students of crime today lay little stress upon the older and elaborate attempts to classify crimes (as for example, crimes against property, crimes against persons, crimes of passion, and accidental crimes). The majority of serious crimes other than sex crimes are, in original intent at least, crimes against property. The personal physical violence that results is usually incidental and unwished for by the criminal and the victim alike. No criminal, unless he be insane or feeble-minded, wishes to add liability for murder to the penalty for theft or burglary. Aside from gang killings and the murder and other physical violence incidental to burglary and robbery (usually due to the haste, fear, or excitement of the criminal), most criminal violence is a result of temporary anger or of the morbid compulsions growing out of a psychopathic personality.

The actual number of deaths produced by crime, although deplorably and scandalously high in the United States, is exaggerated in the public mind. This condition results from the fact that murders are sensational events played up in the newspapers to gain circulation. The annual homicide figure in the United States—less than 9,000 at the present time— is far higher per capita than in any other civilized country and steps should be taken to reduce it. But we rarely consider suicide an important social problem, though there were about 16,354 known suicides in 1948. Homicides pale into insignificance compared to accidental deaths, which now average 100,000 annually in this country. Approximately 4 persons are killed every year in automobile accidents for every one who meets death as a result of homicide. Similarly, homicides are numerically unimpressive when compared with more than 325,000 deaths annually from preventable diseases and from inadequate medical care. Further, most victims of homicide are fortunate, indeed, when compared to the millions who live for many years under conditions that are worse than death as a result of chronic diseases, economic exploitation, impoverishment, and insecurity.

If we supplant sentimentalism by realism, we are compelled to recognize the direct or indirect economic basis of the great majority of crimes— at least of those crimes which are not an outgrowth of literal, if not legal, insanity, emotional disturbances, and mental defects. Need and greed lie at the foundation of the greater portion of contemporary crime. And greed is responsible for the vast majority of the more costly crimes in our day. The latter represent the socially unapproved methods of obtaining something for nothing on a large scale. Most petty crimes may be the result of the necessity for stealing food or clothing or small sums of money to provide these, but the crimes that bring the largest financial losses today are those motivated by greed and a desire to realize the sense of power which wealth provides. We shall have more to say about this later.

Many of the critics of a primarily economic interpretation of crime have based their attitude on a narrow conception of this approach to criminal causation. It is not contended that virtually all criminals commit their delinquent acts to secure sheer necessities of existence or for honorific display and prestige. Economic forces go much further than this. The chief criticism of the economic interpretation of crime has come from those students of the problem who attribute crime to what they call "deviant" or "differential" association, namely, living and associating with persons and groups who are prone to anti-social behavior, especially as promoted by life in slums and delinquency areas. But these very slums and delinquency areas exist primarily because of economic inability to live in better districts. Sub-standard existence is a potent factor in producing those anti-social norms in life patterns that create "deviant" association. We have also frequently pointed out in this book that social and personal disorganization have grown mainly out of the maladjustments due to the impact of modern technology and industrial life upon the social patterns of an agrarian age.

There has, however, recently been an alarming growth of a type of crime that has little or no economic motivation. This has taken the form of various crimes of personal violence: "mugging," physical assaults, knifings, varied types of sex crimes, and the like. These crimes have created a reign of terror in many large cities. Their character and increase have recently been described by Howard Whitman in his startling book, *Terror in the Streets.*[1] There is also some evidence that this type of crime is on the gain in rural areas since the Second World War. Many of these crimes may be attributed to mental instability, but a larger number seem to be motivated by sheer moral irresponsibility and zest for morbid excitement.

THE REVOLUTION IN THE NATURE OF CRIME SINCE THE FIRST WORLD WAR

Popular conception of crime menace. The Federal Bureau of Investigation and the newspapers give us much information regarding the growing menace of crime. In 1949, the FBI stated that 1,686,670 serious crimes were committed in this country, one every 18.7 seconds. A larceny was committed every 30 seconds. Three persons were slain in each 2-hour period. Every day 150 robberies were committed and 255 cases of aggravated assault and rape. In each 24 hours 1,032 places were burglarized, 2,672 larcenies were committed, and 463 automobiles were stolen.

Admittedly this is a serious and alarming record, but it tells us little about the more serious crimes situation in this country today. The total financial cost of the above crimes was under a half-billion dollars, while J. Edgar Hoover estimates the total annual cost of crime to be about 15 billion dollars.

Necessity of readjusting our present perspective on crime. There has been as great a revolution in the nature of the more menacing and dangerous crimes since the First World War as there has been in the character, let us say, of rural life, or transportation. To go on discussing crime as we have dealt with it in the past would be very much like describing farm life without the telephone, automobile, radio, daily newspaper, and gasoline tractor.

---

[1] New York: Dial Press, 1951.

This fact has been evident to the more realistic writers on crime—especially those who have approached it from the angle of journalism—for at least two decades. The more traditional writers on the subject have been slow to adjust themselves to changing realities. But it is high time that all of us who are concerned with the crime question should become thoroughly aware of these changes and should adapt our thinking to current realities.

The traditional discussions of the crime problem were fairly well adapted to conditions as they existed at the close of the First World War. It was natural that these older stereotypes should carry over for a number of years, even though the actual conditions with respect to crime had changed markedly. But there is no longer any excuse for such out-of-date attitudes. To perpetuate such attitudes now is as unfortunate as it would be if authorities on public health were to devote all of their attention and energy to chickenpox and measles, ignoring heart disease, cancer, and mental disorders.

Nature of the crime revolution. The main phases of this striking revolution in crime, which has been implied in the preceding paragraphs, have been the increasing scope and cost of what we call white-collar crime, the development of organized crime and racketeering, and the marked tendency since about 1940 for the overlords of the underworld and organized crime to transfer their activities to an ever increasing extent into "fixed" gambling enterprises conducted by large syndicates. We shall describe all of these recently developed forms of big crime later.

The nature and significance of this revolution in crime may be illustrated by the estimated cost to the public of traditional crimes, organized crime and racketeering, and syndicated gambling. It has been estimated that the total annual cost of crime in the United States today, including the damage done by criminals, and the expense of apprehending, convicting, and confining them, is at least 15 billion dollars. Of this, the cost of organized crime, racketeering, and white-collar crime is at least 6 billion; the cost of traditional crimes—robbery, burglary, larceny, forgery, and theft—does not exceed 500 million dollars. The estimated annual bill for gambling, mainly conducted by organized syndicates, is between 15 and 21 billion dollars. This, of course, dwarfs even the economic cost of organized crime and racketeering.

Main patterns and trends in twentieth-century crime. In the evolution of the crime picture in the United States in the twentieth century, there have been three main stages or patterns: (1) the period before the First World War, when the crime scene was dominated by traditional crimes like robbery, burglary, larceny, forgery and assault; (2) the spectacular rise of "big crime"—organized crime and racketeering—between the First World War and the end of Prohibition; and (3) the remarkable growth of organized and "fixed" gambling since about 1940, and the shifting of more and more of the big criminal and underworld operators into the gambling field to obtain the advantages of its greater gains and reduced risks.

There are lesser but important trends in crime which have developed chiefly since the Second World War. One is the marked increase in rural crime. The trend in rural criminality is away from crimes against persons to crimes against property. Another new development, at least in frequency, is the above-mentioned growth of physical violence and terrorism in cities, taking the form of varied sex crimes and morbid pathological acts of violence.

THE SOCIAL ECOLOGY OF DELINQUENCY AND DELINQUENT TYPES

Ecological distribution of crime. Before taking up in detail the more characteristic types of crimes and criminals in our day, we may well devote some attention to the social, cultural, and historical elements which contribute to criminality and explain the spatial distribution and prevalence of certain typical crimes in given areas of the country. It is, of course, taken for granted that there are more crimes in cities than in the country, but it is usually assumed that there are about as many crimes of all types in one big city as in another.

Urban basis of organized crime. Students of crime have demonstrated, however, that crime and criminals are not distributed in helter-skelter fashion over the country, being about the same in number and character everywhere. Rather, the major crimes are relatively prevalent in particular regions, according to the nature of the social background and the culture of the area. There are preponderant patterns of crime in each main section of the country. This important fact has been presented in an illuminating fashion by Stuart Lottier.[2]

It is obvious that organized crime on a large scale, racketeering and syndicated gambling, which are the more important crimes of our day, are concentrated mainly in the great cities of the urban North. They have also spread to such midwestern metropolitan areas as Chicago and St. Louis, a few metropolitan centers of the Pacific Coast, and New Orleans. This fact results not only from the obviously greater opportunities for loot in these urban centers but also from the more direct contact with the something-for-nothing psychology of the leisure class, big business, speculative finance, and the like. Lottier puts it: "In no small measure is organized crime in the north related to emulation of the men and methods of large-scale business and to the readily available and approved rationalization of the same dominant class."

Crimes of physical violence most numerous in South. Far and away the greatest prevalence of murder and assault—crimes of violence—is to be found in the southern states, especially those of the southeast and the Gulf area. This is the natural outgrowth of Negro trends in crime, of a caste society given to lynching to preserve social discipline, and of the feudist tradition among families in the mountainous areas:

From the plantation economy of the south sprang a tradition of sharp caste discrimination between landed gentry and the Negroes or poor whites whom they exploited. Castes engendered characteristic criminal offenses. One expression of the maintenance of rigid social stratification is lynching which has been confined to the southern and southwestern states. Also, family feuds developed in the isolated and thinly settled areas of the southern mountains "where self-help was once the dominating necessity and where decentralized judicial administration has enfeebled the enforcement of the law." It is true that lynching and feuds are hardly significant numerically but they symbolize extremes of conditions which are territorially circumscribed.[3]

The above generalization might now have to be modified because of the recent growth of crimes of violence and physical terrorism in American cities generally, in northern areas as well as in the south.

Robbery and banditry in the West. When we come to robbery and banditry—crimes against property—we find that these are by far most common in the western part of the United States. In 1931 over half of all the bank robberies in the country were committed in California, Missouri, Illinois, Kansas, Texas, and Oklahoma. Each of these states had more bank robberies than had Connecticut, Maine, Massachusetts, Rhode Island, New York, New Jersey, Pennsylvania, Maryland, and Virginia combined. This seems to be due to the frontier lawlessness, vigilantism,

---

2 "Distribution of Criminal Offenses in Sectional Regions," *Journal of Criminal Law and Criminology,* September-October, 1938.

3 *Ibid.,* p. 332.

and excessive individualism which characterized this part of the country until very recent times:

> In the west, as a counterpart of immature settlement, flourished the frontier tradition of intense individualism and the readiness of the westerner to take the matter of control into his own hands. The west was free, its land and its people, and it was unsettled culturally as well as it was unsettled territorially. Laws were few, and the vigilantes utilized the same violence in enforcing them as the outlaw desperados who broke them.[4]

Practical significance of crime ecology. These facts are of more than academic interest. They represent the indispensable foundation of any really scientific program of crime control and prevention:

> It is submitted that one of the first steps in a program for the prevention of crime and the apprehension of criminals in the United States is the elementary procedure of dividing the country into natural regions of crime. The larger units would take into account sectional differences in culture, for areas of homogeneous culture would have common problems of crime control.[5]

Although this regional ecology of criminality, as described by Lottier, is still generally correct, there is little doubt that some modifications have been effected by the extensive migrations of Americans as a result of the dust bowl and other calamities of the 1930's, and of the industrial demands of the Second World War. The effects of the war on personal habits, changes in the character of crime in the last 15 years, and the activities of the Federal Bureau of Investigation and other law enforcement agencies have also probably produced other minor modifications.

Delinquency areas. In addition to this consideration of the proclivity of certain regions of our country to typical forms of criminality, we need to examine the social background of criminality in urban centers. Here we find a definite social basis for the prevalence and concentration of criminality. The most important contribution to our understanding of this problem has been made by Clifford R. Shaw and his associates in studies made of delinquency in Chicago and other areas. Shaw believes that he has demonstrated the existence of true "delinquency areas"— certain districts of the city where criminality is largely concentrated. These delinquency areas are urban slum districts bordering on the business and industrial centers which are undergoing a transition from residential uses to business and industry. They are, therefore, in a state of disintegration which carries with it a lack of adequate social control. Foreign elements settle in these areas and further complicate the social complexities of the situation. In short, these delinquency areas are districts in which we find the maximum of the social disorganization that promotes the personal disorganization of which delinquency is one manifestation. Criminologists have related the delinquency area facts to a general theory of criminal conduct. The social disorganization of such

---

4 *Ibid.*, p. 332.
5 *Ibid.*, p. 344.

delinquency areas produces many types of non-social, a-social, and anti-social behavior patterns and group norms. The main cause of delinquency, according to this school, is personal association with these socially deviant groups. Anti-social habits, the most serious of which are criminal acts, are produced by this "deviant" or "differential" association. Shaw thus summarizes his conception of the nature, location, and causes of delinquency areas in the city of Chicago:

This study has indicated that school truancy, juvenile delinquency, and adult crime rather than being distributed uniformly throughout the city of Chicago are largely concentrated in certain areas. The highest rates are found in the areas adjacent to the central business districts and the large industrial centers, while the lowest rates occur in outlying residential communities.

The areas in which the greatest concentrations and highest rates are found have many characteristics which differentiate them from the outlying residential communities. As indicated previously, these areas are in a process of transition from residence to business and industry and are characterized by physical deterioration, decreasing population, and the disintegration of the conventional neighborhood culture and organization.

Since delinquents are largely concentrated in these characteristic areas, it may be assumed that delinquent behavior is very closely related to certain community situations which arise in the process of city growth. The way the elements in these situations become involved in the development of delinquent behavior trends can be understood only after thorough studies of community backgrounds have been made.

Under pressure of the disintegrative forces which act when business and industry invade a community, the community thus invaded ceases to function effectively as a means of social control. Traditional norms and standards of the conventional community weaken and disappear. Resistance on the part of the community to delinquent and criminal behavior is low, and such behavior is tolerated and may even become accepted and approved.

Moreover, many of the people who come into the deteriorating section are European immigrants or southern Negroes. All of them come from cultural and social backgrounds which differ widely from the situations in the city. In the conflict of the old with the new the former cultural and social controls in these groups tend to break down. This, together with the fact that there are few constructive community forces at work to reestablish a conventional order, makes for continued social disorganization.

Many of the boys' groups that are indigenous to these disorganized areas are unconventional or delinquent in their traditions and norms. It is probably significant that most of the boys appearing in the Juvenile Court are members of delinquent gangs. The study of detailed case histories indicates that many delinquent careers have their origin in the activities of these delinquent groups.

It has been quite common in discussions of delinquency to attribute causal significance to such conditions as poor housing, overcrowding, low living standards, low educational standards, and so on. But these conditions themselves probably reflect a type of community life. By treating them one treats only symptoms of more basic processes. Even the disorganized family and the delinquent gang, which are often thought of as the main factors in delinquency, probably reflect community situations.

In short, with the process of growth of the city the invasion of residential communities by business and industry causes a disintegration of the community as a unit of social control. This disorganization is intensified by the influx of foreign national and racial groups whose old cultural and social controls break down in the new cultural and racial situation of the city. In this state of social disorganization, community resistance is low. Delinquent and criminal patterns arise and are transmitted socially just as any other cultural and social pattern is transmitted. In time these delinquent patterns may become dominant and shape the attitudes and behavior of persons living in the area. Thus the section becomes an area of delinquency.[6]

One important qualification must be kept in mind in regard to estimating the heavy concentration of crime in these delinquency areas. The very poor who inhabit such areas are at a distinct disadvantage when it comes to probability of arrest, ability to get charges dismissed, and availability of good legal aid. The rich and their children are often able to talk the police or prosecutor out of arrest, or to get cases settled out of court. Failing this, they can hire an able counsel who may win a verdict of "not guilty." The police rarely hesitate to arrest a poor suspect and are not much influenced by his relatives in hushing up cases, nor are other authorities. Moreover, the poor are rarely able to hire competent criminal lawyers. Hence, there are always a disproportionate number of reported crimes, arrests, and convictions in those urban areas inhabited by the poverty-stricken.

Luxuriant habitats of leaders of organized crime. It should be kept in mind, moreover, that the criminality to which Shaw refers represents primarily conventional and, from an economic point of view, the more petty types of delinquency. We shall make clear in some detail later that the more dangerous or costly types of criminality today are organized crime and syndicated gambling. Those who engage in this type of criminality, with the exception of their gangster subsidiaries, do not live in the districts described by Shaw. They dwell in the most aristocratic portions of metropolitan areas—for example, Park Avenue in New York. They do business in the heart of the business and financial centers of our great cities and in the hangouts of the political leaders with whom they consort and connive. Martin Mooney thus describes the location of such business offices of the moguls of organized crime and racketeering:

In New York City the board of directors of Crime, Incorporated, holds its executive sessions high up in a building in Times Square. In every town they hold similar executive sessions, always in a building in the center of the greatest activity. In San Francisco it is in a building in the Montgomery Street financial district; in Chicago it is on Dearborn Street, always where other big business foregathers.[7]

Rural crimes. If cities today produce their special crime trends—notably organized crime, racketeering, and gambling syndicates—rural criminality long exhibited its own peculiar patterns—chiefly that of crimes of physical violence against persons. This was due to the lesser amount of money and moveable property in the country that thieves and robbers could make away with, and also to the smaller and more scattered population of the country and its greater inaccessibility. This special phase of rural crime before the Second World War was well portrayed by Stewart H. Holbrook in *Murder Out Yonder*.

[6] C. R. Shaw, *et al.*, *Delinquency Areas*. Chicago: University of Chicago Press, 1929, pp. 204-206.

[7] Martin Mooney, *Crime, Incorporated*. New York: McGraw-Hill, 1935, p. 38.

Since the Second World War there has been a marked change in rural crime. Together with a general shift of "big crime" from more violent and desperate acts to "fixed" syndicated gambling, this ranks as one of the two most notable trends in crime at the mid-century. Though the rural crime rate per capita is still far lower than the urban rate, the increase of criminality since 1945 has been far greater in the country than in cities, and the largest growth of postwar rural crime has been in the field of crimes against property. For example, in 1946, rural robbery increased by 48.4 per cent over 1945; and auto thefts increased by 34.3 per cent, as against a 23.9 per cent increase in rural assault cases. This trend is still continuing. In 1949, crime increased by 2.7 per cent in cities, and by 7.6 per cent in rural areas. Burglaries and larcenies increased in cities by only 4.4 per cent and 3.3 per cent, respectively, over 1948, but they increased by 13.1 per cent and 8.8 per cent, respectively, in rural districts. On the other hand, assault cases rose by 4.4 per cent in cities, whereas they gained only 3.8 per cent in the rural regions. Trends in 1950 were roughly similar.

There has been no definite study of the reasons for this remarkable transformation in the nature and extent of rural crime since 1945. It is, probably, the result of a complex combination of circumstances—the increasing impact of urban influences on rural life, the experiences of rural youth in wartime, the disruption of rural living conditions and social controls by the war, the relatively defective character of rural crime control and repression, and the recent increase of prosperity and property in rural areas. It is, fundamentally, a reflection of a rather general breakdown in morality and social control since the war.

HISTORICAL BACKGROUND OF ORGANIZED CRIME, RACKETEERING, AND GAMBLING

The El Dorado complex and easy money. In order to understand the nature of the truly menacing crime of our day, it is necessary to back off and get some historical perspective on the problem. Organized crime and gambling syndicates simply represent the latest and most dangerous manifestation of the something-for-nothing complex which has dominated a large sector of American life since the era of discoveries. Many of the early explorers of America came here because they hoped to find great quantities of gold and precious stones. Nothing but sheer starvation, as in the case of Virginia, was able ultimately to discourage this hope. But a sort of substitute was soon found in the lucrative fur trade and other methods for swindling the Indians. The next manifestation of this "El Dorado" complex appeared in the land speculation which prevailed from the close of the French and Indian War to the Civil War. Indeed, it persisted thereafter in connection with the land scandals associated with the building of the transcontinental railroads. The public lottery craze of the 1820's and 1830's helped on the mania for easy money.

Gold, banditry, and stock-jobbing. Gold was finally discovered in California in 1848 and the rush for easy money took on a new vigor, although in many cases the gold was obtained only after terrific personal hardships and after many had died on their way to the gold fields. Another manifestation of the something-for-nothing attitude appeared when bands of outlaws relieved the successful miners of the precious ore which they were taking back to the East, usually on stagecoaches.

Then came the stock-jobbing in connection with American railroad development. For a half century after the Civil War many of our railroads were more earnestly regarded by their owners or directors as the basis for successful stock gambling than as a means of transportation. The plight of the American railroad has been due as much to the deliberate financial chicanery of Jay Gould and his associates and successors as it is to the competition of the automobile, bus, and truck. When the railroads had been milked dry, the same methods were applied even more cleverly and effectively to our great electric utility empire and urban real estate developments.

The "small fry" catch on. In due time this something-for-nothing psychology seeped down from the upper crust of American economic society into the lives and ideas of the lesser lights. As one writer has observed rather caustically, we ultimately "Americanized the small fry." The small fry were, for the most part, the descendants of immigrants. Their parents had earned an honest living by hard work as unskilled laborers, as push-cart operators, as clothes cleaners, or as shoeshiners. The younger generation, however, eagerly embraced the current American slogan that "only saps work." They had no desire to break their backs in hard labor, as their parents had done. So, for example, instead of pushing a cart full of bananas and other fruits or vegetables, they organized rackets which controlled and exploited the distribution of these commodities to entire urban centers.

Also joining in with this crowd of urban racketeers and gangsters were many rural youth. As we have seen, the discipline and social control operating in rural communities were upset by technological advances and social changes in these areas. Moreover, farm machinery threw many young men in country districts out of work. The movies, the sensational newspapers and magazines, and other agencies for the dissemination of information brought to rural youth lurid and glamorous accounts of the easy money which the city gangsters were accumulating. It is from these two groups, urban and rural, that the army of organized criminals and racketeers has been recruited.

The "Noble Experiment" stimulates organized crime. As if by divine, or perhaps diabolic, intervention, the "Noble Experiment" of Prohibition came along about the same time that this sweeping revolution in economic and ethical theory was beginning to affect an ever larger number of American youth. The provision of illicit liquor for millions of American customers provided a perfect training ground for the evolution of the ideals and techniques of racketeering and organized crime. Moreover, it was a type of remunerative criminal activity which was peculiarly difficult to control by ethical inhibitions or the force of public opinion.

Violation of the Volstead Act was looked upon in many quarters as respectable and smart—indeed, indispensable in the service of American needs. Even law enforcement was often rather perfunctory. Bootleggers were even viewed by some responsible publicists as spiritual descendants of those who framed the Declaration of Independence and fought against British tyranny. One eminent American libertarian even predicted that a hundred years hence statues of Al Capone would dot our public parks along with those of Nathan Hale and Thomas Jefferson.

Prohibition and the opportunities for illicit distribution of liquor provided the first great training ground for organized crime and racketeering. But, even before repeal, the liquor racketeers had branched out into many other fields, particularly the related realms of vice and dope. The speculative orgy enlarged the possibilities in the way of marketing bogus stocks and bonds. The notable lowering of public morale with respect to economic and political chicanery in the era of Harding and Coolidge naturally encouraged every form of endeavor to get easy money, facilitated the unholy alliance between financial criminals and politicians, and dulled the public conscience with regard to the doings of both groups. After repeal it was natural that our organized criminals and racketeers, with their improved training and experience, would show increased energy in other lines of activity. The various forms of organized criminality, together with the multifarious rackets and powerful gambling syndicates which we shall later describe, have been the natural and inevitable result.

Crime on advice of counsel. Important developments in the legal fraternity contributed their quota to this trend. The law profession became more and more crowded with practicing members who had to earn a living. At the same time, the corporate practice of law, particularly with respect to civil and financial cases, became more prevalent, thus cutting down the possibilities of remunerative work by individual lawyers. Trust companies took over much work previously associated with estate and inheritance problems. Hence, needy lawyers could be more readily tempted by the fat fees offered by the organized criminals and racketeers. The latter had learned a lesson from the great moguls of finance capitalism—namely, that it is wise to consult a lawyer before taking any important action. In the old days, the smart criminal saw a good lawyer after he had committed his crime. Today the clever crook usually plans his crime with the aid and counsel of a competent attorney.[8]

Factors favoring organized gambling. The vast popularity of stock gambling during the last 30 years, and especially in the 1920's, brought a tremendous stimulus to the aspiration to get much for little. Legislative efforts to bring purity by statute had temporarily restricted the petty

---

[8] See Mooney, *op. cit.*, pp. 12, 40-41; Sheldon Glueck, *Crime and Justice.* Boston: Little, Brown, 1936, pp. 149 ff.; and H. S. Cummings, "The Lawyer Criminal," *American Bar Association Journal*, Vol. XX (1934).

gambling methods of more primitive stages of American development—lotteries, race-track bets, pools, and the like. This helped along a universal interest in the one great legalized realm of national gambling, the stock exchange. The stenographer has here rubbed shoulders with the millionaire manipulator. When various New Deal laws seriously curbed the grosser forms of stock gambling and security swindling, the organized criminal gangs that had been produced by the Prohibition era stood ready to exploit the gambling spirit which had been whetted and developed during the great stock gambling era of the 1920's. This, together with the greater gains and lesser risks associated with syndicated gambling, as compared with the more violent forms of organized crime, goes far to explain our present tremendous organized gambling enterprise that involves at least 15 billion dollars annually.

Alliance of organized crime with crooked politics. How is it possible for a network of well-organized crime to exist in modern America? The answer lies in the fact that organized crime in the United States is closely allied with party politics. Many public officials know the real leaders of organized crime, but they are either unwilling or powerless to move against them. In many cases, the underworld makes large payments to dishonest public officials to buy their friendship and protection. This is particularly true in cities and states where dishonest political machines are in control of the government.

At the funeral of one prominent Chicago "big shot" criminal, the honorary pallbearers included 21 judges, nine attorneys, a special state prosecutor, several city officials, and a number of union officials. The most prominent gambling magnate in New York City held a "charitable" conference early in 1948; present at his "command" were many prominent public officials, judges, and political leaders.

That the situation had not changed greatly in 20 years was further shown by the conduct of the Senatorial investigation of organized crime and gambling in 1950-1951. Much comment was devoted to the fact that, when the official investigators began to question the "big shots" in the gambling world, the latter were treated by the investigators with respect bordering on awe. Though later on the crime and gambling moguls were momentarily handled a little more harshly and realistically, many of the more dangerous leaders of organized crime were virtually ignored. There was also good reason for feeling that the investigation was brought to a close as a result of political pressure, growing out of a fear of the political damage which might result. Even a superficial investigation of the situation in Chicago in 1950 cost the Democrat party the Senatorial election in that year.

WHITE-COLLAR CRIME

The nature and antiquity of white-collar crime. What is now coming to be known rather generally among criminologists as *white-collar crime* comprises those forms of antisocial activities that are normally associated with the prevailing political and economic ideals and practices of any era. Edwin H. Sutherland, our leading student of the subject, defined white-collar crime as "crime committed by a person of high respectability and high social status *in the course of his occupation.*" The particular form that white-collar crime takes in any age will be determined by the nature of such ideals and practices. For example, the dominant white-collar crime during the Middle Ages was the robbery of merchant caravans by the feudal barons. Its counterpart in our time has been such practices as the depredations wrought by the manipulators of holding companies.

In the preceding section we indicated the long history and tradition of white-collar crime in the United States, associated as it has been with the most successful efforts to get something for nothing in the various stages of our economic and social development. But white-collar crime goes back about as far as our historical records. Respectable fraud in relation to land and flocks was common among the pastoral peoples of the ancient Near East, and piracy was rife on the seas at this early period.

Many of the Greeks were notorious grafters, and the Romans developed a great diversity of rackets, such as the combined arson and real estate racket which helped to build up the enormous fortune of Crassus. The medieval robber barons gained their income from organized criminality at the expense of medieval merchants. The English buccaneers of the age of exploration and colonization developed maritime robbery to the point of unprecedented income and respectability, and the English monarchs welcomed their share of boodle. The names of Drake, Frobisher and Hawkins come to mind in this connection. The slave traders of early modern times maintained for centuries a shocking enterprise in organized criminality which, for callous cruelty and brutality, makes the modern white-slave kings seem almost philanthropists by comparison. Francis Bacon was only the best known among the numerous grafting judges of the early modern period. The taxation and confiscation rackets were developed into a fine art by the Bourbon court in the century previous to the French Revolution. Thus, we see that there was a large historical heritage in the way of white-collar criminality which was passed on to the New World.

Political graft. One of the oldest and most persistent types of white-collar crime has been political graft and corruption. This has existed from the earliest historic times. In our own day it has chiefly assumed the form of the graft and financial corruption associated with the great political machines of our metropolitan communities. Since we have already described this in the discussion of city government, we need not go into the matter further at this point.

Political graft is not only in itself one of the oldest and most reputable forms of white-collar crime, but it is also a powerful agency for facilitating and perpetuating what criminologists regard as the more conventional types of white-collar criminality. Politicians have provided the lax laws under which nearly all forms of white-collar criminality operate, and, in collusion with white-collar criminals, they have frequently successfully withstood the reformers who have sought to correct such abuses. In its more overt and common forms, white-collar criminality could not exist for long without the protection afforded to it through various forms of political collusion and corruption.

Corporate chicanery. Probably the most extensive—and in many ways the most disastrous—methods whereby white-collar criminals have sought to get something for nothing have been provided by the more shady practices of finance capitalism.

Great investment banks gained control of the major forms of our economic life and directed and managed them primarily for the purpose of financial exploitation. The formula of many of these bankers was: (1) launch a concern by selling stock, mainly watered, to the mass of citizens; (2) build the enterprise expensively, in order to profit through the operations of the construction and supply companies also controlled by the big banks; (3) administer the concern expensively, with much mismanagement; and (4) wreck the enterprise ultimately, throw it into receivership, and seize ownership of the reorganized concern. At every stage some form of financial return was derived at the expense of the stockholders, and, in the end, at the expense of the bondholders as well.

The governing clique could afford to do this because of the almost complete separation of control and management from ownership. Since the governing group of officers and directors rarely owned as much as 5 per cent of the stock of a holding company or supercorporation, they suffered little directly from the depredations and manipulations and were well-nigh immune from the losses sustained.

The holding company has all too often been a particularly effective device for legalized robbery. If a petty criminal goes to the safe of an industrial concern with his can of nitroglycerine, opens the safe, and takes out a few hundred dollars, he renders himself liable to a long prison sentence. But if ambitious promoters organize a holding company which annually syphons off a million dollars of earnings into the pockets of those who do not directly contribute to the production of a single unit of goods, they may not be punished at all. Indeed, they may be praised for their ingenuity, held in esteem in the local community, and rewarded by important public office. Such antisocial practices as these of conventional finance capitalism have not usually been regarded as white-collar crime, even by the few criminologists who have studied the subject, unless they have led to conviction in the courts (as in the case of the conviction of Howard Hopson, of the Associated Gas and Electric Company).

Corporate white-collar crime, when discussed by criminologists, is generally restricted to those corporate practices which are actually contrary to law and which are prosecuted by public authorities (for example, the Attorney-General of the United States and his subordinates). Such practices are illegal restraint of trade, infringement of patents, misleading advertisements, rebate practices, and unfair labor practices. These forms of corporate chicanery are, however, infinitely less damaging to society than are the general practices of finance capitalism and holding companies. But they are important and they constitute the central theme of Sutherland's recent pioneer book, *White Collar Crime*.[9]

Banking abuses and losses. Similar abuses have been typical of our banking system, too. One cynical veteran journalist once remarked that bank robbers must be feeble-minded. Otherwise, he stated, they would organize banks and let the people bring the money in to them. Unfortunately, there is altogether too much truth in this wisecrack, as well as that made by an eminent economic historian who observed that the burglar alarms in banks should not be put on the vaults but on the doors of the directors' offices.

Between 1921 and 1932 some 11,800 American banks closed their doors, the failures involving deposits of more than five billion dollars. The majority of these bank failures were most surely due to financial chicanery. The United States offers the greatest opportunity for safe and profitable banking to be found anywhere in the world. But the fact is that our banking record has been an international scandal. In the Dominion of Canada, where banking is much more difficult and hazardous, and where bank failures would be much more understandable, there has been only one bank failure since 1914—and that a small collapse involving 20 million dollars. In England there has not been a bank failure in modern times.

Security speculation. The shrinkage of security values on the New York Stock Exchange alone amounted to nearly 100 billion dollars between October, 1929, and March, 1933. Even the enormous burden of rackets and organized crime pales into insignificance by comparison with this. Moreover, the deaths and suicides which directly resulted from the collapse of security values ran close to the homicide record during these years. It is obvious that no social stigma was attached to those responsible for these tremendous financial losses in banks and on the stock exchange, aside from the public antipathy vented upon a few subordinate employees who were made the goats for the evil deeds of their superiors.

War profiteering. The Second World War brought us face to face once more with a particularly reprehensible type of crime that usually goes unpunished—profiteering on war contracts. Billions were stolen from the government and from the American people in this way during the First World War, and almost no one was punished. Indeed, high government officials, including a future Vice-President of the United States, were able to prevent a thorough investigation of war profiteering in postwar days. Similar scandals in the Second World War have been revealed, with black-market criminal operations especially prevalent. It has been estimated that during the Second World War at least half of all American

---

9 New York: Dryden Press, 1950. For a good review of the various phases of white-collar and organized crime and the manner in which our society and culture encourage them, see Albert Deutsch, *Our Rejected Children*. Boston: Little, Brown, 1950, Chap. 28: "Our Crime-Breeding Culture." The whole panorama of mercenary, white-collar crime is well presented in the symposium edited by Ernest D. MacDougall, *Crime for Profit*. Boston: Statford Co., 1933.

businessmen were involved in some kind of violation of laws affecting price controls and priority regulations.

Frauds, swindles, and embezzlements. Less impressive in volume, but still serious in the amount of injury they cause innocent persons, are the more overt forms of financial crookedness, fraud and swindling. It would be difficult to estimate the total amount of money filched from the public by fake enterprises each year. Before the great stock market crash of 1929, the sale of worthless stocks and bonds brought swindlers more than one-half billion dollars every year. Investors in one large investment trust lost 580 million dollars between 1929 and 1935. Swindles involving worthless merchandise have at times reached an annual volume of 500 million dollars. A single fake real estate enterprise took over 100 million dollars from the "suckers" of Washington, D. C., in one year. Embezzlement is a common form of white-collar crime. In only four cases, in 1931, the losses amounted to 9 million dollars. Virgil W. Peterson, an expert on the subject, estimated the annual losses from embezzlement in the United States to be about 400 million dollars. The public loses far more —probably twice as much—each year through swindles and embezzlement than all the robbers, burglars, and pickpockets are able to collect. Ironically enough, these frauds and swindles result in part from the investors' desire to get something for nothing.

Fraud and extortion in labor union circles. It is well to make it clear that not all swindling is done by crooked business. There are plenty of crooks and racketeers in the labor unions. They fleece the poor workers, frequently confiscate union funds, betray the union workers, and blackmail and cajole employers. William Bioff and George E. Browne were accused and convicted of extorting $500,000 from four large moving-picture companies by threatening to call a strike and tie up production. George Scalise was convicted of stealing $60,000 from the International Building Service Union, of which he was president. Joseph S. Fay, international vice-president of the Union of Operating Engineers, and James Bove, international vice-president of the Hod Carriers Union, were convicted of extorting a vast sum from contractors who built the Delaware Aqueduct for New York City. For years, these men and their associates had tyrannized construction work in the metropolitan area. It is not unknown for union crooks both to call unwise strikes, thus injuring the workers, and then to furnish strikebreakers to employers to help break these strikes.

Sundry other forms of white-collar crime. There are various other types of white-collar criminals, among them the loan sharks, who defy the laws against usury and filch large sums from the poor and others in desperate need of funds by charging outrageous interest rates. Others defraud reckless or needy persons through profiteering excessively on installment sales. Fraudulent advertising and the sale of worthless nostrums are other types of white-collar crime; worthless patent medicines and the services of quacks cost the country more than 600 million dollars a year. Fee collectors, both public and private, often gouge their victims severely. With the increase of taxes, a popular type of crime or quasi-criminality is tax evasion, aided and abetted by tax evasion services. The enormous increase of taxes during and since the Second World War has probably increased this type of borderline criminality.

The swindling and fraudulent motivation of the white-collar level has seeped down to the overalls and mechanic group as well. Nation-wide surveys by *Reader's Digest* indicated that 80 per cent of garage mechanics and 60 per cent of radio repairmen commonly defraud their customers in various ways. And surely these two groups are not unique in their attitudes and operations.

ORGANIZED CRIME

Criminal gangs dominate large-scale crime operations. In the United States the "lone wolf" or independent criminal plays only a minor rôle in the complex pattern of present-day crime. The larger portion of serious criminal activity is directed by criminal gangs. During the Prohibition period, criminal gangs were able to develop a large-scale and highly profitable business in bootlegging liquor, since many American citizens were not in sympathy with Prohibition and demanded their liquor. The huge profits from bootlegging enabled the illicit liquor moguls to organize their operations on a comprehensive and efficient basis. When the bootlegging industry became well developed, another form of lucrative criminality connected with illicit liquor sprang up: the hijacking or robbing of the conveyances used by bootleggers in transporting their liquor.

The rôle of Al Capone in organized crime and racketeering. "Scarface" Al Capone was the first important criminal leader to raise organized crime to the level of "big business." He developed a reputation in the New York underworld at an early age, and, in 1925, became the leader of a bootleg ring in Chicago. During the next five years there were numerous dramatic and bloody battles between Capone's henchmen and other gangs for the control of the Chicago liquor trade. Capone finally achieved supreme power by a bloody massacre of his opponents on St. Valentine's Day, 1929. It is estimated that, at the height of his power, Capone controlled bootlegging in four states and that *his gross income from the liquor racket was six million dollars a week*. He and his associates also branched out into the vice and gambling fields.

Capone maintained his power by two means—through the use of a private army of mobsters and killers, and through his association with, and control over, politicians. His killers gave him power over the underworld, and his influence with politicians kept him safe from prosecution. His career did not come to an end until the Federal government sent him to prison—for not paying income taxes on his huge revenue from crime. Amusingly enough, it is said that Capone's prosecution actually grew out of the fact that his carousals in his Miami "palace" had annoyed President-elect Hoover, who, during the winter of 1928-1929, was visiting a friend in Florida.

When the repeal of Prohibition put an end to the bootlegging of liquor, the big criminals turned their efficient organizations to other uses. They entered such forms of organized crime as well-planned bank robberies and thefts from warehouses, docks, railroads, and trucks. Kidnapping was another field to which gangsters turned, but the FBI soon made this form of criminal enterprise risky and unprofitable. At the present time, many organized criminal gangs devote themselves to safer and more lucrative forms of activity like gambling syndicates.

Later crime leaders develop a smoother technique. Although Al Capone was the first important and well-known American to put crime on a business basis, he must be looked upon as only a crude beginner. Later gang leaders have gone into numerous other fields of more vital and immediate concern to the average American citizen than the liquor and vice business. Their methods have become more "refined," and every attempt is made to see to it that the game is worked as smoothly as possible, with little violence. The more sophisticated racketeers have come to realize that the crude and "impolite" methods of a Capone stir up an unnecessary amount of public excitement and may lead to annoying demands for the investigation and suppression of their activities. This trend toward more polish and shrewdness in big crime has been well described by Albert Deutsch:

> Organized crime has graduated from the underworld. Its lords no longer seek the protection of dark alleys, but operate their enterprises from luxurious offices. They hobnob with bankers and industrialists and with famous leaders of the entertainment world. They throw parties and dinners at which judges and other pillars of society appear as if at command performances. They buy and sell judges; they make and break mayors. They control entire local governments. They are powerful influences in state and national politics. They invest in million-dollar real estate enterprises. They have big-name partners and big business fronts.[10]

Operations of criminal gangs. Outside of racketeering, which we shall describe shortly, organized crime falls chiefly into two fields: the operations of criminal gangs, and the activities of criminal syndicates.

Criminal gangs today usually specialize in the theft of merchandise and automobiles, and in bank robberies. Rings of automobile thieves frequently steal and dispose of hundreds of cars before they are caught. One of the largest single items in organized robbery is the wholesale stealing of merchandise from docks, warehouses, trains, and trucks. Losses from these sources are estimated at more than 500 million dollars a year. In 1951, an expert student of the situation estimated that the annual thefts of merchandise from the docks of greater New York City alone amount to at least 140 million dollars. Bank robberies have become more daring, more carefully planned, and more remunerative. The sensational Brink robbery in Boston in 1950 made the largest "haul" on record—over a million dollars. The annual "take" has been as high as 250 million dollars. Bank robbers today can dispose of their thefts in stocks and bonds

---

[10] *Our Rejected Children,* p. 284.

to well-organized business syndicates that specialize in such activities. This is a development of recent years. As Jack Black, the reformed criminal, pointed out:

> Jimmy Hope, the most famous bank burglar of fifty years ago, took a million dollars in bonds out of a Boston bank and couldn't market them. Jimmy dickered and haggled with Mother Mandelbaum, the fence, in her dingy dive, but she would have none of them. Today he could step into a luxurious office and meet a man behind a polished desk who would grubstake him to pull off the burglary and take the bonds off his hands at fifty cents on the dollar the morning after.[11]

Activities of criminal syndicates. There are numerous activities in which criminal syndicates indulge. Arnold Rothstein, one of the founders of the criminal syndicate, and his associated gamblers, "rigged" the crooked baseball World Series of 1919. Criminal syndicates usually "rig" and operate the gambling activities of a city or region. They manage the black market when conditions are favorable to such activities. After the Second World War, the shortage of automobiles and the frenzied demand for them encouraged black-market activities in the purchase and sale of both new and second-hand cars. In 1946, a single black-market car syndicate in South Carolina was discovered to have done 100 million dollars worth of business in this field.

One of the favorite types of syndicate operations is the "confidence game," into which are lured the greedy who may possess considerable wealth and who hope to make vast profits quickly out of what seem to be quasi-legitimate business enterprises. As much as a quarter of a million dollars has been taken from a single victim. Embezzlements are also often engineered by criminal syndicates. As we have already indicated, criminal syndicates have now taken over the operations of our vast organized gambling network. Syndicates also control much of commercialized vice today, as well as the illicit trade in narcotic drugs.

The Ponzi swindle of 1920. Interestingly enough, the most dramatic example of the confidence game in all American history was the work of a lone wolf, Charles Ponzi, of Boston, rather than of a criminal syndicate. Ponzi had a previous criminal record, and 6 months before his great swindle had been a $16-a-week clerk. He organized a confidence concern, the Ponzi Securities Exchange Company, and promised investors 50 per cent on their investments within 90 days. He further agreed to double their money in 6 months. Within 8 months he had induced about 40,000 persons to hand over to him no less than 15 million dollars. He took in as much as 2 million dollars in a single day before he was exposed by the *Boston Post* as an ex-convict and a confidence man. Ponzi's procedure, he asserted, was to buy depreciated foreign currencies with American dollars, to convert the depreciated currency into International Postal Union reply coupons at par, and then to convert the latter into dollars, at a profit of 400 per cent. Actually, he took part of the money paid by one group of "investors" to pay off another group and to keep the game

---

[11] Jack Black, "A Burglar Looks at Laws and Codes," *Harper's Magazine*, February, 1930.

operating. Most of the money "invested" was lost, and Ponzi was sent to prison by the Federal courts for fraudulent use of the mails.

ORGANIZED RACKETEERING

The nature of rackets. After the ideas and practices of organized crime were brought to public attention through articles and books on the subject, it became common practice to designate all forms of organized crime and shady practices as rackets. Indeed, it was not long before one's ordinary occupation came to be called a *racket,* and strangers meeting each other often saluted one another good-naturedly by inquiring: "What's your racket?" Such casual usage may enrich the American language, but it is confusing when applied in the field of scientific criminology.

In more exact terminology, rackets, while a phase of organized criminality, represent a special type of such antisocial activity. Precisely and technically speaking, a racket is a form of criminal behavior which is operated primarily through the technique of extortion, enforced by threats of physical violence and property damage. When violence does take place, it is usually for the purpose of setting up and enforcing the particular racket in question, or to prevent other racketeers from "muscling" into a racket already established. A well-organized and smoothly-operating racket is rarely accompanied by much violence, no matter how great the amount of loot which may be extorted.

Racketeering methods have been introduced into a great diversity of fields. Among these are the arson racket; the rackets in the cleaning, dyeing and laundry industries; the rackets in milk, baked goods, vegetables, fruits, and other types of necessities; labor union rackets and industrial shakedowns; the building trades racket; the dock and wharf racket; the dope racket; taxi dance halls and "shake" joints; the garage and taxi racket; the trucking racket; the venereal disease racket; and many others which were exposed with conspicuous candor and clarity by Courtney Ryley Cooper in his work, *Here's to Crime* (1937).

Organizing a racket. To illustrate how a racket is organized, we may consider a typical form of the laundry racket. A group of ambitious practitioners of the easy-money philosophy decide that here is a field which might profitably be tapped. One of their representatives visits the proprietor of an urban laundry. The racketeer suggests that the latter contribute a sum running, say, from $50 to $500, depending upon the city and the size of the laundry, for "protection." The laundry proprietor may be amazed and entirely aghast at the proposition. He may protest that nobody has ever harmed him and that he sees no logical reason for spending this amount of money to protect himself against imaginary dangers. The representatives of the incipient laundry racket then assure him that even though he has not needed protection in the past he is surely going to be in need of it in the future. The arguments may be sufficiently graphic and concrete to convert him on the spot and to lead him to turn in his payment. Or, the laundryman may be stubborn and skeptical. Shortly thereafter, his delivery truck, with hundreds of dollars worth of newly laundered clothes, may be stopped in a back street or in an alley and oil or acid thrown on the clothes. His windows may be broken and his machinery wrecked. After a few demonstrations like this, the laundryman becomes convinced that it will be cheaper, after all, to pay the sum demanded and render himself secure against future outrages of this sort.

The same method of conversion is applied to other laundrymen in the city, and in due time the laundry racket is safely sewed up and operates smoothly. So far as possible, the laundrymen pass on to the public the costs of their contribution to the racket by means of increased prices. The public, as usual, pays. Much the same technique is followed out in the case of all other forms of typical rackets. Avarice, fear, and intimidation lie at their foundation.

Racketeering methods. The methods pursued in executing and enforcing the various types of rackets may perhaps be better understood if we describe the procedure in certain representative cases. In some instances the racketeers gain a monopolistic control over the methods of distributing various types of necessities of life, such as raw milk, certain types of fresh vegetables, fresh fruit, poultry, and meat. They add a definite sum to the prices charged for these commodities, thus levying a tribute upon consumers. In other cases, they simply compel those who handle such commodities to pay protection money. In the fruit and vegetable racket, for example, the racketeers preserve discipline and keep their victims in line by making it impossible for them to unload their cars or trucks of fruit and vegetables in metropolitan areas unless their account with the rackets is paid up. In the building trades racket, buildings under construction may be seriously wrecked unless the contractors come through with a tribute levied by the racketeers. We have already referred to the operations of Fay and Bove in labor racketeering in metropolitan construction work in New York City and environs. In the dock racket in New York City, merchants operating from the docks had to pay a certain sum, usually based upon the volume of goods handled, for the privilege of using these shipping facilities. In the case of the delivery truck racket, the levy is in proportion to the type and volume of goods carried. For example, a certain sum must be paid for each barrel of flour transported. It has been estimated that this added nearly two million dollars annually to the bread bill paid by the citizens of New York City. Taxi drivers have been brought into a racket in many cities. They have to pay a fixed sum each month for the privilege of driving a taxi. "Big-shot" racketeers also collaborate in the more remunerative phases of organized thievery—such as the 140 million dollar annual dock thefts in greater New York.

Smooth and complex administration of rackets. The skillful racketeer of today not only adopts the methods of big business in the way of the organization and administration of the empire of crime. He has also imitated modern business in making criminal enterprise run smoothly and quietly. Martin Mooney describes this new trend as follows:

The modern racketeer is a suave businessman. His activities are adroitly camou-flaged by hundreds of obviously legitimate corporations. Modern crime has gone big business. And modern crime's bulging kitty is adequately protected by an efficient chamber of commerce.

While the combines in each section of the country are groups that work inde-pendently of others, all of them take counsel from a national association whose slogan is "The public be pleased." Miracles can be accomplished when vile medicine is given that candy taste. That's what is happening in America today . . .

Modern racketeers no longer go to prison because they don't consort with the yeggs their predecessors did. Big business has been shrouded with the mantle of respectability, except for a lobby scandal here and there, and the boys find it profitable to operate their lucrative rackets today under the cloak of big business rather than from behind the barrel of an automatic.[12]

Our contemporary rackets are not managed by ignorant or desperate nitwits. They are now guided by very alert and sagacious businessmen. There is an elaborate centralized control over the major forms of or-ganized racketeering. In each major section of the country there is a sort of central committee, or board of directors, who exert general super-vision and control over this menacing type of criminality. The makeup of this executive committee controlling organized racketeering in the east-ern United States is well described by Mooney on the basis of a fortunate first-hand observation of one of its sessions:

I have witnessed a gathering of the executives of Crime, Incorporated. Through a valuable contact I was tipped off to the time and place that this would occur. . . .

Within an hour Crime, Incorporated, was in executive session, but not in the office of the reputable barrister. The meeting was held on the twelfth floor in a suite of offices ostensibly given over to a real-estate corporation. There, in a simple and bare room with a highly polished floor and comfortable leather chairs grouped around a large table, the directors of Crime, Incorporated, took up unfinished and new business.

A glimpse of those making up this menacing group of super-racketeers or a dictaphone recording of what went on in that room would have shaken the entire country. Revelation of the identities of the crime combine sitting there in the office and manipulating their billion-dollar racketeering activities would have shocked the country as much as the death of a president or the sudden crash of a great bank. . . .

Three of the men in that crime board executive session were important figures in local and national politics. Their names, if revealed, would shake every city in the country and topple scores of state and national politicians.

Another man in that room is the head of a business enterprise that is con-sidered one of the first half dozen in the East. Beside him sat a grayhaired man chewing a cigar who is a lifelong friend and closest confidant of a police official high in the esteem of the city. Across from him was the district leader whose single word could break any office holder in the city. The suave attorney who stood at one of the windows looking far down into the canyon of streets below holds degrees from two of the most esteemed of eastern universities.

The most perfectly groomed and youngest of all present was a gambler. He looked at the most twenty-eight years old. But if one came close, the fine lines around the eyes and the hard line at the corners of the finely molded mouth placed him closer to forty-eight than twenty-eight. His black eyes had a steady look whenever he spoke. Together with the two remaining members of the crime board, this man kept the mobster element used by the racketeers under perfect and complete control. Those two remaining "directors" most closely

---

12 Mooney, *op. cit.,* pp. 5-6.

approximated the picture the public always conjures up when it hears the word "racketeer." One of them was short and wiry, with a sallow face, slightly hunched shoulders, and small light-gray eyes. His teeth were crooked and yellow and he spoke with a husky voice that occasionally broke into a high-pitched register. His companion in the control of gangdom was of medium height, pinkly bald and with burly shoulders.

There they were, the directorate of Crime, Incorporated—representing businessmen, politicians, police protection, crooked lawyers and the newest in gangster tactitians. These were the men controlling the sixteen sinister rackets flourishing in their section of the country. Similar boards, similarly menacing and composed of similar types, hold the same kind of meetings for the same end —illegal gain—in other big cities.[13]

Under this central committee, or board of directors, are special committees with particular functions to perform in maintaining and extending the activities of racketeering. They are also well described by Mooney.

One of these committees is the so-called "new projects" committee. The members of this committee are constantly on the alert to devise or discover new methods of snaring suckers. Old rackets may lose their hold on the public, or they may be temporarily suppressed as a result of public indignation and the work of a courageous prosecutor. In any event, there is always need of new ventures to increase the income and to satisfy the greed of the rulers of the underworld. Another committee handles the secret service work of the racketeers. At its head is always one or more well-trained former detectives who are thoroughly familiar with secret service methods. They assemble all sorts of information concerning important persons in private and public life—especially those in public life. The information which they gather is prized primarily as a means of protecting organized crime against exposure or prosecution. They hope to gather enough embarrassing or incriminating evidence to intimidate any officeholder who might be inclined to doublecross the leaders of the underworld, to cooperate in any campaign to suppress the rackets, or to put on the statute books really effective antiracket laws. And, of course, they frequently dig up juicy material which can be used by those who are conducting the blackmail racket. A third committee deals particularly with new contacts. They seek to get in touch with persons who can be "shaken down" in one way or another through blackmail threats and the like. They also contact promising new recruits who may become valuable associates in the world of rackets.

Finally, there is the lobby committee, which maintains alert contacts with state legislatures, the Federal Congress, and national officials. The lobby committee is active in discouraging legislation which might be effective in suppressing organized crime, gambling, and racketeering. It puts discreet but powerful pressure upon legislators who might otherwise be influenced by a demand for the investigation and punishment of organized criminality. The information which has been gathered about public officials by the secret service committee is especially helpful in

---

13 *Ibid.,* pp. 38-42.

this connection. Further, the politicians have a natural bond with the racketeers, since it is usually the same class of people who demand both a clean-up of crime and the purification of politics. The reformers are the mutual enemies of racketeers and political grafters. Mooney tells us that he knew the head of the underworld lobby in Washington, a venerable and cultivated old gentleman who had many members of Congress at his beck and call over the telephone. Other powerful lobbies sought his services, but he preferred to remain in the employ of "Crime, Incorporated." [14]

This very brief review of the nature and extent of the organization of contemporary racketeering illustrates how far crime has developed beyond the stage of the petty lone wolf who sticks up a local grocer or gasoline station operator or who prowls about in dwellings, seeking the family jewels and silver. To the beginner in this field, these commonplace facts about organized crime and racketeering are likely to appear shocking and amazing—indeed, literally incredible. But they have been set forth in many reputable books. J. Edgar Hoover provided a most enthusiastic commendation of Martin Mooney's *Crime, Incorporated,* and he wrote of Cooper's devastating volume, *Here's to Crime,* that "Courtney Ryley Cooper knows more about crime and criminals than any other writing man in America." Indeed, Cooper actively collaborated with Hoover in the latter's own writings on the crime problem. An extended reading of the more realistic books on crime that have appeared in recent years will convince any fair-minded person that the survey here presented is brief and restrained.

The gangster element and the gunmen, whom the public usually associate with whatever they know of the newer criminality, do not exert any control over organized racketeering. They are simply the paid underlings. They do the "dirty work" for their suave masters. When some rash racketeer, or group of racketeers, attempts to intrude on—that is, "muscle in" on—an already well-organized racket, the gangsters and gunmen have to be summoned to provide impressive discouragement of such audacity and bad taste. Or they are employed to intimidate stubborn converts to a given racket and to enforce discipline therein. But the master minds take no direct part in their bloody work.

Collusion between racketeers and politicians. As we have pointed out several times already, organized criminals and racketeers are at special pains to assure cordial and mutually advantageous relations with organized politics. This fact is well brought out in reports on organized crime and racketeering. It has been made the subject of Dennis T. Lynch's important book, *Criminals and Politicians,* dealing particularly with New York City, and of Fletcher Dobyns' *The Underworld of American Politics,* and Jack Lait and Lee Mortimer's *Chicago Confidential,* which exposed conditions in Chicago. The interrelation of politics and racketeering in a great American metropolitan center is presented in thinly veiled fiction in Stephen Endicott's *Mayor Harding of New York.*

---

[14] *Ibid.,* pp. 47-48.

We have also suggested that machine politicians and the racketeers have a common enemy in the reform element. This gives them a strong bond of "intellectual" and social affinity. The racketeers are sensible enough to recognize that they must render something in return. Hence, they chip in liberally to the campaign funds. They also pay large sums for protection money which finds its way into the pockets of various politicians and public officials. Al Capone is said to have contributed $200,000 to one campaign fund in Chicago, and to have paid, on the average, two million dollars a year for the protection of his liquor operations. And Capone did this when the game was still fairly young and its methods relatively crude. The smoother technique in collusion between politicians and organized criminals, racketeers, and gamblers a quarter of a century after the heyday of Capone is revealed by Lait and Mortimer in *Chicago Confidential*, and *Washington Confidential*.

We have already shown that the materials gathered by the secret service committee of organized crime are extremely cogent and effective in keeping politicians within bounds. Even the gangsters and gunmen are valuable to the politicians. They can be used very handily in discouraging reformers, intimidating honest voters, stuffing the ballot boxes, and performing sundry chores for the political machine.

Public unconscious victims of racketeers. The main reason why the public will patiently and persistently put up with this heavy additional burden imposed by rackets is that it is essentially unaware of their existence. An able journalist, Courtenay Terrett, wrote an interesting book on the New York City rackets under the intriguing title, *Only Saps Work*. In his chapter on "The Home Life of the Sap" he thus describes how the average metropolitan household is unwittingly exploited by the various types of racketeers:

John Henry Smith sat down at the Sunday dinner table and cast an appreciative glance at his helpmeet as she distributed plates of soup—cream of mushrooms, it was—to his place, and hers, and those of the three junior Smiths.

After the soup came fried chicken with green peas and artichokes, and then a salad of alligator pear and a bowl of fresh fruit for dessert. It was, observed Mr. Smith, a mighty fine dinner for a poor man's family to be eating, even on Sunday.

Mrs. Smith was pleased at the tribute, but from long habit she sighed. It did seem, she remarked, that things were getting more and more expensive all the time. Would Mr. Smith believe it, but she paid 46 cents a pound for that chicken and it wasn't so plump either? A good housewife, she inventoried the meal for him: the mushrooms had been 60 cents a pound, and she'd used real cream at 26 cents for a little half-pint carton, and the artichokes had been 15 cents apiece and the peas had cost 25 cents a pound.

Really, she sometimes wondered how they were going to keep it up, if things got any more expensive.

Why, even the fresh tablecloth and napkins, they had used—goodness knows she sent everything to a wet wash laundry because it was so much cheaper than a hand laundry, but even so they never paid below $1.50 a bundle for the wash and sometimes more.

And Edward's suit would simply have to be sent to a cleaner; boys that age were terribly careless. They didn't seem to know or care that even the $1 cleaners charged as much for their suits as for a full-grown man's.

John Henry Smith sighed with her. He supposed it was just the steady rise in commodity costs. If only wages would rise in the same ratio, instead of trailing behind.

But John Henry Smith didn't know for all his masculine informativeness, that what he and his wife found such an oppressive financial burden was man-made and artificial and by no means the result of a fundamental economic condition. What they were paying, with such difficulty, was the racket.

They were paying, in other words, their per capita share of the wages of the thugs who beat up Joseph Blank, a Rivington Street poultry merchant, and poisoned the milk of James Coulter, a Putnam County dairy farmer, and smashed the windows of Jerry Piola's fruit and vegetable store in Greenpoint, and beat up Harry Gersch in his $1 cleaning shop, and threw acid on the bundles of dirty clothes in the cart of the St. Clair Independent Hand Laundry. They were paying their part toward the fees of luxury-loving boss racketeers and expensive lawyers. They were paying a little of the graft that is spent for police protection, for political influence, for fixers in the courts.

There are hundreds of thousands of those Smiths in New York City, in Chicago, in St. Louis, Cleveland, Boston, Philadelphia, Detroit, in nearly all of our big cities and in many of the smaller ones. It is from them—a few cents here, a few cents there, for this and for that a little higher price—that the money comes which adds up to such impressive totals.[15]

Have the racketeers been eliminated? In "Exploded Big Shots," an article in *The New York Times* (January 2, 1942), Meyer Berger maintained that the big shot criminals and racketeers, particularly in New York City, have been eradicated. The truth is that most of the crude boys of the earlier days have been wiped out. In their place, however, we have smoother crooks who conduct the rackets and organized crime with greater finesse and shrewdness. Indeed, it is said on good authority that one single "big shot" operator in New York City today has more power than all the New York racketeers combined had when Thomas E. Dewey began his "crime-busting" career. Prominent politicians and judges do his bidding, and his power extends to many other states throughout the nation.

Not only is the technique of racketeers and big shot criminals smoother than in the days of Al Capone and "Bugs" Moran, but their fields of activities are also becoming less violent and desperate. Instead of participating in organized robbery, bootlegging, kidnapping, and gang murders, they operate criminal syndicates for big swindling enterprises, control illicit gambling or "fix" quasi-legal forms of gambling, run the vice ring, and manage dope smuggling and peddling. As evidence that organized criminality of various kinds has not been eliminated, we may cite the fact that a spectacular gang killing involving top leaders in the Kansas City political machine helped to set off a national Senatorial investigation of organized crime and gambling in the late spring of 1950.

The best answer to Berger's contention that big-shot criminals have been wiped out is contained in the evidence revealed by the Kefauver Senate Crime Investigating Committee in 1950 and 1951. This has brought forth a picture of organized criminality far more impressive than that made public as a result of the Dewey prosecutions nearly 15 years earlier. The main change, aside from better organization, has been

---

15 Courtenay Terrett, *Only Saps Work*. New York: Vanguard, 1930, pp. 75-77.

the shift from cruder and more dangerous operations, such as organized robbery, into various types of gambling, vice, and dope peddling. Indeed, Lait and Mortimer, in *Washington Confidential,* in the chapter on "The Terror from Tennessee" (Chapter 26), and Mortimer, in his article on "Will Kefauver Be President?" in the *American Mercury,* May, 1951, offered much evidence that the material produced by the Kefauver Committee gave a very inadequate and incomplete picture of the extent and operations of organized crime and gambling as it exists at the mid-century.

OUR GAMBLING EMPIRE

Early attitudes toward gambling. Like many of our other social problems, gambling has a past which dates back to the very origin of civilization. In fact, it was very common among primitive peoples. It was closely related to the primitive notions of luck and magic, which determined much primitive thinking and conduct. It was assumed that those whom the good spirits or gods favored would surely be lucky not only in gambling but in all phases of life. Tacitus refers to the marked penchant of the primitive Germans for gambling. Modern anthropologists give us similar reports about existing primitives.

Gambling seems to have been very general after the rise of civilization. Indeed, the first widespread opposition to it was associated with the rise of Protestantism following the early sixteenth century. Puritanical asceticism, particularly as derived from the theories of John Calvin, was basically and bitterly opposed to the whole philosophy of gambling. It was a fundamental contention of the puritanical philosophy of life that property is something to be acquired in a penitential attitude by means of hard work. The acquisition of property is something which is achieved for the glorification of God. Its possession is proof of the indwelling of divine grace. Hence, Protestant asceticism was vehemently opposed to the accumulation of property by means of games of chance and in a light-hearted manner. It is obvious that the sanctified conception of property in Protestant philosophy also made it particularly reprehensible to lose through chance the wealth which had been acquired through the grace of God.

Catholic philosophy, even Catholic asceticism, did not develop this attitude to any such marked degree. This is a partial explanation of what is, to some, the problem of understanding the prevalence of lotteries and other forms of gambling in predominantly Catholic countries. In Catholic portions of Europe and in Latin America, which is predominantly Catholic, there has been far less opposition to gambling than in Protestant states. Therefore, in these countries we find even public lotteries as well as the most varied types of private gambling enterprises. In some countries a considerable portion of the public funds is raised through lotteries, which are regarded as more entertaining and less obnoxious than other forms of more prosaic taxation. In spite of our American Protestantism, there was, however, a large amount of gambling in the West, particularly in the mining towns, where the harsh and unsettled life promoted not only gambling but drinking and prostitution.

Lotteries in our early national history. It took Protestantism some time, indeed, to suppress the common forms of Old World gambling which we inherited. It may surprise some to learn that public lotteries were once very common in this country. Even the colonial clergy sanctioned them. As William Christie MacLeod points out:

> The fathers of our country were participating in public lotteries, and our colonial clergy as a whole did not oppose the lotteries but even joined in their use for the financial benefit of the churches. It is true that from the beginning of the colonial history of our people public lotteries were an integral part of the framework of our public finance and continued to be so during the Revolution and in the post-Revolutionary periods. We acquired from the mother country, along with most of our other institutions, the institution of the public lottery as a means of financing the government itself, in part, and institutions of public necessity such as schools, churches, and public utility promotions.[17]

It may prove even more surprising to learn that the greatest popularity of lotteries in the United States developed between 1820 and 1835, and that they then became the first notable American example of organized gambling. Until about 1820, lotteries in the United States were quiet and periodic affairs conducted by individual communities. After 1820 they came under the control of our first great crop of American gambling promoters, who obtained the lottery concessions from a locality and then marketed lottery tickets all over the entire country. A veritable lottery mania resulted. In the words of MacLeod:

> From about 1820 up until the time of their abolition some thirteen or so years later in these Northeastern states, the sale of lottery tickets, formerly in figures not at all satisfying to the holders of the lottery privileges, reached undreamed of totals. A new big business was developed, and promoters and corrupt politicians made money. Formerly quiet affairs, of no great general interest, held very infrequently, drawings for the lottery became incessant, daily affairs, accompanied by excited popular interest; and the staider citizenry, who once sponsored the dignified affairs of an older day, now avoided them and became alarmed at the wide spread of the gambling fever. High pressure salesmanship along with the interstate distribution of the tickets originating locally accounted for much of the change. The entrepreneur often, like some theater operators today, would sell the tickets of his lotteries in bulk to owners of offices for the sale of lottery tickets, to brokers, and these in turn sent out salesmen into the highways and byways, to the servant's entrance of homes, to the grogshops, out to the country lanes, everywhere. The public had to be made lottery conscious; they do not appear to have become so suddenly of themselves. The everlasting pressure of the salesmen turned the tide in favor of the lotteries, and, needless to say, their commission, paid for spreading the gambling fever over the highways and byways, ate up a very considerable part of the proceeds of the tickets for the lotteries.[18]

The opposition to lotteries at this time was due less to the antagonism of Protestant theology and ethics than to a sense of thrift and economic

---

[17] W. C. MacLeod, "The Truth about Lotteries in American History," *South Atlantic Quarterly*, April, 1936, p. 203.

[18] *Ibid.*, p. 206.

realism. There arose a growing apprehension of the fact that the lotteries were really a "racket" which enriched the promoters rather than the states, cities, and companies under whose auspices the lotteries were launched. The Pennsylvania Canal Company, for example, had to sell 18 million dollars' worth of lottery tickets to realize two million dollars in clear gain from its lottery. Lotteries drained 1½ million dollars annually from Philadelphia, over and above all local proceeds from ticket sales. Another abuse sprang up with the first appearance in this country of the policy, or numbers game, gambling practice. There was widespread betting, promoted by our pioneer racketeers, on the outcome of the lottery drawings. These evils led to a series of laws, beginning with the Pennsylvania Act of 1833, which soon abolished lotteries and ended the first notable gambling epidemic in our country.

American opinion hostile to legalized gambling. In general, the United States has been relatively antagonistic to conventional forms of gambling, though prominent gambling casinos have been maintained at Saratoga, French Lick Springs, Reno, Las Vegas, and other towns. Added to the opposition which grew out of the Protestant philosophy was the righteous indignation against the obvious forms of cheating which often prevail in gambling. This led many who were interested in real games of chance to oppose those gambling enterprises in which the element of luck was virtually eliminated, so that participants would inevitably lose to the operators and be promptly fleeced.

Business practices, reform legislation, and gambling trends. Unfortunately our opposition to gambling in its more overt forms, along with other factors, led to the much more serious gambling in the economic essentials of the nation. This has been more prevalent in the United States than in any other civilized nation in the world. Even before organized gambling was discouraged in the West, the early railroad magnates in the East discovered that more money could be made through gambling in railroad securities than in using dice and poker chips. For generations our railroads were as truly indirect gambling devices as literal transportation facilities. Later, the practice spread into the electric utilities empire and elsewhere. The drive against race-track gambling early in the twentieth century helped still further to concentrate gambling in this country in the stock exchanges. In the 1920's even the white-collar proletariat and the working class had their fling with gambling in the security market, with the calamitous results for all concerned which we know all too well.

Not only has this type of gambling been disastrous to millions of innocents, but it has also tended to degrade and demoralize the essential finance and business of the country. The gambling aspects of the activities of the stock exchange have done more damage to our national economy than thousands of Monte Carlos could have done. And the losses sustained are appalling. The paper losses from dealings on the New York Stock Exchange alone from 1929 to 1933 amounted to about 100 billion dollars—one-third of the direct monetary cost of the First World War. Moreover, the moral repugnance against petty gambling has not been brought to bear upon this institutionalized gambling in securities. It is told that one pious railroad promoter, Daniel Drew, frequently fell on his knees and exhorted God to help him outguess his competitors in reducing railroad finance to the level of a gambling casino. Even one of our most distinguished Federal jurists, who in his earlier days was undoubtedly impelled by honest moral scruples to launch a crusade against racetrack gambling, did not hesitate to act as an attorney for some of our foremost financial speculators.[19]

The attempt to drive gambling out of existence by directly hostile legislation in this country has had the same general effect as the directly repressive legislation against prostitution, liquor, and drugs. In other words, it has thrown organized gambling into the hands of racketeers and organized criminals. From gambling the latter derive an enormous revenue, and they introduce crooked methods which destroy any modicum of chance and luck.

It is estimated that the total gambling turnover of the country is at least 15 billion dollars annually. Of this, not more than one billion can be described as legitimate gambling. About half of the latter takes place through sanctified and quasi-sanctified lotteries, "bingo" parties, and the like, conducted by charitable and religious groups and by public authorities.

Underworld control and "fixing" of gambling today. Racetrack gambling has taken on a new scope and impetus with the development of what is called *pari-mutuel* betting at race tracks, and under the "bookie," or handbook, system in city poolrooms and other gaming emporia. This system, which is too complicated to be described here, is popularly represented as a method of giving the betting public a real "break" in betting on horses, with some good chance of winning.[20] But it does not work out that way in actual practice. Through manipulating the tabulating system, confusing the accounting, doping horses, and fixing jockeys, the promoters can so arrange that the "sap" will never win in the long run.

Other popular methods of underworld gambling controlled by promoters are the numbers game, or the policy "racket," and slot machines —innumerable types of which are used by organized gamblers. The numbers game apparently was first developed in this country by the lottery gamblers a century ago. It was later revived among the Negroes of Harlem, from whom the big shot gamblers took over the system. The first important "czar" was Arthur Flegenheimer, better known as "Dutch Schultz."

The numbers game is a lottery which pays for the successful guessing of certain selected types of numbers, such as the total volume of daily bank clearings, the statement of the United States treasury balance, the

---

[19] See Upton Sinclair, *Upton Sinclair Presents William Fox*. Pasadena: Sinclair, 1933.

[20] For good descriptions of the system and its ramifications, see F. O. Nelson and D. T. Kelliher, "Straight, Place—But No Show," *Ken*, December 1, 1938; and F. B. Warren, "The Billion-Dollar Poolroom Racket," and "The Annenberg Race-Tip Empire," *The Nation*, July 30 and August 6, 1938.

runs scored in baseball games, and the pari-mutuel figures given out at selected racetracks. The results are thoroughly "fixed." To make this more feasible, the numbers which are now most generally used are those given out in connection with pari-mutuel racing. These are given much less publicity and can be more easily manipulated by the gamblers. At the James G. Hines trial in 1938, George Weinberg, Schultz's lieutenant, frankly and fully described the manner in which the numbers game is "fixed" so that the saps can never eventually win.[21]

The average participant in these forms of so-called gambling has no chance of winning in the long run. Everything is fixed and loaded in the interest of the gamblers who control the enterprise. It is determined just how much will be paid out to the suckers in winnings. The sum is just what is believed to be the minimum bait necessary to keep a sufficiently large number of suckers permanently interested in trying their "luck." As Thurman W. Arnold has suggested, the gambling operators may have learned this principle from corporation finance, in which just enough dividends were paid out of corporate earnings to keep a sufficient number of investors interested in purchasing securities.[22]

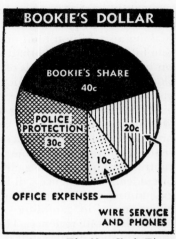

COURTESY *The New York Times.*

Graph illustrating financial operations of bookmakers who conduct much of the race track gambling in the United States.

Since the opportunities for gain in gambling are so much greater than in most forms of organized criminality, and because the risks of life, severe legal penalties, and conviction are so much less, the operators in "big crime" are now tending to shift more and more into gambling. For example, it is said on good authority that the most powerful group controlling racetrack gambling is a remnant of the old Capone gang. It has been alleged that slot machines are controlled mainly by Frank Costello and his underlings. Evidence also indicates that the vice and dope rings are linked with the gambling syndicates and are controlled by Charles "Lucky" Luciano who was convicted by Dewey and then released to take refuge in Italy where he is safe from American law enforcement officers. It is maintained on reasonable authority that Luciano and the notorious Italian *Mafia,* which has revived since the death of Mussolini, actually dominate the underworld of American organized crime, dope syndicates, racketeering, and gambling.

---

[21] For details on the fixing of the numbers game, see Cooper, *Here's to Crime,* Chap. VIII.

[22] *The Folklore of Capitalism.* New Haven: Yale University Press, 1937, pp. 214-215. For details, see Alden Winthrop, *Are You A Stockholder?* New York: Covici Friede, 1937.

Estimates of our gambling bill. There are, naturally, no definite figures of the nation's annual gambling bill, but the best recent studies by experts place it between 15 and 21 billion dollars. One study estimates that three billion dollars are gambled on the 75,000 slot machines in the country; three billion on the policy racket or numbers game; seven billion on horse races; and two billion on other forms of gambling—making a total of 15 billion dollars. Another estimate lists 1.5 billion dollars bet on horses through pari-mutuel betting and 4.5 billion through "bookies"— making a six billion total on horse racing; six billion on baseball games; one billion each on football and basketball games; one-third of a billion on boxing; and two-thirds of a billion on hockey. If the six billion bet on slot machines and the policy games is included, this would give a total gambling bill of 21 billion.[23]

Well-organized gambling reduces ordinary criminality and violence. One interesting and little known aspect of the development of highly-organized and smoothly-operating gambling is the fact that it has notably reduced conventional crime and violence in areas where it is heavily concentrated. The big-shot gambler knows all too well that any crime wave or epidemic of violence will be likely to cause investigations that may even extend to gambling operations. Hence, they give strict orders to the criminal elements in gambling centers to curb, as far as possible, ordinary criminality and violence. They are not always able to achieve complete success in such matters, but it is probable that in leading gambling centers the moguls of the gambling world do more to curb criminality than the police. The worst fears of the big gamblers were confirmed when the underworld got out of hand in the Kansas City murders of 1950 and the resulting violence helped to produce the Senatorial investigation of gambling on a national scale.

Proposed methods of dealing with organized gambling. There are two leading attitudes with respect to desirable and effective methods of suppressing organized gambling. Surely something needs to be done to suppress a type of activity which leads to the partial waste of a sum at least five to six times as great as that which we spend on public education at the present time.

The more traditional approach to the gambling menace recommends strict and fearless enforcement of all the laws against gambling. It is doubtless true that if such enforcement were literally possible, the vast majority of gambling could be eliminated. But this enforcement is extremely difficult in practice, primarily because of the collusion between the gambling syndicates, corrupt politicians, and many enforcement officers. The gamblers have vast sums with which to defeat law enforcement from many angles. It has always proved about as impossible to enforce laws against gambling as it was to carry out the laws supporting Prohibition. In the past, most attempts to suppress gambling have merely produced dramatic and much publicized crusades which tend to subside rather rapidly and quietly.

---

[23] For details on current gambling, see Albert Deutsch, *op. cit.*, pp. 284 ff.

The other approach advocates the legalizing of gambling, accompanied by a long-range campaign of relentless publicity and realistic education as to gambling realities. Such a campaign would seek to make clear the "fixed" character of the great majority of gambling enterprises and to reveal to the average citizen the impossibility of consistent winning in gambling activities. There is much logic in this position, but it has two major defects as a method of eliminating gambling. The first is that it would be difficult to launch and continue an adequate campaign of publicity and education. The second is that, even if citizens were told the facts, the average man would persist in believing that he is the exception to the rule and that he can "beat the game."

Though there is every reason to believe that the legalization of gambling would have little permanent effect in either increasing or decreasing the actual amount of gambling, those who advocate this solution hold that the main evils which result from the gambling situation in the United States today—the organized underworld which controls gambling, and the corruption of public officials and police systems—are a by-product of making gambling unlawful. They maintain that, if gambling were made legal, there would be no need for an underworld to operate it, no basis for the corruption of politicians and police to assure protection for illegal gambling, and no marked increase in gambling.

Those who favor legalization of gambling have recently derived much encouragement from the situation in England. In this country most forms of gambling are legal, notably betting on horses through bookmakers or in person, betting on dog races, and betting on soccer pools and lotteries. About a billion dollars are bet annually. But Britain has virtually no organized underworld, criminals do not control gambling, and neither officials nor police are corrupted by the gambling that takes place. A British Royal Commission was appointed in 1949 to investigate the whole problem of British gambling. It handed in its report in 1951, and this vigorously supported the British system of legal gambling. The Commission maintained that: "We can find no support for the belief that gambling, provided that it is kept within reasonable bounds, does serious harm either to the character of those who take part in it or to their family circle and the community generally. . . . The great majority of those who take part in gambling do not spend money on it recklessly and without regard to the effect of their expenditure on the standard of living of their families." Amazing as this may seem to the average American reader who follows the gambling debate in the United States, the Royal Commission actually recommended that gambling be made easier, so that the little man with only a few pennies of ready cash in his pocket could take part in gambling as well as his more fortunate superiors in the economic scale.

It is extremely unlikely that any such sensible attitude will gain a foothold here and that either the Federal government or the states will legalize gambling. What we may expect is a continuance of the present system, with its vast gambling bill, corruption of public officials and law enforcement agencies, sporadic investigations and crusades, and occasionally some new faces in the rogues' gallery of the top echelons of organized crime and gambling.

SPECIAL CRIMINAL TYPES AND PROBLEMS

The professional or habitual criminal. One of the most dangerous types of criminal is the professional or habitual criminal. Today he usually functions as a member of a criminal gang. The most spectacular recent professional criminals were men like John Dillinger, "Babyface" Nelson, "Prettyboy" Floyd, "Machine-gun" Kelly, and Alvin Karpis, who were dramatically portrayed a number of years ago as the top "public enemies" in the country. But such persons are not the most numerous or typical of professional criminals. We have quiet confidence men, forgers, professional swindlers, and the like, who receive much less publicity but cause far more economic loss than the more dramatic desperadoes.

Personality traits and mental patterns of the professional or habitual criminal. When a man has become a habitual criminal, as a result of various factors which will be described later on, and has been in prison, there is, indeed, a transformation in his personality. Such a person stands apart from normal citizens in his attitude toward law and society. Perhaps the best brief description of the mental attitudes of the habitual criminal ever set forth in brief form is that contained in an article by Jack Black, "A Burglar Looks at Laws and Codes," in *Harper's,* February, 1930.

The ordinary citizen has some respect for the social conventions and the laws of the land. He maintains his status, respectability, and prestige by obeying these laws. He gains distinction, in theory at least, through improving and defending the social order. The force of public opinion is thrown on the side of law observance.

With the habitual criminal all this is completely changed. The criminal gains his social position in the underworld by his success in breaking the law and in avoiding conviction. The bigger and better his crimes and the greater his success in evading the officers of the law, the higher looms the prestige of the criminal. There is a real caste society in the underworld based upon the degree of daring and swagger in criminal activity, and upon skill in evading the law. The criminal has only contempt for ordinary social conventions and the laws of society. Too often, he has good reason for developing this attitude. The public opinion of the underworld thus favors the commission of crimes and the breaking of laws. Scorn, if not bodily injury, may be vented upon the criminal who attempts to reform. He is frequently looked upon by the underworld as a contemptible backslider and quitter.

Although the habitual criminal has no respect for ordinary social morals, there is a code of honor in the underworld which puts that of respectable society to shame. The habitual criminal will seldom reveal to the police the name of another criminal who has mortally wounded him. He may kill a fellow criminal for doublecrossing him or for violating the code of the underworld, but he will rarely betray even the foulest stool-pigeon or double-crosser to the officers of the law. He may take

considerable risk to aid other criminals who have done him favors in
the past.

Difficulty of reforming the professional or habitual criminal. All this
makes it very difficult for the professional criminal to reform. Usually
he does not want to, for reform means accepting and living according to
the despised codes of the upperworld—orderly society. If this initial difficulty is overcome, reform is still almost unattainable. The criminal's
friends are all in the underworld. They will help him there, but they
will only hamper him in any efforts to leave it and go straight. Even
when he does go straight himself, he finds it difficult to keep out of the
hands of the law. He has many friends in the underworld who have
aided and befriended him in the past. They importune him for help and
he finds it hard to refuse. This keeps him in contact with the underworld
and always exposed to the danger of arrest and another conviction. Such
considerations as these throw much light upon the popular illusion that
every convicted criminal ought to want to reform and can easily do so if
he wishes to.

Most criminologists doubt that professional criminals ever reform
except infrequently when one of them leaves his criminal career as a result of physical and mental maturity which improves his social adjustments and lessens his willingness to take the risks involved in criminality.
Even in these cases, it is thought by many that such a reformed criminal
was hardly a true professional criminal.

What we have said about the psychology of the habitual criminal
hardly applies to the successful racketeer and organized criminal. His
ethics and psychology are only a degree removed from that of shady
business and finance. He merely wishes to get a great deal for nothing
and to get it quickly—essentials of the speculative ethics of our day. He
has few relations with what the public regards as the underworld, other
than to hire his gunmen and mobsters from this stratum. He need not
be at all ashamed in society. He associates with political leaders. He lives
in the best urban communities. He is secretly admired by many respectable people who know him. He attends the best night clubs and cabarets.
He has no incentive to reform, since he makes more money than the
doctor, lawyer, or engineer and is usually safer from arrest than the ordinary law-abiding citizen.

Women and criminality. The fact that there are many less women than
men in penal and correctional institutions—6,316 women as compared
with 158,811 men, at the beginning of the year 1950—has given rise to
a widespread opinion that women are inherently less prone to criminal
behavior than men. This common conception will hardly stand up under
analysis.

In the only thorough treatment of the subject in English, Otto Pollak
contends that our erroneous belief is based in part on statistical misconceptions and semantic confusion. Our most reliable criminal statistics
relate to convictions for felonies, but most typical female crimes are
misdemeanors for which women are not sent to prison. Women are prone
to commit crimes of violence under conditions and in situations which

are most favorable to secrecy and avoidance of suspicion of guilt, such as the murder of husbands. In such cases they avoid even arrest. When arrested, they have a better chance than men of escaping conviction in a jury trial.

There are also a number of logical explanations for the small number of incarcerated female felons that in no way imply any lesser proclivity of women to crime. The most frequent expression of female delinquency is prostitution, which is often not officially branded as a crime. Even when so regarded, it is a misdemeanor, not a felony. Moreover, prostitutes are often well protected by police or criminal organizations, and they thus escape arrest. Shoplifting is another common form of female delinquency. Stores usually decline to prosecute in such cases because of undesirable publicity. Blackmail, another form of female criminality, has to remain secret in order to be successful. In such cases it operates entirely beyond the reach of the law. The success of women in evading arrest is shown by the fact that in 1950 the women arrested accounted for only 9.6 per cent of the total arrests. The *Uniform Crime Reports* indicate that more than half of the women arrested are charged with prostitution, petty sex offenses, drunkenness, vagrancy, and petty larceny, which rarely lead to commission to penitentiaries even when convicted.

When need is a cause of crime in a family, it is the husband who usually goes out to steal and rob. Shrewd females realize that it is better to secure a husband or lover to commit crime rather than to engage in it personally. They become "gun molls" rather than killers or robbers, thus getting what benefits come from crime and escaping the more serious penalties. When women do commit conventional crimes, juries are often notoriously lenient with them. One interesting fact is that when it comes to serious crimes, delinquent women are more prone to murder and other crimes of physical violence than men. Women who consort with the moguls of the organized underworld usually become their mistresses rather than direct participants in criminal operations.

Sex criminals. The public is frequently shocked by hideous sex crimes and degenerate sex criminals. Many studies of this type of crime have demonstrated that serious and habitual sexual criminality is nearly always the by-product of a psychoneurotic personality. In other words, sex criminals are emotionally unstable.

Earlier investigations of this problem were recently confirmed by probably the most intensive study of convicted sex offenders yet undertaken —a two-year investigation of 102 sex offenders at Sing Sing Prison by David Abrahamsen, an able professional psychiatrist. He found that all of them were victims of emotional disturbances and that more than half of them belonged in psychiatric hospitals rather than in prison. Over 75 per cent of the group studied were recidivists in sex crimes. Abrahamsen and other recent students of sex criminals are agreed that there is no such thing as a unique sex psychopath who is responsible for most sex crimes. Mentally and emotionally unstable persons who commit sex crimes constitute a highly diversified group of mentally disturbed types.

Cases of sex crimes should be handled by psychiatrists rather than by the police, courts, and prisons. Sex criminals should be segregated in hospitals rather than prisons, and they should be kept there until a cure is effected. Commenting on the findings of the Sing Sing study, F. Lovell Bixby, a trained clinical psychologist and veteran prison administrator, wisely warned that mere routine treatment in either a state or private mental hospital will not suffice to handle the problem of sex criminals. If we wish a high percentage of cures, this must be supplemented by specialized individual and group therapy and by suitable work, recreational, and educational programs. If a cure cannot be effected, sex criminals should be segregated. It is absurd to send them to prisons and then to release them. There is every prospect that their proneness to sexual criminality will be increased rather than reduced by prison life.

A relevant comment here is that the situation in regard to sexual crimes would be improved if many minor sex crimes were removed from the statute books and recognized as a field for psychiatric and social work. By minor sex crimes we mean those which have no serious personal or social consequences, not necessarily those which figure as minor in criminal codes. Heavy penalties are often imposed in criminal codes for sexual irregularities that are of no great social consequence and are severely penalized mainly because of popular prejudice against them.

THE JUVENILE OFFENDER AND THE INCREASING CHALLENGE OF JUVENILE DELINQUENCY

Youth predominates in the crime picture today. One of the most significant and ominous aspects of the crime situation today is the prevalence of minors in the crime picture of our time. This challenge of juvenile crime is underlined by the fact that Sheldon and Eleanor Glueck, in the most extensive study yet made of juvenile delinquents, found that no less than 88.2 per cent of those studied continued their delinquency in adult life. Twenty years ago the Wickersham Committee found that 54.8 per cent of our convicts were under 21 at the time of their first conviction. Juvenile delinquency has increased since that time, especially during the war decade of the 1940's.

We lack precise information on the extent and growth of juvenile delinquency in this country. Writing in *Federal Probation,* September, 1949, I. J. Perlman pointed out that "nation-wide data on the extent of juvenile delinquency are not available." Most of what we know about the matter is contributed by Federal agencies such as the United States Children's Bureau and the Federal Bureau of Investigation. But this is hardly more than extensive sampling. For example, the Children's Bureau reports for 1948 cover only the cases handled in 399 juvenile courts in 17 states. The FBI reports on the number of juvenile delinquents fingerprinted in any year also give a very incomplete picture of the total amount of juvenile delinquency. Many jurisdictions do not fingerprint juveniles, and others that do fail to send the material to the FBI. Even if we knew the exact number of juveniles arrested and convicted each year, this would give us a very incomplete notion of the extent of juvenile delinquency. Albert

Deutsch and other expert students of the problem believe that for every juvenile delinquent who is arrested no less than 20 escape apprehension altogether. We can, however, set down some of the information we do possess.

The FBI reported that the number of girls under 18 arrested increased by 198 per cent between 1939 and 1946. The number of boys under 18 arrested for drunkenness increased by 100 per cent; for assault, 72 per cent; for rape, 70 per cent; for automobile theft, 55 per cent; for homicide, 48 per cent; and for robbery, 39 per cent. In 1945 the largest number of crimes committed by any age-group in the country were the work of

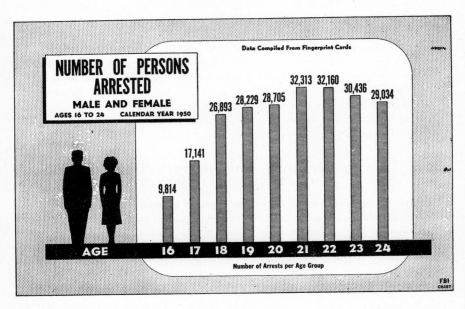

persons 17 years of age. In that year more than 80 per cent of all automobile thefts, 65 per cent of the burglaries, 58 per cent of the robberies, 48 per cent of the rapes, and 40 per cent of the larcenies were committed by persons under 25 years of age. In 1949 persons under 21 accounted for 27.4 per cent of all crimes against property. In 1950, the largest number of persons arrested were 21 years of age, with the years 22, 23, 24, and 25 following in order. Some 31.9 per cent of all those arrested were under 25 years of age. It is estimated that about 275,000 cases of juvenile delinquency reach the courts each year. If there are 20 cases of delinquency to every one brought to the courts, then we would have a figure of over five million crimes committed each year by juveniles.

As to current trends in juvenile delinquency, such sampling as we have indicates that it reached a peak in 1945 and has fallen off somewhat since, though it is at least 25 per cent higher than in 1938. Its continuing prevalence is attested to by the fact that samplings indicate that about half the cases each year represent first offenses. If newspaper accounts afford any basis for judgment, it would appear that juvenile delinquency is again rising at the mid-century.

Increase in juvenile delinquency and laxness indicates prevalence of social and personal disorganization. In recent years our newspapers and periodicals have carried much alarmist material describing the growth of juvenile crime and moral laxity. And there has been a good basis for the alarmist tone, for the depressing picture painted is all too true. Youthful homicide has been on the increase, including many shocking sex crimes committed by juveniles. A disproportionate number of young persons have been implicated in the growth of violence and terrorism in our cities which is described by Howard Whitman in his *Terror in the Streets.* Sensational sex orgies, sometimes involving adult participants, have been repeatedly reported in the press. The greatest increase of venereal disease in recent years has been among "teen-agers." Drunkenness is on the gain in the juvenile group. Drug addiction of various types, even among groups of high school age, has of late become a national scandal. All of this adds up to a striking demonstration of the breakdown of traditional morality and social controls. Social and personal disorganization have grown markedly as the result of many causes, in which wars and uncertainties about the future have played their part. The rural family has disintegrated, city family life is loose and ineffective as a control factor, and community agencies have not developed with sufficient rapidity to provide substitutes for earlier types of guidance and controls for youth.

Juvenile criminal gangs. During recent years organized gangs of juvenile delinquents have appeared in our larger cities. They have not only committed serious crimes but have conducted gang warfare somewhat reminiscent of the old Capone days in Chicago. In June, 1950, *The New York Times* asserted:

There are in New York City between 150 and 180 active teen-age gangs composed of boys and girls who beat up victims, steal, commit sex crimes, smuggle and use narcotics, and sometimes kill. Last year, twelve boys were killed in such gang fighting. In one gang fight in this same month, 105 special policemen were needed to restore order. Most of these gangs are drawn from slum areas, but one of the worst is recruited from upper-income schoolboys who specialize in crashing parties in wealthy homes, breaking up furniture and stealing.

Some reasons for the growth and prevalence of juvenile crime. There are a number of reasons for the alarming amount of juvenile delinquency. As is the case with adult criminality, mental disease, vice, suicide, and all other acute manifestations of social pathology, the growth of juvenile crime can be attributed fundamentally to the increase of social and personal disorganization which, as we have seen, is a product of the sweeping industrial and social changes of the last hundred years.

With the growth of the large city, family discipline has broken down. Even in the rural districts, the restraining influence of family life is not as strong as it was in former days. The importance of the family breakdown is further pointed up by the fact that over one-fourth of all juvenile delinquents come from broken homes—families in which the father or the mother, or both, have deserted their children. Such students of juvenile delinquency as Charles W. Coulter believe that disorganized families—those with chronic quarreling and with defective discipline and training habits—do even more to increase juvenile delinquency than broken homes. Cyril Burt, in England, found that these family defects were seven times as numerous in the homes of delinquents as in those of nondelinquents, and Sheldon Glueck found such deficiencies of discipline in 70 per cent of delinquent homes.

Today there is also more opportunity for young folks to get into mischief. The city is a place of excitement and temptation. With little restraining background of sound family discipline, it is small wonder that many boys have trouble with the law. A large percentage of boys from 16 to 21 cannot find work; others, who do not want to work, hunt for schemes that will bring in money without involving work. Both types are often persuaded to take jobs of a crooked nature offered to them by criminals and racketeers. Many juvenile offenders take the first step toward a life of crime because they need money for amusement or to entertain a girl friend. Once the first downward steps are taken, the juvenile delinquent finds it easier to follow the criminal pattern than to take up a life of hard work and discipline.

In their recent book on juvenile delinquency, *Unravelling Juvenile Delinquency*,[24] Eleanor and Sheldon Glueck emphasize the fact that juvenile delinquents are more likely to be illegitimate children than nondelinquents; that they are more frequently descended from retarded fathers and mothers; that they come preponderantly from disorganized homes, many of them having run away from home; that they early reveal emotional instability and delinquent behavior; that they dislike school experience and discipline and are given to truancy; that they often join street gangs; that they frequent poolrooms, dance halls, and "dives"; and that they crave physical activity and adventure more than noncriminal youths.

Frederic M. Thrasher, in his study of over 1,300 juvenile gangs in the city of Chicago, came to the conclusion that juvenile delinquency centers in the slum areas of large cities, and that the juvenile delinquent's career usually begins with truancy from school and membership in some youthful gang. The children of the slums often have no place to play except in the streets. Here they form bad associations. They raid the corner fruit store, break store windows, and soon are arrested by the patrolman on the beat. They are then on the high road to professional criminality.

In one way, at least, unwise laws contribute to the growth of juvenile delinquency. That is in branding truancy as a crime and bringing truants into the courts and into contact with hardened delinquents. A career of crime may be started or stimulated in this manner. Truancy is a problem which requires the services of social workers, psychiatrists and child-

---

24 New York: Commonwealth Fund, 1950.

guidance clinics rather than of the police, courts, and institutions for delinquents.

The problems created by wayward youths have received serious attention in the last few years because of the enormous increase of juvenile delinquency that accompanied the Second World War. Frequently suggested measures to deal with the growing menace of juvenile delinquency have included better civic and vocational education, family counseling, more ample urban recreational facilities, psychiatric clinics, and wider use of juvenile courts and probation.

CRIMINALS AND CONVICTS

Convicts provide a very inadequate conception of the criminal class. When the average person hears the word *criminal,* he almost invariably thinks of the inmates of penal and reformatory institutions. But the convicts represent only a very small and specialized group within the whole criminal class, and they throw only limited light upon the nature of criminals in general. Today our convicts are chiefly old derelicts and unruly youths. They are, for the most part, the stupid, unlucky, or inexperienced minority of those who commit crime. Moreover, the crimes which they commit are usually the less dangerous and expensive and more traditional types of offenses.

If we were to concentrate our attention upon the contagious section of a charity ward in a city hospital, we would obtain a very restricted and imperfect notion of the problem of health and disease in the population at large. We can obtain no more satisfactory conception of criminality and of criminals by studying convicts—although, of course, we should attempt to learn as much as we possibly can about the convict group, because they are the only criminals we can study. The brighter and more alert element among those who commit even the traditional crimes often escape conviction; indeed, they frequently evade arrest. For the most part, we gather in only the scum of the habitual criminals and inexperienced youth. Let us look realistically at the composition of the criminal class as a whole.

Ranks and grades of criminals. Who are the great criminals? The usual answer given to this question would be to name much publicized desperadoes like John Dillinger. But any such conception would be entirely misleading. Their reputation has been built up by the newspapers, by their prosecutors, and by more sensational writers on crime. Dillinger, at the height of his career, was not even Public Enemy No. 1,000.

The leaders of the criminal world today are the master minds and directors of organized crime, racketeering, and gambling. Since they are rarely convicted, we usually cannot know just who they are. Al Capone was one of them, but he was only one of the crude pioneers in this field. Certain journalists and many politicians know well enough who the leaders of organized crime, racketeering, and gambling actually are, but they have little inclination to tell. They remember all too well the case of Jake Lingle, the Chicago newspaper man, who was unceremoniously "bumped off" because he knew too much and because there was a fear that he might tell some of the things he knew. The files of the secret service committee of organized crime discourage most politicians from divulging any information they possess. The public, then, is mainly in the dark concerning the identity and the actual character of those who control the great empire of organized crime in our day. The Kefauver Committee has recently let in some light on the personnel and operations of that sector of the criminal group which operates organized gambling and related enterprises.

Next below them come such professional desperadoes as Dillinger and his ilk. However spectacular their criminal deeds may be, this type is not numerous and their depredations are relatively unimportant when viewed from the angle of the financial losses involved.

Then, in order, would probably come the gangsters and gunmen who serve the big shot criminals and gamblers, preserve discipline, and protect the local monopoly in organized crime and racketeering. Occasionally one of these is convicted and his name gets into the newspapers, but, as we shall see later, it is relatively difficult to identify and convict even a gangster who is operating subordinately in connection with one of the major rackets.

Continuing down the list, we finally have to consider those criminals who commit the traditional offenses: robbery, burglary, thievery, petty frauds, and the like, and also the crimes of violence which come about incidental to their effort to get something for nothing. With this group we would also have to list those who commit various types of crime, particularly crimes of violence, as a result of psychopathic compulsions and temporary passion. Our convicts are, as we have already suggested, usually the least competent, the least fortunate, or the least experienced members of this last group, the traditional offenders.

It has been estimated that there are about two million criminals in the United States, but at any given time there are only about 160,000 convicts in all Federal and state penal institutions. Many of these are not true criminals at all—at least not until the degenerating influences of prison life have made criminals out of them. Some of them are normal persons like ourselves who have committed an act of violence under stress of great temporary emotion. Another group is made up of those who violated the law through ignorance or accident, but who did not have the influence or money to get cleared by the authorities or the courts. Others are more properly cases for social work or cases which should be handled in institutions for the feeble-minded and the psychopathic.

From what has been said above, it is evident that we must take an altogether different view of the criminal class in the United States from that which has prevailed in conventional descriptions and analyses of American criminals. It is a strange and deplorable state of affairs when we find ourselves at the mercy of unnamed men who are rarely even brought forth and subjected to the condemnation of public opinion, to say nothing of being convicted and incarcerated.

THE CONVICT GROUP

Relatively slight importance of traditional crimes and convicts. We frankly concede that traditional crimes are a nuisance—even a calamity—and that they should be eliminated as speedily as possible. But they do not constitute the essence of the crime problem today. Clarence Darrow once remarked to the writer that he did not think it would make much, if any, difference if the doors of all our prisons, penitentiaries, and reformatories were opened and the inmates were invited to walk out to freedom.

At the time this seemed a very shocking statement. But there was a considerable modicum of truth in the observation. Certainly, Darrow was far closer to the truth than some academic criminologists and the man-on-the-street, who look upon convicts as the only dangerous criminal element in society. Moreover, our prisons are certainly a liability to society, so far as their moral and psychological influence on criminals is concerned. For every criminal who is reformed or made more law-abiding by prison life, probably ten are made habitual criminals or are made more bitter in their attitude toward society and better trained for criminal depredations.

One might legitimately raise the question of how one can logically say, for example, that murder, assault, and robbery do not merit serious attention. We make no such assertion. It may be taken for granted that all the traditional crimes are reprehensible and a loss to the nation. They should be stamped out as rapidly and completely as possible.

It is a fact, however, that a majority of the more serious crimes of physical violence are committed as the result of psychopathic compulsions or as a product of the organized gang warfare associated with large-scale crime and racketeering. The first type of murder and assault cases—those growing out of psychopathic conditions—are a problem for mental hygiene and psychiatry rather than for criminology and penology. The latter group of violent crimes are obviously the outgrowth of organized crime and racketeering. The financial losses from traditional forms of crime are less for the nation as a whole each year than the annual cost of rackets in New York City alone.

These are the sound and substantial reasons why we simply befog the issue and bring about intellectual confusion when we clutter up the treatment of contemporary crime and criminals by concentrating all our attention upon traditional offenses and offenders. Even less defensible is it to consider primarily the convicts, who are, as a rule, the most stupid and least dangerous element in the whole criminal group.

It is desirable, however, to emphasize the fact that recognition of the primary importance today of white-collar organized crime, racketeering, and gambling should not blind us to appropriate apprehensiveness and action in dealing with any novel development of crimes of violence. The most relevant issue here right now is the growth of terrorism in cities carried on by hoodlums, wanton attackers, rapists and other sex criminals, slashers, muggers, and the like. As we have pointed out, the increasing menace of such criminal types has been made clear by Howard Whitman in his book, *Terror in the Streets.*

Extent and relative frequency of traditional crimes. The nature and relative number of traditional crimes committed in the United States, so far as reported, is revealed by the following figures taken from the *Uniform Crime Reports* of the Federal Bureau of Investigation for the period of January to June, 1950:

TOTAL CRIMES

	Urban			Rural	
Crime	Number	Rate per 100,000 of Population	Crime	Number	Rate per 100,000 of Population
Larceny and theft .	296,549	499.1	Larceny and theft .	44,961	113.3
Burglary	125,666	211.5	Burglary	36,611	92.2
Auto theft	51,395	83.8	Auto theft	9,188	23.1
Assault	24,188	39.4	Assault	7,378	18.6
Robbery	18,432	30.0	Robbery	4,009	10.1
Rape	3,702	6.03	Rape	2,383	6.00
Murder and non-negligent man-slaughter	1,691	2.76	Murder and non-negligent man-slaughter	1,123	2.83
Negligent man-slaughter	1,086	1.77	Negligent man-slaughter	903	2.27

The number of persons convicted and sent to prisons and reformatories for the above crimes in a representative year is given in the following table covering Federal and state prisons and reformatories for the year 1946:

	Total received by offenses	Percentage of total
Burglary	10,150	18.0
Larceny	9,693	17.2
Auto theft	5,219	9.2
Robbery	5,207	9.2
Criminal homicide	3,712	6.6
Aggravated assault	3,583	6.3
Rape	2,327	4.1
All other offenses	16,586	29.4

Nature of the average convict group. When we consider the nature of the human beings who commit traditional crimes, we naturally can study only the convicts. Since the brighter, more experienced, and luckier offenders almost never get behind bars, we can seldom investigate their nature and makeup. Therefore, we rarely have a chance to consider any other than the more stupid and unlucky minority of petty criminals who make up our convict group. The convicts are thoroughly compatible with the offenses they commit.

If we were to look over the convict population of any average state

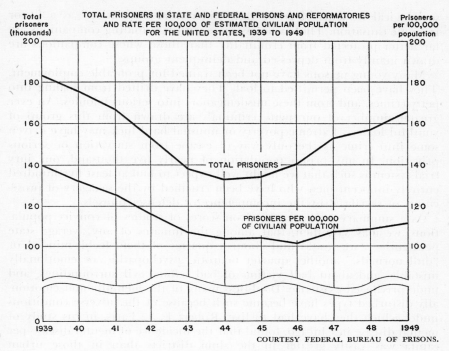

Total prisoners (thousands)

TOTAL PRISONERS IN STATE AND FEDERAL PRISONS AND REFORMATORIES AND RATE PER 100,000 OF ESTIMATED CIVILIAN POPULATION FOR THE UNITED STATES, 1939 TO 1949

Prisoners per 100,000 population

TOTAL PRISONERS

PRISONERS PER 100,000 OF CIVILIAN POPULATION

1939 40 41 42 43 44 45 46 47 48 1949

COURTESY FEDERAL BUREAU OF PRISONS.

Prisoners in state and federal prisons and reformatories.

prison, we would find some men here who are feeble-minded. They have the intelligence of a boy of six to ten years. They are incapable of self-control and are easily influenced by suggestion. Brought up in evil surroundings, they have drifted into crime. There is little hope of reforming them.

Others have glands that are too active or too sluggish in their operation. This condition has helped to make them vicious, abnormal, or unbalanced. Without proper medical attention or decent surroundings, they may turn to crime. Many are psychopathic and neurotic—that is, nervously unbalanced. Some may have superior mentalities but lack stability and self-control. Extreme nervousness may have prevented them from getting and holding a job. Their lack of control leads them to succumb easily to temptation. Some are driven by strong compulsions to commit crimes of violence.

Others, a rather small minority, are physically sick. Their diseases reduce their capacity to labor and their resistance to the strains of life. They may lapse into crime from sheer despair or desperation. A great many more have healthy bodies but have been compelled to live their lives in unhealthy environments—"delinquency areas." They have dwelt in slums. They have been denied healthy recreation. Their communities have swarmed with criminal gangs. Crime has been all around them and they have climbed on the band wagon. They are the victims of what sociological students of crime call "differential association" as a factor in crime causation. Those who associate with law-abiding companions are far better protected from criminality than those whose companions are drawn mainly from depressed and delinquent groups.

Many young persons have not been trained for profitable employment. They have been permitted to loaf. They have drifted from loafing into petty crimes, and from these misdemeanors into serious felonies. An ever greater number of our petty criminals are drawn from this group of youthful loafers. Extreme poverty or unusual hard luck may have driven some into crime as the only way of escape from starvation or serious privation. In any prison population of nearly five thousand, our jury trial system is such that we might well expect to find at least five hundred entirely innocent men who have been crucified by the savagery of prosecutors or sacrificed by the incompetence of defense counsels.

As a summary estimate, based on scores of studies of convict populations, we may say, then, that among the inmates of any average state penitentiary, we would find about a quarter of them feeble-minded or "dull normals," another quarter neurotic, psychopathic, or emotionally unstable, and about half victims of bad habits, evil surroundings, and underprivileged existence. Doubtless many of the mentally and emotionally disturbed types have become such because of the adverse conditions under which they have had to live. Robert E. L. Faris, in his study of mental disease in Chicago, found that the incidence of mental disease per capita was vastly greater in the slum districts than in those urban districts which permitted decent living conditions.

Mental defects and mental disease among convicts. Studies of the intelligence of convict populations by William T. Root, Carl Murchison, E. A. Doll, S. H. Tulchin, and others have thoroughly blasted the once prevalent notion that criminality is chiefly due to feeblemindedness. Such studies of convict mentality have shown that even these convict dregs of the criminal class compare fairly well in respect to intelligence with the general run of the population as sampled by the army mental tests. This fact would certainly imply that the criminal class as a whole, including all the master minds of organized crime, is distinctly superior in native intelligence to the general population. In any event, it is obvious that feeble-mindedness is not a predominant characteristic of criminals. Yet we can not overlook its importance, for it has an effect upon some types of criminality out of proportion to the numerical ratio of the feeble-minded in the population. For example, William Healy found that "the feeble-minded appear among serious delinquents from five to ten times more frequently than in the general population." But even among the serious delinquents, the feeble-minded are greatly outnumbered by the mentally normal. The common notion that the feeble-minded are "naturally" delinquent is absurd. They are simply more susceptible to suggestion than normal types and less able to control their conduct by knowledge and reflection. Therefore, in criminal surroundings they are more easily led into crime.

The same qualifications apply to a somewhat frequent recent inclination to account for criminality mainly on the basis of a mentally diseased or unstable condition, crime being regarded socially as a morbid manifestation of mental and nervous disease. The facts no more support this theory than they do the doctrine that crime is an outgrowth of feeble-mindedness. The studies which have been made in this field reveal that the proportion of psychopathic, neurotic, and emotionally disturbed types among the convicts is about the same as the proportion of feeble-minded. Since we have no accurate census of the psychopathic and emotionally unstable in the general population, we cannot say whether the per capita ratio of these types among convicts is greater than their frequency in the population as a whole. But it would appear rather well established today that not more than a quarter of our convicts go into crime because of mental and nervous disorders. And, as we have suggested above, such disturbances may be rendered acute or aggravated by adverse living conditions.

It is important, however, to emphasize once more the fact that serious mental disease is not the only psychological cause of crime. Lesser mental disturbances, neurotic conditions, bad habits, sexual aberrations, behavior disorders, emotional instability and the like probably account for much more traditional criminal behavior than do psychoses and other serious forms of mental abnormality.

Another important point to remember is that we usually have only those convicted of crime to study when we are trying to discover their mental and emotional states. This means that many of those studied have already served one or more prison terms and that any mentally and emotionally unstable convicts may have been made such, or their condition aggravated, by the psychic ravages of prison life. Therefore, a study of convicts presents a very imperfect method of discovering what mental and emotional factors, if any, led a given convict into a criminal career. The medical director of the Federal Bureau of Prisons estimated that not over 15 per cent of adult felons in our prisons are completely normal mentally and emotionally, and suggested that prison life itself probably accounted for much of this instability of personality.

Economic and social basis of most traditional criminality. Looking at traditional crimes and criminals in a broad way, one may certainly say that economic and social factors are the most potent reasons for the commission of such offenses. It is usually lack of funds, needs, or desperation which originally stimulate the commission of the majority of these crimes, in the same way that greed and ambition urge on the organized criminals, racketeers, and gamblers. It is apparent that poverty, unemployment, life in the slums or other unhealthy habitats, and sundry other evil results of an underprivileged and undernourished existence—all contributing to social and personal disorganization—lie at the basis of most of our traditional criminality other than compulsive crimes of violence. This conclusion need not be taken to imply any Marxian interpretation whatever. It is simply based upon statistical reports and elementary logic. And it fully recognizes the fact that many traditional crimes are committed without any important economic motive at all discernible. And, of course, after some economic motive has once led to criminal conduct, delinquency may become habitual, even if poverty does not remain an impelling factor. We have already indicated how economic factors underlie the slum life and delinquency areas that produce anti-social groups and create the "deviant association" which many criminologists look upon as the main cause of much delinquency.

The above discussion of convicts and the causes of traditional criminality leads naturally to a consideration of the leading theories which have been advanced to explain criminality and the criminal personality.

THEORIES OF CRIMINALITY AND THE CRIMINAL PERSONALITY

Our knowledge of criminals is mainly knowledge of convicts. In the preceding pages of this chapter we have mentioned briefly from time to time the various causes of crime and the nature of criminals. Since theories about the nature of criminals are still a matter of considerable controversy and a large factor in all discussions of the crime problem, we may profitably examine in a brief but comprehensive fashion, the leading types of explanations that have been offered to account for the criminal and his delinquent propensities. It is essential at the outset of this discussion to emphasize once more that all, or most, theories of criminality are based on studies of convicts who furnish a very incomplete picture of the whole criminal class.

Theological conceptions of the criminal. For centuries, the main explanation of criminals was of a religious nature—that criminals are those unbelievers who succumb to the temptations of the Devil. They commit crime because they have deliberately adopted perverse criminal ways. This theory hardly accords with current thought, and it has more recently been specifically discredited because it has been shown that the great majority of criminals profess to have espoused orthodox religious beliefs and to have been reared in the "fold."

Biological conception of the born criminal. The first quasi-scientific approach to the explanation of the criminal personality was that which claimed that the criminal is a definite biological type, afflicted with inferior hereditary physical traits. In other words, the criminal is born to commit crime. The leading apostle of this theory was Cesare Lombroso (1836-1909), who first set forth this doctrine about 75 years ago. Lombroso held that the peculiar physical traits of the born criminal are the result of an atavistic regression to a more primitive or savage type of man. His theories were mainly discredited by the studies of Charles Goring, an eminent English criminologist. We no longer believe that any man is born to commit crime, though we realize that he may inherit personality qualities which make him unusually susceptible to criminal compulsions and temptations.

More recently, the eminent Harvard anthropologist, Earnest A. Hooton, has claimed, in his *Crime and the Man,* that criminals tend to be biologically inferior and that certain races have a special proclivity to particular types of crimes. His theory is not widely accepted, though many critics base their rejection of it on less extensive study than the researches of Hooton, which are embodied in his gigantic statistical treatise, *The American Criminal*. Moreover, much of Hooton's material holds up fairly well if interpreted on the basis of cultural rather than racial traits.

Another interesting biological theory of crime has been developed by William H. Sheldon in his books, *The Varieties of Human Physique* (1940); *The Varieties of Temperament* (1942); and *Varieties of Delinquent Youth* (1949). Sheldon finds a definite physiological basis for the leading physical and personality types, including delinquents. Most criminologists have been no more cordial to this approach than to that of Hooton.

Economic theories of crime. Other students of crime, who hold that crime is chiefly caused by poverty and economic need, attribute crime mainly to economic causes. The outstanding figure in this school of criminological thought was the eminent Dutch criminologist, William A. Bonger. One of the greatest of all criminologists, Enrico Ferri, supported this view in a more moderate version. The distinguished American criminal lawyer and criminologist, Clarence Darrow, was also inclined to accept the view that most criminals commit their crimes because of the pressure exerted by poverty. This doctrine probably does explain much of traditional criminality, if it is broadened to include the reasons why persons find themselves in poverty, embracing even such factors as inadequate vocational education.

Poverty, however, does not explain white-collar crime or crimes committed by organized criminals and racketeers. Here greed and the something-for-nothing motivation come into play, and the chief theorist in this field was the famous American economist, Thorstein Veblen. Veblen's doctrines concerning the predatory origins of capitalism and the something-for-nothing trend in its later and more pathological developments throw more light on white-collar crime and racketeering than any other explanation. The leading expositor of the notion of white-collar criminality was Edwin H. Sutherland, but his own interpretation of criminality was primarily sociopsychological rather than economic.

Psychological and psychiatric interpretations of crime. Psychological theories of the criminal personality date back to nearly a century ago, when Albert Morel explained criminality as due to mental degeneracy and Henry Maudsley regarded criminals as victims of moral insanity. Raffaele Garofalo, a contemporary of Lombroso, contended that criminals are produced by inherited moral degeneracy. But truly scientific psychological interpretations of the criminal personality date from the present century—beginning with the studies of such psychiatrists as William Healy and Bernard Glueck. They have shown that approximately 25 per cent of the usual convict population are psychotic, neurotic, or emotionally unstable, and about an equal number are mentally defective or retarded. Diseased and disturbed mental states do not literally make persons criminals, but they do account for increased susceptibility to temptation to criminal action. These psychiatric studies also help to explain special types of compulsive criminals like kleptomaniacs, pyromaniacs, and sex criminals.

Another psychological approach to crime is that which attributes crime chiefly to feeble-mindedness, which is assumed to be inherited. This doctrine was especially proposed by H. H. Goddard, to whom we owe much of our early scientific knowledge regarding the feeble-minded. It has been greatly limited and modified by later studies which have shown that even convicts compare favorably in intelligence with the noncriminal population and also have proved that at least half of the extant feeble-mindedness is not hereditary.

Carl Murchison, a professional psychologist, concluded that the convict populations he studied manifested a somewhat higher degree of intelligence than the general noncriminal population. But later studies by William H. Root and others seem to indicate that the truth is that convicts are neither more nor less intelligent than the noncriminal element. If one were to include in the criminal class the smarter professional criminals who are rarely caught and convicted, the white-collar criminals, and the master minds in organized crime and racketeering, however, Murchison's theory of the superior intelligence of the criminal class would be amply vindicated. The importance of feeble-mindedness as a causative element in traditional crimes (especially those of physical violence), however, should not be minimized.

Sociological views of crime. Finally, we come to the social, or sociological, explanations of the criminals. The first great sociological interpretation of crime was set forth by the famed French sociologist, Gabriel Tarde (1843-1904). He held that crime is chiefly due to social forces, especially imitation. Although we do not accept this as a complete explanation of all crime, it is valuable in helping us to understand crime waves—extensive repetition of similar crimes. Even more cogent was the suggestion of William I. Thomas, who believed that crime is mainly a product of personal and social disorganization—the breakdown of the social institutions which ordinarily control and limit human actions.

Sociologists, led by Edwin H. Sutherland and others, stress what is known as "deviant" or "differential" association as a cause of crime. Those who associate mainly with law-abiding groups in good living conditions have protection against criminal temptations and habits. The reverse is also true: those who live in depressed areas and in unfortunate social surroundings, and associate with quasi-criminal and criminal companions are more likely to be led into criminal behavior. They are also more likely to be seized by the police and to be more easily convicted, if arrested. They have less prospect of adequate social or legal protection. This helps to explain the greater preponderance of crime in depressed urban districts—the so-called delinquency areas.

A number of sociologists have devoted their study of criminality mainly to the related investigation of the social background and ecology of crime and criminals. Notable here has been the work of Clifford Shaw, Frederic M. Thrasher, and Stuart Lottier.

Cultural interpretation of crime. Closely related to the sociological approach to crime is the cultural interpretation. This explains the prevailing types of crime, the frequency of crime, and the type of punishments meted out for crime as the result of the dominant cultural traits of any period. Georg Rusche and Otto Kirchheimer especially have propounded this theory in their work on *Punishment and the Social Structure* (1939). They show how the crimes and punishments of our time are conditioned, if not determined, by capitalism, the machine age, and the profit motive. The Italian writer, M. A. Vaccaro, has suggested that much crime is a result of inability to adapt to cultural change. Many individuals are unable to do so, become maladjusted, and drift into crime. Thorsten Sellin and others have dealt with the relation between criminality and the increase of cultural conflicts which grow out of the greater mobility of our time. Students of immigration and crime have made it clear that the high crime rate among children of immigrants is mainly due to cultural conflicts. The most menacing criminality of today—organized crime, racketeering, white-collar crime, and the like—is closely associated with the ideals of the shadier side of finance capitalism and financial speculation, as Sutherland and Ernest D. McDougall have demonstrated at length. The cultural interpretation of crime is most completely embodied in the work of Donald R. Taft, *Criminology* (1950).

The individual approach to the criminal. All of these explanations of the criminal help us to understand the nature of the criminal and the causes of crime. But the basic scientific position today is that the criminal is an individual personality and that we can understand what made him a criminal only through a prolonged study of his particular case. This view of the matter was first forcibly stated in the classic work of William Healy, *The Individual Delinquent,* published in 1915. This book has very literally become the "Bible" of truly scientific criminology in our day. Although Healy's approach to the individual delinquent was psychiatric, Clifford Shaw and his associates have studied the individual delinquent through the application of W. I. Thomas' life-history technique in such books as *The Natural History of a Delinquent Career,* and *The Jack Roller.* Today it is generally conceded that each criminal must be studied and treated individually. This conception of the individual approach to the criminal and his treatment has been the basis for our present conception of the necessity of a careful study and classification of criminals and the individualization of treatment in any rational program for the reform of convicts.

Immediately related to this individual and life-history approach to criminality is Sheldon Glueck's famous "maturation" theory of criminality. According to Glueck, criminality is stimulated by the physical vigor, sex urges, adventurous spirit, tensions, and adjustment problems of youth. Although all normal youths are affected by such problems, some react in abnormal and antisocial ways and become delinquents. After the period of youth has passed, there are physical changes, mental adjustments, and social adaptations, which tend to reduce the drive to antisocial behavior, provided that other conditions do not make this impossible. It is Glueck's theory that most cases of so-called reformation of criminals in mid-life are due to maturation rather than to the deterrent influence of punishment and prison life.[25]

THE PREVENTION OF CRIME

Two aspects of crime prevention efforts. In the prevention of crime there are two main fields of possible action. One is the arrest of criminals who have violated the law, their speedy conviction, if guilty, and their scientific treatment until they are reformed, if rehabilitation is possible. England and Canada have made it evident in recent years that a high prospect of arrest and conviction actually does reduce the crime rate. The other logical area of activity in preventing crime lies in various broad social policies and reforms that will prevent persons from becoming criminals. We shall now consider various aspects of the first of the above approaches to crime prevention.

Need for a sane and up-to-date criminal code. The first step in a rational system of criminology and penology is the provision of a scientific and sensible criminal code. We must see to it that all serious forms of antisocial action are listed as crimes. We must eliminate from the code all acts which are not a serious challenge to social well-being. We should remove from the statute books acts which are purely a matter of taste or private morals. Then, and then only, will a man who violates a law be a criminal in fact as well as in name. From that time on, the problem will be narrowed down to the task of apprehending the violator of law and bringing him into the hands of those who may determine what treatment should be accorded to him in the interests of society.

Improvement of police personnel and procedure. An indispensable item in a successful program of crime prevention is a competent, well-trained police force equal to any emergency. We can make little headway with either the punishment or the treatment of criminals unless we apprehend them. Greater certainty of arrest has had a more powerful influence in restraining criminals than have occasional punishments. In a careful study, in 1942, of 610,000 reported offenses, C. C. Van Vechten found that there were arrests for only 25 per cent of the crimes reported, convictions for only 5.5 per cent, and prison sentences for only 3.5 per cent.

In *Uniform Crime Reports,* 1949, the Federal Bureau of Investigation claimed some improvements during the postwar period. It stated that, in 1948, the police made arrests in 28.9 per cent of all known offenses. In the majority of crimes against property there were arrests for only about 25.6 per cent of all reported cases. There were convictions for about 22 per cent of all reported crimes, and for about 15 per cent of serious crimes. In 1949, the police made arrests in the case of 27.9 per cent of all reported crimes—78.7 per cent for crimes against persons and 24.7 per cent for crimes against property.

---

[25] For a good review of the sociological, cultural, and life-history approaches to crime, see Marshall B. Clinard, "Sociologists and American Criminology," in *Journal of Criminal Law and Criminology,* January-February, 1951, pp. 549-577.

Some European countries have milder forms of punishment than ours, but, because they apprehend their criminals, have less crime. We probably get fully as much out of our police as we pay for, but no reasonable price is too great to pay for a competent and independent police force. Greatly needed at present is a sharp differentiation between routine patrolmen and traffic supervisors, on the one hand, and detective personnel, on the other. The latter should be given rigorous professional training and be provided with the latest knowledge and equipment. This type of improvement in police differentiation and training has been accomplished in some of our larger cities, and it has served to reduce the crime rate to a considerable degree. Of course, no reforms in the police area will be effective unless the police, especially the detective branch, are removed from politics, rendered immune to political pressure, and made inaccessible to importuning and temptation by the moguls of organized crime and gambling.

The "third degree" must be eliminated. When the police have arrested their man and submitted their reasons for arrest, they should be considered to have done their work. They may gather evidence, but it is no part of their responsibility to decide the guilt of the accused. At the present time the police of many cities not only do their own job of arresting in incompetent fashion but they also insist upon intruding in another realm of criminal justice where they have no right or duty whatsoever. They try to ascertain the guilt of the person arrested by administering the "third degree"—a reprehensible vestige of medieval and early modern torture in our twentieth-century criminal jurisprudence. Actually, when the police have "got their man," their work is done. It is the function of quite another group to determine guilt.

The average American would regard it as incredible that methods reminiscent of the medieval torture chamber are common-place in our police stations today. Yet this is the fact. Not infrequently men die under the administration of the third degree. Although mental torture is most commonly resorted to, extreme physical torture is not at all unusual.[26]

One of the most objectionable facts about the existence of such barbarism is that these cruelties are visited mainly upon the scum of the petty criminals—often degenerates and psychopaths—who are more logically cases for psychiatrists and social workers than for the police. No "big shot" criminal is ever subjected to the third degree. Police sometimes try to justify the third degree by claiming that "crime is war," and that severe methods must be employed. If police reserved such methods for "big shots," the practice might be a little less repulsive. But most of these warlike methods are visited upon the small fry. It is as if a general ordered his troops to hold their fire against the enemy shock troops and turned the machine guns upon the camp followers and noncombatants.

---

[26] For a brief collection of cases of third degree cruelty, see H. E. Barnes, *The Story of Punishment*. Boston: Stratford, 1930, pp. 15 ff. For more details see E. H. Lavine, *The Third Degree*. New York: Vanguard, 1930; and E. J. Hopkins, *Our Lawless Police*. New York: Viking, 1931, especially pp. 189 ff.

Defects of the jury system. Our present methods of detecting persons guilty of crime have a long historical background. The earliest way was to leave the decision to the gods, through the so-called *ordeal*. Men were compelled to carry a hot stone in their hands or to plunge their arms in boiling water. If their wounds healed quickly, the persons were declared innocent. The rapid healing was viewed as evidence of the aid of the gods. Or the question might be decided by duel or trial by combat. It was believed that God would help the innocent. Still later twelve men swore to the veracity of the accused when the latter protested his innocence. It was believed that God would strike them dead or otherwise punish them if they swore falsely. This device was known as *compurgation*. Torture was also widely used to establish guilt.

Our jury system was slowly introduced in the thirteenth century. It is much more humane than the ordeal or torture, but many believe that its results, in determining guilt or innocence, are no more certain to be accurate than those produced by these ancient devices. On what basis do critics of the jury maintain that a jury verdict is almost as much a matter of chance as the ancient ordeal?

In the first place, it is hard to get high-class and intelligent men to serve on juries. The professional classes are everywhere exempted from service. This means that we rarely get the better persons on the jury. Persons who have read and formed an opinion on a case are excluded from service. In any important case almost every honest and intelligent man in the community would have to confess that he had read about the case and formed an opinion. Seemingly, only liars and illiterates are left for jury service.

The lawyers for the state and defense both want juries as favorable to their side as possible. If the defendant is a Republican, a Protestant, and an interventionist, the defense attorney will wish a jury of Republicans, Protestants and interventionists. The district attorney will try to get a jury of Democrats, Catholics, and traditional isolationists. If the lawyers on the two sides are equally capable and alert, it is impossible to get a jury which is obviously too favorable to one side. Both sides are on their guard against this. They have to content themselves with a colorless and ignorant jury and then trust to their skill and luck in later hypnotizing the jury through the customary courtroom antics and horseplay.

The jury thus selected, along comes the trial. It is supposed to be a careful examinations of the facts in the case. What we really have is a battle of wits and words between the district attorney, who wants a conviction, and the defense counsel, who wants an acquittal. Facts are not seriously considered, except as they may be advantageously used to affect the emotions of the jurymen. Each side tries valiantly to keep out relevant and demonstrable facts opposed to his side of the case. This practice is aided by the rules of legal evidence.

Perhaps the ablest criminal lawyer this country has produced told the writer personally that he rarely considered facts in any case, except with reference to the way in which he might use them to arouse the sympathy of the jury. He said that he was always much more concerned with the personal history and the political, religious, economic, and moral beliefs of the jury and the defendant than with the actual circumstances of the crime committed. And he got results. His technique was to get the jury to identify themselves with the defendant on the sound theory that no man is likely to vote to hang himself. He lost only one important case and this was a result of a political frameup. Other criminal lawyers tried to imitate him. The famous ex-convict, Jack Black, was asked to define an "habitual criminal." He answered: "An habitual criminal is a criminal who habitually gets a poor lawyer." There is all too much truth in this wisecrack.

A trial judge can also exert a strong influence over the course of the trial, and he can do much to color the character of the testimony and its interpretation by the jury.[27] When the judicial prerogative is wisely administered, it exerts a salutary influence upon the courtroom and helps to curtail the vicious effects of the legal horseplay. But when the judge is biased, as is too frequently the case, this only further distorts the situation and increases the difficulty of reaching a verdict in accord with the facts. In one of the most sensational and publicized murder trials of the twentieth century, the trial judge during the trial declared to friends that he was going to "hang the bastards" (the defendants). In spite of his obvious and constant bias in the conduct of the case, the men were executed, though we now know they were not guilty of the murder.

Even after the jury has retired to deliberate, emotional and other influences may intervene to warp the effect of testimony. Debates in the jury room very often have more to do with the verdict to be rendered than with the testimony offered in the courtroom. The foreman of the jury, or an unusually forceful member of the jury, may very deeply influence the discussion of the case by the jury and do much to determine the ultimate decision of the jury. Instances have been reported in which a single juryman has been able to switch an entire jury to his view of the case.

Permanent, professional boards of examiners. The only adequate solution of jury abuses is to do away entirely with the jury trial in criminal cases. Examination as to guilt or innocence should be carried on by a permanent board of high-grade, paid experts who do nothing except examine accused persons. They should be specialists trained in criminal law, psychology, and criminology. They would have no other interest than to learn the facts and to render their verdict accordingly.

With such an examining board in operation, working in conjunction with a competent and honest police force, we would not only apprehend our petty criminals, but we would determine who is guilty. Once we have the guilty in hand, we can proceed to segregate them and treat them intelligently. So long as crafty lawyers can secure the conviction of the

---

27 See Howard Whitman, "Behind the Black Robe," *Ladies' Home Companion*, February, 1948.

innocent or the release of the guilty, the work of even a satisfactory police corps will be very largely wasted.

Rationality of the indeterminate sentence. Successful prison administration and the reformation of convicts depends not only upon better prisons but also upon a thorough overhauling of the practice of sentencing prisoners. In due time we may get rid of the jury trial and conventional sentencing altogether. Expert examination will come to prevail as it now does in handling the insane. In the meantime, we must bring about a sweeping modification of the sentencing power of judges if our prisons are going to protect society or reform convicts. Many nonreformable convicts are now let off with light sentences and then quickly return to crime. In other cases reformable convicts are given such long sentences that it destroys every iota of hope in their breasts and makes their rehabilitation impossible.

No judge in the courtroom can possibly know when a man is going to be ready for release. This can be determined only after a detailed personal examination of each individual convict and prolonged observation of his conduct while in prison or on parole. The only sensible procedure is for the judge to give an indeterminate sentence and then leave it to the prison authorities and parole boards to decide when a prisoner has proved his right to freedom and a new battle with life's responsibilities.

Inasmuch as parole boards can never have that intimate knowledge of convicts which is essential to sound judgment as to when a convict has proved his fitness for release on parole, it is best to give the treatment staff (the classification clinic) of institutions the full and sole power to grant release under parole supervision.

Nuisance of habitual criminal laws. The adoption of the indeterminate sentence would at once do away with one of the chief nuisances in our present sentencing procedure—the habitual criminal acts like the Baumes Law of New York State. In their present operation, such laws are unmitigatedly evil in their effect. They provide imperfect protection to society and demoralize prison discipline. A stupid man convicted of four petty felonies "goes up" for life, while a clever crook who has committed a hundred major felonies may evade prison altogether. The habitual criminal acts do not catch the big fish of the criminal world. Warden Lewis E. Lawes once published a survey of the crimes committed by the men who had been sent to Sing Sing as habitual criminals. Less than two per cent had been guilty of formidable types of crimes. Most of them were stupid and unlucky petty offenders unable to get clever lawyers.

Further, the men under life sentences are rendered hopeless and desperate. They become focal points of infection in planning prison riots and other types of rebellion against prison rules. They have little or nothing to lose if they get killed during a riot. This applies also to men serving long sentences, even though they may not be in for life. Severity in sentencing is bound to demoralize any prison system.

Nor do the habitual criminal acts offer any such protection to society as would a scientific system of rehabilitation. Before any clever and dangerous crook can normally be convicted of four felonies he may have committed from ten to a hundred. Under a scientific system he would be sent to prison for an indefinite term upon his first conviction and kept there until he had given sufficient proof of reformation. If we had an efficient police system, we would apprehend this fellow somewhere near his first offense. Certainty of arrest, expert examination as to guilt, and treatment until reformation is established—these are the main avenues to protection from crime. It cannot be secured through our present hysterical sentencing. That simply adds further fuel to the flames of our already disintegrating system of prison discipline.

Rise of the juvenile court movement. One of the most important advances in providing for a more scientific and humane handling of delinquents has been the juvenile court. The first one was established in Chicago in 1899. Roscoe Pound maintained that the juvenile court is the greatest advance in the administration of justice since the Magna Charta of 1215. Public attention was first directed to the juvenile court through the pioneer work of Judge Benjamin B. Lindsey, of Denver, Colorado, at the turn of the century. Judge Lindsey, a kindly man, did not want to imprison children. Instead, he attempted to get to the bottom of their troubles and to help them straighten out their problems. He also understood the necessity of finding work, play, and proper home surroundings for delinquent children.

More scientific study of juvenile delinquents was provided when William Healy, one of our greatest criminologists, instituted a psychological laboratory in the Chicago Juvenile Court in 1909. In 1917 Healy moved to Boston to work with the Judge Baker Foundation. Healy did much to increase our knowledge of the mental and nervous problems of delinquent children, and he recommended humane treatment of such delinquents. It was in such laboratories as those started by Healy that some of the first really scientific studies were made of the criminal personality, of criminal behavior, and rehabilitation techniques. These studies were possible because public opinion will permit a more humane approach to the problems of delinquent children than it will tolerate in dealing with adult criminals. This pioneer work by Lindsey and Healy aroused widespread interest, and the juvenile court movement grew rapidly. Today all the states have some form of juvenile court.

The juvenile court movement has been mainly responsible for encouraging the wider use of the indeterminate sentence, parole, probation, and the suspended sentence. A sensible juvenile court judge is not eager to send boys and girls who get into trouble to prisons or reformatories. He prefers to give them a chance to become useful citizens. Juvenile court procedure also stimulated the development of child-guidance clinics for problem children, a movement in which Healy was also a pioneer.

Essentials of a comprehensive program. Since all expert students of the crime problem are agreed that both adult and juvenile crime are mainly the result of social and personal disorganization growing out of the declining influence of personal and primary social groups, it is evident that the most fundamental approach to crime prevention lies in the development of various community agencies and activities which can perform the functions of control and guidance once exercised by primary groups. Only in this way can we check the social and personal disorganization which lies at the basis of much of the crime of our day. Certain community projects, such as the Community Coordinating Councils, launched in California in 1932, and the Chicago Area Project directed by Clifford Shaw, give special attention to the prevention of crime, especially juvenile delinquency.

Of all the social agencies for crime prevention, education, if properly understood and administered, can be the most effective and comprehensive force. This will, however, require sweeping changes in our educational program and procedure. We have a serious crime problem primarily because our educational system does not prepare pupils and students for competent and law-abiding citizenship. In view of the fact that white-collar crime, organized crime, racketeering, and gambling constitute far and away the most formidable item in the entire crime picture, it is obvious that education, as an instrument of crime prevention, can be most effective by discrediting the something-for-nothing frame of reference which supports these dangerous types of criminality. We shall not get very far, here, however, as long as we continue—unfortunately and unfairly—to identify this attitude with "the American way of life." We should institute programs of economic and citizenship education that will emphasize the fact that each individual must justify his existence and retain his civic rights on the basis of his constructive contributions to society.

Much greater attention must be given to vocational education, so that our youth will not drift from idleness and shiftlessness into petty crime. It is far more important to teach plumbing or baking effectively than to enable high-grade morons and dull normals to toy futilely with Shakespeare, Milton, or the hortatory subjunctive. But we will accomplish little if we provide few jobs for trained workers. Our economic system must be overhauled in some manner that will assure relatively full employment for all able-bodied citizens.

Religion may well supplement education as a powerful force for crime prevention. Although we must rely upon social science and aesthetics to inform us as to what are desirable forms of good social behavior, the religious impulse could constitute one of the most potent factors impelling us to behave in a law-abiding and altruistic manner. But for religion to accomplish this result means a revamping of religious methods and attitudes. Statistical information indicates that the great majority of convicts have been brought up in conventional religious circles, and studies of the effects of orthodox religion on crime and morals by May, Hartshorne, Hightower, and others clearly reveal that conventional religion is not an effective factor in restraining antisocial acts.

Since we know that many criminals are delinquent because of various grades of mental disturbance and behavior disorders, a sound crime prevention program must lean heavily upon the services of mental hygiene.

There should be more and better child-guidance clinics, and these should be linked up directly with the public school system. In this way we may discover and treat problem children before they drift into crime. A considerable proportion of those who get their first extensive education in crime at reform schools are sent to such schools because of truancy, which is more truly a problem for the child-guidance clinic than for law enforcement officers or a reform school.

We know from readily available statistics that most adult criminals have a record of juvenile delinquency. We further know from the same body of statistics that the great majority of juvenile delinquents come from broken homes and disorganized and bickering families. Hence, crime prevention is directly related to the work of all agencies which can make family life more successful and secure. Marriage and family clinics can be of great assistance in helping to solve this problem. But any comprehensive solution of the family, marriage, and divorce problem will require fundamental improvements in our public policy, economic system, and social habits.

Although we now place no complete faith in the sterilization of the feeble-minded as the cornerstone of crime prevention, we can still agree with the late Justice Oliver Wendell Holmes that "three generations of imbeciles are enough," and that all low-grade morons, imbeciles and idiots should be sterilized.

Since ecological studies of criminality have shown an appallingly high incidence of crime in the congested slum districts of our large cities, one way to attack crime is to clean out slums, to provide good housing facilities, and to create adequate recreational opportunities for underprivileged urban youth.

We cannot logically expect any program of crime prevention to stamp out all crime. Only the direct intervention of the Deity could accomplish this. Crime is a penalty of organized social life, and there is always bound to be an irreducible element of criminality in any human community. But criminologists and penologists have long since agreed upon the essentials of a program which could reduce crime to a tolerable minimum. Unfortunately, however, crime prevention has borne a marked resemblance to the weather in Mark Twain's famous characterization of it as something widely talked about but generally ignored in constructive action.

SUMMARY

Crime is that form of antisocial behavior which is forbidden by law. It may not always be more disastrous in its social consequences than other forms of behavior that are not banned by law. Most crimes (other than sex crimes and other forms of psychopathic behavior) have an economic basis in one way or another.

There has been a great revolution in the nature of crime in the twentieth century, due mainly to the growth and acceptance of the "something-for-nothing" psychology. The bulk of our crime bill today comes from organized crime and racketeering, the economic cost of which greatly transcends that of conventional crime, for organized crime is more efficiently directed and better protected.

Crimes have a rather definite ecological basis; that is, they are spatially distributed approximately in accordance with the social and economic composition and activities of the population. The most notable recent trend here has been the increase in rural crime since the Second World War.

White-collar crime—crime connected with the operations of business—has been receiving increasing attention by criminologists in recent years. Organized crime began on a large scale with Prohibition and has since entered many other and more disastrous fields of operation. The same is true of racketeering. Many of the moguls of crimedom have recently abandoned both organized crime and racketeering and have entered gambling operations because of the greater prospect of gain and the reduced risks of prosecution and punishment.

The professional criminal is usually the product of gradual conditioning to a life of crime, beginning with a record of juvenile delinquency. There is little reason to believe that the professional criminal is a born criminal. But it is extremely difficult to reform a professional criminal, because of his ingrained life habits, obstructive social environment, and lack of scientific treatment in prisons.

Women are not necessarily less given to criminality than men. The fact that there are far fewer women in penal and correctional institutions than men can be explained on other grounds.

Sex criminals are almost invariably emotionally unstable persons and are proper subjects for psychiatric treatment rather than for the police, courts, and prisons.

When we think of criminals we nearly always identify them with convicts—the inhabitants of our penal institutions. But convicts are the small-fry of the criminal class as a whole. They are the more stupid and unlucky of those criminals who commit the traditional crimes that account for far less than 10 per cent of our total crime bill. Unfortunately, however, they are the only criminals we can study. Hence, studies of the convict group provide us with a very imperfect impression of our entire criminal class.

Even the convict group is not inferior mentally to the population at large. One of every four convicts is psychopathic or emotionally unstable; another 25 per cent are mentally defective. The rest are the victims of bad surroundings or bad habits and associations, the latter often being a product of an unfortunate environment.

The many theories offered to explain criminality indicate the necessity of a broad approach to the causes of crime, the treatment of criminals, and the prevention of criminal behavior.

One way to prevent crime is to improve efficiency in the arrest, conviction, segregation, and treatment of criminals. This would involve more efficient police systems; the abolition of the jury trial (and the substitution for it of a board of experts); the use of the indeterminate sentence; and the introduction of good treatment clinics into our penal and correctional institutions.

Even more promising would be the removal of the main causes of crime. This would call for an improved educational system that would discredit something-for-nothing business ethics and would provide better vocational education. It would require the provision of economic security to remove need as a motive for crime. It would involve a wider use of psychiatry, especially in dealing with problem children. It would demand a strengthening of family life to avoid broken or disorganized homes, and it would make necessary the elimination of our slums.

It is, of course, unlikely that even such provisions would eliminate all crime, but they would certainly reduce it to a gratifying minimum.

SELECTED REFERENCES

Abrahamsen, David, *et al., Report on the Study of 102 Sex Offenders at Sing Sing Prison.* Albany: New York State Publications, 1950. One of the most intensive investigations of sex criminals. Rejects the dogma of sex psychopaths and outlines therapeutic and preventive techniques in dealing with sex criminals.

Adams, S. H., *The World Goes Smash.* Boston: Houghton Mifflin, 1938. A fictional analysis of racketeering in New York City, from the extreme developments of which the war may temporarily have delivered us.

Barnes, H. E., and Teeters, N. K., *New Horizons in Criminology.* New York: Prentice-Hall, 1951. The most comprehensive manual on criminology and penology.

Borchard, E. M., *Convicting the Innocent.* New Haven: Yale University Press, 1932. A startling book by an eminent legal scholar revealing many representative cases in which innocent men were convicted on what seemed to be absolutely convincing evidence.

Bromberg, Walter, *Crime and the Mind.* Philadelphia: Lippincott, 1949. One of the best psychiatric studies of the relation of mental and emotional instability to crime.

Cantor, N. F., *Crime and Society.* New York: Holt, 1939. A learned sociological study of the crime problem.

*Cavan, R. S., *Criminology.* New York: Crowell, 1948. A recent, brief, and clear survey of the whole field of criminology.

Cooper, C. R., *Here's to Crime.* Boston: Little, Brown, 1937. A graphic account of organized crime by one of the leading journalistic students of crime.

Frank, Jerome, *Courts on Trial.* Princeton: Princeton University Press, 1949. Admirable recent book on the weaknesses of jury trials and conventional criminal justice by a Federal judge.

*Glueck, Sheldon and Eleanor, *Unravelling Juvenile Delinquency.* New York: Commonwealth Fund, 1950. One of the most recent and authoritative investigations of the causes of juvenile delinquency.

Harding, T. S., *The Popular Practice of Fraud.* New York: 1935. Vivid account of frauds and swindles in merchandising as a phase of white-collar crime.

Holbrook, S. H., *Murder Out Yonder.* New York: Macmillan, 1941. A valuable study of rural crime and violence, a subject usually overlooked in dealing with criminality.

Hopkins, E. J., *Our Lawless Police.* New York: Viking, 1931. The most complete and authoritative account of the third degree and other lawless practices of our police, justifying the assertion of the Wickersham Commission that the lawlessness of our law-enforcing officers is greater than that of the criminals.

Johnson, Malcolm, *Crime on the Labor Front*. New York: McGraw-Hill, 1950. An up-to-date and realistic presentation of the corruption, racketeering, and criminality in certain labor unions.

Kefauver, Estes, and Shallett, Sidney, *Crime in America*. New York: Doubleday, 1951. First hand account of the methods, revelations, and accomplishments of the Kefauver Committee.

Kirby, J. P. (Ed.), *Criminal Justice*. New York: Wilson, 1926. A collection of readings covering nearly every phase of the processes and agencies used in convicting criminals. A very convenient collection.

Kirchbaum, Louis, *America's Labor Dictators*. New York: Industrial Forum, 1940. Good review of racketeering in labor unions.

Lever, Harry, and Young, Joseph, *Wartime Racketeers*. New York: Putnam, 1945. Preliminary study of wartime profiteering, black-market activities, and the like.

*MacDonald, J. C. R., *Crime Is a Business*. Stanford: Stanford University Press, 1939. Popular and vivid portrayal of the nature and operations of the bunco and confidence games and rackets.

McDougall, E. D. (Ed.), *Crime for Profit*. Boston: Stratford, 1933.

———, *Speculation and Gambling*. Boston: Stratford, 1936. Two pioneer books on white-collar crime as associated with shady financial practices.

*Merrill, M. A., *Problems of Child Delinquency*. New York: Houghton Mifflin, 1947. Penetrating discussion of the leading causes of juvenile delinquency and its solution.

*Mooney, Martin, *Crime, Incorporated*. New York: McGraw-Hill, 1935. Probably the best single book on streamlined, organized crime and racketeering prior to the extensive shift of big criminal operators to gambling syndicates.

Neumyer, M. H., *Juvenile Delinquency in Modern Society*. New York: Van Nostrand, 1948. Excellent recent survey of the field.

Pasley, F. D., *Al Capone*. New York: Garden City Publishing Company, 1930. An interesting biography of the first nationally famous "big shot" criminal.

Pollak, Otto, *The Criminality of Women*. Philadelphia: University of Pennsylvania Press, 1950. The only adequate treatment of female criminality. Corrects many current misconceptions of the nature and extent of female criminality.

Raine, W. M., *Guns of the Frontier*. Boston: Houghton Mifflin, 1940. A popular account of lawlessness, outlaws, and gunmen in the West.

Reckless, Walter, *The Crime Problem*. New York: Appleton-Century-Crofts, 1950. Recent basic text, especially notable for its treatment of the reformation of criminals and rehabilitative techniques.

Reeve, A. B., *The Golden Age of Crime*. New York: Mohawk, 1931. Interesting early attempt to estimate the financial losses through organized crime and racketeering.

Rhodes, H. T. F., *The Criminals We Deserve*. New York: Oxford University Press, 1938. Pioneer work on the revolution in the crime picture in England and France.

Seagle, William, *There Ought to Be a Law*. New York: Macaulay, 1933. Entertaining book on the triviality of much law-making and the resulting multiplicity of crimes.

Sheldon, W. H., *Varieties of Delinquent Youth*. New York: Harper, 1950. Massive case-study approach to juvenile delinquency from the bio-psychic viewpoint.

Stalmaster, Irving, *What Price Jury Trials?* Boston: Stratford, 1931. Devastating critique of jury trials by an able lawyer.

Sullivan, E. D., *Rattling the Cup on Chicago Crime.* New York: Vanguard, 1929. Vivid exposure of rackets and organized crime in Chicago.

Sutherland, E. H., *The Principles of Criminology.* Philadelphia: Lippincott, 1947. Long the standard textbook in the field of criminology.

*————, *White Collar Crime.* New York: Dryden, 1949. The long awaited book by a pioneer student of the subject.

Taft, D. R., *Criminology.* New York: Macmillan, 1950. A sane and balanced coverage of the field, stressing cultural causes of crime.

*Tannenbaum, Frank, *Crime and the Community.* Boston: Ginn, 1938. A valuable book, strong on the social causes of crime, and one which takes into consideration recent streamlined crime.

Tappan, P. W., *Juvenile Delinquency.* New York: McGraw-Hill, 1949. Comprehensive recent study of all aspects of juvenile delinquency, including the operations of the juvenile court.

————, *et al.*, *The Habitual Sex Offender.* Trenton: New Jersey State Publications, 1950. Important New Jersey study of sex crimes and criminals, laying special emphasis on treatment and prevention.

*Teeters, N. K., and Reinemann, J. O., *The Challenge of Delinquency.* New York: Prentice-Hall, 1950. The most recent and complete study of all aspects of juvenile delinquency.

Terrett, Courtenay, *Only Saps Work.* New York: Vanguard, 1930. A good study of rackets in New York City, stressing the ignorance of the public on the matter.

Winfield, P. H. (Ed.), *Mental Abnormality and Crime.* New York: Macmillan, 1944. Able symposium by English experts on psychological causes of crime.

Wood, A. E., and Waite, J. B., *Crime and Its Treatment.* New York: American Book Company, 1941. Sane survey of the field, strong on legal aspects of the problem.

CHAPTER 16

The Treatment of Convicted Criminals

IMPOSSIBILITY OF TREATING THE MAJORITY OF WHITE-COLLAR CRIMINALS, ORGANIZED CRIMINALS, RACKETEERS, AND GAMBLERS

The problem of treating convicted criminals. In this chapter we shall consider the various ways in which society has dealt with those convicted of crime. It is obvious from what we have said in the preceding chapter that the main way in which we deal with the most dangerous of our criminals, the white-collar criminals, the organized criminals, the great racketeers, and the master minds of the gambling syndicates, is to allow them to go their way, little impeded by the majesty of the law. Since few such criminals are arrested, and even fewer convicted, we get no opportunity to deal with them either in penal and correctional institutions or outside institutions on probation. Thus, when we refer to our "treatment of criminals" we are actually referring to our treatment of convicts, persons who are, for the most part, convicted of traditional crimes.

Hence, even if we had an extremely rational program in operation for the treatment of criminals, it would apply only to convicts and would not reach the more capable and dangerous criminals, either to restrain them or to reform them. Therefore, any description of our methods of treating convicted criminals is in part travesty and fantasy. The fact is that the great majority of criminals are rarely reached by the law or brought where they can be touched either by punitive measures or by rehabilitative treatment.

The "big shot" criminals usually evade arrest and conviction. From what we have said in the preceding chapter concerning the nature of contemporary criminality, it is obvious that it is extremely difficult to check the depredations of the leaders of organized crime, racketeering, and gambling. These top-notch criminals live peacefully and luxuriantly in lavish metropolitan apartments, enjoying a full sense of security in the knowledge that they are never likely to be disturbed. Prominent politicians share their loot, directly or indirectly, and see to it that the police are never sufficiently unmannerly or misguided as to molest them. In a preceding chapter we called attention to the "social distance" separating the slum dweller from the resident in an exclusive penthouse. The same social distance separates the average "cop" on his beat from the princely contemporary racketeer and gambling mogul. These master minds of crime winter in places like Miami, Havana, Las Vegas, or Palm Springs, and go on serenely gathering in their incalculable revenues. The well-known reformed criminal, Jack Black, wrote a book some years ago called *You Can't Win.*[1] He contended that, in the long run, it is difficult, if not impossible, for the burglar, thief, and other petty criminals to escape the toils of the law. A comparable book, entitled *You Can't Lose,* might almost be written on organized crime and racketeering.

It is almost as difficult to convict one of the henchmen of the great racketeers—the gangsters and gunmen. The police do occasionally arrest one of these mobsters, but it is hard to get even eye-witnesses of their deeds to testify against them because of fear of retaliation. The code of the underworld usually prevents even their victims from revealing their identity. Therefore, both the master minds and their underlings in organized crime and racketeering are relatively immune to the law.

Difficulty of moving against the organized underworld. Many will naturally be skeptical with respect to any such pessimistic view of our essential helplessness before the inroads of the underworld in our day. But the cold facts can easily be driven home by candid examination of just what would be involved in any effective move against organized crime and racketeering.

In the first place, those who would seek to crush the menace must be persons of public importance, who possess a following, and both their public and private career would need to be completely above reproach. There must be nothing in the files of the secret service committee of crookdom which could be used against them. Indeed, even the rare individual of public prominence who had never once "slipped" in public or in private would not be immune today. By various devices, such as trick photography and other ingenious methods, even an Anthony Comstock could now be "framed."

But let us assume that we have a group of prominent reformers of indubitable integrity who escape framing and volunteer to war upon organized crime. Suppose they approach the policemen in their ward and reveal the impressive facts about our crime and racketeering bill, asking immediate action against the offenders. Many of the police have already been paid their protection money and they know that they would face dismissal or some lesser form of discipline if they were to move in and apprehend a criminal mogul. In the first trial of James J. Hines, in the summer of 1938, it was fully and frankly admitted that policemen in New York City were either transferred or disciplined whenever the racketeers complained that they were making some pretense of enforcing the law in any protected district. And even in such cases the police were only annoying the subordinates and underlings in the rackets. Nothing could be done to spur the police into any really effective action.

Then our reformers might proceed, in turn, to the public prosecutor or district attorney. He might listen to their story, look solemn, and admit

---

[1] New York: Macmillan, 1925.

that it is a horrible state of affairs. But there the matter would be likely to end. Most public prosecutors have been trial lawyers and politicians before they enter the office of district attorney. Their often unsavory past is fully tabulated in the files of the secret service committee of organized crime, and they know better than to take any serious steps to drive the latter out of existence. In some of our great metropolitan centers it has, on occasion, been demonstrated that the public prosecutor was himself directly affiliated with the world of racketeering and organized crime. Only very rarely do we get a prosecutor like Thomas E. Dewey, who had not been a political hack and who owed nothing to either major political organization. When we do get a man like Dewey, no time is lost in attempting to promote him to some office in which he will be less annoying to the underworld. Even sincere prosecutors usually hesitate to move against any rackets other than the weaker ones or those about which the public knows most and is most willing to condemn—such as vice and dope. When Dewey prosecuted Hines, it was in connection with numbers-game gambling which probably should not have been branded as criminal in the first place. It was admitted that "Lucky" Luciano was convicted for probably the least serious form of racketeering and organized criminality in which he was engaged.

The reformers may then demand a grand jury investigation of conditions. This is not easy to obtain unless the newspapers take up the cause. Even grand juries may be manned by politicians close to the underworld. In the event that grand juries are sincere and honest, their most startling revelations are likely to be hushed up if newspapers do not force some type of action. And though this press activity is begun, it may die down as the press finds more timely and sensational news.

The reform element may still not be discouraged and may call upon one of the judges in the area. The judge may look even more solemn than did the district attorney when the reforming committee visits him and narrates its sad story. But the judge, as well, is likely to have been a politician before assuming his judicial robes. Indeed, he may have been a public prosecutor. At any rate, he would likely never have been able to get to the bench unless he had been satisfactory to the politicians. Knowing that the latter do not wish any rumpus stirred up concerning the organized underworld, many judges would be highly loath to take any active steps against the racketeers. And they would be relatively limited in the scope of their power and authority even if they were to do so.

So it would go up the political and legal scale, sometimes to the very White House itself. Governors of states are often politicians whose past records are rarely spotless. Their present position and future aspirations may depend upon a political machine which is operating in cahoots with organized gangland. The Attorney General of the United States is not likely to do anything which might bring disgrace upon prominent members of his party. Nor is the President likely to act contrary to the opinion of his Attorney General. Our presidents of late have warmly welcomed the support of some of the most powerful and corrupt political machines in American history.

These elementary considerations will make pretty clear the unlikelihood that we shall be able to deal effectively with the menace of organized crime and racketeering under a regime of partisan politics. Some capitalistic and democratic countries may be able to keep crime within bounds, but it is unlikely that the United States will succeed in doing so.

England and France have a more homogeneous population and a more law-abiding national tradition. Public opinion is more effective in discouraging crime. Moreover, in neither England nor France is there much in the way of the extreme development of finance capitalism and the speculative mania that has taken place in the United States. There has been no bank failure in England in modern times. In France, the Stavisky scandal, which might hardly have raised a flurry in the United States, seriously upset French society and politics for many months. Still, as Henry T. F. Rhodes points out in his important book, *The Criminals We Deserve*, England and France are taking pointers from the United States, and there are dangerous symptoms of racketeering already to be observed in these countries. Indeed, corruption in the higher political circles is far more prevalent in France than in the United States.

Work of Kefauver Committee. For the time being we may well defer judgment as to the final outcome of the investigation of big crime, racketeering and gambling by Senator Estes Kefauver and his Senate Crime Investigating Committee. So far the main result has been to document impressively with up-to-the-minute evidence what we have said about organized crime and gambling in the preceding chapter, and to raise the issue of the wisdom of outlawing gambling and driving it into the hands of the underworld. The political corruption, police "fixing," and other evils which the Committee has revealed may fairly be judged a more serious menace to public weal than any conceivable amount of legal gambling, and there is little evidence that gambling would be any more widespread if it were fully legalized. As *Time* suggests, perhaps the main result of the Committee's work will be to put in a new group of leaders of the underworld:

Estes Kefauver has no notion that all gambling can or should be prohibited. He likes a quiet game of stud poker himself. And most U. S. citizens would hate to give up the right to lose—or the hope of winning—a fast buck. But it would be nice if Estes Kefauver could have it (the underworld) run by a nicer set of fellows.[2]

Long range character of any program adequate to check organized crime. There is little prospect of our being able to check organized crime and racketeering unless we bring about far-reaching changes in the economic and political system that produces this form of behavior and permits it to flourish. It will be necessary to suppress the something-for-

---

[2] *Time*, March 12, 1951, p. 26. Pages 22-26 of this issue of *Time* provide a good summary of the underworld of crime and gambling which the Kefauver Committee has unearthed. For a sensible, critical appraisal of the farce of putting politicians on the track of organized criminals, see W. B. Huie's editorial in the *American Mercury*, June, 1951, pp. 643 ff.

nothing psychology, end widespread poverty, and wipe out the corrupt political machines that dominate party politics and cherish and protect racketeers. Any student of American public affairs must admit that any such body of achievements constitutes a long-time program, even at the very best. It will take many generations to accomplish such results, even if they can be brought about at all. There is, moreover, grave danger that organized crime will be able to improve its methods and to intrench itself firmly—even more rapidly, indeed, than reform measures can be instituted against it.

If we cannot get our major criminals into courts and prisons, then, it would seem that perhaps realistic education represents the only practical immediate mode of approach to crime prevention. This will hardly touch those who are already in the crime ring, but it might gradually dry up the source of supply of racketeers for coming generations. We would have to provide for much more elaborate facilities in the way of manual training in order to make it possible for our youth to earn a living by law-abiding methods. But this would have to be supplemented by more realistic character education, in order that we may undermine the philosophy which leads modern youth to believe that "only saps work." It will do little good to train people for a job if they have no inclination to accept one for which they are prepared. Moreover, we must have a really effective type of civic education which will safeguard us against the grafting complex and the other manifestations of corrupt party politics. Political graft and the "easy-money" philosophy are intimately associated with the something-for-nothing outlook of modern business and finance, and it is only natural that the latter have contributed to both the methods and ideals which are to be found in our organized crime and racketeering. Integrity and efficiency will have to dominate business if the latter is to have any effect in checking criminal tendencies.

IRRATIONALITY AND FUTILITY OF THE PUNISHMENT OF CRIMINALS

Statistical picture of the convict population. Since most of the discussion in this chapter concerns the treatment of convicts, it is expedient here to present the data pertaining to the convict population of the United States in 1949. This is contained in the table on the following page.

The theory of punishment. Our criminal law is still based on the doctrine that we can mete out a punishment which will fit a crime. This punishment is based upon a twofold consideration: the assumed damage of the crime to society and the measure of revenge which society will, accordingly, exact.

What are the basic foundations of the doctrine of punishment? The first is the notion that a man is a free moral agent completely able to choose the line of conduct he will follow. This he can do whether born in the slums or in a palace, whether educated or ignorant, whether diseased or healthy, whether prosperous or poverty-stricken. At any time he may

MOVEMENT OF PRISONERS IN STATE AND FEDERAL PRISONS
AND REFORMATORIES: 1950

Movement of sentenced prisoners	All institutions		
	Total	Male	Female
Prisoners present January 1	165,033	158,746	6,287
Admissions, total	111,487	106,533	4,954
Admitted, except transfers	86,849	82,367	4,482
Received from court	71,978	68,364	3,614
Returned as a conditional-release violator	8,692	8,164	528
Returned from escape	2,282	2,167	115
Other admissions	3,897	3,672	225
Transferred from other institutions	24,638	24,166	472
Discharges, total	109,347	104,119	5,228
Discharged, except transfers	84,790	80,051	4,739
Unconditional and conditional releases	75,088	70,863	4,225
Unconditional	32,555	30,857	1,698
Expiration of sentence	30,469	28,874	1,595
Pardon	54	51	3
Commutation	2,032	1,932	100
Conditional	42,533	40,006	2,527
Parole	33,851	31,712	2,139
Conditional pardon	1,360	1,316	44
Other conditional release	7,322	6,978	344
Death, except execution	782	769	13
Execution	56	56	—
Escape	2,692	2,576	116
Other discharges	6,172	5,787	385
Transferred to other institutions	24,557	24,068	489
Prisoners present December 31	167,173	161,160	6,013

freely decide whether he will deposit money in a bank or forge a check, whether he will go into a church to worship reverently or will stay outside and derisively cast stones through the stained-glass windows. Choosing freely and wilfully to commit a crime, such a person exposes himself to the just revenge of society. Society may be expected to exact a penalty for the damage wilfully done to it.

This doctrine of revenge, as the basis of punishment, was later supplemented by the theory of deterrence. A man is punished not only for revenge but also in order that his pain and misery may be an example to others and may prevent them from committing similar crimes.

Scientific refutation of the punishment complex. The whole body of philosophy supporting the notion of punishing criminals has been undermined both by modern knowledge and by taking note of the actual fruits of punishment in operation. Modern psychology and sociology have clearly shown that we can no longer accept the doctrine that man may freely choose what he will do, regardless of his heredity, his life experiences, and his living conditions. Our attitudes and actions are profoundly affected by all these things. Most criminals are so warped by inherited defects or bad habits that their crimes are as natural an expression for them as law-abiding conduct is for the rest of us.

If a criminal does what is natural for him to do in the light of his background, it is both futile and unjust to punish him as though he could go straight and had deliberately chosen to do otherwise. It would be as foolish to punish him for having contracted tuberculosis. This consideration entirely destroys the justification of social revenge in punishment.

Both the logic and the metaphysics of the free moral agent theory of crime are equally inconsistent with the theory of deterrence. If every person is free to will his conduct irrespective of personal experience, then he is surely able to will criminal conduct in spite of any number of types of punishment.

History also shows us that severe punishments have never succeeded in deterring people from committing crime. For example, in 1800 England had a most brutal criminal code, with more than two hundred capital crimes. Yet England had far more crime per capita in 1800 than she now has with her mild criminal code of today.

Punishment of crimes must be replaced by treatment of criminals. Even more important is the fact that we cannot deal with crime in the abstract. A crime becomes such only when a human being comes into the picture and commits the act which we consider a crime. Hence, what we have to deal with is a delinquent human being. A hundred different types of men may commit the same crime. Thus it is quite impossible to make punishment fit a crime. A sentence that would be just for one criminal might be absurdly light or severe for others.

After all, what we want to do is to protect society from criminals and to prevent crimes from being committed. Hence, we should face the problem rationally. We should not feverishly demand a more frantic application of the same methods which have been tried and found a failure for many centuries. Why expect to end our "crime wave" and prison riots by demanding an extension of exactly the procedure that has permitted our present high crime rate to exist and has incited our riots and fires in the state penitentiaries?

Punishment certainly does not reform men or protect society. Sheldon Glueck examined the records of men discharged from the Massachusetts State Reformatory at Concord. He found that about 80 per cent of them continued their criminal careers after release. The record of many of our state penitentiaries is, naturally, far worse. If we punish a hard-boiled, habitual criminal by giving him a definite time sentence in prison, we offer very imperfect protection to society. As soon as the convict is released, he will return to his life of crime—usually a worse man than before. The average prison term actually served even by convicted adult felons is only about two and one-half years. Punishment thus fails both as a means of reformation and as a way of protecting society.

What is needed is a clear recognition of the fact that we must replace the old slogan of imposing a punishment to fit a crime by the new scientific ideal of finding a type of treatment which will fit a particular criminal. Those who cannot be reformed must be segregated for life, irrespective of the crimes that they have committed. They should be kept in humane quarters and made to be self-supporting through industry. Those who can be reformed should be treated in such a way as to rehabilitate them. But before we know whom to segregate and whom to try to reform, we must carefully examine all convicted criminals. Examination and diagnosis are as important in criminology and penology as they are in medicine.

Capital punishment should be abolished. It is obvious that these elementary considerations with respect to the substitution of treatment for punishment also imply the necessity of abandoning the entire notion of capital punishment—the only important vestige in our day of the era of brutal corporal punishment. There are many who admit the logic of this contention but who maintain that we need the protection of capital punishment in order to prevent an enormous increase in the murder rate. But it has been shown, time and again, that capital punishment has no discernible effect in restraining the homicide rate.

One of the best studies of capital punishment yet made was carried out by Warden Lewis E. Lawes in his book, *Man's Judgment of Death*. There, among other things, he compares the homicide rate in five states which employed capital punishment with the rate in five states which had abolished it. These states were chosen as those presenting cultural similarities, so that disturbing factors would be as nearly absent as possible. The states permitting capital punishment were New Hampshire, Connecticut, Ohio, Missouri, and Indiana. The abolition states were Maine, Rhode Island, Michigan, Kansas, and Minnesota.

What did Lawes discover? He found that over a period of eight years the homicide rate in the capital punishment states averaged 56.5 per million of the population. In the states which had abolished capital punishment the homicide rate averaged 37.9. So much for the notion that where we have capital punishment the homicide rate is low. The leading authority on capital punishment in the English-speaking world was the late E. R. Calvert. In his definitive book on *Capital Punishment in the Twentieth Century*,[3] he wrote: "In no single instance is there evidence of a permanent increase in homicidal crime as a result of abolition (of the death penalty); in many there has been a decided decrease."

MAIN STAGES IN THE TREATMENT OF CONVICTED CRIMINALS

Punishment outside of institutions. There have been four main stages in the manner in which society has dealt with convicted criminals within historic society. The first stage, which dates from primitive society to the close of the eighteenth century, was that in which those convicted of crime were punished *outside* of institutions—by fines or various types of corporal punishment like whipping, branding, and many forms of mutila-

---

[3] New York: Putnam, 1927.

tion. In primitive society, exile was also used, primarily to demonstrate to the gods that the group rejected and expelled those persons who had violated the supposedly revealed folkways and customs of the group. Exile was employed frequently in early historic societies. Institutions for confinement were used mainly to hold suspected criminals prior to trial and for the imprisonment of debtors, political prisoners, heretics, and those held for ransom. It was very rare, indeed, that any convicted criminal was imprisoned for his acts. The main motive was to impose the vengeance of the social group for criminal conduct. There was little idea of reforming criminals, though there was perhaps some hope that the brutal corporal punishment might discourage the repetition of criminal acts and deter others from committing crimes.

Punishing criminals within institutions. The second main stage in society's methods of dealing with convicted criminals was that in which those convicted of crime were punished *within* institutions to which we usually give the name of prisons. Although there were some sporadic beginnings of this practice in the sixteenth and seventeenth centuries, the idea of imprisoning convicts did not take any very effective form until near the close of the eighteenth century. At this time, due mainly to the efforts of John Howard, in England, and the Quakers, in Pennsylvania, the idea arose that convicts could be more effectively punished and society best protected through confining convicts in prisons.

The first true prison system was established in Philadelphia in the last decade of the eighteenth century, and within the next 40 years it evolved into the famous Pennsylvania system of solitary confinement. Dissatisfaction with the Pennsylvania system led to the Auburn, or silent, system of imprisonment, which was established in the prison at Auburn, New York, between 1819 and 1825. The Pennsylvania and Auburn prison systems provided the machinery through which institutions were used to *punish* convicts. These two systems dominated the prison concept during most of the nineteenth century, and despite the formal adoption of the later concept that institutions should be used to reform convicts, the ideals and practices of these two prison systems still prevail in the actual administration of most of the prisons of the United States and Europe at the present time.

It was hoped by those who founded these two prison systems that imprisonment might reform criminals and deter others from committing crimes, but the basic philosophy which dominated during this period from about 1800 to 1870 was that such penal institutions were to be used primarily to punish violators of the law.

The use of institutions to reform convicts. In about 1830, however, the idea arose that institutions should be used primarily to bring about the *reformation* of convicts. This concept first took practical form in the famous Irish prison system established in the 1850's. Here the reform program was applied to adult convicts. American reformers in the 1860's and 1870's endeavored to introduce the Irish prison system into the United States, but they were only successful in having it applied to youthful offenders. Thus applied to criminal youths, the system was here known as the Elmira Reformatory program, because it was first practically established in 1876 at the Elmira Reformatory in New York State. During the next half century, reformers were gradually able to extend the Elmira principles of reform to institutions for adult convicts. This extension constitutes what we generally call *the New Penology*. This is best exemplified today by the institutions in the Federal prison system and in some of the better state systems; for example, those in Massachusetts, Michigan, Wisconsin, New York, New Jersey, Pennsylvania, and California.

Although the philosophy of the Elmira system and the New Penology formally repudiates punishment and embraces reformation as the main aim of imprisonment, the grim character of our Bastille penal institutions and the exaggerated fear of the escape of convicts have produced a type of administration and an institutional atmosphere which makes it all but impossible to reform inmates. The net result is that punishment continues to remain the chief practical effect of the administration of even the best prisons and reformatories in the United States today.

Treating and reforming convicts outside of institutions. The recognition by alert and realistic students of crime that most of our penal and reformatory institutions more or less inevitably perpetuate the punishment program and only rarely bring about the reformation of convicts has led to the fourth stage in dealing with those convicted of crime. This stage, which is only now beginning to emerge and to take form, has grown out of the realization that, if we actually wish to reform convicts, we must do so mainly outside of institutions. Institutions will be retained chiefly to segregate nonreformable convicts and to provide places where other offenders may be studied and prepared for treatment outside of any institution, chiefly through an ever wider use of probation, conditional release, and parole.

Thus far, the most complete development of this program has been embodied in the Youth Correction Authority system that was drafted by the American Law Institute in 1940. It was adopted by California in 1941, by Minnesota and Wisconsin in 1947, by Massachusetts in 1948, and by Texas in 1949. While the states that have adopted this program still employ institutions to a limited extent in their reform efforts, the punitive aspects of institutional administration have been reduced to a minimum, and as many convicted persons as possible are treated outside of institutions through probation and parole.

Although so great a revolution as this fourth stage implies cannot be accomplished in a few years, the results already achieved amply demonstrate the soundness of the philosophy adopted. As yet, it has been employed chiefly with youthful offenders, but in 1944 California extended it in a limited way to adult convicts. What remains to be accomplished is to perfect the program and to extend it to all adult criminals who may be safely handled in this manner. When this is done, we shall have a new penology actually worthy of the name.

PUNISHING CONVICTED CRIMINALS OUTSIDE OF INSTITUTIONS

Primitive punishments. In early society, crimes against the public welfare were punished by summary execution of the culprit, by exile and outlawry, or by corporal punishment, according to the nature of the criminal act and the customary procedure of the group. Private crimes, avenged by kinsmen of the injured, were also punished in a variety of ways, usually by death or enforced slavery. As time passed and punishment was gradually brought under the supervision of the elders of the group, there developed the famous principle of *lex talionis,* the grotesque subjection of the convicted culprit to treatment identical with that which he had given to his victim. This was the eye-for-an-eye doctrine. When the state took over the function of dealing with crime, it adopted these primitive varieties of retaliatory corporal punishment as the more usual method of punishing criminals.

Corporal punishment. Corporal punishment for crime held the field from primitive society to the opening of the nineteenth century. Although persons have been imprisoned from primitive days to our own, the prison was rarely used as a method of punishing convicted criminals until the nineteenth century. Prisons were chiefly used for those held for ransom, debt or trial.

The forms of corporal punishment were many and varied, most of them cruel and barbarous. Mutilation, branding, whipping, the stock and pillory, ducking, public humiliation, and other methods were followed with the greatest variety and ingenuity. The incredible brutality which accompanied some of these measures may be illustrated by characteristic examples of mutilation as a punishment for crime during the Middle Ages. King Canute of England, who developed for himself an unusual reputation for probity and justice, nevertheless gave out the following legislation prescribing mutilation as a method of corporal punishment:

Let the offender's hands be cut off, or his feet, or both, according as the deed may be. And if he have wrought yet greater wrong, then let his eyes be put out and his nose and his ears and his upper lip be cut off, or let him ·be scalped, whichever of these shall counsel those whose duty it is to counsel thereupon, so that punishment may be inflicted and also the soul preserved.

The theory of mutilation as a deterrent example was also well stated in a decree of William the Conqueror:

We decree that no one shall be killed or hung for any misdeeds, but rather that his eyes be plucked out and his feet, hands and testicles cut off, so that whatever part of his body remains will be a living sign to all of his crime and iniquity.

The pain involved in these mutilations, inflicted as they were without any anesthetic, may well be imagined. Further, loss of blood and infection were likely to produce death in the case of major mutilations. Indeed, in a medieval English law it was stated that if a man survived three days unaided after amputation of his legs, he might be nursed back to health and freedom if the bishop of the diocese consented. Brutal mutilation continued, even in England, until after the beginning of the sixteenth century. The cutting off of the ears and hands persisted until the eighteenth century.

Early prisons not used to punish the convicted criminals. Prisons, as places for holding human beings in confinement, have existed since the era of primitive social life. But as a special institution for the confinement of persons convicted of crime, the prison is an innovation which has developed almost entirely within the last 175 years. Until about 1775, in both Europe and America the jails or prisons existed primarily for the confinement of heretics and debtors, or for the safekeeping of those accused of crime, pending their trial. Those who were convicted were normally sentenced either to corporal punishment, or, as became common in England after colonial expansion began, to deportation. Political prisoners were, of course, often incarcerated in prisons.

Transportation of criminals. In addition to the age-old practice of corporal punishment, another phase, intermediate between corporal punishment and the universal use of imprisonment to punish, was the transportation of criminals. Prisoners had been harshly confined on galleys as galley-slaves during the Middle Ages. As soon as English colonies were established in America criminals were sent here, the first batch arriving in 1619. About 50,000 were sent altogether before the Declaration of Independence in 1776 put an end to the practice. For a time thereafter convicts piled up in prison hulks off the shore of England. Then, in 1787, Britain began to send convicts to Australasian areas. This practice lasted until 1852. About 135,000 convicts were sent to Australasia. The French founded penal colonies in French Guiana and New Caledonia, and the Russians in Siberia. Both the French and Russians usually provided prisons for the detention of their transported convicts.

THE RISE OF INSTITUTIONS DESIGNED TO PUNISH CONVICTS

Reforms in the criminal law substitute imprisonment for corporal punishment. During the course of the seventeenth and eighteenth centuries, various reformers became convinced that cruel and brutal forms of corporal punishment fail either to reform criminals or to protect society adequately from their depredations. This led to changes in the criminal law which permitted imprisonment to be substituted for corporal punishment.

The earliest of these reformers were the Quakers of West Jersey and Pennsylvania, whose Christian conscience was revolted at the sight of the universal methods of cruel and bloody corporal punishments then in effect. Therefore, in West Jersey in 1681, and in Pennsylvania in 1682, the Quakers introduced new criminal codes which provided imprisonment rather than corporal punishment for most criminal acts. The English government forced the abandonment of the Quaker system in 1718, and it was not until Pennsylvania gained her independence in 1776 that the Quaker ideas could be permanently realized. Most American states soon followed the example of Pennsylvania in substituting imprisonment for corporal punishment.

Similar ideas were espoused in Europe by such leading reformers of the criminal law as the Italian, Cesare Beccaria, and the English reformers, John Howard, Jeremy Bentham, Sir Samuel Romilly, James Mackintosh, Sir Robert Peel, and Sir Thomas Foxwell Buxton. The reforms of the French Revolution also helped along the trend toward the substitution of imprisonment for corporal punishment. Thus, by the 1830's reform legislation made possible the use of imprisonment rather than corporal punishment. Although all of the early prisons which were established in accordance with this new legislation were primarily interested in punishing rather than in reforming convicts, there was a secondary or residual hope that punishment might also promote reformation.

Some early trends in the establishment of prisons. From the middle of the sixteenth century to the close of the eighteenth, a number of institutions were created which may be fairly regarded as forerunners of the modern prison system, though they were established primarily to deal either with vagrants or with juvenile delinquents. They were more truly workhouses or houses of correction than prisons as we know them today. Representative examples were the so-called English Bridewells, set up in England in the latter part of the sixteenth century; the Amsterdam House of Correction, opened in 1589; the House of Refuge for Children, opened in Florence by Filippo Franci in 1677; the workhouses established in Pennsylvania by William Penn following his reforms in 1682; and the Papal Prison or House of Correction, opened in Rome in 1704 by Pope Clement XI. This Papal Prison was known as the Hospital of St. Michael and was designed for youthful offenders. It was also notable as the first prison which provided for separate or cellular confinement. It introduced the rectangular cell houses later used in the Auburn-Sing Sing type of prison. Another famous early prison was the penal workhouse built by Jean Jacques Philippe Vilain in Ghent and opened in 1773. From it was derived the radial wing construction later used in the Pennsylvania system.

Something closer to the modern prison was provided in England in the last quarter of the eighteenth century, mainly as a result of the efforts of John Howard and Jeremy Bentham. At that time several small cellular prisons were built in England—notably two erected in Sussex in 1775 and 1781, and that opened at Wynondham in Norfolk in 1785 under the direction of Sir Thomas Beevor. These institutions exerted considerable influence on the Quaker reformers in Philadelphia who were then determined to proceed with their program.

The origin of the Pennsylvania prison system. The prison system established by the Pennsylvania Quakers and associated reformers, notably Benjamin Rush, constitutes the actual origin of the modern prison as we have come to know it. These Philadelphia reformers had two leading motives: (1) the realization of their long-delayed aspiration to substitute imprisonment for corporal punishment; and (2) the desire to end the demoralizing association of all types of suspected and convicted criminals in the so-called congregate prisons which were beginning to spring up in several American states. These congregate prisons confined without discrimination in large rooms both those accused of crime and those convicted of crime—men and women, and adult and youthful offenders. The Quakers quite correctly regarded this indiscriminate herding together of all suspected and convicted criminals as utterly demoralizing. This led them to create the Pennsylvania prison system on the basis of solitary confinement.

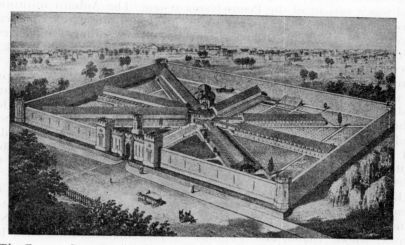

The Eastern State Penitentiary, opened in 1829. Original home of the Pennsylvania system of prison discipline. This picture reveals the radial-wing and outside-cell construction typical of the architecture of the Pennsylvania system.

After 1786, new laws were passed by the state of Pennsylvania ordering imprisonment as the normal method of punishing criminals, and soon afterwards, in 1790, a small block of cells was erected in the yard of the Walnut Street Jail in Philadelphia for the solitary confinement of convicts. This was the first true prison in America for the confinement of adult felons. It was the birthplace of the famous Pennsylvania system of prison discipline, which provided the inspiration, with variations, for all the prison systems of the world during the following century.

Pennsylvania constructed its first state prison at Allegheny, near Pittsburgh, in 1826. This was the first important penal institution to provide for the solitary confinement of all inmates. But the famous Eastern Penitentiary, opened at Cherry Hill in Philadelphia, in 1829, became the classic institution in which the Pennsylvania system of solitary confinement was fully developed.

Under the Pennsylvania system each convict was assigned to a cell and kept there without any association with other convicts until he died or was released. Hence, the Pennsylvania system was known as *the solitary system*. Its chief purpose was punishment, but it was hoped that the convict's meditations might lead to his reformation. It was believed that the prolonged solitude of cellular confinement would stimulate such salutary reflection. The Pennsylvania system thus thoroughly established the second main stage of penology—the idea and practice of using prisons to *punish* convicts. Francis Lieber, a refugee from Germany and a famous political philosopher, was a great admirer of the Pennsylvania system and the foremost advocate of using prisons to *punish* criminals.

Origin of the Auburn prison system. The other great American system of prison discipline and administration was born in Auburn, New York, and was a variant of the Pennsylvania system. The Auburn institution was opened in 1819. From 1821 to 1823, the institution was conducted according to the Pennsylvania system of constant solitary confinement. Because of the small size of the cells ($3\frac{1}{2} \times 7$ feet) and the total lack of exercise, many of the confined convicts either became insane or died. As a result, the Auburn authorities introduced in 1825 what became known as the Auburn system. Under this program, the convicts were segregated individually in cells except during the period of working and eating. They were allowed to leave their cells to work together in prison shops and to eat in a common dining room. But absolute silence was enforced at all times, and any type of communication between convicts was absolutely forbidden. Hence, the Auburn system came to be known as *the silent system.*

From about 1825 to 1850, there was a vigorous conflict between the Pennsylvania and Auburn systems. Though the Pennsylvania system was experimented with briefly in Maryland, Massachusetts, Maine, New Jersey, Rhode Island, and Virginia, by 1850 the Auburn system had triumphed in every state except Pennsylvania.

Two reasons for the ascendancy of the Auburn system in the United States were that institutions on the Auburn plan were more economical to construct and administer, and that the prison shops were also better adapted to the rising mechanical industry than was the solitary cellular confinement of the Pennsylvania system. But perhaps even more important than these was the fact that Louis Dwight, Secretary of the Boston Prison Discipline Society, was an almost fanatical partisan of the Auburn system and carried on very effective propaganda for it whenever the construction of a new prison was under consideration. By the middle of the nineteenth century the Auburn system was thoroughly established, and this marked the complete application of the second great stage of penology: the idea of punishing convicts within institutions.

It is not surprising that few convicts have been reformed by imprisonment. Indeed, Sheldon Glueck has indicated that probably most of those who have led law-abiding lives after release from prison have done so because of the stabilizing influence of physical and mental maturity rather than because of any beneficial influences of imprisonment. This means that the great majority of those discharged from prison resume a life of crime. Therefore, prisons designed almost exclusively to punish inmates have failed to reform them, and have constituted a very inadequate protection of society against criminal acts. This conviction

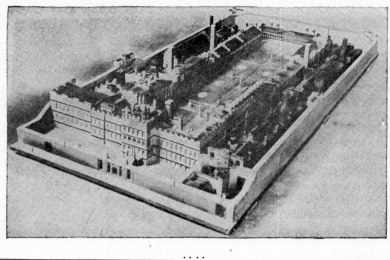

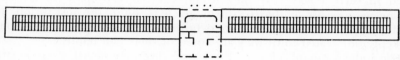

Pictured above is the State Prison at Auburn, New York. Opened in 1819, it is the parent institution of the Auburn system of prison discipline. Diagrammed below are the rectangular flanking cell houses and the inside cell blocks typical of Auburn-Sing Sing Prison design. This type of construction dominated American prison architecture during the hundred year period that followed 1825.

began to take root in the minds of progressive reformers more than a century ago, and it gradually led to the development of prison programs that deliberately sought to make reformation take ascendancy over punishment as the main motive of institutional segregation and treatment.

PENAL INSTITUTIONS DESIGNED TO REFORM CONVICTS

Rise and integration of the program of reformation. Even today, however, most people still adhere to the notion that prisons exist primarily to punish those convicted of crime. Many prison administrators, too, entertain the same concept. Even a majority of those administrators who formally subscribe to the concept that prisons should be mainly devoted to reforming convicts have adopted this view only during relatively recent years.

Actually, however, the belief that institutions should be utilized chiefly to reform inmates was born 175 years ago. Benjamin Rush, of Philadelphia, expressed this idea as far back as 1787, and about 1830, an enlightened French penologist, Charles Lucas, vigorously stated the opinion that men should be sent to prisons to be rehabilitated rather than to be further demoralized.

Perhaps the first notable effort to promote reformation in actual prison administration was introduced by Captain Alexander Maconochie, who was put in charge of the penal colony on Norfolk Island, in the Australasian area of the Pacific. Here he had charge of criminals who had been transported from England. In the place of a flat sentence, he introduced the so-called mark system. The time the prisoner served depended upon the conduct of the prisoner with respect to both discipline and labor. It was believed that this system would promote efforts at reform, since prisoners would presumably be eager for release.

This concept was extended and strengthened by the advocacy of the indeterminate sentence by men like Archbishop Richard Whately, of Dublin, George Combe, and Frederick and Matthew Davenport Hill in Great Britain in the 1830's and the 1840's. Under an indeterminate sentence a convicted person is not given a definite sentence but is incarcerated for a term that depends upon his conduct in the institution and upon the decision of the authorities concerning the time when he has become fit for release. Frederick Hill contended that prisons should be administered in such a way that they would effectively prepare inmates for release as a result of the treatment given them in the institution. He held that prisons should be "moral hospitals" in which inmates should be kept and treated until they are cured of their bad habits.

The indeterminate sentence has usually been employed in connection with the parole system. When a convict is released on an indeterminate sentence, it is customary to have him supervised by parole officers until such time as he is thought to have made a successful transition to a law-abiding existence. In a crude sort of way, the parole system originated in the so-called "ticket of leave" practice used by the British in releasing convicts from the Australasian penal colonies. It was first well defined and forcibly advocated by a French reformer, Bonneville de Marsagny, in the 1840's. It was the first important contribution to those practices which are basic in seeking to reform convicts outside of institutions.

It has long been the conviction of realistic penologists that idleness in prisons exerts a disastrous influence upon convicts, and that productive prison labor will powerfully assist in the program of reformation. This idea was set forth and put into practice in the 1830's and 1840's by Manuel Montesinos, of the Valencia prison in Spain, and by Georg M. Obermaier, a leading prison administrator in Bavaria.

The Irish prison system. The basic principles that prisons should reform rather than punish; that sentences should be commuted for good behavior; that prisoners should have an indeterminate sentence; that this should be supplemented by supervision after release; and that productive and instructive labor is indispensable in any system of reformation, were all brought together in the Irish prison system set up by Sir Joshua Jebb and Sir Walter Crofton in the 1850's. British authorities would not permit so enlightened a system to be established in England, but they were apparently willing to have it tried out on the Irish. In addition to the ideas and principles noted above, the Irish prison system adopted a method of dividing the inmates into classes or grades through which each inmate had to work his way by good conduct and industry before he could be released. His release was on a conditional pardon or ticket-of-leave, the practical origin of the parole system.

Although the Irish prison system did not provide our present day professional assistance to reformation through the introduction of classification clinics, psychiatrists, psychologists, and social workers in the prisons, it was the first prison system that was frankly based upon the motive of reformation rather than punishment. It is significant that it was applied to adult convicts. Not until the twentieth century was a prison system devoted primarily to the reformation of adult convicts set up in the United States, and no such prison exists even yet in England.

Rise of the Elmira Reformatory system in the United States. It was natural that this remarkable Irish prison system would attract the attention of reformers both in Europe and America. Such leaders in American penal reform as Gaylord Hubbell, Franklin B. Sanborn, Enoch C. Wines, and Zebulon R. Brockway made a study of the Irish prison system, and, especially at the famous Cincinnati Prison Congress in 1870, warmly urged its adoption in American penal practice. They desired to have the Irish system applied to all American offenders, both adult and youthful. But the best that they could do at the time was to secure its introduction here for the treatment of youthful offenders between the ages of 16 and 30, and more usually between the ages of 18 and 25. This was provided through the opening of the Elmira Reformatory system in New York State in 1876.

The Elmira system, essentially based on the Irish prison system, emphasized the indeterminate sentence, the classification of inmates, and the institution of vocational education on an unprecedented scale. At the Elmira Reformatory the inmates were divided into three classes or grades. At entry, each inmate was placed in the second grade. At the end of six months of good conduct, he could be promoted to the first grade, and six months of good conduct in this grade entitled him to parole. Misbehavior was punished by demotion to the third grade, where a month's good conduct was required for restoration to the second grade. Incorrigible inmates had to serve the maximum sentence.

Disappointment with the Elmira system. The Elmira system aroused great enthusiasm and was widely adopted by the more progressive states. It was expected that it would reform most inmates. But in the half century following 1876 there was a rather general disillusionment with the practical results of the Elmira system. There was a confirmed feeling among progressive penologists that the Elmira type of institution had degenerated into little more than a conventional prison for delinquent youth. This conviction was further confirmed by the fact that, during this same half century after 1876, the majority of conventional prisons had improved and liberalized their systems of administration and discipline. We may now examine some of the reasons for disappointment concerning the practical value of the Elmira system.

One main reason for the relative failure of the Elmira system lay in the fact that the physical plant of most reformatories resembled the conventional prisons for adults and was utterly unsuited to any such advanced and progressive program as the Elmira system started out to be. The first three important reformatories, those at Elmira, at Concord, Massachusetts, and at Huntingdon, Pennsylvania, had all originally been built as fortress prisons for adult convicts, and most of the reformatories which were later built for youthful offenders were nearly as bad in their grim and forbidding architecture. Not until the Annandale Reformatory in New Jersey was opened in 1929 was a reformatory constructed which was compatible in its architecture with Elmira ideals. But few states have modeled their reformatories after the Annandale plant. Not only do the reformatories have grim and repressive physical surroundings, but they were built to house altogether too many inmates. The majority of reformatories in the larger states, which were the ones that more usually provided reformatories, were built to house between 1,000 and 1,800 inmates, although penologists believe that no satisfactory reformatory can successfully handle more than about 600 inmates.

Another reason for dissatisfaction with the operation of the Elmira system is to be found in the fact that, after the first few years of vivid enthusiasm, most reformatory administrators lost their vision and vigor and settled down to a routine administration not much different from that which dominated the conventional prisons. Even harsh methods of discipline, including corporal punishment, were frequently applied. The military drilling which was common tended to develop habits of acquiescence and obedience rather than to promote inspiration to methods of reform. Hence, those who administered the reformatories did not offer much inspiration or encouragement to reformation on the part of the inmates, thus undermining the fundamental purpose of the reformatory.

The vocational education which the founders of the reformatory system had believed indispensable to the success of the program has rarely been provided for in adequate fashion, though the situation here is better in most reformatories than in prisons. And even where there was a good system of vocational education, it was rarely supplemented by the indispensable civic and social education required for the promotion of good citizenship.

Even the indeterminate sentence and the parole system, which were an integral part of the reformatory complex, were very seldom operated effectively.

We now understand that any really effective program to insure the reformation of a large percentage of convicted criminals must provide a treatment staff of psychiatrists, psychologists, social workers, educators, and others who can bring specialized techniques to bear upon the personal cases and needs of individual inmates. Such a treatment staff was rarely provided in reformatories until after the First World War, and even now only the better reformatories provide such facilities.

Hence, it is not surprising that Sheldon Glueck and other students of the post-release careers of reformatory inmates have convincingly indicated that reformatories rarely bring about the permanent reformation of more than twenty-five per cent of those released from such institutions.

The future of the reformatory movement. What we have just said makes it clear that the Elmira Reformatory system was a relative failure mainly because it was never really given a fair trial in accordance with the ideals and hopes of its founders. It is obvious that this constitutes no basis for repudiating the reformatory. But it does make it clear that if we wish to make the reformatory movement a success, we must recapture the vision of the 1870's and implement it effectively.

The best thought on reformatories today stresses the fact that every large state should build at least two types of reformatories—one a rather secure institution for more difficult inmates, and the other a more open, campus-like institution for the less refractory inmates. Only in this way can the required treatment facilities be made fully available to all inmates of both types of institution. Today, even where we have a good reformatory plant, the administrators are fearful of applying adequately the available treatment facilities to the more difficult types of inmates, and yet it is obvious that these incorrigible or difficult inmates are the ones who need the fullest measure of treatment.

Perhaps even more important than better reformatory architecture is the provision of suitable personnel in the administrative force. This applies both to the custodial staff and the treatment staff. No custodial staff, however efficient, can operate a successful reformatory unless it is more interested in reforming inmates than in jailing them safely. But the finest ideals on the part of the custodial staff will not accomplish reformation unless supplemented by an adequate and professionally trained treatment staff which can examine and deal expertly with the individual behavior problems of each and every reformatory inmate.

The better reformatories of today are beginning to introduce essential improvements in architecture, administration, and treatment. Such reformatories have actually brought about results equal to those hoped for by the founders of the Elmira system. But, as we shall point out more thoroughly later, it is likely that we shall depend less in the future upon even good reformatories. When the conviction that we can reform the reformable far better and much more cheaply outside of institutions than within is widely accepted, it is probable that we shall utilize reformatories chiefly for delinquent youth too dangerous to release for a time, and for the preliminary study and training of those who may be safely dealt with by probation, conditional release, and parole.

The New Penology. Although the experiment with the Elmira Reformatory program has proved a disappointment to many, the ideals of this program have had a beneficial effect upon prisons for adults, especially in the period since the First World War. The net result of this influence of the Elmira program upon our penal institutions has been the creation of what we call *the New Penology,* which dominates the theory underlying the administration of all prisons in enlightened states and has been introduced in practice in some of the better prisons, notably those administered by the Federal government.

The new penology embraces the Elmira principle that the purpose of all penal and correctional institutions is to reform rather than to punish inmates. Further, certain specific aspects of the Elmira administration, such as the classification of inmates, emphasis on education as a rehabilitative measure, and the greater use of parole, have been adopted by the new penology. There has been some progress made in introducing the indeterminate sentence, but so far this has been limited mainly to laws which state the maximum and minimum sentences which a judge may impose for a given crime.

The new penology has also introduced certain progressive features which were not a part of the original Elmira program, though they have also been applied in the better administered reformatories of our day. Some progress has been made in providing professional training for the custodial staff of prisons—the deputy wardens and guards. But in the great majority of cases, even where we have a trained custodial staff, the warden himself remains a political appointee. Often he has had no previous experience in penological matters.

Much more important has been the creation and introduction of the treatment staff. This staff constitutes the classification or behavior clinics that are to be found in all the best penal and correctional institutions. These clinics consist of trained physicians, psychiatrists, psychologists, social workers, sociologists, and educators. Even in the best prisons of a few decades ago there was no such treatment staff. Prison personnel was limited to the custodial staff—a doctor, a chaplain, and perhaps a civilian teacher. The rise of the treatment staff has been due to the growing acceptance of the notion that we must supplant the old ideal of trying to find a punishment to fit a crime by the new conception that we must design individual treatment to fit a particular convict. If this treatment is to be supplied, it is, of course, necessary to provide personnel competent to discover and administer it.

Another phase of progress has been the development of better prison architecture, which we shall describe more thoroughly later. We have already noted that the Elmira program was handicapped by the fact that for more than fifty years after the opening of the Elmira Reformatory most of the reformatories were built with the same gloomy physical plant which dominated the conventional prison picture. Even today we usually build newer and cleaner prisons of the same repressive maximum-security construction that dominated all construction after the rise of the Pennsylvania and Auburn systems. The same type of stone, brick, concrete, and steel cells is provided for all inmates, whether dangerous desperadoes or physically docile forgers and homosexuals. In the Federal system and in some of the better state systems, improved prison architecture has gone as far as to differentiate housing facilities for inmates in accordance with the relative custodial risk. In such states there has also been a tendency to construct medium-security and minimum-security prisons, or correctional institutions, to house convicts who do not require maximum-security prisons for custodial restraint and safety.

Despite the commendable advances in the new penology, the prisons which exist even under this program still remain primarily punitive institutions, and certainly the majority of our prisons have not adopted the new penology in practice. Hence, even in the period of the new penology our penal institutions have generally failed to reform inmates. The reasons for this we shall proceed to make clear by describing the general nature of prison life.

Why prisons cannot reform inmates. It has been the hope that, from the beginning of imprisonment, incarceration would reform prisoners. So powerful has been this conviction that we have resolutely refused to face the hard fact that reformation has rarely been the actual outcome of prison life. Rather, prisons have almost invariably made men worse upon discharge than they were when committed. Indeed, if one were to sit down with pencil and paper and deliberately devise the institution which would most surely degrade and demoralize the human personality, one might unconsciously create our modern prisons. In short, if we desire to punish and destroy a man, our prisons are perfectly designed for that purpose. But if we wish to reform a convict, the typical prison would be the last place to send him. The preposterous nature of the conventional prison as a place for the reformation of the criminal has been strikingly stated by Clair Wilcox in the following paragraphs:

The life of a prisoner is of necessity an abnormal one. He is denied his liberty, held against his will. He is separated from his family, his relatives, and his friends. His companions are all of his own sex and nearly of his own age. He has no contact with women or children. Often he must endure great physical discomfort. He may be housed in a narrow, cold, dark cell, with primitive toilet facilities. He may be forced to share such a cell with one or two others. The prison dietary, though usually ample in quantity, may be so badly planned as to injure his health.

He is oppressed by the monotony of the prison routine. He may be compelled to spend a large part of his day or all of it in idleness. For much of his time he must observe the rule of silence. For many hours he is locked in his cell. He is under the constant surveillance of a guard. If he breaks prison rules, he is subjected to punishment which may be excessively brutal. Around him he finds drug addicts, crazed when deprived of their supply. Sexual vice flourishes on all sides. The lunatic, the hardened criminal, the accidental offender, all are thrown in together. All are treated alike.

The prisoner finds himself branded by society. Usually he is resentful. He meets men who have been given shorter terms than his for an identical offense. He knows of others who have escaped punishment entirely. Rightly or wrongly, he feels a rankling sense of injustice. His one desire is to escape. He looks to good-time allowances or possible pardon or parole as a way out. Then, to check a crime wave, the state may increase sentences, stiffen up on parole release. In desperation he may join in a riot or plot an escape, feeling that he has little to lose, everything to gain.[4]

John L. Gillin has also effectively indicted the contemporary prison:

What monuments to stupidity are these institutions we have built—stupidity not so much of the inmates as of free citizens! What a mockery of science are our prison discipline, our massing of social iniquity in prisons, the good and the bad together in one stupendous *pot-pourri*. How silly of us to think that we can

---

[4] Clair Wilcox, "Prison Conditions and Penal Reform," *Editorial Research Reports,* Vol. 3, No. 6, May 8, 1930, p. 328.

prepare men for social life by reversing the ordinary process of socialization—silence for the only animal with speech; repressive regimentation of men who are in prison because they need to learn how to exercise their activities in constructive ways; outward conformity to rules which repress all efforts at constructive expression; work without the operation of economic motives; motivation by fear of punishment rather than hope of reward or appeal to their higher motives; cringing rather than growth in manliness; rewards secured by the betrayal of a fellow rather than the development of a larger loyalty.[5]

Abnormal sex life in prisons. Although we rarely find the subject mentioned in textbooks, perhaps the worst evil that exists in prison life is the necessarily frustrated and abnormal sex life of convicts. This situation is particularly distressing because it is the one field in which no reform measures are being taken. Even most of the leading prison reformers of our day hesitate even to mention the subject or to suggest remedies.[6] The sex situation in prisons is even worse than in abnormal modes of existence outside, for, in addition to the blocking of normal sexual manifestations, there is little opportunity for sublimation through professional, cultural, or recreational outlets. Hence, the sex urge inevitably finds expression in all sorts of pathological conduct. If we were consciously to plan an institution perfectly designed to promote sexual degeneracy we would envisage the modern prison. Masturbation and homosexuality among prisoners are commonplace.

The vile and degrading conditions which are thus brought about are, after all, the least serious aspect of this abnormal situation. The most deplorable result is the fact that these sex perversions are normally associated with the pathogenesis of many types of psychic abnormality and emotional instability, many of which emerge in definite criminal compulsions. The sexual results of prison life, which have been all but ignored by both conventional criminologists and reformers, would suffice *per se* to create and train a veritable crop of degenerates and potential criminals.

Not only is the sex situation in the modern prison one of the most challenging of the social, psychological, and administrative problems existing in penal institutions; it is also one of the most impossible to deal with in a rational or efficient fashion. With society still medieval in its attitude toward the sexual problem in the general social world outside the prison, there is even less hope that it will be able to handle the sexual problem within prisons in an intelligent or expeditious manner. This fact constitutes an additional argument for the abolition of the present prison system. Pending the time of this achievement, American penologists will do well to study the remarkable success of Latin American prison administrators in dealing with the realities of the prison sex situation, and this in strongly religious countries.

---

[5] From J. L. Gillin, *Taming the Criminal.* New York: Macmillan, 1931, pp. 295-296. By permission of The Macmillan Company, publishers.

[6] Joseph Fulling Fishman has been the only professional penologist who has dared expose in thorough fashion the sexual depravity produced by prison life. See his *Sex Life in Prison.* New York: National Library Press, 1934.

THE RISE OF TECHNIQUES DESIGNED TO REFORM CONVICTS OUTSIDE OF INSTITUTIONS

Failure of prisons to reform inmates leads to new vistas in penological theory and practice. Although the principles of the new penology have stressed rehabilitation rather than punishment, various students of the post-release careers of those discharged from prisons have made it very clear that even the inmates of the better prisons and reformatories are rarely reformed as a result of their incarceration. Recognition of this fact has given rise to the growing conviction that, if we are actually to rehabilitate convicts, this achievement must be accomplished mainly *outside of institutions* through techniques which will combine the protection of the public with the use of methods and facilities that can actually accomplish the rehabilitation of a considerable number of delinquents.

As we noted above, the only complete adoption of this fourth stage of dealing with convicts has been in the Youth Correction Authority program that has developed mainly within the last decade. Down to the present time this has been adopted by no more than a handful of states, and even in these few instances it has been limited chiefly to juvenile delinquents.

The suspended sentence and probation. The only procedure which has been widely followed thus far in trying to reform delinquents outside of institutions and has been applied to adults as well as juveniles is probation, which is used in connection with a suspended sentence.

The use of the suspended sentence along with a sort of informal probation system has existed for a considerable period in England. An offender could be bound over to responsible persons who agreed to produce him at the order of the court. Informal probation preceded specific legislation in this country. Massachusetts was the pioneer in both. Judge Peter O. Thacher of Boston began probation in an informal way in 1831, by handing over convicted persons to the sheriff and other responsible officials. A benign Boston shoemaker by the name of John Augustus induced the court to bail over to him drunkards and others in 1841. He continued his activities with much success for some 18 years and handled over 2,000 cases. The Children's Aid Society of Boston carried on his work. Beginning in 1869, the visiting agents for the Massachusetts State Board of Charities were allowed to take juvenile delinquents and place them in homes. They handled about 4,500 cases in 10 years. Finally, in 1878, Massachusetts passed a law setting up a probation system in Suffolk county, and in 1891 a state-wide probation system was created. Maryland passed a probation law in 1894; Missouri, in 1897; Vermont, in 1898; and Illinois, Minnesota and Rhode Island, in 1899. The Rhode Island system was the first to be administered by the state.

By 1900, then, some seven states had established probation systems, and four of them, Massachusetts, Maryland, Vermont and Rhode Island, permitted the probation of adults. The juvenile court movement, which has always been closely associated with the probation system, was instituted by the Illinois probation law of 1899. Publicized by Benjamin B.

Lindsey in Denver, it spread rather rapidly after 1910. Today all states permit juvenile probation. Some 42 states permit the probation of adult delinquents, and the Federal government established a probation system for Federal prisoners in 1925. About 35 per cent of adult convicts and some 68 per cent of all convicted juvenile delinquents are now put on probation. After a comprehensive study of the subject, N. S. Timasheff concludes that adults respond as successfully to probationary methods as juveniles.

The basic argument in behalf of probation is that it permits the application of rehabilitative techniques to delinquents outside of the demoralizing prison atmosphere. But there are also important special advantages associated with this procedure. In the first place, it is far more economical to handle delinquents on probation than it is to provide maintenance for convicts in prisons and reformatories. Good probation systems cost only about one-tenth as much per capita as the total expense of prison maintenance per prisoner. Offenders on probation usually have to provide for their own support. Another advantage of probation is that it avoids both the stigma of having served a prison sentence and the demoralizing effect of association with hardened convicts.

The person on probation has a strong incentive to do his best to reform in order to remain out of prison. The facilities which may aid in rehabilitation—guidance clinics, public health clinics, social settlements, recreational centers, and night schools—are more numerous and accessible outside institutions than within. Perhaps most important of all is the fact that the person on probation is assisted in making an adjustment to the social environment in which he must live as a free man rather than being induced to be a good convict in the highly artificial and regimented surroundings of a prison or reformatory. Probation may make a man a good citizen; prisons at best can only make him a good convict.

As to just how much use is made of probation today we are not precisely certain because the Bureau of the Census ceased the publication of its figures on this subject in 1946, and no private organization has stepped into the gap to provide this factual information. The latest official statistics of the mid-1940's indicate that about 35 per cent of convicted adult offenders are put on probation under suspended sentences. The proportion differs markedly with the states. Rhode Island uses it for over 60 per cent of adult cases; Ohio, for about 45 per cent; New York and New Jersey, for about 35 per cent; and Iowa and North Dakota, for only about 13 per cent. The percentage is higher with juveniles than with adults. In 1945, 68 per cent of the juvenile cases disposed of by the courts were put on probation. It is generally held that a probation officer should not have more than 50 persons under his supervision; 25 would be better; and even with 10 probation would be cheaper than imprisonment.

Probation has been far more effective than imprisonment in rehabilitating delinquents. This has been due in part to the fact that the least serious criminals are usually put on probation, but it has been mainly a result of the better atmosphere and treatment provided by probationary methods. It is doubtful if the best prisons reform more than 15 per cent of those incarcerated, probably much less, while about 75 per cent of those handled by competent probation systems are rehabilitated. Spectacular success has been achieved at times in the use of probation, even with hardened adult criminals. The Court of General Sessions in New York City, which deals with dangerous felons, puts 25 to 30 per cent of those convicted on probation, and has achieved about 90 per cent success in rehabilitation. The Superior Court of Los Angeles puts about 52 per cent of those convicted on probation and the Inferior Court about 69 per cent; they have obtained as good results as the New York court.

There is no valid criticism of the principle of probation. What is needed is more numerous personnel, better training of probation officers, and complete independence of partisan politics. Another desirable reform is the provision of more state-wide administration of probation systems. At present all too much probation is under the control of local courts.

Rise of the parole system. The aim of probation is to treat convicts without the necessity of their spending any time whatever within an institution. Probation represents the most complete application of the fourth stage of penological theory and practice which holds that convicted delinquents must be reformed, if at all, mainly outside of institutions. What we term *parole* requires a period of incarceration prior to release into the general social environment. It is therefore only a partial manifestation of the program of treating convicts outside of institutions. But to the extent that it enables a delinquent to serve part of his sentence outside of institutions, it represents a great advance over the older practice of compelling a convict to serve his entire sentence within prison walls.

Parole should not be confused with a relatively old and somewhat common practice of commuting a prisoner's sentence for good behavior. Under the commutation system, when a prisoner is discharged, his sentence is ended and he has no official supervision of his conduct by any public authorities. Although good behavior is normally required as a requisite for parole, the time served before parole is usually less than in the case of a man who is released under the commutation system. But more important than this is the fact that under the parole system a released convict is at least supposed to be supervised until the expiration of his sentence by a parole officer whose responsibility it is to aid the parolee in every possible way.

The ideal of parole was born about the same time as probation. The principle of parole was warmly recommended by a French publicist, Bonneville de Marsagny, in the 1840's. First used with adults in the Irish prison system in the 1850's, it was adopted in most western European countries in the latter half of the nineteenth century. Parole came to this country in the law of 1869 which created the Elmira Reformatory. Under this law, parole was used only with the delinquent youths who were admitted to the institution. The first state here to enact a law making adult inmates of penal institutions eligible to parole was Ohio, which passed such an act in 1884. Today all the states and the Federal prison system make use of parole, although, as we shall see, few states have set up a parole system which provides really effective supervision of parolees. About 40,000 convicts are released on parole each year and from 15 to 40 per cent of these are returned for parole violation or other reasons.

Parole is supposed to be operated in conjunction with the indeterminate sentence, but few states have any thoroughgoing indeterminate sentence laws except for juvenile delinquents. For adults the laws usually still provide maximum and minimum sentences, and make convicts legally eligible for parole at the expiration of the minimum sentence.

Purposes and advantages of parole. There are a number of arguments which are advanced in behalf of the parole system. One is the fact that progressive penologists are generally agreed that long prison terms usually help to demoralize the convict and to make him a more serious, determined, and dangerous criminal. In any event, long prison terms tend to make a man unfit for normal social existence. Hence, by shortening the term served in prison, parole tends to reduce the demoralizing influence of prison life upon the convict. Another reason why parole is regarded as helpful lies in the sharp contrast between prison life and normal social existence outside the institution. The discharged convict is in special need of aid and counsel when he is released from the institution. Without a parole system, he is thrown entirely on his own resources as soon as he leaves the prison gate. If there is a good parole system, well-trained and sympathetic parole officers seek to provide the released person with employment, to keep him out of trouble, and to help him adjust himself to normal society. Finally, parole enables a convicted delinquent to serve out a portion of his sentence in the environment to which he must make a satisfactory adjustment if he is to be reformed. In this respect, parole has the advantages we listed above in connection with probationary procedure.

Inadequate nature of most parole systems today. The principle underlying parole is surely above criticism. What is wrong is the fact that what frequently passes for parole is such in name only. Only about a dozen states and the Federal government operate a parole system for adult prisoners that can be correctly regarded as anything approaching parole as it should be administered. And neither the Federal government nor any state has anything like an ideal system.

The following amazing facts were assembled by the Prison Association of New York in a survey of 133 major penal institutions of the country. Some 42 of these prisons had no parole officer at all, though 12,182 convicts were out on parole from these institutions at the time. This is not parole at all; it is only commutation of sentence under a different name. In many of the other prisons studied the situation was little better. Fourteen of the prisons had one parole officer for each 85 parolees; 10 had one officer for each 120; two had one officer for each 128; four had one officer for each 142; 36 had one officer for each 238; five had one officer for each 344; and one had one parole officer for each 682 on parole. There was also a notorious lack of funds for administering the parole system. In Georgia, for example, the only appropriation for parole work was $25 a year for postage. In 1939, James V. Bennett, Director of the Federal

Bureau of Prisons, estimated that, out of 40,000 persons on parole, at least 20,000 were without any effective supervision.

If parole is to mean anything, and if it is to accomplish the results hoped for, it must be a literal parole system. There must be an adequate number of parole officers. They must be experts in criminology and social work. They must be paid enough by the state to hold their loyalty and command their best efforts.

The reorganization and thorough application of the parole system is something more than a potential reform which we may safely await in the distant future. If we intend to be more liberal in paroling men, we must have a better system of parole supervision. If we were to turn loose any great number of convicts and trust to a paper parole scheme, it would be about as unwise as to open the gates of the prisons and invite the men to walk out. Bigger and better parole work is indispensable, but it must be better as well as bigger.

J. Edgar Hoover has led in an attack on parole as an obstacle to crime repression. In the opinion of most authorities, he has exaggerated the case against parole. Only parole violators ever break into the papers and constitute "news." The great majority of parolees, who live law-abiding lives, are never mentioned and are usually overlooked. Moreover, the fact that many parolees are returned to prison need not mean that the parole system is not working. It may mean only very alert and expert supervision and an ideal operation of the plan. Yet the real weakness in the parole system must be faced and eliminated. The New York state parole law, passed in 1930, might well serve as a model for general imitation. But it will do little good to pass the best of parole laws unless enough money is appropriated to operate the system efficiently.

Illogical premises and practices of even good parole systems. Even the better parole systems are operated upon a completely illogical principle —that of letting out the less risky prisoners on parole quickly and of keeping the more dubious inmates incarcerated until near the end of their maximum sentence before admitting them to parole. There is no objection to letting good risks out speedily on parole; the sooner the better, within reason. But it is a great mistake to keep the possibly dangerous types in prison until about the time their sentences will expire. It is, of course, assumed that the obviously or apparently nonreformable convicts will not be admitted to parole at all. They should be detained in prison permanently.

If parole is any aid to rehabilitation, and all good parole is surely this, then it is the more risky types of prisoners who most need parole aid and guidance. The longer they can have it, the better. But, under the present system, these more risky types get only a few months of parole super-vision before their sentences expire. They then become completely free. Moreover, the chances are that the extra years spent in prison will have made them worse risks for parole than they would have been if released on parole as early as feasible. It is likely that, under our present prison system, any average inmate is a better parole risk after one or two years of imprisonment than after 10 years.

Another mistaken procedure that characterizes even the better parole systems is the practice of allowing parole boards, whose members rarely have had any previous contact with inmates, to decide which prisoners should be admitted to parole and when they should be admitted. There is no sound basis for such procedure. The only group qualified to recommend a convict for parole is the trained, professional treatment staff of prisons and reformatories, just as the physicians in a state mental hospital are the sole authorities competent to decide when a patient is safe to discharge.

Conditional release under close supervision. Thus far, the boldest proposal with respect to releasing adult convicts for treatment in the world outside has been one already used with success in several European countries—that of limited conditional release under much closer supervision than is provided by either traditional probation or parole.

The type of inmate to be released under this plan would be one who presumably could not, for the time being, be safely let out on probation or parole, but who does not require complete segregation even in a medium-security institution. Perhaps one-third or more of the inmates of our penal and correctional institutions today would fall within this group. They would require closer inspection and a larger supervisory force than are necessary for probationers or parolees, but, even so, such released convicts could be supervised at far less expense than the cost of their care in an institution. Even with one supervising official to every 10 or 15 conditionally-released convicts, the cost of supervision would be less than that required to support them in institutions. It should, of course, be stipulated that employment must be provided for those released to supervision for any prolonged period.

In countries where this plan has been tried successfully, a start is usually made by letting inmates go home under close supervision during weekends. Subsequently, the period of supervised release may be extended to include working in emergency periods, such as harvest time. If the prisoner's behavior is satisfactory during these short test periods, he may be released indefinitely under supervision. In due time, those who have behaved well under close supervision may be admitted to routine parole, where the extent of supervision would be greatly reduced. This supervised release procedure provides almost the only method of solving the degrading prison sex problem that is virtually ignored in even the most advanced penal treatment programs.

As a general proposition, this conditional release has most of the advantages of probation, except for the fact that the released prisoners bear the stigma of a prison sentence. It is more economical than institutional care, can make use of community facilities for rehabilitation, and brings about the readjustment of the released men in the environment in which we hope they will live as law-abiding citizens. The entire plan is in harmony with the growing conviction that most of the successful rehabilitation of convicts must take place outside of institutions. Indeed, the eminent penologist, Howard B. Gill, who is the leading American exponent of the conditional release program, would limit the rôle of prisons (except in the case of desperate and nonreformable offenders) mainly to the study and classification of inmates before their release under various forms of supervision.[6a]

DEVELOPMENT OF THE YOUTH CORRECTION AUTHORITY PROGRAM

Background of the Youth Correction Authority Act. Earlier in this chapter we made brief reference to the fact that the Youth Correction Authority program represented the most complete adoption to date of the principles and practices underlying the fourth stage in our treatment of convicted criminals—that stage in which we handle as many of them as possible outside of institutions.

The Youth Correction Authority idea grew out of a number of practices and convictions, some of which had been in the minds of progressive penologists for a long time. Belief in the primacy of rehabilitation over punishment in rational penology is more than 100 years old. The notion that we can treat many delinquents more economically and effectively outside of institutions than within them lay at the basis of the development of probation and parole. The juvenile court movement and child guidance clinics demonstrated the value of a scientific approach to juvenile delinquency. In the decade or so prior to the Second World War, a number of careful studies revealed the striking failure of even reformatories and juvenile institutions to rehabilitate their inmates. In the 1930's, there were also a number of scandals exposed in the operation of juvenile institutions, some of which were commonly regarded as among the best in the country. All of these things were favorable to the encouragement of some comprehensive plan to repudiate the futility of the mistakes of the past and to formulate a program which would utilize the best existing knowledge and experience in laying out a future procedure which offered some hope of greater success in dealing with juvenile delinquency.

Although a number of persons were involved in the early developments which led to the formulation of the Youth Correction Authority Act of 1940, two men were especially active and important in this stage of the program. John D. Rockefeller, III, had been profoundly impressed by *Youth in the Toils,* a book by Leonard Harrison and Pryor Grant, published in 1938. This was an especially striking review of the extent of juvenile delinquency and of the signal failure of existing agencies and methods to check its growth. This encouraged Rockefeller to offer funds to help in discovering some way out of the dilemma.

Practical leadership was taken by John B. Waite, of the University of Michigan Law School, long known as one of the most enlightened students of the crime problem in the United States. He had been serving on a committee of the American Bar Association that was dealing with criminal justice. Shortly thereafter the problem of working out a rational plan

---

[6a] "One Hundred Years of Penal Progress," *Prison Journal,* January, 1945.

for handling juvenile delinquents was assigned to the American Law Institute, among the leaders of which were William Draper Lewis, Karl N. Llewellyn, and Leon C. Marshall.

The Youth Correction Authority Act. The Committee of the Institute, of which Waite was a leading member, handed in its report and the draft of a model Youth Correction Authority Act in May, 1940. It was to apply to juvenile delinquents between 16 and 21 years of age. Waite thus summarized the main conceptions involved in the Act:

> The act provides for four things. First, that when a youth is convicted—is found guilty of an offense—there shall be a careful investigation made of the cause of his offense. Second, that anything within the bounds of what is humane shall be put into operation to correct that cause and prevent his further criminality. Third, that when he is released he shall be actively aided to lead an honest life. Fourth, that if he cannot be made safe, he shall be kept in custody for life. That is rather more drastic than the punitive statutes, when you come right down to it.[7]

As a practical procedure, the report and model act proposed to set up a Correction Authority composed of trained experts in the field of juvenile delinquency who would have more or less complete authority over all juvenile delinquents in any state. No fixed sentences would be imposed, and the Authority would be authorized to determine to what extent to use institutional treatment and to what degree it should be entirely dispensed with. As far as compatible with safety and reason, these juvenile delinquents were to be treated on probation outside of institutions. Glen R. Winters thus summarizes the essentials of the Youth Correction Authority Act:

> The Youth Correction Authority Act is beamed at the wayward minor group, ages sixteen to twenty-one. It assumes that they will go through the regular criminal courts of the state up to and including the point of conviction. At that point, unless the youth is merely to be fined, or sentence suspended, or unless he has committed a capital offense, he is committed to the Authority. That is the only sentence pronounced by the judge, and from there on the Authority takes over, makes such investigations as is warranted and administers whatever treatment it considers most appropriate for whatever length of time it deems necessary, the objective being the restoration of the subject to normal, productive life as soon as possible. Treatment may range from probation under supervision of the Authority, through occupational therapy in camps and on farms, to confinement in institutions of various grades of security.[8]

The California Youth Authority. The first state to adopt the Youth Correction program was California. Evidence of serious maladministration of the model institution for juvenile delinquents at Whittier led to the appointment of an investigating committee under the leadership of Benjamin B. Lindsey. This committee handed in its report in December, 1940, and it strongly recommended the adoption of the Youth Correction Authority program. The legislature passed an act in June, 1941, carrying

---

[7] E. T. Stromberg (Ed.), *Crimes of Violence.* Boulder: University of Colorado Press, 1950, p. 92.

[8] *Virginia Law Weekly,* April 21, 1949, p. 1.

out these recommendations, and an appropriation was made to permit operation for two years. A skeleton organization was set up to launch the plan. The program really got under way in 1943, when the legislature transferred the three main institutions for juvenile delinquents to the Youth Correction Authority. A much larger appropriation was made to permit the adequate operation of the program. The title of the new organization entrusted with the administration of the plan was then changed to the Youth Authority.

The California Youth Authority is composed of three members, the Chairman being the chief administrative officer. The other two members have charge of such things as diagnosis, classification, placement of screened delinquents, probation, parole, and discharge. The Authority makes use of the existing staffs of juvenile institutions, probation officers, and parole boards. It has brought about a rather thorough reorganization of both the probation and parole systems of the state.

The Youth Authority has complete control of juvenile delinquents, except in cases where the judge imposes a fine or where the youth has committed a capital crime. In the latter instance, the convicted youth must be sent to a state prison. The original Youth Correction Authority Act of 1940 advocated a complete and thoroughgoing indeterminate sentence. The California law did not go as far as that. It requires the Authority to discharge: "(1) any person committed by a juvenile court when he reaches his twenty-first birthday or two years after commitment, whichever occurs later; (2) any person committed for a misdemeanor by a criminal court, on his twenty-third birthday or at the end of two years, whichever occurs later; and (3) any person committed for a felony by a criminal court, on his twenty-fifth birthday, unless the Authority believes he would be dangerous to the public and petitions the court to transfer the person to a state prison for a period equal to the rest of the maximum term prescribed by law for the offense of which he was convicted."

When a juvenile delinquent is handed over to the Youth Authority by the court, the first step in the procedure is to send the youth to a diagnostic clinic or reception center, where he is studied carefully during a period of four to six weeks. At the outset, the Preston School for Boys was utilized as the diagnostic clinic, but two new reception centers were built, one at Sacramento and one at Los Angeles. The procedure in the diagnostic clinic has been thus described by Winters:

Here takes place the medical examination; the assemblage of a complete social and environmental background picture; psychological diagnosis to learn of possible psychological factors inclining the subject to crime and to uncover clues to constructive interest and activities that will assist in his rehabilitation; and a period of personal observation extending from four to six weeks. At the conclusion of this period all specialists who have participated in the case join in a conference where all findings are brought together and discussed and the most promising type of treatment is agreed upon.

When it is deemed safe to do so as a result of screening at the diagnostic clinic, the delinquent youth is placed on probation. In making use of probation under the Youth Authority, it was necessary to rely upon the probation system of the state of California which was, as usual, under local control. In many parts of the state the probation system was very inadequate, with a single probation officer having as many as 200 children under his charge. The Youth Authority was able to bring about a very considerable improvement of the probation service, but it has never been able to get full control over it. This is one of the main defects of the Youth Authority administration in California.

When it is thought best to send a juvenile delinquent to an institution for temporary study and treatment, the Authority has access to a wide diversity of institutions—from the two state prisons to the new forestry camps which the Authority has established. Mainly, however, it makes use of the three state juvenile institutions—the Schools for Boys at Whittier and Preston, and the Ventura School for Girls—the five forestry camps which it has set up, and the remarkable Fricot Ranch School, which has provisions for about 100 inmates. In all of these institutions every possible effort is made to replace the punitive atmosphere by one of education and helpful treatment. The inmate is made to feel that he or she is receiving sympathetic and affectionate treatment and education rather than "doing time" on a sentence. At the outset, some trouble was experienced with existing staffs, who in some instances were opposed to the new and more enlightened attitude. But the Authority now has this situation well under control, and the staff of each institution has adapted itself to the purposes envisaged in the Authority program.

Perhaps the most notable institutional innovation has been the forestry camps, each with 50 or 75 boys. Such camps are used during the entire year for fire-fighting and reforestation. Inmates are paid about 50 cents daily. Many counties have also established forestry and other work camps for delinquent youth. California has thus taken the lead in establishing camps as custodial and treatment institutions for delinquents —a departure which has received much praise from enlightened penologists.

When a youthful delinquent is released from an institution, he is supervised under parole for a desirable period. As might be expected, parole supervision is extremely important and vital in the Youth Authority picture. In the beginning, the parole system, like the probation service, was defective, but the Youth Authority has remedied this situation and has been able to assume control over the parole system for juvenile delinquents. In 1945 it reorganized the entire parole system for juvenile delinquents, dividing it into five districts with headquarters at Sacramento, San Francisco, Oakland, Fresno, and Los Angeles. The administration of the parole system is centralized under the Chief of the Field Services of the Youth Authority. By 1947 there was a staff of 43 parole officers, with about 80 parolees under each officer. The parole officers were college graduates with professional training, and a pay scale was set up adequate to attract and hold a competent staff.

The results of the work of the Youth Authority have vindicated the hopes of its sponsors. From 1943 through mid-1947, 6,628 juvenile delinquents had been released on parole, and only 992, or 14.9 per cent were rearrested.

The Youth Authority carries on many and sundry activities intended to survey and control the juvenile delinquency situation in California. It conducts crime surveys for the Youth Authority and for the state and the counties. It has set up a Central Juvenile Index under the control of the Probation Department to assemble data concerning all juvenile delinquents in the state. It also helps to organize and guide the community programs of the states in their efforts at crime prevention, especially the prevention of juvenile delinquency.

The logic and success of the California Youth Authority program have induced other states to adopt a similar system. Minnesota and Wisconsin adopted it in 1947, Massachusetts in 1948, and Texas in 1949. To eliminate as far as possible the punitive aspect of the program, Minnesota called its organization *The Youth Conservation Commission;* Wisconsin designated its authority as *The Youth Service Division;* and Massachusetts adopted the name *Youth Service Board.* The Youth Authority plan has also been adopted in a restricted way by New York and New Jersey. As a result of the Kilgore-Walter Act, signed by President Truman on September 30, 1950, the Federal government adopted the Youth Authority system.

If punitive institutional treatment for suitable youthful offenders is to be repudiated and abandoned, we obviously need to give greater attention to educational treatment programs. Perhaps the most interesting experiment along this line is the Highfields Experimental Treatment Project at Hopewell, New Jersey, set up by the New Jersey Department of Institutions and Agencies under the direction of F. Lovell Bixby and Lloyd W. McCorkle, with support from the Vincent Astor Foundation of New York City. Here a small selected group of boys are given intensive social reeducation completely devoid of the traditional punitive patterns.

The California Adult Authority. This Youth Authority plan represents a rather thorough application of the theories and practices of the fourth stage of dealing with delinquents. Naturally, public opinion sanctioned it first for younger delinquents. But California had the vision and courage to take the first step in introducing the same plan, with restrictions, to adults. In February, 1944, the legislature passed a law creating the California Adult Authority; it also provided for a general Prison Reorganization Act. The Adult Authority is headed by the Director of Corrections, who has been Richard McGee, a highly enlightened American penologist who was brought in from New York City to head the new system. The Adult Authority generally adheres to the same concepts and practices that guide the Youth Authority, although its operations are more restricted by legislation, tradition, and public opinion.

The Adult Authority is made up of three members. In sentencing, judges impose only the maximum and minimum limits set by statute for any given crime. Convicted adult delinquents are sent to the two reception centers at San Quentin and Lancaster. Two new centers are being constructed and are known as Guidance Centers. After a period of study and diagnosis at the guidance centers, which requires from four to eight weeks, the Adult Authority imposes the actual sentence to be served. This sentence is usually somewhere between the maximum and minimum statutory sentence. The Adult Authority may reduce this original sentence later for good and sufficient cause. The Adult Authority has the right to parole any sentenced person at any time, with the exception of recidivists, who must be held for a longer period. Most inmates are eligible for parole within a year.

After diagnosis and sentence, the delinquent is sent to an appropriate institution. Every effort is made to eliminate the punitive attitude. The Authority exercises full control over all disciplinary procedure.

If institutional treatment is not regarded as necessary, the Adult Authority may admit the delinquent to probationary treatment at once. The parole system has been greatly improved. By 1947, there were about 90 parolees under each parole officer, and a goal of 75 had been set. A Supervisor of Placement was created who helps parolees to find employment. The industrial situation for adult delinquents was greatly improved. In penal and reformatory institutions, inmates are paid up to 50 cents per day. In the forestry and road camps they are paid between $15 and $50 a month. Each parolee receives $40 "gate money" when admitted to parole. The Adult Authority makes all investigations and recommendations for executive clemency and pardon.

By creating the Adult Authority, California progressed to the fourth stage of treating convicted adult delinquents. Of course, the transition is not yet complete, but the crucial initial steps have been taken. This is the stage to which all states must advance if there is to be any hope of reforming any considerable number of convicted persons. Thus far, no other state has possessed the courage and vision of California in this respect. James V. Bennett, Director of the Federal Bureau of Prisons, has long recommended a similar adult authority for the Federal prison system, but thus far his efforts have not met with success.

MAIN OBSTACLES TO REFORMATION IN PENAL INSTITUTIONS

Great contrast between theory and practice in the treatment of convicts today. In few fields of human endeavor is there a greater contrast between theory and practice than we find today in our penal institutions.

There is an astonishing diversity both in theory and practice between the better and the poorer systems of institutional administration. The accepted theory of enlightened penology is that which envisages the treatment of all convicts except the nonreformable mainly outside of institutions, but this has been attained in practice and only partially in California. In the practical administration of our penological system, the most enlightened practice is still that of the third stage of penological evolution—the use of institutions as the main agency for rehabilitating inmates. In literal operation, even this procedure is found only in the prisons operated by the Federal Bureau of Prisons and by a mere handful of the more enlightened states. This stage of penological theory had been rather fully developed back in the 1850's in the Irish prison system. Therefore, it is not unfair to say that even the best practice in our penal and correctional institutions has only caught up with the best theory of a ceuntry ago. Indeed, the whole theoretical basis of the new penology was set forth by Benjamin Rush in Philadelphia no less than 165 years ago.

In their actual administration, the great majority of American penal and correctional institutions still follow the theory of the second stage of penological development—the utilization of institutions primarily to punish inmates. The custodial staff may, and usually does, give lip service to the ideal of reformation, but the operative administration of the institution is primarily punitive. It offers little opportunity for the application of rehabilitative measures or for the creation of an atmosphere which is favorable to an enthusiastic response by the inmate to such measures.

The reason for this disparity between theory and practice we shall now proceed to explain. It is due primarily to what we call the "convict bogey," the resulting jailing psychosis, and the existence of a code of convict attitude and behavior which is in most cases hostile to rehabilitative measures.

The convict bogey. Curiously and illogically enough, people do not seem to fear criminals until the latter have been pronounced guilty by a jury—certainly a very trivial basis for any such abrupt and sweeping change of attitude. Indeed, if the criminal is sufficiently dangerous and glamorous and has been well-publicized, those financially able to do so are frequently willing to pay a high cover charge at a fashionable night club to get a look at him from a nearby table. But let a man be convicted of even a minor felony and be put safely behind prison bars, where for the time being he cannot be a menace to society, and we suddenly become terror-stricken lest he escape.

The jailing psychosis. As Frank Tannenbaum has made clear in his book, *Wall Shadows,* the convict bogey leads directly to the jailing psychosis which continues to dominate the actual operation of our penal institutions, however much we may give lip service to the nobility of rehabilitative treatment. The fundamental function of a penal and correctional institution is believed to be that of preventing convicts from escaping. The good warden or superintendent is the one who keeps his convict charges safely jailed, even though he never reforms a single one of them—indeed, even though the vast majority are turned out more desperate characters than they were when they were committed to prison.

Because most institutional officials desire to hold their jobs, they have to be extremely solicitous and apprehensive in executing this jailing function. One escape will attract more attention than the rehabilitation of 100 inmates by up-to-date treatment methods. Therefore, rehabilitative treatment, always dominant in rhetoric and theory in any enlightened institution, tends to be either subordinated or discarded altogether in practice. The jailing psychosis demands major emphasis upon high walls, steel cages, machine guns, tear gas, arbitrary inmate routine, and a rigorous punitive discipline. Treatment, on the other hand, stresses the primacy of a flexible program which can be tempered to the needs of the different types of inmates, and which inevitably carries with it some custodial risks. Because secure jailing of convicts promises greater assurance of tenure, administrators—willingly or unwillingly—continue to give most of their concern to safe jailing. They thus persist in punishing convicts, and they devote relatively little attention to an effective treatment program.

Futility and danger of the convict bogey and jailing psychosis. The best answer to the convict bogey and the jailing psychosis is to emphasize the all-important fact that the main danger from convicts is not that they may escape prematurely but that we may fail to reform them before they are released in lawful fashion. The average time served by all inmates of our penal and correctional institutions is only about two years and six months. Even those sentenced for life serve on an average only about 10 years. This means that the average convict will be released every 30 months to proceed once more with his antisocial depredations unless he is reformed while in an institution. This is a far more alarming fact than the possibility that a negligible fraction may escape to resume their criminal activity a few months before they would have been released in the ordinary course of events. These facts make it obvious that our only real protection against convicts is to reform them while they are incarcerated. Making them more bitter, determined, and skillful criminals by locking them in steel cages for a couple of years provides slight protection indeed.

The code of convict behavior also frustrates rehabilitative measures. The atmosphere and administrative procedure created by the convict bogey and the jailing psychosis have developed a type of convict reaction and a code of convict behavior which also strongly militate against the effective operation of rehabilitative measures.[9] The cruelty and regimentation produced by the jailing psychosis have made it difficult for the custodial staff of institutions to be primarily concerned with rehabilitation. Such attitudes and procedures by the staff have developed a type of response on the part of convicts which renders it difficult for the latter to respond enthusiastically to reformative treatment, even when the custodial staff is seriously devoted to rehabilitation and a good treatment staff has been provided.

The atmosphere of the traditional fortress prison, with its tiers of steel cages, creates a depressed attitude on the part of convicts and tends to make them more concerned with escape or release than with reformation. Cruel and brutal regimentation of prisoners by wardens, deputies and

---

[9] On this matter, see Donald Clemmer, *The Prison Community*. New York: Christopher, 1940; and "Observations on Imprisonment as a Source of Criminality," in *Journal of Criminal Law and Criminology*, September-October, 1950.

guards inevitably has led the convict population to develop a code of conduct designed to "beat the game" and secure as much relief as possible from severe institutional discipline. This code is well organized and applied in every important prison—even in the best of them. It is handed down from generation to generation, and every new inmate is thoroughly initiated and indoctrinated. The custodial staff is regarded as the natural enemy of the convict population. Cordial inmate cooperation with the custodial staff is regarded as akin to treason.

All this was entirely understandable, and perhaps pardonable, in institutions devoted primarily to punishment. But it has held over into the present enlightened period of penal administration. It is one of the most powerful obstacles to the application of rehabilitative treatment in any prison. Until prison architecture is improved and the convict population is convinced that treatment rather than punishment is the main motive of institutional administration, it will be difficult to eradicate this convict code which so effectively obstructs any effective rehabilitative program. This has been well understood by the California Youth Authority, and it is the main reason for its effort to induce juvenile delinquents to regard their residence in an institution as a period of training rather than as a term of punishment.

The best proof that this ancient convict code of hostility and non-violent non-cooperation can be broken down in a properly-built and -administered institution is the experience at the Federal minimum-security institution at Seagoville, Texas. Here, with virtually no provisions for safe jailing, there have been a minimum of attempts to escape and inmates have warmly cooperated with the staff in setting up and operating one of the most effective treatment programs to be found in any institution in the world. Comparable success has been achieved by Kenyon Scudder in the model California institution at Chino, near Los Angeles.

The detainer nuisance. Another obstacle to reform in prison that is rarely mentioned but is important is what has been called the detainer nuisance. A detainer is a notice filed with the warden of a prison stating that a given prisoner is wanted for prosecution on another charge, either in the same state or in another. When such a prisoner is brought to the prison vestibule for release at the end of his term, he is picked up by an officer who takes him under guard to the jail where he will be held pending his trial on the charge mentioned in the detainer. About 20 per cent of the inmates of prisons for serious adult delinquents have detainers filed against them. They know this in advance, usually, and the knowledge destroys any effort to reform while in the institution. Such prisoners know they will not regain their freedom and have little or no incentive to reform. They are not eligible for release on parole.

The only sensible procedure is to abolish the detainer system, save perhaps for unusually atrocious cases. If a prisoner has proved his fitness for release while serving a prison sentence, he should be let out on parole and freed at the end of his sentence if his parole record has been good. The detainer system is an especially vicious vestige of the old era of punishment and social revenge and it only serves to demoralize rehabilitative measures. Not only are prisoners who have detainers hanging over their heads likely to be sullen and unruly but they adversely influence the conduct of other inmates with whom they circulate.

CURRENT REALITIES AND PROBLEMS OF PRISON ADMINISTRATION

Discussions of penological practices must deal with existing realities. We have made it clear that the overwhelming majority of American penal and correctional institutions are still actually operating on the basis of punitive measures. We have also shown that all enlightened penologists recognize the vicious menace and complete futility of this punitive prison system. Nevertheless, the actual prison picture in the United States is still much the same as it was at the time of the Civil War, except for the fact that many new structures—some gloomier than ever—have been erected. For example, the most expensive prison ever constructed, which opened in 1929 at Attica, New York, is a far more forbidding and impregnable collection of cages for human beings than was the Eastern Penitentiary of Pennsylvania which had opened exactly a century earlier.

In the light of these facts it is not necessary to repeat here any detailed description of prison life under the repressive punitive system. We have briefly described such conditions earlier in the chapter. We shall now discuss an enlightened program of prison administration and the problems associated with such a program.

The diagnostic clinic or reception center and the study and differentiation of convict types. The first step in the treatment program, after a person has been sentenced by the judge, is to discover the facts relative to the convict in question. If we are going to find a treatment to fit the criminal, we must first acquaint ourselves with this criminal.

This means the invariable establishment in any system of treatment of a reception center or diagnostic clinic well manned with personnel trained in social case work, clinical psychology, psychiatry, medicine, and penology. Such diagnostic clinics would gather every possible relevant fact concerning the life history, personality, and prognosis of the individual delinquent. Before specific treatment can be prescribed, it may also be necessary to observe his behavior in institutional routine. Once the facts are gathered, treatment may be recommended and initiated. Although this treatment must be highly individualized an analysis of convicts usually reveals three major classes or types.

First, there is a considerable group who do not appear to require any institutional segregation. They can be more satisfactorily handled in the general community by probationary methods.

At the other extreme, we find a much smaller group of apparently nonreformable convicts. Among these will be many habitual criminals, psychopaths and degenerates who should never be sent to a conventional penal institution but should be segregated in appropriate special institutions designed for these types of deviates. All apparently nonreformable

convicts should be detained permanently in a secure but humanely designed prison. The Federal Bureau of Prisons has already designed an
institution of this sort to replace the living hell which is Alcatraz. But,
even in the case of these convicts, an appropriate treatment program
should be set up. Persons who respond should be transferred to institutions where a more flexible and liberal program is possible.

The third group represents those for whom there is some hope of
reformation but who require extensive institutional treatment and training. They constitute the real prison problem. The nonreformable, who
must be segregated for life, present a relatively simple situation. Those
on probation fall outside the prison proper.

Of course, we do not contend that these three groups are hard and fast
and that they never overlap. Some of the apparently nonreformable types
may give evidence of possible improvement. Some of those on probation
may need to be sent to prison for treatment inside walls. Some of those
who, at first sight, seem reformable, may turn out to be hopeless. Only
experience and prolonged contact with members of each group will
enable us to check and recheck the results of the preliminary classification.
The best physicians and hospitals make mistakes of diagnosis and treatment. But we need not doubt the soundness of this basic threefold division
of the convict population of any state.

Institutional diversity and assignment. Once convicted delinquents are
carefully studied and screened at a reception center or diagnostic clinic,
the next step is to assign them to a suitable institution for treatment.
One phase of progress in penological practice during the last century
and a half has been the differentiation of institutions according to the
type of convicts to be received. Prisons have been differentiated in
the Federal and the better state systems according to the type of inmates
to be incarcerated: maximum-security prisons, medium-security penitentiaries, and medium- and minimum-security correctional institutions. In
this manner the more enlightened states have been provided with an
amply differentiated group of institutions suitable for most types of
convicted delinquents, with the qualification, of course, that probably
no delinquent type should be kept for long in any institution, with the
exception of those who are clearly nonreformable.

The classification of inmates and the development of a treatment staff.
Like the institutions which house them, institutional inmates, too, have
come to be classified. The first crude step in this direction came with the
separation of convicts into graded classes, based mainly upon their
conduct and prospect for reformation. This first appeared in the Irish
prison system and was a basic procedure in the Elmira Reformatory program. The next trend in this direction came with the introduction of
mental testing and psychiatric studies. Mental tests were administered to
the inmates of New York's Bedford Hills Reformatory for Women in
1913. Bernard Glueck made his pioneer study of the mental state of
selected Sing Sing inmates in 1916. This trend was also stimulated by
the mental and psychiatric tests given to soldiers during the First World
War. The first comprehensive effort to set up a system of classifying

institutional inmates on the basis of their life history, mental states, and outlook for reform was made in New Jersey following the report of the New Jersey Prison Inquiry Committee in 1918. Today the classification system is the basis for all enlightened institutional treatment of delinquents.

The introduction of the principle of classification in the study of delinquents made necessary the development of what we know as the treatment staff of an institution. This treatment staff is frequently called the classification clinic. When it meets to consider disciplinary problems, it is usually designated a behavior clinic. In its most complete form the treatment staff or classification clinic is composed of the following personnel: the superintendent or warden, the identification officer, the disciplinarian, the institution physician, a psychologist, a psychiatrist, the educational director, the chaplain, the industrial director, a social worker, and a sociologist.

The treatment staff makes use of all the data accumulated about each inmate as a result of the studies made at the reception center or diagnostic clinic, before any inmate is sent to a designated institution. On the basis of this information, the treatment staff makes a further intensive study of each delinquent, seeking to ascertain the cause of his delinquency and to recommend the type of individual treatment most likely to rehabilitate him. Such recommendations are checked and rechecked and are altered and modified as the behavior of the inmate in the institution appears to require. On the basis of the criminal's response to treatment, the staff determines his fitness for release on parole, and the desirable time for such release. In short, it is through the operations of the treatment staff of an institution that we put into operation the specialized and individual treatment of all convicts that is the basic ideal of enlightened penology.

Medical care and hygiene. The bad health of a convicted man may have had something to do with his criminal activities. In all too many instances, too little attention is paid to the convict who is physically diseased or who is suffering from mental and nervous disorders. Our better state prisons and the prisons in the Federal system have a competent medical staff and corps of competent technical assistants. But many of the poorer prisons have only a second-rate physician on call, or for routine inspection, aided by convict orderlies.

To have health and efficiency, men must also eat wholesome food; yet, even in some of our better prisons, meals are poorly balanced, poorly prepared, and inferior in quality. Bad food and the bad cooking and serving of food have been the cause of more prison disturbances and riots than any other type of prison abuse. Such rioting even took place at Sing Sing prison under the administration of Lewis E. Lawes, perhaps the most enlightened and humane prison administrator of the present century. Serious rioting at the Stateville prison in Illinois over bad food conditions temporarily paralyzed the institution.

Sanitation, too, is often bad; the cells may be cold and dark or hot and stuffy. With little work to do, the prisoner may sit in his cell all day, idle and shiftless, brooding over his treatment. If the estimate of the Medical Director of the Federal system that 85 per cent of prisoners are mentally disturbed, unbalanced, or defective is even approximately true, then a model prison is in almost as great need of a good staff of psychiatrists and clinical psychologists as is a state hospital for the insane.

The curse of convict idleness. Reformation can rarely be accomplished in idleness. Laws restricting prison labor, especially those passed between 1929 and 1940, introduced wholesale idleness into state prisons. These laws did not affect the prisons in the Federal system. The industrial and labor system in state prisons became so bad by the eve of the Second World War that only a small portion of the inmates could be employed at anything save the chores and drudgery connected with the routine maintenance of the prisons. The entire system of discipline was threatened with demoralization.

There are powerful economic, as well as rehabilitative and disciplinary, grounds for providing a good system of prison industry. It costs over 30 million dollars each year to operate our prisons and reformatories, and a sound system of prison industry should assist in meeting this expense. Indeed, a rational system of prison industry could more than pay for the total cost of operation.

Types of prison labor. There have been several ways of handling convict labor. Formerly, some states allowed contractors to lease the labor of convicts and to work them as they pleased. In many instances, the men were taken out of the prison and put to work on private projects, a system popular in the South. The leasing of convict labor has now been abandoned (Alabama was the last state to give it up, in 1928). More popular was the practice of contracting for the labor of convicts, who remained in prison, supervised by the agents of contractors. Nine states were still using this system when it was outlawed by Federal legislation two decades ago.

Another scheme was the piece-price system, under which the prison was paid by contractors for making, by convict labor, various types of goods at a certain price per unit. In 1932, this system furnished employment for about 9,000 prisoners, who produced goods valued at 10 million dollars. It has been abandoned because of adverse Federal legislation.

A fourth plan was the public-account system, according to which prison authorities took complete charge of prison industry and sold the products in the open market. About 15,000 convicts, or 20 per cent of all gainfully-employed prisoners, were operating under this system in 1932, and they produced 12 million dollars worth of goods. This system, too, was eliminated by Federal laws passed between 1929 and 1940.

Finally, prisons have developed the state-use system, whereby convicts manufacture automobile license plates and other metal products, institutional furniture, bedding, towels, clothing, shoes, and other goods for use in prisons and other state institutions. Some states employ convicts on state roads and public buildings, and prison farms have become more numerous and productive.

Where states now provide for any extensive prison labor, the state-use plan is invariably adopted, for the other systems have been outlawed. Approximately 42 per cent of all productively employed prisoners were involved in the state-use system as early as 1932. The main defect of the state-use system is that the laws establishing it have been notoriously one-sided. Prisons are restricted to manufacturing only for state agencies and institutions, but the latter are rarely restricted to buying only prison-made goods when these are available.

In no plan of prison labor is primary stress laid on helping the prisoner to learn a trade or to acquire a desire to work. With the exception of the Federal prison system and a few of the better state systems, prison labor today is rarely profitable either to the convict or to the prison. Before the paralyzing Federal legislation went into operation in the 1930's and 1940's, states like West Virginia, Minnesota, Wisconsin, Michigan, Missouri, Texas, and California had a large income from prison industries, even though most prisons were rarely self-supporting.

Unwise legislation paralyzes prison labor. In the 1870's there arose strong objections to contract prison labor on the part of unions and industries which feared the competition of cheap, prison-made products. Many laws were therefore passed limiting prison industries to coarse products. Hence, we find that the chief prison-made products between about 1885 and the Second World War were cocoa mats, burlap bags, coarse brushes and brooms, cheap clothing and hosiery, shoes, bricks, and heavy hardware—products that were not highly profitable in the market and offered no industrial training. About all that can be said is that such work kept the convicts from sheer idleness.

In 1929, Congress passed the Hawes-Cooper Act, and, in 1935, the Ashurst-Sumners Act. These laws, which gave the states full power to regulate or suppress entirely both intra- and interstate shipments of prison-made goods, threw thousands of convicts into idleness. The final step came in an act of October 14, 1940, which forbade the shipment of most prison-made products in interstate commerce, thus ending all except state-use prison industry. This restrictive legislation, however, does not apply to prisons in the Federal system.

Opposition to prison-made products is foolish. Even when the contract system was going full blast, 75 years ago, prison-made products did not constitute more than a small fraction of one per cent of the total industrial production of the country. In 1929, they did not make up one-fourth of one per cent of national production.

Through the Prison Industries Reorganization Administration, set up in 1935, the Roosevelt Administration offered aid and counsel to states that wished to reorganize their prison industries on the state-use plan. Only a few states took advantage of the opportunity, but the PIRA made some valuable reports on prison labor conditions.

Second World War revives prison industry. The Second World War was a boon to industry in state prisons. The frantic demand for war materials led to the mobilization of all available manpower, including the thousands of idle and able-bodied men in our state prisons. Maury Maverick organized a Prison War Industries Branch of the War Production Board to enlist and direct the work of prisoners in state prisons on war contracts. Restrictive legislation was waived temporarily, and by 1944 most of the able-bodied prisoners not employed in maintenance operations were at work producing war materials. The Federal prisons, too, shifted much of their industrial activity to the production of war materials.

Altogether, state and Federal prisons produced 138 million dollars' worth of manufactured products for the war effort, together with 75 million dollars' worth of farm products, and prisoner morale was raised to an all-time high. An effort was made to perpetuate the wartime gains and to keep prisoners employed, and the great demand for goods after 1945 made this effort temporarily successful. By the end of 1947, however, the return of millions of service men to normal industrial pursuits had ended the need for convict labor in most fields of industrial activity. With the failure to compel state institutions and agencies to buy all available prison-made products retarding prison industry in peacetime production, our state prisons are headed once more toward demoralizing idleness, though plans have been suggested to get some of them back into armament production in the new defense program.

The Federal prison system, which is not hampered by restrictive legislation, has the most complete and thriving system of prison industry in our country. The industrial operations of the Federal prison system are conducted by a tax-free corporation, Federal Prison Industries, Inc. Since it was established in 1934, it has paid off more than four million dollars in capital investment and handed over about 11 million dollars to the Federal Treasury in dividends. In 1949, it sold 16 million dollars' worth of goods and had a profit of two million dollars.

Wages for prisoners. It has been suggested that convicts should be paid real wages; not just a few cents a day, but enough to make them feel they are really earning money. In this way, they could help their families and save some money for use after their release from prison. Earning power will do a great deal to restore the convict's self-respect, teach him good work habits, and help in his reformation. Warden Lawes once made the sensible suggestion that prisons should pay all employed inmates a wage equal to that paid for comparable work in the outside world. Then, from this wage payment, the cost of maintaining the prisoner could be deducted and the balance paid to his account, to be used to support his dependents and to help him in his adjustment after release. No such rational plan has ever been put into operation. The Federal system and the state of California pay inmates a maximum of $50 a month. Many states pay no wages whatever, and those that do rarely pay more than 30 cents a day.

Prison education. Educational opportunities are also necessary if prisoners are to be reformed. It is difficult for a man without any education to get a job. Thirteen states have no prison schools; in many penitentiaries the school is taught by the chaplain, with the aid of a few convict teachers. Only in an occasional prison and in a few of the better reformatories do we find a comprehensive system of inmate education conducted by trained professional teachers. The excellent Federal system fails to provide adequate educational facilities even for its correctional institutions. Perhaps the best system of institutional education is that at the Rockview medium-security prison in Pennsylvania, which has enjoyed the cooperation of Pennsylvania State College.

Vocational education of prisoners has also been sadly neglected. No released convict has much of a chance to "go straight" if he does not know a trade. No penitentiary in the United States has a thoroughly adequate system of vocational training. Some slight progress has been made along vocational lines in those institutions which employ the state-use system. Prisoners are taught how to manufacture articles like furniture, clothing, and metal products, and some are taught the printing trade. Only in a few of the better reformatories do we find well-developed programs and facilities for vocational education. Even here there is usually little done in the way of finding employment for well-trained inmates when they are discharged from the institution. Moreover, any such efforts usually face the difficulty of inducing labor unions to admit skilled ex-convicts.

Prison recreation. Recreational facilities are greatly needed for an effective program of convict treatment, but they have been generally ignored except in the better juvenile institutions. Adequate convict recreation improves convict health, teaches inmates the essentials of good sportsmanship, and makes them more generally responsive to treatment methods. Most important of all, recreational interests tend more powerfully than anything else to distract the minds of convicts from their otherwise constant obsession with release or escape.

We should begin to spend less for steel cages and high walls and more for gymnasiums, athletic fields, and small playgrounds. Moreover, no system of convict recreation will be adequate where the majority of inmates remain mere spectators. Provision must be made to enable all able-bodied convicts who wish to do so to participate in sports and games.

Self-government for prisoners. Not only have our prisons failed to make convicts healthy and to teach them a useful trade, but, even more important, they have given little time to training convicts to become good citizens. Some convicts have healthy bodies and know a trade, but their ideas about society and government are warped and biased by past criminal experiences. These men did not learn to conform to the best standards of society or to obey the law before they entered prison; they have had little encouragement or opportunity in the past to change their attitude toward life while serving their prison terms. It is the prison's duty, however, to teach them good citizenship. To become an asset to society, the convict must be taught how to control himself and be given some responsibilities in self-government. If a man cannot control himself in a small and simple prison democracy, how can he be expected to control himself in a larger democracy outside the prison?

The idea of convict self-government is not new. It existed in the Boston House of Refuge over a century ago. Calvin Derrick introduced self-government in the Preston, California school for juvenile delinquents in

1912. But the effective introduction of self-government into prison administration and discipline, was mainly the work of the distinguished publicist and philanthropist, Thomas Mott Osborne (1859-1926), who first observed the system at work in the George Junior Republic, a private institution for juveniles at Freeville, New York. In the decade after 1913, Osborne introduced the famous "Mutual Welfare League" in the prisons at Auburn and Sing Sing, New York, and in the United States Naval Prison at Portsmouth, New Hampshire.

Osborne grasped the fundamental truism, neglected by even enlightened prison administrators, that the best an efficient system of repressive prison discipline can do is to turn out a good convict, who may make a very poor citizen. Osborne believed that an inmate should have a chance to learn how to govern himself. He also thought that, if a convict has a part in carrying out prison discipline, he will be more likely to obey prison rules. Thus, although Osborne, by keeping guards on hand, took no chances on a riot or prison break, he put most of the discipline under convict control. The prisoners controlled prison discipline by means of an elected governing council, and they had their own court. The warden kept a general veto power over their decisions.

In spite of criticisms by conservative wardens and the outside world, the Mutual Welfare League operated remarkably well as long as Osborne could personally supervise it. It is, however, unlikely that such a scheme would work perfectly in every prison or for all prisoners. Prisoners who cannot conform should be ruled by guards. But for those who could benefit from the plan, the Mutual Welfare League proved an excellent way to teach good citizenship. A convict should first earn his right to self-government by going through a period of supervision and instruction by prison authorities; he should not be allowed to govern himself or others as soon as he enters prison.

Systems of self-government are not to be recommended unless the warden has the personality and enthusiasm needed to make the experiment a success. Where self-government has been introduced and then neglected, it has tended to degenerate into a system of inmate tyranny, favoritism, corruption, and extortion, and, as in the case of the great riots in the Auburn prison in 1929, a means of plotting and executing mass escape.

MORE RATIONAL INSTITUTIONAL ARCHITECTURE

Little progress in conventional prison architecture. Prison architecture has made more progress in the last quarter of a century than it did in the entire century between 1825 and 1925. In fact, for a hundred years after the building of the Auburn and Sing Sing prisons and the Eastern Penitentiary between 1819 and 1829, there was no fundamental change in prison architecture. Prisons were merely made more secure with a greater array of forbidding tool-resisting steel cages.

The Pennsylvania and Auburn-Sing Sing layout. The Eastern Penitentiary, designed by John Haviland, a distinguished Philadelphia architect, was constructed with radial wings, each containing outside cells. A central corridor ran through each wing, and the cells extended from this corridor to the outside wall of the wing. But, since the great majority of prisons built in the United States were erected on the Auburn pattern, it is the Auburn style of prison architecture which is chiefly of interest to students of American prisons.

The Auburn layout, planned by John Cray, a local architect, discarded the radial wings and adopted in their place long rectangular cell houses, usually flanking the entrance to the institution. Within each of these cell houses, which were lighted by heavily-barred windows in the walls, was the so-called inside-cell block made up of several tiers of cage-like cells. These cells were located back to back, and were surrounded by a corridor extending all the way around the cell block. Because the cell block erected on the Auburn pattern in 1828 at the new Sing Sing prison was much larger and more impressive than the Auburn structure, the great majority of prisons constructed in the United States from 1830 to the present time were based upon this Sing Sing model of long rectangular cell houses enclosing their sombre and ever more escape-proof inside-cell blocks. Hence, the prisons of the United States for more than a century have been architecturally gloomy and oppressive, and a constant frustration of reform efforts on the part of both the staff and the inmates. In short, prison architecture was even more static and brutal than the systems of prison discipline.

The telephone-pole design. The first revolutionary advance over the dreadful Sing Sing pattern of prison architecture came with the opening of the famous telephone-pole prison at Fresnes, France, in 1898, designed by Francisque-Henri Poussin. This split or bisected the long cell houses of the Auburn-Sing Sing pattern into two halves by means of a covered central corridor which extended throughout the length of the whole prison plant. The resulting external appearance roughly represented the arms of a telephone pole, and this gave rise to the name of the new type of prison structure. This prison layout was a great improvement over previous plants. It gave easy and protected access to all parts of the institution, reduced the possibility of escape, lessened the distance over which inmates had to move, made their supervision easier, and facilitated the better lighting of cell blocks.

In 1914 an attempt was made to introduce the telephone-pole prison into the United States at Stillwater Prison in Minnesota. This was a very limited experiment, however, since the majority of the convicts were still housed in long inside-cell blocks of the Auburn-Sing Sing pattern.

The adaptation of the telephone-pole prison to effective prison-designing in the United States was mainly the work of Alfred Hopkins, a professional architect, who, in his mature years, gave ever more attention to prison architecture. He was induced to turn part of his professional attention to prison-designing through the efforts of Orlando F. Lewis and Edward R. Cass, of the New York Prison Association. Hopkins began his work with a new county prison in Westchester, New York, opened in 1916, but his first structures fully illustrating the telephone-pole layout were the Federal penitentiary at Lewisburg, Pennsylvania, and the New York state medium-security prison at Wallkill, both opened in 1932.

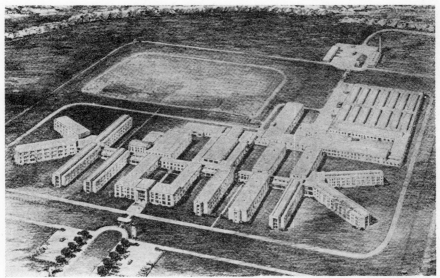

COURTESY FEDERAL BUREAU OF PRISONS.

Army disciplinary barracks at Camp Cooke, California. Latest example of the telephone-pole layout in penal and correctional architecture.

Other architects—notably Robert D. Barnes, senior architect of the Federal Bureau of Prisons—have gone far beyond Hopkins in the perfection of the telephone-pole design, which is best exemplified by the Federal penitentiary at Terre Haute, Indiana, the Federal Correctional Institution at Texarkana, Texas, and the United States Military Penitentiary at Camp Cooke, California. The most notable innovation introduced by Barnes exists in the plans drawn for the Federal super-security prison to supplant Alcatraz. This provides for the elimination of the traditional heavily-barred windows of the cell houses, and substitutes rational and unimpeded skylighting of the cell blocks.

Rational diversification of institutional design. Even more important than the introduction of the telephone-pole design in prison architecture has been the recent tendency to diversify prison construction according to the several types of inmates confined. Under the leadership of the Federal Bureau of Prisons, institutions have been planned to meet the custodial and rehabilitation needs of the great diversity of convicts sent to them.

In the Federal system we have a super-security prison, Alcatraz, for the most desperate criminals; three maximum-security prisons for serious habitual criminals; two mixed-custody penitentiaries for less dangerous adult felons; eight medium-security correctional institutions for inmates who do not need extremely secure prison construction for safe custody; and one minimum-security correctional institution for inmates who show a prospect of speedy reform. Several of the states—New York, New Jersey, Pennsylvania, and California, for example—have also built one or more medium-security institutions, and several others have provided prison farms which are akin in principle and administration.

In medium-security institutions, only about 10 per cent of the inmates are housed in maximum-security inside-cells. The others are placed in outside-cells, dormitories, and honor rooms. Dayrooms, gymnasiums, and other facilities are provided to stimulate reformation. Walls are replaced

COURTESY FEDERAL BUREAU OF PRISONS.

Federal minimum security correctional institution at Seagoville, near Dallas, Texas. America's finest minimum-security plant. Note open, campus-like construction. Despite its apparent lack of secure construction, dangerous criminals have been safely confined here because of an excellent rehabilitation program which eliminates most of the incentive to escape.

by fences. In short, everything compatible with safety is done to create an institutional atmosphere which conforms to the requirements of a program of rehabilitation.

This is carried even further in minimum-security institutions, where there are usually no cells, and where the inmates are housed in single rooms or dormitories. There may be no fence at all around the institution, although it is believed to be good practice to have one in order to check the more or less natural impulse on the part of some inmates to stray away. The rehabilitative program is regarded as the chief means of retaining the inmates in custody. The only thoroughgoing minimum-security institution for adult convicts is the Federal institution at Seagoville, near Dallas, Texas. Although men convicted of serious crimes are sent there, the number of attempted escapes have been few indeed.

Moreover, the rehabilitative record has been gratifying. Of course, minimum-security institutions can only be safe and useful where there is a competent and enthusiastic administrative personnel. Such institutions cannot be safely or successfully administered in perfunctory fashion or by an indifferent or incompetent staff.

Sundry improvements in institution design. The housing facilities are diversified within most Federal institutions. For example, in the Federal mixed-custody penitentiaries at Lewisburg and Terre Haute, not more than 12 per cent of the inmates are housed in maximum-security inside-cells. The rest are satisfactorily detained in outside-cells, dormitories, and honor rooms. This type of diversified prison construction reduces building costs and enables the planners either to save public funds or to put the money saved into various educational and other treatment facilities. There is also a notable tendency to spend less money on expensive walls. The wall of the Attica prison in New York state, opened in 1929, cost $1,275,000. The complete penitentiary at Terre Hause cost only about twice that amount. At Terre Haute heavy wire fences have been found to provide a sufficiently secure enclosure.

Finally, current prison-planning stresses the desirability of building smaller prisons. Although enormous prisons like those at South Lansing, Michigan, and Stateville, Illinois, providing for 3,500 to 5,000 inmates, have been erected since the First World War, the best opinion today would limit prison capacity to not more than 1,200 inmates, approximately the number confined at Lewisburg and at Terre Haute.

Reformatory architecture. In dealing with the subject of reformatories we pointed out that for over fifty years after 1876 they were handicapped by being too large and by being operated within a physical plant identical with, or very much like, the conventional maximum-security prisons. We mentioned the fact that the first institution to be constructed in strict conformity with reformatory ideals was that opened at Annandale, New Jersey, in 1929. The best opinion at present is that each state should have two types of reformatories—one a close-custody institution designed to be relatively secure against escapes but with all modern treatment facilities, and the other an open, campus-like layout, such as at Annandale. Only in this way can the more risky inmates, who most need good treatment facilities, be guaranteed full access to them.

Evolution of juvenile institutions. The design of institutions for juvenile delinquents has shown considerable progress. The first institutions provided in the 1820's—at New York, Philadelphia, and Boston—were no more than conventional prisons for children. Then, for several generations, juveniles were confined in great barrack-like houses of correction. In the last quarter of the nineteenth century some of the more progressive states erected large cottage institutions; in some instances the cottages were four or five stories high. In the present century, the trend has been toward institutions composed of one-story cottages housing from 10 to 25 children each. Model institutions of this sort are those at Whittier, California, and Warwick, New York. Progressive penology today, however, is opposed to erecting many new institutions to house and treat juvenile

delinquents. Greater emphasis is being placed upon the use of probation and speedy parole.

Prison camps. The most extreme departure from conventional prison
architecture has been the construction of camps for convicted delinquents.
These have been used chiefly in connection with forestry, and road and
farm work; California has set up more of these camps than all the other
states combined. The Federal prison system also operates several camps,
the most notable one being that for juveniles at Natural Bridge, Virginia.

Camps are most practical for prisoners who present slight custodial
risks and as places to prepare convicts for release. They are more healthy
and pleasant than the gloomy prison structures. While most suitable for
states which have warm weather throughout the year, camps have proved
practicable even in states with rigorous winter weather.

Investment in archaic plants delays progress. The states have not been
as active in designing and building new penal and correctional institutions as has the Federal government. This has been due to the vast
investment of about 100 million dollars in conventional bastille structures
which the states are loath to demolish. New York state is the most conspicuous example of this unfortunate situation. Here, the richest state in
the nation is afflicted by six large maximum-security hoosegows, either
new or recently reconstructed, but possesses only one small medium-
security prison. Rehabilitation programs will be handicapped for generations by this architectural set-up. Even the Federal government has not
entirely escaped this blight of obsolescent construction. The Federal
prisons at Alcatraz, Leavenworth, Atlanta, and McNeil Island should long
since have been abandoned.

THE TRADITIONAL COUNTY JAIL: AN OBSOLETE NUISANCE

The county jail in the penological picture. Our prisons, according to
some critics, are "universities of crime." In them, offenders receive further
instruction in burglary, safe-cracking, picking pockets, and other phases
of the criminal's trade. We might similarly call our county and city
jails, workhouses, and detention houses "grammar schools of crime." Jails
do not supply as much drama as our prisons; we seldom hear of exciting
jail riots, fires, or escapes. Yet the jail problem is fully as important as
the prison challenge. Many more persons are confined in jails and detention houses than in the prisons of the United States, and living conditions in them are usually far worse. Joseph F. Fishman, former Federal
investigator of prisons and jails, thus describes the typical American
county jail:

An unbelievably filthy institution in which are confined men and women
serving sentence for misdemeanors and crimes, and men and women not under
sentence who are simply awaiting trial. With few exceptions, having no segregation of the unconvicted from the convicted, the well from the diseased, the
youngest and most impressionable from the most degraded and hardened. Usually swarming with bedbugs, roaches, lice and other vermin; has an odor of
disinfectant and filth which is appalling; supports in complete idleness countless
thousands of able-bodied men and women, and generally affords ample time and

opportunity to assure the inmates a complete course in every kind of viciousness and crime. A melting-pot in which the worst elements of the raw material in the criminal world are brought forth, blended and turned out in absolute perfection.[10]

It should not be hard to convince any reasonable person that there is no excuse for an institution of this sort. It is the most obvious and indefensible vestige that has come down to us from the legal and institutional barbarism of the past.

There are 3,152 county jails, workhouses, and city police lockups. From the point of view of construction, cleanliness, food, segregation, and discipline, many of them are not fit for human habitation. A survey by the Federal Bureau of Prisons indicated that three-fourths of the jails of the country do not even measure up to the minimum standards necessary to make them suitable for the safe and humane detention of inmates. Only seven were 80 per cent satisfactory.

Somewhere between one and three million persons go through jails every year, awaiting examination or trial or serving out petty sentences. Perhaps half of those persons, including many held on suspicion or as witnesses for trials, are not guilty of any crime or misdemeanor. There is, also, a most unfortunate mixture of types: from the innocent, held on suspicion, to the hardened criminal and the vicious sex offender. Many young persons are headed toward crime every year as a result of degrading associations in jails.

Inferior administration of most jails. For the most part, our jails are managed inefficiently and corruptly. The average sheriff is far inferior even to the general run of prison wardens in his understanding of the problems of crime and criminals. He often holds his post too briefly to acquire any professional competence; he is usually a politician, without training for his work, and is interested in his position only for the money he can get out of it. One way in which sheriffs add to their income is to underfeed prisoners and to pocket the difference between what they are allowed under the fee system and what they actually spend for food.

Most of our jails are dirty, disorderly, and reeking with filth and vermin. Not only are they degrading and demoralizing but they are not even safe places in which to keep prisoners. The number of escapes from jails amounts to about 3,000 annually.

How to deal with the jail problem. The only solution of the jail problem is to get rid of all jails, as they exist today. We should provide clean and secure detention institutions to house those held as witnesses or awaiting trial. Since, under the Constitution, a person must be considered innocent until he is proved guilty by a fair trial, persons awaiting trial should not be treated like ordinary criminals, as they are in our jails. They should be detained in comfortable and safe houses of detention, entirely separate from jails which house sentenced persons.

The great mass of drunkards, addicts, vagrants, and petty offenders, who make up the bulk of the inmates in our jails, should be placed on

---

[10] *Crucibles of Crime.* New York: Cosmopolis Press, 1923, p. 68.

probation or in scientifically-planned institutions for degenerates, vagrants, and incurables. Those who are convicted of petty crimes and who need temporary segregation should be placed in clean and well-administered jails.

COURTESY FEDERAL BUREAU OF PRISONS.

Model jail designed to house 250 inmates. Ideal structure for large urban counties or for regional jail used by a number of counties, no one of which is able to construct a suitable jail. This structure may be fruitfully compared with the jail structures in the home counties of students.

Since many counties in rural districts cannot afford such institutions, several counties should join in creating suitable regional jails. It is the opinion of progressive penologists that both regional jails and the jails maintained by urban counties should be located in rural areas. There the jail can operate a large farm and thus keep the inmates employed. The operation of simple industries like laundries has also been suggested for county and regional jails.

Virtually no attention has been paid to the rehabilitation of jail inmates, which is a serious mistake because jails are one of the most important feeders of our prisons and reformatories. If any headway is to be made along this way, we require larger jails, at least a skeleton trained treatment staff, and the introduction of an indeterminate sentence for those jail inmates not deemed fit for speedy release or probation after conviction.

SUMMARY

It is extremely difficult to make any effective headway in the matter of curbing the more serious forms of criminality today—organized crime and racketeering—or to convict and treat those who commit such crimes. This type of criminality is enmeshed too firmly in our economic, political, and judicial systems, and the leaders are too well protected against legal action.

In any literal sense, the repression of crime and the treatment of criminals in our day must be limited mainly to traditional crimes and to the convict population which commits such offenses.

Many centuries of experience with punishment as a mode of dealing with crime and criminals have fully demonstrated its futility. It does not adequately deter men from committing crimes and it does not reform many criminals. Capital punishment is equally futile; it does not restrict the homicide rate, and it may frequently lead to the execution of innocent persons.

There have been four main stages in the treatment of convicted criminals: (1) corporal punishment and fines imposed outside of institutions, a stage which lasted from primitive days to the end of the eighteenth century; (2) punishment within institutions, which produced the rise of the modern prison system during the nineteenth century; (3) the effort to reform convicts within institutions, which brought forth the reformatory system and the New Penology of the twentieth century; and (4) the present movement toward plans to reform criminals outside of institutions, which has taken the form of probation, parole, conditional release, and the remarkable Youth Authority program of California and of a few other states.

The New Penology is an enlightened effort to apply scientific methods to the rehabilitation of criminals. It began with the Irish prison system of the 1850's and the Elmira Reformatory movement of the 1870's. But its efforts have been doomed because of the "convict bogey," the jailing psychosis, and the irrational construction of institutions.

Probation, parole, and conditional release offer much hope in the way of more economical and effective treatment of delinquents. What is needed here is mainly an improvement of methods and personnel, both of which are dependent upon more adequate public appropriations for such work.

The most promising trend at the mid-century is the all-out experiment of California in the Youth Authority, set up in 1941. This system assigns delinquent youth to experts for treatment—generally outside of institutions. Even such institutional treatment as is required is shorn of all punitive aspects. This program has been adopted by Minnesota, Wisconsin, Massachusetts, and Texas, and, in a limited way, by some other states. It is, however, necessary to extend this program to adult criminals. A step in this direction has been taken by California, which created an Adult Authority in 1944.

In the interval before such methods become general, the more intelligent efforts to deal with convicted delinquents must be limited to rational treatment within institutions. This involves the classification of convicts by diagnostic clinics, individualized treatment through treatment clinics, better medical care and feeding of prisoners, greater use of self-government plans, improved education, especially better vocational instruction, and adequate facilities for inmate recreation.

One of the most serious problems of prison administration today is that relating to prison industry and labor. After 1929, legislation paralyzed much state prison industry. There was a notable industrial revival during the Second World War, but idleness has again become alarmingly prevalent in state prisons. State-use industry is the only type now open to state prisons and reformatories, and it is handicapped because laws do not compel institutions to buy prison-made goods when available.

Enlightened penology calls for the rational planning and construction of penal and correctional institutions suitable to each main type of delinquent. In the last 100 years the trend has been towards erecting ever more expensive penal cages of stone, brick, concrete, and steel to house *all* convicts. These prisons are needlessly expensive, and the atmosphere they create fatally handicaps rehabilitative measures. The Federal Bureau of Prisons has taken the lead in designing and building model institutions, properly diversified so as to suit all types of delinquents. The state prison systems have been slow in following the lead of the Federal Bureau—in part because of their heavy investment in archaic cages of steel and concrete.

Jails, as we now know them, should be abolished outright. Persons accused of crime should be kept in clean detention stations and should be free from association with convicted culprits. Counties should combine to construct regional jails where the inmates can be kept busy in farming pursuits and simple industries. Many persons who are today detained in jails should actually be sent to specialized institutions for psychopaths and degenerates. An indeterminate sentence should be imposed on jail inmates in order to make possible rehabilitative treatment.

SELECTED REFERENCES

*Barnes, H. E., *The Story of Punishment*. Boston: Stratford, 1930. An introductory survey of the history of the treatment of crime from primitive days to modern psychiatric clinics.

————, *Prisons in Wartime*. Washington: War Production Board, 1944. Survey of the remarkable transformation of state prison industry and morale during the Second World War.

Beard, B. B., *Juvenile Probation*. New York: American Book Company, 1934. A description of the principles and techniques of probation as applied to juvenile delinquents.

*Bennett, J. V., Barnes, R. D., and Barnes, H. E., *Handbook of Correctional Design and Construction*. Washington: Federal Bureau of Prisons, 1950. The most complete work in any language on the history and present nature of prison architecture, from super-security prisons to juvenile detention homes.

Bennett, J. V., *et al.*, *Gearing Prisons to the War Effort*. Washington: Federal Bureau of Prisons, 1946. Account of the wartime industrial operations of the Federal prison system.

Branham, V. C., and Kutash, S. B. (Eds.), *Encyclopedia of Criminology*. New York: Philosophical Library, 1949. Elaborate and up-to-date compilation covering nearly every phase of criminology and penology.

Calvert, E. R., *Capital Punishment in the Twentieth Century*. New York: Putnam, 1930. The best critique of the folly of capital punishment.

Chamberlain, R. W., *There Is No Truce: A Life of Thomas Mott Osborne*. New York: Macmillan, 1935. The best biography of the leading American prison reformer of the twentieth century.

*Clemmer, Donald, *The Prison Community*. New York: Christopher, 1940. A pioneer treatment of convict life, routine, social attitudes, and mental traits.

*Cooley, E. J., *Probation and Delinquency*. New York: Nelson, 1927. The most complete treatment of probation by a leading figure in the probation movement.

*Ellingston, J. R., *Protecting Our Children from Criminal Careers*. New York: Prentice-Hall, 1948. Able and interesting discussion of juvenile delinquency built around the theory and development of the Youth Correction Authority program.

Fishman, J. F., *Sex in Prison*. New York: National Library Press, 1934. The first good book in English on the most serious problem of prison life.

————, *Crucibles of Crime*. New York: Cosmopolis Press, 1923. The best description and criticism of American jails.

Gillin, J. L., *Taming the Criminal*. New York: Macmillan, 1931. An interesting account of some of the typical foreign prisons and prison methods.

————, *Criminology and Penology*. New York: Appleton-Century, 1946. A somewhat traditional, but highly informing and comprehensive, manual.

Glueck, Sheldon (Ed.), *Probation and Criminal Justice*. New York: Macmillan, 1933. Able symposium on probationary ideals and practices.

———— and Eleanor (Eds.), *Preventing Crime*. New York: McGraw-Hill, 1935. Valuable symposium on crime prevention measures, including case studies of crime prevention centers.

*Haynes, F. E., *The American Prison System*. New York: McGraw-Hill, 1939. A valuable factual survey of institutions and penal methods.

Ives, George, *A History of Penal Methods*. London: Stanley Paul, 1914. Perhaps the best book on the history of punishment, including the period before the rise of institutions.

Kirkpatrick, Clifford, *Capital Punishment in the United States*. Philadelphia: Society of Friends, 1925. Good summary of capital punishment trends in this country after the First World War.

*La Roe, Wilbur, *Parole with Honor*. Princeton: Princeton University Press, 1939. The best book on the parole system.

Lawes, L. E., *20,000 Years in Sing Sing*. New York: Long and Smith, 1932. Interesting discussion of prison problems by the best known warden of the twentieth century.

————, *Man's Judgment of Death*. New York: Putnam, 1924. Convincing refutation of the tenets of those who support capital punishment.

Lindner, R. M., and Seliger, R. V. (Eds.), *Handbook of Correctional Psychology*. New York: Philosophical Library, 1947. Symposium on the application of psychiatric techniques to the rehabilitation of prisoners.

*McKelvey, Blake, *American Prisons*. Chicago: University of Chicago Press, 1936. The best general history of American prisons and prison systems.

*Nelson, V. F., *Prison Days and Nights*. Boston: Little, Brown, 1933. A vivid and appalling account of life in an average prison by an intelligent former convict. It is invaluable as a source of information on the abnormal life of prisoners.

Ohlin, L. E., *Selection for Parole*. New York: Russell Sage Foundation, 1951. Important work on methods of selecting inmates for parole, and techniques for predicting success in parole operations.

Robinson, L. N., *Penology in the United States*. Philadelphia: Winston, 1921. Substantial survey of main problems of prison life and administration.

————, *Should Prisoners Work?* Philadelphia: Winston, 1931. Probably the best book on prison labor prior to the restrictive legislation passed in the period from 1929 to 1940.

Scott, G. R., *The History of Capital Punishment*. London: Torchstream Books, 1951. The most recent treatment of the problem of capital punishment, dealing with present issues as well as the history of the death penalty.

*Stromberg, E. T. (Ed.), *Crimes of Violence*. Boulder: University of Colorado Press, 1950. One of the best symposiums on the causes of crime and the treatment of criminals.

Tannenbaum, Frank, *Osborne of Sing Sing*. Chapel Hill: University of North Carolina Press, 1935. Good account of the personality, ideas and achievements of the leading prison reformer of the twentieth century—the founder of the convict self-government idea.

————, *Wall Shadows*. New York: Putnam, 1922. Especially valuable for its treatment of the genesis of the "jailing psychosis" and prison cruelty.

Tappan, P. W. (Ed.), *Contemporary Correction*. New York: McGraw-Hill, 1951. Authoritative symposium covering the whole field of penology and correctional treatment.

Teeters, N. K., *World Prison Systems*. Philadelphia: Pennsylvania Prison Society, 1944. Best brief survey of the main prison systems of the world.

————, *Penology from Panama to Cape Horn*. Philadelphia: University of Pennsylvania Press, 1946. Interesting portrayal of some of the novel elements in Latin American penal theory and practice, especially the efforts made to deal with prison sex problems.

Timasheff, N. S., *One Hundred Years of Probation*. New York: Fordham University Press, 1943. Best historical account of rise and development of probation.

————, *Probation in the Light of Criminal Statistics*. New York: Fordham University Press, 1948. Best summary of the extent and accomplishments of probation.

*Wilson, D. P., *My Six Convicts*. New York: Rinehart, 1951. Quasi-fictional, but one of the most absorbing books ever written on the problems and traits of convict life.

*Wilson, Margaret, *The Crime of Punishment*. New York: Harcourt, Brace, 1931. Good picture of rise and nature of modern prisons, supporting the author's thesis that our prisons are a worse crime than the acts of criminals.

Winning, J. R., *Behind these Walls*. New York: Macmillan, 1933. Another staggering revelation of the horrors of prison life in the average prison. Perhaps even more shocking than Nelson's book.

Young, P. V., *Social Treatment in Probation and Delinquency*. New York: McGraw-Hill, 1951. New edition of a comprehensive treatment of the principles and techniques of probation.

CHAPTER 17

Other Aspects of Social Pathology

PROSTITUTION AS A SOCIAL PROBLEM

Meaning of prostitution. Prostitution, like poverty, is one of our oldest and most venerable social problems. It definitely antedates the dawn of history, and in its present manifestations it is more difficult to control than at any other time during its long history. Geoffrey May thus defines prostitution:

Prostitution may be defined as the practice of habitual or intermittent sexual union, more or less promiscuous, for mercenary inducement. It is thus characterized by three elements: payment, usually involving the passing of money, although gifts or pleasures may constitute equivalent consideration; promiscuity, with the possible exercise of choice; and emotional indifference, which may be inferred from payment and promiscuity.[1]

Prostitution among primitive and oriental groups. Anthropologists have found that prostitution is not uncommon among existing primitive peoples. Thus, it is not unreasonable to assume that it prevailed extensively among prehistoric peoples whose cultures antedated the rise of civilization. Among extant primitive peoples, fathers and husbands frequently hire out their daughters and wives to other men for gain. Indeed, it is not unusual for primitive women to seduce strangers and hand over to their menfolk whatever reward has been obtained for their services. It is also among primitive peoples that we find the earliest manifestations of that sacred prostitution which was so common among the Semitic peoples and Hittites of the ancient Near East.

This religious, sacred, or temple prostitution, about which much has been written, was once extensively practiced in the Near East. The lesser priestesses and other young female devotees offered themselves to male worshippers in religious rites—particularly in the worship of Ishtar, or Astarte, and other major goddesses of fertility. Although this ritual has been condemned by many writers as evidence of gross depravity, it was not so regarded by those who practiced it. Although men might have actual sexual connection with one of the temple prostitutes, or *hierodouli,* more important was the symbolic union with the goddess in whose honor the rites were being conducted. Moreover, these practices were supposed

---

[1] From *The Encyclopedia of the Social Sciences,* Vol. XII, p. 553. By permission of The Macmillan Company, publishers.

to benefit the community by stimulating fertility in women and in plant and animal life, and by promoting virility in men. This whole ritual of sacred prostitution had a fundamentally religious tone. There was, of course, no little private and secular prostitution among the ancient western Asiatic peoples.

The ancient Jews were traditionally bitter against prostitution. But their vehemence was based more on religious than on moral grounds. To them, prostitution symbolized, all too frequently, the worship of a strange enemy god or goddess. Hence, it was a direct affront to the Hebrew god, Yahweh, and to permit it to go on would invite his wrath. But even temple prostitution occasionally crept into Palestine, especially during the more prosperous and corrupt eras. And a large amount of private prostitution flourished in Palestine from the days of the patriarchs to the Diaspora.

Greek and Roman prostitution. Among the ancient Greeks, private prostitution was highly prevalent and relatively respectable. Temple prostitution held over into the Greek period, especially in connection with the rites in honor of Aphrodite in the temple at Corinth and in association with the seasonal fertility rites widely practiced in ancient Greece. The nature and theory of the Greek family encouraged an extensive development of private prostitution in ancient Hellas. The Greek wife was looked upon as a loyal and industrious housekeeper and a breeder of children. To an unusual degree it was believed that the place of Greek housewives was in the home. But the Greek man found little sexual excitement or romance in his home. That he sought outside the domestic hearth. The more prominent and prosperous males associated publicly with what were more truly mistresses than prostitutes, the *hetaerae*. These were relatively superior free-born women, either foreign-born immigrants or middle-class native girls who had an ambition to rise above the social class into which they had been born. Much more numerous were the true prostitutes, some of whom were licensed but many others of whom were of the clandestine and free-lance variety. The term *hetaerae* is frequently incorrectly extended to cover this latter class of true prostitutes among the Greeks. The fact that the Greeks were sea-going people made the port towns particularly popular with prostitutes. Corinth, for example, was a special haven for prostitutes.

Prostitution was extremely prevalent in ancient Rome and in most cities of the empire. Recruits were drawn both from the native women and from slave girls brought in from outside. But prostitution never attained the respectability in Rome that it did in ancient Athens. Prominent Romans consorted freely with prostitutes, but they rarely entered into such public relations with mistresses as that, let us say, of Pericles and Aspasia, though Julius Caesar did bring Cleopatra to Rome and had a child by her. So far as was convenient, prostitutes in Rome were compelled to register, to wear distinctive dress, and to live in special districts. But such regulation was not universally enforceable. The income of prostitutes was taxed, and this constituted a very considerable revenue for the empire. The tax on prostitution continued into the fifth century of the Christian era.

Prostitution in the Middle Ages. The leaders of the early Christian Church rivaled the ancient Hebrew prophets in their glamorous invective against prostitution. Paul and Augustine were particularly conspicuous in this respect. But, in practice, the church was usually more tolerant than the vehement rhetoric of its leaders implied. The medieval friars were among the customers of medieval prostitutes, and the church derived a considerable monetary income from the proceeds of prostitution. The majority of the states of medieval Europe were, like the church, formally antagonistic to prostitution and put it under a legal ban. In practice, however, the control of prostitution was left chiefly to the local cities and towns. The latter were extremely tolerant of the institution and its personnel. It was believed that prostitution increased the immunity of moral women to sexual aggression. Further, prostitution turned a considerable sum of money into the urban treasury. It was held, however, that some regulation of prostitution was desirable in the interest of public order. Hence, prostitution was both common and respectable in medieval towns throughout most of the Middle Ages. Distinguished visitors were frequently entertained in the municipally-regulated brothels, which were often called *lupanars,* a word derived from a Latin term referring to the residence of prostitutes.

The remarkable revolution in the public attitude toward prostitution at the close of the Middle Ages was based upon considerations of public health rather than upon any sweeping moral transformation. An epidemic of syphilis swept over western Europe after 1495 with frightful ravages. According to some estimates, a third of the population of some areas died during the first generation of the epidemic. It was believed necessary to close the *lupanars* and suppress prostitution in order to lessen the prevalence of this dreadful plague.

Influence of Protestantism. The Protestant Reformation added moral zeal to the movement for the suppression of prostitution, but it was not nearly as important as the fear of the spread of syphilis. Harsh measures were passed against prostitution, but it still continued to exist, though with some reduction in numbers and publicity.

Prostitution in the nineteenth century. At the opening of the nineteenth century, partly as a result of the spirit of enlightenment, the belief gradually developed that a rational control of prostitution through the registration of prostitutes and their medical examination was the most sensible way to deal with the problem. This method of control was set up in France in 1800 and was widely followed elsewhere on the continent of Europe during the next half century. Even in Great Britain, which maintained a legal ban on prostitution, some provision was made for medical examination. The promising developments along this line were, however, frustrated mainly through the opposition of the purists and feminists.

Prostitution increased in volume and popularity in Europe during the nineteenth century as a result of changed social conditions, particularly those associated with the growth of cities and the increasing prevalence of urban life. The break-up of family relations, the postponement of marriage on the part of workers, and the increased ease of obscuring prostitution in great urban centers encouraged its growth. A new need was created for it, while its suppression was rendered more difficult. The system of registration, public regulation, and medical examination, though often attacked, was generally continued in western Europe through the period of the First World War.

Current trends and policies in prostitution. Many important changes have taken place with respect to the status and control of prostitution in Europe since the First World War. The establishment of a revised code of sexual ethics in Soviet Russia and the creation of true equality between the sexes, as well as the elimination of the capitalistic system, brought about an almost complete elimination of Russian prostitution. It is probable that Soviet Russia is more thoroughly free of professional prostitution than any important country has been since the dawn of recorded history. The fascist states also tended to frown on prostitution, more for military than for moral reasons. The fascist leaders desired to conserve all sexual energy for reproductive purposes and they regarded prostitution in much the same way as they judged birth control. They wished sexual activity to express itself, as far as possible, in reproduction. Hence, there was a considerable effort on the part of fascist leaders to suppress prostitution.

An attempt to set up some form of international control of prostitution was made by entrusting the League of Nations with supervision over the white slave traffic. The responsible department of the League made important studies and reports on this subject, but it could do little to suppress the traffic or to control prostitution in the modern world. The states in the League tended to look upon the problem as a fit subject for national and local regulation.

Old World trends in prostitution after the Second World War have manifested marked contrasts. In France, Italy, and Japan, where prostitution had been rather openly condoned, though regulated, before 1939, there have been strong movements to curtail it. Due mainly to the activities of a woman fanatic it has been outlawed entirely in Paris, with the result that it has been driven on the streets and also has led to police exploitation and corruption. On the other hand, in Germany, where prostitution was strictly controlled under the Imperial and Republican governments, and virtually eliminated by the Nazis, the destruction and impoverishment wrought by the war have led to a notable increase in prostitution. This increase the occupation forces have made little effort to check.

Prostitution in the United States to 1920. Prostitution has been prevalent in the United States ever since colonial days. Many prostitutes migrated from Europe with other colonial settlers. The sermons of ministers, the criminal laws, the writings of travelers, and reports on jail conditions all attest to the existence and extent of prostitution in colonial America. The more sophisticated Fathers, like Franklin and Jefferson, were thoroughly familiar with prostitution, both in colonial America and Europe, and accepted it as an essential part of the social system.

Jefferson even proposed an orderly and well-regulated house of prostitution as a part of his plan for the new University of Virginia.

Prostitution flourished during the nineteenth century as a result of the growth of the eastern industrial cities and the rise of western mining towns, in both of which there was a large contingent of unmarried males. The European system of frank and candid regulation of prostitution was rarely adopted in this country, though St. Louis experimented with the public regulation of prostitutes from 1870 to 1874. The more general tendency was to herd the prostitutes into segregated areas, the so-called red-light districts. These were frequently very crude in western towns, where the prostitutes lived in small informal dwellings known as "cribs." There was little provision for medical inspection of prostitutes in these segregated districts.

About 1912 a wave of puritanical zeal, set off by the investigation of prostitution in Chicago, swept over the country. Volunteer committees sprang up in many urban centers, gathered information about prostitution, and carried on a vigorous propaganda against segregated districts. Chicago abolished its segregated district in 1912, and many other American cities soon followed suit. Realistic students of the problem believe that this frenzied crusade did far more harm than good and that it actually increased the social dangers of prostitution. Even though there was little regulation and medical inspection in segregated districts, at least segregation made these steps possible when public opinion became sufficiently realistic to demand them. It also kept prostitution off the main city thoroughfares. The crusaders, by wiping out the segregated areas, simply scattered prostitution, often driving it into respectable neighborhoods and apartments. The notable increase in the congestion of cities made prostitution easier to hide. The growing popularity of the automobile and the taxi put much sexual vice on wheels. Particularly did the suppression of segregation increase streetwalking and clandestine prostitution, which is the most dangerous of all types in the spreading of venereal diseases.

Puritanical crusades throw prostitution into the hands of the underworld. After the stamping out of the red-light areas it became impossible for public authorities effectively to regulate and control prostitution. It remained informal and disorganized, though more dangerous than ever to public health. After the First World War the racketeers and organized criminals discerned the great opportunities for gain to be found in prostitution and brought into being the present-day vice syndicates. The attempt to put down interstate traffic in prostitutes, through the Mann Act, was equally ill-fated. It accomplished little that was intended by its sponsors, and it has turned out to be the largest single asset of the present-day blackmail racket.

As we suggested in our earlier treatment of organized crime, the vice syndicate is today one of the most lucrative forms of organized underworld activity. The strictly businesslike organization which dominates the world of large scale crime has been introduced into the control of prostitution. It is managed on a national, or at least upon a regional, basis. The vice ring controls prostitution in all the leading cities. The approved proprietors of houses of prostitution and the prostitutes themselves are carefully listed and rigorously supervised. The prostitutes are frequently shifted from one city to another, and even more often from one locality in a municipality to another. This is done in part to evade the prospect of discovery and prosecution and in part to increase the novelty and appeal of the prostitutes. The latter are kept under thorough control and discipline and intimidated in a manner to prevent the likelihood of desertion and exposure. For the first time in the history of American prostitution, many prostitutes have literally become prisoners in the profession. Any who seem likely to run away and expose the ring are beaten up or quietly disposed of.

Perhaps the only gain that has come from the control of prostitution by the vice syndicates has been the increased introduction of prophylaxis and treatment for venereal disease. The racketeers have elementary business sagacity and recognize that diseased prostitutes or infected customers are bad business. An elementary sense of thrift and greed have thus been able to accomplish more in the way of social protection and the prevention of venereal disease than the moral indignation of the reformers.

One may safely say, looking at the matter broadly, that most prostitution in the United States today is either that controlled by the vice syndicate or the clandestine operations of streetwalkers. But even the more attractive element among the latter are being picked up in ever larger numbers by the vice ring, cleaned up and subjected to medical treatment, and put to work by the syndicate. The ultimate outcome of these current trends cannot be foreseen, but at least it is fairly apparent that the prospect of rational public control and official medical supervision of prostitution in the United States is now indefinitely postponed.

Causes of prostitution. We may now consider some of the more important reasons for the existence of prostitution—particularly the basis of the demand for prostitutes and the reasons why a large number of prostitutes can always be produced to supply this demand.

To understand the demand for prostitutes, we must examine the various reasons why men desire to consort with them. The basic reason, of course, is that prostitution provides an easy, informal, and expeditious gratification of the sex desire of the male. Whatever increases the difficulty of gratifying this desire in a family setting will increase the popularity of prostitution. The increasing prevalence of city life has played a prominent role here. Urban workers and the salaried classes have frequently been compelled to postpone marriage. The hold of family life has been greatly weakened in the contemporary city. There are a large number of bachelors, some of whom never marry. These conditions of city life naturally make for an increase of prostitution. Many married men seek out prostitutes to avoid the responsibility of children. Many males have a definite taste for relations with prostitutes, preferring them to any other women. Sex perverts of the most diversified kinds almost universally patronize prostitutes. Finally, there are a number of unfortunate men so unattractive physically as to find it difficult to secure sexual relief except with prostitutes.

The reasons why women enter prostitution are equally numerous and diverse, in spite of the common belief that they are almost invariably forced into the profession as a result of sheer starvation or innocent betrayal in love. It is very probably true that economic pressure is the most important single factor causing women to enter upon the career of a prostitute. But often this economic pressure does not take the form of sheer necessity. A number of women indulge in part-time prostitution to piece out their income. They may be married women or women otherwise employed. This form of prostitution has been especially common in Paris and some other European cities. Many prostitutes come from the domestic servant class, where the ordinary material needs of life are relatively well provided for. But they live a drab life and their vanity makes them desire some of the better clothes and jewelry which they observe in the possession of the wives and daughters of the families that they serve. Girls employed for long hours and at low wages in the poorer stores decide that they might earn more money with less effort as prostitutes. There are, of course, many instances in which women, in sheer destitution, turn to prostitution to obtain food, clothing, and shelter. The number of women who come into prostitution as highly intelligent and socially superior girls who have been betrayed in their innocence by irresponsible rakes is extremely small indeed, in spite of sentimental convictions to the contrary.

A considerable number of women become prostitutes simply because they are highly sexed and find this type of life the best method of meeting their personal desires. They voluntarily choose this way of life and rarely leave it of their own free will. Wives of impotent men often become occasional prostitutes. Many young girls are raised in slum areas, where at least an informal prostitution is frequently practiced before their very eyes at an early age. They enter the profession through pathological imitation. Not a few homosexual women become prostitutes because in this type of life they can most easily and safely gratify their desire with other prostitutes. Many prostitutes are given to homosexual perversion. This trend is also coming to be more extensively commercialized. Lesbian women, in increasing numbers, are coming to have relations with prostitutes as a relatively safe and convenient method of satisfying their homosexual desires. Shrewd racketeers have capitalized upon this situation. Looking at the matter in a general way, one may agree with Courtney Ryley Cooper that the "Four Horsemen" serving the procurer of prostitutes are vanity, moral weakness, adversity, and romance. To these we might add sexual perversion.

Realistic appraisals of prostitutes. Traditional conceptions of the prostitute are both contradictory and usually far wide of the truth. One type of prostitute, who exists mainly in the realm of imagination and maudlin sentimentality, is the socially superior girl who has been ruthlessly betrayed in innocent love. In desperation and remorse she either voluntarily enters prostitution or is captured and held against her will by conscienceless procurers. Or, the latter pounce down upon helpless virgins and thrust them as virtual prisoners into a life-long career of living death from which there is no possibility of escape.

From other commentators, in some cases ostensibly scientific students of prostitution, we get another picture of the prostitute. It is less emotional but equally wide of the facts. This version tells us that prostitutes are inferior biologically, often degenerate in a purely physical way, usually feeble-minded, and utterly devoid of any decent sentiments. When this interpretation is offered by students of prostitution, they usually draw such deductions from low-grade prostitutes who have been caught and punished. But these are like the convicts among the criminal class; in other words, they are the inferior, stupid, and often more unattractive members of the prostitute class—the proletarians of the profession.

Prostitutes, like women outside of this group, are an extremely diverse lot. Some are very intelligent and others are feeble-minded. Most of them are relatively attractive, considering the class from which they are drawn; otherwise they would gain relatively few customers in their profession. Certain elementary loyalties and virtues are particularly noticeable among prostitutes. They are pathetically devoted to their personal paramours. They resent any special exploitation of their associates. They are notoriously generous with the money they earn. They are usually loyal and devoted to dependent relatives. They easily become "suckers" for those who prey upon their loyalty and generosity. The conventional picture of the prostitute who has a thoroughly mercenary attitude and a heart of stone is true only of certain prostitutes who have been long in the service and who have been rendered thoroughly disillusioned and cynical by prolonged exploitation and betrayal. William J. Robinson gives us the following authentic and sensible portrayal of the typical prostitute:

In short, the attempt to make a special degenerate or criminal class of the prostitute is nonsensical. The prostitute is in every way equal to the average of the stratum from which she derives. There are coarse, vulgar, tough prostitutes; there are decent, gentle, soft-hearted women among them; yes, even truly modest ones. There are some conscienceless grafters among them; so there are among respectable women. On the other hand, their charitableness, their care for a sister in distress or when helpless from disease could well be imitated by women in the respectable walks of life. And the support they give their old parents or needy relatives could also be taken as an example by some women who are proud of their self-righteousness and who consider the prostitute so low a creature that the mere mention of the name gives them a slight shiver (for which shiver, psychoanalytically, perhaps another explanation than the usual one could be found). And when they have a child, to what sacrifices they will go in order to bring it up properly and comfortably—unless indeed they kill it with their own hands, in order that when grown up she may not have to live the same life that they are leading.

So much for the prostitute's moral qualities. As to her mental level, we declare emphatically that the statement that all or almost all prostitutes are morons or near-morons is baseless piffle. They are on the average of the same mental and educational level as are the other women of the stratum from which they come. They often seem to be of a decidedly higher intelligence. There are morons among them? Of course there are. So there are among the novitiates of nunneries and religious orders.[2]

The very common notion that the prostitute is a helpless prisoner, held in a life of shame against her will, and that she has to indulge in relations which are personally abhorrent and humiliating has little foundation in fact. Though there are some who might fit this description, they are, nevertheless, the exceptions. At least, until the vice rings began to move in on prostitution, the average prostitute entered upon her career voluntarily and was relatively free to leave it when she wished to do so. The only restraint or restriction was the question of her ability or willingness to earn a livelihood in some other mode of activity. After their preliminary adjustment to this type of life, the majority of prostitutes prefer their type of work to any other which they might obtain. Not a few of them take an artistic or professional pride in their career.

Equally wide of the truth is the ordinary assumption that prostitutes invariably die in the gutter, the victims of unmentionable diseases and life-long brutalities. Actually a number of them marry advantageously one of their customers, who usually comes from a higher social level than the girl herself. One of the major problems the vice ring has to meet is to prevent their more attractive girls from falling in love with customers and accepting attractive offers of marriage. Before the grip of the syndicate settled down upon such girls, they were free to contract such marriages, and usually did so. A thoroughly realistic description of the prostitute and prostitution before the syndicate era is set forth by H. L. Mencken:

Even the most lowly prostitute is better off, in all worldly ways, than the virtuous woman of her own station in life. She has less work to do, it is less monotonous and dispiriting, she meets a far greater variety of men, and they are of classes distinctly beyond her own. Nor is her occupation hazardous and her ultimate fate tragic.

A dozen or more years ago I observed a somewhat amusing proof of this last. At that time certain sentimental busybodies of the American city in which I lived undertook an elaborate inquiry into prostitution therein, and some of them came to me in advance, as a practical journalist, for advice as to how to proceed. I found that all of them shared the common superstition that the professional life of the average prostitute is only five years long, and that she invariably ends in the gutter. They were enormously amazed when they unearthed the truth.

This truth was to the effect that the average prostitute of that town ended her career, not in the morgue but at the altar of God, and that those who remained unmarried often continued in practice for ten, fifteen, and even twenty years, and then retired on competences. It was established, indeed, that fully eighty per cent married, and that they almost always got husbands who would have been far beyond their reach had they remained virtuous. For one who married a cabman, or petty pugilist there were a dozen who married respectable mechanics, policemen, small shopkeepers and minor officials, and at least two or three who married well-to-do tradesmen and professional men. Among the thousands whose careers were studied there was actually one who ended as the wife of the town's richest banker—that is, one who bagged the best catch in the whole community. This woman had begun as a domestic servant, and abandoned that

[2] The Oldest Profession in the World. New York: Eugenics Publishing Company, 1929, pp. 45-46.

harsh and dreary life to enter a brothel. Her experiences there polished and civilized her, and in her old age she was a *grande dame* of great dignity.

Much of the sympathy wasted upon women of the ancient profession is grounded upon an error as to their own attitude toward it. An educated woman, hearing that a frail sister in a public stew is expected to be amiable to all sorts of bounders, thinks of how she would shrink from such contacts, and so concludes that the actual prostitute suffers acutely. What she overlooks is that these men, however gross and repulsive they may appear to her, are measurably superior to men of the prostitute's own class—say her father and brothers—and that communion with them, far from being disgusting, is often rather romantic. I well remember observing, during my collaboration with the vice-crusaders aforesaid the delight of a lady of joy who had attracted the notice of a police lieutenant; she was intensely pleased by the idea of having a client of such haughty manners, such brilliant dress, and what seemed to her to be so dignified a profession.

It is always forgotten that this weakness is not confined to prostitutes, but runs through the whole female sex. The woman who could not imagine an illicit affair with a wealthy soap manufacturer or even with a lawyer finds it quite easy to imagine herself succumbing to an ambassador or a duke. There are very few exceptions to this rule. In the most reserved of modern societies the women who represent their highest flower are notoriously complaisant to royalty. And royal women, to complete the circuit, not infrequently yield to actors and musicians, i.e., to men radiating a glamour not encountered even in princes.[3]

Mencken's generalizations are thoroughly confirmed in the autobiography of a prostitute, "The Life of a Los Angeles Sporting Girl," published in *Ken* (May 5, 1938), one of the most illuminating and authentic documents on the realities of prostitution ever to see print.

Prostitutes under the control of syndicated vice rings. The failure to provide adequate public regulation and medical inspection of prostitutes in well-supervised segregated districts led to the disorganization and anarchy upon which the vice syndicate capitalized. The latter has brought order out of chaos, made commercialized vice as difficult to get at as other forms of organized crime and racketeering, and has for the first time made the average American prostitute a veritable prisoner. The independence pictured by Mencken cannot continue where the vice ring has intruded. Rather, we have the situation well described by Courtney Ryley Cooper:

There is much wonderment concerning the source of supply for such a big business as syndicate prostitution—which now is linked, city to city, throughout the United States, with sufficient cleverness to make wholesale Federal arrests on Mann Act charges very difficult.

One of the reasons for this latter is that the Syndicate absolutely controls its girls; retribution follows the one who testifies; there is no person so weak financially or morally as a prostitute. Once she has turned against her own kind, she is lost. There is no place to hide, no friend to aid. Her shadow follows her no more closely than her past; there are fine tortures which a Syndicate can devise, such as whispering information about her when she has found a job, arranging her arrest by the Vice Squad if she goes on the street, then laughing at her, when, with her shoes worn through, she begs to come back into a Syndicate house. Only in rare instances are big clearing houses broken up—such as the instance of a "beauty parlor" in Chicago, the workings of which gave an insight into traffic in professional prostitutes.[4]

---

[3] *In Defense of Women*. New York: Alfred A Knopf, 1922, pp. 189-192.

[4] *Here's to Crime*. Boston: Little, Brown, 1937, p. 283.

The control of prostitution by the vice ring has not only subjected the prostitutes to essential servitude but it has also increased the ability of commercialized vice to promote political corruption and to frustrate effective regulation. The syndicate can, all too often, intimidate prosecutors. Or it can stop them short in their tracks by going behind their backs to the political machine which maintains them in power. Moreover, the syndicate has more money to bribe prosecutors and witnesses, as well as to furnish bail for both vice ring leaders and prostitutes. It can also hire able lawyers. The revelations of the Seabury Committee in New York City with respect to prostitution under the dominion of the vice ring brought these facts out in all too clear relief. And the system was much less perfectly developed at that time than it is today. Sexual vice is now truly *commercialized,* and it is in the hands of a group particularly difficult to subject to public control.

Extent and social costs of prostitution. We have no precise and accurate information as to the extent and cost of prostitution in the United States, either before the great clean-up period following 1912 or at present under the regime of the vice syndicate. It is easier to make estimates for the earlier period, when much of the prostitution was carried on in segregated areas where an informal census might be taken by investigators. In 1913, George J. Kneeland of the Bureau of Social Hygiene estimated that there were 15,000 professional prostitutes in New York City. There was probably an equal or greater number of occasional prostitutes and streetwalkers. A figure of one-half million professional and clandestine prostitutes in the United States on the eve of the First World War would be both reasonable and relatively conservative as an estimate. There is no reliable information on the number of prostitutes today. The harsh conditions after 1929 may have increased the number temporarily. There may have been some reduction in recent years due to growth of sex freedom, especially on the part of girls.

As the cost of prostitution, it has been estimated that the total annual income from prostitution and the associated vice, liquor, gambling, and the like, amounted to about 500 million dollars before the beginning of the great drive against prostitution in 1912. The direct receipts from prostitution itself probably did not equal more than half of this sum at the most. It is believed by good authorities that the income derived from prostitution and allied activities after the reign of the vice syndicate was established certainly amounted to more than half a billion dollars annually. Impressive though this bill may be, it should be borne in mind that, in all probability, more money is spent on irregular amorosity and extramarital sex relations with women other than those who are usually regarded as prostitutes. In estimating the total social cost of prostitution and commercialized vice, one must also consider the cost of venereal diseases which arise in part, though not exclusively, from prostitution. We shall deal with venereal diseases later in the chapter.

The moral implications of prostitution are variously assessed, according to the viewpoint of students. Some, looking upon it as inevitable and indispensable in our type of civilization, advocate sensible regulation.

Others regard it as a most repugnant form of social pathology and wish it stamped out altogether. On one point, at least, both schools of thought are united. They agree that the venereal diseases associated with prostitution are an unmitigated menace and should be controlled and eliminated as soon as possible.

Extent of venereal disease among prostitutes. There is, however, a sharp difference of opinion as to the prevalence of venereal diseases among prostitutes, though most students agree that it is more frequent among streetwalkers and clandestine prostitutes than among those in houses of prostitution and the syndicate brothels. There is no doubt that venereal diseases were extremely common among prostitutes until recent times because of the absence of medical knowledge concerning the nature and transmission of venereal diseases and of effective methods of prophylaxis. Even very dolorous figures on the period before 1900 are likely to be all too true. The main difference of opinion exists with respect to the degree to which prophylactic methods are being successfully applied today by prostitutes in freeing themselves from the dangers of infection and the extent to which they have undergone treatment which has cured them of these diseases. Surgeon General Thomas Parran, Jr., stated in 1937 that "50 per cent of all prostitutes, including those new at the business, are infected with syphilis. Eighty per cent have gonorrhea. Eventually all of them become diseased." This exaggerated view is sharply challenged by other writers, among them by W. J. Robinson, in the following passage:

As to venereal infection, we have always protested against the senseless exaggerations, according to which all prostitutes, ninety or one hundred per cent of them, were infected with venereal diseases—one, two or all three of them. The percentage of venereal disease among the controlled or supervised prostitutes is very small—in the neighborhood of two per cent. We have just read a statement that in all the licensed houses of Paris there were found but four cases of syphilis during the entire year. An examination of the thirty inmates of the high class house of prostitution in the Rue Chabanais has not disclosed a single case of venereal disease; not even a suspicious case was discovered. The keepers of those houses are extremely vigilant in this respect, for a case of infection gives the house a black eye and hurts the trade tremendously. On the other hand venereal disease among the clandestine or occasional prostitutes is quite high— to judge by the result of the batches who are now and then taken in and examined, it reaches about thirty per cent. The reason is easy to understand: practicing clandestinely and occasionally, those girls lack the knowledge and the facilities for proper venereal prophylaxis.[5]

The extent of venereal diseases among the prostitutes controlled by the vice syndicate in the United States today is, of course, purely a matter of conjecture; but those who, like Cooper, have investigated the situation, are convinced that it is being markedly reduced through the use of antiseptics and antibiotics which the syndicate prescribes on the basis of ordinary good business sense. Of one thing we may be sure: so far as fanatical efforts to suppress prostitution lead to scattering it and increasing the number of streetwalkers, they bring about conditions which

---

[5] *Op. cit.*, pp. 49, 50.

are extremely favorable to the prevalence and spread of venereal diseases. But even streetwalkers today have some sense of thrift and good business. Moreover, the streetwalker has some regard for her own health and well-being. Since the knowledge of venereal prophylaxis and treatment has now become common property, there is every reason to believe that even clandestine prostitutes are taking greater precautions to protect themselves and their customers against infection. It is not unreasonable, then, to conclude that prostitutes of all classes are becoming freer from venereal diseases than ever before in history. In fact, many students of the subject believe that prostitutes are more alert to the realities of venereal disease and are doing more to check it within their own group than is the body politic at large. There is, however, still an appalling volume of venereal diseases in the United States, a matter which we shall discuss in more detail later. Many contend that much of the venereal disease of today is a result of increasing freedom of sex relations among uninformed and irresponsible youth—that "bobby-sox" girls spread more venereal disease than prostitutes.

Policies in controlling prostitution. As we have already shown, there are two sharply divided schools of thought concerning the problem of prostitution. The moralists and purists attack prostitution head on, without much consideration of underlying causes, or the varied and disastrous aftermath of their clean-up campaigns. They close up segregated districts and houses of prostitution and attempt to drive the streetwalkers from the public thoroughfares. They do nothing to eliminate the causes of prostitution; they simply spread the latter in sections of the city where it can neither be effectively controlled nor inspected. But they cannot really suppress the practice so long as the demand and prospective customers are provided for through taxi drivers, hotel bellboys, and others, and prostitution is quite thoroughly removed from any salutary public scrutiny. In the United States this purist program of attacking prostitution has, as we have seen, had the particularly disastrous result of making it a perfect field for the vice syndicate to invade and organize, just as Prohibition prepared the way for organized bootlegging.

The other school advocates a recognition that we cannot expect to do away with prostitution until the causes which produce it have been undermined and eliminated. Hence, so long as prostitution is bound to prevail, it recommends a policy which will provide the best protection for society. This involves segregated districts, public licensing, thorough medical inspection, the protection of prostitutes from exploitation by irresponsible third parties, and appropriate public health education and measures. To a certain extent, this was the method followed in the European cities, and it seems to have led to a marked curtailment of venereal diseases, organized vice, and political corruption. That it did not produce utopia is evident, but no fair-minded student of the subject can very well deny that it created far better conditions than exist in the case of prostitution in the United States, either before or since the days of the vice racket.

The failure to follow such a method of procedure in the United States has been due mainly to the influence of puritanically minded persons, whose philosophy has had a large influence upon even the American Social Hygiene Association. This resistance to sane regulation was also given powerful support by the very influential work of Abraham Flexner on *Prostitution in Europe*.[6] This was published in 1914 and gave a very critical report on European regulation and medical inspection. It stressed almost entirely the failures in this policy, without adequately calling attention to its obvious achievements and benefits. Moreover, Flexner's work was written before the sweeping recent advances had been made in venereal prophylaxis and treatment of venereal diseases. Yet his book is still taken by many to represent a true picture of the situation with regard to public regulation and medical inspection in Europe a generation later. What we have lost in the way of adequate control of prostitution and social protection against venereal disease through following the lead of puritanical theology rather than sound social and medical science is well summarized by Cooper:

> The accomplishment of such a program by medical supervision would have been a marvelous achievement. Had the originators of the "white slave crusade" followed a carefully prepared plan of procedure there might have been fewer headaches for the future. The commercializing of vice for the profit of exploiters might have been wiped out. Rigid medical and moral supervision might have come about, plus cooperative Federal and State prosecution of a severe nature against anyone who forced a female, by any means whatever, to become a prostitute.
> There might have emerged clean, well-policed, highly segregated districts, operating under the efficient supervision of non-political boards of public health and morals. The earnings of women might have been carefully guarded for their benefit and protection. There might have been laws, rigidly enforced, for the national registration of prostitutes, with fingerprint identifications, cards of identity, and medical inspection. There might also have been the establishment of hospitals designated especially for the treatment of venereal diseases, plus stringent control of all physicians who cater to patients suffering from such maladies.[7]

Whatever the ultimate wisdom of these two conflicting schools of opinion with regard to the regulation of prostitution, it is certain that the methods of the purists have prevailed in this country; and, if we judge them by their fruits, we cannot hold them in very high esteem.

If, in the last 40 years, we had combined the progress of medical knowledge with a realistic social philosophy in dealing with prostitution, we would have been able to reduce venereal diseases to a minimum. The situation in Sweden, to which we shall call attention later, shows what can be done when science rather than archaic sentiment prevails. As a matter of fact, many purists deplore making prostitution free from venereal disease because they believe it would increase its popularity. This would seem to indicate that their criteria and motives are theological rather than sociological or medical. The American Social Hygiene Association has continued its opposition to the regulation and inspection of

---

[6] New York: Century, 1914.

[7] *Op. cit.,* p. 222.

prostitution. Bascom Johnson, associate director of the Association, declared that investigations have shown that such methods are "without any value whatever either for protecting public health or preserving public order." To be sure, one is entitled to his own opinion on this, as upon other matters. But it is necessary to keep clearly in mind the fact that the suppression of "sin" is one thing, and the control and eradication of venereal diseases quite another. The former is a theological consideration; the latter, strictly a sociological and medical problem.

A rational program for handling prostitution. A realistic program of dealing with prostitution in the light of science rather than theology would seem to lead us to the following recommendations: Prostitution should be legalized, the prostitutes segregated in districts where living conditions are healthful, their procedure regulated, gambling and other forms of vice stamped out, the prostitutes rigorously inspected by competent physicians, venereal diseases treated and eradicated, and extended education provided in the use of prophylaxis. The selling of intoxicants in segregated districts should be completely eliminated. No sensible person would expect perfection to result from such measures, but we can reasonably anticipate conditions in every way superior to those which now prevail under a regime of shortsighted repression or syndicate control.

But this would be only the immediate program. A more fundamental effort would be made to eliminate prostitution by dealing with its causes. An effort would be made to promote economic justice and to secure an income for unmarried men and women which would make prostitution and its patronage less necessary. Through sex education, guidance clinics for problem girls, psychiatric treatment for pathological women, and better control of the feeble-minded, we would endeavor to eliminate those causes of prostitution which are essentially of a noneconomic character. An extensive introduction of companionate marriage would provide for the sex needs of normal young persons without any necessity for resorting to prostitution on the part of girls or of recourse to prostitutes in the case of young men.

Any such set of proposals would naturally outrage the purists. But their attitude toward the sex and venereal disease problems is much like the attitude of professional prohibitionists toward the liquor problem. And there is no reason for doubting that their method of handling the sex problem and prostitution has been as shortsighted and ill-founded and as pregnant with evil results as was the Noble Experiment as a method of promoting temperance.

Unfortunately, a policy of sanity and realism might be too late now. The vice syndicates have taken over prostitution for themselves, and have made themselves very solid with the political machines. They are not likely to surrender this lucrative domain until organized crime as a whole is brought to an end. This happy day is likely to be indefinitely postponed in our country. Yet, if we do not like the spectacle of syndicate-controlled prostitution, we have mainly to thank the misguided blunders of the purist fanatics of the past for its existence.

THE CHALLENGE OF VENEREAL DISEASE

Relation of venereal disease problem to prostitution. The close relation of venereal disease to prostitution is entirely evident. Prostitutes have in the past been more frequently infected with venereal diseases than other women and are often the source from which men contract the disease and transmit it to women outside the prostitute class. Much of our venereal disease has been the result of prostitution. But there is every probability that this is becoming much less true in our day.

Today, an even greater amount of venereal disease is being found among women outside of the prostitute class. They acquire it from men who may have consorted with prostitutes or other women. The greater freedom of sex relations, entirely outside of the realm of prostitution, has aggravated this situation. Women outside of the prostitute class are often less alert to the dangers of venereal infection and are all too frequently ignorant of both the need for and means of protecting themselves. The same is true of men who have relations with them. They feel that there is far less danger of venereal infection in relations with nonprostitute women; hence, they are much less careful in providing themselves with protective devices. There are many distinguished medical authorities today who believe that there is more venereal disease transmitted by light-hearted and complaisant but nonprostitute females than by professional prostitutes.

Education only effective solution of venereal disease problem. If this is so, or anything like the situation, we must recognize that the complete suppression of prostitution will not wipe out venereal diseases. This happy result can be achieved only by the most thoroughgoing education of the entire population with respect to the nature, treatment, and prevention of venereal diseases. It has been only recently that anything of the sort has been at all possible. A generation ago no reputable newspaper would even print the names of the leading venereal diseases.

Types of venereal diseases. There are several types of venereal diseases: syphilis; gonorrhea; soft chancre (sometimes also known as chancroid); two relatively rare and recently discovered maladies, *lymphogranuloma inguinale* and *granuloma inguinale;* and crab lice. Of these several forms of venereal diseases, only the first two are of any great medical or social significance. Crab lice are a venereal vermin rather than a true venereal disease.

History of venereal disease. We may first consider the history of venereal diseases. Gonorrhea is far the older of the two in the experience of the race. At least, it appears far earlier than syphilis in the pathological commentaries of Western civilization. As far as we can judge from available evidence, it antedates written history. The disease was known in China more than 5,000 years ago, and there are frequent references to it in the Old Testament. The medical authorities of classical antiquity and the Middle Ages refer to it constantly. There is no means of telling how it first became a contagious disease, contracted and transmitted by members of the human race.

Some medical authorities hold that syphilis possesses an equal antiquity. They maintain that this was the disease which King David contracted from Bathsheba. Although this contention may be true, there is no way of proving it. Physicians and other observers first began to comment widely upon the existence of syphilis at the very close of the fifteenth century. Hence, the great majority of medical historians contend that syphilis was one of the less lovely contributions of the New World to the Old. They believe that it was brought back from the West Indies to Europe by the sailors of Columbus. In fact, there is considerable evidence to support the assertion that Columbus himself died of syphilis in 1506.

The first great epidemic of syphilis in western Europe seems to have spread after the siege of Naples in 1494. Mercenaries had been brought there from all parts of Europe. Prostitutes also came there in large numbers, some of them presumably infected by ex-sailors formerly in the employ of Columbus. These ex-sailors had later entered the army of King Ferdinand of Spain. The syphilitic army harlots spread the disease among the mercenaries at Naples, who later returned to their several homes all over western Europe. A severe epidemic of syphilis followed, and, as we have seen, some recent authorities estimate that one-third of the population of Europe perished as a result during the next 25 years. The disease possessed a virulence and mortality at that time far in excess of anything associated with this malady today. It struck down royalty as well as the peasant and the urban beggar. Among the European monarchs who are known to have contracted syphilis are Henry VIII of England, Charles VIII and Francis I of France, and Ivan the Terrible of Russia. Syphilis was carried from Europe to Asia. Vasco da Gama took it to India in 1498, and other Europeans soon transmitted it to China and Japan. It also made a return trip to America, and an epidemic of syphilis is recorded as having taken place in Boston in 1646.

Certain very eminent medical historians vigorously contest the notion of the American origin of syphilis and maintain that it had been known in Europe long before 1500. They hold that, for some reason, it became more deadly and took on epidemic proportions at the end of the fifteenth century. They also point to the fact that this was the time when the Order of St. Lazarus was abolished and the inmates of some 19,000 leper houses were scattered throughout Europe. It is believed that many of the supposed sufferers from leprosy were, in reality, syphilitics. The majority of medical opinion, however, inclines with good reason to the thesis of the American origin of syphilis.[8]

The main arguments against the thesis that syphilis existed in Europe before the close of the fifteenth century are the following: (1) though its symptoms are easily recognizable, no Greek, Muslim, or Christian physician ever described or discussed the disease before 1494; (2) it was widely described after 1500 by physicians possessing little more knowledge of

---

[8] The eminent historian of science, George Sarton (*Isis*, November, 1938, pp. 406-407), after examining all the recent criticism of the American origin of syphilis by Sudhoff, Holcomb, and others, arrives at the conclusion that they have not proved their case.

medicine; (3) it spread in Europe after 1494 with all the explosive force, virulence, and mortality of a new disease against which no immunity had been gained; and (4) those who deny that it came from America at this date are not able to offer any rational explanation of where it did originate or why it spread like an epidemic after 1494. In any event, both schools of medical thought on the subject agree that it first became a serious malady in the West in 1500.

The lesser venereal diseases are not of sufficient importance to warrant any discussion of their history. Indeed, they have none, since they have been only recently discovered and described.

Historical pathology of venereal disease. In this historical section we should also say a word or two about the history of our knowledge of the germs causing these diseases and of the means whereby their presence in the human body can be demonstrated.

Before the discovery and improvement of the microscope, the weirdest theories of the causes and pathogenesis of venereal diseases prevailed. For a time it was commonly believed that the germs of syphilis and gonorrhea were identical, and that both diseases could come from the same germ. By one of the strangest freaks of all medical history, this dogma was given authority and persistence through the heroism of one of the leading English physicians of the eighteenth century, John Hunter. In 1767 he inoculated himself in two places, in one with pus taken from a case of gonorrhea and in the other with material taken from a case of syphilis. In both infections he developed a syphilitic chancre. This was supposed to settle the question for all time. But we now know that the patient from whom he derived the gonorrhea germs must also have been suffering from syphilis—presumably from the relatively rare intrarurethral chancre. It was not until 1812 that the French physician, Jean Hernandez, upset Hunter's theory and showed that the two diseases are wholly distinct. But so much weight was attributed to the earlier notion and to Hunter's confirmation of it that it was not until 1837 that the most famous specialist of the age in the field of venereal diseases, Philippe Ricord, was finally able to convince the medical profession that these two major venereal diseases were quite different and were derived from distinct forms of bacteria.

The demonstration of this fact was made still clearer when the specific germs causing these diseases were definitely isolated and described. The germ of gonorrhea, the so-called *gonococcus,* was first definitely isolated and observed by Albert Neisser, of Breslau, in 1879. But medical science had to wait another generation before the syphilis germ, *spirochaeta pallida,* was discovered by another German pathologist, Fritz Schaudinn, in 1905. An effective blood test to reveal the presence of the spirochete was devised by August von Wassermann in 1907, and improved tests have been perfected since that time. The electron microscope has recently made the spirochete visible.

Syphilitic infection and symptoms. We may now discuss briefly possible modes of infection with venereal diseases and the symptoms of these diseases. The syphilis germ rarely enters the body except through a break in the skin. But this break need be of only microscopic size to make infection possible. Gonorrhea is rarely contracted except as the result of actual sexual intercourse, but syphilis can be contracted innocently as well as through sexual relations. Indeed, kissing can be more dangerous than sexual intercourse in exposing one to syphilitic infection. This is because a syphilitic may transmit the disease just as readily by kissing as by intercourse, and there is no effective prophylactic device to prevent an infection which takes place through osculation. Syphilis may occasionally be contracted by using cups, eating utensils, towels, toilet seats, and other articles which have been recently touched by syphilitics. Nonsexual infection with syphilis would be much more frequent than it is were it not for the fact that the syphilis germ dies very quickly when exposed to heat and light, especially when the germ is left on a dry surface. Realistic medical experts incline to the belief that noncongenital syphilis is contracted almost entirely through sexual intercourse.

In addition to infection with syphilis through intercourse, kissing, and the like, syphilis may be passed on to a child by a syphilitic mother during the period of pregnancy. This is known as *congenital syphilis*. About 14,000 new cases of congenital syphilis are reported each year. Presumably a far greater number of cases are not reported—particularly in instances where midwives rather than physicians are in attendance during labor. There is no longer any medical excuse for congenital syphilis, since penicillin will almost invariably prevent it.

When syphilis spirochetes have entered the body through a skin abrasion, we have a syphilitic infection and the patient develops the primary symptoms of syphilis. This is the first stage, and the symptoms develop at any time between 12 and 40 days after the exposure. The main symptom of the primary stage of syphilis is the syphilitic sore or chancre, which always forms at the point where the germs have penetrated the skin. It is distinguished from other sores mainly by the fact that it has a hard, or indurated, border, is rarely tender or sore, and heals relatively slowly. It is rare that any serious local or general discomfort is associated with the primary stage of syphilis.

If syphilis is not effectively treated in the primary stage, the symptoms of the secondary stage will usually appear from six weeks to a few months later. A copper-colored rash on various parts of the body, a sore throat with persistent mucous patches, and swollen glands on the throat are among the more obvious of the physical symptoms. Now, for the first time, comes physical discomfort, taking the form of headaches, indigestion, and fever. But even in this stage the patient rarely has to take to bed, and after a few months the secondary symptoms are likely to disappear and the patient will begin to feel relatively normal again. The uninformed victim is all too likely to regard himself as out of all danger.

Lamentably, this is far from true. The more serious—and all the fatal—manifestations of syphilis come in the tertiary stage, the symptoms of which may not manifest themselves until many years after the original infection. These tertiary symptoms assume innumerable forms—the caving in of the bridge of the nose, the falling of the roof of the mouth, serious heart disorders, paralysis of the lower limbs, and syphilitic infection of the brain, or paresis, until recently an incurable and speedily fatal disorder. We have already mentioned in the chapter on public health the high mortality formerly resulting from syphilis.

Contraction and symptoms of gonorrhea. Gonorrhea is a much less complicated disorder. As we have suggested, it can almost never be contracted except as the result of sexual intercourse. The *gonococcus* almost invariably has to be deposited through direct contact. Although it may attack other parts of the body than the genital organs, most notably the eye, gonorrhea is usually restricted to the genitals. In the male it causes an acute inflammation of the urethra. The symptoms appear between three and 10 days after the exposure. They are at first the discharge of a clear, watery fluid, turning to white, and then to a greenish yellow. Discomfort in urination usually accompanies the urethral discharge. The acute stage lasts from a week to a month, depending upon the constitution of the patient and the nature of the treatment he receives. If the malady is not competently treated, the infection may spread to the prostate gland, the seminal vesicles, the bladder, and even to the testicles. In the latter case, serious pain and ultimate sterility may result. In the case of the female, the vagina proper is rarely attacked. The inflammation is more likely to take place in certain glands near the opening of the vagina, in the urethra, or in the cervix. It is rarely as painful locally with women as with men. If not treated promptly, however, the infection may spread into the Fallopian tubes, and may even affect the ovaries.

Although the acute symptoms of gonorrhea are the more immediately painful, the really serious results of this disease are of an indirect and incidental character. It is for this reason that it has been particularly disastrous that the majority of those suffering from gonorrhea have imagined that the disease is solely limited to its acute manifestations, and that it ends when the latter are terminated. Gonorrhea is the most common cause of sterility in both males and females. In the female it may lead to many complications. Some of the most serious female operations, such as the removal of the Fallopian tubes, the ovaries, or both, are most frequently caused by gonorrheal infection. Until recently, at least 30 per cent of all blindness was due to the infection of children at birth by mothers suffering from gonorrhea. This type of blindness has been greatly reduced of late by the almost universal practice of dropping a weak solution of nitrate of silver or of penicillin into the eyes of every child at birth. A serious type of arthritis frequently arises from gonorrheal infection.

Minor venereal diseases. The soft chancre is a local sore which may be differentiated from the syphilitic chancre in a number of ways. In the first place, it usually appears in 10 days or less after exposure. In the second place, it is painful and sore. In the third place, it is soft rather than hard and indurated, as in the case with the syphilitic chancre. It is a purely superficial sore instead of a serious constitutional disease. It may be quickly cured by simple local treatments, such as the application of appropriate salves.

Crab lice represent a type of venereal vermin which are most usually acquired by intercourse with cheap and unclean harlots. They chiefly inhabit the pubic hair and the hair of the arm pits, rarely invading the hair of the head. They are mainly a temporary annoyance, and a few applications of the proper (blue) mercurial ointment will speedily eliminate them. Even more effective are Cuprex and DDT powder. The other forms of venereal diseases are sufficiently rare so that we need not take the space to discuss them.

Extent of venereal disease in the United States. It is difficult to estimate the extent of venereal disease because of the secrecy surrounding it. There is no other field of disease where the statistics vary or conflict so widely. In 1934, the United States Public Health Service made a conscientious effort to ascertain the extent of syphilis and gonorrhea. So far as could be estimated from all available sources, 1,037,000 new cases of gonorrhea and 518,000 new cases of syphilis were reported in 1934. Many new cases were probably not brought to the attention of physicians. In the same year, there were 131,000 new cases of tuberculosis, 7,517 cases of infantile paralysis, and 220,050 cases of scarlet fever. The United States Public Health Service estimated in 1946 that there were about 400,000 new cases of syphilis each year, and about 1,200,000 new cases of gonorrhea. In 1945, there were reported 104,967 new cases of tuberculosis, 13,614 cases of infantile paralysis, 175,398 cases of scarlet fever, and 87,241 cases of pneumonia. About 60 per cent of the new cases of venereal disease today are found in persons in the 15-25-year age group. Clearly the problem of the contraction and spread of venereal disease remains extensive and menacing, despite much reduction in its prevalence since 1945.

Estimates of the number of persons suffering from venereal disease in the United States vary, but the minimum figures still show the problem to be a serious one. The most extreme figure is that offered by Carl Warren, who estimates that about 20 million Americans are suffering from syphilis and gonorrhea at any time. Of this number, six to seven million have syphilis, and the rest gonorrhea. The American Social Hygiene Association estimates that about 5 per cent of the population is infected with syphilis and from 10 to 15 per cent with gonorrhea. In 1947, Walter Clarke estimated that about 13,000,000 Americans were suffering from venereal diseases.

On the other hand, the Committee on the Costs of Medical Care estimated two decades ago that only about one case of venereal disease is under care per 100 of the population. Whether the number suffering from venereal disease is 1, 10 or 15 per cent of the population, the situation is appalling, because even a mere handful of cases are unnecessary from a medical point of view. Moreover, and amazingly enough, venereal disease increased rapidly in the United States for some years after 1940, at the very time when methods of prophylaxis and treatment were being perfected.

Venereal diseases of late appear to be more prevalent, per capita, in rural areas and small cities than in larger urban communities. For example, while the venereal diseases rate in New York City rose by 29 per cent in 1946 over 1945, the rise was 50 per cent in the rest of the state. This is to be explained by the greater difficulty in getting treatment in rural districts, fear of discovery, and ignorance of methods of protection (prophylaxis) against contracting the diseases.

Economic cost of venereal disease. The economic cost of venereal disease is impressive. It has been estimated that 175 million dollars in wages are lost each year by men and women suffering from these diseases. If to this and the cost of medical care is added the expense of supporting those blinded, crippled, or made insane by venereal disease, the amount is staggering; an estimate of half a billion dollars annually would be moderate. Donald Pillsbury, of the Veterans Administration, has estimated that the ultimate cost of caring for the syphilitic veterans of the Second World War alone will run to a billion dollars. At the end of the war there were more than 400,000 syphilitic soldiers. The situation is the more pathetic and lamentable, because there is, medically speaking, almost no excuse for it.

Evolution of treatment of syphilis. One of the most interesting historical aspects of the problem of venereal diseases is the development of methods of treatment. The first important remedy for syphilis to be used by physicians was calomel, or mercury. This was hit upon more or less by accident in the first quarter of the sixteenth century. It was simply a lucky chance that its use was suggested at almost the moment that syphilis first became epidemic in Europe. It is a fairly effective specific against syphilis, but its use is accompanied by various dangers, and the systems of some persons will not tolerate it. It is unfortunate that the experience of Benvenuto Cellini with malarial fever, as a mode of curing syphilis, was not recognized and exploited by physicians at the time. Had it been, syphilotherapy might have been speeded up by several centuries, for quinine soon made its appearance as a method of curing malaria.

Not until 1834 was there any notable improvement in the medical treatment of syphilis, mercury being almost universally relied upon by the most competent doctors. In that year William Wallace, of Dublin, introduced the use of iodide of potassium. This, and improvements in the application of mercury, formed the basis of the battle against syphilis until 1910, when the German chemist and physician, Paul Ehrlich, provided his arsenic preparation, salvarsan, or "606." Another important addition to syphilotherapy came in 1922, when a Paris doctor, Constantin Levaditi, discovered that bismuth, injected intramuscularly, is a valuable supplement to salvarsan. It can also be used on persons whose systems will not tolerate prolonged treatment with either mercury or salvarsan. It has almost no toxic effect upon the human system when given intramuscularly.

A revolutionary advance in dealing with syphilis, especially syphilis of the brain and central nervous system, came in 1918 when the distinguished Austrian physician, Julius Wagner von Jauregg, introduced fever therapy to kill the spirochetes. He used malaria to accomplish this and then treated malaria with quinine. More recently, Charles F.

Kettering, Fred J. Kisling, and Walter M. Simpson have invented electric fever machines which are simpler and less dangerous than malarial treatment. They are now generally used administering fever therapy.

Far and away the greatest discovery in the history of the treatment of syphilis was the demonstration that it yields fairly readily to penicillin. The latter has proved so much more effective than any other remedy that it has virtually superseded all others except in the treatment of neurosyphilitics. Permanent cure of primary syphilis can be accomplished in 8 to 10 days of intensive treatment. The cost of treatment has been enormously reduced—to a mere nominal charge in clinics.

What may prove the most effective of all medical attacks on syphilis was announced late in 1949 by Lee J. Alexander of Dallas, Texas, who for three years had been testing the efficacy of injections of penicillin and bismuth during the incubation period following known exposure to syphilitic infection. By the time the primary chancre of syphilis appears the disease has become firmly implanted in the system. Alexander based his procedure on that followed in giving serum to those bitten by rabid dogs immediately after possible infection. It was shown that treatment by penicillin and bismuth as soon as possible after exposure was almost completely effective in preventing the development of syphilis, while in a comparable "control group" not treated after exposure, some two-thirds developed primary syphilis. If this promising new technique is to be effective, patients must be educated to the necessity of presenting themselves for prophylactic treatment as soon as possible after infection.

Recent success in reducing syphilis. Syphilis can thus be quickly and permanently cured, if treatment is begun in the primary stage. If it is delayed until the secondary stage, the disease can usually be cured, although the cure will take longer. And even in the third stage, a combination of chemicals, antibiotics, and the fever treatment may work wonders in arresting the disease, if the germ has not yet damaged the brain or nerve tissues too severely.

Despite the improvements in prophylaxis and treatment, cases of syphilis continued to gain right down through 1946. Since that time the combination of the more effective penicillin treatment and the increased efforts by various public health agencies have markedly reduced both the new cases and deaths from this disease. The cases of syphilis declined from 362.3 per 100,000 of the population in 1941 to 197.1 in 1949. There were 296,455 cases reported in 1949, a decrease of 14 per cent from 1948. Deaths from syphilis decreased from 15 per 100,000 of the population in 1939 to 8 in 1948. Infant mortality from syphilis in 1948 was one-fifth what it had been in 1939. There was also a notable drop in the admission of cases due to syphilis in mental hospitals. One reason for the greater recent success in combating syphilis than in coping with gonorrhea is that the main efforts have been concentrated on syphilis. Out of a total of 166,066 admitted to treatment centers in 1949, 79 per cent were suffering from syphilis. Only three per cent of those getting treatment were gonorrhea patients. Syphilis cases are also much more adequately reported.

Progress in treatment and cure of gonorrhea. Until recently no progress had been made in the way of discovering a powerful specific against the *gonococcus.* The treatment consisted mainly of lessening the pain in the acute stage and of keeping the patient quiet, so that his natural resistance could assert itself most effectively. Mild irrigations and injections, chiefly argyrol or some silver salt, permanganate of potash, mercurochrome, or chinosol, were most commonly used. But if the infection spread into the prostate gland, the seminal vesicles, or the Fallopian tubes, the physicians were usually helpless to prevent chronic gonorrhea and its aftermaths. The main hope was to start treatment at the first appearance of the symptoms, and, if possible, to prevent the disease from reaching the posterior urethra, the prostatic area, and the Fallopian tubes.

Sulfanilamide revolutionized the treatment of gonorrhea. The newer sulfa drugs, such as sulfadiazine, sulfathiazole, and sulfapyridine, have proved more effective in the treatment of gonorrhea. Their action on the gonococcus is far more decisive and they seem to cause fewer bad aftereffects. Since penicillin has become readily available, it has pretty generally superseded the sulfa drugs in treating gonorrhea, mainly because there are no toxic results or serious after-effects. Today, permanent cure can be achieved by three large injections of penicillin given at intervals of four hours. A new penicillin preparation, known as duracillin, will cure most cases with only one or two injections. It is possible that the technique of Alexander in preventing the development of syphilis by giving penicillin injections during the incubation period may also prove effective in preventing the development of gonorrhea after exposure.

Gonorrhea increased after Pearl Harbor despite medical victories. Despite the effectiveness of the new remedies for venereal disease and the provision of cheap and almost certain methods of prophylaxis, the rate of gonorrhea rose alarmingly after the onset of the Second World War. First cases of civilian gonorrhea reported (no second exposures were reported in these statistics) increased from 191,000 per annum in 1941 to 367,000 in 1946. One reason for this increase is that a great number of cases apparently go without good medical treatment. Although the United States Public Health Service estimates that there are 1,200,000 new cases of gonorrhea each year, private physicians and public clinics report only about 350,000 leaving some 850,000 cases unaccounted for. Many of them are, doubtless, uncured and spread infection. Further, the publicity given to easy cures has made persons more careless about prophylaxis and more ready to rely on self-medication. The increase in the number of promiscuous, uninformed, and careless "teen-age" girls has also been very important in the recent spread of gonorrhea. By the mid-century there was some evidence that the increase in this disorder was being checked, though not as rapidly as syphilis. The number of new cases reported in 1949 was 342,856, the lowest since 1945. In New York City recorded new cases of gonorrhea declined from 24,350 in 1946 to 16,784 in 1950, a drop of 31.1 per cent, as compared with a decline of 59.8 per cent in syphilis.

Importance of prophylactic measures in preventing venereal disease. Important as the progress of remedial measures in dealing with venereal diseases may have been, it is still true that an ounce of prevention is worth a pound of cure, especially in the case of syphilis. Prophylactic measures against the contraction of venereal disease through sexual intercourse are today quite simple and exceedingly effective. It is now merely a matter of getting those who need them to procure them and use them.

The most common prophylactic device is the rubber prophylactic or condom. It is desirable, however, to supplement this by the use of germ-destroying chemicals. The pioneer preparation was developed by Robert Bachmann and is available in a specially devised tube, usually known as a "sanitube." This contains chemicals, mainly calomel and protagol, which are deadly to both the spirochete and the gonococcus. This device is, of course, usable only by males. Douches and vaginal jellies have been provided to protect females against infection. If these prophylactic devices, now available, are used invariably and with care, and the kissing of syphilitics is avoided, there is very slight danger of contracting a venereal disease.

That much progress is being made in the use of prophylactic measures may be discerned from the fact that over 500 million condoms are sold annually in the United States, and over five million chemical devices. The greatest impetus to prophylactic measures in the United States came as the result of their systematic application in the American Expeditionary Force in France during the First World War. The remarkable success achieved there suggested the beneficial effects of following up this practice in civilian life. The soldiers did an important piece of informal educational work along this line in their home localities after they returned from the front.

Purists are alarmed over the increasing knowledge and effectiveness of prophylactic measures, for they fear that they may increase sin. We need not go into the merits of this argument at present. All that we need concern ourselves with is the obvious fact that prophylaxis has greatly reduced possible infection from venereal diseases in the last two decades, and it is likely to accomplish much more in the decades to come. Next to religious and puritanical opposition to prophylaxis, the major obstacle to fairly complete success along this line is intoxication. Many men consort with prostitutes or other infected women when they are under the influence of liquor, and nonprostitute women are most likely to relax and indulge after imbibing. This makes it more difficult to maintain an attitude of apprehensiveness and to take prophylactic measures with promptness.

Another important reason for lack of attention to prophylactic measures has been the increase of male intercourse with nonprostitutes, and the resulting illusion that prophylaxis is not necessary in such cases. Students of the problem believe that this was a chief cause of the alarming increase in venereal disease, especially gonorrhea, during the war decade.

Though venereal disease is one of the main blots on our civilization—"a shadow on the land"—to use the words of former Surgeon General Parran, the only obstacles to its eradication today are social. The medical aspects of the problem have already been successfully mastered. We have the scientific knowledge wherewith to wipe out this scourge in a generation.

Puritanical obstacles to eradication of venereal disease menace. We have already referred to the opposition of purist fanatics to the spread of information with respect to venereal prophylaxis. This attitude on their part may be understood, but it is more difficult to comprehend the attitude of physicians who repudiate the truly medical point of view in favor of puritanical theology. Some of them seem to stand in greater fear of sex sanity than of the specter of venereal diseases. A professor of syphilology and dermatology in one of our leading medical schools once told the writer that he carefully avoided any reference to venereal prophylaxis in his medical lectures lest his students provide themselves with such preparations and engage in sinful behavior.

PUBLIC AGENCIES WORKING TO CONTROL VENEREAL DISEASES

FROM *Prostitution and the War* BY PHILIP S. BROUGHTON, PUBLISHED BY THE PUBLIC AFFAIRS COMMITTEE, INC. CHART BY PICTOGRAPH CORPORATION.

Chart indicating co-operative activities and agencies essential to an effective campaign against venereal disease.

Even men such as former Surgeon General Parran, who conducted a courageous crusade against syphilis, allow nonmedical ethical prejudices to stand in the way of suppressing venereal diseases. Parran supported the very attitude toward prostitution which makes all but impossible its regulation and medical inspection and increases the number of street-walkers who lengthen and darken the "shadow on the land." He was also surprisingly apathetic in his attitude toward prophylaxis. The policy of the American Social Hygiene Association with regard to prostitution was for years opposed to sane medical considerations in the combating of venereal disease. Until we are able to eliminate archaic theological prejudices from the scene, the potentialities of venereal prophylaxis and remedial treatment cannot be thoroughly realized. The soundness of this position is confirmed by Thurman W. Arnold:

> This contrast between two attitudes comes into clearer relief when modern treatment of venereal disease is examined, because these are the only physical epidemics still treated from a medieval point of view. There is no question but that the present ravages of these diseases could be tremendously reduced. Proof of this is found in the record of the United States Army in France. Yet such a solution means that we must recognize an obvious natural fact about human beings which interferes with both reason and morals. To the moral man of the twentieth century, there is a vast difference between smallpox and venereal disease, because smallpox is not the result of sin.[9]

What may be achieved when medicine ousts theology in the control of the campaign against venereal disease may be seen in the case of Sweden. Here, through a system of compulsory treatment and the provision of adequate free public clinics, the number of new cases of syphilis reported annually was reduced from 6,000 to 431 within a five-year period—long before the appearance of the sulfa drugs and penicillin. Even in England, where theological considerations still have some hold, the prevalence of syphilis has been reduced by over 50 per cent since 1920. The achievements in the urban regions of Soviet Russia, where syphilis was most rife before the First World War, have equaled those recorded in Sweden. Nazi Germany virtually obliterated new cases of syphilis.

If we wish to eliminate venereal disease, all that is needed today is a modicum of sex sanity. Prostitution should be segregated and rigorously inspected. Sweeping and candid education should be provided with respect to venereal prophylaxis. Prompt and efficient treatment of venereal disease, at public cost if necessary, should be made completely and easily accessible. Such treatment should not cause any personal embarrassment to the prospective patient. That it does so today is one of the reasons why infected victims consult quacks rather than reputable doctors. If the venereal disease issue could be thoroughly secularized, we would have none of those "soldiers in slime" who run the venereal disease racket which Cooper so thoroughly exposes and roundly condemns.[10]

Since we are now past the period when it might have been possible to regulate and inspect American prostitution, which the vice syndicate has taken over for its own, we shall probably have to concentrate mainly upon prophylactic measures and upon more thorough education concerning adequate treatment of venereal diseases. There is no reason why syphilis and gonorrhea should not be more rare, 10 years from now, than diphtheria is today.

---

9 *The Folklore of Capitalism.* New Haven: Yale University Press, 1937, pp. 86-87.
10 *Here's to Crime,* Chap. XI.

Some signs of growing rationalism in the situation may be discerned in the campaigns against syphilis and in the reduction of its ravages. There were in 1950 about 1,500 treatment and clinical projects for venereal diseases in 36 states. As we have seen, most of their attention was given to syphilis—only three per cent of those treated being gonorrhea patients. Satisfactory community efforts will need to be extended more completely to the latter. In April, 1951, New York City health officials believed that they had venereal disease sufficiently under control so that they could close the Central Social Hygiene Clinic which had treated over 250,000 persons in 34 years. Borough clinics were deemed adequate to care for new cases.

NARCOTIC DRUG ADDICTION

Juvenile addiction brings drug problem to public attention. Though all serious students of the problem of narcotic drugs have long known that the situation has become a national scandal, partly due to fanatical legislation or to fanatical administration of reasonable laws, the public paid little attention to the problem until recently. This lethargy, indifference, and ignorance on the part of the public has recently been upset by the revelation of a shocking amount of addiction among young persons. M. D. Kogel, Commissioner of Hospitals in New York City, stated in January, 1951, that "the influx of juvenile narcotic addicts has become a problem in our hospitals." District Attorney Frank S. Hogan asserted that juvenile addiction in New York City had markedly increased from 1946 to 1949 and had developed in "shocking" fashion after 1949. In 1951, it was estimated that there were at least 15,000 juvenile addicts in New York City. His medical adviser, P. M. Lichtenstein, stated that juvenile addiction in New York City had increased about 200 per cent in 1950 and was gaining in 1951. Similar conditions have been revealed in Chicago, Los Angeles, and other large cities. In May, 1951, the director of the Chicago House of Correction stated that the cells were full of addicts and that if more were sentenced he would have to pile them on the floor. Juvenile patients constituted only three per cent of admissions to the Federal Narcotic Hospital at Lexington, Kentucky, in 1946, but this group had grown to 18 per cent among the new cases admitted in 1950. Only nine were admitted when the institution opened in 1935, and only 11 as late as 1944. Some 52 were admitted in 1948, 210 in 1949, and 440 in 1950.

Long history of use of narcotic drugs. The use of narcotic drugs as a means of achieving personal euphoria and exultation or of producing an exotic calm is as old, apparently, as the use of drugs for the treatment of disease. At least, references to the uses of such drugs go back to the dawn of written history. It seems that the original home of the opium poppy was ancient Mesopotamia, in the Tigris-Euphrates valley. The poppy was used for narcotic purposes by the earliest known dwellers in this region, the Sumerians, among whose writings we have references to the "sleep poppy" and the "joy plant." Opium is frequently mentioned in the Babylonian and Assyrian literature. The Egyptians and Persians appear to have learned of the use of opium from the dwellers in Mesopotamia. It is in Persia that we find the first references to the use of hashish, *cannabis indica,* a hemp-like plant product, the drug effects of which may be attained either by smoking or chewing it. As we shall see later, an American plant producing much the same effects has, in the last few years, become a popular drug (marijuana) now consumed in the United States.

The persistence of the use of narcotic drugs in the area of its origin was revealed by a newspaper report in 1950. On the basis of official sources, this report stated that there are today two million opium addicts in Iran (Persia), and that the opium monopoly nets the government nearly six million dollars annually.

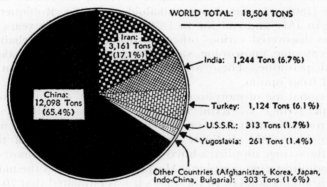

WORLD TOTAL: 18,504 TONS

Iran: 3,161 Tons (17.1%)

India: 1,244 Tons (6.7%)

China: 12,098 Tons (65.4%)

Turkey: 1,124 Tons (6.1%)

U.S.S.R.: 313 Tons (1.7%)

Yugoslavia: 261 Tons (1.4%)

Other Countries (Afghanistan, Korea, Japan, Indo-China, Bulgaria): 303 Tons (16%)

SOURCE: INTERNATIONAL CONCILIATION BULLETIN NO. 441, MAY, 1948. NARCOTIC DRUG CONTROL.

Graph indicating main world sources of opium.

In classical times narcotic drugs derived from opium were very common. They were used by the Greeks and Romans both in medical practice and in personal indulgence. Vergil frequently refers to the opium poppy in his agricultural poems and in the *Aeneid.* In the latter he portrays Queen Dido as putting herself to sleep with poppy juice as a result of her sorrow over the flight of Aeneas from Carthage. The Muslims of the Middle Ages are believed to have carried a knowledge of the opium poppy to India and China. The first reference we have in Chinese literature to opium is from the tenth century, though some authorities have contended that the Chinese were familiar with the opium poppy by the seventh century. But it was apparently not much used there as a narcotic until about 1700.

The opium used by the Chinese was brought in chiefly from India, which became the great source of the opium supply in modern times. The Chinese rulers tried to suppress the opium habit in China as early as 1729, and its importation was definitely forbidden in 1800. The British, who profited mainly from the Indian opium trade, were resentful over this Chinese embargo and, in 1840-1842, 1856-1858, Great Britain fought the notorious Opium Wars against China to protect the Indian opium trade and undermine the Chinese embargo. Opium was also extensively exported from India to western Europe. The Dutch and the English, particularly the latter, controlled this lucrative trade.

The more important narcotic drugs. The easy use of narcotics was made possible by the provision of a number of opium derivatives as a phase of the progress of medical and chemical science in modern times. The famed chemist and physician, Paracelsus (1493-1541), learned to make laudanum and administered it for many diseases. The two most famous physicians of the seventeenth century, Van Helmont and Sydenham, prescribed opiates profusely. About 1700, an English physician, Thomas Dover, produced "Dover's Powders," long a popular opiate, and shortly afterwards a Leyden chemist provided paregoric. A century later Friederich Setürner in Germany and Charles Derosne in France discovered morphine (1803), the first known alkaloid of opium. Robiquet isolated narcotine in 1817 and codeine in 1832. In the following years Pelletier and others discovered various other narcotics: narceine, thebaine, papaverine, cryptopine, gnoscopine, xanthaline, antharaline, apocodeine, dionine, and peronine. These are the more important narcotic drugs developed from opium.

The personal use of morphine was facilitated by the invention of the hypodermic syringe by Rynd and Wood in the middle of the last century. Ironically enough, it was thought that the injection of morphine under the skin would eliminate the habit-forming effects of the drug. Actually, the syringe supplied addicts with what became the most common means of administering morphine. Morphine still remains the most popular narcotic among addicts. In the 1930's it was estimated that 70 per cent of the addicts in Federal institutions for addicts had used morphine.

Some of the most popular of present-day narcotics were, paradoxically enough, produced as a result of the effort to find nonhabit-forming substitutes for morphine. Such, conspicuously, was heroin, an artificial alkaloid (a diacetic ester of morphine), which was discovered by a German chemist, Dreser, in 1898. This has become one of the most widely used of all habit-forming narcotic drugs in our day. The more common methods of administering narcotic drugs by addicts are to smoke opium, to inject morphine by the hypodermic needle, and to snuff heroin.

Cocaine, a dangerous drug, is not a narcotic. Cocaine is commonly supposed to be a form of opiate, but it is quite a different drug. It is not derived from the opium poppy at all but from the coca shrub, which is found in South America and Java. It was used by natives of these areas for centuries but did not become commercialized in Western civilization until the middle of the nineteenth century, after which it became the first important type of local anesthetic used by surgeons and dentists. It has been very generally supplanted in medical and dental practice by novocaine, which, while a less powerful anesthetic, does not have the habit-forming qualities of cocaine.

The effect of cocaine is quite different from that produced by the opiates. While the narcotic drugs derived from opium create a euphoria characterized by psychic calm, cocaine produces marked stimulation and exhilaration.

One of the interesting aspects of narcotic addiction in the case of those who suffer from slavery to the opiates is that the human system develops a tolerance for these drugs, so that ever larger doses must be taken to get the desired euphoria. This is not true of cocaine, at least not to any such degree. Although cocaine addicts often increase the dosage, it is not necessary to do so. The larger dosage consumed is resorted to in order to heighten the effect.

Nature and extent of narcotic addiction in the United States. We may now look into the extent and nature of drug addiction in the United States. The use of opiates by civilians in the United States first became marked during the Civil War. It was so common then that, after the war, drug addiction was commonly referred to as "the army disease." Drug addiction in the United States grew steadily, if slowly, from the period of the Civil War to that of the First World War. The problem is now of great economic importance. The American Association on Drug Addiction asserts that the annual cost of drug addiction in the United States is about $2,750,000,000. Some estimates are even higher. In 1951, it was estimated that the annual revenue from narcotic, cocaine, and marijuana sales was about one billion dollars.

The estimates of the number of drug addicts in the country in our day differ widely. At the time of the passage of the Harrison Act in 1914, Treasury officials estimated that the number of habitual users of narcotic drugs lay somewhere between 60,000 and 100,000. There are certainly far more drug addicts today than there were before the Harrison Narcotic Act was passed in 1914, but they are also more difficult to locate and enumerate. Investigators in 1919 estimated that there were 200,000 drug addicts in New York City alone. In 1931 Arthur Reeve held, on the basis of police estimates, that there were 500,000 drug addicts in New York State. In 1918 a special investigating committee of the U. S. Treasury Department estimated that there were 1.5 million addicts in the country as a whole. Some recent estimates by competent students of the problem go as high as four million. Such generous figures have been vigorously attacked by certain authorities like Thomas S. Blair and Howard Rusk. Those who minimize the extreme estimates place the number of true addicts at about 50,000 to 100,000 in the country as a whole. But any estimate is guesswork, and the victims of drug addiction may be held to be somewhere between 500,000 and three million at the present time. It would be reasonable to hold that there are around 100,000 to 200,000 true addicts and perhaps three million who use narcotic drugs to some extent.

The recent alarming increase in the use of narcotics by American youth has surely produced more addicts, but just how many we do not know.

How drug users become addicts. Before we look into the nature of drug addiction and drug addicts more thoroughly, we should make it clear that most persons who take narcotic drugs chronically are not drug addicts in any technical sense of the word. Those who use these drugs in moderation are comparable to other persons who drink alcohol in moderation or who use tobacco to get relief from nervous tension. The true drug addict, like the real alcoholic addict, is a definitely psychoneurotic type whose addiction is a form of mental disease. This is not true of those

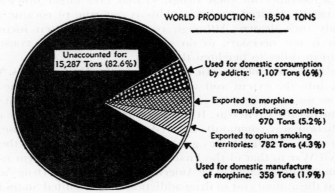

WORLD PRODUCTION: 18,504 TONS

Unaccounted for: 15,287 Tons (82.6%)

Used for domestic consumption by addicts: 1,107 Tons (6%)

Exported to morphine manufacturing countries: 970 Tons (5.2%)

Exported to opium smoking territories: 782 Tons (4.3%)

Used for domestic manufacture of morphine: 358 Tons (1.9%)

SOURCE: INTERNATIONAL CONCILIATION BULLETIN NO. 441, MAY, 1948. NARCOTIC DRUG CONTROL.

Graph indicating world production of opium.

who use narcotic drugs in moderation. A representative case of a chronic moderate user of narcotics is described by Joseph F. Fishman:

Years ago, one of the present writers was overwhelmed with astonishment when, in the Middle-Western home of a physician and quite by accident, he saw his host snuffing some heroin up his nose. The doctor said he had been taking drugs for over twenty-five years. He was a leader in his community, not only among his medical brethren, but otherwise, and was much sought after socially. Since then we have learned from physicians specializing in drug addiction that there are many thousands like him scattered throughout the country.[11]

One of the evils of drastic legislation curbing the use of narcotics is that it has made criminals out of even these mild users of narcotics outside of the medical profession which can obtain the drugs legally. It has led to the lumping of all who use these drugs, either mildly or in extreme degree, in one common class of criminals and addicts. This leads to both confusion and folly.

Accurate knowledge of the causes of the habitual use of narcotics has been supplied mainly by psychiatrists rather than by general practitioners. General practitioners have shown very little insight into the underlying nature of drug addiction, however expert they may be in using such drugs for medical or surgical purposes. It is now definitely demonstrated that most serious cases of true drug addiction are the result of psychoneurotic conditions: mental and nervous disorders growing out of deep-seated mental conflicts in the individual. J. D. Reichard, a specialist on addiction, states this psychiatric view of addiction as follows: "The

11 J. F. Fishman and V. T. Perlman, "The Real Narcotic Addict," *The American Mercury,* January, 1932, p. 104.

more abnormal the individual, the more desirous he is of escape from his own painful sense of reality and the more he tends to use any or all narcotic substances to excess."

The narcotic drug produces a sense of euphoria or well-being, which temporarily releases the sufferer from his mental conflicts and fears. Hence, merely taking away the drug from such an addict in no way produces a cure. The latter cannot be achieved unless the person is subjected to consistent psychiatric treatment which will remove the causes of the mental conflict and eliminate any need for recourse to narcotic drugs. Unless such treatment is available, it may be unwise to take the drug away from the addict, since he may develop further neurotic or psychotic traits far more unfortunate and dangerous than the drug addiction which tends to keep him quiet and satisfied.

There are many ways in which the habitual use of drugs may be acquired. Some get the habit from medical treatment where opiates are prescribed for the relief of physical pain or insomnia. In the days before narcotics became more difficult to obtain, the narcotic drug habit frequently resulted from self-medication, and from the use of numerous patent medicines containing opiates. The drug laws have made it more difficult to market patent medicines containing opiates, but such abuses have not been entirely eliminated. It is not likely, however, that many normal persons will become true addicts, even if they intermittently use powerful narcotics. Chronic addiction is unusual unless the person either is suffering from some deep-seated mental conflict or is living under painful and disturbing conditions from which he desires to make a mental escape by means of the narcotic euphoria.

Many degenerates, prostitutes, and criminals use drugs and alcohol to buoy them up and make them more oblivious to the difficult conditions under which they live. Dejected criminals are taught the drug habit by chronic users who are foolishly committed to prisons either for punishment or for treatment of the habit. Drug users, especially when under the ban of the law, are notoriously prone to seek converts to addiction. The drug habit is not uncommonly brought about by a nefarious type of commercial salesmanship. Dope traffickers may attempt to convert persons to the use of drugs in order to make sales. It is doubtful, however, whether this practice is very important, except in the case of marijuana, since there are usually enough chronic users available to buy up all the narcotics which can be supplied by the dope ring. "Big shot" racketeers and vice kings, while rarely chronic addicts, resort to the use of drugs as a stimulant to their jaded senses.

Not a few authorities claim that more chronic use of drugs is caused by the laws that have been passed to repress it than by any other single factor. The outlawed users wish to secure companions in vice. Hence, they work vigorously to spread the habit not only in the underworld and in prisons but often among innocent and unsuspecting persons. This fact was emphasized by a group of medical specialists appointed by the Mayor of New York City to investigate and report on drug addiction: "Every addict for the sake of companionship or for self-justification ceaselessly

endeavors to make other addicts." [12] They become what Benjamin Karpman calls "missionaries of addiction."

Myth and facts about narcotic drug addiction and addicts. It is commonly believed that chronic use of narcotic drugs lead to speedy physical
disability, if not to death itself. After a careful study of addicts in the
prison population of the United States, and of the New York City prison
on Welfare Island, in particular, Joseph F. Fishman came to the conclusion that this belief finds little substantiation in the actual facts. He
studied 1,166 drug addicts in the New York City prison. He found that
very few had used drugs for less than five years; that half of them had
used drugs for 10 years or more; that 20 to 25 per cent had used drugs
for 15 years; and that 10 per cent had used them for more than 15 years.
Many of the addicts had been chronic users of narcotic drugs for 20 years
or more, and one of them had been a chronic addict for no less than 48
years. Fishman points out that, in his experience as investigator of Federal prisons, it was possible to find addicts who had used narcotic drugs
for 50 years.

Many of the men who had used drugs constantly for 25 years were in
relatively good physical condition. Even those who were not showed
remarkable improvement in health when they were deprived of drugs
and their appetite for food was increased. This indicates that the drugs
had not caused any permanent impairment of physical vigor. Fishman's
findings were confirmed by D. P. Wilson after extended study of addicts
in a Federal institution during the 1930's. Intestinal disorders due to
constipation seem to be the main bad direct physical effect of addiction.[13]
It would seem that it is the mode of life which drug addicts are prone to
live, rather than the drugs themselves, which produces temporary physical
impairment.

With cocaine addicts, however, the situation is somewhat different.
Cocaine is much more toxic in its effect than the opiates and heroin, and
those seriously addicted to cocaine are likely either to die or to abandon
the addiction within a few years. It is, therefore, fortunate that it is much
easier to terminate cocaine addiction than it is to handle addiction to
the opiates.

Drug addiction and criminality. Alarmist literature and the propaganda of the crusaders against drug addiction have created a grotesquely
exaggerated impression concerning the danger to society from the drug
addict. The drug addict is commonly presented as a bold and dangerous
criminal, likely to plan and execute all sorts of violent crimes. Fishman
gives a fair presentation of this conventional conception of the drug
addict, as we meet him in literature and the drama:

Across the stage an emaciated figure slinks. His skin is yellow, his eyes are
feverish, his hands shake. He is in the stage of physical decay which verges on
a complete debâcle, yet presently he will commit the most nervewracking crimes
with a coolness, strength and endurance unknown to healthier normal men.

---

[12] Fishman and Perlman, *loc. cit.,* p. 106.
[13] *My Six Convicts.* New York: Rinehart, 1951, pp. 340-341.

For he is the narcotic addict of romance, and the drug that he takes, it appears, transforms him from a weak, cowardly wreck into a swaggering, brutal, guntoting desperado, who proceeds to shoot indiscriminately anyone whose hands do not reach into the air as high as he thinks they should.[14]

Fishman and Wilson thoroughly debunk this traditional illusion about the narcotic drug addict. Not more than one-fourth of those who are committed to prison because of violation of the narcotic laws are actually criminals. And this criminal fourth are, almost without exception, minor offenders. As Fishman says, "A group of more trivial offenders you could not find anywhere—except in other narcotic cells. All the more shocking and sensational crimes are conspicuous by their absence. Petty thievery, vagrancy, disorderly conduct and various minor offenses—these fill the record." [15] Even the petty thieves steal mainly to get money with which to buy the drugs they so passionately desire. Drug addicts are almost never found among the organized criminals, racketeers, and gangsters, who will have nothing whatever to do with a drug addict because he is notoriously at the mercy of police when they take his narcotic drug away from him. Almost any drug addict will tell all he knows to the police to get more drugs. Moreover, a drug addict does not have the coolness or steadiness of nerve necessary to a modern gunman. Therefore, it is entirely evident that if drug addiction is an evil, it is an evil in itself and not because it incites any considerable number of addicts to serious crimes against either person or property. As Benjamin Karpman puts it, when they can get their drugs "addicts as a group are anything but criminally inclined." [16]

The typical drug addict is usually quite peaceful and law-abiding when provided with the drug he uses. The chronic addict is, however, generally much impaired in his economic and professional efficiency, and hence creates an economic problem for himself and his family. He is rarely a serious personal nuisance or a disturber of the peace, except when deprived of narcotics. Indeed, he is likely to be peaceful and ingratiating when under the influence of the drug. Cocaine addicts are considerably more active and aggressive, but even they are rarely guilty of serious offenses against the peace. As stimulants of crime, the most serious of all drugs are hashish and marijuana, against which we had little or no legal protection until recently. We shall have more to say about this later. In the case of those addicted to morphine, and for the most part to cocaine as well, the evil effects of the drug habit are chiefly the impaired economic usefulness of the addict and the misery and dependency which this may bring to his family. Neither crime nor degeneracy is directly promoted to any notable degree by addiction to the more common narcotic drugs. Most crime and degenerate conduct of which addicts are guilty grow out of their efforts to obtain the drug upon which they rely. As we shall see later, the legislation suppressing the open sale of narcotic drugs

---

14 Fishman and Perlman, *loc. cit.,* p. 100.

15 *Ibid.,* p. 101. Wilson completely agrees with Fishman on this point, *op. cit.,* p. 342.

16 Karpman, "Laws that Cause Crime," *American Mercury,* May, 1931, p. 74.

has probably produced far more criminality than ever resulted from their use.

Treatment and cure of drug addiction. As might be implied from what we have said about the underlying causes of true narcotic drug addiction, there is no really effective cure for the latter, save for recourse to prolonged psychiatric treatment, preferably skilled psychoanalysis, which will remove the motivating psychoneurotic causes of the addiction. Unfortunately, such treatment is extremely rare. Men with means sufficient to pay for psychoanalytic treatment usually have money enough to get all the narcotic drugs they desire. Occasionally, a well-to-do addict has sufficient insight and balance to recognize his plight and to turn to a psychiatrist for aid. In many such cases many gratifying cures have been effected.

The most common types of treatment for narcotic addiction are really no cure at all. They simply constitute different forms of withdrawal of the drugs from the patient. Indeed, the three major types of treatment are classified on the basis of the speed with which the patients are deprived of narcotic drugs. The first type, abrupt withdrawal, often known as the "cold turkey" treatment, consists in abrupt and complete deprivation of narcotics. The second form of treatment is a relatively rapid withdrawal of the drugs. The third mode of handling addicts is that which prescribes a very gradual withdrawal of the narcotic. The second type of procedure is that most commonly employed in the United States, France, and Germany. Frequently, other types of drugs are used temporarily as a substitute for the withdrawn narcotics in the treatment of the addict. Mathadon, or dolphine, produced by the Germans during the Second World War, is the most widely used of such drugs at the present time. Although it is habit-forming, it can be withdrawn from addicts with less suffering than is experienced with deprivation of morphine or heroin.

Since none of these modes of treatment touches the underlying causes of the more serious cases of chronic addiction, it is rare that any permanent cure is effected, and relapses usually result. But relief is frequently provided in the case of mild or early addiction, particularly where this has been the result of ignorance or of accident in the use of habit-forming drugs.

All too often the withdrawal treatment plays into the hands of the addict. As his tolerance for the drug increases, the doses needed to produce euphoria become so great that he can no longer afford to buy the necessary amount of the narcotic required. The withdrawal treatment temporarily reduces the tolerance. When the treatment is over, the patient finds that he can once more provide himself with a sufficient amount of the narcotic to get an adequate "kick" out of it.

A considerable number of addicts who apply to city prisons for treatment do so deliberately with this end in mind. They have no intention of striving valiantly to get rid of their malady. They simply wish to be put into a condition where they can cultivate it more economically. Joseph A. McCann, formerly Warden of the City Penitentiary of New

York, whose experience with addicts was greater than that of any other prison official in the country, reported to Fishman that "many hundreds of self-committed addicts have told him frankly that they were not in the slightest degree desirous of curing themselves of the habit, but merely wanted to reduce its cost." [17]

Withdrawal symptoms. When narcotics are taken away from those addicted to opiates, there may be serious symptoms, particularly if the withdrawal is abrupt. Restlessness, depression, excessive perspiration, nausea, muscular cramps, inactive circulation, nervous exhaustion, and sometimes complete physical collapse may result. There have been some cases of actual death reported as a result of too sudden and complete deprivation of narcotics in long-standing cases of chronic addiction. Wilson's studies of addicts in Federal institutions incline him to discount the reports of serious effects of even the "cold turkey" withdrawal procedure. He believes that many of the serious symptoms are faked to prevent the withdrawal.[18] In the case of cocaine addiction there are almost no distressing withdrawal symptoms, and addicts may be deprived of cocaine without any special medical supervision.

It is obvious that the most serious manifestations of abnormal personal behavior, as a result of drug addiction, appear when the drug is withdrawn rather than when it is available and indulged in. Withdrawal has a more serious effect upon both the mental and physical state of the addict than the use of drugs. Moreover, the addict is rarely aggressive or dangerous to society except when reduced to desperation in his effort to obtain the desired narcotic.

Need for specialized institutions. One indispensable requirement for even superficial treatment of drug addiction is the provision of specialized institutions or separate wards which receive only drug addicts. Because of the well-known tendency of addicts to seek converts to addiction, it is manifestly undesirable to bring them into contact with any other type of institutional inmates, whether sick persons or criminals. Also, those undergoing fake "cures" to reduce their tolerance, as we have pointed out, can spread addiction propaganda among many who have never hitherto followed the habit. The creation of two Federal narcotic farms was definitely a right step in this direction. These have been established at Lexington, Kentucky, and Fort Worth, Texas. Though known as "farms," they are really well-equipped hospitals for narcotic addicts. They are operated by the United States Public Health Service in conjunction with the Federal Bureau of Prisons.

On the whole, however, institutional treatment, even in the enlightened and well-staffed Federal narcotic farms, has proved relatively ineffective in producing real cures. In January, 1951, it was reported that only 20 per cent of those who had taken the full six-months treatment at the Federal farm in Lexington could be proved to have been cured in the

[17] Fishman and Perlman, loc. cit., p. 102.
[18] Op. cit., pp. 332-333.

light of data revealed by a follow-up survey. Some 35 per cent were discovered to be repeaters after this period of treatment, and 45 per cent could not be traced. Many of these were believed to have resumed the habit. Of the 15,000 treated at Lexington since 1935, over 40 per cent have returned for treatment more than once. The record with voluntary patients who left the farm after brief treatment and against medical advice showed virtually no demonstrable cures at all. Whether such treatment as the Yale Clinic Plan provides for alcoholic addicts would prove as effective with narcotic addicts is not known.

In an effort to cure addiction and prevent reversion to the habit, addicts have recently organized to apply group therapy through mutual confessions and resolutions. These have been modeled after "Alcoholics Anonymous." The first group of this sort was founded by patients at Lexington Hospital in 1947. They took the name of "Narcotics Anonymous." The movement is now branching out. A chapter was established in New York City early in 1950, followed by others in Chicago, Los Angeles, and Vancouver.

Legislative and crime enforcement efforts to suppress the use of narcotics. The original basis of Federal procedure in the effort to suppress the drug trade was the Harrison Narcotic Act, passed in December, 1914. It was originally more of a revenue measure than a law designed to promote criminal prosecution of users of narcotic drugs. Prosecution of illegal drug vendors is carried on by the Treasury Department under the authority of the taxing power of the government.

The Harrison Act was originally designed chiefly to eradicate the large-scale smugglers of narcotics, leaving the apprehension and punishment of street vendors and addicts mainly to the states. The act provided that dispensers of narcotic drugs must be registered with the Bureau of Internal Revenue, and that all narcotic drugs sold must bear a revenue stamp. Druggists were also compelled to keep a record of each sale of a narcotic drug, together with the name of the purchaser. Physicians, dentists, and veterinary surgeons were allowed, in professional practice, to dispense narcotic drugs to patients. The Supreme Court, in 1919, interpreted this to mean that a physician can dispense narcotics only in a direct and legitimate effort to cure the patient of the particular disease for which he is being treated. This, of course, leaves a broad loophole for personal interpretation of therapeutic measures by individual physicians.

Even Treasury figures reveal the fact that it was the Harrison Act itself which helped to make the use of narcotics an epidemic. These estimated the number of habitual users of narcotics in 1914 as from 60,000 to 100,000, about half under medical supervision. In 1918, the Treasury estimated the number of narcotic users at 1.5 million, an increase of 1,500 per cent.

Much more drastic than the Harrison Act was the Jones-Miller Act passed by Congress in 1922. This provided a penalty of up to 10 years in prison and a $5,000 fine for any person who imported, concealed, or sold any narcotic drug. The act directed that mere possession of narcotic drugs would suffice to convict unless satisfactorily explained to a jury. This virtually branded every addict a criminal.

Many of the states also proceeded to pass very drastic laws curbing the possession and use of narcotics. Some of them went so far as to make the mere possession of small quantities of narcotic drugs a crime, even though no evidence could be produced that the possessors were engaged in the sale of narcotics. Those arrested in New York City under the New York law are, in at least one-third of the cases, apprehended merely for possessing drugs which are presumably to be used by themselves.

Disastrous effects of antinarcotic legislation. Even though the antinarcotic legislation has not been adequate to suppress the trade, it has been sufficient to drive narcotic vending underground. The result has been the development of a gigantic dope ring, a prominent manifestation of the organized crime which has developed since the First World War. Arnold Rothstein and "Legs" Diamond laid the basis for the narcotics syndicate. It is alleged that the present moguls of the syndicate operate in conjunction with "Lucky" Luciano, now safe from the arms of the law in Italy. It is estimated that the total amount of revenue from illicit narcotic sales amounts to more than a billion dollars annually. This figure may be excessive, but certainly the business runs into the hundreds of millions of dollars each year. It is difficult to suppress the smuggling of drugs. No trucks are needed to transport it. Several hundred thousands of dollars' worth of dope can be brought here in a valise on an airplane.

Alfred R. Lindesmith, a leading student of the narcotic problem, has recently well described the effect of the antinarcotic legislation since 1914. He holds that: "Among the undesirable effects of the legislation are the creation of the illicit traffic, the pauperization and demoralization of addicts, and the stimulation of crime, particularly theft and prostitution." He goes on to say that this legislation "has made the United States the most lucrative market in the world for the illicit trafficker and stimulated the cultivation of the poppy in remote portions of the earth." [19]

Many realistic and well-informed students of the narcotic problem criticize severely all drastic antinarcotic legislation, especially laws which make the mere possession of small quantities of narcotics a crime. They hold that the existing antinarcotic legislation is intellectually and socially on a par with the ill-fated Eighteenth Amendment and the Volstead Act. Such critics list what they regard as a number of outstanding evils of the purely repressive procedure in regard to the narcotic trade and drug addiction.

In the first place, a large number of persons who are in no way real criminals are sent to prison. Here they come into association with habitual criminals and may in time themselves acquire truly criminal habits. In the meantime, they may convert many criminals to drug addiction, the net result being bad for both the noncriminal addicts and the habitual criminals. Next, we have the large expense of caring for addicts who are committed to prisons and other institutions to secure the withdrawal

---

[19] *Opiate Addiction.* Bloomington: Principia Press, 1949, pp. 192, 195.

treatment, without any real intention of making a serious effort to be cured. Further, many who are deprived of narcotic drugs are driven into much more serious neuroses and psychoses. They then become a public charge and are rendered both more expensive and more dangerous to society. Again, the repressive legislation has encouraged the dope rings by making the dispensing of narcotic drugs a crime rather than a legitimate trade. Criminal syndicates, rather than doctors and druggists, are now in charge of the major portion of the drug trade. Finally, putting the matter of drug addiction and its control under the ban of criminal legislation greatly increases the desire of addicts to spread their deplorable habit, and it increases the difficulty of treatment.

Drastic changes needed in antinarcotic legislation and procedures. Realistic students of the narcotic problem recommend the abolition of all criminal legislation relating to the narcotic trade and narcotic drug addiction. They recognize the necessity of suppressing the underworld trade in narcotics, but they are wholeheartedly opposed to making criminals out of a group who are, in reality, only unfortunate invalids, the victims either of their own internal conflicts or of irresponsible medical quacks. Although this point of view is rarely presented in traditional treatments of the problem of drug addiction, it is certainly worthy of serious consideration.

This critical attitude toward existing antinarcotic legislation, already stated by Fishman, is confirmed by such eminent experts in the field as Robert A. Schless and Benjamin Karpman, leading psychiatrists who have made a life study of the problem. Schless says:

I believe that most drug addiction today is due directly to the Harrison Anti-Narcotic Act, which forbids the sale of narcotics without a physician's prescription. Prior to the passage of this act, there was a limited number of drug addicts who went to the corner druggist for their day's or week's supply. They paid a moderate price for the then legitimate article of sale, and the druggist, upheld by professional traditions that are only too often scoffed at, would no more dispense heroin or morphine to a curious adolescent than the old time bartender would sell whisky to a child, especially since the profit was small and the temptation, therefore, not inordinate.[20]

Karpman is even more decisive in his opinion. Until the Harrison Act was passed, "things seemed to run along as smoothly as was possible under the circumstances." There was no greater increase in addiction than in the other neuroses. And few addicts were criminals. When the law was passed, freedom to get drugs disappeared, and users of drugs were compelled to lie, to steal, and to do worse to get them. Our prisons became filled with addicts. Karpman believes that the Harrison Act has produced more criminals than the Volstead Act. It has also created the dope rings. He concludes that: "The law has failed in its proposed effect; indeed, it has been directly responsible for the tremendous increase [in the drug habit] . . . Corrective measures must consist in the repeal of the law and a return to the previous practices." [21]

---

[20] Schless, "The Drug Addict," *American Mercury*, February, 1925, p. 198.
[21] Karpman, *loc. cit.*

Another generation of experience with the antinarcotic legislation has only confirmed the attitude of Schless, Karpman, and Fishman. A. R. Lindesmith, August Vollmer, and D. P. Wilson all agree that the drastic legislation should be repealed. Lindesmith suggests that physicians should be allowed to prescribe narcotics for addicts and that the latter should be as free to buy them as alcoholics to purchase their liquor. Vollmer, a famous police expert and criminologist, recommends Federal control and dispensing of narcotic drugs under the supervision of the United States Public Health Service. Addicts could buy them from this source at cost. Most sensible students of the drug problem will agree that this is far preferable to the present repressive police procedure.[22]

The benefits which might result from the legalization of the sale of narcotic drugs to adults, according to those favoring such action, are the following: drugs would be put back into the drug stores and handled under the control of physicians and pharmacists who would never sell to juveniles; the cost of narcotics would become so slight that it would not be necessary to commit crimes to obtain them and the outlay would not be so great as to take money away from providing the necessities of life; the narcotic ring or syndicate would quickly disappear, for there would be no way to continue its vast illicit profits; political and police corruption to protect the narcotic ring would fade out along with the drug syndicate; the well-trained law enforcement bureaucracy of the Narcotics Department could be transferred to the repression of serious crimes; and the number of addicts would gradually decline.

The marijuana problem. Much publicity has recently been given to the increasing use of marijuana, a drug very similar to hashish which has long been used in the Orient and was introduced into Mexico in modern times. The plant from which marijuana is derived is technically called *cannabis sativa*. Known by the name of "loco weed" and other local terms, it grows wild in many parts of the United States, especially in the Southwest. The drug effect is usually attained through smoking, and the cigarettes which contain marijuana are generally called "reefers." Marijuana addicts are popularly referred to as "floaters."

The effects of the use of marijuana are warmly debated. The alarmists contend that marijuana lowers the sense of restraint and self-control, and that it incites many to crimes of violence and acts of sexual degeneracy. It is alleged to head girls towards prostitution and boys towards activity in criminal gangs and rackets. Others are more reassuring. The noted psychiatrist, Walter Bromberg, appears to doubt many of the alarmist contentions. He writes that: [22a]

In sixty-seven cases involving marijuana from the Court of General Sessions, New York County, it was found in general that early use of the drug apparently did not predispose to crime. No positive relation could be found between violent crime and the use of marijuana in the cases observed in the Psychiatric Clinic.

---

[22] Lindesmith, *op. cit.*, Chap. xii; Wilson, *op. cit.*, Chap. 17.
[22a] Walter Bromberg, "Marijuana: a Psychiatric Study," *Journal of the American Medical Association,* July 1, 1939, pp. 4-12.

No cases of murder or sexual crimes due to marijuana were established.... The present study allows at this time only the statement that the use of marijuana is a "sensual addiction" in the service of the hedonistic elements of the personality.

Though many criminals and degenerates doubtless use marijuana, their criminality and degeneracy may be due to other causes and may have preceded any addiction to marijuana. A real danger from the marijuana habit is that it may lead to the use of powerful narcotics. It is certain that its use by juveniles should be discouraged and prevented, so far as possible.

Health and hygienic aspects of the tobacco habit. Because nicotine is a mild form of narcotic, there has been much discussion of the physical and mental effects of smoking tobacco. Many writers claim that smoking raises the blood pressure, causes serious heart trouble, has a bad effect on digestion, increases infant mortality, and is one of the main causes of tuberculosis.

These assertions have been investigated by eminent medical experts, many of them non-smokers. They find that there seems to be little difference between the blood pressure of those who smoke and those who do not. There seems to be no proof that moderate smoking produces heart ailments, that it seriously affects digestion, or that the children of smoking mothers die as a result of prenatal nicotine poisoning. Smoking does reduce appetite, but it is more likely to prevent excessive eating than to produce malnutrition. Some specialists have recently demonstrated that nicotine contracts the blood vessels of the heart, and have advised heavy smokers to drink moderately, since alcohol dilates the blood vessels. Scientists have shown that smoking has no effect on babies nursed by mothers who smoke. If infants of such mothers die more frequently than others, bad habits often associated with cigarette smoking are responsible, rather than the nicotine itself. Psychiatrists believe that persons often smoke to excess because they are nervous and physically run down. Thus, heavy smoking seems to be the result rather than the cause of nervous or physical disorders. From all available evidence there seems to be no proof that smoking causes tuberculosis. The greatest increase in smoking has occurred within the past 25 years, but during this same period tuberculosis has decreased.

Nicotine, like opiates and alcohol, affects different persons in different ways. Personal tolerance for nicotine varies widely. How much any person should smoke is a matter for individual medical guidance rather than generalized moral exhortation or denunciation.

Economic wastes in tobacco habit. The tobacco habit is, however, expensive. The tobacco bill of the nation runs to about three billion dollars annually, a large expenditure for a product that cannot be classed as a necessity of life. We spend about as much for tobacco as we do for all public education. In addition to the amount spent for tobacco itself, smokers spend a great deal of money each year for accessories, like pipes, smoking stands, cigarette holders, and ash trays. Clothes, cushions, and car seats are often burned, and sometimes even houses are burned down as a result of the careless habits of smokers. While the bad physical effects of moderate smoking are trivial, much of the money spent on smoking, even though it does furnish work and income for thousands engaged in raising tobacco and in making tobacco products, might possibly be used to better advantage.

ALCOHOLISM AS A SOCIAL PROBLEM

Aspects of the alcohol problem. Whatever one's views relative to the ethics of the consumption of alcoholic beverages, the fact remains that the use of alcohol, entirely outside the industrial field, is one of our most important economic and social problems. Aside from the sheer necessities of life, alcohol represents the most important single source of expenditure on the part of the American people, with the sole exception of public taxation. There are few social problems which are not directly and vitally affected by the use of alcohol.

Alcohol as an economic and social problem may be most profitably considered under three headings: (1) the economic social costs; (2) the physical and mental effects of the personal consumption of alcohol in general; and (3) the special problem of chronic alcoholism and alcoholic addiction. The last of these has received most public and medical attention in recent years, but it is far less important than the first.

Economic costs of present alcoholic consumption. The expenditures for alcoholic beverages increased in striking fashion after the repeal of Prohibition. In 1934, the amount spent for this purpose was two billion dollars; in 1940, 3.87 billion; in 1946, 9.5 billion; and in 1950, 8.76 billion. The per capita expenditure grew from $15.80 in 1934 to $67.34 in 1947, but dropped to $58.13 in 1950. The main reason for increased expenditures has, of course, been the tremendous rise in the price of liquor, especially spiritous liquor, due to the great increase in production costs and excise taxes. That the increased expenditures for alcoholic beverages have been caused more by increased liquor costs to the consumer than by the increased consumption can be seen from the fact that while expenditures increased from 3.87 billion dollars in 1940 to 8.76 billion in 1950, the consumption increased only from 1,825,833,000 gallons to 2,897,151,000 gallons. The decrease in expenditures since 1947 has been due mainly to the greater consumption of wine and beer as compared to the more expensive distilled spirits. Entirely aside from the farmers who produce the grain needed, about one million persons are engaged in the manufacture of alcoholic beverages. To these would have to be added the many occupied in the sale and distribution of these beverages.

The money spent for alcoholic beverages is often compared to expenditures for leading personal and social services. The total cost of all medical care and public health is about 8.5 billion dollars annually and of this only about half is paid by the populace for direct medical attention. Our liquor bill is thus twice what we pay for physicians and hospital service. The cost of alcoholic beverages amounts to nearly three times the total expenditure for public education. At the present time the population of the United States spends between 4.5 and 5 per cent of the national income on alcoholic beverages.

In estimating the total economic cost of alcoholic consumption in any year, it would be necessary to add the industrial losses due to the use of alcohol among workers which take the form of wage losses due to drunkenness, decreased worker efficiency, reduction of output, physical damages, and the like. This is fairly estimated to be about one billion dollars annually.

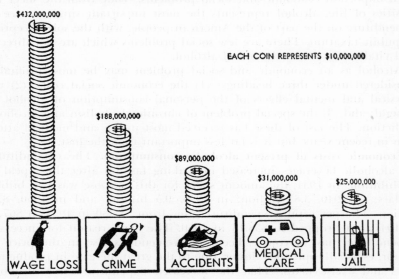

WHAT ALCOHOLISM COST US – 1940

$432,000,000

EACH COIN REPRESENTS $10,000,000

$188,000,000

$89,000,000

$31,000,000

$25,000,000

WAGE LOSS   CRIME   ACCIDENTS   MEDICAL CARE   JAIL

GRAPHIC ASSOCIATES FOR PUBLIC AFFAIRS COMMITTEE, INC.
FROM *Alcoholism Is a Sickness* BY HERBERT YAHRAES.

Comparable figures for 1950 are not available, but the increase in the consumption of liquor and in prices, costs, and wages would certainly justify doubling the figures given in the graph.

Social costs of the use of alcohol. The indirect social costs of the use of alcoholic beverages are also impressive. The minimum cost of crimes in which alcoholism is a contributing cause is a half-billion dollars annually. The cost of accidents due to the use of alcohol cannot be determined with precision, but students of the subject hold that it cannot be less than 100 million dollars each year, and it may be much larger. To these costs we would need to add the decisive contribution of alcoholism to the increase of such aspects of personal and social pathology as mental illness, broken homes, destitution, physical illness and premature deaths, suicide, narcotic addiction, and many others of less social importance.

Decrease in the consumption of absolute alcohol. In spite of considerable increase in the per capita consumption of alcoholic beverages in recent years, there has been a decrease in the per capita consumption of absolute alcohol. In 1850, the per capita consumption of liquor was 7.33 gallons, while in 1950 it stood at 19.30 gallons. Yet, the per capita consumption of absolute alcohol in 1850 was 2.07 gallons and in 1950 it was 1.93 gallons. Similarly, though there was an increase of 35.8 per cent in the number of drinkers between 1940 and 1945, there was an increase of only 4.5 per cent in the per capita consumption of absolute alcohol. Though the consumption of alcoholic beverages increased from 1,825,-833,000 gallons in 1940 to 2,897,151,000 gallons in 1950, the per capita consumption of absolute alcohol only increased from 1.47 gallons to 1.93 gallons in 1950. The per capita consumption of distilled spirits dropped from 2.86 gallons in 1860 to 1.02 gallons in 1949.

The above figures indicate an increasing popularity of malted beverages and wines as compared with the use of spirituous liquors with a high alcoholic content. At present, beer, ale and other malted liquors are growing in popularity and use at the expense of both spirits and wines. These changes in the tastes and demands of consumers since 1940 can be seen from the following table.

APPARENT CONSUMPTION OF ALCOHOLIC BEVERAGES IN THE UNITED STATES, TOTAL AND PER CAPITA OF POPULATION 15 YEARS AND OLDER, IN U.S. GALLONS, 1940 AND 1950.

	Total		Per Capita	
	1940	1950	1940	1950
Distilled Spirits	144,992,000	190,020,000	1.48	1.73
Wine	90,069,000	140,289,000	0.91	1.28
Beer	1,590,772,000	2,566,852,000	16.19	23.38
Absolute alcohol in all three sources.	**	**	1.47	1.93

This trend is partly to be explained by the relatively greater increase in the cost (including taxes) of distilled spirits and wines. At any rate, it probably also means that drunkenness may also have decreased somewhat and more moderate indulgence in alcohol may have been encouraged.

The consumption of alcohol and the drink problem. Alcoholic beverages have been used by mankind as far back as we have any historic records. Their use probably goes back to the origins of agriculture and grain production. The manifold reasons for the consumption of alcoholic beverages have been well stated by Walton H. Hamilton: "To list the reasons why people drink is to recite a catalogue of the ailments, frailties and aspirations to which mortals are subject. To forget the troubles of this world, to ease the strain of existence, to escape from reality, to obtain consolation, to induce sleep, to remove inhibitions—to these ends people drink moderately and temperately." We shall later consider the reasons for excessive alcoholic indulgence.

Types of drinkers. Recent interest in the alcohol problem has stimulated a study of the number of persons who consume alcoholic beverages and of their proper classification in the general category of drinkers. Out of a total population of 150 million, there are about 85 million who do not consume alcoholic beverages at all. Many of these are minors. Out of about 110 million in the drinking age, it is estimated that some 65 million persons use alcoholic beverages to some extent. Contrary to popular impression, only a small percentage (about 6 per cent) of those who drink do so excessively—only about four million of the 65 million who indulge to some degree. But these excessive drinkers affect the lives of perhaps some 20 million others through family or job connections.

Of these four million excessive drinkers there are about 1.75 million alcoholic addicts, that is, those who drink excessively and cannot abandon the habit without external aid, if at all. The number of addicts per capita has fallen off notably in the present century, in spite of increased expenditures for alcoholic beverages. Addiction reached its height about 1910 with a rate of about 1,250 addicts per 100,000 of the population. It has now dropped to about 850. Of this total of 1.75 million addicts some 45 per cent, or about 800,000, are suffering from some psychoneurotic disorder or mental defect. In other words, their addiction is a mental and nervous affliction. In their cases, alcoholism is distinctly a form of illness. This group are known as "compulsive drinkers" or "symptomatic drinkers"—their drinking being symptomatic of a deeper mental disorder. This is the group to whom most attention has been given recently. It is obvious that they cannot be cured merely by depriving them of alcohol.

Personal effect of use of alcohol. Extensive studies of the effect of the use of alcoholic beverages on the bodies and minds of drinkers indicate that moderate drinking seems to have no bad physical or mental effects, so long as it is truly moderate and remains so. Such slight bad effects as moderate drinking may have are probably equalled by the increased pleasures and better adjustments gained from alcoholic indulgence.

There is no decisive proof that moderate drinking has any serious effect on the heart or has notably increased cardiovascular diseases. It does distend the blood vessels, in this way counteracting the effect of nicotine. Alcohol appears to have no serious effect on the kidneys. Only prolonged excessive drinking could produce cirrhosis of the liver and the majority of such cases are not brought about by drinking. Gastritis and other minor stomach disorders are frequently produced by excessive use of spirituous liquors. The development of stomach ulcers may be promoted by aggravating stomach disorders, and drinking seriously impedes the treatment of such ulcers.

On the whole, moderate drinkers appear to have the same life expectancy as non-drinkers. Excessive drinkers have a shorter life expectancy than either, and this may be due mainly to the effect of alcohol. But there are so many other physical and mental factors involved in the make-up and conduct of heavy drinkers that we cannot dogmatize with certainty on this matter.

There is some evidence that the use of alcohol may increase the prevalence of mental and nervous diseases. But this is hard to determine. One illusion here is the common conception that the 800,000 mentally-ill chronic alcoholic addicts are in this condition because of use of alcohol. This precisely puts the cart ahead of the horse. These addicts become excessive alcoholics because of their mental and nervous disorders. If they could not use alcohol their mental illness might well take on more serious forms unless given extended psychiatric treatment.

We have already mentioned the social costs of the use of alcohol in contributing to crime, destitution, broken homes, and the like, and need not mention this further.

Excessive drinkers and alcoholic addicts. We pointed out above that there are about four million excessive drinkers in the country. Of these, 1.75 million are addicts, and of the latter there are around 800,000 mentally-ill or mentally-defective addicts. Among these, it is estimated that 80 per cent are psychoneurotics, 10 per cent psychotics, and 10 per cent mental defectives. This leaves nearly a million addicts who do not appear to be mentally ill or defective. They are persons who for some reason or other have not been able to restrict themselves to moderation. Physical illness, weakness of character, personal worries and disappointments, disasters and deprivations all play their rôles here.

A common form of addiction not based on mental disorders is what is known as "misery drinking," or "compensatory drinking." This is produced chiefly by an extremely unfortunate and depressing set of living conditions and is usually found among the submerged classes. The sheer economic realities of life are all but intolerable and the victims resort to excessive alcoholic indulgence in order to achieve a temporary alcoholic euphoria which makes them forget for the moment the harsh conditions of life. Their intoxication provides a welcome and momentary flight from reality.

The approximately 2.25 million excessive drinkers who are not usually listed as addicts are those who have strayed from moderation for many personal and social reasons. They differ from the addicts in presumably being able to stop their excessive drinking if they desire to do so. But they usually need aid if they actually achieve this restraint.

Nature of the mentally-ill addict. We may now look into the nature of the type of alcoholic addict—the "compulsive drinker"—who is clearly the victim of some mental disorder and whose chronic and excessive alcoholism constitutes the core of his psychoneurosis or psychosis.

Although an adverse social environment may be a contributing factor in true or compulsive alcoholic addiction, the vital sources of this malady are personal and individual, rather than broadly social and environmental. Like the true drug addict, the alcoholic addict is the victim of a psychoneurosis produced by serious forms of mental conflict. An alcoholic flight from reality is the means whereby this conflict is temporarily mitigated and resolved. This mental conflict is usually of a very deep-seated and unconscious type, inherited from the period of infantilism or early childhood. The average addict is usually unconscious of the real nature of his difficulty and has no clear understanding of why he seeks alcoholic relief. He may be able to give many good reasons but rarely the real reason. Psychiatric study of addicts shows that most of them have been subjected to unusual deprivations and disappointments in very early life. Or, early severities in parental discipline may have created in them a strong emotional desire for retaliation. In the alcoholic spree the addict gets compensation for his disappointments and avenges his resentments. Karl A. Menninger, a very astute psychiatrist, thus described the situation:

> Such individuals, as children, have endured bitter disappointment, *unforgettable* disappointment, *unforgivable* disappointment! They feel, with justification, that they have been betrayed, and their entire subsequent life is a prolonged, disguised reaction to this feeling.... Drinking [in the sense in which we are now using it] is a typical infantile revenge reaction.[23]

Viewed from another angle, compulsive or symptomatic alcoholic addiction may be regarded as an avenue of escape from the responsibilities and burdens of adult emotional life. Indulgence in alcohol seems to be the only way in which the person afflicted can face the realities of mature normal existence, or at least the more difficult manifestations of reality.

It should be pointed out here that, while this is decidedly a minority opinion, there are some students of alcoholic addiction who deny that it is a psychoneurosis. L. Irwin Wexburg contends that the mental and emotional traits of the addict are the result rather than the cause of addiction. Such an interpretation, however, leaves the cause largely unexplained.

Changed attitude toward excessive alcoholism. As a result of a more rational attitude toward alcoholism we have come to take a new view of excessive drinking and addiction. In the old days it was popularly believed that nearly all drinkers were excessive drinkers and these were approached almost wholly on moralistic grounds. Now we know that only a small minority of those who use alcoholic beverages are chronic alcoholics and we seek to deal with the latter through medicine, mental hygiene, psychiatry and social work rather than by moral exhortations and legal prohibition.

The nature and the extent of treatment needed by excessive drinkers varies with the type. While the 2.25 million heavy drinkers who are not addicts are presumed to be able to regain moderation if they so wish, they would usually be benefited by psychiatric guidance. All addicts require specialized medical treatment and the aid of social workers. The mentally-ill addicts need the same prolonged psychiatric treatment that is required to improve or cure any type of psychoneurosis. This is usually accessible only to fairly well-to-do addicts who can and wish to avail themselves of private psychiatric treatment.

Methods of treating excessive drinkers. The most rational approach to dealing with excessive drinkers who are not addicts is to alter the living conditions and personal and social values which impel them to drink to excess. For those of this group who wish and need treatment the so-called aversion or conditioned-reflex therapy is probably the most rapid and economical. The well-known "Keeley Cure" and "Gold Cure" are examples of this. Along with his liquor the patient is given a drug which will produce violent nausea. This is repeated sufficiently to build up a

---

[23] *Man Against Himself.* New York: Harcourt, Brace, 1938, pp. 169-170.

HOW ALCOHOLICS ARE TOO OFTEN TREATED

GRAPHIC ASSOCIATES FOR PUBLIC AFFAIRS COMMITTEE, INC.
FROM *Alcoholism Is a Sickness* BY HERBERT YAHRAES.

conditioned-reflex that makes the mere thought of liquor repulsive. With stubborn cases the treatment has to be repeated periodically. This aversion treatment is also the most practicable for the million or so addicts who are not suffering from mental illness or defect. With any addicts, however, it is not likely to be successful unless combined with psychotherapy, counselling and occupational readjustment. A new drug, known as antabuse, which produces intolerance for alcohol, may increase the effectiveness of the conditioned-reflex treatment.

For the mentally-ill addict—the compulsive or symptomatic drinker—the only thorough treatment is private psychiatric treatment, but only well-to-do addicts can usually obtain this. Short of this, the best procedure is that which has been worked out by the Yale Clinic, established in 1944. This is a public clinic where treatment costs from $60 to $100 a patient. It is conducted by psychiatrists, clinical psychologists, social workers, and nurses. As much psychiatric advice and social case-work investigation as possible are provided, though not as much can be done in such a clinic as through private psychiatric practice. Improvement has been noted in over 50 per cent of all cases treated, and in 90 per cent of all cases in which the patient cooperated faithfully. This method would appear to have more promise than any other that can be made available to the majority of addicts. These clinics could be made nationally accessible to addicts for far less than the 2.5 billion dollars paid annually in government liquor taxes.

Inspired by the Yale group, the State of Connecticut has taken the lead in establishing such clinics. It created a Commission on Alcoholism in 1945 and allotted to it 9 per cent of the income from state liquor licenses to set up six free clinics and to build an experimental hospital at Hartford. Oregon and Alabama, as well as Connecticut, have established special state agencies to deal with alcoholism. Seattle, Washington, has also set up a model Rehabilitation Center. Some 25 states have taken preliminary steps along this line. The Federal government is giving attention to the subject through the National Institute for Mental Health.

Another interesting effort to help addicts has been the creation and growth of an informal organization of addicts, known as "Alcoholics Anonymous." [24] It was founded in 1935 by a New York City stockbroker and an Akron, Ohio, physician. It has now about 100,000 members in over 1,300 local groups. It has developed a loose national organization through the Alcoholic Foundation located in New York City. It relies chiefly on a strong religious and moral motivation, group therapy, and the cathartic value of confession. Entirely voluntary in membership and participation, those in each group frankly and fully discuss their alcoholic experiences and problems, seeking mutual understanding and insight. It is claimed that about 75 per cent of the members have been cured or notably helped. So far as it is effective, this innovation has the special virtue of economy.

It is probable that the only rational procedure with addicts who are mentally defective is to segregate them, though some may be helped by psychotherapy. And it is obvious that misery or compensatory drinking can be obliterated only by sweeping social and economic reforms which will eliminate the depressed living conditions which give rise to the efforts to achieve a temporary escape through the alcoholic euphoria.

Need for more research and education on the problem of alcoholism. The rational and scientific approach to alcoholism is so new and the problem is so serious that more research and better public education are greatly needed. The scientific study of alcoholism was launched by the Yale Plan of Alcoholic Studies and the Yale Laboratory. Branches have

---

[24] For a good account of this organization and its work, see Joseph Hirsch, *The Problem Drinker*. New York: Duell, Sloan and Pearce, 1949, Chap. VII.

now been established in Fort Worth, Dallas, and San Antonio, Texas. Another important organization of the kind is the Research Council on the Problems, of Alcohol in New York City. The medical schools of Cornell University, New York University, and the University of Washington are also carrying on research in this field, and several large industrial concerns have started to study the problem.

The most effective organization devoted to educating the public relative to the problems of alcoholism is the Committee for Education on Alcoholism directed by Mrs. Marty Mann in cooperation with the Yale Group. Its activities are on a national scale and its program endeavors to drive home the following basic facts about alcoholism: (1) alcoholism is a disease, and the alcoholic is a sick person; (2) alcoholics can be helped and are worth helping; and (3) the problem of alcoholism is a public health problem and a public responsibility. The Committee helps to set up local groups throughout the country to promote its educational program. They have now been established in about 50 cities.

Unfortunately, those interested in research and education relative to alcoholism have only limited funds at present—about $500,000 annually from all sources to deal with 1,750,000 addicts, some 800,000 of whom are medical cases. In contrast to this, the National Foundation for Infantile Paralysis, with about 25,000 cases, collected 22 million dollars in 1948; the National Tuberculosis Association, with 134,000 cases, collected 20 million; and the American Cancer Society, with about 325,000 cases, collected 13 million. As Joseph Hirsch points out, we virtually waste 25 million dollars each year maintaining "drunk tanks" in the jails of the country.

Temperance and moderate drinking only rational approach to liquor problem. Any successful solution of the larger aspects of the alcohol problem must revolve about a rational campaign to encourage true temperance, or social drinking in moderation. To bring about such an attitude we shall require sane education with respect to the nature and consequences of the consumption of alcohol, and more efficient and reasonable control of the source of supply of alcoholic liquors. Appropriate penalties may be prescribed for public intoxication, and, particularly, for driving automobiles while under the influence of liquor. The latter is a matter which especially demands more thoughtful and drastic action today. Greater emphasis also needs to be laid upon the element of good taste and the esthetics of social drinking. Above all, science and reasonableness should supplant ignorance and fanaticism in handling the matter of alcoholic indulgence.

Our experience with Prohibition from 1919 to 1933 and the unfortunate experience of other countries with this mode of approaching the liquor problem have amply demonstrated its unwisdom and futility. There seems little doubt that Prohibition both increased the prevalence of heavy drinking and made it more respectable. It is certain that it increased the amount of drinking among the leading social and intellectual groups in the community. It made alcoholic consumption far more respectable than ever before—even to swilling down large quantities of vile liquor.

It distracted attention from drinking as a matter of pleasant taste and social grace and concentrated the effort on drinking as a matter of principle and sheer indulgence—pouring down some liquid which possessed a "kick," however vile the taste or toxic its aftereffects. These vulgar practices became the "smart" thing to do. Prohibition also tended to reduce the desirable stigma upon public intoxication. As we have seen, it provided the great training ground for the rise of racketeering and organized crime, both in the liquor field and beyond. It was a powerful stimulant to political and legal corruption. Finally, it had the deplorable effect of at least temporarily discrediting any true temperance movement. It would seem reasonable to assert that, aside from the progress in research and medical treatment of addicts, we are today much further from a rational handling of the liquor problem than we were in 1919, while a great number of incidental evils, some of them far worse than alcoholism, have been created.

SOME ASPECTS OF SUICIDE AS A SOCIAL PROBLEM

Failure to recognize importance of suicide as a social problem. We have just surveyed chronic drug addiction and alcoholic addiction as a flight from reality. It was earlier shown that much of so-called insanity is at bottom a flight from an intolerable mental reality. Here we shall consider some of the more important aspects of suicide—the supreme and final flight from reality. We have given some quantitative facts about the extent of suicide in the chapter concerning health, but here we may examine some of the major causes and possible remedies for suicide.

Although the newspapers play up spectacular cases of suicide, the subject is little discussed in serious literature. Indeed, the life insurance companies, which have to be realistic in the matter, have more fully recognized the importance of suicide than have sociologists. Much of the important writing on the subject in the United States has been done by statisticians and others in the employ of insurance companies. But suicide is a far more important problem than many others concerning which there is chronic excitement—for example, murder and our high homicide rate. In 1948, there were 8,536 homicides and 16,354 suicides reported. In addition to the suicides reported, there are an incalculable number which were not reported as such, many being represented as accidental deaths. There is no way of knowing how many cases of attempted suicide there are each year in the United States, but they probably greatly outnumber those which actually result in death. The following table presents the suicide and homicide rates in the United States in recent years.

Suicides actually account for more violent deaths than any other single source except automobile accidents. Today the reported suicides run to about half the deaths from automobile accidents. It is not unreasonable to believe that all suicides, reported and unreported, run annually to something not far from the deaths in automobile accidents, which now reach about 35,000 yearly.

These facts will indicate the importance of the subject in a quantitative sense, though they give little impression of the psychological and social aspects of the problem, with its intense mental suffering prior to the overt act of suicide in many cases, and the bereavement, humiliation, broken families, and economic dependency that constitute the accompaniment and aftermath of suicide.

HOMICIDE AND SUICIDE RATES, 1912-1948

(Per 100,000 of Population)

Year	Homicide	Suicide	Year	Homicide	Suicide
1912	6.6	16.0	1932	9.2	17.4
1920	7.1	10.2	1940	6.2	14.3
1925	8.6	12.1	1945	5.6	11.2
1930	9.0	15.7	1948	5.8	11.2

Social attitudes toward suicide. The attitudes toward suicide have varied and still do vary greatly. In the Orient we find institutionalized and ceremonial forms of suicide which carry with them honor. Such are Japanese suicides on the occasion of the death of the emperor or an insult to him. Japanese soldiers may kill themselves when they and their leader face or suffer defeat. Hindu widows have committed suicide nobly in the so-called *suttee,* burning themselves to death on the funeral pyre of their husbands. In classical times many statesmen and generals committed suicide with honor. Indeed, suicide has rivaled the duel as a method of saving or demonstrating personal honor.

In Christian and Muslim lands there has been an attitude of intense hostility to suicide. Although the teachings of the Old and New Testaments did not specifically prohibit suicide, they were unfavorable to the practice. The Talmud definitely condemned it. Augustine denounced suicide as a sin, and the Christian church has held suicide to be on a par with murder—in some ways even worse than ordinary homicide. Suicides have often been treated with contempt and indignity in Christian lands. In some cases, burial has been forbidden or has been done in such a fashion as to publicize the disgrace. The attitude of Islam has been just as decisive. Indeed, Islam views suicide as more heinous than murder.

The first important reaction against this traditional Christian attitude toward suicide came during the eighteenth century. Such leaders of the humanitarian philosophy of that age as Hume, Montesquieu, Voltaire, and Rousseau protested against the existing savagery in this matter. But the first general change in attitude came in the late nineteenth century, after the rise of religious liberalism and modern science. These lessened the strength of religious dogma. The fear of hell-fire as the reward of the suicide gradually vanished among the educated classes. Personal acts came to be judged mainly with reference to their contribution to individual and social well-being here and now. When the eminent Austrian sociologist, Ludwig Gumplowicz, committed suicide, along with his invalid wife, in order to avoid lingering suffering from an incurable cancer of the throat, Lester F. Ward and other leading sociologists hailed the act as one of personal heroism. Much approval was showered upon the illustrious feminist, Charlotte Perkins Gilman, when she committed suicide in 1935 as the alternative to a long and painful illness from incurable cancer. One may safely say that in enlightened circles in civilized countries today, there is little stigma attached to suicide, but in orthodox religious circles the ban still remains. The social frustration and psychological shock to members of conventional society, caused by suicide, were graphically described in the anonymous article, "What a Suicide Leaves Behind," in *The Forum* (February, 1939).

Factual picture of suicide problem. A few facts about the relation of suicide to race, age-groups, sex, and cultural setting may prove interesting. Negroes are much less prone to suicide than are whites. In 1930 the suicide rate of Negroes in the United States was 5.1, as compared with 15.7 for the whole population. Suicides take place mainly in and after mid-life. More than half of all suicides are committed by persons past 45. Male suicides exceed female suicides by a ratio of a little better than three to one, though between the ages of 15 and 20 approximately as many females as males commit suicide. Suicide is much more common in cities than in rural areas. This would seem to indicate that family, community, and institutional stability play a large rôle in restricting suicidal tendencies. The greater religious orthodoxy of rural regions also exerts some influence on the matter. Catholics commit suicide less frequently than Protestants, Jews, and freethinkers. As to social and economic status, it appears that suicide is most common among the wealthy and those near or below the poverty line. Instability arising from quite different causes seems to be the main explanation in both cases. There appears to be some superficial relation between the seasons of the year and the suicide rate, but it has no importance for the general social picture of the suicide problem.

Some apparent causes of suicide. In determining the causes of suicide, we must differentiate carefully between simple and superficial reasons, such as those given in suicide notes, and the underlying and true explanations. Suicide is a complex social and personal phenomenon and its causes are equally complex. Apparent and superficial correlations must also be examined with care. For example, there was a great rise in suicides after the depression started in 1929. This might seem to indicate that sheer economic loss and privation directly produced suicide. But these economic factors operated indirectly through a large number of psychological and social channels—a blow to pride, defeat of a lifelong ambition, loss of the home, family disruption, and similar misfortunes. Some millionaires committed suicide during the stock market crash, even though they still remained relatively wealthy men and faced no semblance or prospect of privation.

Although such distressing mental troubles as lead to suicide are in large part individual problems, their origins may lie, in part, in general social disorganization. Social disturbances produced by the rapid change from rural to urban life, the growing instability of the family, and the lack of economic security tend to destroy stabilizing social habits and customs and to make adjustment to life more difficult for many individuals. The great French sociologist Émile Durkheim held that anything that tends to break down the intimate contact between an individual and his primary social groups is favorable to suicidal tendencies. Urban life produces just such conditions. All studies of suicide indicate a close correlation between a high suicide rate and social disorganization.

One interesting fact about suicide, most thoroughly expounded by the French sociologist, Maurice Halbwachs, is that the suicide rate falls off markedly in periods of war and other great social crises, provided that the latter are not also economic crises. The explanation appears to be that the group excitement seems to absorb the attention of persons who might commit suicide in normal times and to distract them from their personal frustrations and distress. In other words, the crisis gives them a temporary sociopsychic "lift." Of course, in the wake of war there is likely to be a marked rise in the suicide rate, especially among defeated and devastated nations. Suicide reached epidemic proportions in Germany and Japan after 1945.

Suicide is, thus, the complex result of social and psychological factors. It usually takes place when unusually difficult external events are brought to bear upon a personality already burdened with psychic conflicts and suffering from mental distress. Persons of normal mental makeup are able to bear the greatest shocks, disappointments, and economic blows. Bessie Bunzel well describes the complicated character of the suicide situation:

Suicide is a reaction to problems that apparently cannot be solved in any other way; it is the final response which a human being makes to inner emotional distress. The motives behind it are as varied as the number of people who seek this method of escape. Hardships of various kinds, like unemployment, poverty, hunger and other deprivations; ill health, mental abnormality, physical pain and deformity, often induce thoughts of suicide. The loss of honor, position, freedom or love as well as failure with its accompanying feeling of inadequacy, disgrace, sex difficulties and tangled personal relationships make death seem necessary as an escape. But ordinarily no one of these alone would drive a person to suicide unless he were already harassed by serious emotional conflict. Usually external events merely intensify latent disturbances and provide the immediate provocation in any given case.... Fundamental forces are fear and anxiety, feelings of inferiority, hatred, aggressiveness, revenge, guilt and the other mental disorders that prevent people from attaining emotional maturity.[25]

In one of the most thorough sociological studies that have yet been made of suicide, Ruth Shonle Cavan interprets suicide as the complex result of a general disintegration of the life-pattern of the individual. Crises in the life of the individual are likely to intensify the desire to escape from an intolerable reality by means of self-destruction:

Perhaps the most frequent type of crisis culminating in suicide is that in which a previously satisfactory life-organization has been broken through forces outside the control of the person: through the death of someone important to

25 From "Suicide," *The Encyclopaedia of the Social Sciences*, Vol. XIV, pp. 458-459. By permission of The Macmillan Company, publishers.

him, through illness, through economic failure, through quarrels, and the like. Such disturbances seem more liable to affect a whole system of interests and relationships, rather than merely one interest, and adjustment is correspondingly difficult. . . . The experiences found to lead to disorganization and suicide in Chicago in 1923 include: unemployment and economic failure, arrests, change of location, illness and disease, alcoholism, insanity, the rupture of intimate relations through quarrels, death, or separation.[26]

Reduction and prevention of suicide. The rational methods of preventing suicide are logically indicated by a knowledge of its causes. Any effective attack upon suicide would involve a combined attack by mental hygiene, economic reconstruction, and community organization. Mental hygiene, working through psychiatry, must uncover and relieve the mental conflicts which place a person in a mood to resort to suicide when he is faced by circumstances that would not produce suicide in the stable individual. External reality and the social environment should be made more endurable. Economic security must be provided through such sweeping economic reconstruction as will assure more stable employment or proper support through social insurance. Community organization must supply new social contacts and group interests to replace those which are being destroyed by the transition from a rural to an urban era.

SUMMARY

Prostitution has existed since primitive times. Social attitudes toward it have varied from exploitation of it in religious ritual to purist attempts to suppress it completely. It was virtually universal until the ravages of syphilis set in after 1500. But it remained fairly prevalent in Europe until the close of the Second World War, and in the United States until after the Chicago vice investigation of 1912. Since that time, segregated districts and legalized prostitution have been rather completely extinguished in the United States.

Nevertheless, because of the fact that the causes of prostitution were left much as they were before the campaign against legalized prostitution, the result of attempted suppression has been mainly to scatter prostitutes throughout the large cities, to encourage the corruption of police departments, and to throw the control of other than "free-lance" prostitution into the hands of the underworld. Most prostitution today is handled by the moguls of organized vice.

There are many causes of prostitution, but the most important of all is the economic. Many girls find that prostitution offers the most feasible or attractive way of making a living. Many men cannot afford to marry and support a family, and they find recourse to prostitutes the most practical manner of solving their sexual needs. At least until the rise of organized vice in recent years, there was little foundation for the common belief that prostitutes enter their profession involuntarily and that they are held against their will as virtual slaves or prisoners.

---

[26] R. S. Cavan, *Suicide.* Chicago: University of Chicago Press, 1928, pp. 326-327.

Aside from purist moral prejudices, the main motive for suppressing prostitution has been the conviction that prostitutes spread venereal disease. In reality, venereal disease is spread to a greater extent today by girls of "easy virtue" whose motives are not primarily pecuniary. A majority of these girls are in their "teens."

It has been difficult to cope with the problem of venereal disease because prudery and archaic moralistic attitudes have made it difficult even to discuss the matter intelligently—to say nothing of taking steps to reduce or eradicate these disorders. Medical science, through prophylaxis and curative drugs, is now prepared virtually to wipe out venereal disease, but hostile social attitudes and ignorance have thus far frustrated any such sweeping success in applying medical knowledge to the problem.

Narcotic drugs have been used for centuries. There are many popular illusions about the serious effects of narcotics on physical health and about their influence in producing criminal behavior. The true narcotic addict is almost invariably a psychoneurotic and a fit subject for psychiatric treatment rather than for restraint and punishment by police and prisons.

The Harrison Act of 1914, its amendments, and the Jones-Miller Act of 1922, which have outlawed the open sale of narcotic drugs, are probably as great a mistake as the Eighteenth Amendment and the Volstead Act. Such legislation has driven the drug traffic into the hands of organized underground rings, has transformed a medical problem into a criminal and punitive operation, and has generally made impossible any sane handling of the problem of narcotics. There is little doubt, however, that the sale of cocaine and marijuana should be sharply restricted, for these are dangerous drugs.

The real solution of the narcotic problem lies in adequate education of the public concerning the uses and abuses of narcotics, the provision of specialized psychiatric and hospital treatment for actual addicts, and the legalization of the sale of narcotics under medical and government supervision.

The use of alcoholic beverages is a problem of vast proportions, with respect both to the economic phases of the situation and the social and personal problems connected with the use of alcoholic liquors. We spend annually three times as much for alcoholic beverages as for all public education. No realistic observer, whatever his tolerance for social drinking, can well regard such an outlay as justified.

Most of those who use alcoholic beverages are social or convivial drinkers. Their use of alcohol is usually not personally or socially disastrous, although the rise and universality of automotive transportation raises serious issues even here. Alcoholic addicts are relatively few by comparison with the number of convivial drinkers.

Alcoholic addicts usually require protracted psychiatric treatment to effect a cure. Since this is not available except to rich addicts, the main hope of helping addicts lies in public clinics, where some psychiatric aid can be given to addicts. A voluntary organization, "Alcoholics Anonymous," is reported to have had considerable success in the use of informal group therapy and catharsis. The most notable advance in recent years has been the tendency to supplant traditional moralizing by a medical approach to excessive drinking and alcoholic addiction.

Suicide constitutes a social and personal problem of generally unrecognized extent. At the present time, even the suicides that are reported account for more than double the number of deaths that result from all reported homicides.

Suicide is usually caused both by emotional instability on the part of individuals and by social disorganization, which reduces the forces that would ordinarily hold the tendency to self-destruction in check.

To reduce the suicide rate, we must provide greater personal security, readjust our institutional patterns to the problems of modern living, and provide psychiatric aid for those prone to suicidal attempts.

SELECTED REFERENCES

*Barnes, H. E., *Prohibition versus Civilization*. New York: Viking Press, 1932. A brief attack on all aspects of prohibition and an argument for temperance and civilized drinking.

Binkley, R. C., *Responsible Drinking*. New York: Vanguard, 1930. A sane and telling argument for temperance versus prohibition.

*Carroll, R. S., *What Price Alcohol?* New York: Macmillan, 1941. Comprehensive survey of the medical, moral and social aspects of the alcohol problem. Somewhat traditional in attitude.

*Cavan, R. S., *Suicide*. Chicago: University of Chicago Press, 1928. The best treatment of suicide in English; a clear and sensible book.

*Cooper, C. R., *Designs in Scarlet*. Boston: Little, Brown, 1939. The best account of prostitution under the control of organized vice.

Dublin, L. I., and Bunzel, Bessie, *To Be or Not to Be*. New York: Smith and Haas, 1933. Important for extensive statistical data on suicide.

*Haggard, H. W., and Jellinek, E. M., *Alcohol Explored*. New York: Doubleday, Doran, 1945. Authoritative treatise on the use and effects of alcohol.

*Hirsch, Joseph, *The Problem Drinker*. New York: Duell, Sloan and Pearce, 1949. Excellent and reliable analysis of the problem drinker and chronic alcoholic.

Jellinek, E. M., *Alcohol and Chronic Alcoholism*. New York: Yale University Press, 1942. Survey of the extent and nature of chronic alcoholism by a leading American authority on the subject.

———, *Recent Trends in Alcoholism and Alcohol Consumption*. New Haven: Hillhouse Press, 1947. Authoritative information on addicts and the consumption of alcohol.

*Lindesmith, A. R., *Opiate Addiction*. Bloomington: Principia Press, 1947. An excellent recent treatment of drug addiction, its causes, effects and solution.

Mangold, G. B., *Social Pathology*. New York: Macmillan, 1932. A standard sociological treatise.

*Mann, Marty, *Primer on Alcoholism*. New York: Rinehart, 1951. Good introduction to the personal and social aspects of the problem by a leader in the educational program on alcoholism.

McCarthy, R. G., and Douglass, E. M., *Alcohol and Social Responsibility*. New York: Crowell, 1949. Competent recent treatment of the social and educational aspects of the alcohol problem.

*Menninger, K. A., *Man Against Himself*. New York: Harcourt, Brace, 1938. An invaluable book dealing with chronic alcoholism and other types of personal psychopathology and maladjustment.

Mowrer, E. R., *Disorganization: Personal and Social*. Philadelphia: Lippincott, 1942. Competent study of personal disorganization in modern urban life. Describes the social basis of personality disintegration.

Parran, Thomas, *Shadow on the Land*. New York: Reynal and Hitchcock, 1937.

————, and Vonderlehr, R. A., *Plain Words about Venereal Disease*. New York: Reynal and Hitchcock, 1942. Two earnest books about the ravages of venereal disease. The second deals also with venereal disease as a military problem. Both books are weakened somewhat by intruding moralistic attitudes into a strictly medical issue.

*Powell, Hickman, *Ninety Times Guilty*. New York: Harcourt, Brace, 1939. Contains good account of organized vice, prostitution, and drug addiction in the syndicate era.

Queen, S. A., and Gruener, J. R., *Social Pathology*. New York: Crowell, 1940. A leading textbook in this field.

*Robinson, W. J., *The Oldest Profession in the World*. New York: Eugenics Publishing Company, 1929. Probably the best brief introduction to the nature of the prostitute and prostitution. A sane little book, debunking most of the common illusions about the prostitute.

Seabrook, William, *Asylum*. New York: Harcourt, Brace, 1935. A revealing account of the chronic alcoholic and his efforts to get effective treatment.

*Spalding, W. B., and Montague, J. R., *Alcohol and Human Affairs*. Yonkers: World Book Company, 1949. Excellent introduction to the whole subject.

Strecker, E. A., and Chambers, F. T., *Alcohol: One Man's Meat*. New York: Macmillan, 1947. Readable psychiatric description of the causes, nature and treatment of chronic alcoholism.

Terry, C. E., and Pellens, Mildred, *The Opium Problem*. New York: Bureau of Social Hygiene, 1928. Voluminous coverage of all aspects of the narcotic problem, including control.

*Warren, Carl, *On Your Guard*. New York: Emerson Books, 1937. A good introductory book on venereal disease. Sane in attitude, but a trifle alarmist and exaggerates the extent of venereal disease.

Waterman, W. C., *Prostitution and Its Repression in New York City*. New York: Columbia University Press, 1932. A scholarly and fairly sympathetic study of the repressive police policy in suppressing prostitution in the largest American city.

Williams, H. S., *Drugs against Men*. New York: McBride, 1933.

*————, *Drug Addicts Are Human Beings*. New York: Shaw, 1938. An introduction to the problem of drug addiction by a famous doctor, wisely advocating a medical rather than a police approach to the drug problem.

Index

A

G

Gaines case, 201, 207
Gallipolis colony, Ohio, 628
Galton, Sir Francis, 75-76, 651
Gambling, 439; attitudes toward, 701-702; cost of, 706; immigrants and, 116-117; law enforcement, 706; legalized, 702, 707; legitimate, 704; organized, 685-686: and criminality, 706, dealing with, 706-708; syndicated, 683; trends, 703-704; underworld control of, 704-705
Gangs, 526; criminal, 691; in cities, 437-438; juvenile criminal, 713
Gangsterism, 415
Garbage collection, 246-247
Garden city movement, 452, 479, 549
Garvey, Marcus, 210-211
Gas plants, municipal ownership of, 430, 431
Gauls, invasions by, 90
Geddes, Patrick, 402, 452, 520, 547, 549
Gentlemen's Agreement with Japan, 105, 106, 182
George, Henry, 64-65, 569, 605
Geriopsychoses, 624
German Americans: and politics, 127-128; immigration, 94, 95, 104
Germanic tribes, 90
Germany: birth rate in, 22, 32, 33; British blockade, 31; control of venereal disease, 821; defeat by Russia, 49; eugenics movement in, 76; housing trends, 464; immigrants from, 93; social case work, 584; social insurance, 591-593
Germs, resistance to new drugs, 239
Germ theory of disease, 234-235
Giddings, Franklin Henry, 155
Gigantism, 625
Gilbert Act of 1782, 28
Gill, Howard B., 766-767
Gillin, John L., 561, 759-760
Gilman, Charlotte Perkins, 848
Gini, Corrado, 23, 63, 64, 66
Ginn estate, 479
Girl Scouts, 526, 542
Gist, N. P., 442
Gladstone, W. E., 414
Glandular therapy, 240-241
Glass, D. V., 32
Glueck, Bernard, 723, 777
Glueck, Eleanor, 711, 714
Glueck, Sheldon, 711, 714, 725-726
Gobineau, Count Joseph Arthur de, 150, 158-159, 160, 161
Goddard, Henry H., 651, 655, 724
Goiter, 239, 240, 625
Goldberger, Joseph, 239
Gold Cure, alcoholism, 842
Gold Rush, 134; and crime, 683-684
Gonorrhea, 810; contraction and symptoms of, 814; increase of, after Pearl Harbor, 818; treatment and cure of, 818
Gordon, Hamilton, 585
Gould, Jay, 684

Government: aid to farmers, 347, 357, 363-367; city (see City government); county, 337; federal (see items beginning with Federal); machine, 415-418; rural element in, 337; supervision of large collective farms, 375-376
Graft: in city government, 415-418; political, 570, 687-688
Gramicidin, 236, 238
Granger movement, 132, 338, 344, 345, 346
Grant, Madison, 160-161
Grant, Pryor, 767
Granuloma inguinale, 810
Grave's disease, 625
Great Britain: birth rate, 21-22, 32; blockade of Germany, 31; borough government, 414; charity organization, 517; control of venereal disease, 821; housing, 463-464; immigrants from, 93; Labour Government, 590-591; poor laws, 28-29, 574-575; public health movement, 248-250; social insurance, 590-591; social legislation, 588-590; state medicine, 266-267
Great Depression, 587
Greece: divorce in, 290; family in, 281; rural life in, 327
Greeman, H. Lawrence, 208
Greenback movement, 132, 345-346
Greenbelt, Maryland, 549-550
Greenbelt communities, 452, 454, 504, 548, 549-550
Greenbie, Marjorie Barstow, 131
Greenwich House, New York, 519
Greenwood, H. H., 271
Gresham, Newt, 343
Griffs, F. A., 626
Grimm brothers (Jacob and Wilhelm), 158
Griscom, John, 250, 478
Group clinics and hospitals, 262
Group consciousness, rise of, 513-515
Group Health Association of Washington, D. C., 265
Group medicine: cooperative, 265-266; rural, 265
Groups: and human personality, 13; on national scale, 11-12; social, 10-13
Group therapy, 663
Groves, Ernest R., 299, 338
Gull's disease, 624
Gumplowicz, Ludwig, 153
"Gun molls," 710
Gunpowder, invention of, 91
Guzman, Jessie P., 189

H

Hague, Frank, 418, 421
Halbert, L. A., 442
Halbwachs, Maurice, 849
Hall, G. Stanley, 527, 619, 642, 647
Hamburg-Elberfeld system, outdoor relief, 578, 584
Hamilton, Alexander, 132, 453
Hamilton, Alice, 242
Hamilton, G. B., 299, 317